The Constitution of India

Highlights

Full text of Constitution of India
amended up-to-date

Selective comments by P.M. Bakshi

Constitution of India in a Nutshell

Documents in relation to its
application to Jammu & Kashmir

Important Caselaws on Fundamental Rights

Caselaws declaring Constitutional Amendments
Unconstitutional

Relevant Caselaws/Reports Leading to
Amendment to Constitution

Supreme Court on Validity of Constitutional
Amendments

List of Allied Amending Acts amending
Constitution

Amendments at a Glance

Recent Case Laws

Landmark Judgments

Glossary of Constitutional Terms

Exhaustive Subject Index

More than 1400 Cases and much more...

The daring publisher, Universal Law Publishing Company, among the foremost in the law publishing field and progressive in venturing to bring out rare legal literature of avant garde *character has rightly enriched the* corpus juris *of India*

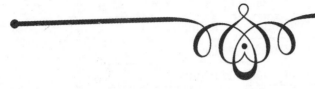

Justice V R Krishna Iyer
Random Reflections, page 14

The Constitution of India

P.M. Bakshi

Former Director, Indian Law Institute
Former Member of the Law Commission of India

Eleventh Edition

Universal
Law Publishing Co.
NEW DELHI - INDIA

First Edition	: 1991	Eighth Edition	: 2007
Second Edition	: 1992	Updated Reprint	: 2008
Third Edition	: 1996	Ninth Edition	: 2009
Fourth Edition	: 2000		
Fifth Edition	: 2002	Tenth Edition	: 2010
Sixth Edition	: 2005	Eleventh Edition	: 2011
Seventh Edition	: 2006	**Updated Reprint**	**: 2012**

Incorporating therein all the amendments upto and including
The Constitution (Ninety-seventh Amendment) Act, 2011

ISBN: 978-93-5035-047-8

© Publishers

Published by
UNIVERSAL LAW PUBLISHING CO. PVT. LTD.
C-FF-1A, Dilkhush Industrial Estate,
(Near Azadpur Metro Station) G.T. Karnal Road,
Delhi-110 033
Tel.: 011-47082254, 27438103, 27215334
Fax : 011-27458529
E-mail *(For sales inquiries)* : unilaw@vsnl.com
E-mail *(For editorial inquiries)* : edit@unilawbooks.com
Website : www.unilawbooks.com

Recommended citation: P.M. Bakshi, *The Constitution of India*,
11th Edn. (New Delhi: Universal Law Publishing Co. Pvt. Ltd., 2011).

Computer Typeset at Aesthetic & *Printed* at Taj Press, NOIDA

CONTENTS AT A GLANCE

Provisions	Part	Article	Page
Preamble	—	—	1 - 6
The Union and its Territory	I	1 to 4	6 - 10
Citizenship	II	5 to 11	10 - 14
Fundamental Rights	III	12 to 35	14 - 98
Directive Principles of State Policy	IV	36 to 51	98 - 109
Fundamental Duties	IVA	51A	109 - 110
The Union	V	52 to 151	110 - 161
The States	VI	152 to 237	162 - 223
The Union Territories	VIII	239 to 242	223 - 228
The Panchayats	IX	243 to 243-O	228 - 234
The Municipalities	IXA	243P to 243ZG	234 - 240A
The Co-operative Societies	IXB	243ZH to 243ZT	240A - 241
The Scheduled and Tribal Areas	X	244 to 244A	241 - 242
Relations between the Union and the States	XI	245 to 263	242 - 256
Finance, Property, Contracts and Suits	XII	264 to 300A	256 - 273
Trade, Commerce and Intercourse within the Territory of India	XIII	301 to 307	273 - 275
Services under the Union and the States	XIV	308 to 323	276 - 298
Tribunals	XIVA	323A to 323B	298 - 301
Elections	XV	324 to 329A	302 - 304
Special Provisions relating to certain classes	XVI	330 to 342	305 - 315
Official Language	XVII	343 to 351	315 - 318
Emergency Provisions	XVIII	352 to 360	319 - 328

Provisions	Part	Article	Page
Miscellaneous	XIX	361 to 367	328 - 334
Amendment of the Constitution	XX	368	334 - 336
Temporary, Transitional and Special Provisions	XXI	369 to 392	336 - 353
Short title, Commencement, Authoritative Text in Hindi and Repeals	XXII	393 to 395	353
Schedules 1 to 12	—	—	354 - 417
The Constitution (Application to Jammu and Kashmir) Order, 1954	—	—	418 - 431
Re-statement, with Reference to the present text of the Constitution, of the exceptions and Modifications subject to which the Constitution applies to the State of Jammu and Kashmir	—	—	432 - 446
Extracts from the Constitution (Forty-fourth Amendment) Act, 1978	—	—	447

CONTENTS
THE CONSTITUTION OF INDIA

Contents at a Glance   v

Table of Cases   xli

List of Statutes Referred   xcvii

Constitution of India in a Nutshell   ci

Important Articles and Schedules at a Glance   cxiv

Important Caselaws on Fundamental Rights   cxiv

Caselaws Declaring Constitutional Amendments Unconstitutional   cxv

Relevant Caselaws/Reports Leading to Amendment to Constitution   cxvi

Supreme Court on Validity of Constitutional Amendments   cxvii

List of Allied Amending Acts Amending Constitution   cxvii

Amendments at a Glance   cxix

PREAMBLE

Abolition of Caste System   1

Basic Structure of Constitution   2

Features of Basic Structure   2

Constitutional Philosophy   2

Duty of Citizen   2

Federal Structure   2

Fundamental Law   3

Idealism   3

Interpretation of Preamble   3

Interpretation of Statutes   3

Parents Patriae   4

Powers from Constitutional Provision   4

Preamble: Part of the Constitution   4

Preamble as Basic Structure   4

Res Extra Commercium   4

Secularism   4

Social Justice   5

Socialistic Concept   5

Sovereign   5

Structural Sources of the Constitution   5

Structure of Government and Fundamental Aspects of Constitution   6

Unity of Nation   6

PART I
THE UNION AND ITS TERRITORY

1. Name and territory of the Union   6

Union of India   6

Acquisition of Foreign Territory   7

Action Subsequent to Acquisition   7

Boundaries of State   7

Law Applicable to Acquired Territory   7

Meaning of Territory of India   7

Territorial Waters   7

Territory of India   8

2. Admission or establishment of new States   8

Admission of New States   8

Formation of New States   8

2A. Sikkim to be associated with the Union.—[Repealed]   8

3. Formation of new States and alteration of areas, boundaries or names of existing States   8

Agreements between India and Bangladesh 9
Effects of Re-organisation of Territory under Existing Laws 9
Inter-State Agreement on Water 9
Reference of Central Bills to States 9

4. **Laws made under articles 2 and 3 to provide for the amendment of the First and the Fourth Schedules and supplemental, incidental and consequential matters** 9
Law in force: Effect of State Reorganisation 9
Legislative Power of State 10
Levy of Penalty 10
New High Court for States 10
Power of Parliament in Respect of New State 10
Scope and Applicability of Article 4 10

PART II
CITIZENSHIP

5. **Citizenship at the commencement of the Constitution** 10
Citizenship at Commencement of Constitution 10
Determination of Citizenship 10
Every Person 11
One Domicile 11

6. **Rights of citizenship of certain persons who have migrated to India from Pakistan** 11
Catch-up Rule 11
Citizenship of Foreign State 11
Migrated to Territory of India 11
Migration: Meaning of 12
Domicile on the Date of Constitution 12

7. **Rights of citizenship of certain migrants to Pakistan** 12
Citizenship of India 12
Scope of Article 7 12
Person Continuing to be in India 12

8. **Rights of citizenship of certain persons of Indian origin residing outside India** 12
Scope of Article 8 and Citizenship 13

9. **Persons voluntarily acquiring citizenship of a foreign State not to be citizens** 13
Citizenship Act, 1955, Section 9(2) 13
Migrants to Pakistan 13
Obtaining Passport 13

10. **Continuance of the rights of citizenship** 13
Citizenship and Domestic Law 13
Procedure Established by Law 13

11. **Parliament to regulate the right of citizenship by law** 13
Question of Citizenship 14
Retrospective Operation of the Citizenship Act, 1955 14
Scope of Article 11 14

PART III
FUNDAMENTAL RIGHTS
General

12. **Definition** 14
Agency outside India 14
Board of Control for Cricket in India (BCCI) 14

Co-operative Societies   14
Examples of Statutory and Other Bodies held to be State   14
Local Authorities: Writ   15
Other Authorities   15
Private Body   16
State   16
State Action   16
13. **Laws inconsistent with or in derogation of the fundamental rights**   16
Act of Parliament   18
Act of State   18
Basic Features   18
Severability   19
Constitution Amendment Acts Declared as Unconstitutional   19
Treaties on Human Rights   19
Voidness of Existing Laws   20
Working of Act   20

Right to Equality

14. **Equality before law**   20
Administrative Order   20
Admission in College and Reservations   20
Arbitrary Action and Discretion   21
Backward Areas   21
Ban on Sex Selection   22
Bias and *mala fide* Allegations   22
Board of Control for Cricket in India (BCCI)   22
Change of Name   22
Citizenship   22
Concept of Equality   22
Defection   22
Discrimination   22
Disinvestment   22
Doctrine of Natural Justice   22
Education   23
Equal Citizens   23
Equal Pay for Equal Work   23
Equality   23
Equality in Promotion   23
Equals and Unequals   23
Executive Action   24
Flexibility   24
Grant-in-aid   24
Illegal Action   24
Illegalities cannot be Perpetuated   24
Interpretation   24
Land Acquisition   24
Land Ceiling   25
Legitimate Expectations   25
Limitations   25
Mala fide   25
Newspapers   25
Panchayat: Removal of Members   25

Pension   25
Principles of Natural Justice   26
Procedural Discrimination   26
Rajasthani Language   26
Reasonable Restriction   26
Reasonableness   26
Right to have Reasoned Order   27
Royalties for Industries   27
Rule for Termination of Service   27
Scheduled Castes   27
Scope of Article 14   27
Service   28
Service Rules   28
Source of Article 14   28
State Policy   29
Tax Exemptions   29
Taxation Laws   29
Taxing Statutes   30
Test of Equality   30
Uncanalised Discretion   30
Zone-wise Merit List for Recruitment   31

15. **Prohibition of discrimination on grounds of religion, race, caste,
    sex or place of birth**   31
Area-wise Reservation   31
Backward Class   31
Constitutional 93rd Amendment 2005   32
Discrimination   32
Discrimination on Grounds of Sex   33
Horizontal and Vertical Reservation   33
Medical Colleges Reservation   33
Relationship to Article 14   33
Reservation for SCs and STs   33
Reservation on the Basis of Domicile   33
Reservation within Reservation   34
Scheduled Caste – Acquiring of Scheduled Caste Status   34
University-wise Reservation   34
Women: Reservation   34
Women and Sexual Harassment   34

16. **Equality of opportunity in matters of public employment**   34
All India Services   35
Appointment   35
Arbitrariness   36
Constitution (Seventy-seventh Amendment) Act, 1995   36
Discrimination   36
Employment   37
Grant of Opportunity of Hearing   37
Medical Colleges   37
Object of Article 16   37
Other Safeguards   37
Pay Scales   38
Qualifying Minimum Marks   38

Relaxation in Standard of Eligibility 38
Recruitment Test 38
Reservation 38
Reservation and Promotion 38
Reservation to Single Post 38
Revision of Pay Scales 38
Right to go anywhere and Live with any Person 39
Scheme of Article 18 39
Seniority 39

17. Abolition of untouchability 39
Object of Article 17 39
Religious Freedom 39

18. Abolition of titles 40
Abolition of Titles 40
Central Civil Service: Pension 40
Equality 40
National Awards, not Titles 40
Title 40

RIGHT TO FREEDOM

19. Protection of certain rights regarding freedom of speech, etc. 41
Aids patient 42
Arbitrariness 42
Ban on Slaughter 42
Bandhs 42
Burden of Proof 42
Business Aspects of the Media 42
Business with Government 42
Constitutionality 43
Contempt of Court 43
Convicts 43
Co-operative Societies Act, 1965 (U.P.) 43
Corporations as Citizens 44
Criteria of Validity of Law 44
False News Item about Judges 44
Freedom of Association 44
Freedom of Expression 45
Freedom of Movement 45
Freedom of Profession 46
Freedom of Residence 46
Government Advertisements 47
Ivory Import 47
Judicial Officers 47
Letter by Employee against the Organisation 47
Licences and Permits for Carrying Trade 47
Press 48
Price Fixation 48
Reasonable Restrictions 48
Relationship with Articles 21 and 22 48
Right of Minority to Administer Educational Institution 49
Right to Know 49
Right to Carry on Business 49

Right to Practise Medicine   49
Right to Pray   50
Right to Practise Profession   50
State Acts: Educational Institution   50
Substantive and Procedural Aspects   50
Test of Reasonableness   50
Total Prohibition   51
Trial by Media   51
Unincorporated Associations   51
20. **Protection in respect of conviction for offences**   52
Applicability   52
Clash between Fundamental Rights   52
Commencement of Protection   52
Compulsion to be a Witness   52
Double Jeopardy   53
Foreign Exchange Regulation Act, 1973   53
No Right in Procedure at Law   53
Penalty not Prescribed   54
Protection against Self-incrimination   54
Scope of Article 20   54
Testimonial Compulsion for the Accused   54
To be a Witness   54
21. **Protection of life and personal liberty**   54
AIDS Patient and Employment   54
Arrest   54
Assault on Child   54
Atomic Energy   55
Bail   55
Beauty Contests   55
Child Offenders   55
Compensation   55
Cruel Punishment   55
Custodial Death   55
Death Sentence   55
Debtor and Article 21   56
Delay in Bringing to Trial   56
Delay in Execution   56
Ecology : Ecological Balance   56
Ecology and "Public Trust" Doctrine   56
Environment   56
Environment: Hazardous Chemicals   56
Environment : Precautionary Principle   57
Fair Procedure   57
Fair Trial   57
Foreign Travel   57
Forests   57
Handcuffing   57
Health   57
Housing   57
Illegal Detention   58
Illegal Encroachment   58

Inhuman Treatment 58
Insane Person 58
Irish Constitution 58
Legal Aid 59
Livelihood 59
Medical aid in Government Hospitals 59
Medical Confidentiality 59
Medical Test 59
Minimum Punishment 60
Natural Justice 60
Non-revision of Pay Scale 60
Obstruction of Movement 60
Oppression of Peasants 60
Passport 60
Paternity of Child 60
Personal Liberty: Women 60
Police Atrocities 61
Position in USA 61
Preventive Detention 61
Prison Restrictions 61
Prisoners: Classification 61
Prisoners: Interview 61
Prisoners: Torture 61
Prisoners: Wrongful Detention 62
Privacy 62
Private Industries and Pollution 62
Prostitution 62
Public Hanging 62
Public Trial 62
Punishment for Attempted Suicide 63
Radiation (X-ray) 63
Right of Appeal 63
Right of Convict 63
Right to Die (Provision in I.P.C.) 63
Right to Life and Personal Liberty 63
Right to Fair Trial 63
Right to Life: Various Rights Included 63
Right to Livelihood or Work 65
Right to Life and Liberty 65
Right to Speedy Trial 65
Right to Work 65
Scope of Article 21 65
Scheduled Tribes Women 66
Sexual Harassment 66
Smoking in Public Place 66
Solitary Confinement 66
Speedy Justice 66
Speedy Trial 66
Summary Dismissal of Appeal 66
Telephone Tapping 66
Traffic Control 67

Undertrial Prisoners   67
Water   67
21A. **Right to education**   67
Right to Education   67
22. **Protection against arrest and detention in certain cases**   67
Analysis of Provision   68
"Arrest": Meaning Thereof   69
Article 21 may Supplement Article 22   69
Consideration of Representation   69
Delay   69
Documents   69
Information about Grounds of Arrest   69
Language   70
Preventive Detention   70
Production of Accused before the Nearest Magistrate   70
Representation: Preventive Detention   70
Right of Detenu   71
Right to Consult and to be Defended by Legal Practitioner
of his Choice   71

Right against Exploitation

23. **Prohibition of traffic in human beings and forced labour**   71
Child Labour   71
Children of Prostitutes   71
Scope   71
Traffic in Human Beings   72
24. **Prohibition of employment of children in factories, etc.**   72
Prohibition of Child Labour   72
Prohibition of Work in Construction Industry   72
Prohibition of Hazardous Employment   72
Random Home and Observation Home   72

Right to Freedom of Religion

25. **Freedom of conscience and free profession, practice and
propagation of religion**   72
Ananda Marg   73
Charity   73
Minority Institutions   73
Priests   73
Regulation by the State   73
Religion   74
Religious Freedom   74
Restrictions that can be Imposed   75
Scope and Object   75
Use of Loudspeaker   75
26. **Freedom to manage religious affairs**   75
Administration of Property of Religious Endowments   75
Affairs of Religion   76
Denomination   76
Directive Principles   76
Right to Own Property   76
Rituals   76

Scope and Object 77

Speedy Trial 77

27. **Freedom as to payment of taxes for promotion of any particular religion** 77

Imposition of Fee 77

28. **Freedom as to attendance at religious instruction or religious worship in certain educational institutions** 77

Religious Instructions 77

Right to Administer Minority Institutions 77

Cultural and Educational Rights

29. **Protection of interests of minorities** 78

Minorities 78

Regional Language 79

30. **Right of minorities to establish and administer educational institutions** 79

Condition as to Admission Fees 79

Conditions for Aid or Recognition 79

Conditions: Void 79

Crucial Words 80

Educational Standards 80

Maladministration 80

Minorities 80

Minorities Based on Religion or Language 81

Regulation by the State 81

Regulatory Laws 81

Requirements of Regulation 82

Right: Not Absolute 82

Right to Receive Aid 82

Scope 82

Standards 83

31. **Compulsory acquisition of property.—[*Repealed*]** 83

Saving of Certain Laws

31A. **Saving of laws providing for acquisition of estates, etc.** 83

Land Reform Legislation 84

31B. **Validation of certain Acts and Regulations** 85

Validity of Article 31B 86

Constitutional Validity of a Statute 86

31C. **Saving of laws giving effect to certain Directive Principles** 86

31D. **Saving of laws in respect of anti-national activities.—[*Repealed*]** 86

Right to Constitutional Remedies

32. **Remedies for enforcement of rights conferred by this Part** 86

Basic Feature of Constitution 87

Certiorari 87

Child Prostitution 87

Closure of Industry 87

Commissioner 87

Compensation 88

Composite Petition 88

Contempt 88

Continuing *Mandamus* 88

Counter-affidavits: Detention 88

Damages 88

Death in Custody   88
Detention   88
Doctrine of *Parens Patriae*   88
Earlier Decision   89
Estoppel against Petitioner   89
Estoppel against State   89
False Plea   89
Infringement of Fundamental Right   89
Introduction of Bill in the Legislature   89
Laches   89
Law Making Power   90
Legislation on Personal Law   90
Limits of Writ Jurisdiction   90
Locus Standi   90
Misuse of PIL   90
Mandamus   90
Natural Justice   91
PIL   91
Pleadings   91
Policy of Government   91
Political Question   91
Pollution   91
Price Fixation   91
Prostitutes' Children   92
Public Interest Litigation   92
Relief   92
Res Judicata   93
Scope of Article 32   93
Service Matters   93
Sovereign Power of Legislature   94
Stock Exchange   94
Supreme Court and High Court: Concurrent Jurisdiction   94
Variety of Other Rights   94
Writ Jurisdiction   95
Writ Petition   95
Writ Petition by Workers in Winding up Proceedings   95
Writ Petition to Determine Age of Chief Justice of India   95
32A. **Constitutional validity of State laws not to be considered in
proceedings under article 32.—[*Repealed*]**   95
33. **Power of Parliament to modify the rights conferred by this Part
in their application to Forces, etc.**   95
Effect   96
Parliamentary Legislation and Fundamental Rights   96
Police Forces (Restriction of Rights) Act, 1966   96
Scope   96
Writs against Courts Martial   96
34. **Restriction on rights conferred by this Part while martial law
is in force in any area**   97
35. **Legislation to give effect to the provisions of this Part**   97
Article 35 and Jammu and Kashmir Constitution   98
Public Safety: Preventive Detention   98

PART IV
DIRECTIVE PRINCIPLES OF STATE POLICY

36. **Definition** 98
    State 98
37. **Application of the principles contained in this Part** 98
    Directive Principles and UN Convention 98
    Effect: The Positive Aspect 98
    Fundamental Rights under Article 37 and Validity of Constitution
        42nd Amendment 99
    Harmony 99
    Scope and Object: The Negative Aspect 99
38. **State to secure a social order for the promotion of welfare of
    the people** 100
    Equality before Law 100
    Casual Labour 100
39. **Certain principles of policy to be followed by the State** 100
    Child Labour: Employment of Parent 101
    Equal Pay for Equal Work 101
    Object of Article 39A 102
    Prices 102
39A. **Equal justice and free legal aid** 102
    Legal Aid 102
40. **Organisation of village panchayats** 103
    Organisation of Village Panchayat 103
41. **Right to work, to education and to public assistance in certain cases** 103
    Reservation 103
    Right to Education 103
42. **Provision for just and humane conditions of work and maternity relief** 103
    Bonded Labour 103
    Maternity Benefits 103
43. **Living wage, etc., for workers** 104
    Casual Labour 104
    Revised Pension Formula 104
43A. **Participation of workers in management of industries** 104
    Non-workman Directors: Banking 104
43B. **Promotion of co-operative societies** 104
44. **Uniform civil code for the citizens** 104
    Personal Law 104
    Religious Freedom 105
    Religious Trusts 105
    Uniform Civil Code 105
45. **Provision for early childhood care and education to children
    below the age of six years** 106
    Right to Education 106
46. **Promotion of educational and economic interests of Scheduled
    Castes, Scheduled Tribes and other weaker sections** 106
47. **Duty of the State to raise the level of nutrition and the standard
    of living and to improve public health** 106
    Grant of Liquor Licence 107
48. **Organisation of agriculture and animal husbandry** 107
    Prohibition on Slaughter of Cows and Calves 107
48A. **Protection and improvement of environment and safeguarding
    of forests and wild life** 107

Environment Protection and Social Development 107
49. **Protection of monuments and places and objects of national importance** 107
    Museum Trust: Public Interest Litigation 108
50. **Separation of judiciary from executive** 108
    Appointment of Judges in Higher Judiciary 108
    Court and Legislature 108
    Separation of Powers 108
51. **Promotion of international peace and security** 108
    Extradition 108
    International Law and National Law (Municipal Law) 108

PART IVA
FUNDAMENTAL DUTIES

51A. **Fundamental duties** 109
    Environment 109
    Fundamental Duties and their Enforcement 110
    Scope 110
    Striving towards Excellence 110
    Use and Interpretation 110

PART V
THE UNION
CHAPTER I
THE EXECUTIVE
The President and Vice-President

52. **The President of India** 110
53. **Executive power of the Union** 111
    Executive Power 111
    Martial Law and Presidential Order 111
54. **Election of President** 111
55. **Manner of election of President** 112
56. **Term of office of President** 112
57. **Eligibility for re-election** 113
58. **Qualifications for election as President** 113
59. **Conditions of President's office** 113
60. **Oath or affirmation by the President** 113
61. **Procedure for impeachment of the President** 113
62. **Time of holding election to fill vacancy in the office of President
    and the term of office of person elected to fill casual vacancy** 114
63. **The Vice-President of India** 114
64. **The Vice-President to be *ex-officio* Chairman of the Council of States** 114
65. **The Vice-President to act as President or to discharge his functions
    during casual vacancies in the office, or during the absence,
    of President** 114
66. **Election of Vice-President** 115
67. **Term of office of Vice-President** 115
68. **Time of holding election to fill vacancy in the office of Vice-President
    and the term of office of person elected to fill casual vacancy** 115
69. **Oath or affirmation by the Vice-President** 116
70. **Discharge of President's functions in other contingencies** 116
71. **Matters relating to, or connected with, the election of a President
    or Vice-President** 116

72. Power of President to grant pardons, etc., and to suspend, remit
    or commute sentences in certain cases 116
    New Commonwealth 117
    Position Elsewhere 118
    Presidential Clemency and Death Sentence 118
    Remission of Sentence 118
    Stay 118
73. Extent of executive power of the Union 118
    Powers of President to Consult Supreme Court 119

Council of Ministers

74. Council of Ministers to aid and advise President 119
    Advice of Cabinet 119
    Cabinet Government 119
    Confidentiality of Cabinet Decisions 120
75. Other provisions as to Ministers 120
    Principle of Collective Responsibility – Object of 121

The Attorney-General for India

76. Attorney-General for India 121

Conduct of Government Business

77. Conduct of business of the Government of India 121
78. Duties of Prime Minister as respects the furnishing of information
    to the President, etc. 122
    Cabinet Secrecy 122

CHAPTER II
PARLIAMENT
General

79. Constitution of Parliament 122
80. Composition of the Council of States 123
81. Composition of the House of the People 123
82. Readjustment after each census 124
83. Duration of Houses of Parliament 125
84. Qualification for membership of Parliament 125
85. Sessions of Parliament, prorogation and dissolution 125
86. Right of President to address and send messages to Houses ... 126
87. Special address by the President 126
88. Rights of Ministers and Attorney-General as respects Houses . 126

Officers of Parliament

89. The Chairman and Deputy Chairman of the Council of States ... 126
90. Vacation and resignation of, and removal from, the office of
    Deputy Chairman 126
91. Power of the Deputy Chairman or other person to perform
    the duties of the office of, or to act as, Chairman 127
92. The Chairman or the Deputy Chairman not to preside while a
    resolution for his removal from office is under consideration 127
93. The Speaker and Deputy Speaker of the House of the People ... 127
94. Vacation and resignation of, and removal from, the offices of
    Speaker and Deputy Speaker 127
95. Power of the Deputy Speaker or other person to perform the
    duties of the office of, or to act as, Speaker 128
96. The Speaker or the Deputy Speaker not to preside while a
    resolution for his removal from office is under consideration 128

97. Salaries and allowances of the Chairman and Deputy Chairman
     and the Speaker and Deputy Speaker   128
98. Secretariat of Parliament   128

Conduct of Business

99. Oath or affirmation by members   128
100. Voting in Houses, power of Houses to act notwithstanding
     vacancies and quorum   129

Disqualifications of Members

101. Vacation of seats   129
102. Disqualifications for membership   130
        Code of Conduct   130
        Material Date   130
        Office of Profit   131
        Principle Debarring Holders of Office of Profit   131
103. Decision on questions as to disqualifications of members   131
        Office of Profit   131
104. Penalty for sitting and voting before making oath or affirmation
     under article 99 or when not qualified or when disqualified   131

Powers, Privileges and Immunities of Parliament and its Members

105. Powers, privileges, etc., of the Houses of Parliament and of the
     members and committees thereof   131
        Constitution (Thirty-third Amendment) Act, 1974   132
        Effect of the Constitution (Forty-second) and (Forty-fourth)
            Amendment Acts   132
        Freedom of Speech   132
        Privileges, Power and Immunities of House of Legislators
            and Members   133
        Publication by or under the Authority of a House   133
        Publication of Proceedings   133
        Scope   133
106. Salaries and allowances of members   133

Legislative Procedure

107. Provisions as to introduction and passing of Bills   133
108. Joint sitting of both Houses in certain cases   134
109. Special procedure in respect of Money Bills   135
110. Definition of "Money Bills"   135
111. Assent to Bills   136

Procedure in Financial Matters

112. Annual financial statement   136
113. Procedure in Parliament with respect to estimates   137
114. Appropriation Bills   137
115. Supplementary, additional or excess grants   137
116. Votes on account, votes of credit and exceptional grants   138
117. Special provisions as to financial Bills   138

Procedure Generally

118. Rules of procedure   139
119. Regulation by law of procedure in Parliament in relation to
     financial business   139
120. Language to be used in Parliament   139
121. Restriction on discussion in Parliament   140
122. Courts not to inquire into proceedings of Parliament   140

CHAPTER III
LEGISLATIVE POWERS OF THE PRESIDENT
123. Power of President to promulgate Ordinances during recess of
Parliament 140
Effect of Duration 140
Re-promulgation 141
Scope 141

CHAPTER IV
THE UNION JUDICIARY
124. Establishment and Constitution of Supreme Court 141
Appointment of Judge 142
Consultation 143
125. Salaries, etc., of Judges 143
126. Appointment of acting Chief Justice 144
127. Appointment of *ad hoc* Judges 144
128. Attendance of retired Judges at sittings of the Supreme Court 144
129. Supreme Court to be a court of record 144
Contempt of Supreme Court 144
Contempt Power 144
Income-tax Tribunal 145
130. Seat of Supreme Court 145
131. Original jurisdiction of the Supreme Court 145
Dispute between Two States 145
Scope and Nature of Article 31 145
131A. Exclusive jurisdiction of the Supreme Court in regard to questions
as to constitutional validity of Central Laws.—[*Repealed*] 145
132. Appellate jurisdiction of Supreme Court in appeals from
High Courts in certain cases 145
133. Appellate jurisdiction of Supreme Court in appeals from
High Courts in regard to civil matters 147
Application of Constitutional Right 147
Building Plan 147
Interlocutory Appeal 147
Jurisdiction of Supreme Court 147
134. Appellate jurisdiction of Supreme Court in regard to criminal matters 147
Appeal against Conviction 148
Appellate Jurisdiction of Supreme Court: Quashing of F.I.R. 148
134A. Certificate for appeal to the Supreme Court 148
135. Jurisdiction and powers of the Federal Court under existing law
to be exercisable by the Supreme Court 149
136. Special leave to appeal by the Supreme Court 149
Appeal 149
Criminal Cases 149
Effect 149
Fraud 150
Grounds 150
Interference of Supreme Court in Service Matter 150
Maintenance Claim by Illegitimate Child 150
Power of Supreme Court 150
Question of Fact 150
Re-appreciation of Evidence 151

Relief   151
Remand of Matter   151
Scope   151
Service Matters   151
Special Leave Petition   151
When Leave may be Granted   151
When Leave may be Refused   152
137. **Review of judgments or orders by the Supreme Court**   **152**
Application for Review   152
Grounds   152
Review   152
Scope   152
Third Party   153
138. **Enlargement of the jurisdiction of the Supreme Court**   **153**
139. **Conferment on the Supreme Court of powers to issue certain writs** **153**
139A. **Transfer of certain cases**   **153**
Scope   153
140. **Ancillary powers of Supreme Court**   **153**
141. **Law declared by Supreme Court to be binding on all courts**   **154**
Binding Jurisdiction of the Supreme Court   154
Doctrine of *Stare Decisis*   154
Foreign Case Law – Precedent   154
Judicial Discipline   154
Law Declared   154
Obiter Dicta   155
Precedent   155
President: Observations made in Judgment   155
Procedure Value of a Decision   155
Reconsideration   155
Retrospective Operation   156
Scope   156
Stare Decisis   156
142. **Enforcement of decrees and orders of Supreme Court and orders**
as to discovery, etc.   **157**
Complete Justice   157
Elasticity   157
Power to do Complete Justice   157
Scope of the Relief   157
143. **Power of President to consult Supreme Court**   **157**
144. **Civil and judicial authorities to act in aid of the Supreme Court** **158**
144A. **Special provisions as to disposal of questions relating to**
constitutional validity of laws.—[*Repealed*]   **158**
145. **Rules of Court, etc.**   **158**
146. **Officers and servants and the expenses of the Supreme Court**   **160**
147. **Interpretation**   **160**

CHAPTER V
COMPTROLLER AND AUDITOR-GENERAL OF INDIA

148. **Comptroller and Auditor-General of India**   **160**
149. **Duties and powers of the Comptroller and Auditor-General**   **161**
150. **Form of accounts of the Union and of the States**   **161**
151. **Audit reports**   **161**

PART VI
THE STATES
CHAPTER I
GENERAL

152. Definition   162

CHAPTER II
THE EXECUTIVE
The Governor

153. Governors of States   162
154. Executive power of State   162
     Central Govt.'s Executive Power   162
155. Appointment of Governor   162
156. Term of office of Governor   162
157. Qualifications for appointment as Governor   163
158. Conditions of Governor's office   163
159. Oath or affirmation by the Governor   163
160. Discharge of the functions of the Governor in certain contingencies 163
161. Power of Governor to grant pardons, etc., and to suspend, remit
     or commute sentences in certain cases   163
162. Extent of executive power of State   164
     Duty of High Officers   164
     Executive Instructions   165

Council of Ministers

163. Council of Ministers to aid and advise Governor   165
     Classification of Orders   165
     Existing Ministry to Continue Until its Successor Assumes Charge   165
     Governor and the Cabinet   165
164. Other provisions as to Ministers   166

The Advocate-General for the State

165. Advocate-General for the State   167
     Appointment of Advocate-General   167

CONDUCT OF GOVERNMENT BUSINESS

166. Conduct of business of the Government of a State   167
167. Duties of Chief Minister as respects the furnishing of information
     to Governor, etc.   167
     Individual Officers   168

CHAPTER III
THE STATE LEGISLATURE
General

168. Constitution of Legislatures in States   168
169. Abolition or creation of Legislative Councils in States   169
170. Composition of the Legislative Assemblies   169
171. Composition of the Legislative Councils   170
172. Duration of State Legislatures   171
173. Qualification for membership of the State Legislature   172
174. Sessions of the State Legislature, prorogation and dissolution   172
     Dissolution of Assembly   172
     Endorsement of Legislative Bill   173
     Ground for Dissolution of Assembly – Immorality   173
     Meaning of Expression "The House" or "Either House"   173

175. Right of Governor to address and send messages to the
     House or Houses   173
176. Special address by the Governor   173
177. Rights of Ministers and Advocate-General as respects the Houses 174

                    Officers of the State Legislature

178. The Speaker and Deputy Speaker of the Legislative Assembly   174
179. Vacation and resignation of, and removal from, the offices of
     Speaker and Deputy Speaker   174
180. Power of the Deputy Speaker or other person to perform the
     duties of the office of, or to act as, Speaker   174
181. The Speaker or the Deputy Speaker not to preside while a
     resolution for his removal from office is under consideration   175
182. The Chairman and Deputy Chairman of the Legislative Council   175
183. Vacation and resignation of, and removal from, the offices of
     Chairman and Deputy Chairman   175
184. Power of the Deputy Chairman or other person to perform the
     duties of the office of, or to act as, Chairman   175
185. The Chairman or the Deputy Chairman not to preside while a
     resolution for his removal from office is under consideration   175
186. Salaries and allowances of the Speaker and Deputy Speaker and
     the Chairman and Deputy Chairman   176
187. Secretariat of State Legislature   176

                    Conduct of Business

188. Oath or affirmation by members   176
189. Voting in Houses, power of Houses to act notwithstanding
     vacancies and quorum   176

                    Disqualifications of Members

190. Vacation of seats   177
191. Disqualifications for membership   178
192. Decision on questions as to disqualifications of members   178
     Election Commission's Opinion   179
193. Penalty for sitting and voting before making oath or affirmation
     under article 188 or when not qualified or when disqualified   179

     Powers, Privileges and Immunities of State Legislatures and their Members

194. Powers, privileges, etc., of the House of Legislatures and of the
     members and committees thereof   179
     Powers and Privileges of Member of Legislature   179
195. Salaries and allowances of members   179

                    Legislative Procedure

196. Provisions as to introduction and passing of Bills   180
197. Restriction on powers of Legislative Council as to Bills other
     than Money Bills   180
198. Special procedure in respect of Money Bills   181
199. Definition of "Money Bills"   181
200. Assent to Bills   182
     Governor's Assent to Bills   182
201. Bills reserved for consideration   182

                    Procedure in Financial Matters

202. Annual financial statement   183
203. Procedure in Legislature with respect to estimates   183

204. Appropriation Bills 184
205. Supplementary, additional or excess grants 184
206. Votes on account, votes of credit and exceptional grants 184
207. Special provisions as to financial Bills 185

Procedure Generally

208. Rules of procedure 185
209. Regulation by law of procedure in the Legislature of the State
in relation to financial business 186
210. Language to be used in the Legislature 186
211. Restriction on discussion in the Legislature 186
212. Courts not to inquire into proceedings of the Legislature 186
    Defects of Competence 187
    Scope 187

CHAPTER IV
LEGISLATIVE POWER OF THE GOVERNOR

213. Power of Governor to promulgate Ordinances during recess of
Legislature 187

CHAPTER V
THE HIGH COURTS IN THE STATES

214. High Courts for States 188
215. High Courts to be courts of record 189
    Contempt Power 189
216. Constitution of High Courts 189
217. Appointment and conditions of the office of a Judge of a High Court 189
    Status of Additional Judge 190
218. Application of certain provisions relating to Supreme Court to
High Courts 191
219. Oath or affirmation by Judges of High Courts 191
220. Restriction on practice after being a permanent Judge 191
221. Salaries etc., of Judges 191
222. Transfer of a Judge from one High Court to another 191
    Transfer of High Court Judges 192
223. Appointment of acting Chief Justice 192
224. Appointment of additional and acting Judges 192
224A. Appointment of retired Judges at sittings of High Courts 192
225. Jurisdiction of existing High Courts 192
226. Power of High Courts to issue certain writs 193
    Acquiescence 194
    Administrative Action 194
    Allotment of Land 194
    Alternative Remedy 195
    Amenability 195
    Arbitrariness 195
    Arrest 195
    Bail 195
    Bias 195
    Cases of Non-statutory Matters 195
    Certiorari 195
    Certiorari and Prohibition 195
    Civil Consequences 198
    Code of Civil Procedure 198

Compensation   198
Concession: Withdrawal   199
Consumer Disputes Redressal Commission   199
Court Martial   199
Criminal Investigation   199
Delay and Lachas   199
Discretion   199
Discrimination   200
Domestic Inquiry   200
Education: Medical Colleges   200
Encroachment and Natural Justice   200
Enforcement of an Act   201
Error of Law   201
Exercise of Power   201
Exercise of Writ Jurisdiction   201
Extraordinary Jurisdiction   201
Facts   201
Factual Inaccuracy   202
Fairness   202
Fraud   202
Futile Writ   202
Geographical Limits   202
Habeas Corpus   202
Illegal Order   204
Image of Judiciary   204
Interim Orders   204
Joint Petitions   204
Judicial Activism   204
Judicial Review *vis-à-vis* Legislative Policy   204
Jurisdiction   204
Jurisdiction of High Court   204
Jurisdictional Limitations   205
Laches   205
Legal Assistance   205
Legal Binding   205
Legitimate Expectation   205
Local Authority   205
Locus Standi   206
Mala Fides   206
Maintenance of Internal Security   206
Mandamus   206
Mining Lease   207
Natural Justice   207
Nemo Judex in *Causa Sua*   208
Notification   208
Order of Arbitral Tribunal   208
Particular Writs   208
Parties   208
Plea before Single Judge of High Court   208
Policy and Discretion   208
Pollution: Disposal of Petition by Consent   209

Premature Petition 209
Preventive Detention 209
Preventive Detentions: Stay 209
Prisons 209
Prohibition 209
\Promissory Estoppel 210
Public Interest Litigation 210
Public Interest Legislation 211
Quasi-judicial Authority 211
Quo Warranto 211
Reasonableness 211
Registered or Unregistered Association 212
Relief 212
Remedy: Extraordinary and Discretionary 212
Res Judicata 213
Restoration of Writ Petition 213
Scope of Article 226: High Court Power 213
Service Matters 214
State Government 214
Statutory Authority 214
Statutory Instrument 214
Suppression of Facts 214
Tender Forms 214
Tribunal 214
Unincorporated Association 214
Violation of Fundamental Rights 215
Writ Petition – Maintainability 215

Students and article 226

Circumstantial Evidence 215
Cross-examination 215
Difference from Criminal Trials 215
Disciplinary Action 215
Disciplinary Proceedings 215
Discretion of the Institution 216
Examinations 216
Illustrations of *Quasi*-judicial Acts 216
Inquiry when not Necessary 216
Natural Justice 216
Procedure 217
Punishment 217
Standard of Proof 217
Writ Jurisdiction 217

226A. **Constitutional validity of Central laws not to be considered in proceedings under Article 226.—[*Repealed*]** 217
227. **Power of superintendence over all courts by the High Court** 217
Correction of Facts 218
Jurisdiction of Court 219
Jurisdictional Defects 219
Locus Standi 219
Reasons 219
Scope and Nature of Article 227 219

Supervisory Jurisdiction   219
Writ Petition – Maintainability   219
228. Transfer of certain cases to High Court   219
228A. Special provisions as to disposal of questions relating to constitutional
      validity of State Laws.—[*Repealed*]   220
229. Officers and servants and the expenses of High Courts   220
230. Extension of jurisdiction of High Courts to Union territories   220
231. Establishment of a common High Court for two or more States   221
232. Interpretation.—[*Repealed*]   221

CHAPTER VI
SUBORDINATE COURTS

233. Appointment of district judges   221
      Appointment of District Judges   221
      Control of High Court Over Subordinate Judiciary   221
233A. Validation of appointments of, and judgments, etc., delivered by,
      certain district judges   221
234. Recruitment of persons other than district judges to the judicial service 222
235. Control over subordinate courts   222
      Adverse Remarks against Subordinate Judicial Officer   222
236. Interpretation   223
237. Application of the provisions of this Chapter to certain class or
      classes of magistrates   223

PART VII
THE STATES IN PART B OF THE FIRST SCHEDULE

238. Application of provisions of Part VI to States in Part B of the
      First Schedule.—[*Repealed*]   223

PART VIII
THE UNION TERRITORIES

239. Administration of Union territories   223
239A. Creation of local Legislatures or Council of Ministers or both for
      certain Union territories   223
239AA. Special provisions with respect to Delhi   224
239AB. Provision in case of failure of constitutional machinery   225
239B. Power of administrator to promulgate Ordinances during recess
      of Legislature   226
240. Power of President to make regulations for certain Union territories 227
241. High Courts for Union territories   228
242. Coorg.—[*Repealed*]   228

PART IX
THE PANCHAYATS

243. Definitions   228
243A. Gram Sabha   229
243B. Constitution of Panchayats   229
243C. Composition of Panchayats   229
243D. Reservation of seats   230
243E. Duration of Panchayats, etc.   230
243F. Disqualifications for membership   231
243G. Powers, authority and responsibilities of Panchayats   231
243H. Powers to impose taxes by, and Funds of, the Panchayats   231
243-I. Constitution of Finance Commission to review financial position   232
243J. Audit of accounts of Panchayats   232
243K. Elections to the Panchayats   232
243L. Application to Union territories   233

243M. Part not to apply to certain areas 233
243N. Continuance of existing laws and Panchayats 233
243-O. Bar to interference by courts in electoral matters 234
　　　Election Process: Gram Panchayats 234

PART IXA
THE MUNICIPALITIES

243P. Definitions 234
243Q. Constitution of Municipalities 235
243R. Composition of Municipalities 235
243S. Constitution and composition of Wards Committees, etc. 236
243T. Reservation of seats 236
243U. Duration of Municipalities, etc. 236
243V. Disqualifications for membership 237
243W. Powers, authority and responsibilities of Municipalities, etc. 237
243X. Power to impose taxes by, and Funds of, the Municipalities 237
243Y. Finance Commission 238
243Z. Audit of accounts of Municipalities 238
243ZA. Elections to the Municipalities 238
243ZB. Application to Union territories 238
243ZC. Part not to apply to certain areas 239
243ZD. Committee for district planning 239
243ZE. Committee for Metropolitan planning 240
243ZF. Continuance of existing laws and Municipalities 240
243ZG. Bar to interference by courts in electoral matters 240A

PART IXB
THE CO-OPERATIVE SOCIETIES

243ZH. Definitions 240A
243ZI. Incorporation of co-operative societies 240A
243ZJ. Number and term of members of board and its office bearers 240B
243ZK. Election of members of board 240B
243ZL. Supersession and suspension of board and interim management 240B
243ZM. Audit of accounts of co-operative societies 240C
243ZN. Convening of general body meetings 240C
243ZO. Right of a member to get information 240D
243ZP. Returns 240D
243.ZQ. Offences and penalties 240D
243ZR. Application to multi-State co-operative societies 240D
243ZS. Application to Union territories 241
243ZT. Continuance of existing laws 241

PART X
THE SCHEDULED AND TRIBAL AREAS

244. Administration of Scheduled Areas and Tribal Areas 241
244A. Formation of an autonomous State comprising certain tribal areas
　　　in Assam and creation of local Legislature or Council of Ministers
　　　or both therefor 241

PART XI
RELATIONS BETWEEN THE UNION AND THE STATES
CHAPTER I
LEGISLATIVE RELATIONS
Distribution of Legislative Powers

245. Extent of laws made by Parliament and by the Legislatures of States 242
　　　Conditional Legislation 242
　　　Conflict between Statutes 243

Constitutional Validity of Law   243
Excessive Delegation   243
Incidental Provisions   243
Legislation as the will of the People   243
Legislation Overriding Decision   243
Legislative Competence of State   244
Legislative Powers of Parliament and State Legislatures   244
Motive of Legislature   245
Power of Legislature   245
Rule-making Power   245
Sub-judice   245
Transgression of Limits of Power by Legislature   245
Validating Act   245

246. **Subject-matter of laws made by Parliament and by the Legislatures
of States**   245
Co-operative Societies   246
Doctrine of Pith and Substance   246
Effect of Declaration   247
Effect of the Words 'subject to'   247
Entry of Goods   247
Essential Commodities   247
Industries   248
Legislative List: Entries   248
Mala Fides   248
Mines   248
Preventive Detention   248
Reconciliation   249
Stamp Duties   249

247. **Power of Parliament to provide for the establishment of
certain additional courts**   249
248. **Residuary powers of legislation**   249
Constitutionality of   249
249. **Power of Parliament to legislate with respect to a matter in
the State List in the national interest**   249
250. **Power of Parliament to legislate with respect to any matter in
the State List if a Proclamation of Emergency is in operation**   250
251. **Inconsistency between laws made by Parliament under articles 249
and 250 and laws made by the Legislatures of States**   250
252. **Power of Parliament to legislate for two or more States by consent
and adoption of such legislation by any other State**   250
253. **Legislation for giving effect to international agreements** 251
254. **Inconsistency between laws made by Parliament and laws made
by the Legislatures of States**   251
Repugnancy   251
Union and State Legislation   252
255. **Requirements as to recommendations and previous sanctions
to be regarded as matters of procedure only**   253

CHAPTER II
ADMINISTRATIVE RELATIONS
General

256. **Obligation of States and the Union**   253
Comply with Article 256   253
257. **Control of the Union over States in certain cases**   254
257A. **Assistance to States by deployment of armed forces or other forces
of the Union.—[Repealed]**   254

258. Power of the Union to confer powers, etc., on States in certain cases 254
258A. Power of the States to entrust functions to the Union 255
259. Armed Forces in States in Part B of the First Schedule.—[*Repealed*] 255
260. Jurisdiction of the Union in relation to territories outside India 255
261. Public acts, records and judicial proceedings 255

Disputes relating to Waters

262. Adjudication of disputes relating to waters of inter-State rivers or river valleys 255

Co-ordination between States

263. Provisions with respect to an inter-State Council 255

PART XII
FINANCE, PROPERTY, CONTRACTS AND SUITS
CHAPTER I
FINANCE
General

264. Interpretation 256
265. Taxes not to be imposed save by authority of law 256
Fee 257
266. Consolidated Funds and public accounts of India and of the States 257
267. Contingency Fund 257

Distribution of Revenues between the Union and the States

268. Duties levied by the Union but collected and appropriated by the States 258
268A. Service tax levied by Union and collected and appropriated by the Union and the States 258
269. Taxes levied and collected by the Union but assigned to the States 258
270. Taxes levied and distributed between the Union and the States 259
271. Surcharge on certain duties and taxes for purposes of the Union 260
272. Taxes which are levied and collected by the Union and may be distributed between the Union and the States.—[*Repealed*] 260
273. Grants in lieu of export duty on jute and jute products 260
274. Prior recommendation of President required to Bills affecting taxation in which States are interested 260
275. Grants from the Union to certain States 261
276. Taxes on professions, trades, callings and employments 262
277. Savings 262
278. Agreement with States in Part B of the First Schedule with regard to certain financial matters.—[*Repealed*] 262
279. Calculation of "net proceeds", etc. 262
280. Finance Commission 262
281. Recommendations of the Finance Commission 263

Miscellaneous Financial Provisions

282. Expenditure defrayable by the Union or a State out of its revenues 263
283. Custody, etc., of Consolidated Funds, Contingency Funds and moneys credited to the public accounts 263
284. Custody of suitors' deposits and other moneys received by public servants and courts 264
285. Exemption of property of the Union from State taxation 264
286. Restrictions as to imposition of tax on the sale or purchase of goods 264
287. Exemption from taxes on electricity 265
288. Exemption from taxation by States in respect of water or electricity in certain cases 266
289. Exemption of property and income of a State from Union taxation 266
290. Adjustment in respect of certain expenses and pensions 266

290A. Annual payment to certain Devaswom Funds   267
291. Privy purse sums of Rulers.—[*Repealed*]   267

CHAPTER II
BORROWING

292. Borrowing by the Government of India   267
293. Borrowing by States   267

CHAPTER III
PROPERTY, CONTRACTS, RIGHTS, LIABILITIES,
OBLIGATIONS AND SUITS

294. Succession to property, assets, rights, liabilities and obligations
     in certain cases   267
295. Succession to property, assets, rights, liabilities and obligations
     in other cases   268
296. Property accruing by escheat or lapse or as bona vacantia   268
297. Things of value within territorial waters or continental shelf and
     resources of the exclusive economic zone to vest in the Union   269
298. Power to carry on trade, etc.   269
         Extra-territorial Operation   269
         Trade or Business   269
299. Contracts   269
         Doctrine of Indoor Management   270
300. Suits and proceedings   271
         Government Liability in Tort   271

CHAPTER IV
RIGHT TO PROPERTY

300A. Persons not to be deprived of property save by authority of law   271
         Deprivation of Property   272
         Nature of the Right   272
         Requisitioning   272
         Right to Property   272
         State Finance Corporations Act, 1951   273

PART XIII
TRADE, COMMERCE AND INTERCOURSE WITHIN
THE TERRITORY OF INDIA

301. Freedom of trade, commerce and intercourse   273
         Freedom of Inter-state & Intra-state Trade & Commerce   273
302. Power of Parliament to impose restrictions on trade, commerce
     and intercourse   273
303. Restrictions on the legislative powers of the Union and of the
     States with regard to trade and commerce   273
304. Restrictions on trade, commerce and intercourse among States   274
         Regulation and Prohibition must be Distinguished from Each Other   274
305. Saving of existing laws and laws providing for State monopolies   275
306. Power of certain States in Part B of the First Schedule to impose
     restrictions on trade and commerce.—[*Repealed*]   275
307. Appointment of authority for carrying out the purposes of
     articles 301 to 304   275

PART XIV
SERVICES UNDER THE UNION AND THE STATES
CHAPTER I
SERVICES

308. Interpretation   276

309. Recruitment and conditions of service of persons serving the
Union or a State   276
    Administrative Instructions   276
    Adverse Remarks in Confidential Report   276
    Appointment   277
    Armed Forces   277
    Compulsory Retirement   277
    Copywriters   277
    Criminal Proceedings   277
    Discrimination   277
    Examination   277
    Exploitation   278
    Gratuity   278
    High Court   278
    Interpretation   278
    Interview   278
    Lien   278
    Mandamus   279
    Officiating Post   279
    Privacy   279
    Promissory Estoppel   279
    Promotion   279
    Provident Fund   279
    Qualification   280
    Quota   280
    Railways   280
    Recruitment   280
    Retrenchment   280
    Rules   281
    Rule-making Power   281
    Salary   281
    Seniority   281
    Service Matters: Judicial Interference   282
    Temporary Service   282
    Termination   282
    Transfer   282
    Vacancies   282
310. Tenure of office of persons serving the Union or a State   283
    Contract   283
    Expiry of Term   283
    Pleasure: Doctrine of   283
311. Dismissal, removal or reduction in rank of persons employed in
civil capacities under the Union or a State   284
    Abolition of Post   284
    Adverse Remarks   285
    Administrative Tribunal   285
    Appeal   285
    Civil Post   285
    Compulsory Retirement   286
    Confirmation   286
    Copy of Report   286
    Criminal Proceedings   286

Date of Birth   286
Disciplinary Enquiry   287
Disciplinary Proceedings   287
Dismissal   287
Double Jeopardy   287
Fresh Inquiry   287
Inquiry   287
Legal Assistance   288
Malice   288
Misconduct   288
Opportunity   288
Penal Order   288
Reinstated Employee   289
Relief by Supreme Court   289
Removal   289
Seniority   289
Temporary Appointment   289
Tenure Post   290
Term : Expiry of   290
312. **All-India Services**   290
Central Staffing Scheme   290
312A. **Power of Parliament to vary or revoke conditions of service of officers of certain services**   290
High Court Judge belonging to Indian Civil Service: Pension   291
313. **Transitional provisions**   291
Dismissal of High Court Staff   292
Promotion to Posts of Assistant Commissioner of Income Tax   292
314. **Provision for protection of existing officers of certain services.— [Repealed]**   292

CHAPTER II
PUBLIC SERVICE COMMISSIONS
315. **Public Service Commissions for the Union and for the States**   292
Essential Qualification for Appointment   292
Seniority   292
316. **Appointment and term of office of members**   293
317. **Removal and suspension of a member of a Public Service Commission**   293
Misconduct   294
Object   295
Proportion   295
318. **Power to make regulations as to conditions of service of members and staff of the Commission**   295
319. **Prohibition as to the holding of offices by members of Commission on ceasing to be such members**   295
320. **Functions of Public Service Commissions**   296
321. **Power to extend functions of Public Service Commissions**   297
322. **Expenses of Public Service Commissions**   297
323. **Reports of Public Service Commissions**   298

PART XIVA
TRIBUNALS
323A. **Administrative tribunals**   298
Co-operative Societies   299

Interference by the Tribunal   299
323B. **Tribunals for other matters**   **299**
All Courts   301
Appeal to Supreme Court   301
Scope   301
Tribunals and Writs   301

PART XV
ELECTIONS

324. **Superintendence, direction and control of elections to be vested
in an Election Commission**   **302**
Articles 174 viz-a-viz Article 324—Scope   303
325. **No person to be ineligible for inclusion in, or to claim to be included
in a special, electoral roll on grounds of religion, race, caste or sex**   **303**
326. **Elections to the House of the People and to the Legislative
Assemblies of States to be on the basis of adult suffrage**   **303**
327. **Power of Parliament to make provision with respect to elections
to Legislatures**   **304**
Power of Parliament to Legislate Election Laws   304
328. **Power of Legislature of a State to make provision with respect
to elections to such Legislature**   **304**
329. **Bar to interference by courts in electoral matters**   **304**
329A. **Special provision as to elections to Parliament in the case of Prime
Minister and Speaker.—[*Repealed*]**   **304**

PART XVI
SPECIAL PROVISIONS RELATING TO CERTAIN CLASSES

330. **Reservation of seats for Scheduled Castes and Scheduled Tribes
in the House of the People**   **305**
331. **Representation of the Anglo-Indian community in the House
of the People**   **305**
332. **Reservation of seats for Scheduled Castes and Scheduled Tribes
in the Legislative Assemblies of the States**   **306**
333. **Representation of the Anglo-Indian community in the Legislative
Assemblies of the States**   **307**
334. **Reservation of seats and special representation to cease after
seventy years**   **307**
335. **Claims of Scheduled Castes and Scheduled Tribes to services and posts**   **308**
336. **Special provision for Anglo-Indian community in certain services**   **308**
337. **Special provision with respect to educational grants for the
benefit of Anglo-Indian community**   **309**
338. **National Commission for Scheduled Castes**   **309**
339. **Control of the Union over the administration of Scheduled
Areas and the welfare of Scheduled Tribes**   **312**
340. **Appointment of a Commission to investigate the conditions
of backward classes**   **312**
341. **Scheduled Castes**   **313**
342. **Scheduled Tribes**   **313**
Conversion   314
Finality of Presidential Order   314
Migrants Tribals   315
Scheduled Tribe –Acquisition of Status   315

PART   XVII
OFFICIAL   LANGUAGE
CHAPTER   I
LANGUAGE   OF   THE   UNION

343. Official language of the Union   315
344. Commission and Committee of Parliament on official language   315

CHAPTER II
REGIONAL LANGUAGES

345. Official language or languages of a State   316
     Language for Right to Information   317
346. Official language for communication between one State and
     another or between a State and the Union   317
347. Special provision relating to language spoken by a section of
     the population of a State   317

CHAPTER III
LANGUAGE OF THE SUPREME COURT, HIGH COURTS, ETC.

348. Language to be used in the Supreme Court and in the High Courts
     and for Acts, Bills, etc.   317
349. Special procedure for enactment of certain laws relating to language 318

CHAPTER IV
SPECIAL DIRECTIVES

350. Language to be used in representations for redress of grievances   318
350A. Facilities for instruction in mother-tongue at primary stage   318
350B. Special Officer for linguistic minorities   318
351. Directive for development of the Hindi language   318

PART XVIII
EMERGENCY PROVISIONS

352. Proclamation of Emergency   319
     Proclamation of Emergency   321
353. Effect of Proclamation of Emergency   321
354. Application of provisions relating to distribution of revenues
     while a Proclamation of Emergency is in operation   321
355. Duty of the Union to protect States against external aggression
     and internal disturbance   321
356. Provisions in case of failure of constitutional machinery in States   321
357. Exercise of legislative powers under Proclamation issued under
     article 356   324
     Judicial Review   324
     Judicial Review of Proclamation under Article 356   325
358. Suspension of provisions of article 19 during emergencies   325
359. Suspension of the enforcement of the rights conferred by
     Part III during emergencies   326
     Application of Article 359   327
359A. Application of this Part to the State of Punjab.—[*Repealed*]   327
360. Provisions as to financial emergency.—[*Repealed*]   327

PART XIX
MISCELLANEOUS

361. Protection of President and Governors and Rajpramukhs.—[*Repealed*] 328
361A. Protection of publication of proceedings of Parliament and
      State Legislatures   328

361B. Disqualification for appointment on remunerative political post   329
 362. Rights and privileges of Rulers of Indian States.—[*Repealed*]   329
 363. Bar to interference by courts in disputes arising out of certain
      treaties, agreements, etc.   329
          Dispute Arising Out of Treaties   330
363A. Recognition granted to Rulers of Indian States to cease and
      privy purses to be abolished   330
 364. Special provisions as to major ports and aerodromes   330
 365. Effect of failure to comply with, or to give effect to, directions
      given by the Union   330
 366. Definitions   331
          Clause (10): 'Existing Law'   333
          Clause (17)   334
          Clause (29A)   334
 367. Interpretation   334

PART XX
AMENDMENT OF THE CONSTITUTION
 368. Power of Parliament to amend the Constitution and procedure therefor 334
          Basic Features   335
          Object of this Proviso is to Give Effect to the Federal Principle 336

PART XXI
TEMPORARY, TRANSITIONAL AND SPECIAL PROVISIONS
 369. Temporary power to Parliament to make laws with respect to certain
      matters in the State List as if they were matters in the Concurrent List 336
 370. Temporary provisions with respect to the State of Jammu and Kashmir 337
 371. Special provision with respect to the States of Maharashtra and Gujarat 338
371A. Special provision with respect to the State of Nagaland   338
371B. Special provision with respect to the State of Assam   341
371C. Special provision with respect to the State of Manipur   341
371D. Special provisions with respect to the State of Andhra Pradesh   342
371E. Establishment of Central University in Andhra Pradesh   345
371F. Special provisions with respect to the State of Sikkim   345
371G. Special provision with respect to the State of Mizoram   347
371H. Special provision with respect to the State of Arunachal Pradesh   347
371-I. Special provision with respect to the State of Goa   348
 372. Continuance in force of existing laws and their adaptation   348
          Expression: "All the Laws in Force"   349
372A. Power of the President to adapt laws   349
 373. Power of President to make order in respect of persons under
      preventive detention in certain cases   349
 374. Provisions as to Judges of the Federal Court and proceedings
      pending in the Federal Court or before His Majesty in Council   350
 375. Courts, authorities and officers to continue to function subject
      to the provisions of the Constitution   350
 376. Provisions as to Judges of High Courts   350
 377. Provisions as to Comptroller and Auditor-General of India   351
 378. Provisions as to Public Service Commissions   351
378A. Special provisions as to duration of Andhra Pradesh
      Legislative Assembly   351

379. Provisions as to provincial Parliament and the Speaker and
     Deputy Speaker thereof.—[*Repealed*]   351
380. Provisions as to President.—[*Repealed*]   351
381. Council of Ministers of the President.—[*Repealed*]   351
382. Provisions as to provisional Legislatues for States in Part A of
     the First Schedule.—[*Repealed*]   352
383. Provisions as to Governors of Provinces.—[*Repealed*]   352
384. Council of Ministers of Governors.—[*Repealed*]   352
385. Provisions as to provisional Legislatures in States in Part B of
     the First Schedule.—[*Repealed*]   352
386. Council of Ministers for States in Part B of the First Schedule.—
     [*Repealed*]   352
387. Special provision as to determination of population for the
     purposes of certain elections.—[*Repealed*]   352
388. Provisions as to the filling of casual vacancies in the provisional
     Parliament and provisional Legislature of the States.—[*Repealed*] 352
389. Provisions as to Bills pending in the Dominion Legislature and
     in the Legislatures of Provinces and Indian States.—[*Repealed*] 352
390. Moneys received or raised or expenditure incurred between the
     commencement of the Constitution and the 31st day of
     March, 1950.—[*Repealed*]   352
391. Power of the President to amend the First and Fourth Schedules
     in certain contingencies.—[*Repealed*]   352
392. Power of the President to remove difficulties   352
     Adaptations to Provisions of the Constitution   352
     Provision for President   352

PART XXII
SHORT   TITLE,   COMMENCEMENT,   AUTHORITATIVE
TEXT   IN   HINDI   AND   REPEALS

393. Short title   353
394. Commencement   353
394A. Authoritative text in the Hindi language   353
395. Repeals   353
     Appeal Maintainable to Federal Court: Suit filed before Adoption
         of Constitution: Right of Appeal   353
FIRST SCHEDULE   354
   I. THE STATES   354
  II. THE UNION TERRITORIES   358
SECOND SCHEDULE   360
   PART A.— PROVISIONS AS TO THE PRESIDENT AND THE
           GOVERNORS OF STATES   360
   PART B.— [*Omitted*]   360
   PART C.— PROVISIONS AS TO THE SPEAKER AND THE DEPUTY
           SPEAKER OF THE HOUSE OF THE PEOPLE AND THE
           CHAIRMAN AND THE DEPUTY CHAIRMAN OF THE
           COUNCIL OF STATES AND THE SPEAKER AND THE
           DEPUTY SPEAKER OF THE LEGISLATIVE ASSEMBLY
           AND THE CHAIRMAN AND THE DEPUTY CHAIRMAN
           OF THE LEGISLATIVE COUNCIL OF A STATE   360
   PART D.— PROVISIONS AS TO THE JUDGES OF THE SUPREME COURT
           AND OF THE HIGH COURTS   361

PART E.— PROVISIONS AS TO THE COMPTROLLER AND
　　　　　AUDITOR-GENERAL OF INDIA　　　　　　　　363
THIRD SCHEDULE　　　　　　　　　　　　　　　　364
　　Forms of Oaths or Affirmations　　　　　　　　364
FOURTH SCHEDULE　　　　　　　　　　　　　　　366
　　Allocation of seats in the Council of States　　　366
FIFTH SCHEDULE　　　　　　　　　　　　　　　　368
　　Provisions as to the Administration and Control of Scheduled
　　Areas and Scheduled Tribes　　　　　　　　　　368
　　PART A.— General　　　　　　　　　　　　　　368
　　PART B.— ADMINISTRATION AND CONTROL OF SCHEDULED
　　　　　　AREAS AND SCHEDULED TRIBES　　　　369
　　PART C.— SCHEDULED AREAS　　　　　　　　　370
　　PART D.—AMENDMENT OF THE SCHEDULE　　　370
SIXTH SCHEDULE　　　　　　　　　　　　　　　　371
　　Provisions as to the Administration of Tribal Areas in the States
　　of Assam, Meghalaya, Tripura and Mizoram　　371
　　1. Autonomous districts and autonomous regions　371
　　2. Constitution of District Councils and Regional Councils　372
　　3. Powers of the District Councils and Regional Councils to make laws　374
　　4. Administration of justice in autonomous districts and
　　　autonomous regions　　　　　　　　　　　　375
　　5. Conferment of powers under the Code of Civil Procedure, 1908,
　　　and the Code of Criminal Procedure, 1898,2 on the Regional and
　　　District Councils and on certain courts and officers for the trial
　　　of certain suits, cases and offences　　　　　　378
　　6. Powers of the District Council to establish primary schools, etc.　379
　　7. District and Regional Funds　　　　　　　　379
　　8. Powers to assess and collect land revenue and to impose taxes　379
　　9. Licences or leases for the purpose of prospecting for, or extraction
　　　of, minerals　　　　　　　　　　　　　　　380
　10. Power of District Council to make regulations for the control of
　　　money-lending and trading by non-tribals　　　380
　11. Publication of laws, rules and regulations made under the Schedule　381
　12. Application of Acts of Parliament and of the Legislature of the
　　　State of Assam to autonomous districts and autonomous
　　　regions in the State of Assam　　　　　　　　381
　12A. Application of Acts of Parliament and of the Legislature of the
　　　State of Meghalaya to autonomous districts and autonomous
　　　regions in the State of Meghalaya　　　　　　382
　12AA. Application of Acts of Parliament and of the Legislature of the
　　　State of Tripura to the autonomous district and autonomous
　　　regions in the State of Tripura　　　　　　　382
　12B. Application of Acts of Parliament and of the Legislature of the
　　　State of Mizoram to autonomous districts and autonomous
　　　regions in the State of Mizoram　　　　　　　383
　13. Estimated receipts and expenditure pertaining to autonomous
　　　districts to be shown separately in the annual financial statement　383
　14. Appointment of Commission to inquire into and report on the
　　　administration of autonomous districts and autonomous regions　384

15. Annulment or suspension of acts and resolutions of District
    and Regional Councils 384
16. Dissolution of a District or a Regional Council 385
17. Exclusion of areas from autonomous districts in forming
    constituencies in such districts 386
18. [Omitted] 386
19. Transitional provisions 386
20. Tribal areas 387
20A. Dissolution of the Mizo District Council 388
20B. Autonomous regions in the Union territory of Mizoram to be
    autonomous districts and transitory provisions consequent thereto 389
20C. Interpretation 390
21. Amendment of the Schedule 390
SEVENTH SCHEDULE 391
    List I—Union List 391
    List II—State List 395
    List III—Concurrent List 399
EIGHTH SCHEDULE 401
    Languages 401
NINTH SCHEDULE 402
TENTH SCHEDULE 413
    Provisions as to disqualification on ground of defection 413
1. Interpretation 413
2. Disqualification on ground of defection 414
3. [Omitted] 414
4. Disqualification on ground of defection not to apply in case of merger 415
5. Exemption 415
6. Decision on questions as to disqualification on ground of defection 415
7. Bar of jurisdiction of courts 415
8. Rules 415
ELEVENTH SCHEDULE 416
TWELFTH SCHEDULE 417
APPENDIX I
    THE CONSTITUTION (APPLICATION TO JAMMU
    AND KASHMIR) ORDER, 1954 418
APPENDIX II
    RE-STATEMENT, WITH REFERENCE TO THE PRESENT
    TEXT OF THE CONSTITUTION, OF THE EXCEPTIONS
    AND MODIFICATIONS SUBJECT TO WHICH THE
    CONSTITUTION APPLIES TO THE STATE OF
    JAMMU AND KASHMIR 432
APPENDIX III
    EXTRACTS FROM THE CONSTITUTION (FORTY-FOURTH
    AMENDMENT) ACT, 1978 447

Subject Index 448
Recent Case-Laws on Constitution 461
Select Landmark Judgments 462
Salary of Five Pillars of India appointed by President under his Hand and Seal 469
Glossary of Constitutional Terms 470

TABLE OF CASES

A

A. Hansavani v. State of Tamil Nadu, JT 1994 (4) SC 651   93
A. Periakaruppan (Minor) v. State of Tamil Nadu, AIR 1971 SC 2303:
    (1971) 2 SCR 430: 1971 (2) SCJ 222: (1971) 2 Andh WR (SC) 65:
    (1971) 2 Mad LJ (SC) 65   37
A. Sanjeevi Naidu v. State of Madras, (1970) 1 SCC 443: (1970) 3 SCR 505:
    AIR 1970 SC 1102   166
A. Suresh v. State of Tamil Nadu, AIR 1997 SC 1889: (1997) 1 SCC 319:
    1997 AIR SCW 1640: 1998 BRLJ 102: 1997 (1) CTC 463: JT 1996 (10) SC 542:
    1997 (2) Mad LJ 23: 1997 (2) Mad LW 551: 1997 (2) Supreme 56   42
A. Thangal Kunju Musaliar v. M. Venkatachalam Potti, (1955) 2 SCR 1196:
    AIR 1956 SC 246: (1956) 29 ITR 349: 1956 SCA 259: 1956 SCJ 323   29
A.A. Mulla v. State of Maharashtra, AIR 1997 SC 1441: (1996) 11 SCC 606   54
A.B.K. Singh v. Union of India, AIR 1981 SC 298: (1981) 1 SCC 246: (1981) 2 SCR 185   37
A.D.M. Jabalpur v. Shukla, AIR 1976 SC 1207: (1976) 2 SCC 521: 1976 Cr LJ 945   97
A.I.I.M.S. Students Union v. A.I.I.M.S., AIR 2001 SC 3262: 2001 AIR SCW 3143:
    2001 (4) All WC 2886: JT 2001 (7) SC 12: (2002) 1 SCC 428: 2001 (4) SCJ 590:
    2001 (4) SCT 150: (2001) 5 SCALE 430: (2001) 4 Serv LR 134:
    2001 (6) Supreme 367   103
A.I.S.B.O.F. v. Union of India, (1990) Supp SCC 336: 1991 SCC (L&S) 429   89
A.K. Bindal v. Union of India, AIR 2003 SC 2189: (2003) 5 SCC 163:
    (2003) SCC (L&S) 620: (2003) 2 LLN 1122   60
A.K. Roy v. Union of India, AIR 1982 SC 710: (1982) 1 SCC 271:
    1982 Cr LJ 340   61, 141, 201, 324
A.M. Mathur v. Pramod, (1990) 1 UJ SC 595: (1990) 2 SCC 533: AIR 1990 SC 1737   151
A.P.S.E.B. v. Azami, (1992) Supp 1 SCC 660: (1992) 19 ATC 862:
    AIR 1992 SC 1542: (1992) 1 LLN 381   345
A.R. Antulay v. R.S. Nayak, AIR 1988 SC 1531: (1988) 2 SCC 602:
    1988 SCC (Cri) 372   157
Aashirwad Films v. Union of India, (2007) 6 SCC 624: 2007 AIR SCW 3603   95
Abdul Ghani v. State of Jammu and Kashmir, AIR 1971 SC 1217: (1971) 3 SCR 275   98
Abdul Hakim v. State of Bihar, (1961) SCR 610: AIR 1961 SC 448: (1961) 1 Cr LJ 573   91
Abdul Kadir v. State of Kerala, AIR 1976 SC 182: (1976) 3 SCC 219:
    1976 Tax LR 1293   253
Abdul Latif v. State of Bihar, AIR 1964 Pat 393: ILR 45 Pat 127   32
Abdul Sattar Haji Ibrahim Patel v. State of Gujarat, AIR 1965 SC 810:
    (1964) 5 Guj LR 439: 1964 Cur LJ (SC) 200: 1964 (2) SCJ 461:
    1964 Mad LJ (Cri) 542: (1965) 1 Cr LJ 759: 1965 SCD 976   12
Abdul Shakur v. Rikhab Chand (Election Tribunal, Ajmer), AIR 1958 SC 52:
    1958 SCR 387: 1958 SCA 279: 1958 SCJ 329: (1958) 1 Mad LJ (SC) 88   131
Abhay v. Bhave, 1991 (1) SCJ 607: (1991) 1 SCC 500: AIR 1991 SC 397   209
Acharya Jagadishwarananda Avadhuta v. Commissioner of Police, Calcutta,
    AIR 1990 Cal 336: 1990 (2) Cal LT 212   76
Acharya Jagdishwaranand Avadhuta v. Commissioner of Police, Calcutta,
    AIR 1984 SC 51: (1983) 4 SCC 522: 1983 Cr LJ 1872: 1984 Cr LR (SC) 37:
    1984 SCC (Cri) 1: 1984 (1) Crimes 318: 1984 Cr App R (SC) 185   73, 76
Acharya Maharajshri Narendra Prasadji Anandprasadji Maharaj v. State of Gujarat,
    AIR 1974 SC 2098: (1975) 1 SCC 11: (1975) 2 SCR 317   73
Achudan v. Union of India, 1976 1 SCWR 80: (1976) 2 SCC 780:
    AIR 1976 SC 1179: (1976) 2 SCR 769   96
Additional District Magistrate, Jabalpur v. Shivakant Shukla, AIR 1976 SC 1207:
    (1976) 2 SCC 521: 1976 Cr LJ 945: 1976 UJ (SC) 610: 1976 SC Cr R 277:
    1976 SCC (Cri) 448: 1976 Cr App R (SC) 298: (1976) 3 SCR 929:
    1976 Supp SCR 172   2, 71, 111, 206, 243, 254, 327, 336
Additional Secretary v. Alka Subhash Gadia, (1990) 2 SCALE 1352:
    (992) Supp 1 SCC 496: 1992 SCC (Cri) 301   203

xli

Additional Secretary v. Gadia, 1991 (1) SCJ 200: (1992) Supp 1 SCC 496:
    1992 SCC (Cri) 301   209
Advisory Board v. State of Kerala, (1991) 2 SCC 1   87
Advocate M.L. George v. High Court of Kerala, AIR 2010 Ker 134   179
Aggarwal v. Union of India, (1992) 2 UJ SC 266: AIR 1992 SC 1872:
    1992 Lab IC 1807: (1992) 4 SLR 583   283, 288, 290
Agricultural Market Committee v. Shalimar Chemical Works Ltd.,
    AIR 1997 SC 2502: (1997) 5 SCC 516: 1997 AIR SCW 2443: 1997 (3) APLJ 10:
    JT 1997 (5) SC 272: (1997) 4 SCALE 93: 1997 (4) Supreme 575   243
Ahmed Noormohmed Bhatti v. State of Gujarat, AIR 2005 SC 2115:
    2005 Cr LJ 2157: 2005 AIR SCW 1923: 2005 (29) All Ind Cas 746:
    2005 (2) BLJR 901: 2005 (2) Crimes 26: JT 2005 (3) SC 484: 2005 (31) OCR 24:
    (2005) 3 SCC 647: (2005) 3 SCALE 300: 2005 (2) Supreme 643   27
Ahmedabad Municipal Corporation v. Nawab Khan Gulab Khan,
    AIR 1997 SC 152: (1997) 11 SCC 121: 1996 AIR SCW 4315:
    1997 (1) All MR 537: 1997 (1) Guj LH 438: JT 1996 (10) SC 485   58, 200
Ahmedabad St. Xavier College Society v. State of Gujarat, (1974) 1 SCC 717:
    AIR 1974 SC 1389: 1974 (2) SCJ 381: (1975) 1 SCR 173   78, 81, 83
Ahmedabad Women Action Group (AWAG) v. Union of India,
    (1997) 3 SCC 573: AIR 1997 SC 3614: 1997 AIR SCW 1620:
    JT 1997 (3) SC 171: 1997 (3) SCJ 107: (1997) 2 SCR 389:
    (1997) 2 SCALE 381: 1997 (2) Supreme 670: 1997 (1) UJ (SC) 548   90, 105
Air India Statutory Corporation v. United Labour Union, AIR 1997 SC 645:
    (1997) 9 SCC 377: 1977 Lab IC 365: (1997) 1 LLJ 1113   65, 98
Air India v. Nerqesh Mirza, (1981) 4 SCC 335: AIR 1981 SC 1829:
    (1981) 2 LLJ 314: 1981 Lab IC 1313   28
Ajay Hasia v. Khalid Mujib, AIR 1981 SC 487: (1981) 1 SCC 722:
    (1981) 2 SCR 79: (1981) 1 LLJ 103   15
Ajay Kumar Agrawal (Dr.) v. State of Uttar Pradesh, AIR 1991 SC 498:
    1991 (17) All LR 452: JT 1991 (1) SC 168: (1991) 1 SCC 636:
    1991 (1) Serv LR 776: 1991 (1) UJ (SC) 54   88
Ajay Kumar Mittal v. Haryana Agricultural University, Hissar, AIR 1984 P&H 278   20
Ajay Kumar v. Chandigarh Administration Union Territory, Chandigarh,
    AIR 1983 P&H 8: ILR (1983) 2 P&H 297   20
Ajay Kumar v. State of Bihar, JT 1994 (3) SC 662: (1994) 4 SCC 401:
    1994 AIR SCW 2515   33
Ajeet Singh Singhvi v. State of Rajasthan, (1991) Supp 1 SCC 343:
    1991 SCC (L&S) 1026: (1991) 16 ATC 935   278
Ajit Singh v. State of Punjab, AIR 1967 SC 856: (1967) 2 SCR 143   21
Ajit Singh v. State of Punjab, AIR 1999 SC 3471: (1999) 7 SCC 209:
    1999 SCC (L&S) 1239   38
Akbar v. Union of India, AIR 1962 SC 70: (1962) 1 SCR 779: 1962 MPLJ 277   13
Akhil Bharatiya Soshit Karamchari Sangh (Railway) v. Union of India,
    AIR 1981 SC 298: (1981) 1 SCC 246: 1980 Lab IC 1325: (1981) 1 LLJ 209:
    (1981) 1 LLN 27: 1981 SCC (Lab) 50: 1981 Serv LJ 734: (1981) 2 SCR 185   99
Aldo Maria Patroni v. E.G. Kesavan, AIR 1965 Ker 75: 1964 Ker LT 791:
    ILR (1964) 2 Ker 478: 1964 Ker LJ 1055: (1964) 2 Ker LR 67   81
Ali Johad Naqvi v. Allahabad Development Authority, AIR 2001 All 172:
    2001 All LJ 1340: 2001 (1) All Rent Cas 524: 2001 (43) All LR 190:
    2001 (2) All WC 890   213
Alka Ceramics, Piplodi, Himatnagar v. Gujarat State Financial Corporation,
    Ahmedabad, AIR 1990 Guj 105 (DB)   273
All Delhi Cycle Rickshaw Operators Union v. Municipal Corporation of Delhi,
    AIR 1987 SC 648: (1987) 1 SCC 371: JT 1987 (1) SC 66: 1986 (4) Supreme 461:
    (1987) 4 (1) IJ Rep 38: 1987 (1) Land LR 297: 1987 (1) SCJ 114:
    (1987) 1 UJ (SC) 496: (1987) 1 MCC 19   48
All India Bank Employees' Association v. National Industrial Tribunal, AIR 1962 SC 171:
    (1962) 3 SCR 269: (1962) 32 Comp Cas 414: (1961) 2 LLJ 385   45, 51

All India Bank Officers' Confederation *v.* Union of India, AIR 1989 SC 2045   104
All India Council for Technical Education *v.* Ombir Kaushik,
   AIR 2006 (NOC) 496 (Del)   204
All India Railway Institute Employees' Association *v.* Union of India,
   AIR 1990 SC 952: (1990) 2 SCC 542: (1990) 13 ATC 691   280
All India Reserve Bank Retired Officers Assocn. *v.* Union of India,
   AIR 1992 SC 767: (1992) Supp 1 SCC 664: 1992 Lab IC 633   280
All Saints High School *v.* Government of Andhra Pradesh, AIR 1980 SC 1042:
   (1980) 2 SCC 478: (1980) 1 Serv LR 716: 1980 (2) SCJ 273   80, 81, 83
Altemesh Rein *v.* Union of India, AIR 1988 SC 1768: (1988) 4 SCC 54:
   1988 SCC (Cri) 900   57
Amar Singh *v.* State of Rajasthan, (1955) 2 SCR 803   246
Amarinder Singh (Capt) *v.* Parkash Singh Badal, (2009) 6 SCC 260   63
Ambica Mills *v.* Bhatt, AIR 1961 SC 970: (1961) 3 SCR 220: (1961) 1 LLJ 1   198
Ameerunnissa Begum *v.* Mahboob Begum, (1953) SCR 404: AIR 1953 SC 91:
   ILR 1953 Hyd 98: 1953 SCJ 61: 1953 SCA 565   30
Amina (in re:), AIR 1992 Bom 214: 1991 (3) Bom CR 531: 1992 (1) Mah LR 873   349
Amrit Banaspati Co. Ltd. *v.* State of Punjab, (1992) 2 SCC 411: AIR 1992 SC 1075:
   1992 AIR SCW 953: (1992) 2 SC 217: (1992) 2 SCR 13:
   1992 (85) STC 493: 1992 (110) Taxation 60: 1992 (1) UJ SC 599   279
Amrit Lal Ambalal Patel *v.* Himathbai Gomanbhai Patel, AIR 1968 SC 1455:
   (1969) 1 SCR 277   130
Amritsar Municipality *v.* State of Punjab, AIR 1969 SC 1100: (1969) 1 SCC 475:
   1969 3 SCR 447   44
Anamalai University *v.* Secretary of Govt. Inf. and Tourism Department,
   (2009) 4 SCC 590   243
Anand Prakash *v.* State of Uttar Pradesh, AIR 1990 SC 516: (1990) 1 SCC 291:
   1990 SCC (Cri) 96   88
Ananda *v.* Chief Secretary, AIR 1966 SC 657: (1966) 2 SCR 406: 1966 Cr LJ 586   122
Andhra Steel Corporation Ltd. *v.* Andhra Pradesh State Electricity Board,
   (1991) 3 SCC 263: AIR 1991 SC 1456: 1991 AIR SCW 1358:
   JT 1991 (2) SC 581: (1991) 2 SCR 624: 1991 (2) UJ (SC) 244   198, 199, 210
Andhra Steel Corporation *v.* Commissioner of Commercial Taxes in Karnataka,
   AIR 1990 SC 1912: 1990 Supp SCC 617: JT 1990 (2) SC 380   275
Andhra Sugars Ltd. *v.* State of Andhra Pradesh, AIR 1968 SC 599:
   (1968) 1 SCR 705: 21 STC 212: (1968) 1 SCA 213:
   (1968) 1 Mad LJ (SC) 117: 1968 (1) SCJ 694   273
Anil *v.* Dean, Government Medical College, Nagpur, AIR 1985 Bom 153   32
Animal and Environment Legal Defence Fund *v.* Union of India, (1997) 3 SCC 549:
   AIR 1997 SC 1071: 1997 AIR SCW 1078: JT 1997 (3) SC 298: 1997 (2) Jab LJ 1:
   1997 (1) SCJ 522: (1997) 2 SCR 728: (1997) 2 SCALE 493: 1997 (2) Supreme 713   56
Anjan Kumar *v.* Union of India, AIR 2006 SC 1177: 2006 AIR SCW 888:
   2006 (3) Jab LJ 42: (2006) 3 SCC 257: 2006 (2) SCJ 472: 2006 (3) SRJ 414:
   (2006) 2 SCALE 327: (2006) 2 Serv LR 487: 2006 (2) Supreme 59   315
Anuj Garg *v.* Hotel Association of India, AIR 2008 SC 663: 2007 AIR SCW 7772:
   ILR 2008 Kant (SC) 697: 2008 (1) Rec Civ R 240: (2008) 3 SCC 1:
   2008 (2) All MR 59 (NOC): 2008 (1) SCT 80: (2007) 13 SCALE 762:
   2008 (2) Serv LR 472   4, 243
Anvaruddin *v.* Shakoor, AIR 1990 SC 1242: (1990) 3 SCC 266: 1990 Cr LJ 1269:
   1990 All LJ 281: JT 1990 (2) SC 83   149
Aramachine and Lakri Vikreta Sangh, Nagpur *v.* State of Rajasthan,
   AIR 1992 Raj 7: 1991 (2) Raj LW 598   275
Arjun *v.* Jamnadas, 1990 (1) SCJ 59: (1989) 4 SCC 612: AIR 1989 SC 1599   201
Arti Sapru *v.* State of Jammu & Kashmir, AIR 1981 SC 1009: (1981) 2 SCC 484:
   1981 Srignar LJ (SC) 1 (SC): 1981 Cur LJ (Civ) 175: 1981 UJ (SC) 333:
   (1981) 3 SCR 34: 1981 SCC (Lab) 398   32, 91
Article 143 of the Constitution of India, AIR 1965 SC 745: (1965) 1 SCR 413:
   1965 (1) SCJ 847: (1965) 1 SCA 441   132

Article 317(1) of the Constitution of India (in re:), JT 1994 (2) SC 63:
    (1994) 4 Supp 2 SCC 166   295
Arton No. 2 (in re:), (1896) 1 QB 509   108
Arumugam v. State of Tamil Nadu, (1991) Supp 1 SCC 199: (1991) 17 ATC 407   279
Arun Kumar Rai Chaudhary v. Union of India, AIR 1992 All 1: 1992 All LJ 290   325
Arun Tewari v. Zila Mansavi Shikshak Sangh, AIR 1998 SC 331:
    1997 AIR SCW 4310: JT 1997 (9) SC 593: 1998 (1) Jab LJ 114:
    (1998) 2 SCC 332: 1998 SCC (L&S) 541: 1998 (1) SCT 533:
    (1997) 7 SCALE 461: 1997 (10) Supreme 281   243
Arun v. State of Bihar, AIR 1991 SC 1514: (1991) Supp 1 SCC 287:
    (1991) 16 ATC 931: (1991) 2 LLN 59   152
Aruna Roy (Ms) v. Union of India, AIR 2002 SC 3176: 2002 AIR SCW 3670:
    2002 (6) Andh LD 66: JT 2002 (7) SC 103: (2002) 7 SCC 368: 2002 (4) SCJ 235:
    2002 (9) SRJ 116: (2002) 6 SCALE 408: 2002 (6) Supreme 437   77
Arya Samaj Education Trust, Delhi v. Director of Education,
    Delhi Administration, Delhi, AIR 1976 Del 207: ILR (1976) 2 Del 93   81
Ashok Kumar Bhattacharyya v. Ajoy Biswas, AIR 1985 SC 211: (1985) 1 SCC 154:
    1985 UJ (SC) 7: (1984) 2 MCC 285: (1985) 1 Cur CC 339: (1985) 2 SCR 50:
    1985 Cur Civ LJ (SC) 316   131
Ashok Lenka v. Rishi Dikshit, AIR 2006 SC 2382: 2006 AIR SCW 3058:
    (2006) 9 SCC 90: 2006 (6) SCJ 650: 2006 (7) SRJ 162:
    (2006) 4 SCALE 519: 2006 (106) Supreme 230   107
Ashok Nagar Welfare Association v. R.K. Sharma, AIR 2002 SC 335:
    (2002) 1 SCC 749: 2001 AIR SCW 5105: JT 2001 (2) SC (Supp) 24:
    2001 (5) SCJ 254: 2002 (2) SRJ 449: (2001) 8 SCALE 503:
    2001 (8) Supreme 647: 2002 (1) UJ (SC) 163   151
Ashok v. Collector, AIR 1980 SC 112: (1980) 1 SCC 180: (1980) 1 SCR 491   205
Ashok v. Union of India, AIR 1991 SC 1792: (1991) 3 SCC 498:
    (1991) 3 Crimes 185: 1991 Cr LJ 2483: (1992) 20 ATC 501 (Pat)   245, 285
Ashoka Kumar Thakur v. Union of India, 2008 AIR SCW 2899:
    AIR 2008 SC (Supp) 1   32
Ashwani v. P.C.D.F., (1992) 4 SCC 17   299
Ashwinder Kaur v. Punjab University, AIR 1989 P&H 190   20
Assam Sillimanite Ltd. v. Union of India, AIR 1990 SC 1417: (1990) 3 SCC 182:
    JT 1990 (2) SC 248   207
Assam Sillimanite v. Union of India, AIR 1992 SC 938: (1992) Supp 1 SCC 692:
    1992 AIR SCW 754: 1992 (1) Comp LJ SC 165: JT 1992 (3) SC 434:
    1992 (1) SCJ 423: 1992 (1) UJ (SC) 288   86
Assistant Collector of Central Excise, Chandan Nagar, W.B. v. Dunlop India Ltd.,
    (1985) 1 SCC 260: AIR 1985 SC 330: 1985 (1) Land LR 443: 1985 SCC (Tax) 75:
    1985 UJ (SC) 368: (1985) 58 Comp Cas 145: (1985) 2 SCR 190   156
Assistant Customs Collector v. Melwani, AIR 1970 SC 962: (1969) 2 SCR 438:
    1970 Cr LJ 885   53
Associated Cement Companies Ltd., Kymore v. Commissioner of Sales Tax,
    Indore, (1991) Supp 1 SCC 251: AIR 1991 SC 1122: 1991 AIR SCW 1102:
    1991 BRLJ 199: 1991 (5) Cor LA 374: JT 1991 (2) SC 144:
    (1991) 2 SCR 250: 1991 (82) STC 1   265
Associated Provincial Picture Houses Ltd. v. Wednesbury Corporation,
    (1948) 1 KB 223: (1947) 2 All ER 680   21
Association of the Residents of Mhow v. Union of India, AIR 2010 MP 40   330
Atam Prakash v. State of Haryana, AIR 1986 SC 859: (1986) 2 SCC 249:
    1986 Punj LJ 191: (1986) 1 Cur CC 641: 1986 (1) Land LR 478:
    1986 (1) Supreme 628: 1986 Sim LC 132: 1986 UJ (SC) 642:
    1986 Cur Civ LJ (SC) 490: (1986) 1 PLR 329   3, 30
Atiabari Tea Co. Ltd. v. State of Assam, AIR 1961 SC 232: (1961) 1 SCR 809:
    ILR (1961) 13 Assam 257   273
Attorney-General of India v. Amratlal Pranjivandas, JT 1994 (3) SC 583:
    (1994) 5 SCC 54: AIR 1994 SC 2179   248

Attorney-General of India *v.* Lachma Devi, AIR 1986 SC 467: 1986 Cr LJ 364:
(1986) 1 Rec Cri R 424: 1986 Cur Cr J 143 (2): 1986 (1) SCJ 166:
1986 Cal Cr LR (SC) 15: 1989 Supp (1) SCC 264   62
Automobile Transport (Rajasthan) Ltd. *v.* State of Rajasthan, AIR 1962 SC 1406:
(1963) 1 SCR 491: (1962) 2 SCA 35   273
Avinash Mehrotra *v.* Union of India, (2009) 6 SCC 398   67
Avinder Singh *v.* State of Punjab, AIR 1979 SC 321: (1979) 1 SCC 137:
1979 (1) SCJ 937: 1979 SCWR 372: (1979) 1 SCR 845: 1979 UPTC 461   21

B

B. Basavalingappa *v.* D. Munichinnappa, AIR 1965 SC 1269: (1965) 1 SCR 316:
1965 (2) SCJ 153   314
B. Hassan Ali Khan *v.* Director of Higher Education, Andhra Pradesh,
(1987) 4 Reports 198 (AP)   15
B. Krishna Bhat *v.* Union of India, (1990) 3 SCC 65   90
B. Viswanathiah & Co. *v.* State of Karnataka, (1991) 3 SCC 358:
1991 AIR SCW 455   246, 247, 248
B.L. Wadehra (Dr.) *v.* Union of India, AIR 1996 SC 2969: (1996) 2 SCC 594:
1996 AIR SCW 1185: 1997 (1) Cur LJ (CCR) 28: JT 1996 (3) SC 38:
(1996) 3 SCR 80: 1996 (2) UJ (SC) 26   64, 67
B.R. Enterprises *v.* State of Uttar Pradesh, AIR 1999 SC 1867: (1999) 9 SCC 700:
1999 AIR SCW 1526: JT 1999 (3) SC 431: 1999 (7) SRJ 95: 2000 (120) STC 302:
1999 SC Cr R 526: 1999 (4) Supreme 472   269
B.R. Ramabhadriah *v.* Secretary, Food and Agriculture Department, A.P.,
AIR 1981 SC 1653: (1981) 3 SCC 528: 1981 Lab IC 1114: 1981 SCC (Lab) 530:
(1981) 2 Serv LJ 263: 1981 UJ (SC) 591: (1981) 2 Lab LJ 263   212
B.S.E.S. Ltd. (now Reliance Energy Ltd.) *v.* Fenner India Ltd., AIR 2006 SC 1148:
2006 AIR SCW 721: (2006) 2 SCC 728: 2006 (3) SCJ 9: 2006 (3) SRJ 389:
(2006) 2 SCALE 186: 2006 (2) Supreme 106   154
Babu Lal *v.* State of Haryana, (1991) 2 SCC 335: (1991) 16 ATC 481:
AIR 1991 SC 1310: (1991) 1 SLR 756   285, 288
Babulal *v.* State of Bombay, AIR 1960 SC 51: (1960) 1 SCR 605: 62 Bom LR 58   9
Bachhittar Singh *v.* State of Punjab, AIR 1963 SC 395: (1962) Supp 3 SCR 713:
1962 All WR (HC) 746   168
Baijnath Kedia *v.* State of Bihar, AIR 1970 SC 1436: (1969) 3 SCC 838:
(1969) 2 SCA 335: 1970 (1) SCJ 913: (1970) 2 SCR 100: 1970 Pat LJR 661   248
Baikuntha *v.* C.D.M.O., AIR 1992 SC 1020: (1992) 2 SCC 299:
(1992) 21 ATC 649: (1992) 1 LLN 902: (1992) 1 LLJ 784   276, 277, 286, 288, 299
Bailey *v.* Conole, (1931) 34 WALR 18   21
Bajiban Chauhan *v.* U.P.S.R.T.C., (1990) Supp SCC 769   103
Bal Kishan *v.* Delhi Administration, AIR 1990 SC 100: (1989) Supp 2 SCC 351:
(1989) 58 FLR 687   27
Bal Patil *v.* Union of India, (2005) 6 SCC 690: AIR 2005 SC 3172:
2005 AIR SCW 3762: 2005 (4) JCR SC 60: 2005 (6) SCJ 171: 2005 (6) SLT 251:
(2005) 6 SCALE 374: 2005 (5) Supreme 669: 2005 (2) UJ (SC) 1249   5, 73
Bal Ram Bali *v.* Union of India, AIR 2007 SC 3074: 2007 AIR SCW 5551:
2007 (58) All Ind Cas 109: (2007) 6 SCC 805: (2007) 10 SCALE 277:
2007 (6) Supreme 409   108
Balaji Raghavan *v.* Union of India, AIR 1996 SC 770: (1996) 1 SCC 361:
1996 AIR SCW 86: 1996 (1) LS SC 54: 1996 (1) UJ (SC) 197   40
Balaji *v.* State of Mysore, AIR 1963 SC 649: (1983) 1 SCC 305: (1983) 1 LLJ 104   30
Balakrishna *v.* Matha, (1991) Cr LJ 691: (1991) 2 SCC 203: (1991) 1 Crimes 448 (SC)   151
BALCO Employees' Union *v.* Union of India, AIR 2002 SC 350: (2002) 2 SCC 333:
(2002) 108 Comp Cas 193: (2002) 100 FJR 152   22
Balkishan *v.* State of Maharashtra, AIR 1981 SC 379: (1980) 4 SCC 600:
1981 SCC (Cri) 62: 1980 Cr LJ 1424   52
Bandhua Mukti Morcha *v.* Union of India, AIR 1984 SC 802: (1984) 3 SCC 161:
1984 Lab IC 560: 1984 SCC (Lab) 389: (1984) 2 Lab LN 60   63

Bandhua Mukti Morcha *v.* Union of India, AIR 1997 SC 2218:
    1997 AIR SCW 2083: 1997 All LJ 1186: JT 1997 (5) SC 285:
    (1997) 10 SCC 549: 1997 SCD 755: 1998 (3) SCJ 353:
    (1997) 2 SCR 379: 1997 (3) SCT 397: 1997 (4) Supreme 609   71, 72
Bangalore Medical Trust *v.* B.S. Muddappa, AIR 1991 SC 1902: (1991) 4 SCC 54:
    1991 AIR SCW 2082: JT 1991 (3) SC 172: (1991) 3 SCR 102:
    1991 (2) UJ (SC) 415   205
Bank of India *v.* O.P. Swaranakar, AIR 2003 SC 858: (2003) 2 SCC 721:
    (2003) 1 LLJ 819: (2003) 1 SLR 1   14
Bansal *v.* Union of India, AIR 1993 SC 978: (1992) Supp 2 SCC 318:
    (1992) 21 ATC 503: (1992) 4 SLR 445   281
Banwasi Sewa Ashram *v.* State of Uttar Pradesh, (1986) 4 SCC 753:
    AIR 1987 SC 374: 1987 Cr LR (SC) 2: 1987 (1) SCJ 203:
    1987 SC Cr R 73: 1987 East Cr C 430   57, 110
Bapna *v.* Union of India, (1992) 3 SCC 512: 1992 SCC (Cri) 683   87
Bar Council of Uttar Pradesh *v.* State of Uttar Pradesh, AIR 1973 SC 231:
    (1973) 1 SCC 261: (1973) 2 SCR 1073   249, 253
Barium Chemicals *v.* Company Law Board, AIR 1967 SC 295:
    1966 Supp SCR 311: (1966) 36 Comp Cas 639   44
Basanta *v.* Emperor, AIR 1944 FC 86   244
Bennett Coleman and Co. Ltd. *v.* Union of India, AIR 1973 SC 106:
    (1972) 2 SCC 788: 1973 (1) SCJ 177   44, 48
Berubari Union (in re:), AIR 1960 SC 845: (1960) 3 SCR 250: 1960 SCJ 933:
    (1961) 1 SCA 22   7, 10, 109
Bhabani Prasad Jena *v.* Convenor Secretary, Orissa State Commission
    for Women, AIR 2010 SC 2851   60
Bhagat *v.* State of Himachal Pradesh, AIR 1983 SC 454: (1983) 2 SCC 442:
    (1983) 2 LLJ 1   97
Bhagwan Dass *v.* Punjab State Electricity Board, AIR 2008 SC 990:
    2008 AIR SCW 534: 2008 (1) All WC 827: 2008 (2) Lab LN 1:
    2008 (2) Mad LJ 79: 2008 (2) Mad LW 866: (2008) 1 SCC 579:
    2008 (2) SRJ 76: (2008) 1 SCALE 64: 2008 (2) Serv LR 32   23
Bhagwati Prasad *v.* D.S.M.D.C., 1990 (1) SCJ 433: (1990) 1 SCC 361:
    AIR 1990 SC 371: 1990 Lab IC 126   93, 211
Bhagwati *v.* Rajeev, AIR 1986 SC 1534: (1986) 4 SCC 78: 1986 SCC (Cri) 399   131
Bhaiya Lal *v.* Harikishan Singh, AIR 1965 SC 1557: (1965) 2 SCR 877:
    (1965) 1 SCWR 840: 1965 MPLJ 669: 1965 Jab LJ 860:
    (1965) 2 SCA 721: 1966 (2) SCJ 77   314
Bhaiya Ram Munda *v.* Anirudh Patar, (1971) 1 SCR 804: AIR 1971 SC 2533:
    (1970) 2 SCC 825   314
Bhandara District Central Co-operative Bank Ltd. *v.* State of Maharashtra,
    AIR 1993 SC 59: (1993) Supp 3 SCC 259: 1992 AIR SCW 2574:
    JT 1993 (Supp) SC 428: (1992) 4 SCR 501: 1993 (1) UJ (SC) 14   150
Bhanushankar Jatashankar Bhatt *v.* Kamal Tara Builders Pvt. Ltd., AIR 1990 Bom 140:
    1989 Mah LJ 440: (1989) 2 Bom CR 526: 1989 Mah LR 1526 (DB)   248
Bharat Coking Coal *v.* State of Bihar, (1990) 4 SCC 557: JT 1990 (3) SC 533:
    (1990) 3 SCR 744   165
Bharat Seva Ashram *v.* State of Gujarat, AIR 1987 SC 494: (1986) 4 SCC 51:
    (1986) 1 ATC 348: 1996 SCC (L&S) 723   182
Bharat Sewa Sansthan *v.* U.P. Electronic Corpn. Ltd., (2007) 7 SCC 737:
    2007 AIR SCW 5399: 2007 (3) All Rent Cas 379: 2007 (4) All WC 3565:
    2007 (3) Arb LR 299: 2007 (4) Rec Civ R 98: 2007 (2) Ren CR 315:
    2007 (2) Rent LR 388: (2007) 10 SCALE 446   157
Bhaskar *v.* State of Andhra Pradesh, (1993) 24 ATC 842   89
Bhatnagar *v.* Union of India, (1991) 1 SCC 544: (1991) 16 ATC 501:
    (1991) 1 SLR 191: (1991) 1 CLR 70   281
Bhattacharya *v.* Union of India, AIR 1991 SC 468: (1991) Supp 2 SCC 109:
    (1991) 17 ATC 355   92

Bhavani River - Sakthi Sugars Ltd. (in re:), AIR 1998 SC 2578:
    (1998) 6 SCC 335: 1998 AIR SCW 2609: 1998 (4) Civ LJ 820:
    JT 1998 (5) SC 214: 1998 (3) SCJ 239: (1998) 3 SCR 929:
    (1998) 4 SCALE 322: 1998 (6) Supreme 169   209
Bhavnagar University *v.* Palitana Sugar Mill Pvt. Ltd., AIR 2003 SC 511:
    (2003) 2 SCC 111: (2003) 2 Guj LR 1154   155
Bhim Singh, MLA *v.* State of Jammu & Kashmir, AIR 1986 SC 494:
    1986 Cr LJ 192: 1986 All LJ 653: (1985) 4 SCC 677: 1986 SC Cr R 20:
    1986 SCC (Cri) 47: 1986 UJ (SC) 458: 1986 Cr LR (SC) 66:
    (1986) 1 APLJ (SC) 36: 1986 Mad LJ (Cri) 32   55, 61
Bhim Singhji *v.* Union of India, AIR 1981 SC 234: (1981) 1 SCC 166:
    1981 Raj LR 39: (1981) 19 DLT 185: 1981 All CJ 38   3, 18, 85, 335
Bhoop *v.* Union of India, AIR 1992 SC 1414: (1992) 3 SCC 136:
    (1992) 21 ATC 675: (1992) 4 SLR 761: 1992 Lab IC 1464   299
Bhopal Sugar Industry *v.* I.T.O., AIR 1961 SC 182: (1961) 1 SCR 474:
    (1960) 40 ITR 618   213
Bhupendrakumar Singhal *v.* Dr. P.R. Mehta, AIR 1990 Guj 48   195
Bhuri Nath *v.* State of Jammu & Kashmir, AIR 1997 SC 1711: (1997) 2 SCC 745:
    1997 AIR SCW 869: JT 1997 (1) SC 546: 1997 (1) SCJ 218: (1997) 1 SCR 138:
    (1997) 1 SCALE 250: 1997 (1) Supreme 358   73
Bidi, Bidi Leaves and Tobacco Merchants' Association, Gondia *v.*
    State of Bombay, AIR 1962 SC 486: (1962) Supp 1 SCR 381:
    (1961-62) 21 FJR 331: (1961) 2 LLJ 663: 64 Bom LR 375   212
Bihar Eastern Gangetic Fishermen Co-operative Society Ltd. *v.* Sipahi Singh,
    AIR 1977 SC 2149: (1977) 4 SCC 145: 1978 Pat LJR 60: 1978 BLJR 22:
    (1978) 1 SCWR 268: 1978 BLJ 60   270
Bihar Public Service Commission *v.* Dr. Shiv Jatan Thakur,
    (1994) Supp 2 SCC 220: AIR 1994 SC 2466: 1994 AIR SCW 3484:
    JT 1994 (4) SC 681: 1994 SCC (L&S) 1247: 1994 (3) SCJ 337:
    1994 (4) SCT 416: (1994) Supp 3 SCC 220: (1995) 1 Serv LJ SC 55:
    1994 Writ LR 881   204, 295
Bihar School Examination Board *v.* Subhas Chandra Sinha,
    (1970) 1 SCC 648: AIR 1970 SC 1269: 1970 Pat LJR 508:
    1970 (2) SCJ 549: (1970) 3 SCR 963   155, 215, 216
Bihar School Examination Board *v.* Suresh Prasad Sinha, AIR 2010 SC 93   155
Bihar State Harijan Kalyan Prishad *v.* Union of India, (1985) 2 SCC 644:
    1985 SCC (L&S) 523: (1985) 2 LLJ 173: AIR 1985 SC 983   78
Bihar State Madarsa Board *v.* Madarsa Hanafia, AIR 1990 SC 695:
    (1990) 1 SCC 428: (1990) 1 BLJR 504   82
Bijoe Emmanuel *v.* State of Kerala, (1986) 3 SCC 615: AIR 1987 SC 748:
    1986 KLT 1037   42, 45
BIMA Office Premises Co-operative Society *v.* Kalamboli Village Panchayat,
    AIR 2001 Bom 83: 2001 (1) Mah LJ 806: 2001 (2) Mah LR 262   235
Bishamber Dayal Chandra Mohan *v.* State of Uttar Pradesh, AIR 1982 SC 33:
    (1982) 1 SCC 39: 1982 SCC (Cri) 53: 1982 Cr LR (SC) 99:
    (1982) 1 SCR 1137: 1982 IJR 67: 1982 UJ (SC) 802   272
Bishan Das *v.* State of Punjab, AIR 1961 SC 1570: (1962) 2 SCR 69: 1963 (1) SCJ 405   94
Bishwanath *v.* Union of India, (1991) 16 ATC 912 (Cal) (FB)   277
Biswas *v.* State Bank of India, (1991) 2 UJ SC 567:AIR 1991 SC 2039:
    (1991) Supp 2 SCC 354   277, 278
Board of Control of Cricket, India *v.* Netaji Cricket Club, AIR 2005 SC 592:
    2005 AIR SCW 230: 2005 (2) All CJ 1283: 2005 (2) All WC 1965:
    JT 2005 (1) SC 235: (2005) 4 SCC 741: 2005 (1) SCJ 725:
    (2005) 1 SCALE 121: 2005 (1) Supreme 507: 2005 (1) UJ (SC) 334   22
Board of Education *v.* Rice, (1911) AC 179: 80 LJ KB 796   197
Board of High School and Intermediate Education, U.P. Allahabad *v.* Ghanshyam
    Das Gupta, AIR 1962 SC 1110: (1962) Supp 3 SCR 36: 64 Punj LR 575:
    1962 All LJ 776: ILR (1962) 2 All 661: 1963 (2) SCJ 509   215, 216

Board of High School and Intermediate Education, U.P. Allahabad *v.*
    Bagleshwar Prasad, (1963) 3 SCR 767: AIR 1966 SC 875: (1963) 7 FLR 415   216, 217
Board of High School and Intermediate Education, U.P. *v.* Kumari Chittra
    Srivastava, AIR 1970 SC 1039: (1970) 1 SCC 121: 1970 SCD 222   215, 216
Board of Muslim Wakfs *v.* Hadi Begum, (1993) Supp 1 SCC 192:
    AIR 1992 SC 1083: 1992 AIR SCW 968: JT 1992 (2) SC 385:
    1992 (2) SCJ 139: 1992 (1) UJ (SC) 627   201
Boddula Krishnaiah *v.* State Election Commissioner, Andhra Pradesh,
    AIR 1996 SC 1595: 1996 AIR SCW 1856: JT 1996 (4) SC 156:
    1996 (2) Land LR 535: (1996) 3 SCC 416: (1996) 3 SCR 687   234
Body Builders Ltd. *v.* City of Ottawa, (1964) 45 DLR (2d) 211   21
Bombay Dyeing & Mfg. Co. Ltd. *v.* Bombay Environmental Action Group,
    AIR 2006 SC 1489: 2006 AIR SCW 1392: 2006 (1) LACC 456:
    (2006) 3 SCC 434: 2006 (2) SCJ 705: 2006 (4) SRJ 170: (2006) 3 SCALE 1   204
Bongaigaon Refinery & Petrochemicals Ltd. *v.* Girish Chandra Sharma,
    (2007) 7 SCC 206   208
Bonham's case (1610) 8 Co Rep 1142: 77 ER 646   208
Brahma Prakash *v.* State of Uttar Pradesh, (1953) SCR 1169: AIR 1954 SC 10:
    1954 Cr LJ 238   145
Builders Association *v.* State of Karnataka, AIR 1993 SC 991:
    (1993) 1 SCC 409: (1993) 88 STC 248   334
Burns and Township of Haldimand (in re:), (1966) 52 DLR (2d) 1014   21

C

C. Sampath Kumar *v.* Enforcement Officer, Enforcement Directorate, Madras,
    AIR 1998 SC 16: (1997) 8 SCC 358: 1997 AIR SCW 3959: JT 1997 (8) SC 135:
    (1997) 6 SCALE 140: 1998 SCC (Cri) 74: 1997 (8) Supreme 268:
    1997 (2) UJ (SC) 749   53
C. Surekha (Dr.) *v.* Union of India, AIR 1989 SC 44: (1988) 3 ITJ 694:
    (1988) 4 SCC 526: 1988 (3) SCJ 514: (1988) 2 UJ (SC) 539   344
C.A. Abraham *v.* I.T.O., AIR 1961 SC 609: (1961) 2 SCR 765: (1961) 41 ITR 425   212
C.A. Rajendran *v.* Union of India, AIR 1968 SC 507: (1968) 1 SCR 721:
    (1968) 1 SCA 202: (1968) 1 SCWR 574: 1968 (2) SCJ 19: 1968 SCD 714:
    (1968) 2 LLJ 407   37
C.K. Daphtary *v.* O.P. Gupta, AIR 1971 SC 1132: (1971) 1 SCC 626:
    1971 SCC (Cri) 286: 1971 Cr LJ 844   145
C.M.C. Vellore Association *v.* Govt. of India (1983) 1 Lab LN 373   82
C.S.I.R. *v.* Labour Court, (1992) 19 ATC 414   285
C.S.O. *v.* Singasan, (1991) 1 SCC 729: AIR 1991 SC 1043: (1991) 16 ATC 453   287
Calcutta Discount Co. *v.* I.T.O., AIR 1961 SC 372: (1961) 2 SCR 241:
    (1961) 41 ITR 191   212
Calcutta Gas Company (Proprietary) Ltd. *v.* State of West Bengal,
    AIR 1962 SC 1044: (1962) Supp 3 SCR 1: (1962) 2 SCA 147: 1963 (1) SCJ 106   213
Cannanore District Muslim Educational Association, Kanpur *v.* State of Kerala,
    AIR 2010 SC 1955   25
Carltona Ltd. *v.* Commissioners of Works, (1943) 2 All ER 560   21
Central Bank of India *v.* State of Kerala, (2009) 4 SCC 94   251
Central Bank *v.* Bernard, (1991) 1 SCC 319: (1991) 15 ATC 720: (1991) 1 LLN 1111   286
Central Board of Dawoodi Bohra Community *v.* State of Maharashtra,
    AIR 2005 SC 752: 2005 AIR SCW 349: JT 2005 (1) SC 97: (2005) 2 SCC 673:
    2005 SCC (L&S) 246: (2004) 10 SCALE 501: 2005 SCC (Cri) 546   154
Central Inland Water Transport Corporation Ltd. *v.* Brojo Nath Ganguly,
    (1986) 3 SCC 156: 1986 Lab IC 1312: 1986 (2) Supreme 479:
    1986 SCC (Lab) 429: (1986) 2 LLJ 171: 1986 (2) SCJ 201:
    (1986) 2 LLN 382: (1986) 3 Comp LJ 1   28
Chairman, Railway Board *v.* C.R. Raugadharniah, (1994) 4 SLR 759   26
Champaklal *v.* Union of India, AIR 1964 SC 1854: (1964) 5 SCR 190:
    (1964) 1 LLJ 752   37

Chandavarkar Sita Ratna Rao *v.* Ashalata S. Guram, (1986) 4 SCC 447:
AIR 1987 SC 117: JT 1986 SC 619: (1986) 88 Bom LR 600:
1986 Mah LJ 955: 1986 (4) Supreme 442: (1987) 1 Ren CJ 321:
1987 Mah LR 1: 1987 Bom RC 276: (1987) 1 Rent LR 684   218
Chandra Bhawan Boarding and Lodging, Bangalore *v.* State of Mysore,
AIR 1970 SC 2042: (1969) 3 SCC 84: 19 Fac LR 325: 38 FJR 1:
(1970) 2 Lab LJ 403: (1970) 2 SCR 600   3, 4, 99
Chandra Rajakumari *v.* Police Commissioner, Hyderabad, AIR 1998 AP 302:
1998 (1) Andh LD 810: 1998 (1) Andh LT 329: 1998 (4) Rec Cr R 631   55
Chandrakant Hargovindas Shah *v.* Deputy Commissioner of Police, (2009) 7 SCC 186   151
Charan Lal Sahu *v.* Union of India, (1990) 1 SCC 613: AIR 1990 SC 1480:
(1989) Supp 2 SCR 597: 1989 Supp SCALE 1   4, 20, 60, 88, 195
Charan Singh *v.* State of Punjab, AIR 1997 SC 1052: 1997 AIR SCW 1050:
1997 (3) LJR 600: (1997) 1 SCC 151: 1997 (1) Supreme 23: 1997 (1) UJ (SC) 277   100
Charles Sobraj *v.* Supdt. Central jail, Tihar, New Delhi, AIR 1978 SC 1514:
(1978) Cr LJ 1534: (1978) 4 SCC 104: 1978 SCC (Cri) 542: 1978 SC Cr R 416   57, 61
Charoria *v.* State of Maharashtra, AIR 1988 SC 938   54
Chatterji *v.* Sub Area Commandant, AIR 1951 Mad 77   96
Chennugadu (in re:), ILR (1955) Mad 92   117
Chhetriya Samiti *v.* State of Uttar Pradesh, 1991 (1) SCJ 130:
(1990) 4 SCC 449: AIR 1990 SC 2060   211
Chief Engineer *v.* Jagdish, AIR 1991 SC 2000: (1991) Supp 2 SCC 1:
(1991) 17 ATC 398   278
Chief Justice *v.* Dikshitulu, (1979) 2 SCC 34: AIR 1979 SC 193: 1978 Lab IC 1672   99
Chikkusappa *v.* State of Karnataka, AIR 2006 (NOC) 472 (Kar)   154
Chintamanrao *v.* State of Madhya Pradesh, (1950) SCR 759: AIR 1951 SC 118:
1950 SCJ 571: 64 MLW 370: 1951 ALJ (SC) 82: ILR 1951 Hyd 221   42, 50
Chiranjit Lal *v.* Union of India, (1950) SCR 869: AIR 1951 SC 41:
(1951) 21 Comp Cas 33   30
Choki *v.* State of Rajasthan, AIR 1957 Raj 10: 1955 Cr LJ 567: 1955 Raj LW 567   34
Cholamandalam Investments & Finance Co. Pvt. Ltd. *v.* Radhika Synthetics,
AIR 1996 SC 1098: (1996) 2 SCC 109: 1996 AIR SCW 628:
1996 (2) Civ LJ 1: JT 1996 (1) SC 372: (1996) 1 SCR 495   153
Chopra *v.* Union of India, AIR 1987 SC 357: (1987) 1 SCC 422: (1987) 1 LLJ 255   26
Christian Medical College Hospital Employees' Union *v.* C.M.C. Vellore
Association, (1987) 4 SCC 691: AIR 1988 SC 37: 1988 SCC (L&S) 53   82
Church of God (Full Gospell) in India *v.* K.K.R. Majestic Colony Welfare
Association, AIR 2000 SC 2773: (2000) 7 SCC 282: 2000 SCC (Cri) 1350   75
Citizens for Democracy *v.* State of Assam, AIR 1996 SC 2193: 1996 Cr LJ 3247:
1996 AIR SCW 2815: JT 1995 (4) SC 475: 1995 (2) Mad LJ 66:
1995 (2) OCR 174: (1995) 3 SCC 743: 1995 (2) SCJ 308:
(1995) 3 SCR 943: 1996 SC Cr R 37: 1995 SCC (Cri) 600   57
City Industrial Development Corporation *v.* Dosu Aardeshir Bhiwandiwala,
(2009) 1 SCC 168: AIR 2009 SC 571: 2008 AIR SCW 7706: 2009 (1) Andh LD 24:
2009 (1) CTC 174: 2009 (3) Mad LJ 137: (2008) 14 SCALE 23   201
Civil Rights Vigilance Committee, S.L.S.R.C. College of Law, Bangalore *v.*
Union of India, AIR 1983 Kant 85: (1982) 2 Kant LJ 208   109
Collector of Customs *v.* Pednekar, AIR 1976 SC 1408: (1976) 3 SCC 790:
(1976) 3 SCR 971   198
Collector of Malabar *v.* Hajee, (1957) SCR 970: AIR 1957 SC 688: (1957) 32 ITR 124   69
Commander Ranvir Kumar Sinha *v.* Union of India, 1991 Cr LJ 1729 (Bom):
1991 (2) Bom CR 28   199
Commissioner of Customs and Excise *v.* Cure and Dooley Ltd., (1962) 1 QB 340   21
Commissioner of Income-tax *v.* Sun Engineering Works (P.) Ltd., AIR 1993 SC 43:
(1992) 4 SCC 363: 1992 AIR SCW 2600: 1992 (3) Comp LJ SC 193:
1992 (198) ITR 297: JT 1992 (5) SC 543: (1992) 4 SCR 733   154
Commissioner of Police *v.* Acharya Jagdishwarananda Abadhuta,
AIR 1991 Cal 263: (1991) 1 Cal HN 18   156

Committee of Management *v.* Vice-Chancellor, AIR 2009 SC 1159: 2009 AIR SCW 398:
    2009 (1) LLN 774: 2009 (3) Mad LJ 323: (2009) 2 SCC 630: 2009 (1) SCT 423:
    (2008) 16 SCALE 310: 2009 (3) Serv LJ 57 (SC)   195
Common Cause *v.* Union of India, AIR 1996 SC 929: 1996 AIR SCW 333:
    1996 (1) BLJ 560: 1996 (1) Civ LJ 742: JT 1996 (1) SC 38: (1996) 1 SCC 753:
    1996 (1) SCJ 422: (1996) 1 SCR 89: (1997) 3 SCALE Supp 21:
    1996 (1) UJ (SC) 404   64
Common Cause, A Registered Society *v.* Union of India, AIR 1997 SC 1539:
    1997 Cr LJ 195: 1997 AIR SCW 290: 1997 (1) MPLJ 4: 1997 (12) OCR 232:
    (1996) 6 SCC 775: 1997 SCC (Cri) 42   64
Communist Party of India (M) *v.* Bharat Kumar, AIR 1998 SC 184:
    (1998) 1 SCC 201: (1998) 1 MLJ 99 (SC)   42
Comptroller & Auditor General of India *v.* Mohan, AIR 1991 SC 2288:
    (1992) 1 SCC 20: (1992) 1 LLJ 335: (1992) 1 SLJ 1   276
Comptroller and Auditor General *v.* Jagannathan, AIR 1987 SC 537:
    (1986) 2 SCC 679: (1986) 2 LLN 11: (1986) 1 SLR 712: (1986) 1 ATC 1   32, 38, 308
Conscientious Group *v.* Mohammad Yunus, AIR 1987 SC 1451: (1987) 3 SCC 89:
    1987 Cr LJ 1182   43
Corporation Bank *v.* Saraswati Abharansala, (2009) 1 SCC 540   30
Corporation of Calcutta *v.* Liberty Cinema, AIR 1965 SC 1107:
    1965 1 SCA 657: 1965 2 SCR 477   257
Corporation of City of Nagpur *v.* N.E.L. & Power Co., AIR 1958 Bom 498   15, 206

D

D.A.V. College, Bhatinda *v.* State of Punjab, AIR 1971 SC 1731:
    (1971) 2 SCC 261: 1971 (Supp) SCR 677   45, 78, 81
D.A.V. College, Jullundur *v.* State of Punjab, AIR 1971 SC 1737:
    (1971) 2 SCC 269: 1971 (Supp) SCR 688   45, 78, 81
D.C. Wadhwa (Dr.) *v.* State of Bihar, AIR 1987 SC 579: (1987) 1 SCC 378:
    JT 1987 (1) SC 70: 1986 (4) Supreme 465: 1987 BBCJ (SC) 46:
    1987 IJR 116   92, 141, 188, 210, 244
D.K. Basu *v.* State of West Bengal, AIR 1997 SC 610: (1997) 1 SCC 416:
    1997 SCC (Cri) 92: 1996 (9) SCALE 298   55, 61
D.K. Nabhirajiah *v.* State of Mysore, (1952) SCR 744: AIR 1952 SC 339:
    1952 SCJ 490: 1952 SCA 598: ILR 1953 Mys 142   20
D.N. Banerjee *v.* Mukherjee, (1953) SCR 302: AIR 1953 SC 58: (1953) 1 LLJ 195   218
D.N. Chanchala *v.* State of Mysore, AIR 1971 SC 1762: (1971) 2 SCC 293:
    (1971) Supp SCR 608   21
D.S. Garewal *v.* State of Punjab, AIR 1959 SC 512: 1959 SCJ 399:
    1959 SCA 364: ILR 1959 Punj 827: (1959) Supp 1 SCR 792   352
D.S. Nakara *v.* Union of India, AIR 1983 SC 130: (1983) 1 SCC 305:
    1983 Lab IC 1: (1983) 1 LLJ 104: 1983 SCC (Lab) 145:
    1983 UJ (SC) 217: 1983 BLJR 122: (1983) 1 SCWR 390:
    (1983) 15 Lawyer 51: 1983 (1) SCJ 188   3, 5, 26, 30, 92, 104
D.S. Sharma *v.* Union of India, AIR 1970 Del 250   122
D.T.C. *v.* Mazdoor Congress, AIR 1991 SC 101: (1991) Supp 1 SCC 600:
    1991 SCC (L&S) 1213: (1991) 1 LLJ 395   16, 27, 30, 36, 42, 87
Dahanu Taluka Environment Protection Group *v.* Bombay Suburban
    Electricity Supply Company Ltd., (1991) 2 SCC 539: 1991 AIR SCW 910   213
Dalbir *v.* State of Punjab, AIR 1962 SC 1106: (1962) Supp 3 SCR 25:
    (1962) 68 Cr LJ 247   75
Dalpat Abasaheb Solunke *v.* Dr. B.S. Mahajan, (1990) 1 SCC 305   277
Daryao *v.* State of Uttar Pradesh, AIR 1961 SC 1457: (1962) 1 SCR 574:
    (1961) 2 SCA 591: 1962 (1) SCJ 702: (1962) 2 Andh WR (SC) 16:
    (1962) 2 MLJ (SC) 16   93
Dasappa & Brothers, Bangalore *v.* Election Commission, New Delhi,
    AIR 1992 Kant 230: ILR 1991 Kant 3038: (1992) 1 Kant LJ 152   303
Dasarathi (Dr.) *v.* State of Andhra Pradesh, AIR 1985 AP 136: (1984) 2 Andh WR 449   110

Dastagir *v.* State of Madras, AIR 1960 SC 756: (1960) 3 SCR 116: 1960 Cr LJ 1159   52
Dattatraya Mahadev Nadkarni *v.* Corporation of Greater Bombay,
   (1992) 2 SCC 547: AIR 1992 SC 786: (1992) 1 SCR 785   289
Dattatraya *v.* State of Bombay, AIR 1953 Bom 311: 55 BM LR 323: (1953) Bom 842   34
David John Hopkins *v.* Union of India, AIR 1997 Mad 366: 1997 Writ LR 681   22
Deep Chand *v.* State of Uttar Pradesh, AIR 1959 SC 648: (1959) Supp 2 SCR 8:
   1959 SCA 377: 1959 SCJ 1069: ILR (1959) 1 All 293   99, 252
Deepak *v.* State of Bihar, AIR 1982 Pat 126: 1982 BBCJ (HC) 295: 1982 BLJ 340:
   1982 BLJR 433: 1982 Pat LJR 267   32
Deewan Singh *v.* Rajendra Pd. Ardevi, AIR 2007 SC 767   98
Dehri Rohtas Light Railway Company Limited *v.* District Board, Bhojpur,
   (1992) 2 SCC 598: AIR 1993 SC 802: 1992 AIR SCW 3181: 1992 (2) All CJ 825:
   1993 (2) BLJ 300: JT 1992 (3) SC 573: (1992) 2 SCR 155: 1992 (2) UJ (SC) 26   90
Delhi Administration *v.* Madan Lal Nangia, AIR 2003 SC 4672:
   (2003) 10 SCC 321: (2003) 107 DLT 646   151, 206
Delhi Cloth and General Mills Co. Ltd. *v.* Union of India, AIR 1983 SC 937:
   (1983) 9 SCC 166: 1983 Tax LR 2584: (1983) 2 Comp LJ 281:
   1983 UJ (SC) 699: (1983) 54 Comp Cas 674   246
Delhi Development Authority *v.* Skipper Construction Company (P) Ltd.,
   AIR 1996 SC 2005: (1996) 4 SCC 622: 1996 AIR SCW 2401:
   1996 (2) CTC 557: JT 1996 (4) SC 679: 1996 (4) SCJ 24   157
Delhi Judicial Service Association, Tis Hazari Court, Delhi *v.* State of Gujarat,
   (1991) 4 SCC 406: AIR 1991 SC 2176: 1991 Cr LJ 3086: 1991 AIR SCW 2419:
   1991 (3) Crimes 232: JT 1991 (3) SC 617: 1991 (3) Rec Cr R 566:
   (1991) 3 SCR 936   87, 336
Delhi Police Non-Gazetted Karmchari Sangh *v.* Union of India,
   AIR 1987 SC 379: (1987) 1 SCC 115: JT 1986 SC 920: 1987 (1) Supreme 9:
   (1987) 1 Serv LJ 213: (1987) 1 LLJ 121: (1987) 2 ATC 194:
   (1987) 1 UJ (SC) 234: (1987) 1 Cur LR 344: 1987 (1) SCJ 144   45, 96
Dental Council of India *v.* Subharti K.K.B. Charitable Trust, AIR 2001 SC 2151:
   2001 AIR SCW 1883: 2001 All LJ 1130: JT 2001 (1) SC (Supp) 435:
   (2001) 5 SCC 486: 2001 (5) SCJ 82: 2001 (2) SCT 1110:
   (2001) 3 SCALE 492: 2001 (3) Supreme 529: 2001 (2) UJ (SC) 898   103
Deputy Inspector General of Police, North Range, Waltair *v.* D. Rajaram,
   AIR 1960 AP 259: (1959) 2 Andh WR 526: 1959 Andh LT 916:
   1960 Cr LJ 565: ILR (1959) AP 1294   117
Deva Ram *v.* Ishwar Chand, AIR 1996 SC 378: (1995) 6 SCC 733:
   1995 AIR SCW 4210: JT 1995 (7) SC 641: 1997 SCFBRC 84: 1995 (4) SCJ 245   148
Devarajiah *v.* B. Padmauna, AIR 1958 Mys 84   39
Devarakonda Rajesh Babu *v.* Nizam Institute of Medical Sciences, AIR 1998 AP 162:
   1998 (1) AP LJ 463: 1998 (1) Andh LD 53: 1997 (6) Andh LT 290 (FB)   31
Devdutta *v.* State of Madhya Pradesh, (1992) 19 ATC 154:
   (1991) Supp 2 SCC 553: (1991) 1 LLJ 492: (1991) 1 SLJ 168 (SC)   282
Dhan Singh *v.* State of Haryana, (1991) 2 Supp SCC 190: (1991) 17 ATC 317:
   AIR 1991 SC 1047: (1991) 2 LLN 8   277, 281
Dharam *v.* Administrator, (1991) 17 ATC 925: AIR 1991 SC 1924:
   (1991) Supp 2 SCC 635: 1991 Lab IC 1695   282
Dharti Pakar Madan Lal Agarwal *v.* K.R. Narayanan, (1997) 8 SCC 766:
   AIR 1998 SC 1462: 1998 AIR SCW 224: 1998 (2) Civ LJ 565:
   (1997) 7 SCALE 201: 1997 (10) Supreme 42   88
Dharwad District P.W.D. Leterate Daily Wage Employees Association *v.*
   State of Karnataka, (1990) 2 SCC 396: AIR 1990 SC 883:
   1990 Lab IC 625   3, 101, 282
Dhiraj Ghosh *v.* Union of India, AIR 1991 SC 73: (1991) Supp 2 SCC 203:
   1990 Lab IC 1956: 1993 (24) ATC 541: 1993 SCC (L&S) 671:
   1994 (2) SCT 736: (1993) 3 Serv LR 18   286, 289
Dhirendra Kumar Mandal *v.* Superintendent and Legal Remembrancer of
   Legal Affairs, (1955) 1 SCR 224: AIR 1954 SC 424: (1954) 2 MLJ 128   30

Dilip S. Dahanukar *v.* Kotak Mahindra Co. Ltd., (2007) 6 SCC 528:
    2007 AIR SCW 2425: 2007 (137) Com Cas 1: 2007 (2) Crimes 435:
    2008 (1) Mah LJ 22: (2007) 5 SCALE 452: 2007 (3) SCC (Cri) 209:
    2007 (3) Supreme 379   63
Dilip *v.* State of Madhya Pradesh, AIR 1976 SC 133: (1976) 1 SCC 560:
    (1976) 2 SCR 289   130
Dimple Gupta (Minor) *v.* Rajiv Gupta, AIR 2008 SC 239: 2007 AIR SCW 6651:
    2007 (4) JCC 3095: (2007) 10 SCC 30: (2007) 12 SCALE 176:
    2008 (1) SCC (Cri) 567: 2007 (8) Supreme 141   150
Dina *v.* Narayan Singh, (1968) 38 ELR 212   314
Dinesh Kumar (Dr.) *v.* Motilal Nehru Medical College, Allahabad,
    AIR 1986 SC 1877: (1986) 3 SCC 727: JT 1986 SC 97   20
Dinesh Trivedi M.P. *v.* Union of India, (1997) 4 SCC 306: JT 1997 (4) SC 237   49
Dinesh *v.* Motilal Nehru Medical College, (1990) 4 SCC 627:
    AIR 1990 SC 2030: (1990) 5 SLR 68   158
Direct Recruit Class-II Engineering Officers' Association *v.* State of Maharashtra,
    (1990) 2 SCC 715: AIR 1990 SC 1607: (1990) 13 ATC 348   213, 280
Director of Industries and Commerce, Government of A. P. Hyderabad *v.*
    V. Venkata Reddy, AIR 1973 SC 827: (1972) 2 Andh LT 243:
    (1973) 1 SCC 99: (1972) 2 LLJ 486: 1973 (1) SCJ 241:
    (1973) 1 Mad LJ (SC) 49: 1973 SCC (Lab) 75   10
Director *v.* Sitadevi, AIR 1991 SC 308: (1991) Supp 2 SCC 378: (1991) 1 LLN 578   287
Divisional Forest Officer *v.* Bishwanath Tea Co. Ltd., AIR 1981 SC 1368:
    (1981) 3 SCC 238: 1981 UJ (SC) 470   44
Divyadarsan Rajendra Ramdassji Varu *v.* State of Andhra Pradesh,
    AIR 1970 SC 181: (1970) 1 SCC 844: (1969) 2 SCA 529: 1970 (1) SCJ 334:
    (1970) 1 MLJ (SC) 86: (1970) 1 Andh WR (SC) 86: (1970) 1 SCR 103   74
Dubey *v.* M.P.S.R.T.C., (1991) Supp 1 SCC 426: AIR 1991 SC 276:
    (1991) 16 ATC 939: (1991) 1 LLN 339   282
Durgadas *v.* Empl., AIR 1979 All 148 (FB)   203
Durgah Committee, Ajmer *v.* Syed Hussain Ali, AIR 1961 SC 1402:
    (1962) 1 SCR 383: (1961) 2 SCA 171   74
Dvijendra Nath (Dr.) *v.* Director of Medical Education, Uttar Pradesh,
    Lucknow, AIR 1990 All 131: 1990 (2) All WC 896   200
Dwarka Prasad Laxmi Narain *v.* State of Uttar Pradesh, (1954) SCR 803:
    AIR 1954 SC 224: 1954 All LJ 203: 1954 SCJ 238: 1954 SCA 204   47, 50
Dwarka Nath *v.* I.T.O., AIR 1966 SC 81: (1965) 3 SCR 536: (1965) 57 ITR 349   212
Dwarka Nath Sharma *v.* Union of India, AIR 1990 SC 428:
    (1989) Supp 2 SCC 225: (1989) 2 LLN 711: (1989) 2 CLR 522   212

E

East Coast Railway *v.* Mahadev Appa Rao, AIR 2010 SC 2794   20
East India Commercial Co. Ltd. Calcutta *v.* Collector of Customs, Calcutta,
    AIR 1962 SC 1893: (1963) 3 SCR 338: (1963) 1 SCA 622   205
Ebrahim *v.* State of Bombay, Regional Transport Authority, (1954) SCR 933:
    AIR 1954 SC 229: (1953) SCR 290: 56 Bom LR 768   46
Ekta Shakti Foundation *v.* Govt. of NCT of Delhi, AIR 2006 SC 2609:
    2006 AIR SCW 3601: 2006 (64) All LR 907: 2006 (3) Ker LT 601:
    2006 (4) Mad LW 864: 2006 (8) SRJ 393: (2006) 7 SCALE 179:
    2006 (6) Supreme 372   24, 194
Election Commission of India *v.* Dr. Subramanian Swamy, (1996) 4 SCC 104:
    AIR 1996 SC 1810: 1996 AIR SCW 2100: JT 1996 (4) SC 463:
    1996 (2) Mad LJ 65: 1996 (2) RRR 572   179
Election Commission of India *v.* St. Mary's School, AIR 2008 SC 655:
    2007 AIR SCW 7761: 2008 (1) LLN 105: 2008 (1) Mad LJ 1062:
    (2008) 2 SCC 390: 2008 (1) SCT 151: 2008 (1) SRJ 561: (2007) 13 SCALE 777   147
Elizebath Samuel Aaron *v.* State of Kerala, AIR 1991 Ker 162: 1992 (75) Comp Cas 377:
    ILR (1991) 2 Ker 113: 1991 (1) Ker LJ 626: 1991 (1) Ker LT 475 (FB)   86, 272

Emperor *v.* Sibnath Banerjee, AIR 1943 FC 75: 1945 FCR 195   204
Emperor *v.* Sibnath Banerjee, AIR 1946 PC 158: 72 IA 241   204
English M.S.I.A. *v.* State of Karnataka, (1994) UJSC 291: (1994) 1 SCC 550:
     AIR 1994 SC 1702   91
Eskayef *v.* C.C.E., (1990) 4 SCC 680: (1990) 49 ELT 649   24
Eureka Engineers Co-operative Society Ltd. *v.* Superintending Engineer,
     Mahananda Barrage Circle, AIR 1998 Cal 12   214
Excel Wear *v.* Union of India, AIR 1979 SC 25: (1978) 4 SCC 224: (1978) 2 LLJ 527   3, 4
Executive Engineer Bhadrak (Rand B) Division, Orissa *v.* Rangadhar Mallik,
     (1992) 2 UJ SC 453: (1993) Supp 1 SCC 763: (1993) 23 ATC 807:
     1993 Lab IC 425   287
Ex-Naik Sardar Singh *v.* Union of India, (1991) 2 UJ SC 466: (1991) 3 SCC 213:
     AIR 1992 SC 417: (1991) 2 Crimes 674   199
Express Newspapers Pvt. Ltd. *v.* Union of India, AIR 1986 SC 872: (1986) 1 SCC 133:
     1986 SCFBRC 72: (1986) 29 DLT 131: (1986) 2 MCC 171:
     1986 Cur Civ LJ (SC) 268: 1986 Recent Laws 7   48
Express Newspapers *v.* Union of India, AIR 1958 SC 578: 1959 SCR 12:
     (1961) 1 LLJ 339   48, 87

F

F.C.J. *v.* Narendra, (1993) 1 UJ SC 572   156
Farooq *v.* Union of India, (1990) 2 SCJ 225: AIR 1990 SC 1597: 1990 Cr LJ 1622   69
Faruk *v.* State of Madhya Pradesh, AIR 1970 SC 93: (1969) 1 SCC 853: 1969 MLLJ 950   47
Fatehchand Himatlal *v.* State of Maharashtra, AIR 1977 SC 1825:
     (1977) 2 SCC 670: (1977) 2 SCR 828   51
Father Thomas Shingare *v.* State of Maharashtra, (2002) 1 SCC 758:
     AIR 2002 SC 463: 2002 SCC (Cri) 273   79
Fazal Ghafoor (Dr.) *v.* Union of India, AIR 1989 SC 48: JT 1988 (3) SC 698:
     (1988) 2 UJ (SC) 613   344
Fedco (P) Ltd. *v.* S.N. Bilgrami, (1960) SCJ 235: AIR 1960 SC 415: (1960) 1 SCA 369:
     (1960) 1 Mad LJ (SC) 71: (1960) 2 SCR 408: (1960) 1 Andh WR (SC) 71:
     (1960) 62 Bom LR 293: 1960 Mad LJ (Cri) 184   47
Federation of Bar Association in Karnataka *v.* Union of India, AIR 2000 SC 2544:
     (2000) 6 SCC 715: 2000 AIR SCW 2626: JT 2000 (2) SC (Supp) 303:
     2000 (7) SRJ 344: (2000) 5 SCALE 269: 2000 (2) UJ (SC) 1149   189
Federation of Hotel and Restaurant Association of India *v.* Union of India,
     JT 1989 (Supp) 168: (1989) 178 ITR 97: AIR 1990 SC 1637:
     (1989) 3 SCC 634: (1989) 74 STC 102   29, 245, 249
Fernandez *v.* State of Maharashtra, (1964) 66 Bom LR 185   49
Fertilizer Corporation of India *v.* Union of India, AIR 1981 SC 344:
     (1981) 1 SCC 568: (1981) 2 SCR 52: (1981) 1 LLJ 193   92, 94, 211
Food Corporation of India Workers Union *v.* Food Corporation of India,
     (1990) Supp SCC 296: AIR 1990 SC 2178: (1990) 2 LLN 664:
     (1990) 4 SLR 745   90, 93, 94, 101
Forum, Prevention of Envn. & Sound Pollution *v.* Union of India, AIR 2006 SC 348:
     2005 AIR SCW 5890: 2006 (62) All LR 339: 2006 (1) All MR 248:
     2006 (1) All WC 5: 2006 (1) Cal LJ 99: 2006 (1) JCR SC 90: JT 2005 (9) SC 319:
     2005 (4) Ker LT 824: 2006 (1) Mad LJ 49: (2005) 8 SCC 796: 2005 (8) SCJ 233:
     (2005) 9 SCALE 69: 2005 (7) Supreme 504   26
Fram Naserwanji *v.* State of Bombay, AIR 1951 Bom 216   99
Francis Coralie Mullin *v.* Administrator, Union Territory of Delhi,
     AIR 1981 SC 746: (1981) 1 SCC 608: 1981 Cr LJ 306   63, 65
Francis John *v.* Director of Education, AIR 1990 SC 423:
     (1989) Supp 2 SCC 598: 1990 SCC (L&S) 105   195
Frank Anthony Public School Employees' Association *v.* Union of India,
     AIR 1987 SC 311: (1986) 4 SCC 707: 1986 JT 861: (1987) 1 LLN 53:
     (1987) 54 FLR 353: 1987 Mah LJ 1: 1987 MPLJ 1: (1987) 1 SCWR 86:
     (1987) 2 ATC 35   79, 81

G

G. Beena v. Andhra Pradesh University of Health Sciences, AIR 1990 AP 247:
    (1990) 2 Andh LT 67   23
G.B. Mahajan v. Jalgaon Municipal Council, (1991) 3 SCC 91:
    AIR 1991 SC 1153: 1991 (3) Bom CR 139: JT 1991 (1) SC 605   208, 212
G.B. Pant University of Agriculture and Technology v. State of Uttar Pradesh,
    AIR 2000 SC 2695: (2000) 7 SCC 109: (2000) 1 LLJ 1109: 2000 All LJ 2420   5
G.P. Doval v. Chief Secretary, Govt. of U.P., AIR 1984 SC 1527:
    (1984) 4 SCC 329: 1984 Lab IC 1304: (1984) 2 Serv LJ 166: (1984) 2 LLN 517   94
Gandhi & Co. v. State of Maharashtra, AIR 1990 Bom 218:
    1989 Mah LR 1708: (1989) 2 Bom CR 380   200
Gandhi Faiz-e-am College, Shahjahanpur v. Agra University, AIR 1975 SC 1821:
    (1975) 2 SCC 283: (1975) 3 SCR 810: 1976 (3) SCJ 74   80
Gannon Dunkerly & Co. v. State of Rajasthan, (1993) 1 SCC 364:
    (1993) 88 STC 204: 1993 AIR SCW 2621   334
Garg v. State of Uttar Pradesh, (1991) 2 UJ SC 571   206
Garg v. Union of India, AIR 1981 SC 2138: (1981) 4 SCC 675: (1982) 133 ITR 239   141
Garhwal Jal Sansthan v. State of Uttar Pradesh, AIR 1997 SC 2143:
    (1997) 4 SCC 24: 1997 All LJ 1175   102
Garikapati Veeraya v. N. Subbiah Choudhry, AIR 1957 SC 540: 1957 SCA 495:
    1957 SCJ 439: (1957) 2 Mad LJ (SC) 1: (1957) 2 Andh WR (SC) 1: 1957 SCR 399 353
Gasket Radiators v. E.S.I.C., AIR 1985 SC 79: (1985) 2 SCC 68:
    (1985) 1 LLJ 506: 1985 Lab IC 682   156
Gaurav Jain v. Union of India, AIR 1990 SC 292: 1990 Supp SCC 709   71, 92
Gaurav Jain v. Union of India, AIR 1997 SC 3021: (1997) 8 SCC 114:
    1997 AIR SCW 3055: 1997 (3) Crimes 40: JT 1997 (6) SC 305: 1997 (2) SCJ 334:
    (1997) 4 SCALE 657: 1998 SCC (Cri) 25: 1997 (6) Supreme 394   62, 71
Gauri Shanker Sharma v. State of Uttar Pradesh, AIR 1990 SC 709:
    1990 Supp SCC 656: JT 1990 (1) SC 6   149
Gauri Shanker v. Union of India, JT 1994 (5) SC 634: (1994) 6 SCC 349:
    AIR 1995 SC 55: 1995 (1) SCT 56: 1994 AIR SCW 4059:
    1994 (2) Ren CJ 391: 1994 (2) Rent LR 283: 1994 SCFBRC 356   57
Gaurya v. Thakur, AIR 1986 SC 1140: (1986) 2 SCC 709: 1986 Cr LJ 1074   156
Gazi Khan v. State of Rajasthan, AIR 1990 SC 1361: (1990) 3 SCC 459:
    1990 Cr LJ 1420   88
General Manager Southern Railway v. Rangachari, AIR 1962 SC 36:
    (1962) 2 SCR 586: 1961 2 Mad LJ (SC) 71: (1961) 2 Andh WR (SC) 71:
    1961 (2) SCJ 424: (1961) 2 SCA 460   30, 36
Ghulam Nabi v. State of Jammu & Kashmir, AIR 1990 J&K 20   47
Gian Kaur v. State of Punjab, AIR 1996 SC 1257: (1996) 2 SCC 648:
    1996 SCC (Cri) 374   63
Girdhar v. State, AIR 1953 MB 147: 1953 MB LJ 529   34
Giridharilal Soni v. Municipal Commission, Calcutta Municipal Corporation,
    AIR 2001 Cal 12: 2000 (2) Cal HN 578: 2001 CWN 310   272
Gladhurst Co-op. Housing Society Ltd. v. Dr. (Mrs.) V.B. Shah,
    AIR 2006 (NOC) 1217 (Bom)   155
Godse v. State of Maharashtra, AIR 1961 SC 600: (1961) 3 SCC 440:
    (1961) 1 Cr LJ 736   117
Goodyear India Ltd. v. State of Haryana, AIR 1990 SC 781:
    (1990) 2 SCC 712: JT 1989 (4) SC 229   259, 273
Gopal v. Union of India, AIR 1987 SC 413: 1986 Supp SCC 501: (1987) 2 ATC 495   96
Gopalan v. State of Madras, (1950) SCR 88: AIR 1950 SC 27: (1950) 1 MLJ 42   69, 71
Gopalanachari v. Administrator, State of Kerala, AIR 1981 SC 674:
    1980 Supp SCC 649: 1981 Cr LJ 337   65
Gopi Aqua Farms v. Union of India, AIR 1997 SC 3519: (1997) 6 SCC 577:
    1997 AIR SCW 3614: JT 1997 (7) SC 75: (1997) 5 SCALE 273:
    1997 (7) Supreme 253: 1997 UJ (SC) 499   89

Gopi Chand *v.* Delhi Administration, AIR 1959 SC 609: (1959) Supp 2 SCR 87:
1959 Cr LJ 782   24
Governing Council of Kidwai Memorial Institute of Oncology, Bangalore *v.*
Dr. Pandurang Godwalkar, (1992) 4 SCC 719: AIR 1993 SC 392:
1992 AIR SCW 3297: 1993 (23) ATC 389: (1993) 1 LLJ 308:
1993 SCC (L&S) 1: 1993 (1) SCT 267: (1993) 2 Serv LJ SC 174   299
Government of Andhra Pradesh *v.* A. Suryanarayanarao, AIR 1991 SC 2113:
(1991) Supp 2 SCC 367: 1991 AIR SCW 2404: JT 1991 (4) SC 206:
1992 SCC (L&S) 62: (1991) Supp 2 SCC 367: (1991) 2 UJ (SC) 623   344
Government of Andhra Pradesh *v.* Hindustan Machine Tools Ltd.,
AIR 1975 SC 2037: (1975) 2 SCC 274: (1975) 1 APLJ (SC) 41:
1975 Tax LR 2013: (1975) 2 SCWR 293: 1975 Supp SCR 394   244
Government of Andhra Pradesh *v.* Maharshi Publishers Pvt. Ltd.,
AIR 2003 SC 296: (2003) 1 SCC 95: 2002 AIR SCW 4771: JT 2002 (9) SC 277:
2002 (10) SRJ 457: (2002) 8 SCALE 291: 2002 (7) Supreme 570   27
Government of Andhra Pradesh *v.* Syed Md., AIR 1962 SC 1778:
(1962) Supp 3 SCR 288: (1963) 2 MLJ (SC) 62   13
Government of India *v.* Nambudri, AIR 1991 SC 1261: (1991) 3 SCC 38:
1991 SCC (L&S) 813: (1991) 17 ATC 104   285
Government of the Federal Republic of Germany *v.* Sotiaridis, (1974) CLYB 1665   108
Govind *v.* State of Madhya Pradesh, AIR 1975 SC 1378: (1975) 1 All LR 752:
1975 Cr LJ 1111: (1975) 2 SCC 148: 1975 SCC (Cri) 468: (1975) 3 SCR 946   45, 62, 63
Govind *v.* State of Maharashtra, (1990) 4 SCC 718: (1990) 2 Crimes 256   208
Gracy *v.* State of Kerala, AIR 1991 SC 1090: (1991) 2 SCC 1: 1991 SCC (Cri) 467   69, 88
Gramophone Co. *v.* Birendra, AIR 1984 SC 667: (1984) 2 SCC 534: 1984 SCC (Cri) 313   109
Green View Tea & Industries *v.* Collector, Golaghat, (2002) 1 SCC 109:
AIR 2002 SC 180: 2001 AIR SCW 4788: JT 2001 (9) SC 497:
(2001) 8 SCALE 163: 2001 (8) Supreme 202   152
Grid Corporation of Orissa *v.* Rasananda Das, AIR 2003 SC 4599:
(2003) 10 SCC 297: 2003 Lab IC 3690: 2003 AIR SCW 5390:
2004 (2) LLJ 1053: 2004 (1) LLN 65: 2004 SCC (L&S) 214: 2004 (1) SCT 412:
(2003) 8 SCALE 129: 2004 (1) Serv LJ 259 SC: 2003 (6) Supreme 938   38
Grih Kalyan Kendra Workers' Union *v.* Union of India, (1991) 1 SCC 619:
AIR 1991 SC 1173: 1991 AIR SCW 194: JT 1991 (1) SC 60: 1991 (1) LLJ 349:
1991 (1) LLN 319: 1991 SCC (L&S) 621: 1991 SCD 146: (1991) 1 SCR 15:
1991 (1) Serv LR 618: 1991 (1) UJ (SC) 468   93, 99, 101
Gujarat Agricultural University *v.* Rathod Labhu Bechar, AIR 2001 SC 706:
2001 AIR SCW 351: JT 2001 (2) SC 16: (2001) 3 SCC 574: 2001 SCC (L&S) 613:
2001 (2) SCJ 46: 2001 (2) SCT 394: (2001) 1 SCALE 270: (2001) 1 Serv LR 519:
2001 (1) Supreme 239: 2001 (2) UJ (SC) 922   100
Gujarat Electricity Board *v.* Thakar Hasmukhhai Khelshanker,
AIR 2006 Guj 16: 2006 (1) AIR Jhar (NOC) 129   215, 219
Gujarat University *v.* Shri Krishna, AIR 1963 SC 703: (1963) Supp 1 SCR 112:
(1963) 4 Guj LR 450   78
Gulam *v.* State of Uttar Pradesh, AIR 1981 SC 2198: (1982) 1 SCC 71:
(1981) 1 SCR 107   16
Gulshan Prakash *v.* State of Haryana, AIR 2010 SC 288   33
Gupta Sugar Works *v.* State of Uttar Pradesh, AIR 1987 SC 2351:
(1987) Supp SCC 476: JT 1987 (5) SC 154   91
Gupta *v.* U.P.S.E.B., AIR 1991 SC 1309: (1991) 2 SCC 263   152
Gurbachan *v.* State of Bombay, (1952) SCR 737: AIR 1952 SC 221:
54 Bom LR 849: 1952 Cr LJ 1147   46, 50
Guwahati University *v.* Raj Konwar, (1970) Assam LR 1   215, 217

H

H. Anraj *v.* State of Maharashtra, AIR 1984 SC 781: (1984) 2 SCC 292:
(1984) 1 SCWR 293: 1984 UJ (SC) 909   269

H.C. Puttaswamy A. *v.* Chief Justice of Karnataka High Court, AIR 1991 SC 295:
    (1991) Supp 2 SCC 421: (1991) 1 LLN 352: (1991) 1 CLR 362   220
H.H. Maharajadhiraja Madhav Rao Jivaji Rao Scindia Bahadur *v.* Union of India,
    AIR 1971 SC 530: (1971) 1 SCC 85: (1971) 3 SCR 9: 1971 (1) SCJ 295:
    1971 Mer LR 78: (1971) 2 SCA 257   111
H.P. Public Service Commission *v.* Mukesh Thakur, AIR 2010 SC 2620   38
H.R. Adanthaya *v.* Sandoz, JT 1994 (5) SC 176: (1994) 5 SCC 737:
    1994 SCC (L&S) 1283: AIR 1994 SC 2608: (1994) 69 FLR 593   156
H.S. Srinivasa Raghavachar *v.* State of Karnataka, AIR 1987 SC 1518:
    (1987) 2 SCC 692: (1987) 4 (1) IJ (Rep) 220: JT 1987 (4) SC 26:
    ILR (1987) Kant 2059: 1987 (1) Supreme 642: (1987) 2 Cur CC 166:
    1987 (2) SCJ 611: (1987) 2 UJ (SC) 427: 1987 (2) Land LR 530   19, 102, 252
H.S. Vankani *v.* State of Gujarat, AIR 2010 SC 1714   39
H.S.S.K. Niyami *v.* Union of India, (1990) 4 SCC 516: AIR 1990 SC 2128   48, 86
Haji Esmail Noor Mohammad and Co. *v.* Competent Officer, Lucknow,
    AIR 1967 SC 1244: (1967) 3 SCR 134: (1967) 1 SCA 497   93
Haji Usmanbhai Hasanbhai Qureshi *v.* State of Gujarat, AIR 1986 SC 1213:
    (1986) 3 SCC 12: (1986) 1 MCC 163: 1986 Cr LR (SC) 370:
    1986 (3) Supreme 250: 1986 (2) SCJ 447   30
Hansmukh *v.* State of Gujarat, AIR 1981 SC 28: (1981) 2 SCC 175: (1981) 1 SCR 353 69
Hanuman Vitamins Foods Pvt. Ltd. *v.* State of Maharashtra, AIR 1990 Bom 204:
    1989 Bank J 377: 1989 Mah LJ 935: (1989) 2 Bom CR 460 (DB)   249
Har Shankar *v.* Deputy Excise and Taxation Commissioner, AIR 1975 SC 1121:
    (1975) 1 SCC 737: 1975 Tax LR 1569: (1975) 3 SCR 254   46
Haradhan Shah *v.* State of West Bengal, AIR 1974 SC 2154: (1975) 3 SCC 198:
    1974 Cr LJ 1479: 1974 SCC (Cri) 816: (1975) 1 SCR 778   49
Harakchand Ratanchand Banthia *v.* Union of India, AIR 1970 SC 1453:
    (1969) 2 SCC 166: 1969 Pat LJR (SC) 744: (1970) 1 SCR 479:
    (1970) 2 SCA 436: 1969 Mer LR 17   47
Harbans *v.* State of Uttar Pradesh, AIR 1982 SC 849: (1982) 2 SCC 101:
    1982 Cr LJ 795   117
Hardwari Lal *v.* Ch. Bhajan Lal, AIR 1993 P&H 3: ILR 1993 (1) P&H 184:
    1992 (2) Land LR 228: 1992 Punj LJ 146: (1992) 2 SCT 226   178
Hargovind *v.* Raghukul, AIR 1979 SC 1109: (1979) 4 SCC 358: 1979 Lab IC 818   294
Hari Jai Singh (in re:), AIR 1997 SC 73: (1996) 6 SCC 466: 1997 Cr LJ 58:
    1996 AIR SCW 4227: 1997 (1) BLJR 907: JT 1996 (8) SC 332:
    1997 (12) OCR 399: 1997 (1) Pat LJR 18: 1997 SC Cr R 364   44
Harish Uppal *v.* Union of India, AIR 2003 SC 739: (2003) 2 SCC 45:
    (2003) 1 KLT 192   159
Harivansh *v.* State of Maharashtra, (1971) 2 SCC 54: AIR 1971 SC 1130: 1971 Cr LJ 842 7
Harjinder Singh *v.* Punjab State Warehousing Corporation, AIR 2010 SC 1116   2
Hasmattulah *v.* State of Madhya Pradesh, AIR 1996 SC 2076: (1996) 4 SCC 391:
    1996 AIR SCW 2498: 1996 (3) ICC 255: JT 1996 (5) SC 295: 1996 Jab LJ 406:
    1996 (3) SCJ 113: 1996 (2) UJ (SC) 478   42
Hathising Manufacturing Co. *v.* Union of India, AIR 1960 SC 923:
    (1960) 3 SCR 928: (1960) 2 LLJ 1   46
High Court of Judicature at Allahabad *v.* Raj Kishore, AIR 1997 SC 1186:
    (1997) 3 SCC 11: 1997 All LJ 795   189
High Court of Judicature at Bombay *v.* Shirish Kumar Rangrao Patil,
    AIR 1997 SC 2631: (1997) 6 SCC 339: (1997) 4 SLR 321: 1997 SCC (L&S) 1486 222
Himmat Lal *v.* State of Madhya Pradesh, AIR 1954 SC 403: 1954 SCR 1122:
    (1954) 5 STC 115   87
Hindi Hitrakshak Samiti *v.* Union of India, AIR 1990 SC 851:
    (1990) 2 SCC 352: (1990) 4 SLR 4   79, 90, 91
Hindu Religious Endowments, Commissioner, Madras *v.* Lakshmindra
    Thirtha Swamiar of Sri Shirur Mutt, (1954) SCR 1005: AIR 1954 SC 282:
    1954 SCJ 335: (1954) 1 Mad LJ 596: 20 Cut LT 250: 1954 SCA 415:
    1954 Mad WN 363   74, 75

Hindustan Antibiotics *v.* Workmen, (1967) 1 SCR 652: AIR 1967 SC 948:
    30 FJR 461: (1967) 1 LLJ 114: 14 FLR 37: (1967) 1 SCWR 361:
    (1967) 1 SCA 669: 1967 (1) SCJ 12   29
Hindustan Machine Tools *v.* M. Rangareddy, AIR 2000 SC 3287:
    2000 AIR SCW 3586: JT 2000 (1) SC (Supp) 267: (2000) 7 SCC 741:
    2000 SCC (L&S) 1039: 2001 (1) SCT 267: (2000) 6 SCALE 614:
    2000 (6) Supreme 535   100, 104
Hindustan Paper Corporation Ltd. *v.* Government of Kerala, (1986) 3 SCC 398:
    AIR 1986 SC 1541: 1986 Comp LJ 238: (1986) 2 Cur CC 689:
    1986 (3) Supreme 273: (1986) 2 UJ (SC) 551: (1986) 19 STL 61: 1986 (2) SCJ 436   29
Hindustan Times *v.* State of Uttar Pradesh, AIR 2003 SC 250:
    (2003) 1 SCC 591: (2003) 1 LLJ 206: (2002) 258 ITR 469   25
Hira Nath Mishra *v.* The Principal, Rajendra Medical College, Ranchi,
    AIR 1973 SC 1260: (1973) 1 SCC 805: (1973) 2 LLJ 111 (SC):
    (1973) UJ SC 83   196, 215
Hoechst Pharmaceuticals Ltd. *v.* State of Bihar, AIR 1983 SC 1019:
    (1983) 4 SCC 45: 1983 UJ (SC) 617: 1983 SCC (Tax) 248:
    (1983) 8 STL (SC) 1   182, 253
Hotel Balaji *v.* State of Andhra Pradesh, AIR 1993 SC 1048:
    (1993) Supp 4 SCC 536: (1993) 88 STC 98   245
Hukam Singh *v.* State of Punjab, AIR 1975 P&H 148: 1975 Cr LJ 902:
    ILR (1975) 1 P&H 619: 78 Punj LR 28: (1976) 3 Cr LT 1   117
Hundraj Kanyalal Sajnani *v.* Union of India, AIR 1990 SC 1106:
    1990 Supp SCC 577: 1990 Lab IC 890: (1990) 2 SLR 400   101, 248
Hussainara (I) *v.* Home Secretary, State of Bihar, AIR 1979 SC 1360:
    (1980) 1 SCC 81: 1979 Cr LJ 1036: (1980) 1 SCC 93:
    1980 SCC (Cri) 35   9, 55, 60, 66, 67, 102
Hussainara Khatoon *v.* Home Secretary, State of Bihar, Patna,
    AIR 1979 SC 1369: 1979 Cr LJ 1045: 1979 Pat LJR 410:
    (1979) 3 SCR 532: (1980) 1 SCC 98: 1980 SCC (Cri) 40   59, 60, 66, 67, 102
Hussainara *v.* Home Secretary, State of Bihar, AIR 1979 SC 1377:
    (1980) 1 SCC 108: 1980 SCC (Cri) 50: 1980 MLJ (Cr) 93: 1979 Cr LJ 1052   59, 66, 67
Hussainara *v.* Home Secretary, State of Bihar, AIR 1980 SC 1819:
    (1980) 1 SCC 115: 1979 Cr LJ 1134   66, 67

I

I. Nelson *v.* Kallayam Pastorate, AIR 2007 SC 1337: 2007 AIR SCW 1512:
    2007 (1) All WC 162: 2007 (1) Andh LD 9: (2006) 11 SCC 624:
    2006 (10) SRJ 334: (2006) 9 SCALE 245: 2006 (8) Supreme 856   73
I.A.C. *v.* Shukla, (1993) 23 ATC 407 (SC): (1993) 1 SCC 17: (1993) 1 LLJ 215   94
I.D.P.L., Officers and Supervisors *v.* Chairman and M.D., I.D.P.L.,
    AIR 2003 SC 2870: (2003) 6 SCC 490: 2003 SCC (L&S) 916: (2003) 3 LLN 870   39
I.I.T. *v.* Union of India, (1991) Supp 2 SCC 12: 1991 SCC (L&S) 1137:
    (1991) 17 ATC 352   288
I.R. Coelho *v.* State of Tamil Nadu, AIR 2007 SC 861: 2007 AIR SCW 611:
    2007 (1) All WC 689: 2007 (2) Andh LT 1: 2007 (3) Civ LJ 589:
    2007 (2) JCR SC 148: 2007 (1) Ker LT 623: 2007 (3) Mad LJ 423:
    (2007) 2 SCC 1: (2007) 1 SCALE 197: 2007 (1) Supreme 137   1
I.T. Appellate Tribunal *v.* V.K. Agarwal, AIR 1999 SC 452: (1999) 1 SCC 16:
    1999 SCC (Cri) 252: 1999 Cr LJ 441   145
I.T.O. *v.* N. Takin Roy Rymbai, (1976) 103 ITR 82: (1976) 1 SCC 916:
    AIR 1976 SC 670   29
Imkong Imchen *v.* Union of India, AIR 2006 Gau 1: 2006 (1) ALJ (NOC) 151:
    2006 (1) AIR Jhar (NOC) 126: 2005 Gau LT (supp) 75   22
Inderjeet *v.* State of Uttar Pradesh, AIR 1979 SC 1867: (1979) 4 SCC 246:
    1979 UJ (SC) 679: 1979 All Cr R 428: 1979 Cr LJ 1410: (1980) 1 SCWR 33:
    1979 SCC (Cri) 966: 1979 All Cr C 350: ILR 1979 HP 148   55, 60

Inderpreet Singh Kahlon v. State of Punjab, AIR 2006 SC 2571:
    2006 AIR SCW 3346: 2006 (3) All CJ 1826: ILR 2006 Kant SC 1 SN:
    2006 (6) SCJ 107: 2006 (3) SCT 25: (2006) 5 SCALE 273:
    2006 (3) SCT 25: 2006 (7) SRJ 432: 2006 (4) Supreme 8   25, 206
Indian Cement v. State of Andhra Pradesh, AIR 1988 SC 567:
    (1988) 1 SCC 743: (1988) 69 STC 305   274
Indian Council for Enviro-legal Action v. Union of India, AIR 1996 SC 1446:
    1996 AIR SCW 1069: 1996 (2) Comp LJ SC 385: JT 1996 (2) SC 196:
    (1996) 3 SCC 212: (1996) 2 SCR 503: 1998 (5) Supreme 226   62, 64
Indian Drugs and Pharmaceuticals Ltd. v. Workman, Indian Drugs and
    Pharmaceuticals Ltd., (2007) 1 SCC 408: 2006 AIR SCW 5994: 2007 (1) ALJ 505   65
Indian Express Newspapers (Bombay) Private Ltd. v. Union of India,
    AIR 1986 SC 515: (1985) 1 Comp LJ 115: 1985 Cr LR (SC) 79:
    (1985) 1 SCC 641: 1985 SCC (Tax) 121: 1985 Cur Cr LJ (SC) 140:
    (1985) 2 SCR 287: (1986) 159 ITR 856   24, 48, 93
Indian Ex-Service League v. Union of India, AIR 1991 SC 1182: (1991) 2 SCC 104:
    (1991) 16 ATC 488: (1991) 1 LLN 387: (1991) 1 SLR 745   277, 281
Indian Handicrafts Emporium v. Union of India, AIR 2003 SC 3240:
    (2003) 7 SCC 589: (2003) 106 DLT 350   47, 272
Indian Oil Corporation v. Municipal Corporation, Jullunder,
    AIR 1990 P&H 99: 1989 (2) Land LR 192   247
Indira Nehru Gandhi v. Raj Narain, AIR 1975 SC 2299: 1975 Supp SCC 1:
    (1976) 2 SCR 347   2, 19, 86, 126, 173, 187, 244, 304, 335, 336
Indira Sawhney v. Union of India, AIR 1993 SC 477: 1992 AIR SCW 3682:
    JT 1992 (6) SC 273: 1993 (1) SCJ 353: 1993 (1) SCT 448:
    (1992) Supp 3 SCC 217: 1992 SCC (L&S) Supp 1:
    (1992) 22 ATC 385   27, 39, 40, 92, 91, 156, 308, 336
Indira Sawhney v. Union of India, AIR 2000 SC 498: (2000) 1 SCC 168:
    2000 SCC (L&S) 1   23
Indira v. Union of India, (1999) Supp 5 SCC 557   87
Indore Municipal Corporation v. Dr. Hemalata, AIR 2010 SC 1758   147
Indore Vikas Pradhikaran, Chairman v. Pure Industrial Coke & Chemicals Ltd.,
    (2007) 8 SCC 705: AIR 2007 SC 2458: 2007 AIR SCW 4387:
    2007 (4) MPHT 1: (2007) 8 SCALE 110   272
Indu Bhushan Dwivedi v. State of Jharkhand, AIR 2010 SC 2472   287
Inspector General of Registrations and Stamps, Hyderabad v.
    Andhra Pradesh State Document Writers' Associations,
    AIR 2003 AP 193: (2003) 4 Andh LD 141: (2002) 3 Andh LT 245   50
Intellectuals Forum, Tirupathi v. State of Andhra Pradesh, AIR 2006 SC 1350:
    2006 AIR SCW 1309: 2006 (2) CTC 71: 2006 (4) Comp LJ 513 SC:
    (2006) 3 SCC 549: 2006 (2) SCJ 293: 2006 (4) SRJ 101: 2006 (2) Supreme 292   107
International Airports Authority of India v. Municipal Corporation of Delhi,
    AIR 1991 Del 302: 1991 (1) Comp LJ 337 Del: ILR 1991 (2) Del 265   264
Iron & Metal Traders v. Haskiel, AIR 1984 SC 629: (1984) 1 SCC 304:
    (1983) 2 LLJ 504: 1984 Lab IC 182   24
Islamia Karimia Society, Indore v. Devi Ahilya Vishwavidyalaya Indore,
    AIR 1988 MP 22: 1988 MPLJ 151: 1988 CCLJ (MP) 81   80
Issac Babu v. Union of India, (1990) 4 SCC 135: 1990 SCC (Cri) 564   69
Izhar Ahmad Khan v. Union of India, AIR 1962 SC 1052: (1962) 2 Cr LJ 215:
    1963 BLJR 99: (1963) 1 SCA 136: (1962) Supp 3 SCR 235   14

J

J. Ranga Swamy v. Government of Andhra Pradesh, AIR 1990 SC 535:
    (1990) 1 SCC 288: 1990 SCC (L&S) 76: (1990) 1 LLJ 526   153
J.K. Aggarwal v. Haryana Seeds Development Corporation Ltd., (1991) 2 SCC 283:
    AIR 1991 SC 1221: 1991 (16) ATC 480: JT 1991 (5) SC 191:
    (1991) 2 Lab LJ 412: 1992 LLR 21: 1991 Lab IC 1008:
    1991 SCC (L&S) 483: (1991) 3 Serv LJ SC 161: (1991) 1 UJ (SC) 633   205, 288

J.K. Jute Mills Co. Ltd. *v.* State of Uttar Pradesh, AIR 1961 SC 1534:
    1961 (12) STC 429: (1962) 2 SCR 1   245
J.P. Bansal *v.* State of Rajasthan, AIR 2003 SC 1405: (2003) 5 SCC 134:
    (2003) 3 SCR 50: (2003) 2 LLN 405   168, 283
Jacab *v.* Kerala Water Authority, (1991) 1 SCC 28: AIR 1990 SC 2228:
    (1990) 2 KLT 673   103
Jagdev Singh Sidhanti *v.* Pratap Singh Daulta, AIR 1965 SC 183:
    (1964) 6 SCR 750: 1964 Cur LJ (SC) 231: 1964 (2) SCJ 633: (1965) 1 SCA 72   78
Jagdish Saran (Dr.) *v.* Union of India, AIR 1980 SC 820: (1980) 2 SCC 768:
    (1980) 12 Lawyer 21: ILR 1980 HP 61   21
Jai Shankar Prasad *v.* State of Bihar, (1993) 2 SCC 597: AIR 1993 SC 1906:
    (1993) 2 SCR 357: (1993) 24 ATC 584: (1993) 3 SLJ 32   293, 295
Jai Singh Rathi *v.* State of Haryana, AIR 1970 P&H 379   187
Jain Studios Ltd. *v.* Shin Satellite Public Co. Ltd., AIR 2006 SC 2686:
    2006 AIR SCW 3592: 2006 (5) Andh LD 71: (2006) 5 SCC 501:
    2006 (8) SRJ 266: (2006) 7 SCALE 34: 2006 (5) Supreme 369   152
Jaipur Development Authority, Secretary *v.* Daulat Mal Jain, (1997) 1 SCC 35:
    JT 1996 (8) SC 387   168
Jaiswal *v.* Debi, (1992) 1 UJ SC 731   281
Jalan Trading Co. (P) Ltd. *v.* D.M. Aney, AIR 1979 SC 233: 1978 Lab IC 1772:
    (1979) 3 SCC 220   99
Jalan Trading Co. *v.* Mill Mazdoor Sabha, AIR 1967 SC 691: (1967) 1 SCR 15:
    (1966) 2 LLJ 546   19
Jarnail *v.* Secretary, (1993) 1 SCC 47: AIR 1994 SC 1484: (1993) 1 LLJ 962:
    (1993 1 SCR 23   334
Jasbhai Motibhai Desai *v.* Roshan Kumar, Haji Bashir Ahmed, AIR 1976 SC 578:
    (1976) 1 SCC 671: (1976) 3 SCR 58   212
Jasbir Rani *v.* State of Punjab, AIR 2002 SC 60: (2002) 1 SCC 124:
    2002 SCC (L&S) 107: (2002) 1 SLR 124   39
Jaswant Kaur *v.* State of Haryana, AIR 1977 P&H 221: 1977 Punj LJ 230:
    1977 Cur LJ (Civ) 324: 1977 Rev LR 418: ILR (1977) 2 P&H 116   252
Jaswant Rai *v.* State of Punjab, AIR 1967 P&H 155: 1967 Cr LJ 577:
    ILR (1967) 2 P&H 244: (1967) 69 Punj LR 1024   117
Jaswant *v.* State of Punjab, (1991) Supp 1 SCC 313: (1991) 1 LLJ 580:
    (1991) 16 ATC 932   277
Jatish Chandra Ghose *v.* Harisadhan Mukherjee, AIR 1956 Cal 433: (1956) 60 CWN 971 133
Jatish Chandra Ghose *v.* Harisadhan Mukherjee, AIR 1961 SC 613:
    (1961) 3 SCR 486: (1961) 1 Cr LJ 443   133
Javed *v.* State of Maharashtra, AIR 1985 SC 231: (1985) 1 SCC 275:
    1984 SCC (Cri) 653   61, 62
Jawala Ram *v.* State of Pepsu, AIR 1962 SC 1246: (1962) 2 SCR 503:
    (1962) 2 Cr LJ 303   53
Jaya Bachchan *v.* Union of India, AIR 2006 SC 2119: 2006 AIR SCW 2601:
    2006 (34) OCR 837: (2006) 5 SCC 266: 2006 (5) SCJ 1: 2006 (7) SRJ 330:
    (2006) 5 SCALE 511: 2006 (4) Supreme 378   131
Jesuratnam *v.* Chief of Air Staff, (1976) Cr LJ 65   96
Jesuratnam *v.* Union of India, (1990) Supp SCC 640: 1990 SCC (L&S) 370   278
Jilubhai Nanbhai Khachar *v.* State of Gujarat, JT 1994 (4) SC 473: AIR 1995 SC 142:
    1994 (72) Taxman 435: 1994 (1) UPTC 603: 1994 AIR SCW 4181   272
Jindal Stainless Ltd. *v.* State of Haryana, AIR 2006 SC 2550: 2006 AIR SCW 3396:
    2006 (2) All CJ 1216: 2006 (283) ITR 1: (2006) 7 SCC 241: (2006) 4 SCALE 300:
    2006 (3) Supreme 593: 2006 (194) Taxation 525   273
Jitendra Panchal *v.* Intelligence Officer, NCB, AIR 2009 SC 1938:
    2009 AIR SCW 1559: 2009 (1) Crimes 338: 2009 (3) Mad LJ (Cri) 333:
    (2009) 3 SCC 57: (2009) 2 SCALE 202: 2009 (1) SCC (Cri) 986   53
Joginder Kumar *v.* State of Uttar Pradesh, (1994) 4 SCC 260: AIR 1994 SC 1349:
    1994 Cr LJ 1981: 1994 AIR SCW 1886: 1994 (2) BLJR 975: 1994 (2) Crimes 106:
    JT 1994 (3) SC 423: 1994 (2) Ker LJ 97: 1994 (1) Ker LT 919: 1994 (2) SCJ 230:
    (1994) 3 SCR 661: 1994 SCC (Cri) 1172   54

John Vallamattom *v.* Union of India, AIR 2003 SC 2902: 2003 AIR SCW 3536:
   2003 (4) JCR SC 44: JT 2003 (6) SC 37: (2003) 6 SCC 611: 2003 (9) SRJ 209:
   (2003) 5 SCALE 384: 2003 (5) Supreme 229: (2003) 3 KLT 66   23, 33, 73, 105
Jolly Verghese *v.* Bank of Cochin, AIR 1980 SC 470: (1980) 2 SCC 360:
   (1980) 2 SCR 913   56
Jose Da Costa *v.* Bascora Sadashiva Sinai Narcornin, AIR 1975 SC 1843:
   (1976) 2 SCC 917   7
Joseph *v.* Narayana, AIR 1964 SC 1552: (1964) 7 SCR 137: (1963) 34 Comp Cas 546   52
Jumman *v.* State of Uttar Pradesh, (1991) Cr LJ 439: (1991) 1 SCC 752:
   AIR 1991 SC 345: 1991 SCC (Cri) 283   149
Justice S.S. Sandhawalia *v.* Union of India, AIR 1990 P&H 198:
   (1990) 1 Serv LR 637(2): ILR 1991 (1) P&H 194: 1990 (1) Punj LR 580   191

K

"K" A Judicial Officer, AIR 2001 SC 972: (2001) 3 SCC 54: 2001 Cr LJ 1157:
   (2001) 1 SCR 581   222
"K" A Judicial Officer *v.* Registrar General, High Court of Andhra Pradesh,
   AIR 2010 SC 2801   219
K. Ashok Reddy *v.* Government of India, JT 1994 (1) SC 40: AIR 1994 SC 1207:
   (1994) 2 SCC 303   192
K. Thimmappa *v.* Chairman, Central Board of Directors, State Bank of India,
   AIR 2001 SC 467: (2001) 2 SCC 259: (2001) 1 LLN 814   30
K. Vasudavan Nair *v.* Union of India, AIR 1990 SC 2295: (1991) Supp 2 SCC 134:
   (1991) 17 ATC 362: (1991) 2 LLJ 420: (1990) 3 SLJ 124   161
K. Venkatachalam *v.* A. Swamickan, AIR 1999 SC 1723: (1999) 4 SCC 526:
   1999 AIR SCW 1353: JT 1999 (3) SC 242: 1999 (5) SRJ 293:
   (1999) 3 SCALE 12: 1999 (4) Supreme 333: (1999) 2 UJ (SC) 1064   304
K.C. Vasanth Kumar *v.* State of Karnataka, AIR 1985 SC 1495:
   (1985) Supp SCC 714: (1985) Supp 1 SCR 352   32, 38
K.L. Rathee *v.* Union of India, AIR 1997 SC 2763: (1997) 6 SCC 7:
   (1997) 4 SLR 545: 1997 Lab IC 2853   26
K.L. Tripathi *v.* State Bank of India, (1984) 1 SCC 43: AIR 1984 SC 273:
   1983 Lab IC 1680: (1983) 2 Serv LJ 623: (1983) 63 FJR 312:
   (1984) 1 LLJ 2: 1984 SCC (Lab) 62: (1984) 48 FLR 38:
   (1984) 1 LLN 19: (1984) 1 SCWR 150: (1984) 16 Lawyers 76   28
K.M. Abdulla Kumhi and B.L. Abdul *v.* Union of India, AIR 1991 SC 574:
   (1991) 1 SCC 476: 1991 Cr LJ 790 (CB)   69
K.M. Ibrahim *v.* K.P. Mohammed, AIR 2010 SC 276   150
K.M. Sharma *v.* Devi Lal, AIR 1990 SC 528: (1990) 1 SCC 438: JT 1990 (1) SC 5   121
K.N. Guruswamy *v.* State of Mysore, AIR 1954 SC 592: (1955) 1 SCR 305:
   1954 SCJ 644: ILR 1955 Mys 279   202
K.P. Hafsath Beevi *v.* State of Kerala, AIR 2010 Ker 103   50
K.P. Sen *v.* State of West Bengal, AIR 1966 Cal 356: (1966) 2 LLJ 861:
   71 CWN 622   294
K.P. Sudhakaran *v.* State of Kerala, AIR 2006 SC 2138: 2006 AIR SCW 2700:
   2006 (4) LLN 120: (2006) 5 SCC 386: 2006 SCJ 723: 2006 (3) SCT 60:
   (2006) 6 SCALE 92: 2006 (5) Supreme 31   165
K.R. Ramaswamy *v.* State, AIR 2008 Mad 25: 2008 (2) ALJ (NOC) 348:
   2007 (5) CTC 113: 2007 (5) Mad LJ 486: 2007 (4) Mad LW 60   49
K.S. Bhoir *v.* State of Maharashtra, AIR 2002 SC 444: (2001) 10 SCC 264:
   (2002) 2 SLR 765   194
K.S. Ramamurthy Reddiar *v.* Chief Commissioner, Pondicherry,
   AIR 1963 SC 1464: (1964) 1 SCR 656: (1964) 1 SCA 108   16
K.T. Alagappa Chettiar *v.* Collector, Tiruvannamalai, AIR 1990 Mad 181:
   1989 TLNJ 452   199
Kalawati *v.* State of Himachal Pradesh, (1953) SCR 546: AIR 1953 SC 131:
   1953 Cr LJ 668: 1953 Mad WN 219: 1953 SCJ 144:
   1953 All WR (Supp) 52: 1953 SCA 660   53

Kalyan Singh *v.* State of Uttar Pradesh, AIR 1962 SC 1183: (1962) Supp 2 SCR 76:
    1962 All LJ 523: ILR (1962) 1 All 906: 1963 (1) SCJ 50   122
Kalyani Stores *v.* State of Orissa, AIR 1966 SC 1686: (1966) 1 SCR 865:
    (1966) 2 SCA 36: 1966 (2) SCJ 367: 1967 SCD 303: 33 Cut LT 356   274
Kamaladevi *v.* State of Punjab, AIR 1984 SC 1895: (1985) 1 SCC 41: 1985 Cr LJ 356   67
Kamla *v.* State of Maharashtra, AIR 1981 SC 814: (1981) 1 SCC 748: 1981 Cr LJ 353   69
Kamra *v.* N.I.A., (1992) 2 SCC 36: AIR 1992 SC 1072: (1992) 1 LLN 401:
    (1992) 1 LLJ 630   285
Kanhaiya Lal Sethia *v.* Union of India, (1997) 6 SCC 573: AIR 1998 SC 365:
    1997 AIR SCW 4348: JT 1997 (7) SC 289: 1997 (3) SCJ 224:
    (1997) 5 SCALE 341: 1997 (7) Supreme 127: 1997 UJ (SC) 457   26, 89
Kanta Kathuria *v.* Manak Chand Surana, AIR 1970 SC 694: (1969) 3 SCC 268:
    1970 (2) SCJ 232: (1970) 2 SCR 835   131
Kanu Sanyal *v.* District Magistrate, AIR 1973 SC 2684: (1973) 2 SCC 674:
    (1974) 1 SCR 621: 1973 Cr LJ 1818   203
Kanubhai Brahmbhatt *v.* State of Gujarat, AIR 1987 SC 1159:
    (1989) Supp 2 SCC 310: (1987) 2 SCR 314   94
Kanyaiya Lal *v.* Income Tax Commissioner, AIR 1975 SC 255   54
Karamshi Jethabhai Somayya *v.* State of Bombay, AIR 1964 SC 1714:
    (1964) 6 SCR 984: 1965 (2) SCJ 568   270
Kartar Singh Gerwal *v.* State of Punjab, (1991) 2 SCC 635: AIR 1991 SC 1067:
    1991 AIR SCW 951: JT 1992 (1) SC 124: 1992 (2) LLJ 30: 1991 (2) LLN 54:
    1991 SCC (L&S) 780: 1991 (1) UJ (SC) 587   151
Kartar Singh *v.* State of Punjab, JT 1994 (2) SC 423: (1994) 3 SCC 569:
    1994 Cr LJ 3139   66, 120, 195
Kashinath G. Jalmi (Dr.) *v.* Speaker, (1993) 2 SCC 703: AIR 1993 SC 1873:
    1993 AIR SCW 1578: JT 1993 (3) SC 594: (1993) 2 SCR 820: 1993 (2) UJ (SC) 113   89
Kasim Maraikkayar *v.* Haji Kathija Beevi Trust, Nagapattinam,
    AIR 2008 Mad 91: 2008 AIHC 384 (NOC): 2008 (3) ALJ (NOC) 591:
    2008 (2) AKAR (NOC) 186: 2008 (1) CTC 190: 2008 (2) Mad LJ 392   27
Kastha Niwarak G.S.S. Maryadit, Indore *v.* President, Indore Development
    Authority, AIR 2006 SC 1142: 2006 AIR SCW 712: 2006 (2) All WC 1139:
    2006 (3) JCR SC 75: (2006) 2 SCC 604: 2006 (2) SCJ 361: 2006 (3) SRJ 367:
    (2006) 2 SCALE 274: 2006 (2) Supreme 121   22
Kasturi Lal Ralia Ram Jain *v.* State of Uttar Pradesh, AIR 1965 SC 1039:
    (1965) 1 SCR 375: ILR (1965) 2 Mad LJ (SC) 15: 1965 (2) SCJ 318:
    (1965) 1 SCWR 995: (1965) 1 SCA 809: (1965) 2 Cr LJ 144:
    1966 SCD 383: (1966) 2 LLJ 583   25, 92, 271
Kathi Raning Rawat *v.* State of Saurashtra, (1952) SCR 435: AIR 1952 SC 123:
    1952 SCJ 168: 1952 Cr LJ 805: 1952 Mad WN 762: 1952 Mad WN (Cri) 210:
    1952 SCA 245   26, 32
Kedar Nath *v.* State of West Bengal, AIR 1953 SC 404: (1954) 1 SCR 30:
    1953 Cr LJ 1621   53
Kehar Singh *v.* Union of India, JT 1988 (4) SC 693: AIR 1989 SC 653: 1989 Cr LJ 941   117
Kennedy & Arnold *v.* Ireland, 1987 IR 587   58
Kerala Education Bill (in re:), AIR 1958 SC 956: 1959 SCR 995:
    (1958) Ker 1167   78, 79, 81, 82, 99
Kerala Hotel and Restaurant Association *v.* State of Kerala,
    JT 1990 1 SC 324: AIR 1990 SC 913: (1990) 2 SCC 502   29
Kerala State Electricity Board, Thiruvananthapuram *v.* Siniya Mol C.S.,
    AIR 2008 (NOC) 730 (Ker)   33
Keshav Ram Pal (Dr.) *v.* Uttar Pradesh Higher Education Services Commission,
    (1986) 1 SCC 671: 1986 SCC (L&S) 195: AIR 1986 SC 597:
    (1986) 1 LLJ 311: 1986 Lab IC 553   297
Keshavan *v.* State of Bombay, (1951) SCR 228: AIR 1951 SC 128: 53 Bom LR 458   20
Keshavananda Bharati Sripadgalvaru *v.* State of Kerala, (1973) 4 SCC 225:
    AIR 1973 SC 1461: 1973 Supp SCR 1   2, 3, 4, 17, 18, 19, 51, 85, 86, 99, 335

Kesoram Industries Ltd. (Textile Division) *v.* Coal India Ltd.,
    AIR 1993 Cal 78: 1993 (1) CHN 488: 1993 (1) Cal LJ 13 (DB)   301
Kesoram Rayon Workmen's Union *v.* Registrar of Trade Unions,
    AIR 1967 Cal 507: *33 FJR 23: (1968) 1 LLJ 335   45
Kharak Singh *v.* State of Uttar Pradesh, AIR 1963 SC 1295: (1964) 1 SCR 332:
    1963 2 Cr LJ 329: 1963 All LJ 711: 1964 (2) SCJ 107   45, 46, 94
Khare *v.* State of Delhi, (1950) SCR 519: AIR 1950 SC 211: (1951) 52 Cr LJ 550   45, 50
Khatki *v.* Limdi Municipality, AIR 1979 SC 418: (1979) 1 SCC 248: (1979) 2 SLR 338   47
Khatri *v.* State of Bihar, AIR 1981 SC 928: (1981) 1 SCC 627:
    1981 SCC (Cri) 228   59, 102
Khazan Singh *v.* State of Uttar Pradesh, AIR 1974 SC 669: (1974) 1 SCC 295:
    (1974) 2 SCR 562   269
Khimji Vidhu *v.* Premier High School, AIR 2000 SC 3495: (1999) 9 SCC 264:
    2000 AIR SCW 2333: (2000) 3 All MR 663: (2000) 2 Mah LR 693   219
Khoday Brewing and Distilling Industries Ltd. *v.* State of Tamil Nadu,
    AIR 1990 Mad 124   44
Khudi Ram *v.* State of West Bengal, AIR 1975 SC 550: (1975) 2 SCC 81:
    (1975) 2 SCR 832   49
Kihota Hollohan *v.* Zachillhu, AIR 1993 SC 412: (1992) Supp (2) SCC 651:
    1992 AIR SCW 3497: JT 1992 (1) SC 600: (1992) 1 SCR 686   19, 87, 179, 187, 336
Kihoto Hollohon *v.* Zachilhu, (1992) 1 SCC 309   415
Kiran Pasha *v.* Government of Andhra Pradesh, (1990) 1 SCC 328: 1990 SCC (Cri) 110   88
Kishan *v.* State of Rajasthan, AIR 1990 SC 2269: 1990 Supp SCC 742:
    (1990) 183 ITR 433   243
Kishore Kumar Khaitan *v.* Praveen Kumar Singh, AIR 2006 SC 1474:
    2006 AIR SCW 1077: 2006 (3) JCR SC 162: 2006 (3) Land LR 300:
    (2006) 3 SCC 312: 2006 (2) SCJ 585: 2006 (3) SRJ 400:
    (2006) 2 SCALE 304: 2006 (2) Supreme 75   218
Kishore *v.* State of Himachal Pradesh, (1991) 1 SCC 286: AIR 1990 2140:
    1990 Cr LJ 2289   103
Kishori Mohan Bera *v.* State of West Bengal, AIR 1972 SC 1749:
    (1972) 3 SCC 845: 1972 SCD 805: 1973 SCC (Cri) 30   204
Kochunni *v.* State of Madras, AIR 1959 SC 725: (1959) Supp 2 SCR 316:
    1959 Ker LJ 464   94
Krishan *v.* State of Andhra Pradesh, (1975) UJ (SC) 951   117
Krishena *v.* Union of India, (1990) 4 SCC 207: AIR 1990 SC 1782:
    (1990) 4 SLR 716 (CB)   155, 279
Krishna Bhimrao Deshpande *v.* Land Tribunal, Dharwad, AIR 1993 SC 883:
    (1993) 1 SCC 287: 1992 AIR SCW 3407: 1993 Bom CJ 576:
    JT 1992 (6) SC 149: 1992 (3) SCJ 693   251
Krishna *v.* Shobha, (1990) 1 UJ SC 71: (1989) 4 SCC 131: AIR 1989 SC 2097   150
Kruse *v.* Jhonson, (1898) 2 QB 91: 14 TLR 416   21
Kubic Darusz *v.* Union of India, 1990 (2) SCJ 132: (1990) 1 SCC 568:
    AIR 1990 SC 605   70, 209
Kulathil Mammu *v.* State of Kerala, AIR 1966 SC 1614: 1966 Cr LJ 1217:
    1967 SCD 101: (1967) 1 SCA 322: (1967) 3 SCR 706:
    1967 Mad LJ (Cri) 817: 1967 (2) SCJ 653   12
Kuldeep Kumar Gupta *v.* Himachal Pradesh State Electricity Board,
    AIR 2001 SC 308: (2001) 1 SCC 475: 2001 Lab IC 409: (2001) 1 LLN 842   39
Kuldip Nayar *v.* Union of India, AIR 2006 SC 3127: 2006 AIR SCW 4394:
    2006 (4) Cur CC 62: (2006) 7 SCC 1: 2006 (6) SCJ 702:
    (2006) 8 SCALE 257: 2006 (7) Supreme 44   18
Kuljit *v.* Lt. Governor, AIR 1982 SC 774: (1982) 1 SCC 417: 1982 Cr LJ 624   117
Kulkarni *v.* State of Bombay, AIR 1954 SC 73: 1954 SCR 384: (1954) 1 MLJ 83:
    1954 Cr LJ 351   44
Kumaon Mandal Vikas Nigam Ltd. *v.* Girja Shankar Pant, AIR 2001 SC 24:
    (2001) 1 SCC 182: 2001 Lab IC 11   22

Kumari Anjali Saxena *v.* Chairman, Professional Examination Board, Bhopal,
    AIR 1990 MP 253: 1990 Jab LJ 77 (DB)   200
Kumari K.S. Jayasree *v.* State of Kerala, AIR 1976 SC 2381: (1976) 3 SCC 730:
    1976 UJ (SC) 805: (1977) 1 SCWR 3: 1977 (1) SCJ 101: (1977) 1 SCR 194:
    (1977) 9 Lawyer 115   32
Kunga Nima Lepcha *v.* State of Sikkim, AIR 2010 SC 1671   95
Kunnikkal Narayanan *v.* State of Kerala, AIR 1973 Ker 97: 1973 Ker LT 125:
    1973 Ker LJ 178: ILR (1973) 1 Ker 258: 1973 Cr LJ 866   49
Kuriakose *v.* State of Kerala, AIR 1977 SC 1509: (1977) 2 SCC 728: (1977) 2 LLJ 13   93

L

L. Chandra Kumar *v.* Union of India, AIR 1997 SC 1125: (1997) 3 SCC 261:
    (1997) 1 CLR 778: 1997 Lab IC 1069: (1977) 2 SCR 1   301
L. Muhammed Aslam *v.* State of Kerala, (2009) 7 SCC 382   150
L.C. Golak Nath *v.* State of Punjab, AIR 1967 SC 1643: (1967) 2 SCR 762:
    1967 All LJ 813: 1967 (2) SCJ 486: 1967 BLJR 818: (1967) 2 SCA 642:
    1967 MPWR 553: (1967) 2 SCWR 1006   17, 19
L.K. Koolwal *v.* State of Rajasthan, AIR 1988 Raj 2: (1987) 4 Reports 53:
    (1987) 1 Raj LR 334: 1987 MCC 431   49
L.T.C. *v.* State of Karnataka, (1985) Supp SCC 476   253
Labourers Working on Salal Hydro-Project *v.* State of Jammu and Kashmir,
    AIR 1984 SC 177: (1983) 2 SCC 181: (1983) 1 LLJ 494: 1983 SCC (Lab) 289:
    (1983) 2 LLN 20: 1983 UJ (SC) 582: (1983) 2 SCWR 202:
    1983 Cr App R (SC) 438: (1983) 2 SCR 473   72
Lakhan Lal *v.* State of Orissa, AIR 1977 SC 722: (1976) 4 SCC 660: (1977) 1 SCR 811   46
Lakshmikant *v.* Union of India, (1997) 4 SCC 739   51
Lal Babu Hussain *v.* Electoral Registration Officer, AIR 1995 SC 1189:
    1995 AIR SCW 1254: (1995) 3 SCC 100   10, 14
Lal Kamlendra Pratap Singh *v.* State of Uttar Pradesh, (2009) 4 SCC 437   54
Larson & Toubro Ltd. *v.* State Consumer Disputes Redressal Commission,
    AIR 1998 Cal 313: 1999 CWN 252: 1999 (33) Cor LA 456: 1999 (2) ICC 749   199
Laxmi Devi *v.* Satya Narayan, (1994) 5 SCC 545: 1994 SCC (Cri) 1566:
    1994 AIR SCW 3408   156
Laxmi Kant *v.* Union of India, AIR 1987 SC 232: (1987) 1 SCC 66: 1987 SCC (Cri) 33   99
Laxmi Shanker Pandey *v.* Union of India, AIR 1991 SC 1070:
    (1991) 2 SCC 488: (1991) 16 ATC 524   214
Laxmi *v.* State of Uttar Pradesh, AIR 1981 SC 873: (1981) 2 SCC 600:
    (1981) 3 SCR 92   50
Laxmi *v.* Union of India, (1991) 2 SCJ 86   97
Laxmikant V. Patel *v.* Chetanbhai Shah, AIR 2002 SC 275: (2002) 3 SCC 65:
    (2002) 110 Comp Cas 5182   147
Leila David *v.* State of Maharashtra, (2009) 4 SCC 578: AIR 2010 SC 862   144
Lena Khan *v.* Union of India, (1987) 2 SCC 402: AIR 1987 SC 1515:
    (1987) 2 LLN 777: 1987 SCC (L&S) 127: 1987 Lab IC 1035   14, 28
Leo Roy Frey *v.* Superintendent, District Jail, Amritsar, AIR 1958 SC 119:
    1958 SCR 822: 1958 Cr LJ 260: 1958 Mad LJ (Cri) 289:
    1958 SCA 240: 1958 SCJ 301   53
Life Insurance Corporation *v.* Professor Manubhai D. Shah, AIR 1993 SC 171:
    (1992) 3 SCC 637: 1992 AIR SCW 3099: 1993 (1) BLJR 431:
    1992 (2) Civ LJ 636: JT 1992 (4) SC 181: 1992 (3) SCJ 84:
    (1992) 3 SCR 595: 1992 (2) UJ (SC) 480   45, 47
Lily Kurian *v.* St. Levina, AIR 1979 SC 52: (1979) 2 SCC 127: (1979) 1 SCR 820   81
Lingappa Pochanna Appelwar *v.* State of Maharashtra, AIR 1985 SC 389:
    (1985) 1 SCC 479: (1985) 87 Bom LR 65: 1985 GOC (SC) 41:
    (1985) 2 SCR 224: 1985 Cur Civ LJ (SC) 387   5, 99, 106, 253
Literate Association *v.* State of Karnataka, (1990) 2 SCC 396: AIR 1990 SC 883:
    1990 SCC (L&S) 274: 1990 Lab IC 625   99
Local Govt. Board *v.* Arlidge, (1915) AC 120: 84 LJ KB 72: 111 LT 905 (HL)   197

Lucy R. D'Souza *v.* State of Goa, AIR 1990 Bom 355: (1990) 1 Goa LT 36:
    1990 MLLJ 713   42
Lynch *v.* Tilden Produce Co., (1923) 265 US 315: 68 Law Ed 1034   21

M

M. Ahamedkutty *v.* Union of India, (1990) 2 SCC 1: JT 1990 (1) SC 143:
    1990 SCC (Cri) 258   69
M. Hasan *v.* Government of Andhra Pradesh, AIR 1998 AP 35:
    1997 (6) Andh LD 826: 1997 (6) Andh LT 209: 1998 (1) Rec Cr R 255   43
M. Jahangir Bhatusha *v.* Union of India, JT 1989 (2) SC 465:
    (1989) Supp 1 SCC 201: AIR 1989 SC 1713   29
M. Karunanidhi *v.* Union of India, AIR 1979 SC 898: (1979) 3 SCC 431:
    1979 Cr LJ 773   251
M. Nagaraj *v.* Union of India, AIR 2007 SC 71: 2006 AIR SCW 5482:
    2006 (4) All WC 4054: 2007 (1) JCR SC 147: 2006 (6) Kant LJ 529:
    2006 (4) Pat LJR 319: (2006) 8 SCC 212: 2006 (8) SCJ 457:
    (2006) 10 SCALE 301: 2006 (8) Supreme 89   3, 11
M.A. Khan, Applicant *v.* State of Maharashtra, AIR 1967 Bom 254:
    68 Bom LR 576: 1966 Mah LJ 793: 1967 Cr LJ 964: ILR (1967) Bom 158   49
M.C. Mehta *v.* Kamal Nath, (1997) 1 SCC 388: 1997 (2) Civil LJ 1   56
M.C. Mehta *v.* Kamal Nath, AIR 2000 SC 1997: (2000) 6 SCC 213:
    2000 AIR SCW 1854: JT 2000 (7) SC 19: 2000 (7) SRJ 210:
    (2000) 5 SCALE 69: 2000 (4) Supreme 391: 2000 (2) UJ (SC) 1196   57
M.C. Mehta *v.* State of Tamil Nadu, AIR 1991 SC 417: (1991) 1 SCC 283:
    1991 Lab IC 231: 1991 AIR SCW 60: JT 1990 (4) SC 263:
    1991 (1) LLN 19: 1991 (1) Mad LJ 44: 1991 SCC (L&S) 299:
    1990 (6) Serv LR 51: 1991 (1) UJ (SC) 169   92
M.C. Mehta *v.* State of Tamil Nadu, AIR 1997 SC 699: (1996) 6 SCC 756:
    1997 Lab IC 563: 1997 AIR SCW 407: 1997 (2) LLJ 724: 1997 (1) LLN 12:
    1997 SCC (L&S) 49: 1997 (1) Supreme 207: 1997 (1) UJ (SC) 243   71, 101
M.C. Mehta *v.* Union of India, (1987) Supp SCC 131: AIR 1987 SC 1086:
    (1987) 1 Comp LJ 99: (1987) 1 ACC 157: (1987) 1 SCC 395:
    1987 (1) Supreme 65: 1987 SCC (L&S) 37: JT 1987 (1) SC 1:
    1987 ACJ 386   16, 55, 56, 63, 92
M.C. Mehta *v.* Union of India, (1992) Supp 2 SCC 85   107
M.C. Mehta *v.* Union of India, (1997) 3 SCC 715   57
M.C. Mehta *v.* Union of India, AIR 1998 SC 186: (1998) 1 SCC 363:
    1997 AIR SCW 4149: 1998 (2) Civ LJ 440: JT 1997 (9) SC 213: 1998 (1) SCJ 523:
    (1997) 7 SCALE 97: 1997 (9) Supreme 418: 1998 (1) UJ (SC) 282   67
M.C. Mehta *v.* Union of India, AIR 1999 SC 2583: (1999) 6 SCC 237:
    1999 AIR SCW 2754: 1999 (3) Comp LJ 371 SC: JT 1999 (5) SC 114:
    1999 (4) LRI 140: 1999 (8) SRJ 255: (1999) 4 SCALE 267:
    1999 (6) Supreme 265: 1999 (2) UJ (SC) 1254   91
M.C. Valsala *v.* State of Kerala, AIR 2006 Ker 1: 2006 (1) AIR Kar R 92:
    2005 (36) All Ind Cas 750: 2006 (5) Bom CR 1 JS: ILR (2005) 4 Ker 122:
    2006 (1) LLN 682: 2006 (2) SCT 749   33, 38
M.H. Devendrappa *v.* Karnataka State Small Industries Development Corporation,
    AIR 1998 SC 1064: (1998) 3 SCC 732: (1998) 2 LLN 419   47
M.H. Hoskot *v.* State of Maharashtra, AIR 1978 SC 1548: (1978) Cr LJ 1678:
    (1978) 3 SCC 544: 1978 SCC (Cri) 468   59, 64, 102
M.I. Shahdad *v.* Mohd. Abdullah Mir, AIR 1967 J&K 120: 1967 Kash LJ 251   34
M.K. Gopalan *v.* State of Madhya Pradesh, (1955) 1 SCR 168: AIR 1954 SC 362:
    1954 Cr LJ 1012: 1954 SCA 557: 1954 SCJ 534: (1954) 2 Mad LJ 76:
    1954 All WR (HC) 392   94
M.K. Sharma *v.* Bharat Electronics Ltd., (1987) 3 SCC 231: AIR 1987 SC 1792:
    (1987) Cr LJ 1908   63
M.P. Oil Extraction *v.* State of Madhya Pradesh, (1997) 7 SCC 592: AIR 1998 SC 145:
    1997 AIR SCW 4104: JT 1997 (6) SC 97: 1997 (2) Jab LJ 214: (1997) 4 SCALE 515:
    1997 (7) Supreme 267: 1997 (2) UJ (SC) 438   21, 22, 27

M.P. Sugar Mills *v.* State of Uttar Pradesh, AIR 1979 SC 627:
1980 Supp SCC 157: 1979 Cr LJ 1027   270
M.R. Balaji *v.* State of Mysore, AIR 1963 SC 649: (1963) Supp 1 SCR 439:
(1963) 2 SCA 1   32, 37
M.S.M. Sharma *v.* Sri Krishna Sinha, AIR 1959 SC 395: (1959) Supp 1 SCR 806:
(1959) 2 MLJ (SC) 125   48, 133
M.S.M. Sharma *v.* Sri Krishna Sinha, AIR 1960 SC 1186: (1961) 1 SCR 96:
(1961) 1 Ker LR 8   187
M.V.AL. Quamar *v.* Tsavliris Salvage (International) Ltd., AIR 2000 SC 2826:
(2000) 8 SCC 278: 2000 AIR SCW 3101: JT 2000 (9) SC 184:
2000 (3) SCJ 464: 2000 (8) SRJ 405: (2000) 5 SCALE 618: 2000 (5) Supreme 688   193
Machindra *v.* King, AIR 1950 FC 129   204
Mackinnon Mackenzie & Co. Ltd. *v.* Audrey D. Costa, AIR 1987 SC 1281:
(1987) 2 SCC 469: (1987) 11 LJ 536   101
Madhosingh Daulatsingh *v.* State of Bombay, AIR 1960 Bom 285:
1959 Nag LJ 441: 61 Bom LR 1537: ILR (1959) Bom 1846: (1960) 1 LLJ 291   284
Madhu Kishwar *v.* State of Bihar, (1996) 5 SCC 125: AIR 1996 SC 1864:
1996 AIR SCW 2178: 1996 (2) BLJ 327: 1996 (1) Hindu LR 610:
JT 1996 (4) SC 379: 1996 (2) Pat LJR 133   64, 66
Madhu Limaye (in re:), AIR 1969 SC 1014: (1969) 1 SCC 292: 1969 Cr LJ 1440   69
Madhu Limaye *v.* Sub Divisional Magistrate, Monghyr, AIR 1971 SC 2486:
(1970) 3 SCC 446: (1972) 1 SCA 45: (1971) 2 SCR 711: 1971 Cr LJ 1721:
1971 (2) SCJ 479: 1971 MLJ (Cri) 629   45
Madhuwanti *v.* State, AIR 1983 Bom 443: 1984 MLLJ 23   21
Madras High Court Advocates' Association *v.* Dr. A.S. Anand, Hon'ble Chief
Justice of India, AIR 2001 SC 970: (2001) 3 SCC 19: 2001 SCC (Cri) 422   95
Mafatlal Industries *v.* Union of India, (1997) 5 SCC 536: JT 1996 (11) SC 283:
1997 (1) Supreme 684: (1996) 9 SCALE 457: (1997) 99 ELT 247:
1997 (68) ECR 209   29
Maganbhai Ishwarbhai Patel *v.* Union of India, (1970) 3 SCC 400:
AIR 1969 SC 783: (1969) 3 SCR 254   5, 109, 111
Maganlal Chaganlal (P) Ltd. *v.* Municipal Corporation of Greater Bombay,
AIR 1975 SC 648: (1975) 1 SCC 339: (1976) 1 SCR 648   214
Maganlal Changalal (P.) Ltd. *v.* Municipal Corporation of Greater Bombay,
(1974) 2 SCC 402: AIR 1974 SC 2009: (1975) 1 SCR I   21
Mahabir Auto Stores *v.* Indian Oil Corporation Ltd., AIR 1989 Del 315   269
Mahabir Auto Stores *v.* Indian Oil Corporation, (1990) 3 SCC 752:
AIR 1990 SC 1031: (1990) 2 SLR 69   16, 269, 270
Mahabir Prasad Jalan *v.* State of Bihar, AIR 1991 Pat 40: (1991) 2 BLJR 915:
1991 BBCJ 227   247
Mahant Moti Das *v.* S.P. Sahi, AIR 1959 SC 942: (1959) Supp 2 SCR 563:
1959 SCJ 1144: (1959) 2 SCA 432: ILR 38 Pat 639   74, 77
Mahant Ram Kishan Dass *v.* State of Punjab, AIR 1981 SC 1576:
(1983) 1 SCC 377: 1980 Land LR 182   76
Maharaja Tourist Service *v.* State of Gujarat, AIR 1991 SC 1650:
(1992) Supp 1 SCC 489: 1991 AIR SCW 1643: 1991 (2) Cur CC 479:
(1991) 2 SCR 524: 1991 (2) UJ (SC) 251   273
Maharashtra Ekta Hawkers Union *v.* Municipal Corporation, Greater Mumbai,
AIR 2004 SC 416: (2004) 1 SCC 625: 2003 AIR SCW 6814:
2004 (3) Bom CR 612: 2004 (3) Mah LJ 437: (2003) 10 SCALE 561:
2004 (1) Supreme 107: 2004 (1) UJ (SC) 676   49
Maharashtra State Board of Secondary and Higher Secondary Education
v. K.S. Gandhi, (1991) 2 SCC 716: 1991 AIR SCW 879   201, 205, 207, 215, 285
Maharishi Advadhesh *v.* Union of India, (1994) Supp 1 SCC 713   105, 106
Maharishi *v.* State of Uttar Pradesh, AIR 1990 All 52   90
Maharshi Avadhesh *v.* State of Uttar Pradesh, AIR 1991 All 52   206, 207
Mahendran *v.* State of Karnataka, (1990) 1 SCC 411: AIR 1990 SC 405:
1990 Lab IC 369   280

Mahesh Chander v. State of Delhi, (1991) Cr LJ 1703: (1991) Supp 1 SCC 257:
    AIR 1991 SC 1108   149, 150
Makbool v. State of Bombay, (1953) SCR 730: AIR 1953 SC 325: 56 Bom LR 13   53
Malak v. State of Punjab, AIR 1981 SC 760: (1981) 1 SCC 420: (1981) 2 SCR 311   46
Malaya v. Sukumar Mukherjee, AIR 2010 SC 1162   25
Managing Director v. V. Muthulakshmi, AIR 2008 (NOC) 381 (Mad)   62
Manchegowda v. State of Karnataka, AIR 1984 SC 1151: (1984) 3 SCC 301:
    (1984) 3 Kant LJ 1   99
Maneka Gandhi v. Union of India, AIR 1978 SC 597: (1978) 1 SCC 248:
    (1978) 2 SCR 621: 1978 (2) SCJ 312   13, 46, 57, 60, 65
Mangal Singh v. Union of India, AIR 1967 SC 944: (1967) 1 SCWR 491:
    (1967) 2 SCR 109: 1967 SCD 1116: 1968 (1) SCJ 240   8, 10
Manganese Ore v. Chandil, AIR 1991 SC 520: (1991) Supp 2 SCC 465:
    (1991) 1 LLN 304: (1991) 1 CLR 357   157
Manhattan General Equipment Co. v. Commissioner, (1935) 297 US 129   21
Mani Nariman Daruwala and Bharucha v. Phiroz N. Bhatena, AIR 1991 SC 1494:
    (1991) 3 SCC 141: 1991 AIR SCW 1441: JT 1991 (5) SC 357:
    (1991) 1 Ren CJ 675: 1992 (1) Rent LR 576: (1991) 2 UJ (SC) 277   219
Manish Goel v. Rohini Goel, AIR 2010 SC 1099   157
Manjeet v. E.S.I.C., AIR 1990 SC 1104: (1990) 2 SCC 367: (1990) 13 ATC 686:
    (1990) 1 CLR 777   278
Manohar Harries Walters v. Basel Mission Higher Education Centre, Dharwad,
    AIR 1991 SC 2230: (1992) Supp 2 SCC 301: 1991 AIR SCW 2562:
    1992 (1) Cur LR 407: 1993 (66) FLR 986: 1992 (1) LLJ 279:
    1992 (1) LLN 387: 1992 SCC (L&S) 747: (1992) Supp 2 SCC 301   82
Manoj Kumar v. Board of Revenue, AIR 2008 MP 22: 2008 (1) AIR Kar R 353:
    2008 (1) Jab LJ 76: 2007 (4) MPHT 545: 2008 (1) MPLJ 152   217
Manoranjan Das v. State of West Bengal, AIR 1998 Cal 22: 1998 CWN 47   22
Maru Ram v. Union of India, AIR 1980 SC 2147: (1981) 1 SCC 107:
    1980 Cr LJ 1440: (1981) 1 SCR 1196   117
Matajog v. Bhari, AIR 1956 SC 44: (1955) 2 SCR 925: (1955) 28 ITR 941   30
Mathew v. State of Bihar, AIR 1984 SC 1854: (1985) 2 SCC 102: 1985 Cr LJ 357   67
Maya v. C.I.T., (1986) 1 SCC 445: AIR 1986 SC 293: 157 IIR 330   54
McEldowner v. Forde, (1971) AC 632 (HL)   21
Md. Joynal Abedin v. State of West Bengal, AIR 1990 Cal 193: (1989) 2 Cal LJ 362   83
Medimpex (India) Pvt. Ltd. v. Drug Controller-cum-Chief Licensing Authority,
    AIR 1990 SC 544: (1989) Supp 2 SCC 665: 1990 Cr LJ 475: 1990 (1) BLJR 159:
    1990 (1) Cr LC 523: 1990 East Cr C 380: 1990 (1) SCJ 168   151
Meenakshi Mills v. Vishwanath, AIR 1955 SC 13: (1955) 1 SCR 787: (1954) 261 TR 713   21
Meera Kanwaria v. Sunita, AIR 2006 SC 597: 2005 AIR SCW 6243:
    2006 (38) All Ind Cas 457: 2006 (62) All LR 464: 2006 (1) All WC 678:
    2006 (2) Bom CR 566: JT 2005 (10) SC 429: (2006) 1 SCC 344:
    2006 (1) SCJ 242: 2006 (1) SCT 126: (2005) 10 SCALE 39: 2006 (1) Supreme 166   34
Meera Nireshwalia v. State of Tamil Nadu, (1991) Cr LJ 2395 (Mad)   58
Mehboob Khan Nawab Khan Pathan v. Commissioner of Police, Ahmedabad,
    AIR 1989 SC 1803: (1989) 3 SCC 568: 1989 Cr LJ 2111: 1990 (1) Guj LR 142   70
Mehtab Singh v. State of Gujarat, (1991) Cr LJ 2325: (1991) Supp 2 SCC 391:
    AIR 1991 SC 1925   150
Merugu Satyanarayana v. State of Andhra Pradesh, AIR 1982 SC 1543:
    1982 Cr LJ 2357: (1982) 3 SCC 301   70
Meskill v. CIE, 1973 IR 121   58
Minerva Mills Ltd. v. Union of India, AIR 1980 SC 1789: (1980) 3 SCC 625:
    1980 Ker LT 573: 1980 UJ (SC) 727   2, 3, 18, 19, 49, 85, 86, 99, 321, 335
Minerva Mills Ltd. v. Union of India, AIR 1986 SC 2030: (1986) 4 SCC 222:
    1986 JT 375: 1986 (3) Supreme 432: (1986) 2 Cur CC 880   85
Mini v. State of Kerala, AIR 1980 SC 838: (1980) 2 SCC 216: (1980) 2 SCR 829   21
Mirza Ali Akbar Kashani v. United Arab Republic, AIR 1966 SC 230:
    (1966) 1 SCR 319: (1965) 2 SCA 590: (1965) 2 SCWR 893: 1966 (2) SCJ 25   109

Misri Lal *v.* State of Orissa, AIR 1977 SC 1686: (1977) 3 SCC 212:
    (1977) 3 SCR 714   244
Mithu *v.* State of Punjab, AIR 1983 SC 473: (1983) 2 SCC 277: 1983 SCC (Cri) 405   55
Mixnam Properties Ltd. *v.* Chertsey U.D.C., (1965) AC 735   21
Mobarik Ali Ahmed *v.* State of Bombay, AIR 1957 SC 857: 1957 Cr LJ 1346:
    1958 SCJ 111: 1958 Mad LJ (Cri) 42: 1958 SCA 665: 1958 SCR 328:
    61 Bom LR 58   12
Mohal *v.* Sr. Supdt., (1991) Supp 2 SCC 503: AIR 1991 SC 328: (1991) 1 LLN 301   289
Mohan Bir Singh Chawla *v.* Punjab University, Chandigarh, AIR 1997 SC 788:
    (1997) 2 SCC 171: 1997 AIR SCW 609: 1997 (1) Cur CC 76: 1997 (2) ESC 1015:
    1996 (3) Serv LR 766: 1997 (1) Supreme 332: 1997 (1) UJ (SC) 339   34
Mohan Lal Arya *v.* Union of India, AIR 2003 All 11   207
Mohan *v.* Union of India, (1992) Suppl 1 SCC 594: AIR 1992 SC 1:
    (1992) 19 ATC 881   110
Mohd. Hanif Quareshi *v.* State of Bihar, (1959) SCR 629: AIR 1958 SC 731:
    1958 SCA 783: 1958 SCJ 975: 1958 Mad LJ (Cri) 727   50, 74
Mohd. Ibrahim Mohd. Sasin *v.* State of Maharashtra, (1987) Supp SCC 32:
    1987 SCC (Cri) 630   61
Mohd. Yunus *v.* Mohd. Mustaqim, AIR 1984 SC 38: (1983) 4 SCC 566:
    1984 UJ (SC) 132: 1984 Cur Civ LJ (SC) 74   218
Molay Kumar Acharya *v.* Chairman-cum-Managing Director, W.B. State
    Electricity Distribution Co. Ltd., AIR 2008 Cal 47: 2008 AIHC 307 (NOC):
    2008 (2) ALJ (NOC) 495: 2008 (3) AKAR (NOC) 380: 2008 (3) Cal HN 27   65
Moran M. Baselios Marthona Mathews *v.* State of Kerala, (2007) 6 SCC 517   208
Moses Wilson *v.* Kasturiba, AIR 2008 SC 379: 2007 AIR SCW 7058:
    2007 (59) All Ind Cas 238: 2007 (69) All LR 309: 2008 (1) Andh LD 102:
    2007 (2) CLR 851: 2008 (1) Mad LJ 1049: (2007) 11 SCALE 405   66
Moti Lal *v.* State of Uttar Pradesh, AIR 1951 All 257: (1957) 1 All 269 (FB)   108
Moti Ram Deka *v.* General Manager, North East Frontier Railway,
    AIR 1964 SC 600: (1964) 5 SCR 683: (1964) 2 SCA 372: (1964) 2 LLJ 467:
    ILR (1964) 2 All 717: ILR (1964) 16 Assam 81   156, 284
Motilal Nehru Medical College *v.* Dr. Vandana Singh, AIR 1991 SC 792:
    1990 Supp SCC 343: JT 1990 (3) SC 679: (1990) 5 Serv LR 83:
    1990 (2) UJ (SC) 616   200
Mukerian Papers Ltd. *v.* State of Punjab, (1991) 2 SCC 580: 1991 AIR SCW 553   259
Mukesh *v.* State of Madhya Pradesh, AIR 1985 SC 537   99
Mukhtiar Singh *v.* State of Punjab, AIR 1991 P&H 20   211
Mulgaonkar (in re:), AIR 1978 SC 727: (1978) 3 SCC 339: 1978 SCC (Cri) 402   43
Mullaperiyar Environmental Protection Forum *v.* Union of India, AIR 2006 SC 1428:
    2006 AIR SCW 1241: 2006 (1) Arb LR 374: ILR (2006) 2 Ker SC 347:
    (2006) 3 SCC 643: 2006 (3) SCJ 196: 2006 (4) SRJ 268: 2006 (2) Supreme 579   9, 10
Mumbai Kamgar Sabha *v.* Abdulbhai, AIR 1976 SC 1455: (1976) 3 SCC 832:
    (1976) 2 LLJ 186   110
Municipal Corporation of Delhi *v.* Female Workers (Muster Roll),
    AIR 2000 SC 1274: 2000 AIR SCW 969: JT 2000 (3) SC 13: (2000) 3 SCC 224:
    2000 SCC (L&S) 331: 2000 (3) SCJ 180: 2000 (2) SCT 258: (2000) 2 SCALE 269:
    2000 (2) Supreme 179: 2000 (2) UJ (SC) 800   103
Municipal Corporation of Delhi *v.* Gurnam Kaur, (1989) 1 SCR 101:
    AIR 1989 SC 38: JT 1988 (4) SC 11: (1988) 23 Reports 139: 1988 Raj LR 579:
    1988 (3) SCJ 674: (1988) 2 UJ (SC) 713: (1989) 1 SCC 101   155
Municipal Corporation of Greater Bombay *v.* Thukral Anjali Deokumar,
    AIR 1989 SC 1194: (1989) 2 SCC 249: JT 1989 (1) SC 468   20
Municipal Corporation of the City of Ahmedabad *v.* New Shrock Spg. and
    Wvg. Co. Ltd., AIR 1970 SC 1292: (1970) 2 SCC 280: (1971) 1 SCR 288   244
Municipal Corporation *v.* Shiv Shankar, AIR 1971 SC 815: (1971) 1 SCC 442:
    1971 Cr LJ 680   251
Municipal Council, Khurai *v.* Kamal Kumar, AIR 1965 SC 1321: (1965) 2 SCR 653:
    1965 MPLJ 237: 1965 Jab LJ 225: 1965 Mah LJ 632: (1965) 1 SCWR 847   213

Munindra Nath Upadhyaya *v.* State of Uttar Pradesh, (1993) Supp 1 SCC 437:
    AIR 1992 SC 566: 1992 AIR SCW 184: 1992 All LJ 1112: 1993 (2) All CJ 749   207
Munisami Naidu *v.* C. Ranganathan, (1991) 2 SCC 139: AIR 1991 SC 492:
    1991 (1) All CJ 647: 1991 (2) Civ LJ 77: 1991 (1) Mad LJ 42:
    1991 (1) Ren CR 676   152
Murli Manohar & Co. *v.* State of Haryana, (1991) 1 SCC 377: JT 1990 (4) SC 189   265
Murli S. Deora *v.* Union of India, AIR 2002 SC 40: (2001) 8 SCC 765:
    2001 AIR SCW 4505: 2002 (1) JCR SC 5: JT 2001 (9) SC 364:
    2002 (22) OCR 118: 2002 (1) SCJ 85: 2002 SC Cr R 10:
    (2001) 8 SCALE 6: 2001 (8) Supreme 326   66
Musheer Khan *v.* State of Madhya Pradesh, AIR 2010 SC 762   149
MX of Bombay Indian Inhabitant *v.* M/s. ZY, AIR 1997 Bom 406   54
Mysore S.R.T.C. *v.* Devraj, AIR 1976 SC 1027   16
Mythili *v.* T. Padnia, Andhra Pradesh University of Health Service,
    AIR 1990 (NOC) 113 (AP): (1989) 2 APLJ 288   200

N

N. Adithayan *v.* Travancore Devaswom Board, AIR 2002 SC 3538:
    2002 AIR SCW 4146: 2003 (1) All Ind Cas 765: 2003 (1) Andh LD 28:
    JT 2002 (8) SC 51: 2002 (4) LRI 578: 2003 (1) Mad LW 97: (2002) 8 SCC 106:
    2002 (4) SCJ 606: (2002) 7 SCALE 280: 2002 (7) Supreme 242   39
N. Kannadasan *v.* Ajay Khose, (2009) 7 SCC 1   190
N. Masthan Sahib *v.* Chief Commissioner, Pondicherry, AIR 1962 SC 797:
    (1962) Supp 1 SCR 981: (1962) 2 SCA 401   7, 8, 16
N.P.T. Co. *v.* N.S.T. Co., (1957) SCR 98: AIR 1957 SC 232: (1957) 1 MLJ (Cri) 157   197
N.T. Devin Katti *v.* Karnataka Public Service Commission, (1990) 3 SCC 157:
    AIR 1990 SC 1233: 1990 Lab IC 1009   277
Nagaraj *v.* State of Andhra Pradesh, AIR 1985 SC 551: (1985) 1 SCC 523:
    (1985) 1 LLJ 444   141
Nagaraj *v.* Syndicate Bank, (1991) 2 UJ SC 217   214
Nagarjuna University *v.* St. Anthony Educational Society, AIR 1998 AP 271:
    1998 (1) APLJ 349: 1998 (3) Andh LD 42: 1998 (2) Andh LT 696:
    1998 (1) LS AP 474 (DB)   199
Nagina Devi *v.* Union of India, AIR 2010 Pat 117   10
Nagpur Improvement Trust *v.* Vithal Rao, AIR 1973 SC 689: (1973) 1 SCC 500:
    1973 SCD 43: (1973) 1 SCWR 127: 1973 Mah LJ 373   26
Nagraj *v.* State of Mysore, AIR 1964 SC 269: (1964) 2 SCR 671:
    (1963) 2 SCWR 231: (1964) 1 Cr LJ 161: 1964 SCD 35:
    (1964) 1 Andh LT 370: ILR 1964 Mys 1   215, 217
Nain Singh *v.* State of Uttar Pradesh, (1991) 2 SCC 432: 1991 SCC (Cri) 241   150
Nair Service Society *v.* State of Kerala, AIR 2007 SC 2891: 2007 AIR SCW 5276:
    2007 (2) Guj LH 358: 2007 (2) Ker LT 77: (2007) 4 SCC 1: 2007 (2) SCT 259:
    (2007) 4 SCALE 106: 2007 (3) Supreme 598   100
Nally *v.* State of Bihar, (1990) 2 SCC 48: (1990) 2 LLJ 211: (1990) 1 LLN 755   202
Namboodripad *v.* Nambiar, AIR 1970 SC 2015: (1970) 2 SCC 325: 1970 SCC (Cri) 451   145
Nanavati *v.* State of Bombay, AIR 1961 SC 112: (1961) 1 SLR 497: (1961) 1 Cr LJ 173   117
Nand Kishore Saraf *v.* State of Rajasthan, AIR 1965 SC 1992: (1965) 3 SCR 173:
    (1965) 2 SCWR 578: 1966 (2) SCJ 194   202
Nand *v.* State of Orissa, AIR 1991 SC 1724: (1991) 2 SCC 698: 1991 Lab IC 1527:
    (1991) 2 CLR 370   200
Nandini *v.* Dani, AIR 1978 SC 1025: (1978) 2 SCC 424: 1978 Cr LJ 968:
    1978 SCC (Cri) 236   52
Nanjanayaka *v.* State of Karnataka, AIR 1990 Kant 97: (1989) 2 Kant LJ 202   248
Narayan *v.* Purshottam, (1993) 1 UJ SC 297: (1993) Supp 2 SCC 90:
    AIR 1993 SC 1698   303
Narendra Kumar *v.* State of Haryana, JT 1994 (2) SC 94: (1994) 4 SCC 460:
    1994 SCC (L&S) 882: 1994 (68) FLR 942: AIR 1995 SC 519   59

Narendra Pratap Narain Singh *v.* State of Uttar Pradesh, (1991) 2 SCC 623:
AIR 1991 SC 1394: 1991 Cr LJ 1816: 1991 AIR SCW 1230:
1991 (2) Crimes 183: JT 1991 (2) SC 86: (1991) 2 SCR 88: 1991 SCC (Cri) 482   150
Narendra *v.* State of Gujarat, AIR 1974 SC 2092: (1975) 3 SCC 185: 1975 Cr LJ 556   76
Narendra *v.* State of Gujarat, AIR 1974 SC 2098: (1975) 1 SCC 11:
(1975) 2 SCR 317   76, 77
Narendra *v.* Union of India, (1990) Supp SCC 440: AIR 1989 SC 2138:
(1989) 3 SCR 43   205
Naresh K. Aggarwala & Co. *v.* Canbank Financial Services Ltd., AIR 2010 SC 2722   22
Narinderjit Singh Sahni *v.* Union of India, (2002) 2 SCC 210: AIR 2001 SC 3810:
2001 AIR SCW 4249: JT 2001 (8) SC 477: 2001 (5) SCJ 107: 2001 (10) SRJ 318:
2002 SC Cr R 770: (2001) 7 SCALE 189: 2001 (7) Supreme 593:
2002 (1) UJ (SC) 178   90
Narmada Bachao Andolan *v.* Union of India, AIR 2000 SC 3751:
(2000) 10 SCC 664: 2000 AIR SCW 4809: 2001 (1) Guj LR 434:
JT 2000 (2) SC (Supp) 6: 2000 (4) LRI 696: 2000 (4) SCJ 261:
(2000) 7 SCALE 34   90, 215
Narpat Singh *v.* Rajasthan Financial Corporation, AIR 2008 SC 77:
2007 AIR SCW 6109: 2007 (6) Mad LJ 1761: (2007) 11 SCALE 459   147
National Human Rights Commission *v.* State of Arunachal Pradesh, AIR 1996 SC 1234:
(1996) 1 SCC 742: 1996 AIR SCW 1274: 1996 (1) Cur CC 69: JT 1996 (1) SC 163:
1996 (2) SCJ 135: (1996) 1 SCR 278: 1996 SC Cr R 403: 1996 (1) UJ (SC) 370   64
Navjyoti Co-operative Group Housing Society *v.* Union of India,
AIR 1993 SC 155: (1992) 4 SCC 477: 1992 AIR SCW 3075:
JT 1992 (5) SC 621: 1993 (1) SCJ 4: (1992) 4 SCR 709: 1993 (1) UJ (SC) 94   208
Nayar *v.* Union of India, AIR 1992 SC 1574: (1992) Supp 2 SCC 508:
(1992) 21 ATC 695   281
Nayyar *v.* State, AIR 1979 SC 602: (1979) 2 SCC 593: 1979 SCC (Cri) 549   54
Neelima Misra *v.* Dr. Harinder Kaur Paintal, AIR 1990 SC 1402:
(1990) 2 SCC 746: 1990 Lab IC 1229: JT 1990 (2) SC 103   207
Neelima *v.* State of Haryana, AIR 1987 SC 169: (1986) 4 SCC 268:
1986 SCC (L&S) 759   297
Neera Mathur *v.* L.I.C., (1992) 1 SCC 286: (1992) 19 ATC 31: AIR 1992 SC 392:
(1992) 1 LLJ 322   279
Nelson *v.* Union of India, AIR 1992 SC 1981: (1992) 4 SCC 711:
(1992) 5 SCR 394   287, 289
New Barrackppore Mini Bus Owners' Association *v.* District Magistrate,
AIR 1990 Cal 268   272
New India Industries Ltd. *v.* Union of India, AIR 1990 Bom 239:
1990 Mah LJ 5: (1990) 1 Bom CR 515 (FB)   257
New Manek Chowk Spg. and Wvg. Mills Co. Ltd. *v.* Municipal Corporation
of the City of Ahmedabad, AIR 1967 SC 1801: (1967) 2 SCR 679:
1967 Cr LJ 1705: 1968 (1) SCJ 332: 9 Guj LR 390: 14 Law Rep 304   26
New Marine Coal Co. (Bengal) Private Ltd. *v.* Union of India, AIR 1964 SC 152:
(1964) 2 SCR 859: 1964 (1) SCA 491: (1964) 2 SCR 859   270
Nibaran *v.* Mahendra, AIR 1963 SC 1895: (1963) Supp 2 SCR 570:
(1963) 1 Ker LR 353   218
Nilabati *v.* State of Orissa, (1993) 2 SCC 746: AIR 1993 SC 1960: 1993 Cr LJ 2899   61, 88
Nirmal *v.* Union of India, (1991) Supp 2 SCC 363: (1991) 1 LLN 316:
(1991) 1 SLR 761   281
Nishi Maghu *v.* State of Jammu & Kashmir, AIR 1980 SC 1975:
(1980) 4 SCC 95: 1980 Srinagar LJ (SC) 13   32
Nityanandakar *v.* State of Orissa, AIR 1991 SC 1134: (1991) Supp 2 SCC 516:
1991 Lab IC 782   94
Nizzar Rawther *v.* Varghese Mathew, AIR 1992 Ker 312: ILR 1991 (3) Ker 514:
(1991) 2 Ker LJ 178: (1991) 2 Ker LT 223: 1991 (2) Ren CJ 638:
(1992) 1 Ren CR 411   219

Northern Corporation *v.* Union of India, (1990) 4 SCC 239: AIR 1991 SC 764:
    (1990) 49 ELT 332   90
Northern India Caterers (Private) Ltd. *v.* State of Punjab, AIR 1967 SC 1581:
    (1967) 3 SCR 399: 13 Law Rep 713: 1968 (1) SCJ 475   26

O

O.K. Ghosh *v.* Joseph, AIR 1963 SC 812: (1963) Supp 1 SCR 789: (1962) 2 LLJ 615   44
O.N. Mohindroo *v.* Bar Council of Delhi, AIR 1968 SC 888: (1968) 2 SCR 709:
    (1968) 1 SCA 618: (1968) 1 SCWR 986: 1968 Ker LJ 373: 1968 SCD 605:
    1968 (2) SCJ 448   252
O.P. Bhandari *v.* I.T.D.C., (1986) 4 SCC 337: AIR 1987 SC 111: (1986) 2 LLJ 509   28
Official Liquidator *v.* Dayanand, (2008) 10 SCC 1: AIR 2008 SC (Supp) 1177   2, 3
Oil and Natural Gas Commission *v.* Association of Natural Gas Consuming
    Industries of Gujarat, AIR 1990 SC 1851: 1990 Supp SCC 397:
    JT 1990 (2) SC 516   102, 208
Olga Tellis *v.* Bombay Municipal Corporation, AIR 1986 SC 180:
    (1985) 3 SCC 545: (1985) 2 Bom CR 434: 1986 Cr LR (SC) 23:
    1986 Cur Civ LJ (SC) 230   60, 65
Om Prakash Poplai *v.* Delhi Stock Exchange Association, JT 1994 (1) SC 114:
    (1994) 2 SCC 117: (1994) 79 Comp Cas 756   94
Om Prakash Shrivastava *v.* State of Madhya Pradesh, AIR 2005 SC 2453:
    2005 AIR SCW 2397: JT 2005 (4) SC 602: (2005) 11 SCC 488:
    2005 (4) SCJ 323: 2005 (2) SCT 665: 2005 (5) SRJ 567:
    (2005) 4 SCALE 358: 2005 (4) Supreme 169   281
Om Prakash *v.* State of Uttar Pradesh, (1991) Supp 2 SCC 436:
    AIR 1991 SC 425: 1991 Lab IC 303   285
Onkar Lal Bajaj *v.* Union of India, AIR 2003 SC 2562: (2003) 2 SCC 673:
    2003 AIR SCW 2757: 2003 (1) Cal LJ 1: 2003 (1) LRI 190:
    2003 (3) SRJ 200: (2002) 9 SCALE 501: 2003 (1) Supreme 402   23
Orient Paper and Industries Ltd. *v.* State of Orissa, AIR 1991 SC 672:
    (1991) Supp 1 SCC 81: JT 1990 (4) SC 267: (1991) 1 UJ (SC) 75   243
Oriental Insurance Co. Ltd. *v.* Laxmi Rani Biswas, AIR 2008 Gau 13:
    2008 AIHC 104 (NOC): 2008 (2) ALJ (NOC) 369:
    2008 (2) AIR Bom R 213 (NOC): 2007 (4) Gau LT 450: 2008 (1) Gau LR 588   155
Orissa Cement Ltd. *v.* State of Orissa, (1991) Supp 1 SCC 430: AIR 1991 SC 1676:
    1991 AIR SCW 1375: 1991 (34) ECR 497: (1991) 2 SCR 105:
    (1991) Supp 1 SCC 430   247, 252
Orissa J.S.A. *v.* State of Orissa, AIR 1991 SC 382: (1992) Supp 1 SCC 187:
    (1992) 19 ATC 229   280
Ouseph Mathai *v.* M. Abdul Khadir, AIR 2002 SC 110: (2002) 1 SCC 319:
    (2002) 1 KLT 3   218

P

P&O Steam Navigation Co. *v.* Secretary of State, (1861) 5 Bom HCR App A   271
P. Bhaskaran *v.* Additional Secretary, Agricultural (Co-operation) Department,
    Trivandrum, AIR 1988 Ker 75: (1987) 2 Ker LT 903: (1988) 2 Lab LJ 307:
    ILR (1988) 1 Ker 217: 1987 Ker LJ 1461: (1988) 19 Reports 636   14
P. Nalla Thampy Terah (Dr.) *v.* Union of India, AIR 1985 SC 1133:
    1985 Supp SCC 189   63
P. Rathinam Nagbhusan Patnaik *v.* Union of India, JT 1994 (3) SC 392:
    (1994) 3 SCC 394: 1994 SCC (Cri) 740: 1994 Cr LJ 1605   63
P. Sagar *v.* State of Andhra Pradesh, AIR 1968 AP 165: (1968) 1 AWR 116   34
P. Sivaswamy *v.* State of Andhra Pradesh, AIR 1988 SC 1863   103
P.A. Inamdar *v.* State of Maharashtra, (2005) 6 SCC 537: AIR 2005 SC 3226:
    2005 AIR SCW 3923: 2005 (4) CTC 81: JT 2005 (7) SC 313: 2005 (5) SCJ 746:
    2005 (3) SCT 697: (2005) 6 SCALE 471: 2005 (5) Serv LR 409:
    2005 (5) Supreme 544: 2005 (2) UJ (SC) 1176   1
P.G.I.M.R. *v.* K.L. Narasimhan, (1997) 6 SCC 283: 1997 SCC (L&S) 1449:
    1997 Lab IC 2317: JT 1997 (5) SC 313   38

P.K. Jaiswal (Dr.) *v.* Debi Mukherjee, AIR 1992 SC 749: 1992 Lab IC 580:
    1992 AIR SCW 432: JT 1992 (1) SC 315l: (1992) 2 SCC 148: 1992 SCC (L&S) 377:
    (1992) 1 SCR 1: (1992) 1 Serv LR 593: (1992) 1 UJ (SC) 731   297
P.L. Lakhanpal *v.* State of Jammu and Kashmir, AIR 1956 SC 197:
    1956 Cr LJ 421(2): 1956 SCJ 236: 1956 SCA 706: (1955) 2 SCR 1101   98
P.L.O. Corp. *v.* Labour Court, (1990) 3 SCC 632 (CB)   156
P.M. Ashwathanarayana Setty *v.* State of Karnataka, (1989) Supp 1 SCC 696:
    AIR 1989 SC 100: 1988 Raj LR 611: JT 1988 (4) SC 639:
    (1988) 23 Reports 210: ILR (1989) Kant 1: (1989) 1 Bom CLR 169   29
P.N. Duda *v.* P. Shiv Shankar, AIR 1988 SC 1208: (1988) 3 SCC 167:
    1988 SCC (Cri) 589   43
P.N. Kumar *v.* Municipal Corporation of Delhi, (1987) 4 SCC 609: 1988 SCC (L&S) 80   94
P.R. Transport Agency Agency *v.* Union of India, AIR 2006 All 23: 2005 All LJ 3568:
    2005 (61) All LR 408: 2006 (1) All WC 504: 2007 (1) CTLJ 384   204
P.S. Doshi *v.* State of Madhya Pradesh, AIR 1990 MP 171 (DB)   20
P.T. Services *v.* S.I. Court, AIR 1963 SC 114: (1963) 3 SCR 650: (1965) 2 LLJ 360   198
P.U. Abdul Rahiman *v.* Union of India, AIR 1991 SC 336: (1991) Supp 2 SCC 274:
    1991 Cr LJ 430   69
P.V. Kapoor *v.* Union of India, (1992) Cr LJ 140 (Del)   58
P.V. Srinivasa *v.* Comptroller Auditor General, (1993) 1 SCC 419:
    AIR 1993 SC 1321: 1993 Lab IC 421: (1993) 1 LLJ 824   287
P.V. Sundara Rajan *v.* Union of India, AIR 2000 SC 3387: 2000 AIR SCW 1677:
    2000 (86) FLR 59: JT 2000 (5) SC 175: 2000 (3) LLJ 997: 2000 (2) LLN 890:
    (2000) 4 SCC 469: 2000 SCC (L&S) 660: 2000 (2) SCT 771:
    (2000) 4 SCALE 48: 2000 (5) Supreme 83: 2000 (2) UJ (SC) 937   40
Palani, (in re:), AIR 1955 Mad 495: 56 Cr LJ 1197   53
Pallow Sheth *v.* Custodian, AIR 2001 SC 2763: (2001) 7 SCC 549:
    (2001) 107 Comp Cas 76   189
Paltu Dutta *v.* S.M. Nibedita Roy, AIR 1990 Cal 262: (1989) 2 Cal HN 338   218
Pannalal Bansilal Patil *v.* State of Andhra Pradesh, AIR 1996 SC 1023:
    (1996) 2 SCC 498: 1996 AIR SCW 507: 1996 (2) APLJ 24:
    1996 (1) Andh LD 18: 1996 (3) Andh LT 1: 1996 (1) Hindu LR 176:
    JT 1996 (1) SC 516: (1996) 1 SCR 603: 1996 (1) UJ (SC) 265   104, 105
Pannalal Binjraj *v.* Union of India, (1957) SCR 233: AIR 1957 SC 397:
    (1957) 31 ITR 565: 1957 SCA 660   20, 29, 205
Parenteral Drugs India Ltd. *v.* State of Himachal Pradesh, AIR 2008 (NOC) 380 (HP)   29
Parkash Singh Badal *v.* State of Punjab, (2007) 1 SCC 1: AIR 2007 SC 1274:
    2007 AIR SCW 1415: 2006 (4) Crimes 388: 2007 SC Cr R 488:
    (2006) 13 SCALE 54: 2007 (1) SCC (Cri) 193: 2006 (8) Supreme 964   221
Parmanand Katara *v.* Union of India, AIR 1989 SC 2039: (1990) Cr LJ 671:
    (1989) 4 SCC 286: 1989 SCC (Cri) 721   59
Parmatma Sharan *v.* Chief Justice Rajasthan High Court, AIR 1964 Raj 13:
    1963 Raj LW 246: ILR (1963) 13 Raj 215: (1965) 1 Lab LJ 221   16
Parsram *v.* Shivchand, AIR 1969 SC 597: (1969) 1 SCC 20: (1969) 2 SCR 997   314
Parveen Hans *v.* Registrar, AIR 1990 (NOC) 107 (P&H): (1990) 1 Serv LR 808   20
Paschim Banga Khet Mazdoor Samity *v.* State of West Bengal,
    AIR 1996 SC 2426: 1996 Lab IC 2054: 1996 AIR SCW 2964:
    1996 (2) APLJ 33: JT 1996 (6) SC 43: (1996) 4 SCC 37:
    1996 (3) SCJ 25: 1996 (4) SCT 28: 1996 (6) Serv LR 346   59, 64
Pashupati Nath Sukul *v.* Nem Chandra Jain, (1984) 2 SCC 404:
    AIR 1984 SC 399: 1984 All LJ 215: 1984 UJ (SC) 179   130
Pavadai Gounder *v.* State of Madras, AIR 1973 Mad 458: (1973) 2 Mad LJ 517   39
Payal Sharma alias Kamla Sharma alias Payal Katara *v.* Superintendent,
    Nari Niketan Kalindri Vihar, Agra, AIR 2001 All 254:
    2001 (2) All CJ 964: 2001 (44) All LR 146: 2001 (3) All WC 1778:
    2001 (3) East Cr C 143: 2001 (2) Marri LJ 391   39
Pedda Narayana *v.* State of Uttar Pradesh, AIR 1975 SC 1252:
    (1975) 4 SCC 153: 1975 Cr LJ 1062: (1975) 12 ACC 201   146

People's Union for Civil Liberties *v.* Union of India, AIR 2004 SC 456:
   2003 AIR SCW 7233: 2004 (1) CTC 241: (2004) 9 SCC 580:
   (2003) 10 SCALE 967: 2005 SCC (Cri) 1905: 2003 (8) Supreme 756   93
People's Union for Democratic Rights *v.* State of Bihar, AIR 1987 SC 355:
   (1987) Cr LJ 528: (1987) 1 SCC 265: 1987 SCC (Cri) 58   59, 60
People's Union for Democratic Rights *v.* Union of India, AIR 1982 SC 1473:
   1982 Lab IC 1646: (1982) 45 FLR 140: 1982 UJ (SC) 657:
   (1982) 3 SCC 235: 1982 BLJR 401: (1982) 2 LLN 642:
   (1982) 2 SCWR 202: (1982) 14 Lawyer 57: (1982) 2 LLJ 454   40, 72, 211
Peoples Union for Civil Liberties (PUCL) *v.* Union of India, AIR 2003 SC 2363:
   (2003) 4 SCC 399: 2003 AIR SCW 2353: JT 2003 (2) SC 528: 2003 (2) LRI 13:
   2003 (3) Mah LR 797: (2003) 2 SCR 1136: 2003 (5) SRJ 197:
   (2003) 3 SCALE 263: 2003 (3) Supreme 93   49
Peoples Union for Civil Liberties *v.* Union of India, AIR 1997 SC 568:
   (1997) 1 SCC 301: 1997 AIR SCW 113: 1997 (1) ICC 682: JT 1997 (1) SC 288:
   1996 (3) Raj LW 126: 1996 (4) SCJ 565: 1997 (1) UJ (SC) 187   61, 64, 67, 72
Peoples Union for Democratic Rights *v.* Police Commr., Delhi Police Headquarters,
   (1989) 4 SCC 730: (1989) 1 SCALE 598: 1990 SCC (Cri) 75: 1990 ACC CJ 192   61
Periakaruppan *v.* State of Tamil Nadu, AIR 1971 SC 2303: (1971) 3 SCC 38:
   (1971) 2 MLJ 65 (SC)   32
Point of Ayr. Collieries Ltd. *v.* Lloyd George, (1943) 2 All ER 546   21
Pokhar Singh *v.* State of Punjab, AIR 1958 Punj 294: 1958 Cr LJ 1084   53
Police Commissioner, Delhi *v.* Registrar, Delhi High Court, AIR 1997 SC 95:
   (1996) 6 SCC 323: 1996 SCC (Cri) 1325   57, 64
Poona City Municipal Corporation *v.* Dattatraya Nagesh Deodhar, AIR 1965 SC 555:
   (1964) 8 SCR 178: 1965 MPLJ 69: 1965 Mah LJ 105: (1965) 1 SCWR 221:
   1965 (1) SCJ 626   244
Poonam *v.* Wadhwan, AIR 1987 SC 1383: (1987) 3 SCC 347: 1987 Cr LJ 1130   88
Poorvanchal Caterers *v.* Indian Railway Catering and Tourism Corporation Ltd.,
   AIR 2006 (NOC) 455 (Del)   201
Post and Telegraph Board *v.* Murthy, (1992) 2 SCC 317:(1992) 21 ATC 664:
   AIR 1992 SC 1368: (1992) 1 LLN 948   286
Prabha Dutt *v.* Union of India, (1982) 1 SCC 1: (1982) Cr LJ 148: AIR 1982 SC 6   61
Prabha *v.* Union of India, AIR 1982 SC 6: (1982) 1 SCC 1: 1982 SCC (Cri) 41   48
Prabhakar *v.* State of Andhra Pradesh, AIR 1986 SC 210: 1985 Supp SCC 432:
   1986 SCC (L&S) 49   37
Prabhuswamy *v.* K.S.R.T.C., AIR 1991 SC 1789: (1991) 19 ATC 266:
   (1991) Supp 2 SCC 433 (SC)   289
Prabodh Verma *v.* State of Uttar Pradesh, AIR 1985 SC 167: (1984) 4 SCC 251:
   1984 All LJ 931: 1984 SCC Lab 704: 1984 UPSC 576: 1984 UPLBEC 771:
   1985 Cur Civ LJ (SC) 128: (1985) 1 SCR 216   91
Pradeep Jain (Dr.) *v.* Union of India, AIR 1984 SC 1420: (1984) 3 SCC 654:
   1984 Ed Cas 237: (1984) 3 SCR 942   1, 11, 21, 30
Pradip Chandra Parija *v.* Pramod Chandra Pattnaik, AIR 2002 SC 296:
   (2002) 1 SCC 1: (2002) 254 ITR 99   160
Pradyat Kumar Bose *v.* Hon'ble Chief Justice of Calcutta High Court,
   AIR 1956 SC 285: 1956 SCA 79: 1956 SCJ 259: (1955) 2 SCR 1331:
   1956 SCC 402   292
Prafulla *v.* Bank of Commerce, AIR 1947 PC 60   246
Prafulla *v.* State of Maharashtra, AIR 1992 SC 2209: (1993) Supp 1 SCC 564:
   (1993) 23 ATC 675: (1993) 1 LLJ 171   286
Prakash Warehousing Co. *v.* Municipal Corpn., (1991) 1 UJ SC 553: (1991) 2 SCC 304, 152
Prakasha *v.* C.C.T., (1990) 2 SCC 259: AIR 1990 SC 997: (1990) SCC (L&S) 235:
   (1990) 4 SLR 215   345
Pramatha Nath Talukdar *v.* Saroj Ranjan Sarkar, AIR 1962 SC 876:
   (1962) Supp 2 SCR 297: (1962) 1 Cr LJ 770   193
Pramod Kumar Joshi (Dr.) *v.* Medical Council of India, (1991) 1 UJ SC 400:
   (1991) 2 SCC 179: 1991 AIR SCW 744   89, 91

Pramod v. Medical Council, (1991) 1 UJ SC 400: (1991) 2 SCC 179   92
Pranatosh Roy (Dr.) v. University of Calcutta, AIR 1998 Cal 181:
    1997 (2) Cal LJ 294: 1997 CWN 372: 1997 (3) Serv LR 633   34
Prasanna Dinkar Sohale v. Director-in-charge, Laxminarayan Institute of
    Technology, Nagpur, AIR 1982 Bom 176   20
Prasanna Kumar Roy Karmakar v. State of West Bengal, AIR 1996 SC 1517:
    (1996) 3 SCC 403: 1996 AIR SCW 1585: JT 1996 (3) SC 647:
    1996 (2) Ori LR 105: 1996 SCFBRC 507: (1996) 3 SCR 912: 1996 (2) UJ (SC) 468 148
Prasant Pattajoshy v. Principal, Lingaraj Law College, AIR 1977 Ori 107:
    (1976) 2 Cut WR 919: ILR (1977) Cut 33   216
Pratap Pharma (P) Ltd. v. Union of India, AIR 1997 SC 2648: (1997) 5 SCC 87:
    (1997) 2 BLJR 1076   51
Pratapsingh Raojirao Rane v. Governor of Goa, AIR 1999 Bom 53:
    1999 (1) Bom CR 574: 1998 (3) Bom LR 173 (DB)   165
Prathibha R.C.C. Spun, Pipe and Cement Products v. State of Karnataka,
    AIR 1991 Kant 205: ILR (1990) Kant 2672   164
Pratibha Co-operative Housing Society Ltd. v. State of Maharashtra,
    AIR 1991 SC 1453: (1991) 3 SCC 341: 1991 AIR SCW 1354:
    1992 (1) Bom CR 453: JT 1991 (2) SC 543: 1991 (2) Land LR 382:
    1991 (2) Mah LR 646: (1991) 2 SCR 745: (1991) 2 UJ (SC) 196   213
Pratima Paul v. Competent Authority, AIR 1990 Cal 185: (1989) 1 Cal LJ 425:
    (1989) 1 Cal HN 433: (1989) 2 Cal LT (HC) 80: (1989) 93 CWN 1146 (DB)   25
Prem Chand Somchand Shah v. Union of India, (1991) UJ (SC) 690   93
Prem Nath Kaul v. State of Jammu & Kashmir, AIR 1959 SC 749:
    (1959) Supp 2 SCR 270: (1959) 2 SCA 65: 1959 SCJ 797   253
Prem Prakash Kaluniya v. Punjab University, AIR 1972 SC 1408:
    (1973) 3 SCC 424   216, 217
Prem Shanker Shukla v. Delhi Administration, AIR 1980 SC 1535:
    1980 Cr LJ 930: (1980) 3 SCC 526: 1980 SCC (Cri) 815   57
Prem v. Chhabra, (1984) 2 SCC 302: 1984 SCC (Cri) 233: 1984 Cr LJ 668   246
Premium Granites v. State of Tamil Nadu, JT 1994 (1) SC 374:
    (1994) 2 SCC 691: AIR 1994 SC 2233   24
Premji Bhai v. Delhi Development Authority, AIR 1980 SC 738: (1980) 2 SCC 129 16
Presidential Reference (in re:), AIR 1999 SC 1: 1998 AIR SCW 3400:
    JT 1998 (7) SC 304: (1998) 7 SCC 739: 1998 (4) SCJ 200:
    1998 (4) SCT 696: (1998) 5 SCALE 629: 1998 (8) Supreme 140   142
Printers Mysore v. Assistant Commercial Law Officer, JT 1994 (1) SC 692:
    (1994) 2 SCC 434: (1994) 53 DLT 662   48
Prithi Pal Singh Bedi (Lt. Col.) v. Union of India, AIR 1982 SC 1413:
    (1982) 3 SCC 140: 1982 SCC (Cri) 642: 1982 UJ (SC) 695: (1982) 2 Serv LJ 582 11, 96
Pt. Parmanand Katara v. Union of India, AIR 1989 SC 2039: (1989) 4 SCC 286:
    1990 Cr LJ 671 (SC): 1989 All LJ 1111: 1990 (1) ACC 3: 1990 (1) BLJ 233:
    1990 Jab LJ 37: 1990 (1) Pat LJR 26   64
Pt. Ramprashad s/o Nandlalji Purohit v. State Transport Appellate Tribunal,
    M.P., AIR 1993 MP 92: 1993 (1) ACC 378: 1993 MPLJ 34 (DB)   219
Public Service Commission, Uttaranchal v. Mamta Bisht, AIR 2010 SC 2613   33
Punjab Traders v. State of Punjab, AIR 1990 SC 2300: (1991) 1 SCC 86   275
Purshottam v. Union of India, AIR 1958 SC 36: 1958 SCR 828: (1958) 1 LLJ 544 284
Purushotham v. State of Kerala, AIR 1962 SC 694: (1962) Supp 1 SCR 753:
    (1962) 1 MLJ (SC) 180   182
Pushpa v. Union of India, AIR 1979 SC 1953: 1980 Supp SCC 391: 1979 Cr LJ 1314 70
Puthiyadath Jayamathy Avva v. K.J. Naga Kumar, AIR 2001 Ker 38   182
Puttaswamy v. Chief Justice, AIR 1991 SC 295: (1991) Supp 2 SCC 421:
    (1991) 1 LLN 352   278
Puttawwa (in re:), AIR 1959 Mys 116: 1959 Cr LJ 617   117
Pyare Lal v. New Delhi Municipal Committee, AIR 1968 SC 133: (1967) 3 SCR 747:
    (1968) 70 Punj LR (D) 153: 1968 (2) SCJ 393: (1967) 2 SCWR 894   46

R

R. Chitralekha *v.* State of Mysore, AIR 1964 SC 1823: (1964) 6 SCR 368:
  1965 1 SCA 132   30
R. *v.* Governor of Ashford Remand Centre, (1973) Current Law Year Book 1434   108
R. *v.* Governor of Ashford Remand Centre, The Times, July 14, 1987,
  Current Law (August, 1987)   108
R. *v.* Middlesex II, (1952) 2 All ER 312   197
R. *v.* Northumberland Compensation Tribunal, (1952) 1 KB 338   197, 198
R.B.I. *v.* R.B.I. Staff, (1991) 2 UJ SC 546: (1991) 4 SCC 132: 1991 SCC (L&S) 1090:
  (1991) 17 ATC 295: AIR 1992 SC 485   200
R.C. Poudyal *v.* Union of India, AIR 1993 SC 1804: 1993 AIR SCW 1620:
  JT 1993 (2) SC 1: (1993) 1 SCR 891: (1994) Supp 1 SCC 324   8
R.D. CCB *v.* Dinkar, (1993) Supp 1 SCC 9   219
R.D. Shetty *v.* International Airport Authority of India, (1979) 3 SCR 1014:
  (1979) 3 SCC 489: AIR 1979 SC 1628   29
R.K. Dalmia *v.* Delhi Admn., AIR 1962 SC 1821: (1963) 1 SCR 253: (1962) 2 Cr LJ 805 52
R.S. Pandey *v.* State of Uttar Pradesh, AIR 1996 SC 717: (1995) 6 SCC 464:
  (1995) 31 ATC 735   204
Rabindra *v.* Union of India, AIR 1970 SC 470: (1970) 1 SCC 84: (1970) 2 SCR 697   20
Radha Mohan Singh @ Lal Saheb *v.* State of Uttar Pradesh, AIR 2006 SC 951:
  2006 Cr LJ 1121: 2006 AIR SCW 421: (2006) 2 SCC 450: 2006 (3) SCJ 466:
  (2006) 1 SCALE 369: 2006 SCC (Cri) 661: 2006 (1) Supreme 371   151
Radhakrishna Agarwal *v.* State of Bihar, AIR 1977 SC 1496: (1977) 3 SCC 457:
  (1977) 3 SCR 249   196
Radhey Shyam Singh *v.* Union of India, AIR 1997 SC 1610: (1997) 1 SCC 60:
  (1997) 1 LLJ 972: 1997 SCC (L&S) 136   31
Raghubir *v.* State of Haryana, AIR 1981 SC 2037: (1981) 4 SCC 210: 1981 Cr LJ 1497 251
Raghunath *v.* State of Karnataka, AIR 1992 SC 81: (1992) 1 SCC 335:
  (1992) 19 ATC 507   281
Raghunathrao Ganpatrao *v.* Union of India, AIR 1993 SC 1267: 1993 AIR SCW 1044:
  (1994) Supp 1 SCC 191: JT 1993 (1) SC 374: (1993) 1 SCR 480 (CB)   336
Rai Sahib Ram Jawaya Kapur *v.* State of Punjab, (1955) 2 SCR 225:
  AIR 1955 SC 549: 1955 SCA 577: 1955 SCJ 504:
  (1955) 2 Mad LJ (SC) 59: 57 Punj LR 444: 1955 Mad WN 973   43, 111, 166
Raj Deo Sharma *v.* State of Bihar, AIR 1998 SC 3281: (1999) 7 SCC 507:
  1998 Cr LJ 4596: 1998 AIR SCW 3208: 1998 (4) Crimes 53: JT 1998 (7) SC 1:
  1999 (2) SCJ 140: 1999 (1) SRJ 72: (1998) 5 SCALE 477: 1998 SCC (Cri) 1692:
  1998 (7) Supreme 556: 1999 (1) UJ (SC) 136   66
Raja Narayan Lal Bansilal *v.* Manek Phioz Mistry, AIR 1961 SC 29:
  (1961) 1 SCR 417: (1960) 30 Comp Cas 644   53, 54
Rajasthan Chapter of Indian Association of Lawyers *v.* Union of India,
  AIR 2008 (NOC) 533 (Raj)   204
Rajasthan Pradesh V.S. Sardar Shahar *v.* Union of India, AIR 2010 SC 2221   49
Rajendra *v.* State of Madhya Pradesh, (1992) Supp 2 SCC 513: (1992) 21 ATC 699   289
Rajendran *v.* Union of India, AIR 1968 SC 507: (1968) 1 SCR 721: (1968) 2 LLJ 407   32
Rajesh Arjunbhai Patel *v.* State of Maharashtra, AIR 1990 Bom 114: 1990 Mah LJ 55   315
Rajesh Kumar Gupta *v.* State of Uttar Pradesh, AIR 2005 SC 2540:
  2005 Lab IC 2087: 2005 All LJ 1915: 2005 (106) FLR 411: 2005 (3) LLN 1041:
  (2005) 5 SCC 172: 2005 SCC(L&S) 668: 2005 (2) SCT 827:
  (2005) 4 SCALE 657: 2005 (5) Serv LR 1: 2005 (4) Supreme 262   34
Rakesh Kumar *v.* State of Punjab, AIR 1965 Punj 507   216
Rakhi Ray *v.* High Court of Delhi, AIR 2010 SC 932   35, 221
Ram and Shyam Company *v.* State of Haryana, AIR 1985 SC 1147:
  (1985) 3 SCC 267: (1985) Supp 1 SCR 541   43
Ram Badan Rai *v.* Union of India, AIR 1999 SC 166: 1998 AIR SCW 3525:
  1998 All LJ 2637: 1999 (1) All WC 430: JT 1998 (7) SC 478:
  (1999) 1 SCC 705: 1998 (4) SCJ 153: (1998) 6 SCALE 71: 1998 (8) Supreme 342   7

Ram Beli *v.* District Panchayat Rajadhukari, AIR 1998 SC 1222:
  (1998) 1 SCC 680: 1998 All LJ 832   25
Ram Bhagat Singh *v.* State of Haryana, (1997) 11 SCC 417: (1990) 2 SCR 329:
  (1991) 3 SLR 15: (1990) 2 SLJ 107   38
Ram Ekbal Sharma *v.* State of Bihar, AIR 1990 SC 1368: (1990) 3 SCC 504:
  1990 SCC (L&S) 491: (1990) 2 SLJ 98   286
Ram Krishna Paul *v.* Government of West Bengal, AIR 1972 SC 863:
  (1972) 1 SCC 570: 1972 Cr LJ 649   70
Ram Kumar Kashyap *v.* Union of India, AIR 2010 SC 1151   37
Ram Kumar *v.* State of Madhya Pradesh, AIR 1975 SC 1026: (1975) 3 SCC 815:
  (1975) 3 SCR 519: 1975 Cr LJ 870   146
Ram Prasad *v.* State of Uttar Pradesh, AIR 1988 All 309: (1988) 14 All LR 497:
  1988 All WC 1082 (DB)   110
Ram Saran *v.* State of Punjab, (1991) 2 SCC 253: (1991) 16 ATC 484:
  (1991) 1 LLJ 585   278
Ram Sarup *v.* Union of India, AIR 1965 SC 247: (1964) 5 SCR 931:
  1964 Cur LJ (SC) 169: 1964 SCD 661: 1964 (2) SCJ 619:
  1964 Mad LJ (Cri) 626: (1965) 1 Cr LJ 236   96
Ram Swarup *v.* State of Uttar Pradesh, AIR 1958 All 119: 1958 Cr LJ 134   52
Rama Dass Ram *v.* State of Bihar, AIR 1987 SC 1333: (1987) Cr LJ 1055:
  (1987) Supp SCC 143   62
Rama Dayal Markarha *v.* State of Madhya Pradesh, AIR 1978 SC 921:
  (1978) 2 SCC 630: 1978 SCC (Cri) 327   43
Rama Murthy *v.* State of Karnataka, (1997) 2 SCC 642: 1997 SCC (Cri) 386:
  AIR 1997 SC 1739: 1997 Cr LJ 1508   209
Ramakant Shripad Sinai Advalpalkar *v.* Union of India, AIR 1991 SC 1145:
  (1991) Supp 2 SCC 733: 1992 SCC (L&S) 115: 1993 (3) SCT 586:
  1992 (6) Serv LR 290   279
Ramakrishna Hegde *v.* State of Karnataka, AIR 1993 Kant 54: ILR 1992 Kant 3028   178
Ramalingam *v.* Daily Thanthi, AIR 1975 Mad 209   133
Ramana *v.* International Airport Authority of India, AIR 1979 SC 1628:
  (1979) 3 SCC 489   16
Ramanaiah *v.* Supdt., Central Jail, AIR 1974 SC 31: (1974) 3 SCC 531: 1974 Cr LJ 150   117
Ramchandra Shankar Deodhar *v.* State of Maharashtra, AIR 1974 SC 259:
  1974 Lab IC 165: 1974 SCC (Lab) 137: (1974) 1 SCC 317:
  (1974) 1 LLJ 221: (1974) 2 SCR 216   89
Ramchandra *v.* Andhra Pradesh Regional Committee, AIR 1965 AP 305   187
Ramchandra *v.* Union of India, AIR 1984 SC 541: (1984) 2 SCC 141: (1984) 1 LLJ 314 101
Ramesh Birch *v.* Union of India, AIR 1990 SC 560: (1989) Supp 1 SCC 430:
  JT 1989 (2) SC 483: (1989) 2 All RC 273: (1989) 2 Rec CR 79:
  (1989) 2 Rent LR 164   154
Ramesh Kumar Singh *v.* State of Bihar, (1987) Supp SCC 335: 1988 SCC (Cri) 89   67
Rameshwar Prasad *v.* Union of India, AIR 2006 SC 980: 2006 AIR SCW 494:
  2006 (3) CTC 209: (2006) 2 SCC 1: 2006 (1) SCJ 477: 2006 (3) SRJ 399:
  (2006) 1 SCALE 385: 2006 (1) Supreme 393   91, 172, 173, 325
Ramji Lal Modi *v.* State of Uttar Pradesh, AIR 1957 SC 620: 1957 SCR 860:
  1957 Cr LJ 1006: (1957) 2 Mad LJ (SC) 65: 1957 SCJ 522: 1957 SCC 334:
  1957 BLJR 723: (1957) 1 Mad LJ (Cri) 771: 1958 SCA 157   73, 75
Ramsharan Autyanuprasi *v.* Union of India, AIR 1989 SC 549:
  JT 1988 (4) SC 577: (1989) Supp 1 SCC 251: (1988) 2 SCALE 1399   108
Ranchod *v.* State of Gujarat, AIR 1974 SC 1143: (1974) 3 SCC 581: 1974 Cr LJ 799   59
Randhir Singh *v.* Union of India, AIR 1982 SC 879: (1982) 1 SCC 618: (1982) 1 LLJ 344   3
Randhir *v.* Union of India, AIR 1982 SC 879: (1982) 1 SCC 618: (1982) 1 LLJ 344 101
Rangaswamy *v.* Government of Andhra Pradesh, AIR 1990 SC 535:
  (1990) 1 SCC 288: 1991 Lab IC 296: (1990) 1 LLJ 526   280
Ranital Chowk Vyapari Sangh, Jabalpur *v.* State of Madhya Pradesh,
  AIR 2006 (NOC) 299 (MP)   58

Ranjit Singh v. Union Territory of Chandigarh, AIR 1991 SC 2296: (1991) 4 SCC 304:
    1991 SCC (Cri) 965   87
Ranjit Thakur v. Union of India, AIR 1987 SC 2386: (1987) 4 SCC 611:
    1988 SCC (L&S) 1   97
Ranvir v. Union of India, (1991) Cr LJ 1791 (Bom)   97
Rao Shiv Bahadur Singh v. State of Vindhya Pradesh, AIR 1953 SC 394:
    (1953) SCR 1188: 1953 Cr LJ 1480: 1953 SCA 803: 1953 SCJ 563   53
Rashbihari v. State of Orissa, AIR 1969 SC 1081: (1969) 1 SCC 414:
    (1969) 35 Cut LJ 479   202
Rasiklal v. Kishore Khanchand Wadhwani, AIR 2009 SC 1341: 2009 Cr LJ 1887:
    2009 AIR SCW 1945: 2009 (2) Chand Cr C 288: 2009 (4) MPHT 1:
    2009 (43) OCR 28: 2009 (1) Raj LW 580: (2009) 4 SCC 446:
    (2009) 3 SCALE 9: 2009 (2) SCC (Cri) 338   26
Ratan Singh v. State of Rajasthan, AIR 2006 (NOC) 129 (Raj)   213
Ratilal Panachand Gandhi v. State of Bombay, (1954) SCR 1055: AIR 1954 SC 388:
    1954 SCJ 480: (1954) 1 Mad LJ 718: 1954 SCA 538: 56 Bom LR 1184   73, 76
Ratlam Municipality v. Vardichan, AIR 1980 SC 1622: (1980) 4 SCC 162:
    1980 Cr LJ 1075   92, 211
Ravi Naik v. Union of India, JT 1994 (1) SC 551: (1994) Supp 2 SCC 641:
    AIR 1994 SC 1558   178
Ravinder Pal Singh Sidhu v. Punjab Public Service Commission,
    AIR 2003 SC 788: (2003) 2 SCC 147: 2003 SCC (L&S) 143   295
Rayala M. Bhuvaneswari v. Nagaphanender Rayala, AIR 2008 AP 98:
    2008 AIHC 356 (NOC): 2008 (3) ALJ (NOC) 624: 2008 (2) AIR Jhar (NOC) 429:
    2008 (64) All Ind Cas 860: 2008 (1) Andh LT 613   62
Reference under article 317(1), AIR 1983 SC 996: (1983) 4 SCC 258:
    (1983) 2 Serv LJ 411: 1983 BLJR 529: 1983 UJ (SC) 860:
    (1983) 2 Serv LR 759: (1983) 47 FLR 371   294
Rev. Father W. Proost v. State of Bihar, AIR 1969 SC 465: (1969) 2 SCR 73   79, 82
Revenue Officer v. Prafulla Kumar Pati, AIR 1990 SC 727: JT 1990 (1) SC 155   315
Reynold Rajamani v. Union of India, AIR 1982 SC 1261: (1982) 2 SCC 474:
    1982 East LR 304: 1982 UJ (SC) 570: 1982 (8) All LR 649:
    1982 Marriage LJ 498: 1982 Cr App R (SC) 223   106
Robert Baird. L.D. City of Glasgow, (1936) AC 32   21
Rohtas Industries Ltd., Workers v. Rohtas Industries Ltd., AIR 1990 SC 481:
    (1989) Supp 2 SCC 481: 1990 Lab IC 146   87
Rohtas Industries Ltd., Workers v. Rohtas Industries, AIR 1996 SC 467:
    (1995) Supp 4 SCC 5: 1996 SCC (L&S) 125   95
Roshan Deen v. Preeti Lal, (2002) 1 SCC 100: 2002 SCC (L&S) 97:
    AIR 2002 SC 33: (2002) 1 LLN 11   158, 201
Roshan v. S.R.C. Mills, AIR 1990 SC 1881: (1990) 2 SCC 636: 1990 Cr LJ 1770   157
Rudul Shah v. State of Bihar, AIR 1983 SC 1086: (1983) 4 SCC 141:
    1983 Cr LJ 1644   55, 56
Rupinder v. Union of India, AIR 1983 SC 65: (1983) 1 SCC 140: 1983 SCC (Cri) 136 60
Ruqmani v. Achuthan, (1991) Supp 1 SCC 520: AIR 1991 SC 983   202
Rural Litigation and Entitlement Kendra v. State of Uttar Pradesh,
    AIR 1989 SC 594: (1989) Supp 1 SCC 537: JT 1988 (4) SC 710   93
Rural Litigation and Entitlement Kendra v. State of Uttar Pradesh, AIR 1987 SC 359:
    1986 Supp SCC 517: JT 1986 SC 1118: 1986 (4) Supreme 324:
    (1987) 1 Cur CC 200: (1987) 13 All LR 139: (1987) 1 UJ (SC) 132:
    1987 (1) SCJ 337: 1987 Cur Civ LJ (SC) 209   109
Rural Litigation and Entitlement Kendra v. State of Uttar Pradesh,
    AIR 1987 SC 2426: (1987) Supp SCC 487: JT 1987 (5) SC 122   110
Rustom Cowasji Cooper v. Union of India, AIR 1970 SC 564: (1970) 1 SCC 248:
    (1970) 40 Comp Cas 325: 1970 (3) SCR 530   141

S

S. Azeez Basha v. Union of India, AIR 1968 SC 662: (1968) 1 SCR 833   76, 80

S. Narayan Iyer *v.* Union of India, AIR 1976 SC 1986: (1976) 3 SCC 428: (1976) 2 SCWR 13: 1976 UJ (SC) 569: 1976 SCC (Tax) 325: 1976 Supp SCR 486: 1977 (1) SCJ 193   196

S. Raghbir Singh Gill *v.* S. Gurcharan Singh Tohra, AIR 1980 SC 1362: 1980 Supp SCC 53: (1980) 3 SCR 1302   353

S. Rama Krishna *v.* S. Rammi Reddy, AIR 2008 SC 2066   77

S.B. Dogra *v.* State of Himachal Pradesh, (1992) 4 SCC 455   289

S.B. Minerals *v.* M/s. MSPL Ltd., AIR 2010 SC 1137   151

S.B. Narasimha Prakash *v.* State of Karnataka, (1997) 11 SCC 425   47

S.B.P. & Co. *v.* Patel Engineering Ltd., AIR 2006 SC 450: 2005 AIR SCW 5932: 2005 CLC 1546: 2006 (1) JCR SC 190: JT 2005 (9) SC 219: (2005) 8 SCC 618: 2005 (7) SCJ 461: 2006 (1) SRJ 25: (2005) 9 SCALE 1: 2005 (7) Supreme 610   208

S.C. Employees Association *v.* Union of India, (1989) 4 SCC 187: AIR 1990 SC 334: (1989) 2 LLJ 506   90

S.K. Dutta, I.T.O. *v.* Lawrence Singh Ingty, (1968) 68 ITR 272   29

S.M. Mukherjee *v.* Union of India, AIR 1990 SC 1984: (1990) 4 SCC 594: 1990 Cr LJ 2148   93

S.M.D. Kiran Pasha *v.* Government of Andhra Pradesh, 1990 (1) SCJ 282: (1990) 1 SCC 328: 1990 SCC (Cri) 110   213

S.N. Mukherjee *v.* Union of India, 1990 (3) SCJ 193: (1990) 4 SCC 594: AIR 1990 SC 1984: 1990 Cr LJ 2148   97, 199

S.N.J. Abdul Hakeem *v.* Assisrathul Musthakeem Etheemkhana Trust, AIR 2006 Mad 67: 2006 AIHC 53 (NOC): 2005 (2) Mad LJ 533: 2005 (2) Mad LW 621   195

S.P. Gupta *v.* President of India, AIR 1982 SC 149: 1982 Raj LR 389: 1981 Supp SCC 87   1, 18, 120, 143, 210

S.P. Mittal *v.* Union of India, AIR 1983 SC 1: (1983) 1 SCC 51: (1983) 1 East LR 53: 1983 (1) SCJ 45: (1983) 1 SCR 729   74

S.P. Sampath Kumar *v.* Union of India, AIR 1987 SC 386: (1987) 1 SCC 124: (1987) 1 SLR 182: (1987) 2 ATC 82: 1987 Lab IC 222: (1987) 1 LLJ 128   18, 299, 335

S.R. Bommai *v.* Union of India, (1994) 3 SCC 1: AIR 1994 SC 1918: 1994 AIR SCW 2946: JT 1994 (2) SC 215: (1994) 2 SCR 644: JT 1994 (2) SC 215   5, 173, 325

S.R. Bommai *v.* Union of India, AIR 1990 Kant 5: ILR 1989 Kant 2425 (FB)   324

S.S. Balu *v.* State of Kerala, AIR 2009 SC 1994: 2009 Lab IC 1454: 2009 AIR SCW 1644: 2009 (3) JCR SC 63: (2009) 2 LLN 28: (2009) 2 SCC 479: 2009 (2) SCT 73: (2009) 2 Serv LJ 480 SC   206

S.S. Bola *v.* B.D. Sardana, AIR 1997 SC 3127: (1997) 8 SCC 522: 1997 AIR SCW 3172: 1997 (5) SCJ 278: 1997 (3) SCT 645: (1997) 5 SCALE 90: 1997 (7) Supreme 427   243

S.S. Dhanoa *v.* Union of India, AIR 1991 SC 1745: (1991) 3 SCC 567: (1991) 2 LLN 428   285, 302, 303

Sabhajit *v.* Union of India, AIR 1975 SC 1329: (1975) 1 SCC 485: (1975) 1 LLJ 374   16

Sachdev *v.* Union of India, (1991) 1 SCC 605: AIR 1991 SC 311: 1991 Cr LJ 392   88, 92

Sachidanand Pandey *v.* State of West Bengal, AIR 1987 SC 1109: (1987) 2 SCC 295: (1987) 1 Comp LJ 211: JT 1987 (1) SC 425: 1987 (2) SCJ 70: 1987 (1) Supreme 492: (1987) 1 UJ (SC) 641   92, 110

Sadhana Devi *v.* State of Uttar Pradesh, AIR 1997 SC 1120: (1997) 3 SCC 90: 1997 All LJ 677   38

Sadhuram Bansal *v.* Pulin Behari Sarkar, AIR 1984 SC 1471: (1984) 3 SCC 410   5

Saghir Ahmad *v.* State of Uttar Pradesh, AIR 1954 SC 728: (1955) 1 SCR 707: 1954 SCA 1218: (1954) 2 MLJ 622: 1954 SCJ 819: 1954 All WR 23: 68 Mad LW 8: 1955 All LJ 38   42

Saheli *v.* Commissioner of Police, AIR 1990 SC 513: (1990) 1 SCC 422: (1990) 1 SCJ 300: 1990 SCC (Cri) 145   54, 88, 271

Sakal Papers (P) Ltd. *v.* Union of India, AIR 1962 SC 305: (1962) 3 SCR 842: 1962 (2) SCJ 400   48

Salonah Tea Co. Ltd. *v.* Superintendent of Taxes, Nowgong, AIR 1990 SC 772:
(1988) 1 SCC 401: (1988) 69 STC 290: (1988) 173 ITR 42	257
Samatha *v.* State of Andhra Pradesh, AIR 1997 SC 3297: (1997) 8 SCC 199:
1997 AIR SCW 3361: JT 1997 (6) SC 449: 1997 (2) SCJ 539:
(1997) 4 SCALE 746: 1997 (6) Supreme 530	66
Sambamurthy *v.* Union of India, AIR 1987 SC 66: (1987) 1 SCC 362:
(1987) 2 ATC 502: (1987) 1 LLJ 221	19
Sampat Prakash *v.* State of Jammu and Kashmir, AIR 1970 SC 1118:
(1969) 2 SCR 365: 1970 Lab IC 873	98
Sampat *v.* State of Jammu & Kashmir, AIR 1969 SC 1153: (1969) 1 SCC 562:
1969 Cr LJ 1555	69
Samsher Singh *v.* State of Punjab, AIR 1974 SC 2192: (1974) 2 SCC 831:
(1974) 2 LLJ 465: (1974) 1 SCR 814: 1974 Lab IC 1380	119, 122, 222
Sanaboina Satyanarayan *v.* Government of Andhra Pradesh,
AIR 2003 SC 3074: (2003) 10 SCC 78: 2003 Cr LJ 3854	164
Sand Carrier's Owners' Union *v.* Board of Trustees for the Port of Calcutta,
AIR 1990 Cal 176: (1989) 1 Cal LT (HC) 437: (1989) 1 Cal HN 474:
(1989) 2 Cal LJ 201: (1989) 93 CWN 1095	214
Sangita *v.* State of Uttar Pradesh, (1992) Supp 1 SCC 715	87
Sanjay Kumar Manjul *v.* Chairman, U.P.S.C., AIR 2007 SC 254:
2006 AIR SCW 6023: (2006) 8 SCC 42: 2006 (4) SCT 329:
2006 (10) SRJ 386: (2006) 9 SCALE 232: 2006 (7) Supreme 304	292
Sanjay Mehrotra (Dr.) *v.* G.S.V.M. Medical College, Kanpur, AIR 1989 SC 775:
(1989) 1 SCC 559: JT 1989 (1) SC 274: 1989 All WC 653:
(1989) 1 UPLBEC 431: 1989 Ed Cas 50	20
Sanjeev Coke Manufacturing Company *v.* Bharat Cooking Coal, AIR 1983 SC 239:
(1983) 1 SCC 147: 1983 UJ (SC) 81: 1983 (1) SCJ 233: (1983) 1 SCR 1000	85, 102
Sanjeevi *v.* State of Madras, AIR 1970 SC 1102: (1970) 1 SCC 443:
1970 SCC (Cri) 196	111, 168
Sanjit *v.* State of Rajasthan, AIR 1983 SC 328: (1983) 1 SCC 525: (1983) 1 LLJ 220	72
Santosh Sood *v.* Gajendra Singh, AIR 2010 SC 593	211
Sarada Bai *v.* Shakuntala Bai, AIR 1993 AP 20: 1992 (2) Andh LT 660: 1992 MCC 426	219
Saraswati Industrial Syndicate Ltd. *v.* Union of India, AIR 1975 SC 460:
(1974) 2 SCC 630: (1975) 1 SCR 956	196
Sarat Chandra Rabha *v.* Khagendranath Nath, AIR 1961 SC 334:
(1961) 2 SCR 133: (1961) 2 SCA 326: 1963 (1) SCJ 796: ILR (1961) 13 Assam 1	117
Sardar Sarup Singh *v.* State of Punjab, AIR 1959 SC 860: (1959) Supp 2 SCR 499:
1959 SCJ 1115: (1960) 1 SCA 163	74, 76
Sardar Syedna Taher Saifuddin Saheb *v.* State of Bombay, AIR 1962 SC 853:
(1962) Supp 2 SCR 496: (1962) 2 SCA 192: 1963 (2) SCJ 519	73, 74, 76
Sardara Singh *v.* State of Punjab, AIR 1991 SC 2248: (1991) 4 SCC 555:
1991 SCC (L&S) 1357	278
Sarvjeet Kumar *v.* Union of India, AIR 2008 Del 37: 2008 (3) AKAR (NOC) 383	119
Sasanka Sekhar Maity *v.* Union of India, AIR 1981 SC 522: (1980) 4 SCC 716:
(1980) 3 SCR 1209	335
Sat Pal Chopra *v.* Director-cum-Joint Secretary, AIR 1991 SC 970: 1991 AIR SCW 270:
(1991) Supp 2 SCC 352: 1991 Lab IC 441: JT 1991 (5) SC 89	150
Satish *v.* State of Uttar Pradesh, (1992) Supp 2 SCC 94	107
Satpal *v.* Lt. Governor, AIR 1979 SC 1550: (1979) 4 SCC 232: 1979 Tax LR 2486	141
Satpal *v.* State of Haryana, AIR 2000 SC 1702: (2000) 5 SCC 170:
2000 SCC (Cri) 920: 2000 Cr LJ 2297	164
Satrucharla Vijaya Rama Raju *v.* Nimmaka Jaya Raju, AIR 2006 SC 543:
2005 AIR SCW 6197: JT 2005 (9) SC 545: (2006) 1 SCC 212: 2005 (8) SCJ 238:
2006 (1) SRJ 109: (2005) 8 SCALE 745: 2005 (8) Supreme 433	155
Satvir Singh *v.* Baldeva, AIR 1997 SC 169: (1996) 8 SCC 593: 1997 Cr LJ 66:
1996 AIR SCW 4331: 1996 (2) Crimes 138: 1996 (2) East Cr C 280:
1996 SCC (Cri) 725	153

Satwant Singh Sawhney *v.* D. Ramarathnam, AIR 1967 SC 1836:
    (1967) 3 SCR 525: (1968) 70 Bom LR 1   57
Satwant *v.* State of Punjab, AIR 1960 SC 266: (1960) 2 SCR 89: 1960 Cr LJ 410   53
Satya Narain Shukla *v.* Union of India, AIR 2006 SC 2511: 2006 AIR SCW 2665:
    2006 (4) ALJ 276: (2006) 9 SCC 69: 2006 (6) SCJ 272: 2006 (3) SCT 305:
    (2006) 5 SCALE 627: 2006 (5) Supreme 417   162, 290
Saurabh Chaudri *v.* Union of India, AIR 2004 SC 361: (2003) 11 SCC 146:
    2003 AIR SCW 6392: 2004 (3) Bom CR 796: 2004 (1) JCR SC 140:
    JT 2003 (8) SC 296: 2003 (4) SCT 867: (2003) 9 SCALE 272: 2004 (1) Supreme 26   33
Sawhney *v.* L.I.C., (1991) 2 SCC 318: 1991 SCC (L&S) 480: 1991 Lab IC 648   152
Scientific Adviser *v.* Daniel, (1990) Supp SCC 374: 1991 SCC (L&S) 355:
    (1990) 2 LLJ 275   149
Scott *v.* Glasgow Corporation, (1989) AC 470   21
Sebastian Hongray *v.* Union of India, AIR 1984 SC 571: (1984) 1 SCC 339:
    1984 Cr LJ 289   55
Secretary to Government of Madras *v.* P.R. Sriramulu, AIR 1996 SC 676:
    (1996) 1 SCC 345: 1995 AIR SCW 4691: 1996 (1) CTC 235:
    JT 1995 (8) SC 305: 1996 (1) Mad LW 1: 1996 (1) UJ (SC) 612   257
Selvi *v.* State of Karnataka, AIR 2010 SC 1974   1, 54, 59
Seshanmal *v.* State of Tamil Nadu, AIR 1972 SC 1586: (1972) 3 SCR 815:
    (1972) 2 SCC 1: (1973) 1 MLJ 58 (SC)   73, 76
Shafiq *v.* D.M., (1989) 8 SCJ 568: (1984) 4 SCC 556: AIR 1990 SC 200   69
Shaik Fakruddin *v.* Shaik Mohammed Hasan, AIR 2006 AP 48:
    2006 (1) ALJ (EE) 148: 2006 (54) All Cr C 14 SOC: 2006 (37) All Ind Cas 197:
    2005 (6) Andh LD 179: 2005 (6) Andh LT 97: 2006 (3) Civ LJ 13   60
Sham Sunder *v.* Puran, (1990) 4 SCC 731: AIR 1991 SC 8: 1990 Cr LJ 2600:
    1991 (1) Crimes 165: JT 1990 (4) SC 165: 1991 SCC (Cri) 38:
    (1991) Supp 1 SCC 68: 1990 (2) UJ (SC) 695   150
Shankar *v.* Vice Admiral, (1991) 2 SCC 209: (1991) 16 ATC 470: (1991) 1 LLN 579   198
Shankaran *v.* Union of India, (1991) 3 SCC 47: (1991) 17 ATC 95:
    AIR 1991 SC 1612: (1991) 62 FLR 981: (1991) 2 LLN 65   283
Shankari Prasad Singh Deo *v.* Union of India, AIR 1951 SC 458: 64 MLW 1005:
    1951 ALJ 740: (1951) 2 MLJ 683: 88 Cal LJ 281: 1951 SCJ 775: 30 Pat 1176:
    1952 SCR 89   353
Shanno Devi *v.* Mangal Sain, AIR 1961 SC 58: 1961 (1) SCJ 201:
    (1961) 1 SCR 576: ILR (1961) 1 Punj 234: 22 Ele LR 469   11
Shantistar Builders *v.* Narayan Khimalal Totame, AIR 1990 SC 630:
    (1990) 1 SCC 520: 1990 Jab LJ 209: JT 1990 (1) SC 106   106
Shantistar *v.* Narayanan, (1990) 2 SCJ 10   57
Sharma Transport *v.* Government of Andhra Pradesh, AIR 2002 SC 322:
    (2002) 2 SCC 188: 2001 AIR SCW 4958: 2002 (1) ACC 85:
    2002 (1) Andh LD 66: 2002 (1) Arb LR 231: JT 2001 (2) SC (Supp) 1:
    2002 (1) SCJ 67: 2002 (2) SRJ 96: (2001) 8 SCALE 417: 2001 (8) Supreme 496   30
Sharma *v.* Satish, (1954) SCR 1077: (1954) 1 MLJ 680: 1954 Cr LJ 865   54
Sharma *v.* Union of India, AIR 1981 SC 588: (1981) 1 SCC 397: (1981) 1 SCR 1184   91
Shashikant Laxman Kale *v.* Union of India, JT 1990 (3) SC 267:
    AIR 1990 SC 2114: 1990 Tax LR 877   29
Sheela Barse *v.* Secretary, Children Aid Society, AIR 1987 SC 656:
    JT 1987 (1) SC 58: 1987 Cr LR (SC) 29: 1987 (1) SCJ 584: (1987) 3 SCC 50:
    (1987) 1 UJ (SC) 516: 1987 SCC (Cri) 458: 1987 Mah LR 906   15, 72
Sheela Barse *v.* State of Maharashtra, AIR 1983 SC 378: (1983) Cr LJ 642:
    (1983) 2 SCC 96: 1983 SCC (Cri) 353   55, 61
Sheela Barse *v.* Union of India, AIR 1986 SC 1773: (1986) 3 SCC 596:
    1986 All LJ 1369: 1986 Cr LJ 1736: 1986 SCC (Cri) 337:
    JT 1986 (53) SC 136: 1986 BBCJ (SC) 116: 1986 Cur Cr J (SC) 249   55, 92
Sheela Barse *v.* Union of India, AIR 1988 SC 2211:
    (1988) 4 SCC 2261 (1988) 3 Crimes 269   210

Sheetal Prasad Gupta v. State of Bihar, AIR 1990 Pat 64: 1990 (1) Pat LJR 133 (FB)   246
Sher Singh v. State of Punjab, AIR 1983 SC 465: (1983) 2 SCC 344:
    1983 Cr LJ 803   56, 62, 66
Sheshrao Jungluji Bagle v. Govindrao, AIR 1991 SC 76: (1991) Supp 1 SCC 367:
    (1991) 16 ATC 938: (1991) 2 LLJ 109   279
Shiba Shankar Mohapatra v. State of Orissa, AIR 2010 SC 706   199
Shikshan Prasarak Mandal, Pune v. State of Maharashtra, AIR 2010 Bom 39   67
Shilpi v. State of Bihar, (1991) Supp 2 SCC 659: AIR 1991 SC 532: 1991 Lab IC 360   282
Shiv Charan v. State of Mysore, AIR 1965 SC 280: (1967) 2 LLJ 246: 15 FLR 224   37
Shiv Kumar Sharma v. Santosh Kumari, AIR 2008 SC 171: 2007 AIR SCW 6384:
    2007 (6) Andh LD 116: 2007 (5) CTC 453: 2008 (3) Mah LJ 593:
    2007 (4) Rec Civ R 515: (2007) 8 SCC 600: (2007) 11 SCALE 303:
    2007 (6) Supreme 347   204
Shivajirao Nilangekar Patil v. Dr. Mahesh Madhav Gosavi, AIR 1987 SC 294:
    (1987) 1 SCC 227: JT 1986 SC 1071: (1987) 89 Bom LR 65: (1987) 1 UJ (SC) 88:
    1987 (2) SCJ 1: (1987) 1 Cur LJ (Civ and Cri) 460: 1987 (2) Supreme 97   211
Shri Krishna Rangnath Mudholkar v. Gujarat University, AIR 1962 Guj 88:
    (1962) 3 Guj LR 204 (FB)   80, 81
Shri Kumar v. Union of India, (1992) 2 SCC 428: AIR 1992 SC 1213:
    (1992) 20 ATC 239: (1992) 1 LLN 951   336
Shri Sita Ram Sugar Co. Ltd. v. Union of India, AIR 1990 SC 1277:
    (1990) 3 SCC 223: JT 1990 (1) SC 462   21, 27, 92, 164, 208
Shridhar v. Nagar Palika, 1990 (1) SCJ 383: 1990 Supp SCC 157:
    AIR 1990 SC 307: (1990) 2 LLN 970   198
Shrilekha v. State of Uttar Pradesh, (1991) 1 SCC 212: (1991) SCC (L&S) 742:
    AIR 1991 SC 537   211, 282
Shyam Sundar v. State of Rajasthan, AIR 1974 SC 890: (1974) 1 SCC 690:
    (1974) 3 SCR 549   25, 271
Shyamal Ranjan Mukherjee v. Nirmal Ranjan Mukherjee, AIR 2008 (NOC) 568 (All)   74
Siddha Raj Dhadda v. State of Rajasthan, AIR 1990 Raj 34:
    (1989) 1 Raj LR 355: 1990 (1) Civ LJ 179   207
Sidhrajbhai v. State of Gujarat, AIR 1963 SC 540: (1963) 3 SCR 837:
    1962 Ker LJ 135 (SC)   80, 82
Simranjit Singh Mann v. Union of India, (1993) 1 UJ SC 32: (1992) 4 SCC 653:
    AIR 1993 SC 280: 1993 Cr LJ 37: 1992 AIR SCW 3133: JT 1992 (5) SC 441:
    (1992) 4 SCR 592: 1993 SCC (Cri) 22   89
Sita Ram v. State of Uttar Pradesh, AIR 1979 SC 745: (1979) 2 SCC 656:
    1979 Cr LJ 659   62
Sita Ram v. State of Uttar Pradesh, AIR 1983 SC 65   66
Sitaram v. Ramjibhai, AIR 1987 SC 1293: (1987) 2 SCC 262: (1987) 3 ATC 515   130
Sitharmachary v. Senior Deputy Inspector, AIR 1958 AP 78   45
Society of St. Joseph's College v. Union of India, (2002) 1 SCC 273:
    AIR 2002 SC 195: (2002) 1 KLT 438   79
Sodhi v. Union of India, AIR 1991 SC 1617: (1991) 1 LLN 365:
    (1991) 2 SCC 382: 1991 SCC (Cri) 357: 1991 Cr LJ 1947   97, 194
Sohan Lal Baid v. State of West Bengal, AIR 1990 Cal 168: (1989) 2 Cal HN 474:
    (1989) 2 Cal LJ 433 (DB)   193
Som Prakash v. Union of India, AIR 1981 SC 212: (1981) 1 SCC 449:
    (1981) 1 LLJ 79: (1981) 1 LLN 322   16
Soosai v. Union of India, AIR 1986 SC 733: 1985 Supp SCC 590:
    1986 UJ (SC) 39: 1986 (1) Supreme 207: (1985) 87 Bom LR 652   314
Sophia Gulam Mohd. Bham v. State of Maharashtra, AIR 1999 SC 3051:
    (1999) 6 SCC 593   69
Southern Pharmaceuticals & Chemicals, Trichur v. State of Kerala,
    AIR 1981 SC 1863: (1981) 4 SCC 391: 1981 Tax LR 2838: (1982) 1 SCR 519   246
Special Courts Bill, 1978 (in re:), AIR 1979 SC 478: (1979) 1 SCC 380:
    1979 (2) SCJ 35: (1979) 2 SCR 476   26, 30

Special Deputy Collector (L.A.) *v.* N. Vasudeva Rao, AIR 2008 SC 944:
  2008 AIR SCW 435: 2008 (62) All Ind Cas 270: 2008 (70) All LR 488:
  2008 (5) All MR 8 (NOC): 2008 (1) ICC 729: (2007) 13 SCALE 508:
  2008 (8) Supreme 631   154
Special Reference of 1956, AIR 1965 SC 745 (762): (1965) 1 SCR 413:
  1965 (1) SCJ 847: (1965) 1 SCA 441   7
Special Ref. No. 1 of 2002, (under article 143(1) of the Constitution), AIR 2003 SC 87:
  (2002) 8 SCC 237: 2002 AIR SCW 4492: JT 2002 (8) SC 389: 2002 (4) LRI 169:
  2002 (6) SLT 599: (2002) 7 SCALE 614: 2002 (7) Supreme 437   173, 303
Sree Jain Swetamber Terapanthi Vidyalaya *v.* State of West Bengal,
  AIR 1982 Cal 101: (1982) 86 CWN 84: (1982) 1 Cal HN 247   81
Sri Adi Visheshwara of Kashi Vishwanath Temple, Varanasi *v.* State of Uttar Pradesh,
  (1997) 4 SCC 606: JT 1997 (4) SC 124: (1997) 3 SCALE 1   76
Srimad Perarulala Ethiraja Ramanuja Jeeyar Swami *v.* State of Tamil Nadu,
  AIR 1972 SC 1586: 1973 (1) SCJ 346: (1973) 1 Mad LJ (SC) 58:
  (1973) 1 Andh WR (SC) 58: (1972) 3 SCR 815   74, 76
Srinivasa *v.* State of Karnataka, AIR 1987 SC 1518: (1987) 2 SCC 692   85
Srish Kumar Chouhay *v.* State of Tripura, AIR 1990 SC 991: 1990 Supp SCC 220:
  1990 Lab IC 707   314
St. John's Teacher Training Institute (for Women), Madurai *v.* State of Tamil Nadu,
  AIR 1994 SC 43: 1 (1993) 3 SCC 595: 1993 AIR SCW 3089: JT 1993 (4) SC 78:
  1993 (2) Mad LW 218: 1993 (3) SCJ 1: (1993) 3 SCR 985: 1993 (4) SCT 33:
  1993 (2) UJ (SC) 490   82
St. Stephen's College *v.* University of Delhi, (1992) 1 SCC 558: AIR 1992 SC 1630:
  1992 AIR SCW 1792: JT 1991 (4) SC 548: 1992 (1) SCJ 624   23, 82, 83
St. Xavier's College *v.* State of Gujarat, AIR 1974 SC 1389: (1974) 1 SCC 717:
  (1975) 1 SCR 173   79, 81
Stainislaus *v.* State of Madhya Pradesh, AIR 1977 SC 908: (1977) 1 SCC 677:
  1977 Cr LJ 551   74, 75
Star Co. *v.* Union of India, AIR 1987 SC 179: (1986) 4 SCC 246: 1986 SCC (Cri) 431   156
Star Enterprises *v.* City and Industrial Development Corpn. of Maharashtra,
  (1990) 3 SCC 280: (1990) 2 Punj LR 264: (1990) 2 KLT 37   16
State Consumer Disputes Redressal Commission, Uttarakhand *v.*
  Uttarakhand State Information Commission, AIR 2010 Uttra 55   317
State of Andhra Pradesh *v.* Abdul Khader, AIR 1961 SC 1467: (1961) 2 Cr LJ 573:
  (1961) 63 Punj LR 751: 1961 Andh LT 816: 1961 All Cr R 347:
  (1961) 2 SCA 643: (1962) 1 Mad LJ (SC) 65: (1962 1 Andh WR (SC) 65:
  1962 (1) SCJ 100: (1962) 1 SCR 737   13
State of Andhra Pradesh *v.* Lavu Narendra Nath, AIR 1971 SC 2560:
  (1971) 1 SCC 607: (1971) 3 SCR 699   168
State of Andhra Pradesh *v.* Muralidhar, AIR 1992 SC 922: (1992) 2 SCC 241:
  (1992) 20 ATC 226: 1992 Lab IC 855   282
State of Assam *v.* P.C. Mishra, AIR 1996 SC 430: (1995) Supp 4 SCC 139:
  1995 AIR SCW 4287: 1996 (32) ATC 103: JT 1995 (8) SC 23:
  1996 SCC (L&S) 169: 1995 (4) SCJ 560: 1996 (1) SCT 520   164
State of Assam *v.* Ranga Mohammed, AIR 1967 SC 903: (1967) 1 SCR 454:
  (1968) 1 LLJ 282   222
State of Bihar *v.* Bal Mukund Sah, AIR 2000 SC 1296: 2000 AIR SCW 1180:
  JT 2000 (3) SC 221: (2000) 4 SCC 640: 2000 SCC (L&S) 489: 2000 (2) SCJ 599:
  2000 (3) SCT 459: (2000) 2 SCALE 415: 2000 (2) Supreme 409   276
State of Bihar *v.* Bhabapritananda Ojha, AIR 1959 SC 1073: 1961 BLJR 653:
  1959 SCJ 1197: ILR 38 Pat 834: (1960) 1 SCA 245: (1959) Supp 2 SCR 624   77
State of Bihar *v.* Bihar Distillery Ltd., AIR 1997 SC 1511: (1997) 2 SCC 453:
  1997 AIR SCW 259: 1997 (2) BLJ 640: 1997 (1) BLJR 551:
  JT 1996 (10) SC 854: 1997 (1) Supreme 121   243
State of Bihar *v.* Charusila Dasi, AIR 1959 SC 1002: (1959) Supp 2 SCR 601:
  (1959) 2 SCA 369: 1959 SCJ 1193: 1959 BLJR 785: 1960 Pat LR (SC) 1   244

State of Bihar *v.* Industrial Corporation Pvt. Ltd., AIR 2004 SC 1151:
    2003 AIR SCW 5874: 2003 (8) ACE 218: 2004 (1) BLJR 54:
    2003 (4) JLJR 162: 2003 (4) Pat LJR 231: (2003) 11 SCC 465:
    2003 (6) SLT 556: (2003) 9 SCALE 169: 2003 (7) Supreme 681   10
State of Bihar *v.* Kameshwar Singh, AIR 1952 SC 252: 1952 SCR 889: 31 Pat 565   19
State of Bihar *v.* Kamla Kant Misra, AIR 1971 SC 1667: (1969) 3 SCC 337:
    (1970) 3 SCR 181: ILR 49 Pat 467: 1969 Pat LJR (SC) 93 A: (1970) 2 SCA 574:
    1971 Mad LW (Cri) 24: 1971 (1) SCJ 621: 1971 Mad LJ (Cri) 305   45
State of Bihar *v.* Kumar Amar Singh, AIR 1955 SC 282: 1955 SCA 376:
    34 Pat 274: 1955 SCJ 311: 1955 All LJ 351: 1955 SCR 1259   12
State of Bihar *v.* P.P. Sharma, AIR 1991 SC 1260: (1992) Supp 1 SCC 222:
    1992 SCC (Cri) 192   87, 206
State of Bihar *v.* Sanjay, AIR 1990 SC 749: (1990) 4 SCC 624: (1990) 1 SLR 858   212
State of Bombay *v.* Bombay Education Society, (1955) 1 SCR 568:
    AIR 1954 SC 561: 56 Bom LR 1211   78
State of Bombay *v.* Kathi Kalu, AIR 1961 SC 1808: (1962) 3 SCR 10:
    64 Bom LR 240: (1961) 2 Cr LJ 856   52, 53
State of Bombay *v.* R.M.D. Chamarbaugwala, AIR 1957 SC 699:
    (1957) SCR 874: 52 Bom LR 945   51
State of Bombay *v.* S.L. Apte, AIR 1961 SC 578: (1961) 3 SCR 107:
    63 Bom LR 491: (1961) 1 Ker LR 452: (1961) 2 SCA 446:
    (1961) 1 AndhWR (SC) 210: 1961 (1) SCJ 685: 1961 Mad LJ (SC) 210:
    (1961) 1 Cr LJ 725: 1961 MPLJ 1108   53
State of Gujarat *v.* Ambica Mills Ltd., Ahmedabad, (1974) 4 SCC 656:
    AIR 1974 SC 1300: 1974 Lab IC 841: 45 FJR 381: 1974 SCC (Lab) 381:
    1974 (2) SCJ 211: (1974) 3 SCR 760   43
State of Gujarat *v.* Kasturchand Chhotalal Shah, AIR 1991 SC 695:
    (1991) Supp 2 SCC 345: 1991 (1) Guj LH 382: JT 1991 (5) SC 419:
    1991 (80) STC 394   154
State of Gujarat *v.* Mirzapur Moti Kureshi Kassab Jamat, AIR 2006 SC 212:
    2005 AIR SCW 5723: 2006 (1) All MR 32 (NOC): 2006 (1) Guj LR 294:
    2006 (2) JCR SC 272: (2005) 8 SCC 534: 2005 (7) SCJ 701:
    (2005) 8 SCALE 661: 2005 (8) Supreme 697   48, 107
State of Gujarat *v.* P.J. Kampavat, (1992) 3 SCC 226: AIR 1992 SC 1685:
    1992 AIR SCW 1866: JT 1992 (Supp) 102: 1992 SCC (L&S) 654:
    1992 (2) SCJ 404: (1992) 2 SCR 845: 1993 (1) SCT 231: 1992 Lab IC 1687:
    (1992) 21 ATC 112: (1992) 5 Serv LR 524: (1992) 2 UJ SC 78   283
State of Gujarat *v.* R.L. Patel, AIR 1992 Guj 42: 1991 (1) Civ LJ 128:
    (1990) 2 Guj LH 1: (1990) 2 Guj LR 1163: (1992) 1 LLJ 721:
    (1990) 6 Serv LR 782   315
State of Gujarat *v.* Shri Ambica Mills Ltd., (1974) 4 SCC 656:
    AIR 1974 SC 1300: (1974) 3 SCR 760: 1924 Lab IC 841   44
State of Gujarat *v.* Turabali Gulamhussain Hirani, AIR 2008 SC 86:
    2007 AIR SCW 6122: 2007 (4) Crimes 122: (2007) 11 SCALE 556:
    2007 (7) Supreme 129: 2007 (4) JLJR 199: 2007 (4) Ker LT 656:
    2008 (1) Mad LJ (Cri) 1045: 2007 (38) OCR 619   201
State of Haryana *v.* Amar Nath Bansal, AIR 1997 SC 718: (1997) 10 SCC 700:
    1997 Lab IC 550: (1997) 1 SLR 55   18
State of Haryana *v.* Bhajan, (1991) 2 SCJ 351: (1992) Supp 1 SCC 335:
    AIR 1992 SC 604: 1992 Cr LJ 527   199
State of Haryana *v.* Charanjit Singh, AIR 2006 SC 161: 2005 AIR SCW 5632:
    (2006) 9 SCC 321: 2005 (7) SCJ 536: 2006 (3) SCT 170: 2005 (9) SRJ 520:
    (2005) 8 SCALE 482: (2005) 6 Serv LR 693: 2005 (7) Supreme 193   101
State of Haryana *v.* Jagdish, AIR 2010 SC 1690   63, 118
State of Haryana *v.* Manoj Kumar, AIR 2010 SC 1779   219
State of Haryana *v.* Piara, (1992) 4 SCC 118: AIR 1992 SC 2130:
    (1992) 21 ATC 403: 1992 Lab IC 2168   278, 281, 282

State of Haryana *v.* Prem, AIR 1990 SC 538: (1990) 1 SCC 249:
1990 SCC (Cri) 93: 1990 Cr LJ 454   149
State of Haryana *v.* Ram Kishan, AIR 1988 SC 1301: (1988) 3 SCC 416   207
State of Haryana *v.* Ram Kumar, JT 1997 (8) SC 171: (1997) 3 SCC 321:
1997 Lab IC 1541   204
State of Haryana *v.* Smt. Darshana Devi, AIR 1979 SC 855: (1979) 2 SCC 236:
1979 UJ (SC) 389: 1979 Raj LR 311: 1979 Rev LR 312: 1979 ACJ 205:
81 Punj LR 472: 1979 TAC 285   102
State of Haryana *v.* Surinder Kumar, AIR 1997 SC 2129: (1997) 3 SCC 633:
1997 Lab IC 2096   102
State of Himachal Pradesh *v.* A Parent of a Student of Medical College,
Shimla, AIR 1985 SC 910: (1985) 3 SCC 169: (1985) 2 SCWR 48:
(1985) 11 All LR 487: (1985) 2 Cur CC 239   211
State of Himachal Pradesh *v.* Ganesh Wood Products, AIR 1996 SC 149:
(1995) 6 SCC 363: 1995 AIR SCW 3847: 1995 (5) Comp LJ SC 1:
JT 1995 (6) SC 485   164
State of Himachal Pradesh *v.* Paras Ram, AIR 2008 SC 930: 2008 Cr LJ 1026:
2008 AIR SCW 373: (2008) 3 SCC 655: (2008) 1 SCALE 6:
2008 (2) SCC (Cri) 117   154
State of Himachal Pradesh *v.* Raja Mahendra Pal, AIR 1999 SC 1786: (1999) 4 SCC 43   59
State of Himachal Pradesh *v.* Umed Ram Sharma, (1986) 2 SCC 68:
AIR 1986 SC 847: 1986 (1) SCJ 322: 1986 UJ (SC) 478: 1986 (2) Supreme 58   46
State of Jammu & Kashmir *v.* A.R. Zakki, AIR 1992 SC 1546:
(1992) Supp 1 SCC 548: (1992) 20 ATC 285: (1992) 1 LLJ 891   201
State of Karnataka *v.* Appa Balu Ingale, AIR 1993 SC 1126: 1993 Cr LJ 1029:
1993 AIR SCW 337: 1993 (1) Chand Cr C 147: 1992 (3) Crimes 1104:
1993 IJR 58: JT 1992 SC (Supp) 588: 1993 (1) SCJ 189: (1992) 3 SCR 284:
1994 SCC (Cri) 1762: (1995) Supp 4 SCC 469   40
State of Karnataka *v.* N.A. Nagendrappa, AIR 1991 Kant 317:
ILR (1991) Kant 1057: (1991) 2 Kant LJ 172 (FB)   206
State of Karnataka *v.* Southern India Plywood Co., AIR 1991 SC 1307:
(1991) Supp 1 SCC 212   151
State of Karnataka *v.* Union of India, (1977) 4 SCC 608: AIR 1978 SC 68:
(1978) 2 SCR 1: 1978 (2) SCJ 190   121, 133, 145
State of Karnataka *v.* Vishwabarathi House Building Co-operative Society,
AIR 2003 SC 1043: (2003) 2 SCC 412: (2003) 11 Comp Cas 536   301
State of Kerala *v.* A. Lakshmikutty, AIR 1987 SC 331: (1986) 4 SCC 632:
1987 Lab IC 447: JT 1986 SC 819: (1986) 12 All LR 699: (1987) 1 LLN 31:
(1986) 1 ATC 735: (1987) 1 Serv LJ 245   168
State of Kerala *v.* A.B. Abdul Khadir, AIR 1970 SC 1912: (1970) SCR 700:
1969 KLT 649   273
State of Kerala *v.* Mother Provincial, AIR 1970 SC 2079: (1970) 2 SCC 417:
1970 KLT 630   82
State of Kerala *v.* N.M. Thomas, AIR 1976 SC 490: (1976) 2 SCC 310:
1976 Lab IC 395: (1976) 1 Serv LR 805: (1976) 1 LLJ 376:
1976 SCC (Lab) 227: (1976) 1 SCR 906: 1976 SCWR 207   3, 32, 38, 51, 99
State of Kerala *v.* R. Sudarsan Babu, AIR 1984 Ker 1: 1983 Ker LT 764:
ILR (1983) 2 Ker 661   132, 187
State of Kerala *v.* Very. Rev. Mother Provincial, AIR 1970 SC 2079:
(1970) 2 SCC 417: 1970 KLT 630 (1971) 1 SCR 734   81, 83
State of Madhya Pradesh *v.* Bani, (1990) Supp SCC 736: AIR 1990 SC 1308:
(1990) 1 LLN 780   276
State of Madhya Pradesh *v.* Bhailal Bhai, AIR 1964 SC 1006: (1964) 6 SCR 261:
1964 Jab LJ 115: (1964) 15 STC 450: 1964 MPLJ 705: 1964 Mah LJ 601:
(1964) 1 SCWR 793   212
State of Madhya Pradesh *v.* Kumari Nivedita Jain, AIR 1981 SC 2045:
(1981) 4 SCC 296: (1982) 1 SCR 759   32, 168

State of Madhya Pradesh *v.* Nandlal Jaiswal, AIR 1987 SC 251: (1986) 4 SCC 566:
1987 Tax LR 1830: JT 1986 (2) SC 701: 1986 (4) Supreme 81: 1987 Jab LJ 53:
(1987) 20 STL 83: 1987 Cr LR (SC) 128: 1987 MPLJ 250   48, 122
State of Madhya Pradesh *v.* Orient Paper, (1990) 1 UJ SC 232: (1990) 1 SCC 176   150
State of Madhya Pradesh *v.* Peer Mohd., AIR 1963 SC 645: (1963) 1 Cr LJ 617:
(1963) 1 SCA 649: 1963 (2) SCJ 655: 1963 Mad LJ (Cri) 609:
(1963) Supp 1 SCR 429   12
State of Madhya Pradesh *v.* Shobharam, AIR 1966 SC 1910: 1966 Cr LJ 1521:
1966 Supp SCR 239   71
State of Madhya Pradesh *v.* Thakur Bharat Singh, AIR 1967 SC 1170:
(1967) 2 SCR 454: 1967 Jab LJ 493: 1967 Mah LJ 541: 1967 MPLJ 433:
(1967) 2 SCA 246: 1968 (1) SCJ 173: 1967 MPWR 64: 1968 Mad LJ (Cri) 24   46
State of Madras *v.* Champakam Dorairajan, (1951) SCR 525: AIR 1951 SC 226:
1951 SCJ 313: 1951 KLT (SC) 41: (1951) 1 MLJ 621: 1951 MWN 470:
1951 ALJ (SC) 107   78, 99
State of Madras *v.* N.K. Nataraja Mudaliar, AIR 1969 SC 147:
(1968) 3 SCR 829: (1968) 22 STC 376   273, 274
State of Maharashtra *v.* Abdul Hamid Haji Mohammed, JT 1994 (2) SC 1:
(1994) Supp 1 SCC 579: 1994 SCC (Cri) 723   195
State of Maharashtra *v.* Basantibai Mohanlal Khetan, AIR 1986 SC 1466:
(1986) 2 SCC 516: 1986 (1) SCJ 566: 1986 (2) Supreme 399:
(1986) 88 Bom LR 205: 1986 Mah LR 650: (1986) 1 MCC 73: 1986 UJ (SC) 715 49, 85
State of Maharashtra *v.* Champalal, AIR 1981 SC 1675: (1981) 3 SCC 610:
1981 SCC (Cri) 762: 1981 Cr LJ 1273   56, 60
State of Maharashtra *v.* Himmatbhai, AIR 1970 SC 1157: (1969) 2 SCR 392:
73 Bom LR 75   50
State of Maharashtra *v.* Manubhai Pragaji Vashi, AIR 1996 SC 1: (1995) 5 SCC 730:
1995 AIR SCW 3701: JT 1995 (6) SC 119: 1997 (1) Mah LR 153:
1995 (3) SCJ 610: 1995 (4) SCT 547: 1996 (1) Serv LJ SC 1   24, 65
State of Maharashtra *v.* Maruti Sharipati Dubal, AIR 1997 SC 411:
(1996) 6 SCC 42: 1996 SCC (Cri) 1116   63
State of Maharashtra *v.* Narayan Shamrao Puranic, AIR 1982 SC 1198:
1982 UJ (SC) 368: (1982) 2 SCC 440   10
State of Maharashtra *v.* Prabhakar, AIR 1966 SC 424: (1966) 1 SCR 702:
1966 Cr LJ 311: 1966 MLJ 141   11, 49
State of Maharashtra *v.* Rajendra Jawanmal Gandhi, (1997) 8 SCC 386:
AIR 1997 SC 3986: 1997 Cr LJ 4657: 1997 AIR SCW 3923:
1997 (3) Crimes 285: JT 1997 (8) SC 43: 1997 (3) SCJ 175:
1998 SC Cr R 1: 1998 SC (Cri) 76: 1997 (8) Supreme 129   51
State of Maharashtra *v.* Ravi Kant, (1991) 2 UJ SC 188: (1991) 2 SCC 373:
1991 SCC (Cri) 656   198
State of Maharashtra *v.* Sau Shobha Vitthal Kolte, AIR 2006 Bom 44:
2006 (1) ALJ (NOC) 92: 2006 (2) AKAR (NOC) 190: 2006 (1) All MR 188:
2006 (1) Bom CR 468   65
State of Maharashtra *v.* Union of India, JT 1994 (4) SC 423:
1994 AIR SCW 3305: (1994) 5 SCC 244   27
State of Mysore *v.* Sivabasappa, AIR 1963 SC 375: (1963) 2 SCR 943:
1963 MLLJ 284: (1963) 1 LLJ 24   217
State of Orissa *v.* Balaram Sahu, AIR 2003 SC 33: 2002 AIR SCW 4421:
2003 (1) JCR SC 49: JT 2002 (8) SC 477: 2002 (3) LLJ 1115: (2003) 1 SCC 250:
2003 SCC (L&S) 65: 2002 (4) SCT 902: (2002) 8 SCALE 178:
2002 (7) Supreme 518: 2002 (2) UJ (SC) 1535   23
State of Orissa *v.* Bhupendra, AIR 1962 SC 945: (1962) Supp 2 SCR 380:
(1962) 28 Cut LT 273   141
State of Orissa *v.* Dhirendranath, AIR 1961 SC 1715   26, 284
State of Orissa *v.* Hari Narayan, AIR 1972 SC 1816: (1972) 2 SCC 36: (1972) 3 SCR 784 43
State of Orissa *v.* M.M.T.C., JT 1994 (4) SC 628: (1994) 3 SCC 109: (1994) 95 STC 80 265

State of Orissa *v.* Madan Gopal Rungta, (1952) SCR 28: AIR 1952 SC 12:
    (1951) 2 Mad LJ 645: 1952 Mad WN 13: 1951 SCJ 764: 18 Cut LT 45:
    ILR 1951 Cut 637   213
State of Orissa *v.* Rajkishore Nanda, AIR 2010 SC 2100   35
State of Punjab *v.* Ajaib Singh, (1953) SCR 254: AIR 1953 SC 10: 1953 Cr LJ 180   69
State of Punjab *v.* Balbir, AIR 1977 SC 629: (1976) 3 SCC 242:
    (1976) 2 LLJ 4: 1977 Lab IC 281   9
State of Punjab *v.* Col. Kuldeep Singh, AIR 2010 SC 1937   23
State of Punjab *v.* Joginder, AIR 1990 SC 1396: (1990) 2 SCC 661:
    1990 SCC (Cri) 419: 1990 Cr LJ 1464   117, 164
State of Punjab *v.* Mahinder Singh Chawla, AIR 1997 SC 1225: (1997) 2 SCC 83:
    1997 SCC (L&S) 294   57
State of Punjab *v.* Manjit Singh, AIR 2003 SC 4580: (2003) 11 SCC 559:
    (2003) 6 SLR 63   297
State of Punjab *v.* Mohar Singh, AIR 1955 SC 84: (1955) 1 SCR 893: 1955 Cr LJ 254   141
State of Punjab *v.* Mohinder Singh Chawla, AIR 1997 SC 1225: (1997) 2 SCC 83:
    1997 AIR SCW 1260: JT 1997 (1) SC 416: 1997 (3) LLN 262:
    1997 SCC (L&S) 294: 1996 (4) SCJ 391: 1997 (1) SCT 716:
    (1997) 1 SCALE 135: 1997 (2) Serv LJ 25 SC: 1997 (1) Supreme 546   64
State of Punjab *v.* Raja Ram, (1981) 2 SCC 66: AIR 1981 SC 1694: (1981) 2 SCR 712   16
State of Punjab *v.* Ram, AIR 1992 SC 2188: (1992) 4 SCC 54:
    1992 SCC (L&S) 793: (1992) 21 ATC 435   287, 288
State of Punjab *v.* Satya Pal Dang, AIR 1969 SC 903: (1969) 1 SCR 478   188
State of Punjab *v.* Sodhi Sukhdev Singh, AIR 1961 SC 493: (1961) 1 SCA 434:
    1961 Mad LJ (Cri) 731: 1961 (2) SCJ 691: (1961) 2 Mad LJ (SC) 203:
    (1961) 2 SCR 371   122
State of Punjab *v.* Sukhpal Singh, AIR 1990 SC 231: (1990) 1 SCC 35:
    1990 Cr LJ 584   69, 88
State of Rajasthan *v.* Ashok Kumar Gupta, AIR 1989 SC 177:
    (1988) 1 SCC 93: JT 1988 (4) SC 176   20
State of Rajasthan *v.* Bhawani Singh, (1993) Supp 1 SCC 306: AIR 1992 SC 1018:
    1992 AIR SCW 930: 1993 (1) All CJ 717: JT 1992 (3) SC 531:
    (1993) Supp 1 SCC 306: 1992 (1) UJ (SC) 491   201, 213
State of Rajasthan *v.* G. Chawla, (1959) Supp 1 SCR 904: AIR 1959 SC 544:
    1959 Cr LJ 660: 1959 SCJ 585: 1959 Mad LJ (Cri) 309   75, 246
State of Rajasthan *v.* Gurcharan, (1990) Supp SCC 778: AIR 1990 SC 1760:
    (1990) 2 LLN 278: (1990) 1 SLJ 151   279
State of Rajasthan *v.* Hat Singh, AIR 2003 SC 791: (2003) 2 SCC 152:
    2003 SCC (Cri) 451   52
State of Rajasthan *v.* Jagdish Narain Chaturvedi, AIR 2010 SC 157   155
State of Rajasthan *v.* Karamchand Thappar and Bros, AIR 1965 SC 913:
    (1965) 16 STC 412: (1964) 2 SCWR 593   212
State of Rajasthan *v.* Mangilal, (1969) 2 SCC 710   274
State of Rajasthan *v.* Mohan Lal Vyas, AIR 1971 SC 2068: (1971) 3 SCC 705:
    (1971) UJ 222   46
State of Rajasthan *v.* Prem Raj, AIR 1997 SC 1081: (1997) 10 SCC 317:
    1997 SCC (L&S) 1688   26
State of Rajasthan *v.* Rajasthan Pensioner Samaj, AIR 1991 SC 1743:
    (1991) Supp 2 SCC 141: (1991) 17 ATC 342: 1991 Lab IC 1651   280
State of Rajasthan *v.* Sukhpal, AIR 1984 SC 207: (1983) 1 SCC 393: 1983 SCC (Cri) 213 56
State of Rajasthan *v.* Union of India, AIR 1977 SC 1361: (1977) 3 SCC 592:
    (1978) 1 SCR 1: 1978 (1) SCJ 78   120, 141, 324
State of Rajasthan *v.* Vidhyawati, AIR 1962 SC 933: (1962) Supp 2 SCR 989:
    (1962) 2 SCA 362: (1963) 1 MLJ 70 (SC)   25, 271
State of Sikkim *v.* Sonam, (1991) Supp 1 SCC 179: AIR 1991 SC 534:
    (1991) 17 ATC 257   277
State of Sikkim *v.* Surendra Prasad Sharma, JT 1994 (3) SC 372:
    (1994) 5 SCC 282: AIR 1994 SC 2342: (1994) 1 SLR 685   33, 36

State of Tamil Nadu *v.* Hind Stone, AIR 1981 SC 711: (1981) 2 SCC 205:
(1981) 2 SCR 742   248
State of Tamil Nadu *v.* J.T.T.I., (1991) 2 UJ SC 162   208
State of Tamil Nadu *v.* Joseph, (1991) 3 SCC 87: (1991) 2 SLR 605   80
State of Tamil Nadu *v.* K. Sabanayagam, AIR 1998 SC 344: 1997 AIR SCW 4325:
(1998) 1 SCC 318: 1998 SCC (L&S) 260: 1998 (2) SCJ 373: 1998 (1) SCT 354:
(1997) 7 SCALE 170: 1997 (10) Supreme 324   242
State of Tamil Nadu *v.* L. Abu Kavur Bai, AIR 1984 SC 326:
(1984) 1 SCC 515: (1984) 1 SCR 725   102
State of Tamil Nadu *v.* M.R. Alagappan, AIR 1997 SC 2006: (1997) 4 SCC 401:
1997 AIR SCW 1793: JT 1997 (4) SC 515: 1997 SCC (L&S) 1080:
(1997) 3 SCR 717: 1997 (2) SCT 531: (1997) 3 SCALE 464:
1997 (2) Serv LR 554: 1997 (4) Supreme 67   102
State of Tamil Nadu *v.* Pari, 1991 (3) SCJ 302   282
State of Tamil Nadu *v.* Sanjeetha Trading Co., AIR 1993 SC 237:
(1993) 1 SCC 236: 1992 AIR SCW 2934: 1993 (2) EFR 115:
JT 1992 (Supp) 695: 1992 (3) SCJ 293: (1992) 4 SCR 840   275
State of Tamil Nadu *v.* State of Karnataka, (1991) 2 UJ SC 134:
(1991) Supp 1 SCC 240   214, 256
State of Uttar Pradesh *v.* Abdul Samad, AIR 1962 SC 1506:
(1962) Supp 3 SCR 915: (1962) 2 Cr LJ 499: ILR (1962) 2 All 547:
1962 All Cr R 440: 1962 BLJR 952: (1963) 1 SCA 122: 1963 SCD 885   69, 70
State of Uttar Pradesh *v.* Bijoy, AIR 1982 SC 1234: (1982) 2 SCC 365: 1982 All LJ 582   43
State of Uttar Pradesh *v.* C.O.D. Chheoke Employees Co-operative Society Ltd.,
AIR 1997 SC 1413: (1997) 3 SCC 681: 1997 All LJ 576   43
State of Uttar Pradesh *v.* Committee of Management, AIR 2010 SC 402   22
State of Uttar Pradesh *v.* Devi Dayal, AIR 1959 All 421: 1959 Cr LJ 803   193
State of Uttar Pradesh *v.* Dr. K.U. Ansari, AIR 2002 SC 208: (2002) 1 SCC 616:
(2002) 1 SLR 301: (2002) 92 FLR 513   38
State of Uttar Pradesh *v.* Kaushal, (1991) 1 SCC 691: 1991 SCC (L&S) 587:
(1991) 16 ATC 498: (1991) 1 SCR 606: (1991) 1 SLR 606   281, 289
State of Uttar Pradesh *v.* Kaushaliya, AIR 1964 SC 416: (1964) 4 SCR 1002:
(1964) 1 Cr LJ 304   47
State of Uttar Pradesh *v.* Man Mohan Nath Sinha, AIR 2010 SC 137   287
State of Uttar Pradesh *v.* Pradhan Sangh Kshettra Samiti, AIR 1995 SC 1512:
1995 AIR SCW 2303: 1995 All LJ 1689: (1995) Supp 2 SCC 305   103
State of Uttar Pradesh *v.* Rafiquddin, AIR 1988 SC 162: 1988 Lab IC 344:
JT 1987 (5) SC 251: 1987 Supp SCC 401: (1988) 19 Reports 28:
1988 SCC (Lab) 183: (1988) 1 Serv LR 491: 1988 (2) SCJ 170:
1988 SCC (L&S) 153   292, 297
State of Uttar Pradesh *v.* Ram Sajivan, AIR 2010 SC 1738   1
State of Uttar Pradesh *v.* Roshan, (1969) 2 SCWR 232   13
State of Uttar Pradesh *v.* Sani, (1992) 19 ATC 264 (SC)   289
State of Uttar Pradesh *v.* Shah Muhammad, AIR 1969 SC 1234:
(1969) 2 SCA 539: (1969) 3 SCR 1006   11, 13, 14
State of Uttar Pradesh *v.* Synthetics and Chemicals Ltd., (1991) 4 SCC 139:
JT 1991 (3) SC 268   155, 252
State of Uttar Pradesh *v.* U.S.V. Balaram, AIR 1972 SC 1375: (1972) 1 SCC 660:
(1972) 1 SCA 214: (1972) 3 SCR 247   32
State of Uttar Pradesh *v.* Vam Organic Chemicals Ltd., AIR 2003 SC 4650:
(2004) 1 SCC 225: 2003 AIR SCW 5463: JT 2003 (8) SC 1: 2004 (2) SRJ 125:
(2003) 8 SCALE 775: 2003 (8) Supreme 165   257
State of Uttaranchal *v.* Balwant Singh Chaufal, AIR 2010 SC 2550   90, 167
State of West Bengal *v.* Anwar Ali, (1952) SCR 284: AIR 1952 SC 75:
1952 Cr LJ 510   21, 26, 30
State of West Bengal *v.* Atul Krishna Shaw, (1991) Supp 1 SCC 414:
AIR 1990 SC 2205: (1990) Supp 1 SCR 91   219

State of West Bengal *v.* B.K. Mondal & Sons, AIR 1962 SC 779:
  (1962) Supp 1 SCR 876: (1962) 2 SCA 375   270
State of West Bengal *v.* Debdas, (1991) 1 SCC 138: (1991) 17 ATC 261:
  1991 SCC (L&S) 841   279
State of West Bengal *v.* S.K. Ghose, AIR 1963 SC 255: (1963) 2 SCR 111:
  (1963) Cr LJ 252   53
State of West Bengal *v.* S.K. Nurul Amin, AIR 2010 SC 2271   23
State of West Bengal *v.* Union of India, (1964) 1 SCR 371: AIR 1963 SC 1241:
  (1963) 2 SCA 448   29
State of West Bengal *v.* West Bengal Regn. Copy Writers Assocn., AIR 2010 SC 2184   277
State through SPE and CBI, A.P. *v.* M. Krishna Mohan, AIR 2008 SC 368:
  2007 AIR SCW 7044: 2007 (4) Crimes 327: 2007 (4) JCC 3294:
  2008 (1) Mad LJ (Cri) 1417: 2008 (39) OCR 276: (2007) 12 SCALE 618:
  2007 (8) Supreme 205   54
Subash Chander *v.* State of Haryana, AIR 1992 P&H 20: 1991 (2) LJR 580:
  1992 (1) RRR 50: 1991 (2) RevLR 431   257
Sub-Committee of Judicial Accountability *v.* Union of India, AIR 1992 SC 320:
  (1991) 4 SCC 699: 1991 AIR SCW 3049: JT 1991 (6) SC 184   294
Subhash Kumar *v.* State of Bihar, AIR 1991 SC 420: (1991) 1 SCC 598:
  1991 AIR SCW 121: 1991 (1) All CJ 424: 1991 (1) BLJR 550:
  1991 (1) Civ LJ 719: JT 1991 (1) SC 77: 1991 (1) Pat LJR 69:
  1991 (1) SCJ 564: (1991) 1 SCR 5: 1991 (1) UJ (SC) 533   56, 91, 107, 211
Subhesh Sharma *v.* Union of India, AIR 1991 SC 631: (1991) Supp 1 SCC 574:
  1991 AIR SCW 128: 1991 (2) Civ LJ 532: JT 1990 (4) SC 245:
  (1990) 6 Serv LR 36: 1991 (2) UPLBEC 826   336
Subodhaya Chit Fund (P) Ltd. *v.* Director of Chits, Madras, AIR 1991 SC 998:
  (1991) Supp 2 SCC 131: 1991 AIR SCW 271: 1991 (2) Bank CLR 243:
  1993 (76) Comp Cas 873   275
Subramaniam *v.* Union of India, (1990) Supp SCC 775   92
Suchitra Srivastava *v.* Chandigarh Administration, AIR 2010 SC 235   60
Sudama Pandey *v.* State of Bihar, (2002) 1 SCC 679: AIR 2002 SC 693:
  2002 Cr LJ 582   149
Sudarshan Trading Company Ltd. *v.* PP. Saffiya, AIR 1991 SC 716:
  (1991) Supp 2 SCC 498   152
Sudhir Chandra Sarkar *v.* Tata Iron and Steel Company, (1984) 3 SCC 369:
  AIR 1984 SC 1064: 1984 Lab IC 790: (1984) 1 Serv LJ 575: (1984) 65 FJR 61:
  (1984) 49 Fac LR 1: 1984 SCC (Lab) 540: (1984) 2 LLN 229: (1984) 2 LLJ 223   28
Suganthi Suresh Kumar *v.* Jagdeeshan, (2002) 2 SCC 420: AIR 2002 SC 681:
  2002 Cr LJ 1003: 2002 SCC (Cri) 344   154
Sujal Atul Munshi *v.* State of Gujarat, AIR 1996 Guj 170   37
Suk Das *v.* Union Territory of Arunachal Pradesh, AIR 1986 SC 991:
  1986 Cr LJ 1084: 1986 All LJ 774: 1986 SCC (Cri) 166: (1986) 1 SCWR 219:
  (1986) 2 SCC 401: 1986 (2) Crimes 40: 1986 Cr LR (SC) 188:
  1986 (2) Supreme 1: 1986 Cal Cr LR (SC) 83   59, 64, 102
Sukhdev *v.* Bhagatram, AIR 1975 SC 1331: (1975) 1 SCC 421: (1975) 1 LLJ 399   16
Sukhnandan Saran Dinesh Kumar *v.* Union of India, AIR 1982 SC 902:
  (1982) 2 SCC 150: 1982 UJ (SC) 503: 1982 (2) SCJ 13   47
Sukhnandan *v.* State of Bihar, AIR 1957 Pat 617: ILR 35 Pat 1   37
Sukhwant Singh *v.* State of Punjab, (2009) 7 SCC 559   63
Sulthan *v.* Jt. Secy., 1991 (1) SCJ 239: (1991) 1 SCC 144: AIR 1990 SC 2222:
  1990 Cr LJ 2473   209
Sumakiran Mallena *v.* Secretary, Medical & Health Secretariat Building, Saifabad,
  AIR 2008 (NOC) 374 AP   63
Suman Gupta *v.* State of Jammu & Kashmir, AIR 1983 SC 1235: (1983) 4 SCC 339:
  1983 UJ (SC) 897   24
Sumedha Kalia *v.* State of Haryana, AIR 1990 P&H 239: ILR 1991 (2) P&H 498:
  1990 (4) Serv LR 122   200

Sundarjas Kanyalal Bhathija *v.* Collector, Thane, Maharashtra, AIR 1990 SC 261:
    (1989) 3 SCC 396: JT 1989 (3) SC 57: (1989) 2 RRR 111: (1989) 25 ECR 129   156
Suneel Jatley *v.* State of Haryana, AIR 1984 SC 1534: (1984) 4 SCC 296   20
Sunil Batra *v.* Delhi Administration, AIR 1978 SC 1675: (1978) 4 SCC 494:
    1978 Cr LJ 1741   11, 60, 62, 66
Sunil Gupta *v.* State of Madhya Pradesh, (1990) 3 SCC 119: 1990 SCC (Cri) 440:
    JT 1990 (2) SC 372   57
Supreme Court Advocates-on-Records Association *v.* Union of India,
    AIR 1994 SC 268: 1993 AIR SCW 4101: JT 1993 (5) SC 479:
    (1993) 4 SCC 441: 1993 (5) Serv LR 337   1, 91, 108, 156, 192
Supreme Court Employees' Welfare Association *v.* Union of India,
    AIR 1990 SC 334: (1989) 4 SCC 187: 1989 SCC (L&S) 569:
    (1989) 2 LLJ 506: (1989) 1 SLR 3: 1990 Lab IC 324   23, 155., 160, 206, 214
Suraj *v.* Bharat, (1990) 1 UJ SC 135: AIR 1990 SC 753: (1989) Supp 2 SCC 456   150
Surendra *v.* Naba Krishna, AIR 1958 Ori 168   133
Suresh Koshy George *v.* University of Kerala, AIR 1969 SC 198:
    (1969) 1 SCR 317: 1969 Ker LJ 197   215, 216, 197, 217
Suresh *v.* Punit, AIR 1951 Cal 176   133
Suresh Seth *v.* Commissioner, Indore Municipal Corporation, AIR 2006 SC 767:
    2005 AIR SCW 6380: JT 2005 (9) SC 210: (2005) 13 SCC 287: 2005 (7) SCJ 629:
    2005 (9) SRJ 473: (2005) 8 SCALE 514: 2005 (7) Supreme 134   94
Suresh Swami *v.* State of Rajasthan, AIR 2001 Raj 244: 2001 (2) Raj LW 1232   45
Suresh *v.* Defence Secretary, AIR 1991 SC 483: (1991) 2 SCC 198: (1991) 16 ATC 486   93
Suresh *v.* R.C.D., (1991) UJ SC 343   208
Surinder *v.* Delhi Administration, (1990) Supp SCC 610: 1991 SCC (Cri) 154   150
Surya Narain Choudhary *v.* Union of India, AIR 1982 Raj 1: 1981 WLN 198:
    1981 Raj LW 490   110
Surya Pal Singh *v.* State of Uttar Pradesh, (1952) SCR 1056: AIR 1952 SC 252:
    1952 SCJ 354: 1953 SCA 53   73, 76, 187
Sushil Kumar *v.* Rakesh Kumar, AIR 2004 SC 230: (2003) 8 SCC 673:
    2003 AIR SCW 6005: 2004 (1) JLJR 261: 2004 (1) Pat LJR 261:
    (2003) 8 SCALE 659: 2003 (8) Supreme 149   172
Sushilabai Laxminarayan Mudliyar *v.* Nihalchand Waghajibhai Shaha,
    (1993) Supp 1 SCC 11: AIR 1992 SC 185: 1991 AIR SCW 2896:
    (1993) 1 Andh LT 60: 1991 Mah LJ 1288   219
Syed Yakoob *v.* K.S. Radhakrishnan, AIR 1964 SC 477: (1964) 5 SCR 64   196, 197
Synthetics & Chemicals Ltd. *v.* State of Uttar Pradesh, (1990) 1 SCC 109:
    AIR 1990 SC 1927: JT 1989 (4) SC 267   4, 5, 156, 243, 257

T

T. Barai *v.* Henry, AIR 1983 SC 150: (1983) 1 SCC 177: 1983 Cr LJ 164   253
T. Deen Dayal *v.* Union of India, AIR 1991 AP 307: (1991) 2 Andh LT 373:
    1991 (2) APLJ 83: 1992 (1) Civ LJ 614: 1992 (1) Serv LR 555   228
T. Devadasan *v.* Union of India, AIR 1964 SC 179: (1964) 4 SCR 680: (1965) 2 LLJ 560 37
T. Devaki *v.* Government of Tamil Nadu, 1990 (3) SCJ 303: (1990) 2 SCC 456:
    AIR 1990 SC 1086: 1990 Cr LJ 140   70, 209
T. Sham Bhat *v.* Union of India, JT 1994 (5) SC 165: (1994) Supp 3 SCC 340:
    (1994) 4 SLR 598   28
T. Subbiah *v.* S.K.D. Ramaswamy Nadar, AIR 1970 Mad 85:
    1969 Mad LW (Cri) 117: 1970 Cr LJ 254   53
T. Venkata Reddy *v.* State of Andhra Pradesh, AIR 1985 SC 724:
    (1985) 3 SCC 193: 1985 SCC (L&S) 632   141
T.C. Basappa *v.* T. Nagappa, (1955) 1 SCR 250: AIR 1954 SC 440:
    1954 SCA 620: 67 Mad LW 613: 1954 SCJ 695: ILR 1954 Mys 235   196, 198
T.M.A. Pai Foundation *v.* State of Karnataka, AIR 2003 SC 355: (2002) 8 SCC 481:
    2002 AIR SCW 4957: JT 2002 (9) SC 1: 2003 (1) Kant LJ 1: 2002 (4) LRI 329:
    2003 (2) SCT 385: 2003 (1) SRJ 271: (2002) 8 SCALE 1: 2002 (6) Serv LR 627:
    2002 (8) Supreme 62   77, 81

T.N. Cauvery Neerppasana Vilaiporulgal Vivasayigal Nala Urimai
Padhugappu Sangam *v.* Union of India, AIR 1990 SC 1316:
(1990) 3 SCC 440: 1990 (2) SCJ 547: JT 1990 (2) SC 397   89, 145, 255, 256
T.N. Panchayat Development Officers Association, Madras *v.* Secretary
to Govt. of T.N., Rural Development and Local Administration
Dept., Madras, AIR 1989 Mad 224: 1990 (1) LJR 488 (FB)   212
T.N. Rugmani *v.* C. Achutha Menon, AIR 1991 SC 983: (1991) Supp 1 SCC 520:
JT 1991 (1) SC 265: 1991 (1) UJ (SC) 422   90
T.V. Vatheeswaran *v.* State of Tamil Nadu, AIR 1983 SC 361: (1983) Cr LJ 482:
(1983) 2 SCC 68   57
Tajinder Singh *v.* Bharat Petroleum Corpn. Ltd., (1986) 4 SCC 237: 1986 JT 405:
(1986) 2 Cur LR 319: (1986) 4 SCC 237: (1986) 2 Cur CC 862:
1986 (3) Supreme 414: 1986 SCC (Lab) 765: 1986 (3) SCJ 556:
(1987) 1 UJ (SC) 1: (1987) 2 LLJ 225   16
Tamil Nadu Nursery, Matriculation and Higher Secondary Schools
Association, Chennai *v.* State of Tamil Nadu, AIR 2010 Mad 142   50
Tarun Bharat Sangh, Alwar *v.* Union of India, (1992) Supp 2 SCC 448:
AIR 1992 SC 514: 1992 AIR SCW 102   107
Tashi Delek Gaming Solutions Ltd. *v.* State of Karnataka, AIR 2006 SC 661   145
Tata Engineering and Locomotive Co. Ltd. *v.* State of Bihar, AIR 1965 SC 40:
(1964) 34 Com Cas 458: (1964) 1 Comp LJ 280: 1964 (1) SCJ 666:
1964 BLJR 834: (1965) 1 SCWR 26: (1965) 1 SCA 365: (1964) 6 SCR 885   44
Tata Iron & Steel Co. *v.* Sarkar, AIR 1961 SC 65: (1961) 1 SCR 379:
(1960) 11 STC 655   94
Tata Iron & Steel Co. *v.* State of Bihar, AIR 1958 SC 452: 1958 SCR 1355:
(1958) 9 STC 267   244
Tej Kiran Jain *v.* M. Sanjiva Reddy, AIR 1970 SC 1573: (1970) 2 SCC 272:
(1971) 1 SCR 612   133
Tej Pal *v.* State of Uttar Pradesh, (1986) 3 SCC 604: AIR 1986 SC 1814:
1986 SCC (L&S) 688   222
Tej Singh Rao *v.* State of Maharashtra, (1992) Supp 2 SCC 554: AIR 1993 SC 1227:
1992 AIR SCW 3228: JT 1992 (4) SC 520: 1993 (2) Mah LR 693:
1992 (3) SCJ 483: (1992) 3 SCR 929: (1992) 2 UJ (SC) 677   333, 349
Tekraj *v.* Union of India, AIR 1988 SC 469: (1988) 1 SCC 236:
1988 SCC (L&S) 300: 1988 Lab IC 961   15
Temjenkaba *v.* Temjenwati, AIR 1992 Gau 8: 1991 (2) Gau LR 200   341
Thakur Amar Singhji *v.* State of Rajasthan, AIR 1955 SC 504: 1954 KLT 273:
1955 SCA 766: 1955 SCJ 523: (1955) 2 SCR 303   7, 8
Thirumala Tirupati Devasthanams *v.* Thallappaka Anantha Charyulu,
AIR 2003 SC 3290: (2003) 8 SCC 134: 2003 AIR SCW 4847: JT 2004 (6) SC 425:
2003 (10) SRJ 375: (2003) 7 SCALE 352: 2003 (6) Supreme 684   210
Thirumuruga Kirupananda Variyar Thavathiru Sundara Swamigal Medical
Educational and Charitable Trust *v.* State of Tamil Nadu, AIR 1996 SC 2384:
(1996) 3 SCC 15: 1996 AIR SCW 926: JT 1996 (2) SC 692:
1996 (2) Mad LJ 10: (1996) 2 SCR 422   252
Tika Ramji *v.* State of Uttar Pradesh, (1956) SCR 393: AIR 1956 SC 676:
1956 SCA 979: 1956 SCJ 625: 1956 All WR (HC) 657   251, 274
Tilak Raj *v.* Reg., AIR 1979 All 28   203
Tilkayat Shri Govindlalji Maharaj *v.* State of Rajasthan, AIR 1963 SC 1638:
(1964) 1 SCR 561: (1963) 2 SCA 518   76
Tinsukhia Electric Supply Co. Ltd. *v.* State of Assam, AIR 1990 SC 123:
(1989) 3 SCC 709: JT 1989 (2) SC 217: (1989) 45 Taxman 29:
(1989) 2 Comp LJ 377   243, 272
Tirath Ram Saini *v.* State of Punjab, JT 1994 (1) SC 420: (1994) Supp 2 SCC 16:
1994 SCC (Cri) 675   92
Tirath Ram *v.* State of Uttar Pradesh, AIR 1973 SC 405: (1973) 3 SCC 585:
1973 Tax LR 1951: (1973) 2 CTR 123 (SC)   244

Tokugha Yepthomo (Dr.) *v.* Apollo Hospital, JT 1998 (7) SC 626: AIR 1999 SC 495:
1998 AIR SCW 3662: 1998 (3) CPJ 12: 1999 (1) Comp LJ 23 SC:
1999 (1) Mah LR 750: (1998) 8 SCC 296: 1999 (1) SRJ 88: (1998) 6 SCALE 230:
1998 (9) Supreme 220: 1999 (1) UJ (SC) 232   59
Trans Yamuna Cement Dealers Association *v.* Lt. Governor of Delhi,
AIR 1988 Del 247: 1988 Raj LR 134: (1988) 21 Reports 537:
(1988) 14 DRJ 275: (1988) 25 STL 25   247
Trilok Chand *v.* Munshi, AIR 1970 SC 898: (1969) 1 SCC 110: (1969) 2 SCR 824   89
Trilok *v.* DM, AIR 1976 SC 1988: (1976) 3 SCC 726: (1976) 3 SCR 942   209
Triloki Nath *v.* State of Jammu & Kashmir, AIR 1967 SC 1283:
(1967) 2 SCR 265: 14 FLR 282   37
Triveni *v.* State of Uttar Pradesh, AIR 1992 SC 496: (1992) Supp 1 SCC 524:
1992 (1) SCJ 27: (1992) 19 ATC 931: (1992) 1 LLN 889:
(1992) 2 LLJ 23   280, 278, 289, 290
Triveniben *v.* State of Gujarat, (1990) Cr LJ 273: 1990 Cr LR Guj 17:
AIR 1989 SC 1335: (1989) 1 SCC 678   118
Tulsipur Sugar Co. Ltd. *v.* Notified Area Committee, Tulsipur,
AIR 1980 SC 882: (1980) 2 SCC 295: 1980 All LJ 401   196

U

U.N.R. Rao *v.* Indira Gandhi, AIR 1971 SC 1002: (1971) 2 SCC 63:
(1971) 1 Civ Ap J (SC) 176: 1971 (Supp) SCR 46   111, 126, 165
U.P.S.E. Board *v.* Hari, AIR 1979 SC 65: (1978) 4 SCC 16: (1978) 2 LLJ 399   99
Uduman *v.* Astam, AIR 1991 SC 1020: (1991) 1 SCC 412: (1991) 1 MLJ (SC) 46   151
Ujagar Prints (II) *v.* Union of India, AIR 1989 SC 516: (1989) 3 SCC 488:
(1989) 179 ITR 317: (1989) 74 STC 401   248
Ukha *v.* State of Maharashtra, AIR 1963 SC 1531: (1964) 1 SCR 926:
(1963) 2 Cr LJ 418: 65 Bom LR 793   253
Uktal Highways *v.* State of Chhattisgarh, AIR 2006 Chhat 29   195
Umaji Keshao Meshram *v.* Smt. Radhikabai, AIR 1986 SC 1272:
1986 Supp SCC 401: 1986 (2) Supreme 417: 1986 Cur Civ LJ (SC) 393:
(1986) 2 Cur CC 273: 1986 (1) SCJ 624: (1986) 2 UJ (SC) 319:
(1986) 88 Bom LR 432   218
Umesh Chand Vinod Kumar *v.* Krishi Utpadan Mandi Samiti, Bharthana,
AIR 1984 All 46 (FB): 1983 UPLBEC 756: 1983 All CJ 600:
1983 All WC 881: (1984) 10 All LR 136: (1984) 1 Serv LR 532   212
Umesh Chandra Sinha *v.* V.N. Singh, AIR 1968 Pat 3 (9): ILR 46 Pat 616:
1967 BLJR 798   16
Union of India *v.* A.L. Rallia Ram, AIR 1963 SC 1685: (1964) 3 SCR 164   270
Union of India *v.* Alok Kumar, AIR 2010 SC 2735   287
Union of India *v.* Amrik, (1991) 1 SCC 654: (1991) 16 ATC 497:
AIR 1991 SC 564: 1991 Cr LJ 664   198, 208
Union of India *v.* Ashok Kumar, AIR 2006 SC 124: 2005 AIR SCW 5590:
2005 (107) FLR 840: (2005) 8 SCC 760: 2005 (8) SCJ 124: 2005 (4) SCT 610:
(2005) 8 SCALE 397: (2006) 1 Serv LJ 312 SC: 2005 (7) Supreme 239   206
Union of India *v.* Bijan Ghosh, AIR 1997 SC 3019: (1997) 6 SCC 535:
1997 AIR SCW 3052: JT 1997 (7) SC 198: (1997) 5 SCALE 329:
1997 (7) Supreme 10: 1997 (2) UJ (SC) 409   40
Union of India *v.* Central Electrical and Mechanical Engineering Service
Group A (Direct Recruits) Association, CPWD, AIR 2008 SC 3:
2007 AIR SCW 6986: 2008 (2) All MR 38 (NOC): 2008 (2) LLN 705:
(2008) 1 SCC 354: (2007) 13 SCALE 23: 2007 (8) Supreme 73   165
Union of India *v.* Chajju Ram, AIR 2003 SC 2339: (2003) 5 SCC 568:
2003 AIR SCW 2322: 2003 (51) All LR 534: 2003 (3) All MR 766:
2003 (3) Civ LJ 247: JT 2003 (4) SC 161: 2003 (1) LACC 595:
2003 (7) SRJ 71: (2003) 4 SCALE 155: 2003 (3) Supreme 661   24
Union of India *v.* Chhida, (1991) Supp 2 SCC 16: 1991 SCC (L&S) 1362   285

Union of India *v.* Cynamide India Ltd., AIR 1987 SC 1802: (1987) 2 SCC 720:
  JT 1987 (3) SC 107: (1987) 2 Comp LJ 10: (1987) 12 ECR 199:
  (1987) 2 UJ (SC) 198   91
Union of India *v.* Darshna Devi, AIR 1997 SC 166: (1996) 2 SCC 681:
  1996 AIR SCW 4314: 1996 (2) Civ LJ 592: JT 1996 (1) SC 622:
  1996 (1) Land LR 323: (1996) 1 SCR 839   157
Union of India *v.* Deep, (1992) 4 SCC 432: AIR 1993 SC 382:
  (1993) 23 ATC 356: 1993 SCC (L&S) 21   87, 285, 301
Union of India *v.* E.G. Nambudri, AIR 1991 SC 1216: (1991) 3 SCC 38:
  (1991) 17 ATC 104: (1991) 62 FLR 850: 1993 UJ (SC) 303:
  1993 SCC (L&S) 813: 1993 SLR 615   195, 198, 202, 207, 276, 285
Union of India *v.* Gopal, AIR 1978 SC 694: (1978) 2 SCC 301: (1978) 1 LLJ 492   132
Union of India *v.* Graphic Industries, JT 1994 (5) SC 237: (1994) 5 SCC 398:
  AIR 1995 SC 409   272
Union of India *v.* Harbhajan Singh Dhillon, AIR 1972 SC 1061:
  (1971) 2 SCC 779: (1972) 2 SCR 33: (1972) 83 ITR 582   249
Union of India *v.* Hemraj Singh Chauhan, AIR 2010 SC 1682   23
Union of India *v.* K.F.C., (1991) 2 UJ SC 617   211
Union of India *v.* K.P. Prabhakaran, (1997) 11 SCC 638: 1998 SCC (L&S) 327   34
Union of India *v.* K.V. Jankiraman, AIR 1991 SC 2010: (1991) 4 SCC 109:
  1991 Lab IC 2045: 1991 AIR SCW 2276: JT 1991 (3) SC 527:
  1991 (2) LLJ 570: 1992 (1) LLN 24: 1993 SCC (L&S) 387: (1991) 3 SCR 790   279
Union of India *v.* Kamalakshi, (1991) 2 UJ SC 617   206
Union of India *v.* Kashikar, AIR 1986 SC 431: (1986) 1 SCC 458: (1986) 1 LLJ 435   37
Union of India *v.* Komal, AIR 1992 SC 1479: (1992) Supp 3 SCC 186:
  1992 Lab IC 1549: (1992) 4 SLR 575   301
Union of India *v.* M.P. Singh, AIR 1990 SC 1098: 1990 Supp SCC 701:
  (1990) Lab IC 910: (1990) 2 LLN 297   151, 152
Union of India *v.* Majji Jangammayya, AIR 1977 SC 757: 1977 Lab IC 295:
  1977 Serv LJ 90: 1977 SCC (Lab) 191: 1977 SLWR 163: (1977) 1 SCC 606:
  (1977) 2 SCR 28   292
Union of India *v.* Miss. Pritilata Nanda, AIR 2010 SC 2821   36
Union of India *v.* More, AIR 1962 SC 630: (1961) 2 LLJ 427: (1961) 3 FLR 313   284
Union of India *v.* P.K. Roy, AIR 1968 SC 850: (1968) 2 SCR 186:
  (1968) 2 SCWR 41: 1968 (2) SCJ 503: (1970) 1 LLJ 633   197
Union of India *v.* Partap, AIR 1992 SC 1363: (1992) 3 SCC 268:
  (1992) 20 ATC 756: (1992) 1 LLJ 446   301
Union of India *v.* Prakash P. Hinduja, AIR 2003 SC 2562: (2003) 6 SCC 195:
  2003 SCC (Cri) 1314   245
Union of India *v.* Rakesh Kumar, AIR 2001 SC 1877: (2000) 4 SCC 309:
  2001 SCC (L&S) 707   25
Union of India *v.* Mohd. Ramzan Khan, (1991) 1 SCC 588: (1991) 16 ATC 505:
  AIR 1991 SC 471   286, 288
Union of India *v.* Ramesh Ram, AIR 2010 SC 2691   35
Union of India *v.* Reddy, AIR 1990 SC 563   277
Union of India *v.* S.P. Anand, AIR 1998 SC 2615: (1998) 6 SCC 466:
  1998 AIR SCW 2656: JT 1998 (5) SC 359: (1998) 3 SCR 1046:
  1999 (1) SRJ 110: (1998) 4 SCALE 433: 1998 (6) Supreme 309:
  1998 (2) UJ (SC) 483: 1999 Writ LR 1   205
Union of India *v.* Sankalchand Seth, AIR 1977 SC 2328: (1977) 4 SCC 193:
  1977 Lab IC 1857: 1977 SCC (L&S) 435   143
Union of India *v.* Sharma, AIR 1992 SC 1188: (1992) 2 SCC 728:
  (1992) Lab IC 1136: (1992) 2 SCR 373   301
Union of India *v.* Sripati, (1976) 1 SCWR 173: (1975) 4 SCC 699: AIR 1975 SC 1755   122
Union of India *v.* State of Punjab, AIR 1990 P&H 183   264
Union of India *v.* Sugrabai Wife of Abdul Majid, AIR 1969 Bom 13:
  70 Bom LR 212: 1968 Mah LJ 468: ILR (1968) Bom 998   271

Union of India *v.* Sukumar Pyne, AIR 1966 SC 1206: (1966) 2 SCR 34: 1966 Cr LJ 946 53
Union of India v. Sukumar Sengupta, AIR 1990 SC 1692: JT 1990 (2) SC 297:
  1990 (Supp) SCC 545 9
Union of India *v.* Sunil Kumar Sarkar, AIR 2001 SC 1092: (2001) 3 SCC 414:
  2001 Lab IC 1114: 2001 SCC (L&S) 600 287
Union of India *v.* Syed, (1992) 1 UJ SC 590: (1992) Supp 2 SCC 534:
  AIR 1994 SC 605: (1992) 2 CLR 38 280
Union of India *v.* T.R. Verma, AIR 1957 SC 882: 1958 SCR 499: (1958) 2 LLJ 259 205
Union of India *v.* Tajinder Singh, (1991) 4 SCC 129: 1991 SCC (L&S) 387:
  (1986) 2 SCALE 860 279
Union of India *v.* Tejram Parashramji Bombhate, AIR 1992 SC 570:
  (1991) 3 SCC 11: (1991) 2 LLJ 263: (1991) 16 ATC 556 102, 208
Union of India *v.* Tulsi Ram Patel, (1985) 3 SCC 398: AIR 1985 SC 1416:
  1985 Lab IC 1393: 1985 SCC (Lab) 672: (1985) 2 LLJ 206:
  (1985) 2 LLN 488: (1985) 2 Cur LR 117: (1985) 3 Comp LJ 45 28
Union of India *v.* V.B. Raju, AIR 1982 SC 1174: 1982 Lab IC 1487:
  1982 UJ (SC) 312: (1982) 2 SCC 326: (1982) 1 Serv LJ 602:
  1982 SCC (Lab) 247: (1982) 2 LLN 640 291
Union of India *v.* Vasanbharthi, AIR 1990 SC 1216: (1990) 2 SCC 275: 1990 Cr LJ 1244 61
Union Territory of Goa, Daman & Diu *v.* Lakshmibai Narayan Patil,
  AIR 1990 SC 1771: (1990) 4 SCC 102 85
United Provinces *v.* Atiqua Begum, AIR 1941 FC 16 246
University of Calcutta *v.* Dipa Pal, AIR 1952 Cal 594 216
University of Delhi *v.* Raj Singh, JT 1994 (6) SC 1: (1994) Supp 3 SCC 576:
  (1994) 28 ATC 541: AIR 1995 SC 336 249
University of Jodhpur *v.* Purohit, (1990) 1 UJ SC 235: (1989) Supp 2 SCC 586:
  1990 SCC (L&S) 117: (1991) 16 ATC 176 152
University of Kerala *v.* Council Principals, Colleges, Kerala, AIR 2010 SC 2532 108
Unni Krishnan, J.P. *v.* State of Andhra Pradesh, AIR 1993 SC 2178: (1993) 1 SCC 645:
  1993 AIR SCW 863: JT 1993 (1) SC 474: (1993) 1 SCR 594: 1993 (2) SCT 511:
  1993 (1) Serv LR 743: 1993 (1) UJ (SC) 721 64, 106
Usha *v.* Palisetty Mohan Rao, AIR 2002 SC 400: 2001 AIR SCW 5196:
  2001 (1) DMC 584: 2001 (2) Marri LJ 385: (2002) 10 SCC 544:
  2001 (5) Supreme 400 153
Utkal Contractors and Joinery (P) Ltd. *v.* State of Orissa, AIR 1987 SC 2310:
  1987 Supp SCC 751: JT 1987 (5) SC 1: 1987 Raj LR 652 253
Uttar Pradesh Avas Evam Vikas Parishad *v.* Friends Co-op. Housing Society Ltd.,
  AIR 1996 SC 114: (1995) Supp 3 SCC 456: 1995 AIR SCW 3800:
  1995 All LJ 2066: 1995 (2) Rent LR 33: 1995 (2) SCJ 255: (1995) 3 SCR 729 58, 64
Uttar Pradesh Junior Doctors' Action Committee *v.* Dr. B. Sheetal Nandwani,
  (1990) 4 SCC 633: AIR 1991 SC 909: JT 1990 (3) SC 690:
  1990 (2) UJ (SC) 671: 1990 (2) UPLBEC 1321 202, 207
Uttar Pradesh Public Service Commission *v.* Suresh, AIR 1987 SC 1953:
  (1987) 4 SCC 176: 1987 Lab IC 1644: (1987) 55 FLR 461 166, 168, 294
Uttar Pradesh Rajkiya Nirman Nigam Ltd. *v.* Indure Pvt. Ltd., AIR 1996 SC 1373:
  (1996) 2 SCC 667: 1996 AIR SCW 980: JT 1996 (2) SC 322:
  1996 (1) LJR 323: 1996 (2) RRR 31: (1996) 2 SCR 386: 1996 (2) UJ (SC) 48 271
Uttar Pradesh State Road Transport Corporation *v.* Mohammed Ismail,
  (1991) 3 SCC 239: AIR 1991 SC 1099: (1991) 17 ATC 234: (1991) 2 LLJ 332 199, 206
Uttar Pradesh State Road Transport Corporation *v.* Mahesh Kumar Mishra,
  AIR 2000 SC 1151: (2000) 3 SCC 450: (2000) 2 SCR 435: 2000 All LJ 865 217
Uttar Pradesh State Sugar Corpn. Ltd. *v.* Sant Raj Singh, AIR 2006 SC 2296:
  2006 AIR SCW 3013: 2006 (4) ALJ 590: 2006 (3) LLJ 509: 2006 (4) LLN 163:
  (2006) 9 SCC 82: 2006 (7) SCJ 30: 2006 (3) SCT 56: (2006) 6 SCALE 205:
  2006 (6) Supreme 174: (2006) 4 Serv LR 788 23, 27, 101
Uttaranchal Jal Sansthan, General Manager *v.* Laxmi Devi, (2009) 7 SCC 205:
  AIR 2009 SC 3121: 2009 Lab IC 3613: 2009 AIR SCW 5014:
  2009 (6) ALJ 451: 2009 (121) FLR 1000: (2009) 8 SCALE 503 23

V

V. Jagannadha Rao *v.* State of Andhra Pradesh, AIR 2002 SC 77:
(2001) 10 SCC 401: (2002) 92 FLR 512 — 344

V. Parukutty Mannadissiar *v.* State of Kerala, AIR 1990 SC 817:
1990 Supp SCC 245: JT 1989 (3) SC 572 — 214

V. Subramaniam *v.* Rajesh Raghuvandra Rao, AIR 2009 SC 1858:
2009 AIR SCW 3329: 2009 (3) All MR 418: 2009 (3) Bom CR 790:
2009 (4) Mad LJ 120: 2009 (3) Mah LJ 946: 2009 (5) Mah LJ 120:
(2009) 5 SCC 608: (2009) 4 SCALE 459 — 272

V.R. Katarki *v.* State of Karnataka, AIR 1991 SC 1241: (1991) Supp 1 SCC 267:
(1991) 16 ATC 555 — 214

V.T. Khanzode *v.* R.B.I., AIR 1982 SC 917: (1982) 2 SCC 7: (1982) 1 LLJ 465 — 94

V.V.S. Rama Sharma *v.* State of Uttar Pradesh, (2009) 7 SCC 234 — 245

Vadamalai *v.* Syed Thastha Keer, AIR 2009 SC 1956: 2009 AIR SCW 1583:
2009 (1) Crimes 361: 2009 (2) JCR SC 90: (2009) 3 SCC 454:
(2009) 2 SCALE 475: 2009 (2) SCC (Cri) 142 — 148

Vakil Prasad Singh *v.* State of Bihar, AIR 2009 SC 1822: 2009 Cr LJ 1731:
2009 AIR SCW 1418: 2009 (1) Cur Cr R 282: 2009 (42) OCR 680:
(2009) 3 SCC 355: (2009) 2 SCALE 22: 2009 (2) SCC (Cri) 95 — 65

Vamuzo *v.* Union of India, 1988 (2) GLJ 468 — 173

Vareli Weaves Pvt. Ltd. *v.* Union of India, AIR 1996 SC 1543: (1996) 3 SCC 318 — 208

Varghese *v.* Bank of Cochin, AIR 1980 SC 470: (1980) 2 SCC 360:
(1980) 2 SCR 913 — 109

Vasantakumar Radhakisan Vora *v.* Board of Trustees of the Port of Bombay,
AIR 1991 SC 14: (1991) 1 SCC 761: 1991 (2) All CJ 743: JT 1990 (3) SC 609:
1991 (1) Land LR 45: 1990 (2) Ren CR 454: 1992 (1) Rent LR 83 — 210

Vashisht Narain Karwaria *v.* State of Uttar Pradesh, AIR 1990 SC 1272:
(1990) 2 SCC 629: 1990 Cr LJ 1311 reversing (1990) Cr LJ (NOC) 36 (All) — 70

Vasudev Shenoy *v.* Government of India, (1994) 1 KLT 389 — 201

Vasudevan *v.* Union of India, AIR 1990 SC 2295: (1991) Supp 2 SCC 134:
(1991) 2 LLJ 420 — 101

Vatheeswaran *v.* State of Tamil Nadu, AIR 1983 SC 361: (1983) 2 SCC 68:
1983 Cr LJ 481 — 49

Vedprakash Devkinandan Chiripal *v.* State of Gujarat, AIR 1987 Guj 253:
(1987) 1 Crimes 440: 1987 EFR 347 (FB) — 203

Veena *v.* State of Bihar, AIR 1983 SC 339: (1982) 2 SCC 583: 1982 SCC (Cri) 511 — 58

Veera Ibrahim *v.* State of Maharashtra, AIR 1976 SC 1167: (1976) 2 SCC 302:
1976 SCC (Cri) 278: 1976 Cr LJ 860 — 52

Veeramani *v.* State of Tamil Nadu, JT 1994 (1) SC 350: 1995 Cr LJ 2644:
1995 AIR SCW 1730: 1994 (1) Crimes 617: (1994) 2 SCC 337:
1994 (2) SCJ 41: (1994) 1 SCR 616: 1994 SCC (Cri) 482: 1994 (1) UJ (SC) 524 — 70

Vellore Citizens Welfare Forum *v.* Union of India, AIR 1996 SC 2715:
(1996) 5 SCC 647: 1996 AIR SCW 3399: 1996 (5) Comp LJ SC 40:
JT 1996 (7) SC 375 — 56, 64

Venkataramana Devaru *v.* State of Mysore, AIR 1958 SC 255: 1958 SCR 895:
1958 SCJ 382: (1958) 1 Andh WR (SC) 109: (1958) 1 Mad LJ (SC) 109 — 73, 75

Venkateswara *v.* Government of Andhra Pradesh, AIR 1966 SC 828 — 204

Vidadala Harinadhababu *v.* N.T. Ramarao, AIR 1990 AP 20 (FB) — 130

Video Electronics Pvt Ltd. *v.* State of Punjab, AIR 1990 SC 820:
(1990) 3 SCC 87: (1989) Supp 2 SCR 731 — 274, 275

Vijay Kumar Kathuria (Dr.) *v.* State of Haryana, AIR 1983 SC 622:
(1983) 3 SCC 333: 1983 UJ (SC) 454: 1983 IJR (Civ) 57 — 214

Vijay Kumar *v.* Union of India, AIR 1990 SC 1184: (1990) 1 SCC 606:
1990 SCC (Cri) 247 — 70

Vijay Sharma *v.* Union of India, AIR 2008 Bom 29: 2008 (3) ALJ (NOC) 652:
2008 (2) AKAR (NOC) 244: 2007 (6) AIR Bom R 625: 2007 (6) All MR 336:
2007 (5) Bom CR 710 — 22

Vijaynagar Industrial Workers Housing Co-operative Society Ltd. *v.*
   State of Karnataka, AIR 1998 Kant 361: ILR 1998 Kant 2479:
   1998 (4) Kant LJ 117   194
Vijeta Gajra *v.* State of NCT of Delhi, AIR 2010 SC 2712   148
Vikramjit Saha *v.* State of West Bengal, AIR 1998 Cal 316 (DB)   202
Vimla *v.* State of Uttar Pradesh, (1990) Supp SCC 770: 1991 Supp SCC (L&S) 704:
   (1991) 16 ATC 479   207
Vimlabai Deshpande *v.* Emp., AIR 1945 Nag 8   204
Vineet Narain *v.* Union of India, AIR 1998 SC 889: (1998) 1 SCC 226:
   1998 SCC (Cri) 307: 1998 Cr LJ 1208   62, 88
Vinodkumar Shantilal Gosalia *v.* Gangadhar Narsingdas Agarwal,
   AIR 1981 SC 1946: (1981) 4 SCC 226: (1982) 1 SCR 392   7
Virender *v.* Avinash, AIR 1991 SC 958: (1990) 3 SCC 472: (1991) 14 ATC 732   278
Virendra Mohan Rai Khangar (Dr.) *v.* Union of India, AIR 1992 All 147:
   1991 AWC 1089: 1992 (1) All CJ 193   314, 315
Virendra Nath *v.* Delhi, (1990) 2 SCC 307: AIR 1990 SC 1148: 1990 Lab IC 929   81
Virendra *v.* State of Punjab, AIR 1957 SC 896: (1958) 1 SCR 308: 1958 SCJ 88:
   1958 SCA 891: 1958 SCC 1   48, 50, 75
Virendra *v.* State of Uttar Pradesh, (1955) 1 SCR 415: AIR 1954 SC 447:
   (1954) 2 MLJ 369   271
Vishaka *v.* State of Rajasthan, AIR 1997 SC 3011: 1997 AIR SCW 3043:
   1998 (1) BLJR 228: 1997 (3) Crimes 188JT 1997 (7) SC 384:
   1997 (13) OCR 305: (1997) 6 SCC 241: 1997 (3) SCJ 584:
   (1997) 5 SCALE 453: 1997 SCC (Cri) 932: 1997 (7) Supreme 323:
   1997 Writ LR 823   13, 34, 66
Vishal Jeet *v.* Union of India, AIR 1990 SC 1412: (1990) 3 SCC 318:
   1990 Cr LJ 1469   71, 72, 87
Vishal Properties Pvt. Ltd. *v.* State of Uttar Pradesh, AIR 2008 SC 183:
   2007 AIR SCW 6540: 2008 (1) ALJ 32: 2007 (60) All Ind Cas 219:
   2008 (1) Land LR 140: (2007) 11 SCC 172: 2008 (2) SCT 352:
   (2007) 12 SCALE 32: 2008 (4) Serv LR 66: 2007 (7) Supreme 432   24
Vishundas Hundumal *v.* State of Madhya Pradesh, AIR 1981 SC 1636:
   (1981) 2 SCC 410: 1981 UJ (SC) 306: 1981 BBCJ (SC) 150: 1981 SCC (Tax) 278   24
Vishwas Anna Sawant *v.* Municipal Corporation of Greater Bombay,
   JT 1994 (3) SC 573: (1994) 4 SCC 434: (1994) 27 ATC 600:
   AIR 1994 SC 2408   36, 106
Vishwas Nagar Evacuee Plot Purchasers Association *v.* Under Secretary,
   Delhi Admn., AIR 1990 SC 849: (1990) 2 SCC 268: JT 1990 (2) SC 176   205
Viswan *v.* Union of India, AIR 1983 SC 658: (1983) 3 SCC 401: (1983) 2 LLJ 157   96
Vrajlal Manilal & Co. *v.* State of Madhya Pradesh, AIR 1970 SC 129:
   (1969) 2 SCC 248: (1969) 2 SCA 413: 1970 MPWR 193:
   (1970) 1 SCR 400: 1970 MPLJ 518   42

W

Waman Rao *v.* Union of India, AIR 1981 SC 271: (1981) 2 SCC 362:
   1980 Ker LT 573: 1980 UJ (SC) 742: (1981) 2 SCR 1   3, 18, 85, 335
Welcome Hotel *v.* State of Andhra Pradesh, AIR 1983 SC 1015:
   (1983) 4 SCC 575: 1983 SCC (Cri) 872   214
Welfare Assocn. A.R.P., Maharashtra *v.* Ranjit P. Gohil, AIR 2003 SC 1266:
   2003 AIR SCW 1663: JT 2003 (2) SC 335: (2003) 9 SCC 358:
   (2003) 2 SCR 139: 2003 (4) SRJ 381: (2003) 2 SCALE 288   247
West Bengal Head Masters' Association *v.* Union of India, AIR 1983 Cal 448:
   (1983) 87 CWN 597   110
Western Coalfields Ltd. *v.* Special Area Development Authority, Korba,
   AIR 1982 SC 697: (1982) 1 SCC 125: 1982 (2) SCJ 1: (1982) 2 Comp LJ 793   251
Workmen *v.* Hindustan Steel Ltd., (1984) Supp SCC 554: AIR 1985 SC 251:
   1985 SCC (L&S) 260   28

X

X *v.* Hospital Z, AIR 1999 SC 495: (1998) 9 SCC 296: 1998 AIR SCW 3662: JT 1998 (7) SC 626: 1999 (1) SRJ 88: (1998) 6 SCALE 230: 1998 (9) Supreme 220: 1999 (1) UJ (SC) 232   52

Y

Y. Theclamma *v.* Union of India, (1987) 2 SCC 516: AIR 1987 SC 1210: (1987) Lab IC 907   82

Yadlapati Venkateswarlu *v.* State of Andhra Pradesh, AIR 1991 SC 704: (1992) Supp 1 SCC 74: 1991 (190) ITR 375: JT 1990 (4) SC 19   245

Yajnapurusdasji *v.* Muldas, AIR 1966 SC 1119: (1966) 3 SCR 242: 1967 MLLJ 289   74

Yates (Arthur) & Co. Ltd. *v.* Vegetable Seeds Committee, (1945-46) 72 CIR 37   21

Yusuf *v.* State of Bombay, AIR 1954 SC 321: (1954) 1 SCR 930: 56 Bom LR 1176: 1954 Cr LJ 886   30, 34

Z

Zameer Ahmed Latifur Rehman Sheikh *v.* State of Maharashtra, AIR 2010 SC 2633   244

Zaverbhai *v.* State of Bombay, AIR 1954 SC 752: (1955) 1 SCR 799: 1954 Cr LJ 1822   251

Zee Telefilms Ltd. *v.* Union of India, AIR 2005 SC 2677: 2005 AIR SCW 2985: 2005 (4) Comp LJ 283 SC: JT 2005 (2) SC 8: (2005) 4 SCC 649: 2005 (2) SCJ 121: 2005 (3) SRJ 67: (2005) 1 SCALE 666.2: 2005 (1) Supreme 886   14

LIST OF STATUTES REFERRED

A.P. Hindu Religious and Charitable Endowments Act, *1987*, 105

A.P. Panchayati Raj Engineering Service Rules, *1963*, 344

Abolition of Privy Council Jurisdiction Act, *1949*, 353

Acquired Territories (Merger) Act, *1960*, 356

Administrative Tribunals Act, *1985*, 285, 299, 301

Advocates Act, *1961*, 252

All India Services (Death-cum-Retirement) Rules, *1958*, 286

All India Services Act, *1951*, 290

Andhra Pradesh and Madras (Alteration of Boundaries) Act, *1959*, 354, 355

Andhra Pradesh and Mysore (Transfer of Territory) Act, *1968*, 354, 356

Andhra State Act, *1953*, 354, 355

Arbitration and Conciliation Act, *1996*, 157

Army Act, *1950*, 208

Assam (Alteration of Boundaries) Act, *1951*, 354

Assam Forest Regulation, *1891*, 374

Banking Companies (Acquisition and Transfer of Undertakings) Act, *1970*, 104

Bar Council Act, *1926*, 252

Bengal Cess Act, *1880*, 301

Bihar and Uttar Pradesh (Alteration of Boundaries) Act, *1968*, 354, 356

Bihar and West Bengal (Transfer of Territories) Act, *1956*, 354, 357

Bihar Hindu Religious Trusts Act, *1951*, 77

Bihar Reorganisation Act, *2000*, 354, 358

Bombay Money-Lenders Act, *1946*, 248

Bombay Reorganisation Act, *1960*, 355

Bombay Stamp Act, *1958*, 249

Bonded Labour System (Abolition) Act, *1976*, 103

Central Civil Services (Classification and Control and Appeal) Rules, *1965*, 287

Chandernagore (Merger) Act, *1954*, 357

Citizenship Act, *1955*, 13, 14

Civil Services (Temporary) Rules, *1949*, 289

Code of Civil Procedure, 154

Code of Criminal Procedure, 150, 399

Colonial Courts of Admiralty (India) Act, *1891*, 193

Colonial Courts of Admiralty Act, *1890*, 193

Conservation of Foreign Exchange and Prevention of Smuggling Activities Act, *1974*, 61, 70

Constitution (Application to Jammu and Kashmir) Order, *1954*, 418

Constitution (Application to Jammu and Kashmir) Amendment Order, *1960*, 422, 437

Constitution (Application to Jammu and Kashmir) Amendment Order, *1989*, 431, 446

Constitution (Application to Jammu and Kashmir) Order, *1950*, 418

Constitution (Application to Jammu and Kashmir) Order, *1954*, 98, 418, 420, 423, 426, 432, 434, 438, 439, 442, 443, 444

Constitution (Application to Jammu and Kashmir) Second Amendment Order, *1974*, 421, 422, 436, 437

Constitution of India, *1950*, 14, 25, 33, 39, 50, 105, 173, 202, 252, 295, 364, 365, 366

Contempt of Courts Act, *1971*, 43

Co-operative Societies Act, *1965*, 43

Defence of India Act, *1971*, 24

Delhi Cement and Licensing and Control Order, *1982*, 247

Delimitation Act, 1972, 421, 435, 436

Dissolution of Muslim Marriages Act, *1939*, 105

Election Laws (Amendment) Act, *1975*, 446

Essential Commodities Act, *1955*, 21, 247

Evidence Act, 120

Fatal Accidents Act, *1855*, 88

Federal Court (Enlargement of Jurisdiction) Act, *1947*, 353

Foreign Exchange Regulation Act, *1973*, 53

Foreigners Act, *1946*, 12

General Clauses Act, *1897*, 53, 334

Goa, Daman and Diu Reorganisation Act, *1987*, 358, 359

Government of India Act, *1915*, 5, 6, 11, 12, 160, 190, 193, 246, 332, 349, 352, 353

Government of Union Territories Act, *1963*, 389

Haryana and Uttar Pradesh (Alteration of Boundaries) Act, *1979*, 356, 357

Hindu Marriage Act, *1955*, 105

Income Tax Act, *1961*, 29, 248

Indecent Representation of Women Act, *1986*, 55

Indian Administrative Services (Second Amendment) Regulation, *1989*, 28

Indian Contract Act, *1872*, 270

Indian Divorce Act, *1869*, 106

Indian Evidence Act, *1872*, 54

Indian Forest Act, *1927*, 110

Indian Independence Act, *1947*, 160, 353

Indian Medical Council Act, *1956*, 251

Indian Penal Code, *1860*, 34, 148, 164, 378, 399

Indian Telegraphs Act, *1885*, 67

Industrial Disputes Act, *1947*, 90, 156

Industries (Development and Regulation) Act, *1951*, 247

Inter State Water Disputes Act, *1956*, 255

Jammu and Kashmir Constitution Act, *1996*, 428

Jammu and Kashmir Debtor's Relief Act, *1976*, 430, 446

Jammu and Kashmir Restitution of Mortgaged Properties Act, *1976*, 430, 446

Judges (Inquiry) Act, *1968*, 294

Karnataka Land Reforms Act, *1961*, 252

Land Acquisition Act, *1894*, 24

Land Acquisition Act, *1948*, 205

Limitation Act, *1963*, 341

Madhya Pradesh Reorganisation Act, *2000*, 355, 358

Maintenance of Internal Security Act, *1971*, 446

Maternity Benefit Act, *1961*, 103

Mines and Minerals (Regulation and Development) Act, *1957*, 248

Motor Vehicles Act, *1988*, 67

Muslim Women's Protection of Rights on Divorce Act, *1986*, 105

National Security Act, *1980*, 70

Negotiable Instruments Act, *1881*, 150

North-Eastern Areas (Reorganisation) Act, *1971*, 354, 358, 387

Passports Act, *1967*, 60

Police Forces (Restriction of Rights) Act, *1966*, 96

Prevention of Publication of Objectionable Matter Act, *1976*, 446

Prevention of Terrorism Act, *2002*, 93

Punjab Panchayat Secretaries (Recruitment and Conditions of Services) Rules, *1993*, 39

Punjab Reorganisation Act, *1966*, 356, 357, 359

Qualitative Requirements and Finance Act, *1981*, 29

Rajasthan and Madhya Pradesh (Transfer of Territories) Act, *1959*, 355, 356

Representation of People Act, *1951*, 304

Representation of the People (Amendment) Act, *1974*, 446

Representation of the People Act, *1951*, 78, 446

Specific Relief Act, *1963*, 285

State Finance Corporations Act, *1951*, 273

State of Nagaland Act, *1962*, 341, 354, 357

States Reorganisation Act, *1956*, 351, 354, 355, 356, 359

Sugar Control Order, *1966*, 196

Supreme Court Rules, 149

Tamil Nadu Prevention of Dangerous Activities of Bootleggers, Drug Offenders, Forest Offenders, Immoral Traffic Offenders and Slum Grabbers Act, *1982*, 70

Territorial Waters, Continental Shelf, Exclusive Economic Zone and other Maritime Zones Act, *1976*, 7

Tripura Tribal Areas Autonomous District Council Act, *1979*, 387

U.P. Co-operative Societies Act, *1965*, 43

U.P. Panchayat Raj Act, *1947*, 25

U.P. Sales Tax Act, *1948*, 274

U.P. Town Areas Act, *1914*, 196

University Grants Commission Act, *1956*, 249

Untouchability (Offences) Act, *1955*, 39

Urban Land (Ceiling and Regulation) Act, *1976*, 25

Uttar Pradesh Reorganisation Act, *2000*, 356, 358

Uttar Pradesh Tea Validation Act, *1958*, 245

Validity of the Police Forces (Restriction of Rights) Act, *1966*, 96

W.B. Primary Education Act, *1973*, 301

W.B. Rural Employment and Production Act, *1976*, 301

W.B. Taxation Tribunal Act, *1987*, 301

Wealth-tax Act, 249

West Bengal Requisition of Vehicles Act, *1979*, 272

CONSTITUTION OF INDIA IN A NUTSHELL

BASICS OF CONSTITUTION

Constitution is a complex document and not to be construed as mere law, but as the machinery by which laws are made. It provides for the democratic function of the Government of India. Our Constitution is a written Constitution. It was adopted on 26th November, 1949 and Articles 5, 6, 7, 8, 9, 60, 324, 366, 367, 379, 380, 388, 391, 392, 393, and 394 came into force on 26 November, 1949 and other articles came into force on 26th January, 1950.

The Constitution defines and determines the relation between:

    (a) various institutions and the areas of government,

    (b) executive, the legislature and the judiciary,

    (c) Central government, State governments and the local governments,

    (d) people and the government,

    (e) political, social and economic issues.

Ours is a longest Constitution of the world. It has XXII (22) Parts with 395 original Articles. [Total No. of present Articles 448] Out of these Articles, many contain number of exceptions and limitations and it is added with 12 Schedules. Upto January, 2012 it has gone through 97 amendments.

In our Constitution the federal system has been discussed in detail. It prescribes the Constitution for the Union and the State governments along with clear-cut and well defined division of power of Union and State Governments and jurisdiction and powers of Union and State Governments. The Chapters like legislative relations, administrative relations, financial relations and inter-state trade and commerce discuss the detailed and elaborate approach to these issues.

PREAMBLE

The Preamble is the basic structure of the Constitution. The Preamble says that people are the ultimate authority and the Constitution emerges from them.

In fact the Preamble contains with the declaration that "to secure to all citizens justice, social, economic and political, liberty of thought, expression, belief, faith and worship - equality of status and of opportunity.

The Preamble emphasises the unity of Nation and it proceeds further to define the objectives of the Indian Republic. The Preamble has been amended once in 1976. The Preamble contains a specified objective that is the basic structure. The Preamble may be invoked to determine the ambit of the fundamental rights, and directive principles of State Policy. It is the soul of the Constitution and as such is the precious part of the Constitution. Preamble says that the Constitution was adopted on 26th November, 1949 which is observed as the Law Day though it came into force from 26th January, 1950;

UNION OF INDIA

Article 1 of the Constitution states India, that is Bharat and it is Union of States. At present India is the Union of 28 States and 7 Union Territories. The names of States and the names of Union Territories are specified in Schedule I. The latest three new States i.e. Uttaranchal (now changed as Uttarakhand), Jharkhand and Chhatisgarh were formed in the year 2000. The territory of India comprises, the territories of States, Union Territories and other territories which can be acquired from time to time. After all, the Union of India is a federal one, with distribution of powers. The judiciary is the interpreter of Constitution and other laws. Though there is controversy whether India is or is not a federation some writers have called it "quasi-federal" hence it would seem that, essentially Constitution is a federal one.

CITIZENSHIP

Under the Constitution, there is only one domicile i.e., domicile of the country and there is no separate domicile for a State. In the popular meaning of domicile, it means a person must be having permanent home at any place in India. The Part II also deals with rights of citizenship of certain persons who have migrated to India from Pakistan, right of citizenship of certain migrants to Pakistan, right of citizenship of certain persons of Indian origin residing outside India, persons voluntarily acquiring citizenship of a foreign State are not citizens and continuance of the rights of citizenship. Persons of Indian origin who voluntarily acquire citizenship of a foreign State are no longer citizens of India. This Part has given the Parliament of India to regulate the right of citizenship by law. The Citizenship Act of 1955 regulates the provisions for the citizenship.

Central Government has exclusive jurisdiction to determine the question of citizenship of a person. The court has no power in this subject. In 2003, the Central Government amended the Citizenship Act. This amendment provided for dual citizenship of People of Indian Origin in 16 specified countries. The Citizenship Act of 1955 says about the acquisition and termination of citizenship.

FUNDAMENTAL RIGHTS

The fundamental rights always remain controversial till date. The fundamental rights are basics and basic freedoms guaranteed to the individual. Articles 12 to 35 deal with the fundamental rights. There are six fundamental rights excluding right to basic education. The fundamental rights are freedoms guaranteed but these freedoms are not absolute, but are justiciable. Justiciable here means judicially enforceable. The fundamental rights are different from legal rights. The legal rights are protected and enforced by ordinary law, on the contrary fundamental right is protected and guaranteed by the Constitution. Constitution 86th amendment in the year 2002, inserted Article 21A for the right to education. Generally it falls under the right to freedom.

These fundamental rights are:
   (1) Right to equality (Articles 14 to 18)
   (2) Right to freedom (Articles 19 to 22)
   (3) Right against exploitation (Articles 23 and 24)
   (4) Right to freedom of religion (Articles 25 to 28)
   (5) Right to cultural and educational rights (Articles 29 to 30)
   (6) Right to constitutional remedies (Article 32).

Before 44th Amendment in 1978 the right to property was a Fundamental right under Article 31, but now it is the legal and Constitutional right under Article 300A.

Article 13 makes all laws and administrative actions which abridge fundamental rights *ipso facto* null and void.

Article 14 guarantees to all, equality before law and equal protection of laws. The President and the Governor are an exception to the equality mandate.

Article 15 prohibits discrimination against any citizen on grounds of religion, race, caste, sex or place of birth or any of them. This article was amended by 93rd Amendment, 2005 for providing reservations in admission for SCs, STs and Backward Classes in private unaided educational institutions.

Article 16 provides for equality of opportunity in the matters of public employment.

Article 17 abolishes untouchability.

Article 18 abolishes titles. But it does not prevent other institutions to confer titles or honours.

Article 19 guarantees freedom of speech, freedom to assemble peacefully without arms, to form associations or unions, to move throughout the territory of India, to reside and settle in any part of the territory of India, to practice any profession, or to carry on any occupation, trade or business.

Article 20 provides that no person shall be convicted for any offence except the violation of a law in force, no person shall be punished for the same offence more than once, no person shall be compelled to be a witness against himself.

Article 21 guarantees that no person shall be deprived of his life and personal liberty except according to procedure established by law.

Article 21A provides for free and compulsory education to children of the age of six to fourteen years.

Article 22 provides that the person shall be informed of the grounds of his arrest, he shall have legal practitioner of his choice and that he must be produced before the nearest magistrate within 24 hours of his arrest.

Article 23 prohibits traffic in human beings and forced labour.

Article 24 prohibits employing children below the age of 14 in any hazardous employment.

Article 25 prohibits freedom of conscience and free profession, practice and propagation of religion, subject to public order, morality and health.

Article 26 provides freedom to manage religious affairs.

Article 27 gives freedom as to payment of taxes for promotion of any religious affairs.

Article 28 prohibits religious instruction in educational institutions maintained by the State.

Article 29 states that citizens having a distinct language, script or culture shall have right to conserve the same and no citizen will be denied admission into educational institution maintained by State on the ground of religion, race, caste, language etc.

Article 30 gives rights to minorities to establish and administer educational institutions.

Article 31A, 31B and 31C validate and save certain laws which otherwise may turn out to be violative of fundamental rights.

Article 32 gives a right to every individual to move the Supreme Court directly in case of violation of his fundamental rights.

Under Article 33 the Parliament can modify the application of fundamental rights to the Armed Forces or police forces so as to ensure proper discharge of their duties and maintenance of discipline among them.

Article 34 provides that when martial law is in force in any part of India, Parliament may by law indemnify any person in the service of the Union or State for any act done by him in connection with the maintenance or restoration of law and order in such area or validate any sentence passed or act done when martial law was in force.

DIRECTIVE PRINCIPLES OF STATE POLICY

Articles 36 to 51 deals with the Directive Principles of State Policy.

These Principles are as follows:

Article 36 defines the State.

Article 37 provides that provision of the directive principles shall not be enforceable by any court.

Article 38 provides that State shall secure social order for promotion of welfare of the people.

Article 39 states that the State shall regulate ownership and control of the means of production and distribution, prevent concentration of wealth and income, ensure their more equitable distribution and enact laws to protect the interests of the workers.

Article 39A provides for equal justice and free legal aid.

Article 40 provides for organisation of village Panchayats.

Article 41 provides for right to work, right to education and right to public assistance in cases of unemployment, old age, sickness and disablement, etc.

Article 42 provides for just and humane conditions of work and maternity relief.

Article 43 provides for living wage, conditions of work ensuring the descent standard of life and full enjoyment of leisure, social and culture, opportunities for all workers, agricultural, industrial or otherwise and provision for the promotion of cottage industries in rural areas.

Article 43A provides for participation of workers in management of industries.

Article 44 makes the provision for uniform civil code for the citizens.

Article 45 makes the provision for free and compulsory education to children below the age of 14 years.

Article 46 makes the provision for the promotion of educational and economic interests of Scheduled Castes, Scheduled Tribes and other weaker sections.

Article 47 states about the duty of State to raise the level of nutrition and the standard of living and to improve public health.

Article 48 provides for organisation of agriculture and animal husbandary.

Article 48A provides for protection and improvement of environment and safeguarding of forests and wild life.

Article 49 makes the provision for protection of monuments and places and objects of national importance.

Article 50 provides for separation of judiciary from executive.

Article 51 provides for promotion of international peace and security.

FUNDAMENTAL DUTIES

Articles 51A deals with the fundamental duties. This provision was introduced by the 42nd Amendment of Constitution in the year 1976 by inserting Part IVA in the Constitution. These duties cannot be enforced by writs. They can be promoted by Constitutional methods.

There are 11 fundamental duties *viz-a-viz*:

(1) to abide by the Constitution and, respect its ideals and institutions, the National Flag and the National Anthem. [Article 51A(a)]

(2) to cherish and follow the noble ideals which inspired our national struggle for freedom. [Article 51A(b)]

(3) to uphold and protect the sovereignty, unity and integrity of India. [Article 51A(c)]

(4) to defend the country and render national service when called upon to do so. [Article 51A(d)]

(5) to promote harmony and the spirit of common brotherhood amongst all the people of India transcending religious, linguistic and regional or sectional diversities and to renounce practices derogatory to the dignity of women. [Article 51A(e)]

(6) to value and preserve the rich heritage of our composite culture. [51A(f)]

(7) to protect and improve the natural environment including forests, lakes, rivers and wild life, and to have compassion for living creatures. [Article 51A(g)]

(8) to develop the scientific temper, humanism and the spirit of inquiry and reform. [Article 51A(h)]

(9) to safeguard public property and to abjure violence. [Article 51A(i)]

(10) to strive towards excellence in all spheres of individual and collective activity so that the nation constantly rises to higher levels of endeavour and achievement. [Article 51A(j)]

(11) the parent or guardian to provide opportunities for education to his child or, as the case may be, ward between the age of 6 to 14 years. [Article 51A(k)]

PRESIDENT OF INDIA

The Union Executive consists of the President of India, the Lok Sabha and Rajya Sabha. According to the Article 53, the executive power of the Union is vested in the President of India. He exercises such power either directly or through officers subordinate to him.

The President shall be elected by the members of an electoral college. The electoral college consists of elected members of both the Houses of Parliament and the elected members of the Legislative Assemblies of the States and there shall be uniformity in the scale of representation of the different States at the election of President. The election of President is held in accordance with proportional representation by single transferable secret ballot system. The President holds office for 5 years from the date he enters into office and he can be re-elected. A person to be eligible for President's election should be citizen of India and must have completed 35 years of age and must be qualified to be a member of Lok Sabha.

The President takes oath from Chief Justice of India and in his absence from the senior most Judge of the Supreme Court. [Article 60]

The President can only be impeached if he violates the provisions of the Constitution and such charge shall be preferred either in Lok Sabha or in Rajya Sabha. [Article 61]

Functions and Powers of President of India:

(1) He appoints Prime Minister of India and on his advice, the Council of Ministers.

(2) He makes rules for the more convenient transaction of business of the Government and allocates among ministries for such business.

(3) He must be informed of all decisions of Council of Ministers.

(4) No bill can become an Act, without the President's signature. Except money Bills, he can return other Bills for reconsideration of the Parliament.

(5) When two Houses do not agree on the provisions of a Bill, he may summon them to a joint sitting.

(6) When the Parliament is not in Session, he may promulgate Ordinances.

(7) When the security of India is threatened, he can proclaim emergency. He can also promulgate the President's rule in States as also the Financial Emergency.

(8) He appoints judges of Supreme Court and High Courts, Chief Election Commissioner, Comptroller and Auditor General, members of Union Public Service Commission. He also appoints Ambassadors and other diplomatic representatives of India abroad, the Commissioners of SCs and STs, Backward Classes and Minorities, Governors of States and Lt. Governors, Chief Commissioner and Administrators of Union Territories, members of Finance Commission and inter-State Council. Moreover every appointment in the Union Government is made in the name of President or under his authority.

(9) He is the Supreme Commander of the Indian defence forces.

(10) He summons, prorogues and addresses the Parliament. He also dissolves the Lok Sabha.

(11) He can grant pardons, reprieves, respites or remissions of punishments.

Legislative Powers of the President.—When both the Houses of Parliament are not in session and if the President is satisfied that circumstances exist which render it necessary for him to take immediate action, he may promulgate Ordinances. The Ordinances after promulgation by President of India have become the same force and effect as an Act of Parliament.

The Ordinance after promulgation is laid before both the Houses of Parliament and shall cease to operate at the expiration of 6 weeks from the re-assembly of Parliament, or, if before the expiration of that period resolutions disapproving it are passed by both Houses, upon the passing of those resolutions and the ordinances may be withdrawn any time by the President. [Article 123]

VICE-PRESIDENT OF INDIA

The Vice-President is *ex-officio* Chairman of Rajya Sabha *i.e.* Council of States but when he performs the duty of President in his absence, he is seized to be *ex-officio* Chairman of the Rajya Sabha.

The Vice-President acts as President or discharges his functions during casual vacancies or during absence of President. The Vice-President is elected by the members of electoral college of members of both Lok Sabha and Rajya Sabha in accordance with the System of proper representations by means of single transferable secret ballot system.

The Vice-President can be removed from his office on resolution by majority of members of Rajya Sabha and such resolution must be agreed upon by the Lok Sabha but subject to 14 days notice regarding such resolution, he can hold his office until his successor enters into his office. The Vice-President takes oath from President of India or from any other authority appointed on his behalf.

PRIME MINISTER

Prime Minister of India is the leader of the majority party in Lok Sabha. He is the head of the Council of Ministers. His functions include to aid and advise the President in the exercise of his functions.

Office of Prime Minister (The PM House).—It is the secretariat of the Prime Minister. His office includes liaison with the union ministries and the State Governments on matters in which the Prime Minister may be interested. The Prime Minister becomes the Chairman of the Planning Commission in India. Prime Minister is the head of the Council of Ministers.

The Prime Minister after being elected unanimously by his political party in Lok Sabha, is appointed by the President and the other ministers are appointed by President on the advice of the Prime Minister. He communicates to the President all decisions of the Council of Ministers relating to the administration of the affairs of the union and proposals for legislation. [Article 78]

ATTORNEY-GENERAL FOR INDIA

The Attorney-General for India is the first law officer of the country. He is appointed by the President and holds office during the pleasure of the President. A person to be qualified to be the Attorney-General must be eligible for the post of a Judge of Supreme Court. The Attorney-General gives advice to the Central Government on legal matters. He can take part in the proceedings of Parliament without the right to vote. [Article 76]

PARLIAMENT OF INDIA

The constitution of Parliament includes composition of Council of States (Rajya Sabha), composition of the House of People (Lok Sabha) and President of India.

The Rajya Sabha consist of 12 members who are nominated by President and upto 238 representatives of States and of the Union territories.

The allocation of seats in the Council of States to be filled by representatives of the States and of the Union territories.

The representatives of each State in the Council of States shall be elected by the elected members of the Legislative Assembly of the State in accordance with system of proportional representation by means of single transferable vote.

The representatives of the Union Territories in Rajya Sabha (Council of States) are chosen under any law made by the Parliament.

The Lok Sabha consists of 500 members. Two members are nominated by the President to represent the Anglo-Indian community.

The Constitution's 91st Amendment of 2003 says that the total number of ministers including the Prime Minister in Lok Sabha shall not exceed 15% of the total number of members of Lok Sabha.

POWERS OF LOK SABHA AND RAJYA SABHA

In the matter of Ordinary Bills, Lok Sabha and Rajya Sabha do not stand in distinctive root. In case of Money Bills, Lok Sabha enjoys a pre-eminent position. A Money Bill cannot be introduced in Rajya Sabha and it has no power to amend or reject. Rajya Sabha has two special powers. It empowers Parliament to make legislations with respect to a matter in the State List and it empowers Parliament to create new All India Services.

MONEY BILL

The Money Bill deals with borrowings of the Government of India, custody and maintenance of Consolidated Fund, Contingent Fund or Public Accounts of India and audit of accounts of Union and States. It also deals with imposition and abolition of tax. The important point is that the Bill is Money Bill or not, depends upon the Speaker of Lok Sabha. The Money Bill originates in Lok Sabha on recommendation of President. When the Money Bill is sent to Rajya Sabha and Rajya Sabha fails to recommend it within 14 days when it is sent after passing in Lok Sabha and sent to Rajya Sabha, then it is considered that the Bill has been passed by both the Lok Sabha and Rajya Sabha and then is finally sent to President for his assent. [Articles 109 and 110]

ORDINARY BILL

Any Bill except Money Bill is introduced in either House and passes through three various stages like first reading, second reading, committee stages and report stage and third reading. After its passing in the Lok Sabha it is sent to Rajya Sabha and after its passing in Rajya Sabha it is sent to President for his assent and after the President gives his assent, it becomes the law.

QUALIFICATION FOR MEMBERSHIP OF PARLIAMENT

A person must be citizen of India, he must not be less than 25 years in case of Lok Sabha membership and must not be less than 30 years in case of Rajya Sabha.

GROUNDS FOR DISQUALIFICATION OF MEMBERS OF PARLIAMENT

A member of Parliament can be disqualified if he:
  (a) holds any office of profit, [Article 102(1)(a)]
  (b) is declared of unsound mind by a competent court, [Article 102(1)(b)]
  (c) is an undischarged insolvent, [Article 102(1)(c)]
  (d) ceases to be a citizen of India, [Article 102(1)(d)]
  (e) if he absents himself for 60 days (from Parliament in case he is a member of Parliament) without permission of Parliament.

The matter of disqualification is decided by the President in accordance with the advice of Election Commission of India. [Article 103]

ANTI-DEFECTION

The provision for Anti-Defection is contained in 10th Schedule to the Constitution which was introduced by the 52nd Amendment to the Constitution in the year 1985. If a member defects from his party to some other party he is disqualified by the Speaker but his disqualification is subject to the judicial review.

There are two exceptions in which case no disqualification occurs:
  (a) no member can be disqualified if a group of 1/3 of members of party decide to split.
  (b) or if a group of 2/3 of the total members of a party decide to merge with some other party.

PRIVILEGES AND IMMUNITIES OF PARLIAMENT AND ITS MEMBERS

The Constitution guarantees freedom of speech in Parliament and freedom of publication of its proceedings. The Parliament also has the power to punish any person for violating its privileges. The Members of Parliament (MPs) are immune from arrest in civil cases while the Parliament is in Session and for 40 days before and after. In criminal cases, they cannot be arrested while House is in Session.

PARLIAMENTARY COMMITTEES

The Parliamentary committees are device for effective control over the executive. In this context, the following three committees are important because of excercising financial control:
  (1) *Public Accounts Committee.*—It consists of 22 members (15 from Lok Sabha + 7 from Rajya Sabha). It ensures that the government spends money in accordance with the

sanction of the Parliament. It is headed by an opposition member. The Comptroller and Auditor General (CAG) of India assists the Committee.

(2) *Estimates Committee.*—It consists of 30 members all of whom are drawn from Lok Sabha. It reports on what committees or administrative reforms can be effective to ensure efficiency of administration.

(3) *Committee on Public Undertakings.*—It consists of 22 members (15 from Lok Sabha + 7 from Rajya Sabha). It examines the accounts of public undertakings and sees whether they are being run on sound business principles.

SESSIONS OF PARLIAMENT

Between two Sessions of Parliament, there should not be more than six months gap. In case of pendency of Bills and other business of the House the Bills do not lapse on the prorogation of a Session. When it meets after prorogation, the House takes up these pending matters. A fresh House is reconstituted after the dissolution of House. It may be noted that only Lok Sabha dissolves after expiry of its normal term of five years or in any other case during such tenure, but the Rajya Sabha is a permanent House. The President is authority to dissolve Lok Sabha on the advice of Prime Minister. If any Bill is pending in Rajya Sabha but not passed in Lok Sabha it does not lapse at the dissolution of Lok Sabha but other Bills lapse.

The President may address either House of Parliament or both Houses assembled together. At the commencement of first Session after each general election to the House of People and at the commencement of the first Session of each year the President shall address both the Houses of Parliament.

The Vice-President of India is the *ex-officio* Chairman of the Council of States.

JOINT SESSION OF PARLIAMENT

In a case, where a Bill passed by one House is rejected by other House and in case where the amendment proposed to a Bill in one House is rejected by other House and also in case the other House does not take any action into a Bill for continuous 6 months, then President can call a Joint Session of both Lok Sabha and Rajya Sabha. The Joint Session is presided by Speaker of Lok Sabha. His decision becomes final if it receives the majority opinion of members present.

COMPTROLLER AND AUDITOR-GENERAL OF INDIA

The CAG is appointed by the President under his own hand and seal. [Article 148]

The Comptroller and Auditor-General exercises the powers in relation to the accounts of the Union and of the States and of any other authority or body prescribed by the Parliament. [Article 149]

The Comptroller and Auditor-General of India in case of accounts of Union submits the report to the President of India who shall cause them to be laid before both Lok Sabha and Rajya Sabha.

The report of Comptroller and Auditor-General of India in relation to the accounts of States is submitted to the Governor of State and such report is laid before the Legislature of that State. [Article 151]

The Comptroller and Auditor-General is the guardian of public purse and is called the Fourth Pillar of Indian Constitution. His term is 6 years or upto the age 65 years. He guides the Public Accounts Committee of the Parliament.

GOVERNORS OF STATES

The Governor is the Chief Executive of State. The same person can be appointed by President for two or more States. The Governor holds office during the pleasure of President and he holds office for a term of 5 years from the date he enters into his office.

A person is eligible for appointment as a Governor if he is a citizen of India and has completed the age of 35 years. [Article 157]

The Governor can grant pardons, suspend, remit or commute sentences in certain cases. [Article 161]

The Governor appoints Chief Minister and also other ministers of that State on the advice of the Chief Minister. [Article 164]

The total number of ministers, including Chief Minister in the Council of Ministers shall not exceed 15% of total number of members of Legislative Assembly of that State. [Article 164(1A)]

The Governor of a State appoints the Advocate General for that State who holds office during the pleasure of Governor. [Article 165]

All executive action of a State is taken in the name of the Governor. [Article 166]

Legislative Power of Governor.—The Governor promulgates Ordinances if he thinks to take immediate action on any circumstances only when the Legislative Assembly or Legislative Council if any is/are not in session. [Article 213]

SUPREME COURT OF INDIA

The Supreme Court consists of Chief Justice of India and 25 other judges. The Chief Justice and other judges are appointed by the President of India and they hold office upto the age of 65 years. [Article 124(1) and (2)]

A judge addresses his resignation to the President. A person to be a judge of Supreme Court must be a citizen of India, must be a judge for at least 5 years in any High Court, must have been an advocate for at least 10 years in any High Court. [Article 124(2) and (3)]

A judge of Supreme Court can be impeached by an order of President passed after an address by each House of Parliament supported by a majority of the total membership of that House or by a majority of not less than 2/3 of members of the House present and voting has been presented to President in the same session for such removal on the ground of proved misbehaviour or incapacity. [Article 124(4)]

A Judge of Supreme Court after his retirement and during his tenure in the Supreme Court cannot practise in any Court or in any authority throughout India. [Article 124(7)]

A Supreme Court is the court of record and has power to punish for its own contempt. [Article 129]

The Supreme Court has the original jurisdiction in any dispute between the Government of India and one or more States between the Government of India and any State or States on one side and one or more other States on the other or between two or more States. [Article 131]

An appeal shall also lie to the Supreme Court from any judgment, decree or final order of a High Court if the matter involves a substantial question of law. [Article 132]

An appeal shall also lie to the Supreme Court from any judgment, decree or final order in a civil proceeding of a High Court, if the case involves a substantial question of law. [Article 133]

An appeal shall also lie to the Supreme Court from any judgment, final order or sentence in a criminal proceeding of a High Court. [Article 134]

The Supreme Court can in its discretion grant special leave to appeal from any judgment, decree, determination, sentence or order in any cause or matter passed or made by any court or tribunal. [Article 136]

The Supreme Court has power to review its own judgment. [Article 137]

Law declared by Supreme Court is binding on all courts in India. [Article 141]

Where in case a question of law and fact arises and if the President of India thinks proper, he can refer the matter to it for consideration and the Supreme Court if it thinks fit can report to the President about its opinion. [Article 143]

All civil and judicial authorities shall act in aid of Supreme Court. [Article 144]

Supreme Court has power to make rules from time to time with the previous approval of the President of India for the practice and procedure of the court (Supreme Court). [Article 145]

STATE LEGISLATURE

States legislature consists of Governor and Legislative Assembly but where there are two Houses like in Bihar, Maharashtra, Karnataka and Uttar Pradesh then the legislature consists of Governor, Legislative Council and Legislative Assembly. [Article 168]

Parliament can abolish the legislative council in the States. [Article 169]

The Legislative Assembly of a State shall consist of 500 members maximum and 60 members in minimum elected, directly by the people of their territorial constituencies. [Article 170]

Members of Legislative Council shall not exceed $1/3$rd of total number of members in the Legislative Assembly in that State but the total number of members in Legislative Council shall not be less than 40. [Article 171]

Duration of State Legislature is 5 years from the date of its first meeting. [Article 172]

A person to be qualified for being a member of Legislative Assembly must be a citizen of India, must be of 25 years of age and in case of member of Legislative Council the minimum age is 30 years at the time of membership. [Article 173]

According to the Constitution 91st Amendment in 2003 the total number of ministers including Chief Minister shall not exceed 15% of the total number of members in the Legislative Assembly.

Speaker and Deputy Speaker of the Legislative Assembly.—The Speaker and Deputy Speaker are appointed by the Legislative Assembly of State. [Article 178]

Every member of Legislative Assembly or Legislative Council takes oath from the Governor. [Article 188]

The decision for disqualifications of members rests upon Governor. [Article 192]

A money bill is not introduced in legislative council, it is introduced in the Legislative Assembly. [Article 198]

A Bill is money bill or not is provided in Article 199.

A Bill to be converted into an Act is presented to Governor for his assent, after being passed by Legislative Assembly or by the Legislative Assembly and Legislative Council if there are bicameral system like in States of Bihar, Karnataka, Maharashtra and Uttar Pradesh. [Article 200]

HIGH COURTS IN THE STATES

In each State there is one High Court. [Article 214]

Every High Court is the Court of Record and shall have all the powers of such a court including the power for contempt. [Article 215]

Every High Court consists of Chief Justice and some other Judges as per President's discretion. [Article 216]

Every Judge of High Court is appointed by President of India and holds office upto the age of 62 years. A Judge addresses his resignation to the President of India. [Article 217]

A Judge of a High Court takes oath from the Governor of that State. [Article 219]

A retired judge of a High Court cannot practice in same High Court but he can practise in the other High Courts and in the Supreme Court. [Article 220]

The High Court has power to issue to any person or authority, any direction, order or writs including writs in nature of *habeas corpus, mandamus*, prohibition, *quo warranto* and *certiorari* for the enforcement of any fundamental rights. [Article 226]

Every High Court has power of superintendence over all courts and tribunals throughout its territories of that State. [Article 227]

SUBORDINATE COURTS

The District Judge is appointed by the Governor in consultation with High Court. His appointment is subject to recommendation of High Court. [Article 233]

Other judicial officers, other than District Judges are appointed by the Governor in consultation with the State Public Service Commission and the High Court. [Article 234]

UNION TERRITORIES

Every Union territory is administered by President of India through the administrator appointed by him with such designation as he may specify. [Article 239]

Parliament has power to create the local legislatures or Council of Ministers or both, for certain Union territories. [Article 239A]

After 69th Amendment of the Constitution in the year 1991 the Union Territory of Delhi is called the National Capital Territory of Delhi and the administrator is designated as Lieutenant Governor.

In Delhi there is Legislative Assembly and the members of such Assembly are directly elected by the people from territorial constituencies in NCT of Delhi. [Article 239AA]

Parliament constitutes a High Court for a Union Territory or declares any court in any such territory to be a High Court. [Article 241]

PANCHAYATS

There are Panchayats at the village, intermediate and at the district levels. But the Panchayats at the intermediate level may not be constituted in a State where the population does not exceed 20 lakhs. [Article 243B]

State Legislature has power to make provisions by various enactments for the composition of Panchayats in that State. [Article 243C]

Some seats are reserved to SCs and STs in the States. [Article 243D]

Every Panchayat is continued for a period of 5 years unless it is dissolved under any law for time being in force. [Article 243E]

A person can be disqualified from being a member of Panchayat if he is so desqualified by or under any law. [Article 243F]

The powers, authority and responsibilities of Panchayat are laid down under the law by the State Government. [Article 243G]

The Panchayats can impose taxes and raise funds. [Article 243H]

The State Election Commission is vested with powers of superintendence, direction and control of the preparation of electoral rolls for the conduct of all elections to the Panchayats. [Article 243K]

MUNICIPALITIES

In every State, a Nagar Panchayat, Municipal Councils and Municipal Corporation are constituted for a transitional area for smaller urban area and for larger urban area accordingly. [Article 243Q]

All the seats in a Municipality are filled by direct election from the territorial constituencies in Municipal area. [Article 243R].

Where in an area there is more than 3 lakhs or more population, the wards committees are constituted. [Article 243S].

The seats are reserved for the Scheduled Castes and Scheduled Tribes in every Municipality in a State. [Article 243T]

Every Municipality unless it is dissolved by any law, continues till 5 years. [Article 243U].

The State Government may by law endow the Municipalities with such powers and authority and responsibilities and makes provisions for such purpose. [Article 243W]

The State Governments make laws for the provision to impose taxes, raise funds by the Municipalities. [Article 243X]

The Finance Commission constituted by the Governor of a State under Article 243-I reviews the financial position of the Municipalities and make recommendations to the Governor. [Article 243Y]

Powers of superintendence, direction and control of the preparation of electoral rolls for the conduct of elections to the Municipalities is vested in the State Election Commission. [Article 243ZA]

A District Planning Committee is constituted in every State to consolidate the plans prepared by Panchayats and the Municipalities in the District and to prepare a draft development plan for the district. [Article 243ZD]

The State Government makes the provision for Constitution of Metropolitan Planning Committee for preparing draft development plan for Metropolitan Area. [Article 243ZE]

THE SCHEDULED AND TRIBAL AREAS

The provisions of Fifth Schedule shall apply to the administrative control of the Scheduled Areas and Scheduled Tribes in any State except the States of Assam, Meghalaya, Tripura and Mizoram. In these States the provisions of Sixth Schedule apply. [Article 244]

Parliament has formed an autonomous State in the State of Assam. [Article 244A]

RELATION BETWEEN THE UNION AND THE STATES

The Parliament may make the law for the whole or any part of the territory of India and the State Legislature makes the law for the whole or any part of the State. [Article 245]

Parliament has power to make any law for the whole of India or any part of India for implementing any international treaty, international agreement or conventions. [Article 253]

There is a provision for administrative relations between States and Centre. [Articles 256 to 261]

Parliament by law provides for the adjudication of disputes relating to waters of inter-State river or river valleys. [Article 262]

President by order establishes the inter-State Council if he thinks that the public interest shall be served by such Council. [Article 263]

Provision has been made for consolidated funds and public accounts of India and States. [Article 266]

Provision has been made for Contingency Fund of India. [Article 267]

Stamp duties and duties on medicinal and toilet preparations mentioned in Union List is levied by Government of India and collected and appropriated by States. [Article 268]

Service tax is levied by Government of India, collected and appropriated by the Union of India and the States. [Article 268A]

Taxes on sale and purchase of goods and taxes on consignment of goods are levied and collected by the Government of India and is assigned to State Governments. [Article 269]

Taxes mentioned in Union List are levied and distributed between the Union of India and States. [Article 270]

Grants are given by the Union to certain States. [Article 275]

Provision for taxes on professions, trades, callings and employments have been made. [Article 276]

President at the expiration of every 5th year or earlier, by order constitutes the Finance Commission. [Article 280]

President causes every recommendation of Finance Commission to be laid before each House of Parliament. [Article 281]

The custody of the consolidated Fund of India and the Contingency Fund of India, and the payment of money into such funds and the withdrawal of moneys therefrom, the custody of public moneys other than those credited such funds received by or on behalf of Government of India, etc. are regulated by rules made by Parliament. [Article 283]

Provision has been made for custody of Suitor's deposits and other moneys received by public servants and courts. [Article 284]

The property of the Union is exempted from all taxes imposed by State or by any authority within a State. [Article 285]

Adjustments can be made in respect of certain expenses and pensions. [Article 290]

The executive power of the Union expands to borrowing upon security of the consolidated fund of India within limit of Parliament's discretion and guarantee to that limits. [Article 292]

The executive power of a State extends to borrowing within the India upon the security of the consolidated fund of State as limit fixed by State Legislature and subject to limit of guarantee. [Article 293]

Provisions have been made for property contracts, rights, liabilities, obligations and suits. [Articles 294 to 300]

All contracts made in exercise of the executive power of the Union or of a State. [Article 299]

The Government of India may sue or be sued in the name of Union of India. [Article 300]

RIGHT TO PROPERTY

No person shall be deprived of his property save by authority of law. [Article 300A]

FREEDOM OF TRADE, COMMERCE AND INTERCOURSE

The trade, commerce and intercourse throughout the territory of India are free. [Article 301]

Parliament has power to impose restrictions on trade, commerce and intercourse between one State and another. [Article 302]

Parliament and the State Legislature has no power to make laws giving or authorising the giving of any preference to one State over another, or making or authorising the making of any discrimination between one State and another. [Article 303]

Restrictions on trade, commerce and intercourse among States are made under Article 304.

SERVICES

Parliament may by law provide for the creation of one or more all-India Services. [Article 312(1)]

PUBLIC SERVICE COMMISSIONS

There is provision for Public Service Commissions for the Union and States. [Article 315]

The Chairman and other members of the Public Service Commission are appointed by the President in case of Union Public Service Commission and in case of State Public Service Commission they are appointed by Governor of that State. [Article 316]

The President and Governors have powers to make regulations as to their number and conditions of service of members and staff of the Commission in case of Union and States respectively. [Article 318]

ADMINISTRATIVE TRIBUNALS

The law provides for the adjudication or trial by administrative tribunals of disputes and complaints with respect to recruitment and conditions of service of persons appointed to public services and posts, etc. [Article 323A], and Tribunals for other matters. [Article 323B]

ELECTIONS

The Superintendence, direction and control of the preparation of the electoral rolls for the conduct of all elections to Parliament and State Legislature and for the offices of President and Vice-President are vested in the Election Commission of India. [Article 324]

A person is not to be ineligible for inclusion in or to claim to be included in a special, electoral roll on grounds of religion, race, caste or sex. [Article 325]

Elections to the House of the People and to the Legislative Assemblies of States are made on the basis of adult suffrage. [Article 326]

The validity of any law relating to the delimitation of constituencies or the allotment of seats to such constituencies, made or purporting to be made under Article 327 or Article 328 shall not be called upon in question in any court. [Article 329]

RESERVATION OF SEATS FOR SCs AND STs

The seats are reserved for SCs and STs except to STs in autonomous districts of Assam and STs in the autonomous districts of Assam. [Article 330]

The President nominates upto two members of the Anglo-Indian Community to Lok Sabha. [Article 331]

The State Governments reserve appropriate number of seats for the SCs and STs except STs in the autonomous districts of Assam. [Article 332]

The Governor nominates one member of the Anglo-Indian Community to the Legislative Assembly. [Article 333]

The claims of SCs and STs to services and posts can be taken into considerations. [Article 335]

Appointment of members of Anglo-Indian Community of certain services shall be made as same basis as immediately before 15th August, 1947. [Article 336]

Special provision has been made with respect to educational grants for the benefit of Anglo-Indian Community. [Article 337]

There shall be a National Commission for Scheduled Castes with power to regulate its own procedure. [Article 338]

There shall be separate National Commission for Scheduled Tribes. [Article 338A]

Provision has been made for control of Union over the administration of Scheduled Areas and the Welfare of Scheduled Tribes in the States. [Article 339]

The President, by order appoints a Commission to report to Union Government regarding appointment of a Commission to investigate the conditions of backward classes within the territory of India. [Article 340]

The President after consultations with Governors of States, by public notification, specify the castes, races, tribes, parts or groups within castes, races and tribes to be the Scheduled Castes. [Article 341]

President after consultation with the Governors of States, by public notification, specify the tribes or tribal community or parts or groups within tribes or tribal communities to be the Scheduled Tribes. [Article 342]

LANGUAGE OF THE UNION

The official language of the Union shall be Hindi in Devnagari Script. [Article 343]

The official language or languages of a State, shall be as the State Legislature adopt. [Article 345]

The English language shall be used in the Supreme Court and High Courts. [Article 348]

The special officers for linguistic minorities are appointed by President. [Article 350B]

EMERGENCY PROVISIONS

President has power to proclaim the Emergency in case when the security of India is threatened by internal or, external aggression. [Article 352]

During the proclamation of emergency the executive power of the union shall extend to States and Parliament has power to make laws and impose duties and authorities. [Article 353]

President may effect the application of provisions relating to distribution of revenues while a proclamation of emergency is in operation, if he thinks fit. [Article 354].

It is the duty of the union to protect States against external aggression and internal disturbance. [Article 355]

If the President, on receipt of report from the Governor of a State that a situation has arisen in which the Government of State cannot be carried on, the President if thinks fit declares the State emergency for that State. [Article 356]

The provisions of Article 19, *i.e.* protection of rights regarding freedom of speech, can be suspended during emergency. [Article 358]

MISCELLANEOUS PROVISIONS

The President and Governors and Rajpramukhs of States cannot be answerable for their duties of their offices. [Article 361]

Provision has been made for protection of publications of proceedings of Parliament and State Legislatures. [Article 361A]

Any disqualified member of political party, shall be disqualified from appointment on remunerative political post. [Article 361B]

Special provisions as to major ports and aerodromes. [Article 364]

If any State fails to comply with, or to give effect to, the directions given by the Union President can hold that Government of that State cannot be carried on. [Article 365]

AMENDMENT OF CONSTITUTION

Parliament has power to amend the Constitution. [Article 368]

TEMPORARY, TRANSITIONAL AND SPECIAL PROVISIONS

Parliament has temporary power to make laws with respect to certain matters in the State List as if they were matters in the Concurrent List. [Article 369]

SPECIAL PROVISIONS WITH RESPECT TO THE STATE OF JAMMU AND KASHMIR

The provisions of Article 238 shall not apply to the State of Jammu and Kashmir and the power of Parliament is limited to make laws for the State on some transitory matter. [Article 370]

SPECIAL PROVISIONS FOR SOME STATES

Special provisions have been made for the States of Maharashtra and Gujarat under Article 371, State of Nagaland under Article 371A, State of Assam under Article 371B, State of Manipur under Article 371C, State of Andhra Pradesh under Article 371D, State of Sikkim under Article 371F, State of Mizoram under Article 371G, State of Arunachal Pradesh under Article 371H and State of Goa under Article 371-I, respectively.

SPECIAL POWER OF PRESIDENT

The President enjoys the power to make order in respect of persons under the preventive detention in certain cases. [Article 373]

SCHEDULES TO THE CONSTITUTION

First Schedule	—	Territorial demarcations of States and Union Territories (28 States and 7 Union Territories).
Second Schedule	—	President and Governors of States.
Third Schedule	—	Form of oath or affirmations.
Fourth Schedule	—	Allocation of seats in Rajya Sabha (Total 233 seats).
Fifth Schedule	—	Administration and control of Scheduled Areas and Scheduled Tribes.
Sixth Schedule	—	Administration of Tribal Areas in North-Eastern States.
Seventh Schedule	—	Union List, State List and Concurrent List (Distribution of Legislative Subjects between Union and States).
Eighth Schedule	—	Languages (Now 22 languages, 92nd Amendment to the Constitution added Maithili, Santhali, Bodo and Dogri as four new languages).
Ninth Schedule	—	Allied laws and regulations saved for judicial review.
Tenth Schedule	—	Disqualification on the ground of defection (This Schedule followed latest developments by 91st amendment to the Constitution in 2003).
Eleventh Schedule	—	Panchayats.
Twelfth Schedule	—	Urban and Local self governments.

IMPORTANT ARTICLES AND SCHEDULES AT A GLANCE

Article 1	— Name and Territory of Union of India,
Article 2	— New States,
Article 5	— Citizenship,
Article 14	— Equality before law,
Article 15	— Prohibition of discrimination,
Article 17	— Abolition of untouchability,
Article 19	— Freedom of speech,
Article 21	— Protection of life and personal liberty,
Article 21A	— Right to education,
Article 32	— Right to move Supreme Court for enforcement of fundamental rights,
Article 39	— Directive Principles of State Policy,
Article 39A	— Equal justice and free legal aid,
Article 41	— Right to work,
Article 44	— Uniform Civil Code,
Article 45	— Provision for free and compulsory education,
Article 48A	— Protection of environment,
Article 51A	— Fundamental duties,
Article 75(1A)	— Number of Ministers of Union,
Article 123	— Ordinance by President,
Article 124	— Supreme Court,
Article 141	— Law declared by Supreme Court to be binding by all courts,
Article 164(1A)	— Number of ministers in a State,
Article 215	— High Court is the Court of Record,
Article 300A	— Right to property,
Articles 341 and 342	— Scheduled Castes and Scheduled Tribes,
Article 352	— Emergency Provisions,
Article 370	— Special Provision for State of J&K.
Schedule 1	— Names of States and union territories,
Schedule 7	— Union List, State List and Concurrent List,
Schedule 8	— Languages,
Schedule 10	— Disqualification on the ground of defection.

IMPORTANT CASELAWS ON FUNDAMENTAL RIGHTS

Right	Caselaw	Citation
Right to go abroad	*Satwant Singh Sawhney* v. *D. Ramaratnam, A.P.O., New Delhi*	(1967) 3 SCR 525: AIR 1967 SC 1836
Right to privacy	*Govind* v. *State of Madhya Pradesh*	(1975) 2 SCC 148: AIR 1975 SC 1378
Right against solitary confinement	*Sunil Batra* v. *Delhi Administration*	(1978) 4 SCC 494: AIR 1978 SC 1675
Right against bar fetters	*Charles Sobhraj* v. *Suptd., Central Jail*	(1978) 4 SCC 104: AIR 1978 SC 1514
Right to legal aid	*M.H. Hoskot* v. *State of Maharashtra*	(1978) 3 SCC 544: AIR 1978 SC 1548

Right	Caselaw	Citation
Right to speedy trial	Hussainara Khatoon v. Home Secretary, State of Bihar	(1980) 1 SCC 81: AIR 1979 SC 1360
Right against handcuffing	Prem Shankar Shukla v. Delhi Administration	(1980) 3 SCC 526: AIR 1980 SC 1535
Right against delayed execution	T.V. Vatheeswaram v. State of Tamil Nadu	(1983) 2 SCC 68: AIR 1983 SC 361
Right against custodial violence	Sheela Barse v. State of Maharashtra	(1983) 2 SCC 96: AIR 1983 SC 378
Right against public hanging	A.G. of India v. Lachma Devi	(1989) Supp (1) SCC 264
Right against doctor's assistance	Parmanand Katra v. Union of India	(1989) 4 SCC 286
Right to shelter	Shantistar Builders v. N.K. Totame	(1990) 1 SCC 520: AIR 1990 SC 630
Right to information	Peoples' Union for Civil Liberties v. Union of India	AIR 2004 SC 1442: (2004) 2 SCC 476
	Dattaprasad Co-operative Housing Society Ltd., Bangalore v. Karnataka State Chief Information Commissioner.	AIR 2009 Karn 1

CASELAWS DECLARING CONSTITUTIONAL AMENDMENTS UNCONSTITUTIONAL

ARTICLE	AMENDMENT	YEAR	CASELAW
13(2)	17th Amendment	1964	L.C. Golok Nath v. State of Punjab, AIR 1967 SC 1643
31C	25th Amendment	1971	Keshavananda Bharati v. State of Kerala, AIR 1973 SC 1461
371 (1)	32nd Amendment	1973	P. Sambamurthy v. Union of India, AIR 1987 SC 663
329	36th Amendment	1975	Indira Nehru Gandhi v. Raj Narain, AIR 1975 SC 2299
368(4) & (5)	42nd Amendment	1972	Minerva Mills Ltd. v. Union of India, AIR 1980 SC 1789
10th Schedule Para 7	42nd Amendment	1972	Kihota v. Zachilhu, AIR 1993 SC 412.

RELEVANT CASELAWS/REPORTS LEADING TO
AMENDMENT TO CONSTITUTION

Caselaw	Amendment	Year
Saghir Ahmed v. *State of Uttar Pradesh,* AIR 1954 SC 728	4th Amendment	1955
State of Bombay v. *United Motors India (P) Limited,* AIR 1953 SC 252	6th Amendment	1956
Bengal Immunity Company Ltd. v. *State of Bihar,* AIR 1955 SC 661	6th Amendment	1956
L.C. Golak Nath v. *State of Punjab,* AIR 1967 SC 1643	24th Amendment	1971
R.C. Cooper v. Union of India, (1970) 3 SCR 530: AIR 1970 SC 564	25th Amendment	1971
Misrilal Jain v. *State of Orissa,* AIR 1977 SC 1686	43rd Amendment	1977
State of Madras v. *M/s. Gannon Dunkerley & Co., Madras,* AIR 1958 SC 560	46th Amendment	1982
State of Himachal Pradesh v. *Associated Hotels of India Ltd.,* AIR 1972 SC 1131	46th Amendment	1982
New India Suger Mills v. *Commissioner of Sales Tax, Bihar,* AIR 1963 SC 1207	46th Amendment	1982
Oil and Natural Gas Commission v. *State of Bihar,* AIR 1976 SC 2478	46th Amendment	1982
Vishu Agencies v. *Commercial Tax Officer,* AIR 1978 SC 449	46th Amendment	1982
Northern India Caterers (India) Ltd. v. *Lt. Governor of Delhi,* AIR 1978 SC 1581	46th Amendment	1982
Prabha Karan Nair v. *State of Tamil Nadu,* (1985) 1 SCC 290	75th Amendment	1993
Indira Sawhney v. *Union of India,* AIR 1993 SC 447	76th Amendment	1994
Indra Sawhney v. *Union of India,* (2000) 1 SCC 168: JT (1999) 9 SC 557	81st Amendment	2000
S. Vinod Kumar v. *Union of India,* (1996) 6 SCC 580	82nd Amendment	2000
Indira Sawhney v. *Union of India,* AIR 1993 SC 477	82nd Amendment	2000
Union of India v. *Virpal Singh Chauhan,* (1995) 6 SCC 684	85th Amendment	2001
Ajit Singh Januja v. *State of Punjab,* (1996) 2 SCC 715	85th Amendment	2001
Committee on Electoral Reforms (Dinesh Goswany Committee) 1990	91st Amendment	2003
170th Law Commission of India Report on "Reform of Electoral Laws" 1999	91st Amendment	2003
National Commission to Review the Working of Constitution (Venkatachaliah Report) (NCRWC) 2002	91st Amendment	2003

SUPREME COURT ON VALIDITY OF CONSTITUTIONAL AMENDMENTS

Caselaw	Amendment	year
Akadasi Pradhan v. *State of Orissa*, AIR 1963 SC 1047	1st Amendment (Validity)	1951
Indra Sawhney v. *Union of India*, AIR 1993 SC 477	1st Amendment (Constitutionality)	1951
Bengal Immunity Company Ltd v. *State of Bihar*, AIR 1955 SC 661	6th Amendment (Concern on procedure for Amendment)	1956
L.C. Golakanath v. *State of Punjab*, AIR 1967 SC 1643	24th Amendment (Procedure for Amendment)	1971
Keshavananda Bharati v. *State of Kerala*, AIR 1973 SC 1461	7th and 26th Amendment (Validity)	1956 & 1971
P. Sambamurthy v. *State of Andhra Pradesh*, AIR 1987 SC 663	32nd Amendment (Unconstitutionality)	1973
Minerva Mills Ltd v. *Union of India*, AIR 1980 SC 1789 *Misrilal Jain* v. *Sate of Orissa*, AIR 1977 SC 1686	42nd Amendment (Validity)	1976

LIST OF ALLIED AMENDING ACTS AMENDING CONSTITUTION

1951:   Assam (Alteration of Boundaries) Act

1953:   Andhra State Act

1954:   Lushai Hills District (Change of Name) Act

1954:   Himanchal Pradesh and Bilaspur (New State) Act

1954:   Chandernagore (Merger) Act

1956:   States Reorganisation Act

1956:   Bihar and West Bengal (Transfer of Territories) Act

1959:   Rajasthan and Madhya Pradesh (Transfer of Territories) Act

1959:   Andhra Pradesh and Madras (Alteration of Territories) Act

1960:   Bombay Reorganisation Act

1960:   Acquired Territories (Merger) Act

1962:   State of Nagaland Act

1966:   Punjab Reoganisation Act

1968:   ·Bihar and Uttar Pradesh (Alteration of Boundaries) Act

1968:   Andhra Pradesh and Mysore (Transfer of Territory) Act

1968:   Madras State (Alteration of Name) Act

1969:   West Bengal Legislative Council (Abolition) Act

1969:   Punjab Legislative Council (Abolition) Act

1969:	Assam Reoganisation (Meghalaya) Act
1970:	State of Himachal Pradesh Act
1971:	North-Eastern Areas (Reorganisation) Act
1971:	Government of Union Territories (Amendment) Act
1973:	Mysore State (Alteration of Name) Act
1973:	Laccadive Minicoy and Amindevi Islands (Alteration of Name) Act
1974:	Repealing and Amending Act
1976:	Fifth Schedule to the Constitution (Amendment) Act
1979:	Haryana and Uttar Pradesh (Alteration of Boundaries) Act
1985:	Andhra Pradesh Legislative Council (Abolition) Act
1986:	State of Mizoram Act
1986:	Tamil Nadu Legislative Council (Abolition) Act
1986:	State of Arunachal Pradesh Act
1987:	Goa, Daman and Diu Reorganisation Act
1988:	Sixth Schedule to the Constitution (Amendment) Act
1995:	Sixth Schedule to the Constitution (Amendment) Act
2000:	Bihar Reorganisation Act
2000:	Madhya Pradesh Reorganisation Act
2000:	Uttar Pradesh Reorganisation Act
2006:	Uttranchal (Alteration of Name) Act, 2006 (52 of 2006)
2006:	Pondicherry (Alteration of Name) Act, 2006 (44 of 2006)
2008:	President's (Emoluments and Pension Amendment) Act, 2008 (28 of 2008)
2008:	Governer's (Emoluments, Allowances and Privileges Amendment) Act, 2008 (1 of 2009)
2009:	High Court and Supreme Court Judges (Salaries and Conditions of Service) Amendment Act, 2009 (23 of 2009)
2010:	Tamil Nadu Legislative Council Act, 2010 (18 of 2010).
2011:	The Orissa (Alteration of Name) Act, 2011 (15 of 2011).

AMENDMENTS (TO CONSTITUTION) AT A GLANCE

Amendment No./Year	Date of Assent	Article amended	Article inserted	Article substituted	Article omitted	Sch. added	Sch. amended*/subs.**	Sch. inserted	Amendment of Part
1st (1951)	18th June, 1951	15, 19, 85, 87, 174, 176, 341, 342, 372, 376	31A, 31B	–	–	9th	–	–	–
2nd (1952)	1st May, 1953	81	–	–	–	–	–	–	
3rd (1954)	22nd February, 1955	–	–	–	–	–	7th	–	
4th (1955)	27th April, 1955	31, 31A	–	305	–	–	9th	–	
5th (1955)	24th December, 1955	3	–	–	–	–	–	–	
6th (1956)	11th September, 1956	269, 286	–	–	–	–	7th	–	
7th (1956)	19th October, 1956	1, 3, 16, 31A, 58, 66, 72, 73, 101, 112, 131, 143, 151, 152, 153, 158, 168, 171, 214, 216, 217, 219, 222, 239, 241, 244, 246, 254, 255, 267, 268, 270, 280, 283, 291, 299, 304, 308, 309, 310, 311, 315, 316, 317, 318, 320, 323, 324, 330, 332, 333, 337, 339, 341, 342, 348, 356, 361, 362, 366, 367, 368	258A, 290A, 350A, 350B, 372A, 378A	81, 82, 170, 220, 224, 230, 231, 232, 239, 240, 264, 298, 371	242, 243, 259, 278, 306, 379 to 391	–	1st, 2nd, IVth, Vth, VIth, VIIth & VIIIth	–	Part VI Part IX
8th (1959)	5th January, 1960	334	–	–	–	–	–	–	

Amendment No./Year	Date of Assent	Article amended	Article inserted	Article substituted	Article omitted	Sch. added	Sch. amended*/subs.**	Sch. inserted	Amendment of Part
9th (1960)	28th December, 1960	—	—	—	—	—	1st	—	—
10th (1961)	16th August, 1961	240	—	—	—	—	1st	—	—
11th (1961)	19th December, 1961	66, 71	—	—	—	—	—	—	—
12th (1962)	27th March, 1962	240	—	—	—	—	1st	—	—
13th (1962)	28th December, 1962	—	—	—	—	371A	—	—	XXI
14th (1962)	28 December, 1962	81, 240	239A	—	—	—	1st, 4th	—	—
15th (1963)	5th October, 1963	124, 128, 217, 222, 224, 226, 297, 311, 316	224A	—	—	—	7th	—	—
16th (1963)	5th October, 1963	19, 84, 173	—	—	—	—	3rd	—	—
17th (1964)	20th June, 1964	31A	—	—	—	—	9th	—	—
18th (1966)	27th August, 1966	3	—	—	—	—	—	—	—

Amendment No./Year	Date of Assent	Article amended	Article inserted	Article substituted	Article omitted	Sch. added	Sch. amended*/subs.**	Sch. inserted	Amendment of Part
19th (1966)	11th December, 1966	324	—	—	—	—	—	—	—
20th (1966)	22nd December, 1966	—	233A	—	—	—	—	—	—
21st (1967)	10th April, 1967	—	—	—	—	—	8th	—	—
22nd (1969)	25th September, 1969	275	244A, 371B	—	—	—	—	—	—
23rd (1969)	23rd January, 1970	330, 332, 333, 334	—	—	—	—	—	—	—
24th (1971)	5th November, 1971	13, 368	—	—	—	—	—	—	—
25th (1971)	20th April, 1972	31	31C	—	—	—	—	—	—
26th (1971)	28th December, 1971	366	363A	—	291 & 362	—	—	—	—
27th (1971)	30th December, 1971	239A, 240	239B, 371C	—	—	—	—	—	—
28th (1972)	27th August, 1972	—	312A	—	314	—	—	—	—

Amendment No./Year	Date of Assent	Article amended	Article inserted	Article substituted	Article omitted	Sch. added	Sch. amended*/subs.**	Sch. inserted	Amendment of Part
29th (1972)	9th June, 1972	–	–	–	–	–	9th	–	–
30th (1972)	22nd February, 1973	133	–	–	–	–	–	–	–
31st (1973)	17th October, 1973	81, 330, 332	–	–	–	–	–	–	–
32nd (1973)	3rd May, 1974	371	371D, 371E	–	–	–	7th	–	–
33rd (1974)	19th May, 1974	101, 190	–	–	–	–	–	–	–
34th (1974)	7th September, 1974	–	–	–	–	–	9th	–	–
35th (1974)	2nd February, 1975	80, 81	2A	–	–	10th	–	10th	–
36th (1975)	16th May, 1975	80, 81	371F	–	2A	–	1st, 4th* 10th**	–	–
37th (1975)	3rd May, 1975	–	239A, 240	–	–	–	–	–	–
38th (1975)	1st August, 1975	123, 213, 239B, 352, 356, 359, 360	–	–	–	–	–	–	–

Amendment No./Year	Date of Assent	Article amended	Article inserted	Article substituted	Article omitted	Sch. added	Sch. amended*/subs.**	Sch. inserted	Amendment of Part
39th (1975)	10th August, 1975	329	329A	71	–	–	9th	–	–
40th (1976)	27th May, 1976	–	–	297	–	–	9th	–	–
41st (1976)	7th September, 1976	316	–	–	–	–	–	–	–
42nd (1976)	18th December, 1976	* 31C, 39, 55, 74, 77, 81, 82, 83, 100, 102, 105, 118, 145, 166, 170, 172, 189, 191, 194, 208, 217, 225, 227, 228, 311, 312, 330, 352, 353, 356, 357, 358, 359, 366, 368, 371F	sub-heading after article 31, 31D, 32A, 39A, 43A, 48A, 51A, 131A, 139A, 144A, 226A, 228A, 257A, 323A, 323B	103, 150, 192, 226	–	–	7th	–	Part-IVA and Part-XIVA inserted
43rd (1977)	13th April, 1978	145, 226, 228, 366	–	–	31D, 32A, 131A, 144A, 226A, 228A				
44th (1978)**	30th April, 1979	19, 22, 30, 31A, 31C, 38, 74, 77, 83, 105, 123, 132, 133, 134, 139A, 150, 166, 172, 194, 213, 217, 225, 226, 227, 239B, 329, 352, 356, 358, 359, 360, 371F	134A, 300A, 361A	71, 103, 192	sub-heading after article 30, 31, 257A, 329A		9th	–	Chapter-IV in Part-XII inserted

* Preamble amended.

** In the Constitution (Forty-Second Amendment) Act, 1976, section 18, 19, 21, 22, 31, 32, 34, 35, 58 and 59 omitted.

Amendment No./Year	Date of Assent	Article amended	Article inserted	Article substituted	Article omitted	Sch. added	Sch. amended*/subs.**	Sch. inserted	Amendment of Part
45th (1980)	14th April, 1980	334	—	—	—	—	—	—	—
46th (1982)	2nd February, 1983	269, 286, 366	—	—	—	—	7th	—	—
47th (1984)	26th August, 1984	—	—	—	—	—	9th	—	—
48th (1984)	26th August, 1984	356	—	—	—	—	—	—	—
49th (1984)	11th September, 1984	244	—	—	—	—	5th, 6th	—	—
50th (1984)	11th September, 1984	—	—	13	—	—	—	—	—
51st (1984)	29th April, 1985	330, 332	—	—	—	—	—	—	—
52nd (1985)	15th February, 1985	101, 102, 190, 191	—	—	—	10th	—	—	—
53rd (1986)	14th August, 1986	—	371G	—	—	—	—	—	—
54th (1986)	14th March, 1987	125, 221	—	—	—	—	2nd	—	—

Amendment No./Year	Date of Assent	Article amended	Article inserted	Article substituted	Article omitted	Sch. added	Sch. amended*/subs.**	Sch. inserted	Amendment of Part
55th (1986)	23rd December, 1986	—	371H	—	—	—	—	—	—
56th (1987)	23rd May, 1987	—	371-I	—	—	—	—	—	—
57th (1987)	15th September, 1987	—	Clause 3A in article 332	—	—	—	—	—	—
58th (1987)	9th December, 1987		394A	—	—	—	—	—	Heading of Part-XXII
59th (1988)	30th March, 1988	356	359A	—	—	—	—	—	—
60th (1988)	20th December, 1988	276	—	—	—	—	—	—	—
61st (1988)	28th March, 1989	326	—	—	—	—	—	—	—
62nd (1989)	25th January, 1990	334	—	—	—	—	—	—	—
63rd (1989)	6th January, 1990	356	—	—	359A	—	—	—	—
64th (1990)	16th April, 1990	356	—	—	—	—	—	—	—

Amend-ment No./ Year	Date of Assent	Article amended	Article inserted	Article substituted	Article omitted	Sch. added	Sch. amended*/ subs.**	Sch. inserted	Amendment of Part
65th (1990)	7th June, 1990	338	–	–	–	–	–	–	–
66th (1990)	7th June, 1990	–	–	–	–	–	9th	–	–
67th (1990)	4th October, 1990	356	–	–	–	–	–	–	–
68th (1991)	12th March, 1991	356	–	–	–	–	–	–	–
69th (1991)	21st December, 1991	–	239AA, 239AB	–	–	–	–	–	–
70th (1992)	12th August, 1992	54, 239AA	–	–	–	–	–	–	–
71st (1992)	31st August, 1992	–	–	–	–	–	8th	–	–
72nd (1992)	4th December, 1992	332	–	–	–	–	–	–	–
73rd (1992)	20th April, 1993	280	243, 243A to 243-O	–	–	11th	–	–	IX inserted
74th (1992)	20th April, 1993	280	243P to 243Z 243ZA to 243ZE	–	–	12th	–	–	IXA inserted

Amendment No./Year	Date of Assent	Article amended	Article inserted	Article substituted	Article omitted	Sch. added	Sch. amended*/subs.**	Sch. inserted	Amendment of Part
75th (1993)	5th February, 1994	323B	—	—	—	—	—	—	—
76th (1994)	31st August, 1994	—	—	—	—	—	9th	—	—
77th (1995)	17th June, 1995	16	—	—	—	—	—	—	—
78th (1995)	30th August, 1995	—	—	—	—	—	9th	—	—
79th (1999)	21st January, 2000	334	—	—	—	—	—	—	—
80th (2000)	9th June, 2000	269	—	270	272	—	—	—	—
81st (2000)	9th June, 2000	16	—	—	—	—	—	—	—
82nd (2000)	8th September, 2000	335	—	—	—	—	—	—	—
83rd (2000)	8th September, 2000	243M	—	—	—	—	—	—	—
84th (2001)	21st February, 2002	55, 81, 82, 170, 330, 332	—	—	—	—	—	—	—
85th (2001)	4th January, 2002	16	—	—	—	—	—	—	—
86th (2002)	12th December, 2002	51A	21A	45	—	—	—	—	—

Amendment No./Year	Date of Assent	Article amended	Article inserted	Article substituted	Article omitted	Sch. added	Sch. amended*/subs.**	Sch. inserted	Amendment of Part
87th (2003)	22nd June, 2003	81, 82, 170, 330	—	—	—	—	—	—	—
88th (2003)	15th January, 2004	270	268A	—	—	—	7th	—	—
89th (2003)	28th September, 2003	338	338A	—	—	—	—	—	—
90th (2003)	28th September, 2003	332	—	—	—	—	—	—	—
91st (2003)	1st January, 2004	75, 164	361B	—	—	—	10th	—	—
92nd (2003)	7th January, 2004	—	—	—	—	—	8th	—	—
93rd (2005)	20th January, 2006	15	—	—	—	—	—	—	—
94th (2006)	12th June, 2006	164	—	—	—	—	—	—	—
95th (2009)	18th January, 2010	334	—	—	—	—	8th	—	—
96th (2011)	23rd September, 2011	—	—	—	—	—	—	—	—
97th (2011)	12th January, 2012	19	43B, 243ZH to 243ZT	—	—	—	—	—	IXB inserted

Notes.—(i)   The Fifth Schedule to the Constitution was amended by the Fifth Schedule to the Constitution (Amendment) Act, 1976 (101 of 1976) (w.e.f. 17-9-1976).

(ii)   The Sixth Schedule to the Constitution was amended by the Sixth Schedule to the Constitution (Amendment) Act, 1988 (67 of 1988) in its application to the States of Tripura and Mizoram (w.e.f. 16-12-1988).

THE CONSTITUTION OF INDIA

PREAMBLE

WE, THE PEOPLE OF INDIA, having solemnly resolved to constitute India into a [1][SOVEREIGN SOCIALIST SECULAR DEMOCRATIC REPUBLIC] and to secure to all its citizens:

JUSTICE, social, economic and political;

LIBERTY of thought, expression, belief, faith and worship;

EQUALITY of status and of opportunity;

and to promote among them all

FRATERNITY assuring the dignity of the individual and the [2][unity and integrity of the Nation];

IN OUR CONSTITUENT ASSEMBLY this twenty-sixth day of November, 1949, do HEREBY ADOPT, ENACT AND GIVE TO OURSELVES THIS CONSTITUTION.

Notes on Preamble

Preamble is controlled Constitution not framed by Parliament; *I.R. Coelho* v. *State of Tamil Nadu*, AIR 2007 SC 861: 2007 AIR SCW 611: 2007 (1) All WC 689: 2007 (2) Andh LT 1: 2007 (3) Civ LJ 589: 2007 (2) JCR SC 148: 2007 (1) Ker LT 623: 2007 (3) Mad LJ 423: (2007) 2 SCC 1: (2007) 1 SCALE 197: 2007 (1) Supreme 137.

Constitution is what the judges say it is; *Supreme Court Advocates-on-Records Association* v. *Union of India*, AIR 1994 SC 268: 1993 AIR SCW 4101: JT 1993 (5) SC 479: (1993) 4 SCC 441: 1993 (5) Serv LR 337.

It is well accepted by thinkers, philosphers and academicians that if JUSTICE, LIBERTY, EQUALITY and FRATERNITY, including social, economic and political justice, the golden goals set out in the PREAMBLE OF THE CONSTITUTION, are to be achieved, the Indian polity has to be educated and educated with excellence; *P.A. Inamdar* v. *State of Maharashtra*, (2005) 6 SCC 537: AIR 2005 SC 3226: 2005 AIR SCW 3923: 2005 (4) CTC 81: JT 2005 (7) SC 313: 2005 (5) SCJ 746: 2005 (3) SCT 697: (2005) 6 SCALE 471: 2005 (5) Serv LR 409: 2005 (5) Supreme 544: 2005 (2) UJ (SC) 1176.

Preamble of the Constitution is framed with the great care and deliberation so that it reflects the high purpose and noble objective of the Constitution makers; *Pradeep Jain (Dr.)* v. *Union of India*, AIR 1984 SC 1420: (1984) 3 SCC 654: 1984 Ed Cas 237: (1984) 3 SCR 942.

The task of legislature to arrive at a pragmatic balance between the often competing interests of "personal liberty" and "public safety"; *Selvi* v. *State of Karnataka*, AIR 2010 SC 1974.

Abolition of Caste System

It is absolutely imperative to abolish the caste system as expeditiously as possible for the smooth functioning of Rule of Law and Democracy in our country; *State of Uttar Pradesh* v. *Ram Sajivan*, AIR 2010 SC 1738.

Independence of judiciary is a basic structure of Constitution; *S.P. Gupta* v. *President of India*, AIR 1982 SC 149: 1982 Raj LR 389: 1981 Supp SCC 87.

---

1. Subs. by the Constitution (Forty-second Amendment) Act, 1976, sec. 2(a), for "SOVEREIGN DEMOCRATIC REPUBLIC" (w.e.f. 3-1-1977).

2. Subs. by the Constitution (Forty-second Amendment) Act, 1976, sec. 2(b), for "unity of the Nation" (w.e.f. 3-1-1977).

Basic Structure of Constitution

The objectives specified in the Preamble contain the basic structure of our Constitution, which cannot be amended in exercise of the power under article 368 of the Constitution. For the theory of "basic structure". *See* the following judgments of the Supreme Court:

(i) *Keshavananda Bharati Sripadgalvaru* v. *State of Kerala*, AIR 1973 SC 1461: (1973) 4 SCC 225: (1973) Supp SCR 1, paragraphs 292, 437, 599, 682 and 1164.

(ii) *Indira Nehru Gandhi* v. *Raj Narain*, AIR 1975 SC 2299: 1975 Supp SCC 1: (1976) 2 SCR 347 paragraphs 251-252 (Khanna, J.), paragraphs 664, 665 and 691 (Chandrachud, J.), paragraphs 555 and 575 (Beg, J.) (3 Judges view out of 5).

(iii) *Minerva Mills Ltd.* v. *Union of India*, AIR 1980 SC 1789: (1980) 3 SCC 625: 1980 Ker LT 573: 1980 UJ (SC) 727 (majority view).

(iv) *Addl. Distt. Magistrate, Jabalpur* v. *Shivakant Shukla*, AIR 1976 SC 1207: (1976) 2 SCC 521: 1976 Cr LJ 945: 1976 UJ (SC) 610: 1976 SC Cr R 277: 1976 SCC (Cri) 448: 1976 Cr App R (SC) 298: (1976) 3 SCR 929: 1976 Supp SCR 172.

Features of Basic Structure

1. Supremacy of Constitution
2. Republican and Democratic form of Government
3. Secular Character of Constitution
4. Separation of Powers between the Legislature, the Executive and the Judiciary
5. Federal Character of Constitution; *Keshavananda Bharati Sripadgalvaru* v. *State of Kerala*, AIR 1973 SC 1461: (1973) 4 SCC 225: (1973) Supp SCR 1 (Justice Sikri).

Constitutional Philosophy

The approach of courts must be compatible with constitutional philosophy of which Directive Principles of State Policy constitute an integral part; *Harjinder Singh* v. *Punjab State Warehousing Corporation*, AIR 2010 SC 1116.

Duty of Citizen

In the constitutional set-up every citizen is under a duty to abide by the Constitution and respect its ideals and institutions; *Official Liquidator* v. *Dayanand*, (2008) 10 SCC 1: AIR 2008 SC (Supp) 1177.

Federal Structure

The Indian Constitution is basically federal in form and is marked by the traditional characteristics of a federal system, namely, supremacy of the Constitution, division of power between the Union and State Governments, existence of an independent judiciary and a rigid procedure for the amendment of the Constitution. It establishes a duly polity, *with* clearly defined spheres of authority between the Union and the States, to be exercised in fields assigned to them respectively. There is an independent judiciary to determine issues between the Union and the States, to be exercised in fields assigned to them respectively. There is an independent judiciary to determine issues between the Union and the States, or between one State and another. An amendment in the respective jurisdictions of the Union and the States can be brought about only by invoking a special procedure in Parliament and ratification by a majority of the States. However, there are marked differences between the American federation (which is the classical federal model) and the Indian federation. First, in America, there is a dual citizenship, whereas, in India, there is only one citizenship. Indian citizens, wherever they reside, are equal in the eye of the law. Secondly, the States in America have a right to make their own constitutions, whereas no such power is given to the States in India. Thirdly, the Indian Constitution exhibits a centralising tendency in several of its provisions, *e.g.*, the adoption of a lengthy Concurrent List, the power of Parliament to re-organise the political structure of the country, supremacy of Parliament over State Legislatures if there is a direct conflict between their respective jurisdictions, vesting of the residuary legislative power in Parliament, and powers of Governors to reserve Bills for the consideration of the President of the Republic. Fourthly, in certain circumstances, the Union is empowered to supersede the authority of the State or to exercise powers otherwise vested in the States.

Fundamental Law

The Constitution operates as a fundamental law. The governmental organs owe their origin to the Constitution and derive their authority from, and discharge their responsibilities within the framework of the Constitution. The Union Parliament and the State Legislature are not sovereign, The validity of a law, whether Union or State, is judged with reference to their respective jurisdictions as defined in the Constitution. The Judiciary has power to declare a law unconstitutional, if the law is found to have contravened any provision of the Constitution.

Idealism

The ideals of socialism, secularism and democracy are elaborated by the enacting provisions. *See* the undermentioned decisions:

(i) *Bhim Singhji* v. *Union of India*, AIR 1981 SC 234: (1981) 1 SCC 166: 1981 Raj LR 39: 1981 All CJ 38, paragraphs 39, 71-72.

(ii) *State of Kerala* v. *N.M. Thomas*, AIR 1976 SC 490 (531): (1976) 2 SCC 310: (1976) 1 LLJ 376; *Waman Rao* v. *Union of India*, AIR 1981 SC 271: (1981) 2 SCC 362: 1980 Ker LT 573: 1980 UJ (SC) 742: (1981) 2 SCR 1.

(iii) *Official Liquidator* v. *Dayanand*, (2008) 10 SCC 1: AIR 2008 SC (Supp) 1177.

The word "socialist", read with articles 14 and 16, enabled the Court to deduce a fundamental right to equal pay for equal work, the same word, when read with article 14, enabled the Court to strike down a statute which failed to achieve the socialist goal to the fullest extent. Undermentioned decisions are relevant on this point:

(i) *Excel Wear* v. *Union of India*, AIR 1979 SC 25: (1978) 4 SCC 224: (1978) 2 LLJ 527, paragraph 24.

(ii) *Atam Prakash* v. *State of Haryana*, AIR 1986 SC 859: (1986) 2 SCC 249: 1986 Punj LJ 191: (1986) 1 Cur CC 641: 1986 (1) Land LR 478: 1986 (1) Supreme 628: 1986 Sim LC 132: 1986 UJ (SC) 642: 1986 Cur Civ LJ (SC) 490, paragraph 5.

(iii) *Randhir Singh* v. *Union of India*, AIR 1982 SC 879: (1982) 1 SCC 618: (1982) 1 LLJ 344, paragraph 8.

(iv) *D.S. Nakara* v. *Union of India*, AIR 1983 SC 130: (1983) 1 SCC 305: (1983) 1 LLJ 104, paragraphs 33-34.

(v) *Minerva Mills Ltd.* v. *Union of India*, AIR 1980 SC 1789: (1980) 3 SCC 625: 1980 Ker LT 573: 1980 UJ (SC) 727, paragraphs 62 and 111.

(vi) *Dharwad Employees* v. *State of Karnataka*, (1990) 2 SCC 396: AIR 1990 SC 883: 1990 Lab IC 625, paragraphs 14-17.

Interpretation of Preamble

The Preamble may be invoked to determine the ambit of—

(a) Fundamental rights; and

(b) Directive Principles of State Policy.

See the undermentioned decisions:

(i) *Keshavananda Bharati Sripadgalvaru* v. *State of Kerala*, AIR 1973 SC 1461: (1973) 4 SCC 225: 1973 Supp SCR 1.

(ii) *Chandra Bhawan Boarding and Lodging, Bangalore* v. *State of Mysore*, AIR 1970 SC 2042: 19 Fac LR 325: 38 FJR 1: (1970) 2 Lab LJ 403: (1970) 2 SCR 600, paragraph 13.

(iii) *Dharwad District P.W.D. Leterate Daily Wage Employees Association* v. *State of Karnataka*, (1990) 2 SCC 396: AIR 1990 SC 883: 1990 Lab IC 625, paragraphs 14-27.

Interpretation of Statutes

Constitution must be construed in wide and liberal manner so that constitutional provision does not get fossilized but remains flexible enough to meet newly emerging problems and challenges; *M. Nagaraj* v. *Union of India*, AIR 2007 SC 71: 2006 AIR SCW 5482: 2007 (1) JCR SC 147: 2006 (6) Kant LJ 529: 2006 (4) Pat LJR 319: (2006) 8 SCC 212: 2006 (8) SCJ 457: (2006) 10 SCALE 301: 2006 (8) Supreme 89 (Para 19).

Parents Patriae

The doctrine of *parents patriae* can be invoked by reason of sovereignty; *Charan Lal Sahu* v. *Union of India*, (1990) 1 SCC 613: AIR 1990 SC 1480: (1989) Supp 2 SCR 597: 1989 (Supp) SCALE 1, paragraphs 35-37, 63, 74 and 10.

Powers from Constitutional Provision

Powers must be derived from specific provisions of the Constitution; *Synthetics & Chemicals Ltd.* v. *State of Uttar Pradesh*, (1990) 1 SCC 109: AIR 1990 SC 1927: JT 1989 (4) SC 267 (7 Judges Bench).

Preamble: Part of the Constitution

The Preamble is part of the Constitution; *Keshavananda Bharati Sripadgalvaru* v. *State of Kerala*, AIR   1973 SC 1461: (1973) 4 SCC 225: 1973 Supp SCR 1.

Preamble as Basic Structure

The objectives specified in the Preamble contain the basic structure of the Constitution.

  (i) *Keshavananda Bharati Sripadgalvaru* v. *State of Kerala*, AIR 1973 SC 1461: (1973) 4 SCC 225: 1973 Supp SCR 1, paragraphs 292, 599, 682, 1164, 1437 (majority view).

 (ii) *Excel Wear* v. *Union of India*, AIR 1979 SC 25: (1978) 4 SCC 224: (1988) 2 LLJ 527, paragraph 24.

The Preamble may therefore be pressed into service to interpret the provisions as to:

  (i) fundamental rights — *Keshavananda Bharati Sripadgalvaru* v. *State of Kerala*, AIR 1973 SC 1461: (1973) 4 SCC 225: (1973) Supp SCR 1.

 (ii) directive principles — *Chandra Bhavan* v. *State of Mysore*, AIR 1970 SC 2042: (1969) 3 SCC 84: (1990) 2 LLJ 403, paragraph 13.

Res Extra Commercium

The doctrine of *res extra commercium* cannot be extended to prohibit employment of women in Hotels and Bars serving liquor; *Anuj Garg* v. *Hotel Association of India*, AIR 2008 SC 663: 2007 AIR SCW 7772: ILR 2008 Kant (SC) 697: 2008 (1) Rec Civ R 240: (2008) 3 SCC 1: 2008 (1) SCT 80: (2007) 13 SCALE 762: 2008 (2) Serv LR 472.

Secularism

The Constitution of India stands for a secular State. The State has no official religion. Secularism pervades its provisions which give full opportunity to all persons to profess, practise and propagate religion of their choice. The Constitution not only guarantees a person's freedom of religion and conscience, but also ensures freedom for one who has no religion, and it scrupulously restrains the State from making any discrimination on grounds of religion. A single citizenship is assured to all persons irrespective of their religion.

Dr. Radhakrishnan, former President of India, has in his book *Recovery of Faith*, page 184, explained secularism in this country, as follows:

> "When India is said to be a Secular State, it does not mean that we reject the reality of an unseen spirit or the relevance of religion to life or that we exalt irreligion. It does not mean that secularism itself becomes a positive religion or that the State assumes divine prerogatives ... We hold that not one religion should be given preferential status ... This view of religious impartiality, or comprehension and forbearance, has a prophetic role to play within the National and International life."

Most important components of secularism are as under:

  (i) *samanata* (equality) is incorporated in article 14;

 (ii) prohibition against discrimination on the ground of religion, caste, *etc.*, is incorporated in articles 15 and 16;

(iii) freedom of speech and expression and all other important freedoms of all the citizens are conferred under articles 19 and 21;

 (iv) right to practise religion is conferred under articles 25 to 28;

(v) fundamental duty of the State to enact uniform civil laws treating all the citizens as equal, is imposed by article 44;

(vi) sentiment of majority of the people towards the cow and against its slaughter was incorporated in articles 48. [*See* Basu, Constitutional Law of India].

An eminent writer [Basu, Constitutional Law of India, 1998, page 4, footnote] has described the expression "secular" as vague. He has further stated that it would be a correct summary of the provisions of articles 25-30 to say that the expression "Republic" as qualified by the expression "secular" means a republic in which there is equal respect for all religions.

This was the proposal in the 45th Constitutional Amendment Bill, which was passed by the Lok Sabha but defeated in the Rajya Sabha, because of oppositions of the Congress Party. Secularism (whatever it may mean) is a basic feature of the Constitution; *S.R. Bommai* v. *Union of India*, (1994) 3 SCC 1: AIR 1994 SC 1918: 1994 AIR SCW 2946: JT 1994 (2) SC 215: (1994) 2 SCR 644, paragraph 153.

The concept of secularism to put it in a nutshell is that the "State" will have no religion; *Bal Patil* v. *Union of India*, (2005) 6 SCC 690: AIR 2005 SC 3172: 2005 AIR SCW 3762: 2005 (4) JCR SC 60: 2005 (6) SCJ 171: 2005 (6) SLT 251: (2005) 6 SCALE 374: 2005 (5) Supreme 669: 2005 (2) UJ (SC) 1249.

Social Justice

Social justice enables the courts to uphold legislation—

(a) to remove economic unequalities;

(b) to provide a decent standard of living to the working people;

(c) to protect the interests of the weaker sections of the society.

See the undermentioned decisions:

(i) *Lingappa Pochanna Appealwar* v. *State of Maharashtra*, AIR 1985 SC 389: (1985) 1 SCC 479: (1985) 87 Bom LR 65: 1985 GOC (SC) 41: (1985) 2 SCR 224: 1985 Cur Civ LJ (SC) 387, paragraphs 14, 16, 18 and 20.

(ii) *Nakara* v. *Union of India*, AIR 1983 SC 130: (1983) 1 SCC 305: (1983) 1 LLJ 104, paragraphs 33-34.

(iii) *Sadhuram Bansal* v. *Pulin Behari Sarkar*, AIR 1984 SC 1471: (1984) 3 SCC 410, paragraphs 29, 70 and 73.

Socialistic Concept

Democratic socialism aims to end poverty, ignorance, disease and inequality of opportunity. This socialistic concept ought to be implemented in the true spirit of the Constitution; *G.B. Pant University of Agriculture and Technology* v. *State of Uttar Pradesh*, AIR 2000 SC 2695: (2000) 7 SCC 109: (2000) 1 LLJ 1109: 2000 All LJ 2420.

Sovereign

The word "sovereign" means that the State has power to legislate on any subject in conformity with constitutional limitations; *Synthetics & Chemicals Ltd.* v. *State of Uttar Pradesh*, (1990) 1 SCC 109: AIR 1990 SC 1927: JT 1989 (4) SC 267, paragraphs 35-37, 56-64, 106-108.

Being a sovereign State, India is free from any type of external control. It can acquire foreign territory and, if necessary, cede a part of the territory in favour of a foreign State, subject to certain constitutional requirements; *Maganbhai Ishwarbhai Patel* v. *Union of India*, (1970) 3 SCC 400: AIR 1969 SC 783: (1969) 3 SCR 254.

Structural Sources of the Constitution

Sources of the Indian Constitution can be best explained with reference to its principal parts. The structural part of the Constitution is, to a large extent, derived from the Government of India Act, 1935. The philosophical part of the Constitution has other sources. Part III on Fundamental Rights partly derives its inspiration from the Bill of Rights, enshrined in the American Constitution, and so also Part IV on Directive Principles of State Policy from the Irish Constitution. The political part (the principle of Cabinet Government and the relations between the executive and the Legislature) have been largely drawn from the British experience.

The Union-State relations find a similarity in the Act of 1935 and also in the Canadian Constitution, though the expanded concurrent list in the Seventh Schedule has a model in the Australian Constitution. Part XIII, dealing with trade, commerce and intercourse, also appears to derive inspiration from the Australian Constitution. Some indigenous institutions like "panchayats" have been specifically encouraged and new ideals, such as, promotion of international peace and security, have been woven into the fabric of the Constitution. The Constitution specifically provides for the privileges of the members of Parliament and of the State Legislature, to some extent following the Australian model.

Structure of Government and Fundamental Aspects of Constitution

The Indian Constitution, adopted by the Constituent Assembly on November 26, 1949 is a comprehensive document containing 395 articles and several Schedules. Besides dealing with the structure of Government the Constitution makes detailed provisions for the rights of citizens and other persons in a number of entrenched provisions, and for the principles to be followed by the State in the governance of the country, labelled as "Directive Principles of State Policy".

Historical and geographical factors have been responsible for the build of the Constitution, which is the largest Constitution in the world. The framers of the Constitution were keen to preserve the democratic values to which Indians had attached the highest importance in their struggle for freedom. But they were also keen to make provisions considered to be necessary in the light of the social and economic backwardness of certain sections of society. They had also before them the precedent of the Government of India Act, 1935 whose detailed provisions were found suitable for adoption in the interests of continuity and certainty. Some precautions for the constitutional image being distorted or being impaired in its essential features, were also required. All this has contributed to the length of the Indian Constitution.

Unity of Nation

The Preamble declares India to be a sovereign, socialist, secular, democratic republic. It is declared that the Constitution has been "given by the people to themselves", thereby affirming the republican character of the polity and the sovereignty of the people. The democratic character of the Indian polity is illustrated by the provisions conferring, on the adult citizens, the right to vote, and by the provisions for elected representatives and responsibility of the executive to the Legislature.

PART I

THE UNION AND ITS TERRITORY

1. Name and territory of the Union.—(1) India, that is Bharat, shall be a Union of States.

[1][(2) The States and the territories thereof shall be as specified in the First Schedule.]

(3) The territory of India shall comprise—

(a) The territories of the States;

[2][(b) the Union territories specified in the First Schedule; and]

(c) such other territories as may be acquired.

Notes on Article 1

Union of India

The Constitution describes India as a Union of States, thereby implying the indestructible nature of its unity. No unit constituting the Indian Union can secede from it [VII Constituent

---

1. Subs. by the Constitution (Seventh Amendment) Act, 1956, sec. 2(1)(a), for clause (2) (w.e.f. 1-11-1956).

2. Subs. by the Constitution (Seventh Amendment) Act, 1956, sec. 2(1)(b), for sub-clause (b) (w.e.f. 1-11-1956).

Assembly Debates 43]. The country is divided into several units, known as States or Union Territories, and the Constitution lays down not only the structure of the Union Government, but also the structure of the State Governments.

The Union of India is a federal Union, with a distribution of powers, of which the judiciary is the interpreter. Although there has been considerable controversy whether India is or is not a federation and although some writers have called it "quasi federal", it would seem that essentially the Indian Constitution is a federal one; *Special Reference of 1956*, AIR 1965 SC 745 (762): (1965) 1 SCR 413: 1965 (1) SCJ 847: (1965) 1 SCA 441.

Acquisition of Foreign Territory

Acquisition of foreign territory does not fall within article 1. It is governed by international law; *Jose Da Costa* v. *Bascora Sadashiva Sinai Narcornin*, AIR 1975 SC 1843: (1976) 2 SCC 917, paragraph 24.

Article 1 does not confer power to acquire foreign territories; *In re Berubari Union and Exchange of Enclaves*, AIR 1960 SC 845: 1960 SCJ 933: (1961) 1 SCA 22: (1960) 3 SCR 250.

Action Subsequent to Acquisition

Foreign territories which become part of India on acquisition may (i) either be admitted into the Union, or (ii) constituted into new States under article 2, or (iii) merged into an existing State under article 3(a) or 3(b), or (iv) formed into a Union territory. Of course, a foreign territory would not come under article 1(3)(c) until there is legal transfer of territory to India, so as to constitute its "acquisition" in international law. *See* the undermentioned decisions:

  (i) *Harivansh* v. *State of Maharashtra*, (1971) 2 SCC 54: AIR 1971 SC 1130: 1971 Cr LJ 842.

  (ii) *N. Masthan Sahib* v. *Chief Commissioner, Pondicherry*, AIR 1962 SC 797: (1962) Supp 1 SCR 981: (1962) 2 SCA 401.

  (iii) *Thakur Amar Singhji* v. *State of Rajasthan*, AIR 1955 SC 504: 1954 KLT 273: 1955 SCA 766: 1955 SCJ 523: (1955) 2 SCR 303.

Boundaries of State

Territories of States as on commencement of Constitution *i.e.*, 26-1-1950 was not frozen and the Constitution provided for prospective changes including alteration of boundaries; *Ram Badan Rai* v. *Union of India*, AIR 1999 SC 166: 1998 AIR SCW 3525: 1998 All LJ 2637: 1999 (1) All WC 430: JT 1998 (7) SC 478: (1999) 1 SCC 705: 1998 (4) SCJ 153: (1998) 6 SCALE 71: 1998 (8) Supreme 342.

Law Applicable to Acquired Territory

On acquisition of territory, the pre-acquisition laws and the rights acquired therein may continue, only if the new Government chooses to recognise them unequivocally; *Vinodkumar Shantilal Gosalia* v. *Gangadhar Narsingdas Agarwal*, AIR 1981 SC 1946: (1981) 4 SCC 226: (1982) 1 SCR 392, paragraphs 29-30.

Meaning of Territory of India

The term "territory of India" has been used in several articles of the Constitution and in every article where these phraseology is employed it means the territory of India for the time being as falls within article 1(3), but the phrase cannot mean different territories in different articles; *N. Masthan Sahib* v. *Chief Commissioner, Pondicherry*, AIR 1962 SC 797: (1962) Supp 1 SCR 981: (1962) 2 SCA 401.

Territorial Waters

Section 3(2) of the Territorial Waters, Continental Shelf, Exclusive Economic Zone and other Maritime Zones Act, 1976 now provides that the limit of the territorial waters is the line, every point of which is at a distance of twelve nautical miles from the nearest point of the appropriate base line. Another notification of the Government dated 15 January, 1977 has extended the "exclusive economic zone" of India upto a distance of 200 nautical miles into the sea from the shore base line. This has been done under the Territorial Waters, Continental Shelf, Exclusive Economic Zone and other Maritime Zones Act, 1976, passed after the Constitution (40th Amendment) Act, 1976.

Territory of India

The expression "territory of India", wherever used, means the territory which, for the time being, falls within article 1(3). *See* the undermentioned decisions:

(i) *Thakur Amar Singhji* v. *State of Rajasthan*, AIR 1955 SC 504: 1954 KLT 273: 1955 SCA 766: 1955 SCJ 523: (1955) 2 SCR 303.

(ii) *N. Masthan Sahib* v. *Chief Commissioner, Pondicherry*, AIR 1962 SC 797: (1962) Supp 1 SCR 981: (1962) 2 SCA 401.

2. Admission or establishment of new States.—Parliament may by law admit into the Union, or establish, new States on such terms and conditions as it thinks fit.

Notes on Article 2

Admission of New States

The power to admit new States into the union under article 2 is, no doubt, in the very nature of the power, very wide and its exercise necessarily guided by political issues of considerable complexity many of which may not be judicially manageable; *R.C. Poudyal* v. *Union of India*, AIR 1993 SC 1804: 1993 AIR SCW 1620: JT 1993 (2) SC 1: (1993) 1 SCR 891: (1994) Supp 1 SCC 324.

Formation of New States

The power with which the Parliament is invested by article 2 is power to admit, establish or form new States which conform to democratic pattern envisaged by constitutional power which Parliament can exercise under article 4 is supplemental, incidental or consequential to the admission, establishment or formation of State contemplated by Constitution; *Mangal Singh* v. *Union of India*, AIR 1967 SC 944: (1967) 1 SCWR 491: (1967) 2 SCR 109: 1967 SCD 1116: 1968 (1) SCJ 240.

[1][**2A. Sikkim to be associated with the Union.**—[*Rep. by the Constitution (Thirty-sixth Amendment) Act, 1975, sec. 5(a) (w.e.f. 26-4-1975).*]]

3. Formation of new States and alteration of areas, boundaries or names of existing States.—Parliament may by law—

(a) form a new State by separation of territory from any State or by uniting two or more States or parts of States or by uniting any territory to a part of any State;

(b) increase the area of any State;

(c) diminish the area of any State;

(d) alter the boundaries of any State;

(e) alter the name of any State:

[2][Provided that no Bill for the purpose shall be introduced in either House of Parliament except on the recommendation of the President and unless, where the proposal contained in the Bill affects the area, boundaries or name of any of the States [3][***], the Bill has been referred by the President to the Legislature of that State for expressing its views thereon within such period as may be specified in the

---

1. Article 2A was earlier inserted by the Constitution (Thirty-fifth Amendment) Act, 1974, sec. 2 (w.e.f. 1-3-1975).

2. Subs. by the Constitution (Fifth Amendment) Act, 1955, sec. 2, for the proviso (w.e.f. 24-12-1955).

3. The words and letters "specified in Part A or Part B of the First Schedule" omitted by the Constitution (Seventh Amendment) Act, 1956, sec. 29 and Sch. (w.e.f. 1-11-1956).

reference or within such further period as the President may allow and the period so specified or allowed has expired.]

[1][*Explanation I.*—In this article, in clauses (a) to (e), "State" includes a Union territory, but in the proviso, "State" does not include a Union territory.]

[1][*Explanation II.*—The power conferred on Parliament by clause (a) includes the power to form a new State or Union territory by uniting a part of any State or Union territory to any other State or Union territory.]

Notes on Article 3

Agreements between India and Bangladesh

The lease agreement in perpetuity of some area at Teen Bigha (Indian Territory) to Bangladesh did not amount to lease or surrender of sovereignty. It amounts to survitude suffered by India; *Union of India* v. *Sukumar Sengupta*, AIR 1990 SC 1692: JT 1990 (2) SC 297.

Effects of Re-organisation of Territory under Existing Laws

The principles relating to a change of sovereignty in international law are not applicable to a re-organisation of territory of a State under article 3. When such an adjustment or re-organisation of territories takes place, the existing laws as well as administrative orders in a particular territory continue to be in force and continue to be binding upon the successor State, so long as they are not modified, changed or repudiated by the successor State. *See* the undermentioned decision; *State of Punjab* v. *Balbir*, AIR 1977 SC 629: (1976) 3 SCC 242: (1976) 2 LLJ 4: 1977 Lab IC 281, paragraphs 13-14.

Inter-State Agreement on Water

The State cannot claim to have legislative powers over right to receive and utilize water; *Mullaperiyar Environmental Protection Forum* v. *Union of India*, AIR 2006 SC 1428: 2006 AIR SCW 1241: 2006 (1) Arb LR 374: ILR (2006) 2 Ker SC 347: (2006) 3 SCC 643: 2006 (3) SCJ 196: 2006 (4) SRJ 268: 2006 (2) Supreme 579.

Reference of Central Bills to States

Once the original Bill is referred to the State or States, the purpose of the proviso is served and no fresh reference is required every time an amendment to the Bill is moved and accepted according to the Rules of Procedure in Parliament. Parliament is not bound to accept or act upon the views of the State Legislature, even if those views are received in time; *Babulal* v. *State of Bombay*, AIR 1960 SC 51 (54): (1960) 1 SCR 605: 62 Bom LR 58.

4. Laws made under articles 2 and 3 to provide for the amendment of the First and the Fourth Schedules and supplemental, incidental and consequential matters.—(1) Any law referred to in article 2 or article 3 shall contain such provisions for the amendment of the First Schedule and the Fourth Schedule as may be necessary to give effect to the provisions of the law and may also contain such supplemental, incidental and consequential provisions (including provisions as to representation in Parliament and in the Legislature or Legislatures of the State or States affected by such law) as Parliament may deem necessary.

(2) No such law as aforesaid shall be deemed to be an amendment of this Constitution for the purposes of article 368.

Notes on Article 4

Law in force: Effect of State Reorganisation

The effect of reorganisation of States made under articles 3 and 4 of making Telengana a Part of new State of Andhra Pradesh must be ignored under article 35(b), hence the Mukti Rules continue in force, even after constitution of the State of Andhra Pradesh under the Reorganisation

---

1. Ins. by the Constitution (Eighteenth Amendment) Act, 1966, sec. 2 (w.e.f. 27-8-1966).

of States Act, 1956; *Director of Industries and Commerce, Government of A. P. Hyderabad* v. *V. Venkata Reddy*, AIR 1973 SC 827: (1972) 2 Andh LT 243: (1973) 1 SCC 99: (1972) 2 LLJ 486: 1973 (1) SCJ 241: (1973) 1 Mad LJ (SC) 49: 1973 SCC (Lab) 75.

Legislative Power of State

State cannot claim to have legislative powers over waters in question; *Mullaperiyar Environmental Protection Forum* v. *Union of India*, AIR 2006 SC 1428: 2006 AIR SCW 1241: 2006 (1) Arb LR 374: ILR (2006) 2 Ker SC 347: (2006) 3 SCC 643: 2006 (3) SCJ 196: 2006 (4) SRJ 268: 2006 (2) Supreme 579.

Levy of Penalty

State has power to levy of penalty; *State of Bihar* v. *Industrial Corporation Pvt. Ltd.*, AIR 2004 SC 1151: 2003 AIR SCW 5874: 2003 (8) ACE 218: 2004 (1) BLJR 54: 2003 (4) JLJR 162: 2003 (4) Pat LJR 231: (2003) 11 SCC 465: 2003 (6) SLT 556: (2003) 9 SCALE 169: 2003 (7) Supreme 681.

New High Court for States

The power to appoint the sittings of the Judges and Division Courts of the High Court for a new State at places other than the place of the principal seat is in the unquestioned domain of the Chief Justice, the only condition being that he must act with the approval of Governor; *State of Maharashtra* v. *Narayan Shamrao Puranic*, AIR 1982 SC 1198: 1982 UJ (SC) 368: (1982) 2 SCC 440.

Power of Parliament in Respect of New State

The power with which the Parliament is invested by articles 2 and 3 is power to admit, establish or form new States which conform to democratic pattern envisaged by Constitution; *Mangal Singh* v. *Union of India*, AIR 1967 SC 944: (1967) 1 SCWR 491: (1967) 2 SCR 109: 1967 SCD 1116: 1968 (1) SCJ 240.

Scope and Applicability of Article 4

The effect of article 4 is that the laws relatable to article 2 or article 3 are not to be treated as constitutional amendments for the purpose of article 368, which means that if legislation is competent under article 3 in respect of the topic, it would be unnecessary to invoke article 368; *In re Berubari Union and Exchange of Enclaves*, AIR 1960 SC 845: 1960 SCJ 933: (1961) 1 SCA 22: (1960) 3 SCR 250.

PART II

CITIZENSHIP

5. Citizenship at the commencement of the Constitution.—At the commencement of this Constitution every person who has his domicile in the territory of India and—

(a) who was born in the territory of India; or

(b) either of whose parents was born in the territory of India; or

(c) who has been ordinarily resident in the territory of India for not less than five years immediately preceding such commencement,

shall be a citizen of India.

Notes on Article 5

Citizenship at Commencement of Constitution

The person must have her domicile in India at time of commencement of Constitution. Where a person was born much after commencement of Constitution *i.e.*, in 1958, the question of his/her domicile in India at time of commencement of Constitution does not arise; *Nagina Devi* v. *Union of India*, AIR 2010 Pat 117.

Determination of Citizenship

The question about the determination of citizenship even after the limited purpose of certain other law has to be done by authority in light of constitutional provisions and provisions of Citizenship Act of 1955; *Lal Babu Hussain* v. *Electoral Registration Officer*, AIR 1995 SC 1189: 1995 AIR SCW 1254: (1995) 3 SCC 100.

Every Person

The expression "every person" includes—

(a) a prisoner;

(b) a member of the armed forces (but subject to article 33).

See the undermentioned decisions:

(i) *State of Maharashtra* v. *Prabhakar,* AIR 1966 SC 424 (426): (1966) 1 SCR 702: 1966 Cr LJ 311.

(ii) *Sunil Batra* v. *Delhi Administration,* AIR 1978 SC 1675: (1978) 4 SCC 494: 1978 Cr LJ 1741.

(iii) *Prithi Pal Singh Bedi (Lt. Col.)* v. *Union of India,* AIR 1982 SC 1413: (1982) 3 SCC 140: 1982 SCC (Cri) 642, paragraph 45.

One Domicile

Under the Indian Constitution, there is only one domicile *viz.* the domicile of the country and there is no separate domicile for a State; *Pradeep Jain (Dr.)* v. *Union of India,* AIR 1984 SC 1420: (1984) 3 SCC 654: 1984 Ed Cas 237, paragraphs 8-9.

6. Rights of citizenship of certain persons who have migrated to India from Pakistan.—Notwithstanding anything in article 5, a person who has migrated to the territory of India from the territory now included in Pakistan shall be deemed to be a citizen of India at the commencement of this Constitution if—

(a) he or either of his parents or any of his grand-parents was born in India as defined in the Government of India Act, 1935 (as originally enacted); and

(b) (i) in the case where such person has so migrated before the nineteenth day of July, 1948, he has been ordinarily resident in the territory of India since the date of his migration, or

(ii) in the case where such person has so migrated on or after the nineteenth day of July, 1948, he has been registered as a citizen of India by an officer appointed in that behalf by the Government of the Dominion of India on an application made by him therefor to such officer before the commencement of this Constitution in the form and manner prescribed by that Government:

Provided that no person shall be so registered unless he has been resident in the territory of India for at least six months immediately preceding the date of his application.

Notes on Article 6

Catch-up Rule

Obligation of the "Catch-up" rule or insertion of the concept of "Consequential Seniority Code" violates the basic structure of the Equality Code enshrined in articles 14, 15 and 16 of Constitution; *M. Nagaraj* v. *Union of India,* AIR 2007 SC 71: 2006 AIR SCW 5482: 2006 (4) All WC 4054: 2007 (1) JCR SC 147: 2006 (6) Kant LJ 529: 2006 (4) Pat LJR 319: (2006) 8 SCC 212: 2006 (8) SCJ 457: (2006) 10 SCALE 301: 2006 (8) Supreme 89.

Citizenship of Foreign State

Article 9 deals with cases when citizenship of foreign State has been acquired by Indian citizens prior to Constitution and means that he cannot claim citizenship of India by virtue of articles 5, 6 and 8; *State of Uttar Pradesh* v. *Shah Muhammad,* AIR 1969 SC 1234: (1969) 2 SCA 539: (1969) 3 SCR 1006.

Migrated to Territory of India

Migration must be with intention to reside permanently in India. Such intention may be formed even later; *Shanno Devi* v. *Mangal Sain,* AIR 1961 SC 58: 1961 (1) SCJ 201: (1961) 1 SCR 576: ILR (1961) 1 Punj 234: 22 Ele LR 469.

Migration: Meaning of

Movement should be voluntary and not for a limited period; *Kulathil Mammu* v. *State of Kerala,* AIR 1966 SC 1614: 1966 Cr LJ 1217: 1967 SCD 101: (1967) 1 SCA 322: (1967) 3 SCR 706: 1967 Mad LJ (Cri) 817: 1967 (2) SCJ 653.

Domicile on the Date of Constitution

Where an accused under section 14 of the Foreigners Act, 1946 claims that he was domiciled in India and was residing in India when Constitution came into force, then the burden is upon him and he should be given a chance to prove it; *Abdul Sattar Haji Ibrahim Patel* v. *State of Gujarat,* AIR 1965 SC 810: (1964) 5 Guj LR 439: 1964 Cur LJ (SC) 200: 1964 (2) SCJ 461: 1964 Mad LJ (Cri) 542: (1965) 1 Cr LJ 759: 1965 SCD 976.

7. Rights of citizenship of certain migrants to Pakistan.—Notwithstanding anything in articles 5 and 6, a person who has after the first day of March, 1947, migrated from the territory of India to the territory now included in Pakistan shall not be deemed to be a citizen of India:

Provided that nothing in this article shall apply to a person who, after having so migrated to the territory now included in Pakistan, has returned to the territory of India under a permit for resettlement or permanent return issued by or under the authority of any law and every such person shall for the purposes of clause (b) of article 6 be deemed to have migrated to the territory of India after the nineteenth day of July, 1948.

Notes on Article 7

Citizenship of India

Article 7 clearly overrides article 5. It is peremptory in its scope and makes no exception for a case of the wife migrating to Pakistan leaving her husband in India. Even such a wife must be deemed not to be a citizen of India unless the particular facts bring her case within proviso to article 7; *State of Bihar* v. *Kumar Amar Singh*, AIR 1955 SC 282: 1955 SCA 376: 34 Pat 274: 1955 SCJ 311: 1955 All LJ 351: 1955 SCR 1259.

Scope of Article 7

Article 7 refers to migration taking place between 1-3-1947 to 26-1-1950; *State of Madhya Pradesh* v. *Peer Mohd.*, AIR 1963 SC 645: (1963) 1 Cr LJ 617: (1963) 1 SCA 649: 1963 (2) SCJ 655: 1963 Mad LJ (Cri) 609: (1963) Supp 1 SCR 429.

Person Continuing to be in India

Where a person continued to be in India till July, 1950 *prima facie* by virtue of article 5 read with article 7 he was a citizen of India on the date of Constitution and continued to be so at the date of the offence committed by him in July – August 1951; *Mobarik Ali Ahmed* v. *State of Bombay*, AIR 1957 SC 857: 1957 Cr LJ 1346: 1958 SCJ 111: 1958 Mad LJ (Cri) 42: 1958 SCA 665: 1958 SCR 328: 61 Bom LR 58.

8. Rights of citizenship of certain persons of Indian origin residing outside India.—Notwithstanding anything in article 5, any person who or either of whose parents or any of whose grand-parents was born in India as defined in the Government of India Act, 1935 (as originally enacted), and who is ordinarily residing in any country outside India as so defined shall be deemed to be a citizen of India if he has been registered as a citizen of India by the diplomatic or consular representative of India in the country where he is for the time being residing on an application made by him therefor to such diplomatic or consular representative, whether before or after the commencement of this Constitution, in the form and manner prescribed by the Government of the Dominion of India or the Government of India.

Notes on Article 8

Scope of Article 8 and Citizenship

Article 9 deals with cases when citizenship of foreign State had been acquired by Indian citizen prior to Constitution and States that he cannot claim citizenship of India by virtue of articles 5 and 6 or 8; *State of Uttar Pradesh* v. *Shah Muhammad,* AIR 1969 SC 1234: (1969) 2 SCA 539: (1969) 3 SCR 1006.

9. Persons voluntarily acquiring citizenship of a foreign State not to be citizens.—No person shall be a citizen of India by virtue of article 5, or be deemed to be a citizen of India by virtue of article 6 or article 8, if he has voluntarily acquired the citizenship of any foreign State.

Notes on Article 9

Citizenship Act, 1955, Section 9(2)

A State Government has no jurisdiction to determine question of citizenship unless the function is delegated by the Central Government, under article 258 of the Constitution. Undermentioned decisions support the above propositions:

   (i) *Government of Andhra Pradesh* v. *Syed Md.,* AIR 1962 SC 1778: (1962) Supp 3 SCR 288: (1963) 2 MLJ (SC) 62; *State of Uttar Pradesh* v. *Roshan,* (1969) 2 SCWR 232 (233).

   (ii) *Akbar* v. *Union of India,* AIR 1962 SC 70 (72): (1962) 1 SCR 779: 1962 MPLJ 277.

Migrants to Pakistan

Migration contemplated by article 9 is one before 26-1-1950 and not one thereafter; *State of Andhra Pradesh* v. *Abdul Khader,* AIR 1961 SC 1467: (1961) 2 Cr LJ 573: (1961) 63 Punj LR 751: 1961 Andh LT 816: 1961 All Cr R 347: (1961) 2 SCA 643: (1962) 1 Mad LJ (SC) 65: (1962 1 Andh WR (SC) 65: 1962 (1) SCJ 100: (1962) 1 SCR 737.

Obtaining Passport

Mere proof of the fact that the person has obtained a passport from a foreign country is not sufficient to sustain an order for deportation or prosecution, unless there has been a decision of the Central Government under section 9(2) of the Citizenship Act, 1955. The inquiry by the Central Government under section 9(2) of the Citizenship Act is quasi-judicial. *See* the undermentioned decision.

   Government of Andhra Pradesh v. *Syed Md.,* AIR 1962 SC 1778: (1962) Supp 2 SCR 288: (1963) 2 MLJ (SC) 62; *State of Uttar Pradesh* v. *Roshan,* (1969) 2 SCWR 232 (233).

10. Continuance of the rights of citizenship.—Every person who is or is deemed to be a citizen of India under any of the foregoing provisions of this Part shall, subject to the provisions of any law that may be made by Parliament, continue to be such citizen.

Notes on Article 10

Citizenship and Domestic Law

It is accepted rule of judicial construction that regard must be had to International Conventions and norms for construing domestic law when there is no inconsistency between them and there is a void in domestic law; *Vishaka* v. *State of Rajasthan,* AIR 1997 SC 3011: 1997 AIR SCW 3043: 1998 (1) BLJR 228: 1997 (3) Crimes 188: JT 1997 (7) SC 384: 1997 (13) OCR 305: (1997) 6 SCC 241: 1997 (3) SCJ 584: (1997) 5 SCALE 453: 1997 SCC (Cri) 932: 1997 (7) Supreme 323: 1997 Writ LR 823.

Procedure Established by Law

Procedure for impounding passport is procedure established by law in respect of right to go abroad; *Maneka Gandhi* v. *Union of India,* AIR 1978 SC 597: (1978) 1 SCC 248: (1978) 2 SCR 621: 1978 (2) SCJ 312.

11. Parliament to regulate the right of citizenship by law.—Nothing in the foregoing provisions of this Part shall derogate from the power of Parliament to make any provision with respect to the acquisition and termination of citizenship and all other matters relating to citizenship.

Notes on Article 11

Question of Citizenship

The question about determination even for limited purpose of some other law has to be done by authority in light of constitutional provisions and provisions of Citizenship Act, 1955; *Lal Babu Hussain* v. *Electoral Registration Officer*, AIR 1995 SC 1189: 1995 AIR SCW 1254: (1995) 3 SCC 100.

Retrospective Operation of the Citizenship Act, 1955

Pending suit involving questions falling within provisions of section 9(2) of Citizenship Act, 1955 outsted the jurisdiction of civil courts; *State of Uttar Pradesh* v. *Shah Muhammad*, AIR 1969 SC 1234: (1969) 2 SCA 539: (1969) 3 SCR 1006.

Scope of Article 11

The scheme of the relevant articles of Part II of Constitution, which deals with citizenship, clearly suggests that the status of citizenship can be adversely affected by a statute made by Parliament in exercise of its legislative powers; *Izhar Ahmad Khan* v. *Union of India*, AIR 1962 SC 1052: (1962) 2 Cr LJ 215: 1963 BLJR 99: (1963) 1 SCA 136: (1962) Supp 3 SCR 235.

PART III

FUNDAMENTAL RIGHTS

General

12. Definition.—In this part, unless the context otherwise requires, "the State" includes the Government and Parliament of India and the Government and the Legislature of each of the States and all local or other authorities within the territory of India or under the control of the Government of India.

Notes on Article 12

Agency outside India

An instrumentality or agency of the State having operations outside India must comply with Indian labour legislation; *Lena Khan* v. *Union of India*, AIR 1987 SC 1515: (1987) 2 SCC 402: (1987) Lab IC 1035: (1987) 1 LLN 777.

Board of Control for Cricket in India (BCCI)

BCCI is not financially, functionally or administratively dominated by Government nor it is under Control of Government, therefore not a State; *Zee Telefilms Ltd.* v. *Union of India*, AIR 2005 SC 2677: 2005 AIR SCW 2985: 2005 (4) Comp LJ 283 SC: JT 2005 (2) SC 8: (2005) 4 SCC 649: 2005 (2) SCJ 121: 2005 (3) SRJ 67: (2005) 1 SCALE 666.2: 2005 (1) Supreme 886.

Co-operative Societies

The statutory regulation or restriction in the functioning of the societies is not "an imprint of the State under article 12". Hence no writ will lie against a co-operative society governed by the Kerala Co-operative Societies Act; *P. Bhaskaran* v. *Additional Secretary, Agricultural (Co-operation) Department, Trivandrum*, AIR 1988 Ker 75: (1987) 2 Ker LT 903: (1988) 2 Lab LJ 307: ILR (1988) 1 Ker 217: 1987 Ker LJ 1461: (1988) 19 Reports 636.

Examples of Statutory and Other Bodies held to be State

The State Bank of India as also the nationalised Banks are 'States' within the meaning of article12 of the Constitution of India. The service of the workman are also governed by several standing orders and bipartite settlements which have the force of law. The Banks, therefore, cannot take recourse to 'hire and fire' for the purpose of terminating the services of the employees; *Bank of India* v. *O.P. Swaranakar*, AIR 2003 SC 858: (2003) 2 SCC 721: (2003) 1 LLJ 819: (2003) 1 SLR 1.

The Children Aid Society should be treated as a State within the meaning of article 12, as it is undoubtedly an instrumentality of State; *Sheela Barse* v. *Secretary, Children Aid Society*, AIR 1987 SC 656: (1987) 3 SCC 50: 1987 SCC (Cri) 458 (P.N. Bhagwati, C.J. and R.S. Pathak, J.).

There are tests formulated by several cases of the Supreme Court to find out whether an institution is a "State". There cannot indeed be a straight jacket formula; *Tekraj* v. *Union of India*, AIR 1988 SC 469: (1988) 1 SCC 236: 1988 SCC (L&S) 300: 1988 Lab IC 961.

Local Authorities: Writ

A local authority having a legal grievance may be able to take out a writ. Thus, a writ was issued on the petition of a local authority against a public utility concern, for the latter's failure to fulfil its statutory obligation to supply power to the local authority, a consumer; *Corporation of City of Nagpur* v. *N.E.L. & Power Co.*, AIR 1958 Bom 498.

Other Authorities

What is, and what is not a "State" has been the subject-matter of rich case law under article 12. From the numerous decisions on the subject, a judgment of the Andhra Pradesh High Court has culled out certain propositions; *B. Hassan Ali Khan* v. *Director of Higher Education, Andhra Pradesh*, (1987) 4 Reports 198 (AP). The judgment says that the essential tests to determine whether a particular institution is "other authority" within the meaning of article 12 are substantial financial aid, control by the Government, performance of public functions and entrustment of governmental activities. All of these are not essential, and, in a particular case, one or a combination of more than one of them may suffice. In the leading case of *Ajay Hasia* v. *Khalid Mujib*, AIR 1981 SC 487: (1981) 1 SCC 722: (1981) 2 SCR 79: (1981) 1 LLJ 103 (Registered Society), the Regional Engineering College was held to be a "State". P.N. Bhagwati, J. observed as under in that case:

> The constitutional philosophy of a democratic socialist republic requires the Government to undertake a multitude of socio-economic operations and the Government, having regard to the practical advantages of functioning through the legal device of a corporation embarks on myriad commercial and economic activities by resorting to the instrumentality or agency of a corporation, but this contrivance of carrying on such activities through a corporation cannot exonerate the Government from its basic obligation to respect the Fundamental Rights and not to override them. The mandate of a corporation may be adopted in order to free the Government from the inevitable constrains of red tapism and slow motion but by doing so, the Government cannot be allowed to play truant with the basic human rights. Otherwise, it would be the easiest thing for the Government to assign to a plurality of corporations almost every State business such as Post and Telegraph, TV and Radio, Rail, Road and Telephones—in short every economic activity—and thereby cheat the people of India out of the Fundamental Rights guaranteed to them.

In the above judgment of the Supreme Court, Mr. Justice Bhagwati enunciated the following test for determining whether an entity is an instrumentality or agency of the State:—

(1) One thing is clear that if the entire share capital of the corporation is held by Government, it would go a long way towards indicating that the corporation is an instrumentality or agency or Government.

(2) Where the financial assistance of the State is so much as to meet almost entire expenditure of the corporation, it would afford some indication of the corporation being impregnated with governmental character.

(3) It may also be a relevant factor whether the corporation enjoys monopoly status which is the State conferred or State protected.

(4) Existence of deep and pervasive State control may afford an indication that the corporation is a State agency or instrumentality.

(5) If the functions of the corporation of public importance and closely related to governmental functions, it would be a relevant factor in classified the corporation as a instrumentality or agency of Government.

(6) Specifically, if a department of Government is transferred to a corporation, it would be a strong factor supportive of this inference of the corporation being an instrumentality or agency of Government.

The Delhi Transport Corporation is "State"; *D.T.C.* v. *Mazdoor Congress*, AIR 1991 SC 101: (1991) Supp 1 SCC 600: 1991 SCC (L&S) 1213: (1991) 1 LLJ 395.

Undermentioned decisions may be seen in this connections:

(i) *Som Prakash* v. *Union of India*, AIR 1981 SC 212: (1981) 1 SCC 449: (1981) 1 LLJ 79: (1981) 1 LLN 322; *Tajinder Singh* v. *Bharat Petroleum Corpn. Ltd.*, (1986) 4 SCC 237: 1986 JT 405: (1986) 2 Cur LR 319: (1986) 4 SCC 237: (1986) 2 Cur CC 862: 1986 (3) Supreme 414: 1986 SCC (Lab) 765: 1986 (3) SCJ 556: (1987) 1 UJ (SC) 1: (1987) 2 LLJ 225.

(ii) *State of Punjab* v. *Raja Ram*, (1981) 2 SCC 66: AIR 1981 SC 1694: (1981) 2 SCR 712, paragraphs 9-10.

(iii) *Sukhdev* v. *Bhagatram*, AIR 1975 SC 1331 (1342): (1975) 1 SCC 421: (1975) 1 LLJ 399.

(iv) *K.S. Ramamurthy Reddiar* v. *Chief Commissioner, Pondicherry*, AIR 1963 SC 1464: (1964) 1 SCR 656: (1964) 1 SCA 108.

(v) *Umesh Chandra Sinha* v. *V.N. Singh*, AIR 1968 Pat 3 (9): ILR 46 Pat 616: 1967 BLJR 798.

(vi) *Parmatma Sharan* v. *Chief Justice Rajasthan High Court*, AIR 1964 Raj 13: 1963 Raj LW 246: ILR (1963) 13 Raj 215: (1965) 1 Lab LJ 221.

(vii) *Sabhajit* v. *Union of India*, AIR 1975 SC 1329: (1975) 1 SCC 485: (1975) 1 LLJ 374; *Mysore S.R.T.C.* v. *Devraj*, AIR 1976 SC 1027, paragraph 14; *Premji Bhai* v. *Delhi Development Authority*, AIR 1980 SC 738: (1980) 2 SCC 129, paragraphs 8, 9.

(viii) *N. Masthan Sahib* v. *Chief Commissioner, Pondicherry*, AIR 1962 SC 797: (1962) Supp 1 SCR 981: (1962) 2 SCA 401.

Private Body

A private body which is an agency of the State may be a *"State"; Star Enterprises* v. *City and Industrial Development Corpn. of Maharashtra*, (1990) 3 SCC 280: (1990) 2 Punj LR 264: (1990) 2 KLT 37.

State

The definition of "State" is not confined to a Government Department and the Legislature, but extends to any action—administrative (whether statutory or non-statutory), judicial or quasi-judicial, which can be brought within the fold of 'State action' being action which violates a fundamental right. *See* the undermentioned decisions:

(i) *Ramana* v. *International Airport Authority of India*, AIR 1979 SC 1628 (1638): (1979) 3 SCC 489, paragraphs 14-16; *State of Punjab* v. *Raja Ram*, AIR 1981 SC 1694: (1981) 2 SCC 66: (1981) 2 SCR 712, paragraph 5.

(ii) *Gulam* v. *State of Uttar Pradesh*, AIR 1981 SC 2198: (1982) 1 SCC 71: (1981) 1 SCR 107, paragraph 23.

(iii) *Som Prakash* v. *Union of India*, AIR 1981 SC 212: (1981) 1 SCC 449: (1981) 1 LLJ 79, paragraphs 34, 37.

Even a private body may be "State"; *Mahabir Auto Stores* v. *Indian Oil Corporation*, (1990) 3 SCC 752: AIR 1990 SC 1031: (1990) 2 SLR 69.

State Action

The historical context in which the doctrine of "State action" evolved in the U.S. is irrelevant for India. But the principle behind the doctrine (State aid, control and regulation so impregnating a private activity as to give it the colour of "State action") is of interest to us to the limited extent to which it can be Indianised and harmoniously blended with our constitutional jurisprudence; *M.C. Mehta* v. *Union of India*, AIR 1987 SC 1086: (1987) 1 SCC 395: 1987 SCC (L&S) 37.

13. Laws inconsistent with or in derogation of the fundamental rights.— (1) All laws in force in the territory of India immediately before the commencement of this Constitution, in so far as they are inconsistent with the provisions of this Part, shall, to the extent of such inconsistency, be void.

(2) The State shall not make any law which takes away or abridges the rights conferred by this Part and any law made in contravention of this clause shall, to the extent of the contravention, be void.

(3) In this article, unless the context otherwise requires,—

(a) "law" includes any Ordinance, order, bye-law, rule, regulation, notification, custom or usage having in the territory of India the force of law;

(b) "laws in force" includes laws passed or made by a Legislature or other competent authority in the territory of India before the commencement of this Constitution and not previously repealed, notwithstanding that any such law or any part thereof may not be then in operation either at all or in particular areas.

[1][(4) Nothing in this article shall apply to any amendment of this Constitution made under article 368.]

Notes on Article 13

The main object of article 13 is to secure the paramountcy of the Constitution in regard to fundamental rights. The first clause relates to the laws already existing in force and declares that pre-Constitution laws are void to the extent to which they are inconsistent with the fundamental rights. The second clause relates to post-Constitution laws and prohibits the State from making a law which either takes away totally or abrogates in part a fundamental right. The expression "the State" is to be construed in conformity with article 12 as judicially interpreted. The ambit of the expression "law" is defined in article 13(3)(a) itself, so as to ensure that the paramountcy of the Constitution extends also to:—

(a) temporary laws, such as Ordinances, Acts as well as permanent laws;

(b) statutory instruments in the nature of subordinate legislation, specifically described as "order, bye-law, rule, regulation, notification" having in the territory of India the force of law;

(c) non-legislative sources of law, that is to say, custom or usage having in the territory of India the force of law.

The object of the definition in article 13 is to ensure that instruments emanating from any source of law—permanent or temporary, legislative or judgment or any other source—will pay homage to the constitutional provision relating to fundamental rights. At the same time, clause (4) seeks to ensure that a constitutional amendment does not fall within the definition of law in article 13, and its validity cannot be challenged on the ground that it violates a fundamental right. But it should be noted that fundamental rights as such, while not immune from constitutional amendment, may, in some cases, form part of the theory of basic features, enunciated in certain decisions by the Supreme Court. The chronology of important Supreme Court decisions on the subject is as under:

(i) *L.C. Golak Nath* v. *State of Punjab*, AIR 1967 SC 1643: (1967) 2 SCR 762: 1967 All LJ 813: 1967 (2) SCJ 486: 1967 BLJR 818: (1967) 2 SCA 642: 1967 MPWR 553: (1967) 2 SCWR 1006.

(ii) *Keshavananda Bharati Sripadgalvaru* v. *State of Kerala*, AIR 1973 SC 1461: (1973) 4 SCC 225: 1973 Supp SCR 1, which, while upholding the validity of the Constitution (24th Amendment) by which article 13(4) was inserted, laid down (by majority) the theory that there were certain basic features which could not be amended under the amending power.

---

1. Ins. by the Constitution (Twenty-fourth Amendment) Act, 1971, sec. 2 (w.e.f. 5-11-1971).

(iii) *Minerva Mills Ltd.* v. *Union of India*, AIR 1980 SC 1789: (1980) 3 SCC 625: 1980 Ker LT 573: 1980 UJ (SC) 727, which declared that even though the 42nd Amendment sought to amend article 368 (relating to the amending power) there shall be no limitation whatsoever on the Constituent power of Parliament to amend, by way of addition, variation or repeal, the provisions of the Constitution under article 368, a Constitutional amendment which relates to a basic feature (*e.g.*, total exclusion of judicial review) would be void.

(iv) *Waman Rao* v. *Union of India*, AIR 1981 SC 271: (1981) 2 SCC 362: 1980 Ker LT 573: 1980 UJ (SC) 742: (1981) 2 SCR 1, paragraph 15, re-affirming the above limitation on the constituent power.

(v) *Bhim Singhji* v. *Union of India*, AIR 1981 SC 234: (1981) 1 SCC 166: 1981 Raj LR 39: (1981) 19 DLT 185: 1981 All CJ 38.

(vi) *S.P. Gupta* v. *Union of India*, AIR 1982 SC 149: 1982 Raj LR 389: 1981 Supp SCC 87 and *S.P. Sampath Kumar* v. *Union of India*, AIR 1987 SC 386: (1987) 1 SCC 124: (1987) 1 LLJ 128: (1987) 1 SLR 182, both being decisions which, while upholding the validity of a particular amendment, impliedly proceed on the proposition that a constitutional amendment cannot override a basic feature.

Act of Parliament

The Doctrine of Basic Feature in the context of our Constitution does not apply to ordinary legislation which has only a dual criteria to meet:

(i) It should relate to a matter within its competence

(ii) It should not be void under article 13 as being an unreasonable restriction on a fundamental right or as being repugnant to an express constitutional prohibition. The basic structure theory imposes limitation on power of the Parliament to amend the Constitution. An amendment to the Constitution under article 368 could be challenged on the ground of violation of the Basic Structure of the Constitution. An ordinary legislation cannot be challenged; *Kuldip Nayar* v. *Union of India*, AIR 2006 SC 3127: 2006 AIR SCW 4394: 2006 (4) Cur CC 62: (2006) 7 SCC 1: 2006 (6) SCJ 702: (2006) 8 SCALE 257: 2006 (7) Supreme 44.

Act of State

In *State of Haryana* v. *Amar Nath Bansal*, AIR 1997 SC 718: (1997) 10 SCC 700: 1997 Lab IC 550: (1997) 1 SLR 55 (paragraph 10) it has been held that as a result of the Convenant entered into by the Rulers of the States there was the establishment of a new sovereign over the territories comprising the States of the Rulers. The Covenant is, therefore, an act of the State. With regard to the act of the State, the law is settled. The residents of the territories which are acquired do not carry with them the rights which they possessed as subjects of the ex-sovereign. As subjects of the new sovereign they possess only such rights as are granted or recognised by him.

Basic Features

The "basic features" of the Constitution cannot be amended by exercising the power of amendment under article 368. The Constitution (Forty-second Amendment) Act, 1976, which inserted in article 368(5) a provision that there is no limitation on the constituent power of the Parliament to amend the Constitution, has been invalidated by the Supreme Court, adhering to the doctrine of basic features. Though fundamental rights, as such, are not immune from amendment *en bloc*, particular rights or parts thereof may be held as basic features. *See* the undermentioned cases:

(i) *Keshavananda Bharati Sripadgalvaru* v. *State of Kerala*, AIR 1973 SC 1461: (1973) 4 SCC 225: 1973 Supp SCR 1, paragraphs 759, 850, 1574, 1582, 1595, 1840, 1916, 2079 (overruling *Golaknath Case*).

(ii) *Minerva Mills Ltd.* v. *Union of India*, AIR 1980 SC 1789: (1980) 3 SCC 625: 1980 Ker LT 573: 1980 UJ (SC) 727.

(iii) *Waman Rao* v. *Union of India*, AIR 1981 SC 271: (1981) 2 SCC 362: 1980 Ker LT 573: 1980 UJ (SC) 742: (1981) 2 SCR 1, paragraph 15.

(iv) *H.S. Srinivasa Raghavachar* v. *State of Karnataka*, AIR 1987 SC 1518: (1987) 2 SCC 692: (1987) 4 (1) IJ (Rep) 220: JT 1987 (4) SC 26: ILR (1987) Kant 2059: 1987 (1) Supreme 642: (1987) 2 Cur CC 166: 1987 (2) SCJ 611: (1987) 2 UJ (SC) 427: 1987 (2) Land LR 530.

Severability

When a particular provision of an enactment (or of subordinate legislation) is found to be void as violating a constitutional provision (*e.g.*, a provision as to fundamental rights) the question may arise as to what is the impact of such finding on the other provisions of the Act, etc. The answer to this question depends on the answer to another question, namely:— Is the other provision so intimately connected with the void provision—

(a) that each is inextricably to bound up with the other, or

(b) it can be assumed that the legislature would not have enacted the one without enacting the other? If the answer under (a) or (b) above is in the affirmative then the other provision also becomes void. See undertimed cases.

(i) *State of Bihar* v. *Kameshwar Singh*, AIR 1952 SC 252 (277): 1952 SCR 889: 31 Pat 565.

(ii) *Jalan Trading Co.* v. *Mill Mazdoor Sabha*, AIR 1967 SC 691 (711): (1967) 1 SCR 15: (1966) 2 LLJ 546.

(iii) *Kihota Hollohan* v. *Zachillhu*, (1992) Supp 2 SCC 651: AIR 1993 SC 412: 1992 AIR SCW 3497 : JT 1992 (1) SC 600: (1992) 1 SCR 686: (1992) Supp 2 SCC 651.

Constitution Amendment Acts Declared as Unconstitutional

Amendment Act	Relevant ruling
(1) Seventeenth Amendment (in part)	*L.C. Golak Nath* v. *State of Punjab*, AIR 1967 SC 1643: (1967) 2 SCR 762: 1967 All LJ 813: 1967 (2) SCJ 486: 1967 BLJR 818: (1967) 2 SCA 642: 1967 MPWR 553: (1967) 2 SCWR 1006.
(2) Twenty-fifth Amendment (article 31C)	*Keshavananda Bharati Sripadgalvaru* v. *State of Kerala*, AIR 1973 SC 1461: (1973) 4 SCC 225: 1973 Supp SCR 1.
(3) Thirty-second Amendment	*Sambamurthy* v. *Union of India*, AIR 1987 SC 66: (1987) 1 SCC 362: (1987) 2 ATC 502: (1987) 1 LLJ 221 (Rule of law).
(4) Thirty-sixth Amendment (article 329)	*Indira Nehru Gandhi* v. *Raj Narain*, AIR 1975 SC 2299: 1975 Supp SCC 1, para 251.
[The relevant article 329A was repealed by the Forty-fourth Amendment]	
(5) Article 368 (Amendment power)	*Minerva Mills Ltd.* v. *Union of India*, AIR 1980 SC 1789: (1980) 3 SCC 625: 1980 Ker LT 573: 1980 UJ (SC) 727.
(6) Fifty-second Amendment (10th	*Kihota Hollohan* v. *Zachillhu*, (1992) Supp 2 SCC 651: AIR 1993 SC 412: 1992 AIR SCW 3497 : JT 1992 (1) SC 600: (1992) 1 SCR 686: (1992) Supp 2 SCC 651.

Treaties on Human Rights

The most remarkable institutional development in human rights has been the evolution of an international multilateral treaty regime, with appropriate monitoring bodies. At the time of the only previous World Conference on Human Rights that held in Teheran in 1968 not a single human rights treaty body existed. By the time of the world conference in Vienna, several treaty bodies had come into existence under seven treaties namely the International Covenant on Civil and Political Rights, 1977 the International Covenant on Economic, Social and Cultural Rights, 1966 the Convention on the Elimination of all Forms of Racial Discrimination, 1966 the Convention on the Suppression and Punishment of the Crime of Apartheid, 1973 the Convention on the Elimination of Discrimination against Torture, and the Convention on the Rights of the

Child, 1989. At the time of the Vienna Conference 168 States were parties to these treaties, all plugged into their monitoring procedures.

Voidness of Existing Laws

Clause (1) of article 13 provides that the existing laws which clash with the exercise of the fundamental rights conferred by Part III of the Constitution shall, to that extent, be void; *Keshavan* v. *State of Bombay*, (1951) SCR 228: AIR 1951 SC 128: 53 Bom LR 458.

But they are not void *ab initio*. Existing laws which are inconsistent with any provision of Part III are rendered void only with effect from the commencement of the Constitution.

(i) *D.K. Nabhirajiah* v. *State of Mysore*, (1952) SCR 744: AIR 1952 SC 339: 1952 SCJ 490: 1952 SCA 598: ILR 1953 Mys 142.

(ii) *Pannalal Biniraj* v. *Union of India*, AIR 1957 SC 397 (412): 1957 SCR 233: (1957) 31 ITR 565.

(iii) *Rabindra* v. *Union of India*, AIR 1970 SC 470 (479): (1970) 1 SCC 84: (1970) 2 SCR 697.

Working of Act

How an Act has been worked may be looked at for assessing validity; *Charan Lal Sahu* v. *Union of India*, (1990) 1 SCC 613 (667): AIR 1990 SC 1480: (1989) Supp 2 SCR 597: 1989 Supp SCALE 1.

Right to Equality

14. Equality before law.—The State shall not deny to any person equality before the law or the equal protection of the laws within the territory of India.

Notes on Article 14

Administrative Order

The reasons must be stated in order or official file contemporaneously maintained; *East Coast Railway* v. *Mahadev Appa Rao*, AIR 2010 SC 2794.

Admission in College and Reservations

For admission to LL.B. course in the Department of Laws in the Punjab University, reservation of seats for employees of the University and their wards is unconditional. It has no reasonable nexus with the object of selection; *Parveen Hans* v. *Registrar*, AIR 1990 NOC 107 (P&H): (1990) 1 Serv LR 808. Such reservations cannot be made as a measure of welfare. Following decisions were referred:

(i) *Prasanna Dinkar Sohale* v. *Director-in-charge, Laxminarayan Institute of Technology, Nagpur*, AIR 1982 Bom 176.

(ii) *Ajay Kumar* v. *Chandigarh Administration Union Territory, Chandigarh*, AIR 1983 P&H 8: ILR (1983) 2 P&H 297.

(iii) *Ajay Kumar Mittal* v. *Haryana Agricultural University, Hissar*, AIR 1984 P&H 278.

(iv) *Ashwinder Kaur* v. *Punjab University*, AIR 1989 P&H 190.

(v) *P.S. Doshi* v. *State of Madhya Pradesh*, AIR 1990 MP 171 (185, 186) (DB) (V.D. Gyani & A.G. Qureshi, JJ.,).

On the question of reservation in educational institutions (particularly medical institutions) *see* further the following cases:—

(i) *State of Rajasthan* v. *Ashok Kumar Gupta*, AIR 1989 SC 177: (1988) 1 SCC 93: JT 1988 (4) SC 176.

(ii) *Sanjay Mehrotra (Dr.)* v. *G.S.V.M. Medical College, Kanpur*, AIR 1989 SC 775: (1989) 1 SCC 559: JT 1989 (1) SC 274: 1989 All WC 653: (1989) 1 UPLBEC 431: 1989 Ed Cas 50.

(iii) *Municipal Corporation of Greater Bombay* v. *Thukral Anjali Deokumar*, AIR 1989 SC 1194: (1989) 2 SCC 249: JT 1989 (1) SC 468.

(iv) *Dinesh Kumar (Dr.)* v. *Motilal Nehru Medical College, Allahabad*, AIR 1986 SC 1877: (1986) 3 SCC 727: JT 1986 SC 97.

(v) *Suneel Jatley* v. *State of Haryana*, AIR 1984 SC 1534: (1984) 4 SCC 296.

(vi) *Pradeep Jain (Dr.)* v. *Union of India*, AIR 1984 SC 1420: (1984) 3 SCC 654: 1984 Ed Cas 237: (1984) 3 SCR 942.

(vii) *Madhuwanti* v. *State*, AIR 1983 Bom 443: 1984 MLLJ 23.

(viii) *Mini* v. *State of Kerala*, AIR 1980 SC 838: (1980) 2 SCC 216: (1980) 2 SCR 829.

(ix) *Jagdish Saran (Dr.)* v. *Union of India*, AIR 1980 SC 820: (1980) 2 SCC 768: (1980) 12 Lawyer 21: ILR 1980 HP 61.

(x) *D.N. Chanchala* v. *State of Mysore*, AIR 1971 SC 1762: (1971) 2 SCC 293: (1971) Supp SCR 608.

Arbitrary Action and Discretion

Legislation which give a wide power to the executive to select cases for special treatment, without indicating the policy, may be set aside as violative of equality. On the one hand, provisions which lay down policy are likely to be upheld. But, on the other hand, provisions which fail to give such guidance are likely to be invalidated. Important judicial decisions on this subject are:

(i) *State of West Bengal* v. *Anwar Ali*, (1952) SCR 284: AIR 1952 SC 75: 1952 Cr LJ 510.

(ii) *Meenakshi Mills* v. *Vishwanath*, AIR 1955 SC 13: (1955) 1 SCR 787: (1954) 261 TR 713.

(iii) *Avinder Singh* v. *State of Punjab*, AIR 1979 SC 321: (1979) 1 SCC 137: 1979 (1) SCJ 937: 1979 SCWR 372: (1979) 1 SCR 845: 1979 UPTC 461, paragraph 9.

(iv) *Ajit Singh* v. *State of Punjab*, AIR 1967 SC 856 (886) : (1967) 2 SCR 143.

The law provides for special treatment to Government or other public bodies was held not to be discriminatory, but from that it does not follow that every law which gives differential treatment to Govt. or other public bodies is necessarily immune from challenge on the ground of discrimination; *Maganlal Changalal (P.) Ltd.* v. *Municipal Corpn. of Greater Bombay*, (1974) 2 SCC 402: AIR 1974 SC 2009: (1975) 1 SCR I.

In *Shri Sita Ram Sugar Co. Ltd.* v. *Union of India*, AIR 1990 SC 1277 (1297): (1990) 3 SCC 223, the Supreme Court (Mr. Justice Thommen) has laid down, that "any act of the repository of power, whether legislative or administrative or quasi judicial is open to challenge, if it is in conflict with the Constitution or the governing Act or the general principles of the law of the land, or if it is so arbitrary or unreasonable that no fair minded authority could ever have made it".

These observations were made in the context of a challenge to an order for the price fixation of levy sugar under the Essential Commodities Act, 1955. In Footnote 8 to paragraph 52 of the judgment, the following English and American cases as well as Canadian and Australian cases, have been collected:—

See the observations of Lord Russell in *Kruse* v. *Jhonson*, (1898) 2 QB 91: 14 TLR 416, and that of Lord Greene. M.R. in *Associated Provincial Picture Houses Ltd.* v. *Wednesbury Corporation*, (1948) 1 KB 223: (1947) 2 All ER 680. *See* also *Mixnam Properties Ltd.* v. *Chertsey U.D.C.*, (1965) AC 735; *Commissioner of Customs and Excise* v. *Cure and Dooley Ltd.*, (1962) 1 QB 340; *McEldowner* v. *Forde*, (1971) AC 632 (HL); *Carltona Ltd.* v. *Commissioners of Works*, (1943) 2 All ER 560 (564); *Point of Ayr. Collieries Ltd.* v. *Lloyd George*, (1943) 2 All ER 546; *Scott* v. *Glasgow Corporation*, (1989) AC 470 (492); *Robert Baird. L.D. City of Glasgow*, (1936) AC 32 (42); *Manhattan General Equipment Co.* v. *Commissioner*, (1935) 297 US 129 (134); *Yates (Arthur) & Co. Ltd.* v. *Vegetable Seeds Committee*, (1945-46) 72 CIR 37; *Bailey* v. *Conole*, (1931) 34 WALR 18; *Body Builders Ltd.* v. *City of Ottawa*, (1964) 45 DLR (2d) 211; *Re Burns and Township of Haldimand*, (1966) 52 DLR (2d) 1014 and *Lynch* v. *Tilden Produce Co.*, (1923) 265 US 315 (320-322): 68 Law Ed 1034.

Backward Areas

Discrimination in favour of persons residing in backward areas is permissible *M.P. Oil Extraction* v. *State of Madhya Pradesh*, (1997) 7 SCC 592: AIR 1998 SC 145: 1997 AIR SCW 4104: JT 1997 (6) SC 97: 1997 (2) Jab LJ 214: (1997) 4 SCALE 515: 1997 (7) Supreme 267: 1997 (2) UJ (SC) 438.

Industrial units were set up in backward areas at the instance of State Government. Special treatment was given to them assuring supply of Sal seeds at concessional rates for oil extraction.

It was held that the distinction was reasonable; *M.P. Oil Extraction* v. *State of Madhya Pradesh*, (1997) 7 SCC 592: AIR 1998 SC 145: 1997 AIR SCW 4104: JT 1997 (6) SC 97: 1997 (2) Jab LJ 214: (1997) 4 SCALE 515: 1997 (7) Supreme 267: 1997 (2) UJ (SC) 438.

Ban on Sex Selection

A prospective mother who does not want to bear a child of a particular sex cannot be equated with a mother who wants to terminate the pregnancy not because of the sex of the child but because of other circumstances laid down under the Medical Termination of Pregnancy Act; *Vijay Sharma* v. *Union of India*, AIR 2008 Bom 29: 2008 (3) ALJ (NOC) 652: 2008 (2) AKAR (NOC) 244: 2007 (6) AIR Bom R 625: 2007 (6) All MR 336: 2007 (5) Bom CR 710.

Bias and *mala fide* Allegations

Bias and *mala fide* allegations are to be proved, by cogent and clear evidence; *Naresh K. Aggarwala & Co.* v. *Canbank Financial Services Ltd.*, AIR 2010 SC 2722.

Board of Control for Cricket in India (BCCI)

BCCI enjoys monopoly status as regards to regulation of sport of cricket in India. It exercises enormous public functions, hence is bound to follow doctrine of fairness and good faith in all its activities; *Board of Control of Cricket, India* v. *Netaji Cricket Club*, AIR 2005 SC 592: 2005 AIR SCW 230: 2005 (2) All CJ 1283: 2005 (2) All WC 1965: JT 2005 (1) SC 235: (2005) 4 SCC 741: 2005 (1) SCJ 725: (2005) 1 SCALE 121: 2005 (1) Supreme 507: 2005 (1) UJ (SC) 334.

Change of Name

In a Calcutta case, the Management of a School passed a resolution to change the name of the school after accepting a donation. Board accepted the resolution and the procedure adopted was in accordance with relevant statutory provisions. It was held that the action was taken for development of the institution and was valid; *Manoranjan Das* v. *State of West Bengal*, AIR 1998 Cal 22: 1998 CWN 47.

Citizenship

Foreigners do not have a fundamental right to obtain Indian Citizenship; *David John Hopkins* v. *Union of India*, AIR 1997 Mad 366: 1997 Writ LR 681.

Concept of Equality

Concept of equality cannot be pressed to commit another wrong; *Kastha Niwarak G. S. S. Maryadit, Indore* v. *President, Indore Development Authority*, AIR 2006 SC 1142: 2006 AIR SCW 712: 2006 (2) All WC 1139: 2006 (3) JCR SC 75: (2006) 2 SCC 604: 2006 (2) SCJ 361: 2006 (3) SRJ 367: (2006) 2 SCALE 274: 2006 (2) Supreme 121.

Defection

Defection – Para 2(2) of Tenth Schedule of Constitution prohibiting independent candidates from joining any political party after his election as an independent candidate is not discriminatory; *Imkong Imchen* v. *Union of India*, AIR 2006 Gau 1: 2006 (1) ALJ (NOC) 151: 2006 (1) AIR Jhar (NOC) 126: 2005 Gau LT (supp) 75.

Discrimination

Action of State creating class within class violates article 14; *State of Uttar Pradesh* v. *Committee of Management*, AIR 2010 SC 402.

Disinvestment

In the matter of the policy decision of the Government in respect of economic matter, the court cannot interfere unless such policy is contrary to the Act or Constitution. The appropriate forum for testing the policy is the court, *BALCO Employees' Union* v. *Union of India*, AIR 2002 SC 350: (2002) 2 SCC 333: (2002) 108 Comp Cas 193: (2002) 100 FJR 152.

Doctrine of Natural Justice

This doctrine is termed as a synonym of fairness in the concept of justice and stands as the most accepted methodology of a governmental action; *Kumaon Mandal Vikas Nigam Ltd.* v. *Girja Shankar Pant*, AIR 2001 SC 24: (2001) 1 SCC 182: 2001 Lab IC 11.

Education

Rules of admission (to medical courses) specifying length of service for purposes of claiming admission in the quota reserved for children of ex-servicemen, are valid; *G. Beena v. Andhra Pradesh University of Health Sciences*, AIR 1990 AP 247: (1990) 2 Andh LT 67, paragraph 16 (Full Bench of 5 judges). "The reservation made in favour of the children of ex-servicemen is not one of the categories mentioned in article 15(4) of the Constitution. But such reservations have been upheld by the courts on the ground of reasonable classification."

Equal Citizens

The superiors of disabled employees are duty bound to follow law and it is not open to them to allow their bias to defeat their lawful rights.

What the law permits to them is no charity or largess but their right as equal citizens of the country; *Bhagwan Dass v. Punjab State Electricity Board*, AIR 2008 SC 990: 2008 AIR SCW 534: 2008 (1) All WC 827: 2008 (2) Lab LN 1: 2008 (2) Mad LJ 79: 2008 (2) Mad LW 866: (2008) 1 SCC 579: 2008 (2) SRJ 76: (2008) 1 SCALE 64: 2008 (2) Serv LR 32.

Equal Pay for Equal Work

The doctrine of equal pay for equal work postulates equal pay for equal work for those who are equally placed in all respects, *Uttar Pradesh Sugar Corpn. Ltd. v. Sant Raj Singh*, AIR 2006 SC 2296: 2006 AIR SCW 3013: 2006 (4) ALJ 590: 2006 (3) LLJ 509: 2006 (4) LLN 163: 2006 (4) MLJ 618: (2006) 9 SCC 82: 2006 (7) SCJ 30: 2006 (3) SCT 56: (2006) 6 SCALE 205: 2006 (6) Supreme 174; *Supreme Court Employees Welfare Assocn. v. Union of India*, AIR 1990 SC 334: 1990 Lab IC 324: (1989) 4 SCC 187; *State of Orissa v. Balaram Sahu*, AIR 2003 SC 33: 2002 AIR SCW 4421: 2003 (1) JCR SC 49: JT 2002 (8) SC 477: 2002 (3) LLJ 1115: (2003) 1 SCC 250: 2003 SCC (L&S) 65: 2002 (4) SCT 902: (2002) 8 SCALE 178: 2002 (7) Supreme 518: 2002 (2) UJ (SC) 1535.

Equality

The equality clause enshrined in article 14 is of wide import. It guarantees equality before the law or the equal protection of the laws within the territory of India; *John Vallamattom v. Union of India*, AIR 2003 SC 2902: (2003) 6 SCC 611: (2003) 3 KLT 66.

The equality clause in article 14 has positive concept and such equality cannot be claimed in illegality; *State of Punjab v. Col. Kuldeep Singh*, AIR 2010 SC 1937.

Equality cannot be applied when it arises out of illegality; *General Manager, Uttaranchal Jal Sansthan v. Laxmi Devi*, (2009) 7 SCC 205: AIR 2009 SC 3121: 2009 Lab IC 3613: 2009 AIR SCW 5014: 2009 (6) ALJ 451: 2009 (121) FLR 1000: (2009) 8 SCALE 503 (Para 34).

Claim for equality; *State of West Bengal v. S.K. Nurul Amin*, AIR 2010 SC 2271.

Equality in Promotion

Right of eligible employees to be considered for promotion is virtually part of fundamental right of employees; *Union of India v. Hemraj Singh Chauhan*, AIR 2010 SC 1682.

Equals and Unequals

Unequals are not only permitted to be treated unequally but also they have to be so treated; *St. Stephen's College v. University of Delhi*, (1992) 1 SCC 558: AIR 1992 SC 1630: 1992 AIR SCW 1792: JT 1991 (4) SC 548: 1992 (1) SCJ 624, paragraphs 97-100.

The 'creamy layer' in the Backward Class is to be treated 'on par' with the forward classes and is not entitled to benefits of reservation. If the 'creamy layer' is not excluded, there will be discrimination and violation of articles 14 and 16(1) in as much as equals (forwards and creamy layer of Backward Classes) cannot be treated unequally. Again, non-exclusion of creamy layer will also be violative of articles 14, 16(1) and 16(4) since unequals (the creamy layer) cannot be treated as equals that is to say, equal to the rest of the Backward Class; *Indra Sawhney v. Union of India*, AIR 2000 SC 498: (2000) 1 SCC 168: 2000 SCC (L&S) 1.

The equal treatment to unequals is nothing but inequality. To put both categories—tainted and the rest—at par is wholly unjustified, arbitrary, unconstitutional being violative of article 14 of the Constitution; *Onkar Lal Bajaj v. Union of India*, AIR 2003 SC 2562: (2003) 2 SCC 673: 2003 AIR SCW 2757: 2003 (1) Cal LJ 1: 2003 (1) LRI 190: 2003 (3) SRJ 200: (2002) 9 SCALE 501: 2003 (1) Supreme 402.

Executive Action

Occasionally, administrative action which violates equality comes up for scrutiny before the courts. Such action may be based on statute or may be purely executive action of an administrative nature, that is, of non-statutory character. In either case, a statutory or non-statutory order of the executive which is arbitrary may be set aside.

 (i) *Gopi Chand* v. *Delhi Administration*, AIR 1959 SC 609: (1959) Supp 2 SCR 87: 1959 Cr LJ 782.

 (ii) *Iron & Metal Traders* v. *Haskiel*, AIR 1984 SC 629: (1984) 1 SCC 304: (1983) 2 LLJ 504: 1984 Lab IC 182.

 (iii) *Vishundas Hundumal* v. *State of Madhya Pradesh*, AIR 1981 SC 1636: (1981) 2 SCC 410: 1981 UJ (SC) 306: 1981 BBCJ (SC) 150: 1981 SCC (Tax) 278.

 (iv) *Indian Express Newspapers (Bombay) Private Ltd.* v. *Union of India*, AIR 1986 SC 515: (1985) 1 Comp LJ 115: 1985 Cr LR (SC) 79: (1985) 1 SCC 641: 1985 SCC (Tax) 121: 1985 Cur Cr LJ (SC) 140: (1985) 2 SCR 287: (1986) 159 ITR 856.

 (v) *Suman Gupta* v. *State of Jammu & Kashmir*, AIR 1983 SC 1235: (1983) 4 SCC 339: 1983 UJ (SC) 897, paragraph 6.

Here the courts are not concerned with the validity of the Parent Act, but with the mode of exercise of power thereunder.

Flexibility

Article 14 has an in built flexibility to allow reasonable classification passed on an objective basis; *Premium Granites* v. *State of Tamil Nadu*, JT 1994 (1) SC 374: (1994) 2 SCC 691: AIR 1994 SC 2233

Grant-in-aid

Non-extension of the grant-in-aid by the State to non-Government law colleges but the grant of such benefit to non-Government colleges with other faculties, is patently discriminatory; *State of Maharashtra* v. *Manubhai Pragaji Vashi*, AIR 1996 SC 1: (1995) 5 SCC 730: 1995 AIR SCW 3701: JT 1995 (6) SC 119: 1997 (1) Mah LR 153: 1995 (3) SCJ 610: 1995 (4) SCT 547: 1996 (1) Serv LJ SC 1, paragraphs 10, 12.

Illegal Action

Equality clause cannot be applied to legitimise an illegal action; *Ekta Shakti Foundation* v. *Govt. of NCT of Delhi*, AIR 2006 SC 2609: 2006 AIR SCW 3601: 2006 (64) All LR 907: 2006 (3) Ker LT 601: 2006 (4) Mad LW 864: 2006 (8) SRJ 393: (2006) 7 SCALE 179: 2006 (6) Supreme 372.

Illegalities cannot be Perpetuated

Where unauthorised construction by appellant in violation of building bye-laws and terms and conditions in lease deed prejudicially affecting proper planning of industrial area, he cannot claim that benefit extended to others though illegally should be extended to him. Article 14 provides for positive equality and not negative equality; *Vishal Properties Pvt. Ltd.* v. *State of Uttar Pradesh*, AIR 2008 SC 183: 2007 AIR SCW 6540: 2008 (1) ALJ 32: 2007 (60) All Ind Cas 219: 2008 (1) Land LR 140: (2007) 11 SCC 172: 2008 (2) SCT 352: (2007) 12 SCALE 32: 2008 (4) Serv LR 66: 2007 (7) Supreme 432.

Interpretation

There is no discrimination where, owing to wrong interpretation some producers are exempted; *Eskayef* v. *C.C.E.*, (1990) 4 SCC 680: (1990) 49 ELT 649.

Land Acquisition

The classification sought to be made for determination of the amount of compensation for acquisition of the land under the Defence of India Act, 1971 *vis-a-vis* the Land Acquisition Act, 1894 is a reasonable and valid one. The said classification is found on intelligible differentia and has a rational relation with the object sought to be achieved by the legislation in question; *Union of India* v. *Chajju Ram*, AIR 2003 SC 2339: (2003) 5 SCC 568: 2003 AIR SCW 2322: 2003 (51) All

LR 534: 2003 (3) All MR 766: 2003 (3) Civ LJ 247: JT 2003 (4) SC 161: 2003 (1) LACC 595: 2003 (7) SRJ 71: (2003) 4 SCALE 155: 2003 (3) Supreme 661.

Land Ceiling

Section 4(7) of Urban Land (Ceiling and Regulation) Act, 1976, is not unconstitutional on the ground that it makes certain special provisions regarding Hindu undivided families. Such a family is not a "person", and is not to be treated as a single unit for the purpose of ceiling limit. Under section 4(7) each individual member, major or minor, has a separate ceiling; *Pratima Paul v. Competent Authority,* AIR 1990 Cal 185: (1989) 1 Cal LJ 425: (1989) 1 Cal HN 433: (1989) 2 Cal LT (HC) 80: (1989) 93 CWN 1146 (DB) (A.M. Bhattacharjee, J.).

Legitimate Expectations

There is legitimate expectations to get permission to run minority institution; *Secretary, Cannanore District Muslim Educational Association, Kanpur v. State of Kerala,* AIR 2010 SC 1955.

Premium stature of services available to patients by doctors raises a legitimate expectation; *Malaya v. Sukumar Mukherjee,* AIR 2010 SC 1162.

Limitations

Broadly speaking, judicial decisions interpreting article 14 while recognising the paramount nature of the fundamental rights, recognise the need on considerations of reality to have certain limitations. It is often stated that equality before the law guaranteed by the first part of article 14, is a negative concept while the second part is a more positive concept. Neither part of the article is above the recognition of exceptions and qualifications on special grounds. Thus, while the first part which is mentioned by Dicey (Dicey, Law of the Constitution, 9th Edition, page 202) as a second corollary of the rule of law would rule out any special 'privilege' for any authority or person. But Constitution does give certain privileges to the President and the Governors (and also to Members of Parliament and State Legislatures). Moreover some of its provisions, as interpreted, result in a certain element of discrimination. For example, the liability of the State in tort is even today in India not necessarily the same as the liability of any private employer. According to current theory, no suit lies against the Government for an injury in the course of exercise of the 'sovereign' functions of the Government; *State of Rajasthan v. Vidyawati,* AIR 1962 SC 933 (935): (1962) Supp 2 SCR 989: (1963) 1 MLJ 70 (SC); *Kasturi Lal v. State of Uttar Pradesh,* AIR 1965 SC 1039: (1965) 1 SCR 375: (1966) 2 LLJ 583: (1965) 2 Cr LJ 144; *Shyam Sundar v. State of Rajasthan,* AIR 1974 SC 890: (1974) 1 SCC 690: (1974) 3 SCR 549, paragraph 21.

Mala fide

Action taken by State in undue haste may be held to be *mala fide; Inderpreet Singh Kahlon v. State of Punjab,* AIR 2006 SC 2571: 2006 AIR SCW 3346: 2006 (3) All CJ 1826: ILR 2006 Kant SC 1 SN: 2006 (6) SCJ 107: 2006 (3) SCT 25: (2006) 5 SCALE 273: 2006 (4) Supreme 8.

Newspapers

The State cannot in view of the equality doctrine contained in article 14 of the Constitution of India, resort to the theory of "take it or leave it". The bargaining power of the State and the newspaper in matters of release of advertisements is unequal. Any unjust condition thrust upon by the State would attract the wrath of article 14; *Hindustan Times v. State of Uttar Pradesh,* AIR 2003 SC 250: (2003) 1 SCC 591: (2003) 1 LLJ 206: (2002) 258 ITR 469.

Panchayat: Removal of Members

U.P. Panchayat Raj Act, 1947, section 14, is valid. It empowers members of the Gram Panchayat to remove the Pradhan of Gram Sabha by a motion of no confidence. It is not unconstitutional, as infringing (a) democracy or (b) article 14; *Ram Beli v. District Panchayat Rajadhukari,* AIR 1998 SC 1222: (1998) 1 SCC 680: 1998 All LJ 832.

Pension

By erroneous interpretation of the rules if pensionary benefits are granted to someone it would not mean that the said mistake should be perpetuated by the direction of the court; *Union of India v. Rakesh Kumar,* AIR 2001 SC 1877: (2000) 4 SCC 309: 2001 SCC (L&S) 707.

The decision in *D.S. Nakara* v. *Union of India*, AIR 1983 SC 130: (1983) 1 SCC 305: 1983 Lab IC 1: (1983) 1 LLJ 104: 1983 SCC (Lab) 145: 1983 UJ (SC) 217: 1983 BLJR 122: (1983) 1 SCWR 390: (1983) 15 Lawyer 51: 1983 (1) SCJ 188, can be invoked so as to give liberalised pension to those who had already retired prior to liberalisation; *State of Rajasthan* v. *Prem Raj*, AIR 1997 SC 1081: (1997) 10 SCC 317: 1997 SCC (L&S) 1688.

But it cannot be applied irrespective of the facts of the case; *K.L. Rathee* v. *Union of India*, AIR 1997 SC 2763: (1997) 6 SCC 7: (1997) 4 SLR 545: 1997 Lab IC 2853.

Retrospective reduction of pension that had already become payable to employees is unreasonable and void; *Chairman Railway Board* v. *C.R. Raugadharniah*, (1994) 4 SLR 759.

Principles of Natural Justice

Court is not bound to issue notice to complainant and hear him is relation to release of person accused of bailable offence such as defamation. The cancellation of bail on ground that the complainant was not heard is not proper; *Rasiklal* v. *Kishore Khanchand Wadhwani*, AIR 2009 SC 1341: 2009 Cr LJ 1887: 2009 AIR SCW 1945: 2009 (2) Chand Cr C 288: 2009 (4) MPHT 1: 2009 (43) OCR 28: 2009 (1) Raj LW 580: (2009) 4 SCC 446: (2009) 3 SCALE 9: 2009 (2) SCC (Cri) 338.

Procedural Discrimination

Article 14 forbids discrimination in matters of procedure also.

 (i) *State of West Bengal* v. *Anwar Ali*, (1952) SCR 284 (314, 328-357): AIR 1952 SC 75: 1952 Cr LJ 510.

 (ii) *State of Orissa* v. *Dhirendranath*, AIR 1961 SC 1715.

 (iii) *Kathi Raning Rawat* v. *State of Saurashtra*, (1952) SCR 435: AIR 1952 SC 123: 1952 SCJ 168: 1952 Cr LJ 805: 1952 Mad WN 762: 1952 Mad WN (Cri) 210: 1952 SCA 245.

 (iv) *Special Courts Bill (In re:)*, AIR 1979 SC 478: (1979) 1 SCC 380: (1979) 2 SCR 476.

 (v) *Chopra* v. *Union of India*, AIR 1987 SC 357: (1987) 1 SCC 422: (1987) 1 LLJ 255.

Rajasthani Language

Non-inclusion of Rajasthani language in the Eighth Schedule to the Constitution does not violate article 14. Such policy matters have to be left to the State. Judicial interference is uncalled for in the absence of *mala fides*; *Kanhaiya Lal Sethia* v. *Union of India*, (1997) 6 SCC 573: AIR 1998 SC 365: 1997 AIR SCW 4348: JT 1997 (7) SC 289: 1997 (3) SCJ 224: (1997) 5 SCALE 341: 1997 (7) Supreme 127: 1997 UJ (SC) 457.

Reasonable Restriction

A limited power of exemption from the operation of noise rules granted by the Central Government in exercise of its statutory powers is not unreasonable. The power to grant exemption is a reasonable restriction placed in public interest; *Forum, Prevention of Envn. & Sound Pollution* v. *Union of India*, AIR 2006 SC 348: 2005 AIR SCW 5890: 2006 (62) All LR 339: 2006 (1) All MR 248: 2006 (1) All WC 5: 2006 (1) Cal LJ 99: 2006 (1) JCR SC 90: JT 2005 (9) SC 319: 2005 (4) Ker LT 824: 2006 (1) Mad LJ 49: (2005) 8 SCC 796: 2005 (8) SCJ 233: (2005) 9 SCALE 69: 2005 (7) Supreme 504.

Reasonableness

An important consequence of the rights to equality is the element of reasonableness. Classification which is unreasonable is open to challenge and to this extent the policy of legislation is open to judicial review. This aspect is illustrated *inter alia*, in the following decisions:—

 (i) *Northern India Caterers (Private) Ltd.* v. *State of Punjab*, AIR 1967 SC 1581: (1967) 3 SCR 399: 13 Law Rep 713: 1968 (1) SCJ 475.

 (ii) *New Manek Chowk Spg. and Wvg. Mills Co. Ltd.* v. *Municipal Corporation of the City of Ahmedabad*, AIR 1967 SC 1801 (1810): (1967) 2 SCR 679: 1967 Cr LJ 1705: 1968 (1) SCJ 332: 9 Guj LR 390: 14 Law Rep 304.

 (iii) *Nagpur Improvement Trust* v. *Vithal Rao*, AIR 1973 SC 689 (694): (1973) 1 SCC 500: 1973 SCD 43: (1973) 1 SCWR 127: 1973 Mah LJ 373.

Any act of the repository of power whether legislative or administrative or quasi judicial is open to challenge if it is in conflict with Constitution or the governing Act or the general principles of the law of the land or if it is so arbitrary or unreasonable that no fair-minded authority could ever have made it; *Shri Sita Ram Sugar Co. Ltd.* v. *Union of India*, AIR 1990 SC 1277 (1297): (1990) 3 SCC 223: JT 1990 (1) SC 462.

Right to have Reasoned Order

The Courts though are not liable to furnish the information like public bodies are still expected to reveal reasons in order; *Kasim Maraikkayar* v. *Haji Kathija Beevi Trust, Nagapattinam*, AIR 2008 Mad 91: 2008 AIHC 384 (NOC): 2008 (3) ALJ (NOC) 591: 2008 (2) AKAR (NOC) 186: 2008 (1) CTC 190: 2008 (2) Mad LJ 392.

Royalties for Industries

Government decisions in matters of policy, if *prima facie* based on a plausible rationale, are generally upheld by the courts. A certain element of discretion is thus allowed to be exercised by the executive; *M.P. Oil Extraction* v. *State of Madhya Pradesh*, AIR 1998 SC 145: (1997) 7 SCC 592: 1997 AIR SCW 4104: JT 1997 (6) SC 97: 1997 (2) Jab LJ 214: (1997) 4 SCALE 515: 1997 (7) Supreme 267: 1997 (2) UJ (SC) 438.

Rule for Termination of Service

Rule for termination of service of permanent employee without reason is void; *D.T.C.* v. *Mazdoor Congress*, AIR 1991 SC 101: (1991) Supp 1 SCC 600: (1991) 1 LLJ 395, paragraphs 199, 244, 257, 262-264, 267.

In service, there could be only one norm for confirmation or promotion of persons belonging to the same cadre. No junior shall be confirmed or promoted without considering the case of his senior. Any deviation from this principle will have demoralising effect in service, apart from being contrary to article 16(1) of the Constitution.

Where the High Court directed that an employee be confirmed with reference to a particular date and because of the faulty implementation of the High Court's order he was given promotions superseding many of his seniors even though they were eligible and suitable for promotion, the promotion given to him being totally unjustified and arbitrary, the Government could rectify the same, refix the seniority and consequently revert him; *Bal Kishan* v. *Delhi Administration*, AIR 1990 SC 100: (1989) Supp 2 SCC 351: (1989) 58 FLR 687 (K. Jagannatha Shetty and A.M. Ahmadi, JJ.).

Scheduled Castes

Denial of benefits to migrating members of Scheduled Castes and Scheduled Tribes does not violate article 14 or article 19; *State of Maharashtra* v. *Union of India*, JT 1994 (4) SC 423: 1994 AIR SCW 3305 : (1994) 5 SCC 244.

Scope of Article 14

Article 14 has a positive concept. No body can claim equality in illegality; *Uttar Pradesh State Sugar Corpn. Ltd.* v. *Sant Raj Singh*, AIR 2006 SC 2296: 2006 AIR SCW 3013: 2006 (4) ALJ 590: 2006 (3) LLJ 509: 2006 (4) LLN 163: (2006) 9 SCC 82: 2006 (7) SCJ 30: 2006 (3) SCT 56: (2006) 6 SCALE 205: 2006 (6) Supreme 174.

Article 14 is to be understood in the light of directive principles; *Indra Sawhney* v. *Union of India*, AIR 1993 SC 477: (1992) Supp 3 SCC 217: 1992 SCC (L&S) Supp 1, paragraph 4.

Article 14 guarantees equal treatment to persons who are equally situated; *Government of Andhra Pradesh* v. *Maharshi Publishers Pvt. Ltd.*, AIR 2003 SC 296: (2003) 1 SCC 95: 2002 AIR SCW 4771: JT 2002 (9) SC 277: 2002 (10) SRJ 457: (2002) 8 SCALE 291: 2002 (7) Supreme 570.

Power granted by a provision may be abused and cannot merely be ground to declare provision unconstitutional; *Ahmed Noormohmed Bhatti* v. *State of Gujarat*, AIR 2005 SC 2115: 2005 Cr LJ 2157: 2005 AIR SCW 1923: 2005 (29) All Ind Cas 746: 2005 (2) BLJR 901: 2005 (2) Crimes 26: JT 2005 (3) SC 484: 2005 (31) OCR 24: (2005) 3 SCC 647: (2005) 3 SCALE 300: 2005 (2) Supreme 643.

Service

Indian Administrative Services (Second Amendment) Regulation, 1989 which brings about classification of officers which is arbitrary and unreasonable, is unconstitutional; *T. Sham Bhat* v. *Union of India*, JT 1994 (5) SC 165: (1994) Supp 3 SCC 340: (1994) 4 SLR 598.

Service Rules

On the question whether service rules would violate article 14, the undermentioned decisions may be seen:

   (i) *Air India* v. *Narqesh Mirza*, (1981) 4 SCC 335: AIR 1981 SC 1829: (1981) 2 LLJ 314.

   (ii) *Sudhir Chandra Sarkar* v. *Tata Iron and Steel Company*, (1984) 3 SCC 369: AIR 1984 SC 1064: 1984 Lab IC 790: (1984) 1 Serv LJ 575: (1984) 65 FJR 61: (1984) 49 Fac LR 1: 1984 SCC (Lab) 540: (1984) 2 LLN 229: (1984) 2 LLJ 223.

   (iii) *K. L. Tripathi* v. *State Bank of India*, (1984) 1 SCC 43: AIR 1984 SC 273: 1983 Lab IC 1680: (1983) 2 Serv LJ 623: (1983) 63 FJR 312: (1984) 1 LLJ 2: 1984 SCC (Lab) 62: (1984) 48 FLR 38: (1984) 1 LLN 19: (1984) 1 SCWR 150: (1984) 16 Lawyers 76.

   (iv) *Union of India* v. *Tulsi Ram Patel*, (1985) 3 SCC 398 (453): AIR 1985 SC 1416: 1985 Lab IC 1393: 1985 SCC (Lab) 672: (1985) 2 LLJ 206: (1985) 2 LLN 488: (1985) 2 Cur LR 117: (1985) 3 Comp LJ 45, paragraphs 72 and 95.

   (v) *Workmen* v. *Hindustan Steel Ltd.*, (1984) Supp SCC 554: AIR 1985 SC 251: 1985 SCC (L&S) 260.

   (vi) *Central Inland Water Transport Corporation Ltd.* v. *Brojo Nath Ganguly*, (1986) 3 SCC 156: 1986 Lab IC 1312: 1986 (2) Supreme 479: 1986 SCC (Lab) 429: (1986) 2 LLJ 171: 1986 (2) SCJ 201: (1986) 2 LLN 382: (1986) 3 Comp LJ 1.

   (vii) *O.P. Bhandari* v. *I.T.D.C.*, (1986) 4 SCC 337: AIR 1987 SC 111: (1986) 2 LLJ 509.

   (viii) *Lena Khan* v. *Union of India*, (1987) 2 SCC 402: AIR 1987 SC 1515: 1987 Lab IC 1035.

Air Hostesses and Deputy Chief Air Hostesses belong to the same class, in view of the duties performed by them. However, as the Air India Corporation had already adopted the policy of avoiding discrimination, the writ petition had become infructuous; *Lena Khan* v. *Union of India*, (1987) 2 SCC 402: AIR 1987 SC 1515: 1987 SCC (L&S) 127: 1987 Lab IC 1035 [case subsequent to *Air India* v. *Nerqesh Mirza*, (1981) 4 SCC 335: AIR 1981 SC 1829: (1981) 2 LLJ 314: 1981 Lab IC 1313.

Source of Article 14

The source of article 14 lies in the American and the Irish Constitutions. It may be mentioned that the Preamble to the Indian Constitution speaks of equality of status and of opportunity and this article gives effect to that principle in the text of the Constitution. In a sense, the demand for equality is linked up with the history of the freedom movement in India. Indians wanted the same rights and privileges that their British masters enjoyed in India and the desire for civil rights was implicit in the formation of the Indian National Congress in 1885. The Commonwealth of India Bill, 1925, in clause 8 demanded, *inter alia* equality before the law and provided especially that there was to be "no disqualification or disability on the ground only of sex", along with the provision that all persons were to have equal right to the use of "roads, courts of justice and all other places of business or resort dedicated to the public". *See* Chakravarty and Bhattacharya, Congress in Evolution, (1940), page 27. The right to equality finds place in the report drawn up by Motilal Nehru as Chairman of the Committee appointed to determine principles of the Constitution for India (1928). The Karachi Resolution (March 1931) reiterated, *inter alia*, this right in the resolution on fundamental rights and economic and social change. Chakravarty and Bhattacharya, Congress in Evolution, (1940) page 28. The Sapru Report (1945) incorporating the proposals of the Sapru Committee, while laying emphasis on "minorities" did enunciate the fundamental rights and in page 260 of the report, described the fundamental rights of the proposed new Constitution as a standing warning to all—

> "that what the Constitution demands and expects is perfect equality between one section of the community and another in the matter of political and civic rights, equality of

liberty and security in the enjoyment of the freedom of religion, worship, and the pursuit of the ordinary applications of life."

State Policy

Issuance of notification/circulars giving concessions to entrepreneurs for rapid industrialisation cannot be said to be against provisions of law; *Parenteral Drugs India Ltd.* v. *State of Himachal Pradesh*, AIR 2008 (NOC) 380 (HP).

Tax Exemptions

The Supreme Court has upheld the validity of section 10 (10C) of the Income-tax Act, 1961, which grants certain tax exemptions to employees in the Public Sector who retire voluntarily. An objection was raised against this provision in *Shashikant Laxman Kale* v. *Union of India*, JT 1990 (3) SC 267: AIR 1990 SC 2114: 1990 Tax LR 877 (Judgment dated 20 July, 1990), on the ground that article 14 had been violated. But it was held that there is a rational nexus between the legislation and its object. A number of Public Sector Undertakings who had formulated a scheme for Qualitative Requirements and Finance Act, 1981 had introduced this scheme to exempt payment received by them. In accordance with the approved scheme compensation package in public sector is much lower than that of private sector undertaking and for this reason discrimination was justified. moreover, one of the afflictions of the public sector were surplus staff which are to be streamlined. the scheme was ultimately beneficial to health, prosperity of the Public Sector.

Cases referred to:

(i) *Kerala Hotel and Restaurant Association* v. *State of Kerala*, JT 1990 1 SC 324: AIR 1990 SC 913: (1990) 2 SCC 502.

(ii) *M. Jahangir Bhatusha* v. *Union of India*, JT 1989 (2) SC 465: (1989) Supp 1 SCC 201: AIR 1989 SC 1713.

(iii) *P.M. Ashwathanarayana Setty* v. *State of Karnataka*, (1989) Supp 1 SCC 696: AIR 1989 SC 100: 1988 Raj LR 611: JT 1988 (4) SC 639: (1988) 23 Reports 210: ILR (1989) Kant 1: (1989) 1 Bom CLR 169.

(iv) *Federation of Hotel and Restaurant Association of India* v. *Union of India*, JT 1989 (Supp) 168: (1989) 179 ITR 94: AIR 1990 SC 1637: (1989) 3 SCC 634.

(v) *Hindustan Paper Corporation Ltd.* v. *Government of Kerala*, (1986) 3 SCC 398: AIR 1986 SC 1541: 1986 Comp LJ 238: (1986) 2 Cur CC 689: 1986 (3) Supreme 273: (1986) 2 UJ (SC) 551: (1986) 19 STL 61: 1986 (2) SCJ 436.

(vi) *R.D. Shetty* v. *International Airport Authority of India*, (1979) 3 SCR 1014: (1979) 3 SCC 489: AIR 1979 SC 1628.

(vii) *I.T.O.* v. *N. Takin Roy Rymbai*, (1976) 103 ITR 82: (1976) 1 SCC 916: AIR 1976 SC 670.

(viii) *S.K. Dutta, I.T.O.* v. *Lawrence Singh Ingty*, (1968) 68 ITR 272 – Distinguished.

(ix) *Hindustan Antibiotics* v. *Workmen*, (1967) 1 SCR 652: AIR 1967 SC 948: 30 FJR 461: (1967) 1 LLJ 114: 14 FLR 37: (1967) 1 SCWR 361: (1967) 1 SCA 669: 1967 (1) SCJ 12 – Distinguished.

(x) *State of West Bengal* v. *Union of India*, (1964) 1 SCR 371: AIR 1963 SC 1241: (1963) 2 SCA 448.

(xi) *Pannalal Binjraj* v. *Union of India*, (1957) SCR 233: AIR 1957 SC 397: (1957) 31 ITR 565: 1957 SCA 660.

(xii) *A. Thangal Kunju Musaliar* v. *M. Venkatachalam Potti*, (1955) 2 SCR 1196: AIR 1956 SC 246: (1956) 29 ITR 349: 1956 SCA 259: 1956 SCJ 323.

Legislature can choose a method of taxing if it is not arbitrary; *Kerala Hotel* v. *State*, (1990) 2 SCC 502: AIR 1990 SC 913: (1990) 1 KLT 825.

Taxation Laws

In the matter of taxation, the court permits great latitude to the legislature. The legislature can make reasonable discrimination and make a choice in respect of districts, objects, persons, methods and even rates of taxation; *Mafatlal Industries* v. *Union of India*, (1997) 5 SCC 536: JT

1996 (11) SC 283: 1997 (1) Supreme 684: (1996) 9 SCALE 457: (1997) 99 ELT 247: 1997 (68) ECR 209.

The cancellation of benefit of concessional rate of tax available to tourist buses cannot be said to be discriminatory, *Sharma Transport* v. *Government of Andhra Pradesh*, AIR 2002 SC 322: (2002) 2 SCC 188: 2001 AIR SCW 4958: 2002 (1) ACC 85: 2002 (1) Andh LD 66: 2002 (1) Arb LR 231: JT 2001 (2) SC (Supp) 1: 2002 (1) SCJ 67: 2002 (2) SRJ 96: (2001) 8 SCALE 417: 2001 (8) Supreme 496.

Taxing Statutes

The duty of State is to act reasonably having regard to equality clause in article 14; *Corporation Bank* v. *Saraswati Abharansala*, (2009) 1 SCC 540.

Test of Equality

In determining the validity of the statutory provisions, courts in India have followed the general principle that equal protection of the laws means the right to equal treatment in similar circumstances, courts have upheld legislation containing apparently discriminatory provisions where the discrimination is based on a reasonable basis. By 'reasonable', it is meant that the classification must not be arbitrary but must be rational. The classical test as judicially enunciated requires the fulfilment of two conditions, namely:—

(1) The classification must be founded on an intelligible differential which distinguishes those that are grouped together from others.

(2) The differential must have a rational relation to the object sought to be achieved by the law under challenge. Judicial decisions laying down the important propositions on the subject are the following:—

  (i) *Chiranjit Lal* v. *Union of India*, (1950) SCR 869: AIR 1951 SC 41: (1951) 21 Comp Cas 33.

 (ii) *State of West Bengal* v. *Anwar Ali*, (1952) SCR 284: AIR 1952 SC 75: 1952 Cr LJ 510.

(iii) *Dhirendra Kumar Mandal* v. *Superintendent and Legal Remembrancer of Legal Affairs*, (1955) 1 SCR 224: AIR 1954 SC 424: (1954) 2 MLJ 128.

 (iv) *Ameerunnissa Begum* v. *Mahboob Begum*, (1953) SCR 404 (414): AIR 1953 SC 91: ILR 1953 Hyd 98: 1953 SCJ 61: 1953 SCA 565.

  (v) *Yusuf* v. *State of Bombay*, AIR 1954 SC 321: (1954) 1 SCR 930: 1954 Cr LJ 886.

 (vi) *R. Chitralekha* v. *State of Mysore*, AIR 1964 SC 1823 (1827): (1964) 6 SCR 368: 1965 1 SCA 132.

(vii) *Special Courts Bill, 1978 (in re:)*, AIR 1979 SC 478: (1979) 1 SCC 380: 1979 (2) SCJ 35: (1979) 2 SCR 476, paragraphs 74, 78, 80 to 89.

(viii) *General Manager Southern Railway* v. *Rangachari*, AIR 1962 SC 36: (1962) 2 SCR 586: 1961 2 Mad LJ (SC) 71: (1961) 2 Andh WR (SC) 71: 1961 (2) SCJ 424: (1961) 2 SCA 460.

 (ix) *Balaji* v. *State of Mysore*, AIR 1963 SC 649 (664): (1983) 1 SCC 305: (1983) 1 LLJ 104.

  (x) *D.S. Nakara* v. *Union of India*, AIR 1983 SC 130: (1983) 1 SCC 305: 1983 Lab IC 1: (1983) 1 LLJ 104: 1983 SCC (Lab) 145: 1983 UJ (SC) 217: 1983 BLJR 122: (1983) 1 SCWR 390: (1983) 15 Lawyer 51: 1983 (1) SCJ 188, paragraph 14.

 (xi) *Matajog* v. *Bhari*, AIR 1956 SC 44: (1955) 2 SCR 925: (1955) 28 ITR 941.

(xii) *Atam Prakash* v. *State of Haryana*, AIR 1986 SC 859: (1986) 2 SCC 249: (1986) 1 PLR 329.

(xiii) *Pradeep Jain (Dr.)* v. *Union of India*, AIR 1984 SC 1420: (1984) 3 SCC 654: 1984 Ed Cas 237: (1984) 3 SCR 942.

(xiv) *Haji Usmanbhai Hasanbhai Qureshi* v. *State of Gujarat*, AIR 1986 SC 1213: (1986) 3 SCC 12: (1986) 1 MCC 163: 1986 Cr LR (SC) 370: 1986 (3) Supreme 250: 1986 (2) SCJ 447.

 (xv) *K. Thimmappa* v. *Chairman, Central Board of Directors, State Bank of India*, AIR 2001 SC 467: (2001) 2 SCC 259: (2001) 1 LLN 814.

Uncanalised Discretion

Uncanalised discretion vested in an administrative authority is not permissible; *D.T.C.* v. *Mazdoor Union*, AIR 1991 SC 101: (1991) Supp 1 SCC 600: (1991) 1 LLJ 395, paragraphs 276, 279, 280.

Zone-wise Merit List for Recruitment

Preparation of zone-wise merit list of candidates for recruitment to All India Service is unconstitutional (even if tests are held in different zones); *Radhey Shyam Singh* v. *Union of India,* AIR 1997 SC 1610: (1997) 1 SCC 60: (1997) 1 LLJ 972: 1997 SCC (L&S) 136.

15. Prohibition of discrimination on grounds of religion, race, caste, sex or place of birth.—(1) The State shall not discriminate against any citizen on grounds only of religion, race, caste, sex, place of birth or any of them.

(2) No citizen shall, on grounds only of religion, race, caste, sex, place of birth or any of them, be subject to any disability, liability, restriction or condition with regard to—

(a) access to shops, public restaurants, hotels and places of public entertainment; or

(b) the use of wells, tanks, bathing ghats, roads and places of public resort maintained wholly or partly out of State funds or dedicated to the use of general public.

(3) Nothing in this article shall prevent the State from making any special provision for women and children.

[1][(4) Nothing in this article or in clause (2) of article 29 shall prevent the State from making any special provision for the advancement of any socially and educationally backward classes of citizens or for the Scheduled Castes and the Scheduled Tribes.]

[2][(5) Nothing in this article or in sub-clause (g) of clause (1) of article 19 shall prevent the State from making any special provision, by law, for the advancement of any socially and educationally backward classes of citizens or for the Scheduled Castes or the Scheduled Tribes in so far as such special provisions relate to their admission to educational institutions including private educational institutions, whether aided or unaided by the State, other than the minority educational institutions referred to in clause (1) of article 30.]

Notes on Article 15

To promote the educational advancement of the socially and educationally backward classes of citizens, *i.e.,* the OBCs or of the Scheduled Castes and Scheduled Tribes in matters of admission of students belonging to these categories in unaided educational institutions, other than the minority educational institutions referred to in clause (1) of article 30 of the Constitution, in article 15 clause (5) has been inserted after clause (4). The new clause (5) shall enable the Parliament as well as the State Legislatures to make appropriate laws for the purposes mentioned above.

Area-wise Reservation

Area-wise reservation (article 371D) prevails over reservation under article 15(4); *Devarakonda Rajesh Babu* v. *Nizam Institute of Medical Sciences,* AIR 1998 AP 162: 1998 (1) AP LJ 463: 1998 (1) Andh LD 53: 1997 (6) Andh LT 290 (FB).

Backward Class

Clause (4) of article 15 may at the first sight appear to be a blanket provision, protecting any kind of beneficial discrimination in the nature of special provisions for the benefit of the classes mentioned therein. However, apart from questions as to when a particular class can be legitimately regarded as backward class, discriminatory provisions of such a nature may be struck down as unreasonable in the circumstances. This is on the basis that the general right of

---

1. Added by the Constitution (First Amendment) Act, 1951, sec. 2 (w.e.f. 18-6-1951).

2. Ins. by the Constitution (Ninety-third Amendment) Act, 2005, sec. 2 (w.e.f. 20-1-2006).

equality guaranteed by article 14, would override the special provision under article 15(4), in such circumstances. Hence, reservation of an excessively high percentage of seats in technical institutions for each classes would be void. In fact, ordinarily speaking, reservation in excess of 50 per cent of available seats may not be upheld. The undermentioned decisions may be seen on this point:

(i) *State of Uttar Pradesh* v. *U.S.V. Balaram*, AIR 1972 SC 1375 (1395): (1972) 1 SCC 660: (1972) 1 SCA 214: (1972) 3 SCR 247.

(ii) *Rajendran* v. *Union of India*, AIR 1968 SC 507: (1968) 1 SCR 721: (1968) 2 LLJ 407.

(iii) *M.R. Balaji* v. *State of Mysore*, AIR 1963 SC 649 (662): (1963) Supp 1 SCR 439: 1962 Ker LT (SC) 145: (1963) 2 SCA 1.

(iv) *Kumari K.S. Jayasree* v. *State of Kerala*, AIR 1976 SC 2381: (1976) 3 SCC 730: 1976 UJ (SC) 805: (1977) 1 SCWR 3: 1977 (1) SCJ 101: (1977) 1 SCR 194: (1977) 9 Lawyer 115.

(v) *Periakaruppan* v. *State of Tamil Nadu*, AIR 1971 SC 2303: (1971) 3 SCC 38: (1971) 2 MLJ 65 (SC).

(vi) *Abdul Latif* v. *State of Bihar*, AIR 1964 Pat 393 (395): ILR 45 Pat 127.

(vii) *Anil* v. *Dean, Govt. Medical College, Nagpur*, AIR 1985 Bom 153, paragraph 6.

In making reservation by executive order by virtue of article 15(4), the State has to take care that it is not unduly wide. Apart from Scheduled Castes and Scheduled Tribes, the other classes eligible for reservation, if made by the State, is the category of "socially and educationally backward classes of citizens". Undermentioned decisions may be seen on the above aspect:

(i) *K.C. Vasanthkumar* v. *State of Karnataka*, AIR 1985 SC 1495: 1985 Supp SCC 714, paragraphs 36, 57, 88 and 148 to 151.

(ii) *Comptroller and Auditor-General* v. *Jagannathan*, AIR 1987 SC 537: (1986) 2 SCC 679: (1986) 2 LLN 11: (1986) 1 SLR 712, paragraphs 21-22 and 30-31.

(iii) *Deepak* v. *State of Bihar*, AIR 1982 Pat 126: 1982 BBCJ (HC) 295: 1982 BLJ 340: 1982 BLJR 433: 1982 Pat LJR 267, paragraph 12.

(iv) *Arti Sapru* v. *State of Jammu & Kashmir*, AIR 1981 SC 1009: (1981) 2 SCC 484: 1981 Srignar LJ (SC) 1 (SC): 1981 Cur LJ (Civ) 175: 1981 UJ (SC) 333: 1981 SCC (Lab) 398, paragraphs 7 and 9.

(v) *Nishi Maghu* v. *State of Jammu & Kashmir*, AIR 1980 SC 1975: (1980) 4 SCC 95: 1980 Srinagar LJ (SC) 13.

(vi) *State of Madhya Pradesh* v. *Kumari Nivedita Jain*, AIR 1981 SC 2045: (1981) 4 SCC 296: (1982) 1 SCR 759, paragraph 25.

(vii) *State of Kerala* v. *N.M. Thomas*, AIR 1976 SC 490: (1976) 2 SCC 310: (1976) 1 LLJ 376.

Constitutional 93rd Amendment 2005

Act of 2005 introducing article 15(5) does not interfere with executive power of State and not invalid for not following procedure under article 368; *Ashoka Kumar Thakur* v. *Union of India*, 2008 AIR SCW 2899: AIR 2008 SC (Supp) 1 (Para 193). K.G. Balakrishnan CJI.

Discrimination

The crucial word in this article is 'discrimination', which means 'making an adverse distinction with regard to' or 'distinguishing unfavourably from others'; *Kathi Raning Rawat* v. *State of Saurashtra*, (1952) SCR 435 (442): AIR 1952 SC 123: 1952 Cr LJ 805. Another crucial word is 'only' so that if the discrimination is based on some ground not connected with religion, *etc.*, but with some other rational factor, the discrimination would be valid.

The discrimination forbidden by article 15 is only such discrimination as is based, *inter alia*, on the ground that a person belongs to a particular religion. The said right conferred by clause (1) of article 15 being only on a 'citizen', the same is an individual right by way of a guarantee which may not be subjected to discrimination in the matter of rights, privileges and immunities pertaining to him as a citizen. In other words, the right conferred by article 15 is personal. A statute, which restricts a right of a class of citizens in the matter of testamentary disposition who may belong to a particular religion would, therefore, not attract the wrath of clause (1) of article 15 of the Constitution of India; *John Vallamattom* v. *Union of India*, AIR 2003 SC 2902: (2003) 6 SCC 611: (2003) 3 KLT 66.

Discrimination on Grounds of Sex

The exclusion of women not exclusively based on sex but taking into consideration peculiar nature of duties to be performed by electricity workers is not violative of article 15 of Constitution; *Kerala State Electricity Board, Thiruvananthapuram* v. *Siniya Mol C.S.*, AIR 2008 (NOC) 730 (Ker).

Horizontal and Vertical Reservation

The principle that reserved category candidate getting appointed against non-reserved post will not be counted against reserved quota. It applies only to vertical reservations, but not to horizontal reservation for women and handicapped persons; *Public Service Commission, Uttaranchal* v. *Mamta Bisht*, AIR 2010 SC 2613.

Medical Colleges Reservation

Reservation in medical colleges is permitted; *Ajay Kumar* v. *State of Bihar*, JT 1994 (3) SC 662: (1994) 4 SCC 401: 1994 AIR SCW 2515.

Relationship to Article 14

In a sense, the general and abstract principle of equality laid down in article 14 is spelt out for certain situations in greater detail in article 15 and in some of the succeeding articles. But it should be noted that article 15 is limited to citizens, while article 14 extends to all persons. Secondly, article 15, clause (1) and article 15(2) are both limited to discrimination on the ground of religion, race, sex, place of birth or any of them. Thirdly, the article permits the State to make special provisions for women and children. Fourthly, the article also permits the State to make any special provision for the following:—

(a) Socially and educationally backward classes of citizens;

(b) Scheduled Castes; and

(c) Scheduled Tribes.

Article 14 prohibits the State from denying to any person equality before the law, etc. articles 15(1) and 16(2) protect the citizen against discrimination; *State of Sikkim* v. *Surendra Prasad Sharma*, JT 1994 3 SC 372: (1994) 5 SCC 282: AIR 1994 SC 2342: (1994) 2 SLR 685.

Reservation for SCs and STs

The State Government is competent authority to decide the question of reservation of seats for SCs and STs in medical colleges; *Gulshan Prakash* v. *State of Haryana*, AIR 2010 SC 288.

Children born to inter-caste marriage of which either father or mother belongs to SC/ST category can claim reservation benefits only on proof that he is subjected to some handicap and disadvantages having been born as member of SC/ST; *M.C. Valsala* v. *State of Kerala*, AIR 2006 Ker 1: 2006 (1) AIR Kar R 92: 2005 (36) All Ind Cas 750: 2006 (5) Bom CR 1 JS: ILR (2005) 4 Ker 122: 2006 (1) LLN 682: 2006 (2) SCT 749.

Reservation on the Basis of Domicile

The term 'place of birth' occurs in clause (1) of article 15 but not 'domicile'. If a comparison is made between article 15 (1) and article 16 (2), it would appear that whereas the former refers to 'place of birth' alone, the latter refers to both 'domicile' and 'residence' apart from 'place of birth'. A distinction, therefore, has been made by the makers of the Constitution themselves to the effect that the expression 'place of birth' is not synonymous to the expression 'domicile' and they reflect two different concepts. It may be true, that both the expression appeared to be synonymous to some of the members of the Constitutent Assembly but the same cannot be a guiding factor. Reservation on the basis of domicile is not impermissible in terms of clause (1) of article 15 of the Constitution of India; *Saurabh Chaudri* v. *Union of India*, AIR 2004 SC 361: (2003) 11 SCC 146: 2003 AIR SCW 6392: 2004 (3) Bom CR 796: 2004 (1) JCR SC 140: JT 2003 (8) SC 296: 2003 (4) SCT 867: (2003) 9 SCALE 272: 2004 (1) Supreme 26.

Reservation within Reservation

Allotment of a quota of seats (in post graduate medical course) for candidates to be selected out of persons in Government service sponsored by the State Government is not a "reservation". It amounts to laying down a source for filling up the seats and is "classification" within article 15(1). Hence, reservation for SC/ST in the Government quota is not reservation within reservation. It is permissible; *Pranatosh Roy (Dr.)* v. *University of Calcutta*, AIR 1998 Cal 181: 1997 (2) Cal LJ 294: 1997 CWN 372: 1997 (3) Serv LR 633.

Scheduled Caste – Acquiring of Scheduled Caste Status

A person by reason of marriage alone cannot *ipso facto* become a member of Scheduled Caste or Scheduled Tribe; *Meera Kanwaria* v. *Sunita*, AIR 2006 SC 597: 2005 AIR SCW 6243: 2006 (38) All Ind Cas 457: 2006 (62) All LR 464: 2006 (1) All WC 678: 2006 (2) Bom CR 566: JT 2005 (10) SC 429: (2006) 1 SCC 344: 2006 (1) SCJ 242: 2006 (1) SCT 126: (2005) 10 SCALE 39: 2006 (1) Supreme 166.

University-wise Reservation

(a) University-wise preference is valid if it is reasonable.

(b) Domicile-wise preference is valid if it does not exceed reasonable limits.

(c) College-wise preference is bad

Mohan Bir Singh Chawla v. *Punjab University, Chandigarh*, AIR 1997 SC 788: (1997) 2 SCC 171: 1997 AIR SCW 609: 1997 (1) Cur CC 76: 1997 (2) ESC 1015: 1996 (3) Serv LR 766: 1997 (1) Supreme 332: 1997 (1) UJ (SC) 339.

Women: Reservation

Reservation of 50% of posts in favour of female candidates not arbitrary; *Rajesh Kumar Gupta* v. *State of Uttar Pradesh*, AIR 2005 SC 2540: 2005 Lab IC 2087: 2005 All LJ 1915: 2005 (106) FLR 411: 2005 (3) LLN 1041: (2005) 5 SCC 172: 2005 SCC(L&S) 668: 2005 (2) SCT 827: (2005) 4 SCALE 657: 2005 (5) Serv LR 1: 2005 (4) Supreme 262.

Reservation of certain posts exclusively for women is valid under article 15(3), article 15 covers every sphere of State action; *Union of India* v. *K.P. Prabhakaran*, (1997) 11 SCC 638: 1998 SCC (L&S) 327.

Clause (3) of article 15, which permits special provision for women and children, has been widely resorted to and the courts have upheld the validity of special measures in legislation or executive orders favouring women. In particular, provisions in the criminal law, in favour of women, or in the procedural law discriminating in favour of women, have been upheld. The following decisions may be seen in this context:—

(i) *Girdhar* v. *State*, AIR 1953 MB 147: 1953 MB LJ 529. (Section 354, Indian Penal Code).

(ii) *Yusuf* v. *State of Bombay*, AIR 1954 SC 321 (322): (1954) 1 SCR 930: 56 Bom LR 1176: 1954 Cr LJ 886. (Section 497, Indian Penal Code).

(iii) *Choki* v. *State of Rajasthan*, AIR 1957 Raj 10: 1955 Cr LJ 567: 1955 Raj LW 567 (Bail).

(iv) *M.I. Shahdad* v. *Mohd. Abdullah Mir*, AIR 1967 J&K 120 (127): 1967 Kash LJ 251. (Service of summons on men only in civil cases).

Similarly, provisions providing for reservation of seats for women in local bodies or in educational institutions are valid. Undermentioned decisions may be seen:

(i) *Dattatraya* v. *State of Bombay*, AIR 1953 Bom 311: 55 BM LR 323: (1953) Bom 842.

(ii) *P. Sagar* v. *State of Andhra Pradesh*, AIR 1968 AP 165 (174): (1968) 1 AWR 116.

Women and Sexual Harassment

Sexual harassment of working women amounts to violation of the rights guaranteed by articles 14, 15 and 23 (equality and dignity), the court issued detailed directions on the subject; *Vishakha* v. *State of Rajasthan*, AIR 1997 SC 3011: (1997) 6 SCC 241: 1997 SCC (Cri) 932.

16. Equality of opportunity in matters of public employment.—(1) There shall be equality of opportunity for all citizens in matters relating to employment or appointment to any office under the State.

(2) No citizen shall, on grounds only of religion, race, caste, sex, descent, place of birth, residence or any of them, be ineligible for, or discriminated against in respect of, any employment or office under the State.

(3) Nothing in this article shall prevent Parliament from making any law prescribing, in regard to a class or classes of employment or appointment to an office [1][under the Government of, or any local or other authority within, a State or Union territory, any requirement as to residence within that State or Union territory] prior to such employment or appointment.

(4) Nothing in this article shall prevent the State from making any provision for the reservation of appointments or posts in favour of any backward class of citizens which, in the opinion of the State, is not adequately represented in the services under the State.

[2][(4A) Nothing in this article shall prevent the State from making any provision for reservation [3][in matters of promotion, with consequential seniority, to any class] or classes of posts in the services under the State in favour of the Scheduled Castes and the Scheduled Tribes which, in the opinion of the State, are not adequately represented in the services under the State.]

[4][(4B) Nothing in this article shall prevent the State from considering any unfilled vacancies of a year which are reserved for being filled up in that year in accordance with any provision for reservation made under clause (4) or clause (4A) as a separate class of vacancies to be filled up in any succeeding year or years and such class of vacancies shall not be considered together with the vacancies of the year in which they are being filled up for determining the ceiling of fifty per cent. reservation on total number of vacancies of that year.]

(5) Nothing in this article shall affect the operation of any law which provides that the incumbent of an office in connection with the affairs of any religious or denominational institution or any member of the governing body thereof shall be a person professing a particular religion or belonging to a particular denomination.

Notes on Article 16

All India Services

The reserved category candidates belonging to OBC, SC and ST categories who are selected on merit and placed in the list of general/unreserved category candidates can choose to migrate to the respective reserved category at the time of allocation of services; *Union of India* v. *Ramesh Ram,* AIR 2010 SC 2691.

Appointment

The appointment over and above post advertised offends article 16; *Rakhi Ray* v. *High Court of Delhi,* AIR 2010 SC 932.

The select listed candidates do not get indefeasible right to get appointment. The select list is not a reservoir for appointment; *State of Orissa* v. *Rajkishore Nanda,* AIR 2010 SC 2100.

---

1. Subs. by the Constitution (Seventh Amendment) Act, 1956, sec. 29 and Sch., for certain words (w.e.f. 1-11-1956).
2. Ins. by the Constitution (Seventy-seventh Amendment) Act, 1995, sec. 2 (w.e.f. 17-6-1995).
3. Subs. by the Constitution (Eighty-fifth Amendment) Act, 2001, sec. 2, for "in matters of promotion to any class" (w.r.e.f. 17-6-1995).
4. Ins. by the Constitution (Eighty-first Amendment) Act, 2000, sec. 2 (w.e.f. 9-6-2000).

The sponsorship from employment exchange is made essential but such requirement cannot be construed as mandatory; *Union of India* v. *Miss. Pritilata Nanda*, AIR 2010 SC 2821.

Arbitrariness

Article 16 is a spread of article 14. Hence non-arbitrariness is a part of article 16; *D.T.C.* v. *Mazdoor Congress*, AIR 1991 SC 101: (1991) Supp 1 SCC 600: 1991 SCC (L&S) 1213: (1991) 1 LLJ 395, paragraphs 258-280.

M, was given promotion when he approached the High Court. He was an employee belonging to backward classes. Another employee who was similarly placed was denied promotion. It was held that the discrimination was illegal; *Vishwas Anna Sawant* v. *Municipal Corporation of Greater Bombay*, JT 1994 (3) SC 573: (1994) 4 SCC 434: AIR 1994 SC 2408.

Article 14 guarantees to all persons equality before the law. Articles 15(1) and 16(2) protect citizens against discrimination; *State of Sikkim* v. *Surendra Prasad Sharma*, JT 1994 (3) SC 372: (1994) 5 SCC 282: AIR 1994 SC 2342: (1994) 1 SLR 685.

Scheduled Caste or Scheduled Tribe status is not carried by a member when he migrates to another State; JT 1994 (4) SC 423.

Constitution (Seventy-seventh Amendment) Act, 1995

The Scheduled Castes and the Scheduled Tribes had been enjoying the facility of reservation in promotion since 1995. The Supreme Court, in its judgment dated 16th November, 1992, in the case of *Indra Sawhney* v. *Union of India*, however, observed that reservation of appointments or posts under article 16(4) of the Constitution is confined to the *initial appointment* and cannot extend to reservation in the matter of promotion. This ruling of the Supreme Court was considered to adversely affect the interests of the Scheduled Castes and the Scheduled Tribes. Since the representation of the Scheduled Castes and the Scheduled Tribes in services in the States had not reached the required level, it was thought necessary to continue the existing dispensation of providing reservation in promotion in the case of Scheduled Castes and Scheduled Tribes. In view of its commitment to protect the interests of the Scheduled Castes and the Scheduled Tribes, the Government decided to continue the existing policy of reservation in promotion for the Scheduled Castes and the Scheduled Tribes. To carry out this, it was necessary to amend article 16 of the Constitution by inserting a new clause (4A) to provide for reservation in promotion for the Scheduled Castes and Scheduled Tribes. The Constitution (Seventy-seventh Amendment) Act, 1995 seeks to achieve the aforesaid object.

Section 2 of this Act inserts a new clause (4 A) in article 16 of the Constitution, empowering the State to make a provision for reservation in matters of promotion to any class or classes of posts in the services under the State in favour of the Scheduled Castes and the Scheduled Tribes which in the opinion of the State, are not adequately represented in the services under the State, notwithstanding anything contrary contained in article 16.

Discrimination

Besides the right to equality of opportunity in general terms, article 16(2) prohibits discrimination against a citizen on the ground of—

    (a) religion,

    (b) race,

    (c) caste,

    (d) sex,

    (e) descent,

    (f) place of birth, and

    (g) residence, subject, of course to article 16(3).

In case of this particular article, the courts have held that the general right given by the first two clauses should be construed liberally and the exceptions may be construed strictly. Decisions on this point are;

    (i) *General Manager Southern Railway* v. *Rangachari*, AIR 1962 SC 36 (44) : (1962) 2 SCR 586: 1961 2 Mad LJ (SC) 71: (1961) 2 Andh WR (SC) 71: 1961 (2) SCJ 424: (1961) 2 SCA 460.

(ii) *C.A. Rajendran* v. *Union of India*, AIR 1968 SC 507: (1968) 1 SCR 721: (1968) 1 SCA 202: (1968) 1 SCWR 574: 1968 (2) SCJ 19: 1968 SCD 714: (1968) 2 LLJ 407.

(iii) *M.R. Balaji* v. *State of Mysore*, AIR 1963 SC 649 (662): (1963) Supp 1 SCR 439: (1963) 2 SCA 1.

(iv) *Triloki Nath* v. *State of Jammu & Kashmir*, AIR 1967 SC 1283: (1967) 2 SCR 265: 14 FLR 282.

(v) *A. Periakaruppan Minor* v. *State of Tamil Nadu*,AIR 1971 SC 2303: (1971) 2 SCR 430: 1971 (2) SCJ 222: (1971) 2 Andh WR (SC) 65: (1971) 2 Mad LJ (SC) 65.

Employment

The words 'employment or appointment' are wide enough to include tenure, duration, emoluments and duties and obligations, whether the employment is temporary or permanent. They cover amongst themselves not merely the initial appointment, but also salary, increments, revision of pay, promotion, gratuity, leave, pension and age of superannuation. Decisions relevant to this point are:

(i) *Sukhnandan* v. *State of Bihar*, AIR 1957 Pat 617: ILR 35 Pat 1.

(ii) *Champaklal* v. *Union of India*, AIR 1964 SC 1854: (1964) 5 SCR 190: (1964) 1 LLJ 752.

(iii) *Shiv Charan* v. *State of Mysore*, AIR 1965 SC 280 (282): (1967) 2 LLJ 246: 15 FLR 224.

(iv) *Union of India* v. *Kashikar*, AIR 1986 SC 431: (1986) 1 SCC 458: (1986) 1 LLJ 435, paragraph 8.

(v) *Prabhakar* v. *State of Andhra Pradesh*, AIR 1986 SC 210: 1985 Supp SCC 432: 1986 SCC (L&S) 49, paragraph 22.

Grant of Opportunity of Hearing

Public Service Commission being constitutional creation, the principles of service law are not applicable. The opportunity of hearing need not be given in respect of order of suspension passed against members of Public Service Commission; *Ram Kumar Kashyap* v. *Union of India*, AIR 2010 SC 1151.

Medical Colleges

Although the Indian Constitution permits reservation of seats (and other similar special privileges) for persons belonging to Scheduled Castes and Tribes, it does not make it *obligatory* that such reservation should be made in every case for Government service or for admission to educational institutions. It is because of this position, that the Gujarat High Court held in *Sujal Atul Munshi* v. *State of Gujarat*, AIR 1996 Guj 170, that Government is not bound to reserve seats for such persons in payment seats for admission to medical educations.

Object of Article 16

The main object of article 16 is to create a constitutional right to equality of opportunity and employment in public offices. This article is confined to citizens as distinguished from other persons. Further, it is confined to employment or appointment to an office 'under the State'.

Other Safeguards

On the question whether article 16(4) is subject to any safeguard, it is relevant to point out that courts has insisted that it must be read with article 335 which directs that in taking into consideration the claim of members of the Scheduled Castes and Scheduled Tribes, the State should bear in mind that the claim should be consistent with the maintenance of efficiency of administration. This incidentally calls upon the judiciary to read together articles 16, 46, 335. Decisions on this point are:

(i) *T. Devadasan* v. *Union of India*, AIR 1964 SC 179: (1964) 4 SCR 680: (1965) 2 LLJ 560, paragraph 1.

(ii) *M.R. Balaji* v. *State of Mysore*, AIR 1963 SC 649 (662): (1963) Supp 1 SCR 439: (1963) 2 SCA 1.

(iii) *A.B.K. Singh* v. *Union of India*, AIR 1981 SC 298: (1981) 1 SCC 246: (1981) 2 SCR 185.

(iv) *State of Kerala* v. *N.M. Thomas*, AIR 1976 SC 490: (1976) 2 SCC 310: 1976 Lab IC 395, paragraphs 168 and 179.

(v) *K.C. Vasanth Kumar* v. *State of Karnataka*, AIR 1985 SC 1495: (1985) Supp SCC 714: (1985) Supp 1 SCR 352, paragraphs 36, 57, 88 and 148 to 151.

(vi) *Comptroller and Auditor-General* v. *Jagannathan*, AIR 1987 SC 537: (1986) 2 SCC 679: (1986) 2 LLN 11: (1986) 1 SLR 712.

Pay Scales

When the employees continue to work up to the retirement age of 60 years their pay scales cannot be reduced for the period between 58 to 60 years. There cannot be two types of pay scales one for the purpose of continuing in service upto the age of retirement and the other for the period between 58 to 60 years. It must be kept in mind that pension is not a bounty but it is hard-earned benefit for long service, which cannot be taken away; *Grid Corporation of Orissa* v. *Rasananda Das*, AIR 2003 SC 4599: (2003) 10 SCC 297: 2003 Lab IC 3690: 2003 AIR SCW 5390: 2004 (2) LLJ 1053: 2004 (1) LLN 65: 2004 SCC (L&S) 214: 2004 (1) SCT 412: (2003) 8 SCALE 129: 2004 (1) Serv LJ 259 SC: 2003 (6) Supreme 938.

Qualifying Minimum Marks

Government cannot totally dispense with minimum qualifying marks for Post-Graduate medical courses for Scheduled Castes *etc.* candidates; *Sadhana Devi* v. *State of Uttar Pradesh*, AIR 1997 SC 1120: (1997) 3 SCC 90: 1997 All LJ 677.

However reservation for the in Post-Graduate Courses is not itself inconsistent with efficiency; *P.G.I.M.R.* v. *K.L. Narasimha*, JT 1997 (5) SC 313: (1997) 6 SCC 283: 1997 Lab IC 2317.

Relaxation in Standard of Eligibility

Relaxation in shape of lower standards of eligibility is permissible for Scheduled Caste candidates *etc.* But relaxation should be consistent with eligibility; *Ram Bhagat Singh* v. *State of Haryana*, (1997) 11 SCC 417: (1990) 2 SCR 329: (1991) 3 SLR 15: (1990) 2 SLJ 107.

Recruitment Test

The Court in absence of provision for re-evaluation of answer sheets, cannot direct so; *H.P. Public Service Commission* v. *Mukesh Thakur*, AIR 2010 SC 2620.

Reservation

Children born to inter-caste marriage of which either father or mother belongs to SC/ST category can claim reservation benefits only on proof that he is subjected to some handicap and disadvantages having been born as member of SC/ST; *M.C. Valsala* v. *State of Kerala*, AIR 2006 Ker 1: 2006 (1) AIR Kar R 92: 2005 (36) All Ind Cas 750: 2006 (5) Bom CR 1 JS: ILR (2005) 4 Ker 122: 2006 (1) LLN 682: 2006 (2) SCT 749.

Reservation and Promotion

Article 16(4) and article 16(4A) do not confer any fundamental rights nor do they impose any constitutional duties but are only in the nature of enabling provision vesting a discretion in the State to consider providing reservation of the circumstances mentioned in those articles so warranted; *Ajit Singh* v. *State of Punjab*, AIR 1999 SC 3471: (1999) 7 SCC 209: 1999 SCC (L&S) 1239.

It is well-settled position that while making entries in the character roll proper assessment on the basis of objective standards should be made since character role is a primary material which forms the basis for further progress of the employee in his service career; *State of Uttar Pradesh* v. *Dr. K.U. Ansari*, AIR 2002 SC 208: (2002) 1 SCC 616: (2002) 1 SLR 301: (2002) 92 FLR 513.

Reservation to Single Post

Reservation to single post cadre (even through rotation or roaster) is void as it creates 100 per cent reservation; *P.G.I.M.R.* v. *K.L. Narasimhan*, (1997) 6 SCC 283: 1997 SCC (L&S) 1449: 1997 Lab IC 2317.

Revision of Pay Scales

Being employees of the companies, it is responsibility of the companies to pay them salary and if the company is sustaining losses continuously over a period and does not have the financial capacity to revise or enhance the pay scale, the petitioners, cannot claim any legal right to ask for a direction to the Central Government to meet the additional expenditure which may be incurred on account of revision of pay scales; *I.D.P.L. Officers and Supervisors* v. *Chairman and M.D., I.D.P.L.*, AIR 2003 SC 2870: (2003) 6 SCC 490: 2003 SCC (L&S) 916: (2003) 3 LLN 870.

Right to go anywhere and Live with any Person

A man and a woman, even without getting married can live together if they wish. This may be regarded immoral by society but it is not illegal. There is a difference between law and morality; *Payal Sharma* alias *Kamla Sharma* alias *Payal Katara* v. *Superintendent, Nari Niketan Kalindri Vihar, Agra*, AIR 2001 All 254: 2001 (2) All CJ 964: 2001 (44) All LR 146: 2001 (3) All WC 1778: 2001 (3) East Cr C 143: 2001 (2) Marri LJ 391.

Scheme of Article 18

Article 16(4) is not an exception to article 16 but gives a permissible basis; *Indra Sawhney* v. *Union of India*, AIR 1993 SC 477: (1992) Supp 3 SCC 217: 1992 SCC (L&S) Supp 1.

This is in the largest interest of the administration that it is the employer, who is best suited to decide the percentage of posts in the promotional cadre, which can be earmarked for different category of persons. This provision actually effectuates the constitutional mandate engrafted in article 16(1), as it would offer equality of opportunity in the matters relating to employment and it would not be the monopoly of a specified category of persons in the feeder category to get promotions. There is no infraction of the constitutional provision engrafted in article 16(4) while providing a quota in promotional cadre; *Kuldeep Kumar Gupta* v. *Himachal Pradesh State Electricity Board*, AIR 2001 SC 308: (2001) 1 SCC 475: 2001 Lab IC 409: (2001) 1 LLN 842.

Prescribing a cut-off date prior to the date of appointment for the purpose of satisfying the eligibility qualifications pertaining to age is permissible under the Punjab Panchayat Secretaries (Recruitment and Conditions of Services) Rules, 1993; *Jasbir Rani* v. *State of Punjab*, AIR 2002 SC 60: (2002) 1 SCC 124: 2002 SCC (L&S) 107: (2002) 1 SLR 124.

Seniority

The seniority plays a vital role in employee's service career. Unsetting the seniority leads to resentment, hostility and loss of enthusiasm to do quality work; *H.S. Vankani* v. *State of Gujarat*, AIR 2010 SC 1714.

17. Abolition of untouchability.—"Untouchability" is abolished and its practice in any form is forbidden. The enforcement of any disability arising out of "Untouchability" shall be an offence punishable in accordance with law.

Notes on Article 17

Object of Article 17

Article 17 has been implemented by the Protection of Civil Rights Act, 1955 whose earlier title was "The Untouchability (Offences) Act, 1955". The principal object of article 17 is to ban the practice of untouchability in any form. This expression refers to the social disabilities imposed on certain classes of persons by reason of their birth in certain castes and does not cover social boycott based on conduct; *Devarajiah* v. *B. Padmauna*, AIR 1958 Mys 84. A curious question was raised in a Madras case. The State Legislature passed a law to improve the conditions of living of untouchables, by providing for the acquisition of land to construct a colony for them. The argument was advanced that such a construction would result in the segregation of those persons and would not be in conformity with article 17, but the argument was not accepted; *Pavadai Gounder* v. *State of Madras*, AIR 1973 Mad 458: (1973) 2 Mad LJ 517.

Religious Freedom

The religious freedom is subject to public order, health, morality and other provisions of Part III of Constitution of India including article 17; *N. Adithayan* v. *Travancore Devaswom Board*, AIR 2002 SC 3538: 2002 AIR SCW 4146: 2003 (1) All Ind Cas 765: 2003 (1) Andh LD 28: JT 2002 (8) SC 51: 2002 (4) LRI 578: 2003 (1) Mad LW 97: (2002) 8 SCC 106: 2002 (4) SCJ 606: (2002) 7 SCALE 280: 2002 (7) Supreme 242.

See also undermentioned cases:

(i) Protection of civil rights; *State of Karnataka* v. *Appa Balu Ingale*, AIR 1993 SC 1126: 1993 Cr LJ 1029: 1993 AIR SCW 337: 1993 (1) Chand Cr C 147: 1992 (3) Crimes 1104: 1993 IJR 58: JT 1992 SC (Supp) 588: 1993 (1) SCJ 189: (1992) 3 SCR 284: 1994 SCC (Cri) 1762: (1995) Supp 4 SCC 469.

(ii) Violation of fundamental rights; *People's Union for Democratic Rights* v. *Union of India*, AIR 1982 SC 1473: 1982 Lab IC 1646: (1982) 45 FLR 140: 1982 UJ (SC) 553: (1982) 2 SCC 494: 1982 BLJR 401: (1982) 2 LLN 410: (1982) 2 SCWR 202: (1982) 14 Lawyer 57: (1982) 2 LLJ 454.

18. Abolition of titles.—(1) No title, not being a military or academic distinction, shall be conferred by the State.

(2) No citizen of India shall accept any title from any foreign State.

(3) No person who is not a citizen of India shall, while he holds any office of profit or trust under the State, accept without the consent of the President any title from any foreign State.

(4) No person holding any office of profit or trust under the State shall, without the consent of the President, accept any present, emolument, or office of any kind from or under any foreign State.

Notes on Article 18

Abolition of Titles

(i) *Union of India* v. *Bijan Ghosh*, AIR 1997 SC 3019: 1997 AIR SCW 3052: JT 1997 (7) SC 198: (1997) 6 SCC 535: (1997) 5 SCALE 329: 1997 (7) Supreme 10: 1997 (2) UJ (SC) 409.

(ii) *Balaji Raghavan* v. *Union of India*, AIR 1996 SC 770: 1996 AIR SCW 86: 1996 (1) LS SC 54: (1996) 1 SCC 361: 1996 (1) UJ (SC) 197.

Central Civil Service: Pension

Where the Central Government employee abserved in public sector undertaking, commuted 100% pension then he is entitled to dearness relief on 1/3rd portion of commuted pension which is restored but not entitled to dearness relief on full pension. Time of 3 months allowed by court to Central Government to pay the amount; *P.V. Sundara Rajan* v. *Union of India*, AIR 2000 SC 3387: 2000 AIR SCW 1677: 2000 (86) FLR 59: JT 2000 (5) SC 175: 2000 (3) LLJ 997: 2000 (2) LLN 890: (2000) 4 SCC 469: 2000 SCC (L&S) 660: 2000 (2) SCT 771: (2000) 4 SCALE 48: 2000 (5) Supreme 83: 2000 (2) UJ (SC) 937.

Equality

Doctrine of Equality is also envisaged under article 18; *Indra Sawhney* v. *Union of India*, AIR 1993 SC 477: 1992 AIR SCW 3682: JT 1992 (6) SC 273: 1993 (1) SCJ 353: 1993 (1) SCT 448: (1992) Supp 3 SCC 217.

National Awards, not Titles

It has been held that the Awards, Bharat Ratna, Padma Vibhushan, Padma Bhushan and Padma Shri called as "The National Awards" would not amount to "title" within the meaning of article 18(1) and they should not be used as suffixes or prefixes. If this is done, the defaulter should forfeit the National Award conferred on him or her, by following the procedure laid down in Regulation 10 of each of the four notifications creating the National Awards; *Balaji Raghavan* v. *Union of India*, AIR 1996 SC 770: (1996) 1 SCC 361: 1996 AIR SCW 86: 1996 (1) LS SC 54: 1996 (1) UJ (SC) 197 (paragraphs 32, 35).

Title

Where an award is not yet formally conferred and the Government communique relating thereto is cancelled on account of sentiments expressed by family members of the proposed deceased recipient, writ would not be issued for formal annulment of conferment of national award; *Union of India* v. *Bijan Ghosh*, AIR 1997 SC 3019: (1997) 6 SCC 535: 1997 AIR SCW 3052: JT 1997 (7) SC 198: (1997) 5 SCALE 329: 1997 (7) Supreme 10: 1997 (2) UJ (SC) 409.

Right to Freedom

19. Protection of certain rights regarding freedom of speech, etc.—(1) All citizens shall have the right—

(a) to freedom of speech and expression;

(b) to assemble peaceably and without arms;

(c) to form associations or unions [1][or co-operative societies];

(d) to move freely throughout the territory of India;

(e) to reside and settle in any part of the territory of India; [2][and]

[3][***]

(g) to practise any profession, or to carry on any occupation, trade or business.

[4][(2) Nothing in sub-clause (a) of clause (1) shall affect the operation of any existing law, or prevent the State from making any law, in so far as such law imposes reasonable restrictions on the exercise of the right conferred by the said sub-clause in the interests of [5][the sovereignty and integrity of India,] the security of the State, friendly relations with Foreign States, public order, decency or morality or in relation to contempt of court, defamation or incitement to an offence.]

(3) Nothing in sub-clause (b) of the said clause shall affect the operation of any existing law in so far as it imposes, or prevent the State from making any law imposing, in the interests of [6][the sovereignty and integrity of India or] public order, reasonable restrictions on the exercise of the right conferred by the said sub-clause.

(4) Nothing in sub-clause (c) of the said clause shall affect the operation of any existing law in so far as it imposes, or prevent the State from making any law imposing, in the interests of [6][the sovereignty and integrity of India or] public order or morality, reasonable restrictions on the exercise of the right conferred by the said sub-clause.

(5) Nothing in [7][sub-clauses (d) and (e)] of the said clause shall affect the operation of any existing law in so far as it imposes, or prevent the State from making any law imposing, reasonable restrictions on the exercise of any of the rights conferred by the said sub-clauses either in the interests of the general public or for the protection of the interests of any Scheduled Tribe.

(6) Nothing in sub-clause (g) of the said clause shall affect the operation of any existing law in so far as it imposes, or prevent the State from making any law imposing, in the interests of the general public, reasonable restrictions on the exercise of the right conferred by the said sub-clause, and, in particular, [8][nothing

---

1. Ins. by the Constitution (Ninety-seventh Amendment) Act, 2011, sec. 2 (w.e.f. 15-2-2012).
2. Ins. by the Constitution (Forty-fourth Amendment) Act, 1978, sec. 2(a)(i) (w.e.f. 20-6-1979).
3. Sub-clause (f) omitted by the Constitution (Forty-fourth Amendment) Act, 1978, sec. 2(a)(ii) (w.e.f. 20-6-1979).
4. Subs. by the Constitution (First Amendment) Act, 1951, sec. 3(a), for clause (2) (with retrospective effect).
5. Ins. by the Constitution (Sixteenth Amendment) Act, 1963, sec. 2(a) (w.e.f. 5-10-1963).
6. Ins. by the Constitution (Sixteenth Amendment) Act, 1963, sec. 2(b) (w.e.f. 5-10-1963).
7. Subs. by the Constitution (Forty-fourth Amendment) Act, 1978, sec. 2(b), for "sub-clauses (d), (e) and (f)" (w.e.f. 20-6-1979).
8. Subs. by the Constitution (First Amendment) Act, 1951, sec. 3(b), for certain words (w.e.f. 18-6-1951).

in the said sub-clause shall affect the operation of any existing law in so far as it relates to, or prevent the State from making any law relating to,—

(i) the professional or technical qualifications necessary for practising any profession or carrying on any occupation, trade or business, or

(ii) the carrying on by the State, or by a corporation owned or controlled by the State, of any trade, business, industry or service, whether to the exclusion, complete or partial, of citizens or otherwise].

Notes on Article 19

AIDS Patient

A person suffering from AIDS can be restricted in his movements by law; *Lucy R. D'Souza* v. *State of Goa*, AIR 1990 Bom 355: (1990) 1 Goa LT 36: 1990 MLLJ 713, paragraphs 7-8 (law made by State Legislature).

Arbitrariness

Where policy is laid down, discretion is not of reasonableness—arbitrary; *D.T.C.* v. *Mazdoor Congress*, AIR 1991 SC 101: (1991) Supp 1 SCC 600: (1991) 1 LLJ 395: 1991 SCC (L&S) 1213.

Ban on Slaughter

Ban on slaughter of bulls below 16 years of age would be a reasonable restriction. But total ban on slaughter of bulls would be unreasonable; *Hasmattulah* v. *State of Madhya Pradesh*, AIR 1996 SC 2076: (1996) 4 SCC 391: 1996 AIR SCW 2498: 1996 (3) ICC 255: JT 1996 (5) SC 295: 1996 Jab LJ 406: 1996 (3) SCJ 113: 1996 (2) UJ (SC) 478.

Bandhs

"*Bandhs*" do not fall within the fundamental right of speech. A Bandh is a warning to a citizen that he goes for work or opens his shop he would be prevented. Even if legislature does not prohibit them courts should intervene to protect the right to work or right to study; *Communist Party of India (M)* v. *Bharat Kumar*, AIR 1998 SC 184: (1998) 1 SCC 201: (1998) 1 MLJ 99 (SC).

Burden of Proof

The scheme of article 19, broadly speaking, is that once a law *prima facie* violates a right guaranteed by any clause of the article, then the State must show how the legislation or other State action falls within the permissible limits allowed by clauses (2) to (6) of the article and to place proper material to support that argument. The decisions in support of this proposition are the following:—

(i) *Vrajlal Manilal & Co.* v. *State of Madhya Pradesh*, AIR 1970 SC 129: (1969) 2 SCC 248: (1969) 2 SCA 413: 1970 MPWR 193: (1970) 1 SCR 400: 1970 MPLJ 518.

(ii) *Saghir Ahmad* v. *State of Uttar Pradesh*, AIR 1954 SC 728: (1955) 1 SCR 707: 1954 SCA 1218: (1954) 2 MLJ 622: 1954 SCJ 819: 1954 All WR 23: 68 Mad LW 8: 1955 All LJ 38.

(iii) *Chintamanrao* v. *State of Madhya Pradesh*, (1950) SCR 759: AIR 1951 SC 118: 1950 SCJ 571: 64 MLW 370: 1951 ALJ (SC) 82: ILR 1951 Hyd 221.

(iv) *Bijoe Emmanuel* v. *State of Kerala*, (1986) 3 SCC 615: AIR 1987 SC 748: 1986 KLT 1037.

Business Aspects of the Media

Where an activity involves questions of freedom of speech as well as questions of freedom to carry on a business, profession or vocation, then it is legitimate for the State to regulate the business aspect in terms of article 19(1)(g); *A. Suresh* v. *State of Tamil Nadu*, AIR 1997 SC 1889: (1997) 1 SCC 319: 1997 AIR SCW 1640: 1998 BRLJ 102: 1997 (1) CTC 463: JT 1996 (10) SC 542: 1997 (2) Mad LJ 23: 1997 (2) Mad LW 551: 1997 (2) Supreme 56.

Business with Government

There is no right to carry on business with the Government as such; nor is there a right that one's product (*e.g.* text books) must be recognised by the Government. Nor there is any right that at a public auction or in tenders invited by the Government, the highest bid or the lowest tender must be accepted. But by virtue of article 14, it is now established that rejection of the highest bid or the lowest tender by Government must not be arbitrary. Decisions in support of these propositions are the following:—

(i) *Rai Sahib Ram Jawaya Kapur* v. *State of Punjab*, (1955) 2 SCR 225 (240): AIR 1955 SC 549: 1955 SCA 577: 1955 SCJ 504: (1955) 2 Mad LJ (SC) 59: 57 Punj LR 444: 1955 Mad WN 973 (Text books).

(ii) *State of Orissa* v. *Hari Narayan*, AIR 1972 SC 1816: (1972) 2 SCC 36: (1972) 3 SCR 784 (Auctions).

(iii) *State of Uttar Pradesh* v. *Bijoy*, AIR 1982 SC 1234: (1982) 2 SCC 365: 1982 All LJ 582.

(iv) *Ram and Shyam Company* v. *State of Haryana*, AIR 1985 SC 1147: (1985) 3 SCC 267: (1985) Supp 1 SCR 541, paragraphs 13 and 14 (Rejection of highest bid).

Constitutionality

One to whom the application of a statute is constitutional will not be heard to attack the statute on the ground that it must also be taken as applying to other persons or other situations in which its appilcation might be unconstitutional; *State of Gujarat* v. *Ambica Mills Ltd., Ahmedabad*, (1974) 4 SCC 656: AIR 1974 SC 1300: 1974 Lab IC 841: 45 FJR 381: 1974 SCC (Lab) 381: 1974 (2) SCJ 211: (1974) 3 SCR 760.

Contempt of Court

Guidelines for the use of contempt of court law have been suggested in the case of *Mulgaonkar (in re:)*, AIR 1978 SC 727: (1978) 3 SCC 339: 1978 SCC (Cri) 402.They are as under:

(1) Economic use of this jurisdiction is desirable.

(2) Harmonisation between free criticism and the judiciary should be the goal.

(3) Confusion between personal protection of a libelled judge and prevention of obstruction of public justice should be avoided.

(4) Press should be given free play within reasonable limits, even when the focus of its critical attention is the court.

(5) Judges should not be hypersensitive, even where distortions and criticism overstep the limits.

(6) If after taking into account all these considerations, the court finds contempt of court beyond condonable limits, then the strong arm of the law must be used in the name of public interest and public justice.

Lastly, Mr. Justice K. Iyer stated "Justice" and not judge should be the keynote and creative legal journalism and activist statesmanship for judicial reform cannot be jeopardized by an undefined apprehension of contempt action.

The Supreme Court did try to restrain the use of the Contempt of Courts Act, 1971 when it stated in *Rama Dayal Markarha* v. *State of Madhya Pradesh*, AIR 1978 SC 921: (1978) 2 SCC 630: 1978 SCC (Cri) 327, that the path of justice is not strewn with roses and justice being not a cloistered virtue, it must be allowed to suffer the scrutiny and respectful, even though outspoken, comments of ordinary man. The Supreme Court in *Conscientious Group* v. *Mohammad Yunus*, AIR 1987 SC 1451: (1987) 3 SCC 89: 1987 Cr LJ 1182 and in *P.N. Duda* v. *P. Shiv Shankar*, AIR 1988 SC 1208: (1988) 3 SCC 167: 1988 SCC (Cri) 589 adopted a liberal attitude towards contempt of court.

Convicts

If a convict is prepared to give an interview to journalists and videographers, the facility should be allowed to the latter. Position of a person sentenced to death is in this respect not inferior to that of a citizen; *M. Hasan* v. *Government of Andhra Pradesh*, AIR 1998 AP 35: 1997 (6) Andh LD 826: 1997 (6) Andh LT 209: 1998 (1) Rec Cr R 255.

Co-operative Societies Act, 1965 (U.P.)

Though article 19(1)(c) guaranteed freedom to form an association the freedom is subject to certain permissible restrictions imposed by law. Provisions of the U.P. Co-operative Societies Act, 1965 do not infringe this freedom. Court cannot interfere with policy of the Government; *State of Uttar Pradesh* v. *C.O.D. Chheoke Employees Co-operative Society Ltd.*, AIR 1997 SC 1413: (1997) 3 SCC 681: 1997 All LJ 576, paragraph 16.

Corporations as Citizens

The freedoms under article 19 are limited to citizens and if literally construed these freedoms would not be available to corporations, because corporations cannot be talked of as having or possessing citizenship. But it has been held that shareholders can challenge the validity of a law on the ground of violation of their fundamental rights and the company may be joined in such proceeding with proper pleading. The decisions relevant to this point are the following:—

(i)   *Amritsar Municipality* v. *State of Punjab*, AIR 1969 SC 1100 (1106): (1969) 1 SCC 475: 1969 3 SCR 447.

(ii) *Barium Chemicals* v. *Company Law Board*, AIR 1967 SC 295 (305): 1966 Supp SCR 311: (1966) 36 Comp Cas 639.

(iii) *Tata Engineering and Locomotive Co. Ltd.* v. *State of Bihar*, AIR 1965 SC 40 (48): (1964) 34 Com Cas 458: (1964) 1 Comp LJ 280: 1964 (1) SCJ 666: 1964 BLJR 834: (1965) 1 SCWR 26: (1965) 1 SCA 365: (1964) 6 SCR 885.

(iv) *Bennett Coleman and Co. Ltd.* v. *Union of India*, AIR 1973 SC 106: (1972) 2 SCC 788: 1973 (1) SCJ 177.

(v)   *Divisional Forest Officer* v. *Bishwanath Tea Co. Ltd.*, AIR 1981 SC 1368: (1981) 3 SCC 238: 1981 UJ (SC) 470, paragraph 7.

(vi) *State of Gujarat* v. *Shri Ambica Mills Ltd.*, (1974) 4 SCC 656: AIR 1974 SC 1300: (1974) 3 SCR 760: 1924 Lab IC 841.

A company is not a "citizen" and cannot invoke article 19(1)(g). Dealing in intoxicants is not "trade" or business; *Khoday Brewing and Distilling Industries Ltd.* v. *State of Tamil Nadu*, AIR 1990 Mad 124.

Criteria of Validity of Law

The considerations which generally prevail in judging the validity of a law in the context of this article are:

(a) whether the law imposes a restriction on the freedom in question;

(b) whether the restrictions have been imposed by law;

(c) whether the restrictions are reasonable; and

(d) whether the restriction besides being reasonable, is imposed for one of the specified purposes relevant to the freedom in question as enumerated in the applicable clause out of clauses (2) to (6) of the article.

Each of these conditions must be satisfied.

False News Item about Judges

A newspaper published a news item, stating that two sons of a senior Judge of the Supreme Court and two sons of the Chief Justice of India had been favoured by allotment of petrol outlets from the discretionary quota of the Petroleum Minister. Falsity of the news item was later admitted by the concerned editor, publisher and newspaper. They said that it had been published inadvertently. It was held that they could not escape responsibility for careless publication. However, as they had tendered unqualified apology, the apology was accepted with a warning to be careful in future; *Hari Jai Singh (in re:)*, AIR 1997 SC 73: (1996) 6 SCC 466: 1997 Cr LJ 58: 1996 AIR SCW 4227: 1997 (1) BLJR 907: JT 1996 (8) SC 332: 1997 (12) OCR 399: 1997 (1) Pat LJR 18: 1997 SC Cr R 364.

Freedom of Association

The right to freedom of association covers a variety of right, so long as the association is for a lawful purpose. The right includes the right to start or continue an association subject to reasonable restrictions in the interest of sovereignty or integrity of India, public order and morality. Decisions relevant to this right are the following:—

(i) *Kulkarni* v. *State of Bombay*, AIR 1954 SC 73: 1954 SCR 384: (1954) 1 MLJ 83: 1954 Cr LJ 351.

(ii) *O.K. Ghosh* v. *Joseph*, AIR 1963 SC 812 (815): (1963) Supp 1 SCR 789: (1962) 2 LLJ 615.

(iii) *D.A.V. College, Jullundur* v. *State of Punjab*, (1971) 2 SCC 269 (281): AIR 1971 SC 1737: (1971) Supp SCR 688.

(iv) *Delhi Police Sangh* v. *Union of India*, AIR 1987 SC 379: (1987) 1 SCC 115: (1987) 1 LLJ 121.

(v) *All India Bank Employees' Association* v. *National Industrial Tribunal*, AIR 1962 SC 171 (179): (1962) 3 SCR 269: (1962) 32 Comp Cas 414.

(vi) *Sitharmachary* v. *Senior Deputy Inspector*, AIR 1958 AP 78 (right of an individual to refuse to be member of an association Upheld).

(vii) *State of Bihar* v. *Kamla Kant Misra*, AIR 1971 SC 1667: (1969) 3 SCC 337: (1970) 3 SCR 181: ILR 49 Pat 467: 1969 Pat LJR (SC) 93 A: (1970) 2 SCA 574: 1971 Mad LW (Cri) 24: 1971 (1) SCJ 621: 1971 Mad LJ (Cri) 305 (procedural aspect).

(viii) *Madhu Limaye* v. *Sub Divisional Magistrate, Monghyr*, AIR 1971 SC 2486: (1970) 3 SCC 446: (1972) 1 SCA 45: (1971) 2 SCR 711: 1971 Cr LJ 1721: 1971 (2) SCJ 479: 1971 MLJ (Cri) 629.

(ix) *Kesoram Rayon Workmen's Union* v. *Registrar of Trade Unions*, AIR 1967 Cal 507 (508): 33 FJR 23: (1968) 1 LLJ 335.

Right to form an Association or Union being a fundamental right of every citizen including the students of the colleges, that right can only be curtailed or put under cloud by legislative action. State Government has no authority to pass executive orders regarding amendment or alteration in the eligibility criteria for contesting the elections of the Student's Unions or Associations; *Suresh Swami* v. *State of Rajasthan*, AIR 2001 Raj 244: 2001 (2) Raj LW 1232.

Freedom of Expression

State cannot prohibit criticism of executive action; *L.I.C.* v. *Professor Manubhai D. Shah*, AIR 1993 SC 171: (1992) 3 SCC 637: 1992 AIR SCW 3099: 1993 (1) BLJR 431: 1992 (2) Civ LJ 636: JT 1992 (4) SC 181: 1992 (3) SCJ 84: (1992) 3 SCR 595: 1992 (2) UJ (SC) 480, paragraph 23.

Expulsion of the three children from the school for the reason that because of their conscientiously held religious faith, they do not join the singing of the National Anthem in the morning assembly though they do stand up respectfully when the anthem is sung, is a violation of their fundamental right to freedom of conscience and freely to profess, practise and propagate religion – Fundamental rights of the appellate under articles 19(1)(a) and 25(1) have been infringed and they are entitled to be protected; *Bijoe Emmanuel* v. *State of Kerala*, (1986) 3 SCC 615: AIR 1987 SC 748: 1986 KLT 1037.

Freedom of Movement

The freedom of movement guaranteed by clause (d) of article 19(1) is in addition to the right to personal liberty guaranteed under article 21. Orders of externment and internment violate this right unless they fall within the permissible restrictions. While judicial decisions confine this article to physical movement, the intangible aspect of freedom may receive protection under article 21. For example, domiciliary visits by the police at night disturbing a person's sleep infringe personal liberty under article 21 and may not be constitutionally valid, except in the case of surveillance needed for the legitimate purpose of prevention of crime. In particular, entries in the 'Bad Character Register' at a police station, if *mala fide*, are subject to judicial scrutiny. A combined reading of article 19(1)(d) and article 21 has led to the proposition that residents of hilly areas have a right to be provided access to the roads, which access is necessary for the proper exercise of the right of life. Generally, a person proposed to be extreme must be given a hearing. A permanent restriction on the freedom of movement is *prima facie* suspect. Decisions ringing out these propositions are the following:—

(i) *Khare* v. *State of Delhi*, (1950) SCR 519: AIR 1950 SC 211: (1951) 52 Cr LJ 550.

(ii) *Kharak Singh* v. *State of Uttar Pradesh*, AIR 1963 SC 1295 (1303): (1964) 1 SCR 332: 1963 2 Cr LJ 329: 1963 All LJ 711: 1964 (2) SCJ 107.

(iii) *Govind* v. *State of Madhya Pradesh*, AIR 1975 SC 1378: (1975) 2 SCC 148: 1975 SCC (Cri) 468: 1975 Cr LJ 1111.

(iv) *State of Madhya Pradesh* v. *Thakur Bharat Singh*, AIR 1967 SC 1170: (1967) 2 SCR 454: 1967 Jab LJ 493: 1967 Mah LJ 541: 1967 MPLJ 433: (1967) 2 SCA 246: 1968 (1) SCJ 173: 1967 MPWR 64: 1968 Mad LJ (Cri) 24.

(v) *Malak* v. *State of Punjab*, AIR 1981 SC 760: (1981) 1 SCC 420: (1981) 2 SCR 311, paragraphs 7, 9 and 10.

(vi) *Maneka Gandhi* v. *Union of India*, AIR 1978 SC 597: (1978) 1 SCC 248: (1978) 2 SCR 621, paragraph 54.

(vii) *State of Himachal Pradesh* v. *Umed Ram Sharma*, (1986) 2 SCC 68: AIR 1986 SC 847: 1986 (1) SCJ 322: 1986 UJ (SC) 478: 1986 (2) Supreme 58 (cases relating to hilly areas).

(viii) *Gurbachan* v. *State of Bombay*, (1952) SCR 737: AIR 1952 SC 221: 1952 Cr LJ 1147.

Freedom of Profession

The right guaranteed by clause (g) of article 19(1), namely, freedom of profession, trade or business, is intended to ensure that citizens' right to business does not depend on grant by the State and that the State cannot prevent a citizen from carrying on a business, except by a law imposing a reasonable restriction in the interest of the general public. Of course, there is no right where the business is dangerous or immoral; such a business may be absolutely prohibited or may be required to be licensed. Moreover, there is no right to carry on a business at any place or at any time restrictions may be imposed in that regard. A citizen cannot be compelled to do a certain business. Relevant cases are:

(i) *Pyare Lal* v. *New Delhi Municipal Committee*, AIR 1968 SC 133 (138): (1967) 3 SCR 747: (1968) 70 Punj LR (D) 153: 1968 (2) SCJ 393: (1967) 2 SCWR 894. (Business on the streets).

(ii) *Ebrahim* v. *Regional Transport Authority*, (1953) SCR 290 (299): AIR 1954 SC 229: 56 Bom LR 768. (Reasonable restrictions for public convenience).

(iii) *Hathising Manufacturing Co.* v. *Union of India*, AIR 1960 SC 923 (928): (1960) 3 SCR 928: (1960) 2 LLJ 1. (Right not to carry on a business).

(iv) *Har Shankar* v. *Deputy Excise and Taxation Commissioner*, AIR 1975 SC 1121: (1975) 1 SCC 737: 1975 Tax LR 1569: (1975) 3 SCR 254. (Absolute prohibition for harmful trades).

(v) *Lakhan Lal* v. *State of Orissa*, AIR 1977 SC 722: (1976) 4 SCC 660: (1977) 1 SCR 811. (Dangerous trade).

(vi) *State of Rajasthan* v. *Mohan Lal Vyas*, AIR 1971 SC 2068: (1971) 3 SCC 705: (1971) UJ 222 (Right cannot be surrendered).

Freedom of Residence

Denial of benefits to migrating members of Scheduled Castes and Scheduled Tribes does not violate article 19; *See* JT 1994 (4) SC 423.

Freedom to reside and settle in any part of India guaranteed by clause (e) of article 19(1) is subject to reasonable restrictions in the interest of the general public or for the protection of interest of Scheduled Tribes. In general, substantive as well as procedural reasonableness would be required. This freedom is said to be intended to remove internal barriers in India or between any of its parts, but is limited to citizens. Moreover, even citizens can be subjected to reasonable restrictions such as passport regulations. Besides this, certain areas may be banned for certain kinds of persons, such as prostitutes. These propositions bear support from the following decisions:—

(i) *State of Madhya Pradesh* v. *Thakur Bharat Singh*, AIR 1967 SC 1170 (1172): (1967) 2 SCR 454: 1967 Jab LJ 493: 1967 Mah LJ 541: 1967 MPLJ 433: (1967) 2 SCA 246: 1968 (1) SCJ 173: 1967 MPWR 64: 1968 Mad LJ (Cri) 24.

(ii) *Kharak Singh* v. *State of Uttar Pradesh*, AIR 1963 SC 1295 (1303): (1964) 1 SCR 332: 1963 2 Cr LJ 329: 1963 All LJ 711: 1964 (2) SCJ 107.

(iii) *Ebrahim* v. *State of Bombay*, (1954) SCR 933 (950): AIR 1954 SC 229: 56 Bom LR 768. (Passport).

(iv) *State of Uttar Pradesh* v. *Kaushaliya*, AIR 1964 SC 416 (423): (1964) 4 SCR 1002: (1964) 1 Cr LJ 304. (Prostitutes).

Government Advertisements

Government advertisements should be given to newspapers under a definite policy or uniform guidelines (Guidelines set out in the judgment); *Ghulam Nabi* v. *State of Jammu & Kashmir*, AIR 1990 J&K 20 (21), for Rights of reply see *L.I.C.* v. *Professor Manubhai D. Shah*, AIR 1993 SC 171: (1992) 3 SCC 637: 1992 AIR SCW 3099: 1993 (1) BLJR 431: 1992 (2) Civ LJ 636: JT 1992 (4) SC 181: 1992 (3) SCJ 84: (1992) 3 SCR 595: 1992 (2) UJ (SC) 480.

Ivory Import

Dealing in imported ivory so long the law permits may be a fundamental right but if the statute prohibits it, it must be held to be a law within the meaning of clause (6) of article 19 in terms whereof reasonable restriction is imposed. A trade which is dangerous to ecology may be regulated or totally prohibited; *Indian Handicrafts Emporium* v. *Union of India*, AIR 2003 SC 3240: (2003) 7 SCC 589.

Judicial Officers

The right is conferred by article 19(1)(a) of the Constitution, on all citizens. Undoubtedly, the word "citizens" includes Government officers, including judicial officers. In one case, which went up to the Supreme Court, the question arose whether a judicial officer can be prohibited from writing or publishing legal works during the tenure of his office. Such a prohibition was laid down in rule 9 of the Karnataka Civil Services (Conduct) Rules. It was held that the refusal of the High Court of Karnataka to permit a judicial officer to publish a commentary on the Karnataka Rent Control Act was not illegal; *S.B. Narasimha Prakash* v. *State of Karnataka*, (1997) 11 SCC 425.

Letter by Employee against the Organisation

An employee of a public sector organisation wrote to the Governor a letter, making against the head of the Corporation certain allegations of mismanagement. It was held that such an employee can be dismissed and he cannot claim the protection of any fundamental right, to justify such conduct; *M.H. Devendrappa* v. *Karnataka State Small Industries Development Corporation*, AIR 1998 SC 1064: (1998) 3 SCC 732: (1998) 2 LLN 419.

Licences and Permits for Carrying Trade

In the context of licences and permits required for carrying on a business or trade, the grant of such licence cannot depend upon the absolute discretion of an administrative authority. The policy must be laid down on which the discretion is to be exercised. Further, in general, the discretion must be exercised on relevant consideration. In short, if the law imposing licensing does not set out the consideration, the law would be void, if the consideration are set out in the law, but are departed from by the competent authority while administering the law then the order of the competent authority would be void, even though the law itself may be valid. Generally, an existing licence cannot be revoked without giving the licensee an opportunity of hearing. The undermentioned decisions bear out these propositions:

(i) *Dwarka Prasad Laxmi Narain* v. *State of Uttar Pradesh*, (1954) SCR 803: AIR 1954 SC 224: 1954 All LJ 203: 1954 SCJ 238: 1954 SCA 204

(ii) *Faruk* v. *State of Madhya Pradesh*, AIR 1970 SC 93 (96): (1969) 1 SCC 853: 1969 MLLJ 950.

(iii) *Fedco (P) Ltd.* v. *S.N. Bilgrami*, (1960) SCJ 235 (249): AIR 1960 SC 415: (1960) 1 SCA 369: (1960) 1 Mad LJ (SC) 71: (1960) 2 SCR 408: (1960) 1 Andh WR (SC) 71: (1960) 62 Bom LR 293: 1960 Mad LJ (Cri) 184 (Hearing before cancellation of licence).

(iv) *Sukhnandan Saran Dinesh Kumar* v. *Union of India*, AIR 1982 SC 902: (1982) 2 SCC 150: 1982 UJ (SC) 503: 1982 (2) SCJ 13, paragraph 23 (Hearing before cancellation of licence).

(v) *Harakchand Ratanchand Banthia* v. *Union of India*, AIR 1970 SC 1453: (1969) 2 SCC 166: 1969 Pat LJR (SC) 744: (1970) 1 SCR 479: (1970) 2 SCA 436: 1969 Mer LR 17.

(vi) *Khatki* v. *Limdi Municipality*, AIR 1979 SC 418: (1979) 1 SCC 248: (1979) 2 SLR 338.

(vii) *All Delhi Cycle Rickshaw Operators Union* v. *Municipal Corporation of Delhi*, AIR 1987 SC 648: (1987) 1 SCC 371: JT 1987 (1) SC 66: 1986 (4) Supreme 461: (1987) 4 (1) IJ Rep 38: 1987 (1) Land LR 297: 1987 (1) SCJ 114: (1987) 1 UJ (SC) 496: (1987) 1 MCC 19 (Reasonable restrictions are permissible).

(viii) *State of Madhya Pradesh* v. *Nandlal Jaiswal*, AIR 1987 SC 251: (1986) 4 SCC 566: 1987 Tax LR 1830: JT 1986 (2) SC 701: 1986 (4) Supreme 81: 1987 Jab LJ 53: (1987) 20 STL 83: 1987 Cr LR (SC) 128: 1987 MPLJ 250, paragraphs 4, 32 and 33 (Requirements of State policy).

Press

The press is not immune from the general law of liability for defamation (civil and criminal); *Printers Mysore* v. *Assistant Commercial Law Officer*, JT 1994 (1) SC 692: (1994) 2 SCC 434: (1994) 53 DLT 662.

Freedom of the press is not expressly mentioned in article 19 but has been held to flow from the general freedom of speech and expression guaranteed to all citizens. As judicially construed, this freedom now includes not merely the freedom to write and publish what the writer considers proper (subject to reasonable restrictions imposed by law for specific purpose), but also the freedom to carry on the business so that information may be disseminated and excessive and prohibitive burden restricting circulation may be avoided. Decisions relevant to these aspects of freedom of press are the following:—

(i) *Virendra* v. *State of Punjab*, AIR 1957 SC 896: (1958) 1 SCR 308: 1958 SCJ 88: 1958 SCA 891: 1958 SCC 1: 1958 SCJ 88.

(ii) *Express Newspapers* v. *Union of India*, AIR 1958 SC 578: 1959 SCR 12: (1961) 1 LLJ 339.

(iii) *Bennett Coleman and Co. Ltd.* v. *Union of India*, AIR 1973 SC 106: (1972) 2 SCC 788: 1973 (1) SCJ 177.

(iv) *Prabha* v. *Union of India*, AIR 1982 SC 6: (1982) 1 SCC 1: 1982 SCC (Cri) 41.

(v) *Indian Express Newspapers* v. *Union of India*, AIR 1986 SC 515: (1985) 1 SCC 641: 1985 Tax LR 2451.

(vi) *Sakal Papers (P) Ltd.* v. *Union of India*, AIR 1962 SC 305: (1962) 3 SCR 842: 1962 (2) SCJ 400.

(vii) *Express Newspapers Pvt. Ltd.* v. *Union of India*, AIR 1986 SC 872: (1986) 1 SCC 133: 1986 SCFBRC 72: (1986) 29 DLT 131: (1986) 2 MCC 171: 1986 Cur Civ LJ (SC) 268: 1986 Recent Laws 7.

(viii) *M.S.M. Sharma* v. *Sri Krishna Sinha*, AIR 1959 SC 395: (1959) Supp 1 SCR 806: (1959) 2 MLJ (SC) 125.

Price Fixation

Price fixation being a legislative act, prior consultation is not required; *H.S.S.K. Niyami* v. *Union of India*, (1990) 4 SCC 516: AIR 1990 SC 2128, paragraph 12.

Reasonable Restrictions

Directive Principles are also relevant consideration in deciding reasonableness of restrictions imposed on Fundamental Rights; *State of Gujarat* v. *Mirzapur Moti Kureshi Kassab Jamat*, AIR 2006 SC 212: 2005 AIR SCW 5723: 2006 (1) All MR 32 (NOC): 2006 (1) Guj LR 294: 2006 (2) JCR SC 272: (2005) 8 SCC 534: 2005 (7) SCJ 701: (2005) 8 SCALE 661: 2005 (8) Supreme 697.

Relationship with Articles 21 and 22

Article 19 is available against State action for the protection of freedoms enumerated in the article. Some controversy existed in the past as to whether the operation of this article is ruled out where articles 21 and 22 apply; but the current trend is not to regard these articles as mutually exclusive. Thus to take one example, a person whose freedom of movement has been taken away by imprisonment or detention does not thereby lose his freedom of expression, so long as it is exercised within the valid conditions relating to imprisonment or detention. Hence a detenue cannot be prevented from sending outside the jail for publication, matter which contains nothing prejudicial to the grounds for which he had been detained. The undermentioned decisions are relevant on the aspect.

   (i)   *State of Maharashtra* v. *Prabhakar,* AIR 1966 SC 424: (1966) 1 SCR 702: 1966 MLJ 141.

   (ii)   *Fernandez* v. *State of Maharashtra,* (1964) 66 Bom LR 185.

   (iii)   *M.A. Khan, Applicant* v. *State of Maharashtra,* AIR 1967 Bom 254: 68 Bom LR 576: 1966 Mah LJ 793: 1967 Cr LJ 964: ILR (1967) Bom 158.

   (iv)   *Kunnikkal Narayanan* v. *State of Kerala,* AIR 1973 Ker 97: 1973 Ker LT 125: 1973 Ker LJ 178: ILR (1973) 1 Ker 258: 1973 Cr LJ 866.

   (v)   *Haradhan Shah* v. *State of West Bengal,* AIR 1974 SC 2154: (1975) 3 SCC 198: 1974 Cr LJ 1479: 1974 SCC (Cri) 816: (1975) 1 SCR 778, paragraphs 32 and 33.

   (vi)   *State of Maharashtra* v. *Basantibai Mohanlal Khetan,* AIR 1986 SC 1466: (1986) 2 SCC 516: 1986 (1) SCJ 566: 1986 (2) Supreme 399: (1986) 88 Bom LR 205: 1986 Mah LR 650: (1986) 1 MCC 73: 1986 UJ (SC) 715.

   (vii)   *Minerva Mills Ltd.* v. *Union of India,* AIR 1980 SC 1789: (1980) 3 SCC 625: 1980 Ker LT 573: 1980 UJ (SC) 727.

   (viii)   *Khudi Ram* v. *State of West Bengal,* AIR 1975 SC 550: (1975) 2 SCC 81: (1975) 2 SCR 832, paragraph 12.

   (ix)   *Vatheeswaran* v. *State of Tamil Nadu,* AIR 1983 SC 361: (1983) 2 SCC 68: 1983 Cr LJ 481.

Right of Minority to Administer Educational Institution

Right of minority to administer educational institution is not infringed by making Tamil as compulsory subject in school syllabi. It does not restric minority students to learn his mother-tongue as well; *K.R. Ramaswamy* v. *State,* AIR 2008 Mad 25: 2008 (2) ALJ (NOC) 348: 2007 (5) CTC 113: 2007 (5) Mad LJ 486: 2007 (4) Mad LW 60.

Right to Know

A citizen has a right to know about the activities of the State, the instrumentalities, the departments and the agencies of the State. The privilege of secrecy which existed in old times, (namely) that the State is not bound to disclose the facts to the citizens or the State cannot be compelled by the citizens to disclose the facts, does not survive now to a great extent. Under article 19 there exists the right of freedom of speech. Freedom of speech is based on the foundation of freedom of right to know. The State can impose and should impose reasonable restrictions in the rights where it affects the national security or any other matter affecting the nation's integrity. But the right is limited and particularly in the matter of sanitation and other allied matters, every citizen has a right to know how the State is functioning and why the State is withholding such information in such matters; *L.K. Koolwal* v. *State of Rajasthan,* AIR 1988 Raj 2: (1987) 4 Reports 53: (1987) 1 Raj LR 334: 1987 MCC 431.

Citizens have a right to know about affairs of Government. But the right is not absolute, *Secrecy* can be *legitimately* claimed in respect of transactions with repercussions on public security; *Dinesh Trivedi M.P.* v. *Union of India,* (1997) 4 SCC 306: JT 1997 (4) SC 237 (case relating to Vohra Committee Report); *Peoples Union for Civil Liberties (PUCL)* v. *Union of India,* AIR 2003 SC 2363: (2003) 4 SCC 399: 2003 AIR SCW 2353: JT 2003 (2) SC 528: 2003 (2) LRI 13: 2003 (3) Mah LR 797: (2003) 2 SCR 1136: 2003 (5) SRJ 197: (2003) 3 SCALE 263: 2003 (3) Supreme 93.

Right to Carry on Business

The hawkers have a right under article 19(1)(g). This right, however, is subject to reasonable restrictions under article 19(6); *Maharashtra Ekta Hawkers Union* v. *Municipal Corporation, Greater Mumbai,* AIR 2004 SC 416: (2004) 1 SCC 625: 2003 AIR SCW 6814: 2004 (3) Bom CR 612: 2004 (3) Mah LJ 437: (2003) 10 SCALE 561: 2004 (1) Supreme 107: 2004 (1) UJ (SC) 676.

Right to Practise Medicine

The restriction placed on right of holders of degree or diploma of "vaidya visharad" and Ayurved Ratna from Hindi Sahitya Sammelan, does not offend article 19(1)(g); *Rajasthan Pradesh V.S. Sardar Shahar* v. *Union of India,* AIR 2010 SC 2221.

Right to Pray

Restriction from offering cures for illness on basis of prayers is reasonable restrictions imposed on ground of public health, morality etc.; *K.P. Hafsath Beevi* v. *State of Kerala*, AIR 2010 Ker 103.

Right to Practise Profession

The properties enclosed within the compound walls of the Sub-Registrars' offices are the properties of the State. It is not the case of document writers that there exist contracts between them and the State as per which they are entitled to carry on their profession within the compound of the Sub-Registrars' offices. If that is the factual position, the right of ownership exercised by the State and State authorities prohibiting the document writers from practising their profession within the enclosures of the Government properties would not violate the fundamental right guaranteed to the document writers under article 19(1)(g) of the Constitution of India; *Inspector General of Registrations and Stamps, Hyderabad* v. *Andhra Pradesh State Document Writers' Associations*, AIR 2003 AP 193: (2003) 4 Andh LD 141: (2002) 3 Andh LT 245.

State Acts: Educational Institution

The State Act strikes a balance between autonomy of institutions and measures to be taken to prevent commercialisation of education; *Tamil Nadu Nursery, Matriculation and Higher Secondary Schools Association, Chennai* v. *State of Tamil Nadu*, AIR 2010 Mad 142.

Substantive and Procedural Aspects

Reasonableness in this context covers substantive reasonableness, as well as procedural reasonableness. Thus, in ordinary circumstances, it will be unreasonable to make the exercise of a fundamental right depend on the subjective satisfaction of the executive. Decisions on this point are:

    (a)   *Khare* v. *State of Delhi*, (1950) SCR 519: AIR 1950 SC 211: (1951) 52 Cr LJ 550.

    (b)   *Gurbachan* v. *State of Bombay*, (1952) SCR 737 (742): AIR 1952 SC 221: 54 Bom LR 849.

    (c)   *Virendra* v. *State of Punjab*, AIR 1957 SC 896: (1958) 1 SCR 308: 1958 SCJ 88: 1958 SCA 891: 1958 SCC 1.

Test of Reasonableness

In applying the test of reasonableness (which is the most crucial consideration), the broad criterion is whether the law strikes a proper balance between social control on the one hand and the rights of the individual on the other hand. The court must take into account the following aspects:—

    (a)   nature of the right infringed;

    (b)   underlying purpose of the restriction imposed;

    (c)   evils sought to be remedied by the law, its extent and urgency;

    (d)   how far the restriction is or is not proportionate to the evil; and

    (e)   prevailing conditions at the time.

Decisions relevant to these propositions are the following:—

    (i)   *Chintaman Rao* v. *State of Madhya Pradesh*, (1950) SCR 759: AIR 1951 SC 118: (1951) Hyd 221.

    (ii)   *Khare* v. *State of Delhi*, (1950) SCR 519: AIR 1950 SC 211: 52 Cr LJ 550.

    (iii)   *Mohd. Hanif Quareshi* v. *State of Bihar*, (1959) SCR 629: AIR 1958 SC 731: 1958 SCA 783: 1958 SCJ 975: 1958 Mad LJ (Cri) 727.

    (iv)   *Dwarka Prasad Laxmi Narain* v. *State of Uttar Pradesh*, (1954) SCR 803: AIR 1954 SC 224: 1954 All LJ 203: 1954 SCJ 238: 1954 SCA 204.

    (v)   *State of Maharashtra* v. *Himmatbhai*, AIR 1970 SC 1157: (1969) 2 SCR 392: 73 Bom LR 75.

    (vi)   *Laxmi* v. *State of Uttar Pradesh*, AIR 1981 SC 873: (1981) 2 SCC 600: (1981) 3 SCR 92.

The Supreme Court has considered the question of reasonableness on several occasions and has laid down several tests and guidelines, to indicate what, in particular circumstances, can be retarded as a reasonable restriction. One of the tests is to bear in mind the directive Principles of State Policy.

(i) *Keshavananda Bharati Sripadgalvaru* v. *State of Kerala*, AIR 1973 SC 1461: (1973) Supp SCR 1: (1973) 4 SCC 225.

(ii) *State of Kerala* v. *N.M. Thomas*, AIR 1976 SC 490: (1976) 2 SCC 310: 1976 Lab IC 395: (1976) 1 Serv LR 805: (1976) 1 LLJ 376: 1976 SCC (Lab) 227: (1976) 1 SCR 906: 1976 SCWR 207.

(iii) *State of Bombay* v. *R.M.D. Chamarbaugwala*, AIR 1957 SC 699: (1957) SCR 874: 52 Bom LR 945.

(iv) *Fatehchand Himatlal* v. *State of Maharashtra*, AIR 1977 SC 1825: (1977) 2 SCC 670: (1977) 2 SCR 828.

Total Prohibition

Total prohibition can be imposed against manufacture of drugs or preparations which are injurious to health. Decisions on this subject are:

(i) *Pratap Pharma (P) Ltd.* v. *Union of India*, AIR 1997 SC 2648: (1997) 5 SCC 87: (1997) 2 BLJR 1076.

(ii) *Lakshmikant* v. *Union of India*, (1997) 4 SCC 739.

Trial by Media

Questions are often raised as to "trial by media". When a sensational criminal case comes to be tried before the court, public curiosity experiences an upsurge. Newspapers — most of them — compete with each other, in publishing their own version of the facts. Some of them employ their own reporters, to unearth details not otherwise available. This enthusiasm is understandable. The thirst for sensational news is a natural human desire. However, investigatory journalism has its risks. The law does not prohibit it in the abstract. But the law does require the players in this activity to keep within certain limits. These limits primarily flow from:

(a) the right to reputation;

(b) the right to privacy; and

(c) the law of contempt of court.

Right to reputation requires that an allegation casting an adverse reflection on the character of an individual should not be published, unless the publication falls within one of the exceptional situations, recognised in this regard by the law. If the situation does not fall within this list of "privileged" or protected situations, then the publisher would be guilty of defamation.

The law of contempt of court operates on a slightly different plane. The paramount considerations hear are — dignity of the court and fairness of trial. Hence, it follows, that once a case has reached the court, no one is allowed to publish his own version of the facts. Violation of this rule amounts to contempt of court. This rule, evolved judicially, is supplemented by special statutory provisions, which prohibit the publication, even of certain matters actually taking place in the course of trial. For example, the name of a victim of rape cannot be published, without permission of the court.

Now, the question may arise whether this negative approach of the law is, in any respect, inconsistent with the constitutionally guaranteed right of freedom of speech and expression. In this connection, it may be pointed out that the Constitution, in article 19(2), expressly saves the operation of the law of contempt of court (apart from recognising other permissible heads of restriction on the freedom of speech and expression). The matter came up before the Supreme Court in *State of Maharashtra* v. *Rajendra Jawanmal Gandhi*, (1997) 8 SCC 386: AIR 1997 SC 3986: 1997 Cr LJ 4657: 1997 AIR SCW 3923: 1997 (3) Crimes 285: JT 1997 (8) SC 43: 1997 (3) SCJ 175: 1998 SC Cr R 1: 1998 SC (Cri) 76: 1997 (8) Supreme 129.

Unincorporated Associations

An unincorporated association cannot also be citizen and cannot claim these rights; *All India Bank Employees' Association* v. *National Industrial Tribunal*, AIR 1962 SC 171 (180): (1962) 3 SCR 269: (1962) 32 Comp Cas 414: (1961) 2 LLJ 385.

20. Protection in respect of conviction for offences.—(1) No person shall be convicted of any offence except for violation of a law in force at the time of the commission of the act charged as an offence, nor be subjected to a penalty greater than that which might have been inflicted under the law in force at the time of the commission of the offence.

(2) No person shall be prosecuted and punished for the same offence more than once.

(3) No person accused of any offence shall be compelled to be a witness against himself.

Notes on Article 20

Applicability

To attract applicability of article 20(2) there must be a second prosecution and punishment for the same offence for which the accused has been prosecuted and punished previously. A subsequent trial or a prosecution and punishment are not barred if the ingredients of the two offences are distinct; *State of Rajasthan* v. *Hat Singh*, AIR 2003 SC 791: (2003) 2 SCC 152: 2003 SCC (Cri) 451.

Clash between Fundamental Rights

Where there is a clash of two fundamental rights, the right which would advance the public morality or public interest, would alone be enforced through the process of court, for the reason that moral considerations cannot be kept at bay and the judges are not expected to sit mute but have to be sensitive; *Mr. X* v. *Hospital Z*, AIR 1999 SC 495: (1998) 9 SCC 296: 1998 AIR SCW 3662: JT 1998 (7) SC 626: 1999 (1) SRJ 88: (1998) 6 SCALE 230: 1998 (9) Supreme 220: 1999 (1) UJ (SC) 232.

Commencement of Protection

The protection given to the accused commences as soon as a formal accusation is made, whether before or during prosecution. It follows that the lodging of a First Information Report, the filing of a complaint in court or the issue of a show-cause notice under a special criminal statute brings article 20(3) into play. But there must be a proceeding contemplating action against a particular person. Important cases on this point are the following:—

(i) *Dastagir* v. *State of Madras*, AIR 1960 SC 756 (761): (1960) 3 SCR 116: 1960 Cr LJ 1159.

(ii) *State of Bombay* v. *Kathi Kalu*, AIR 1961 SC 1808 (1816): (1962) 3 SCR 10: (1961) 2 Cr LJ 856.

(iii) *R.K. Dalmia* v. *Delhi Admn.*, AIR 1962 SC 1821 (1870): (1963) 1 SCR 253: (1962) 2 Cr LJ 805.

(iv) *Joseph* v. *Narayana*, AIR 1964 SC 1552 (1556): (1964) 7 SCR 137: (1963) 34 Comp Cas 546.

(v) *Veera Ibrahim* v. *State of Maharashtra*, AIR 1976 SC 1167: (1976) 2 SCC 302: 1976 SCC (Cri) 278: 1976 Cr LJ 860.

(vi) *Nandini* v. *Dani*, AIR 1978 SC 1025: (1978) 2 SCC 424: 1978 Cr LJ 968: 1978 SCC (Cri) 236, paragraph 30.

(vii) *Balkishan* v. *State of Maharashtra*, AIR 1981 SC 379: (1980) 4 SCC 600: 1981 SCC (Cri) 62: 1980 Cr LJ 1424, paragraph 70.

Compulsion to be a Witness

(a) The immunity under article 20(3) does not extend to compulsory production of material objects or compulsion to give specimen writing, specimen signature, finger impression or compulsory exhibition of the body or giving of blood specimens. Following cases may be seen on this point:—

(i) *Dastagir* v. *State of Madras*, AIR 1960 SC 756: (1960) SCR 116: 1960 Cr LJ 1159.

(ii) *Ram Swarup* v. *State of Uttar Pradesh*, AIR 1958 All 119 (126): 1958 Cr LJ 134.

(iii) *Palani, (in re:)*, AIR 1955 Mad 495: 56 Cr LJ 1197.

(iv) *T. Subbiah* v. *S.K.D. Ramaswamy Nadar*, AIR 1970 Mad 85: 1969 Mad LW (Cri) 117: 1970 Cr LJ 254.

(v) *Pokhar Singh* v. *State of Punjab*, AIR 1958 Punj 294: 1958 Cr LJ 1084.

(b) Compulsion regarding documents is prohibited only if the documents convey the personal knowledge of the accused relating to the charge; *State of Bombay* v. *Kathi Kalu*, AIR 1961 SC 1808 (1816): (1962) 2 SCR 10: 64 Bom LR 240.

Double Jeopardy

As regards article 20(2) dealing with double jeopardy what it bars is prosecution and punishment after an earlier punishment for the same offence. 'Offence' here means an offence as defined in section 3(38) of the General Clauses Act, 1897 applied to the Constitution by article 367. Important decisions interpreting this clause of article 20 are the following:—

(i) *Makbool* v. *State of Bombay*, (1953) SCR 730: AIR 1953 SC 325: 56 Bom LR 13

(ii) *Kalawati* v. *State of Himachal Pradesh*, (1953) SCR 546: AIR 1953 SC 131: 1953 Cr LJ 668: 1953 Mad WN 219: 1953 SCJ 144: 1953 All WR (Supp) 52: 1953 SCA 660.

(iii) *State of Bombay* v. *S.L. Apte*, AIR 1961 SC 578: (1961) 3 SCR 107: 63 Bom LR 491: (1961) 1 Ker LR 452: (1961) 2 SCA 446: (1961) 1 AndhWR (SC) 210: 1961 (1) SCJ 685: 1961 Mad LJ (SC) 210: (1961) 1 Cr LJ 725: 1961 MPLJ 1108.

(iv) *Raja Narayan Lal Bansilal* v. *Manek Phioz Mistry*, AIR 1961 SC 29: (1961) 1 SCR 417: (1960) 30 Comp Cas 644.

(v) *Leo Roy Frey* v. *Superintendent, District Jail, Amritsar*, AIR 1958 SC 119 (121): 1958 SCR 822: 1958 Cr LJ 260: 1958 Mad LJ (Cri) 289: 1958 SCA 240: 1958 SCJ 301.

(vi) *Assistant Customs Collector* v. *Melwani*, AIR 1970 SC 962: (1969) 2 SCR 438: 1970 Cr LJ 885.

The offences for which accused was tried and convicted in foreign country and for which he is tried in India are distinct and separate; *Jitendra Panchal* v. *Intelligence Officer, NCB*, AIR 2009 SC 1938: 2009 AIR SCW 1559: 2009 (1) Crimes 338: 2009 (3) Mad LJ (Cri) 333: (2009) 3 SCC 57: (2009) 2 SCALE 202: 2009 (1) SCC (Cri) 986.

Foreign Exchange Regulation Act, 1973

Where a person is summoned and examined under section 40 of the Foreign Exchange Regulation Act, 1973, it cannot be presumed that the statement was obtained under pressure or duress. The statement cannot be attacked on the ground of infringement of the constitutional guarantee of protection against self incrimination under article 20(3) of the Constitution; *C. Sampath Kumar* v. *Enforcement Officer, Enforcement Directorate, Madras*, AIR 1998 SC 16: (1997) 8 SCC 358: 1997 AIR SCW 3959: JT 1997 (8) SC 135: (1997) 6 SCALE 140: 1998 SCC (Cri) 74: 1997 (8) Supreme 268: 1997 (2) UJ (SC) 749.

No Right in Procedure at Law

It should be noted that while substantive law imposing liability or penalty cannot be altered to the prejudice of the person supposed to be guilty with retrospective effect, there is no vested right in procedure. Besides this, the thrust of article 20(1) is in the field of criminal law only, since the word 'offence' as defined in article 367 read with the General Clauses Act, 1897 can only denote an act or omission punishable by law. Important decisions on the above aspect are the following:—

(i) *Rao Shiv Bahadur Singh* v. *State of Vindhya Pradesh*, AIR 1953 SC 394: (1953) SCR 1188: 1953 Cr LJ 1480: 1953 SCA 803: 1953 SCJ 563.

(ii) *Kedar Nath* v. *State of West Bengal*, AIR 1953 SC 404: (1954) 1 SCR 30: 1953 Cr LJ 1621.

(iii) *Jawala Ram* v. *State of Pepsu*, AIR 1962 SC 1246: (1962) 2 SCR 503: (1962) 2 Cr LJ 303.

(iv) *State of West Bengal* v. *S.K. Ghose*, AIR 1963 SC 255: (1963) 2 SCR 111: (1963) Cr LJ 252.

(v) *Satwant* v. *State of Punjab*, AIR 1960 SC 266: (1960) 2 SCR 89: 1960 Cr LJ 410.

(vi) *Union of India* v. *Sukumar*, AIR 1966 SC 1206: (1966) 2 SCR 34: 1966 Cr LJ 946.

(vii) *Nayyar* v. *State*, AIR 1979 SC 602: (1979) 2 SCC 593: 1979 SCC (Cri) 549.

(viii) *Kanyaiya Lal* v. *Income Tax Commissioner*, AIR 1975 SC 255.

(ix) *Maya* v. *C.I.T.*, (1986) 1 SCC 445: AIR 1986 SC 293: 157 IIR 330, paragraphs 11 and 12.

Penalty not Prescribed

Article 20(3) does not apply where there is no penalty prescribed for the contravention in question; *A.A. Mulla* v. *State of Maharashtra*, AIR 1997 SC 1441: (1996) 11 SCC 606, paragraphs 21, 22.

Protection against Self-incrimination

Test results of polygraph and brain fingerprinting tests are testimonial compulsions. Bar of article 20(3) applies; *Selvi* v. *State of Karnataka*, AIR 2010 SC 1974 (Paras 123, 136, 149, 160, 161).

Scope of Article 20

The prohibitions imposed by article 20 are directly relevant to the criminal process. While clause (1) is concerned with the substantive law of criminal liability and penalty, clauses (2) and (3) are concerned mainly with the stage of procedure. In the jurisprudence of constitutional law, article 20(1) incorporates a prohibition against '*ex post facto penal law*', article 20(2) incorporates a prohibition against 'double jeopardy' article 20(3) gives protection against 'testimonial compulsion'. Because of the word 'person' used in each clause, the article must be regarded as applicable to a corporation which is accused, prosecuted, convicted or punished for an offence; *Sharma* v. *Satish*, (1954) SCR 1077: (1954) 1 MLJ 680: 1954 Cr LJ 865. Thus, article 20 is not confined to individuals.

Testimonial Compulsion for the Accused

The protection against compulsion 'to be a witness' is confined to persons 'accused of an offence'. There is no constitutional protection for witnesses (*i.e.* persons other than the accused). However, the Indian Evidence Act, 1872, in sections 132 and 148, confers a limited protection against self-incrimination to witness in civil and criminal courts. Important cases on the above limitation of article 20(3) are the following:—

(i) *Raja Narayanlal Bansilal* v. *Maneck Phiroz Mistry*, AIR 1961 SC 29: (1961) 2 SCR 417: (1960) 30 Comp Cas 644.

(ii) *Charoria* v. *State of Maharashtra*, AIR 1988 SC 938 (947).

To be a Witness

Taking specimen fingerprints and handwritings from accused is not hit by article 20(3) as being "witness against himself"; *State through SPE and CBI, A.P.* v. *M. Krishna Mohan*, AIR 2008 SC 368: 2007 AIR SCW 7044: 2007 (4) Crimes 327: 2007 (4) JCC 3294: 2008 (1) Mad LJ (Cri) 1417: 2008 (39) OCR 276: (2007) 12 SCALE 618: 2007 (8) Supreme 205.

21. Protection of life and personal liberty.—No person shall be deprived of his life or personal liberty except according to procedure established by law.

Notes on Article 21

AIDS Patient and Employment

It has been held that a person cannot be regarded as medically unfit and denied employment, merely on the ground that he is found to be HIV positive; *MX of Bombay Indian Inhabitant* v. *M/s. ZY*, AIR 1997 Bom 406.

Arrest

Arrest is not must in all cases of cognizable offences; *Lal Kamlendra Pratap Singh* v. *State of Uttar Pradesh*, (2009) 4 SCC 437; *see* also *Joginder Kumar* v. *State of Uttar Pradesh*, (1994) 4 SCC 260: AIR 1994 SC 1349: 1994 Cr LJ 1981: 1994 AIR SCW 1886: 1994 (2) BLJR 975: 1994 (2) Crimes 106: JT 1994 (3) SC 423: 1994 (2) Ker LJ 97: 1994 (1) Ker LT 919: 1994 (2) SCJ 230: (1994) 3 SCR 661: 1994 SCC (Cri) 1172

Assault on Child

In *Saheli* v. *Commissioner of Police*, AIR 1990 SC 513: (1990) 1 SCC 422: 1990 SCC (Cri) 145, police officers had, at the behest of the landlord, beaten up lady tenant "K" and her minor son

"N". The son succumbed to the injuries. The mother was held entitled to compensation against the Delhi Administration. The compensation so awarded included:

(a) solatium for mental pain;

(b) solatium for distress and indignity;

(c) damages for loss of liberty;

(d) damages for death.

It was further directed that the Delhi Administration may recover the amount from the officers responsible for the beating.

Atomic Energy

Under articles 21 and 32, the court has directed that the Gamma Chambers housed in Jawaharlal Nehru University, Delhi, be sent to Bhabha Atomic Research Centre, Bombay for recharging; *M.C. Mehta* v. *Union of India*, AIR 1987 SC 1086: (1987) 1 SCC 395: 1987 SCC (L&S) 37.

Bail

Pre-trial release on personal bond (*i.e.,* without surety) should be allowed where the person to be released on bail is indigent and there is no substantial risk of his absconding; *Hussainara* v. *Home Secretary, State of Bihar,* AIR 1979 SC 1360: (1980) 1 SCC 93: 1980 SCC (Cri) 35: 1979 Cr LJ 1036.

Beauty Contests

It has been held that beauty contests, in their true form, are not objectionable. But, if there is indecent representation of the figure of a woman or if there is any matter derogatory of women, then it would offend the Indecent Representation of Women Act, 1986, and also article 21; *Chandra Rajakumari* v. *Police Commissioner, Hyderabad,* AIR 1998 AP 302: 1998 (1) Andh LD 810: 1998 (1) Andh LT 329: 1998 (4) Rec Cr R 631.

Child Offenders

Child offenders are entitled to speedy trial; *Sheela Barse* v. *Union of India,* AIR 1986 SC 1773: (1986) 3 SCC 596: 1986 SCC (Cri) 337, paragraph 12.

Compensation

Rudul Shah v. *State of Bihar,* AIR 1983 SC 1086: (1983) 4 SCC 141: 1983 Cr LJ 1644 was the first case in which compensation was awarded by the writ court. *Sebastian Hongray* v. *Union of India,* AIR 1984 SC 571: (1984) 1 SCC 339: 1984 Cr LJ 289 and *Bhim Singh, MLA* v. *State of Jammu & Kashmir,* AIR 1986 SC 494: 1986 Cr LJ 192: 1986 All LJ 653: (1985) 4 SCC 677: 1986 SC Cr R 20: 1986 SCC (Cri) 47: 1986 UJ (SC) 458: 1986 Cr LR (SC) 66: (1986) 1 APLJ (SC) 36: 1986 Mad LJ (Cri) 32 were later cases, in the same directions.

Cruel Punishment

A punishment which is too cruel or torturesome is unconstitutional; *Inderjeet* v. *State of Uttar Pradesh,* AIR 1979 SC 1867: (1979) 4 SCC 246: 1979 Cr LJ 1410.

Custodial Death

For custodial death, the writ court can award compensation. Custodial death has been described as "one of the worst crimes in a civilised society, governed by the rule of law"; *D.K. Basu* v. *State of West Bengal,* AIR 1997 SC 610: (1997) 1 SCC 416: 1997 SCC (Cri) 92, paragraph 36.

The right against custodial violence arises from article 21; *Sheela Barse* v. *State of Maharashtra,* AIR 1983 SC 378: (1983) Cr LJ 642: (1983) 2 SCC 96: 1983 SCC (Cri) 353.

Death Sentence

Compulsory death sentence for murder committed by a life convict undergoing the sentence of imprisonment for life (section 303, I.P.C.) is unconstitutional; *Mithu* v. *State of Punjab,* AIR 1983 SC 473: (1983) 2 SCC 277: 1983 SCC (Cri) 405, paragraphs 23-25.

Debtor and Article 21

A debtor can be put in civil prison for non-payment of decretal debt, only if there is—

   (i) wilful default by him, notwithstanding his having sufficient means to pay, or

  (ii) some other element of bad faith, going beyond mere indifference; *Jolly Verghese* v. *Bank of Cochin*, AIR 1980 SC 470: (1980) 2 SCC 360: (1980) 2 SCR 913, paragraph 10.

Delay in Bringing to Trial

Inordinate delay by the State in bringing an accused to trial or in preferring an appeal against his acquittal, violates article 21, if there is no fault by the accused. *See* the under-mentioned decisions:

   (i) *State of Maharashtra* v. *Champalal*, AIR 1981 SC 1675: (1981) 3 SCC 610: 1981 SCC (Cri) 762, paragraph 2.

  (ii) *State of Rajasthan* v. *Sukhpal*, AIR 1984 SC 207: (1983) 1 SCC 393: 1983 SCC (Cri) 213.

 (iii) *Rudul Shah* v. *State of Bihar*, AIR 1983 SC 1086: (1983) 4 SCC 141: 1983 Cr LJ 1644.

Delay in Execution

Unjustifiable delay in execution of death sentence violates article 21; *Sher Singh* v. *State of Punjab*, AIR 1983 SC 465: (1983) 2 SCC 344: 1983 Cr LJ 803, paragraphs 13, 16 and 19.

Ecology : Ecological Balance

Every attempt should be made to preserve the fragile ecology of the forest area and to protect the Tiger Reserve and the right of tribals in the State of Madhya Pradesh; *Animal and Environment Legal Defence Fund* v. *Union of India*, (1997) 3 SCC 549: AIR 1997 SC 1071: 1997 AIR SCW 1078: JT 1997 (3) SC 298: 1997 (2) Jab LJ 1: 1997 (1) SCJ 522: (1997) 2 SCR 728: (1997) 2 SCALE 493: 1997 (2) Supreme 713, paragraph 11.

Ecology and "Public Trust" Doctrine

The Supreme Court has enunciated the doctrine of "Public Trust", based on the legal theory of the ancient Roman Empire. The idea of this theory was that certain common properties such as rivers, seashores, forests and the air, were held by the Government in trusteeship for the free and unimpeded use of the general public. The resources like air, sea, waters and the forests have such a great importance to the people as a whole, that it would be totally unjustified to make them a subject of private ownership. The concept "environment" bears a very close relationship to this doctrine. The doctrine enjoins upon the resources for the enjoyment of the general public, rather to permit their use for private ownership or commercial purposes. It was thus held that the State Government committed breach of public trust, by leasing the ecologically fragile land to the Motel management; *M.C. Mehta* v. *Kamal Nath*, (1997) 1 SCC 388: 1997 (2) Civil LJ 1.

Environment

Chemical or other hazardous industries which are essential for economic development may have to be set up. But measures should be taken to reduce the risk of hazard or risk to the community by taking all necessary steps for locating such industries in a manner that would pose the least risk or danger to the community and for maximizing safety requirements in such industries. The Supreme Court directed the High Court to set up a Green Bench; *Vellore Citizens Welfare Forum* v. *Union of India*, AIR 1996 SC 2715: (1996) 5 SCC 647: 1996 AIR SCW 3399: 1996 (5) Comp LJ SC 40: JT 1996 (7) SC 375.

Environment: Hazardous Chemicals

Certain directions regarding hazardous chemicals were given by the Supreme Court in *M.C. Mehta* v. *Union of India*, (1987) Supp SCC 131: AIR 1987 SC 1086: (1987) 1 Comp LJ 99: (1987) 1 ACC 157: (1987) 1 SCC 395: 1987 (1) Supreme 65: 1987 SCC (Lab) 37: JT 1987 (1) SC 1: 1987 ACJ 386, relying partly on article 21. In the above judgment, there are dicta that life, public health and ecology have priority over unemployment and loss of revenue.

Right to pollution free air falls within article 21; *Subhash Kumar* v. *State of Bihar*, AIR 1991 SC 420: (1991) 1 SCC 598: 1991 AIR SCW 121: 1991 (1) All CJ 424: 1991 (1) BLJR 550: 1991 (1) Civ LJ 719: JT 1991 (1) SC 77: 1991 (1) Pat LJR 69: (1991) 1 SCR 5: 1991 (1) UJ (SC) 533, paragraph 7.

Any disturbance of the basic environment elements, namely air, water and soil, which are necessary for "life", would be hazardous to "life" within the meaning of article 21 of the Constitution; *M.C. Mehta* v. *Kamal Nath*, AIR 2000 SC 1997: (2000) 6 SCC 213: 2000 AIR SCW 1854: JT 2000 (7) SC 19: 2000 (7) SRJ 210: (2000) 5 SCALE 69: 2000 (4) Supreme 391: 2000 (2) UJ (SC) 1196.

Environment : Precautionary Principle

The "precautionary principle" requires the State to anticipate, prevent and attack the causes of environmental degradation; *M.C. Mehta* v. *Union of India*, (1997) 3 SCC 715.

Fair Procedure

Subsequent to *Maneka Gandhi's* case, AIR 1978 SC 597: (1978) 1 SCC 248: (1978) 2 SCR 621 so many aspects of fair procedure or reasonable and just procedure in the context of article 21 have come up before the court. The stream is endless and the case law can be surveyed only in a full fledged commentary. Some important points laid down in the case law are mentioned in the succeeding paragraphs, by way of illustrations. For convenience of reference, the topics to which the cases relate have been arranged alphabetically as far as possible, in the following paragraphs.

Fair Trial

Assurance of a fair trial is the first imperative of the dispensation of justice; *Police Commr., Delhi* v. *Registrar Delhi High Court*, AIR 1997 SC 95: (1996) 6 SCC 323: 1996 SCC (Cri) 1325 (paragraphs 15, 23)

Foreign Travel

Right to go abroad forms part of article 21; *Satwant Singh Sawhney* v. *D. Ramarathnam*, AIR 1967 SC 1836: (1967) 3 SCR 525: (1968) 70 Bom LR 1.

Forests

In one case the court gave directions regarding declaring disputed areas as reserved forests; *Banwasi Sewa Ashram* v. *State of Uttar Pradesh*, (1986) 4 SCC 753: AIR 1987 SC 374: 1987 Cr LR (SC) 2: 1987 (1) SCJ 203: 1987 SC Cr R 73: 1987 East Cr C 430.

Handcuffing

The Supreme Court has given directions to the Union of India to frame rules or guidelines as regards the circumstances in which handcuffing of the accused should be resorted to. *See* the following cases:—

 (i) *Prem Shanker Shukla* v. *Delhi Administration*, AIR 1980 SC 1535: 1980 Cr LJ 930: (1980) 3 SCC 526: 1980 SCC (Cri) 815.

 (ii) *Altemesh Rein* v. *Union of India*, AIR 1988 SC 1768: (1988) 4 SCC 54: 1988 SCC (Cri) 900.

 (iii) *Citizens for Democracy* v. *State of Assam*, AIR 1996 SC 2193: 1996 Cr LJ 3247: 1996 AIR SCW 2815: JT 1995 (4) SC 475: 1995 (2) Mad LJ 66: 1995 (2) OCR 174: (1995) 3 SCC 743: 1995 (2) SCJ 308: (1995) 3 SCR 943: 1996 SC Cr R 37: 1995 SCC (Cri) 600.

 (iv) *Charles Sobraj* v. *Supdt. Central jail, Tihar, New Delhi*, AIR 1978 SC 1514: (1978) Cr LJ 1534: (1978) 4 SCC 104: 1978 SCC (Cri) 542: 1978 SC Cr R 416.

 (v) *T. Vatheeswaran* v. *State of Tamil Nadu*, AIR 1983 SC 361(2): (1983) Cr LJ 482: (1983) 2 SCC 68.

Handcuffing is permitted only in extraordinary circumstances; *Sunil Gupta* v. *State of Madhya Pradesh*, (1990) 3 SCC 119: 1990 SCC (Cri) 440: JT 1990 (2) SC 372.

Health

The right to life includes the right to health; *State of Punjab* v. *Mahinder Singh Chawla*, AIR 1997 SC 1225: (1997) 2 SCC 83: 1997 SCC (L&S) 294.

Housing

Dicta in *Shantistar* v. *Narayanan*, (1990) 2 SCJ 10, paragraphs 8 and 13, speaks of a right to housing. Later it was been held that shelter is not a fundamental right; *Gauri Shanker* v. *Union of India*, JT 1994 (5) SC 634: (1994) 6 SCC 349: AIR 1995 SC 55: 1995 (1) SCT 56: 1994 AIR SCW 4059: 1994 (2) Ren CJ 391: 1994 (2) Rent LR 283: 1994 SCFBRC 356.

However, the following propositions emerge from a Supreme Court judgment relating to encroachments:—

(a) There is no right to encroach on public paths, etc.

(b) But the State and Municipal Corporations have constitutional as well as statutory duty to provide to poor and indigent weaker sections, residential accommodation by utilising urban vacant land available under the Urban Land Ceiling Act.

(c) But is not obligatory for the State or the Municipal Corporation to provide alternative accommodation in *every case*.

(d) In view of the consistent influx of rural population into urban areas and consequent growth of encroachments, local bodies should also prepare plans in accordance with articles 243G and 243W of the Constitution.

Ahmedabad Municipal Corporation v. *Nawab Khan Gulab Khan*, AIR 1997 SC 152: (1997) 11 SCC 121: 1996 AIR SCW 4315: 1997 (1) All MR 537: 1997 (1) Guj LH 438: JT 1996 (10) SC 485.

It has been held that the right to shelter is a fundamental right. It springs from:—

(a) right to residence [article 19(1)a] and

(b) right to life [article 21]

Uttar Pradesh Avas Evam Vikas Parishad v. *Friends Co-op. Housing Society Ltd.*, AIR 1996 SC 114: (1995) Supp 3 SCC 456: 1995 AIR SCW 3800: 1995 All LJ 2066: 1995 (2) Rent LR 33: 1995 (2) SCJ 255: (1995) 3 SCR 729, paragraph 7.

Illegal Detention

In a Madras case, the State of Tamil Nadu was ordered to pay compensation (Rs. 50,000) to a lady who was illegally detained; *Meera Nireshwalia* v. *State of Tamil Nadu*, (1991) Cr LJ 2395 (Mad).

Illegal Encroachment

An encroacher has no right whatsoever to put forth a claim that he has the protection of article 21 of the Constitution; *Ranital Chowk Vyapari Sangh, Jabalpur* v. *State of Madhya Pradesh*, AIR 2006 (NOC) 299 (MP).

Inhuman Treatment

In a Delhi case, the High Court came to the conclusion that, having regard to the inhuman manner in which the deceased had been treated by the police compensation should be awarded. The High Court further held that the fact that the matter was under investigation on an FIR Registered with the police, could not come in the way of compensation being awarded in writ jurisdiction; *P.V. Kapoor* v. *Union of India*, (1992) Cr LJ 140 (Del).

Insane Person

Imprisonment of a person is unconstitutional after that person in declared insane; *Veena* v. *State of Bihar*, AIR 1983 SC 339: (1982) 2 SCC 583: 1982 SCC (Cri) 511.

Irish Constitution

Under the Constitution of Ireland, (1937), article 4.3.1, the Judges are invested with the obligation of protecting and enforcing the rights of individuals and provisions of the Bunchreacht in proceedings before them.

[*See*, Andrew S. Butler, "Constitutional Rights in Private Litigation: A Critique and Comparative Analysis" (1993) 16 Anglo American Law L. REV. 1 (1993)]. A person can directly invoke, the Bunchreacht, so as to sue for the violation of constitutionally guaranteed rights.

[*Meskill* v. *CIE*, 1973 IR 121, *Kennedy & Arnold* v. *Ireland*, 1987 IR 587, here an unjustified phone tape was redressed with damages]. These developments have given rise to the evolution of a theory of constitutional torts that have been enabling the judiciary to vindicate and protect the rights of an Irish Citizen, by ordering the payment of compensation for the infringement of rights.

See also, W. Binchy, "Constitutional Remedies and the Law of Torts" in J.O. Reilly (ed.) Constitutional Remedies and the Law of Torts: Essays in Honour of Brian Walsh (1992), 201.

Compensation was awarded to the dependents of persons killed in firing on persons of backward classes and also to persons injured in the firing; *People's Union for Democratic Rights* v. *State of Bihar*, AIR 1987 SC 355: (1987) Cr LJ 528: (1987) 1 SCC 265: 1987 SCC (Cri) 58.

Legal Aid

An accused person at least where the charge is of an offence punishable with imprisonment, is entitled to be offered legal aid, if he is too poor to afford counsel. Further, counsel for the accused must be given sufficient time and facility for preparing the defence. Breach of these safeguards of fair trial would invalidate the trial and conviction, even if the accused did not ask for legal aid. *See* the undermentioned cases:

   (i) *Hussainara* v. *Home Secretary, State of Bihar*, AIR 1979 SC 1377: (1980) 1 SCC 108: 1980 SCC (Cri) 50: 1980 MLJ (Cr) 93.

  (ii) *Hussainara Khatoon* v. *Home Secretary, State of Bihar, Patna*, AIR 1979 SC 1369: (1980) 1 SCC 98: 1979 Cr LJ 1045: 1979 Pat LJR 410: (1979) 3 SCR 532: 1980 SCC (Cri) 40.

 (iii) *Khatri* v. *State of Bihar*, AIR 1981 SC 928: (1981) 1 SCC 627: 1981 SCC (Cri) 228.

  (iv) *Suk Das* v. *Union Territory of Arunachal Pradesh*, AIR 1986 SC 991: 1986 Cr LJ 1084: 1986 All LJ 774: 1986 SCC (Cri) 166: (1986) 1 SCWR 219: (1986) 2 SCC 401: 1986 (2) Crimes 40: 1986 Cr LR (SC) 188: 1986 (2) Supreme 1: 1986 Cal Cr LR (SC) 83.

   (v) *Ranchod* v. *State of Gujarat*, AIR 1974 SC 1143: (1974) 3 SCC 581: 1974 Cr LJ 799.

  (vi) *M.H. Hoskot* v. *State of Maharashtra*, AIR 1978 SC 1548: (1978) Cr LJ 1678: (1978) 3 SCC 544.

Livelihood

Right to livelihood is an integral facet of the right to life; *Narendra Kumar* v. *State of Haryana*, JT 1994 (2) SC 94: (1994) 4 SCC 460: 1994 SCC (L&S) 882: 1994 (68) FLR 942: AIR 1995 SC 519.

The violation of the right to livelihood is required to be remedied. But the right to livelihood as contemplated under article 21 of the Constitution cannot be so widely construed which may result in the defeating the purpose sought to be achieved by the aforesaid article. It is also true that the right to livelihood would include all attributes of life but the same cannot be extended to the extent that it may embrace or take within its ambit all sorts of claim relating to the legal or contractual rights of parties completely ignoring the person approaching the court and the alleged violation of the said right; *State of Himachal Pradesh* v. *Raja Mahendra Pal*, AIR 1999 SC 1786: (1999) 4 SCC 43.

Medical aid in Government Hospitals

Failure on the part of a government hospital to provide timely medical treatment to a patient in need of such treatment amounts to violation of the right to life. *See* the undermentioned cases:

   (i) *Paschim Banga Khet Mazdoor Samity* v. *State of West Bengal*, AIR 1996 SC 2426: 1996 Lab IC 2054: 1996 AIR SCW 2964: 1996 (2) APLJ 33: JT 1996 (6) SC 43: (1996) 4 SCC 37: 1996 (3) SCJ 25: 1996 (4) SCT 28: 1996 (6) Serv LR 346, paragraphs 9, 15, 16.

  (ii) *Parmanand Katara* v. *Union of India*, AIR 1989 SC 2039: (1990) Cr LJ 671: (1989) 4 SCC 286: 1989 SCC (Cri) 721.

Medical Confidentiality

The Supreme Court has held that if a prospective spouse has an apprehension that the other (prospective) spouse is suffering from AIDS, the former has a right to seek information about the latter's disease from the hospital where blood reports of the latter are available. This right is part of the right to life; *Tokugha Yepthomo (Dr.)* v. *Apollo Hospital*, JT 1998 (7) SC 626: AIR 1999 SC 495: 1998 AIR SCW 3662: 1998 (3) CPJ 12: 1999 (1) Comp LJ 23 SC: 1999 (1) Mah LR 750: (1998) 8 SCC 296: 1999 (1) SRJ 88: (1998) 6 SCALE 230: 1998 (9) Supreme 220: 1999 (1) UJ (SC) 232.

Medical Test

The test results of polygraph and BEAP/Brain fingerprinting test amount to testimonial compulsions and it hence violates right against self-incrimination and personal liberty under article 21; *Selvi* v. *State of Karnataka*, AIR 2010 SC 1974.

The Court has power to order a person to undergo medical test and such an order would not be in violation of the right of personal liberty under article 21 of the Constitution; *Shaik Fakruddin* v. *Shaik Mohammed Hasan,* AIR 2006 AP 48: 2006 (1) ALJ (EE) 148: 2006 (54) All Cr C 14 SOC: 2006 (37) All Ind Cas 197: 2005 (6) Andh LD 179: 2005 (6) Andh LT 97: 2006 (3) Civ LJ 13.

Minimum Punishment

Minimum punishment provided by statute for anti-social offences is not *per se* unconstitutional; *Inderjeet* v. *State of Uttar Pradesh,* AIR 1979 SC 1867: (1979) 4 SCC 246: 1979 UJ (SC) 679: 1979 All Cr R 428: 1979 Cr LJ 1410: (1980) 1 SCWR 33: 1979 SCC (Cri) 966: 1979 All Cr C 350: ILR 1979 HP 148 (Food adulteration).

Natural Justice

Natural justice is implicit in article 21. *See* the undermentioned cases:

   (i) *Maneka Gandhi* v. *Union of India,* AIR 1978 SC 597: (1978) 1 SCC 248: (1978) 2 SCR 621, paragraph 56.

  (ii) *Sunil Batra* v. *Delhi Administration,* AIR 1978 SC 1675: (1978) 4 SCC 494: 1978 Cr LJ 1741.

 (iii) *Hussainara* v. *Home Secretary, State of Bihar,* AIR 1979 SC 1369: (1980) 1 SCC 98: 1979 Cr LJ 1045.

  (iv) *State of Maharashtra* v. *Champalal,* AIR 1981 SC 1675: (1981) 3 SCC 610: 1981 Cr LJ 1273.

   (v) *Olga Tellis* v. *Bombay Municipal Corporation,* AIR 1986 SC 180: (1985) 3 SCC 545: (1985) 2 Bom CR 434: 1986 Cr LR (SC) 23: 1986 Cur Civ LJ (SC) 230, paragraph 31.

Whether the procedure laid down in a particular case is fair, depends on the facts of each case; *Charan Lal Sahu* v. *Union of India,* (1990) 1 SCC 613: AIR 1990 SC 1480: (1989) Supp 2 SCR 597: 1989 Supp SCALE 1.

Non-revision of Pay Scale

To hold that mere non-revision of pay scale would amount to a violation of fundamental right guaranteed under article 21 would be stretching it too far and cannot be countenanced; *A.K. Bindal* v. *Union of India,* AIR 2003 SC 2189: (2003) 5 SCC 163: (2003) SCC (L&S) 620: (2003) 2 LLN 1122.

Obstruction of Movement

Obstruction of movement along highway by the police is constitutional, provided the obstruction is reasonable and in the interest of public order; *Rupinder* v. *Union of India,* AIR 1983 SC 65: (1983) 1 SCC 140: 1983 SCC (Cri) 136.

Oppression of Peasants

In *Peoples Union for Democratic Rights* v. *State of Bihar,* AIR 1987 SC 355: (1987) Cr LJ 528: (1987) 1 SCC 265: 1987 SCC (Cri) 58 the People's Union filed a writ petition complaining that about 600 peasants who had assembled peacefully were harassed by the police. The Supreme Court awarded compensation of Rs. 20,000 in case of death and Rs. 5,000 in case of injury.

Passport

A citizen's passport cannot be impounded for an indefinite period of time; *Maneka Gandhi* v. *Union of India,* AIR 1978 SC 597: (1978) 1 SCC 248: (1978) 2 SCR 621, paragraphs 68, 84, 135, 143.

The requirement of natural justice being implicit in article 21, the Passports Act, 1967 would be construed by the court as requiring hearing before taking prejudicial action; *Maneka Gandhi* v. *Union of India,* AIR 1978 SC 597: (1978) 1 SCC 248: (1978) 2 SCR 621, paragraph 56.

Paternity of Child

The use of DNA Test is to be resorted to only if such test is eminently needed; *Bhabani Prasad Jena* v. *Convenor Secretary, Orissa State Commission for Women,* AIR 2010 SC 2851.

Personal Liberty: Women

The personal liberty includes right of women to make reproductive choices. She can refuse to participate in sexual act; *Suchitra Srivastava* v. *Chandigarh Administration,* AIR 2010 SC 235.

Police Atrocities

In *Peoples Union for Democratic Rights* v. *Police Commr., Delhi Police Headquarters*, (1989) 4 SCC 730: (1989) 1 SCALE 598: 1990 SCC (Cri) 75: 1990 ACC CJ 192, under article 32, compensation was awarded to victims of police atrocities.

When the constitutional and legal rights of a person are invaded with a mischievous or malicious intent, the court has jurisdiction to compensate the victim, by awarding suitable monetary compensation; *Bhim Singh* v. *State of Jammu & Kashmir*, 1986 Cr LJ 192: (1985) 4 SCC 677: AIR 1986 SC 494 (paragraphs 2, 3). *Nilabati* v. *State of Orissa*, (1993) 2 SCC 746: AIR 1993 SC 1960: 1993 Cr LJ 2899; *D.K. Basu* v. *State of West Bengal*, 1996 (9) SCALE 298: (1997) 1 SCC 416: AIR 1997 SC 610; *People's Union of Civil Liberties* v. *Union of India*, AIR 1997 SC 568: (1997) 1 SCC 301.

Position in USA

In the United States of America, a constitutional tort is redressed in two ways. There is available a statutory cause of action under the Civil Rights Act of 1871, for a violation of the constitutional rights and other rights based on common law principles. American courts have made some important progress in this regard. T. Eisenberg & S. Schwab, "The Reality of Constitutional tort Litigation, (1987) 67 IOWA L. Rev. 641; J. C. Love, "damages: A Remedy for violation of Constitutional Rights, (1979) 67 CAL IF L. REV 1242.

Preventive Detention

A State Government ordered preventive detention immediately after revoking the earlier order on the report of the Advisory Board. It failed to defend its action, in court despite two adjournments. Its action was held to violate articles 21 and 22 of the Constitution in the circumstances; *Mohd. Ibrahim Mohd. Sasin* v. *State of Maharashtra*, (1987) Supp SCC 32: 1987 SCC (Cri) 630.

Where a person is detained under the Conservation of Foreign Exchange and Prevention of Smuggling Activities Act, 1974 the members of the family of the detenu must be informed about the passing of the order of detention and the place of detention. *See* the undermentioned cases:

(i) *A.K. Roy* v. *Union of India*, AIR 1982 SC 710: (1982) 1 SCC 271: (1982) Cr LJ 340.

(ii) *Union of India* v. *Vasanbharthi*, AIR 1990 SC 1216: (1990) 2 SCC 275: 1990 Cr LJ 1244.

Prison Restrictions

Prison restrictions amounting to torture, pressure or infliction, beyond that awarded by the court must pass the test of scrutiny with reference to article 21. *See* the undermentioned cases;

(i) *Sheela Barse* v. *State of Maharashtra*, AIR 1983 SC 378: (1983) 2 SCC 96: 1983 Cr LJ 642.

(ii) *Javed* v. *State of Maharashtra*, AIR 1985 SC 231: (1985) 1 SCC 275: 1984 SCC (Cri) 653.

Prisoners: Classification

Classification of prisoners (under prison rules) on the basis of ordinary or dangerous prisoners and prisoners under sentence of death is valid; *Charles Sobraj* v. *Supdt. Central jail, Tihar, New Delhi*, AIR 1978 SC 1514: (1978) Cr LJ 1534: (1978) 4 SCC 104: 1978 SCC (Cri) 542: 1978 SC Cr R 416.

Prisoners: Interview

Public spirited citizens should be allowed to interview prisoners in order to ascertain how far article 21 is being complied with. But the interview has to be subject to reasonable restrictions which themselves are subject to judicial review. Special permission should be obtained for tape recording the interview. *See* the undermentioned cases:

(i) *Prabha Dutt* v. *Union of India*, (1982) 1 SCC 1: (1982) Cr LJ 148: AIR 1982 SC 6.

(ii) *Sheela Barse* v. *State of Maharashtra*, AIR 1983 SC 378: (1983) 2 SCC 96: 1983 Cr LJ 642.

Prisoners: Torture

An undertrial or convicted prisoner cannot be subjected to a physical or mental restraint—

(a) which is not warranted by the punishment awarded by the court, or

(b) which is in excess of the requirements of prisoners discipline, or

(c) which constitutes human degradation.

See the undermentioned cases on the above point

(i) *Sunil Batra* v. *Delhi Administration*, AIR 1978 SC 1675: (1978) 4 SCC 494: 1978 Cr LJ 1741.

(ii) *Sita Ram* v. *State of Uttar Pradesh*, AIR 1979 SC 745: (1979) 2 SCC 656: 1979 Cr LJ 659.

(iii) *Sunil Batra* v. *Delhi Administration*, AIR 1978 SC 1675: (1978) 4 SCC 494: 1978 Cr LJ 1741, paragraphs 31 and 42.

(iv) *Javed* v. *State of Maharashtra*, AIR 1985 SC 231: (1985) 1 SCC 275: 1984 SCC (Cri) 653, paragraph 4.

(v) *Sher Singh* v. *State of Punjab*, AIR 1983 SC 465: (1983) 2 SCC 344: 1983 Cr LJ 803.

Prisoners: Wrongful Detention

A prisoner already in jail for 8 years (who would have served out the maximum punishment for the offence) cannot be detained on the basis of a production warrant issued with the application of mind; *Rama Dass Ram* v. *State of Bihar*, AIR 1987 SC 1333: (1987) Cr LJ 1055: (1987) Supp SCC 143.

Privacy

Right to privacy is a part of article 21; *Govind* v. *State of Madhya Pradesh*, AIR 1975 SC 1378: (1975) 2 SCC 148: 1975 Cr LJ 1111.

The act of recording conversation of his wife by husband without her knowledge would amount to infringement of her right to privacy; *Rayala M. Bhuvaneswari* v. *Nagaphanender Rayala,* AIR 2008 AP 98: 2008 AIHC 356 (NOC): 2008 (3) ALJ (NOC) 624: 2008 (2) AIR Jhar (NOC) 429: 2008 (64) All Ind Cas 860: 2008 (1) Andh LT 613.

Right to privacy *vis-a-vis* freedom of press is available as long as privacy is maintained by parties; *Managing Director* v. *V. Muthulakshmi*, AIR 2008 (NOC) 381 (Mad).

Private Industries and Pollution

If an industry is established without requisite permission and in blatant disregard of law to the detriment of citizens' right to life, the Supreme Court can interfere to project right to life — Rule of absolute liability applies in such cases; *Indian Council for Enviro-legal Action* v. *Union of India*, AIR 1996 SC 1446: 1996 AIR SCW 1069: 1996 (2) Comp LJ SC 385: JT 1996 (2) SC 196: (1996) 3 SCC 212: (1996) 2 SCR 503: 1998 (5) Supreme 226, paragraphs 55, 56.

Prostitution

In a case dealing with the plight of prostitutes the Supreme Court placed emphasis on the need to provide to prostitutes opportunities for education and training so as to facilitate their rehabilitation; *Gaurav Jain* v. *Union of India*, AIR 1997 SC 3021 (3035, 3036): (1997) 8 SCC 114: 1997 AIR SCW 3055: 1997 (3) Crimes 40: JT 1997 (6) SC 305: 1997 (2) SCJ 334: (1997) 4 SCALE 657: 1998 SCC (Cri) 25: 1997 (6) Supreme 394.

Public Hanging

Public hanging (the execution of death sentence) is violation of article 21, which mandates the observance of a just, fair and reasonable procedure; *Attorney-General of India* v. *Lachma Devi*, AIR 1986 SC 467: 1986 Cr LJ 364: (1986) 1 Rec Cri R 424: 1986 Cur Cr J 143 (2): 1986 (1) SCJ 166: 1986 Cal Cr LR (SC) 15.

An order passed by the High Court of Rajasthan for public hanging was set aside by the Supreme Court on the ground *inter alia*, that it was violative of article 21; *Attorney-General of India* v. *Lachma Devi*, AIR 1986 SC 467: 1986 Cr LJ 364: (1986) 1 Rec Cri R 424: 1986 Cur Cr J 143 (2): 1986 (1) SCJ 166: 1986 Cal Cr LR (SC) 15.

Public Trial

The requirement of public hearing in court, as a component of fair trial that is subject to the need to hold proceedings in camera, in order to safeguard the public interest and to avoid prejudice to the accused; *Vineet Narain* v. *Union of India*, AIR 1998 SC 889: (1998) 1 SCC 226: 1998 Cr LJ 1208.

Punishment for Attempted Suicide

Punishment for attempted suicide has been held to be unconstitutional by the Supreme Court on the reasoning that a person cannot be forced to enjoy the right to life to his detriment, disadvantage or dislike; *P. Rathinam Nagbhusan Patnaik* v. *Union of India*, JT 1994 (3) SC 392: (1994) 3 SCC 394: 1994 SCC (Cri) 740: 1994 Cr LJ 1605.

Radiation (X-ray)

In a case filed by the workers of a public sector undertaking claiming compensation for being exposed to the ill-effects of X-ray radiation, the court issued directions as to check and safeguards to be adopted to guard against radiation; *M.K. Sharma* v. *Bharat Electronics Ltd.*, (1987) 3 SCC 231: AIR 1987 SC 1792: (1987) Cr LJ 1908.

Right of Appeal

The right of appeal from a judgment of conviction as under section 374 of Cr. P.C. is a fundamental right. It is obvious. Neither can be inferred with or impaired nor can it be subjected to any condition; *Dilip S. Dahanukar* v. *Kotak Mahindra Co. Ltd.*, (2007) 6 SCC 528: 2007 AIR SCW 2425: 2007 (137) Com Cas 1: 2007 (2) Crimes 435: 2008 (1) Mah LJ 22: (2007) 5 SCALE 452: 2007 (3) SCC (Cri) 209: 2007 (3) Supreme 379.

Right of Convict

The right of convict to claim remission of sentence is limited to consideration of his case as per relevant rules and short sentencing schemes existing at the time of his conviction. He cannot claim premature claim of release as a matter of right; *State of Haryana* v. *Jagdish*, AIR 2010 SC 1690.

Right to Die (Provision in I.P.C.)

Punishing the attempt to commit suicide does not violate article 21; *Gian Kaur* v. *State of Punjab*, AIR 1996 SC 1257: (1996) 2 SCC 648: 1996 SCC (Cri) 374, paragraphs 19, 21, 22, 27, 31, 41, 42.

See also

(i) *Govind* v. *State of Madhya Pradesh*, AIR 1975 SC 1378: (1975) 1 All LR 752: 1975 Cr LJ 1111: (1975) 2 SCC 148: 1975 SCC (Cri) 468: (1975) 3 SCR 946.

(ii) *State of Maharashtra* v. *Maruti Sharipati Dubal*, AIR 1997 SC 411: (1996) 6 SCC 42: 1996 SCC (Cri) 1116.

Right to Life and Personal Liberty

Reputation of a person is his valuable asset and is a facet of his right under article 21; *Sukhwant Singh* v. *State of Punjab*, (2009) 7 SCC 559.

Right to Fair Trial

The assurance of fair trial, uninfluenced by extraneous considerations is first imperative of dispensation of justice; *Amarinder Singh (Capt)* v. *Parkash Singh Badal*, (2009) 6 SCC 260.

Right to Life: Various Rights Included

Declaring that the right to life included the "finer graces of human civilisation", the Supreme Court in *Dr. P. Nalla Thampy Terah* v. *Union of India*, AIR 1985 SC 1133: 1985 Supp SCC 189, virtually rendered this fundamental right a repository of various human rights.

Thus, it includes:

(a) the right to live with human dignity; *Francis Coralie Mullin* v. *Administrator, Union Territory of Delhi*, AIR 1981 SC 746: (1981) 1 SCC 608: 1981 Cr LJ 306.

(b) right to healthy environment; *M.C. Mehta* v. *Union of India*, (1987) Supp SCC 131: AIR 1987 SC 1086: (1987) 1 Comp LJ 99: (1987) 1 ACC 157: (1987) 1 SCC 395: 1987 (1) Supreme 65: 1987 SCC (Lab) 37: 1987 JT 1: 1987 ACJ 386; *Bandhua Mukti Morcha* v. *Union of India*, AIR 1984 SC 802: (1984) 3 SCC 161: 1984 Lab IC 560: 1984 SCC (Lab) 389: (1984) 2 Lab LN 60

(c) **Donation of Organ.**—Donation of organ by husband to his ailing father cannot be objected to by wife on ground of violation of her fundamental right to life; *Sumakiran Mallena* v. *Secretary, Medical & Health Secretariat Building, Saifabad*, AIR 2008 (NOC) 374 AP.

This right [healthy environment], itself includes the following:—

    (i) Pollution free water and air; *Dr. B.L. Wadehra* v. *Union of India*, AIR 1996 SC 2969: (1996) 2 SCC 594: 1996 AIR SCW 1185: 1997 (1) Cur LJ (CCR) 28: JT 1996 (3) SC 38: (1996) 3 SCR 80: 1996 (2) UJ (SC) 26; *Indian Council for Enviro-legal Action* v. *Union of India*, AIR 1996 SC 1446: 1996 AIR SCW 1069: 1996 (2) Comp LJ SC 385: JT 1996 (2) SC 196: (1996) 3 SCC 212: (1996) 2 SCR 503: 1998 (5) Supreme 226, paragraphs 55, 65.

    (ii) Protection against hazardous industries; *Vellore Citizens Welfare Forum* v. *Union of India*, AIR 1996 SC 2715: (1996) 5 SCC 647: 1996 AIR SCW 3399: 1996 (5) Comp LJ SC 40: JT 1996 (7) SC 375.

  (c) Free education upto 14 years of age; *Unni Krishnan, J.P.* v. *State of Andhra Pradesh*, AIR 1993 SC 2178: (1993) 1 SCC 645: 1993 AIR SCW 863: JT 1993 (1) SC 474: (1993) 1 SCR 594: 1993 (2) SCT 511: 1993 (1) Serv LR 743: 1993 (1) UJ (SC) 721.

  (d) Emergency medical aid; *Pt. Parmanand Katara* v. *Union of India*, AIR 1989 SC 2039: (1989) 4 SCC 286: 1990 Cr LJ 671 (SC): 1989 All LJ 1111: 1990 (1) ACC 3: 1990 (1) BLJ 233: 1990 Jab LJ 37: 1990 (1) Pat LJR 26.

  (e) Right to health; *State of Punjab* v. *Mohinder Singh Chawla*, AIR 1997 SC 1225: (1997) 2 SCC 83: 1997 AIR SCW 1260: JT 1997 (1) SC 416: 1997 (3) LLN 262: 1997 SCC (L&S) 294: 1996 (4) SCJ 391: 1997 (1) SCT 716: (1997) 1 SCALE 135: 1997 (2) Serv LJ 25 SC: 1997 (1) Supreme 546.

  (f) Privacy; *Peoples Union for Civil Liberties* v. *Union of India*, AIR 1997 SC 568: (1997) 1 SCC 301: 1997 AIR SCW 113: 1997 (1) ICC 682: JT 1997 (1) SC 288: 1996 (3) Raj LW 126: 1996 (4) SCJ 565: 1997 (1) UJ (SC) 187.

  (g) Right to shelter; *Uttar Pradesh Avas Evam Vikas Parishad* v. *Friends Co-op. Housing Society Ltd.*, AIR 1996 SC 114: (1995) Supp 3 SCC 456: 1995 AIR SCW 3800: 1995 All LJ 2066: 1995 (2) Rent LR 33: 1995 (2) SCJ 255: (1995) 3 SCR 729, paragraph 7.

  (h) Right to livelihood, which includes right of succession; *Madhu Kishwar* v. *State of Bihar*, (1996) 5 SCC 125: AIR 1996 SC 1864: 1996 AIR SCW 2178: 1996 (2) BLJ 327: 1996 (1) Hindu LR 610: JT 1996 (4) SC 379: 1996 (2) Pat LJR 133.

  (i) Timely medical treatment in Government Hospital; *Paschim Banga Khet Mazdoor Samity* v. *State of West Bengal*, AIR 1996 SC 2426: (1996) 4 SCC 37: 1996 Lab IC 2054: 1996 AIR SCW 2964: 1996 (2) AP LJ 33: JT 1996 (6) SC 43: 1996 (3) SCJ 25: 1996 (4) SCT 28: 1996 (6) Serv LR 346, paragraphs 9, 15, 16.

  (j) Right, not to be driven out of a State; *National Human Rights Commission* v. *State of Arunachal Pradesh*, AIR 1996 SC 1234: (1996) 1 SCC 742: 1996 AIR SCW 1274: 1996 (1) Cur CC 69: JT 1996 (1) SC 163: 1996 (2) SCJ 135: (1996) 1 SCR 278: 1996 SC Cr R 403: 1996 (1) UJ (SC) 370, paragraphs 16, 20, 21.

  (k) Right to fair trial; *Police Commissioner, Delhi* v. *Registrar, Delhi High Court*, AIR 1997 SC 95: (1996) 6 SCC 323: 1996 SCC (Cri) 1325, paragraphs 15, 23.

  (l) Right to speedy trial; *Common Cause* v. *Union of India*, AIR 1996 SC 929: 1996 AIR SCW 333: 1996 (1) BLJ 560: 1996 (1) Civ LJ 742: JT 1996 (1) SC 38: (1996) 1 SCC 753: 1996 (1) SCJ 422: (1996) 1 SCR 89: (1997) 3 SCALE Supp 21: 1996 (1) UJ (SC) 404 and *Common Cause, A Registered Society* v. *Union of India*, AIR 1997 SC 1539: 1997 Cr LJ 195: 1997 AIR SCW 290: 1997 (1) MPLJ 4: 1997 (12) OCR 232: (1996) 6 SCC 775: 1997 SCC (Cri) 42, paragraph 1.

  (m) Right to free legal aid, where conviction for an offence may involve loss of life or personal liberty.

    (i) *Suk Das* v. *Union Territory of Arunachal Pradesh*, AIR 1986 SC 991: (1986) 2 SCC 401: 1986 Cr LJ 1084.

    (ii) *M.H. Hoskot* v. *State of Maharashtra*, AIR 1978 SC 1548: (1978) 3 SCC 544: 1978 Cr LJ 1678.

   (iii) *State of Maharashtra* v. *Manubhai Pragaji Vashi*, AIR 1996 SC 1: (1995) 5 SCC 730: 1995 AIR SCW 3701: JT 1995 (6) SC 119: 1997 (1) Mah LR 153: 1995 (3) SCJ 610: 1995 (4) SCT 547: 1996 (1) Serv LJ SC 1, paragraph 16.

Right to Livelihood or Work

Article 21 cannot be stretched so far as to mean that everyone must be given a job. Article 41 has been deliberately kept by the Founding Fathers in the directive principles chapters and hence made unenforceable; *Indian Drugs and Pharmaceuticals Ltd.* v. *Workman, Indian Drugs and Pharmaceuticals Ltd.*, (2007) 1 SCC 408: 2006 AIR SCW 5994: 2007 (1) ALJ 505.

Right to Life and Liberty

Right to electricity is also right to life and liberty in terms of article 21 because no one in the modern days can survive without electricity; *Molay Kumar Acharya* v. *Chairman-cum-Managing Director, W.B. State Electricity Distribution Co. Ltd.*, AIR 2008 Cal 47: 2008 AIHC 307 NOC: 2008 (2) ALJ (NOC) 495: 2008 (3) AKAR (NOC) 380: 2008 (3) Cal HN 27.

Right to Speedy Trial

Constitutional guarantee of speedy trial investigation and trial was violated in a case where through the accused had committed serious offence facing delay of 17 years in investigation and trial by prosecution; *Vakil Prasad Singh* v. *State of Bihar*, AIR 2009 SC 1822: 2009 Cr LJ 1731: 2009 AIR SCW 1418: 2009 (1) Cur Cr R 282: 2009 (42) OCR 680: (2009) 3 SCC 355: (2009) 2 SCALE 22: 2009 (2) SCC (Cri) 95.

Right to Work

Right to work can be considered as fundamental right only in cases where legislative guarantee is given in the form of legislation; *State of Maharashtra* v. *Sau. Shobha Vitthal Kolte*, AIR 2006 Bom 44: 2006 (1) ALJ (NOC) 92: 2006 (2) AKAR (NOC) 190: 2006 (1) All MR 188: 2006 (1) Bom CR 468.

Right to work is not a fundamental right. But it can be claimed after employment; *Air India Statutory Corporation* v. *United Labour Union*, AIR 1997 SC 645: (1997) 9 SCC 377: (1997) 1 LLJ 1113.

Scope of Article 21

Article 21, if read literally, is a colourless article and would be satisfied, the moment it is established by the State that there is a law which provides a procedure which has been followed by the impugned action. But the expression 'procedure established by law' in article 21 has been judicially construed as meaning a procedure which is reasonable, fair and just. Read with article 39A, it would further imply legal aid being made available to the indigent accused and a prisoner. The concept of 'fairness', so evolved, has been imported into article 22(3) also, so that a prison regulation which arbitrarily deprives a detenu of opportunity to interview his relatives or friends or a lawyer is invalid. *See* the undermentioned cases as to the scope of article 21 on above points:

   (i) *Maneka Gandhi* v. *Union of India*, AIR 1978 SC 597: (1978) 1 SCC 248: (1978) 2 SCR 621, paragraph 56. (The basic case).

   (ii) *Gopalanachari* v. *Administrator, State of Kerala*, AIR 1981 SC 674: 1980 Supp SCC 649: 1981 Cr LJ 337, paragraph 6.

   (iii) *Francis Coralie Mullin* v. *Union Territory of Delhi*, (1981) Cr LJ 306 (SC): (1981) 1 SCC 608: AIR 1981 SC 746, paragraphs 6-8.

   (iv) *Olga Tellis* v. *Bombay Municipal Corporation*, AIR 1986 SC 180: (1985) 3 SCC 545: (1985) 2 Bom CR 434: 1986 Cr LR (SC) 23: 1986 Cur Civ LJ (SC) 230, paragraph 31.

The right to life and the right to personal liberty in India have been guaranteed by a constitutional provision, which has received the widest possible interpretation. Under the canopy of article 21 of the Constitution, so many rights have found shelter, growth and nourishment. An intelligent citizen would like to be aware of the developments in this regard, as they have evolved from judicial decisions.

Article 21 lays down that no person shall be deprived of life or personal liberty, except according to procedure established by law. "Life", in article 21 is not merely the physical act of breathing; *Samatha* v. *State of Andhra Pradesh*, AIR 1997 SC 3297: (1997) 8 SCC 199: 1997 AIR SCW 3361: JT 1997 (6) SC 449: 1997 (2) SCJ 539: (1997) 4 SCALE 746: 1997 (6) Supreme 530.

Scheduled Tribes Women

Denial of right of succession to women of Scheduled Tribes amounts to deprivation of their right to livelihood under article 21; *Madhu Kishwar* v. *State of Bihar*, (1996) 5 SCC 125: AIR 1996 SC 1864: 1996 AIR SCW 2178: 1996 (2) BLJ 327: 1996 (1) Hindu LR 610: JT 1996 (4) SC 379: 1996 (2) Pat LJR 133.

Sexual Harassment

Sexual harassment in the workplace is a violation of articles 15 and 21 of the Constitution. (The court gave detailed directions on the subject, which guidelines are to be strictly observed by all employers, public or private, until suitable legislation is enacted on the subject; *Vishakha* v. *State of Rajasthan*, AIR 1997 SC 3011: (1997) 6 SCC 241: 1997 SCC (Cri) 932.

Smoking in Public Place

In any case, there is no reason to compel non-smokers to be helpless victims of air pollution, *Murli S. Deora* v. *Union of India*, AIR 2002 SC 40: (2001) 8 SCC 765: 2001 AIR SCW 4505: 2002 (1) JCR SC 5: JT 2001 (9) SC 364: 2002 (22) OCR 118: 2002 (1) SCJ 85: 2002 SC Cr R 10: (2001) 8 SCALE 6: 2001 (8) Supreme 326.

Solitary Confinement

Solitary confinement violates the fundamental right guaranteed by article 21; *Sunil Batra* v. *Delhi Administration*, AIR 1978 SC 1675: (1978) Cr LJ 1741: (1978) 4 SCC 494.

Speedy Justice

In the matter of denial of speedy justice, the court expressed the concern at delay in disposal of cases. The concerned authorities were directed to do needful in the matter urgently before situation goes totally out of control; *Moses Wilson* v. *Kasturiba*, AIR 2008 SC 379: 2007 AIR SCW 7058: 2007 (59) All Ind Cas 238: 2007 (69) All LR 309: 2008 (1) Andh LD 102: 2007 (2) CLR 851: 2008 (1) Mad LJ 1049: (2007) 11 SCALE 405.

Speedy Trial

A procedural law is void if it does not provide for speedy trial. *See* the undermentioned cases:

   (i) *Sher Singh* v. *State Punjab*, AIR 1983 SC 465: (1983) 2 SCC 344: (1983) Cr LJ 803 (Delay in execution).

   (ii) *Hussainara (I)* v. *Home Secretary, State of Bihar*, AIR 1979 SC 1360: (1980) 1 SCC 81: 1979 Cr LJ 1036.

   (iii) *Hussainara Khatoon* v. *Home Secretary, State of Bihar, Patna*, AIR 1979 SC 1369: 1979 Cr LJ 1045: 1979 Pat LJR 410: (1979) 3 SCR 532: (1980) 1 SCC 98: 1980 SCC (Cri) 40.

   (iv) *Hussainara* v. *Home Secretary, State of Bihar*, AIR 1979 SC 1377: (1980) 1 SCC 108: 1979 Cr LJ 1052.

   (v) *Hussainara* v. *Home Secretary, State of Bihar*, AIR 1980 SC 1819: (1980) 1 SCC 115: 1979 Cr LJ 1134.

Speedy trial is a component of personal liberty; *Kartar Singh* v. *State of Punjab*, JT 1994 (2) SC 423: (1994) 3 SCC 569: 1994 Cr LJ 3139; *Raj Deo Sharma* v. *State of Bihar*, AIR 1998 SC 3281: (1999) 7 SCC 507: 1998 Cr LJ 4596: 1998 AIR SCW 3208: 1998 (4) Crimes 53: JT 1998 (7) SC 1: 1999 (2) SCJ 140: 1999 (1) SRJ 72: (1998) 5 SCALE 477: 1998 SCC (Cri) 1692: 1998 (7) Supreme 556: 1999 (1) UJ (SC) 136.

Summary Dismissal of Appeal

A provision for summary dismissal of criminal appeal is not unfair if certain safeguards against arbitrary dismissal are incorporated; *Sita Ram* v. *State of Uttar Pradesh*, AIR 1983 SC 65.

Telephone Tapping

Telephone tapping would infringe article 21 of the Constitution, unless it is permitted "under procedure established by law". The court issued guidelines for the exercise of power of interception of telegrams under section 5(2) of the Indian Telegraphs Act, 1885; *Peoples Union for Civil Liberties* v. *Union of India*, AIR 1997 SC 568: (1997) 1 SCC 301: 1997 AIR SCW 113: 1997 (1) ICC 682: JT 1997 (1) SC 288: 1996 (3) Raj LW 126: 1996 (4) SCJ 565: 1997 (1) UJ (SC) 187.

Traffic Control

Taking into account the need to have proper management and control of traffic, which is a matter of public safety and falls within the ambit of article 21 of the Constitution, the Supreme Court empowered the authorities under the Motor Vehicles Act, 1988 to delegate their authority to responsible persons, including members of the public; *M.C. Mehta* v. *Union of India*, AIR 1998 SC 186: (1998) 1 SCC 363: 1997 AIR SCW 4149: 1998 (2) Civ LJ 440: JT 1997 (9) SC 213: 1998 (1) SCJ 523: (1997) 7 SCALE 97: 1997 (9) Supreme 418: 1998 (1) UJ (SC) 282.

Undertrial Prisoners

(a) An undertrial prisoner kept in jail for a period exceeding the maximum prison term awardable on conviction must be released. *See* the undermentioned cases:

   (i) *Hussainara* v. *Home Secretary, State of Bihar*, AIR 1979 SC 1369: (1980) 1 SCC 98: 1979 Cr LJ 1045.

   (ii) *Hussainara* v. *Home Secretary, State of Bihar*, AIR 1979 SC 1377: (1980) 1 SCC 108: 1979 Cr LJ 1052.

   (iii) *Hussainara* v. *Home Secretary, State of Bihar*, AIR 1980 SC 1819: (1980) 1 SCC 115: 1979 Cr LJ 1134.

(b) Persons kept in jail without trial or without charge must be released. *See* the undermentioned cases:

   (i) *Mathew* v. *State of Bihar*, AIR 1984 SC 1854: (1985) 2 SCC 102: 1985 Cr LJ 357.

   (ii) *Kamaladevi* v. *State of Punjab*, AIR 1984 SC 1895: (1985) 1 SCC 41: 1985 Cr LJ 356.

   (iii) *Hussainara* v. *State of Bihar*, AIR 1980 SC 1819: (1980) 1 SCC 115: 1979 Cr LJ 1134.

(c) Non-production of the accused (an undertrial prisoner) before the court on dates of trial after obtaining judicial remand is improper. Matter was disposed of, on an assurance given by the State Government. Accused was not entitled to be released on bail merely on above ground but costs were awarded to him; *Ramesh Kumar Singh* v. *State of Bihar*, (1987) Supp SCC 335: 1988 SCC (Cri) 89.

Water

Right to life under article 21 includes the right to enjoyment of pollution-free water; *Dr. B.L. Wadehra* v. *Union of India*, AIR 1996 SC 2969: (1996) 2 SCC 594: 1996 AIR SCW 1185: 1997 (1) Cur LJ (CCR) 28: JT 1996 (3) SC 38: (1996) 3 SCR 80: 1996 (2) UJ (SC) 26.

[1][**21A. Right to education.**—The State shall provide free and compulsory education to all children of the age of six to fourteen years in such manner as the State may, by law, determine.]

Notes on Article 21A

Right to Education

The condition of not permitting new school within radius of 5 kms. of existing school is not mandatory; *Shikshan Prasarak Mandal, Pune* v. *State of Maharashtra*, AIR 2010 Bom 39.

Right to education includes right to safe education; *Avinash Mehrotra* v. *Union of India*, (2009) 6 SCC 398.

[2]**22. Protection against arrest and detention in certain cases.**—(1) No person who is arrested shall be detained in custody without being informed, as soon as

---

1. Ins. by the Constitution (Eighty-sixth Amendment) Act, 2002, sec. 2 (w.e.f. 1-4-2010).

2. On the enforcement of section 3 of the Constitution (Forty-fourth Amendment) Act, 1978, article 22 shall stand amended as directed in section 3 of that Act. (**Ed.**—So far no date has been notified for the enforcement of section 3).

may be, of the grounds for such arrest nor shall he be denied the right to consult, and to be defended by, a legal practitioner of his choice.

(2) Every person who is arrested and detained in custody shall be produced before the nearest magistrate within a period of twenty-four hours of such arrest excluding the time necessary for the journey from the place of arrest to the court of the magistrate and no such person shall be detained in custody beyond the said period without the authority of a magistrate.

(3) Nothing in clauses (1) and (2) shall apply—

(a) to any person who for the time being is an enemy alien; or

(b) to any person who is arrested or detained under any law providing for preventive detention.

(4) No law providing for preventive detention shall authorise the detention of a person for a longer period than three months unless—

(a) an Advisory Board consisting of persons who are, or have been, or are qualified to be appointed as, Judges of a High Court has reported before the expiration of the said period of three months that there is in its opinion sufficient cause for such detention:

Provided that nothing in this sub-clause shall authorise the detention of any person beyond the maximum period prescribed by any law made by Parliament under sub-clause (b) of clause (7); or

(b) such person is detained in accordance with the provisions of any law made by Parliament under sub-clauses (a) and (b) of clause (7).

(5) When any person is detained in pursuance of an order made under any law providing for preventive detention, the authority making the order shall, as soon as may be, communicate to such person the grounds on which the order has been made and shall afford him the earliest opportunity of making a representation against the order.

(6) Nothing in clause (5) shall require the authority making any such order as is referred to in that clause to disclose facts which such authority considers to be against the public interest to disclose.

(7) Parliament may by law prescribe—

(a) the circumstances under which, and the class or classes of cases in which, a person may be detained for a period longer than three months under any law providing for preventive detention without obtaining the opinion of an Advisory Board in accordance with the provisions of sub-clause (a) of clause (4);

(b) the maximum period for which any person may in any class or classes of cases be detained under any law providing for preventive detention; and

(c) the procedure to be followed by an Advisory Board in an inquiry under sub-clause (a) of clause (4).

Notes on Article 22

Analysis of Provision

Article 22 consists of two parts. Clauses (1) and (2) apply to persons arrested or detained under a law otherwise than a preventive detention law. Clauses (4) to (7) apply to persons arrested or detained under a preventive detention law.

The word "grounds" used in clause (5) of article 22 means not only the narration or conclusions of facts, but also all materials on which those facts or conclusions which constitute grounds are based; *Sophia Gulam Mohd. Bham* v. *State of Maharashtra*, AIR 1999 SC 3051: (1999) 6 SCC 593.

"Arrest": Meaning Thereof

It should be noted that 'arrest' and 'detention' in articles 22(1) and 22(2) do not cover civil arrest, or deportation of an alien or action by the court itself. *See* the undermentioned cases:

(i) *Madhu Limaye (in re:)*, AIR 1969 SC 1014 (1019): (1969) 1 SCC 292: 1969 Cr LJ 1440.

(ii) *Collector of Malabar* v. *Hajee*, (1957) SCR 970: AIR 1957 SC 688: (1957) 32 ITR 124.

(iii) *State of Uttar Pradesh* v. *Abdul Samad*, AIR 1962 SC 1506: (1962) Supp 3 SCR 915: (1962) 2 Cr LJ 499: ILR (1962) 2 All 547: 1962 All Cr R 440: 1962 BLJR 952: (1963) 1 SCA 122: 1963 SCD 885.

(iv) *State of Punjab* v. *Ajaib Singh*, (1953) SCR 254: AIR 1953 SC 10: 1953 Cr LJ 180.

Article 21 may Supplement Article 22

It is now well settled that article 21 may also supplement the various requirements laid down in article 22; *Kamla* v. *State of Maharashtra*, AIR 1981 SC 814: (1981) 1 SCC 748: 1981 Cr LJ 353; *Sampat* v. *State of Jammu & Kashmir*, AIR 1969 SC 1153: (1969) 1 SCC 562: 1969 Cr LJ 1555.

Consideration of Representation

Consideration by the Board is an additional safeguard. It is not a substitute for consideration by the Central Government; *Gracy* v. *State of Kerala*, AIR 1991 SC 1090: (1991) 2 SCC 1: 1991 SCC (Cri) 467.

If a representation is sent to the Chairman, Advisory Board through the Superintendent of the jail, the Central Government must consider it, Even when the detenu's representation under the COFEPOSA Act is received after the order is confirmed by Government, the Government must consider it; *K.M. Abdulla Kumhi and B.L. Abdul* v. *Union of India*, AIR 1991 SC 574: (1991) 1 SCC 476: 1991 Cr LJ 790 (CB), paragraphs 19-20.

Government cannot delay consideration of the representation on the ground that it awaits the Board's advice; *Issac Babu* v. *Union of India*, (1990) 4 SCC 135: 1990 SCC (Cri) 564 (Delay of 11 months).

Delay

Real test for article 22(4) is whether delay is explained; *State of Punjab* v. *Sukhpal*, AIR 1990 SC 231: (1990) 1 SCC 35.

Time taken in investigating may excuse delay; *Farooq* v. *Union of India*, (1990) 2 SCJ 225: AIR 1990 SC 1597: 1990 Cr LJ 1622; *Shafiq* v. *D.M.*, (1989) 8 SCJ 568: (1984) 4 SCC 556: AIR 1990 SC 200.

Documents

Every document casually referred to in the order of detention need not be supplied. Only a document relied on by the detaining authority need be given; *Farooq* v. *Union of India*, (1990) 2 SCJ 225: AIR 1990 SC 1597: 1990 Cr LJ 1622, paragraph 10.

Detention is vitiated, if the following documents are not supplied—

(a) documents which are considered by the detaining authority, or

(b) documents which are vital, though not considered by the detaining authority; *P.U. Abdul Rahiman* v. *Union of India*, AIR 1991 SC 336: (1991) Supp 2 SCC 274: 1991 Cr LJ 430, paragraph 9 (3 Judge Bench).

Documents, which are vital, should be supplied; *M. Ahamedkutty* v. *Union of India*, (1990) 2 SCC 1: JT 1990 (1) SC 143: 1990 SCC (Cri) 258.

Information about Grounds of Arrest

Information about grounds of arrest is mandatory under clause (1). *See* undermentioned cases:

(a) *Gopalan* v. *State of Madras*, (1950) SCR 88: AIR 1950 SC 27: (1950) 1 MLJ 42.

(b) *Hansmukh* v. *State of Gujarat*, AIR 1981 SC 28: (1981) 2 SCC 175: (1981) 1 SCR 353.

Language

Where the grounds of detention are served in the detenue's language, there is no irregularity even if the order is not in his language; *Kubic Darusz* v. *Union of India,* 1990 (2) SCJ 132: AIR 1990 SC 605: (1990) 1 SCC 568, paragraphs 11 and 14.

Preventive Detention

A detention order (for preventive detention) is not void, merely because it does not specify the period, if the parent Act under which it is made does not require that the order should specify the period. In such a case, the order is deemed to be for the maximum period for which detention is authorised. The case was under the Tamil Nadu Prevention of Dangerous Activities of Bootleggers, Drug Offenders, Forest Offenders, Immoral Traffic Offenders and Slum Grabbers Act, 1982 (T.N. Act 14 of 1882). Section 3(1) of the Act reads as under:—

(1) The state Government may, if satisfied with respect to any bootlegger or drug offender (or forest offender) or goonda or immoral traffic offender of slum grabber that with a view to prevent him from acting in any manner prejudicial to the maintenance of public order it is necessary so to do make an order directing that such person to be detained; *T. Devaki* v. *Government of Tamil Nadu,* AIR 1990 SC 1086 (1097): (1990) 2 SCC 456: 1990 Cr LJ 1140, paragraphs, 18 and 19.

A detention order passed under the Conservation of Foreign Exchange and Prevention of Smuggling Activities Act, 1974, section 3 (in the Gurumukhi version), stated that detention was necessary to prevent the detenu from abetting smuggling. But the grounds of detention spoke of "concealing *etc.*" of smuggled goods. The order of detention was held to be void; *Vijay Kumar* v. *Union of India,* AIR 1990 SC 1184: (1990) 1 SCC 606: 1990 SCC (Cri) 247 reversing (1989) 4 Delhi Lawyers 298. (The reason is, that in such cases, the detenu cannot make an effective representation). In this case, there was also a variance between the English version and the Gurumukhi version of the order of detention.

Extraneous matters mentioned in the documents annexed to the detention order were not referred to, in the grounds of detention. These might have influenced the decision of the detaining authority. Detention was held to be void; *Vashisht Narain Karwaria* v. *State of Uttar Pradesh,* AIR 1990 SC 1272: (1990) 2 SCC 629: 1990 Cr LJ 1311 reversing (1990) Cr LJ NOC 36 (All). (This was a case under the National Security Act, 1980).

In the above case, particulars of offences referred to in the enclosed documents were also not supplied and hence the detenu could not make an effective representation; *Mehboob Khan Nawab Khan Pathan* v. *Police Commissioner, Ahmedabad,* AIR 1989 SC 1803: (1989) 3 SCC 568: (1989) Cr LJ 2111 followed.

On the question of extraneous matter, *see* the undermentioned cases:

(i) *Ram Krishna Paul* v. *Government of West Bengal,* AIR 1972 SC 863: (1972) 1 SCC 570: 1972 Cr LJ 649.

(ii) *Pushpa* v. *Union of India,* AIR 1979 SC 1953: 1980 Supp SCC 391: 1979 Cr LJ 1314.

(iii) *Merugu Satyanarayana* v. *State of Andhra Pradesh,* AIR 1982 SC 1543: 1982 Cr LJ 2357: (1982) 3 SCC 301.

(iv) *Mehboob Khan Nawab Khan Pathan* v. *Commissioner of Police, Ahmedabad,* AIR 1989 SC 1803: (1989) 3 SCC 568: 1989 Cr LJ 2111: 1990 (1) Guj LR 142.

Production of Accused before the Nearest Magistrate

To produce an accused before the nearest magistrate is mandatory; *State of Uttar Pradesh* v. *Abdul Samad,* AIR 1962 SC 1506: (1962) Supp 3 SCR 915: (1962) 2 Cr LJ 499 Compare section 57 of the Code of Criminal Procedure, 1973.

Representation: Preventive Detention

Representation in case of preventive detention is to be made to the competent authority. To ascertain who is the competent authority, the scheme relating to the authority is to be examined; *Veeramani* v. *State of Tamil Nadu,* JT 1994 (1) SC 350: 1995 Cr LJ 2644: 1995 AIR SCW 1730: 1994 (1) Crimes 617: (1994) 2 SCC 337: 1994 (2) SCJ 41: (1994) 1 SCR 616: 1994 SCC (Cri) 482: 1994 (1) UJ (SC) 524.

Right of Detenu
There are two rights of detenu: (i) one is fundamental right (ii) statutory right; *Addl. Distt. Magistrate, Jabalpur* v. *Shivakant Shukla*, AIR 1976 SC 1207: (1976) 2 SCC 521: 1976 Cr LJ 945: 1976 UJ (SC) 610: 1976 SC Cr R 277: 1976 SCC (Cri) 448: 1976 Cr App R (SC) 298: (1976) 3 SCR 929: 1976 Supp SCR 172.

Right to Consult and to be Defended by Legal Practitioner of his Choice
This is also mandatory; *Gopalan* v. *State of Madras*, (1950) SCR 88: AIR 1950 SC 27: (1950) 2 MLJ 42; *State of Madhya Pradesh* v. *Shobharam*, AIR 1966 SC 1910 (1917): 1966 Cr LJ 1521: 1966 Supp SCR 239 Besides this, there is a right to legal aid, flowing from article 21, even where section 304 of the Code of Criminal Procedure, 1973 does not apply.

Right against Exploitation

23. Prohibition of traffic in human beings and forced labour.—(1) Traffic in human beings and begar and other similar forms of forced labour are prohibited and any contravention of this provision shall be an offence punishable in accordance with law.

(2) Nothing in this article shall prevent the State from imposing compulsory service for public purposes, and in imposing such service the State shall not make any discrimination on grounds only of religion, race, caste or class or any of them.

Notes on Article 23

Child Labour
The Supreme Court has issued elaborate guidelines to child labour. Child labour shall not be engaged in hazardous employment. There shall be set up child labour rehabilitation welfare fund in which offending employer should deposit Rs. 20,000. Adult member of such child should be given employment; *M.C. Mehta* v. *State of Tamil Nadu*, AIR 1997 SC 699: (1996) 6 SCC 756: 1997 Lab IC 563: 1997 AIR SCW 407: 1997 (2) LLJ 724: 1997 (1) LLN 12: 1997 SCC (L&S) 49: 1997 (1) Supreme 207: 1997 (1) UJ (SC) 243.

Supreme Court has further directions as to education, health and nutrition of child labour. The judgment is a sequee to the judgment in—

(i) *M.C. Mehta* v. *State of Tamil Nadu*, AIR 1997 SC 699: (1996) 6 SCC 756: 1997 Lab IC 563: 1997 AIR SCW 407: 1997 (2) LLJ 724: 1997 (1) LLN 12: 1997 SCC (L&S) 49: 1997 (1) Supreme 207: 1997 (1) UJ (SC) 243.

(ii) *Bandhua Mukti Morcha* v. *Union of India*, AIR 1997 SC 2218: (1997) 10 SCC 549: 1997 All LJ 1186.

Children of Prostitutes
Directions were issued by the Supreme Court in public interest litigation, as to the children of prostitutes. *See* the undermentioned cases:

(i) *Vishal Jeet* v. *Union of India*, AIR 1990 SC 1412: (1990) 3 SCC 318: 1990 Cr LJ 1469, paragraphs 3, 7 and 18.

(ii) *Gaurav Jain* v. *Union of India*, AIR 1990 SC 292: 1990 Supp SCC 709.

(iii) *Gaurav Jain* v. *Union of India*, AIR 1997 SC 3021: (1997) 8 SCC 114: 1997 AIR SCW 3055: 1997 (3) Crimes 40: JT 1997 (6) SC 305: 1997 (2) SCJ 334: (1997) (4) SCALE 657: 1998 SCC (Cri) 25: 1997 (6) Supreme 394.

Scope
This article prohibits—

(a) traffic in human beings;

(b) begar; and

(c) other similar forms of forced labour.

An exception is made for compulsory service for public purposes, under clause (2). Although clause (2) does not say so, obviously the imposition of such service has to be by law, as a mere executive order of the State would not suffice for the purpose. It has been held that even if remuneration is paid for the labour still, if it is 'forced', then it is unconstitutional. Judicial decisions in support of these propositions are:

(i) *People's Union* v. *Union of India*, AIR 1982 SC 1473: (1982) 3 SCC 235: (1982) 2 LLJ 454.

(ii) *Sanjit* v. *State of Rajasthan*, AIR 1983 SC 328: (1983) 1 SCC 525: (1983) 1 LLJ 220 .

Traffic in Human Beings

Traffic in human beings includes *devadasis*; *Vishal Jeet* v. *Union of India*, AIR 1990 SC 1412: (1990) 3 SCC 318: 1990 Cr LJ 1469.

24. Prohibition of employment of children in factories, etc.—No child below the age of fourteen years shall be employed to work in any factory or mine or engaged in any other hazardous employment.

Notes on Article 24

Prohibition of Child Labour

Directions given by Supreme Court to implement constitutional mandates needs speedy implementation; *Bandhua Mukti Morcha* v. *Union of India*, AIR 1997 SC 2218: 1997 AIR SCW 2083: 1997 All LJ 1186: JT 1997 (5) SC 285: (1997) 10 SCC 549: 1997 SCD 755: 1998 (3) SCJ 353: (1997) 2 SCR 379: 1997 (3) SCT 397: 1997 (4) Supreme 609.

Prohibition of Work in Construction Industry

The prohibition of employment of children in construction industry is not a bar; *People's Union for Democratic Rights* v. *Union of India*, AIR 1982 SC 1473: 1982 Lab IC 1646: (1982) 45 FLR 140: 1982 UJ (SC) 657: (1982) 3 SCC 235: 1982 BLJR 401: (1982) 2 LLN 642: (1982) 2 SCWR 202: (1982) 14 Lawyer 57: (1982) 2 LLJ 454.

Prohibition of Hazardous Employment

Child below the age of 14 years cannot be allowed to be employed in hazardous employment; *Labourers Working on Salal Hydro-Project* v. *State of Jammu and Kashmir*, AIR 1984 SC 177: (1983) 2 SCC 181: (1983) 1 LLJ 494: 1983 SCC (Lab) 289: (1983) 2 LLN 20: 1983 UJ (SC) 582: (1983) 2 SCWR 202: 1983 Cr App R (SC) 438: (1983) 2 SCR 473.

Random Home and Observation Home

The special trained judicial officers should be appointed for juvenile courts; *Sheela Barse* v. *Secretary, Children Aid Society*, AIR 1987 SC 656: JT 1987 (1) SC 58: 1987 Cr LR (SC) 29: 1987 (1) SCJ 584: (1987) 3 SCC 50: (1987) 1 UJ (SC) 516: 1987 SCC (Cri) 458: 1987 Mah LR 906.

Right to Freedom of Religion

25. Freedom of conscience and free profession, practice and propagation of religion.—(1) Subject to public order, morality and health and to the other provisions of this Part, all persons are equally entitled to freedom of conscience and the right freely to profess, practise and propagate religion.

(2) Nothing in this article shall affect the operation of any existing law or prevent the State from making any law—

(a) regulating or restricting any economic, financial, political or other secular activity which may be associated with religious practice;

(b) providing for social welfare and reform or the throwing open of Hindu religious institutions of a public character to all classes and sections of Hindus.

Explanation I.—The wearing and carrying of *kirpans* shall be deemed to be included in the profession of the Sikh religion.

Explanation II.—In sub-clause (b) of clause (2), the reference to Hindus shall be construed as including a reference to persons professing the Sikh, Jaina or

Buddhist religion, and the reference to Hindu religious institutions shall be construed accordingly.

Notes on Article 25

Ananda Marg

Ananda Margis have a right to perform *"tandava"*; *Acharya Jagadiswarananda Avadhuta* v. *Commissioner of Police, Calcutta*, AIR 1984 SC 51: (1983) 4 SCC 522: 1984 SCC (Cri) 1.

Charity

Article 25 merely protects the freedom to practise rituals and ceremonies etc. which are only the integral parts of the religion. A disposition towards making gift for charitable or religious purpose may be a pious act of a person but the same cannot be said to be an integral part of any religion; *John Vallamattom* v. *Union of India*, AIR 2003 SC 2902: (2003) 6 SCC 611: (2003) 3 KLT 66.

Minority Institutions

The court is empowered to oversee the functions of minority institutions in case of missmanagement; *I Nelson* v. *Kallayam Pastorate*, AIR 2007 SC 1337: 2007 AIR SCW 1512: 2007 (1) All WC 162: 2007 (1) Andh LD 9: (2006) 11 SCC 624: 2006 (10) SRJ 334: (2006) 9 SCALE 245: 2006 (8) Supreme 856; *Bal Patil* v. *Union of India*, (2005) 6 SCC 690: AIR 2005 SC 3172: 2005 AIR SCW 3762: 2005 (4) JCR SC 60: 2005 (6) SCJ 171: (2005) 6 SCALE 374: 2005 (5) Supreme 669: 2005 (2) UJ (SC) 1249.

Priests

Service of a priest is a secular activity and can be regulated by the State under article 25(2); *Bhuri Nath* v. *State of Jammu & Kashmir*, AIR 1997 SC 1711: (1997) 2 SCC 745: 1997 AIR SCW 869: JT 1997 (1) SC 546: 1997 (1) SCJ 218: (1997) 1 SCR 138: (1997) 1 SCALE 250: 1997 (1) Supreme 358.

Regulation by the State

Article 25, clause 2(a) saves the power of the State to regulate or restrict secular activities associated with religious practice. These restrictions or regulations should be primarily concerned with the *secular* aspects of religious practice rather than with the essentials of religion as per judicial pronouncement. This view, enunciated for the first time in *Ratilal* v. *State of Bombay*, (1954) SCR 1055: AIR 1954 SC 388: (1954) 1 MLJ 718: 56 Bom LR 1184, has been followed in all later cases though the test is not easy to apply. What is the dividing line between the two is for the court to determine. But, subject to that, the religious denomination is entitled to lay down its rites and ceremonies—an aspect illustrated by *Sehanmal* v. *State of Tamil Nadu*, AIR 1972 SC 1586: (1972) 2 SCC 1: (1972) 3 SCR 815.

As the various limbs of article 25, particularly article 25(1) and article 25(2)(a) are interconnected, it is advisable to study a number of cases when a concrete question arises. The following list of cases would be helpful:—

   (i) *Ratilal Panachand Gandhi* v. *State of Bombay*, (1954) SCR 1055: AIR 1954 SC 388: 1954 SCJ 480: (1954) 1 Mad LJ 718: 1954 SCA 538: 56 Bom LR 1184 (Legislation on public trusts).

   (ii) *Ramji Lal Modi* v. *State of Uttar Pradesh*, AIR 1957 SC 620: 1957 SCR 860: 1957 Cr LJ 1006: (1957) 2 Mad LJ (SC) 65: 1957 SCJ 522: 1957 SCC 334: 1957 BLJR 723: (1957) 1 Mad LJ (Cri) 771: 1958 SCA 157 (Section 153A of the I.P.C.).

   (iii) *Sardar Syedna Taher Saifuddin Saheb* v. *State of Bombay*, AIR 1962 SC 853 (863): (1962) Supp 2 SCR 496: (1962) 2 SCA 192: 1963 (2) SCJ 519 (Excommunication).

   (iv) *Venkataramana Devaru* v. *State of Mysore*, AIR 1958 SC 255: 1958 SCR 895: 1958 SCJ 382: (1958) 1 Andh WR (SC) 109: (1958) 1 Mad LJ (SC) 109 (Religious practices).

   (v) *Surya Pal Singh* v. *State of Uttar Pradesh*, (1952) SCR 1056 (1090): AIR 1952 SC 252: 1952 SCJ 354: 1953 SCA 53.

   (vi) *Acharya Maharajshri Narendra Prasadji Anandprasadji Maharaj* v. *State of Gujarat*, AIR 1974 SC 2098: (1975) 1 SCC 11: (1975) 2 SCR 317, paragraph 25.

 (vii) *Commissioner, Hindu Religious Endowments, Madras* v. *Lakshmindra Thirtha Swamiar of Sri Shirur Mutt*, (1954) SCR 1005: AIR 1954 SC 282: 1954 SCJ 335: (1954) 1 Mad LJ 596: 20 Cut LT 250: 1954 SCA 415: 1954 Mad WN 363 (Religious trusts).

(viii) *Divyadarsan Rajendra Ramdassji Varu* v. *State of Andhra Pradesh*, AIR 1970 SC 181 (188): (1970) 1 SCC 844: (1969) 2 SCA 529: 1970 (1) SCJ 334: (1970) 1 MLJ (SC) 86: (1970) 1 Andh WR (SC) 86: (1970) 1 SCR 103 (Day to day administration of religious trust).

 (ix) *Stainislaus* v. *State of Madhya Pradesh*, AIR 1977 SC 908: (1977) 1 SCC 677: 1977 Cr LJ 551 (Freedom of conscience).

  (x) *Srimad Perarulala Ethiraja Ramanuja Jeeyar Swami* v. *State of Tamil Nadu*, AIR 1972 SC 1586: 1973 (1) SCJ 346: (1973) 1 Mad LJ (SC) 58: (1973) 1 Andh WR (SC) 58: (1972) 3 SCR 815 (Scrutiny of essentials of religion).

 (xi) *Mohd. Hanif Quareshi* v. *State of Bihar*, (1959) SCR 629: AIR 1958 SC 731: 1958 SCA 783: 1958 SCJ 975: 1958 Mad LJ (Cri) 727 (Ban on cow slaughter).

(xii) *Sardar Sarup Singh* v. *State of Punjab*, AIR 1959 SC 860 (866): (1959) Supp 2 SCR 499: 1959 SCJ 1115: (1960) 1 SCA 163 (Committee of administration).

(xiii) *Mahant Moti Das* v. *S.P. Sahi*, AIR 1959 SC 942 (949): (1959) Supp 2 SCR 563: 1959 SCJ 1144: (1959) 2 SCA 432: ILR 38 Pat 639 (Administration of religious endowment).

(xiv) *S.P. Mittal* v. *Union of India*, AIR 1983 SC 1: (1983) 1 SCC 51: (1983) 1 East LR 53: 1983 (1) SCJ 45: (1983) 1 SCR 729, paragraphs 119, 122 and 123 (Aurobindo University).

 (xv) *Sardar Syedna Taher Saifuddin Saheb* v. *State of Bombay*, AIR 1962 SC 853 (863): (1962) Supp 2 SCR 496: (1962) 2 SCA 192: 1963 (2) SCJ 519 (Essentials and non-essentials of religion).

(xvi) *Durgah Committee, Ajmer* v. *Syed Hussain Ali*, AIR 1961 SC 1402 (1415): (1962) 1 SCR 383: (1961) 2 SCA 171 (Judicial scrutiny).

(xvii) *Yajnapurusdasji* v. *Muldas*, AIR 1966 SC 1119 (1127): (1966) 3 SCR 242: 1967 MLLJ 289.

Religion
 (a) 'Religion' is a matter of faith but belief in God is not essential to constitute religion.
 (b) Doctrines of each religion constitute its essential part, but the court is competent to examine them.
 (c) 'Philosophy' is different from religion.

Following decisions support the above propositions as to the scope of 'religion':—

  (i) *Commissioner, Hindu Religious Endowments, Madras* v. *Lakshmindra Thirtha Swamiar of Sri Shirur Mutt*, (1954) SCR 1005: AIR 1954 SC 282: 1954 SCJ 335: (1954) 1 Mad LJ 596: 20 Cut LT 250: 1954 SCA 415: 1954 Mad WN 363.

 (ii) *Divyadarsan Rajendra Ramdassji Varu* v. *State of Andhra Pradesh*, AIR 1970 SC 181 (188): (1970) 1 SCC 844: (1970) 1 MLJ 86.

(iii) *Mohd. Hanif Quareshi* v. *State of Bihar*, (1959) SCR 629: AIR 1958 SC 731: 1958 SCA 783: 1958 SCJ 975: 1958 Mad LJ (Cri) 727.

 (iv) *Srimad Perarulala Ethiraja Ramanuja Jeeyar Swami* v. *State of Tamil Nadu*, AIR 1972 SC 1586: 1973 (1) SCJ 346: (1973) 1 Mad LJ (SC) 58: (1973) 1 Andh WR (SC) 58: (1972) 3 SCR 815.

  (v) *Sardar Sarup Singh* v. *State of Punjab*, AIR 1959 SC 860 (866): (1959) Supp 2 SCR 499: 1959 SCJ 1115: (1960) 1 SCA 163.

 (vi) *Mahant Moti Das* v. *S.P. Sahi*, AIR 1959 SC 942 (949): (1959) Supp 2 SCR 563: 1959 SCJ 1144: (1959) 2 SCA 432: ILR 38 Pat 639.

(vii) *S.P. Mittal* v. *Union of India*, AIR 1983 SC 1: (1983) 1 SCC 51: (1983) 1 East LR 53: 1983 (1) SCJ 45: (1983) 1 SCR 729, paragraphs 119, 122 and 123

Religious Freedom
Where temples and other religious institutions of Hindus are affected by frequent communal violence, the State is duty-bound to maintain public order; *Shyamal Ranjan Mukherjee* v. *Nirmal Ranjan Mukherjee*, AIR 2008 (NOC) 568 (All).

Restrictions that can be Imposed

By article 25(1), the Constitution itself makes freedom of religion subject to—

(a) public order.

(b) morality.

(c) health.

(d) 'other provisions of this Part'—which, *inter alia*, includes clause (b) of article 25(2) itself; *Venkataramana Devaru* v. *State of Mysore*, AIR 1958 SC 255: 1958 SCR 895: 1958 SCJ 382: (1958) 1 Andh WR (SC) 109: (1958) 1 Mad LJ (SC) 109.

The expression 'public order' occurs elsewhere in the Constitution—*e.g.*, article 19(2)—and should bear the same meaning here also. For the meaning of 'public order' under the Constitution, *See* the undermentioned cases:

(i) *Virendra* v. *State of Punjab*, AIR 1957 SC 896: (1958) 1 SCR 308: 1958 SCJ 88: 1958 SCA 891: 1958 SCC 1.

(ii) *Ramji Lal Modi* v. *State of Uttar Pradesh*, AIR 1957 SC 620: 1957 SCR 860: 1957 Cr LJ 1006: (1957) 2 Mad LJ (SC) 65: 1957 SCJ 522: 1957 SCC 334: 1957 BLJR 723: (1957) 1 Mad LJ (Cri) 771: 1958 SCA 157 (Discusses article 25 also).

(iii) *State of Rajasthan* v. *G. Chawla*, (1959) Supp 1 SCR 904: AIR 1959 SC 544: 1959 Cr LJ 660: 1959 SCJ 585: 1959 Mad LJ (Cri) 309 (Use of loudspeakers).

(iv) *Dalbir* v. *State of Punjab*, AIR 1962 SC 1106: (1962) Supp 3 SCR 25: (1962) 68 Cr LJ 247.

Scope and Object

With article 25 begins a group of provisions which ensure equality of all religions, thereby promoting secularism. The emphasis in this article is on the practice of religious freedom by individuals. The emphasis in article 26 is on the establishment of institutions. But article 25 may be available even where the practice of religion by individuals is through institutions.

The freedom guaranteed by article 25 is to 'profess, practice and propagate' religion. The act of 'practice' is concerned primarily with religious worship, ritual and observations. Propagation is concerned with right to communicate beliefs to another person or to expound the tenets of one's religion, but does not include a right to forcible conversions; *Stainislaus* v. *State of Madhya Pradesh*, AIR 1977 SC 908: (1977) 1 SCC 677: 1977 Cr LJ 551.

The logic underlying the constitutional guarantee regarding 'practice' of religion is that religious practices are as such a part of religion as religious faith or doctrines; *Commissioner, Hindu Religious Endowment* v. *Lakshmindra Tirtha Swamiyar of Sri Shirur Mutt*, (1954) SCR 1005: AIR 1954 SC 282: (1954) 1 MLJ 596.

Use of Loudspeaker

No religion prescribes that prayers should be performed by disturbing the peace of others nor does it preach that they should be through voice-amplifiers or beating of drums. In any case if there is such practice, it should not adversely affect the rights of others including that of being not disturbed in their activities; *Church of God (Full Gospell) in India* v. *K.K.R. Majestic Colony Welfare Association*, AIR 2000 SC 2773: (2000) 7 SCC 282: 2000 SCC (Cri) 1350.

26. Freedom to manage religious affairs.—Subject to public order, morality and health, every religious denomination or any section thereof shall have the right—

(a) to establish and maintain institutions for religious and charitable purposes;

(b) to manage its own affairs in matters of religion;

(c) to own and acquire movable and immovable property; and

(d) to administer such property in accordance with law.

Notes on Article 26

Administration of Property of Religious Endowments

The broad principle is that a State made law can regulate the administration of property of religious endowment, but the law cannot take away the right of administration altogether. *See* the undermentioned decisions:

(i) *Ratilal Panachand Gandhi* v. *State of Bombay*, (1954) SCR 1055: AIR 1954 SC 388: 1954 SCJ 480: (1954) 1 Mad LJ 718: 1954 SCA 538: 56 Bom LR 1184

(ii) *Tilkayat Shri Govindlalji Maharaj* v. *State of Rajasthan*, AIR 1963 SC 1638: (1964) 1 SCR 561: (1963) 2 SCA 518.

(iii) *Sardar Syedna Taher Saifuddin Saheb* v. *State of Bombay*, AIR 1962 SC 853 (863): (1962) Supp 2 SCR 496: (1962) 2 SCA 192: 1963 (2) SCJ 519.

(iv) *Mahant Ram Kishan Dass* v. *State of Punjab*, AIR 1981 SC 1576: (1983) 1 SCC 377: 1980 Land LR 182.

(v) *Narendra* v. *State of Gujarat*, AIR 1974 SC 2092: (1975) 3 SCC 185: 1975 Cr LJ 556.

(vi) *S. Azeez Basha* v. *Union of India*, AIR 1968 SC 662: (1968) 1 SCR 833.

Affairs of Religion

As under article 25, under article 26 also, courts have made a distinction between the essentials of religion and non-essentials. *See* the undermentioned decisions:

(i) *Ratilal Panachand Gandhi* v. *State of Bombay*, (1954) SCR 1055: AIR 1954 SC 388: 1954 SCJ 480: (1954) 1 Mad LJ 718: 1954 SCA 538: 56 Bom LR 1184.

(ii) *Sardar Sarup Singh* v. *State of Punjab*, AIR 1959 SC 860 (866): (1959) Supp 2 SCR 499: 1959 SCJ 1115: (1960) 1 SCA 163.

(iii) *Srimad Perarulala Ethiraja Ramanuja Jeeyar Swami* v. *State of Tamil Nadu*, AIR 1972 SC 1586: 1973 (1) SCJ 346: (1973) 1 Mad LJ (SC) 58: (1973) 1 Andh WR (SC) 58: (1972) 3 SCR 815.

(iv) *Acharya Jagdishwaranand Avadhuta* v. *Commissioner of Police, Calcutta*, AIR 1984 SC 51: (1983) 4 SCC 522: 1983 Cr LJ 1872: 1984 Cr LR (SC) 37: 1984 SCC (Cri) 1: 1984 (1) Crimes 318: 1984 Cr App R (SC) 185.

Denomination

In the case of a denomination tenets are important, thus distinguishing it from an individual; *Acharya Jagadishwarananda Avadhuta* v. *Commissioner of Police, Calcutta*, AIR 1990 Cal 336: 1990 (2) Cal LT 212.

Directive Principles

In this context, courts have also relied on the Directive Principles of State Policy (particularly article 37), and have taken the view, that property of a religious institution can be acquired under article 31A(1)(a), for effecting agrarian reform. It may also be acquired, if it exceeds the ceiling allowed by the relevant legislation. But the core of the religious institution should not be interfered with; *Narendra* v. *State of Gujarat*, AIR 1974 SC 2098: (1975) 1 SCC 11: (1975) 2 SCR 317.

Right to Own Property

The right to own and administer property is not an absolute right. It is subject to reasonable regulation by the State, the important condition being that such regulation should not affect the survival of the religious institution itself; *Narendra* v. *State of Gujarat*, AIR 1974 SC 2098: (1975) 1 SCC 11: (1975) 2 SCR 317.

On this basis, acquisition of its property (under the authority of law), is valid, subject to the condition mentioned above; *Surya Pal Singh* v. *State of Uttar Pradesh*, (1952) SCR 1056 (1090): AIR 1952 SC 252: 1952 SCJ 354: 1953 SCA 53.

Rituals

Articles 25 and 26 extend to rituals also and are not confined to doctrine. However, courts have to be pragmatic. Right to manage a temple is not an integral part of religion. It can be regulated by law; *Sri Adi Visheshwara of Kashi Vishwanath Temple, Varanasi* v. *State of Uttar Pradesh*, (1997) 4 SCC 606: JT 1997 (4) SC 124: (1997) 3 SCALE 1.

Where the ritual in a temple cannot be performed except by a person belongings to a denomination, the purpose of worship will be defeated; *Seshanmal* v. *State of Tamil Nadu*, AIR 1972 SC 1586: (1972) 3 SCR 815: (1973) 1 MLJ 58 (SC).

Scope and Object

Article 26 protects—(i) religious denominations, and (ii) selections thereof. The four rights guaranteed by the article are subject to 'public order, morality and health'—as in article 25. But article 26 is not subject to other provisions of Part III—an aspect noticed in *Narendra v. State of Gujarat*, AIR 1974 SC 2098: (1975) 1 SCC 11: (1975) 2 SCR 317.

The right under clause (a) of article 26(a) is a group right and is available to very religious denomination or any section thereof, be it of majority or any section thereof. It is evident from the opening words of article 26 that this right is subject to public order, morality and health; *T.M.A. Pai Foundation v. State of Karnataka*, AIR 2003 SC 355 (440): (2002) 8 SCC 481: 2002 AIR SCW 4957: JT 2002 (9) SC 1: 2003 (1) Kant LJ 1: 2002 (4) LRI 329: 2003 (2) SCT 385: 2003 (1) SRJ 271: (2002) 8 SCALE 1: 2002 (6) Serv LR 627: 2002 (8) Supreme 62.

Speedy Trial

The complainant cannot allow the case for an indefinite period; *S. Rama Krishna v. S. Rammi Reddy*, AIR 2008 SC 2066.

27. Freedom as to payment of taxes for promotion of any particular religion.— No person shall be compelled to pay any taxes, the proceeds of which are specifically appropriated in payment of expenses for the promotion or maintenance of any particular religion or religious denomination.

Notes on Article 27

Imposition of Fee

The imposition of fee under section 70 of the Bihar Hindu Religious Trusts Act is not tax, and such imposition is not hit by article 27; *Mahant Moti Das v. S.P. Sahi*, AIR 1959 SC 942 (949): (1959) Supp 2 SCR 563: 1959 SCJ 1144: (1959) 2 SCA 432: ILR 38 Pat 639. The Bihar Hindu Religious Trusts Act, 1951 does not infringe article 27; *State of Bihar v. Bhabapritananda Ojha*, AIR 1959 SC 1073: 1961 BLJR 653: 1959 SCJ 1197: ILR 38 Pat 834: (1960) 1 SCA 245: (1959) Supp 2 SCR 624.

28. Freedom as to attendance at religious instruction or religious worship in certain educational institutions.—(1) No religious instruction shall be provided in any educational institution wholly maintained out of State funds.

(2) Nothing in clause (1) shall apply to an educational institution which is administered by the State but has been established under any endowment or trust which requires that religious instruction shall be imparted in such institution.

(3) No person attending any educational institution recognised by the State or receiving aid out of State funds shall be required to take part in any religious instruction that may be imparted in such institution or to attend any religious worship that may be conducted in such institution or in any premises attached thereto unless such person or, if such person is a minor, his guardian has given his consent thereto.

Notes on Article 28

Religious Instructions

Recommending that students be acquainted with basics of all religions, the values inherited therein and also a comparative study of philosophy of all religions does not offend article 28; *Aruna Roy (Ms) v. Union of India*, AIR 2002 SC 3176: 2002 AIR SCW 3670: 2002 (6) Andh LD 66: JT 2002 (7) SC 103: (2002) 7 SCC 368: 2002 (4) SCJ 235: 2002 (9) SRJ 116: (2002) 6 SCALE 408: 2002 (6) Supreme 437.

Right to Administer Minority Institutions

The admission cannot be denied on ground of race, religion, language or caste. Articles 28 and 29 relate to any institutions receiving aid. On receipt of aid both articles would apply to minority institutions; *T.M.A. Pai Foundation v. State of Karnataka*, AIR 2003 SC 355 (440): (2002) 8 SCC

481: 2002 AIR SCW 4957: JT 2002 (9) SC 1: 2003 (1) Kant LJ 1: 2002 (4) LRI 329: 2003 (2) SCT 385: 2003 (1) SRJ 271: (2002) 8 SCALE 1: 2002 (6) Serv LR 627: 2002 (8) Supreme 62.

Cultural and Educational Rights

29. Protection of interests of minorities.—(1) Any section of the citizens residing in the territory of India or any part thereof having a distinct language, script or culture of its own shall have the right to conserve the same.

(2) No citizen shall be denied admission into any educational institution maintained by the State or receiving aid out of State funds on grounds only of religion, race, caste, language or any of them.

Notes on Article 29

The leading cases on article 29 are:

(i) *Kerala Education Bill (in re:)*, AIR 1958 SC 956: 1959 SCR 995: (1958) Ker 1167.

(ii) *Ahmedabad St. Xaviers College Society* v. *State of Gujarat*, AIR 1974 SC 1389: (1974) 1 SCC 717: (1975) 1 SCR 173.

(iii) *State of Bombay* v. *Bombay Education Society*, (1955) 1 SCR 568: AIR 1954 SC 561: 56 Bom LR 1211.

(iv) *Gujarat University* v. *Shri Krishna*, AIR 1963 SC 703: (1963) Supp 1 SCR 112: (1963) 4 Guj LR 450.

(v) *D.A.V. College, Jullundur* v. *State of Punjab*, AIR 1971 SC 1737: (1971) 2 SCC 269: 1971 (Supp) SCR 688.

Although, commonly article 29(1) is assumed to relate to minorities, its scope is not necessarily so confined, as it is available to "any section of citizens resident in the territory of India". This may well include the majority, as Ray, C.J. pointed out in the *Ahmedabad St Xaviers College Society* v. *State of Gujarat*, AIR 1974 SC 1389: (1974) 1 SCC 717: (1975) 1 SCR 173.

As regards article 29(2), it should be read subject to article 15(4), (as inserted in 1951), permitting special provision for backward classes, thus overriding the earlier decision in *State of Madras* v. *Champakam Dorairajan*, (1951) SCR 525: AIR 1951 SC 226: 1951 SCJ 313: 1951 KLT (SC) 41: (1951) 1 MLJ 621: 1951 MWN 470: 1951 ALJ (SC) 107. *See Bihar State Harijan Kalyan Prishad* v. *Union of India*, (1985) 2 SCC 644: 1985 SCC (L&S) 523: (1985) 2 LLJ 173: AIR 1985 SC 983.

An important consequence of the 'right to conserve' one's script is that citizens have the right to agitate for the protection of their language. 'Political' speeches for the conservation of the language of a section of the citizens cannot, therefore, be regarded as a corrupt practice within the meaning of section 123(3) of the Representation of the People Act, 1951; *Jagdev Singh Sidhanti* v. *Pratap Singh Daulta*, AIR 1965 SC 183 (188): (1964) 6 SCR 750: 1964 Cur LJ (SC) 231: 1964 (2) SCJ 633: (1965) 1 SCA 72.

Minorities

Although the word 'minorities' occurs in the marginal note to article 29, it does not occur in the text. The original proposal of the Advisory Committee in the Constituent Assembly recommended the following:—

"(1) *Minorities* in every unit shall be protected in respect of their language, script and culture and no laws or regulations may be enacted that may operate oppressively or prejudicially in this respect." [B. Siva Rao, "Select Documents" (1957) Vol. 2, page 281.]

But after the clause was considered by the Drafting Committee on 1st November, 1947, it emerged with substitute of 'section of citizens'. [B. Siva Rao, Select Documents (1957) Vol. 3 pages, 525-26, clause 23, Draft Constitution]. It was explained that the intention had always been to use 'minority' in a wide sense, so as to include (for example) Maharashtrians who settled in Bengal. (7 C.A.D. pages 922-23].

Regional Language

Not holding an entrance examination (pre-medical test), in any particular language *viz.* Hindi or any regional language, does not violate article 29(2); *Hindi Hitrakshak Samiti* v. *Union of India*, AIR 1990 SC 851: (1990) 2 SCC 352: (1990) 4 SLR 4, paragraph 6.

30. Right of minorities to establish and administer educational institutions.— (1) All minorities, whether based on religion or language, shall have the right to establish and administer educational institutions of their choice.

[1][(1A) In making any law providing for the compulsory acquisition of any property of an educational institution established and administered by a minority, referred to in clause (1), the State shall ensure that the amount fixed by or determined under such law for the acquisition of such property is such as would not restrict or abrogate the right guaranteed under that clause.]

(2) The State shall not, in granting aid to educational institutions, discriminate against any educational institution on the ground that it is under the management of a minority, whether based on religion or language.

Notes on Article 30

Condition as to Admission Fees

It is legal position is that the State cannot impose any restriction on the right of the minorities to administer educational institution so long as such institutions are unaided by the State, except to the limited extent that regulations can be made for ensuring excellence in education; *Father Thomas Shingare* v. *State of Maharashtra*, (2002) 1 SCC 758: AIR 2002 SC 463: 2002 SCC (Cri) 273.

Article 30(1A) requires a State, that is to say, Parliament in the case of a central legislation or a State legislature in the case of a State legislation, to make a specific law to provide for the compulsory acquisition of the property of minority educational institutions, the provisions of which law should ensure that the amount payable to the such institution or the acquisition of its property will not be such as will in many manner impair the functioning of educational institutions; *Society of St. Joseph's College* v. *Union of India*, (2002) 1 SCC 273: AIR 2002 SC 195: (2002) 1 KLT 438.

Conditions for Aid or Recognition

As a condition of granting aid or recognition to an institution coming under article 30(1), the State may impose reasonable regulations for the purpose of ensuring sanitation, competence of teachers, maintenance of discipline and the like. *See* the following cases:—

  (i) *Kerala Education Bill (in re:)*, AIR 1958 SC 956: 1959 SCR 995: (1958) Ker 1167.

  (ii) *Rev. Father W. Proost* v. *State of Bihar*, AIR 1969 SC 465: (1969) 2 SCR 73.

Conditions: Void

Thus, the State cannot prescribe a condition that if an institution, including one entitled to the protection of article 30(1), seeks to receive State aid, it must submit to the condition that the State may take over the management of the institution or acquire it, under certain conditions. Such a condition would completely destroy the right of the community to "administer" the institution; *St. Xavier's College* v. *State of Gujarat*, AIR 1974 SC 1389: (1974) 1 SCC 717: (1975) 1 SCR 173, paragraphs 6, 73, 124.

Similarly, there is no constitutional or other right for an institution to receive State recognition, and the State may impose reasonable conditions for receiving its recognition, *e.g.* as to the qualifications or pay of teachers or qualifications of governing bodies. *See* the undermentioned cases:—

  (i) *Frank Anthony Public School Employees' Association* v. *Union of India*, AIR 1987 SC 311: (1986) 4 SCC 707: 1986 JT 861: (1987) 1 LLN 53: (1987) 54 FLR 353: 1987 Mah LJ 1: 1987 MPLJ 1: (1987) 1 SCWR 86, paragraphs 13, 15-17.

---

1. Ins. by the Constitution (Forty-fourth Amendment) Act, 1978, sec. 4 (w.e.f. 20-6-1979).

(ii) *Gandhi Faiz-e-am College, Shahjahanpur* v. *Agra University,* AIR 1975 SC 1821: (1975) 2 SCC 283: (1975) 3 SCR 810: 1976 (3) SCJ 74.

But the State cannot impose conditions which are of such a nature, that the acceptance thereof would virtually deprive a minority community of the right guaranteed by article 30(1); *Sidhrajbhai* v. *State of Gujarat,* AIR 1963 SC 540: (1963) 3 SCR 837: 1962 Ker LJ 135 (SC).

Crucial Words

In article 30(1), the crucial words are:

(a) minorities;

(b) establish and administer;

(c) educational institutions;

(d) of their own choice.

The words 'of their own choice' are important; *Shri Krishna Rangnath Mudholkar* v. *Gujarat University,* AIR 1962 Guj 88: (1962) 3 Guj LR 204 (FB). The word 'establish' has been construed by Wanchoo, C.J. in *S. Azeez Basha* v. *Union of India,* AIR 1968 SC 662: (1968) 1 SCR 833.

Educational Standards

Right of a minority to administer educational institution has been dealt with by the Madhya Pradesh High Court. It has been held that the provisions contained in paragraph 17(1) of statute 28, Devi Ahilya University, in regard to the Constitution of the Selection Committee in the case of teaching posts [except in so far as they provide in sub-clause (a) that the *Kulpati* or his nominee shall be Chairman of such Committee] are aimed at ensuring educational standards and maintaining excellence thereof and cannot be said to be in violation of article 30(1) of the Constitution. The same is the position with regard to clause (1) of the said paragraph 17(1), which deals with the constitution of a Selection Committee in the case of Principal. Sub-clause (a), which provides that the *Kulpati* (or his nominee), shall be the Chairman, is void. But the other sub-clauses do not offend article 30(1) of the Constitution, inasmuch as they have apparently been enacted for ensuring educational standards and maintaining excellence thereof; *Islamia Karimia Society, Indore* v. *Devi Ahilya Vishwavidyalaya Indore,* AIR 1988 MP 22: 1988 MPLJ 151: 1988 CCLJ (MP) 81.

Reasonable regulations can be made to prescribe the syllabus; *State of Tamil Nadu* v. *Joseph,* (1991) 3 SCC 87: (1991) 2 SLR 605.

Maladministration

Maladministration would defeat the very object of article 30, which is to promote excellence of minority institutions in the field of education; *All Saints High School* v. *Government of Andhra Pradesh,* AIR 1980 SC 1042: (1980) 2 SCC 478: (1980) 1 Serv LR 716: 1980 (2) SCJ 273, paragraphs 12, 65.

Minorities

The word 'minority' has not been defined in the Constitution. The Motilal Nehru Report (1928) showed a prominent desire to afford protection to minorities, but did not define the expression. The Sapru Report (1945) also proposed, *inter alia,* a Minorities Commission but did not define *minority.* The Year Book on Human Rights (1950), page 490. The U.N. Sub-Commission on Prevention of Discrimination and Protection of Minorities has defined 'minority' (by an inclusive definition), as under:

(i) The term 'minority' includes only those non-document groups in a population which possess and wish to preserve stable ethnic, religious or linguistic traditions or characteristics markedly different from those of the rest of the population; (ii) such minorities should properly include a number of persons sufficient by themselves to preserve such traditions or characteristics; and (iii) such minorities must be loyal to the State of which they are nationals.

Article 27 of the International Covenant on Civil and Political Rights does not define the expression but gives the following right to them:—

In those States in which ethnic, religious or linguistic minorities exist, persons belonging to such minorities shall not be denied the right, in community with the other members of their group, to enjoy their own culture, to profess and practise their own religion or to use their own language.

The word 'minority' is not defined in the Constitution but literally it means 'a non-dominant' group. It is a relative term and is referred to, to represent the smaller of two numbers, sections or group called 'majority'. In that sense, there may be political minority, religious minority, linguistic minority, etc.; *T.M.A. Pai Foundation* v. *State of Karnataka*, AIR 2003 SC 355 (440): (2002) 8 SCC 481: 2002 AIR SCW 4957: JT 2002 (9) SC 1: 2003 (1) Kant LJ 1: 2002 (4) LRI 329: 2003 (2) SCT 385: 2003 (1) SRJ 271: (2002) 8 SCALE 1: 2002 (6) Serv LR 627: 2002 (8) Supreme 62.

Minorities Based on Religion or Language

Backward classes are not minorities within article 30. As K.M. Munshi [5 C.A.D. page 227] pointed out, "The Harijans generally known as the Scheduled Castes, are neither a racial minority nor a linguistic minority... The Harijans are part and parcel of Hindu community." Following judicial decisions are relevant as to the concept of 'minorities':—

(i) *Kerala Education Bill (in re:)*, AIR 1958 SC 956 (976, 977): 1959 SCR 995: (1958) Ker 1167.

(ii) *Shri Krishna Rangnath Mudholkar* v. *Gujarat University*, AIR 1962 Guj 88: (1962) 3 Guj LR 204 (Shelat, C.J.) (A judgment worth perusal).

(iii) *Aldo Maria Patroni* v. *E.G. Kesavan*, AIR 1965 Ker 75: 1964 Ker LT 791: ILR (1964) 2 Ker 478: 1964 Ker LJ 1055: (1964) 2 Ker LR 67 (M.S. Menon, C.J.).

(iv) *Sree Jain Swetamber Terapanthi Vidyalaya* v. *State of West Bengal*, AIR 1982 Cal 101 (111): (1982) 86 CWN 84: (1982) 1 Cal HN 247 (B.C. Ray, J.).

(v) *D.A.V. College, Bhatinda* v. *State of Punjab*, AIR 1971 SC 1731: (1971) 2 SCC 261: 1971 (Supp) SCR 677 (Reddy, J.).

(vi) *Arya Samaj Education Trust, Delhi* v. *Director of Education, Delhi Administration, Delhi*, AIR 1976 Del 207 (218): ILR (1976) 2 Del 93.

Regulation by the State

The "regulation" by the State cannot go to the length of annihilating the right guaranteed by article 30(1). Regulation must be related to the interests of the institution as an educational institution (and not merely in the interests of the general public); *St. Xavier's College* v. *State of Gujarat*, AIR 1974 SC 1389: (1974) 1 SCC 717: (1975) 1 SCR 173, paragraphs 6, 73, 124.

Regulatory Laws

The right under article 30(1) is subject to the regulatory power of the State. Article 30(1) is not a charter for maladministration. Legislation for social welfare and similar regulatory measure do not constitute an infringement of article 30(1). So long as the minority is not deprived of the actual management of the institution, a law regulating certain matters concerning industrial relation, academic matters and the like does not infringe article 30(1); *Virendra Nath* v. *Delhi*, (1990) 2 SCC 307: AIR 1990 SC 1148: 1990 Lab IC 929.

The above broad statement of the legal position is illustrated by, and draws support from, the following cases:—

(i) *Kerala Education Bill (in re:)*, AIR 1958 SC 956: 1959 SCR 995: (1958) Ker 1167.

(ii) *State of Kerala* v. *Very Rev. Mother Provincial*, AIR 1970 SC 2079: (1970) 2 SCC 417: (1971) 1 SCR 734.

(iii) *Ahmedabad St. Xavier College Society* v. *State of Gujarat*, (1974) 1 SCC 717: AIR 1974 SC 1389: 1974 (2) SCJ 381: (1975) 1 SCR 173.

(iv) *Lily Kurian* v. *St. Levina*, AIR 1979 SC 52: (1979) 2 SCC 127: (1979) 1 SCR 820.

(v) *All Saints High School* v. *Government of Andhra Pradesh*, AIR 1980 SC 1042: (1980) 2 SCC 478: (1980) 1 Serv LR 716: 1980 (2) SCJ 273.

(vi) *Frank Anthony Public School Employees' Association* v. *Union of India*, (1986) 4 SCC 707: (1987) 2 ATC 35: AIR 1987 SC 311.

(vii) *Christian Medical College Hospital Employees' Union* v. *C.M.C. Vellore Association*, (1987) 4 SCC 691 (708, 812, 717): AIR 1988 SC 37: 1988 SCC (L&S) 53 [Reversing *C.M.C. Vellore Association* v. *Govt. of India* (1983) 1 Lab LN 373].

(viii) *Y. Theclamma* v. *Union of India*, (1987) 2 SCC 516 (527, 528): AIR 1987 SC 1210: (1987) Lab IC 907.

(ix) *Bihar State Madarsa Board* v. *Madarsa Hanafia*, AIR 1990 SC 695: (1990) 1 SCC 428: (1990) 1 BLJR 504.

(x) *St. Stephen's College* v. *University of Delhi*, (1992) 1 SCC 558: AIR 1992 SC 1630: 1992 AIR SCW 1792: JT 1991 (4) SC 548: 1992 (1) SCJ 624, paragraphs 97-100.

Requirements of Regulation

In order to be consonant with article 30(1), a regulation imposed by the State upon a minority institution should satisfy the following requirements:—

(a) it must be reasonable;

(b) it must be regulative of the educational character of the institution;

(c) it must be conducive to making the institution an effective vehicle of education for the minority community or other persons who resort to it.

Sidhrajbhai v. *State of Gujarat*, AIR 1963 SC 540: (1963) 3 SCR 837: 1962 Ker LJ 135 (SC).

(d) It must not annihilate the institution.

(i) *Sidhrajbhai* v. *State of Gujarat*, AIR 1963 SC 540: (1963) 3 SCR 837: 1962 Ker LJ 135 (SC).

(ii) *St. John's Teacher Training Institute (for Women), Madurai* v. *State of Tamil Nadu*, AIR 1994 SC 43: 1 (1993) 3 SCC 595: 1993 AIR SCW 3089: JT 1993 (4) SC 78: 1993 (2) Mad LW 218: 1993 (3) SCJ 1: (1993) 3 SCR 985: 1993 (4) SCT 33: 1993 (2) UJ (SC) 490, paragraph 6.

(iii) *Manohar Harries Walters* v. *Basel Mission Higher Education Centre, Dharwad*, AIR 1991 SC 2230: (1992) Supp 2 SCC 301: 1991 AIR SCW 2562: 1992 (1) Cur LR 407: 1993 (66) FLR 986: 1992 (1) LLJ 279: 1992 (1) LLN 387: 1992 SCC (L&S) 747: (1992) Supp 2 SCC 301.

(iv) *State of Kerala* v. *Mother Provincial*, AIR 1970 SC 2079: (1970) 2 SCC 417: 1970 KLT 630.

Right: Not Absolute

The right under article 30 is not absolute. The State has power to regulate the administration of the institutions established by the minority communities. State has the right to regulate the administration or religious institutions. Right to "administer" does not include right to maladminister. *See* the following cases:—

(i) *Kerala Education Bill (in re:)*, AIR 1958 SC 956: 1959 SCR 995: (1958) Ker 1167.

(ii) *Rev. Father Proost* v. *State of Bihar*, AIR 1969 SC 465: (1969) 2 SCR 73.

Right to Receive Aid

There is no constitutional right to receive State aid outside article 337. But if the State does, in fact, grant aid to educational institutions, it cannot impose upon the right to receive such aid such conditions as would virtually deprive the members of a religious or linguistic community of their right under article 30(1); *St. Stephen's College* v. *University of Delhi*, (1992) 1 SCC 558: AIR 1992 SC 1630: 1992 AIR SCW 1792: JT 1991 (4) SC 548: 1992 (1) SCJ 624, paragraphs 97-100.

Scope

Article 30 is confined to minorities—whether based on religion or language—and unlike article 29(1), it cannot be availed of by any 'section of citizens'. At the same time, article 30(1) is not confined to the conservation of language, script or culture—unlike article 29(1). It may be, that the right given by article 29(1) is fortified, as regards minorities, by article 30(1). But the two rights are separate; *Rev. Father Proost* v. *State of Bihar*, AIR 1969 SC 465: (1969) 2 SCR 73. The right to establish an educational institution under article 30 is not confined to the conservation of language, script or culture. This was pointed out by Mathew, J. in *Ahmedabad St. Xavier College Society* v. *State of Gujarat,* (1974) 1 SCC 717: AIR 1974 SC 1389: 1974 (2) SCJ 381: (1975) 1 SCR 173.

Article 30 confers two rights:

(a) right to establish an institution, and

(b) right to administer it.

The former means the right to create the institution, while the latter (right to administer) means that the management of the affairs of the institution must be free of external control, so that the founders or their nominees can manage the institution as they think fit and in accordance with their ideas of how best the interest of the community in general and the institution in particular will be served; *Md. Joynal Abedin* v. *State of West Bengal,* AIR 1990 Cal 193 (201, 202): (1989) 2 Cal LJ 362, paragraphs 12 and 13.

Autonomy of a minority institution cannot be completely taken away; *St. Stephen's College* v. *University of Delhi,* (1992) 1 SCC 558: AIR 1992 SC 1630: 1992 AIR SCW 1792: JT 1991 (4) SC 548: 1992 (1) SCJ 624, paragraphs 97-100.

Standards

A "standard" of education is not a part of "Management" as such; *All Saints High School* v. *Government of Andhra Pradesh,* AIR 1980 SC 1042: (1980) 2 SCC 478: (1980) 1 Serv LR 716: 1980 (2) SCJ 273, paragraphs 12, 65.

The minority institutions cannot be allowed to fall below the standards of excellence expected of educational institutions; *State of Kerala* v. very. Rev. *Mother Provincial,* AIR 1970 SC 2079 (2082): (1970) 2 SCC 417: 1970 KLT 630 (1971) 1 SCR 734.

[1][***]

[2][**31. Compulsory acquisition of property.**—[*Rep. by the Constitution (Forty-fourth Amendment) Act, 1978, sec. 6 (w.e.f. 20-6-1979).*]]

[3][*Saving of Certain Laws*]

[4][**31A. Saving of laws providing for acquisition of estates, etc.—** [5][(1) Notwithstanding anything contained in article 13, no law providing for—

(a) the acquisition by the State of any estate or of any rights therein or the extinguishment or modification of any such rights, or

(b) the taking over of the management of any property by the State for a limited period either in the public interest or in order to secure the proper management of the property, or

(c) the amalgamation of two or more corporations either in the public interest or in order to secure the proper management of any of the corporations, or

(d) the extinguishment or modification of any rights of managing agents, secretaries and treasurers, managing directors, directors or managers of corporations, or of any voting rights of shareholders thereof, or

---

1. The sub-heading *"Right to Property"* omitted by the Constitution (Forty-fourth Amendment) Act, 1978, sec. 5 (w.e.f. 20-6-1979).

2. Article 31 was earlier amended by the Constitution (Fourth Amendment) Act, 1955, sec. 2 (w.e.f. 27-4-1955) and by the Constitution (Twenty-fifth Amendment) Act, 1971, sec. 2 (w.e.f. 20-4-1972).

3. Ins. by the Constitution (Forty-second Amendment) Act, 1976, sec. 3 (w.e.f. 3-1-1977).

4. Ins. by the Constitution (First Amendment) Act, 1951, sec. 4 (with retrospective effect).

5. Subs. by the Constitution (Fourth Amendment) Act, 1955, sec. 3(a), for clause (1) (with retrospective effect).

(e) the extinguishment or modification of any rights accruing by virtue of any agreement, lease or licence for the purpose of searching for, or winning, any mineral or mineral oil, or the premature termination or cancellation of any such agreement, lease or licence,

shall be deemed to be void on the ground that it is inconsistent with, or takes away or abridges any of the rights conferred by [1][article 14 or article 19]:

Provided that where such law is a law made by the Legislature of a State, the provisions of this article shall not apply thereto unless such law, having been reserved for the consideration of the President, has received his assent:]

[2][Provided further that where any law makes any provision for the acquisition by the State of any estate and where any land comprised therein is held by a person under his personal cultivation, it shall not be lawful for the State to acquire any portion of such land as is within the ceiling limit applicable to him under any law for the time being in force or any building or structure standing thereon or appurtenant thereto, unless the law relating to the acquisition of such land, building or structure, provides for payment of compensation at a rate which shall not be less than the market value thereof.]

(2) In this article,—

[3][(a) the expression "estate" shall, in relation to any local area, have the same meaning as that expression or its local equivalent has in the existing law relating to land tenures in force in that area and shall also include—

(i) any *jagir, inam* or *muafi* or other similar grant and in the States of [4][Tamil Nadu] and Kerala, any *janmam* right;

(ii) any land held under *ryotwari* settlement;

(iii) any land held or let for purposes of agriculture or for purposes ancillary thereto, including waste land, forest land, land for pasture or sites of buildings and other structures occupied by cultivators of land, agricultural labourers and village artisans;]

(b) the expression "rights", in relation to an estate, shall include any rights vesting in a proprietor, sub-proprietor, under-proprietor, tenure-holder, [5][*raiyat, under-raiyat*] or other intermediary and any rights or privileges in respect of land revenue.]

Notes on Article 31A

Land Reform Legislation

(1) Laws providing for acquisition of estates, take over of corporation, etc., have been saved by article 31A against challenge on the ground of alleged infringement of article 14 or article 19.

---

1. Subs. by the Constitution (Forty-fourth Amendment) Act, 1978, sec. 7, for "article 14, article 19 or article 31" (w.e.f. 20-6-1979).
2. Ins. by the Constitution (Seventeenth Amendment) Act, 1964, sec. 2(i) (w.e.f. 20-6-1964).
3. Subs. by the Constitution (Seventeenth Amendment) Act, 1964, sec. 2(ii), for sub-clause (a) (with retrospective effect). Earlier clause (a) was amended by the Constitution (Fourth Amendment) Act, 1955, sec. 3(b)(i) (with retrospective effect) and by the Constitution (Seventh Amendment) Act, 1956, sec. 29 and Sch. (w.e.f. 1-11-1956).
4. Subs. by the Madras State (Alteration of Name) Act, 1968 (53 of 1968), sec. 4, for "Madras" (w.e.f. 14-1-1969).
5. Ins. by the Constitution (Fourth Amendment) Act, 1955, sec. 3(b)(ii) (with retrospective effect).

(2) By article 31B, Acts and Regulations specified in the Ninth Schedule have been saved against challenge on the ground of inconsistency with, taking away or abridging any *fundamental right*. However, after the decision in *Keshavananda's* case, inclusion in the Ninth Schedule of any law is open to challenge on the ground of damage to the basic structure of the Constitution; *Keshavananda Bharati Sripadgalvaru* v. *State of Kerala*, AIR 1973 SC 1461: (1973) 4 SCC 225: 1973 Supp SCR 1; *Waman Rao* v. *Union of India*, AIR 1981 SC 271: (1981) 2 SCC 362: (1981) 2 SCR 1; *Srinivasa* v. *State of Karnataka*, AIR 1987 SC 1518: (1987) 2 SCC 692, paragraphs 6-7. Article 31C, inserted by The Constitution (Twenty-fifth Amendment) Act, 1971, protected laws giving effect to the Directive Principles in article 39(b) and 39(c) from unconstitutionality on the ground of contravention of articles 14, 19 and 31. By the 42nd (Amendment) Act, 1976, the protection was extended to legislation for implementation of any directive principle. But the Supreme Court in 1980 (by majority) held this extension of the protection to be unconstitutional on the ground that such an omnibus withdrawal of legislation from judicial review would undermine the basic structure of the Constitution. In 1983, the Supreme Court has declared the relevant observation in its 1980 judgment to be obiter. *See* the following cases:—

(i)   *Minerva Mills Ltd.* v. *Union of India*, AIR 1986 SC 2030: (1986) 4 SCC 222: 1986 JT 375: 1986 (3) Supreme 432: (1986) 2 Cur CC 880.

(ii) *Minerva Mills Ltd.* v. *Union of India*, AIR 1980 SC 1789: (1980) 3 SCC 625: 1980 Ker LT 573: 1980 UJ (SC) 727, paragraphs 30, 64 70 and 80.

(iii) *Sanjeev Coke Manufacturing Co.* v. *Bharat Coking Coal Ltd.*, AIR 1983 SC 239: (1983) 1 SCC 147: 1983 UJ (SC) 81: 1983 (1) SCJ 233: (1983) 1 SCR 1000, paragraphs 13, 14.

Article 31C in its main paragraph, second part (as amended by The Constitution (Twenty-fifth Amendment) Act, 1971) provides as under:

and no law containing a declaration that it is for giving effect so such policy shall be called in question in any court on the ground that it does not give effect to such policy.

In 1973, the Supreme Court struck down this portion as unconstitutional on the ground that it was beyond the competence of the Constitution (Twenty-fifth Amendment) Act, 1971 (Which introduced article 31C), to take away the power of judicial review to question whether a particular law which professed to give effect to a Directive Principles was, in reality, a law having that object or whether that was only its colourable purpose; *Keshavananda Bharati Sripadgalvaru* v. *State of Kerala*, AIR 1973 SC 1461: (1973) 4 SCC 225: 1973 Supp SCR 1.

It follows that the court can still consider whether a particular law purporting to implement any directive principle is valid if it finds that the nexus between that law and the Directive Principle relied on is illusory or colourable or whether it has 'direct and reasonable' nexus with the directive principle in article 39(b) or article 39(c); *Bhim Singhji* v. *Union of India*, AIR 1981 SC 234: (1981) 1 SCC 166: 1981 Raj LR 39: 1981 All CJ 38; *State of Maharashtra* v. *Basantibai*, (1986) 2 SCC 516, paragraph 13: AIR 1986 SC 1466: 1986 (1) SCJ 566: 1986 (2) Supreme 399: (1986) 88 Bom LR 205: 1986 Mah LR 650: (1986) 1 MCC 73: 1986 UJ (SC) 715, paragraph 2.

A law providing for agrarian reform need not provide for land ceilings; *Union Territory of Goa, Daman & Diu* v. *Lakshmibai Narayan Patil*, AIR 1990 SC 1771: (1990) 4 SCC 102, paragraph 9.

[1][**31B. Validation of certain Acts and Regulations.**—Without prejudice to the generality of the provisions contained in article 31A, none of the Acts and Regulations specified in the Ninth Schedule nor any of the provision thereof shall be deemed to be void, or ever to have become void, on the ground that such Act, Regulation or provision is inconsistent with, or takes away or abridges any of the rights conferred by, any provisions of this Part, and notwithstanding any judgment, decree or order of any court or tribunal to the contrary, each of the said Acts and Regulations shall, subject to the power of any competent Legislature to repeal or amend it, continue in force.]

---

1. Ins. by the Constitution (First Amendment) Act, 1951, sec. 5 (w.e.f. 18-6-1951).

Notes on Article 31B

Article 31B saves conflict with any fundamental right, including the right guaranteed by article 19(1)(g); *H.S.S.K. Niyami* v. *Union of India*, AIR 1990 SC 2128: (1990) 4 SCC 516.

Validity of Article 31B

All Constitutional amendments made after the decision in *Keshavananda Bharati's* case (AIR 1973 SC 1461). Would have to be tested by reference to the basic structure doctrine and constitutional validity should be tested with relation to such doctrine; *Minerva Mills Ltd.* v. *Union of India*, AIR 1980 SC 1789: (1980) 3 SCC 625: 1980 Ker LT 573: 1980 UJ (SC) 727.

Constitutional Validity of a Statute

The Constitutional validity of a statute depends entirely on the existence of the legislative power and the express provision in article 13; *Indira Nehru Gandhi* v. *Raj Narain*, AIR 1975 SC 2299: 1975 Supp SCC 1: (1976) 2 SCR 347.

[1][**31C. Saving of laws giving effect to certain Directive Principles.**— Notwithstanding anything contained in article 13, no law giving effect to the policy of the State towards securing [2][all or any of the principles laid down in Part IV] shall be deemed to be void on the ground that it is inconsistent with, or takes away or abridges any of the rights conferred by [3][article 14 or article 19] [4][*and no law containing a declaration that it is for giving effect to such policy shall be called in question in any court on the ground that it does not give effect to such policy*]:

Provided that where such law is made by the Legislature of a State, the provisions of this article shall not apply thereto unless such law, having been reserved for the consideration of the President, has received his assent.]

Notes on Article 31C

As to effect of article 31C on article 19 see *Elizebath Samuel Aaron* v. *State of Kerala*, AIR 1991 Ker 162: 1992 (75) Com Cas 377: ILR (1991) 2 Ker 113: 1991 (1) Ker LJ 626: 1991 (1) Ker LT 475 (FB).

Article 31C does not bar judicial review to examine the nexus between impugned law and article 39; *Assam Sillimanite* v. *Union of India*, AIR 1992 SC 938: (1992) Supp 1 SCC 692: 1992 AIR SCW 754: 1992 (1) Comp LJ SC 165: JT 1992 (3) SC 434: 1992 (1) SCJ 423: 1992 (1) UJ (SC) 288.

[5][**31D. Saving of laws in respect of anti-national activities.**—[*Rep. by the Constitution (Forty-third Amendment) Act, 1977, section 2 (w.e.f. 13-4-1978).*]]

Right to Constitutional Remedies

32. Remedies for enforcement of rights conferred by this Part.—(1) The right to move the Supreme Court by appropriate proceedings for the enforcement of the rights conferred by this Part is guaranteed.

---

1. Ins. by the Constitution (Twenty-fifth Amendment) Act, 1971, sec. 3 (w.e.f. 20-4-1972).

2. Subs. by the Constitution (Forty-second Amendment) Act, 1976, sec. 4, for "the principles specified in clause (b) or clause (c) of article 39" (w.e.f. 3-1-1977). Section 4 has been declared invalid by the Supreme Court in *Minerva Mills Ltd.* v. *Union of India*, (1980) 2 SCC 591.

3. Subs. by the Constitution (Forty-fourth Amendment) Act, 1978, sec. 8, for "article 14, article 19 or article 31" (w.e.f. 20-6-1979).

4. In *Keshavananda Bharati Sripadgalvaru* v. *State of Kerala*, 1973 Supp SCR 1: (1973) 4 SCC 225: AIR 1973 SC 1461, the Supreme Court held the provision in italics to be invalid.

5. Article 31D was earlier inserted by the Constitution (Forty-second Amendment) Act, 1976, sec. 5 (w.e.f. 3-1-1977).

(2) The Supreme Court shall have power to issue directions or orders or writs, including writs in the nature of *habeas corpus, mandamus*, prohibition, *quo warranto* and *certiorari*, whichever may be appropriate, for the enforcement of any of the rights conferred by this Part.

(3) Without prejudice to the powers conferred on the Supreme Court by clauses (1) and (2), Parliament may by law empower any other court to exercise within the local limits of its jurisdiction all or any of the powers exercisable by the Supreme Court under clause (2).

(4) The right guaranteed by this article shall not be suspended except as otherwise provided for by this Constitution.

Notes on Article 32

Basic Feature of Constitution
Judicial review under articles 32 and 226 is a basic feature of the Constitution beyond the pale of amendability; *Kihota Hollohan* v. *Zachillhu*, AIR 1993 SC 412: (1992) Supp 2 SCC 651: 1992 AIR SCW 3497 : JT 1992 (1) SC 600: (1992) 1 SCR 686, paragraphs 26, 85 and 107.

Certiorari
(a) *Certiorari* may be issued where the law under which the decision was given is void; *Himmat Lal* v. *State of Madhya Pradesh*, AIR 1954 SC 403: 1954 SCR 1122: (1954) 5 STC 115.

(b) the decision itself violates a fundamental right (*see* below); or

(c) the decision violates the law or is without jurisdiction; *Ranjit Singh* v. *Union Territory of Chandigarh*, AIR 1991 SC 2296: (1991) 4 SCC 304: 1991 SCC (Cri) 965.

(d) the decision is against natural justice, *mala fide*, perverse or based on non-applicability of avenue.

Decisions violating fundamental rights—category (b) above, are illustrated by situations where fundamental rights violated are those created under: (i) article 14—*D.T.C.* v. *Mazdoor Congress*, AIR 1991 SC 101: (1991) Supp 1 SCC 600: 1991 SCC (L&S) 1213; (ii) article 19(1)(g)—*Express Newspapers* v. *Union of India*, AIR 1958 SC 578: 1959 SCR 12: (1961) 1 LLJ 339 paragraphs 226; (iii) article 16—*Indra* v. *Union of India*, (1999) Supp 5 SCC 557 (559); (iv) article 21—*Sangita* v. *State of Uttar Pradesh*, (1992) Supp 1 SCC 715; *State of Bihar* v. *P.P. Sharma*, AIR 1991 SC 1260: (1991) Supp 1 SCC 222; (v) article 22—*Bapna* v. *Union of India*, (1992) 3 SCC 512: 1992 SCC (Cri) 683; *Advisory Board* v. *State of Kerala*, (1991) 2 SCC 1. Mere misapplication of law is not a ground for *certiorari*; *Union of India* v. *Deep*, (1992) 4 SCC 432: AIR 1993 SC 382: (1993) 23 ATC 356.

Child Prostitution
Supreme Court has issued directions to check the evil of child prostitution; *Vishal Jeet* v. *Union of India*, (1990) 3 SCC 318: AIR 1990 SC 1412: 1990 Cr LJ 1469, paragraph 16.

Closure of Industry
Supreme Court issued directions for revival of a company (viable units) having regard to the fact that living had been denied to 10,000 workers for five years; *Workers of M/s. Rohtas Industries Ltd.* v. *Rohtas Industries Ltd.*, AIR 1990 SC 481: (1989) Supp 2 SCC 481: 1990 Lab IC 146.

Commissioner
Court may appoint a person to act as Commissioner to inquire into allegations made against Government officers for breach of fundamental right. A request made after an objective inquiry would not be rejected unless good reasons are shown to exist for rejection; *Delhi Judicial Service Association, Tis Hazari Court, Delhi* v. *State of Gujarat*, (1991) 4 SCC 406: AIR 1991 SC 2176: 1991 Cr LJ 3086: 1991 AIR SCW 2419: 1991 (3) Crimes 232: JT 1991 (3) SC 617: 1991 (3) Rec Cr R 566: (1991) 3 SCR 936.

Compensation

For deprivation of right to life and personal liberty, compensation may be awarded; *Saheli* v. *C.P.*, (1990) 1 SCJ 300: (1990) 1 SCC 422: AIR 1990 SC 513, paragraphs 11-14.

Composite Petition

Election petition and writ petition cannot be combined; *Dharti Pakar Madan Lal Agarwal* v. *K.R. Narayanan*, (1997) 8 SCC 766: AIR 1998 SC 1462: 1998 AIR SCW 224: 1998 (2) Civ LJ 565: (1997) 7 SCALE 201: 1997 (10) Supreme 42.

Contempt

Wilful non-compliance with court order under article 32 is contempt of court; *Sachdev* v. *Union of India*, (1991) 1 SCC 605: AIR 1991 SC 311: 1991 Cr LJ 392, paragraphs 6-8 and 11.

Instead of proceeding in contempt court may award exemplary costs; *Dr. Ajay Kumar Agrawal* v. *State of Uttar Pradesh*, AIR 1991 SC 498: 1991 (17) All LR 452: JT 1991 (1) SC 168: (1991) 1 SCC 636: 1991 (1) Serv LR 776: 1991 (1) UJ (SC) 54, paragraph 4.

Continuing *Mandamus*

Where the mere issue of (one-time) *mandamus* would be futile against a public agency guilty of continuous inertia then 'continuing' *mandamus*' can be issued; *Vineet Narain* v. *Union of India*, AIR 1998 SC 889: (1998) 1 SCC 226: 1998 SCC (Cri) 307: 1998 Cr LJ 1208.

Counter-affidavits: Detention

Counter affidavits filed as in reply to allegations of (i) *mala fide,* (ii) abuse of power, or (iii) bias, should be filed by the detaining authority himself; *Gazi Khan* v. *State of Rajasthan*, AIR 1990 SC 1361 (1367): (1990) 3 SCC 459: 1990 Cr LJ 1420, paragraphs 9-14.

Damages

For breach of *public law* duty the court may award against the wrong doer exemplary damages, *Nilabati* v. *State of Orissa*, (1993) 2 SCC 746: AIR 1993 SC 1960: 1993 Cr LJ 2899, paragraphs 11, 20, 32, 34, 35 and 36.

Death in Custody

Compensation may be awarded for death in police custody; *Nilabati* v. *State of Orissa*, (1993) 2 SCC 746: AIR 1993 1960: 1993 Cr LJ 2899 (3 Judges bench).

Detention

In case of preventive detention, main ground of interference is breach of article 22(5); *Gracy* v. *State of Kerala*, AIR 1991 SC 1090: (1991) 2 SCC 1: 1991 SCC (Cri) 467, paragraphs 9-10.

Court may order release of a detenue if he is not given opportunity to appear before the Board within the statutory period; *State of Punjab* v. *Sukhpal Singh*, AIR 1990 SC 231: (1990) 1 SCC 35: 1990 Cr LJ 584.

Court may order the release of a detenue if there is failure to obtain Government approval within statutory period; *Kiran Pasha* v. *Government of Andhra Pradesh*, (1990) 1 SCC 328: 1990 SCC (Cri) 110.

Inordinate delay in passing detention order may entail release of the detenue; *Anand Prakash* v. *State of Uttar Pradesh*, AIR 1990 SC 516: (1990) 1 SCC 291: 1990 SCC (Cri) 96.

Court cannot reduce the period of detention; *Poonam* v. *Wadhwan*, AIR 1987 SC 1383: (1987) 3 SCC 347: 1987 Cr LJ 1130, paragraph 12.

Doctrine of *Parens Patriae*

The Supreme Court in *Charan Lal Sahu* v. *Union of India*, (1990) 1 SCC 613: AIR 1990 SC 1480: (1989) Supp 2 SCR 597: 1989 Supp SCALE 1 has Upheld the validity of the Bhopal Gas Disaster (Processing of Claims) Act, 1985. The judgment discusses the doctrine of *parens patriae*. It also takes note of the fact that the legislation in question related to "actionable wrong" under the Seventh Schedule, Concurrent list, entry 8. It also contains a suggestion (in para 129) to lay down certain norms and standards in regard to the industries dealing with materials which are of dangerous potentialities. In the judgment of Mr. Justice Ranganathan, there is a suggestion that either the Fatal Accidents Act, 1855 should be amended or fresh legislation enacted to deal with victims of mass disaster; *Inter alia*, the suggested legislation should deal with the following matters:—

(i) Fixed minimum compensation on no fault basis, pending filing adjudication of the case.

(ii) Creation of a special forum with specific power to grant interim relief in appropriate cases.

(iii) Evaluation of a procedure to be followed by such (special) forum, which will be conducive to the determination of the claims and avoid high degree of formalism in proceedings.

(iv) A provision requiring industries and concerns engaged in hazardous activities to take out compulsory insurance against third party risk.

The court did not uphold the argument that the Act was against article 14 of the Constitution.

Earlier Decision

Writ petition cannot be filed to circumvent an earlier decision of the Supreme Court; *Gopi Aqua Farms* v. *Union of India*, AIR 1997 SC 3519: (1997) 6 SCC 577: 1997 AIR SCW 3614: JT 1997 (7) SC 75: (1997) 5 SCALE 273: 1997 (7) Supreme 253: 1997 UJ (SC) 499.

Estoppel against Petitioner

Petitioner who has voluntarily accepted benefit under a statute, cannot object to its validity; *Dr. Pramod Kumar Joshi* v. *Medical Council of India*, (1991) 1 UJ SC 400: (1991) 2 SCC 179: 1991 AIR SCW 744.

Estoppel against State

Where a State party supports a petition on the merits, it cannot be allowed to raise a technical plea after a long lapse of time; *T.N. Cauvery Neerppasana Vilaiporulgal Vivasayigal Nala Urimai Padhugappu Sangam* v. *Union of India*, AIR 1990 SC 1316: (1990) 3 SCC 440: JT 1990 (2) SC 397, paragraph 6.

False Plea

A petition may be dismissed at any stage (even after *rule nisi* is issued) if petitioner has made a false plea; *A.I.S.B.O.F.* v. *Union of India*, (1990) Supp SCC 336: 1991 SCC (L&S) 429, paragraphs 12-13.

Infringement of Fundamental Right

Threat of infringement of fundamental right is enough to justify issue of writ; *Simranjit Singh Mann* v. *Union of India*, (1993) 1 UJ SC 32: (1992) 4 SCC 653: AIR 1993 SC 280: 1993 Cr LJ 37: 1992 AIR SCW 3133: JT 1992 (5) SC 441: (1992) 4 SCR 592: 1993 SCC (Cri) 22, paragraph 7.

Introduction of Bill in the Legislature

Writ-petition cannot be filed to seek introduction of Bill for Rajasthani language being included in the Eighth Schedule; *Kanhaiya Lal Sethia* v. *Union of India*, AIR 1998 SC 365: 1997 AIR SCW 4348: JT 1997 (7) SC 289: 1997 (3) SCJ 224: (1997) 5 SCALE 341: 1997 (7) Supreme 127: 1997 UJ (SC) 457: (1997) 6 SCC 573.

Laches

Laches or unreasonable delay in instituting writ petition may bar the remedy; *Trilok Chand* v. *Munshi*, AIR 1970 SC 898: (1969) 1 SCC 110: (1969) 2 SCR 824; *Ramchandra Shankar Deodhar* v. *State of Maharashtra*, AIR 1974 SC 259 (265): 1974 Lab IC 165: 1974 SCC (Lab) 137: (1974) 1 SCC 317: (1974) 1 LLJ 221: (1974) 2 SCR 216.

Unexplained delay may entail refusal to issue a writ; *Bhaskar* v. *State of Andhra Pradesh*, (1993) 24 ATC 842.

But delay is no bar to *quo warranto*; *Dr. Kashinath G. Jalmi* v. *Speaker*, (1993) 2 SCC 703: AIR 1993 SC 1873: 1993 AIR SCW 1578: JT 1993 (3) SC 594: (1993) 2 SCR 820: 1993 (2) UJ (SC) 113, paragraphs 34-36.

Where the Government in view of the policy decision to construct dam (Sardar Sarovar Project) on river Narmada, had granted the environment clearance after conducting studies, the petition opposing the construction of dam filed by way of public interest litigation after commencement of execution of project would be barred by laches; *Narmada Bachao Andolan* v. *Union of India*, AIR 2000 SC 3751: (2000) 10 SCC 664: 2000 AIR SCW 4809: 2001 (1) Guj LR 434: JT 2000 (2) SC (Supp) 6: 2000 (4) LRI 696: 2000 (4) SCJ 261: (2000) 7 SCALE 34.

Recently refusal for delay has been described as a rule of practice; *Dehri Rohtas Light Railway Company Limited* v. *District Board, Bhojpur*, (1992) 2 SCC 598: AIR 1993 SC 802: 1992 AIR SCW 3181: 1992 (2) All CJ 825: 1993 (2) BLJ 300: JT 1992 (3) SC 573: (1992) 2 SCR 155: 1992 (2) UJ (SC) 26.

Law Making Power

Court can not issue direction for making of law or subordinate legislation; *S.C. Employees Association* v. *Union of India*, (1989) 4 SCC 187: AIR 1990 SC 334: (1989) 2 LLJ 506.

Legislation on Personal Law

Writ petition is not maintainable to challenge legislation on personal law, where policy matters are involved; *Ahmedabad Women Action Group (AWAG)* v. *Union of India*, (1997) 3 SCC 573: AIR 1997 SC 3614: 1997 AIR SCW 1620: JT 1997 (3) SC 171: 1997 (3) SCJ 107: (1997) 2 SCR 389: (1997) 2 SCALE 381: 1997 (2) Supreme 670: 1997 (1) UJ (SC) 548.

Limits of Writ Jurisdiction

There must be a clear breach of fundamental right not involving disputed questions of fact; *Northern Corporation* v. *Union of India*, (1990) 4 SCC 239: AIR 1991 SC 764: (1990) 49 ELT 332.

Non-justifiable and political matters cannot be dealt with under the guise of public interest litigation; *Maharishi* v. *State of Uttar Pradesh*, AIR 1990 All 52, paragraph 18.

Policy preferences not involving fundamental rights cannot be agitated under article 32 "Articles of the Constitution cannot be a means to indicate policy preference"; *Hindi Hitarakshak Samiti* v. *Union of India*, (1990) 1 SCJ 617: AIR 1990 SC 851 (853, 856): (1990) 2 SCC 352: (1990) 4 SLR 4, paragraphs 6-7.

Government policy cannot be enforced by writ under article 32; *Hindi Hitarakshak Samiti* v. *Union of India*, AIR 1990 SC 851: (1990) 2 SCC 352: (1990) 4 SLR 4.

A directive principle cannot be enforced by writ under article 32; *B. Krishna Bhat* v. *Union of India*, (1990) 3 SCC 65.

A question that can be agitated under the Industrial Disputes Act, 1947 will not be normally allowed to be agitated under article 32; *Food Corporation of India Workers Union* v. *Food Corporation of India*, (1990) Supp SCC 296: AIR 1990 SC 2178: (1990) 2 LLN 664, paragraph 11.

Locus Standi

Any person complaining of infraction of any fundamental right guaranteed by the Constitution is at liberty to move to the Supreme Court but the rights that could be invoked under article 32 must ordinarily be the rights of the person who complains of the infraction of such rights and approaches the court for relief and the proper subject for investigation would however be as to the nature of the rights that is stated to have been infringed; *Narinderjit Singh Sahni* v. *Union of India*, (2002) 2 SCC 210: AIR 2001 SC 3810: 2001 AIR SCW 4249: JT 2001 (8) SC 477: 2001 (5) SCJ 107: 2001 (10) SRJ 318: 2002 SC Cr R 770: (2001) 7 SCALE 189: 2001 (7) Supreme 593: 2002 (1) UJ (SC) 178.

Locus standi to file a particular petition under article 32 depends on the facts as they existed at the time when the petition was filed; *T.N. Rugmani* v. *C. Achutha Menon*, AIR 1991 SC 983: (1991) Supp 1 SCC 520: JT 1991 (1) SC 265: 1991 (1) UJ (SC) 422.

Misuse of PIL

The prevention petition by a practising lawyer challenging the appointment of Advocate-General on ground that appointee was beyond 62 years of age amounts to misuse of PIL as law in this respect is already settled; *State of Uttaranchal* v. *Balwant Singh Chaufal*, AIR 2010 SC 2550.

Mandamus

(a) *Mandamus* should be issued under article 32 where a fundamental right is infringed by a statute.

(b) statutory order.

(c) executive order (non-statutory); *Prabodh Verma* v. *State of Uttar Pradesh*, AIR 1985 SC 167: (1984) 4 SCC 251: 1984 All LJ 931: 1984 SCC Lab 704: 1984 UPSC 576: 1984 UPLBEC 771: 1985 Cur Civ LJ (SC) 128: (1985) 1 SCR 216, paragraphs 38 and 50; *Abdul Hakim* v. *State of Bihar*, (1961) SCR 610: AIR 1961 SC 448: (1961) 1 Cr LJ 573. However, according to some decisions, it is discretionary; *Dr. Pramod Kumar Joshi* v. *Medical Council of India*, (1991) 1 UJ SC 400: (1991) 2 SCC 179: 1991 AIR SCW 744.

Natural Justice

It is not always necessary for the court to strike down an order merely because the order has been passed against the petitioner in breach of natural justice. The court can under article 32 or article 226 refuse to exercise its discretion of striking down the order if such striking down will result in restoration of another order passed earlier in favour of the petitioner and against the opposite party, in violation of principles of natural justice or is otherwise not in accordance with law; *M.C. Mehta* v. *Union of India*, AIR 1999 SC 2583: (1999) 6 SCC 237: 1999 AIR SCW 2754: 1999 (3) Comp LJ 371 SC: JT 1999 (5) SC 114: 1999 (4) LRI 140: 1999 (8) SRJ 255: (1999) 4 SCALE 267: 1999 (6) Supreme 265: 1999 (2) UJ (SC) 1254.

PIL

Public Interest Litigation cannot be entertained where stand taken was contrary to stand taken by those who are affected by any action; *Rameshwar Prasad* v. *Union of India*, AIR 2006 SC 980: 2006 AIR SCW 494: 2006 (3) CTC 209: (2006) 2 SCC 1: 2006 (1) SCJ 477: 2006 (3) SRJ 399: (2006) 1 SCALE 385: 2006 (1) Supreme 393.

Pleadings

Court will not give relief if the pleadings are not specific; *Arti* v. *State of Jammu & Kashmir*, AIR 1981 SC 1009: (1981) 2 SCC 484: (1981) 3 SCR 34; *Sharma* v. *Union of India*, AIR 1981 SC 588: (1981) 1 SCC 397: (1981) 1 SCR 1184.

Policy of Government

Court cannot—

(a) *enforce* implementation of a Government policy unless fundamental right is involved; *Hindi Hitrakshak Samiti* v. *Union of India*, AIR 1990 SC 851: (1990) 2 SCC 352: (1990) 4 SLR 4.

(b) *interfere* in the implementation of Government policy; *English M.S.I.A.* v. *State of Karnataka*, (1994) UJSC 291: (1994) 1 SCC 550: AIR 1994 SC 1702, paragraph 23.

Political Question

Where a fundamental right is involved the doctrine of non-justifiability of political question has no application; *Indra Sawhney* v. *Union of India*, (1992) Supp 3 SCC 217: 1992 SCC (L&S) Supp 1: AIR 1993 SC 477: (1992) 22 ATC 385, paragraphs 557-559 (9 Judges); *Supreme Court Advocates-on-Record Association* v. *Union of India*, (1993) 4 SCC 441: AIR 1994 SC 268: 1993 AIR SCW 4101: JT 1993 (5) SC 479: 1993 (5) Serv LR 337, paragraphs 273 and 328 (9 Judges).

Pollution

Directions can be issued to control pollution; *Subhash Kumar* v. *State of Bihar*, AIR 1991 SC 420: (1991) 1 SCC 598: 1991 AIR SCW 121: 1991 (1) Civ LJ 719: JT 1991 (1) SC 77: (1991) 1 SCR 5: 1991 (1) UJ (SC) 533, paragraph 7.

Price Fixation

Price fixation is not within the province of the court. Judicial review is exhausted when there is found to be a rational basis for the conclusions reached by the concerned authority. *See* the undermentioned decisions:

(i) *Union of India* v. *Cynamide India Ltd.*, AIR 1987 SC 1802 (1807): (1987) 2 SCC 720 (736): JT 1987 (3) SC 107: (1987) 2 Comp LJ 10: (1987) 12 ECR 199: (1987) 2 UJ (SC) 198.

(ii) *Gupta Sugar Works* v. *State of Uttar Pradesh*, AIR 1987 SC 2351: (1987) Supp SCC 476 (481): JT 1987 (5) SC 154.

(iii) *Shri Sita Ram Sugar Co. Ltd.* v. *Union of India*, AIR 1990 SC 1277 (1297): (1990) 3 SCC 223: JT 1990 (1) SC 462, paragraphs 8 and 58.

Prostitutes' Children

Segregating children of prostitutes by locating separate schools and providing separate hostels, would not be in the interest of such children. Once children are born to prostitutes, it is in the interest of such children and of society at large, that the children of prostitutes should not be segregated from their mothers and be allowed to mingle with others and become part of the society; *Gaurav Jain* v. *Union of India*, AIR 1990 SC 292: 1990 Supp SCC 709 (Ranganath Misra, M.N. Venkatachaliah and P.B. Sawant, JJ.).

Public Interest Litigation

The development of public interest litigation during the last decade has largely modified the traditional rule as to standing to litigate in constitutional matters. The following decisions may be particularly seen in this context:—

(i) *Ratlam Municipality* v. *Vardichan*, AIR 1980 SC 1622: (1980) 4 SCC 162: 1980 Cr LJ 1075.

(ii) *Fertiliser Corporation of India* v. *Union of India*, AIR 1981 SC 344: (1981) 1 SCC 568: (1981) SCR 52, paragraphs 43, 44 and 48.

(iii) *Sheela Barse* v. *Union of India*, AIR 1986 SC 1773: (1986) 3 SCC 596: 1986 All LJ 1369: 1986 Cr LJ 1736: 1986 SCC (Cri) 337: JT 1986 (53) SC 136: 1986 BBCJ (SC) 116: 1986 Cur Cr J (SC) 249, paragraphs 8 and 9.

(iv) *D.S. Nakara* v. *Union of India*, AIR 1983 SC 130: (1983) 1 SCC 305: (1983) 1 LLJ 104, paragraph 64.

(v) *Dr. D.C. Wadhwa* v. *State of Bihar*, AIR 1987 SC 579: (1987) 1 SCC 378: JT 1987 (1) SC 70: 1986 (4) Supreme 465: 1987 BBCJ (SC) 46: 1987 IJR 116, paragraph 3.

(vi) *Sachidanand Pandey* v. *State of West Bengal*, AIR 1987 SC 1109: (1987) 2 SCC 295: (1987) 1 Comp LJ 211: JT 1987 (1) SC 425: 1987 (2) SCJ 70: 1987 (1) Supreme 492: (1987) 1 UJ (SC) 641, paragraph 60.

(vii) *M.C. Mehta* v. *Union of India*, (1987) 1 SCC 395: AIR 1987 SC 1086: 1987 SCC (L&S) 37.

A public interest litigation may be transferred to the appropriate High Court; *Kasturi Lal Ralia Ram Jain* v. *State of Uttar Pradesh*, AIR 1965 SC 1039: (1965) 1 SCR 375: ILR (1965) 2 Mad LJ (SC) 15: 1965 (2) SCJ 318: (1965) 1 SCWR 995: (1965) 1 SCA 809: (1965) 2 Cr LJ 144: 1966 SCD 383: (1966) 2 LLJ 583.

A petition in public interest litigation filed before the Supreme Court may be transferred to the appropriate High Court; *Subramaniam* v. *Union of India*, (1990) Supp SCC 775.

A letter in public interest litigation should be addressed to the court and not to an individual judge; *Sachdev* v. *Union of India*, (1991) 1 SCC 605: AIR 1991 SC 311: 1991 Cr LJ 392, paragraph 1.

Relief

There is no theoretical limit to the relief to be granted. Court gave direction for insurance of workers in match factories; *M.C. Mehta* v. *State of Tamil Nadu*, AIR 1991 SC 417: (1991) 1 SCC 283: 1991 Lab IC 231: 1991 AIR SCW 60: JT 1990 (4) SC 263: 1991 (1) LLN 19: 1991 (1) Mad LJ 44: 1991 SCC (L&S) 299: 1990 (6) Serv LR 51: 1991 (1) UJ (SC) 169.

Where two persons were detained by the Punjab police and political rivalry was alleged, the Supreme Court directed the District Judge, Ludhiana to conduct an inquiry; *Tirath Ram Saini* v. *State of Punjab*, JT 1994 (1) SC 420: (1994) Supp 2 SCC 16: 1994 SCC (Cri) 675.

Relief given up in the High Court may be disallowed under article 32; *Bhattacharya* v. *Union of India*, AIR 1991 SC 468: (1991) Supp 2 SCC 109: (1991) 17 ATC 355, paragraph 6.

Court may refuse relief to a person who has voluntarily accepted benefit under a challenged statute and files the challenge after considerable lapse of time; *Pramod Kumar Joshi* v. *Medical Council of India*, (1991) 1 UJ SC 400: (1991) 2 SCC 179.

Even where the court does not grant relief as prayed for on the merits, it may give orders to do justice to petitioner who might otherwise suffer by reason of delay in granting interim relief; *Prem Chand Somchand Shah* v. *Union of India*, (1991) UJ (SC) 690 paragraph 19.

Res Judicata

If the petition is dismissed *in limine* without passing a speaking order then such dismissal cannot be treated as creating a ban of *res judicata*. It is true that, *prima facie*, dismissal *in limine* even without passing a speaking order in that behalf may strongly suggest that the court took the view that there was no substance in the petition at all; but in the absence of speaking order it would not be easy to decide what factors weighed in the mind of the court and that makes it difficult and unsafe to hold that such a summary dismissal is a dismissal on merits and as such constitutes a ban of *res judicata* against a similar petition filed under Art. 32. If the petition is dismissed as withdrawn it cannot be ban to a subsequent petition under Art. 32, because in such a case there has been no decision on the merits by the court; *Daryao* v. *State of Uttar Pradesh*, AIR 1961 SC 1457: (1962) 1 SCR 574: (1961) 2 SCA 591: 1962 (1) SCJ 702: (1962) 2 Andh WR (SC) 16: (1962) 2 MLJ (SC) 16.

Res judicata applies in writ petitions generally (though not in public interest litigation); *Grih Kalyan Kendra Workers' Union* v. *Union of India*, (1991) 1 SCC 619: AIR 1991 SC 1173: (1991) 1 LLJ 349, paragraph 11; *Rural Litigation and Entitlement Kendra* v. *State of Uttar Pradesh*, AIR 1989 SC 594: (1989) Supp 1 SCC 537: JT 1988 (4) SC 710.

Scope of Article 32

Only fundamental rights falling within category (a) above can be enforced under article 32. Cases illustrating this proposition about the scope of article 32 are the following:—

   (i) *Haji Esmail Noor Mohammad and Co.* v. *Competent Officer, Lucknow*, AIR 1967 SC 1244: (1967) 3 SCR 134: (1967) 1 SCA 497.

   (ii) *Kuriakose* v. *State of Kerala*, AIR 1977 SC 1509: (1977) 2 SCC 728: (1977) 2 LLJ 13.

Supreme Court cannot determine an issue not involving fundamental right; *Indian Express Newspapers* v. *Union of India*, (1986) 1 SCC 641, paragraphs 200 and 207.

Supreme Court cannot go into and examine the 'need' of Prevention of Terrorism Act, 2002 (POTA). It is a matter of policy. Once legislation is passed the Government has an obligation to exercise all available options to prevent terrorism within the bounds of the Constitution; *People's Union for Civil Liberties* v. *Union of India*, AIR 2004 SC 456: 2003 AIR SCW 7233: 2004 (1) CTC 241: (2004) 9 SCC 580: (2003) 10 SCALE 967: 2005 SCC (Cri) 1905: 2003 (8) Supreme 756.

Service Matters

Where the petitioner's fundamental rights are impaired by legislation or rules, or Government orders, the court can interfere even if it is a matter concerning service; *Food Corporation of India Workers* v. *Food Corporation of India*, AIR 1990 SC 2178: 1990 Supp SCC 296: (1990) 4 SCR 745.

Similarly, the court may interfere where the fundamental rights of a public sector employee are infringed; *Bhagwati* v. *D.S.M.D.C.*, (1990) 1 SCJ 433: (1990) 1 SCC 361: AIR 1990 SC 371, paragraph 6.

Denial of equal pay for equal work becomes irrational classification for the purposes of article 14; *Grih Kalyan Kendra Workers' Union* v. *Union of India*, (1991) 1 SCC 619: AIR 1991 SC 1173: (1991) 1 LLJ 349, paragraph 6.

If the fundamental rights of a member of the Armed Forces are violated or if there is a jurisdictional error, judicial review is available; *S.M. Mukherjee* v. *Union of India*, AIR 1990 SC 1984: (1990) 4 SCC 594: 1990 Cr LJ 2148.

However, if *mala fides* are alleged, there must be proper pleading; *Suresh* v. *Defence Secretary*, AIR 1991 SC 483: (1991) 2 SCC 198: (1991) 16 ATC 486.

Direction under article 32 would not be issued to the opposite party to regulate the services of the petitioner in the post of helper where petitioner does not approve the Commission set up for the purpose; *A. Hansavani* v. *State of Tamil Nadu*, JT 1994 (4) SC 651.

For violation of fundamental right (this includes observance of natural justice) in service matters writ is available under article 32. This is illustrated by violation of article from—

(a) unconstitutional statute—*Nityanandakar* v. *State of Orissa*, AIR 1991 SC 1134: (1991) Supp 2 SCC 516: 1991 Lab IC 782, paragraph 13.

(b) Rule or order—*Food Corporation of India Workers Union* v. *Food Corporation of India*, AIR 1990 SC 2178: 1990 Supp SCC 296: (1990) 4 SLR 745, paragraphs 18-20.

(c) arbitrary, perverse or *mala fide* decision; *G.P. Doval* v. *Chief Secretary, Govt. of U.P.*, AIR 1984 SC 1527: (1984) 4 SCC 329: 1984 Lab IC 1304: (1984) 2 Serv LJ 166: (1984) 2 LLN 517; *V.T. Khanzode* v. *R.B.I.*, AIR 1982 SC 917: (1982) 2 SCC 7: (1982) 1 LLJ 465. (Public Sector Corporation).

A candidate who has been illegally denied selection can approach, the court for quashing the selection and issuing directions for selection, but court cannot be evaluator of the fitness; *I.A.C.* v. *Shukla*, (1993) 23 ATC 407 (SC): (1993) 1 SCC 17: (1993) 1 LLJ 215, paragraph 9.

Sovereign Power of Legislature

Court cannot direct legislature to make particular enactment; *Suresh Seth* v. *Commissioner, Indore Municipal Corporation*, AIR 2006 SC 767: 2005 AIR SCW 6380: JT 2005 (9) SC 210: (2005) 13 SCC 287: 2005 (7) SCJ 629: 2005 (9) SRJ 473: (2005) 8 SCALE 514: 2005 (7) Supreme 134.

Stock Exchange

Increase in the number or members of the Delhi Stock Exchange is a matter of policy. Court would not issue a mandate in such matters; *Om Prakash Poplai* v. *Delhi Stock Exchange Association*, JT 1994 (1) SC 114: (1994) 2 SCC 117: (1994) 79 Comp Cas 756.

Supreme Court and High Court: Concurrent Jurisdiction

(a) On the text of articles 32 and 226, where a fundamental right is involved, a party should be free to approach either of the two courts. And this, in fact, has been the earlier judicial approach; *M.K. Gopalan* v. *State of Madhya Pradesh*, (1955) 1 SCR 168 (174): AIR 1954 SC 362: 1954 Cr LJ 1012: 1954 SCA 557: 1954 SCJ 534: (1954) 2 Mad LJ 76: 1954 All WR (HC) 392. In fact, some decisions have pointed out that since the remedy under article 32(1) is itself a fundamental right, the Supreme Court is under duty to grant relief for violation of a substantive fundamental right. *See* the undermentioned cases:

(i) *Kochunni* v. *State of Madras*, AIR 1959 SC 725 (729): (1959) Supp 2 SCR 316: 1959 Ker LJ 464.

(ii) *Tata Iron & Steel Co.* v. *Sarkar*, AIR 1961 SC 65: (1961) 1 SCR 379: (1960) 11 STC 655.

(iii) *Bishan Das* v. *State of Punjab*, AIR 1961 SC 1570: (1962) 2 SCR 69: 1963 (1) SCJ 405.

(iv) *Kharak Singh* v. *State of Uttar Pradesh*, AIR 1963 SC 1295: (1964) 1 SCR 332 (1963) 2 Cr LJ 329.

Even still stronger are decisions holding article 32 to be a basic feature of the Constitution which cannot be taken away by even amending the Constitution; *Fertiliser Corporation of India* v. *Union of India*, AIR 1981 SC 344: (1981) 1 SCC 568: (1981) 2 SCR 52, paragraph 11.

(b) Notwithstanding the above position, the Supreme Court has, in the following decisions stated that where relief through High Court is available under article 226, the party should first approach the High Court:—

(i) *P.N. Kumar* v. *Municipal Corporation of Delhi*, (1987) 4 SCC 609 (610, 611): 1988 SCC (L&S) 80.

(ii) *Kanubhai Brahmbhatt* v. *State of Gujarat*, AIR 1987 SC 1159: (1989) Supp 2 SCC 310: (1987) 2 SCR 314.

It is submitted with great respect that this view goes against the intendment of the Constitution and is contrary to earlier case law.

Variety of Other Rights

Right given by law or recognized by law can be analysed into the following categories:—

(a) fundamental rights given by the Constitution;

(b) constitutional rights not having the status of fundamental rights;

(c) statutory rights;

(d) rights flowing from subordinate legislation;

(e) rights based on case law;

(f) customary rights;

(g) contractual rights.

Writ Jurisdiction

The directions for investigation cannot be given by Supreme Court in exercise of writ jurisdiction where statutory remedies are available; *Kunga Nima Lepcha* v. *State of Sikkim*, AIR 2010 SC 1671.

Writ Petition

The writ petition under article 32 against the contravention of article 351 is not maintainable; *Aashirwad Films* v. *Union of India*, (2007) 6 SCC 624: 2007 AIR SCW 3603.

Writ Petition by Workers in Winding up Proceedings

The Supreme Court had entertained a writ petition with the object of rival of an undertaking and rehabilitation of workers. In spite of the best efforts, revival was not feasible. The court then directed resumption of winding up proceedings; *Workers of M/s. Rohtas Industries* v. *Rohtas Industries*, AIR 1996 SC 467: (1995) Supp 4 SCC 5: 1996 SCC (L&S) 125 (paragraphs 15, 17, 19).

Writ Petition to Determine Age of Chief Justice of India

Writ petition filed under article 32 to determine the age of Chief Justice of India (Dr. Justice A.S. Anand) by declaring that he was born on 1-11-1934 and then declare that he had attained the age of superannuation on 31-10-1999. President of India already had determined relating to age of Chief Justice of India in 1991 which has attained finality. Supreme Court has held that the writ petition filed by the petitioner is an abuse of the process of the Court. Apart from the non-disclosure of what fundamental right of the petitioner has been infringed or to be enforced by the writ petition, it is a reckless action to malign and scandalise the highest judicial institution of this country; *Madras High Court Advocates' Association* v. *Dr. A.S. Anand, Hon'ble Chief Justice of India*, AIR 2001 SC 970: (2001) 3 SCC 19: 2001 SCC (Cri) 422.

[1][**32A. Constitutional validity of State laws not to be considered in proceedings under article 32.**—[*Rep. by the Constitution (Forty-third Amendment) Act, 1977, sec. 3 (w.e.f. 13-4-1978).*]]

[2][**33. Power of Parliament to modify the rights conferred by this Part in their application to Forces, etc.**—Parliament may, by law, determine to what extent any of the rights conferred by this Part shall, in their application to,—

(a) the members of the Armed Forces; or

(b) the members of the Forces charged with the maintenance of public order; or

(c) persons employed in any bureau or other organisation established by the State for purposes of intelligence or counter intelligence; or

(d) persons employed in, or in connection with, the telecommunication systems set up for the purposes of any Force, bureau or organisation referred to in clauses (a) to (c),

be restricted or abrogated so as to ensure the proper discharge of their duties and the maintenance of discipline among them.]

---

1. Article 32A was earlier inserted by the Constitution (Forty-second Amendment) Act, 1976, sec. 6 (w.e.f. 1-2-1977).

2. Subs. by the Constitution (Fiftieth Amendment) Act, 1984, sec. 2, for article 33 (w.e.f. 11-9-1984).

Notes on Article 33

Effect

The article empowers Parliament to restrict or abrogate the application of fundamental rights in relation to armed forces, para military forces, the police *etc.*; *Achudan* v. *Union of India*, 1976 1 SCWR 80: (1976) 2 SCC 780: AIR 1976 SC 1179: (1976) 2 SCR 769; *Gopal* v. *Union of India*, AIR 1987 SC 413: 1986 Supp SCC 501: (1987) 2 ATC 495.

The article does not, itself, abrogate any rights; *Chatterji* v. *Sub Area Commandant*, AIR 1951 Mad 77. Its operation is dependent on Parliamentary legislation. Of course, such legislation need not refer to article 33 in so many words; *Ram Sarup* v. *Union of India*, AIR 1965 SC 247 (251): (1964) 5 SCR 931: (1965) 1 Cr LJ 236. A law passed by virtue of article 33 can override articles 21 and 22; *Prithi Pal Singh Bedi (Lt. Col.)* v. *Union of India*, AIR 1982 SC 1413: (1982) 3 SCC 140: 1982 SCC (Cri) 642, paragraphs 13-18. Parliament may empower Government to impose restrictions: *Viswan* v. *Union of India*, AIR 1983 SC 658: (1983) 3 SCC 401: (1983) 2 LLJ 157 paragraphs 7, 9 and 10.

Parliamentary Legislation and Fundamental Rights

Such legislation may restrict the operation of any fundamental right, such as,—

(a) equality; *Jesuratnam* v. *Chief of Air Staff*, (1976) Cr LJ 65.

(b) freedom of expression; *Lt. Col. Prithi Pal Singh Bedi* v. *Union of India*, AIR 1982 SC 1413: (1982) 3 SCC 140: 1982 UJ (SC) 695: (1982) 2 Serv LJ 582.

(c) freedom of association; *Achudan* v. *Union of India*, (1976) 1 SCWR 80: (1976) 2 SCC 780: AIR 1976 SC 1179.

(d) personal liberty; *Lt. Col. Prithi Pal Singh Bedi* v. *Union of India*, AIR 1982 SC 1413: (1982) 3 SCC 140: 1982 UJ (SC) 695: (1982) 2 Serv LJ 582.

Police Forces (Restriction of Rights) Act, 1966

Validity of the Police Forces (Restriction of Rights) Act, 1966 has been upheld, as a valid exercise of Parliament's power under that part of article 33 which applies to armed forces; *Delhi Police Sangh* v. *Union of India*, AIR 1987 SC 379: (1987) 1 SCC 115: (1987) 2 ATC 194.

Scope

Article 33 (which was extensively amended in 1984) enables Parliament to modify fundamental rights in relation to military and para-military forces, police forces and analogous forces. The reaction can be only by law. The undermentioned decisions illustrate the wide scope of this article:

(i) *Achudan* v. *Union of India*, (1976) 1 SCWR 80: (1976) 2 SCC 780: AIR 1976 SC 1179 (Right of association).

(ii) *Ram Sarup* v. *Union of India*, AIR 1965 SC 247: (1964) 5 SCR 931: 1964 Cur LJ (SC) 169: 1964 SCD 661: 1964 (2) SCJ 619: 1964 Mad LJ (Cri) 626: (1965) 1 Cr LJ 236 (General scope).

(iii) *Delhi Police Sangh* v. *Union of India*, (1987) 2 ATC 194: AIR 1987 SC 379: (1987) 1 SCC 115 (122, 124) (De-recognition of Employees Union).

The decision in *Delhi Police Non-Gazetted Karmchari Sangh* v. *Union of India*, AIR 1987 SC 379: (1987) 1 SCC 115: JT 1986 SC 920: 1987 (1) Supreme 9: (1987) 1 Serv LJ 213 (SC): (1987) 1 LLJ 121 (SC): (1987) 1 UJ (SC) 234: (1987) 1 Cur LR 344: 1987 (1) SCJ 144, is concerned with the Police Forces (Restriction of Rights) Act, 1966 and rules framed thereunder. The rules cannot be challenged on the ground of violation of article 19(1)(c), because of article 33.

Writs against Courts Martial

Articles 136(2) and 227(4) exclude the appellate jurisdiction of the Supreme Court and the supervisory jurisdiction of the High Court in relation to court martial. But they do not exclude the operation of articles 32 and 226. Hence, unless the substantive fundamental right itself has been excluded by a law made under article 33, the right services and consequentially the remedy of writ also survives. Hence the general principles for grant of relief in writ and grounds for interference, as generally applicable to quasi-judicial proceedings, apply in relation to courts martial also. Accordingly, case law furnishes illustrations of judicial review of proceedings of courts martial on the basis of—

(i) bias; *Ranjit Thakur* v. *Union of India,* AIR 1987 SC 2386: (1987) 4 SCC 611: 1988 SCC (L&S) 1.

(ii) other breaches of natural justice; *Laxmi* v. *Union of India,* (1991) 2 SCJ 86.

(iii) error of jurisdiction or error of law apparent on the face of the record; *S.N. Mukherjee* v. *Union of India,* (1990) 3 SCJ 193: (1990) 4 SCC 594: AIR 1990 SC 1984; *Ranvir* v. *Union of India,* (1991) Cr LJ 1791 (Bom).

The Supreme Court may interfere if the sentence imposed by the courts martial is disproportionate to the crime; *Ranjit Thakur* v. *Union of India,* AIR 1987 SC 2386: (1987) 4 SCC 611: 1988 SCC (L&S) 1.

Supreme Court will not enter into—

(a) questions of fact which are disputed; *Sodhi* v. *Union of India,* AIR 1991 SC 1617: (1991) 2 SCC 382: 1991 Cr LJ 1947.

(b) irregularities not causing injustice; *Bhagat* v. *State of Himachal Pradesh,* AIR 1983 SC 454 (460): (1983) 2 SCC 442: (1983) 2 LLJ 1.

34. Restriction on rights conferred by this Part while martial law is in force in any area.—Notwithstanding anything in the foregoing provisions of this Part, Parliament may by law indemnify any person in the service of the Union or of a State or any other person in respect of any act done by him in connection with the maintenance or restoration of order in any area within the territory of India where martial law was in force or validate any sentence passed, punishment inflicted, forfeiture ordered or other act done under martial law in such area.

Notes on Article 34

Article 34 is primarily concerned with granting indemnity by law in respect of acts done during operation of martial law. The Constitution does not have a provision authorising proclamation of martial law. Declaration of martial law does not *ipso facto* result in suspension of the writ of *habeas corpus*; *A.D.M. Jabalpur* v. *Shukla,* AIR 1976 SC 1207: (1976) 2 SCC 521: 1976 Cr LJ 945, paragraph 535.

35. Legislation to give effect to the provisions of this Part.—Notwithstanding anything in this Constitution,—

(a) Parliament shall have, and the Legislature of a State shall not have, power to make laws—

(i) with respect to any of the matters which under clause (3) of article 16, clause (3) of article 32, article 33 and article 34 may be provided for by law made by Parliament; and

(ii) for prescribing punishment for those acts which are declared to be offences under this Part,

and Parliament shall, as soon as may be after the commencement of this Constitution, make laws for prescribing punishment for the acts referred to in sub-clause (ii);

(b) any law in force immediately before the commencement of this Constitution in the territory of India with respect to any of the matters referred to in sub-clause (i) of clause (a) or providing for punishment for any act referred to in sub-clause (ii) of that clause shall, subject to the terms thereof and to any adaptations and modifications that may be made therein under article 372, continue in force until altered or repealed or amended by Parliament.

Explanation.—In this article, the expression "law in force" has the same meaning as in article 372.

Notes on Article 35

Article 35 and Jammu and Kashmir Constitution

The introduction of provision contained in article 35(c), when applying to the Constitution to State of Jammu and Kashmir, does not in any way affect the right of citizen of Jammu and Kashmir; *Abdul Ghani* v. *State of Jammu and Kashmir*, AIR 1971 SC 1217: (1971) 3 SCR 275; See also *Sampat Prakash* v. *State of Jammu and Kashmir*, AIR 1970 SC 1118: (1969) 2 SCR 365: 1970 Lab IC 873.

Public Safety: Preventive Detention

Section 8 of Jammu and Kashmir Preventive Detention Act is not in excess of or inconsistent with the provisions of clause (c) added to article 35 of Constitution by Constitution (Application to Jammu and Kashmir) Order, 1954; *P.L. Lakhanpal* v. *State of Jammu and Kashmir*, AIR 1956 SC 197: 1956 Cr LJ 421(2): 1956 SCJ 236: 1956 SCA 706: (1955) 2 SCR 1101.

PART IV

DIRECTIVE PRINCIPLES OF STATE POLICY

36. Definition.—In this Part, unless the context otherwise requires, "the State" has the same meaning as in Part III.

Notes on Article 36

State

A statutory authority, cannot in absence of the provisions of a statute, be treated to be an agency of the State. It is one thing to say that the State exercises statutory control over the functions of a statute but it is another thing to say thereby an agency is created which would be separate in entity over which the State exercises control. Agency of a State would ordinarily mean an instrumentality of a State. It must be separate legal entity. A statutory authority does not answer the description of an agency under the control of the State; *Deewan Singh* v. *Rajendra Pd. Ardevi*, AIR 2007 SC 767.

37. Application of the principles contained in this Part.—The provisions contained in this Part shall not be enforceable by any court, but the principles therein laid down are nevertheless fundamental in the governance of the country and it shall be the duty of the State to apply these principles in making laws.

Notes on Article 37

Directive Principles and UN Convention

The directive principles have been described as forerunners of the U.N. Convention on Right to Development as an inalienable human right; *Air India Statutory Corporation* v. *United Labour Union*, AIR 1997 SC 645: (1997) 9 SCC 377: 1997 Lab IC 365 paragraph 38 (observations that they stand elevated to human rights).

Effect: The Positive Aspect

At the same time, the Directive Principles have, according to later decisions of the Supreme Court, a positive aspect. Thus, the Directives have been held to supplement fundamental rights in achieving a Welfare State. Parliament can amend fundamental rights for implementing the Directives, so long as the amendment does not touch the basic features. Legislation enacted to implement the Directive Principles should be upheld, as far as possible. In fact, when necessary, even constitutional provisions as to fundamental rights should be adjusted in their ambit so as to give effect to the Directive Principles. Even legislative entries may (within the limits of the total federal scheme) be given a wide interpretation for effecting Directive Principles. Constitutional provisions (apart from fundamental rights) may be construed in the light of Directive Principles. Undermentioned decisions illustrative the above propositions:

(i) *Chandra Bhawan Boarding and Lodging, Bangalore* v. *State of Mysore,* AIR 1970 SC 2042: (1969) 3 SCC 84: 19 Fac LR 325: 38 FJR 1: (1970) 2 Lab LJ 403: (1970) 2 SCR 600, paragraph 13.

(ii) *State of Kerala* v. *N.M. Thomas,* AIR 1976 SC 490: (1976) 2 SCC 310: (1976) 1 LLJ 376.

(iii) *Lingappa Pochanna Appealwar* v. *State of Maharashtra,* AIR 1985 SC 389: (1985) 1 SCC 479: (1985) 87 Bom LR 65: 1985 GOC (SC) 41: (1985) 2 SCR 224: 1985 Cur Civ LJ (SC) 387.

(iv) *Sri Manchegowda* v. *State of Karnataka,* AIR 1984 SC 1151: (1984) 3 SCC 301: (1984) 3 Kant LJ 1.

(v) *Chief Justice* v. *Dikshitulu,* (1979) 2 SCC 34: AIR 1979 SC 193: 1978 Lab IC 1672.

(vi) *Jalan Trading Co. (P) Ltd.* v. *D. M. Aney,* AIR 1979 SC 233: 1978 Lab IC 1772: (1979) 3 SCC 220

(vii) *Mukesh* v. *State of Madhya Pradesh,* AIR 1985 SC 537.

(viii) *Laxmi Kant* v. *Union of India,* AIR 1987 SC 232: (1987) 1 SCC 66: 1987 SCC (Cri) 33.

(ix) *Akhil Bharatiya Soshit Karamchari Sangh (Railway)* v. *Union of India,* AIR 1981 SC 298 (335): (1981) 1 SCC 246: 1980 Lab IC 1325: (1981) 1 LLJ 209: (1981) 1 LLN 27: 1981 SCC (Lab) 50: 1981 Serv LJ 734: (1981) 2 SCR 185.

Fundamental Rights under Article 37 and Validity of Constitution 42nd Amendment

Section 4 of the Constitution 42nd Amendment is void as it destroys the basic structure of Constitution.

Further the fundamental rights occupy a unique place in the lives of civilised societies and have been variously described in judgments of Supreme Court as "transdental", "inalienable" and 'primordial"; *Minerva Mills Ltd.* v. *Union of India,* AIR 1980 SC 1789: (1980) 3 SCC 625: 1980 Ker LT 573: 1980 UJ (SC) 727.

Harmony

Directive principles and fundamental rights are to be harmoniously construed; *Grih Kalyan Kendra Workers' Union* v. *Union of India,* (1991) 1 SCC 619: AIR 1991 SC 1173: 1991 AIR SCW 194: JT 1991 (1) SC 60: 1991 (1) LLJ 349: 1991 (1) LLN 319: 1991 SCC (L&S) 621: 1991 SCD 146: (1991) 1 SCR 15: 1991 (1) Serv LR 618: 1991 (1) UJ (SC) 468, paragraph 6; *Literate Association* v. *State of Karnataka,* (1990) 2 SCC 396: AIR 1990 SC 883: 1990 SCC (L&S) 274: 1990 Lab IC 625.

Scope and Object: The Negative Aspect

The object of Directive Principles is to embody the concept of a welfare State; *Keshavananda Bharati Sripadgalvaru* v. *State of Kerala,* (1973) 4 SCC 225: AIR 1973 SC 1461: 1973 Supp SCR 1 paragraphs 134, 139, 174. However, the Directives do not confer any enforceable rights and their alleged breach does not invalidate a law, not does it entitle a citizen to complain of its violation by the State so as to seek mandatory relief against the State. Similarly, if a legislative power does not exist in a particular legislature, then the legislature cannot seek to rely on a Directive Principle for claiming that power. Undermentioned decisions support the above propositions:

(i) *Kerala Education Bill (in re:),* AIR 1958 SC 956: 1959 SCR 995: (1958) Ker 1167.

(ii) *Deep Chand* v. *State of Uttar Pradesh,* AIR 1959 SC 648: (1959) Supp 2 SCR 8: 1959 SCA 377: 1959 SCJ 1069: ILR (1959) 1 All 293.

(iii) *State of Madras* v. *Champakam Dorairajan,* (1951) SCR 525: AIR 1951 SC 226: 1951 SCJ 313: 1951 KLT (SC) 41: (1951) 1 MLJ 621: 1951 MWN 470: 1951 ALJ (SC) 107.

(iv) *Fram Naserwanji* v. *State of Bombay,* AIR 1951 Bom 216.

(v) *U.P.S.E. Board* v. *Hari,* AIR 1979 SC 65: (1978) 4 SCC 16: (1978) 2 LLJ 399, paragraph 4A.

38. State to secure a social order for the promotion of welfare of the people.—
[1][(1)] The State shall strive to promote the welfare of the people by securing and protecting as effectively as it may a social order in which justice, social, economic and political, shall inform all the institutions of the national life.

[2][(2) The State shall, in particular, strive to minimise the inequalities in income, and endeavour to eliminate inequalities in status, facilities and opportunities, not only amongst individuals but also amongst groups of people residing in different areas or engaged in different vocations.]

Notes on Article 38

Equality before Law
  (i) The "equality before law" has many facets and is a dynamic concept. The law seeking to achieve the said purpose is to be interpreted not only on anvil of articles 14, 16 but also having regards to international laws; *Nair Service Society* v. *State of Kerala*, AIR 2007 SC 2891: 2007 AIR SCW 5276: 2007 (2) Guj LH 358: 2007 (2) Ker LT 77: (2007) 4 SCC 1: 2007 (2) SCT 259: (2007) 4 SCALE 106: 2007 (3) Supreme 598.
 (ii) Economic empowerment of weaker sections; *Charan Singh* v. *State of Punjab*, AIR 1997 SC 1052: 1997 AIR SCW 1050: 1997 (3) LJR 600: (1997) 1 SCC 151: 1997 (1) Supreme 23: 1997 (1) UJ (SC) 277.
(iii) Regularisation of daily wage workers; *Gujarat Agricultural University* v. *Rathod Labhu Bechar*, AIR 2001 SC 706: 2001 AIR SCW 351: JT 2001 (2) SC 16: (2001) 3 SCC 574: 2001 SCC (L&S) 613: 2001 (2) SCJ 46: 2001 (2) SCT 394: (2001) 1 SCALE 270: (2001) 1 Serv LR 519: 2001 (1) Supreme 239: 2001 (2) UJ (SC) 922.

Casual Labour
Where the casual workers who were rendering services similar to regular employees to government company for over a decade on daily wage basis for almost 10 years continuously discharging duties similar to those of regular employees of company then the company should frame scheme for absorption of casual labour as regular employees; *Hindustan Machine Tools* v. *M. Rangareddy*, AIR 2000 SC 3287: 2000 AIR SCW 3586: JT 2000 (1) SC (Supp) 267: (2000) 7 SCC 741: 2000 SCC (L&S) 1039: 2001 (1) SCT 267: (2000) 6 SCALE 614: 2000 (6) Supreme 535.

39. Certain principles of policy to be followed by the State.—The State shall, in particular, direct its policy towards securing—
  (a) that the citizens, men and women equally, have the right to an adequate means of livelihood;
  (b) that the ownership and control of the material resources of the community are so distributed as best to subserve the common good;
  (c) that the operation of the economic system does not result in the concentration of wealth and means of production to the common detriment;
  (d) that there is equal pay for equal work for both men and women;
  (e) that the health and strength of workers, men and women, and the tender age of children are not abused and that citizens are not forced by economic necessity to enter avocations unsuited to their age or strength;
[3][(f) that children are given opportunities and facilities to develop in a healthy manner and in conditions of freedom and dignity and that childhood and

---

  1. Article 38 renumbered as clause (1) thereof by the Constitution (Forty-fourth Amendment) Act, 1978, sec. 9 (w.e.f. 20-6-1979).
  2. Ins. by the Constitution (Forty-fourth Amendment) Act, 1978, sec. 9 (w.e.f. 20-6-1979).
  3. Subs. by the Constitution (Forty-second Amendment) Act, 1976, sec. 7, for clause (f) (w.e.f. 3-1-1977).

youth are protected against exploitation and against moral and material abandonment.]

Notes on Article 39

Child Labour: Employment of Parent

Provisions of articles 39(e), 39(f), 41 and 47 can be pressed into service to make suitable provisions regarding child labour.

Accordingly, the Supreme Court has issued directions to the State to see that an adult member of the family whose child is in employment in a factory, mine or hazardous employment gets employment anywhere, in lieu of the child; *M.C. Mehta* v. *State of Tamil Nadu*, AIR 1997 SC 699: (1996) 6 SCC 756: 1997 SCC (L&S) 49, paragraphs 29, 30, 31.

Equal Pay for Equal Work

Person employed on contract cannot claim equal pay on the basis of equal pay for equal work; *State of Haryana* v. *Charanjit Singh*, AIR 2006 SC 161: 2005 AIR SCW 5632: (2006) 9 SCC 321: 2005 (7) SCJ 536: 2006 (3) SCT 170: 2005 (9) SRJ 520: (2005) 8 SCALE 482: (2005) 6 Serv LR 693: 2005 (7) Supreme 193.

The doctrine of equal pay for equal work postulates equal pay for equal work for those who are equally placed in all respects, *Uttar Pradesh Sugar Corpn. Ltd.* v. *Sant Raj Singh*, AIR 2006 SC 2296: 2006 AIR SCW 3013: (2006) 9 SCC 82: 2006 (7) SCJ 30: 2006 (3) SCT 56: (2006) 6 SCALE 205: (2006) 4 Serv LR 788: 2006 (6) Supreme 174.

Denial of equal pay for equal work becomes irrational classification within article 14; *Grih Kalayan Kendra Workers' Union* v. *Union of India*, (1991) 1 SCC 619: AIR 1991 SC 1173: (1991) 1 LLJ 349 paragraph 6.

Difference in duties justifies difference in pay; *Hundraj Kanyalal Sajnani* v. *Union of India*, AIR 1990 SC 1106: 1990 Supp SCC 577: (1990) 2 SLR 400, paragraph 44.

Differences in duties justifies discrimination in pay; *Vasudevan* v. *Union of India*, AIR 1990 SC 2295: (1991) Supp 2 SCC 134: (1991) 2 LLJ 420, paragraphs 18-19.

Writ can be to enforce the principle of equal work if article 14 is infringed; *Food Corporation of India Union* v. *Food Corporation of India*, AIR 1990 SC 2178: 1990 Supp SCC 296: (1990) 4 SLR 745 paragraph 20; *See* undermentioned cases as to equal pay:

    (i) *Randhir* v. *Union of India*, AIR 1982 SC 879: (1982) 1 SCC 618: (1982) 1 LLJ 344.

    (ii) *Ramchandra* v. *Union of India*, AIR 1984 SC 541: (1984) 2 SCC 141: (1984) 1 LLJ 314, paragraph 17.

Also see *Dharwad District P.W.D. Literate Daily Wage Employees' Association* v. *State of Karnataka*, (1990) 2 SCC 396: AIR 1990 SC 883: 1990 Lab IC 625.

Whether a particular work is same or similar in nature to another work, can be determined on three considerations:

    (i) The Authority should take a broad view;

    (ii) In ascertaining whether any differences are of practical importance, the authority should take an equally broad approach, for the very concept of similar work implies differences in detail. These small deference however, should not defeat a claim of equality on trivial grounds;

    (iii) One should look at the duties actually performed, and not at those theoretically possible.

In making a comparison the Authority should look at the duties generally performed by men and women. Both men and women work at inconvenient times, there is no requirement that all those who work, *e.g.*, at night, shall be paid the same basic rate as those who work normal day shifts. Thus, a woman who works in a day cannot claim equality with a man at a higher basic rate for working nights if, in fact there are women working in nights at that rate too, and the applicant herself would be entitled to that rate if she changed the shifts; *Mackinnon Mackenzie & Co. Ltd.* v. *Audrey D. Costa*, AIR 1987 SC 1281: (1987) 2 SCC 469: (1987) 11 LJ 536.

See the undermentioned cases:

   (i) *Union of India* v. *Tejram Parashramji Bombhate,* AIR 1992 SC 570: (1991) 3 SCC 11: (1991) 2 LLJ 263, paragraphs 4-5.

  (ii) *State of Tamil Nadu* v. *M.R. Alagappan,* AIR 1997 SC 2006: (1997) 4 SCC 401: 1997 AIR SCW 1793: JT 1997 (4) SC 515: 1997 SCC (L&S) 1080: (1997) 3 SCR 717: 1997 (2) SCT 531: (1997) 3 SCALE 464: 1997 (2) Serv LR 554: 1997 (4) Supreme 67, paragraph 13.

 (iii) *State of Haryana* v. *Surinder Kumar,* AIR 1997 SC 2129: (1997) 3 SCC 633: 1997 Lab IC 2096, paragraph 5.

 (iv) *Garhwal Jal Sansthan* v. *State of Uttar Pradesh,* AIR 1997 SC 2143: (1997) 4 SCC 24: 1997 All LJ 1175, paragraph 10.

Object of Article 39A

This article has been described as having the object of securing a Welfare State and may be utilised for construing provisions as to fundamentals rights. *See* the undermentioned decisions:

   (i) *H.S. Srinivasa Raghavachar* v. *State of Karnataka,* AIR 1987 SC 1518: (1987) 2 SCC 692: JT 1987 (4) SC 26: ILR 1987 Kant 2059: 1987 (1) Supreme 642: 1987 (2) SCJ 611: (1987) 2 UJ (SC) 427: 1987 (2) Land LR 530.

  (ii) *Kesavananda Bharati Sripadgalvaru* v. *State of Kerala,* AIR 1973 SC 1461: (1973) 4 SCC 225: (1973) Supp SCR 1.

 (iii) *State of Tamil Nadu* v. *L. Abu Kavur Bai,* AIR 1984 SC 326: (1984) 1 SCC 515: (1984) 1 SCR 725.

 (iv) *Sanjeev Coke Manufacturing Company* v. *Bharat Cooking Coal,* AIR 1983 SC 239: (1983) 1 SCC 147: 1983 UJ (SC) 81: 1983 (1) SCJ 233: (1983) 1 SCR 1000.

Prices

A statutory corporation (even if it is not a public utility) must comply with article 39 and charge only fair prices; *Oil and Natural Gas Commission* v. *Association of Natural Gas Consuming Industries of Gujarat,* AIR 1990 SC 1851: 1990 Supp SCC 397: JT 1990 (2) SC 516, paragraphs 15 and 30.

[1][**39A. Equal justice and free legal aid.**—The State shall secure that the operation of the legal system promotes justice, on a basis of equal opportunity, and shall, in particular, provide free legal aid, by suitable legislation or schemes or in any other way, to ensure that opportunities for securing justice are not denied to any citizen by reason of economic or other disabilities.]

Notes on Article 39A

Legal Aid

An important impact of article 39A read with article 21 has been to reinforce the right of a person involved in a criminal proceeding to legal aid. The article has been thus used to interpret (and even expand) the right conferred by section 304 of the Code of Criminal Procedure, 1973; *See* the undermentioned cases:

   (i) *Hussainara* v. *Home Secretary, State of Bihar,* AIR 1979 SC 1369: (1980) 1 SCC 98: 1979 Cr LJ 1045.

  (ii) *M.H. Hoskot* v. *State of Maharashtra,* AIR 1978 SC 1548: (1978) 3 SCC 544: 1978 SCC (Cri) 468.

 (iii) *State of Haryana* v. *Smt. Darshana Devi,* AIR 1979 SC 855: (1979) 2 SCC 236: 1979 UJ (SC) 389: 1979 Raj LR 311: 1979 Rev LR 312: 1979 ACJ 205: 81 Punj LR 472: 1979 TAC 285.

 (iv) *Khatri (II)* v. *State of Bihar,* AIR 1981 SC 928: (1981) 1 SCC 627: 1981 SCC (Cri) 228.

  (v) *Sukh Das* v. *Union Territory,* AIR 1986 SC 991: (1986) 2 SCC 401: 1986 Cr LJ 1084.

---

1. Ins. by the Constitution (Forty-second Amendment) Act, 1976, sec. 8 (w.e.f. 3-1-1977).

Legal aid may be treated as a part of the right created under article 21; *Kishore* v. *State of Himachal Pradesh*, (1991) 1 SCC 286: AIR 1990 2140: 1990 Cr LJ 2289.

In a suitable case, Supreme Court may direct District Judge to arrange legal aid; *Bajiban Chauhan* v. *U.P.S.R.T.C.*, (1990) Supp SCC 769.

40. Organisation of village panchayats.—The State shall take steps to organise village panchayats and endow them with such powers and authority as may be necessary to enable them to function as units of self-government.

Notes on Article 40

Organisation of Village Panchayat

Article 40 does not give guidelines for organising village panchayats. All that they require is that the village panchayats howsoever organised have to be equipped with such powers and authority as may be necessary to enable them to function as units of self-government; *State of Uttar Pradesh* v. *Pradhan Sangh Kshettra Samiti*, AIR 1995 SC 1512: 1995 AIR SCW 2303: 1995 All LJ 1689: (1995) Supp 2 SCC 305.

41. Right to work, to education and to public assistance in certain cases.—The State shall, within the limits of its economic capacity and development, make effective provision for securing the right to work, to education and to public assistance in cases of unemployment, old age, sickness and disablement, and in other cases of undeserved want.

Notes on Article 41

Court should so interpret an Act as to advance article 41; *Jacab* v. *Kerala Water Authority*, (1991) 1 SCC 28: AIR 1990 SC 2228: (1990) 2 KLT 673.

Reservation

Reservation other than constitutional reservation is subversion of fraternity, unity, integrity and dignity of individual. Extending reservation beyond undergraduate medical education is keeping the crippled, crippled for ever; *A.I.I.M.S. Students Union* v. *A.I.I.M.S.*, AIR 2001 SC 3262: 2001 AIR SCW 3143: 2001 (4) All WC 2886: JT 2001 (7) SC 12: (2002) 1 SCC 428: 2001 (4) SCJ 590: 2001 (4) SCT 150: (2001) 5 SCALE 430: (2001) 4 Serv LR 134: 2001 (6) Supreme 367.

Right to Education

The jurisdiction of court to interfere with the discretion exercised by expert's body like Medical Council of India or Dental Council of India is limited even though right to education is concommitant to the fundamental rights; *Dental Council of India* v. *Subharti K.K.B. Charitable Trust*, AIR 2001 SC 2151: 2001 AIR SCW 1883: 2001 All LJ 1130: JT 2001 (1) SC (Supp) 435: (2001) 5 SCC 486: 2001 (5) SCJ 82: 2001 (2) SCT 1110: (2001) 3 SCALE 492: 2001 (3) Supreme 529: 2001 (2) UJ (SC) 898.

42. Provision for just and humane conditions of work and maternity relief.— The State shall make provision for securing just and humane conditions of work and for maternity relief.

Notes on Article 42

Bonded Labour

After Repatriation to State of origin of bonded labour the effective rehabilitation is necessary for fulfilment of purpose of Bonded Labour System (Abolition) Act, 1976; *P. Sivaswamy* v. *State of Andhra Pradesh*, AIR 1988 SC 1863.

Maternity Benefits

The Maternity Benefit Act, 1961 is not applicable to Municipal Corporation; *Municipal Corporation of Delhi* v. *Female Workers (Muster Roll)*, AIR 2000 SC 1274: 2000 AIR SCW 969: JT 2000 (3) SC 13: (2000) 3 SCC 224: 2000 SCC (L&S) 331: 2000 (3) SCJ 180: 2000 (2) SCT 258: (2000) 2 SCALE 269: 2000 (2) Supreme 179: 2000 (2) UJ (SC) 800.

43. Living wage, etc., for workers.—The State shall endeavour to secure, by suitable legislation or economic organisation or in any other way, to all workers, agricultural, industrial or otherwise, work, a living wage, conditions of work ensuring a decent standard of life and full enjoyment of leisure and social and cultural opportunities and, in particular, the State shall endeavour to promote cottage industries on an individual or co-operative basis in rural areas.

Notes on Article 43

Casual Labour

Where casual workers who were rendering services similar to govt. to regular employer to company for over a decade should be regularised; *Hindustan Machine Tools* v. *M. Rangareddy*, AIR 2000 SC 3287: 2000 AIR SCW 3586: JT 2000 (1) SC (Supp) 267: (2000) 7 SCC 741: 2000 SCC (L&S) 1039: 2001 (1) SCT 267: (2000) 6 SCALE 614: 2000 (6) Supreme 535.

Revised Pension Formula

Classification is revised pension formula between pensioners on basis of date of retirement is arbitrary and violative of article 14; *D.S. Nakara* v. *Union of India*, AIR 1983 SC 130: (1983) 1 SCC 305: 1983 Lab IC 1: (1983) 1 LLJ 104: 1983 SCC (Lab) 145: 1983 UJ (SC) 217: 1983 BLJR 122: (1983) 1 SCWR 390: (1983) 15 Lawyer 51: 1983 (1) SCJ 188.

[1][**43A. Participation of workers in management of industries.**—The State shall take steps, by suitable legislation or in any other way, to secure the participation of workers in the management of undertakings, establishments or other organisations engaged in any industry.]

Notes on Article 43A

Non-workman Directors: Banking

The object of section 9 of the Banking Companies (Acquisition and Transfer of Undertakings) Act, 1970 is to empower the Central Government to make a scheme for the Constitution of the Board of Directors so as to include representatives of the employees and other specified categories; *All India Bank Officers' Confederation* v. *Union of India*, AIR 1989 SC 2045.

[2][**43B. Promotion of co-operative societies.**—The State shall endeavour to promote voluntary formation, autonomous functioning, democratic control and professional management of co-operative societies.]

44. Uniform civil code for the citizens.—The State shall endeavour to secure for the citizens a uniform civil code throughout the territory of India.

Notes on Article 44

Uniform law for all persons may be desirable. But its enactment in one go may be counter-productive to the unity of the nation; *Pannalal Bansilal Patil* v. *State of Andhra Pradesh*, AIR 1996 SC 1023: (1996) 2 SCC 498: 1996 AIR SCW 507: 1996 (2) APLJ 24: 1996 (1) Andh LD 18: 1996 (3) Andh LT 1: 1996 (1) Hindu LR 176: JT 1996 (1) SC 516: (1996) 1 SCR 603: 1996 (1) UJ (SC) 265 paragraph 12.

Personal Law

The Supreme Court of India has, in a large number of cases, rejected attempts (through public interest litigation) to seek the issue of writs:—

  (a) praying for the introduction of uniform civil code: or
  (b) declaring certain enactments relating to family law (alleged to be discriminatory) as unconstitutional.

Certain petitioners prayed as under:

  (a) to declare Muslim Personal Law which allows polygamy as void, as offending articles 14 and 15 of the Constitution;
  (b) to declare Muslim Personal Law which enables a Muslim male to give a unilateral *Talaq* to his wife without her consent and without resort to judicial process of courts, as void, offending articles 13, 14 and 15 of the Constitution;

---

  1. Ins. by the Constitution (Forty-second Amendment) Act, 1976, sec. 9 (w.e.f. 3-1-1977).
  2. Ins. by the Constitution (Ninety-seventh Amendment) Act, 2011, sec. 3 (w.e.f. 15-2-2012).

(c) to declare that the mere fact that a muslim husband takes more than one wife is an act of cruelty within the meaning of sub-section (8) of section 2 of the Dissolution of Muslim Marriages Act, 1939.

In another writ petition, the reliefs prayed for were the following:—

(a) to declare sections 2(2), 5(ii) and (iii), 6 and *Explanation* to section 30 of the Hindu Succession Act, 1956, as void, as offending articles 14 and 15 read with article 13 of the Constitution of India;

(b) to declare section 2 of as the Hindu Marriage Act, 1955, as void, offending articles 14 and 15 of the Constitution of India.

The court stated at the very outset that the petitions mentioned above did not deserve disposal on the merits, as the issues involved were matters of policy with which the Supreme Court would not ordinarily have concern. (The court cited numerous earlier cases, adopting the same approach).

Further, the issue regarding Muslim Women *etc.* Act was already pending before another Bench. The above judgment shows that the court is somewhat reluctant to interfere in matters of personal law. There have been other decisions exhibiting the same approach; *Ahmedabad Women Action Group (AWAG)* v. *Union of India*, (1997) 3 SCC 573: AIR 1997 SC 3614: 1997 AIR SCW 1620: JT 1997 (3) SC 171: 1997 (3) SCJ 107: (1997) 2 SCR 389: (1997) 2 SCALE 381: 1997 (2) Supreme 670: 1997 (1) UJ (SC) 548.

Religious Freedom

The premises behind article 44 is that there is no necessary connection between religion and personal law in civilised society; *John Vallamattom* v. *Union of India*, AIR 2003 SC 2902: 2003 AIR SCW 3536: 2003 (4) JCR SC 44: JT 2003 (6) SC 37: (2003) 6 SCC 611: 2003 (9) SRJ 209: (2003) 5 SCALE 384: 2003 (5) Supreme 229.

Religious Trusts

In *Pannalal Bansilal* v. *State of Andhra Pradesh*, AIR 1996 SCW 507 (515): (1996) 2 SCC 498: AIR 1996 SC 1023 the Supreme Court (with reference to the A.P. Hindu Religious and Charitable Endowments Act, 1987) rejected the challenge based on the argument, that the law should apply to persons professing all religions.

The court made these observations—

In a pluralist society like India, in which people have faith in their respective religious beliefs or tenets propounded by different religions or their offshoots, the founding fathers, while making the Constitution, were confronted with problems to unify and integrate people of India professing different religious faiths, born in different castes, creeds or sub-sections in the society, speaking different languages and dialects in different regions and provided a secular Constitution to integrate all sections of the society as a united *Bharat*. The directive principles of the Constitution themselves visualise diversity and attempt to foster uniformity among people of different faiths. A uniform law, though it is highly desirable, enactment thereof in one go perhaps may be counter-productive to unity and integrity of the nation. In a democracy governed by the rule of law, gradual progressive change and order should be brought about. Making law or amendment to a law is a slow process and the legislature attempts to remedy where the need is felt most acute. It would, therefore, be inexpedient and incorrect to think that all laws have to be made uniformly applicable to all people in one go. The mischief of defect which is most acute can be remedied by process of law at stages.

Uniform Civil Code

In *Maharishi Avadhesh* v. *Union of India*, (1994) 1 Supp SCC 713, the Supreme Court dismissed a petition seeking a writ of *mandamus* against the Government of India to introduce a Common Civil Code. The court took the view that it was a matter for the legislature. "The court cannot legislate in these matters".

In the same petition, the Supreme Court declined to grant a declaration nullifying the Muslim Women's Protection of Rights on Divorce Act, 1986.

The court also dismissed the prayer to direct the Government, not to enact a Shariat Act so as to affect the rights of Muslim women; *Maharishi Advadhesh* v. *Union of India*, (1994) Supp 1 SCC 713.

In *Reynold Rajamani* v. *Union of India*, AIR 1982 SC 1261 (1263, 1264): (1982) 2 SCC 474: 1982 East LR 304: 1982 UJ (SC) 570: 1982 (8) All LR 649: 1982 Marriage LJ 498: 1982 Cr App R (SC) 223 the court rejected a prayer to remove the discrimination between men and women under section 10 of the Indian Divorce Act, 1869 (applicable to Christians). the court based its approach on the "limits" of the courts' jurisdiction. It held that when a legislative provision enumerates the grounds of divorce, those grounds limit the courts' jurisdiction and the court cannot re-write the law, so as to add grounds of divorce not permissible under the section.

[1][**45. Provision for early childhood care and education to children below the age of six years.**—The State shall endeavour to provide early childhood care and education for all children until they complete the age of six years.]

Notes on Article 45

Right to Education

In respect of the right to education, the contents and parameters is to be determined in right of articles 41, 45 and 46. It means free education upto 14 years of age to every child and after 14 years of age right gets circumscribed by limits of economic capacity of State; *Unni Krishnan, J.P.* v. *State of Andhra Pradesh*, AIR 1993 SC 2178: (1993) 1 SCC 645: 1993 AIR SCW 863: JT 1993 (1) SC 474: (1993) 1 SCR 594: 1993 (2) SCT 511: 1993 (1) Serv LR 743: 1993 (1) UJ (SC) 721.

46. Promotion of educational and economic interests of Scheduled Castes, Scheduled Tribes and other weaker sections.—The State shall promote with special care the educational and economic interests of the weaker sections of the people, and, in particular, of the Scheduled Castes and the Scheduled Tribes, and shall protect them from social injustice and all forms of exploitation.

Notes on Article 46

A law prohibiting transfer of land belonging to a member of a Scheduled Tribes to a non-tribals is valid; *Lingappa Pochanna Appealwar* v. *State of Maharashtra*, AIR 1985 SC 389: (1985) 1 SCC 479: (1985) 87 Bom LR 65: 1985 GOC (SC) 41: (1985) 2 SCR 224: 1985 Cur Civ LJ (SC) 387.

Regarding the expression "weaker sections of the Society", the Supreme Court has directed the Central Government to lay down appropriate guidelines; *Shantistar Builders* v. *Narayan Khimalal Totame*, AIR 1990 SC 630: (1990) 1 SCC 520: 1990 Jab LJ 209: JT 1990 (1) SC 106, paragraphs 12-13.

An employee belonging to backward classes has a fundamental right to be considered for promotion on the basis of article 16 read with article 46. M, an employee in the backward class category, was granted promotion when he approached the High Court. It was held that promotion could not be denied to another employee, who was similarly placed; *Vishwas Anna Sawant* v. *Municipal Corporation of Greater Bombay*, JT 1994 (3) SC 573: (1994) 4 SCC 434: (1994) 27 ATC 600: AIR 1994 SC 2408.

47. Duty of the State to raise the level of nutrition and the standard of living and to improve public health.—The State shall regard the raising of the level of nutrition and the standard of living of its people and the improvement of public health as among its primary duties and, in particular, the State shall endeavour to bring about prohibition of the consumption except for medicinal purposes of intoxicating drinks and of drugs which are injurious to health.

---

1. Subs. by the Constitution (Eighty-sixth Amendment) Act, 2002, sec. 3, for article 45 (w.e.f. 1-4-2010).

Notes on Article 47

Grant of Liquor Licence

All information supplied by applicants must undergo and satisfy "strict scrutiny test". The state should not treat its right of parting with its privilege only as a means of earning more and more revenue. The importance of regulation of liquor *vis-à-vis* public health should be noted; Ashok Lenka v. *Rishi Dikshit*, AIR 2006 SC 2382: 2006 AIR SCW 3058: (2006) 9 SCC 90: 2006 (6) SCJ 650: 2006 (7) SRJ 162: (2006) 4 SCALE 519: 2006 (106) Supreme 230.

48. Organisation of agriculture and animal husbandry.—The State shall endeavour to organise agriculture and animal husbandry on modern and scientific lines and shall, in particular, take steps for preserving and improving the breeds, and prohibiting the slaughter of cows and calves and other milch and draught cattle.

Notes on Article 48

Prohibition on Slaughter of Cows and Calves

Having specifically spoken of cows and calves, the framers of Constitution in to article 48 chose not to catalogue the list of other cattles and felt satisfied by employing a general expression "other milch and draught cattle" which in their opinion any reader of the Constitution would understand in the context of words "cows and calves"; *State of Gujarat* v. *Mirzapur Moti Kureshi Kassab Jamat*, AIR 2006 SC 212: 2005 AIR SCW 5723: 2006 (1) All MR 32 (NOC): 2006 (1) Guj LR 294: 2006 (2) JCR SC 272: (2005) 8 SCC 534: 2005 (7) SCJ 701: (2005) 8 SCALE 661: 2005 (8) Supreme 697.

[1][**48A. Protection and improvement of environment and safeguarding of forests and wild life.**—The State shall endeavour to protect and improve the environment and to safeguard the forests and wild life of the country.]

Notes on Article 48A

Articles 14, 21 and 51A(g) are to be read together; *Subhash Kumar* v. *State of Bihar*, AIR 1991 SC 420: (1991) 1 SCC 598: 1991 AIR SCW 121: 1991 (1) All CJ 424: 1991 (1) BLJR 550: 1991 (1) Civ LJ 719: JT 1991 (1) SC 77: 1991 (1) Pat LJR 69: (1991) 1 SCR 5: 1991 (1) UJ (SC) 533.

Through public interest litigation brought by an institution in the locality on the basis of article 21, the duty under article 48A can be enforced; *Satish* v. *State of Uttar Pradesh*, (1992) Supp 2 SCC 94, paragraph 1; *Tarun Bharat Sangh, Alwar* v. *Union of India*, (1992) Supp 2 SCC 448: AIR 1992 SC 514: 1992 AIR SCW 102, paragraph 12.

Duty under article 48A can be enforced through a letter, based on article 21; *M.C. Mehta* v. *Union of India*, (1992) Supp 2 SCC 85 (633, 637).

Environment Protection and Social Development

Merely asserting an intention for development is not enough to sanction destruction of local ecological resources; *Intellectuals Forum, Tirupathi* v. *State of Andhra Pradesh*, AIR 2006 SC 1350: 2006 AIR SCW 1309: 2006 (2) CTC 71: 2006 (4) Comp LJ 513 SC: (2006) 3 SCC 549: 2006 (2) SCJ 293: 2006 (4) SRJ 101: 2006 (2) Supreme 292.

49. Protection of monuments and places and objects of national importance.—It shall be the obligation of the State to protect every monument or place or object of artistic or historic interest, [2][declared by or under law made by Parliament] to be of national importance, from spoilation, disfigurement, destruction, removal, disposal or export, as the case may be.

---

1. Ins. by the Constitution (Forty-second Amendment) Act, 1976, sec. 10 (w.e.f. 3-1-1977).

2. Subs. by the Constitution (Seventh Amendment) Act, 1956, sec. 27, for "declared by Parliament by law" (w.e.f. 1-11-1956).

Notes on Article 49

Museum Trust: Public Interest Litigation

The petition under article 32 asserting it to be public interest litigation alleging arbitrary manner of running trust by maharaja of Jaipur State is not maintainable. It does not violate article 49; *Ramsharan Autyanuprasi* v. *Union of India,* AIR 1989 SC 549: JT 1988 (4) SC 577: (1989) Supp 1 SCC 251: (1988) 2 SCALE 1399.

50. Separation of judiciary from executive.—The State shall take steps to separate the judiciary from the executive in the public services of the State.

Notes on Article 50

Appointment of Judges in Higher Judiciary

In appointment of Supreme Court and High Court judges the opinion of Chief Justice of India has primacy; *Supreme Court Advocates-on-Records Association* v. *Union of India,* AIR 1994 SC 268: 1993 AIR SCW 4101: JT 1993 (5) SC 479: (1993) 4 SCC 441: 1993 (5) Serv LR 337.

Court and Legislature

Court cannot direct legislature to enact particular kind of laws. The prohibition of slaughter of cows, buffaloes and horses cannot be imposed by court. It is a matter of policy of govt.; *Bal Ram Bali* v. *Union of India,* AIR 2007 SC 3074: 2007 AIR SCW 5551: 2007 (58) All Ind Cas 109: (2007) 6 SCC 805: (2007) 10 SCALE 277: 2007 (6) Supreme 409.

Separation of Powers

The separation of power has to be viewed through prison of constitutionalism and for upholding goals of justice in its full magnitude; *University of Kerala* v. *Council Principals, Colleges, Kerala,* AIR 2010 SC 2532.

51. Promotion of international peace and security.—The State shall endeavour to—

(a) promote international peace and security;

(b) maintain just and honourable relations between nations;

(c) foster respect for international law and treaty obligations in the dealings of organised peoples with one another; and

(d) encourage settlement of international disputes by arbitration.

Notes on Article 51

Extradition

Extradition treaty is a contract—

(i) *Arton No. 2 (in re:),* (1896) 1 QB 509.

(ii) *R.* v. *Governor of Ashford Remand Centre,* (1973) Current Law Year Book 1434.

(iii) *Government of the Federal Republic of Germany* v. *Sotiaridis,* (1974) CLYB 1665.

(iv) *R.* v. *Governor of Ashford Remand Centre,* The Times, July 14, 1987, Current Law (August, 1987).

International Law and National Law (Municipal Law)

The following propositions should be noted:—

(a) International treaties do not automatically become part of national law. They have to be incorporated into the legal system by appropriate law.

(b) However, national courts generally interpret statutes so as to maintain harmony with rules of international law.

(c) National legislation, even if contrary of international law, has to be respected.

(d) Power to implement treaties belongs exclusively to the Union under article 253.

Following cases support the above propositions:—

(i) *Moti Lal* v. *State of Uttar Pradesh,* AIR 1951 All 257: (1957) 1 All 269 (FB).

(ii) *Berubari Union (in re:)*, AIR 1960 SC 845: (1960) 3 SCR 250: 1960 SCJ 933: (1961) 1 SCA 22.

(iii) *Mirza Ali Akbar Kashani* v. *United Arab Republic*, AIR 1966 SC 230: (1966) 1 SCR 319: (1965) 2 SCA 590: (1965) 2 SCWR 893: 1966 (2) SCJ 25.

(iv) *Maganbhai* v. *Union of India*, AIR 1969 SC 783: (1970) 3 SCC 400: (1969) 3 SCR 254.

(v) *Varghese* v. *Bank of Cochin*, AIR 1980 SC 470: (1980) 2 SCC 360: (1980) 2 SCR 913.

(vi) *Civil Rights Vigilance Committee, S.L.S.R.C. College of Law, Bangalore* v. *Union of India*, AIR 1983 Kant 85: (1982) 2 Kant LJ 208.

(vii) *Gramophone Co.* v. *Birendra*, AIR 1984 SC 667: (1984) 2 SCC 534: 1984 SCC (Cri) 313.

[1][PART IVA

FUNDAMENTAL DUTIES

51A. Fundamental duties.—It shall be the duty of every citizen of India—

(a) to abide by the Constitution and respect its ideals and institutions, the National Flag and the National Anthem;

(b) to cherish and follow the noble ideals which inspired our national struggle for freedom;

(c) to uphold and protect the sovereignty, unity and integrity of India;

(d) to defend the country and render national service when called upon to do so;

(e) to promote harmony and the spirit of common brotherhood amongst all the people of India transcending religious, linguistic and regional or sectional diversities; to renounce practices derogatory to the dignity of women;

(f) to value and preserve the rich heritage of our composite culture;

(g) to protect and improve the natural environment including forests, lakes, rivers and wild life, and to have compassion for living creatures;

(h) to develop the scientific temper, humanism and the spirit of inquiry and reform;

(i) to safeguard public property and to abjure violence;

(j) to strive towards excellence in all spheres of individual and collective activity so that the nation constantly rises to higher levels of endeavour and achievement.]

[2][(k) who is a parent or guardian to provide opportunities for education to his child or, as the case may be, ward between the age of six and fourteen years.]

Notes on Article 51A

Environment

Fundamental duties have been particularly invoked in litigation concerning the environment. *See* the undermentioned cases:

(i) *Rural Litigation and Entitlement Kendra* v. *State of Uttar Pradesh*, AIR 1987 SC 359: 1986 Supp SCC 517: JT 1986 SC 1118: 1986 (4) Supreme 324: (1987) 1 Cur CC 200: (1987) 13 All LR 139: (1987) 1 UJ (SC) 132: 1987 (1) SCJ 337: 1987 Cur Civ LJ (SC) 209.

---

1. Part IVA (containing article 51A) ins. by the Constitution (Forty-second Amendment) Act, 1976, sec. 11 (w.e.f. 3-1-1977).
2. Added by the Constitution (Eighty-sixth Amendment) Act, 2002, sec. 4 (w.e.f. 1-4-2010).

   (ii) *Shri Sachidanand Pandey* v. *State of West Bengal*, AIR 1987 SC 1109: (1987) 2 SCC 295: (1987) 1 Comp LJ 211: JT 1987 (1) SC 425: 1987 (2) SCJ 70: 1987 (1) Supreme 492: (1987) 1 UJ (SC) 641, paragraph 60.

Fundamental Duties and their Enforcement

Provisions as to fundamental duties cannot be enforced by writs. They can be promoted only by constitutional methods. But they can be used for interpreting ambiguous statutes. *See* undermentioned cases:

   (i) *Mumbai Kamgar Sabha* v. *Abdulbhai*, AIR 1976 SC 1455: (1976) 3 SCC 832: (1976) 2 LLJ 186.

   (ii) *Surya Narain Choudhary* v. *Union of India*, AIR 1982 Raj 1: 1981 WLN 198: 1981 Raj LW 490.

   (iii) *West Bengal Head Masters' Association* v. *Union of India*, AIR 1983 Cal 448: (1983) 87 CWN 597.

   (iv) *Dr. Dasarathi* v. *State of Andhra Pradesh*, AIR 1985 AP 136: (1984) 2 Andh WR 449.

Where the constitutionality of an Act is challenged the court may look at article 51A to uphold it; *Mohan* v. *Union of India*, (1992) Suppl 1 SCC 594: AIR 1992 SC 1: (1992) 19 ATC 881, paragraphs 41 and 42.

Scope

Article 51A is confined to "citizens" unlike some of the articles relating to fundamental rights (*e.g.* article 21) which extend to "all persons".

Striving towards Excellence

In a case in which the High Court of Allahabad quashed a notification issued under the Land Acquisition Act as *mala fide*, the High Court discussed the significance of article 51A(g) and pointed out that a new chapter had been inserted in the Constitution to regulate behaviour and to bring about excellence. Article 51A is in a positive form with a view to striving towards excellence. People should not conduct themselves in a blameworthy manner. 'Excellence' means surpassing merit, virtue, honest performance. Constitutional law givers have provided that the citizens of this great nation shall perform their duties in an excellent way rather than perform them half heartedly; The performance of these duties falls within Constitutional law; *Ram Prasad* v. *State of Uttar Pradesh*, AIR 1988 All 309: (1988) 14 All LR 497: 1988 All WC 1082 (DB).

Use and Interpretation

The courts may look at the fundamental duties while interpreting equivocal statutes which admit of two constructions. On the principle that as the duties are obligatory on citizens, the State should also observe them, the Supreme Court has, with reference to article 51A(g), issued oral orders stopping quarrying operations at certain places in UP. Similarly, it has issued directions regarding declaring disputed areas as 'reserved forests' under section 20 of the Indian Forest Act, 1927; *See* the undermentioned cases:

   (i) *Mumbai Kamgar Sabha* v. *Abdulbhai*, AIR 1976 SC 1455: (1976) 3 SCC 832: (1976) 2 LLJ 186, paragraph 29.

   (ii) *Rural Litigation and Entitlement Kendra* v. *State of Uttar Pradesh*, AIR 1987 SC 2426: (1987) Supp SCC 487: JT 1987 (5) SC 122 (Quarrying).

   (iii) *Banwasi Sewa Ashram* v. *State of Uttar Pradesh*, (1986) 4 SCC 753: AIR 1987 SC 374: 1987 Cr LR (SC) 2: 1987 (1) SCJ 203: 1987 SC Cr R 73: 1987 East Cr C 430 (Forests).

PART V

THE UNION

CHAPTER I

THE EXECUTIVE

The President and Vice-President

52. The President of India.—There shall be a President of India.

53. Executive power of the Union.—(1) The executive power of the Union shall be vested in the President and shall be exercised by him either directly or through officers subordinate to him in accordance with this Constitution.

(2) Without prejudice to the generality of the foregoing provision, the supreme command of the Defence Forces of the Union shall be vested in the President and the exercise thereof shall be regulated by law.

(3) Nothing in this article shall—

(a) be deemed to transfer to the President any functions conferred by any existing law on the Government of any State or other authority; or

(b) prevent Parliament from conferring by law functions on authorities other than the President.

Notes on Article 53

Executive Power

The following propositions are worth noting:—

(a) Executive power must be exercised in accordance with the Constitution—including, in particular, the provisions of article 14.

   (i) *U.N.R. Rao* v. *Indira Gandhi*, AIR 1971 SC 1002: (1971) 2 SCC 63: (1971) 1 Civ Ap J (SC) 176: 1971 (Supp) SCR 46.

   (ii) *Sanjeevi* v. *State of Madras*, AIR 1970 SC 1102: (1970) 1 SCC 443: 1970 SCC (Cri) 196.

(b) Executive power (so long as it does not violate the Constitution or the law) may be exercised without prior legislative support.

   (i) *Maganabhai* v. *Union of India*, AIR 1969 SC 783: (1969) 3 SCR 254: (1970) 3 SCC 400.

   (ii) *Rai Sahib Ram Jawaya Kapur* v. *State of Punjab*, (1955) 2 SCR 225 (240): AIR 1955 SC 549: 1955 SCA 577: 1955 SCJ 504: (1955) 2 Mad LJ (SC) 59: 57 Punj LR 444: 1955 Mad WN 973.

(c) Executive power is the residue of functions of Government, which are not legislative or judicial; *H.H. Maharajadhiraja Madhav Rao Jivaji Rao Scindia Bahadur* v. *Union of India*, AIR 1971 SC 530: (1971) 1 SCC 85: (1971) 3 SCR 9: 1971 (1) SCJ 295: 1971 Mer LR 78: (1971) 2 SCA 257, paragraphs 94, 96.

Martial Law and Presidential Order

A Presidential Order would ordinarily have a wider range and effect throughout the country than the existence of martial law in any particular part of the country. The presidential proclamations are meant generally to cover at country as a whole. The "martial law" is generally of a locally restricted application. Another difference is that the martial law may prevail result in taking over by military courts of power even to try offences and ordinary and civil courts will not interfere with this special jurisdiction under extraordinary conditions. Such a taking over by military courts is certainly outside the provisions of article 359(1) taken by itself. It perhaps fall under presidential powers under articles 53 and 73 read with 355; *Addl. Distt. Magistrate, Jabalpur* v. *Shivakant Shukla*, AIR 1976 SC 1207: (1976) 2 SCC 521: 1976 Cr LJ 945: 1976 UJ (SC) 610: 1976 SC Cr R 277: 1976 SCC (Cri) 448: 1976 Cr App R (SC) 298: (1976) 3 SCR 929: 1976 Supp SCR 172.

54. Election of President.—The President shall be elected by the members of an electoral college consisting of—

(a) the elected members of both Houses of Parliament; and

(b) the elected members of the Legislative Assemblies of the States.

[Explanation.—In this article and in article 55, "State" includes the National Capital Territory of Delhi and the Union Territory of Pondicherry.][1]

55. Manner of election of President.—(1) As far as practicable, there shall be uniformity in the scale of representation of the different States at the election of the President.

(2) For the purpose of securing such uniformity among the States *inter se* as well as parity between the States as a whole and the Union, the number of votes which each elected member of Parliament and of the Legislative Assembly of each State is entitled to cast at such election shall be determined in the following manner:—

(a) every elected member of the Legislative Assembly of a State shall have as many votes as there are multiples of one thousand in the quotient obtained by dividing the population of the State by the total number of the elected members of the Assembly;

(b) if, after taking the said multiples of one thousand, the remainder is not less than five hundred, then the vote of each member referred to in sub-clause (a) shall be further increased by one;

(c) each elected member of either House of Parliament shall have such number of votes as may be obtained by dividing the total number of votes assigned to the members of the Legislative Assemblies of the States under sub-clauses (a) and (b) by the total number of the elected members of both Houses of Parliament, fractions exceeding one-half being counted as one and other fractions being disregarded.

(3) The election of the President shall be held in accordance with the system of proportional representation by means of the single transferable vote and the voting at such election shall be by secret ballot.

[Explanation.—In this article, the expression "population" means the population as ascertained at the last preceding census of which the relevant figures have been published:][2]

Provided that the reference in this *Explanation* to the last preceding census of which the relevant figures have been published shall, until the relevant figures for the first census taken after the year [2026][3] have been published, be construed as a reference to the 1971 census.]

56. Term of office of President.—(1) The President shall hold office for a term of five years from the date on which he enters upon his office:

Provided that—

(a) the President may, by writing under his hand addressed to the Vice-President, resign his office;

(b) the President may, for violation of the Constitution, be removed from office by impeachment in the manner provided in article 61:

(c) the President shall, notwithstanding the expiration of his term, continue to hold office until his successor enters upon his office.

---

1. Ins. by the Constitution (Seventieth Amendment) Act, 1992, sec. 2 (w.e.f. 1-6-1995).
2. Subs. by the Constitution (Forty-second Amendment) Act, 1976, sec. 12, for the *Explanation* (w.e.f. 3-1-1977).
3. Subs. by the Constitution (Eighty-fourth Amendment) Act, 2001, sec. 2, for "2000" (w.e.f. 21-2-2002).

(2) Any resignation addressed to the Vice-President under clause (a) of the proviso to clause (1) shall forthwith be communicated by him to the Speaker of the House of the People.

57. Eligibility for re-election.—A person who holds, or who has held, office as President shall, subject to the other provisions of this Constitution, be eligible for re-election to that office.

58. Qualifications for election as President.—(1) No person shall be eligible for election as President unless he—

(a) is a citizen of India,

(b) has completed the age of thirty-five years, and

(c) is qualified for election as a member of the House of the People.

(2) A person shall not be eligible for election as President if he holds any office of profit under the Government of India or the Government of any State or under any local or other authority subject to the control of any of the said Governments.

Explanation.—For the purposes of this article, a person shall not be deemed to hold any office of profit by reason only that he is the President or Vice-President of the Union or the Governor [1][***] of any State or is a Minister either for the Union or for any State.

59. Conditions of President's office.—(1) The President shall not be a member of either House of Parliament or of a House of the Legislature of any State, and if a member of either House of Parliament or of a House of the Legislature of any State be elected President, he shall be deemed to have vacated his seat in that House on the date on which he enters upon his office as President.

(2) The President shall not hold any other office of profit.

(3) The President shall be entitled without payment of rent to the use of his official residences and shall be also entitled to such emoluments, allowances and privileges as may be determined by Parliament by law and, until provision in that behalf is so made, such emoluments, allowances and privileges are specified in the Second Schedule.

(4) The emoluments and allowances of the President shall not be diminished during his term of office.

60. Oath or affirmation by the President.—Every President and every person acting as President or discharging the functions of the President shall, before entering upon his office, make and subscribe in the presence of the Chief Justice of India or, in his absence, the seniormost Judge of the Supreme Court available, an oath or affirmation in the following form, that is to say—

"I, A.B., do $\dfrac{\text{swear in the name of God}}{\text{solemnly affirm}}$ that I will faithfully execute the office of

President (or discharge the functions of the President) of India and will to the best of my ability preserve, protect and defend the Constitution and the law and that I will devote myself to the service and well-being of the people of India."

61. Procedure for impeachment of the President.—(1) When a President is to be impeached for violation of the Constitution, the charge shall be preferred by either House of Parliament.

---

1. The words "or Rajpramukh or Uparajpramukh" omitted by the Constitution (Seventh Amendment) Act, 1956, sec. 29 and Sch. (w.e.f. 1-11-1956).

(2) No such charge shall be preferred unless—

(a) the proposal to prefer such charge is contained in a resolution which has been moved after at least fourteen days' notice in writing signed by not less than one-fourth of the total number of members of the House has been given of their intention to move the resolution, and

(b) such resolution has been passed by a majority of not less than two-thirds of the total membership of the House.

(3) When a charge has been so preferred by either House of Parliament, the other House shall investigate the charge or cause the charge to be investigated and the President shall have the right to appear and to be represented at such investigation.

(4) If as a result of the investigation a resolution is passed by a majority of not less than two-thirds of the total membership of the House by which the charge was investigated or caused to be investigated, declaring that the charge preferred against the President has been sustained, such resolution shall have the effect of removing the President from his office as from the date on which the resolution is so passed.

62. Time of holding election to fill vacancy in the office of President and the term of office of person elected to fill casual vacancy.—(1) An election to fill a vacancy caused by the expiration of the term of office of President shall be completed before the expiration of the term.

(2) An election to fill a vacancy in the office of President occurring by reason of his death, resignation or removal, or otherwise shall be held as soon as possible after, and in no case later than six months from, the date of occurrence of the vacancy; and the person elected to fill the vacancy shall, subject to the provisions of article 56, be entitled to hold office for the full term of five years from the date on which he enters upon his office.

63. The Vice-President of India.—There shall be a Vice-President of India.

64. The Vice-President to be *ex-officio* Chairman of the Council of States.— The Vice-President shall be *ex-officio* Chairman of the Council of States and shall not hold any other office of profit:

Provided that during any period when the Vice-President acts as President or discharges the functions of the President under article 65, he shall not perform the duties of the office of Chairman of the Council of States and shall not be entitled to any salary or allowance payable to the Chairman of the Council of States under article 97.

65. The Vice-President to act as President or to discharge his functions during casual vacancies in the office, or during the absence, of President.—(1) In the event of the occurrence of any vacancy in the office of the President by reason of his death, resignation or removal, or otherwise, the Vice-President shall act as President until the date on which a new President elected in accordance with the provisions of this Chapter to fill such vacancy enters upon his office.

(2) When the President is unable to discharge his functions owing to absence, illness or any other cause, the Vice-President shall discharge his functions until the date on which the President resumes his duties.

(3) The Vice-President shall, during, and in respect of, the period while he is so acting as, or discharging the functions of, President, have all the powers and immunities of the President and be entitled to such emoluments, allowances and privileges as may be determined by Parliament by law and, until provision in that behalf is so made, such emoluments, allowances and privileges as are specified in the Second Schedule.

66. Election of Vice-President.—(1) The Vice-President shall be elected by the [1][members of an electoral college consisting of the members of both Houses of Parliament] in accordance with the system of proportional representation by means of the single transferable vote and the voting at such election shall be by secret ballot.

(2) The Vice-President shall not be a member of either House of Parliament or of a House of the Legislature of any State, and if a member of either House of Parliament or of a House of the Legislature of any State be elected Vice-President, he shall be deemed to have vacated his seat in that House on the date on which he enters upon his office as Vice-President.

(3) No person shall be eligible for election as Vice-President unless he—

    (a) is a citizen of India;

    (b) has completed the age of thirty-five years; and

    (c) is qualified for election as a member of the Council of States.

(4) A person shall not be eligible for election as Vice-President if he holds any office of profit under the Government of India or the Government of any State or under any local or other authority subject to the control of any of the said Governments.

Explanation.—For the purposes of this article, a person shall not be deemed to hold any office of profit by reason only that he is the President or Vice-President of the Union or the Governor [2][***] of any State or is a Minister either for the Union or for any State.

67. Term of office of Vice-President.—The Vice-President shall hold office for a term of five years from the date on which he enters upon his office:

Provided that—

    (a) a Vice-President may, by writing under his hand addressed to the President, resign his office;

    (b) a Vice-President may be removed from his office by a resolution of the Council of States passed by a majority of all the then members of the Council and agreed to by the House of the People; but no resolution for the purpose of this clause shall be moved unless at least fourteen days' notice has been given of the intention to move the resolution;

    (c) a Vice-President shall, notwithstanding the expiration of his term, continue to hold office until his successor enters upon his office.

68. Time of holding election to fill vacancy in the office of Vice-President and the term of office of person elected to fill casual vacancy.—(1) An election to fill a

---

1. Subs. by the Constitution (Eleventh Amendment) Act, 1961, sec. 2, for "members of both Houses of Parliament assembled at a joint meeting" (w.e.f. 19-12-1961).

2. The words "or Rajpramukh or Uparajpramukh" omitted by the Constitution (Seventh Amendment) Act, 1956, sec. 29 and Sch. (w.e.f. 1-11-1956).

vacancy caused by the expiration of the term of office of Vice-President shall be completed before the expiration of the term.

(2) An election to fill a vacancy in the office of Vice-President occurring by reason of his death, resignation or removal, or otherwise shall be held as soon as possible after the occurrence of the vacancy, and the person elected to fill the vacancy shall, subject to the provisions of article 67, be entitled to hold office for the full term of five years from the date on which he enters upon his office.

69. Oath or affirmation by the Vice-President.—Every Vice-President shall, before entering upon his office, make and subscribe before the President, or some person appointed in that behalf by him, an oath or affirmation in the following form, that is to say—

"I, A.B., do $\dfrac{\text{swear in the name of God}}{\text{solemnly affirm}}$ that I will bear true faith, and allegiance to the Constitution of India as by law established and that I will faithfully discharge the duty upon which I am about to enter."

70. Discharge of President's functions in other contingencies.—Parliament may make such provision as it thinks fit for the discharge of the functions of the President in any contingency not provided for in this Chapter.

[1][**71. Matters relating to, or connected with, the election of a President or Vice-President.**—(1) All doubts and disputes arising out of or in connection with the election of a President or Vice-President shall be inquired into and decided by the Supreme Court whose decision shall be final.

(2) If the election of a person as President or Vice-President is declared void by the Supreme Court, acts done by him in the exercise and performance of the powers and duties of the office of President or Vice-President, as the case may be, on or before the date of the decision of the Supreme Court shall not be invalidated by reason of that declaration.

(3) Subject to the provisions of this Constitution, Parliament may by law regulate any matter relating to or connected with the election of a President or Vice-President.

(4) The election of a person as President or Vice-President shall not be called in question on the ground of the existence of any vacancy for whatever reason among the members of the electoral college electing him.]

72. Power of President to grant pardons, etc., and to suspend, remit or commute sentences in certain cases.—(1) The President shall have the power to grant pardons, reprieves, respites or remissions of punishment or to suspend, remit or commute the sentence of any person convicted of any offence—

(a) in all cases where the punishment or sentence is by a Court Martial;

(b) in all cases where the punishment or sentence is for an offence against any law relating to a matter to which the executive power of the Union extends;

(c) in all cases where the sentence is a sentence of death.

---

1. Subs. by the Constitution (Forty-fourth Amendment) Act, 1978, sec. 10, for article 71 (w.e.f. 20-6-1979). Earlier article 71 was amended by the Constitution (Eleventh Amendment) Act, 1961, sec. 3 (w.e.f. 19-12-1961) and was substituted by the Constitution (Thirty-ninth Amendment) Act, 1975, sec. 2 (w.e.f. 10-8-1975).

(2) Nothing in sub-clause (a) of clause (1) shall affect the power conferred by law on any officer of the Armed Forces of the Union to suspend, remit or commute a sentence passed by a Court martial.

(3) Nothing in sub-clause (c) of clause (1) shall affect the power to suspend, remit or commute a sentence of death exercisable by the Governor [1][***] of a State, under any law for the time being in force.

Notes on Article 72

The effect of a series of decisions of the Supreme Court (and of some High Courts) is as under:—

  (a) The exercise of the power by the president under article 72 is primarily a matter for his discretion and the courts would not interfere with his actual decision on the merits.

  (b) But courts exercise a very limited power of judicial review, to ensure that the President considers all relevant materials before coming to his decision.

  (c) The President can, in the exercise of this power, examine the evidence afresh. In doing so, he is not sitting as a court of appeal. His power is independent of the judiciary. He can, therefore, afford relief not only from a sentence which he regards as unduly harsh., but also from an evident mistake.

  (d) The President is not bound to hear a petitioner for mercy before he rejects the petition.

The undermentioned decisions support the above propositions:

  (i) *Nanavati* v. *State of Bombay*, AIR 1961 SC 112: (1961) 1 SLR 497: (1961) 1 Cr LJ 173.

  (ii) *Ramanaiah* v. *Supdt., Central Jail*, AIR 1974 SC 31: (1974) 3 SCC 531: 1974 Cr LJ 150.

  (iii) *Godse* v. *State of Maharashtra*, AIR 1961 SC 600: (1961) 3 SCC 440: (1961) 1 Cr LJ 736.

  (iv) *Sarat Chandra Rabha* v. *Khagendranath Nath*, AIR 1961 SC 334: (1961) 2 SCR 133: (1961) 2 SCA 326: 1963 (1) SCJ 796: ILR (1961) 13 Assam 1.

  (v) *Krishan* v. *State of Andhra Pradesh*, (1975) UJ (SC) 951.

  (vi) *Maru Ram* v. *Union of India*, AIR 1980 SC 2147: (1981) 1 SCC 107: 1980 Cr LJ 1440: (1981) 1 SCR 1196, paragraphs 59-60, 72 and 100.

  (vii) *Kuljit* v. *Lt. Governor*, AIR 1982 SC 774: (1982) 1 SCC 417: 1982 Cr LJ 624.

  (viii) *Harbans* v. *State of Uttar Pradesh*, AIR 1982 SC 849: (1982) 2 SCC 101: 1982 Cr LJ 795.

  (ix) *Chennugadu (in re:)*, ILR (1955) Mad 92.

  (x) *Deputy Inspector General of Police, North Range, Waltair* v. *D. Rajaram*, AIR 1960 AP 259: (1959) 2 Andh WR 526: 1959 Andh LT 916: 1960 Cr LJ 565: ILR (1959) AP 1294.

  (xi) *Puttawwa (in re:)*, AIR 1959 Mys 116: 1959 Cr LJ 617.

  (xii) *Jaswant Rai* v. *State of Punjab*, AIR 1967 P&H 155: 1967 Cr LJ 577: ILR (1967) 2 P&H 244: (1967) 69 Punj LR 1024.

  (xiii) *Hukam Singh* v. *State of Punjab*, AIR 1975 P&H 148: 1975 Cr LJ 902: ILR (1975) 1 P&H 619: 78 Punj LR 28: (1976) 3 Cr LT 1.

  (xiv) *Kehar Singh* v. *Union of India*, JT 1988 (4) SC 693: AIR 1989 SC 653: 1989 Cr LJ 941.

  (xv) *State of Punjab* v. *Joginder Singh*, AIR 1990 SC 1396: (1990) 2 SCC 661: 1990 Cr LJ 1464.

New Commonwealth

Some years ago, De Smith, a reputed scholar of constitutional law, studied the 'New Commonwealth'—*i.e.*, the group of countries especially comprising African, Caribbean and Far East members of the Commonwealth. He noted at that time in Malaysia, there is a Pardons Board—a Body with an unofficial and potentially non-political majority—to tender advice to the Head of the State. In Sierra Leone the Prime Minister assumes the responsibility. He must consult

---

  1. The words "or Rajpramukh" omitted by the Constitution (Seventh Amendment) Act, 1956, sec. 29 and Sch. (w.e.f. 1-11-1956).

a Committee of the Cabinet for capital cases, but is not bound to accept their advice. Advisory Committees, including the Attorney General, exist in a few other countries of the New Commonwealth. Nigeria had an Advisory Committee with a medical practitioner as one of its members. Incidentally, the Ceylon Constitution of 1947-48 envisaged that the Governor-General shall not grant a pardon, respite or remission to an offender without first receiving, in every case, the advice of one of his Ministers. Further, where any offender shall have been condemned to suffer death by the sentence of any court, the Governor-General shall cause a report to be made by the judge who tried the case and also obtain the Attorney General's advice thereon. The report and the advice should then be sent to the Minister who is to advise the Governor-General.

Position Elsewhere

Consistent with the democratic principle that the people are the source of all political power, the Constitutions of the various States in the United States designate the institution that will wield the clemency power. The Advisory Board (wherever created) may have the Governor as a member, or may sit separately and send its recommendation to the Governor. In some States (*e.g.* Arizona, Delaware, Louisiana, Pennsylvania, Texas), the State Constitution prohibits the Governor from granting clemency where the Advisory Board has made an unfavourable recommendation. In a few States, the Constitution of the State vests the power exclusively in the Advisory Board. To this category belong Connecticut, Georgia, Idaho and Utah. Where Advisory Boards have been constituted, the Boards are, in some cases, staffed by elected officials while in others the Board is composed of members appointed by the Governor. In some States (*e.g.* Oklahoma, South Dakota, Texas), the nominations to the Board are made by a variety of agencies—namely, the Governor, the Chief Justice of the State Supreme Court and the President of the Court of Criminal Appeals.

Should India adopt a system of having an Advisory Board for advising the President in exercising the prerogative of mercy? There are some basic difficulties here. The advice of the Board cannot be made binding on the President without amending the Constitution. If the President rejects its advice, controversies are likely to be raised. Again, if the Board is to consist of persons other than sitting judges, the Board would find it embarrassing to reconsider and review matters considered by the high judiciary. If the Board is to consist of non-judicial personnel, it may often be found inadvisable to communicate to several persons the reasons for proposed exercise of prerogative of mercy.

It should, however, be mentioned that there is nothing to prevent the President from consulting the Attorney General. The terms of article 6(2) of the Constitution are wide enough to enable him to do so. In an exceptional case, the President can even refer the matter for opinion to the Supreme Court. Here again, the terms of article 143 of the Constitution are wide enough.

Presidential Clemency and Death Sentence

From time to time, the questions of the President's power to commute the sentence of death into a lesser sentence comes up for discussion before the public. This is not a purely legal matter and involves several ethical and social implications. Unfortunately, a few misconceptions prevail on the subject, because of the failure to appreciate several important socio-legal aspects.

Remission of Sentence

The power of President and Governor to grant remission of sentence is absolute and unfettered; *State of Haryana* v. *Jagdish*, AIR 2010 SC 1690.

Stay

Where the earlier petition for mercy has been rejected by the President, stay cannot be obtained by filing another petition; *Triveniben* v. *State of Gujarat*, (1990) Cr LJ 273: 1990 Cr LR Guj 17: AIR 1989 SC 1335: (1989) 1 SCC 678, paragraph 7.

73. Extent of executive power of the Union.—(1) Subject to the provisions of this Constitution, the executive power of the Union shall extend—

(a) to the matters with respect to which Parliament has power to make laws; and

(b) to the exercise of such rights, authority and jurisdiction as are exercisable by the Government of India by virtue of any treaty or agreement:

Provided that the executive power referred to in sub-clause (a) shall not, save as expressly provided in this Constitution or in any law made by Parliament, extend in any State [1][***] to matters with respect to which the Legislature of the State has also power to make laws.

(2) Until otherwise provided by Parliament, a State and any officer or authority of a State may, notwithstanding anything in this article, continue to exercise in matters with respect to which Parliament has power to make laws for that State such executive power or functions as the State or officer or authority thereof could exercise immediately before the commencement of this Constitution.

Notes on Article 74

Powers of President to Consult Supreme Court

The text of "123 Agreement" between India and United States of America on Nuclear Co-operation released. The Court cannot assume power and jurisdiction to itself of issuing *mandamus* to Union to make reference to President of India to exercise power vested under provisions of article 143. It is for President to determine whether and what questions should be referred under article 143; *Sarvjeet Kumar* v. *Union of India*, AIR 2008 Del 37: 2008 (3) AKAR (NOC) 383.

Council of Ministers

74. Council of Ministers to aid and advise President.—[2][(1) There shall be a Council of Ministers with the Prime Minister at the head to aid and advise the President who shall, in the exercise of his functions, act in accordance with such advice:]

[3][Provided that the President may require the Council of Ministers to reconsider such advice, either generally or otherwise, and the President shall act in accordance with the advice tendered after such reconsideration.]

(2) The question whether any, and if so what, advice was tendered by Ministers to the President shall not be inquired into in any court.

Notes on Article 74

Advice of Cabinet

By the peremptory provisions of article 74(1) as it now stands (*i.e.*, after the 42nd and 44th Amendments) the President is bound in every case to act on the advice of the Cabinet. The amendment incorporates the view taken in *Samsher* v. *State of Punjab*, AIR 1974 SC 2192: (1974) 2 SCC 831: 1974 Lab IC 1380: (1974) 2 LLJ 465. For the latest English practice, *see*—

(i) Halsbury, 4th Ed., Vol. 8, paragraph 938.

(ii) Hood Philips, Constitutional and Administrative Law (1978), pages 148-49.

Cabinet Government

Basu, Constitutional Law of India, (1998) page 153, points out that the following propositions will appear to have been well-established by convention in UK, with reference to Cabinet Government—

---

1. The words and letters "specified in Part A or Part B of the First Schedule" omitted by the Constitution (Seventh Amendment) Act, 1956, sec. 29 and Sch. (w.e.f. 1-11-1956).

2. Subs. by the Constitution (Forty-second Amendment) Act, 1976, sec. 13, for clause (1) (w.e.f. 3-1-1977).

3. Ins. by the Constitution (Forty-fourth Amendment) Act, 1978, sec. 11 (w.e.f. 20-6-1979).

(1) The dissolution of the House of Commons is a "prerogative" of the Crown; but, since the advent of the Cabinet Government, the Crown has to exercise this prerogative on the advice of the Prime Minister. The theory behind the Prime Minister's right to advise dissolution is that when he loses the confidence of the House, he may, instead of resigning, assert that the House itself has ceased to reflect the will of the Electorate which constitutes, the "political sovereign". A dissolution has thus become a "privilege" of the Prime Minister, to appeal from the House of Parliament to the Electorate.

(2) But, a defeated Prime Minister has to elect between either of two alternatives, either to resign or to advise dissolution; he *cannot have both. "Either* the Government will resign and the Opposition come into power ......, or the Government will advise the Queen to dissolve Parliament". [Jennings, "Law and the Constitution" 5th Ed. p. 184].

Basu refers also to Stephen's Commentaries, 20th Ed. Vol I. p. 403; Parry, British Government 1969, p. 93; de Smith, "Constitutional Law 1971, p. 105; Wade & Phillips, Constitutional Law, 8th Ed., p. 121; Hood Phillips, Constitutional and Administrative Law, 6th Ed. 1978, pp. 144 - 151, in this context—

(3) The reason for the above view is, that no question of appeal to the Electorate from the Lok Sabha arises, where the Prime Minister has bowed down to the will of the Lok Sabha and has resigned. It would, therefore, be contrary to British conventions, (on which the power of dissolution rests), to urge that an advice of dissolution from a *resigning* Prime Minister would still be binding on the President.

(4) According to Basu, if the Prime Minister, who is defeated in the House or who loses the confidence of the House, refuses to resign, the President may dismiss him (which power, though obsolete in England, is confided in article 75(2) of the Indian Constitution);

(5) If the Prime Minister does resign, the President should at once offer an opportunity to the opposition to form a Government, in which case, the outgoing prime Minister can have no right to advise dissolution, and no right to retain office as the head of a care taker Government.

Confidentiality of Cabinet Decisions

See *S.P. Gupta* v. *President of India,* AIR 1982 SC 149: 1982 Raj LR 389: 1981 Supp SCC 87, paragraphs 60-61 and *State of Rajasthan* v. *Union of India,* AIR 1977 SC 1361: (1977) 3 SCC 592: (1978) 1 SCR 1: 1978 (1) SCJ 78, paragraphs 82-83. *See* also notes on article 78.

Article 74(2) does not bar scrutiny of advice tendered by the Council of Ministers to the President.

Courts are justified in looking into the basis of the advice subject to the provisions of section 123 of the Evidence Act, *Kartar Singh* v. *State of Punjab,* JT 1994 (2) SC 423: (1994) 3 SCC 569: 1994 Cr LJ 3139.

75. Other provisions as to Ministers.—(1) The Prime Minister shall be appointed by the President and the other Ministers shall be appointed by the President on the advice of the Prime Minister.

[1][(1A) The total number of Ministers, including the Prime Minister, in the Council of Ministers shall not exceed fifteen per cent. of the total number of members of the House of the People.]

[1][(1B) A member of either House of Parliament belonging to any political party who is disqualified for being a member of that House under paragraph 2 of the Tenth Schedule shall also be disqualified to be appointed as a Minister under clause (1) for duration of the period commencing from the date of his disqualification till the date on which the term of his office as such member would expire or where he contests any election to either House of Parliament before the

---

1. Ins. by the Constitution (Ninety-first Amendment) Act, 2003, sec. 2 (w.e.f. 1-1-2004).

expiry of such period, till the date on which he is declared elected, whichever is earlier.]

(2) The Ministers shall hold office during the pleasure of the President.

(3) The Council of Ministers shall be collectively responsible to the House of the People.

(4) Before a Minister enters upon his office, the President shall administer to him the oaths of office and of secrecy according to the forms set out for the purpose in the Third Schedule.

(5) A Minister who for any period of six consecutive months is not a member of either House of Parliament shall at the expiration of that period cease to be a Minister.

(6) The salaries and allowances of Ministers shall be such as Parliament may from time to time by law determine and, until Parliament so determines, shall be as specified in the Second Schedule.

Notes on Article 75

Describing a person as Deputy Prime Minister is descriptive only, and such description does not confer on him any powers of Prime Minister, Hence, oath as Deputy Prime Minister is not invalid; *K.M. Sharma* v. *Devi Lal*, AIR 1990 SC 528: (1990) 1 SCC 438: JT 1990 (1) SC 5 (Ranga Nath Misra & M.M. Punchhi, JJ.).

Principle of Collective Responsibility – Object of

The object of collective responsibility is to make the whole body of persons holding ministerial office collectively, or, if one may so put it, "vicariously responsible for such acts of the others as are referable to their collective violation so that, even if an individual may not be personally responsible for it, yet, he will be deemed to share the responsibility with those who may have actually committed some wrong; *State of Karnataka* v. *Union of India*, AIR 1978 SC 68: (1977) 4 SCC 608: (1978) 2 SCR 1.

The Attorney-General for India

76. Attorney-General for India.—(1) The President shall appoint a person who is qualified to be appointed a Judge of the Supreme Court to be Attorney-General for India.

(2) It shall be the duty of the Attorney-General to give advice to the Government of India upon such legal matters, and to perform such other duties of a legal character, as may from time to time be referred or assigned to him by the President, and to discharge the functions conferred on him by or under this Constitution or any other law for the time being in force.

(3) In the performance of his duties the Attorney-General shall have right of audience in all courts in the territory of India.

(4) The Attorney-General shall hold office during the pleasure of the President, and shall receive such remuneration as the President may determine.

Conduct of Government Business

77. Conduct of business of the Government of India.—(1) All executive action of the Government of India shall be expressed to be taken in the name of the President.

(2) Orders and other instruments made and executed in the name of the President shall be authenticated in such manner as may be specified in rules[1] to be

---

1. *See* Notification No. S.O. 2297, dated the 3rd November, 1958, Gazette of India, Extra., 1958, Pt. II, Sec. 3(ii), p. 1315, as amended from time-to-time.

made by the President, and the validity of an order or instrument which is so authenticated shall not be called in question on the ground that it is not an order or instrument made or executed by the President.

(3) The President shall make rules for the more convenient transaction of the business of the Government of India, and for the allocation among Ministers of the said business.

¹[***]

Notes on Article 77

Article 77, as per judicial decisions, applied to all *executive* action of the Government of India, including constitutional or statutory functions, and even including quasi-judicial powers. *See* the undermentioned decisions:

   (i) *Samsher Singh* v. *State of Punjab*, AIR 1974 SC 2192: (1974) 2 SCC 831: (1974) 2 LLJ 465.

  (ii) *Union of India* v. *Sripati*, (1976) 1 SCWR 173: (1975) 4 SCC 699: AIR 1975 SC 1755.

 (iii) *Kalyan Singh* v. *State of Uttar Pradesh*, AIR 1962 SC 1183: (1962) Supp 2 SCR 76: 1962 All LJ 523: ILR (1962) 1 All 906: 1963 (1) SCJ 50.

 (iv) *D.S. Sharma* v. *Union of India*, AIR 1970 Del 250.

  (v) *Ananda* v. *Chief Secretary*, AIR 1966 SC 657: (1966) 2 SCR 406: 1966 Cr LJ 586.

78. Duties of Prime Minister as respects the furnishing of information to the President, etc.—It shall be the duty of the Prime Minister—

  (a) to communicate to the President all decisions of the Council of Ministers relating to the administration of the affairs of the Union and proposals for legislation;

  (b) to furnish such information relating to the administration of the affairs of the Union and proposals for legislation as the President may call for; and

  (c) if the President so requires, to submit for the consideration of the Council of Ministers any matter on which a decision has been taken by a Minister but which has not been considered by the Council.

Notes on Article 78

Cabinet Secrecy

Resolutions or other deliberations at meetings of State Cabinet and advice finally tendered in pursuance of such deliberations, are privileged from disclosure in court. But if Government produces them without any objection, the court can look into them. *See* the undermentioned decisions:

   (i) *State of Punjab* v. *Sodhi Sukhdev Singh*, AIR 1961 SC 493 (512, 532): (1961) 1 SCA 434: 1961 Mad LJ (Cri) 731: 1961 (2) SCJ 691: (1961) 2 Mad LJ (SC) 203: (1961) 2 SCR 371.

  (ii) *State of Madhya Pradesh* v. *Nandlal Jaiswal*, AIR 1987 SC 251: (1986) 4 SCC 566: JT 1986 (2) SC 701: 1986 (4) Supreme 81: 1987 Jab LJ 53: (1987) 20 STL 83: 1987 Cr LR (SC) 128: 1987 MPLJ 250.

See also Notes on article 74.

CHAPTER II

PARLIAMENT

General

79. Constitution of Parliament.—There shall be a Parliament for the Union which shall consist of the President and two Houses to be known respectively as the Council of States and the House of the People.

---

1. Clause (4) omitted by the Constitution (Forty-fourth Amendment) Act, 1978, sec. 12 (w.e.f. 20-6-1979). Earlier clause (4) was inserted by the Constitution (Forty-second Amendment) Act, 1976, sec. 14 (w.e.f. 3-1-1977).

80. Composition of the Council of States.—(1) [1][[2][***] The Council of States] shall consist of—

(a) twelve members to be nominated by the President in accordance with the provisions of clause (3); and

(b) not more than two hundred and thirty-eight representatives of the States [3][and of the Union territories].

(2) The allocation of seats in the Council of States to be filled by representatives of the States [4][and of the Union territories] shall be in accordance with the provisions in that behalf contained in the Fourth Schedule.

(3) The members to be nominated by the President under sub-clause (a) of clause (1) shall consist of persons having special knowledge or practical experience in respect of such matters as the following, namely:—

Literature, science, art and social service.

(4) The representatives of each State [5][***] in the Council of States shall be elected by the elected members of the Legislative Assembly of the State in accordance with the system of proportional representation by means of the single transferable vote.

(5) The representatives of the [6][Union Territories] in the Council of States shall be chosen in such manner as Parliament may by law prescribe.

[7][**81. Composition of the House of the People.**—(1) [8][Subject to the provisions of article 331 [9][***],] the House of the People shall consist of—

(a) not more than [10][five hundred and thirty members] chosen by direct election from territorial constituencies in the States, and

---

1. The words and figure "Subject to the provisions of paragraph 4 of the Tenth Schedule, the Council of States" subs. by the Constitution (Thirty-fifth Amendment) Act, 1974, sec. 3, for "The Council of States" (w.e.f. 1-3-1975).

2. The words "Subject to the provisions of paragraph 4 of the Tenth Schedule," omitted by the Constitution (Thirty-sixth Amendment) Act, 1975, sec. 5(b) (w.e.f. 26-4-1975).

3. Added by the Constitution (Seventh Amendment) Act, 1956, sec. 3(1)(a) (w.e.f. 1-11-1956).

4. Added by the Constitution (Seventh Amendment) Act, 1956, sec. 3(1)(b) (w.e.f. 1-11-1956).

5. The words and letters "specified in Part A or Part B of the First Schedule" omitted by the Constitution (Seventh Amendment) Act, 1956, sec. 3(1)(c) (w.e.f. 1-11-1956).

6. Subs. by the Constitution (Seventh Amendment) Act, 1956, sec. 3(1)(d), for "States specified in Part C of the First Schedule" (w.e.f. 1-11-1956).

7. Subs. by the Constitution (Seventh Amendment) Act, 1956, sec. 4, for article 81 (w.e.f. 1-11-1956). Earlier article 81 was amended by the Constitution (Second Amendment) Act, 1952, sec. 2 (w.e.f. 1-5-1953).

8. Subs. by the Constitution (Thirty-fifth Amendment) Act, 1974, sec. 4, for "Subject to the provisions of article 331" (w.e.f. 1-3-1975).

9. The words and figure "and paragraph 4 of the Tenth Schedule" omitted by the Constitution (Thirty-sixth Amendment) Act, 1975, sec. 5(c) (w.e.f. 26-4-1975).

10. Subs. by the Goa, Daman and Diu Reorganisation Act, 1987 (18 of 1987), sec. 63, for "five hundred and twenty-five members" (w.e.f. 30-5-1987). Earlier the words "five hundred and twenty-five members" were substituted by the Constitution (Thirty-first Amendment) Act, 1973, sec. 2(a)(i), for the words "five hundred members" (w.e.f. 17-10-1973).

(b) not more than [1][twenty members] to represent the Union territories, chosen in such manner as Parliament may by law provide.

(2) For the purposes of sub-clause (a) of clause (1)—

(a) there shall be allotted to each State a number of seats in the House of the People in such manner that the ratio between that number and the population of the State is, so far as practicable, the same for all States; and

(b) each State shall be divided into territorial constituencies in such manner that the ratio between the population of each constituency and number of seats allotted to it is, so far as practicable, the same throughout the State:

[2][Provided that the provisions of sub-clause (a) of this clause shall not be applicable for the purpose of allotment of seats in the House of the People to any State so long as the population of that State does not exceed six millions.]

(3) In this article, the expression "population" means the population as ascertained at the last preceding census of which the relevant figures have been published:

[3][Provided that the reference in this clause to the last preceding census of which the relevant figures have been published shall, until the relevant figures for the first census taken after the year [4][2026] have been published, [5][be construed,—

(i) for the purposes of sub-clause (a) of clause (2) and the proviso to that clause, as a reference to the 1971 census; and

(ii) for the purposes of sub-clause (b) of clause (2) as a reference to the [6][2001] census.]]

[7][**82. Readjustment after each census.**—Upon the completion of each census, the allocation of seats in the House of the People to the States and the division of each State into territorial constituencies shall be readjusted by such authority and in such manner as Parliament may by law determine:

Provided that such readjustment shall not affect representation in the House of the People until the dissolution of the then existing House:]

[8][Provided further that such readjustment shall take effect from such date as President may, by order, specify and until such readjustment takes effect, any election to the House may be held on the basis of the territorial constituencies existing before such readjustment:

---

1. Subs. by the Constitution (Thirty-first Amendment) Act, 1973, sec. 2(a)(ii), for "twenty-five members" (w.e.f. 17-10-1973). Earlier the words "twenty-five members" were substituted by the Constitution (Fourteenth Amendment) Act, 1962, sec. 2, for the words "twenty members" (w.e.f. 28-12-1962).

2. Ins. by the Constitution (Thirty-first Amendment) Act, 1973, sec. 2(b) (w.e.f. 17-10-1973).

3. Ins. by the Constitution (Forty-second Amendment) Act, 1976, sec. 15 (w.e.f. 3-1-1977).

4. Subs. by the Constitution (Eighty-fourth Amendment) Act, 2001, sec. 3(i), for "2000" (w.e.f. 21-2-2002).

5. Subs. by the Constitution (Eighty-fourth Amendment) Act, 2001, sec. 3(ii), for "be construed as a reference to the 1971 census" (w.e.f. 21-2-2002).

6. Subs. by the Constitution (Eighty-seventh Amendment) Act, 2003, sec. 2, for '1991' (w.e.f. 22-6-2003).

7. Subs. by the Constitution (Seventh Amendment) Act, 1956, sec. 4, for article 82 (w.e.f. 1-11-1956).

8. Ins. by the Constitution (Forty-second Amendment) Act, 1976, sec. 16 (w.e.f. 3-1-1977).

Provided also that until the relevant figures for the first census taken after the year [1][2026] have been published, it shall not be necessary to [2][readjust—

(i) the allocation of seats in the House of the People to the States as readjusted on the basis of the 1971 census; and

(ii) the division of each State into territorial constituencies as may be readjusted on the basis of the [3][2001] census,

under this article.]]

83. Duration of Houses of Parliament.—(1) The Council of States shall not be subject to dissolution, but as nearly as possible one-third of the members thereof shall retire as soon as may be on the expiration of every second year in accordance with the provisions made in that behalf by Parliament by law.

(2) The House of the People, unless sooner dissolved, shall continue for [4][five years] from the date appointed for its first meeting and no longer and the expiration of the said period of [4][five years] shall operate as a dissolution of the House:

Provided that the said period may, while a Proclamation of Emergency is in operation, be extended by Parliament by law for a period not exceeding one year at a time and not extending in any case beyond a period of six months after the Proclamation has ceased to operate.

84. Qualification for membership of Parliament.—A person shall not be qualified to be chosen to fill a seat in Parliament unless he—

[5][(a) is a citizen of India, and makes and subscribes before some person authorised in that behalf by the Election Commission an oath or affirmation according to the form set out for the purpose in the Third Schedule;]

(b) is, in the case of a seat in the Council of States, not less than thirty years of age and, in the case of a seat in the House of the People, not less than twenty-five years of age; and

(c) possesses such other qualifications as may be prescribed in that behalf by or under any law made by Parliament.

[6][**85. Sessions of Parliament, prorogation and dissolution.**—(1) The President shall from time to time summon each House of Parliament to meet at such time and place as he thinks fit, but six months shall not intervene between its last sitting in one session and the date appointed for its first sitting in the next session.

---

1. Subs. by the Constitution (Eighty-fourth Amendment) Act, 2001, sec. 4(i), for "2000" (w.e.f. 21-2-2002).

2. Subs. by the Constitution (Eighty-fourth Amendment) Act, 2001, sec. 4(ii), for certain words (w.e.f. 21-2-2002).

3. Subs. by the Constitution (Eighty-seventh Amendment) Act, 2003, sec. 3, for '1991' (w.e.f. 22-6-2003).

4. Subs. by the Constitution (Forty-fourth Amendment) Act, 1978, sec. 13, for "six years" (w.e.f. 20-6-1979). Earlier the words "six years" were substituted by the Constitution (Forty-second Amendment) Act, 1976, sec. 17(i), for the words "five years"(w.e.f. 3-1-1977). •

5. Subs. by the Constitution (Sixteenth Amendment) Act, 1963, sec. 3, for clause (a) (w.e.f. 5-10-1963).

6. Subs. by the Constitution (First Amendment) Act, 1951, sec. 6, for article 85 (w.e.f. 18-6-1951).

(2) The President may from time to time—

(a) prorogue the Houses or either House;

(b) dissolve the House of the People.]

Notes on Article 85

See the undermentioned cases:

  (i) *U.N.R. Rao* v. *Indira Gandhi*, AIR 1971 SC 1002: (1971) 2 SCC 63: (1971) 1 Civ Ap J (SC) 176: (1971) Supp SCR 46.

  (ii) *Indira Nehru Gandhi* v. *Raj Narain*, AIR 1975 SC 2299: 1975 Supp SCC 1: (1976) 2 SCR 347.

86. Right of President to address and send messages to Houses.—(1) The President may address either House of Parliament or both Houses assembled together, and for that purpose require the attendance of members.

(2) The President may send messages to either House of Parliament, whether with respect to a Bill then pending in Parliament or otherwise, and a House to which any message is so sent shall with all convenient despatch consider any matter required by the message to be taken into consideration.

87. Special address by the President.—(1) At the commencement of ¹[the first session after each general election to the House of the People and at the commencement of the first session of each year] the President shall address both Houses of Parliament assembled together and inform Parliament of the causes of its summons.

(2) Provision shall be made by the rules regulating the procedure of either House for the allotment of time for discussion of the matters referred to in such address ²[***].

88. Rights of Ministers and Attorney-General as respects Houses.—Every Minister and the Attorney-General of India shall have the right to speak in, and otherwise to take part in the proceedings of, either House, any joint sitting of the Houses, and any committee of Parliament of which he may be named a member, but shall not by virtue of this article be entitled to vote.

Officers of Parliament

89. The Chairman and Deputy Chairman of the Council of States.—(1) The Vice-President of India shall be *ex-officio* Chairman of the Council of States.

(2) The Council of States shall, as soon as may be, choose a member of the Council to be Deputy Chairman thereof and, so often as the office of Deputy Chairman becomes vacant, the Council shall choose another member to be Deputy Chairman thereof.

90. Vacation and resignation of, and removal from, the office of Deputy Chairman.—A member holding office as Deputy Chairman of the Council of States—

(a) shall vacate his office if he ceases to be a member of the Council;

(b) may at any time, by writing under his hand addressed to the Chairman, resign his office; and

---

1. Subs. by the Constitution (First Amendment) Act, 1951, sec. 7(1), for "every session" (w.e.f. 18-6-1951).

2. The words "and for the precedence of such discussion over other business of the House" omitted by the Constitution (First Amendment) Act, 1951, sec. 7(2) (w.e.f. 18-6-1951).

(c) may be removed from his office by a resolution of the Council passed by a majority of all the then members of the Council:

Provided that no resolution for the purpose of clause (c) shall be moved unless at least fourteen days' notice has been given of the intention to move the resolution.

91. Power of the Deputy Chairman or other person to perform the duties of the office of, or to act as, Chairman.—(1) While the office of Chairman is vacant, or during any period when the Vice-President is acting as, or discharging the functions of, President, the duties of the office shall be performed by the Deputy Chairman, or, if the office of Deputy Chairman is also vacant, by such member of the Council of States as the President may appoint for the purpose.

(2) During the absence of the Chairman from any sitting of the Council of States the Deputy Chairman, or, if he is also absent, such person as may be determined by the rules of procedure of the Council, or, if no such person is present, such other person as may be determined by the Council, shall act as Chairman.

92. The Chairman or the Deputy Chairman not to preside while a resolution for his removal from office is under consideration.—(1) At any sitting of the Council of States, while any resolution for the removal of the Vice-President from his office is under consideration, the Chairman, or while any resolution for the removal of the Deputy Chairman from his office is under consideration, the Deputy Chairman, shall not, though he is present, preside, and the provisions of clause (2) of article 91 shall apply in relation to every such sitting as they apply in relation to a sitting from which the Chairman, or, as the case may be, the Deputy Chairman, is absent.

(2) The Chairman shall have the right to speak in, and otherwise to take part in the proceedings of, the Council of States while any resolution for the removal of the Vice-President from his office is under consideration in the Council, but, notwithstanding anything in article 100 shall not be entitled to vote at all on such resolution or on any other matter during such proceedings.

93. The Speaker and Deputy Speaker of the House of the People.—The House of the People shall, as soon as may be, choose two members of the House to be respectively Speaker and Deputy Speaker thereof and, so often as the office of Speaker or Deputy Speaker becomes vacant, the House shall choose another member to be Speaker or Deputy Speaker, as the case may be.

94. Vacation and resignation of, and removal from, the offices of Speaker and Deputy Speaker.—A member holding office as Speaker or Deputy Speaker of the House of the People—

(a) shall vacate his office if he ceases to be a member of the House of the People;

(b) may at any time, by writing under his hand addressed, if such member is the Speaker, to the Deputy Speaker, and if such member is the Deputy Speaker, to the Speaker, resign his office; and

(c) may be removed from his office by a resolution of the House of the People passed by a majority of all the then members of the House:

Provided that no resolution for the purpose of clause (c) shall be moved unless at least fourteen days' notice has been given of the intention to move the resolution:

Provided further that, whenever the House of the People is dissolved, the Speaker shall not vacate his office until immediately before the first meeting of the House of the People after the dissolution.

95. Power of the Deputy Speaker or other person to perform the duties of the office of, or to act as, Speaker.—(1) While the office of Speaker is vacant, the duties of the office shall be performed by the Deputy Speaker or, if the office of Deputy Speaker is also vacant, by such member of the House of the People as the President may appoint for the purpose.

(2) During the absence of the Speaker from any sitting of the House of the People the Deputy Speaker or, if he is also absent, such person as may be determined by the rules of procedure of the House, or, if no such person is present, such other person as may be determined by the House, shall act as Speaker.

96. The Speaker or the Deputy Speaker not to preside while a resolution for his removal from office is under consideration.—(1) At any sitting of the House of the People, while any resolution for the removal of the Speaker from his office is under consideration, the Speaker, or while any resolution for the removal of the Deputy Speaker from his office is under consideration, the Deputy Speaker, shall not, though he is present, preside, and the provisions of clause (2) of article 95 shall apply in relation to every such sitting as they apply in relation to a sitting from which the Speaker, or, as the case may be, the Deputy Speaker, is absent.

(2) The Speaker shall have the right to speak in, and otherwise to take part in the proceedings of, the House of the People while any resolution for his removal from office is under consideration in the House and shall, notwithstanding anything in article 100, be entitled to vote only in the first instance on such resolution or on any other matter during such proceedings but not in the case of an equality of votes.

97. Salaries and allowances of the Chairman and Deputy Chairman and the Speaker and Deputy Speaker.—There shall be paid to the Chairman and the Deputy Chairman of the Council of States, and to the Speaker and the Deputy Speaker of the House of the People, such salaries and allowances as may be respectively fixed by Parliament by law and, until provision in that behalf is so made, such salaries and allowances as are specified in the Second Schedule.

98. Secretariat of Parliament.—(1) Each House of Parliament shall have a separate secretarial staff:

Provided that nothing in this clause shall be construed as preventing the creation of posts common to both Houses of Parliament.

(2) Parliament may by law regulate the recruitment, and the conditions of service of persons appointed, to the secretarial staff of either House of Parliament.

(3) Until provision is made by Parliament under clause (2), the President may, after consultation with the Speaker of the House of the People or the Chairman of the Council of States, as the case may be, make rules regulating the recruitment, and the conditions of service of persons appointed, to the secretarial staff of the House of the People or the Council of States, and any rules so made shall have effect subject to the provisions of any law made under the said clause.

Conduct of Business

99. Oath or affirmation by members.—Every member of either House of Parliament shall, before taking his seat, make and subscribe before the President, or some person appointed in that behalf by him, an oath or affirmation according to the form set out for the purpose in the Third Schedule.

100. Voting in Houses, power of Houses to act notwithstanding vacancies and quorum.—(1) Save as otherwise provided in this Constitution, all questions at any sitting of either House or joint sitting of the Houses shall be determined by a majority of votes of the members present and voting, other than the Speaker or person acting as Chairman or Speaker.

The Chairman or Speaker, or person acting as such, shall not vote in the first instance, but shall have and exercise a casting vote in the case of an equality of votes.

(2) Either House of Parliament shall have power to act notwithstanding any vacancy in the membership thereof, and any proceedings in Parliament shall be valid notwithstanding that it is discovered subsequently that some person who was not entitled so to do sat or voted or otherwise took part in the proceedings.

(3) Until Parliament by law otherwise provides, the quorum to constitute a meeting of either House of Parliament shall be one-tenth of the total number of members of the House.

(4) If at any time during a meeting of a House there is no quorum, it shall be the duty of the Chairman or Speaker, or person acting as such, either to adjourn the House or to suspend the meeting until there is a quorum.

Disqualifications of Members

101. Vacation of seats.—(1) No person shall be a member of both Houses of Parliament and provision shall be made by Parliament by law for the vacation by a person who is chosen a member of both Houses of his seat in one House or the other.

(2) No person shall be a member both of Parliament and of a House of the Legislature of a State [1][***], and if a person is chosen a member both of Parliament and of a House of the Legislature of [2][a State], then, at the expiration of such period as may be specified in rules[3] made by the President, that person's seat in Parliament shall become vacant, unless he has previously resigned his seat in the Legislature of the State.

(3) If a member of either House of Parliament—

(a) becomes subject to any of the disqualifications mentioned in [4][clause (1) or clause (2) of article 102], or

[5][(b) resigns his seat by writing under his hand addressed to the Chairman or the Speaker, as the case may be, and his resignation is accepted by the Chairman or the Speaker, as the case may be,]

his seat shall thereupon become vacant:

---

1. The words and letters "specified in Part A or Part B of the First Schedule" omitted by the Constitution (Seventh Amendment) Act, 1956, sec. 29 and Sch. (w.e.f. 1-11-1956).
2. Subs. by the Constitution (Seventh Amendment) Act, 1956, sec. 29 and Sch., for "such a State" (w.e.f. 1-11-1956).
3. *See* the Prohibition of Simultaneous Membership Rules, 1950, published with the Ministry of Law Notification No. F. 46/50-C, dated the 26th January, 1950, Gazette of India, Extraordinary, p. 678.
4. Subs. by the Constitution (Fifty-second Amendment) Act, 1985, sec. 2 for "clause (1) of article 102" (w.e.f. 1-3-1985).
5. Subs. by the Constitution (Thirty-third Amendment) Act, 1974, sec. 2(1), for sub-clause (b) (w.e.f. 19-5-1974).

[1][Provided that in the case of any resignation referred to in sub-clause (b), if from information received or otherwise and after making such inquiry as he thinks fit, the Chairman or the Speaker, as the case may be, is satisfied that such resignation is not voluntary or genuine, he shall not accept such resignation.]

(4) If for a period of sixty days a member of either House of Parliament is without permission of the House absent from all meetings thereof, the House may declare his seat vacant:

Provided that in computing the said period of sixty days no account shall be taken of any period during which the House is prorogued or is adjourned for more than four consecutive days.

102. Disqualifications for membership.—(1) A person shall be disqualified for being chosen as, and for being, a member of either House of Parliament—

(a) if he holds any office of profit under the Government of India or the Government of any State, other than an office declared by Parliament by law not to disqualify its holder;

(b) if he is of unsound mind and stands so declared by a competent court;

(c) if he is an undischarged insolvent;

(d) if he is not a citizen of India, or has voluntarily acquired the citizenship of a foreign State, or is under any acknowledgement of allegiance or adherence to a foreign State;

(e) if he is so disqualified by or under any law made by Parliament.

[2][*Explanation.*—For the purposes of this clause] a person shall not be deemed to hold an office of profit under the Government of India or the Government of any State by reason only that he is a Minister either for the Union or for such State.

[3][(2) A person shall be disqualified for being a member of either House of Parliament if he is so disqualified under the Tenth Schedule.]

Notes on Article 102

Code of Conduct

Code of conduct has no statutory force, *Vidadala Harinadhababu* v. *N.T. Ramarao*, AIR 1990 AP 20 (FB).

Material Date

Material date is the date of scrutiny of nomination, subject to the qualification that when a conviction is set aside on appeal, the appellate order has retrospective effect. *See* the undermentioned cases:

(i) *Amrit Lal Ambalal Patel* v. *Himathbai Gomanbhai Patel*, AIR 1968 SC 1455: (1969) 1 SCR 277.

(ii) *Dilip* v. *State of Madhya Pradesh*, AIR 1976 SC 133: (1976) 1 SCC 560: (1976) 2 SCR 289.

(iii) *Sitaram* v. *Ramjibhai*, AIR 1987 SC 1293: (1987) 2 SCC 262: (1987) 3 ATC 515.

(iv) *Pashupati Nath Sukul* v. *Nem Chandra Jain*, (1984) 2 SCC 404: AIR 1984 SC 399: 1984 All LJ 215: 1984 UJ (SC) 179, paragraphs 18 and 42.

---

1. Ins. by the Constitution (Thirty-third Amendment) Act, 1974, sec. 2(2) (w.e.f. 19-5-1974).

2. Subs. by the Constitution (Fifty-second Amendment) Act, 1985, sec. 3(a), for "(2) For the purposes of this article" (w.e.f. 1-3-1985).

3. Ins. by the Constitution (Fifty-second Amendment) Act, 1985, sec. 3(b) (w.e.f. 1-3-1985).

Office of Profit

If the 'pecuniary gain' is 'receivable' in connection with the office then it becomes an office of profit, irrespective of whether such pecuniary gain is actually received or not; *Jaya Bachchan* v. *Union of India*, AIR 2006 SC 2119: 2006 AIR SCW 2601: 2006 (34) OCR 837: (2006) 5 SCC 266: 2006 (5) SCJ 1: 2006 (7) SRJ 330: (2006) 5 SCALE 511: 2006 (4) Supreme 378.

The office of profit must be under the Government, Contrast articles 58(2) and 66(4) covering local and other authorities, *See* the undermentioned cases:

(i) *Abdul Shakur* v. *Rikhab Chand (Election Tribunal, Ajmer)*, AIR 1958 SC 52 (55): 1958 SCR 387: 1958 SCA 279: 1958 SCJ 329: (1958) 1 Mad LJ (SC) 88.

(ii) *Kanta Kathuria* v. *Manak Chand Surana*, AIR 1970 SC 694: (1969) 3 SCC 268: 1970 (2) SCJ 232: (1970) 2 SCR 835.

(iii) *Ashok Kumar Bhattacharyya* v. *Ajoy Biswas*, AIR 1985 SC 211: (1985) 1 SCC 154: 1985 UJ (SC) 7: (1984) 2 MCC 285: (1985) 1 Cur CC 339: (1985) 2 SCR 50: 1985 Cur Civ LJ (SC) 316.

(iv) *Bhagwati* v. *Rajeev*, AIR 1986 SC 1534: (1986) 4 SCC 78: 1986 SCC (Cri) 399.

Principle Debarring Holders of Office of Profit

The principle debarring holders of office of profit 'under the Government' from being a member of Parliament is that such a person cannot exercise his functions independently of the executive of which he is a part. The principle can be traced to developments in English constitution history, in the course of which it came to be established that the Crown and its officers shall have no say in Parliament.

[1][**103. Decision on questions as to disqualifications of members.**—(1) If any question arises as to whether a member of either House of Parliament has become subject to any of the disqualifications mentioned in clause (1) of article 102, the question shall be referred for the decision of the President and his decision shall be final.

(2) Before giving any decision on any such question, the President shall obtain the opinion of the Election Commission and shall act according to such opinion.]

Notes on Article 103

Office of Profit

If the 'pecuniary gain' is 'receivable' in connection with the office then it becomes an office of profit, irrespective of whether such pecuniary gain is actually received or not; *Jaya Bachchan* v. *Union of India*, AIR 2006 SC 2119: 2006 AIR SCW 2601: 2006 (34) OCR 837: (2006) 5 SCC 266: 2006 (5) SCJ 1: 2006 (7) SRJ 330: (2006) 5 SCALE 511: 2006 (4) Supreme 378.

104. Penalty for sitting and voting before making oath or affirmation under article 99 or when not qualified or when disqualified.—If a person sits or votes as a member of either House of Parliament before he has complied with the requirements of article 99, or when he knows that he is not qualified or that he is disqualified for membership thereof, or that he is prohibited from so doing by the provisions of any law made by Parliament, he shall be liable in respect of each day on which he so sits or votes to a penalty of five hundred rupees to be recovered as a debt due to the Union.

Powers, Privileges and Immunities of Parliament and its Members

105. Powers, privileges, etc., of the Houses of Parliament and of the members and committees thereof.—(1) Subject to the provisions of this Constitution and to

---

1. Subs. by the Constitution (Forty-fourth Amendment) Act, 1978, sec. 14, for article 103 (w.e.f. 20-6-1979). Earlier article 103 was substituted by the Constitution (Forty-second Amendment) Act, 1976, sec. 20 (w.e.f. 3-1-1977).

the rules and standing orders regulating the procedure of Parliament, there shall be freedom of speech in Parliament.

(2) No member of Parliament shall be liable to any proceedings in any court in respect of anything said or any vote given by him in Parliament or any committee thereof, and no person shall be so liable in respect of the publication by or under the authority of either House of Parliament of any report, paper, votes or proceedings.

(3) In other respects, the powers, privileges and immunities of each House of Parliament, and of the members and the committees of each House, shall be such as may from time to time be defined by Parliament by law, and, until so defined, [1][shall be those of that House and of its members and committees immediately before the coming into force of section 15 of the Constitution (Forty-fourth Amendment) Act, 1978].

(4) The provisions of clauses (1), (2) and (3) shall apply in relation to persons who by virtue of this Constitution have the right to speak in, and otherwise to take part in the proceedings of, a House of Parliament or any committee thereof as they apply in relation to members of Parliament.

Notes on Article 105

Constitution (Thirty-third Amendment) Act, 1974

By the Amendment Act of 1974—

(i) power has been given to the Speaker or Chairman, to inquire into the genuineness of a letter of resignation coming from a member, and

(ii) the termination of membership by resignation has been made dependent upon the *acceptance* of such resignation by the Speaker or Chairman. A member of the Union or a State Legislature has thus lost the privilege which constitutional functionaries enjoy, namely, the termination of his office by unilateral action, and the resignation has been made dependent upon acceptance, as in the case of ordinary Government servants; *Union of India* v. *Gopal*, AIR 1978 SC 694: (1978) 2 SCC 301: (1978) 1 LLJ 492, paragraphs 84-85.

So long as the resignation is not accepted, it may be withdrawn or revoked by the member, by addressing a letter to that effect, to the Speaker or Chairman; *Union of India* v. *Gopal*, AIR 1978 SC 694: (1978) 2 SCC 301: (1978) 1 LLJ 492, paragraphs 84-85.

Effect of the Constitution (Forty-second) and (Forty-fourth) Amendment Acts

Basu has pointed out (Constitutional Law, page 215) that the changes made in the text of article 105(3) make it clear that, so long as the Legislature is not able to define its privileges by making a law, there cannot be a vacuum. It is provided in clause (3) of article 105 as well as in article 194 (as amended), that till such legislation is enacted, each House and its committees shall have those privileges which they had at the commencement of the Constitution (Forty-fourth Amendment) Act. In other words, the existing privileges shall continue, until they are replaced by privileges defined by law. *Cf. Ref. Article 143 of Constitution of India*, AIR 1965 SC 745: (1965) 1 SCR 413: 1965 (1) SCJ 847: (1965) 1 SCA 441; *State of Kerala* v. *R. Sudarsan Babu*, AIR 1984 Ker 1: 1983 Ker LT 764: ILR (1983) 2 Ker 661, paragraph 29.

Freedom of Speech

Clause (1) confers the freedom of speech in Parliament, but this is subject to the provisions of the Constitution and to the rules and standing orders of Parliament. *See* in Particular, articles 118, 121, 208 and 211 and the case mentioned below:

---

1. Subs. by the Constitution (Forty-fourth Amendment) Act, 1978, sec. 15, for certain words (w.e.f. 20-6-1979).

M.S.M. Sharma v. *Sri Krishna Sinha*, AIR 1959 SC 395 (409): (1959) Supp 1 SCR 806: (1959) 2 MLJ (SC) 125.

Privileges, Power and Immunities of House of Legislators and Members

A House of Parliament or State Legislature cannot try anyone or any case directly, as a Court of Justice can, but it can proceed quasi judicially in case of contempts of its authority and take up motions concerning its 'privileges and immunities' because, in doing so, it only seeks removal of obstructions to the due performance of its legislative functions. But, if any question of jurisdiction arises as to whether a matter falls here or not, it has to be decided by the ordinary courts in appropriate proceedings; *State of Karnataka* v. *Union of India*, (1977) 4 SCC 608: AIR 1978 SC 68: (1978) 2 SCR 1: 1978 (2) SCJ 190.

Publication by or under the Authority of a House

The immunity under article 105(2) was previously confined to publication by or under the authority of a House; *Jatish Chandra Ghose* v. *Harisadhan Mukherjee*, AIR 1961 SC 613: (1961) 3 SCR 486: (1961) 1 Cr LJ 443 affirming *Jatish Chandra Ghose* v. *Harisadhan Mukherjee*, AIR 1956 Cal 433: (1956) 60 CWN 971.

Publication of Proceedings

Immunity from liability as regards speeches in parliament and as regards publication thereof under the authority of the House is conferred by clause (2). This immunity is not subject to the provisions of the Constitution.

The underlying principle has been stated to be this, namely, that people's representatives should be free to express themselves without fear of legal consequences. Of course, the immunity is confined to what is said within the House. For publications by persons other than those authorised by the House, see article 361A, inserted by the Constitution (Forty-fourth Amendment) Act, 1978. The undermentioned cases may be seen as to liability for publication:

(i) *Jatish Chandra Ghose* v. *Harisadhan Mukherjee*, (1956) 60 CWN 971; on appeal, AIR 1961 SC 613: (1961) 3 SCR 486: (1961) 1 Cr LJ 443.

(ii) *Surendra* v. *Naba Krishna*, AIR 1958 Ori 168 (175) (Qualified privilege for publication by member outside House).

(iii) *Ramalingam* v. *Daily Thanthi*, AIR 1975 Mad 209.

(iv) *Suresh v Punit*, AIR 1951 Cal 176 (Member not liable for publication by newspaper of its own).

(v) *Tej Kiran Jain* v. *M. Sanjiva Reddy*, AIR 1970 SC 1573: (1970) 2 SCC 272: (1971) 1 SCR 612.

Scope

Parliamentary privileges is the subject-matter of this article with which one should compare article 194 concerned with privileges of Members of State Legislatures. Although the expression 'privileges' occurs in article 105(3) and article 194(3) and is historically correct, having regard to the terminology used in England, it should be pointed out that the current opinion in England is not in favour of retaining the word 'privilege'.

106. Salaries and allowances of members.—Members of either House of Parliament shall be entitled to receive such salaries and allowances as may from time to time be determined by Parliament by law and, until provision in that respect is so made, allowances at such rates and upon such conditions as were immediately before the commencement of this Constitution applicable in the case of members of the Constituent Assembly of the Dominion of India.

Legislative Procedure

107. Provisions as to introduction and passing of Bills.—(1) Subject to the provisions of articles 109 and 117 with respect to Money Bills and other financial Bills, a Bill may originate in either House of Parliament.

(2) Subject to the provisions of articles 108 and 109, a Bill shall not be deemed to have been passed by the Houses of Parliament unless it has been agreed to by both Houses, either without amendment or with such amendments only as are agreed to by both Houses.

(3) A Bill pending in Parliament shall not lapse by reason of the prorogation of the Houses.

(4) A Bill pending in the Council of States which has not been passed by the House of the People shall not lapse on a dissolution of the House of the People.

(5) A Bill which is pending in the House of the People, or which having been passed by the House of the People is pending in the Council of States, shall, subject to the provisions of article 108, lapse on a dissolution of the House of the People.

108. Joint sitting of both Houses in certain cases.—(1) If after a Bill has been passed by one House and transmitted to the other House—

(a) the Bill is rejected by the other House; or

(b) the Houses have finally disagreed as to the amendments to be made in the Bill; or

(c) more than six months elapse from the date of the reception of the Bill by the other House without the Bill being passed by it,

the President may, unless the Bill has lapsed by reason of a dissolution of the House of the People, notify to the Houses by message if they are sitting or by public notification if they are not sitting, his intention to summon them to meet in a joint sitting for the purpose of deliberating and voting on the Bill:

Provided that nothing in this clause shall apply to a Money Bill.

(2) In reckoning any such period of six months as is referred to in clause (1), no account shall be taken of any period during which the House referred to in sub-clause (c) of that clause is prorogued or adjourned for more than four consecutive days.

(3) Where the President has under clause (1) notified his intention of summoning the Houses to meet in a joint sitting, neither House shall proceed further with the Bill, but the President may at any time after the date of his notification summon the Houses to meet in a joint sitting for the purpose specified in the notification and, if he does so, the Houses shall meet accordingly.

(4) If at the joint sitting of the two Houses the Bill, with such amendments, if any, as are agreed to in joint siting, is passed by a majority of the total number of members of both Houses present and voting, it shall be deemed for the purposes of this Constitution to have been passed by both Houses:

Provided that at a joint sitting—

(a) if the Bill, having been passed by one House, has not been passed by the other House with amendments and returned to the House in which it originated, no amendment shall be proposed to the Bill other than such amendments (if any) as are made necessary by the delay in the passage of the Bill;

(b) if the Bill has been so passed and returned, only such amendments as aforesaid shall be proposed to the Bill and such other amendments as are relevant to the matters with respect to which the Houses have not agreed, and the decision of the person presiding as to the amendments which are admissible under this clause shall be final.

(5) A joint sitting may be held under this article and a Bill passed thereat, notwithstanding that a dissolution of the House of the People has intervened since the President notified his intention to summon the Houses to meet therein.

109. Special procedure in respect of Money Bills.—(1) A Money Bill shall not be introduced in the Council of States.

(2) After a Money Bill has been passed by the House of the People it shall be transmitted to the Council of States for its recommendations and the Council of States shall within a period of fourteen days from the date of its receipt of the Bill return the Bill to the House of the People with its recommendations and the House of the People may thereupon either accept or reject all or any of the recommendations of the Council of States.

(3) If the House of the People accepts any of the recommendations of the Council of States, the Money Bill shall be deemed to have been passed by both Houses with the amendments recommended by the Council of States and accepted by the House of the People.

(4) If the House of the People does not accept any of the recommendations of the Council of States, the Money Bill shall be deemed to have been passed by both Houses in the form in which it was passed by the House of the People without any of the amendments recommended by the Council of States.

(5) If a Money Bill passed by the House of the People and transmitted to the Council of States for its recommendations is not returned to the House of the People within the said period of fourteen days, it shall be deemed to have been passed by both Houses at the expiration of the said period in the form in which it was passed by the House of the People.

110. Definition of "Money Bills".—(1) For the purposes of this Chapter, a Bill shall be deemed to be a Money Bill if it contains only provisions dealing with all or any of the following matters, namely:—

(a) the imposition, abolition, remission, alteration or regulation of any tax;

(b) the regulation of the borrowing of money or the giving of any guarantee by the Government of India, or the amendment of the law with respect to any financial obligations undertaken or to be undertaken by the Government of India;

(c) the custody of the Consolidated Fund or the Contingency Fund of India, the payment of moneys into or the withdrawal of moneys from any such Fund;

(d) the appropriation of moneys out of the Consolidated Fund of India;

(e) the declaring of any expenditure to be expenditure charged on the Consolidated Fund of India or the increasing of the amount of any such expenditure;

(f) the receipt of money on account of the Consolidated Fund of India or the public account of India or the custody or issue of such money or the audit of the accounts of the Union or of a State; or

(g) any matter incidental to any of the matters specified in sub-clauses (a) to (f).

(2) A Bill shall not be deemed to be a Money Bill by reason only that it provides for the imposition of fines or other pecuniary penalties, or for the demand or

payment of fees for licences or fees for services rendered, or by reason that it provides for the imposition, abolition, remission, alteration or regulation of any tax by any local authority or body for local purposes.

(3) If any question arises whether a Bill is a Money Bill or not, the decision of the Speaker of the House of the People thereon shall be final.

(4) There shall be endorsed on every Money Bill when it is transmitted to the Council of States under article 109, and when it is presented to the President for assent under article 111, the certificate of the Speaker of the House of the People signed by him that it is a Money Bill.

111. Assent to Bills.—When a Bill has been passed by the Houses of Parliament, it shall be presented to the President, and the President shall declare either that he assents to the Bill, or that he withholds assent therefrom:

Provided that the President may, as soon as possible after the presentation to him of a Bill for assent, return the Bill if it is not a Money Bill to the Houses with a message requesting that they will reconsider the Bill or any specified provisions thereof and, in particular, will consider the desirability of introducing any such amendments as he may recommend in his message, and when a Bill is so returned, the Houses shall reconsider the Bill accordingly, and if the Bill is passed again by the Houses with or without amendment and presented to the President for assent, the President shall not withhold assent therefrom.

Procedure in Financial Matters

112. Annual financial statement.—(1) The President shall in respect of every financial year cause to be laid before both the Houses of Parliament a statement of the estimated receipts and expenditure of the Government of India for that year, in this Part referred to as the "annual financial statement".

(2) The estimates of expenditure embodied in the annual financial statement shall show separately—

(a) the sums required to meet expenditure described by this Constitution as expenditure charged upon the Consolidated Fund of India; and

(b) the sums required to meet other expenditure proposed to be made from the Consolidated Fund of India,

and shall distinguish expenditure on revenue account from other expenditure.

(3) The following expenditure shall be expenditure charged on the Consolidated Fund of India—

(a) the emoluments and allowances of the President and other expenditure relating to his office;

(b) the salaries and allowances of the Chairman and the Deputy Chairman of the Council of States and the Speaker and the Deputy Speaker of the House of the People;

(c) debt charges for which the Government of India is liable including interest, sinking fund charges and redemption charges, and other expenditure relating to the raising of loans and the service and redemption of debt;

(d) (i) the salaries, allowances and pensions payable to or in respect of Judges of the Supreme Court,

(ii) the pensions payable to or in respect of Judges of the Federal Court,

(iii) the pensions payable to or in respect of Judges of any High Court which exercises jurisdiction in relation to any area included in the territory of India or which at any time before the commencement of this Constitution exercised jurisdiction in relation to any area included in ¹[a Governor's Province of the Dominion of India];

(e) the salary, allowances and pension payable to or in respect of the Comptroller and Auditor-General of India;

(f) any sums required to satisfy any judgment, decree or award of any court or arbitral tribunal;

(g) any other expenditure declared by this Constitution or by Parliament by law to be so charged.

113. Procedure in Parliament with respect to estimates.—(1) So much of the estimates as relates to expenditure charged upon the Consolidated Fund of India shall not be submitted to the vote of Parliament, but nothing in this clause shall be construed as preventing the discussion in either House of Parliament of any of those estimates.

(2) So much of the said estimates as relates to other expenditure shall be submitted in the form of demands for grants to the House of the People, and the House of the People shall have power to assent, or to refuse to assent, to any demand, or to assent to any demand subject to a reduction of the amount specified therein.

(3) No demand for a grant shall be made except on the recommendation of the President.

114. Appropriation Bills.—(1) As soon as may be after the grants under article 113 have been made by the House of the People, there shall be introduced a Bill to provide for the appropriation out of the Consolidated Fund of India of all moneys required to meet—

(a) the grants so made by the House of the People; and

(b) the expenditure charged on the Consolidated Fund of India but not exceeding in any case the amount shown in the statement previously laid before Parliament.

(2) No amendment shall be proposed to any such Bill in either House of Parliament which will have the effect of varying the amount or altering the destination of any grant so made or of varying the amount of any expenditure charged on the Consolidated Fund of India, and the decision of the person presiding as to whether an amendment is inadmissible under this clause shall be final.

(3) Subject to the provisions of articles 115 and 116, no money shall be withdrawn from the Consolidated Fund of India except under appropriation made by law passed in accordance with the provisions of this article.

115. Supplementary, additional or excess grants.—(1) The President shall—

(a) If the amount authorised by any law made in accordance with the provisions of article 114 to be expended for a particular service for the

---

1. Subs. by the Constitution (Seventh Amendment) Act, 1956, sec. 29 and Sch., for certain words (w.e.f. 1-11-1956).

current financial year is found to be insufficient for the purposes of that year or when a need has arisen during the current financial year for supplementary or additional expenditure upon some new service not contemplated in the annual financial statement for that year, or

(b) if any money has been spent on any service during a financial year in excess of the amount granted for that service and for that year,

cause to be laid before both the Houses of Parliament another statement showing the estimated amount of that expenditure or cause to be presented to the House of the People a demand for such excess, as the case may be.

(2) The provisions of articles 112, 113 and 114 shall have effect in relation to any such statement and expenditure or demand and also to any law to be made authorising the appropriation of moneys out of the Consolidated Fund of India to meet such expenditure or the grant in respect of such demand as they have effect in relation to the annual financial statement and the expenditure mentioned therein or to a demand for a grant and the law to be made for the authorisation of appropriation of moneys out of the Consolidated Fund of India to meet such expenditure or grant.

116. Votes on account, votes of credit and exceptional grants.— (1) Notwithstanding anything in the foregoing provisions of this Chapter, the House of the People shall have power—

(a) to make any grant in advance in respect of the estimated expenditure for a part of any financial year pending the completion of the procedure prescribed in article 113 for the voting of such grant and the passing of the law in accordance with the provisions of article 114 in relation to that expenditure;

(b) to make a grant for meeting an unexpected demand upon the resources of India when on account of the magnitude or the indefinite character of the service the demand cannot be stated with the details ordinarily given in an annual financial statement;

(c) to make an exceptional grant which forms no part of the current service of any financial year,

and Parliament shall have power to authorise by law the withdrawal of moneys from the Consolidated Fund of India for the purposes for which the said grants are made.

(2) The provisions of articles 113 and 114 shall have effect in relation to the making of any grant under clause (1) and to any law to be made under that clause as they have effect in relation to the making of a grant with regard to any expenditure mentioned in the annual financial statement and the law to be made for the authorisation of appropriation of moneys out of the Consolidated Fund of India to meet such expenditure.

117. Special provisions as to financial Bills.—(1) A Bill or amendment making provision for any of the matters specified in sub-clauses (a) to (f) of clause (1) of article 110 shall not be introduced or moved except on the recommendation of the President and a Bill making such provision shall not be introduced in the Council of States:

Provided that no recommendation shall be required under this clause for the moving of an amendment making provision for the reduction or abolition of any tax.

(2) A Bill or amendment shall not be deemed to make provision for any of the matters aforesaid by reason only that it provides for the imposition of fines or other pecuniary penalties, or for the demand or payment of fees for licences or fees for services rendered, or by reason that it provides for the imposition, abolition, remission, alteration or regulation of any tax by any local authority or body for local purposes.

(3) A Bill which, if enacted and brought into operation, would involve expenditure from the Consolidated Fund of India shall not be passed by either House of Parliament unless the President has recommended to that House the consideration of the Bill.

Procedure Generally

118. Rules of procedure.—(1) Each House of Parliament may make rules for regulating, subject to the provisions of this Constitution, its procedure [1][***] and the conduct of its business.

(2) Until rules are made under clause (1), the rules of procedure and standing orders in force immediately before the commencement of this Constitution with respect to the Legislature of the Dominion of India shall have effect in relation to Parliament subject to such modifications and adaptations as may be made therein by the Chairman of the Council of States or the Speaker of the House of the People, as the case may be.

(3) The President, after consultation with the Chairman of the Council of States and the Speaker of the House of the People, may make rules as to the procedure with respect to joint sittings of, and communications between, the two Houses.

(4) At a joint sitting of the two Houses the Speaker of the House of the People, or in his absence such person as may be determined by rules of procedure made under clause (3), shall preside.

119. Regulation by law of procedure in Parliament in relation to financial business.—Parliament may, for the purpose of the timely completion of financial business, regulate by law the procedure of, and the conduct of business in, each House of Parliament in relation to any financial matter or to any Bill for the appropriation of moneys out of the Consolidated Fund of India, and, if and so far as any provision of any law so made is inconsistent with any rule made by a House of Parliament under clause (1) of article 118 or with any rule or standing order having effect in relation to Parliament under clause (2) of that article, such provision shall prevail.

120. Language to be used in Parliament.—(1) Notwithstanding anything in Part XVII, but subject to the provisions of article 348, business in Parliament shall be transacted in Hindi or in English:

Provided that the Chairman of the Council of States or Speaker of the House of the People, or person acting as such, as the case may be, may permit any member who cannot adequately express himself in Hindi or in English to address the House in his mother-tongue.

---

1. The words "(including the quorum to constitute a meeting of the House)" omitted by the Constitution (Forty-fourth Amendment) Act, 1978, sec. 45. Earlier the words "(including the quorum to constitute a meeting of the House)" were inserted by the Constitution (Forty-second Amendment) Act, 1976, sec. 22 which had not been brought into force till then.

(2) Unless Parliament by law otherwise provides, this article shall, after the expiration of a period of fifteen years from the commencement of this Constitution, have effect as if the words "or in English" were omitted therefrom.

121. Restriction on discussion in Parliament.—No discussion shall take place in Parliament with respect to the conduct of any Judge of the Supreme Court or of a High Court in the discharge of his duties except upon a motion for presenting an address to the President praying for the removal of the Judge as hereinafter provided.

122. Courts not to inquire into proceedings of Parliament.—(1) The validity of any proceedings in Parliament shall not be called in question on the ground of any alleged irregularity of procedure.

(2) No officer or member of Parliament in whom powers are vested by or under this Constitution for regulating procedure or the conduct of business, or for maintaining order, in Parliament shall be subject to the jurisdiction of any court in respect of the exercise by him of those powers.

CHAPTER III
LEGISLATIVE POWERS OF THE PRESIDENT

123. Power of President to promulgate Ordinances during recess of Parliament.—(1) If at any time, except when both Houses of Parliament are in session, the President is satisfied that circumstances exist which render it necessary for him to take immediate action, he may promulgate such Ordinances as the circumstances appear to him to require.

(2) An Ordinance promulgated under this article shall have the same force and effect as an Act of Parliament, but every such Ordinance—

(a) shall be laid before both Houses of Parliament and shall cease to operate at the expiration of six weeks from the reassembly of Parliament, or, if before the expiration of that period resolutions disapproving it are passed by both Houses, upon the passing of the second of those resolutions; and

(b) may be withdrawn at any time by the President.

Explanation.—Where the Houses of Parliament are summoned to reassemble on different dates, the period of six weeks shall be reckoned from the later of those dates for the purposes of this clause.

(3) If and so far as an Ordinance under this article makes any provision which Parliament would not under this Constitution be competent to enact, it shall be void.

[1][***]

Notes on Article 123

Effect of Duration

As pointed out above, the law making power of the President is co-extensive as regards all matters except duration, with the law-making power of Parliament, it follows that the power is subject to constitutional provisions, particularly those regarding fundamental rights. In respect of the subject-matter of Ordinances, the position is the same as applies to Parliament under the

---

1. Clause (4) omitted by the Constitution (Forty-fourth Amendment) Act, 1978, sec. 16 (w.e.f. 20-6-1979). Earlier clause (4) was inserted by the Constitution (Thirty-eighth Amendment) Act, 1975, sec. 2 (retrospectively).

constitutional scheme of distribution of legislative powers between the Union and the States undermentioned decisions illustrate these aspects:

   (i) *State of Punjab* v. *Mohar Singh*, AIR 1955 SC 84: (1955) 1 SCR 893: 1955 Cr LJ 254.

  (ii) *Garg* v. *Union of India*, AIR 1981 SC 2138: (1981) 4 SCC 675: (1982) 133 ITR 239.

 (iii) *T. Venkata Reddy* v. *State of Andhra Pradesh*, AIR 1985 SC 724: (1985) 3 SCC 193: 1985 SCC (L&S) 632.

 (iv) *Nagaraj* v. *State of Andhra Pradesh*, AIR 1985 SC 551: (1985) 1 SCC 523: (1985) 1 LLJ 444.

  (v) *State of Orissa* v. *Bhupendra*, AIR 1962 SC 945 (955): (1962) Supp 2 SCR 380: (1962) 28 Cut LT 273.

Re-promulgation

While no case has gone to the Supreme Court regarding re-promulgation of Ordinances by the Union, notice must be taken of the Supreme Court judgment holding that successive repromulgation of Ordinances with the same text by the Governor of Bihar, without any attempt to get the Bills passed by the State Assembly while it was in session, coupled with the habitual practice of proroguing the Assembly merely in order to enable the Governor to repromulgate an Ordinance in a routine manner would be a fraud on the Constitution, and the Ordinance so repromulgated is liable to be struck down; *Dr. D.C. Wadhwa* v. *State of Bihar*, AIR 1987 SC 579: (1987) 1 SCC 378: JT 1987 (1) SC 70: 1986 (4) Supreme 465: 1987 BBCJ (SC) 46: 1987 IJR 116.

Scope

This article is intended to enable the President to promulgate Ordinances during the recess of Parliament. The President's power is no higher and no lower than that of the law-making power of the Parliament. The satisfaction of the President must be as to the existence of circumstances which render it necessary for him to take immediate action and such satisfaction has to be on the advice of the Cabinet. Undermentioned decisions illustrate these propositions:

   (i) *Rustom Cowasji Cooper* v. *Union of India*, AIR 1970 SC 564: (1970) 1 SCC 248: (1970) 40 Comp Cas 325: 1970 (3) SCR 530.

  (ii) *A.K. Roy* v. *Union of India*, AIR 1982 SC 710: (1982) 1 SCC 271: 1982 Cr LJ 340.

 (iii) *State of Rajasthan* v. *Union of India*, AIR 1977 SC 1361: (1977) 3 SCC 592: (1978) 1 SCR 1: 1978 (1) SCJ 78.

 (iv) *T. Venkata Reddy* v. *State of Andhra Pradesh*, AIR 1985 SC 724: (1985) 3 SCC 193: 1985 SCC (L&S) 632.

  (v) *Nagaraj* v. *State of Andhra Pradesh*, AIR 1985 SC 551: (1985) 1 SCC 523: (1985) 1 LLJ 444.

 (vi) *Satpal* v. *Lt. Governor*, AIR 1979 SC 1550: (1979) 4 SCC 232: 1979 Tax LR 2486.

CHAPTER IV

THE UNION JUDICIARY

124. Establishment and constitution of Supreme Court.—(1) There shall be a Supreme Court of India consisting of a Chief Justice of India and, until Parliament by law prescribes a larger number, of not more than seven[1] other Judges.

(2) Every Judge of the Supreme Court shall be appointed by the President by warrant under his hand and seal after consultation with such of the Judges of the Supreme Court and of the High Courts in the States as the President may deem necessary for the purpose and shall hold office until he attains the age of sixty-five years:

Provided that in the case of appointment of a Judge other than the Chief Justice, the Chief Justice of India shall always be consulted:

---

1. Now "thirty", *vide* the Supreme Court (Number of Judges) Amendment Act, 2008 (11 of 2009). Earlier it was "twenty-five", *vide* the Supreme Court (Number of Judges) Amendment Act, 1986 (22 of 1986).

Provided further that—

(a) a Judge may, by writing under his hand addressed to the President, resign his office;

(b) a Judge may be removed from his office in the manner provided in clause (4).

[1][(2A) The age of a Judge of the Supreme Court shall be determined by such authority and in such manner as Parliament may by law provide.]

(3) A person shall not be qualified for appointment as a Judge of the Supreme Court unless he is a citizen of India and—

(a) has been for at least five years a Judge of a High Court or of two or more such Courts in succession; or

(b) has been for at least ten years an advocate of a High Court or of two or more such courts in succession; or

(c) is, in the opinion of the President, a distinguished jurist.

Explanation I.—In this clause "High Court" means a High Court which exercises, or which at any time before the commencement of this Constitution exercised, jurisdiction in any part of the territory of India.

Explanation II.—In computing for the purpose of this clause the period during which a person has been an advocate, any period during which a person has held judicial office not inferior to that of a district Judge after he became an advocate shall be included.

(4) A Judge of the Supreme Court shall not be removed from his office except by an order of the President passed after an address by each House of Parliament supported by a majority of the total membership of that House and by a majority of not less than two-thirds of the members of the House present and voting has been presented to the President in the same session for such removal on the ground of proved misbehaviour or incapacity.

(5) Parliament may by law regulate the procedure for the presentation of an address and for the investigation and proof of the misbehaviour or incapacity of a Judge under clause (4).

(6) Every person appointed to be a Judge of the Supreme Court shall, before he enters upon his office, make and subscribe before the President, or some person appointed in that behalf by him, an oath or affirmation according to the form set out for the purpose in the Third Schedule.

(7) No person who has held office as a Judge of the Supreme Court shall plead or act in any court or before any authority within the territory of India.

Notes on Article 124

Appointment of Judge

A nine Judges Bench of the Supreme Court *In re Presidential Reference,* AIR 1999 SC 1: 1998 AIR SCW 3400: JT 1998 (7) SC 304: (1998) 7 SCC 739: 1998 (4) SCJ 200: 1998 (4) SCT 696: (1998) 5 SCALE 629: 1998 (8) Supreme 140, has held that recommendations made by the Chief Justice of India without complying with the "norms and requirements of the consultation process" were not binding on the Central Government.

In July 1998, the President has sought the Court's opinion on nine issues relating to the appointment of Apex Court judges and transfer of High Court Judges. The 11th Presidential

---

1. Ins. by the Constitution (Fifteenth Amendment) Act, 1963, sec. 2 (w.e.f. 5-10-1963).

Reference sought clarification on certain doubts over the consultation process to be adopted by the Chief Justice of India as stipulated in the 1993 case relating to judges appointment and transfer opinion.

The following propositions were laid down:—

(a) As to the appointment of the Supreme Court Judges, the Chief Justice of India should consult a collegium of four seniormost Judges of the Apex Court. Even if two judges give an adverse opinion, the CJI should not send the recommendation to the Government.

(b) Giving primacy to the CJI's opinion as laid down in the 1983 judgment, the judges said, "The collegium should make the decision in consensus and unless the opinion of the collegium is in conformity with that of the Chief Justice of India, no recommendation is to be made."

(c) Regarding the transfer of High Court judges, in addition to the collegium of four seniormost Judges, the Chief Justice of India was obliged to consult the Chief Justice of the two High Courts (one from which the Judge was transferred and the other receiving him).

(d) In regard to the appointment of High Court Judges, the CJI was required to consult only two seniormost Judges of the Apex Court.

(e) The consultation process requires "consultation of plurality of Judges." The sole opinion of the CJI does not constitute the "consultation" process.

(f) The transfer of puisne Judges of the High Courts was judicially reviewable, only if the CJI had recommended the transfers without consulting four seniormost Judges of the Apex Court and two Chief Justices of the High Courts concerned.

(g) The requirement of consultation by the CJI with his colleagues does not exclude consultation with those Judges who are conversant with the affairs of the High Court concerned — either as a parent court (the High Court from where the transfer is made) or who have occupied the office of a Judge or Chief Justice of that Court on transfer from his parent High Court or any other court.

(h) Strong and cogent reasons must exist regarding a person's name not being recommended. Only positive reasons may be given. The views of the other Judges consulted by the CJI should be in writing and the same should be conveyed to the Government, along with the recommendation by the CJI. (Judgment dated 28th October, 1998).

Consultation

Consultation must be effective, and implies exchange of views after examining the merits, but does not mean concurrence. *See* the undermentioned cases:

(i) *S.P. Gupta* v. *President of India*, AIR 1982 SC 149: 1982 Raj LR 389: 1981 Supp SCC 87.

(ii) *Union of India* v. *Sankalchand Seth*, AIR 1977 SC 2328: (1977) 4 SCC 193: 1977 Lab IC 1857: 1977 SCC (L&S) 435.

125. Salaries, etc., of Judges.—[1][(1) There shall be paid to the Judges of the Supreme Court such salaries as may be determined by Parliament by law and, until provision in that behalf is so made, such salaries as are specified in the Second Schedule.]

(2) Every Judge shall be entitled to such privileges and allowances and to such rights in respect of leave of absence and pension as may from time to time be determined by or under law made by Parliament and, until so determined, to such privileges, allowances and rights as are specified in the Second Schedule:

---

1. Subs. by the Constitution (Fifty-fourth Amendment) Act, 1986, sec. 2, for clause (1) (w.r.e.f. 1-4-1986).

Provided that neither the privileges nor the allowances of a Judge nor his rights in respect of leave of absence or pension shall be varied to his disadvantage after his appointment.

126. Appointment of acting Chief Justice.—When the office of Chief Justice of India is vacant or when the Chief Justice is, by reason of absence or otherwise, unable to perform the duties of his office, the duties of the office shall be performed by such one of the other Judges of the Court as the President may appoint for the purpose.

127. Appointment of *ad hoc* Judges.—(1) If at any time there should not be a quorum of the Judges of the Supreme Court available to hold or continue any session of the Court, the Chief Justice of India may, with the previous consent of the President and after consultation with the Chief Justice of the High Court concerned, request in writing the attendance at the sittings of the Court, as an *ad hoc* Judge, for such period as may be necessary, of a Judge of a High Court duly qualified for appointment as a Judge of the Supreme Court to be designated by the Chief Justice of India.

(2) It shall be the duty of the Judge who has been so designated, in priority to other duties of his office, to attend the sittings of the Supreme Court at the time and for the period for which his attendance is required, and while so attending he shall have all the jurisdiction, powers and privileges, and shall discharge the duties, of a Judge of the Supreme Court.

128. Attendance of retired Judges at sittings of the Supreme Court.— Notwithstanding anything in this Chapter, the Chief Justice of India may at any time, with the previous consent of the President, request any person who has held the office of a Judge of the Supreme Court or of the Federal Court [1][or who has held the office of a Judge of a High Court and is duly qualified for appointment as a Judge of the Supreme Court] to sit and act as a Judge of the Supreme Court, and every such person so requested shall, while so sitting and acting, be entitled to such allowances as the President may by order determine and have all the jurisdiction, powers and privileges of, but shall not otherwise be deemed to be, a Judge of that Court:

Provided that nothing in this article shall be deemed to require any such person as aforesaid to sit and act as a Judge of that Court unless he consents so to do.

129. Supreme Court to be a court of record.—The Supreme Court shall be a court of record and shall have all the powers of such a court including the power to punish for contempt of itself.

Notes on Article 129

Contempt of Supreme Court

Supreme Court as a guardian of right to personal liberty, cannot do anything by which that right is taken away or abridged, especially when Supreme Court is acting *suo motu* as in proceedings for its own contempt; *Leila David* v. *State of Maharashtra*, (2009) 4 SCC 578: AIR 2010 SC 862.

Contempt Power

The power of contempt of court has come up before the Supreme Court on numerous occasions, but most of the important propositions will be found discussed in the undermentioned cases:

---

1. Ins. by the Constitution (Fifteenth Amendment) Act, 1963, sec. 3 (w.e.f. 5-10-1963).

(i)   *C.K. Daphtary* v. *O.P. Gupta*, AIR 1971 SC 1132: (1971) 1 SCC 626: 1971 SCC (Cri) 286: 1971 Cr LJ 844.

(ii) *Namboodripad* v. *Nambiar*, AIR 1970 SC 2015: (1970) 2 SCC 325: 1970 SCC (Cri) 451.

(iii) *Brahma Prakash* v. *State of Uttar Pradesh*, (1953) SCR 1169: AIR 1954 SC 10: 1954 Cr LJ 238.

Income-tax Tribunal

Supreme Court has jurisdiction to punish for contempt of Income Tax Appellate Tribunal. It is a national tribunal; *I.T. Appellate Tribunal* v. *V.K. Agarwal*, AIR 1999 SC 452: (1999) 1 SCC 16: 1999 SCC (Cri) 252: 1999 Cr LJ 441.

130. Seat of Supreme Court.—The Supreme Court shall sit in Delhi or in such other place or places, as the Chief Justice of India may, with the approval of the President, from time to time, appoint.

131. Original jurisdiction of the Supreme Court.—Subject to the provisions of this Constitution, the Supreme Court shall, to the exclusion of any other court, have original jurisdiction in any dispute—

(a)   between the Government of India and one or more States; or

(b)   between the Government of India and any State or States on one side and one or more other States on the other; or

(c)   between two or more States,

if and in so far as the dispute involves any question (whether of law or fact) on which the existence or extent of a legal right depends:

[1][Provided that the said jurisdiction shall not extend to a dispute arising out of any treaty, agreement, covenant, engagement, *sanad* or other similar instrument which, having been entered into or executed before the commencement of this Constitution, continues in operation after such commencement, or which provides that the said jurisdiction shall not extend to such a dispute.]

Notes on Article 131

Dispute between Two States

Article 131 will not be applicable where citizens or private bodies are parties either jointly or in alternative with State; *Tashi Delek Gaming Solutions Ltd.* v. *State of Karnataka*; AIR 2006 SC 661.

Scope and Nature of Article 31

When differences arises between the representatives of the State and those of the whole people of India an question of interpretation of the Constitution, which must affect the welfare of the whole people, and particularly that of the people of the State concerned; *State of Karnataka* v. *Union of India*, (1977) 4 SCC 608: AIR 1978 SC 68: (1978) 2 SCR 1: 1978 (2) SCJ 190.

In inter-State water disputes, jurisdiction is excluded; *T.N. Cauvery Sangam* v. *Union of India*, 1990 (2) SCJ 547: (1990) 3 SCC 440: AIR 1990 SC 1316.

[2][**131A. Exclusive jurisdiction of the Supreme Court in regard to questions as to constitutional validity of Central Laws.**—[*Rep. by the Constitution (Forty-third Amendment) Act, 1977, sec. 4 (w.e.f. 13-4-1978).*]]

132. Appellate jurisdiction of Supreme Court in appeals from High Courts in certain cases.—(1) An appeal shall lie to the Supreme Court from any judgment, decree or final order of a High Court in the territory of India, whether in a civil,

---

1. Subs. by the Constitution (Seventh Amendment) Act, 1956, sec. 5, for the proviso (w.e.f. 1-11-1956).

2. Article 131A was earlier inserted by the Constitution (Forty-second Amendment) Act, 1976, sec. 23 (w.e.f. 1-2-1977).

criminal or other proceeding, [1][if the High Court certifies under article 134A] that the case involves a substantial question of law as to the interpretation of this Constitution.

[2][***]

(3) Where such a certificate is given, [3][***] any party in the case may appeal to the Supreme Court on the ground that any such question as aforesaid has been wrongly decided [4][***].

Explanation.—For the purposes of this article, the expression "final order" includes an order deciding an issue which, if decided in favour of the appellant, would be sufficient for the final disposal of the case.

Notes on Articles 132 to 136

Article 132 deals with the appellate jurisdiction of the Supreme Court in constitutional cases. It must be read with article 134A [inserted by the Constitution (Forty-fourth Amendment) Act, 1978] under which, *inter alia*, if a substantial question of interpretation of the Constitution is involved, the High Court must grant a certificate. Unlike article 133(1)(a), article 132(1) does not require that the question must be of general importance.

Article 133 deals with the appellate jurisdiction of the Supreme Court from High Courts in civil cases. As amended by the Constitution (Thirtieth Amendment) Act, 1972, the article allows such appeal if (i) the case involves a substantial question of law of general importance, and (ii) in the opinion of the High Court, the said question needs to be decided by the Supreme Court. The certificate is issued under article 134A.

Article 134(1) allowed criminal appeals to the Supreme Court from High Courts in the specified cases. Clauses (a) and (b) involve a death sentence. Clause (c) is much wider. If the High Court certifies under article 134A that the case is a fit one for appeal to the Supreme Court, then the appeal is competent.

As regards article 134(2), *see* the following:—

  (i) Supreme Court (Enlargement of Criminal Appellate Jurisdiction) Act, 1970.

 (ii) Section 379 of the Code of Criminal Procedure, 1973.

(iii) *Ram Kumar* v. *State of Madhya Pradesh*, AIR 1975 SC 1026: (1975) 3 SCC 815: (1975) 3 SCR 519: 1975 Cr LJ 870, paragraph 4.

(iv) *Pedda Narayana* v. *State of Uttar Pradesh*, AIR 1975 SC 1252: (1975) 4 SCC 153: 1975 Cr LJ 1062: (1975) 12 ACC 201.

Article 135 saves jurisdiction under existing law, conferred on the Federal Court, which will not be exercised by the Supreme Court.

Article 136 confers on the Supreme Court jurisdiction to entertain by special leave appeal.

The jurisdiction is of the widest amplitude as regards—

(a) the court from whose decision the appeal may be entertained (but courts martial are excluded);

(b) the nature of the decision that may be appealed from;

(c) the nature of the proceeding in which appeal may be entertained;

(d) the grounds that may be allowed to be raised for seeking such special leave.

---

1. Subs. by the Constitution (Forty-fourth Amendment) Act, 1978, sec. 17(a), for "if the High Court certifies" (w.e.f. 1-8-1979).

2. Clause (2) omitted by the Constitution (Forty-fourth Amendment) Act, 1978, sec. 17(b) (w.e.f. 1-8-1979).

3. The words "or such leave is granted, " omitted by the Constitution (Forty-fourth Amendment) Act, 1978, sec. 17(c) (w.e.f. 1-8-1979).

4. The words "and, with the leave of the Supreme Court, on any other ground" omitted by the Constitution (Forty-fourth Amendment) Act, 1978, sec. 17(c) (w.e.f. 1-8-1979).

133. Appellate jurisdiction of Supreme Court in appeals from High Courts in regard to civil matters.—[1][(1) An appeal shall lie to the Supreme Court from any judgment, decree or final order in a civil proceeding of a High Court in the territory of India [2][if the High Court certifies under article 134A—]

(a) that the case involves a substantial question of law of general importance; and

(b) that in the opinion of the High Court the said question needs to be decided by the Supreme Court.]

(2) Notwithstanding anything in article 132, any party appealing to the Supreme Court under clause (1) may urge as one of the grounds in such appeal that a substantial question of law as to the interpretation of this Constitution has been wrongly decided.

(3) Notwithstanding anything in this article, no appeal shall, unless Parliament by law otherwise provides, lie to the Supreme Court from the judgment, decree or final order of one Judge of a High Court.

Notes on Article 133

Application of Constitutional Right

The question in regard to application of constitutional right and in particular fundamental right cannot be thwarted only by reason of a concession made by a counsel; *Election Commission of India* v. *St. Mary's School*, AIR 2008 SC 655: 2007 AIR SCW 7761: 2008 (1) LLN 105: 2008 (1) Mad LJ 1062: (2008) 2 SCC 390: 2008 (1) SCT 151: 2008 (1) SRJ 561: (2007) 13 SCALE 777.

Building Plan

The extension of Constitution is question of fact. Where the High Court after examining records concluded that there was no excess construction, the Supreme Court cannot re-examine the said question of fact; *Indore Municipal Corporation* v. *Dr. Hemalata*, AIR 2010 SC 1758.

Interlocutory Appeal

Interlocutory application is maintainable only during pendency of case but not after case is finally disposed of. Except for correcting clerical or accidental mistakes; *Narpat Singh* v. *Rajasthan Financial Corporation*, AIR 2008 SC 77: 2007 AIR SCW 6109: 2007 (6) Mad LJ 1761: (2007) 11 SCALE 459.

Jurisdiction of Supreme Court

The Supreme Court would not ordinarily interfere with the exercise of discretion in the matter of grant of temporary injunction by the High Court and the trial court and substitute its own discretion therefor, except where the discretion has been shown to have been exercised arbitrarily or capriciously or perversely or where the order of the court under scrutiny ignores the settled principles of law regulating grant or refusal of interlocutory injunction; *Laxmikant V. Patel* v. *Chetanbhai Shah*, AIR 2002 SC 275: (2002) 3 SCC 65: (2002) 110 Comp Cas 5182.

134. Appellate jurisdiction of Supreme Court in regard to criminal matters.— (1) An appeal shall lie to the Supreme Court from any judgment, final order or sentence in a criminal proceeding of a High Court in the territory of India if the High Court—

(a) has on appeal reversed an order of acquittal of an accused person and sentenced him to death; or

---

1. Subs. by the Constitution (Thirtieth Amendment) Act, 1972, sec. 2, for clause (1) (w.e.f. 27-2-1973).

2. Subs. by the Constitution (Forty-fourth Amendment) Act, 1978, sec. 18, for "if the High Court certifies—" (w.e.f. 1-8-1979).

(b) has withdrawn for trial before itself any case from any court subordinate to its authority and has in such trial convicted the accused person and sentenced him to death; or

(c) [1][certifies under article 134A] that the case is a fit one for appeal to the Supreme Court:

Provided that an appeal under sub-clause (c) shall lie subject to such provisions as may be made in that behalf under clause (1) of article 145 and to such conditions as the High Court may establish or require.

(2) Parliament may by law confer on the Supreme Court any further powers to entertain and hear appeals from any judgment, final order or sentence in a criminal proceeding of a High Court in the territory of India subject to such conditions and limitations as may be specified in such law.

Notes on Articles 133 and 134

There is no ground for restricting the expression "civil proceeding" (in article 133) to those proceedings which arise out of civil suits (or proceedings which are tried as civil suits); nor is there any rational basis for excluding, from its purview, proceedings instituted and tried in the High Court in exercise of its jurisdiction under article 226, where the aggrieved party seeks the relief against infringement of civil rights by authorities purporting to act in the exercise of the powers conferred upon them by revenue statutes, or disputes between landlord and tenant; *Prasanna Kumar Roy Karmakar* v. *State of West Bengal*, AIR 1996 SC 1517: (1996) 3 SCC 403: 1996 AIR SCW 1585: JT 1996 (3) SC 647: 1996 (2) Ori LR 105: 1996 SCFBRC 507: (1996) 3 SCR 912: 1996 (2) UJ (SC) 468 (paragraphs 11, 12).

Question of limitation cannot be said to be a pure question of law as, it will require investigation into facts, to ascertain the exact dates of accrual of the cause of action. The Supreme Court declined to entertain the plea of limitation. Plea of *res judicata* cannot be raised for the first time; *Deva Ram* v. *Ishwar Chand*, AIR 1996 SC 378: (1995) 6 SCC 733: 1995 AIR SCW 4210: JT 1995 (7) SC 641: 1997 SCFBRC 84: 1995 (4) SCJ 245 (paragraph 30).

Appeal against Conviction

Non-filing of appeal by co-accused cannot be treated as a factor against accused. It would not be in any event take away right of accused to file appeal; *Vadamalai* v. *Syed Thastha Keer*, AIR 2009 SC 1956: 2009 AIR SCW 1583: 2009 (1) Crimes 361: 2009 (2) JCR SC 90: (2009) 3 SCC 454: (2009) 2 SCALE 475: 2009 (2) SCC (Cri) 142.

Appellate Jurisdiction of Supreme Court: Quashing of F.I.R.

Where the accused is fostor sister and is not relative of husband by blood, marriage or adoption, then she cannot be tried for offence under section 498A of Indian Penal Code. The FIR can be quashed; *Vijeta Gajra* v. *State of NCT of Delhi*, AIR 2010 SC 2712.

[2][**134A. Certificate for appeal to the Supreme Court.**—Every High Court, passing or making a judgment, decree, final order, or sentence, referred to in clause (1) of article 132 or clause (1) of article 133, or clause (1) of article 134—

(a) may, if it deems fit so to do, on its own motion; and

(b) shall, if an oral application is made, by or on behalf of the party aggrieved, immediately after the passing or making of such judgment, decree, final order or sentence,

determine, as soon as may be after such passing or making, the question whether a certificate of the nature referred to in clause (1) of article 132, or clause (1) of article

---

1. Subs. by the Constitution (Forty-fourth Amendment) Act, 1978, sec. 19, for "certifies" (w.e.f. 1-8-1979).

2. Ins. by the Constitution (Forty-fourth Amendment) Act, 1978, sec. 20 (w.e.f. 1-8-1979).

133 or, as the case may be, sub-clause (c) of clause (1) of article 134, may be given in respect of that case.]

Notes on Article 134A
See notes under article 132.

135. Jurisdiction and powers of the Federal Court under existing law to be exercisable by the Supreme Court.—Until Parliament by law otherwise provides, the Supreme Court shall also have jurisdiction and powers with respect to any matter to which the provisions of article 133 or article 134 do not apply if jurisdiction and powers in relation to that matter were exercisable by the Federal Court immediately before the commencement of this Constitution under any existing law.

136. Special leave to appeal by the Supreme Court.—(1) Notwithstanding anything in this Chapter, the Supreme Court may, in its discretion, grant special leave to appeal from any judgment, decree, determination, sentence or order in any cause or matter passed or made by any court or tribunal in the territory of India.

(2) Nothing in clause (1) shall apply to any judgment, determination, sentence or order passed or made by any court or tribunal constituted by or under any law relating to the Armed Forces.

Notes on Article 136

Appeal

Where the High Court takes plausible view in acquitting accused from charge of murder, the Supreme Court need not incline to take different view in exercise of jurisdiction under article 136; *Musheer Khan* v. *State of Madhya Pradesh,* AIR 2010 SC 762 (Para 56).

Criminal Cases

In criminal cases under O. XL, r. 7 of the Supreme Court Rules, no review lies except on ground of error apparent on the face of the record; *State of Haryana* v. *Prem,* AIR 1990 SC 538: (1990) 1 SCC 249: 1990 SCC (Cri) 93: 1990 Cr LJ 454, paragraphs 2-6.

In case of appeal against conviction, the Supreme Court does not interfere with the findings of the lower courts, *Sudama Pandey* v. *State of Bihar,* (2002) 1 SCC 679: AIR 2002 SC 693: 2002 Cr LJ 582.

In an appeal against acquittal the Supreme Court would be justified to interfere when approach of the High Court is far from satisfactory; *Anvaruddin* v. *Shakoor,* AIR 1990 SC 1242: (1990) 3 SCC 266: 1990 Cr LJ 1269: 1990 All LJ 281: JT 1990 (2) SC 83.

Where the High Court has completely misdirected itself in reversing the order of conviction by the trial court; *Gauri Shanker Sharma* v. *State of Uttar Pradesh,* AIR 1990 SC 709: 1990 Supp SCC 656: JT 1990 (1) SC 6.

Where the conclusion arrived by the court below is such as to shake the conscience, the Supreme Court would strike it down whether the judgment is one of conviction or acquittal; *Mahesh* v. *State of Delhi,* (1991) Cr LJ 1703: (1991) Supp 1 SCC 257: AIR 1991 SC 1108, paragraph 11.

Even after a death sentence has been confirmed and is not open to review, the Supreme Court may, in a petition under article 32 read with article 21 commute the sentence of death into one of life imprisonment on the ground of undue delay in execution of the death since it was confirmed, because a sentence of death is one thing and the sentence of death followed by lengthy imprisonment prior to execution is another; *Jumman* v. *State of Uttar Pradesh,* (1991) Cr LJ 439: (1991) 1 SCC 752: AIR 1991 SC 345: 1991 SCC (Cri) 283, paragraph 15.

Effect

Dismissal of a special leave petition *in limine* does not preclude Supreme Court considering the point in subsequent appeal; *Scientific Adviser* v. *Daniel,* (1990) Supp SCC 374: 1991 SCC (L&S) 355: (1990) 2 LLJ 275.

Fraud

Where the petitioner obtained a special leave by suppressing the fact that an earlier petition by him was dismissed, the court directed recall of the order releasing him on bail; *Suraj* v. *Bharat*, (1990) 1 UJ SC 135: AIR 1990 SC 753: (1989) Supp 2 SCC 456, paragraph 3.

Similarly, bail was recalled on the basis of fraud practised upon the court; *Surinder* v. *Delhi Administration*, (1990) Supp SCC 610: 1991 SCC (Cri) 154.

Court may refuse relief to a petitioner who has taken reckless steps without recourse to law; *Krishna* v. *Shobha*, (1990) 1 UJ SC 71: (1989) 4 SCC 131: AIR 1989 SC 2097, paragraph 10.

Grounds

Where the High Court has dismissed a writ petition *in limine* the scope of appeal to the Supreme Court is limited to the grounds set forth in the petition; *Sat Pal Chopra* v. *Director-cum-Joint Secretary*, AIR 1991 SC 970: (1991) Supp 2 SCC 352: 1991 Lab IC 441: 1991 AIR SCW 270: JT 1991 (5) SC 89, paragraph 3.

Interference of Supreme Court in Service Matter

When High Court has properly understood purport, object and purpose of a government order and arrived at a correct conclusion, the Supreme Court's interference is not warranted; *L. Muhammed Aslam* v. *State of Kerala*, (2009) 7 SCC 382.

Maintenance Claim by Illegitimate Child

The illegitimate child has no other right except right to claim maintenance under section 125 of Cr. P.C.; *Dimple Gupta (Minor)* v. *Rajiv Gupta*, AIR 2008 SC 239: 2007 AIR SCW 6651: 2007 (4) JCC 3095: (2007) 10 SCC 30: (2007) 12 SCALE 176: 2008 (1) SCC (Cri) 567: 2007 (8) Supreme 141.

Power of Supreme Court

In respect of compounding of offence of dishonour of cheques the Supreme Court is empowered to pass appropriate order in line with section 328 of Criminal Procedure Code in application under section 147 of Negotiable Instruments Act, 1881; *K.M. Ibrahim* v. *K.P. Mohammed*, AIR 2010 SC 276.

Question of Fact

Where the High Court has completely missed the real points requiring determination and has on erroneous grounds discredited the evidence, the Supreme Court would be justified in going into the evidence to avoid grave injustice; *Sham Sunder* v. *Puran*, (1990) 4 SCC 731: AIR 1991 SC 8: 1990 Cr LJ 2600: 1991 (1) Crimes 165: JT 1990 (4) SC 165: 1991 SCC (Cri) 38: (1991) Supp 1 SCC 68: 1990 (2) UJ (SC) 695.

The Supreme Court will not reassess the evidence at large and come to a fresh opinion as to the innocence or guilt of the accused, so as to interfere with a concurrent finding of fact by the court below, except where there is some serious infirmity in the appreciation of evidence, and the finding is perverse; *Narendra Pratap Narain Singh* v. *State of Uttar Pradesh*, (1991) 2 SCC 623: AIR 1991 SC 1394: 1991 Cr LJ 1816: 1991 AIR SCW 1230: 1991 (2) Crimes 183: JT 1991 (2) SC 86: (1991) 2 SCR 88: 1991 SCC (Cri) 482, paragraphs 28-29.

  (i) *Mahesh Chander* v. *State of Delhi*, (1991) Cr LJ 1703: (1991) Supp 1 SCC 257: AIR 1991 SC 1108, paragraph 11.

  (ii) *Nain Singh* v. *State of Uttar Pradesh*, (1991) 2 SCC 432: 1991 SCC (Cri) 241, paragraph 24.

In the absence of perversity concurrent finding of fact is not disturbed; *Mehtab Singh* v. *State of Gujarat*, (1991) Cr LJ 2325: (1991) Supp 2 SCC 391: AIR 1991 SC 1925, paragraph 2.

Supreme Court will not ordinarily interfere with appreciation of the evidence by High Court; *State of Madhya Pradesh* v. *Orient Paper*, (1990) 1 UJ SC 232: (1990) 1 SCC 176, paragraph 2.

Mixed questions of fact and law not argued before the lower courts cannot be raised before Supreme Court; *Bhandara District Central Co-operative Bank Ltd.* v. *State of Maharashtra*, AIR 1993 SC 59: (1993) Supp 3 SCC 259: 1992 AIR SCW 2574: JT 1993 (Supp) SC 428: (1992) 4 SCR 501: 1993 (1) UJ (SC) 14, paragraph 10.

Questions of fact can not be raised for the first time before the Supreme Court; *State of Karnataka* v. *Southern India Plywood Co.*, AIR 1991 SC 1307: (1991) Supp 1 SCC 212; *Uduman* v. *Astam*, AIR 1991 SC 1020: (1991) 1 SCC 412: (1991) 1 MLJ (SC) 46, paragraph 19.

Re-appreciation of Evidence

Re-appreciation of evidence is permissible only if an error of law or procedure and conclusions arrived at are perverse; *Radha Mohan Singh @ Lal Saheb* v. *State of Uttar Pradesh*, AIR 2006 SC 951: 2006 Cr LJ 1121: 2006 AIR SCW 421: (2006) 2 SCC 450: 2006 (3) SCJ 466: (2006) 1 SCALE 369: 2006 SCC (Cri) 661: 2006 (1) Supreme 371.

Relief

Apart from the merits of an appeal, the Supreme Court would expunge derogatory remarks, or aspersions made in a High Court judgment against a party or lawyer, which are not absolutely necessary for the decision of the case before the court, and that, without giving him an opportunity of explaining his conduct; *A.M. Mathur* v. *Pramod*, (1990) 1 UJ SC 595: (1990) 2 SCC 533: AIR 1990 SC 1737.

It is well settled that article 136 does not confer a right of appeal on any party, but it confers a discretionary power on the Supreme Court to interfere in suitable cases; *Ashok Nagar Welfare Association* v. *R.K. Sharma*, AIR 2002 SC 335: (2002) 1 SCC 749: 2001 AIR SCW 5105: JT 2001 (2) SC (Supp) 24: 2001 (5) SCJ 254: 2002 (2) SRJ 449: (2001) 8 SCALE 503: 2001 (8) Supreme 647: 2002 (1) UJ (SC) 163.

Remand of Matter

The court would not pass any order which would make a statutory authority to comply with only useless formalities; *Chandrakant Hargovindas Shah* v. *Deputy Commissioner of Police*, (2009) 7 SCC 186.

Scope

Supreme Court would not grant special leave to appeal from a decision of the Central Administrative Tribunal directing re-fixation of seniority on a particular basis, where there is no substantial injustice. The court observed: "What is baffling is the filing of the Special Leave Petition by the Union Government, not because of injustice to Assistant Military Estate Officers as that has been taken care of by the Tribunal by protecting all those who are working, but because if it works out seniority of Assistant Military Estates Officer (Technical) from back date, it may have to pay substantial amount and creation of supernumerary posts may further entail cost. *Justice is alert to difference and sensitive to discrimination.* It cannot be measured in terms of money"; *Union of India* v. *M.P. Singh*, AIR 1990 SC 1098 (1103): 1990 Supp SCC 701: (1990) Lab IC 910: (1990) 2 LLN 297, paragraph 8; *Medimpex (India) Pvt. Ltd.* v. *Drug Controller-cum-Chief Licensing Authority*, AIR 1990 SC 544: (1989) Supp 2 SCC 665: 1990 Cr LJ 475: 1990 (1) BLJR 159: 1990 (1) Cr LC 523: 1990 East Cr C 380: 1990 (1) SCJ 168.

If a Special Leave Petition is summarily dismissed such a dismissal does not bar other parties from filing a Special Leave Petition against the same judgment; *Delhi Administration* v. *Madan Lal Nangia*, AIR 2003 SC 4672: (2003) 10 SCC 321.

Service Matters

Ordinarily, Supreme Court does not interfere in punishment in service matters. But in exceptional cases it may do so; *Kartar Singh Gerwal* v. *State of Punjab*, (1991) 2 SCC 635: AIR 1991 SC 1067: 1991 AIR SCW 951: JT 1992 (1) SC 124: 1992 (2) LLJ 30: 1991 (2) LLN 54: 1991 SCC (L&S) 780: 1991 (1) UJ (SC) 587.

Special Leave Petition

The special leave petition against order admitting second appeal is not maintainable. Such order does not decide any issue; *S.B. Minerals* v. *M/s. MSPL Ltd.*, AIR 2010 SC 1137.

When Leave may be Granted

Where the judgment is tainted with serious legal infirmities, or is founded on a legal construction which is wrong; *Balakrishna* v. *Matha*, (1991) Cr LJ 691: (1991) 2 SCC 203: (1991) 1 Crimes 448 (SC), paragraph 11.

If the High Court sets aside a finding of fact by a tribunal, the Supreme Court will interfere; *Prakash Warehousing Co.* v. *Municipal Corpn.*, (1991) 1 UJ SC 553: (1991) 2 SCC 304, paragraph 12.

Petition for leave would be granted where approach of the court whose judgment is under appeal is wrong in law; *Munisami Naidu* v. *C. Ranganathan*, (1991) 2 SCC 139: AIR 1991 SC 492, paragraph 9: 1991 (1) All CJ 647: 1991 (2) Civ LJ 77: 1991 (1) Mad LJ 42: 1991 (1) Ren CR 676.

When Leave may be Refused
Where granting the petition would mean multiple claim on same cause of action, court may disallow the petition; *Sawhney* v. *L.I.C.*, (1991) 2 SCC 318: 1991 SCC (L&S) 480: 1991 Lab IC 648, paragraphs 2 and 10.

Unnecessary appeal by Government may be discouraged where only one party's liability is involved; *Union of India* v. *M.P. Singh*, AIR 1990 SC 1098: 1990 Supp SCC 701: (1990) 2 LLN 297.

An order of the High Court will not be set aside if it has not caused any prejudice to petitioner even though no notice was given to the petitioner; *Gupta* v. *U.P.S.E.B.*, AIR 1991 SC 1309: (1991) 2 SCC 263, paragraphs 4-5.

Supreme Court would be reluctant to interfere with an administrative decision as to the needs of the department; *Arun* v. *State of Bihar*, AIR 1991 SC 1514: (1991) Supp 1 SCC 287: (1991) 16 ATC 931: (1991) 2 LLN 59, paragraph 13 (Case of appointment).

An appointment made on the recommendation of Selection Committee cannot be set aside by the High Court without valid reasons; *University of Jodhpur* v. *Purohit*, (1990) 1 UJ SC 235: (1989) Supp 2 SCC 586: 1990 SCC (L&S) 117: (1991) 16 ATC 176, paragraph 11.

137. Review of judgments or orders by the Supreme Court.—Subject to the provisions of any law made by Parliament or any rules made under article 145, the Supreme Court shall have power to review any judgment pronounced or order made by it.

Notes on Article 137

Application for Review
Where the previous order was not an adjudicatory one but was disposed of on concession and the party subsequently applies for modification of that order, the application is not one for review; *Sudarshan Trading Company Ltd.* v. *PP. Saffiya*, AIR 1991 SC 716: (1991) Supp 2 SCC 498, paragraph 8.

Grounds
Article 137 does not limit the grounds for review. However, these may be limited by—

(a) Parliamentary legislation, or

(b) Rules made by the Supreme Court.

Review
Order passed by Chief Justice of India or his nominee under section 11(6) of Arbitration Act is 'order' within meaning of article 137 and is subject to review; *Jain Studios Ltd.* v. *Shin Satellite Public Co. Ltd.*, AIR 2006 SC 2686: 2006 AIR SCW 3592: 2006 (5) Andh LD 71: (2006) 5 SCC 501: 2006 (8) SRJ 266: (2006) 7 SCALE 34: 2006 (5) Supreme 369.

Scope
The law in regard to review of an order of the Supreme Court is too well settled to justify an elaborate discussion on the point. Suffice it to observe that the finality of the order of the apex court of the country should not lightly be unsettled; *Green View Tea & Industries* v. *Collector, Golaghat*, (2002) 1 SCC 109: AIR 2002 SC 180: 2001 AIR SCW 4788: JT 2001 (9) SC 497: (2001) 8 SCALE 163: 2001 (8) Supreme 202.

Writ petition and Civil Appeal were dismissed by the Supreme Court—Review petition was also dismissed. Matter was disposed of after a consideration of all points. Another petition (virtually by way of second review) raising same contentions is not maintainable; *J. Ranga Swamy v. Government of Andhra Pradesh*, AIR 1990 SC 535: (1990) 1 SCC 288: 1990 SCC (L&S) 76: (1990) 1 LLJ 526.

Third Party

Review petition by a third party is not maintainable, *Satvir Singh* v. *Baldeva*, AIR 1997 SC 169: (1996) 8 SCC 593: 1997 Cr LJ 66: 1996 AIR SCW 4331: 1996 (2) Crimes 138: 1996 (2) East Cr C 280: 1996 SCC (Cri) 725.

138. Enlargement of the jurisdiction of the Supreme Court.—(1) The Supreme Court shall have such further jurisdiction and powers with respect to any of the matters in the Union List as Parliament may by law confer.

(2) The Supreme Court shall have such further jurisdiction and powers with respect to any matter as the Government of India and the Government of any State may by special agreement confer, if Parliament by law provides for the exercise of such jurisdiction and powers by the Supreme Court.

139. Conferment on the Supreme Court of powers to issue certain writs.— Parliament may by law confer on the Supreme Court power to issue directions, orders or writs, including writs in the nature of *habeas corpus, mandamus, prohibition, quo warranto* and *certiorari*, or any of them, for any purposes other than those mentioned in clause (2) of article 32.

[1][**139A. Transfer of certain cases.**—[2][(1) Where cases involving the same or substantially the same questions of law are pending before the Supreme Court and one or more High Courts or before two or more High Courts and the Supreme Court is satisfied on its own motion or an application made by the Attorney-General of India or by a party to any such case that such questions are substantial questions of general importance, the Supreme Court may withdraw the case or cases pending before the High Court or the High Courts and dispose of all the cases itself:

Provided that the Supreme Court may after determining the said questions of law return any case so withdrawn together with a copy of its judgment on such questions to the High Court from which the case has been withdrawn, and the High Court shall on receipt thereof, proceed to dispose of the case in conformity with such judgment.]

(2) The Supreme Court may, if it deems it expedient so to do for the ends of justice, transfer any case, appeal or other proceedings pending before any High Court to any other High Court.]

Notes on Article 139A

Scope

Article 139A does not whittle down powers of the court under articles 136 and 142; *Cholamandalam Investments & Finance Co. Pvt. Ltd.* v. *Radhika Synthetics*, AIR 1996 SC 1098: (1996) 2 SCC 109: 1996 AIR SCW 628: 1996 (2) Civ LJ 1: JT 1996 (1) SC 372: (1996) 1 SCR 495.

The matrimonial case can be transferred by the Supreme Court to a court having no jurisdiction under the Hindu Marraige Act; *Usha* v. *Palisetty Mohan Rao*, AIR 2002 SC 400: 2001 AIR SCW 5196: 2001 (1) DMC 584: 2001 (2) Marri LJ 385: (2002) 10 SCC 544: 2001 (5) Supreme 400.

140. Ancillary powers of Supreme Court.—Parliament may by law make provision for conferring upon the Supreme Court such supplemental powers not

---

1. Ins. by the Constitution (Forty-second Amendment) Act, 1976, sec. 24 (w.e.f. 1-2-1977).

2. Subs. by the Constitution (Forty-fourth Amendment) Act, 1978, sec. 21, for clause (1) (w.e.f. 1-8-1979).

inconsistent with any of the provisions of this Constitution as may appear to be necessary or desirable for the purpose of enabling the court more effectively to exercise the jurisdiction conferred upon it by or under this Constitution.

141. Law declared by Supreme Court to be binding on all courts.—The law declared by the Supreme Court shall be binding on all courts within the territory of India.

Notes on Article 141

Binding Jurisdiction of the Supreme Court

It is impermissible for the High Court to overrule the decision of the Apex Court on the ground that the Supreme Court laid down the legal position without considering any other point. It is not only a matter of discipline for the High Courts in India, it is mandate of the Constitution as provided in article 141 that the law declared by the Supreme Court shall be binding on all courts within the territory of India, *Suganthi Suresh Kumar* v. *Jagdeeshan*, (2002) 2 SCC 420: AIR 2002 SC 681: 2002 Cr LJ 1003: 2002 SCC (Cri) 344.

Where a State Government is a party and is duly represented before the Supreme Court, the decision of the court declaring a State Act to be *ultra vires* shall be binding on that State Government. Even a notice, as required by the Civil Procedure Code, was not served upon the Advocate General; *State of Gujarat* v. *Kasturchand Chhotalal Shah*, AIR 1991 SC 695: (1991) Supp 2 SCC 345: 1991 (1) Guj LH 382: JT 1991 (5) SC 419: 1991 (80) STC 394.

A ruling making specific reference to earlier binding precedent may or may not be correct; *Central Board of Dawoodi Bohra Community* v. *State of Maharashtra*, AIR 2005 SC 752: 2005 AIR SCW 349: JT 2005 (1) SC 97: (2005) 2 SCC 673: 2005 SCC (L&S) 246: (2004) 10 SCALE 501: 2005 SCC (Cri) 546.

Doctrine of *Stare Decisis*

Decision cannot be considered as binding authority in view of statutory provisions having undergone legislative changes; *Chikkusappa* v. *State of Karnataka*, AIR 2006 (NOC) 472 (Kar).

Foreign Case Law – Precedent

When law in India is clear and settled no occasion arises to rely upon foreign case laws laying down a wider proposition; *BSES Ltd. (now Reliance Energy Ltd.)* v. *Fenner India Ltd.*, AIR 2006 SC 1148: 2006 AIR SCW 721: (2006) 2 SCC 728: 2006 (3) SCJ 9: 2006 (3) SRJ 389: (2006) 2 SCALE 186: 2006 (2) Supreme 106.

Judicial Discipline

(i) The judicial discipline to abide by Supreme Court decision cannot be forsaken under any pretext by any authority or court, be it even High Court; *State of Himachal Pradesh* v. *Paras Ram*, AIR 2008 SC 930: 2008 Cr LJ 1026: 2008 AIR SCW 373: (2008) 3 SCC 655: (2008) 1 SCALE 6: 2008 (2) SCC (Cri) 117.

(ii) High Court distinguishing the judgment of Apex Court on ground that there was no elaborate discussion and therefore, no reason is discernible, is clearly violative of judicial discipline; *Special Deputy Collector (L.A.)* v. *N. Vasudeva Rao*, AIR 2008 SC 944: 2008 AIR SCW 435: 2008 (62) All Ind Cas 270: 2008 (70) All LR 488: 2008 (5) All MR 8 (NOC): 2008 (1) ICC 729: (2007) 13 SCALE 508: 2008 (8) Supreme 631.

Law Declared

It is immaterial that the conclusion of the majority was arrived at by the several judges on different grounds or different processes of reasoning; *Ramesh Birch* v. *Union of India*, AIR 1990 SC 560: (1989) Supp 1 SCC 430: JT 1989 (2) SC 483: (1989) 2 All RC 273: (1989) 2 Rec CR 79: (1989) 2 Rent LR 164, paragraph 20.

What is binding is the ratio of the decision and not any finding on facts, or the opinion of the court on any question which was not required to be decided in a particular case, it is the principle found out upon a reading of the judgment as a whole in the light of the questions before the court, and not particular words or sentences; *Commissioner of Income-tax* v. *Sun Engineering Works*

(P.) Ltd., AIR 1993 SC 43: (1992) 4 SCC 363: 1992 AIR SCW 2600: 1992 (3) Comp LJ SC 193: 1992 (198) ITR 297: JT 1992 (5) SC 543: (1992) 4 SCR 733, paragraph 39.

The later court would not be bound by those reasons or propositions which were not necessary for the deciding the previous case; conversely, the later court should not unnecessarily expand the scope and authority of the precedent; *Krishena* v. *Union of India*, (1990) 4 SCC 207: AIR 1990 SC 1782: (1990) 4 SLR 716 (CB), paragraphs 19, 20.

There is no law declared where the court gives no reasons; *Supreme Court Employees* v. *Union of India*, AIR 1990 SC 334: (1989) 4 SCC 187: 1989 SCC (L&S) 569: (1989) 2 LLJ 506: (1989) 1 SLR 3, paragraph 22.

Obiter Dicta

The Supreme Court has laid down that the following categories of decisions of the Supreme Court have no binding force:—

(a) *Obiter dicta*, i.e., statements which are not part of the *ratio decidendi*.

(b) A decision *per incurium*, i.e., a decision given in ignorance of the terms of a statute or rule having the force of a statute.

(c) A decision passed *sub-silentio*, i.e., without any argument or debate on the relevant question.

(d) An order made with the consent of the parties, and with the reservation that it should not be treated as a precedent.

See the undermentioned cases:

(i) *Municipal Corporation of Delhi* v. *Gurnam Kaur*, (1989) Supp (2) SCR 929: AIR 1989 SC 38: JT 1988 (4) SC 11: (1988) 23 Reports 139: 1988 Raj LR 579: 1988 (3) SCJ 674: (1988) 2 UJ (SC) 713: (1989) 1 SCC 101 (paragraphs 10-11);

(ii) *State of Uttar Pradesh* v. *Synthetics and Chemicals Ltd.*, (1991) 4 SCC 139: JT 1991 (3) SC 268.

Precedent

Decision in election petition cannot be treated to be a judicial precedent; *Satrucharla Vijaya Rama Raju* v. *Nimmaka Jaya Raju*, AIR 2006 SC 543: 2005 AIR SCW 6197: JT 2005 (9) SC 545: (2006) 1 SCC 212: 2005 (8) SCJ 238: 2006 (1) SRJ 109: (2005) 8 SCALE 745: 2005 (8) Supreme 433.

Supreme Court decision is binding on lower courts. It cannot be distinguished mere because some facts allegedly escaped its attention, more so when Supreme Court had before it the factual aspects in toto; *Gladhurst Co-op. Housing Society Ltd.* v. *Dr. (Mrs.) V.B. Shah*, AIR 2006 (NOC) 1217 (Bom).

The precedents are to be a binding authority or precedent on any specific issue, must be at least raised and answered directly or by implication; *Oriental Insurance Co. Ltd.* v. *Laxmi Rani Biswas*, AIR 2008 Gau 13: 2008 AIHC 104 (NOC): 2008 (2) ALJ (NOC) 369: 2008 (2) AIR Bom R 213 (NOC): 2007 (4) Gau LT 450: 2008 (1) Gau LR 588.

President: Observations made in Judgment

The observations made in judgment is not to be applied mechanically; *Bihar School Examination Board* v. *Suresh Prasad Sinha*, AIR 2010 SC 93; *See* also *State of Rajasthan* v. *Jagdish Narain Chaturvedi*, AIR 2010 SC 157.

Procedure Value of a Decision

A decision, as is well known, is an authority for which it is decided and not what can logically be deduced therefrom. It is also well settled that a little difference in facts or additional facts may make a lot of difference in the precedential value of a decision; *Bhavnagar University* v. *Palitana Sugar Mill Pvt. Ltd.*, AIR 2003 SC 511: (2003) 2 SCC 111: (2003) 2 Guj LR 1154.

Reconsideration

The court would not depart from a long-settled interpretation solely depending upon the facts of a given case. Where, however, there has been no uniformity in previous decisions, the later court would examine the principle in the light of the scheme of the Constitution and the materials placed before it; *Indra Sawhney* v. *Union of India*, AIR 1993 SC 477: (1992) Supp 3 SCC 217: 1992 SCC (L&S) Supp I: (1992) 22 ATC 385, paragraph 26A.

A Division Bench of two Judges cannot over turn the decision of another Bench of two Judges. If they are unable to agree, they should refer it to a larger Bench; *Sundarjas Kanyalal Bhathija* v. *Collector, Thane, Maharashtra*, AIR 1990 SC 261: (1989) 3 SCC 396: JT 1989 (3) SC 57: (1989) 2 RRR 111: (1989) 25 ECR 129, paragraphs 16-20.

In reviewing an earlier decision, however, the court would take into consideration the fact that the said decision has been followed in a large number of cases. It would be particularly slow to disturb a unanimous decision of a Bench of five Judges.

Where, in a subsequent petition under article 32, the Supreme Court directs the petitioner to go before the High Court and directs the High Court to reconsider the matter, the High Court would not be fettered by the previous judgment of the High Court; *Commissioner of Police* v. *Acharya Jagdishwarananda Abadhuta*, AIR 1991 Cal 263: (1991) 1 Cal HN 18, paragraph 9.

The Supreme Court directed the State Government to treat the complaint as an industrial dispute and to refer the same under section 10(1)(d) of the Industrial Disputes Act, 1947 to the Industrial Tribunal; *H.R. Adanthaya* v. *Sandoz*, JT 1994 (5) SC 176: (1994) 5 SCC 737: 1994 SCC (L&S) 1283: AIR 1994 SC 2608: (1994) 69 FLR 593.

The Supreme Court awarded compensation to the wife (appellant) whose husband was living with another woman though there was no proof of a second marriage; *Laxmi Devi* v. *Satya Narayan*, (1994) 5 SCC 545: 1994 SCC (Cri) 1566: 1994 AIR SCW 3408.

Retrospective Operation

Where the Supreme Court has expressly made its ratio prospective, the High Court cannot give it retrospective operation; *F.C.J.* v. *Narendra*, (1993) 1 UJ SC 572, paragraph 7.

Scope

As to the scope of article 141, the most important judgments of the Supreme Court are the following:—

   (i) *Moti Ram Deka* v. *General Manager, North East Frontier Railway*, AIR 1964 SC 600: (1964) 5 SCR 683: (1964) 2 SCA 372: (1964) 2 LLJ 467: ILR (1964) 2 All 717: ILR (1964) 16 Assam 81 (As to the effect of *obiter dicta*).

  (ii) *Gasket Radiators* v. *E.S.I.C.*, AIR 1985 SC 79: (1985) 2 SCC 68: (1985) 1 LLJ 506: 1985 Lab IC 682 (Meaning of the expression on law declared).

 (iii) *Assistant Collector of Central Excise, Chandan Nagar, W.B.* v. *Dunlop India Ltd.*, (1985) 1 SCC 260: AIR 1985 SC 330: 1985 (1) Land LR 443: 1985 SCC (Tax) 75: 1985 UJ (SC) 368: (1985) 58 Comp Cas 145: (1985) 2 SCR 190 (As to the effect of the expression binding).

 (iv) *Star Co.* v. *Union of India*, AIR 1987 SC 179: (1986) 4 SCC 246: 1986 SCC (Cri) 431 (Binding nature of judgment).

  (v) *Gaurya* v. *Thakur*, AIR 1986 SC 1140: (1986) 2 SCC 709: 1986 Cr LJ 1074 (Binding nature).

 (vi) *Synthetics & Chemicals Ltd.* v. *State of Uttar Pradesh*, (1990) 1 SCC 109: AIR 1990 SC 1927: JT 1989 (4) SC 267, paragraphs 3, 74, 80, 82, (Social changes and Supreme Court decisions).

This article 141 recognises the role of the Supreme Court to alter the law, in course of its function to interpret legislation, in order to bring the law in harmony with social changes; *P.L.O. Corp.* v. *Labour Court*, (1990) 3 SCC 632 (CB), paragraphs 59, 81.

Stare Decisis

Stare decisis is not inflexible rule. It has less relevance in constitutional cases; *Supreme Court Advocates-on-Records Association* v. *Union of India*, AIR 1994 SC 268: 1993 AIR SCW 4101: JT 1993 (5) SC 479: (1993) 4 SCC 441: 1993 (5) Serv LR 337.

142. Enforcement of decrees and orders of Supreme Court and orders as to discovery, etc.—(1) The Supreme Court in the exercise of its jurisdiction may pass such decree or make such order as is necessary for doing complete justice in any cause or matter pending before it, and any decree so passed or order so made shall be enforceable throughout the territory of India in such manner as may be prescribed by or under any law made by Parliament and, until provision in that behalf is so made, in such manner as the President may by order[1] prescribe.

(2) Subject to the provisions of any law made in this behalf by Parliament, the Supreme Court shall, as respects the whole of the territory of India, have all and every power to make any order for the purpose of securing the attendance of any person, the discovery or production of any documents, or the investigation or punishment of any contempt of itself.

Notes on Article 142

Complete Justice

The court can grant equitable relief to eradicate injustice. There should be question of law of general importance; *Manish Goel* v. *Rohini Goel*, AIR 2010 SC 1099.

Supreme Court can extend the benefit of its judgment to a case not in appeal; *Manganese Ore* v. *Chandil*, AIR 1991 SC 520: (1991) Supp 2 SCC 465: (1991) 1 LLN 304: (1991) 1 CLR 357 paragraph 19; *Roshan* v. *S.R.C. Mills*, AIR 1990 SC 1881: (1990) 2 SCC 636: 1990 Cr LJ 1770.

Elasticity

While considering the nature and ambit of article 142, the Supreme Court in *Delhi Development Authority* v. *Skipper Construction Company (P) Ltd.*, AIR 1996 SC 2005: (1996) 4 SCC 622: 1996 AIR SCW 2401: 1996 (2) CTC 557: JT 1996 (4) SC 679: 1996 (4) SCJ 24 observed that it is advisable to leave this power undefined and uncatalogued, so that it remains elastic enough, to be moulded to suit the given situation.

Power to do Complete Justice

The Supreme Court cannot bypass the provisions of the Arbitration and Conciliation Act, 1996 while exercising power under article 142; *Bharat Sewa Sansthan* v. *U.P. Electronic Corpn. Ltd.*, (2007) 7 SCC 737: 2007 AIR SCW 5399: 2007 (3) All Rent Cas 379: 2007 (4) All WC 3565: 2007 (3) Arb LR 299: 2007 (4) Rec Civ R 98: 2007 (2) Ren CR 315: 2007 (2) Rent LR 388: (2007) 10 SCALE 446.

Scope of the Relief

The Supreme Court can grant appropriate relief—

(a) where there is some manifest illegality, or

(b) where there is manifest want of jurisdiction, or

(c) where some palpable injustice is shown to have resulted.

Such a power can be traced, either to—

(i) article 142, or

(ii) powers inherent in the court as guardian of the Constitution.

A.R. Antulay v. *R.S. Nayak*, AIR 1988 SC 1531: (1988) 2 SCC 602: 1988 SCC (Cri) 372, paragraph 190.

Cf. Union of India v. *Darshna Devi*, AIR 1997 SC 166: (1996) 2 SCC 681: 1996 AIR SCW 4314: 1996 (2) Civ LJ 592: JT 1996 (1) SC 622: 1996 (1) Land LR 323: (1996) 1 SCR 839.

143. Power of President to consult Supreme Court.—(1) If at any time it appears to the President that a question of law or fact has arisen, or is likely to arise, which is of such a nature and of such public importance that it is expedient to obtain the

---

1. *See* the Supreme Court (Decrees and Orders) Enforcement Order, 1954 (C.O. 47).

opinion of the Supreme Court upon it, he may refer the question to that Court for consideration and the Court may, after such hearing as it thinks fit, report to the President its opinion thereon.

(2) The President may, notwithstanding anything in [1][***] the proviso to article 131, refer a dispute of the kind mentioned in the [2][said proviso] to the Supreme Court for opinion and the Supreme Court shall, after such hearing as it thinks fit, report to the President its opinion thereon.

144. Civil and judicial authorities to act in aid of the Supreme Court.—All authorities, civil and judicial, in the territory of India shall act in aid of the Supreme Court.

Notes on Article 144

Supreme Court may award exemplary costs against defaulting Government; *Dinesh* v. *Motilal Nehru Medical College*, (1990) 4 SCC 627: AIR 1990 SC 2030: (1990) 5 SLR 68, paragraph 6.

The direction of Supreme Court is required for completion of the even course of justice, *Roshan Deen* v. *Preeti Lal*, (2002) 1 SCC 100: 2002 SCC (L&S) 97: AIR 2002 SC 33: (2002) 1 LLN 11.

[3][**144A. Special provisions as to disposal of questions relating to constitutional validity of laws.**—[*Rep. by the Constitution (Forty-third Amendment) Act, 1977, sec. 5 (w.e.f. 13-4-1978).*]]

145. Rules of Court, etc.—(1) Subject to the provisions of any law made by Parliament, the Supreme Court may from time to time, with the approval of the President, make rules for regulating generally the practice and procedure of the Court including—

(a) rules as to the persons practising before the Court;

(b) rules as to the procedure for hearing appeals and other matters pertaining to appeals including the time within which appeals to the Court are to be entered;

(c) rules as to the proceedings in the Court for the enforcement of any of the rights conferred by Part III;

[4][(cc) rules as to the proceedings in the Court under [5][article 139A];]

(d) rules as to the entertainment of appeals under sub-clause (c) of clause (1) of article 134;

(e) rules as to the conditions subject to which any judgment pronounced or order made by the Court may be reviewed and the procedure for such review including the time within which applications to the Court for such review are to be entered;

---

1. The words, brackets and figure "clause (i) of" omitted by the Constitution (Seventh Amendment) Act, 1956, sec. 29 and Sch. (w.e.f. 1-11-1956).

2. Subs. by the Constitution (Seventh Amendment) Act, 1956, sec. 29 and Sch., for "said clause" (w.e.f. 1-11-1956).

3. Article 144A was earlier inserted by the Constitution (Forty-second Amendment) Act, 1976, sec. 25 (w.e.f. 1-2-1977).

4. Ins. by the Constitution (Forty-second Amendment) Act, 1976, sec. 26(a) (w.e.f. 1-2-1977).

5. Subs. by the Constitution (Forty-third Amendment) Act, 1977, sec. 6(a), for "articles 131A and 139A" (w.e.f. 13-4-1978).

(f) rules as to the costs of and incidental to any proceedings in the Court and as to the fees to be charged in respect of proceedings therein;

(g) rules as to the granting of bail;

(h) rules as to stay of proceedings;

(i) rules providing for the summary determination of any appeal which appears to the Court to be frivolous or vexatious or brought for the purpose of delay;

(j) rules as to the procedure for inquiries referred to in clause (1) of article 317.

(2) Subject to the [1][provisions of [2][***] clause (3)], rules made under this article may fix the minimum number of Judges who are to sit for any purpose, and may provide for the powers of single Judges and Division Courts.

(3) [3][4][***] The minimum number] of Judges who are to sit for the purpose of deciding any case involving a substantial question of law as to the interpretation of this Constitution or for the purpose of hearing any reference under article 143 shall be five:

Provided that, where the Court hearing an appeal under any of the provisions of this Chapter other than article 132 consists of less than five Judges and in the course of the hearing of the appeal the Court is satisfied that the appeal involves a substantial question of law as to the interpretation of this Constitution the determination of which is necessary for the disposal of the appeal, such Court shall refer the question for opinion to a Court constituted as required by this clause for the purpose of deciding any case involving such a question and shall on receipt of the opinion dispose of the appeal in conformity with such opinion.

(4) No judgment shall be delivered by the Supreme Court save in open Court, and no report shall be made under article 143 save in accordance with an opinion also delivered in open Court.

(5) No judgment and no such opinion shall be delivered by the Supreme Court save with the concurrence of a majority of the Judges present at the hearing of the case, but nothing in this clause shall be deemed to prevent a Judge who does not concur from delivering a dissenting judgment or opinion.

Notes on Article 145

Article 145 gives to the Supreme Court power to frame rules including rules regarding condition on which a person (including an Advocate) can practice in the Supreme Court. Such a rule would be valid and binding on all. Such a rule if framed would not have anything to do with the disciplinary jurisdiction of Bar Councils; *Harish Uppal* v. *Union of India*, AIR 2003 SC 739: (2003) 2 SCC 45: (2003) 1 KLT 192.

---

1. The words, figures, letter and brackets "provisions of article 144A and clause (3)" subs. by the Constitution (Forty-second Amendment) Act, 1976, sec. 26(b), for "provisions of clause (3)" (w.e.f. 1-2-1977).

2. The words, figures and letter "article 144A and of" omitted by the Constitution (Forty-third Amendment) Act, 1977, sec. 6(b) (w.e.f. 13-4-1978).

3. The words, figures and letter "Subject to the provisions of article 144B, the minimum number" subs. by the Constitution (Forty-second Amendment) Act, 1976, sec. 26(c), for "The minimum number" (w.e.f. 1-2-1977).

4. The words, figures and letter "Subject to the provisions of article 144A, " omitted by the Constitution (Forty-third Amendment) Act, 1977, sec. 6(c) (w.e.f. 13-4-1978).

The only situation when a two judge bench may refer a matter directly to a Constitution Bench is when the provisions of clause (3) of article 145 are attracted; *Pradip Chandra Parija* v. *Pramod Chandra Pattnaik,* AIR 2002 SC 296: (2002) 1 SCC 1: (2002) 254 ITR 99.

146. Officers and servants and the expenses of the Supreme Court.—(1) Appointments of officers and servants of the Supreme Court shall be made by the Chief Justice of India or such other Judge or officer of the Court as he may direct:

Provided that the President may by rule require that in such cases as may be specified in the rule, no person not already attached to the Court shall be appointed to any office connected with the Court, save after consultation with the Union Public Service Commission.

(2) Subject to the provisions of any law made by Parliament, the conditions of service of officers and servants of the Supreme Court shall be such as may be prescribed by rules made by the Chief Justice of India or by some other Judge or officer of the Court authorised by the Chief Justice of India to make rules for the purpose:

Provided that the rules made under this clause shall, so far as they relate to salaries, allowances, leave or pensions, require the approval of the President.

(3) The administrative expenses of the Supreme Court, including all salaries, allowances and pensions payable to or in respect of the officers and servants of the Court, shall be charged upon the Consolidated Fund of India, and any fees or other moneys taken by the Court shall form part of that Fund.

Notes on Article 146

Power under article 146(2) is of legislative nature; *Supreme Court Employees' Welfare Association* v. *Union of India,* AIR 1990 SC 334: (1989) 4 SCC 187: 1989 SCC (L&S) 569: (1989) 2 LLJ 506, paragraph 46.

147. Interpretation.—In this Chapter and in Chapter V of Part VI, references to any substantial question of law as to the interpretation of this Constitution shall be construed as including references to any substantial question of law as to the interpretation of the Government of India Act, 1935 (including any enactment amending or supplementing that Act), or of any Order in Council or order made thereunder, or of the Indian Independence Act, 1947, or of any order made thereunder.

CHAPTER V

COMPTROLLER AND AUDITOR-GENERAL OF INDIA

148. Comptroller and Auditor-General of India.—(1) There shall be a Comptroller and Auditor-General of India who shall be appointed by the President by warrant under his hand and seal and shall only be removed from office in like manner and on the like grounds as a Judge of the Supreme Court.

(2) Every person appointed to be the Comptroller and Auditor-General of India shall, before he enters upon his office, make and subscribe before the President, or some person appointed in that behalf by him, an oath or affirmation according to the form set out for the purpose in the Third Schedule.

(3) The salary and other conditions of service of the Comptroller and Auditor-General shall be such as may be determined by Parliament by law and, until they are so determined, shall be as specified in the Second Schedule:

Provided that neither the salary of a Comptroller and Auditor-General nor his rights in respect of leave of absence, pension or age of retirement shall be varied to his disadvantage after his appointment.

(4) The Comptroller and Auditor-General shall not be eligible for further office either under the Government of India or under the Government of any State after he has ceased to hold his office.

(5) Subject to the provisions of this Constitution and of any law made by Parliament, the conditions of service of persons serving in the Indian Audit and Accounts Department and the administrative powers of the Comptroller and Auditor-General shall be such as may be prescribed by rules made by the President after consultation with the Comptroller and Auditor-General.

(6) The administrative expenses of the office of the Comptroller and Auditor-General, including all salaries, allowances and pensions payable to or in respect of persons serving in that office, shall be charged upon the Consolidated Fund of India.

Notes on Article 148

Article 148(5) does not preclude the President from referring the matter to the Pay Commission provided the final rules are made after consulting the Comptroller and Auditor-General of India; *K. Vasudavan Nair* v. *Union of India*, AIR 1990 SC 2295: (1991) Supp 2 SCC 134: (1991) 17 ATC 362: (1991) 2 LLJ 420: (1990) 3 SLJ 124, Para 10.

149. Duties and powers of the Comptroller and Auditor-General.—The Comptroller and Auditor-General shall perform such duties and exercise such powers in relation to the accounts of the Union and of the States and of any other authority or body as may be prescribed by or under any law made by Parliament and, until provision in that behalf is so made, shall perform such duties and exercise such powers in relation to the accounts of the Union and of the States as were conferred on or exercisable by the Auditor-General of India immediately before the commencement of this Constitution in relation to the accounts of the Dominion of India and of the Provinces respectively.

[1][**150. Form of accounts of the Union and of the States.**—The accounts of the Union and of the States shall be kept in such form as the President may, [2][on the advice of] the Comptroller and Auditor-General of India, prescribe.]

151. Audit reports.—(1) The reports of the Comptroller and Auditor-General of India relating to the accounts of the Union shall be submitted to the President, who shall cause them to be laid before each House of Parliament.

(2) The reports of the Comptroller and Auditor-General of India relating to the accounts of a State shall be submitted to the Governor [3][***] of the State, who shall cause them to be laid before the Legislature of the State.

---

1. Subs. by the Constitution (Forty-second Amendment) Act, 1976, sec. 27, for article 150 (w.e.f. 1-4-1977).
2. Subs. by the Constitution (Forty-fourth Amendment) Act, 1978, sec. 22, for "after consultation with" (w.e.f. 20-6-1979).
3. The words "or Rajpramukh" omitted by the Constitution (Seventh Amendment) Act, 1956, sec. 29 and Sch. (w.e.f. 1-11-1956).

PART VI
THE STATES [1][***]

CHAPTER I
GENERAL

152. Definition.—In this Part, unless the context otherwise requires, the expression "State" [2][does not include the State of Jammu and Kashmir].

CHAPTER II
THE EXECUTIVE
The Governor

153. Governors of States.—There shall be a Governor for each State:

[3][Provided that nothing in this article shall prevent the appointment of the same person as Governor for two or more States.]

154. Executive power of State.—(1) The executive power of the State shall be vested in the Governor and shall be exercised by him either directly or through officers subordinate to him in accordance with this Constitution.

(2) Nothing in this article shall—

(a) be deemed to transfer to the Governor any functions conferred by any existing law on any other authority; or

(b) prevent Parliament or the Legislature of the State from conferring by law functions on any authority subordinate to the Governor.

Notes on Article 154

Central Govt.'s Executive Power

The Central Govt.'s executive power extends to the same subjects and to the same extent as that of the Parliament; *Satya Narain Shukla* v. *Union of India,* AIR 2006 SC 2511: 2006 AIR SCW 2665: 2006 (4) ALJ 276: (2006) 9 SCC 69: 2006 (6) SCJ 272: 2006 (3) SCT 305: (2006) 5 SCALE 627: 2006 (5) Supreme 417.

155. Appointment of Governor.—The Governor of a State shall be appointed by the President by warrant under his hand and seal.

156. Term of office of Governor.—(1) The Governor shall hold office during the pleasure of the President.

(2) The Governor may, by writing under his hand addressed to the President, resign his office.

(3) Subject to the foregoing provisions of this article, a Governor shall hold office for a term of five years from the date on which he enters upon his office:

Provided that a Governor shall, notwithstanding the expiration of his term, continue to hold office until his successor enters upon his office.

---

1. The words "IN PART A OF THE FIRST SCHEDULE" omitted by the Constitution (Seventh Amendment) Act, 1956, sec. 29 and Sch. (w.e.f. 1-11-1956).

2. Subs. by the Constitution (Seventh Amendment) Act, 1956, sec. 29 and Sch., for "means a State specified in Part A of the First Schedule" (w.e.f. 1-11-1956).

3. Added by the Constitution (Seventh Amendment) Act, 1956, sec. 6 (w.e.f. 1-11-1956).

157. Qualifications for appointment as Governor.—No person shall be eligible for appointment as Governor unless he is a citizen of India and has completed the age of thirty-five years.

158. Conditions of Governor's office.—(1) The Governor shall not be a member of either House of Parliament or of a House of the Legislature of any State specified in the First Schedule, and if a member of either House of Parliament or of a House of the Legislature of any such State be appointed Governor, he shall be deemed to have vacated his seat in that House on the date on which he enters upon his office as Governor.

(2) The Governor shall not hold any other office of profit.

(3) The Governor shall be entitled without payment of rent to the use of his official residences and shall be also entitled to such emoluments, allowances and privileges as may be determined by Parliament by law and, until provision in that behalf is so made, such emoluments, allowances and privileges as are specified in the Second Schedule.

[1][(3A) Where the same person is appointed as Governor of two or more States, the emoluments and allowances payable to the Governor shall be allocated among the States in such proportion as the President may by order determine.]

(4) The emoluments and allowances of the Governor shall not be diminished during his term of office.

159. Oath or affirmation by the Governor.—Every Governor and every person discharging the functions of the Governor shall, before entering upon his office, make and subscribe in the presence of the Chief Justice of the High Court exercising jurisdiction in relation to the State, or, in his absence, the senior most Judge of that Court available, an oath or affirmation in the following form, that is to say—

"I, A.B., do $\dfrac{\text{swear in the name of God}}{\text{solemnly affirm}}$ that I will faithfully execute the office of

Governor (or discharge the functions of the Governor) of .... (name of the State) and will to the best of my ability preserve, protect and defend the Constitution and the law and that I will devote myself to the service and well-being of the people of .... (name of the State)."

160. Discharge of the functions of the Governor in certain contingencies.—The President may make such provision as he thinks fit for the discharge of the functions of the Governor of a State in any contingency not provided for in this Chapter.

161. Power of Governor to grant pardons, etc., and to suspend, remit or commute sentences in certain cases.—The Governor of a State shall have the power to grant pardons, reprieves, respites or remissions of punishment or to suspend, remit or commute the sentence of any person convicted of any offence against any law relating to a matter to which the executive power of the State extends.

---

1. Ins. by the Constitution (Seventh Amendment) Act, 1956, sec. 7 (w.e.f. 1-11-1956).

Notes on Article 161

The Power under article 161 is a statutory power which cannot be fettered by position such as sections 432, 433, 433A of the Indian Penal Code, 1860; *State of Punjab* v. *Joginder*, AIR 1990 SC 1396: (1990) 2 SCC 661: 1990 SCC (Cri) 419: 1990 Cr LJ 1464.

The remission proposed in commemoration of the 50 years of Indian Republic itself is a boon and concession to which no one had any vested right. As to what classes of persons or category of offenders to whom the remission has to be extended is a matter of policy particularly when it is also a Constitutent power conferred upon the Constitutional functionary and Head of the State Government, larger area of latitude is to be conceded in favour of such authority to decide upon the frame and limits of its exercise under article 161 itself; *Sanaboina Satyanarayan* v. *Government of Andhra Pradesh*, AIR 2003 SC 3074: (2003) 10 SCC 78: 2003 Cr LJ 3854.

The power of granting pardon under article 161 is very wide and do not contain any limitation as to the time on which and the occasion on which and the circumstances in which the said power could be exercised. But the said power being a constitutional power is amenable to judicial review on certain limited grounds. The court, therefore, would be justified in interfering with an order passed by the Governor in exercise of power under article 161 of the Constitution. If the Governor is found to have exercised the power himself without being advised by the Government or if the Governor transgresses the jurisdiction in exercising the same or it is established that the Governor has passed the order without application of mind or the order in question is a *mala fide* one or the Governor has passed the order on some extraneous consideration; *Satpal* v. *State of Haryana*, AIR 2000 SC 1702: (2000) 5 SCC 170: 2000 SCC (Cri) 920: 2000 Cr LJ 2297.

162. Extent of executive power of State.—Subject to the provisions of this Constitution, the executive power of a State shall extend to the matters with respect to which the Legislature of the State has power to make laws:

Provided that in any matter with respect to which the Legislature of a State and Parliament have power to make laws, the executive power of the State shall be subject to, and limited by, the executive power expressly conferred by this Constitution or by any law made by Parliament upon the Union or authorities thereof.

Notes on Article 162

Since the executive power of the State Executive is co-extensive with that of the State Legislature, it follows that the State Executive may make rules regulating any matter within the legislative competence of the State Legislature, without prior legislative authority, except where a law is required because the Rules so framed would violate any provision of the Constitution which requires legislation, *e.g.*, articles 265 and 302; *Prathibha R.C.C. Spun, Pipe and Cement Products* v. *State of Karnataka*, AIR 1991 Kant 205: ILR (1990) Kant 2672, paragraph 10.

In general, the court, would not exercise its power of judicial review to interfere with a policy made by the Government in exercise of its power under article 162, particularly where it involves technical, scientific or economic expertise; *Shri Sitaram Sugar Co. Ltd.* v. *Union of India*, AIR 1990 SC 1277: (1990) 3 SCC 223: JT 1990 (1) SC 462, paragraph 56.

Duty of High Officers

Proper functioning of State administration should not be jeopardised owing to ego clashes between high officers. Such officers should be aware that power should be exercised for public good, and not for personal benefit; *State of Assam* v. *P.C. Mishra*, AIR 1996 SC 430: (1995) Supp 4 SCC 139: 1995 AIR SCW 4287: 1996 (32) ATC 103: JT 1995 (8) SC 23: 1996 SCC (L&S) 169: 1995 (4) SCJ 560: 1996 (1) SCT 520, paragraph 11.

The Government is entitled to lay down policies and is empowered to refuse approval for setting U.P. Katha industry; *State of Himachal Pradesh* v. *Ganesh Wood Products*, AIR 1996 SC 149: (1995) 6 SCC 363: 1995 AIR SCW 3847: 1995 (5) Comp LJ SC 1: JT 1995 (6) SC 485, paragraphs 24, 26.

Executive Instructions

Where statutory rules govern the field, prior executive instructions cease to apply; *K.P. Sudhakaran* v. *State of Kerala*, AIR 2006 SC 2138: 2006 AIR SCW 2700: 2006 (4) LLN 120: (2006) 5 SCC 386: 2006 SCJ 723: 2006 (3) SCT 60: (2006) 6 SCALE 92: 2006 (5) Supreme 31.

Executive instructions can only fill in gaps not covered by rules and cannot be in derogation of statutory rules; *Union of India* v. *Central Electrical and Mechanical Engineering Service Group A (Direct Recruits) Association, CPWD*, AIR 2008 SC 3: 2007 AIR SCW 6986: 2008 (2) All MR 38 (NOC): 2008 (2) LLN 705: (2008) 1 SCC 354: (2007) 13 SCALE 23: 2007 (8) Supreme 73.

Council of Ministers

163. Council of Ministers to aid and advise Governor.—(1) There shall be a Council of Ministers with the Chief Minister as the head to aid and advise the Governor in the exercise of his functions, except in so far as he is by or under this Constitution required to exercise his functions or any of them in his discretion.

(2) If any question arises whether any matter is or is not a matter as respects which the Governor is by or under this Constitution required to act in his discretion, the decision of the Governor in his discretion shall be final, and the validity of anything done by the Governor shall not be called in question on the ground that he ought or ought not to have acted in his discretion.

(3) The question whether any, and if so what, advice was tendered by Ministers to the Governor shall not be inquired into in any court.

Notes on Article 163

Where an entry in the State list, is expressly made subject to Parliamentary legislation (State List entry 23) the State ceases to have both legislative and executive power in respect of the matter to which the Parliamentary law relates; *Bharat Coking Coal* v. *State of Bihar*, (1990) 4 SCC 557: JT 1990 (3) SC 533: (1990) 3 SCR 744.

Classification of Orders

The orders passed by the Governor of a State (article 163) fall in four broad categories:
   (i) The exercise of executive power in accordance with the provisions of the Constitution, by or under the order of the Governor, wherein full judicial review is available;
  (ii) Orders passed by the Governor, on the aid and advice of the Council of Ministers headed by the Chief Minister, wherein full judicial review is available;
 (iii) Orders like the grant of pardon under article 161 and the orders passed by the President on the report submitted by the Governor under article 356, on account of which limited judicial review is available; and
 (iv) Where the Governor acts without the aid and advice of the Council of Ministers (headed by the Chief Minister) and acts in his own discretion. (Here no judicial review is permissible).

Pratapsingh Raojirao Rane v. *Governor of Goa*, AIR 1999 Bom 53 (91): 1999 (1) Bom CR 574: 1998 (3) Bom LR 173 (DB), paragraphs 29, 36.

Existing Ministry to Continue Until its Successor Assumes Charge

A Council of Ministers must always exist to advise the Governor, (even after dissolution of the Legislature or resignation of a Council of Ministers). Hence, the existing ministry may continue in the office until its successor assumes charge of office; *U.N.R. Rao* v. *Indira Gandhi*, AIR 1971 SC 1002: (1971) 2 SCC 63: (1971) 1 Civ Ap J (SC) 176: 1971 (Supp) SCR 46.

Governor and the Cabinet

The Governor is required to act in his discretion in the following cases:—
   (a) the powers of the Governor of Assam under paragraph 9 of the 6th Schedule;
   (b) the functions of a Governor appointed to be administrator of a Union Territory, under article 239(2);
   (c) the functions under articles 371(2), 371 A (1) (b); 371 C (1); 371 F (g).

In other cases the Governor is to act on the advice of ministers.

(i) *Rai Sahib Ram Jawaya Kapur* v. *State of Punjab*, (1955) 2 SCR 225 (240): AIR 1955 SC 549: 1955 SCA 577: 1955 SCJ 504: (1955) 2 Mad LJ (SC) 59: 57 Punj LR 444: 1955 Mad WN 973.

(ii) *A. Sanjeevi Naidu* v. *State of Madras*, (1970) 1 SCC 443: (1970) 3 SCR 505: AIR 1970 SC 1102.

The function of hearing appeal against Public Service Commission is also to be exercised on cabinet advice; *U.P. Public Service Commission* v. *Suresh*, AIR 1987 SC 1953: (1987) 4 SCC 176: 1987 Lab IC 1644: (1987) 55 FLR 461.

Because of its very nature, the report of the Governor, under article 356 (1), cannot be given on the advice of the Council of Ministers when such a report may lead to the fall of that body.

164. Other provisions as to Ministers.—(1) The Chief Minister shall be appointed by the Governor and the other Ministers shall be appointed by the Governor on the advice of the Chief Minister, and the Ministers shall hold office during the pleasure of the Governor:

Provided that in the States of [1][Chattisgarh, Jharkhand], Madhya Pradesh and [2][Odisha], there shall be a Minister in charge of tribal welfare who may in addition be in charge of the welfare of the Scheduled Castes and backward classes or any other work.

[3][(1A) The total number of Ministers, including the Chief Minister, in the Council of Ministers in a State shall not exceed fifteen per cent. of the total number of members of the Legislative Assembly of that State:

Provided that the number of Ministers, including the Chief Minister, in a State shall not be less than twelve:

Provided further that where the total number of Ministers, including the Chief Minister, in the Council of Ministers in any State at the commencement of the Constitution (Ninety-first Amendment) Act, 2003 exceeds the said fifteen per cent. or the number specified in the first proviso, as the case may be, then the total number of Ministers in that State shall be brought in conformity with the provisions of this clause within six months from such date as the President may by public notification* appoint.]

[3][(1B) A member of the Legislative Assembly of a State or either House of the Legislature of a State having Legislative Council belonging to any political party who is disqualified for being a member of that House under paragraph 2 of the Tenth Schedule shall also be disqualified to be appointed as a Minister under clause (1) for duration of the period commencing from the date of his disqualification till the date on which the term of his office as such member would expire or where he contests any election to the Legislative Assembly of a State or either House of the Legislature of a State having Legislative Council, as the case may be, before the expiry of such period, till the date on which he is declared elected, whichever is earlier.]

(2) The Council of Ministers shall be collectively responsible to the Legislative Assembly of the State.

---

1. Subs. by the Constitution (Ninety-fourth Amendment) Act, 2006, sec. 2, for "Bihar" (w.e.f. 12-6-2006).
2. Subs. by the Orissa (Alteration of Name) Act, 2011 (15 of 2011), sec. 4, for "Orissa" (w.e.f. 1-11-2011, *vide* G.S.R. 791(E), dated 1st November, 2011).
3. Ins. by the Constitution (Ninety-first Amendment) Act, 2003, sec. 3 (w.e.f. 1-1-2004).
* 7th January, 2004, *vide* S.O. 21(E), dated 7th Janaury, 2004.

(3) Before a Minister enters upon his office, the Governor shall administer to him the oaths of office and of secrecy according to the forms set out for the purpose in the Third Schedule.

(4) A Minister who for any period of six consecutive months is not a member of the Legislature of the State shall at the expiration of that period cease to be a Minister.

(5) The salaries and allowances of Ministers shall be such as the Legislature of the State may from time to time by law determine and, until the Legislature of the State so determines, shall be as specified in the Second Schedule.

The Advocate-General for the State

165. Advocate-General for the State.—(1) The Governor of each State shall appoint a person who is qualified to be appointed a Judge of a High Court to be Advocate-General for the State.

(2) It shall be the duty of the Advocate-General to give advice to the Government of the State upon such legal matters, and to perform such other duties of a legal character, as may from time to time be referred or assigned to him by the Governor, and to discharge the functions conferred on him by or under this Constitution or any other law for the time being in force.

(3) The Advocate-General shall hold office during the pleasure of the Governor, and shall receive such remuneration as the Governor may determine.

Notes on Article 165

Appointment of Advocate-General
The person beyond age of 62 years can be appointed as advocate-general; *State of Uttaranchal* v. *Balwant Singh Chauful*, AIR 2010 SC 2550.

Conduct of Government Business

166. Conduct of business of the Government of a State.—(1) All executive action of the Government of a State shall be expressed to be taken in the name of the Governor.

(2) Orders and other instruments made and executed in the name of the Governor shall be authenticated in such manner as may be specified in rules to be made by the Governor, and the validity of an order or instrument which is so authenticated shall not be called in question on the ground that it is not an order or instrument made or executed by the Governor.

(3) The Governor shall make rules for the more convenient transaction of the business of the Government of the State, and for the allocation among Ministers of the said business in so far as it is not business with respect to which the Governor is by or under this Constitution required to act in his discretion.

[1][***]

167. Duties of Chief Minister as respects the furnishing of information to Governor, etc.—It shall be the duty of the Chief Minister of each State—

    (a) to communicate to the Governor of the State all decisions of the Council of Ministers relating to the administration of the affairs of the State and proposals for legislation;

---

1. Clause (4) omitted by the Constitution (Forty-fourth Amendment) Act, 1978, sec. 23 (w.e.f. 20-6-1979). Earlier clause (4) was inserted by the Constitution (Forty-second Amendment) Act, 1976, sec. 28 (w.e.f. 3-1-1977).

(b) to furnish such information relating to the administration of the affairs of the State and proposals for legislation as the Governor may call for; and

(c) if the Governor so requires, to submit for the consideration of the Council of Ministers any matter on which a decision has been taken by a Minister but which has not been considered by the Council.

Notes on Articles 162 to 167

By article 162, the executive power of the State is made co-extensive with the legislative power of the State, as to which see article 246(2) and 246(3). This power, however, is subject to the limitation contained in the proviso to article 162. Of course, executive power cannot be so exercised as to conflict with a law. *See* the undermentioned cases:

(i) *State of Andhra Pradesh* v. *Lavu Narendra Nath*, AIR 1971 SC 2560: (1971) 1 SCC 607: (1971) 3 SCR 699.

(ii) *State of Madhya Pradesh* v. *Kumari Nivedita Jain*, AIR 1981 SC 2045: (1981) 4 SCC 296: (1982) 1 SCR 759.

Article 163 (Council of Ministers in the State) follows to a large extent article 74 (Council of Ministers in the Union), but, unlike article 74(1) as amended, article 163 does not expressly require the Governor to accept the Cabinet's advice. However, (except where the Governor is to exercise his functions in his discretion), the Governor has to accept the advice of the State Council of Ministers, as per the rulings in (i) *Sanjeevi* v. *State of Madras*, AIR 1970 SC 1102: (1970) 1 SCC 443: 1970 SCC (Cri) 196 and (ii) *U.P. Public Service Commission* v. *Suresh*, AIR 1987 SC 1953: (1987) 4 SCC 176: 1987 Lab IC 1644.

Article 166, though concerned primarily with conduct of business, has considerable constitutional importance. The principle that all executive action must be expressed to be taken in the Governor's name, seems to carry the implication that a decision of the Council of Ministers does not become an order of the State Government until it is sent out as the Governor's order; *State of Kerala* v. *A. Lakshmikutty*, AIR 1987 SC 331: (1986) 4 SCC 632: 1987 Lab IC 447: JT 1986 SC 819: (1986) 12 All LR 699: (1987) 1 LLN 31: (1986) 1 ATC 735: (1987) 1 Serv LJ 245, paragraph 40; unless it is a purely internal matter for noting on the file; *Bachhittar Singh* v. *State of Punjab*, AIR 1963 SC 395: (1962) Supp 3 SCR 713: 1962 All WR (HC) 746.

The Constitution requires that action must be taken by the authority concerned in the name of the Governor. It is not till this formality is observed that the action can be regarded as that of the State. Constitutionally speaking the Council of Ministers are advisors and as the head of the State, the Governor is to act with the aid or advice of the Council of Ministers. Therefore, till the advice is accepted by the Governor, views of the Council of Ministers does not get crystallised into action of the State; *J.P. Bansal* v. *State of Rajasthan*, AIR 2003 SC 1405: (2003) 5 SCC 134: (2003) 3 SCR 50: (2003) 2 LLN 405.

Individual Officers

Governmental action is routed through individuals. Hence, they should be answerable for illegal acts. Further, a policy directed by the Minister can be examined by the court to see if it is meant for the public good or whether it fritters away public property; *Secretary Jaipur Development Authority* v. *Daulat Mal Jain*, (1997) 1 SCC 35: JT 1996 (8) SC 387.

CHAPTER III

THE STATE LEGISLATURE

General

168. Constitution of Legislatures in States.—(1) For every State there shall be a Legislature which shall consist of the Governor, and

(a) in the States of [1][Andhra Pradesh], Bihar, [2][***], [3][***], [4][***], [5][Maharashtra], [6][Karnataka], [7][Tamil Nadu] [8][***] [9][and Uttar Pradesh], two houses:

(b) in other States, one House.

(2) Where there are two Houses of the Legislature of a State, one shall be known as the Legislative Council and the other as the Legislative Assembly, and where there is only one House, it shall be known as the Legislative Assembly.

169. Abolition or creation of Legislative Councils in States.— (1) Notwithstanding anything in article 168, Parliament may by law provide for the abolition of the Legislative Council of a State having such a Council or for the creation of such a Council in a State having no such Council, if the Legislative Assembly of the State passes a resolution to that effect by a majority of the total membership of the Assembly and by a majority of not less than two-thirds of the members of the Assembly present and voting.

(2) Any law referred to in clause (1) shall contain such provisions for the amendment of this Constitution as may be necessary to give effect to the provisions of the law and may also contain such supplemental, incidental and consequential provisions as Parliament may deem necessary.

(3) No such law as aforesaid shall be deemed to be an amendment of this Constitution for the purposes of article 368.

[10][**170. Composition of the Legislative Assemblies.**—(1) Subject to the provisions of article 333, the Legislative Assembly of each State shall consist of not more than five hundred, and not less than sixty, members chosen by direct election from territorial constituencies in the State.

(2) For the purposes of clause (1), each State shall be divided into territorial constituencies in such manner that the ratio between the population of each constituency and the number of seats allotted to it shall, so far as practicable, be the same throughout the State.

---

1. Ins. by the Andhra Pradesh Legislative Council Act, 2005 (1 of 2006), sec. 3(1) (w.e.f. 30-3-2007). Earlier the words "Andhra Pradesh" were omitted by the Andhra Pradesh Legislative Council (Abolition) Act, 1985 (34 of 1985), sec. 4 (w.e.f. 1-6-1986).
2. The word "Bombay" omitted by the Bombay Reorganisation Act, 1960 (11 of 1960), sec. 20 (w.e.f. 1-5-1960).
3. By the Constitution (Seventh Amendment) Act, 1956, section 8(2) the words "Madhya Pradesh" are to be inserted but no date has been appointed for the insertion of the said words.
4. The words "Tamil Nadu", omitted by the Tamil Nadu Legislative Council (Abolition) Act, 1986 (40 of 1986) sec. 4 (w.e.f. 1-11-1986). Earlier the words "Tamil Nadu" were substituted by the Madras State Alteration of Name) Act, 1968 (53 of 1968), sec. 4, for the word "Madras" (w.e.f. 14-1-1969).
5. Ins. by the Bombay Reorganisation Act, 1960 (11 of 1960), sec. 20 (w.e.f. 1-5-1960).
6. Subs. by the Mysore State (Alteration of Name) Act, 1973 (31 of 1973), sec. 4, for "Mysore" (w.e.f. 1-11-1973). Earlier the word "Mysore" was inserted by the Constitution (Seventh Amendment) Act, 1956, sec. 8(1) (w.e.f. 1-11-1956).
7. Ins. by the Tamil Nadu Legislative Council Act, 2010 (16 of 2010), sec. 3(1).
8. The word "Punjab", omitted by the Punjab Legislative Council (Abolition) Act, 1969 (46 of 1969), sec. 4 (w.e.f. 7-1-1970).
9. Subs. by the West Bengal Legislative Council (Abolition) Act, 1969 (20 of 1969), sec. 4, for "Uttar Pradesh and West Bengal" (w.e.f. 1-8-1969).
10. Subs. by the Constitution (Seventh Amendment) Act, 1956, sec. 9, for article 170 (w.e.f. 1-11-1956).

[Explanation.—In this clause, the expression "population" means the population as ascertained at the last preceding census of which the relevant figures have been published:

Provided that the reference in this *Explanation* to the last preceding census of which the relevant figures have been published shall, until the relevant figures for the first census taken after the year [2026] have been published, be construed as a reference to the [2001] census.]

(3) Upon the completion of each census, the total number of seats in the Legislative Assembly of each State and the division of each State into territorial constituencies shall be readjusted by such authority and in such manner as Parliament may by law determine:

Provided that such readjustment shall not affect representation in the Legislative Assembly until the dissolution of the then existing Assembly:]

[Provided further that such readjustment shall take effect from such date as the President may, by order, specify and until such readjustment takes effect, any election to the Legislative Assembly may be held on the basis of the territorial constituencies existing before such readjustment:

Provided also that until the relevant figures for the first census taken after the year [2026] have been published, it shall not be necessary to [readjust—

(i) the total number of seats in the Legislative Assembly of each State as readjusted on the basis of the 1971 census; and

(ii) the division of such State into territorial constituencies as may be readjusted on the basis of the [2001] census,

under this clause.]]

171. Composition of the Legislative Councils.—(1) The total number of members in the Legislative Council of a State having such a Council shall not exceed [one-third] of the total number of members in the Legislative Assembly of that State:

Provided that the total number of members in the Legislative Council of a State shall in no case be less than forty.

(2) Until Parliament by law otherwise provides, the composition of the Legislative Council of a State shall be as provided in clause (3).

---

1. Subs. by the Constitution (Forty-second Amendment) Act, 1976, sec. 29(a), for the *Explanation* (w.e.f. 3-1-1977).
2. Subs. by the Constitution (Eighty-fourth Amendment) Act, 2001, sec. 5(a), for "2000" (w.e.f. 21-2-2002).
3. Subs. by the Constitution (Eighty-seventh Amendment) Act, 2003, sec. 4(i), for '1991' (w.e.f. 22-6-2003). Earlier the figures "1991" were substituted by the Constitution (Eighty-fourth Amendment) Act, 2001, sec. 5(d), for "1971" (w.e.f. 21-2-2002).
4. Ins. by the Constitution (Forty-second Amendment) Act, 1976, sec. 29(b) (w.e.f. 3-1-1977).
5. Subs. by the Constitution (Eighty-fourth Amendment) Act, 2001, sec. 5(b)(i), for "2000" (w.e.f. 21-2-2002)
6. Subs. by the Constitution (Eighty-fourth Amendment) Act, 2001, sec. 5(b)(ii), for certain words (w.e.f. 21-2-2002).
7. Subs. by the Constitution (Eighty-seventh Amendment) Act, 2003, sec. 4(ii), for '1991' (w.e.f. 22-6-2003).
8. Subs. by the Constitution (Seventh Amendment) Act, 1956, sec. 10, for "one-fourth" (w.e.f. 1-11-1956).

(3) Of the total number of members of the Legislative Council of a State—

(a) as nearly as may be, one-third shall be elected by electorates consisting of members of municipalities, district boards and such other local authorities in the State as Parliament may by law specify;

(b) as nearly as may be, one-twelfth shall be elected by electorates consisting of persons residing in the State who have been for at least three years graduates of any university in the territory of India or have been for at least three years in possession of qualifications prescribed by or under any law made by Parliament as equivalent to that of a graduate of any such university;

(c) as nearly as may be, one-twelfth shall be elected by electorates consisting of persons who have been for at least three years engaged in teaching in such educational institutions within the State, not lower in standard than that of a secondary school, as may be prescribed by or under any law made by Parliament;

(d) as nearly as may be, one-third shall be elected by the members of the Legislative Assembly of the State from amongst persons who are not members of the Assembly;

(e) the remainder shall be nominated by the Governor in accordance with the provisions of clause (5).

(4) The members to be elected under sub-clauses (a), (b) and (c) of clause (3) shall be chosen in such territorial constituencies as may be prescribed by or under any law made by Parliament, and the elections under the said sub-clauses and under sub-clause (d) of the said clause shall be held in accordance with the system of proportional representation by means of the single transferable vote.

(5) The members to be nominated by the Governor under sub-clause (e) of clause (3) shall consist of persons having special knowledge or practical experience in respect of such matters as the following, namely:—

Literature, science, art, co-operative movement and social service.

172. Duration of State Legislatures.—(1) Every Legislative Assembly of every State, unless sooner dissolved, shall continue for [1][five years] from the date appointed for its first meeting and no longer and the expiration of the said period of [1][five years] shall operate as a dissolution of the Assembly:

Provided that the said period may, while a Proclamation of Emergency is in operation, be extended by Parliament by law for a period not exceeding one year at a time and not extending in any case beyond a period of six months after the Proclamation has ceased to operate.

(2) The Legislative Council of a State shall not be subject to dissolution, but as nearly as possible one-third of the members thereof shall retire as soon as may be on the expiration of every second year in accordance with the provisions made in that behalf by Parliament by law.

---

1. Subs. by the Constitution (Forty-fourth Amendment) Act, 1978, sec. 24, for "six years" (w.e.f. 6-9-1979). Earlier the words "six years" were substituted by the Constitution (Forty-second Amendment) Act, 1976, sec. 30(1), for the words "five years" (w.e.f. 3-1-1977).

173. Qualification for membership of the State Legislature.—A person shall not be qualified to be chosen to fill a seat in the Legislature of a State unless he—

[1][(a) is a citizen of India, and makes and subscribes before some person authorised in that behalf by the Election Commission an oath or affirmation according to the form set out for the purpose in the Third Schedule;]

(b) is, in the case of a seat in the Legislative Assembly, not less than twenty-five years of age and in the case of a seat in the Legislative Council, not less than thirty years of age; and

(c) possesses such other qualifications as may be prescribed in that behalf by or under any law made by Parliament.

Notes on Article 173

A person cannot be permitted to occupy an office for which he is disqualified under the Constitution. The endeavour of the court shall therefore be to see that a disqualified person should not hold the office but should not at the same time, unseat a person qualified therefor; *Sushil Kumar* v. *Rakesh Kumar*, AIR 2004 SC 230: (2003) 8 SCC 673: 2003 AIR SCW 6005: 2004 (1) JLJR 261: 2004 (1) Pat LJR 261: (2003) 8 SCALE 659: 2003 (8) Supreme 149.

[2][**174. Sessions of the State Legislature, prorogation and dissolution.**—(1) The Governor shall from time to time summon the House or each House of the Legislature of the State to meet at such time and place as he thinks fit, but six months shall not intervene between its last sitting in one session and the date appointed for its first sitting in the next session.

(2) The Governor may from time to time—

(a) prorogue the House or either House;

(b) dissolve the Legislative Assembly.]

Notes on Article 174

Dissolution of Assembly

Dissolution cannot be resorted to for good governance or cleansing of politics; *Rameshwar Prasad* v. *Union of India*, AIR 2006 SC 980: 2006 AIR SCW 494: 2006 (3) CTC 209: (2006) 2 SCC 1: 2006 (1) SCJ 477: 2006 (3) SRJ 399: (2006) 1 SCALE 385: 2006 (1) Supreme 393.

On the 7th December, 1988, the High Court of Gauhati pronounced an important judgment in the case relating to dissolution of the Nagaland Assembly and held that the report of the Governor recommending dissolution of the Assembly was not acceptable. The writ petition had been filed by Mr. Vamuzo, leader of the Joint Regional Legislative Party, challenging the validity of the Presidential Proclamation of 17th August, 1988 dissolving the Assembly and taking over the Government of the State. Contention of the petitioner was that the petitioner was enjoying support of the majority of 35 members in the 60 members House, and should have been invited to form the Ministry after the split in the Congress-I. His grievance was that in spite of the Speaker's decision that it was a split, the Governor took into account extraneous and irrelevant aspects. Three points were submitted by the Attorney-General opposing the writ petition; *First*, the President acted on the aid and advice of the Council of Ministers and no court could determine what information was made available to the President under article 74(2) of the Constitution; *Secondly*, the Governor was protected under article 361 of the Constitution; *Thirdly*, as the proclamation had been approved by Parliament, no relief could be granted to the

---

1. Subs. by the Constitution (Sixteenth Amendment) Act, 1963, sec. 4, for clause (a) (w.e.f. 5-10-1963).

2. Subs. by the Constitution (First Amendment) Act, 1951, sec. 8, for article 174 (w.e.f. 18-6-1951).

petitioner. It appears that the second contention was not approved by the Division Bench (Chief Justice A. Raghuvir and Mr. Justice B.L. Hansaria), in view of the allegation that the Governor had acted on irrelevant material. In a sense, this judgement qualifies article 361, by holding that action of the Governor based on collateral material is justifiable, notwithstanding the wide protection given by article 361.

There seems to have been a difference of opinion amongst the two Judges on the question of material supporting the President's satisfaction. The Chief Justice accepted the Attorney-General's contention, to the extent that the court could not call for the material on the basis of which the President had formed his satisfaction. But, according to Mr. Justice Hansaria, the proclamation could not have been issued within the parameters of law, relying solely on the report of the Governor, in as much as a very relevant material had not found place in the report. As such, the satisfaction of the president arrived at would be a 'fraud on the power'. Political trick could not bar the court from the judiciability, the judge observed; *Vamuzo* v. *Union of India*, 1988 (2) GLJ 468. *See* also *S.R. Bommai* v. *Union of India*, (1994) 3 SCC 1: AIR 1994 SC 1918: 1994 AIR SCW 2946: JT 1994 (2) SC 215: (1994) 2 SCR 644.

Endorsement of Legislative Bill

Where a Bill is duly endorsed by the Speaker is passed, it cannot be questioned in the courts on the ground that certain members were prevented from attendance owing to detention under Emergency laws; *Indira Nehru Gandhi* v. *Raj Narain*, AIR 1975 SC 2299: 1975 Supp SCC 1: (1976) 2 SCR 347.

Ground for Dissolution of Assembly – Immorality

Immorality is not a ground recognized by Constitution for formation of satisfaction to dissolve assembly; *Rameshwar Prasad* v. *Union of India*, AIR 2006 SC 980: 2006 AIR SCW 494: 2006 (3) CTC 209: (2006) 2 SCC 1: 2006 (1) SCJ 477: 2006 (3) SRJ 399: (2006) 1 SCALE 385: 2006 (1) Supreme 393.

Meaning of Expression "The House" or "Either House"

The expression "The House" or "either House" in clause (2) of article 174 of the Constitution and Legislative Assembly are synonymous and are interchangeable expressions. The use of expression "The House" denotes the skill of Draftsman using appropriate phraseology in the text of the Constitution of India. Further the employment of expressions "The House" or "either House" do not refer to different bodies other than the Legislative Assembly or the Legislative Council, as the case may be, and have no further significance; *Special Ref. No. 1 of 2002, D/28-10-2002 (under article 143 (1) of the Constitution)*, AIR 2003 SC 87: (2002) 8 SCC 237: 2002 AIR SCW 4492: JT 2002 (8) SC 389: 2002 (4) LRI 169: 2002 (6) SLT 599: (2002) 7 SCALE 614: 2002 (7) Supreme 437.

175. Right of Governor to address and send messages to the House or Houses.—(1) The Governor may address the Legislative Assembly or, in the case of a State having a Legislative Council, either House of the Legislature of the State, or both Houses assembled together, and may for that purpose require the attendance of members.

(2) The Governor may send messages to the House or Houses of the Legislature of the State, whether with respect to a Bill then pending in the Legislature or otherwise, and a House to which any message is so sent shall with all convenient despatch consider any matter required by the message to be taken into consideration.

176. Special address by the Governor.—(1) At the commencement of [1][the first session after each general election to the Legislative Assembly and at the

---

1. Subs. by the Constitution (First Amendment) Act, 1951, sec. 9(1), for "every session" (w.e.f. 18-6-1951).

commencement of the first session of each year], the Governor shall address the Legislative Assembly or, in the case of a State having a Legislative Council, both Houses assembled together and inform the Legislature of the causes of its summons.

(2) Provision shall be made by the rules regulating the procedure of the House or either House for the allotment of time for discussion of the matters referred to in such address [***].

177. Rights of Ministers and Advocate-General as respects the Houses.—Every Minister and the Advocate-General for a State shall have the right to speak in, and otherwise to take part in the proceedings of, the Legislative Assembly of the State or, in the case of a State having a Legislative Council, both Houses, and to speak in, and otherwise to take part in the proceedings of, any committee of the Legislature of which he may be named a member, but shall not, by virtue of this article, be entitled to vote.

Officers of the State Legislature

178. The Speaker and Deputy Speaker of the Legislative Assembly.—Every Legislative Assembly of a State shall, as soon as may be, choose two members of the Assembly to be respectively Speaker and Deputy Speakers thereof and, so often as the office of Speaker or Deputy Speaker becomes vacant, the Assembly shall choose another member to be Speaker or Deputy Speaker, as the case may be.

179. Vacation and resignation of, and removal from, the offices of Speaker and Deputy Speaker.—A member holding office as Speaker or Deputy Speaker of an Assembly—

(a) shall vacate his office if he ceases to be a member of the Assembly;

(b) may at any time by writing under his hand addressed, if such member is the Speaker, to the Deputy Speaker, and if such member is the Deputy Speaker, to the Speaker, resign his office; and

(c) may be removed from his office by a resolution of the Assembly passed by a majority of all the then members of the Assembly:

Provided that no resolution for the purpose of clause (c) shall be moved unless at least fourteen days' notice has been given of the intention to move the resolution:

Provided further that, whenever the Assembly is dissolved, the Speaker shall not vacate his office until immediately before the first meeting of the Assembly after the dissolution.

180. Power of the Deputy Speaker or other person to perform the duties of the office of, or to act as, Speaker.—(1) While the office of Speaker is vacant, the duties of the office shall be performed by the Deputy Speaker or, if the office of Deputy Speaker is also vacant, by such member of the Assembly as the Governor may appoint for the purpose.

(2) During the absence of the Speaker from any sitting of the Assembly the Deputy Speaker or, if he is also absent, such person as may be determined by the rules of procedure of the Assembly, or, if no such person is present, such other person as may be determined by the Assembly, shall act as Speaker.

---

1. The words "and for the precedence of such discussion over other business of the House" omitted by the Constitution (First Amendment) Act, 1951, sec. 9(2) (w.e.f. 18-6-1951).

181. The Speaker or the Deputy Speaker not to preside while a resolution for his removal from office is under consideration.—(1) At any sitting of the Legislative Assembly, while any resolution for the removal of the Speaker from his office is under consideration, the Speaker, or while any resolution for the removal of the Deputy Speaker from his office is under consideration, the Deputy Speaker, shall not, though he is present, preside, and the provisions of clause (2) of article 180 shall apply in relation to every such sitting as they apply in relation to a sitting from which the Speaker or, as the case may be, the Deputy Speaker, is absent.

(2) The Speaker shall have the right to speak in, and otherwise to take part in the proceedings of, the Legislative Assembly while any resolution for his removal from office is under consideration in the Assembly and shall, notwithstanding anything in article 189, be entitled to vote only in the first instance on such resolution or on any other matter during such proceedings but not in the case of an equality of votes.

182. The Chairman and Deputy Chairman of the Legislative Council.—The Legislative Council of every State having such Council shall, as soon as may be, choose two members of the Council to be respectively Chairman and Deputy Chairman thereof and, so often as the office of Chairman or Deputy Chairman becomes vacant, the Council shall choose another member to be Chairman or Deputy Chairman, as the case may be.

183. Vacation and resignation of, and removal from, the offices of Chairman and Deputy Chairman.—A member holding office as Chairman or Deputy Chairman of a Legislative Council—

(a) shall vacate his office if he ceases to be a member of the Council;

(b) may at any time by writing under his hand addressed, if such member is the Chairman, to the Deputy Chairman, and if such member is the Deputy Chairman, to the Chairman, resign his office; and

(c) may be removed from his office by a resolution of the Council passed by a majority of all the then members of the Council:

Provided that no resolution for the purpose of clause (c) shall be moved unless at least fourteen days' notice has been given of the intention to move the resolution.

184. Power of the Deputy Chairman or other person to perform the duties of the office of, or to act as, Chairman.—(1) While the office of Chairman is vacant, the duties of the office shall be performed by the Deputy Chairman or, if the office of Deputy Chairman is also vacant, by such member of the Council as the Governor may appoint for the purpose.

(2) During the absence of the Chairman from any sitting of the Council the Deputy Chairman or, if he is also absent, such person as may be determined by the rules of procedure of the Council, or, if no such person is present, such other person as may be determined by the Council, shall act as Chairman.

185. The Chairman or the Deputy Chairman not to preside while a resolution for his removal from office is under consideration.—(1) At any sitting of the Legislative Council, while any resolution for the removal of the Chairman from his office is under consideration, the Chairman, or while any resolution for the removal of the Deputy Chairman from his office is under consideration, the Deputy Chairman, shall not, though he is present, preside, and the provisions of clause (2) of article 184 shall apply in relation to every such sitting as they apply in relation to a sitting from which the Chairman or, as the case may be, the Deputy Chairman is absent.

(2) The Chairman shall have the right to speak in, and otherwise to take part in the proceedings of, the Legislative Council while any resolution for his removal from office is under consideration in the Council and shall, notwithstanding anything in article 189, be entitled to vote only in the first instance on such resolution or on any other matter during such proceedings but not in the case of an equality of votes.

186. Salaries and allowances of the Speaker and Deputy Speaker and the Chairman and Deputy Chairman.—There shall be paid to the Speaker and the Deputy Speaker of the Legislative Assembly, and to the Chairman and the Deputy Chairman of the Legislative Council, such salaries and allowances as may be respectively fixed by the Legislature of the State by law and, until provision in that behalf is so made, such salaries and allowances as are specified in the Second Schedule.

187. Secretariat of State Legislature.—(1) The House or each House of the Legislature of a State shall have a separate secretarial staff:

Provided that nothing in this clause shall, in the case of the Legislature of a State having a Legislative Council, be construed as preventing the creation of posts common to both Houses of such Legislature.

(2) The Legislature of a State may by law regulate the recruitment, and the conditions of service of persons appointed, to the secretarial staff of the House or Houses of the Legislature of the State.

(3) Until provision is made by the Legislature of the State under clause (2), the Governor may, after consultation with the Speaker of the Legislative Assembly or the Chairman of the Legislative Council, as the case may be, make rules regulating the recruitment, and the conditions of service of persons appointed, to the secretarial staff of the Assembly or the Council, and any rules so made shall have effect subject to the provisions of any law made under the said clause.

Conduct of Business

188. Oath or affirmation by members.—Every member of the Legislative Assembly or the Legislative Council of a State shall, before taking his seat, make and subscribe before the Governor, or some person appointed in that behalf by him, an oath or affirmation according to the form set out for the purpose in the Third Schedule.

189. Voting in Houses, power of Houses to act notwithstanding vacancies and quorum.—(1) Save as otherwise provided in this Constitution, all questions at any sitting of a House of the Legislature of a State shall be determined by a majority of votes of the members present and voting, other than the Speaker or Chairman, or person acting as such.

The Speaker or Chairman, or person acting as such, shall not vote in the first instance, but shall have and exercise a casting vote in the case of an equality of votes.

(2) A House of the Legislature of a State shall have power to act notwithstanding any vacancy in the membership thereof, and any proceedings in the Legislature of a State shall be valid notwithstanding that it is discovered

subsequently that some person who was not entitled so to do sat or voted or otherwise took part in the proceedings.

(3) Until the Legislature of the State by law otherwise provides, the quorum to constitute a meeting of a House of the Legislature of a State shall be ten members or one-tenth of the total number of members of the House, whichever is greater.

(4) If at any time during a meeting of the Legislative Assembly or the Legislative Council of a State there is no quorum, it shall be the duty of the Speaker or Chairman, or person acting as such, either to adjourn the House or to suspend the meeting until there is a quorum.

Disqualifications of Members

190. Vacation of seats.—(1) No person shall be a member of both Houses of the Legislature of a State and provision shall be made by the Legislature of the State by law for the vacation by a person who is chosen a member of both Houses of his seat in one House or the other.

(2) No person shall be a member of the Legislatures of two or more States specified in the First Schedule and if a person is chosen a member of the Legislatures of two or more such States, then, at the expiration of such period as may be specified in rules[1] made by the President, that person's seat in the Legislatures of all such States shall become vacant, unless he has previously resigned his seat in the Legislatures of all but one of the States.

(3) If a member of a House of the Legislature of a State—

(a) becomes subject to any of the disqualifications mentioned in [2][clause (1) or clause (2) of article 191]; or

[3][(b) resigns his seat by writing under his hand addressed to the Speaker or the Chairman, as the case may be, and his resignation is accepted by the Speaker or the Chairman, as the case may be,]

his seat shall thereupon become vacant:

[4][Provided that in the case of any resignation referred to in sub-clause (b), if from information received or otherwise and after making such inquiry as he thinks fit, the Speaker or the Chairman, as the case may be, is satisfied that such resignation is not voluntary or genuine, he shall not accept such resignation.]

(4) If for a period of sixty days a member of a House of the Legislature of a State is without permission of the House absent from all meetings thereof, the House may declare his seat vacant:

Provided that in computing the said period of sixty days no account shall be taken of any period during which the House is prorogued or is adjourned for more than four consecutive days.

---

1. *See* the Prohibition of Simultaneous Membership Rules, 1950, published with the Ministry of Law Notification No. F 46/50-C, dated the 26th January, 1950, Gazette of India, Extra., p. 678.

2. Subs. by the Constitution (Fifty-second Amendment) Act, 1985, sec. 4, for "clause (1) of article 191" (w.e.f. 1-3-1985).

3. Subs. by the Constitution (Thirty-third Amendment) Act, 1974, sec. 3(1), for sub-clause (b) (w.e.f. 19-5-1974).

4. Ins. by the Constitution (Thirty-third Amendment) Act, 1974, sec. 3(2) (w.e.f. 19-5-1974).

191. Disqualifications for membership.—(1) A person shall be disqualified for being chosen as, and for being, a member of the Legislative Assembly or Legislative Council of a State—

(a) if he holds any office of profit under the Government of India or the Government of any State specified in the First Schedule, other than an office declared by the Legislature of the State by law not to disqualify its holder;

(b) if he is of unsound mind and stands so declared by a competent court;

(c) if he is an undischarged insolvent;

(d) if he is not a citizen of India, or has voluntarily acquired the citizenship of a foreign State, or is under any acknowledgement of allegiance or adherence to a foreign State;

(e) if he is so disqualified by or under any law made by Parliament.

[1][*Explanation.*—For the purposes of this clause] a person shall not be deemed to hold an office of profit under the Government of India or the Government of any State specified in the First Schedule by reason only that he is a Minister either for the Union or for such State.

[2][(2) A person shall be disqualified for being a member of the Legislative Assembly or Legislative Council of a State if he is so disqualified under the Tenth Schedule.]

Notes on Article 191

An 'office of profit' is an office which is capable of yielding a profit or pecuniary gain. Contrary is the case of an honorary Chairman of a Board of Election, or the office of an M.L.A.; *Ramakrishna Hegde* v. *State of Karnataka*, AIR 1993 Kant 54: ILR 1992 Kant 3028, paragraph 25.

Breach of oath by a member or minister is not a ground of disqualification under this article and no writ of *Quo warranto* can be issued to remove him on this ground; *Hardwari Lal* v. *Ch. Bhajan Lal*, AIR 1993 P&H 3: ILR 1993 (1) P&H 184: 1992 (2) Land LR 228: 1992 Punj LJ 146: (1992) 2 SCT 226, paragraphs 8, 9 and 16.

Disqualification of a member of the State Legislature was ordered by the Speaker, but the decision was by the High Court.

The Speaker disregarded the stay order. It was held that the High Court was not justified in subsequently upholding the Speaker's decision; *Ravi Naik* v. *Union of India*, JT 1994 (1) SC 551: (1994) Supp 2 SCC 641: AIR 1994 SC 1558.

[3][**192. Decision on questions as to disqualifications of members.**—(1) If any question arises as to whether a member of a House of the Legislature of a State has become subject to any of the disqualifications mentioned in clause (1) of article 191, the question shall be referred for the decision of the Governor and his decision shall be final.

(2) Before giving any decision on any such question, the Governor shall obtain the opinion of the Election Commission and shall act according to such opinion.]

---

1. Subs. by the Constitution (Fifty-second Amendment) Act, 1985, sec. 5(a), for "(2) For the purposes of this article" (w.e.f. 1-3-1985).

2. Ins. by the Constitution (Fifty-second Amendment) Act, 1985, sec. 5(b) (w.e.f. 1-3-1985).

3. Subs. by the Constitution (Forty-fourth Amendment) Act, 1978, sec. 25, for article 192 (w.e.f. 20-6-1979). Earlier article 192 was substituted by the Constitution (Forty-second Amendment) Act, 1976, sec. 33 (w.e.f. 3-1-1977).

Notes on Article 192

Election Commission's Opinion

Where two Election Commissioners, do not reach a unanimous decision out of 'necessity' the Chief Election Commissioner has to express his opinion. Majority view would be sent to the Governor; *Election Commission of India* v. *Dr. Subramanian Swamy*, (1996) 4 SCC 104: AIR 1996 SC 1810: 1996 AIR SCW 2100: JT 1996 (4) SC 463: 1996 (2) Mad LJ 65: 1996 (2) RRR 572.

193. Penalty for sitting and voting before making oath or affirmation under article 188 or when not qualified or when disqualified.—If a person sits or votes as a member of the Legislative Assembly or the Legislative Council of a State before he has complied with the requirements of article 188, or when he knows that he is not qualified or that he is disqualified for membership thereof, or that he is prohibited from so doing by the provisions of any law made by Parliament or the Legislature of the State, he shall be liable in respect of each day on which he so sits or votes to a penalty of five hundred rupees to be recovered as a debt due to the State.

Powers, Privileges and Immunities of State Legislatures and their Members

194. Powers, privileges, etc., of the House of Legislatures and of the members and committees thereof.—(1) Subject to the provisions of this Constitution and to the rules and standing orders regulating the procedure of the Legislature, there shall be freedom of speech in the Legislature of every State.

(2) No member of the Legislature of a State shall be liable to any proceedings in any court in respect of anything said or any vote given by him in the Legislature or any committee thereof, and no person shall be so liable in respect of the publication by or under the authority of a House of such a Legislature of any report, paper, votes or proceedings.

(3) In other respects, the powers, privileges and immunities of a House of the Legislature of a State, and of the members and the committees of a House of such Legislature, shall be such as may from time to time be defined by the Legislature by law, and, until so defined, [1][shall be those of that House and of its members and committees immediately before the coming into force of section 26 of the Constitution Forty-fourth Amendment) Act, 1978].

(4) The provisions of clauses (1), (2) and (3) shall apply in relation to persons who by virtue of this Constitution have the right to speak in, and otherwise to take part in the proceedings of a House of, the Legislature of a State or any committee thereof as they apply in relation to members of that Legislature.

Notes on Article 194

The provisions of the Tenth Schedule, paragraph 2 of Constitution are not violative of article 105(1) or 194(1); *Kihota* v. *Zachilhu*, AIR 1993 SC 412: (1992) Supp 2 SCC 651 (CB).

Powers and Privileges of Member of Legislature

The members of legislature being protected by privileges under article 194 are not answerable to Court for voting in a particular manner in legislature. No person can claim any legal right to have a rule framed in a particular manner and rule-making authority does not owe any corresponding duty to do same; *Advocate M.L. George* v. *High Court of Kerala*, AIR 2010 Ker 134.

195. Salaries and allowances of members.—Members of the Legislative Assembly and the Legislative Council of a State shall be entitled to receive such

---

1. Subs. by the Constitution (Forty-fourth Amendment) Act, 1978, sec. 26, for certain words (w.e.f. 20-6-1979).

salaries and allowances as may from time to time be determined, by the Legislature of the State by law and, until provision in that respect is so made, salaries and allowances at such rates and upon such conditions as were immediately before the commencement of the Constitution applicable in the case of members of the Legislative Assembly of the corresponding province.

Legislative Procedure

196. Provisions as to introduction and passing of Bills.—(1) Subject to the provisions of articles 198 and 207 with respect to Money Bills and other financial Bills, a Bill may originate in either House of the Legislature of a State which has a Legislative Council.

(2) Subject to the provisions of articles 197 and 198, a Bill shall not be deemed to have been passed by the Houses of the Legislature of a State having a Legislative Council unless it has been agreed to by both Houses, either without amendment or with such amendments only as are agreed to by both Houses.

(3) A Bill pending in the Legislature of a State shall not lapse by reason of the prorogation of the House or Houses thereof.

(4) A Bill pending in the Legislative Council of a State which has not been passed by the Legislative Assembly shall not lapse on a dissolution of the Assembly.

(5) A Bill which is pending in the Legislative Assembly of a State, or which having been passed by the Legislative Assembly is pending in the Legislative Council, shall lapse on a dissolution of the Assembly.

197. Restriction on powers of Legislative Council as to Bills other than Money Bills.—(1) If after a Bill has been passed by the Legislative Assembly of a State having a Legislative Council and transmitted to the Legislative Council—

(a) the Bill is rejected by the Council; or

(b) more than three months elapse from the date on which the Bill is laid before the Council without the Bill being passed by it; or

(c) the Bill is passed by the Council with amendments to which the Legislative Assembly does not agree;

the Legislative Assembly may, subject to the rules regulating its procedure, pass the Bill again in the same or in any subsequent session with or without such amendments, if any, as have been made, suggested or agreed to by the Legislative Council and then transmit the Bill as so passed to the Legislative Council.

(2) If after a Bill has been so passed for the second time by the Legislative Assembly and transmitted to the Legislative Council—

(a) the Bill is rejected by the Council; or

(b) more than one month elapses from the date on which the Bill is laid before the Council without the Bill being passed by it; or

(c) the Bill is passed by the Council with amendments to which the Legislative Assembly does not agree;

the Bill shall be deemed to have been passed by the Houses of the Legislature of the State in the form in which it was passed by the Legislative Assembly for the second time with such amendments, if any, as have been made or suggested by the Legislative Council and agreed to by the Legislative Assembly.

(3) Nothing in this article shall apply to a Money Bill.

198. Special procedure in respect of Money Bills.—(1) A Money Bill shall not be introduced in a Legislative Council.

(2) After a Money Bill has been passed by the Legislative Assembly of a State having a Legislative Council, it shall be transmitted to the Legislative Council for its recommendations, and the Legislative Council shall within a period of fourteen days from the date of its receipt of the Bill return the Bill to the Legislative Assembly with its recommendations, and the Legislative Assembly may thereupon either accept or reject all or any of the recommendations of the Legislative Council.

(3) If the Legislative Assembly accepts any of the recommendations of the Legislative Council, the Money Bill shall be deemed to have been passed by both Houses with the amendments recommended by the Legislative Council and accepted by the Legislative Assembly.

(4) If the Legislative Assembly does not accept any of the recommendations of the Legislative Council, the Money Bill shall be deemed to have been passed by both Houses in the form in which it was passed by the Legislative Assembly without any of the amendments recommended by the Legislative Council.

(5) If a Money Bill passed by the Legislative Assembly and transmitted to the Legislative Council for its recommendations is not returned to the Legislative Assembly within the said period of fourteen days, it shall be deemed to have been passed by both Houses at the expiration of the said period in the form in which it was passed by the Legislative Assembly.

199. Definition of "Money Bills".—(1) For the purposes of this Chapter, a Bill shall be deemed to be a Money Bill if it contains only provisions dealing with all or any of the following matters, namely:—

(a) the imposition, abolition, remission, alteration or regulation of any tax;

(b) the regulation of the borrowing of money or the giving of any guarantee by the State, or the amendment of the law with respect to any financial obligations undertaken or to be undertaken by the State;

(c) the custody of the Consolidated Fund or the Contingency Fund of the State, the payment of moneys into or the withdrawal of moneys from any such Fund;

(d) the appropriation of moneys out of the Consolidated Fund of the State;

(e) the declaring of any expenditure to be expenditure charged on the Consolidated Fund of the State, or the increasing of the amount of any such expenditure;

(f) the receipt of money on account of the Consolidated Fund of the State or the public account of the State or the custody or issue of such money; or

(g) any matter incidental to any of the matters specified in sub-clauses (a) to (f).

(2) A Bill shall not be deemed to be a Money Bill by reason only that it provides for the imposition of fines or other pecuniary penalties, or for the demand or payment of fees for licences or fees for services rendered, or by reason that it provides for the imposition, abolition, remission, alteration or regulation of any tax by any local authority or body for local purposes.

(3) If any question arises whether a Bill introduced in the Legislature of a State which has a Legislative Council is a Money Bill or not, the decision of the Speaker of the Legislative Assembly of such State thereon shall be final.

(4) There shall be endorsed on every Money Bill when it is transmitted to the Legislative Council under article 198, and when it is presented to the Governor for assent under article 200, the certificate of the Speaker of the Legislative Assembly signed by him that it is a Money Bill.

200. Assent to Bills.—When a Bill has been passed by the Legislative Assembly of a State or, in the case of a State having a Legislative Council, has been passed by both Houses of the Legislature of the State, it shall be presented to the Governor and the Governor shall declare either that he assents to the Bill or that he withholds assent therefrom or that he reserves the Bill for the consideration of the President:

Provided that the Governor may, as soon as possible after the presentation to him of the Bill for assent, return the Bill if it is not a Money Bill together with a message requesting that the House or Houses will reconsider the Bill or any specified provisions thereof and, in particular, will consider the desirability of introducing any such amendments as he may recommend in his message and, when a Bill is so returned, the House or Houses shall reconsider the Bill accordingly, and if the Bill is passed again by the House or Houses with or without amendment and presented to the Governor for assent, the Governor shall not withhold assent therefrom:

Provided further that the Governor shall not assent to, but shall reserve for the consideration of the President, any Bill which in the opinion of the Governor would, if it became law, so derogate from the powers of the High Court as to endanger the position which that Court is by this Constitution designed to fill.

Notes on Article 200

Governor's Assent to Bills

There are four courses open to a Governor to whom a Bill passed by the State Legislature is presented for assent. The Governor—

(i)　assents, or

(ii)　withholds assent, or

(iii)　reserves the Bill for the consideration of the President, or

(iv)　returns the Bill (If not a Money Bill), for re-consideration, with his message. This is to be done "as soon as possible after the presentation" of the Bill (First Proviso).

The Governor's action in this regard has been held to be non-justifiable. *See* the undermentioned cases:

(i)　*Purushotham* v. *State of Kerala*, AIR 1962 SC 694: (1962) Supp 1 SCR 753: (1962) 1 MLJ (SC) 180.

(ii)　*Hoechst Pharmaceuticals Ltd.* v. *State of Bihar*, AIR 1983 SC 1019: (1983) 4 SCC 45: 1983 UJ (SC) 617: 1983 SCC (Tax) 248: (1983) 8 STL (SC) 1.

(iii)　*Bharat Seva Ashram* v. *State of Gujarat*, AIR 1987 SC 494: (1986) 4 SCC 51: (1986) 1 ATC 348: 1996 SCC (L&S) 723.

If the President assents to a State law which has been reserved for consideration under article 200, it will prevail notwithstanding its repugnancy to an earlier law of the Union. Thus even if there is repugnancy, the law made by the Legislature of the State, if it was reserved for consideration of the President and has received the assent, will prevail in the State; *Puthiyadath Jayamathy Avva* v. *K.J. Naga Kumar*, AIR 2001 Ker 38.

201. Bills reserved for consideration.—When a Bill is reserved by a Governor for the consideration of the President, the President shall declare either that he assents to the Bill or that he withholds assent therefrom:

Provided that, where the Bill is not a Money Bill, the President may direct the Governor to return the Bill to the House or, as the case may be, the Houses of the Legislature of the State together with such a message as it mentioned in the first proviso to article 200 and, when a Bill is so returned, the House or Houses shall reconsider it accordingly within a period of six months from the date of receipt of such message and, if it is again passed by the House or Houses with or without amendment, it shall be presented again to the President for his consideration.

Procedure in Financial Matters

202. Annual financial statement.—(1) The Governor shall in respect of every financial year cause to be laid before the House or Houses of the Legislature of the State a statement of the estimated receipts and expenditure of the State for that year, in this Part referred to as the "annual financial statement".

(2) The estimates of expenditure embodied in the annual financial statement shall show separately—

(a) the sums required to meet expenditure described by this Constitution as expenditure charged upon the Consolidated Fund of the State; and

(b) the sums required to meet other expenditure proposed to be made from the Consolidated Fund of the State,

and shall distinguish expenditure on revenue account from other expenditure.

(3) The following expenditure shall be expenditure charged on the Consolidated Fund of each State—

(a) the emoluments and allowances of the Governor and other expenditure relating to his office;

(b) the salaries and allowances of the Speaker and the Deputy Speaker of the Legislative Assembly and, in the case of State having a Legislative Council, also of the Chairman and the Deputy Chairman of the Legislative Council;

(c) debt charges for which the State is liable including interest, sinking fund charges and redemption charges, and other expenditure relating to the raising of loans and the service and redemption of debt;

(d) expenditure in respect of the salaries and allowances of Judges of any High Court;

(e) any sums required to satisfy any judgment, decree or award of any court or arbitral tribunal;

(f) any other expenditure declared by this Constitution, or by the Legislature of the State by law, to be so charged.

203. Procedure in Legislature with respect to estimates.—(1) So much of the estimates as relates to expenditure charged upon the Consolidated Fund of a State shall not be submitted to the vote of the Legislative Assembly, but nothing in this clause shall be construed as preventing the discussion in the Legislature of any of those estimates.

(2) So much of the said estimates as relates to other expenditure shall be submitted in the form of demands for grants to the Legislative Assembly, and the Legislative Assembly shall have power to assent, or to refuse to assent, to any demand, or to assent to any demand subject to a reduction of the amount specified therein.

(3) No demand for a grant shall be made except on the recommendation of the Governor.

204. Appropriation Bills.—(1) As soon as may be after the grants under article 203 have been made by the Assembly, there shall be introduced a Bill to provide for the appropriation out of the Consolidated Fund of the State of all moneys required to meet—

(a) the grants so made by the Assembly; and

(b) the expenditure charged on the Consolidated Fund of the State but not exceeding in any case the amount shown in the statement previously laid before the House or Houses.

(2) No amendment shall be proposed to any such Bill in the House or either House of the Legislature of the State which will have the effect of varying the amount or altering the destination of any grant so made or of varying the amount of any expenditure charged on the Consolidated Fund of the State, and the decision of the person presiding as to whether an amendment is inadmissible under this clause shall be final.

(3) Subject to the provisions of articles 205 and 206, no money shall be withdrawn from the Consolidated Fund of the State except under appropriation made by law passed in accordance with the provisions of this article.

205. Supplementary, additional or excess grants.—(1) The Governor shall—

(a) if the amount authorised by any law made in accordance with the provisions of article 204 to be expended for a particular service for the current financial year is found to be insufficient for the purposes of that year or when a need has arisen during the current financial year for supplementary or additional expenditure upon some new service not contemplated in the annual financial statement for that year, or

(b) if any money has been spent on any service during a financial year in excess of the amount granted for that service and for that year,

cause to be laid before the House or the Houses of the Legislature of the State another statement showing the estimated amount of that expenditure or cause to be presented to the Legislative Assembly of the State a demand for such excess, as the case may be.

(2) The provisions of articles 202, 203 and 204 shall have effect in relation to any such statement and expenditure or demand and also to any law to be made authorising the appropriation of moneys out of the Consolidated Fund of the State to meet such expenditure or the grant in respect of such demand as they have effect in relation to the annual financial statement and the expenditure mentioned therein or to a demand for a grant and the law to be made for the authorisation of appropriation of moneys out of the Consolidated Fund of the State to meet such expenditure or grant.

206. Votes on account, votes of credit and exceptional grants.—(1) Notwithstanding anything in the foregoing provisions of this Chapter, the Legislative Assembly of a State shall have power—

(a) to make any grant in advance in respect of the estimated expenditure for a part of any financial year pending the completion of the procedure prescribed in article 203 for the voting of such grant and the passing of the law in accordance with the provisions of article 204 in relation to that expenditure;

(b) to make a grant for meeting an unexpected demand upon the resources of the State when on account of the magnitude or the indefinite character of the service the demand cannot be stated with the details ordinarily given in an annual financial statement;

(c) to make an exceptional grant which forms no part of the current service of any financial year,

and the Legislature of the State shall have power to authorise by law the withdrawal of moneys from the Consolidated Fund of the State for the purposes for which the said grants are made.

(2) The provisions of articles 203 and 204 shall have effect in relation to the making of any grant under clause (1) and to any law to be made under that clause as they have effect in relation to the making of a grant with regard to any expenditure mentioned in the annual financial statement and the law to be made for the authorisation of appropriation of moneys out of the Consolidated Fund of the State to meet such expenditure.

207. Special provisions as to financial Bills.—(1) A Bill or amendment making provision for any of the matters specified in sub-clauses (a) to (f) of clause (1) of article 199 shall not be introduced or moved except on the recommendation of the Governor, and a Bill making such provision shall not be introduced in a Legislative Council:

Provided that no recommendation shall be required under this clause for the moving of an amendment making provision for the reduction or abolition of any tax.

(2) A Bill or amendment shall not be deemed to make provision for any of the matters aforesaid by reason only that it provides for the imposition of fines or other pecuniary penalties, or for the demand or payment of fees for licences or fees for services rendered, or by reason that it provides for the imposition, abolition, remission, alteration or regulation of any tax by any local authority or body for local purposes.

(3) A Bill which, if enacted and brought into operation, would involve expenditure from the Consolidated Fund of a State shall not be passed by a House of the Legislature of the State unless the Governor has recommended to that House the consideration of the Bill.

Procedure Generally

208. Rules of procedure.—(1) A House of the Legislature of a State may make rules for regulating, subject to the provisions of this Constitution, its procedure and the conduct of its business.

(2) Until rules are made under clause (1), the rules of procedure and standing orders in force immediately before the commencement of this Constitution with respect to the Legislature for the corresponding Province shall have effect in relation to the Legislature of the State subject to such modifications and adaptations as may be made therein by the Speaker of the Legislative Assembly, or the Chairman of the Legislative Council, as the case may be.

(3) In a State having a Legislative Council the Governor, after consultation with the Speaker of the Legislative Assembly and the Chairman of the Legislative Council, may make rules as to the procedure with respect to communications between the two Houses.

209. Regulation by law of procedure in the Legislature of the State in relation to financial business.—The Legislature of a State may, for the purpose of the timely completion of financial business, regulate by law the procedure of, and the conduct of business in, the House or Houses of the Legislature of the State in relation to any financial matter or to any Bill for the appropriation of moneys out of the Consolidated Fund of the State, and, if and so far as any provision of any law so made is inconsistent with any rule made by the House or either House of the Legislature of the State under clause (1) of article 208 or with any rule or standing order having effect in relation to the Legislature of the State under clause (2) of that article, such provision shall prevail.

210. Language to be used in the Legislature.—(1) Notwithstanding anything in Part XVII, but subject to the provisions of article 348, business in the Legislature of a State shall be transacted in the official language or languages of the State or in Hindi or in English:

Provided that the Speaker of the Legislative Assembly or Chairman of the Legislative Council, or person acting as such, as the case may be, may permit any member who cannot adequately express himself in any of the languages aforesaid to address the House in his mother-tongue.

(2) Unless the Legislature of the State by law otherwise provides, this article shall, after the expiration of a period of fifteen years from the commencement of this Constitution, have effect as if the words "or in English" were omitted therefrom:

[1][Provided that in relation to the [2][Legislatures of the States of Himachal Pradesh, Manipur, Meghalaya and Tripura] this clause shall have effect as if for the words "fifteen years" occurring therein, the words "twenty-five years" were substituted:]

[3][Provided further that in relation to the [4][Legislature of the States of [5][Arunachal Pradesh, Goa and Mizoram]], this clause shall have effect as if for the words "fifteen years' occurring therein, the words "forty years" were substituted.]

211. Restriction on discussion in the Legislature.—No discussion shall take place in the Legislature of a State with respect to the conduct of any Judge of the Supreme Court or of a High Court in the discharge of his duties.

212. Courts not to inquire into proceedings of the Legislature.—(1) The validity of any proceedings in the Legislature of a State shall not be called in question on the ground of any alleged irregularity of procedure.

---

1. Ins. by the State of Himachal Pradesh Act, 1970 (53 of 1970), sec. 46 (w.e.f. 25-1-1971).
2. Subs. by the North-Eastern Areas (Reorganisation) Act, 1971 (81 of 1971), sec. 71, for "Legislature of the State of Himachal Pradesh" (w.e.f. 21-1-1972).
3. Ins. by the State of Mizoram Act, 1986 (34 of 1986), sec. 39 (w.e.f. 20-2-1987).
4. Subs. by the State of Arunachal Pradesh Act, 1986 (69 of 1986), sec. 42, for "Legislature of the State of Mizoram" (w.e.f. 20-2-1987).
5. Subs. by the Goa, Daman and Diu Reorganisation Act, 1987 (18 of 1987), sec. 63, for "Arunachal Pradesh and Mizoram" (w.e.f. 30-5-1987).

(2) No officer or member of the Legislature of a State in whom powers are vested by or under this Constitution for regulating procedure or the conduct of business, or for maintaining order, in the Legislature shall be subject to the jurisdiction of any court in respect of the exercise by him of those powers.

Notes on Article 212

Defects of Competence

Of course, want of legislative competence is not cured by article 212; (i) *M.S.M. Sharma v. Sri Krishna Sinha*, AIR 1960 SC 1186: (1961) 1 SCR 96: (1961) 1 Ker LR 8; (ii) *State of Kerala v. R. Sudarsan Babu*, AIR 1984 Ker 1: 1983 Ker LT 764: ILR (1983) 2 Ker 661.

Scope

Article 212 precludes the court from (a) interfering with the presentation of a Bill for assent to the Governor on the ground of non-compliance with the procedure for passing Bills, or from (b) otherwise questioning Bills passed by the House. *See* the undermentioned cases:

  (i) *Ramchandra v. Andhra Pradesh Regional Committee*, AIR 1965 AP 305.

 (ii) *Surya Pal Singh v. State of Uttar Pradesh*, (1952) SCR 1056 (1090): AIR 1952 SC 252: 1952 SCJ 354: 1953 SCA 53.

(iii) *Indira Nehru Gandhi v. Raj Narain*, AIR 1975 SC 2299: 1975 Supp SCC 1: (1976) 2 SCR 347.

 (iv) *Jai Singh Rathi v. State of Haryana*, AIR 1970 P&H 379.

Proceedings inside the legislature cannot be called into question on the ground that they have not been carried on in accordance with the rules of business; *Kihota Hollohan v. Zachillhu*, (1992) Supp 2 SCC 651: AIR 1993 SC 412: 1992 AIR SCW 3497: JT 1992 (1) SC 600: (1992) 1 SCR 686.

CHAPTER IV
LEGISLATIVE POWER OF THE GOVERNOR

213. Power of Governor to promulgate Ordinances during recess of Legislature.—(1) If at any time, except when the Legislative Assembly of a State is in session, or where there is a Legislative Council in a State, except when both Houses of the Legislature are in session, the Governor is satisfied that circumstances exist which render it necessary for him to take immediate action, he may promulgate such Ordinances as the circumstances appear to him to require:

Provided that the Governor shall not, without instructions from the President, promulgate any such Ordinance if—

(a) a Bill containing the same provisions would under this Constitution have required the previous sanction of the President for the introduction thereof into the Legislature; or

(b) he would have deemed it necessary to reserve a Bill containing the same provisions for the consideration of the President; or

(c) an Act of the Legislature of the State containing the same provisions would under this Constitution have been invalid unless, having been reserved for the consideration of the President, it had received the assent of the President.

(2) An Ordinance promulgated under this article shall have the same force and effect as an Act of Legislature of the State assented to by the Governor, but every such Ordinance—

(a) shall be laid before the Legislative Assembly of the State, or where there is a Legislative Council in the State, before both the Houses, and shall cease to operate at the expiration of six weeks from the reassembly of the Legislature,

The Constitution of India

or if before the expiration of that period a resolution disapproving it is passed by the Legislative Assembly and agreed to by the Legislative Council, if any, upon the passing of the resolution or, as the case may be, on the resolution being agreed to by the Council; and

(b) may be withdrawn at any time by the Governor.

Explanation.—Where the Houses of the Legislature of a State having a Legislative Council are summoned to reassemble on different dates, the period of six weeks shall be reckoned from the later of those dates for the purposes of this clause.

(3) If and so far as an Ordinance under this article makes any provision which would not be valid if enacted in an Act of the Legislature of the State assented to by the Governor, it shall be void:

Provided that, for the purposes of the provisions of this Constitution relating to the effect of an Act of the Legislature of a State which is repugnant to an Act of Parliament or an existing law with respect to a matter enumerated in the Concurrent List, an Ordinance promulgated under this article in pursuance of instructions from the President shall be deemed to be an Act of the Legislature of the State which has been reserved for the consideration of the President and assented to by him.

[1][***]

Notes on Article 213

See notes on article 123 (Ordinances issued by the President). The most important case on article 213 is *Dr. D.C. Wadhwa* v. *State of Bihar*, AIR 1987 SC 579: (1987) 1 SCC 378: JT 1987 (1) SC 70: 1986 (4) Supreme 465: 1987 BBCJ (SC) 46: 1987 IJR 116. Dr. Wadhwa's book Repromulgation of Ordinances (Orient Longman, 1985) traces history of the Ordinances "making power in a comprehensive manner. Earlier decisions-such as *State of Punjab* v. *Satya Pal Dang*, AIR 1969 SC 903: (1969) 1 SCR 478 should now be read subject to *Dr. D.C. Wadhwa* v. *State of Bihar*, AIR 1987 SC 579: (1987) 1 SCC 378: JT 1987 (1) SC 70: 1986 (4) Supreme 465: 1987 BBCJ (SC) 46: 1987 IJR 116.

An Ordinance can be challenged if the Governor—

(a) directly violated a constitutional provision, or

(b) exceeded his constitutional power to make an Ordinance, or

(c) has made a colourable use of such power (*e.g.* by successive repromulgation of an Ordinance without getting an Act of the Legislature passed to replace an expiring Ordinance) the court would strike down the Ordinance; *Dr. D.C. Wadhwa* v. *State of Bihar*, AIR 1987 SC 579: (1987) 1 SCC 378: JT 1987 (1) SC 70: 1986 (4) Supreme 465: 1987 BBCJ (SC) 46: 1987 IJR 116, paragraphs 6-8.

CHAPTER V

THE HIGH COURTS IN THE STATES

214. High Courts for States.—[2][***]There shall be a High Court for each State.
[3][***]

---

1. Clause (4) omitted by the Constitution (Forty-fourth Amendment) Act, 1978, sec. 27 (w.e.f. 20-6-1979). Earlier clause (4) was inserted by the Constitution (Thirty-eighth Amendment) Act, 1975, sec. 3 (retrospectively).
2. The brackets and figure "(1)" omitted by the Constitution (Seventh Amendment) Act, 1956, sec. 29 and Sch. (w.e.f. 1-11-1956).
3. Clauses (2) and (3) omitted by the Constitution (Seventh Amendment) Act, 1956, sec. 29 and Sch. (w.e.f. 1-11-1956).

Notes on Article 214

No litigant can claim a fundamental right to have the High Court located within proximal distance of his residence; *Federation of Bar Association in Karnataka* v. *Union of India*, AIR 2000 SC 2544: (2000) 6 SCC 715: 2000 AIR SCW 2626: JT 2000 (2) SC (Supp) 303: 2000 (7) SRJ 344: (2000) 5 SCALE 269: 2000 (2) UJ (SC) 1149.

215. High Courts to be courts of record.—Every High Court shall be a court of record and shall have all the powers of such a court including the power to punish for contempt of itself.

Notes on Article 215

Contempt Power

Jurisdiction in contempt is independent jurisdiction of original nature; *High Court of Judicature at Allahabad* v. *Raj Kishore*, AIR 1997 SC 1186: (1997) 3 SCC 11: 1997 All LJ 795.

There can be no doubt that the Supreme Court and High Courts are Courts of Record and the Constitution has given them the power to punish for contempt. This power cannot be abrogated or stultified. But if the power under article 129 and article 215 is absolute can there be any legislation indicating the manner and to the extent that the power can be exercised? If there is any provision of the law which stultifies or abrogates that power under article 129 and/or article 215 there can be little doubt that such law would not be regarded as having been validly enacted. However, a law providing for the quantum of punishment or what may or may not be regarded as acts of contempt or even providing for a period of limitation for initiating proceedings for contempt cannot be taken to be a provision which abrogates or stultifies the contempt jurisdiction under article 129 or article 215 of the Constitution; *Pallow Sheth* v. *Custodian*, AIR 2001 SC 2763: (2001) 7 SCC 549: (2001) 107 Comp Cas 76.

216. Constitution of High Courts.—Every High Court shall consist of a Chief Justice and such other Judges as the President may from time to time deem it necessary to appoint.

[1][***]

217. Appointment and conditions of the office of a Judge of a High Court.—(1) Every Judge of a High Court shall be appointed by the President by warrant under his hand and seal after consultation with the Chief Justice of India, the Governor of the State, and, in the case of appointment of a Judge other than the Chief Justice, the Chief Justice of the High court, and [2][shall hold office, in the case of an additional or acting Judge, as provided in article 224, and in any other case, until he attains the age of [3][sixty-two years]]:

Provided that—

(a) a Judge may, by writing under his hand addressed to the President, resign his office;

(b) a Judge may be removed from his office by the President in the manner provided in clause (4) of article 124 for the removal of a Judge of the Supreme Court;

(c) the office of a Judge shall be vacated by his being appointed by the President to be a Judge of the Supreme Court or by his being transferred by the President to any other High Court within the territory of India.

---

1. Proviso omitted by the Constitution (Seventh Amendment) Act, 1956, sec. 11 (w.e.f. 1-11-1956).

2. Subs. by the Constitution (Seventh Amendment) Act, 1956, sec. 12, for "shall hold office until he attains the age of sixty years" (w.e.f. 1-11-1956).

3. Subs. by the Constitution (Fifteenth Amendment) Act, 1963, sec. 4(a), for "sixty years" (w.e.f. 5-10-1963).

(2) A person shall not be qualified for appointment as a Judge of a High Court unless he is a citizen of India and—

(a) has for at least ten years held a judicial office in the territory of India; or

(b) has for at least ten years been an advocate of a High Court [1][***] or of two or more such courts in succession; [2][***]

[3][***]

Explanation.—For the purposes of this clause—

[4][(a) in computing the period during which a person has held judicial office in the territory of India, there shall be included any period, after he has held any judicial office, during which the person has been an advocate of a High Court or has held the office of a member of a tribunal or any post, under the Union or a State, requiring special knowledge of law;]

[5][(aa)] in computing the period during which a person has been an advocate of a High Court, there shall be included any period during which the person [6][has held judicial office or the office of a member of a tribunal or any post, under the Union or a State, requiring special knowledge of law] after he became an advocate;

(b) in computing the period during which a person has held judicial office in the territory of India or been an advocate of High Court, there shall be included any period before the commencement of this Constitution during which he has held judicial office in any area which was comprised before the fifteenth day of August, 1947, within India as defined by the Government of India Act, 1935, or has been an advocate of any High Court in any such area, as the case may be.

[7][(3) If any question arises as to the age of a Judge of a High Court, the question shall be decided by the President after consultation with the Chief Justice of India and the decision of the President shall be final.]

Notes on Article 217

Status of Additional Judge

An additional judge holding tenure post, cannot, for all purposes be equated with sitting judge; *N. Kannadasan* v. *Ajay Khose,* (2009) 7 SCC 1.

---

1. The words "in any State specified in the First Schedule" omitted by the Constitution (Seventh Amendment) Act, 1956, sec. 29 and Sch. (w.e.f. 1-11-1956).

2. The word "or" omitted by the Constitution (Forty-fourth Amendment) Act, 1978, sec. 28(a) (w.e.f. 20-6-1979). Earlier the word "or" was inserted by the Constitution (Forty-second Amendment) Act, 1976, sec. 36(a) (w.e.f. 3-1-1977).

3. Clause (c) omitted by the Constitution (Forty-fourth Amendment) Act, 1978, sec. 28(b) (w.e.f. 20-6-1979). Earlier clause (c) was inserted by the Constitution (Forty-second Amendment) Act, 1976, sec. 36(b) (w.e.f. 3-1-1977).

4. Ins. by the Constitution (Forty-fourth Amendment) Act, 1978, sec. 28(c) (w.e.f. 20-6-1979).

5. Clause (a) re-lettered as clause (aa) by the Constitution (Forty-fourth Amendment) Act, 1978, sec. 28(c) (w.e.f. 20-6-1979).

6. Subs. by the Constitution (Forty-second Amendment) Act, 1976, sec. 36(c), for "has held judicial office" (w.e.f. 3-1-1977).

7. Ins. by the Constitution (Fifteenth Amendment) Act, 1963, sec. 4(b) (with retrospective effect).

218. Application of certain provisions relating to Supreme Court to High Courts.—The provisions of clauses (4) and (5) of article 124 shall apply in relation to a High Court as they apply in relation to the Supreme Court with the substitution of references to the High Court for references to the Supreme Court.

219. Oath or affirmation by Judges of High Courts.—Every person appointed to be a Judge of a High Court [1][***] shall, before he enters upon his office, make and subscribe before the Governor of the State, or some person appointed in that behalf by him, an oath or affirmation according to the form set out for the purpose in the Third Schedule.

[2][**220. Restriction on practice after being a permanent Judge.**—No person who, after the commencement of this Constitution, has held office as a permanent Judge of a High Court shall plead or act in any court or before any authority in India except the Supreme Court and the other High Courts.

Explanation.—In this article, the expression "High Court" does not include a High Court for a State specified in Part B of the First Schedule as it existed before the commencement[3] of the Constitution (Seventh Amendment) Act, 1956.]

221. Salaries etc., of Judges.—[4][(1) There shall be paid to the Judges of each High Court such salaries as may be determined by Parliament by law and, until provision in that behalf is so made, such salaries as are specified in the Second Schedule.]

(2) Every Judge shall be entitled to such allowances and to such rights in respect of leave of absence and pension as may from time to time be determined by or under law made by Parliament and, until so determined, to such allowances and rights as are specified in the Second Schedule:

Provided that neither the allowances of a Judge nor his rights in respect of leave of absence or pension shall be varied to his disadvantage after his appointment.

Notes on Article 221

Rights of a Chief Justice of a High Court to receive pension and other benefits, cannot be altered to his disadvantage, after his appointment; *Justice S.S. Sandhawalia* v. *Union of India*, AIR 1990 P&H 198: (1990) 1 Serv LR 637(2): ILR 1991 (1) P&H 194: 1990 (1) Punj LR 580.

222. Transfer of a Judge from one High Court to another.—(1) The President may, after consultation with the Chief Justice of India, transfer a Judge from one High Court to any other High Court [5][***].

[6][(2) When a Judge has been or is so transferred, he shall, during the period he serves, after the commencement of the Constitution (Fifteenth Amendment) Act, 1963, as a Judge of the other High Court, be entitled to receive in addition to his

---

1. The words "in a State" omitted by the Constitution (Seventh Amendment) Act, 1956, sec. 29 and Sch. (w.e.f. 1-11-1956).
2. Subs. by the Constitution (Seventh Amendment) Act, 1956, sec. 13, for article 220 (w.e.f. 1-11-1956).
3. 1st day of November, 1956.
4. Subs. by the Constitution (Fifty-fourth Amendment) Act, 1986, sec. 3, for clause (1) (w.r.e.f. 1-4-1986).
5. The words "within the territory of India" omitted by the Constitution (Seventh Amendment) Act, 1956, sec. 14(a) (w.e.f. 1-11-1956).
6. Ins. by the Constitution (Fifteenth Amendment) Act, 1963, sec. 5 (w.e.f. 5-10-1963). Earlier clause (2) was omitted by the Constitution (Seventh Amendment) Act, 1956, sec. 14(b) (w.e.f. 1-11-1956).

salary such compensatory allowance as may be determined by Parliament by law and, until so determined, such compensatory allowance as the President may by order fix.]

Notes on Article 222

Transfer of High Court Judges

In transfer of High Court judges, the opinion of chief justice of India is determinative; *Supreme Court Advocates-on-Records Association* v. *Union of India*, AIR 1994 SC 268: 1993 AIR SCW 4101: JT 1993 (5) SC 479: (1993) 4 SCC 441: 1993 (5) Serv LR 337.

In regard to transfer of judges, judicial review is necessary to check arbitrariness. But as to *locus standi*, only the judge who is transferred can challenge it; *K. Ashok Reddy* v. *Government of India*, JT 1994 (1) SC 40: AIR 1994 SC 1207: (1994) 2 SCC 303.

223. Appointment of acting Chief Justice.—When the office of Chief Justice of a High Court is vacant or when any such Chief Justice is by reason of absence or otherwise, unable to perform the duties of his office, the duties of the office shall be performed by such one of the other Judges of the court as the President may appoint for the purposes.

¹[**224. Appointment of additional and acting Judges.**—(1) If by reason of any temporary increase in the business of High Court or by reason of arrears of work therein, it appears to the President that the number of the Judges of that Court should be for the time being increased, the President may appoint duly qualified persons to be additional Judges of the Court for such period not exceeding two years as he may specify.

(2) When any Judge of a High Court other than the Chief Justice is by reason of absence or for any other reason unable to perform the duties of his office or is appointed to act temporarily as Chief Justice, the President may appoint a duly qualified person to act as a Judge of that Court until the permanent Judge has resumed his duties.

(3) No person appointed as an additional or acting Judge of a High Court shall hold office after attaining the age of ²[sixty-two years].]

³[**224A. Appointment of retired Judges at sittings of High Courts.**—Notwithstanding anything in this Chapter, the Chief Justice of a High Court for any State may at any time, with the previous consent of the President, request any person who has held the office of a Judge of that Court or of any other High Court to sit and act as a Judge of the High Court for that State, and every such person so requested shall, while so sitting and acting, be entitled to such allowances as the President may by order determine and have all the jurisdiction, powers and privileges of, but shall not otherwise be deemed to be, a Judge of that High Court:

Provided that nothing in this article shall be deemed to require any such person as aforesaid to sit and act as a Judge of that High Court unless he consents so to do.]

225. Jurisdiction of existing High Courts.—Subject to the provisions of this Constitution and to the provisions of any law of the appropriate Legislature made by virtue of powers conferred on that Legislature by this Constitution, the jurisdiction

---

1. Subs. by the Constitution (Seventh Amendment) Act, 1956, sec. 15, for article 224 (w.e.f. 1-11-1956).
2. Subs. by the Constitution (Fifteenth Amendment) Act, 1963, sec. 6, for "sixty years" (w.e.f. 5-10-1963).
3. Ins. by the Constitution (Fifteenth Amendment) Act, 1963, sec. 7 (w.e.f. 5-10-1963).

of, and the law administered in, any existing High Court, and the respective powers of the Judges thereof in relation to the administration of justice in the Court, including any power to make rules of Court and to regulate the sittings of the court and of members thereof sitting alone or in Division Courts, shall be the same as immediately before the commencement of this Constitution:

¹[Provided that any restriction to which the exercise of original jurisdiction by any of the High Courts with respect to any matter concerning the revenue or concerning any act ordered or done in the collection thereof was subject immediately before the commencement of this Constitution shall no longer apply to the exercise of such jurisdiction.]

Notes on Article 225

A High Court Judge's power to hear specified class of cases is derived only from the application of business by the Chief justice. A case not covered by such allocation cannot be heard by a judge sitting singly or in Division Bench (History of Calcutta High Court's jurisdiction traced). The power of the Chief Justice to allocate business is (a) not only derived from section 108(2), Government of India Act, 1915 (which still subsists by virtue of section 223, Government of India Act, 1935 and article 225 of the Constitution) but (b) is also inherent in the Chief Justice; *Pramatha Nath Talukdar* v. *Saroj Ranjan Sarkar*, AIR 1962 SC 876: (1962) Supp 2 SCR 297: (1962) 1 Cr LJ 770 and *State of Uttar Pradesh* v. *Devi Dayal*, AIR 1959 All 421 (423): 1959 Cr LJ 803 cited.); *Sohan Lal Baid* v. *State of West Bengal*, AIR 1990 Cal 168: (1989) 2 Cal HN 474: (1989) 2 Cal LJ 433 (DB).

The three erstwhile Presidency High Courts (in common and popular paralance Chartered High Courts) namely, Calcutta, Bombay and Madras were having the Letters Patent for the conferment of the ordinary original civil jurisdiction and by reason of the provisions contained therein read with the Admiralty Court Act, 1861 and subsequent enactment of Colonial Courts of Admiralty Act, 1890 and Colonial Courts of Admiralty (India) Act, 1891, the admiralty jurisdiction of the three High Courts noticed above can be fairly traced. This special admiralty jurisdiction was saved by the Government of India Act, 1915 as also that of 1935 and subsequently protected in terms of articles 225 of the Constitution; *M.V.AL. Quamar* v. *Tsavliris Salvage (International) Ltd.*, AIR 2000 SC 2826: (2000) 8 SCC 278: 2000 AIR SCW 3101: JT 2000 (9) SC 184: 2000 (3) SCJ 464: (2000) 8 SRJ 405: (2000) 5 SCALE 618: 2000 (5) Supreme 688.

²[**226. Power of High Courts to issue certain writs.**—(1) Notwithstanding anything in article 32 ³[***], every High Court shall have power, throughout the territories in relation to which it exercises jurisdiction, to issue to any person or authority, including in appropriate cases, any Government, within those territories directions, orders or writs, including ⁴[writs in the nature of *habeas corpus, mandamus, prohibition, quo warranto* and *certiorari*, or any of them, for the enforcement of any of the rights conferred by Part III and for any other purpose].

(2) The power conferred by clause (1) to issue directions, orders or writs to any Government, authority or person may also be exercised by any High Court

---

1. Ins. by the Constitution (Forty-fourth Amendment) Act, 1978, sec. 29 (w.e.f. 20-6-1979). Earlier proviso was omitted by the Constitution (Forty-second Amendment) Act, 1976, sec. 37 (w.e.f. 1-2-1977).

2. Subs. by the Constitution (Forty-second Amendment) Act, 1976, sec. 38, for article 226 (w.e.f. 1-2-1977). Earlier article 226 was amended by the Constitution (Fifteenth Amendment) Act, 1963, sec. 8 (w.e.f. 5-10-1963).

3. The words, figures and letters "but subject to the provisions of article 131A and article 226A" omitted by the Constitution (Forty-third Amendment) Act, 1977, sec. 7 (w.e.f. 13-4-1978).

4. Subs. by the Constitution (Forty-fourth Amendment) Act, 1978, sec. 30(a), for certain words (w.e.f. 1-8-1979).

exercising jurisdiction in relation to the territories within which the cause of action, wholly or in part, arises for the exercise of such power, notwithstanding that the seat of such Government or authority or the residence of such person is not within those territories.

[1][(3) Where any party against whom an interim order, whether by way of injunction or stay or in any other manner, is made on, or in any proceedings relating to, a petition under clause (1), without—

(a) furnishing to such party copies of such petition and all documents in support of the plea for such interim order; and

(b) giving such party an opportunity of being heard,

makes an application to the High Court for the vacation of such order and furnishes a copy of such application to the party in whose favour such order has been made or the counsel of such party, the High Court shall dispose of the application within a period of two weeks from the date on which it is received or from the date on which the copy of such application is so furnished, whichever is later, or where the High Court is closed on the last day of that period, before the expiry of the next day afterwards on which the High Court is open; and if the application is not so disposed of, the interim order shall, on the expiry of that period, or, as the case may be, the expiry of the said next day, stand vacated.]

[2][(4)] The power conferred on a High Court by this article shall not be in derogation of the power conferred on the Supreme Court by clause (2) of article 32.]

Notes on Article 226

Acquiescence

Minor violations of the rules of procedures will be no ground for interference where the petitioner has participated in the trial and no prejudice has been caused to him in defence. *Sodhi v. Union of India*, (1991) 2 SCC 382: 1991 SCC (Cri) 357: (1991) 1 LLN 365: 1991 Cr LJ 1947, paragraph 35.

The power conferred on the High Court by virtue of article 226 is to enforce the rule of law and ensure that the State and other statutory authorities act in accordance with law; *K.S. Bhoir v. State of Maharashtra*, AIR 2002 SC 444: (2001) 10 SCC 264: (2002) 2 SLR 765.

Administrative Action

While exercising power of judicial review of administrative action, the Court is not an appellate authority and the Court cannot direct or advise the executive in matter of policy; *Ekta Shakti Foundation* v. *Govt. of NCT of Delhi*, AIR 2006 SC 2609: 2006 AIR SCW 3601: 2006 (64) All LR 907: 2006 (3) Ker LT 601: 2006 (4) Mad LW 864: 2006 (8) SRJ 393: (2006) 7 SCALE 179: 2006 (6) Supreme 372.

Allotment of Land

A Housing Society sought (through writ petition) a direction to the Government to allot certain land in respect of which the Development Authority had passed a resolution. However, it was found that no order of allotment had been communicated to the petitioner society, nor had Government approval been granted. Petition was dismissed; *Vijaynagar Industrial Workers Housing Co-operative Society Ltd.* v. *State of Karnataka*, AIR 1998 Kant 361: ILR 1998 Kant 2479: 1998 (4) Kant LJ 117.

---

1. Subs. by the Constitution (Forty-fourth Amendment) Act, 1978, sec. 30(b), for clauses (3), (4), (5) and (6) (w.e.f. 1-8-1979).

2. Clause (7) renumbered as clause (4) by the Constitution (Forty-fourth Amendment) Act, 1978, sec. 30(c) (w.e.f. 1-8-1979).

Alternative Remedy

The alternative remedy is not an absolute bar; *Committee of Management* v. *Vice-Chancellor*, AIR 2009 SC 1159: 2009 AIR SCW 398: 2009 (1) LLN 774: 2009 (3) Mad LJ 323: (2009) 2 SCC 630: 2009 (1) SCT 423: (2008) 16 SCALE 310: 2009 (3) Serv LJ 57 (SC).

Writ petition once allowed can be dismissed in appeal on facts of case, on ground of alternative remedy; *S.N.J. Abdul Hakeem* v. *Assisrathul Musthakeem Etheemkhana Trust*, AIR 2006 Mad 67: 2006 AIHC 53 (NOC): 2005 (2) Mad LJ 533: 2005 (2) Mad LW 621.

Amenability

Even though a writ would not issue against a non-statutory private body, it should lie against such body when it receives grant from Government and is subject to regulation made by the Government, or against the order of a Government Officer even though it is in relation to the private institution; *Francis John* v. *Director of Education*, AIR 1990 SC 423: (1989) Supp 2 SCC 598: 1990 SCC (L&S) 105, paragraphs 8-9.

Arbitrariness

Emphasis is now being placed on the need to avoid arbitrariness by administrative authority even in spheres where the relevant statute does not lay down any *quasi judicial* obligation; *Union of India* v. *Nambudri*, (1991) 2 UJ SC 303: (1991) 1 SCC 38: AIR 1991 SC 1216: (1991) 17 ATC 104, paragraph 7.

Arrest

A person was arrested under the Terrorists Act and the designated court refused bail. It was held that the High Court in writ jurisdiction could not examine the correctness of the view of the designated court to quash the presentation of the accused; *State of Maharashtra* v. *Abdul Hamid Haji Mohammed*, JT 1994 (2) SC 1: (1994) Supp 1 SCC 579: 1994 SCC (Cri) 723.

Bail

Although the High Court has jurisdiction to entertain prayer for bail in writ jurisdiction, yet, such jurisdiction should be exercised sparingly having regard to judicial discipline and *comity* of courts; *Kartar Singh* v. *State of Punjab*, JT 1994 (2) SC 423: (1994) 3 SCC 569: 1994 Cr LJ 3139.

Bias

When no other person is available to discharge an adjudicatory function, even a person who is disqualified on account of bias may be allowed to function, without the risk of violating natural justice. This doctrine also applies where no quorum can be formed without the disqualified member or where all the members of a tribunal are disqualified; *Charan Lal Sahu* v. *Union of India*, (1990) 1 SCC 613: AIR 1990 SC 1480 (CB): (1989) Supp 2 SCR 597: 1989 Supp SCALE 1, paragraphs 75 and 105.

The main witnesses of an alleged incident of misbehaviour by a student were Professors of the College. They were members of the Inquiry Committee and also members of the Disciplinary Committee. The Principal passed restriction order on the basis of the report of the above Committee. It was held that the decision was vitiated on the ground of bias; *Bhupendrakumar Singhal* v. *Dr. P.R. Mehta*, AIR 1990 Guj 48 (Reviews case law).

Cases of Non-statutory Matters

Writ petition lies only where State or its instrumentality acts in exercise of statutory power under certain Act or Rules made thereunder; *Uktal Highways* v. *State of Chhattisgarh*, AIR 2006 Chhat 29.

Certiorari

In India, certiorari would be available even against administrative bodies, not having any *quasi judicial* obligation, if they *affect* rights of individuals without conforming to the principles of 'fair play'; *Union of India* v. *E.G. Nambudri*, (1991) 2 UJ SC 303: (1991) 3 SCC 38: AIR 1991 SC 1216: (1991) 17 ATC 104, paragraph 9.

Certiorari and Prohibition

The grounds for issuing *certiorari* and *prohibition* are as under:

1. Defect of jurisdiction

(a) Defect of jurisdiction attracts *certiorari*. But *certiorari* would not lie, merely because the decision of a tribunal on a subject-matter within its jurisdiction is considered to be wrong. *See* the undermentioned cases:—

    (i) *T.C. Basappa* v. *T. Nagappa*, (1955) 1 SCR 250 (257-258): AIR 1954 SC 440: 1954 SCA 620: 67 Mad LW 613: 1954 SCJ 695: ILR 1954 Mys 235.

    (ii) *Syed Yakoob* v. *K.S. Radhakrishnan*, AIR 1964 SC 477: (1964) 5 SCR 64.

Illustrations

(1) The State Government leased out some forest land to appellants to collect and exploit sal seeds for 15 years on payment of royalty at a certain rate and when the State, under the terms of leases, revised the rate of royalty and thereafter cancelled the leases for the breach of certain conditions, the appellants challenged the orders of revision of rate and cancellation of leases as illegal by writ proceedings under article 226. Held that the contract did not contain any statutory terms or obligations and no statutory power or obligation which could attract the application of article 14 was involved; *Radhakrishna Agarwal* v. *State of Bihar*, AIR 1977 SC 1496: (1977) 3 SCC 457: (1977) 3 SCR 249.

(2) Clause 7(2) of the Sugar Control Order, 1966, requires the Government to fix the price "having regard to the estimated cost of production of sugar on the basis of the relevant schedule". The expression "having regard to" only obliges the Government to consider as relevant data material to which it must have regard. It is evident that the price fixed is an estimated maximum price chargeable because the manufacturer cannot charge more. Furthermore, it should be noted that the only "adjustment" provided for is before a fixation of the estimated price "having regard" to the basis provided by the relevant schedule, but there is no obligation whatsoever cast upon the Government to make any "adjustment" to compensate for losses due to any previous erroneous fixation; *Saraswati Industrial Syndicate Ltd.* v. *Union of India*, AIR 1975 SC 460: (1974) 2 SCC 630: (1975) 1 SCR 956.

(3) The courts have no jurisdiction under article 226 to go into reasonableness of Telephone Tariff Rates. These rates are decided as policy matter in fiscal planning. There is legislative prescription of rates. Rates are a matter for legislative judgment and not for judicial determination; *S. Narayan Iyer* v. *Union of India*, AIR 1976 SC 1986: (1976) 3 SCC 428: (1976) 2 SCWR 13: 1976 UJ (SC) 569: 1976 SCC (Tax) 325: 1976 Supp SCR 486: 1977 (1) SCJ 193.

(4) A notification issued under section 3 of the U.P. Town Areas Act, 1914, which has the effect of making the Act Applicable to a geographical area is in the nature of a conditional legislation and it cannot be characterised as a piece of subordinate legislation. Therefore, it is not necessary for the State Government to follow the same procedure which is applicable to the promulgation of rules under section 39 of the Act; *Tulsipur Sugar Co. Ltd.* v. *Notified Area Committee, Tulsipur*, AIR 1980 SC 882: (1980) 2 SCC 295: 1980 All LJ 401.

(5) Principles of natural justice are not inflexible and may differ in different circumstances. When a proper inquiry is held by an inquiry committee consisting of three respectable and independent members of the staff as appointed by the principal of a Medical College to inquire into the complaints of the inmates of the girls hostel against certain male students of that college about their indecent behaviour with them in hostel compound itself during odd hours of night, in such case, the rules of natural justice do not require that statement of girl students should be recorded in presence of the male students concerned; *Hira Nath Mishra* v. *The Principal, Rajendra Medical College, Ranchi*, AIR 1973 SC 1260: (1973) 1 SCC 805: (1973) 2 LLJ 111 (SC).

(6) A writ of *certiorari* can be issued for correcting errors of jurisdiction committed by inferior courts or tribunals. A writ can be issued where in exercise of jurisdiction conferred on it, the court or tribunal acts illegally or improperly, as for instance, it decides a question without giving an opportunity to be heard to the party affected by the order, or where the procedure adopted in dealing with the dispute is opposed to principles of natural justice; *Syed Yakoob* v. *Radhakrishnan*, AIR 1964 SC 477: (1964) 5 SCR 64.

(b) *certiorari* will issue if, there is an error of law *apparent* on the face of the record, (as stated above) or if the tribunal acts without sufficient evidence or misdirects itself in considering the evidence.

(c) defect of jurisdiction must be distinguished from error or irregularity in *procedure*. The reason is that—

"In granting ...... *certiorari* the superior court does not review or rewigh the evidence upon which the determination of the inferior Tribunal purports to be based. It demolishes the order which it considers to be without jurisdiction or palpably erroneous but does not substitute its own views for those of the inferior tribunal".

(d) the writ of *certiorari* does not issue to correct a mere erroneous decision; *R.* v. *Middlesex II*, (1952) 2 All ER 312 or irregularity in procedure (except where the error is one of law which is "apparent on the face of the record" or constitutes a denial of natural justice).

(i) *R.* v. *Northumberland Compensation Tribunal*, (1952) 1 KB 338 (357).

(ii) *R.* v. *Middlesex II*, (1952) 2 All ER 312.

Object of *certiorari* is to get rid of a decision which is vitiated by a defect or jurisdiction or a denial of the basic principles of justice—not to substitute a right determination for a wrong one; *R.* v. *Northumberland Compensation Tribunal*, (1952) 1 KB 338 (357).

2. Non-observance of the rules of natural justice

(a) An administrative body vested with quasi judicial power is not bound to follow the rules of *judicial procedure*, such as to examine witnesses or even to hear the parties orally.

(i) *Board of Education* v. *Rice*, (1911) AC 179: 80 LJ KB 796.

(ii) *Local Govt. Board* v. *Arlidge*, (1915) AC 120: 84 LJ KB 72: 111 LT 905 (HL).

(b) But there is a minimum standard to be observed "by any one who decides anything"; *Board of Education* v. *Rice*, (1911) AC 179: 80 LJ KB 796.

(c) The requirements of natural justice vary with the varying Constitution of the different *quasi judicial* authorities and the statutory provisions under which they function.

Hence, the question whether or not any rule of natural justice has been contravened in any particular case should be decided not under any preconceived notions, but in the light of the relevant statutory provisions, the Constitution of the tribunal and circumstances of each case.

(i) *N.P.T. Co.* v. *N.S.T. Co.*, (1957) SCR 98: AIR 1957 SC 232: (1957) 1 MLJ (Cri) 157.

(ii) *Union of India* v. *P.K. Roy*, AIR 1968 SC 850 (858): (1968) 2 SCR 186: (1968) 2 SCWR 41: 1968 (2) SCJ 503: (1970) 1 LLJ 633.

(iii) *Suresh Koshy George* v. *University of Kerala*, AIR 1969 SC 198: (1969) 1 SCR 317: 1969 Ker LJ 197.

The authority competent to decide must "act in good faith and fairly listen to both sides", and "deal with the question referred to it without bias, and give to each of the parties the opportunity of adequately presenting the case made."

(i) *Board of Education* v. *Rice*, (1911) AC 179: 80 LJ KB 796.

(ii) *Local Govt. Board* v. *Arlidge*, (1915) AC 120 (132): 84 LJ KB 72.

3. Errors of law apparent on the face of the record

This means, (i) error of law, (ii) which *apparent* form the record, and (iii) which does not require to be established by evidence comparatively recent decisions in England and India lay down above.

(i) R. v. *Northumberland Compensation Tribunal*, (1952) 1 KB 338 (357).

(ii) *T.C. Basappa* v. *T. Nagappa*, (1955) 1 SCR 250 (257-258): AIR 1954 SC 440: 1954 SCA 620: 67 Mad LW 613: 1954 SCJ 695: ILR 1954 Mys 235.

(iii) *Ambica Mills* v. *Bhatt*, AIR 1961 SC 970 (973): (1961) 3 SCR 220: (1961) 1 LLJ 1.

When it is an error of *law*, and it is apparent, *certiorari* will issue even though the tribunal has not transgressed its "jurisdiction" in any way.

Error in this context means an "error of law", which is apparent.

(i) Where the tribunal stated on the face of the order the grounds on which it made the order and in law these grounds were not such as to warrant the decision to which the tribunal had come, *certiorari* would issue to quash the decision; *P.T. Services* v. *S.I. Court*, AIR 1963 SC 114: (1963) 3 SCR 650: (1965) 2 LLJ 360.

(ii) Where the order cites the provision of law relied upon, but the facts stated do not warrant its application, certiorari would issue; *Collector of Customs* v. *Pednekar*, AIR 1976 SC 1408: (1976) 3 SCC 790: (1976) 3 SCR 971 paragraphs 22, 24.

Civil Consequences

No civil consequence, so as to require an obligation to hear the person to be affected, takes place where such person had no legal right of which he is a mere privilege or concession; *Andhra Steel Corporation Ltd.* v. *Andhra Pradesh State Electricity Board*, (1991) 3 SCC 263: AIR 1991 SC 1456: 1991 AIR SCW 1358: JT 1991 (2) SC 581: (1991) 2 SCR 624: 1991 (2) UJ (SC) 244, paragraph 15.

An instance of civil consequences, is taking away of vested rights, *e.g.*, the removal of an employee's name from a 'select list' for promotion; *Union of India* v. *E.G. Nambudri*, (1991) 2 UJ SC 303: (1991) 3 SCC 38: 1991 SCC (L&S) 813: AIR 1991 SC 1216: (1991) 2 SLR 675, paragraph 7.

An instance of civil consequences, is the taking away of vested rights, *e.g.*, termination of any employment governed by statute; *Shridhar* v. *Nagar Palika*, 1990 (1) SCJ 383: 1990 Supp SCC 157: AIR 1990 SC 307: (1990) 2 LLN 970, paragraphs 7-8.

An instance of civil consequences, is imposing any penalty upon an employee, for misconduct, *e.g.*, making an adverse entry in his service record; *State of Maharashtra* v. *Ravi Kant*, (1991) 2 UJ SC 188: (1991) 2 SCC 373: 1991 SCC (Cri) 656.

No civil consequence, so as to require an obligation to hear the person to be affected, take place where such person had no legal right of which he is going to be deprived, *e.g.*, economical loss caused by the transfer of a Government employee, except where the conditions of his employment indicate that he cannot be transferred without his consent; *Shankar* v. *Vice Admiral*, (1991) 2 SCC 209: (1991) 16 ATC 470: (1991) 1 LLN 579.

Even an administrative order must be made in conformity with the rules of natural justice, if it involves civil consequences, or if it affects any right of citizen which is capable of being enforced by a legal action, including even procedural rights; *Union of India* v. *Amrik*, (1991) 1 SCC 654: AIR 1991 SC 564: 1991 Cr LJ 664, paragraph 4.

Code of Civil Procedure

Certain High Courts have framed Rules attracting the application of the provisions of the Code of Civil Procedure to proceedings under article 226, in matters on which the rules are silent, and in these High Courts it has been held that even after 1976, the provisions of the Code will apply to writ proceedings in so far as they are not inconsistent with the rules, *e.g.* the principle under *Explanation IV* to section 11.

Compensation

In a Madras case, the police entered the premises of a Devasthanam illegally, and prepared non-vegetarian food. The petitioner, who was managing trustee of the temple, sought *mandamus*, directing the police officers to vacate the premises. During the pendency of the proceedings, the police vacated the premises. The writ petition, therefore, became infructuous. But a sum of Rs. 2,000 was ordered to be paid as costs to the petitioner, having regard to the illegality committed by the police; *K.T. Alagappa Chettiar* v. *Collector, Tiruvannamalai*, AIR 1990 Mad 181 (183): 1989 TLNJ 452, paragraph 8.

Concession: Withdrawal

Concession on tariff can be withdrawn without giving opportunity of hearing to consumers, except where promissory estoppel applies; *Andhra Steel Corporation Ltd.* v. *Andhra Pradesh State Electricity Board*, (1991) 3 SCC 263: AIR 1991 SC 1456: 1991 AIR SCW 1358: JT 1991 (2) SC 581: (1991) 2 SCR 624: 1991 (2) UJ (SC) 244, paragraph 15.

Consumer Disputes Redressal Commission

Where the State Consumer Disputes Redressal Commission exercises jurisdiction not conferred by law (*e.g.* entertaining a complaint made by a *seller* of goods) the High Court can quash the order; *Larson & Toubro Ltd.* v. *State Consumer Disputes Redressal Commission*, AIR 1998 Cal 313: 1999 CWN 252: 1999 (33) Cor LA 456: 1999 (2) ICC 749.

Court Martial

Mandamus will issue to prevent courts-martial from exceeding their jurisdiction, but not to interfere with their proper jurisdiction, *e.g.*, on issues of military discipline, except in case of error of law; *Commander Ranvir Kumar Sinha* v. *Union of India*, 1991 Cr LJ 1729 (Bom): 1991 (2) Bom CR 28, paragraph 9.

The Supreme Court under article 32 and a High Court under article 226 can interfere with proceedings before a court-martial and grant appropriate relief where the impugned order has resulted in denial of fundamental rights of the party aggrieved; *S.N. Mukherjee* v. *Union of India*, 1990 (3) SCJ 193: (1990) 4 SCC 594: AIR 1990 SC 1984: 1990 Cr LJ 2148, paragraph 4.

Writ court can interfere with proceedings before a court-martial and grant appropriate relief where the sentence awarded by the court-martial is disproportionate to the offence committed, thereby violating article 14 of the Constitution; *Ex-Naik Sardar Singh* v. *Union of India*, (1991) 2 UJ SC 466: (1991) 3 SCC 213: AIR 1992 SC 417: (1991) 2 Crimes 674, paragraph 6.

Criminal Investigation

While the court should not normally interfere with criminal investigation, it may prohibit the continuance of a criminal proceeding at any stage before its conclusion, in extraordinary cases, *e.g.*, where the proceeding was launched by a person who was not competent to make the F.I.R. or to institute prosecution under the relevant law; *State of Haryana* v. *Bhajan*, (1991) 2 SCJ 351: (1992) Supp 1 SCC 335: AIR 1992 SC 604: 1992 Cr LJ 527, paragraph 144.

Delay and Lachas

Three to four years is reasonable period for challenging seniority. The delay in approaching adjudicatory forum beyond same should be satisfactorily explained; *Shiba Shankar Mohapatra* v. *State of Orissa*, AIR 2010 SC 706.

Discretion

The exercise of a statutory power must not be *ultra vires*. Thus, the discretion must be exercised in furtherance of accomplishment of the purpose for which it had been conferred. Thus, in the case of a public utility organisation, it must be exercised having regard to the consideration of the efficiency of the public service, within the limits of its resources; *U.P.S.R.T.C.* v. *Mohammed Ismail*, (1991) 3 SCC 239: AIR 1991 SC 1099: (1991) 17 ATC 234: (1991) 2 LLJ 332, paragraph 15.

A writ court cannot direct a civil court to act in a particular direction, as held by the High Court of Andhra Pradesh in *Nagarjuna University* v. *St. Anthony Educational Society*, AIR 1998 AP 271: 1998 (1) APLJ 349: 1998 (3) Andh LD 42: 1998 (2) Andh LT 696: 1998 (1) LS AP 474 (DB). In this case, a University had refused to affiliate a college. The High Court held that the role of the Judiciary is very limited in such matters. The University has its due mechanism, with which the court cannot interfere. The law court cannot act as superintendent of an educational institution. In the writ court (single Judge) had directed the trial court to dispose of the suit within 6 months. It had further directed that a certain group shall not take unnecessary adjournments. The Appeal Court held, that such directions are illegal and unjustified.

Where a discriminatory Rule fixing different age for retirement of employees belonging to the same class has been struck down by a court, those who had been wrongly retired at the lower age (say, 58) shall not be entitled to claim salary for the period intervening the higher age (say, 60) during which they did not actually render any service; nevertheless, their pension should be re-fixed by extending (by fiction) their retirement by the intervening period (*i.e.* 2 years) in the given case; *Nand* v. *State of Orissa*, AIR 1991 SC 1724: (1991) 2 SCC 698: 1991 Lab IC 1527: (1991) 2 CLR 370.

Discrimination

An extra payment made to those who were willing to go on transfer to a remote place cannot be challenged as discriminatory by those who were not willing to go to that place; *R.B.I.* v. *R.B.I. Staff*, (1991) 2 UJ SC 546: (1991) 4 SCC 132: 1991 SCC (L&S) 1090: (1991) 17 ATC 295: AIR 1992 SC 485, paragraph 3.

Domestic Inquiry

In a domestic inquiry, the principles of natural justice must be observed. Where there were allegations of acceptance of illegal bets by a runner employed by the petitioner, the licence cannot be cancelled, merely on the statement of one employees, without calling the employee for cross-examination; *Gandhi & Co.* v. *State of Maharashtra*, AIR 1990 Bom 218: 1989 Mah LR 1708: (1989) 2 Bom CR 380.

Education: Medical Colleges

Where, for admission to a medical college certain seats are reserved for the Central Board of Secondary Education, and the Board does not sponsor the candidates so that the seats remain vacant, the seats must be filled from the waiting list. The University cannot say that it has a discretion not to fill the seats.

Making of a provision in the prospectus casts a legal duty on the University to give admission to the students who otherwise fulfil the qualifications. It was further held that the petitioners should not suffer for late admission and that shortage of lectures must be condoned by the University or the college; *Miss Sumedha Kalia* v. *State of Haryana*, AIR 1990 P&H 239: ILR 1991 (2) P&H 498: 1990 (4) Serv LR 122.

Petitioner was wrongly denied admission to M.S. General Surgery. Though 2 years had passed, he could not get relief. His representation was still pending. Court gave direction to admit the petitioner to M.S. Surgery; *Dr. Dvijendra Nath* v. *Director of Medical Education, Uttar Pradesh, Lucknow*, AIR 1990 All 131: 1990 (2) All WC 896.

For admission to medical college, seats were reserved for Scheduled Tribes. Petitioner was described as Scheduled Tribe in Birth Register. Her father (a Government servant) was a member of Scheduled Tribe. It was held, that her application could not be rejected on flimsy grounds; *Mythili* v. *T. Padnia, Andhra Pradesh University of Health Service*, AIR 1990 (NOC) 113 (AP): (1989) 2 APLJ 288.

For admission test to medical course, "Multiple choice" type objective questions were set. Petitioner challenged the key answers. It was held that the burden lay on her to prove that the key answers were wrong (On the facts, the key answers were held to be correct); *Kumari Anjali Saxena* v. *Chairman, Professional Examination Board, Bhopal*, AIR 1990 MP 253: 1990 Jab LJ 77 (DB).

In the case of admission to medical institutions, the rule may be departed from in filling up vacant seats in view of the dearth of qualified doctors in this country. The court would not disturb any practical step adopted by the authorities to tide over a transitional difficulty; *Principal, Motilal Nehru Medical College* v. *Dr. Vandana Singh*, AIR 1991 SC 792: 1990 Supp SCC 343: JT 1990 (3) SC 679: (1990) 5 Serv LR 83: 1990 (2) UJ (SC) 616, paragraph 9.

Encroachment and Natural Justice

Where the encroachment upon public property is recent then natural justice need not be observed; *Ahmedabad Municipal Corporation* v. *Nawab Khan Gulab Khan*, AIR 1997 SC 152: (1997) 11 SCC 121: 1996 AIR SCW 4315: 1997 (1) All MR 537: 1997 (1) Guj LH 438: JT 1996 (10) SC 485.

Enforcement of an Act

Mandamus cannot be issued to seek from the court a direction to the executive to bring into force an enactment. In such a case, there is no duty as such, imposed on the executive to bring the enactment into force.

See the undermentioned cases:

   (i) *A.K. Roy* v. *Union of India*, AIR 1982 SC 710: (1982) 1 SCC 271: 1982 Cr LJ 340.

  (ii) *Vasudev Shenoy* v. *Government of India*, (1994) 1 KLT 389 (390).

 (iii) *State of Jammu & Kashmir* v. *A.R. Zakki*, AIR 1992 SC 1546: (1992) Supp 1 SCC 548: (1992) 20 ATC 285: (1992) 1 LLJ 891.

Error of Law

If justice became the byproduct of an erroneous view of law, the High Court is not expected to erase such justice in the name of "correcting the error of law"; *Roshan Deen* v. *Preeti Lal*, AIR 2002 SC 33: (2002) 1 SCC 100: (2002) 1 LLN 11.

Exercise of Power

The writ court is bound to consider all relevant parameters and authentic facts of the case; *City Industrial Development Corporation* v. *Dosu Aardeshir Bhiwandiwala*, (2009) 1 SCC 168: AIR 2009 SC 571: 2008 AIR SCW 7706: 2009 (1) Andh LD 24: 2009 (1) CTC 174: 2009 (3) Mad LJ 137: (2008) 14 SCALE 23.

Exercise of Writ Jurisdiction

Whether to exercise discretion or not arises only in cases where a mandatory provision of law is said to be violated and not in case of directory provisions which is not enforceable; *Poorvanchal Caterers* v. *Indian Railway Catering and Tourism Corporation Ltd.*, AIR 2006 (NOC) 455 (Del).

Extraordinary Jurisdiction

The power to summon Chief Secretary, Secretary to Government and other Senior Government officials is to be exercised only in rare and exceptional cases. In case higher official has to be and is summoned, he should be shown due respect and should not be made to stand all the time during hearing; *State of Gujarat* v. *Turabali Gulamhussain Hirani*, AIR 2008 SC 86: 2007 AIR SCW 6122: 2007 (4) Crimes 122: (2007) 11 SCALE 556: 2007 (7) Supreme 129: 2007 (4) JLJR 199: 2007 (4) Ker LT 656: 2008 (1) Mad LJ (Cri) 1045: 2007 (38) OCR 619.

Facts

In general, a disputed question of fact is *not* investigated in a proceeding under article 226, particularly where an alternative remedy is available, *e.g.*, the merits of rival claims to property or a disputed question of title; *State of Rajasthan* v. *Bhawani Singh*, (1993) Supp 1 SCC 306: AIR 1992 SC 1018: 1992 AIR SCW 930: 1993 (1) All CJ 717: JT 1992 (3) SC 531: (1993) Supp 1 SCC 306: 1992 (1) UJ (SC) 491.

The High Court may interfere with a finding of fact, if it is shown that the finding is not supported by any evidence, or that the finding is 'perverse' or based upon a view of facts which could never be reasonably entertained; *Arjun* v. *Jamnadas*, 1990 (1) SCJ 59: (1989) 4 SCC 612: AIR 1989 SC 1599, paragraph 15.

A finding based on *no evidence* constitutes an error of law, but an error in appreciation of evidence or in drawing inferences is not, except where it is perverse, that is to say, such a conclusion as no person properly instructed in law could have reached, or it is based on evidence which is legally inadmissible; *Board of Muslim Wakfs* v. *Hadi Begum*, (1993) Supp 1 SCC 192: AIR 1992 SC 1083: 1992 AIR SCW 968: JT 1992 (2) SC 385: 1992 (2) SCJ 139: 1992 (1) UJ (SC) 627, paragraph 17.

If the conclusion on facts is supported by evidence on record, no interference is called for even though the court considers that another view is possible; *Maharashtra State Board of Secondary and Higher Secondary Education* v. *K.S. Gandhi*, (1991) 2 SCC 716: 1991 AIR SCW 879, paragraph 10.

Factual Inaccuracy

A writ petition cannot succeed, if its factual basis is not established. In a Calcutta case, the petitioner sought inspection of his answer scripts at a particular examination on the ground that he had reason to believe that his answer scripts were missing. However, existence of the answer scripts was proved from the order of the controller of Examinations. It was held that writ could not be issued; *Vikramjit Saha* v. *State of West Bengal*, AIR 1998 Cal 316 (DB).

Fairness

The requirement of 'fairness' implies that even an administrative authority must not act arbitrarily or capriciously and must not come to a conclusion which is perverse or is such that no reasonable body of persons properly informed could arrive at; *Nally* v. *State of Bihar*, (1990) 2 SCC 48: (1990) 2 LLJ 211: (1990) 1 LLN 755, paragraphs 13-15, 19.

Once the test of 'fairness' is substituted for a 'hearing' in this area of administrative decisions, it would follow that it cannot require that much of hearing when a person is charged with some offence or misconduct. Notice of the penalty sought to be imposed with an opportunity for making a representation and consideration of that representation in a fair and just manner, would suffice.

Where the administrative function is statutory the court must read into the statute the requirement of *fairness*, which means the minimum principles of natural justice; *Union of India* v. *E.G. Nambudri*, (1991) 2 UJ SC 303: (1991) 3 SCC 38: 1991 SCC (L&S) 813: AIR 1991 SC 1216, paragraph 9.

Fraud

Where a person has obtained an order from the High Court by fraud or false representation, that order as well as all advantages obtained thereunder shall be cancelled. Natural justice is not attracted to such a case; *U.P. Junior Doctors* v. *Nandwani*, AIR 1991 SC 909: (1990) 4 SCC 633, paragraph 5.

A petition filed by the party aggrieved cannot be thrown out on the ground of forgery and fraud, merely because there was a *bona fide* mistake in stating the name of the petitioner in a petition drafted by another person; *Ruqmani* v. *Achuthan*, (1991) Supp 1 SCC 520: AIR 1991 SC 983, paragraph 7.

Futile Writ

Writ will not be granted if, to grant it would be futile. *See* the undermentioned cases:

(i) *Rashbihari* v. *State of Orissa*, AIR 1969 SC 1081 (1088): (1969) 1 SCC 414: (1969) 35 Cut LJ 479.

(ii) *K.N. Guruswamy* v. *State of Mysore*, AIR 1954 SC 592: (1955) 1 SCR 305: 1954 SCJ 644: ILR 1955 Mys 279.

(iii) *Nand Kishore Saraf* v. *State of Rajasthan*, AIR 1965 SC 1992 (1994): (1965) 3 SCR 173: (1965) 2 SCWR 578: 1966 (2) SCJ 194.

Geographical Limits

On a combined reading of clauses (1) and (2) of article 226, one can say that writ can be issued against a Government, person or authority if—

(a) its seat is within the High Court's jurisdiction, or

(b) the cause of action has arisen, wholly or in part, within the High Court's jurisdiction.

Habeas Corpus

The Constitution of India mentions the writ of *habeas corpus* in articles 32 and 226. The writ ordinarily issued is *habeas corpus, ad subjiciendum*, whose object is to secure the release of a person found to be detained illegally. There are also other species of writs, going under the wider fabric of *habeas corpus*.

The various writs are as under:

(a) *Habeas Corpus ad deliberandum et recipiendum.* A writ used to remove a person confined in one place for trial to another place in which the *offence* is alleged to have been committed.

(b) *Habeas Corpus ad faciendum et recipiendum* (also called, *habeas corpus cum causa).* A writ issued in a civil case to remove the case from the trial court to a superior court (having jurisdiction), for disposal.

(c) *Habeas Corpus ad presequendum.* This writ is issued by a court, when it is necessary to bring before the issuing court, for trial, a person who is confined for some other offence.

(d) *Habeas Corpus ad respondendum.* A writ employed in civil cases to remove a person out of the custody or one court into that of another, in order that he may be sued in the latter court and answer the action in that court.

(e) *Habeas Corpus ad satisfaciendum.* A writ which issues when the prisoner has had judgment (in a civil case), against him, in an action and the plaintiff is desirous of bringing him up before a superior court to charge him with the process of execution.

(f) *Habeas Corpus ad subjiciendum.* A writ directed to the person detaining another in his custody and commanding him to produce, before the issuing court, the person so detained. This is the most common form of the writ. Its object is to test the legality of detention of a person and to secure his release if the detention is found to be illegal. Backstone called it "the most celebrated writ in the English law and the great and efficacious writ in all manner of illegal confinement".

[Blackstones Commentaries (29)].

(g) *Habeas Corpus ad testificandum* ("You produce the body for testifying"). The writ is used to bring up a prisoner detained in Jail or prison, to give evidence before the issuing court. [Black's Law Dictionary (1990) pages 709, 710].

History of the writ is also traced in *Kanu Sanyal* v. *District Magistrate,* AIR 1973 SC 2684: (1973) 2 SCC 674: (1974) 1 SCR 621: 1973 Cr LJ 1818.

Generally, the writ of *habeas corpus* is applied for, only after a person has been arrested. However, in exceptional cases, it may be granted even when detention is threatened, (and not yet carried out); *Additional Secretary* v. *Alka Subhash Gadia,* (1990) 2 SCALE 1352: (992) Supp 1 SCC 496: 1992 SCC (Cri) 301.

The exceptional cases in which *threatened* detention may give rise to the writ, are where the court is satisfied about one of the following circumstances:—

(a) the order of detention is not passed under the act under which it purports to be passed;

(b) it is passed against a wrong person;

(c) it is passed for a wrong purpose;

(d) it is passed on vague, extraneous and irrelevant grounds;

(e) the officer purporting to pass the order has no authority, in law, to make the order.

Additional Secretary v. *Alka Subhash Gadia,* (1990) 2 SCALE 1352:(1992) Supp 1 SCC 496: 1992 SCC (Cri) 301.

According to the Gujarat High Court, where the detention order has not been served and there has been no detention, then *mandamus* is the proper remedy; *Vedprakash Devkinandan Chiripal* v. *State of Gujarat,* AIR 1987 Guj 253 (254): (1987) 1 Crimes 440: 1987 EFR 347 (FB).

Habeas corpus is granted, only if the detention is illegal. Principal grounds for challenging the legality of detention are as under:

(a) The law under which the detention order has been issued, is invalid.

(b) The order under which detention has been ordered, is invalid.

(c) Detention is not in compliance with the law mentioned at (a) above or (b) above. This defect may arise (for example) where the law prescribes certain limits of as to period, procedure, etc., which have not been observed or where the officer ordering detention is not competent under the law.

(i) *Durgadas* v. *Empl.,* AIR 1979 All 148 (FB).

(ii) *Tilak Raj* v. *Reg.,* AIR 1979 All 28.

(d) The detention itself is not in conformity with the order mentioned at (b) above.

(e) The order of detention is *mala fide*.

   Vimlabai Deshpande v. *Emp.*, AIR 1945 Nag 8.

(f) The order of detention is based on irrelevant or extraneous considerations.

   Machindra v. *King*, AIR 1950 FC 129.

(g) The order is passed without application of the mind

   (i) *Emperor* v. *Sibnath Banerjee*, AIR 1943 FC 75: 1945 FCR 195, affirmed in;

   (ii) *Emperor* v. *Sibnath Banerjee*, AIR 1946 PC 158: 72 9A 241.

   (iii) *Kishori Mohan Bera* v. *State of West Bengal*, AIR 1972 SC 1749: (1972) 3 SCC 845: 1972 SCD 805: 1973 SCC (Cri) 30.

Illegal Order

Writ will not be issued if the effect of issuing a writ would be to sustain or restore an illegal order; *Venkateswara* v. *Government of Andhra Pradesh*, AIR 1966 SC 828.

Equality clause cannot be invoked to perpetuate an illegal order; *State of Haryana* v. *Ram Kumar*, JT 1997 (8) SC 171: (1997) 3 SCC 321:1997 Lab IC 1541.

Image of Judiciary

Petition by Association of lawyers that court scenes projected in some motion pictures lowers down the image of judiciary is maintainable as PIL; *Rajasthan Chapter of Indian Association of Lawyers* v. *Union of India*, AIR 2008 (NOC) 533 (Raj).

Interim Orders

High Court cannot in writ jurisdiction make interim orders that would make the functioning of constitutional institutions a mockery; *Bihar Public Service Commission* v. *Dr. Shiv Jatan Thakur*, (1994) Supp 2 SCC 220: AIR 1994 SC 2466: 1994 AIR SCW 3484: JT 1994 (4) SC 681: 1994 SCC (L&S) 1247: 1994 (3) SCJ 337: 1994 (4) SCT 416: (1994) Supp 3 SCC 220: (1995) 1 Serv LJ SC 55: 1994 Writ LR 881.

Joint Petitions

Disposal of joint writ petitions on separate issues by one order is not sustainable; *R.S. Pandey* v. *State of Uttar Pradesh*, AIR 1996 SC 717: (1995) 6 SCC 464: (1995) 31 ATC 735 (paragraph 3).

Judicial Activism

Judicial activism should be resorted to in exceptional circumstances when situation forcefully demands it in interest of nation; *All India Council For Technical Education* v. *Ombir Kaushik*, AIR 2006 (NOC) 496 (Del).

Judicial Review *vis-à-vis* Legislative Policy

A policy decision should not be lightly interfered with but it is difficult to accept that courts cannot exercise this power of judicial review at all; *Bombay Dyeing & Mfg. Co. Ltd.* v. *Bombay Environmental Action Group*, AIR 2006 SC 1489: 2006 AIR SCW 1392: 2006 (1) LACC 456: (2006) 3 SCC 434: 2006 (2) SCJ 705: 2006 (4) SRJ 170: (2006) 3 SCALE 1.

Jurisdiction

Ouster clause in contract can oust jurisdiction only of civil court and not of High Court under article 226; *P.R. Transport Agency* v. *Union of India*, AIR 2006 All 23: 2005 All LJ 3568: 2005 (61) All LR 408: 2006 (1) All WC 504: 2007 (1) CTLJ 384.

Jurisdiction of High Court

High Court while deciding appeal is bound to act within four corners of statute. However, while exercising powers of judicial review the High Court exercises a wider jurisdiction; *Shiv Kumar Sharma* v. *Santosh Kumari*, AIR 2008 SC 171: 2007 AIR SCW 6384: 2007 (6) Andh LD 116: 2007 (5) CTC 453: 2008 (3) Mah LJ 593: 2007 (4) Rec Civ R 515: (2007) 8 SCC 600: (2007) 11 SCALE 303: 2007 (6) Supreme 347.

Jurisdictional Limitations

Where the relief sought by a writ petitioner before the High Court is such that it cannot be granted by the High Court (in view of limitations on its jurisdiction), then the High Court should not issue notice to the respondent (Union of India), but should dismiss the petition *in limine.* Writ procedure should not be resorted to, just to seek publicity; *Union of India* v. *S.P. Anand,* AIR 1998 SC 2615: (1998) 6 SCC 466: 1998 AIR SCW 2656: JT 1998 (5) SC 359: (1998) 3 SCR 1046: 1999 (1) SRJ 110: (1998) 4 SCALE 433: 1998 (6) Supreme 309: 1998 (2) UJ (SC) 483: 1999 Writ LR 1.

Laches

Petition under article 226, challenging land acquisition proceedings, which is filed near about 7 years after the notification under section 6 of the Land Acquisition Act, 1948 is issued, is not maintainable, if the delay is not explained; *Vishwas Nagar Evacuee Plot Purchasers Association* v. *Under Secretary, Delhi Admn.,* AIR 1990 SC 849: (1990) 2 SCC 268: JT 1990 (2) SC 176, paragraph 4. (However, as the Government made an offer to make alternative site available, certain directions were issued by the Supreme Court).

Writ for "other purposes" may be refused, if the petitioner has been guilty of laches or acquiescence. *See* undermentioned cases:

   (i) *Ashok* v. *Collector,* AIR 1980 SC 112: (1980) 1 SCC 180: (1980) 1 SCR 491 paragraph 7.

   (ii) *Union of India* v. *T.R. Verma,* AIR 1957 SC 882 (884): 1958 SCR 499: (1958) 2 LLJ 259.

   (iii) *Pannalal* v. *Union of India,* AIR 1957 SC 397 (512): 1957 SCR 233: (1957) 31 ITR 565.

Legal Assistance

Right to be represented by a lawyer is not a necessary ingredient of natural justice but in particular circumstances it may be required as a condition of fair play, *e.g.,* in the case of a departmental proceeding against an employee where the employer is a legally trained mind; *J.K. Agarwal* v. *H.S.D.C.,* (1991) 2 SCC 283: AIR 1991 SC 1221: (1991) 16 ATC 480: 1991 Lab IC 1008, paragraphs 4 and 8.

Right to be represented by a lawyer is not a necessary ingredient of natural justice but in particular circumstances, it may be required as a condition of fair play; *Maharashtra State Board of Secondaryand Higher Secondary Education* v. *K.S. Gandhi,* (1991) 2 SCC 716: 1991 AIR SCW 879, paragraph 17.

Legal Binding

The law declared by the High Court is binding on all subordinate courts within the State; *East India Commercial Co. Ltd. Calcutta* v. *Collector of Customs, Calcutta,* AIR 1962 SC 1893: (1963) 3 SCR 338: (1963) 1 SCA 622.

Legitimate Expectation

Under the doctrine of 'legitimate expectation', even a non-statutory policy or guideline issued by the State would be enforceable against the State if a person can show that he has been led to take certain action on the basis of or on the legitimate expectation that the Government would abide by such policy or guideline. In such a case, deviation from the policy would be arbitrary and involve a violation of article 14; *Narendra* v. *Union of India,* (1990) Supp SCC 440: AIR 1989 SC 2138: (1989) 3 SCR 43, paragraphs 106-107.

Local Authority

The court can interfere with the action of a statutory local body where the action of the local authority is *ultra vires, e.g.,* where a local authority, having the power to approve or disapprove building plans, approves the plan subject to a condition that it has no authority to impose, *mandamus* will issue, commanding it to approve the plan as submitted, *e.g.,* without the *ultra vires* condition; *Bangalore Medical Trust* v. *B.S. Muddappa,* AIR 1991 SC 1902: (1991) 4 SCC 54: 1991 AIR SCW 2082: JT 1991 (3) SC 172: (1991) 3 SCR 102: 1991 (2) UJ (SC) 415.

A local authority having a legal grievance may be able to take out a writ. Thus a writ was issued on the petition of a local authority against a public utility concern, for the latter's failure to fulfil its statutory obligation to supply power to the local authority, which was a consumer of electricity; *Corporation of City of Nagpur* v. *N.E.L. & Power Co.*, AIR 1958 Bom 498.

Locus Standi

It is only a person, who has an interest in the land who can challenge acquisition. When a challenge is made, to an acquisition, at a belated stage, then even if the Court is inclined to allow such a belated challenge, it must first satisfy itself that the person challenging acquisition has title to the land; *Delhi Administration* v. *Madan Lal Nangia*, AIR 2003 SC 4672: (2003) 10 SCC 321: (2003) 107 DLT 646.

Mala Fides

Mala fides should be established only by direct evidence; *Union of India* v. *Ashok Kumar*, AIR 2006 SC 124: 2005 AIR SCW 5590: 2005 (107) FLR 840: (2005) 8 SCC 760: 2005 (8) SCJ 124: 2005 (4) SCT 610: (2005) 8 SCALE 397: (2006) 1 Serv LJ 312 SC: 2005 (7) Supreme 239.

Action taken by State in undue haste may be held to be *mala fide*; *Inderpreet Singh Kahlon* v. *State of Punjab*, AIR 2006 SC 2571: 2006 AIR SCW 3346: 2006 (6) SCJ 107: 2006 (3) SCT 25: 2006 (7) SRJ 432: (2006) 5 SCALE 273: 2006 (4) Supreme 8.

The mere fact that the Investigating Officer ruled out certain documents as irrelevant, is no ground to assume that he acted *mala fide*; *State of Bihar* v. *P.P. Sharma*, AIR 1991 SC 1260: (1992) Supp 1 SCC 222: 1992 SCC (Cri) 192, paragraphs 16 and 23.

Maintenance of Internal Security

The law of Internal Security is valid and it is a rule of evidence and it is not open either to the detenu or to the court to ask for grounds of detention; *Addl. Distt. Magistrate, Jabalpur* v. *Shivakant Shukla*, AIR 1976 SC 1207: (1976) 2 SCC 521: 1976 Cr LJ 945: 1976 UJ (SC) 610: 1976 SC Cr R 277: 1976 SCC (Cri) 448: 1976 Cr App R (SC) 298: (1976) 3 SCR 929: 1976 Supp SCR 172.

Mandamus

Employer has right to fill all posts or not to fill them. The writ of *mandamus* cannot be issued unless discrimination is made in regard to filling up of vacancies; *S.S. Balu* v. *State of Kerala*, AIR 2009 SC 1994: 2009 Lab IC 1454: 2009 AIR SCW 1644: 2009 (3) JCR SC 63: (2009) 2 LLN 28: (2009) 2 SCC 479: 2009 (2) SCT 73: (2009) 2 Serv LJ 480 SC.

Mandamus will issue against an inferior tribunal where an inferior tribunal has refused to carry out the *intra vires* directions of its superior tribunal; *Union of India* v. *Kamalakshi*, (1991) 2 UJ SC 617, paragraph 6.

Mandamus will not issue to direct a subordinate Legislative authority to enact or not to enact a rule, order or notification which it is competent to enact; *Supreme Court Employees* v. *Union of India*, AIR 1990 SC 334: (1989) 4 SCC 187: (1989) 2 LLJ 506: (1989) 1 SLR 3, paragraphs 50-56.

Mandamus would issue to cancel a seniority list or promotion and to make necessary adjustments, which the seniority list has been made in contravention of the statutory rules or making *ad hoc* deviations therefrom; *Garg* v. *State of Uttar Pradesh*, (1991) 2 UJ SC 571, paragraphs 22 and 25.

The existence of a statutory remedy is no bar to *mandamus* where the ground on which relief is sough is beyond the competence of the statutory tribunal to entertain, *e.g.*, where the act or omission complained of, *e.g.*, alternation of delimitation of constituencies, took place at a time *anterior* to the commencement of the electoral process; *State of Karnataka* v. *N.A. Nagendrappa*, AIR 1991 Kant 317: ILR (1991) Kant 1057: (1991) 2 Kant LJ 172 (FB), paragraph 35.

Mandamus will not issue against the Chief Justice of a High Court in the matter of assigning cases to the puisne Judges, in the absence of some clear breach of the rules governing the matter: *Maharshi Avadhesh* v. *State of Uttar Pradesh*, AIR 1991 All 52, paragraph 6.

Mandamus would issue to command a statutory authority to perform its duty to exercise its discretion according to law, but not to exercise its discretion in a particular manner unless that is expressly required by the law; *U.P.S.R.T.C.* v. *Mohammed Ismail*, (1991) 3 SCC 239: AIR 1991 SC 1099: (1991) 17 ATC 234: (1991) 2 LLJ 332, paragraph 12 (3 Judges).

Relief by way of *mandamus* which is discretionary may be refused, when there is no legal or constitutional obligation which is capable of being enforced by *mandamus, e.g.,* to direct any Minister to resign, in the absence of any statutory or constitutional provision; *Maharshi Avadhesh* v. *State of Uttar Pradesh,* AIR 1991 All 52, paragraphs 8, 9 and 10; *Cf. Vimla* v. *State of Uttar Pradesh,* (1990) Supp SCC 770: 1991 Supp SCC (L&S) 704: (1991) 16 ATC 479, paragraph 4.

Where an administrative authority has the duty to exercise a discretion or power, but has failed to exercise it, the court cannot, by issuing a *mandamus,* either direct the authority to make an order in exercise of the discretion in any particular direction nor can the court make the administrative order itself. The proper direction should be that the authority shall make a proper order after exercising his discretion accordingly to the circumstances of the case, *e.g.,* even where the court finds the petitioner to be the highest bidder; *Munindra Nath Upadhyaya* v. *State of Uttar Pradesh,* (1993) Supp 1 SCC 437: AIR 1992 SC 566: 1992 AIR SCW 184: 1992 All LJ 1112: 1993 (2) All CJ 749.

Where irregularities in hospital administration of a Government hospital are alleged, the court can appoint a commissioner to ascertain the facts. But it cannot issue *mandamus* directing the State Government to appoint a commission of inquiry. It is discretionary to set upon a commission of inquiry (unless the legislature passed a resolution). Where there is discretionary jurisdiction, no *mandamus* can be issued; *Siddha Raj Dhadda* v. *State of Rajasthan,* AIR 1990 Raj 34: (1989) 1 Raj LR 355: 1990 (1) Civ LJ 179.

A foreign national has no right to claim that a writ of mandamus be issued by the Supreme Court to command the 'Union of India' (respondents) to decide his application for grant of Indian citizenship to him. Similarly, there is no statutory duty cast upon the Central Government to decide an application moved by a foreign national seeking grant of Indian citizenship; *Mohan Lal Arya* v. *Union of India,* AIR 2003 All 11.

Mining Lease

Petition was filed to quash premature termination of lease for mining. Relief of damages was not claimed. Termination of the lease (premature) was void, because no hearing was given to the lessee. It was held, that it was not proper to ask the petitioner to file suit for compensation. The Supreme Court appointed an arbitrator to determine compensation/ damages; *Assam Sillimanite Ltd.* v. *Union of India,* AIR 1990 SC 1417: (1990) 3 SCC 182: JT 1990 (2) SC 248.

As to premature termination, see *State of Haryana* v. *Ram Kishan,* AIR 1988 SC 1301: (1988) 3 SCC 416.

Natural Justice

The principles of natural justice are applicable even to administrative inquiries, which means that even where the nature of the function (*e.g.* price-fixing) does not require the hearing of the person affected, the authority must nevertheless observe the requirement of reasonableness and fair play, *Union of India* v. *E.G. Nambudri,* (1991) 3 SCC 38: AIR 1991 SC 1216: (1991) 17 ATC 104, paragraph 7.

If a statutory provision either specifically or by necessary implication *excludes* the application of any rule of natural justice, then the court cannot ignore the mandate of the legislature or the statutory authority and read into the concerned provision the principles of natural justice; *Km. Neelima Misra* v. *Dr. Harinder Kaur Paintal,* AIR 1990 SC 1402: (1990) 2 SCC 746: 1990 Lab IC 1229: JT 1990 (2) SC 103.

No obligation to offer an opportunity of being heard arises where a student has secured admission through a *fraudulent device; U.P. Junior Doctors' Action Committee* v. *Dr. B. Sheetal Nandwani,* (1990) 4 SCC 633: AIR 1991 SC 909: JT 1990 (3) SC 690: 1990 (2) UJ (SC) 671: 1990 (2) UPLBEC 1321, paragraph 5.

There would be a sufficient compliance with the requirements of natural justice in cases of disciplinary proceedings against students, if in the given facts, the students have been given a fair deal; *Maharashtra State Board of Secondaryand Higher Secondary Education* v. *K.S. Gandhi,* (1991) 2 SCC 716: 1991 AIR SCW 879, paragraphs 15, 26 and 37.

Natural justice requires that opportunity to be heard must be given to the accused for enhancing the sentence; *Govind* v. *State of Maharashtra*, (1990) 4 SCC 718: (1990) 2 Crimes 256, paragraph 15.

Administrative functions of a legislative nature do not attract the requirements of natural justice; *O.N.G.C.* v. *Assn. N.G.C.*, (1990) Supp SCC 397 (439): AIR 1990 SC 1851; *Shri Sitaram Sugar Co. Ltd.* v. *Union of India*, (1990) 3 SCC 223: AIR 1990 SC 1277, paragraph 44 (CB).

Principles of natural justice are not attracted to the disposal of a petition under section 177(2) of the Army Act, 1950; *Union of India* v. *Amrik*, (1991) 1 SCC 654: (1991) 16 ATC 497: AIR 1991 SC 564: 1991 Cr LJ 664, paragraph 8.

Nemo Judex in Causa Sua

The maxim *"nemo judex in causa sua"* (no one should be a judge in his own cause) is one of the principles of natural justice. It originated in Lord Coke's pronouncement in Dr. *Bonham's* case (1610) 8 Co Rep 1142: 77 ER 646. It prohibits a person from trying a matter, if he has a bias.

Notification

Article 226 confers on the High Courts power to issue appropriate writs to any person or authority within their jurisdiction, in terms absolute and unqualified. Petitioner challenged a notification issued in Delhi. It was held that the Delhi High Court had jurisdiction to entertain and try the writ petition; *Vareli Weaves Pvt. Ltd.* v. *Union of India*, AIR 1996 SC 1543: (1996) 3 SCC 318 (paragraph 5).

Order of Arbitral Tribunal

Orders passed by Arbitral Tribunal are not open to challenge under articles 226, 227; *S.B.P. & Co.* v. *Patel Engineering Ltd.*, AIR 2006 SC 450: 2005 AIR SCW 5932: 2005 CLC 1546: 2006 (1) JCR SC 190: JT 2005 (9) SC 219: (2005) 8 SCC 618: 2005 (7) SCJ 461: 2006 (1) SRJ 25: (2005) 9 SCALE 1: 2005 (7) Supreme 610.

Particular Writs

The matter involving the private law remedy cannot be entertained by High Court except for good reasons; *Moran M. Baselios Marthona Mathews* v. *State of Kerala*, (2007) 6 SCC 517.

Parties

A person who acquires interest during the pendency of a writ proceeding on the express condition that his interest would abide by the decisions in that proceeding, need not be impleaded; *Navjyoti Co-operative Group Housing Society* v. *Union of India*, AIR 1993 SC 155: (1992) 4 SCC 477: 1992 AIR SCW 3075: JT 1992 (5) SC 621: 1993 (1) SCJ 4: (1992) 4 SCR 709: 1993 (1) UJ (SC) 94, paragraph 14.

Plea before Single Judge of High Court

The plea abandoned before the Single Judge in High Court could be raised before Division Bench. Such plea is not barred by estoppel because writ appeal is in continuation of the original order passed by the Single Judge in writ jurisdiction; *Bongaigaon Refinery & Petrochemicals Ltd.* v. *Girish Chandra Sharma*, (2007) 7 SCC 206.

Policy and Discretion

The court will not interfere with an order of an administrative authority or the Government where the order rests on its statutory discretion, unless the order is arbitrary or capricious, or is *ultra vires* of statutory rules or *mala fide* or an abuse of power; *G.B. Mahajan* v. *Jalgaon Municipal Council*, (1991) 3 SCC 91: AIR 1991 SC 1153: 1991 (3) Bom CR 139: JT 1991 (1) SC 605, paragraphs 41, 43 and 45.

The court will not issue directions over the compliance of which it shall have no control; *Suresh* v. *R.C.D.*, (1991) UJ SC 343, paragraph 7.

No court or tribunal can compel the Government to change its policy involving expenditure; *Union of India* v. *Tejram*, (1991) 3 SCC 11: (1991) 16 ATC 556: AIR 1992 SC 570, paragraph 4.

The court cannot direct any party to disobey a statute, even on humanitarian grounds; *State of Tamil Nadu* v. *J.T.T.I.*, (1991) 2 UJ SC 162, paragraph 5.

Pollution: Disposal of Petition by Consent

Where there is unabated pollution of a river, than a petition in respect thereof cannot be disposed of by the High Court merely on the consent of the State Pollution Control Board; *Bhavani River - Sakthi Sugars Ltd. (in re:)*, AIR 1998 SC 2578: (1998) 6 SCC 335: 1998 AIR SCW 2609: 1998 (4) Civ LJ 820: JT 1998 (5) SC 214: 1998 (3) SCJ 239: (1998) 3 SCR 929: (1998) 4 SCALE 322: 1998 (6) Supreme 169.

Premature Petition

Writ cannot be issued where the cause of action has not yet matured that is to say where the petition is still premature; *Trilok* v. *DM*, AIR 1976 SC 1988: (1976) 3 SCC 726: (1976) 3 SCR 942.

Preventive Detention

It is open to the court to consider the facts and circumstances to ascertain whether the detenue was feigning ignorance of the language in which the order had been communicated to him; *Kubic Darusz* v. *Union of India*, 1990 (2) SCJ 132: (1990) 1 SCC 568: AIR 1990 SC 605, paragraph 10.

Where there is no question of legislative competence as above, a solitary act may offer a good ground for the subjective satisfaction of the detaining authority where there are circumstances to lead to the reasonable inference that the person concerned would be likely to repeat that act so as to warrant his detention, *e.g.*, a single act of smuggling (under the COFEPOSA) followed by an attempt to obtain passport in a false name; *Sulthan* v. *Jt. Secy.*, 1991 (1) SCJ 239: (1991) 1 SCC 144: AIR 1990 SC 2222: 1990 Cr LJ 2473, paragraph 7.

Apart from a plain transgression of the terms of the statute authorising the detention, the detention may be illegal by reason of the abuse of the statutory power, non-application of mind: *Abhay* v. *Bhave*, (1991) 1 SCC 500: AIR 1991 SC 397; *T. Devaki* v. *Government of T.N.*, 1990 (3) SCJ 303: (1990) 2 SCC 456: AIR 1990 SC 1086, paragraph 3; *Abhay* v. *Bhave*, 1991 (1) SCJ 607: (1991) 1 SCC 500: AIR 1991 SC 397, paragraph 9.

Preventive Detentions: Stay

The court has jurisdiction to issue an interim order of stay against the execution of an order of preventive detention. But the very object of preventive detention would be defeated if this power is used in every case. It should, therefore, be used sparingly, only in cases where the court is *prima facie* satisfied that the *authority* which passed the order had no authority to do so; *Addl. Secy.* v. *Gadia*, 1991 (1) SCJ 200: (1992) Supp 1 SCC 496: 1992 SCC (Cri) 301, paragraph 19.

Prisons

The literature on prison justice and prison reform shows that there are nine major problems which afflict the system and which need immediate attention. These are (1) overcrowding; (2) delay in trial; (3) torture and ill-treatment; (4) neglect of health and hygiene; (5) insubstantial food and inadequate clothing; (6) prison vices; (7) deficiency in communication; (8) streamlining of jail visits, and (9) management of open-air prisons. The Supreme Court of India has, given directions to remedy the above problems; *Rama Murthy* v. *State of Karnataka*, (1997) 2 SCC 642: 1997 SCC (Cri) 386: AIR 1997 SC 1739: 1997 Cr LJ 1508, paragraphs 14, 51.

Prohibition

The Supreme Court and the High Courts have power to issue writs, including a writ of prohibition. A writ of prohibition is normally issued only when the inferior Court or Tribunal—

(a) proceeds to act without or in excess of jurisdiction,

(b) proceeds to act in violation of rules of natural justice,

(c) proceeds to act under law which is itself *ultra vires* or unconstitutional, or

(d) proceeds to act in contravention of fundamental rights.

The principles, which govern exercise of such power, must be strictly observed. A writ of prohibition must be issued in the rarest of the rare cases. Judicial disciplines of the highest order has to be exercised whilst issuing such writs. It must be remembered that the writ jurisdiction is original jurisdiction distinct from appellate jurisdiction. An appeal cannot be allowed to be disguised in the form of a writ; *Thirumala Tirupati Devasthanams* v. *Thallappaka Anantha Charyulu*, AIR 2003 SC 3290: (2003) 8 SCC 134: 2003 AIR SCW 4847: JT 2004 (6) SC 425: 2003 (10) SRJ 375: (2003) 7 SCALE 352: 2003 (6) Supreme 684.

Promissory Estoppel

The doctrine of promissory estoppel cannot be invoked when the petitioner knew all the facts and there was no question of his being misled by the representation or the authority or the Government was under a legal duty or prohibition to act in a particulate manner, or the application of the doctrine would involve the violation of a statute, or the petitioner failed to substantiate that he had altered his position, relying on he alleged representation or the officer concerned was not competent and acted beyond the scope of his authority, so that the alleged representation was *ultra vires*; *Vasantakumar Radhakisan Vora* v. *Board of Trustees of the Port of Bombay*, AIR 1991 SC 14: (1991) 1 SCC 761: 1991 (2) All CJ 743: JT 1990 (3) SC 609: 1991 (1) Land LR 45: 1990 (2) Ren CR 454: 1992 (1) Rent LR 83.

The doctrine of promissory estoppel would operate where injustice would be caused to the promisee if the promisor would be allowed to go back on the promise. But the facts giving rise to the doctrine must be pleaded; *Andhra Steel Corporation Ltd.* v. *Andhra Pradesh State Electricity Board*, (1991) 3 SCC 263: AIR 1991 SC 1456: 1991 AIR SCW 1358: JT 1991 (2) SC 581: (1991) 2 SCR 624: 1991 (2) UJ (SC) 244, paragraphs 13-15.

Public Interest Litigation

The distinction between private litigation and public interest litigation can be explained in the following words:—

In a public interest litigation, unlike traditional dispute resolution mechanism, there is no determination or adjudication on individual rights. While in the ordinary conventional adjudications, the party structure is merely bi-polar and the controversy pertains to the determination of the legal consequences of past events and the remedy is essentially linked to and limited by the logic of the array of the parties, in a public interest action the proceedings cut across and transcend these traditional forms and inhibitions. The compulsion for the judicial innovation of the technique of a public interest action is the constitutional promise of a social and economic transformation to usher in an egalitarian social order and a welfare State ... The dispute is not comparable to one between private parties, with the result that there is no recognition of the status of a *dominus litis* for any individual or group of individuals to determine the course or destination of the proceedings, except to the extent recognised and permitted by the court. The "rights" of those who bring the action on behalf of the others must necessarily be subordinate to the "interests" of those for whose benefit the action is brought. The grievance in a public interest action, generally speaking, is about the content and conduct of Government action in relation to the Constitutional or statutory rights of segments of society and, in certain circumstances the conduct of Government policies. Necessarily, both the party structure and the matters in controversy are sprawling and amorphous, to be defined and adjusted or re-adjusted as the case may be, *ad hoc*, according as the exigencies of the emerging situations. The proceedings do not partake of predetermined private law litigation models, but are exogenously determined by variations of the themes.

Sheela Barse v. *Union of India*, AIR 1988 SC 2211: (1988) 4 SCC 2261 (1988) 3 Crimes 269, paragraph 6.

Public interest litigation is a proceeding in which an individual or group seeks relief in the interest of the general public and not for its own purpose. The spate of such litigation has enriched the law, modified the traditional doctrine of *locus standi* and led to the devising of new remedies and procedures. Of the numerous cases on the subject, the following are worth study, as illustrating the basic and important features:—

- (i) *S.P. Gupta* v. *President of India*, AIR 1982 SC 149: 1982 Raj LR 389: 1981 Supp SCC 87 (Scope and basic approach).
- (ii) *Dr. D.C. Wadhwa* v. *State of Bihar*, AIR 1987 SC 579: (1987) 1 SCC 378: JT 1987 (1) SC 70: 1986 (4) Supreme 465: 1987 BBCJ (SC) 46: 1987 IJR 116, paragraph 38 (*Locus Standi*).

(iii) *Ratlam Municipality* v. *Vardichand,* AIR 1980 SC 1622: (1980) 4 SCC 162: 1980 Cr LJ 1075 (General).

(iv) *Fertilizer Corporation* v. *Union of India,* AIR 1981 SC 344: (1981) 1 SCC 568: (1981) 2 SCR 52: (1981) 1 LLJ 193 (*Locus Standi*).

(v) *Peoples' Union for Democratic Rights* v. *Union of India,* AIR 1982 SC 1473: (1982) 3 SCC 235: (1981) 2 LLJ 454: 1982 Lab IC 1640 (General).

(vi) *State of Himachal Pradesh* v. *A Parent of a Student of Medical College, Shimla,* AIR 1985 SC 910: (1985) 3 SCC 169: (1985) 2 SCWR 48: (1985) 11 All LR 487: (1985) 2 Cur CC 239 (Mode of entertaining).

(vii) *Shivajirao Nilangekar Patil* v. *Dr. Mahesh Madhav Gosavi,* AIR 1987 SC 294: (1987) 1 SCC 227: JT 1986 SC 1071: (1987) 89 Bom LR 65: (1987) 1 UJ (SC) 88: 1987 (2) SCJ 1: (1987) 1 Cur LJ (Civ and Cri) 460: 1987 (2) Supreme 97, paragraphs 35 and 36 (Mode of entertaining). Regarding public interest litigation a Calcutta case elaborates as under:—

in case of public interest litigation, the persons concerned who move such writ application not for enforcing his personal right but filed by public spirited and individual espousing the cause of large number of people who are suffering under some legal wrong or injury and such person or determinated class of persons is by reason of poverty, helplessness or disability or socially or economically disadvantaged position, unable to approach the court for relief and in such case any member of the public can maintain writ application.

The court should not allow an unscrupulous person to vindicate his personal grudge in the garb of protecting a public or social interest. *See* the undermentioned cases:

(i) *Chhetriya Samiti* v. *State of Uttar Pradesh,* 1991 (1) SCJ 130: (1990) 4 SCC 449: AIR 1990 SC 2060, paragraph 8.

(ii) *Subhash* v. *State of Bihar,* 1991 (1) SCJ 564: (1991) 1 SCC 598: AIR 1991 SC 420, paragraph 7.

Public Interest Legislation

Public interest litigation during pendency of civil suit is not maintainable; *Santosh Sood* v. *Gajendra Singh,* AIR 2010 SC 593.

*Quasi-*judicial Authority

*Quasi-*judicial orders of a superior administrative authority are binding on all subordinate authorities. The High Court would interfere under article 226, in case a subordinate authority fails to follow the superior's order, irrespective of any question of *mala fides; Union of India* v. *K.F.C.,* (1991) 2 UJ SC 617, paragraph 6.

It is not open to the parties before a quasi judicial tribunal (as in the case of courts) to assail its record of proceedings and the statement of facts made therein, as incorrect, unless steps are taken before the same forum; *Bhagwati* v. *D.S.M.D.C.,* 1990 (1) SCJ 433: (1990) 1 SCC 361: AIR 1990 SC 371: 1990 Lab IC 126, paragraph 5.

Quo Warranto

Quo warranto is a discretionary remedy which the court may grant or refuse according to the facts and circumstances of each case. Thus, the court may refuse it where the application was actuated by ill-will or malice, or ulterior motive; *Mukhtiar Singh* v. *State of Punjab,* AIR 1991 P&H 20, paragraph 6.

Reasonableness

Where an administrative action is *prima facie* unreasonable because there is no discernible principle to justify it, the burden is shifted to the State to show that the impugned decision is an informed action, and in such a case, if the reasons are not recorded, the decision will be struck down as violative of article 14 of the Constitution, *Shrilekha* v. *State of Uttar Pradesh,* (1991) 1 SCC 212: (1991) SCC (L&S) 742: AIR 1991 SC 537, paragraphs 18, 23, 29, 31 and 39-40.

In administrative law, 'reasonableness' has not the same meaning as in the law of torts, where the test used is that of a 'reasonable man'. In administrative law, it simply indicates an improper use or *abuse* of power. In this context, the court cannot interfere merely because the court thinks that the administrative action or decision has been unwise; *G.B. Mahajan* v. *Jalgaon Municipal Council*, (1991) 3 SCC 91: AIR 1991 SC 1153: 1991 (3) Bom CR 139: JT 1991 (1) SC 605, paragraphs 41, 43 and 45.

Registered or Unregistered Association

An association of persons (registered or unregistered) can file a writ petition to enforce the members' rights where the members are unable to approach the court because of poverty *etc.* or in case of public interest litigation; *Umesh Chand Vinod Kumar* v. *Krishi Utpadan Mandi Samiti, Bharthana*, AIR 1984 All 46 (FB): 1983 UPLBEC 756: 1983 All CJ 600: 1983 All WC 881: (1984) 10 All LR 136: (1984) 1 Serv LR 532, paragraph 20.

According to the Madras High Court, an unregistered association cannot file a writ petition. *T.N. Panchayat Development Officers Association, Madras* v. *Secretary to Govt. of T.N., Rural Development and Local Administration Dept., Madras*, AIR 1989 Mad 224: 1990 (1) LJR 488 (FB).

Relief

While finding that an educational institution has wrongly interpreted the directions of the court, the court may condone the defect so far as the admissions already made on the basis of the wrong interpretation, in order to save the admitted candidates (who were not at fault, *State of Bihar* v. *Sanjay*, AIR 1990 SC 749: (1990) 4 SCC 624: (1990) 1 SLR 858, paragraph 6.

Equitable considerations weigh with the court partly in adjusting the rights of competing co-employees under the Government, in matters of seniority, promotion and the like; *Dwarka Nath Sharma* v. *Union of India*, AIR 1990 SC 428: (1989) Supp 2 SCC 225: (1989) 2 LLN 711: (1989) 2 CLR 522, paragraphs 11, 13-14.

The relief that may be granted under article 226 may be—

   (a) setting aside an illegal order;

   (b) declaratory;

   (c) restitutionary (Refund of invalid tax);

   (d) other consequential relief.

See the undermentioned cases:

  (i) *Calcutta Discount Co.* v. *I.T.O.*, AIR 1961 SC 372: (1961) 2 SCR 241: (1961) 41 ITR 191.

  (ii) *Bidi, Bidi Leaves and Tobacco Merchants' Association, Gondia* v. *State of Bombay*, AIR 1962 SC 486: (1962) Supp 1 SCR 381: (1961-62) 21 FJR 331: (1961) 2 LLJ 663: 64 Bom LR 375.

  (iii) *State of Madhya Pradesh* v. *Bhailal Bhai*, AIR 1964 SC 1006: (1964) 6 SCR 261: 1964 Jab LJ 115: (1964) 15 STC 450: 1964 MPLJ 705: 1964 Mah LJ 601: (1964) 1 SCWR 793.

  (iv) *Dwarka Nath* v. *I.T.O.*, AIR 1966 SC 81: (1965) 3 SCR 536: (1965) 57 ITR 349.

  (v) *Jasbhai Motibhai Desai* v. *Roshan Kumar, Haji Bashir Ahmed*, AIR 1976 SC 578: (1976) 1 SCC 671: (1976) 3 SCR 58.

  (vi) *B.R. Ramabhadriah* v. *Secretary, Food and Agriculture Department, A.P.*, AIR 1981 SC 1653: (1981) 3 SCC 528: 1981 Lab IC 1114: 1981 SCC (Lab) 530: (1981) 2 Serv LJ 263: 1981 UJ (SC) 591: (1981) 2 Lab LJ 263.

Remedy: Extraordinary and Discretionary

The remedy of writ is—

   (a) extraordinary;

   (b) discretionary (unless a fundamental right is involved);

   (c) dependent on there being a cause of action;

   (d) exercisable only against the parties before the court.

The undermentioned cases illustrate the above aspects:

  (i) *C.A. Abraham* v. *I.T.O.*, AIR 1961 SC 609: (1961) 2 SCR 765: (1961) 41 ITR 425 (Alternative remedy).

  (ii) *State of Rajasthan* v. *Karamchand Thappar and Bros*, AIR 1965 SC 913: (1965) 16 STC 412: (1964) 2 SCWR 593 (Fundamental right).

(iii) *Municipal Council, Khurai* v. *Kamal Kumar*, AIR 1965 SC 1321: (1965) 2 SCR 653: 1965 MPLJ 237: 1965 Jab LJ 225: 1965 Mah LJ 632: (1965) 1 SCWR 847 (Mandatory provision violated).

(iv) *Bhopal Sugar Industry* v. *I.T.O.*, AIR 1961 SC 182: (1961) 1 SCR 474: (1960) 40 ITR 618 (Alternative remedy).

Res Judicata

Where there has been a decision on the merits, the rule of constructive *res judicata* will be applicable to bar a second application founded on the same cause of action or as regards relief, which were asked for but not granted in the previous proceeding under article 226, or as regards a ground which ought to have been taken in the previous application, according to *Explanation* IV to section 11 of the Code of Civil Procedure, 1908; *Direct Recruit Class-II Engineering Officers' Association* v. *State of Maharashtra*, AIR 1990 SC 1607: (1990) 2 SCC 715: (1990) 13 ATC 348, paragraph 35.

Restoration of Writ Petition

Writ petition dismissed for want of prosecution can be restored; *Ratan Singh* v. *State of Rajasthan*, AIR 2006 (NOC) 129 (Raj).

Scope of Article 226: High Court Power

The power of the High Court to issue writs under article 226 is wider than that of the Supreme Court. It is not confined to fundamental rights, but extends to all cases where the breach of a right is alleged. *See* notes on article 32. The writ may be issued for the enforcement of fundamental rights of for "any other purpose"; *State of Orissa* v. *Madan Gopal Rungta*, (1952) SCR 28: AIR 1952 SC 12: (1951) 2 Mad LJ 645: 1952 Mad WN 13: 1951 SCJ 764: 18 Cut LT 45: ILR 1951 Cut 637. Of course, there must be violation of a right; *Calcutta Gas Company (Proprietary) Ltd.* v. *State of West Bengal*, AIR 1962 SC 1044: (1962) Supp 3 SCR 1: (1962) 2 SCA 147: 1963 (1) SCJ 106.

The scope of the power to enforce fundamental right (under article 32 or 226) is *both* protective and remedial. Hence, to reject such petition on the simple ground that it cannot be entertained because of a rule of practice of the court cannot be justified; *S.M.D. Kiran Pasha* v. *Government of Andhra Pradesh*, 1990 (1) SCJ 282: (1990) 1 SCC 328: 1990 SCC (Cri) 110, paragraphs 13-15 and 20.

Court will not permit this extraordinary jurisdiction to be converted into a suit or a criminal proceeding under the ordinary law.

A declaration of title to property; *State of Rajasthan* v. *Bhawani*, (1993) Supp 1 SCC 306: AIR 1992 SC 1018, paragraph 7.

The High Court, under article 226, cannot sit as an appellate court on administrative decisions. It cannot interfere in the absence of illegality, unconstitutionality, want of jurisdiction or *mala fides*; *Pratibha Co-operative Housing Society Ltd.* v. *State of Maharashtra*, AIR 1991 SC 1453: (1991) 3 SCC 341: 1991 AIR SCW 1354: 1992 (1) Bom CR 453: JT 1991 (2) SC 543: 1991 (2) Land LR 382: 1991 (2) Mah LR 646: (1991) 2 SCR 745: (1991) 2 UJ (SC) 196, paragraph 5.

It is primarily for the Government to strike a just balance between two competing objectives. The court's role is restricted to examine whether Government has taken into account all relevant aspects, and can interfere only where the Government has overlooked any material considerations or is influenced by extraneous or immaterial considerations; *Dahanu Taluka Environment Protection Group* v. *Bombay Suburban Electricity Supply Company Ltd.*, (1991) 2 SCC 539: 1991 AIR SCW 910, paragraphs 2 and 3.

The writ jurisdiction under article 226 cannot be invoked for enforcing the contract between the petitioner and the respondent—Allahabad Development Authority; *Ali Johad Naqvi* v. *Allahabad Development Authority*, AIR 2001 All 172: 2001 All LJ 1340: 2001 (1) All Rent Cas 524: 2001 (43) All LR 190: 2001 (2) All WC 890.

Service Matters

In a writ proceeding relating to a service matter, even where the petition is dismissed on the merits, the court may recommend a lesser punishment in view of the meritorious service of the delinquent; *Laxmi Shanker Pandey* v. *Union of India*, AIR 1991 SC 1070: (1991) 2 SCC 488: (1991) 16 ATC 524, paragraphs 5, 7; *V.R. Katarki* v. *State of Karnataka*, AIR 1991 SC 1241: (1991) Supp 1 SCC 267: (1991) 16 ATC 555, paragraph 6.

State Government

Direction given by the High Court under article 226 cannot be altered by the State Government; *V. Parukutty Mannadissiar* v. *State of Kerala*, AIR 1990 SC 817 (819): 1990 Supp SCC 245: JT 1989 (3) SC 572, paragraphs 4-6.

Statutory Authority

The court would interfere where the statutory authority blindly acts in compliance with the direction or advice given by the Government or the Commission; *Nagaraj* v. *Syndicate Bank*, (1991) 2 UJ SC 217, paragraphs 15, 17 and 19.

Statutory Instrument

A statutory instrument may be *ultra vires* if it abuses its power by acting in bad faith; *Supreme Court Employees Welfare Assocn.* v. *Union of India*, AIR 1990 SC 334: 1990 Lab IC 324: (1989) 4 SCC 187, paragraph 105.

Suppression of Facts

Suppression of facts may disentitle a petitioner seeking a writ "for other purposes". *See* the undermentioned cases:

    (i) *Maganlal Chaganlal (P) Ltd.* v. *Municipal Corporation of Greater Bombay*, AIR 1975 SC 648: (1975) 1 SCC 339: (1976) 1 SCR 648.

    (ii) *Welcome Hotel* v. *State of Andhra Pradesh*, AIR 1983 SC 1015: (1983) 4 SCC 575: 1983 SCC (Cri) 872.

    (iii) *Dr. Vijay Kumar Kathuria* v. *State of Haryana*, AIR 1983 SC 622: (1983) 3 SCC 333: 1983 UJ (SC) 454: 1983 IJR (Civ) 57.

Tender Forms

Applicant for a tender form could not show that it was eligible and qualified or satisfied the required conditions for the grant of tender form in its favour. It was held that the authority was not acting arbitrarily in refusing tender form. No relief could be granted to the petitioner; *Eureka Engineers Co-operative Society Ltd.* v. *Superintending Engineer, Mahananda Barrage Circle*, AIR 1998 Cal 12.

Tribunal

Even where the jurisdiction of the courts is excluded by the statute or the Constitution itself, *e.g.*, under article 226(2), the Supreme Court retains its jurisdiction to decide the parameters of the jurisdiction of the Tribunal which depends upon an interpretation of the Constitution or the statute (as the case may be). What is excluded is the power of the courts to sit in judgment over the merits of the Tribunal's decision; *State of Tamil Nadu* v. *State of Karnataka*, (1991) 2 UJ SC 134: (1991) Supp 1 SCC 240.

Unincorporated Association

An unincorporated association does not fall within any of the above categories. Unincorporated associations are not legal "persons" and, as such, writ petitions are not maintainable by them. An association could be formed to protect the interests of consumers, tenants or other groups, with common interest, but such a group cannot move a writ application, if it is not incorporated. Nor can they move writ application as a public interest litigation in a representative capacity; *Sand Carrier's Owners' Union* v. *Board of Trustees for the Port of Calcutta*, AIR 1990 Cal 176: (1989) 1 Cal LT (HC) 437: (1989) 1 Cal HN 474: (1989) 2 Cal LJ 201: (1989) 93 CWN 1095, paragraphs 13 and 14 (Bhagavati Prasad Banerjee, J.).

Violation of Fundamental Rights

On account of construction of dam (Sardar Sarovar) the displacement of the tribals and other persons would not *per se* result in the violation of their fundamental or other rights. The effect is to see that on their rehabilitation at new locations they are better off than what they were. At the rehabilitation sites they will have more and better amenities than which they enjoyed in their tribal hamlets. The gradual assimilation in the main stream of the society will lead to betterment and progress; *Narmada Bachao Andolan v. Union of India,* AIR 2000 SC 3751: (2000) 10 SCC 664: 2000 AIR SCW 4809: 2001 (1) Guj LR 434: JT 2000 (2) SC (Supp) 6: 2000 (4) LRI 696: 2000 (4) SCJ 261: (2000) 7 SCALE 34.

Writ Petition – Maintainability

Writ Petition to rectify grave procedural error is maintainable; *Gujarat Electricity Board v. Thakar Hasmukhhai Khelshanker,* AIR 2006 Guj 16: 2006 (1) AIR Jhar (NOC) 129.

STUDENTS AND ARTICLE 226

Circumstantial Evidence

The court would not interfere on the ground that the decision of the authority is not supported by any evidence, where there is circumstantial evidence to justify it; *Maharashtra State Board of Secondaryand Higher Secondary Education v. K.S. Gandhi,* (1991) 2 SCC 716: 1991 AIR SCW 879, paras 15, 26, 37.

It is not necessary to make a formal inquiry after issuing a show cause notice where the charge was of all the examinees at a centre *en masse* using unfair means as distinguished from the case of any particular examinee being so charged; *Bihar School Education Board v. Subhash C. Sinha,* (1970) 3 SCR 963: (1970) 1 SCC 648: AIR 1970 SC 1269.

Cross-examination

If the above two conditions are satisfied, the proceeding cannot be vitiated on the ground that the delinquent was not given an opportunity of cross-examining the witness examined against him that they were examined in his absence.

(i) *Nagraj v. State of Mysore,* AIR 1964 SC 269: (1964) 2 SCR 671: (1963) 2 SCWR 231: (1964) 1 Cr LJ 161: 1964 SCD 35: (1964) 1 Andh LT 370: ILR 1964 Mys 1.

(ii) *Guwahati University v. Raj Konwar,* (1970) Assam LR 1.

Or that the report of the inquiry Officer was not supplied to him; *Suresh Koshy George v. University of Kerala,* AIR 1969 SC 198 (202): (1969) 1 SCR 317: 1969 Ker LJ 197.

Difference from Criminal Trials

It would not be reasonable to import into such inquiry all considerations which govern criminal trials in courts of law; *Suresh Koshy George v. University of Kerala,* AIR 1969 SC 198 (202): (1969) 1 SCR 317: 1969 Ker LJ 197.

Disciplinary Action

The head of an educational institution has the inherent power to take disciplinary action against students who misbehave. (In this case safety of girl students was involved); *Hiranath Mishra v. Principal,* (1973) UJ SC 83: (1973) 1 SCC 805: AIR 1973 SC 1260: (1973) 2 LLJ 111.

Disciplinary Proceedings

It is settled that a disciplinary proceeding against a student on the ground of some misconduct, *e.g.,* malpractice at an examination, is a *quasi judicial* proceeding.

(i) *Board of High School and Intermediate Education, U. P. Allahabad v. Ghanshyam Das Gupta,* AIR 1962 SC 1110: (1962) Supp 3 SCR 36: 64 Punj LR 575: 1962 All LJ 776: ILR (1962) 2 All 661: 1963 (2) SCJ 509.

(ii) *Board of High School and Intermediate Education, U.P. v. Kumari Chittra Srivastava,* AIR 1970 SC 1039: (1970) 1 SCC 121: 1970 SCD 222.

The principles of natural justice must be observed, in such inquiries; *Board of High School and Intermediate Education, U. P. Allahabad v. Ghanshyam Das Gupta,* AIR 1962 SC 1110: (1962) Supp 3 SCR 36: 64 Punj LR 575: 1962 All LJ 776: ILR (1962) 2 All 661: 1963 (2) SCJ 509.

Discretion of the Institution

Subject to the above *quasi judicial* obligation, it is within the jurisdiction of the educational institution or the tribunal set up by it to decide all relevant questions in the light of the evidence adduced before it; *Suresh Koshy George* v. *University of Kerala*, AIR 1969 SC 198, 202: (1969) 1 SCR 317: 1969 Ker LJ 197.

Examinations

The examination of a candidate or the result thereof cannot be cancelled, without informing him or her of the nature of accusation made.a

   (i) *Board of High School and Intermediate Education, U.P.* v. *Kumari Chittra Srivastava*, AIR 1970 SC 1039: (1970) 1 SCC 121: 1970 SCD 222.

   (ii) *Suresh Koshy George* v. *University of Kerala*, AIR 1969 SC 198 (202): (1969) 1 SCR 317: 1969 Ker LJ 197.

The student must be offered an opportunity of being heard and of defending himself or herself.

   (i) *Board of High School and Intermediate Education, U. P. Allahabad* v. *Bagleshwar Prasad*, (1963) 3 SCR 767: AIR 1966 SC 875: (1963) 7 FLR 415.

   (ii) *Prem Prakash Kaluniya* v. *Punjab University*, AIR 1972 SC 1408: (1973) 3 SCC 424.

This is so, whether there is a statutory obligation to proceed *quasi judicially* or not.

   Board of High School and Intermediate Education, U.P. v. *Kumari Chittra Srivastava*, AIR 1970 SC 1039: (1970) 1 SCC 121: 1970 SCD 222.

Exception exists for cases like mass-copying, where the evidence of unfair means is perfectly plain that transparent; *Bihar School Examination Board* v. *Subhash C. Sinha*, (1970) 3 SCR 963: (1970) 1 SCC 648: AIR 1970 SC 1269.

Illustrations of *Quasi*-judicial Acts

The following acts have been held to be *quasi judicial*, where they are done by the authorities on the ground of misconduct or behaviour of the student:—

   (i) Expulsion; *Board of High School* v. *Ghanshyam*, AIR 1962 SC 1110: (1962) Supp 3 SCR 36: 1962 All LJ 776.

   (ii) Rustication; *Board of High School* v. *Ghanshyam*, AIR 1962 SC 1110: (1962) Supp 3 SCR 36: 1962 All LJ 776.

   (iii) Cancellation of admission; *Prasant Pattajoshy* v. *Principal, Lingaraj Law College*, AIR 1977 Ori 107: (1976) 2 Cut WR 919: ILR (1977) Cut 33.

   (iv) Suspension of a student; *Rakesh Kumar* v. *State of Punjab*, AIR 1965 Punj 507 (509).

   (v) Cancellation of admission to an examination;

   (vi) Disqualified from sitting at examination; *Prem Prakash* v. *Punjab University*, AIR 1972 SC 1408: (1973) 3 SCC 424.

   (vii) Cancellation of examination; *Bihar School Examination Board* v. *Subhas Chandra Sinha*, (1970) 1 SCC 648: AIR 1970 SC 1269: 1970 Pat LJR 508: 1970 (2) SCJ 549.

Inquiry when not Necessary

No inquiry of any sort is necessary where the adoption of unfair means by an examinee is detected by the invigilators at the examination hall and the examinee is expelled from the hall on that ground; *University of Calcutta* v. *Dipa Pal*, AIR 1952 Cal 594.

Similarly, where the identity of wrong answers offers intrinsic evidence of copying them from the same source, the court cannot interfere on the ground that the inquiring authority acted without any evidence.

   (i) *Board of High School* v. *Bagleswar*, (1963) 3 SCR 767: AIR 1966 SC 875: (1963) 7 FLR 415.

   (ii) *Prem Prakash* v. *Punjab University*, AIR 1972 SC 1408: (1973) 3 SCC 424.

Natural Justice

There would be a sufficient compliance of the requirements of natural justice in such case if—

(i) the delinquent student is informed of the charge or the case he has to meet; *Suresh Koshy George* v. *University of Kerala*, AIR 1969 SC 198: (1969) 1 SCR 317: 1969 Ker LJ 197.

(ii) he is given an adequate opportunity of meeting such charges and the materials used against him and of stating his own case.

    (i) *Suresh Koshy George* v. *University of Kerala*, AIR 1969 SC 198: (1969) 1 SCR 317: 1969 Ker LJ 197.

    (ii) *Nagraj* v. *State of Mysore*, AIR 1964 SC 269: (1964) 2 SCR 671: (1963) 2 SCWR 231: (1964) 1 Cr LJ 161: 1964 SCD 35: (1964) 1 Andh LT 370: ILR 1964 Mys 1.

Guwahati University v. *Raj Konwar*, (1970) Assam LR 1.

Procedure

It is open to the domestic tribunal to evolve its own *procedure* for inquiry *etc.*

  (i) *Board of High School* v. *Bagleswar*, (1963) 3 SCR 767: AIR 1966 SC 875: (1963) 7 FLR 415.

  (ii) *Prem Prakash* v. *Punjab University*, AIR 1972 SC 1408: (1973) 3 SCC 424.

  (iii) *State of Mysore* v. *Sivabasappa*, AIR 1963 SC 375: (1963) 2 SCR 943: 1963 MLLJ 284: (1963) 1 LLJ 24.

Punishment

The court under article 226 cannot sit as a court of Appeal over such domestic tribunals, *e.g.*, the matter of quantum of punishment (in the absence of any statutory limitations in that behalf).

The High Court can interfere with the punishment inflicted upon the delinquent employee, if that penalty, shocks the conscience of the Court; *Uttar Pradesh State Road Transport Corporation* v. *Mahesh Kumar Mishra*, AIR 2000 SC 1151: (2000) 3 SCC 450: (2000) 2 SCR 435: 2000 All LJ 865.

Standard of Proof

The court cannot apply the same strict standard as is applicable to criminal charges before a court of law in the case of a domestic body.

  (i) *Board of High School* v. *Bagleswar*, (1963) 3 SCR 767: AIR 1966 SC 875: (1963) 7 SLR 415.

  (ii) *Prem Prakash* v. *Punjab University*, AIR 1972 SC 1408: (1973) 3 SCC 424.

Writ Jurisdiction

The High Courts exercise original jurisdiction under article 226 of the Constitution and supervisory jurisdiction and the power of Superintendence under article 227 of the Constitution; *Manoj Kumar* v. *Board of Revenue*, AIR 2008 MP 22: 2008 (1) AIR Kar R 353: 2008 (1) Jab LJ 76: 2007 (4) MPHT 545: 2008 (1) MPLJ 152.

[1][**226A. Constitutional validity of Central laws not to be considered in proceedings under Article 226.**—[*Rep. by the Constitution (Forty-third Amendment) Act, 1977, sec. 8 (w.e.f. 13-4-1978).*]]

227. Power of superintendence over all courts by the High Court.—[2][(1) Every High Court shall have superintendence over all courts and tribunals throughout the territories in relation to which it exercises jurisdiction.]

(2) Without prejudice to the generality of the foregoing provisions, the High Court may—

(a) call for returns from such courts;

(b) make and issue general rules and prescribe forms for regulating the practice and proceedings of such courts; and

---

1. Article 226A was earlier inserted by the Constitution (Forty-second Amendment) Act, 1976, sec. 39 (w.e.f. 1-2-1977).

2. Subs. by the Constitution (Forty-fourth Amendment) Act, 1978, sec. 31(a), for clause (1) (w.e.f. 20-6-1979). Earlier clause (1) was substituted by the Constitution (Forty-second Amendment) Act, 1976, sec. 40(a) (w.e.f. 1-2-1977).

(c) prescribe forms in which books, entries and accounts shall be kept by the officers of any such courts.

(3) The High Court may also settle tables of fees to be allowed to the sheriff and all clerks and officers of such courts and to attorneys, advocates and pleaders practising therein:

Provided that any rules made, forms prescribed or tables settled under clause (2) or clause (3) shall not be inconsistent with the provision of any law for the time being in force, and shall require the previous approval of the Governor.

(4) Nothing in this article shall be deemed to confer on a High Court powers of superintendence over any court or tribunal constituted by or under any law relating to the Armed Forces.

[1][***]

Notes on Article 227

Interference under article 227 (1) can be *suo motu*, but cannot be resorted to merely because the High Court takes a different view on the merits. Generally, it is limited to want of jurisdiction, errors of law, perverse findings, gross violation of natural justice and so on.

See the undermentioned cases:

(i) *Nibaran* v. *Mahendra*, AIR 1963 SC 1895: (1963) Supp 2 SCR 570: (1963) 1 Ker LR 353.

(ii) *D.N. Banerjee* v. *Mukherjee*, (1953) SCR 302 (304): AIR 1953 SC 58: (1953) 1 LLJ 195.

(iii) *Chandavarkar Sita Ratna Rao* v. *Ashalata S. Guram*, (1986) 4 SCC 447: AIR 1987 SC 117: JT 1986 SC 619: (1986) 88 Bom LR 600: 1986 Mah LJ 955: 1986 (4) Supreme 442: (1987) 1 Ren CJ 321: 1987 Mah LR 1: 1987 Bom RC 276: (1987) 1 Rent LR 684.

(iv) *Mohd. Yunus* v. *Mohd. Mustaqim*, AIR 1984 SC 38: (1983) 4 SCC 566: 1984 UJ (SC) 132: 1984 Cur Civ LJ (SC) 74.

Exercise of power under article 227 may be necessary if it is shown that grave injustice has been done to a party and the case is a fit case, *Ouseph Mathai* v. *M. Abdul Khadir*, AIR 2002 SC 110: (2002) 1 SCC 319: (2002) 1 KLT 3.

West Bengal Act 15 of 1988, sec. 3 (w.e.f. 5-11-1988) has inserted, in the Code of Civil Procedure, 1908, a new section 115A, giving revisional jurisdiction to the District Court. The new section 115A, *inter alia* bars further revision "by the High Court or any other court", by providing that the decision of the District Court on such proceeding shall be final. But the Calcutta High Court has held, that the Act cannot deprive the High Court of its power of superintendence under article 227 of the Constitution. "No legislation—and far less a State legislation—can forfeit, curtail, enlarge or abridge the power under article 227 of the Constitution. By ordinary process of legislation, even the Union Legislature cannot do it"; *Umaji Keshao Meshram* v. *Smt. Radhikabai*, AIR 1986 SC 1272: 1986 Supp SCC 401: 1986 (2) Supreme 417: 1986 Cur Civ LJ (SC) 393: (1986) 2 Cur CC 273: 1986 (1) SCJ 624: (1986) 2 UJ (SC) 319: (1986) 88 Bom LR 432, following *Paltu Dutta* v. *S.M. Nibedita Roy*, AIR 1990 Cal 262 (265): (1989) 2 Cal HN 338, paragraph 11 (A.K. Nandi, J).

Correction of Facts

Finding of fact reached in improper manner can be corrected under article 227; *Kishore Kumar Khaitan* v. *Praveen Kumar Singh*, AIR 2006 SC 1474: 2006 AIR SCW 1077: 2006 (3) JCR SC 162: 2006 (3) Land LR 300: (2006) 3 SCC 312: 2006 (2) SCJ 585: 2006 (3) SRJ 400: (2006) 2 SCALE 304: 2006 (2) Supreme 75.

---

1. Clause (5) omitted by the Constitution (Forty-fourth Amendment) Act, 1978, sec. 31(b) (w.e.f. 20-6-1979). Earlier clause (5) was inserted by the Constitution (Forty-second Amendment), Act, 1976, sec. 40(b) (w.e.f. 1-2-1977).

Jurisdiction of Court

The higher courts should observe restraint in making disparaging remarks against members of lower judiciary; *"K" A Judicial Officer* v. *Registrar General, High Court of Andhra Pradesh*, AIR 2010 SC 2801.

Jurisdictional Defects

Relief under article 227 is granted against inferior tribunals where the tribunal decides wrongly, a question as to its own jurisdiction; *Pt. Ramprashad s/o Nandlalji Purohit* v. *State Transport Appellate Tribunal, M.P.*, AIR 1993 MP 92: 1993 (1) ACC 378: 1993 MPLJ 34 (DB), paragraph 7.

Locus Standi

Any person who is likely to be affected by the impugned order, even though he has no present interest in the property, is entitled to make an application under article 227. In the case of a public injury, even a neighbour has been allowed to apply; *Sarada Bai* v. *Shakuntala Bai*, AIR 1993 AP 20: 1992 (2) Andh LT 660: 1992 MCC 426, paragraph 9.

Reasons

Where a statutory appellate tribunal brushes aside the well-reasoned order of the primary statutory authority, on conjectures and without giving cogent reasons, there is an error apparent on the record, and the High Court may interfere; *State of West Bengal* v. *Atul Krishna Shaw*, (1991) Supp 1 SCC 414: AIR 1990 SC 2205: (1990) Supp 1 SCR 91, paragraph 11.

Scope and Nature of Article 227

Jurisdiction vested in the High Court under article 227 is a revisional jurisdiction and, accordingly, no Letters Patent Appeal is competent from an order passed by a single Judge in exercise of such jurisdiction; *Sushilabai Laxminarayan Mudliyar* v. *Nihalchand Waghajibhai Shaha*, (1993) Supp 1 SCC 11: AIR 1992 SC 185: 1991 AIR SCW 2896: (1993) 1 Andh LT 60: 1991 Mah LJ 1288, paragraph 4; *R.D. CCB* v. *Dinkar*, (1993) Supp 1 SCC 9, paragraph 3.

This power (power under article 227) does not vest the High Court with any unlimited prerogative to correct all species of hardship or wrong decisions made within the limits of the jurisdiction of the court of tribunal; *Nizzar Rawther* v. *Varghese Mathew*, AIR 1992 Ker 312: ILR 1991 (3) Ker 514: (1991) 2 Ker LJ 178: (1991) 2 Ker LT 223: 1991 (2) Ren CJ 638: (1992) 1 Ren CR 411.

The High Court would not interfere with a finding of fact, within the jurisdiction of the inferior tribunal, except where it is perverse or not based on any material whatever, or the conclusion arrived at is such that no reasonable tribunal could possibly have come to, or it has resulted in manifesting injustice; *Mani Nariman Daruwala and Bharucha* v. *Phiroz N. Bhatena*, AIR 1991 SC 1494: (1991) 3 SCC 141: 1991 AIR SCW 1441: JT 1991 (5) SC 357: (1991) 1 Ren CJ 675: 1992 (1) Rent LR 576: (1991) 2 UJ (SC) 277, paragraph 16.

Jurisdiction under article 227 must be sparingly exercised and may be exercised to correct errors of jurisdiction and the like but not to upset pure findings of fact, which falls in the domain of an appellate court only; *Khimji Vidhu* v. *Premier High School*, AIR 2000 SC 3495: (1999) 9 SCC 264: 2000 AIR SCW 2333: (2000) 3 All MR 663: (2000) 2 Mah LR 693.

Supervisory Jurisdiction

Where there is no concurrent findings of fact in question, the High Court can set aside; *State of Haryana* v. *Manoj Kumar*, AIR 2010 SC 1779.

Writ Petition – Maintainability

Writ Petition to rectify grave procedural error is maintainable; *Gujarat Electricity Board* v. *Thakar Hasmukhhai Khelshanker*, AIR 2006 Guj 16: 2006 (1) AIR Jhar (NOC) 129.

228. Transfer of certain cases to High Court.—If the High Court is satisfied that a case pending in a court subordinate to it involves a substantial question of law as to the interpretation of this Constitution the determination of which is necessary for the disposal of the case, [1][it shall withdraw the case and [2][***] may—]

(a) either dispose of the case itself, or

(b) determine the said question of law and return the case to the court from which the case has been so withdrawn together with a copy of its judgment on such question, and the said court shall on receipt thereof proceed to dispose of the case in conformity with such judgment.

[3][**228A. Special provisions as to disposal of questions relating to constitutional validity of State Laws.**—[*Rep. by the Constitution (Forty-third Amendment) Act, 1977, sec. 10 (w.e.f. 13-4-1978).*]]

229. Officers and servants and the expenses of High Courts.—(1) Appointments of officers and servants of a High Court shall be made by the Chief Justice of the Court or such other Judge or officer of the Court as he may direct:

Provided that the Governor of the State [4][***] may by rule require that in such cases as may be specified in the rule no person not already attached to the Court shall be appointed to any office connected with the Court save after consultation with the State Public Service Commission.

(2) Subject to the provisions of any law made by the Legislature of the State, the conditions of service of officers and servants of a High Court shall be such as may be prescribed by rules made by the Chief Justice of the Court or by some other Judge or officer of the Court authorised by the Chief Justice to make rules for the purpose:

Provided that the rules made under this clause shall, so far as they relate to salaries, allowances, leave or pensions, require the approval of the Governor of the State [4][***].

(3) The administrative expenses of a High Court, including all salaries, allowances and pensions payable to or in respect of the officers and servants of the court, shall be charged upon the Consolidated Fund of the State, and any fees or other moneys taken by the Court shall form part of that Fund.

Notes on Article 229

Rule made under article 229 (1) and (2) proviso must be observed. An appointment made by the Chief Justice without consulting the Public Service Commission is not proper; *H.C. Puttaswamy A.* v. *Chief Justice of Karnataka High Court*, AIR 1991 SC 295: (1991) Supp 2 SCC 421: (1991) 1 LLN 352: (1991) 1 CLR 362.

[5][**230. Extension of jurisdiction of High Courts to Union territories.**— (1) Parliament may by law extend the jurisdiction of a High Court to, or exclude the jurisdiction of a High Court from, any Union territory.

---

1. Subs. by the Constitution (Forty-second Amendment) Act, 1976, sec. 41, for "it shall withdraw the case and may—" (w.e.f. 1-2-1977).

2. The words, figure and letter, ", subject to the provisions of article 131A," omitted by the Constitution (Forty-third Amendment) Act, 1977, sec. 9 (w.e.f. 13-4-1978).

3. Article 228A was earlier inserted by the Constitution (Forty-second Amendment) Act, 1976, sec. 42 (w.e.f. 1-2-1977).

4. The words "in which the High Court has its principal seat" omitted by the Constitution (Seventh Amendment) Act, 1956, sec. 29 and Sch. (w.e.f. 1-11-1956).

5. Subs. by the Constitution (Seventh Amendment) Act, 1956, sec. 16, for article 230 (w.e.f. 1-11-1956).

(2) Where the High Court of a State exercises jurisdiction in relation to a Union territory—

(a) nothing in this Constitution shall be construed as empowering the Legislature of the State to increase, restrict or abolish that jurisdiction; and

(b) the reference in article 227 to the Governor shall, in relation to any rules, forms or tables for subordinate courts in that territory, be construed as a reference to the President.]

¹[231. Establishment of a common High Court for two or more States.— (1) Notwithstanding anything contained in the preceding provisions of this Chapter, Parliament may by law establish a common High Court for two or more States or for two or more States and a Union territory.

(2) In relation to any such High Court,—

(a) the reference in article 217 to the Governor of the State shall be construed as a reference to the Governors of all the States in relation to which the High Court exercises jurisdiction;

(b) the reference in article 227 to the Governor shall, in relation to any rules, forms or tables for subordinate courts, be construed as a reference to the Governor of the State in which the subordinate courts are situate; and

(c) the reference in articles 219 and 229 to the State shall be construed as a reference to the State in which the High Court has its principal seat:

Provided that if such principal seat is in a Union territory, the references in articles 219 and 229 to the Governor, Public Service Commission, Legislature and Consolidated Fund of the State shall be construed respectively as references to the President, Union Public Service Commission, Parliament and Consolidated Fund of India.]

232. Interpretation.—[*Rep. by the Constitution (Seventh Amendment) Act, 1956, sec. 16 (w.e.f. 1-11-1956).*]

CHAPTER VI

SUBORDINATE COURTS

233. Appointment of district judges.—(1) Appointments of persons to be, and the posting and promotion of, district judges in any State shall be made by the Governor of the State in consultation with the High Court exercising jurisdiction in relation to such State.

(2) A person not already in the service of the Union or of the State shall only be eligible to be appointed a district judge if he has been for not less than seven years an advocate or a pleader and is recommended by the High Court for appointment.

Notes on Article 233

Appointment of District Judges

Anticipated vacancies cannot be considered when statutory rules do not provide so; *Rakhi Ray* v. *High Court of Delhi*, AIR 2010 SC 932.

Control of High Court Over Subordinate Judiciary

The control of High Court over subordinate judiciary is comprehensive, exclusive and effective and it is to subserve a basic feature of the Constitution *i.e.*, independence of judiciary; *Parkash Singh Badal* v. *State of Punjab*, (2007) 1 SCC 1: AIR 2007 SC 1274: 2007 AIR SCW 1415: 2006 (4) Crimes 388: 2007 SC Cr R 488: (2006) 13 SCALE 54: 2007 (1) SCC (Cri) 193: 2006 (8) Supreme 964.

²[233A. Validation of appointments of, and judgments, etc., delivered by, certain district judges.—Notwithstanding any judgment, decree or order of any court,—

(a) (i) no appointment of any person already in the judicial service of a State or of any person who has been for not less than seven years an advocate or a pleader, to be a district judge in that State, and

(ii) no posting, promotion or transfer of any such person as a district judge,

---

1. Subs. by the Constitution (Seventh Amendment) Act, 1956, sec. 16, for article 231 (w.e.f. 1-11-1956).

2. Ins. by the Constitution (Twentieth Amendment) Act, 1966, sec. 2 (w.e.f. 22-12-1966).

made at any time before the commencement of the Constitution (Twentieth Amendment) Act, 1966, otherwise than in accordance with the provisions of article 233 or article 235 shall be deemed to be illegal or void or ever to have become illegal or void by reason only of the fact that such appointment, posting, promotion or transfer was not made in accordance with the said provisions;

(b) no jurisdiction exercised, no judgment, decree, sentence or order passed or made, and no other act or proceeding done or taken, before the commencement of the Constitution (Twentieth Amendment) Act, 1966 by, or before, any person appointed, posted, promoted or transferred as a district judge in any State otherwise than in accordance with the provisions of article 233 or article 235 shall be deemed to be illegal or invalid or ever to have become illegal or invalid by reason only of the fact that such appointment, posting, promotion or transfer was not made in accordance with the said provisions.]

234. Recruitment of persons other than district judges to the judicial service.— Appointments of persons other than district judges to the judicial service of a State shall be made by the Governor of the State in accordance with rules made by him in that behalf after consultation with the State Public Service Commission and with the High Court exercising jurisdiction in relation to such State.

235. Control over subordinate courts.—The control over district courts and courts subordinate thereto including the posting and promotion of, and the grant of leave to, persons belonging to the judicial service of a State and holding any post inferior to the post of district judge shall be vested in the High Court, but nothing in this article shall be construed as taking away from any such person any right of appeal which he may have under the law regulating the conditions of his service or as authorising the High Court to deal with him otherwise than in accordance with the conditions of his service prescribed under such law.

Notes on Article 235

The leading cases on article 235 are the following:—

(i) *State of Assam* v. *Ranga Mohammed*, AIR 1967 SC 903: (1967) 1 SCR 454: (1968) 1 LLJ 282.

(ii) *Samsher* v. *State of Punjab*, AIR 1974 SC 2192: (1974) 2 SCC 831: (1974) 2 LLJ 465: (1974) 1 SCR 814.

(iii) *Tej Pal* v. *State of Uttar Pradesh*, (1986) 3 SCC 604: AIR 1986 SC 1814: 1986 SCC (L&S) 688.

All these cases elucidate the expressed 'Control' in article 235.

The 'Control' vested in the High Court is a mechanism to ensure independence of the subordinate judiciary; *High Court of Judicature at Bombay* v. *Shirish Kumar Rangrao Patil*, AIR 1997 SC 2631: (1997) 6 SCC 339: (1997) 4 SLR 321: 1997 SCC (L&S) 1486.

Adverse Remarks against Subordinate Judicial Officer

Though the power to make remarks or observations is there but on being questioned, the power must withstand judicial scrutiny on the touchstone of following tests:—(a) whether the party whose conduct is in question is before the court or has an opportunity of explaining or defending himself; (b) whether there is evidence on record bearing on that conduct justifying the remarks; and (c) whether it is necessary for the decision of the case, as an integral part thereof, to animadvert on that conduct.

The overall test is that the criticism or observation must be judicial in nature and should not formally depart from sobriety, moderation and reserve; *In the matter of 'K' a Judicial Officer*, AIR 2001 SC 972: (2001) 3 SCC 54: 2001 Cr LJ 1157: (2001) 1 SCR 581.

236. Interpretation.—In this Chapter—

(a) the expression "district judge" includes judge of a city civil court, additional district judge, joint district judge, assistant district judge, chief judge of a small cause court, chief presidency magistrate, additional chief presidency magistrate, sessions judge, additional sessions judge and assistant sessions judge;

(b) the expression "judicial service" means a service consisting exclusively of persons intended to fill the post of district judge and other civil judicial posts inferior to the post of district judge.

237. Application of the provisions of this Chapter to certain class or classes of magistrates.—The Governor may by public notification direct that the foregoing provisions of this Chapter and any rules made thereunder shall with effect from such date as may be fixed by him in that behalf apply in relation to any class or classes of magistrates in the State as they apply in relation to persons appointed to the judicial service of the State subject to such exceptions and modifications as may be specified in the notification.

PART VII.—**THE STATES IN PART B OF THE FIRST SCHEDULE**

[*Rep. by the Constitution (Seventh Amendment) Act, 1956,
sec. 29 and Sch. (w.e.f. 1-11-1956).*]

238. Application of provisions of Part VI to States in Part B of the First Schedule.—[*Rep. by the Constitution (Seventh Amendment) Act, 1956, sec. 29 and Sch. (w.e.f. 1-11-1956).*]

PART VIII

[1][**THE UNION TERRITORIES**]

[2][**239. Administration of Union territories.**—(1) Save as otherwise provided by Parliament by law, every Union territory shall be administered by the President acting, to such extent as he thinks fit, through an administrator to be appointed by him with such designation as he may specify.

(2) Notwithstanding anything contained in Part VI, the President may appoint the Governor of a State as the administrator of an adjoining Union territory, and where a Governor is so appointed, he shall exercise his functions as such administrator independently of his Council of Ministers.]

[3][**239A. Creation of local Legislatures or Council of Ministers or both for certain Union territories.**—(1) Parliament may by law create [4][for the Union territory of [5][Puducherry]—

---

1. Subs. by the Constitution (Seventh Amendment) Act, 1956, sec. 17(a), for the heading "THE STATES IN PART C OF THE FIRST SCHEDULE" (w.e.f. 1-11-1956).

2. Subs. by the Constitution (Seventh Amendment) Act, 1956, sec. 17(b), for article 239 (w.e.f. 1-11-1956).

3. Ins. by the Constitution (Fourteenth Amendment) Act, 1962, sec. 4 (w.e.f. 28-12-1962).

4. Subs. by the Goa, Daman and Diu Reorganisation Act, 1987 (18 of 1987), sec. 63(c), for certain words (w.e.f. 30-5-1987). Earlier those words were amended by the State of Himachal Pradesh Act, 1970 (53 of 1970), sec. 46(b) (w.e.f. 25-1-1971); by the North Eastern Areas (Reorganisation) Act, 1971 (81 of 1971), sec. 71(b) (w.e.f. 21-1-1972); by the Constitution (Twenty-seventh Amendment) Act, 1971, sec. 2 (w.e.f. 30-12-1971) and by the Constitution (Thirty-seventh Amendment) Act, 1975, sec. 2 (w.e.f. 5-5-1975).

5. Subs. by the Pondicherry (Alteration of Name) Act, 2006 (44 of 2006), sec. 4, for "Pondicherry" (w.e.f. 1-10-2006).

(a) a body, whether elected or partly nominated and partly elected, to function as a Legislature for the Union territory, or

(b) a Council of Ministers,

or both with such Constitution, powers and functions, in each case, as may be specified in the law.

(2) Any such law as is referred to in clause (1) shall not be deemed to be an amendment of this Constitution for the purposes of article 368 notwithstanding that it contains any provision which amends or has the effect of amending this Constitution.]

¹[**239AA. Special provisions with respect to Delhi.**—(1) As from the date of commencement of the Constitution (Sixty-ninth Amendment) Act, 1991*, the Union territory of Delhi shall be called the National Capital Territory of Delhi (hereafter in this Part referred to as the National Capital Territory) and the administrator thereof appointed under article 239 shall be designated as the Lieutenant Governor.

(2) (a) There shall be a Legislative Assembly for the National Capital Territory and the seats in such Assembly shall be filled by members chosen by direct election from territorial constituencies in the National Capital Territory.

(b) The total number of seats in the Legislative Assembly, the number of seats reserved for Scheduled Castes, the division of the National Capital Territory into territorial constituencies (including the basis for such division) and all other matters relating to the functioning of the Legislative Assembly shall be regulated by law made by Parliament.

(c) The provisions of articles 324 to 327 and 329 shall apply in relation to the National Capital Territory, the Legislative Assembly of the National Capital Territory and the members thereof as they apply, in relation to a State, the Legislative Assembly of a State and the members thereof respectively; and my reference in articles 326 and 329 to "appropriate Legislature" shall be deemed to be a reference to Parliament.

(3) (a) Subject to the provisions of this Constitution, the Legislative Assembly shall have power to make laws for the whole or any part of the National Capital Territory with respect to any of the matters enumerated in the State List or in the Concurrent List in so far as any such matter is applicable to Union territories except matters with respect to Entries 1, 2 and 18 of the State List and Entries 64, 65 and 66 of that List in so far as they relate to the said Entries 1, 2, and 18.

(b) Nothing in sub-clause (a) shall derogate from the powers of Parliament under this Constitution to make laws with respect to any matter for a Union territory or any part thereof.

(c) If any provision of a law made by the Legislative Assembly with respect to any matter is repugnant to any provision of a law made by Parliament with respect to that matter, whether passed before or after the law made by the Legislative Assembly, or of an earlier law, other than a law made by the Legislative Assembly, then, in either case, the law made by Parliament, or, as the case may be, such earlier law, shall prevail and the law made by the Legislative Assembly shall, to the extent of the repugnancy, be void:

---

1. Ins. by the Constitution (Sixty-ninth Amendment) Act, 1991, sec. 2 (w.e.f. 1-2-1992).
* 1st February, 1992.

Provided that if any such law made by the Legislative Assembly has been reserved for the consideration of the President and has received his assent, such law shall prevail in the National Capital Territory:

Provided further that nothing in this sub-clause shall prevent Parliament from enacting at any time any law with respect to the same matter including a law adding to, amending, varying or repealing the law so made by the Legislative Assembly.

(4) There shall be a Council of Ministers consisting of not more than ten per cent. of the total number of members in the Legislative Assembly, with the Chief Minister at the head to aid and advise the Lieutenant Governor in the exercise of his functions in relation to matters with respect to which the Legislative Assembly has power to make laws, except in so far as he is, by or under any law, required to act in his discretion:

Provided that in the case of difference of opinion between the Lieutenant Governor and his Ministers on any matter, the Lieutenant Governor shall refer it to the President for decision and act according to the decision given thereon by the President and pending such decision it shall be competent for the Lieutenant Governor in any case where the matter, in his opinion, is so urgent that it is necessary for him to take immediate action, to take such action or to given such direction in the matter as he deems necessary.

(5) The Chief Minister shall be appointed by the President and the other Ministers shall be appointed by the President on the advice of the Chief Minister and the Ministers shall hold office during the pleasure of the President.

(6) The Council of Ministers shall be collectively responsible to the Legislative assembly.

[1][(7)(a)] Parliament may, by law, make provisions for giving effect to, or supplementing the provisions contained in the foregoing clauses and for all matters incidental or consequential thereto.

[2][(b) Any such law as is referred to in sub-clause (a) shall not be deemed to be an amendment of this Constitution for the purposes of article 368 notwithstanding that it contains any provision which amends or has the effect of amending, this Constitution.]

(8) The provisions of article 239B shall, so far as may be, apply in relation to the National Capital Territory, the Lieutenant Governor and the Legislative Assembly, as they apply in relation to the Union territory of [3][Puducherry], the administrator and its Legislature, respectively; and any reference in that article to "clause (1) of article 239A" shall be deemed to be a reference to this article or article 239AB, as the case may be.]

[4][**239AB. Provision in case of failure of constitutional machinery.**—If the President, on receipt of a report from the Lieutenant Governor or otherwise, is satisfied—

---

1. Subs. by the Constitution (Seventieth Amendment) Act, 1992 sec. 3(i), for "(7)" (w.r.e.f. 21-12-1991).
2. Ins. by the Constitution (Seventieth Amendment) Act, 1992, sec. 3(ii) (w.r.e.f. 21-12-1991).
3. Subs. by the Pondicherry (Alteration of Name) Act, 2006 (44 of 2006), sec. 4, for "Pondicherry" (w.e.f. 1-10-2006).
4. Ins. by the Constitution (Sixty-ninth Amendment) Act, 1991, sec. 2 (w.e.f. 1-2-1992).

(a) that a situation has arisen in which the administration of the National Capital Territory cannot be carried on in accordance with the provisions of article 239AA or of any law made in pursuance of that article; or

(b) that for the proper administration of the National Capital Territory it is necessary or expedient so to do,

the President may by order suspend the operation of any provision of article 239AA or of all or any of the provisions of any law made in pursuance of that article for such period and subject to such conditions as may be specified in such law and make such incidental and consequential provisions as may appear to him to be necessary or expedient for administering the National Capital Territory in accordance with the provisions of article 239 and article 239AA.]

¹[**239B. Power of administrator to promulgate Ordinances during recess of Legislature.**—(1) If at any time, except when the Legislature of ²[the Union territory of ³[Puducherry]] is in session, the administrator thereof is satisfied that circumstances exist which render it necessary for him to take immediate action, he may promulgate such Ordinances as the circumstances appear to him to require:

Provided that no such Ordinance shall be promulgated by the administrator except after obtaining instructions from the President in that behalf:

Provided further that whenever the said legislature is dissolved, or its functioning remains suspended on account of any action taken under any such law as is referred to in clause (1) of article 239A, the administrator shall not promulgate any Ordinance during the period of such dissolution or suspension.

(2) An Ordinance promulgated under this article in pursuance of instructions from the President shall be deemed to be an Act of the Legislature of the Union territory which has been duly enacted after complying with the provisions in that behalf contained in any such law as is referred to in clause (1) of article 239A, but every such Ordinance—

(a) shall be laid before the Legislature of the Union territory and shall cease to operate at the expiration of six weeks from the reassembly of the Legislature or if, before the expiration of that period, a resolution disapproving it is passed by the Legislature, upon the passing of the resolution; and

(b) may be withdrawn at any time by the administrator after obtaining instructions from the President in that behalf.

(3) If and so far as an Ordinance under this article makes any provision which would not be valid if enacted in an Act of the Legislature of the Union territory made after complying with the provisions in that behalf contained in any such law as is referred to in clause (1) of article 239A, it shall be void.]

⁴[***]

---

1. Ins. by the Constitution (Twenty-seventh Amendment) Act, 1971, sec. 3 (w.e.f. 30-12-1971).

2. Subs. by the Goa, Daman and Diu Reorganisation Act, 1987 (18 of 1987), sec. 63(d), for "a Union territory referred to in clause (1) of article 239A" (w.e.f. 30-5-1987).

3. Subs. by the Pondicherry (Alteration of Name) Act, 2006 (44 of 2006), sec. 4, for "Pondicherry" (w.e.f. 1-10-2006).

4. Clause (4) omitted by the Constitution (Forty-fourth Amendment) Act, 1978, sec. 32 (w.e.f. 20-6-1979). Earlier clause (4) was inserted by the Constitution (Thirty-eighth Amendment) Act, 1975, sec. 4 (retrospectively).

[1][240. Power of President to make regulations for certain Union territories.—(1) The President may make regulations for the peace, progress and good Government of the Union territory of—

(a) the Andaman and Nicobar Islands;

[2][(b) Lakshadweep;]

[3][(c) Dadra and Nagar Haveli;]

[4][(d) Daman and Diu;]

[5][(e) [6][Puducherry;]

[7][***]

[8][***]

[9][Provided that when any body is created under article 239A to function as a Legislature for the [10][Union territory of [11][6][Puducherry]], the President shall not make any regulation for the peace, progress and good Government of that Union territory with effect from the date appointed for the first meeting of the Legislature:]

[12][Provided further that whenever the body functioning as a Legislature for the Union territory of [11][6][Puducherry]] is dissolved, or the functioning of that body as such Legislature remains suspended on account of any action taken under any such law as is referred to in clause (1) of article 239A, the President may, during the period of such dissolution or suspension, make regulations for the peace, progress and good Government of that Union territory.]

---

1. Subs. by the Constitution (Seventh Amendment) Act, 1956, sec. 17(b), for article 240 (w.e.f. 1-11-1956).

2. Subs. by the Laccadive, Minicoy and Amindivi Islands (Alteration of Name) Act, 1973 (34 of 1973), sec. 4, for entry (b) (w.e.f. 1-11-1973).

3. Ins. by the Constitution (Tenth Amendment) Act, 1961, sec. 3 (w.e.f. 11-8-1961).

4. Subs. by the Goa, Daman and Diu Reorganisation Act, 1987 (18 of 1987), sec. 63(e)(i), for entry (d) (w.e.f. 30-5-1987). Earlier entry (d) was inserted by the Constitution (Twelfth Amendment) Act, 1962, sec. 3 (w.e.f. 20-12-1961).

5. Ins. by the Constitution (Fourteenth Amendment) Act, 1962, secs. 5(a) and 7 (w.r.e.f. 16-8-1962).

6. Subs. by the Pondicherry (Alteration of Name) Act, 2006 (44 of 2006), sec. 4, for "Pondicherry" (w.e.f. 1-10-2006).

7. The entry (f) relating to Mizoram omitted by the State of Mizoram Act, 1986 (34 of 1986), sec. 39 (w.e.f. 20-2-1987). Earlier entry (f) was inserted by the Constitution (Twenty-seventh Amendment) Act, 1971, sec. 4(a)(i) (w.e.f. 15-2-1972), and was amended by the Constitution (Thirty-seventh Amendment) Act, 1975, sec. 4 (w.e.f. 5-5-1975).

8. The entry (g) relating to Arunanchal Pradesh omitted by the State of Arunachal Pradesh Act, 1986 (69 of 1986), sec. 42 (w.e.f. 20-2-1987). Earlier entry (g) was inserted by the Constitution (Twenty-seventh Amendment) Act, 1971, sec. 4(a)(i) (w.e.f. 15-2-1972) and was amended by the Constitution (Thirty-seventh Amendment) Act, 1972, sec. 3 (w.e.f. 5-5-1975).

9. Ins. by the Constitution (Fourteenth Amendment) Act, 1962 sec. 5(b) (w.e.f. 28-12-1962). Earlier the proviso was amended by the Constitution (Twenty-seventh Amendment) Act, 1971, sec. 4(a)(ii).

10. Subs. by the Constitution (Twenty-seventh Amendment) Act, 1971, sec. 4(ii), for "Union territory of Goa, Daman and Diu or Pondicherry" (w.e.f. 15-2-1972).

11. Subs. by the Goa, Daman and Diu Reorganisation Act, 1987 (18 of 1987), sec. 63(e)(ii), for "Goa, Daman and Diu or Pondicherry" (w.e.f. 30-5-1987).

12. Ins. by the Constitution (Twenty-seventh Amendment) Act, 1971, sec. 4(iii) (w.e.f. 15-2-1972).

(2) Any regulation so made may repeal or amend any Act made by Parliament or [1][any other law] which is for the time being applicable to the Union territory and, when promulgated by the President, shall have the same force and effect as an Act of Parliament which applies to that territory.]

241. High Courts for Union territories.—(1) Parliament may by law constitute a High Court for a [2][Union territory] or declare any court in any [3][such territory] to be a High Court for all or any of the purposes of this Constitution.

(2) The provisions of Chapter V of Part VI shall apply in relation to every High Court referred to in clause (1) as they apply in relation to a High Court referred to in article 214 subject to such modifications or exceptions as Parliament may by law provide.

[4][(3) Subject to the provisions of this Constitution and to the provisions of any law of the appropriate Legislature made by virtue of powers conferred on that Legislature by or under this Constitution, every High Court exercising jurisdiction immediately before the commencement of the Constitution (Seventh Amendment) Act, 1956, in relation to any Union territory shall continue to exercise such jurisdiction in relation to that territory after such commencement.]

[4][(4) Nothing in this article derogates from the power of Parliament to extend or exclude the jurisdiction of a High Court for a State to, or from, any Union territory or part thereof.]

Notes on Article 241

By virtue of article 241 read with article 214 subject to Parliamentary modificatious High Court for a Union territory has the same status as High Court for a State (a) as it is a Court of record, (b) its judge is eligible for appointment as a Supreme Court judge; *T. Deen Dayal* v. *Union of India*, AIR 1991 AP 307: (1991) 2 Andh LT 373: 1991 (2) APLJ 83: 1992 (1) Civ LJ 614: 1992 (1) Serv LR 555 paras 7-8.

242. Coorg.—[*Rep. by the Constitution (Seventh Amendment) Act, 1956, sec. 29 and Sch. (w.e.f. 1-11-1956).*]

[5][PART IX
THE PANCHAYATS

243. Definitions.—In this Part, unless the context otherwise requires,—

    (a) "district" means a district in a State;

    (b) "Gram Sabha" means a body consisting of persons registered in the electoral rolls relating to a village comprised within the area of Panchayat at the village level;

---

1. Subs. by the Constitution (Twenty-seventh Amendment) Act, 1971, sec. 4(b), for "any existing law" (w.e.f. 15-2-1972).
2. Subs. by the Constitution (Seventh Amendment) Act, 1956, sec. 29 and Sch., for "State specified in Part C of the First Schedule" (w.e.f. 1-11-1956).
3. Subs. by the Constitution (Seventh Amendment) Act, 1956, sec. 29 and Sch., for "such State" (w.e.f. 1-11-1956).
4. Subs. by the Constitution (Seventh Amendment) Act, 1956, sec. 29 and Sch., for clauses (3) and (4) (w.e.f. 1-11-1956).
5. Part IX (containing articles 243, 243A to 243-O) ins. by the Constitution (Seventy-third Amendment) Act, 1992, sec. 2 (w.e.f. 24-4-1993). Earlier Part IX dealing with territories in Part D of the First Schedule was repealed by the Constitution (Seventh Amendment) Act, 1956, sec. 29 and Sch. (w.e.f. 1-11-1956).

(c) "intermediate level" means a level between the village and district levels specified by the Governor of a State by public notification to be the intermediate level for the purposes of this Part;

(d) "Panchayat" means an institution (by whatever name called) of self-government constituted under article 243B, for the rural areas;

(e) "Panchayat area" means the territorial area of a Panchayat;

(f) "population" means the population as ascertained at the last preceding census of which the relevant figures have been published;

(g) "village" means a village specified by the Governor by public notification to be a village for the purposes of this Part and includes a group of villages so specified.

243A. Gram Sabha.—A Gram Sabha may exercise such powers and perform such functions at the village level as the Legislature of a State may, by law, provide.

243B. Constitution of Panchayats.—(1) There shall be constituted in every State, Panchayats at the village, intermediate and district levels in accordance with the provisions of this Part.

(2) Notwithstanding anything in clause (1), Panchayats at the intermediate level may not be constituted in a State having a population not exceeding twenty lakhs.

243C. Composition of Panchayats.—(1) Subject to the provisions of this Part, the Legislature of a State may, by law, make provisions with respect to the composition of Panchayats:

Provided that the ratio between the population of the territorial area of a Panchayat at any level and the number of seats in such Panchayat to be filled by election shall, so far as practicable, be the same throughout the State.

(2) All the seats in a Panchayat shall be filled by persons chosen by direct election from territorial constituencies in the Panchayat area and, for this purpose, each Panchayat area shall be divided into territorial constituencies in such manner that the ratio between the population of each constituency and the number of seats allotted to it shall, so far as practicable, be the same throughout the Panchayat area.

(3) The Legislature of a State may, by law, provide for the representation—

(a) of the Chairpersons of the Panchayats at the village level, in the Panchayats at the intermediate level or, in the case of a State not having Panchayats at the intermediate level, in the Panchayats at the district level;

(b) of the Chairpersons of the Panchayats at the intermediate level, in the Panchayats at the district level;

(c) of the members of the House of the People and the members of the Legislative Assembly of the State representing constituencies which comprise wholly or partly a Panchayat area at a level other than the village level, in such Panchayat;

(d) of the members of the Council of States and the members of the Legislative Council of the State, where they are registered as electors within—

(i) a Panchayat area at the intermediate level, in Panchayat at the intermediate level;

(ii) a Panchayat area at the district level, in Panchayat at the district level.

(4) The Chairperson of a Panchayat and other members of a Panchayat whether or not chosen by direct election from territorial constituencies in the Panchayat area shall have the right to vote in the meetings of the Panchayats.

(5) The Chairperson of—

(a) a Panchayat at the village level shall be elected in such manner as the Legislature of a State may, by law, provide; and

(b) a Panchayat at the intermediate level or district level shall be elected by, and from amongst, the elected members thereof.

243D. Reservation of seats.—(1) Seats shall be reserved for—

(a) the Scheduled Castes; and

(b) the Scheduled Tribes,

in every Panchayat and the number of seats so reserved shall bear, as nearly as may be, the same proportion to the total number of seats to be filled by direct election in that Panchayat as the population of the Scheduled Castes in that Panchayat area or of the Scheduled Tribes in that Panchayat area bears to the total population of that area and such seats may be allotted by rotation to different constituencies in a Panchayat.

(2) Not less than one-third of the total number of seats reserved under clause (1) shall be reserved for women belonging to the Scheduled Castes or, as the case may be, the Scheduled Tribes.

(3) Not less than one-third (including the number of seats reserved for women belonging to the Scheduled Castes and the Scheduled Tribes) of the total number of seats to be filled by direct election in every Panchayat shall be reserved for women and such seats may be allotted by rotation to different constituencies in a Panchayat.

(4) The offices of the Chairpersons in the Panchayats at the village or any other level shall be reserved for the Scheduled Castes, the Scheduled Tribes and women in such manner as the Legislature of a State may, by law, provide:

Provided that the number of offices of Chairpersons reserved for the Scheduled Castes and the Scheduled Tribes in the Panchayats at each level in any State shall bear, as nearly as may be, the same proportion to the total number of such offices in the Panchayats at each level as the population of the Scheduled Castes in the State or of the Scheduled Tribes in the State bears to the total population of the State:

Provided further that not less than one-third of the total number of offices of Chairpersons in the Panchayats at each level shall be reserved for women:

Provided also that the number of offices reserved under this clause shall be allotted by rotation to different Panchayats at each level.

(5) The reservation of seats under clauses (1) and (2) and the reservation of offices of Chairpersons (other than the reservation for women) under clause (4) shall cease to have effect on the expiration of the period specified in article 334.

(6) Nothing in this Part shall prevent the Legislature of a State from making any provision for reservation of seats in any Panchayat or offices of Chairpersons in the Panchayats at any level in favour of backward class of citizens.

243E. Duration of Panchayats, etc.—(1) Every Panchayat, unless sooner dissolved under any law for the time being in force, shall continue for five years from the date appointed for its first meeting and no longer.

(2) No amendment of any law for the time being in force shall have the effect of causing dissolution of a Panchayat at any level, which is functioning immediately before such amendment, till the expiration of its duration specified in clause (1).

(3) An election to constitute a Panchayat shall be completed—

(a) before the expiry of its duration specified in clause (1);

(b) before the expiration of a period of six months from the date of its dissolution:

Provided that where the remainder of the period for which the dissolved Panchayat would have continued is less than six months, it shall not be necessary to hold any election under this clause for constituting the Panchayat for such period.

(4) A Panchayat constituted upon the dissolution of a Panchayat before the expiration of its duration shall continue only for the remainder of the period for which the dissolved Panchayat would have continued under clause (1) had it not been so dissolved.

243F. Disqualifications for membership.—(1) A person shall be disqualified for being chosen as, and for being, a member of a Panchayat—

(a) if he is so disqualified by or under any law for the time being in force for the purposes of elections to the Legislature of the State concerned:

Provided that no person shall be disqualified on the ground that he is less than twenty-five years of age, if he has attained the age of twenty-one years;

(b) if he is so disqualified by or under any law made by the Legislature of the State.

(2) If any question arises as to whether a member of a Panchayat has become subject to any of the disqualifications mentioned in clause (1), the question shall be referred for the decision of such authority and in such manner as the Legislature of a State may, by law, provide.

243G. Powers, authority and responsibilities of Panchayats.—Subject to the provisions of this Constitution, the Legislature of a State may, by law, endow the Panchayats with such powers and authority and may be necessary to enable them to function as institutions of self-government and such law may contain provisions for the devolution of powers and responsibilities upon Panchayats at the appropriate level, subject to such conditions as may be specified therein, with respect to—

(a) the preparation of plans for economic development and social justice;

(b) the implementation of schemes for economic development and social justice as may be entrusted to them including those in relation to the matters listed in the Eleventh Schedule.

243H. Powers to impose taxes by, and Funds of, the Panchayats.—The Legislature of a State may, by law,—

(a) authorise a Panchayat to levy, collect and appropriate such taxes, duties, tolls and fees in accordance with such procedure and subject to such limits;

(b) assign to a Panchayat such taxes, duties, tolls and fees levied and collected by the State Government for such purposes and subject to such conditions and limits;

(c) provide for making such grants-in-aid to the Panchayats from the Consolidated Fund of the State; and

(d) provide for constitution of such Funds for crediting all moneys received, respectively, by or on behalf of the Panchayats and also for the withdrawal of such moneys therefrom,

as may be specified in the law.

243-I. Constitution of Finance Commission to review financial position.—(1) The Governor of a State shall, as soon as may be within one year from the commencement of the Constitution (Seventy-third Amendment) Act, 1992*, and thereafter at the expiration of every fifth year, constitute a Finance Commission to review the financial position of the Panchayats and to make recommendations to the Governor as to—

(a) the principle which should govern—

    (i) the distribution between the State and the Panchayats of the net proceeds of the taxes, duties, tolls and fees leviable by the State, which may be divided between them under this Part and the allocation between the Panchayats at all levels of their respective shares of such proceeds;

    (ii) the determination of the taxes, duties, tolls and fees which may be assigned to, or appropriated by, the Panchayats;

    (iii) the grants-in-aid to the Panchayats from the Consolidated Fund of the State;

(b) the measures needed to improve the financial position of the Panchayats;

(c) any other matter referred to the Finance Commission by the Governor in the interests of sound finance of the Panchayats.

(2) The Legislature of a State may, by law, provide for the composition of the Commission, the qualifications which shall be requisite for appointment as members thereof and the manner in which they shall be selected.

(3) The Commission shall determine their procedure and shall have such powers in the performance of their functions as the Legislature of the State may, by law, confer on them.

(4) The Governor shall cause every recommendation made by the Commission under this article together with an explanatory memorandum as to the action taken thereon to be laid before the Legislature of the State.

243J. Audit of accounts of Panchayats.—The Legislature of a State may, by law, make provisions with respect to the maintenance of accounts by the Panchayats and the auditing of such accounts.

243K. Elections to the Panchayats.—(1) The superintendence, direction and control of the preparation of electoral rolls for, and the conduct of, all elections to the Panchayats shall be vested in a State Election Commission consisting of a State Election Commissioner to be appointed by the Governor.

(2) Subject to the provisions of any law made by the Legislature of a State, the conditions of service and tenure of office of the State Election Commissioner shall be such as the Governor may by rule determine:

Provided that the State Election Commissioner shall not be removed from his office except in like manner and on the like ground as a Judge of a High Court and the conditions of service of the State Election Commissioner shall not be varied to his disadvantage after his appointment.

(3) The Governor of a State shall, when so requested by the State Election Commission, make available to the State Election Commission such staff as may be necessary for the discharge of the functions conferred on the State Election Commission by clause (1).

---

* 24th April, 1993.

(4) Subject to the provisions of this Constitution, the Legislature of a State may, by law, make provision with respect to all matters relating to, or in connection with, elections to the Panchayats.

243L. Application to Union territories.—The provisions of this Part shall apply to the Union territories and shall, in their application to a Union territory, have effect as if the references to the Governor of a State were references to the Administrator of the Union territory appointed under article 239 and references to the Legislature or the Legislative Assembly of a State were references, in relation to a Union territory having a Legislative Assembly, to that Legislative Assembly:

Provided that the President may, by public notification, direct that the provisions of this Part shall apply to any Union territory or part thereof subject to such exceptions and modifications as he may specify in the notification.

243M. Part not to apply to certain areas.—(1) Nothing in this Part shall apply to the Scheduled Areas referred to in clause (1), and the tribal areas referred to in clause (2), of article 244.

(2) Nothing in this Part shall apply to—

(a) the States of Nagaland, Meghalaya and Mizoram;

(b) the hill areas in the State of Manipur for which District Councils exist under any law for the time being in force.

(3) Nothing in this Part—

(a) relating to Panchayats at the district level shall apply to the hill areas of the District of Darjeeling in the State of West Bengal for which Darjeeling Gorkha Hill Council exists under any law for the time being in force;

(b) shall be construed to affect the functions and powers of the Darjeeling Gorkha Hill Council constituted under such law.

[1][(3A) Nothing in article 243D, relating to reservation of seats for the Scheduled Castes, shall apply to the State of Arunachal Pradesh.]

(4) Notwithstanding anything in this Constitution—

(a) the Legislature of a State referred to in sub-clause (a) of clause (2) may, by law, extend this Part to that State, except the areas, if any, referred to in clause (1), if the Legislative Assembly of that State passes a resolution to that effect by a majority of the total membership of that House and by a majority of not less than two-thirds of the members of that House present and voting;

(b) Parliament may, by law, extend the provisions of this Part to the Scheduled Areas and the tribal areas referred to in clause (1) subject to such exceptions and modifications as may be specified in such law, and no such law shall be deemed to be an amendment of this Constitution for the purposes of article 368.

243N. Continuance of existing laws and Panchayats.—Notwithstanding anything in this Part, any provision of any law relating to Panchayats in force in a State immediately before commencement of the Constitution (Seventy-third Amendment) Act, 1992[†], which is inconsistent with the provisions of this Part, shall continue to be in force until amended or repealed by a competent Legislature or other competent

---

1. Ins. by the Constitution (Eighty-third Amendment) Act, 2000, sec. 2 (w.e.f. 8-9-2000).

† 24th April, 1993.

authority or until the expiration of one year from such commencement, whichever is earlier:

Provided that all the Panchayats existing immediately before such commencement shall continue till the expiration of their duration, unless sooner dissolved by a resolution passed to that effect by the Legislative Assembly of that State or, in the case of a State having a Legislative Council, by each House of the Legislature of that State.

243-O. Bar to interference by courts in electoral matters.—Notwithstanding anything in this Constitution—

(a) the validity of any law relating to the delimitation of constituencies or the allotment of seats to such constituencies, made or purporting to be made under article 243K, shall not be called in question in any court;

(b) no election to any Panchayat shall be called in question except by an election petition presented to such authority and in such manner as is provided for by or under any law made by the Legislature of a State.]

Notes on Article 243-O

Election Process: Gram Panchayats

Once the election process has started, the High Court cannot—

(a) direct the election officer to stall the proceedings or to conduct the election process afresh or

(b) direct him not to declare the result of the election of the gram Panchayat, or

(c) direct him to conduct a fresh poll for 20 persons.

Boddula Krishnaiah v. *State Election Commissioner, Andhra Pradesh*, AIR 1996 SC 1595: 1996 AIR SCW 1856: JT 1996 (4) SC 156: 1996 (2) Land LR 535: (1996) 3 SCC 416: (1996) 3 SCR 687, paragraphs 11, 12.

¹[PART IXA*

THE MUNICIPALITIES

243P. Definitions.—In this Part, unless the context otherwise requires,—

(a) "Committee" means a Committee constituted under article 243S;

(b) "district" means a district in a State;

(c) "Metropolitan area" means an area having a population of ten lakhs or more, comprised in one or more districts and consisting of two or more Municipalities or Panchayats or other contiguous areas, specified by the Governor by public notification to be a Metropolitan area for the purposes of this Part;

(d) "Municipal area" means the territorial area of a Municipality as is notified by the Governor;

---

1. Part IXA (containing articles 243P to 243Z, 243ZA to 243ZG) ins. by the Constitution (Seventy-fourth Amendment) Act, 1992, sec. 2 (w.e.f. 1-6-1993).

* In exercise of the powers conferred by the proviso to article 243ZB of the Constitution, the President, hereby, directs that the provisions of Part IXA of the Constitution shall apply to the Union Territory of Dadra and Nagar Haveli subject to the following exceptions and modifications namely:—

In article 243Y of the Constitution, in clause (1), for the word "Governor", at both the places, the word "President" shall be substituted. [*Vide* S.O. 615(E), dated 21st May, 2004, published in the Gazette of India, Extra., Pt. II, Sec. 3(ii), dated 21st May, 2004].

(e) "Municipality" means an institution of self-government constituted under article 243Q;

(f) "Panchayat" means a Panchayat constituted under article 243B;

(g) "population" means the population as ascertained at the last preceding census of which the relevant figures have been published.

243Q. Constitution of Municipalities.—(1) There shall be constituted in every State,—

(a) a Nagar Panchayat (by whatever name called) for a transitional area, that is to say, an area in transition from a rural area to an urban area;

(b) a Municipal Council for a smaller urban area; and

(c) a Municipal Corporation for a larger urban area,

in accordance with the provisions of this Part:

Provided that a Municipality under this clause may not be constituted in such urban area or part thereof as the Governor may, having regard to the size of the area and the municipal services being provided or proposed to be provided by an industrial establishment in that area and such other factors as he may deem fit, by public notification, specify to be an industrial township.

(2) In this article, "a transitional area", "a smaller urban area" or "a larger urban area" means such area as the Governor may, having regard to the population of the area, the density of the population therein, the revenue generated for local administration, the percentage of employment in non-agricultural activities, the economic importance or such other factors as he may deem fit, specify by public notification for the purposes of this Part.

Notes on Article 243Q

Under clause (2) of article 243Q, Governor has to issue public notification considering the population of the area, density of the population therein with other factors mentioned in the said article for declaring any area as "transitional area". In the absence of such notification issued under the signature of the Governor of the State the said area cannot be treated as "transitional area"; *BIMA Office Premises Co-operative Society* v. *Kalamboli Village Panchayat,* AIR 2001 Bom 83: 2001 (1) Mah LJ 806: 2001 (2) Mah LR 262.

243R. Composition of Municipalities.—(1) Save as provided in clause (2), all the seats in a Municipality shall be filled by persons chosen by direct election from the territorial constituencies in the Municipal area and for this purpose each Municipal area shall be divided into territorial constituencies to be known as wards.

(2) The Legislature of a State may, by law, provide—

(a) for the representation in a Municipality of—

(i) persons having special knowledge or experience in Municipal administration;

(ii) the members of the House of the People and the members of the Legislative Assembly of the State representing constituencies which comprise wholly or partly the Municipal area;

(iii) the members of the Council of States and the members of the Legislative Council of the State registered as electors within the Municipal area;

(iv) the Chairpersons of the Committees constituted under clause (5) of article 243S:

Provided that the persons referred to in paragraph (i) shall not have the right to vote in the meetings of the Municipality;

(b) the manner of election of the Chairperson of a Municipality.

243S. Constitution and composition of Wards Committees, etc.—(1) There shall be constituted Wards Committees, consisting of one or more wards, within the territorial area of a Municipality having a population of three lakhs or more.

(2) The Legislature of a State may, by law, make provision with respect to—

(a) the composition and the territorial area of a Wards Committee;

(b) the manner in which the seats in a Wards Committee shall be filled.

(3) A member of a Municipality representing a ward within the territorial area of the Wards Committee shall be a member of that Committee.

(4) Where a Wards Committee consists of—

(a) one ward, the member representing that ward in the Municipality; or

(b) two or more wards, one of the members representing such wards in the Municipality elected by the members of the Wards Committee,

shall be the Chairperson of that Committee.

(5) Nothing in this article shall be deemed to prevent the Legislature of a State from making any provision for the Constitution of Committees in addition to the Wards Committees.

243T. Reservation of seats.—(1) Seats shall be reserved for the Scheduled Castes and the Scheduled Tribes in every Municipality and the number of seats so reserved shall bear, as nearly as may be, the same proportion to the total number of seats to be filled by direct election in that Municipality as the population of the Scheduled Castes in the Municipal area or of the Scheduled Tribes in the Municipal area bears to the total population of that area and such seats may be allotted by rotation to different constituencies in a Municipality.

(2) Not less than one-third of the total number of seats reserved under clause (1) shall be reserved for women belonging to the Scheduled Castes or, as the case may be, the Scheduled Tribes.

(3) Not less than one-third (including the number of seats reserved for women belonging to the Scheduled Castes and the Scheduled Tribes) of the total number of seats to be filled by direct election in every Municipality shall be reserved for women and such seats may be allotted by rotation to different constituencies in a Municipality.

(4) The offices of Chairpersons in the Municipalities shall be reserved for the Scheduled Castes, the Scheduled Tribes and women in such manner as the Legislature of a State may, by law, provide.

(5) The reservation of seats under clauses (1) and (2) and the reservation of offices of Chairpersons (other than the reservation for women) under clause (4) shall cease to have effect on the expiration of the period specified in article 334.

(6) Nothing in this Part shall prevent the Legislature of a State from making any provision for reservation of seats in any Municipality or offices of Chairpersons in the Municipalities in favour of backward class of citizens.

243U. Duration of Municipalities, etc.—(1) Every Municipality, unless sooner dissolved under any law for the time being in force, shall continue for five years from the date appointed for its first meeting and no longer:

Provided that a Municipality shall be given a reasonable opportunity of being heard before its dissolution.

(2) No amendment of any law for the time being in force shall have the effect of causing dissolution of a Municipality at any level, which is functioning immediately before such amendment, till the expiration of its duration specified in clause (1).

(3) An election to constitute a Municipality shall be completed,—

(a) before the expiry of its duration specified in clause (1);

(b) before the expiration of a period of six months from the date of its dissolution:

Provided that where the remainder of the period for which the dissolved Municipality would have continued is less than six months, it shall not be necessary to hold any election under this clause for constituting the Municipality for such period.

(4) A Municipality constituted upon the dissolution of a Municipality before the expiration of its duration shall continue only for the remainder of the period for which the dissolved Municipality would have continued under clause (1) had it not been so dissolved.

243V. Disqualifications for membership.—(1) A person shall be disqualified for being chosen as, and for being, a member of a Municipality—

(a) if he is so disqualified by or under any law for the time being in force for the purposes of elections to the Legislature of the State concerned:

Provided that no person shall be disqualified on the ground that he is less than twenty-five years of age, if he has attained the age of twenty-one years;

(b) if he is so disqualified by or under any law made by the Legislature of the State.

(2) If any question arises as to whether a member of a Municipality has become subject to any of the disqualifications mentioned in clause (1), the question shall be referred for the decision of such authority and in such manner as the Legislature of a State may, by law, provide.

243W. Powers, authority and responsibilities of Municipalities, etc.—Subject to the provisions of this Constitution, the Legislature of a State may, by law, endow—

(a) the Municipalities with such powers and authority as may be necessary to enable them to function as institutions of self-government and such law may contain provisions for the devolution of powers and responsibilities upon Municipalities, subject to such conditions as may be specified therein, with respect to—

(i) the preparation of plans for economic development and social justice;

(ii) the performance of functions and the implementation of schemes as may be entrusted to them including those in relation to the matters listed in the Twelfth Schedule;

(b) the Committees with such powers and authority as may be necessary to enable them to carry out the responsibility conferred upon them including those in relation to the matters listed in the Twelfth Schedule.

243X. Power to impose taxes by, and Funds of, the Municipalities.—The Legislature of a State may, by law,—

(a) authorise a Municipality to levy, collect and appropriate such taxes, duties, tolls and fees in accordance with such procedure and subject to such limits;

(b) assign to a Municipality such taxes, duties, tolls and fees levied and collected by the State Government for such purposes and subject to such conditions and limits;

(c) provide for making such grants-in-aid to the Municipalities from the Consolidated Fund of the State; and

(d) provide for constitution of such Funds for crediting all moneys received, respectively, by or on behalf of the Municipalities and also for the withdrawal of such moneys therefrom,

as may be specified in the law.

*243Y. Finance Commission.—(1) The Finance Commission constituted under article 243-I shall also review the financial position of the Municipalities and make recommendations to the Governor as to—

(a) the principles which should govern—

　(i) the distribution between the State and the Municipalities of the net proceeds of the taxes, duties, tolls and fees leviable by the State, which may be divided between them under this Part and the allocation between the Municipalities at all levels of their respective shares of such proceeds;

　(ii) the determination of the taxes, duties, tolls and fees which may be assigned to, or appropriated by, the Municipalities;

　(iii) the grants-in-aid to the Municipalities from the Consolidated Fund of the State;

(b) the measures needed to improve the financial position of the Municipalities;

(c) any other matter referred to the Finance Commission by the Governor in the interests of sound finance of the Municipalities.

(2) The Governor shall cause every recommendation made by the Commission under this article together with an explanatory memorandum as to the action taken thereon to be laid before the Legislature of the State.

243Z. Audit of accounts of Municipalities.—The Legislature of a State may, by law, make provisions with respect to the maintenance of accounts by the Municipalities and the auditing of such accounts.

243ZA. Elections to the Municipalities.—(1) The superintendence, direction and control of the preparation of electoral rolls for, and the conduct of, all elections to the Municipalities shall be vested in the State Election Commission referred to in article 243K.

(2) Subject to provisions of this Constitution, the Legislature of a State may, by law, make provision with respect to all matters relating to, or in connection with, elections to the Municipalities.

243ZB. Application to Union territories.—The provisions of this Part shall apply to the Union territories and shall, in their application to a Union territory, have effect

---

* In its application to the Union Territory of Dadra and Nagar Haveli, in clause (1) of article 243Y, for the word "Governor", at both the places, the word "President" shall be substituted. [*Vide* S.O. 615(E), dated 21st May, 2004, published in the Gazette of India, Extra., Pt. II, Sec. 3(ii), dated 21st May, 2004].

as if the references to the Governor of a State were references to the Administrator of the Union territory appointed under article 239 and references to the Legislature or the Legislative Assembly of a State were references in relation to a Union territory having a Legislative Assembly, to that Legislative Assembly:

Provided that the President may, by public notification, direct that the provisions of this Part shall apply to any Union territory or part thereof subject to such exceptions and modifications as he may specify in the notification.

243ZC. Part not to apply to certain areas.—(1) Nothing in this Part shall apply to the Scheduled Areas referred to in clause (1), and the tribal areas referred to in clause (2), of article 244.

(2) Nothing in this part shall be construed to affect the functions and powers of the Darjeeling Gorkha Hill Council constituted under any law for the time being in force for the hill areas of the district of Darjeeling in the State of West Bengal.

(3) Notwithstanding anything in this Constitution, Parliament may, by law, extend the provisions of this Part to the Scheduled Areas and the tribal areas referred to in clause (1) subject to such exceptions and modifications as may be specified in such law, and no such law shall be deemed to be an amendment of this Constitution for the purposes of article 368.

*243ZD. Committee for district planning.—(1) There shall be constituted in every State at the district level a District Planning Committee to consolidate the plans prepared by the Panchayats and the Municipalities in the district and to prepare a draft development plan for the district as a whole.

(2) The Legislature of a State may, by law, make provision, with respect to—

(a) the composition of the District Planning Committees;

(b) the manner in which the seats in such Committees shall be filled:

   Provided that not less than four-fifths of the total number of members of such Committee shall be elected by, and from amongst, the elected members of the Panchayat at the district level and of the Municipalities in the district in proportion to the ratio between the population of the rural areas and of the urban areas in the district;

(c) the functions relating to district planning which may be assigned to such Committees;

(d) the manner in which the Chairpersons of such Committees shall be chosen.

(3) Every District Planning Committee shall, in preparing the draft development plan,—

(a) have regard to—

   (i) matters of common interest between the Panchayats and the Municipalities including spatial planning, sharing of water and other physical and natural resources, the integrated development of infrastructure and environmental conservation;

   (ii) the extent and type of available resources whether financial or otherwise;

(b) consult such institutions and organizations as the Governor may, by order, specify.

---

* The provisions of article 243ZD shall not apply to the National Capital Territory of Delhi, *vide* S.O. 1125(E), dated 12th November, 2001.

(4) The Chairperson of every District Planning Committee shall forward the development plan, as recommended by such Committee, to the Government of the State.

*243ZE. Committee for Metropolitan planning.—(1) There shall be constituted in every Metropolitan area, a Metropolitan Planning Committee to prepare a draft development plan for the Metropolitan area as a whole.

(2) The Legislature of a State may, by law, make provision with respect to—

(a) the composition of the Metropolitan Planning Committees;

(b) the manner in which the seats in such Committees shall be filled:

Provided that not less than two-thirds of the members of such Committee shall be elected by, and from amongst, the elected members of the Municipalities and Chairpersons of the Panchayats in the Metropolitan area in proportion to the ratio between the population of the Municipalities and of the Panchayats in that area;

(c) the representation, in such Committees of the Government of India and the Government of the State and of such organisations and institutions as may be deemed necessary for carrying out the functions assigned to such Committees;

(d) the functions relating to planning and coordination for the Metropolitan area which may be assigned to such Committees;

(e) the manner in which the Chairpersons of such Committees shall be chosen.

(3) Every Metropolitan Planning Committee shall, in preparing the draft development plan,—

(a) have regard to—

(i) the plans prepared by the Municipalities and the Panchayats in the Metropolitan area;

(ii) matters of common interest between the Municipalities and the Panchayats, including co-ordinated spatial planning of the area, sharing of water and other physical and natural resources, the integrated development of infrastructure and environmental conservation;

(iii) the overall objectives and priorities set by the Government of India and the Government of the State;

(iv) the extent and nature of investments likely to be made in the Metropolitan area by agencies of the Government of India and of the Government of the State and other available resources whether financial or otherwise;

(b) consult such institutions and organisations as the Governor may, by order, specify.

(4) The Chairperson of every Metropolitan Planning Committee shall forward the development plan, as recommended by such Committee, to the Government of the State.

243ZF. Continuance of existing laws and Municipalities.—Notwithstanding anything in this Part, any provision of any law relating to Municipalities in force in a State immediately before the commencement of the Constitution (Seventy-fourth Amendment) Act, 1992**, which is inconsistent with the provisions of this Part, shall

---

* The provisions of article 243ZE shall not apply to the National Capital Territory of Delhi, *vide* S.O. 1125(E), dated 12th November, 2001.

** 1st June, 1993.

continue to be in force until amended or repealed by a competent Legislature or other competent authority or until the expiration of one year from such commencement, whichever is earlier:

Provided that all the Municipalities existing immediately before such commencement shall continue till the expiration of their duration, unless sooner dissolved by a resolution passed to that effect by the Legislative Assembly of that State or, in the case of a State having a Legislative Council, by each House of the Legislature of that State.

243ZG. Bar to interference by courts in electoral matters.—Notwithstanding anything in this Constitution,—

(a) the validity of any law relating to the delimitation of constituencies or the allotment of seats to such constituencies, made or purporting to be made under article 243ZA shall not be called in question in any court;

(b) no election to any Municipality shall be called in question except by an election petition presented to such authority and in such manner as is provided for by or under any law made by the Legislature of a State.]

¹[PART IXB

THE CO-OPERATIVE SOCIETIES

243ZH. Definitions.—In this Part, unless the context otherwise requires,—

(a) "authorised person" means a person referred to as such in article 243ZQ;

(b) "board" means the board of directors or the governing body of a co-operative society, by whatever name called, to which the direction and control of the management of the affairs of a society is entrusted to;

(c) "co-operative society" means a society registered or deemed to be registered under any law relating to co-operative societies for the time being in force in any State;

(d) "multi-State co-operative society" means a society with objects not confined to one State and registered or deemed to be registered under any law for the time being in force relating to such co-operatives;

(e) "officer bearer" means a President, Vice-President, Chairperson, Vice-Chairperson, Secretary or Treasurer of a co-operative society and includes any other person to be elected by the board of any co-operative society;

(f) "Registrar" means the Central Registrar appointed by the Central Government in relation to the multi-State co-operative societies and the Registrar for co-operative societies appointed by the State Government under the law made by the Legislature of a State in relation to co-operative societies;

(g) "State Act" means any law made by the Legislature of a State;

(h) "State level co-operative society" means a co-operative society having its area of operation extending to the whole of a State and defined as such in any law made by the Legislature of a State.

243ZI. Incorporation of co-operative societies.—Subject to the provisions of this Part, the Legislature of a State may, by law, make provisions with respect to the

---

1. Part IXB (containing Articles 243ZH to 243ZT) inserted by the Constitution (Ninety-seventh Amendment) Act, 2011, sec. 4 (w.e.f. 15-2-2012).

incorporation, regulation and winding-up of co-operative societies based on the principles of voluntary formation, democratic member-control, member-economic participation and autonomous functioning.

243ZJ. Number and term of members of board and its office bearers.—(1) The board shall consist of such number of directors as may be provided by the Legislature of a State, by law:

Provided that the maximum number of directors of a co-operative society shall not exceed twenty-one:

Provided further that the Legislature of a State shall, by law, provide for the reservation of one seat for the Scheduled Castes or the Scheduled Tribes and two seats for women on board of every co-operative society consisting of individuals as members and having members from such class or category of persons.

(2) The term of office of elected members of the board and its office bearers shall be five years from the date of election and the term of office bearers shall be [1][coterminous] with the term of the board:

Provided that the board may fill a casual vacancy on the board by nomination out of the same class of members in respect of which the casual vacancy has arisen, if the term of office of the board is less than half of its original term.

(3) The Legislature of a State shall, by law, make provisions for co-option of persons to be members of the board having experience in the field of banking, management, finance or specialisation in any other field relating to the objects and activities undertaken by the co-operative society, as members of the board of such society:

Provided that the number of such co-opted members shall not exceed two in addition to twenty-one directors specified in the first proviso to clause (1):

Provided further that such co-opted members shall not have the right to vote in any election of the co-operative society in their capacity as such member or to be eligible to be elected as office bearers of the board:

Provided also that the functional directors of a co-operative society shall also be the members of the board and such members shall be excluded for the purpose of counting the total number of directors specified in the first proviso to clause (1).

243ZK. Election of members of board.—(1) Notwithstanding anything contained in any law made by the Legislature of a State, the election of a board shall be conducted before the expiry of the term of the board so as to ensure that the newly elected members of the board assume office immediately on the expiry of [2][the term of the office] of members of the outgoing board.

(2) The superintendence, direction and control of the preparation of electoral rolls for, and the conduct of, all elections to a co-operative society shall vest in such an authority or body, as may be provided by the Legislature of a State, by law:

Provided that the Legislature of a State may, by law, provide for the procedure and guidelines for the conduct of such election.

243ZL. Supersession and suspension of board and interim management.—(1) Notwithstanding anything contained in any law for the time being in force, no board shall be superseded or kept under suspension for a period exceeding six months:

---

1. Corrected for "conterminous" *vide* corrigendum dated 29th March, 2012, published along with Act 19 of 2012 in the Gazette of India, Extra., Pt. II, Sec. 1, No. 21, dated 29th March, 2012.
2. Corrected for "the office" *vide* corrigendum dated 29th March, 2012, published along with Act 19 of 2012 in the Gazette of India, Extra., Pt. II, Sec. 1, No. 21, dated 29th March, 2012.

Provided that the board may be superseded or kept under suspension in case—
  (i) of its persistent default; or
  (ii) of negligence in the performance of its duties; or
  (iii) the board has committed any act prejudicial to the interests of the co-operative society or its members; or
  (iv) there [1][is a stalement] in the constitution or functions of the board; or
  (v) the authority or body as provided by the Legislature of a State, by law, under clause (2) of article 243ZK, has failed to conduct elections in accordance with the provisions of the State Act:

Provided further that the board of any such co-operative society shall not be superseded or kept under suspension where there is no Government shareholding or loan or financial assistance or any guarantee by the Government:

Provided also that in case of a co-operative society carrying on the business of banking, the provisions of the Banking Regulation Act, 1949 (10 of 1949) shall also apply:

Provided also that in case of a co-operative society, other than a multi-State co-operative society, carrying on the business of banking, the provisions of this clause shall have the effect as if for the words "six months", the words "one year" had been substituted.

(2) In case of supersession of a board, the administrator appointed to manage the affairs of such co-operative society shall arrange for conduct of elections within the period specified in clause (1) and handover the management to the elected board.

(3) The Legislature of a State may, by law, make provisions for the conditions of service of the administrator.

243ZM. Audit of accounts of co-operative societies.—(1) The Legislature of a State may, by law, make provisions with respect to the maintenance of accounts by the co-operative societies and the auditing of such accounts at least once in each financial year.

(2) The Legislature of a State shall, by law, lay down the minimum qualifications and experience of auditors and auditing firms that shall be eligible for auditing accounts of the co-operative societies.

(3) Every co-operative society shall cause to be audited by an auditor or auditing firms referred to in clause (2) appointed by the general body of the co-operative society:

Provided that such auditors or auditing firms shall be appointed from a panel approved by a State Government or an authority authorised by the State Government in this behalf.

(4) The accounts of every co-operative society shall be audited within six months of the close of the financial year to which such accounts relate.

(5) The audit report of the accounts of an apex co-operative society, as may be defined by the State Act, shall be laid before the State Legislature in the manner, as may be provided by the State Legislature, by law.

243ZN. Convening of general body meetings.—The Legislature of a State may, by law, make provisions that the annual general body meeting of every co-operative society shall be convened within a period of six months of close of the financial year to transact the business as may be provided in such law.

---

1. Corrected for "is stalemate" *vide* corrigendum dated 29th March, 2012, published along with Act 19 of 2012 in the Gazette of India, Extra., Pt. II, Sec. 1, No. 21, dated 29th March, 2012.

243ZO. Right of a member to get information.—(1) The Legislature of a State may, by law, provide for access to every member of a co-operative society to the books, information and accounts of the co-operative society kept in regular transaction of its business with such member.

(2) The Legislature of a State may, by law, make provisions to ensure the participation of members in the management of the co-operative society providing minimum requirement of attending meetings by the members and utilising the minimum level of services as may be provided in such law.

(3) The Legislature of a State may, by law, provide for co-operative education and training for its members.

243ZP. Returns.—Every co-operative society shall file returns, within six months of the close of every financial year, to the authority designated by the State Government including the following matters, namely:—

    (a) annual report of its activities;

    (b) its audited statement of accounts;

    (c) plan for surplus disposal as approved by the general body of the co-operative society;

    (d) list of amendments to the bye-laws of the co-operative society, if any;

    (e) declaration regarding date of holding of its general body meeting and conduct of elections when due; and

    (f) any other information required by the Registrar in pursuance of any of the provisions of the State Act.

243.ZQ. Offences and penalties.—(1) The Legislature of a State may, by law, make provisions for the offences relating to the co-operative societies and penalties for such offences.

(2) A law made by the Legislature of a State under clause (1) shall include the commission of the following act or omission as offences, namely:—

    (a) a co-operative society or an officer or member thereof wilfully makes a false return or furnishes false information, or any person wilfully not furnishes any information required from him by a person authorised in this behalf under the provisions of the State Act;

    (b) any person wilfully or without any reasonable excuse disobeys any summons, requisition or lawful written order issued under the provisions of the State Act;

    (c) any employer who, without sufficient cause, fails to pay to a co-operative society amount deducted by him from its employee within a period of fourteen days from the date on which such deduction is made;

    (d) any officer or custodian who wilfully fails to handover custody of books, accounts, documents, records, cash, security and other property belonging to a co-operative society of which he is an officer or custodian, to an authorised person; and

    (e) whoever, before, during or after the election of members of the board or office bearers, adopts any corrupt practice.

243ZR. Application to multi-State co-operative societies.—The provisions of this Part shall apply to the multi-State co-operative societies subject to the modification that any reference to "Legislature of a State", "State Act" or "State Government" shall be construed as a reference to "Parliament", "Central Act" or "the Central Government" respectively.

243ZS. Application to Union territories.—The provisions of this Part shall apply to the Union territories and shall, in their application to a Union territory, having no Legislative Assembly as if the references to the Legislature of a State were a reference to the administrator thereof appointed under article 239 and, in relation to a Union territory having a Legislative Assembly, to that Legislative Assembly:

Provided that the President may, by notification in the Official Gazette, direct that the provisions of this Part shall not apply to any Union territory or part thereof as he may specify in the notification.

243ZT. Continuance of existing laws.—Notwithstanding anything in this Part, any provision of any law relating to co-operative societies in force in a State immediately before the commencement of the Constitution (Ninety-seventh Amendment) Act, 2011, which is inconsistent with the provisions of this Part, shall continue to be in force until amended or repealed by a competent Legislature or other competent authority or until the expiration of one year from such commencement, whichever is less.]

PART X

THE SCHEDULED AND TRIBAL AREAS

244. Administration of Scheduled Areas and Tribal Areas.—(1) The provisions of the Fifth Schedule shall apply to the administration and control of the Scheduled Areas and Scheduled Tribes in any State [1][***] other than [2][the States of Assam [3][,[4][Meghalaya, Tripura and Mizoram]]].

(2) The provisions of the Sixth Schedule shall apply to the administration of the tribal areas in [5][the State of Assam, [3][[6][Meghalaya, Tripura and Mizoram]]].

[7][**244A. Formation of an autonomous State comprising certain tribal areas in Assam and creation of local Legislature or Council of Ministers or both therefor.**— (1) Notwithstanding anything in this Constitution, Parliament may, by law, form within the State of Assam an autonomous State comprising (whether wholly or in part) all or any of the tribal areas specified in [8][Part I] of the table appended to paragraph 20 of the Sixth Schedule and create therefor—

---

1. The words and letters "specified in Part A or Part B of the First Schedule" omitted by the Constitution (Seventh Amendment) Act, 1956, sec. 29 and Sch. (w.e.f. 1-11-1956).
2. The words "the States of Assam and Meghalaya" subs. by the North Eastern Areas (Reorganisation) Act, 1971 (81 of 1971), sec. 71(c)(i), for the words "the State of Assam" (w.e.f. 21-1-1972).
3. The words ", Meghalaya and Tripura" subs. by the Constitution (Forty-ninth Amendment) Act, 1984, sec. 2, for the words "and Meghalaya" (w.e.f. 1-4-1985).
4. The words "Meghalaya, Tripura and Mizoram" subs. by the State of Mizoram Act, 1986 (34 of 1986), sec. 39(d)(i), for the words "Meghalaya and Tripura" (w.e.f. 20-2-1987).
5. The words "the States of Assam and Meghalaya and the Union Territory of Mizoram" subs. by the North-Eastern Areas (Reorganisation) Act, 1971 (81 of 1971), sec. 71(c)(ii), for the words "the State of Assam" (w.e.f. 21-1-1972).
6. The words "Meghalaya, Tripura and Mizoram" subs. by the State of Mizoram Act, 1986 (34 of 1986), sec. 39(d)(ii), for the words "Meghalaya and Tripura and the Union Territory of Mizoram" (w.e.f. 20-2-1987).
7. Ins. by the Constitution (Twenty-second Amendment) Act, 1969, sec. 2 (w.e.f. 25-9-1969).
8. Subs. by the North Eastern Areas (Reorganisation) Act, 1971 (81 of 1971), sec. 71(d), for "Part A" (w.e.f. 21-1-1972).

(a) a body, whether elected or partly nominated and partly elected, to function as a Legislature for the autonomous State, or

(b) a Council of Ministers,

or both with such constitution, powers and functions, in each case, as may be specified in the law.

(2) Any such law as is referred to in clause (1) may, in particular,—

(a) specify the matters enumerated in the State List or the Concurrent List with respect to which the Legislature of the autonomous State shall have power to make laws for the whole or any part thereof, whether to the exclusion of the Legislature of the State of Assam or otherwise;

(b) define the matters with respect to which the executive power of the autonomous State shall extend;

(c) provide that any tax levied by the State of Assam shall be assigned to the autonomous State in so far as the proceeds thereof are attributable to the autonomous State;

(d) provide that any reference to a State in any article of this Constitution shall be construed as including a reference to the autonomous State; and

(e) make such supplemental, incidental and consequential provisions as may be deemed necessary.

(3) An amendment of any such law as aforesaid in so far as such amendment relates to any of the matters specified in sub-clause (a) or sub-clause (b) of clause (2) shall have no effect unless the amendment is passed in each House of Parliament by not less than two-thirds of the members present and voting.

(4) Any such law as is referred to in this article shall not be deemed to be an amendment of this Constitution for the purposes of article 368 notwithstanding that it contains any provision which amends or has the effect of amending this Constitution.]

PART XI

RELATIONS BETWEEN THE UNION AND THE STATES

CHAPTER I

LEGISLATIVE RELATIONS

Distribution of Legislative Powers

245. Extent of laws made by Parliament and by the Legislatures of States.—(1) Subject to the provisions of this Constitution, Parliament may make laws for the whole or any part of the territory of India, and the Legislature of a State may make laws for the whole or any part of the State.

(2) No law made by Parliament shall be deemed to be invalid on the ground that it would have extra-territorial operation.

Notes on Article 245

Conditional Legislation

Where an authority is empowered to exercise the power of conditional legislation, then the duty to hear affected parties does not exist, if the delegate has to act on subjective satisfaction. But such duty exists if he has to be objectively satisfied; *State of Tamil Nadu v. K. Sabanayagam,* AIR 1998 SC 344: 1997 AIR SCW 4325: (1998) 1 SCC 318: 1998 SCC (L&S) 260: 1998 (2) SCJ 373: 1998 (1) SCT 354: (1997) 7 SCALE 170: 1997 (10) Supreme 324.

Conflict between Statutes

One of two Acts of parliament enacted under List I Entry 66 and the other under List III Entry 25 cannot be repugnant to each other; *Anamalai University* v. *Secretary of Govt. Inf. and Tourism Department*, (2009) 4 SCC 590.

Constitutional Validity of Law

The Constitutional validity of law is to be decided as per societal conditions prevalent at relevant time. The changed social psyche and expectations are important factors to be considered in upkeep of law; *Anuj Garg* v. *Hotel Association of India*, AIR 2008 SC 663: 2007 AIR SCW 7772: 2008 (2) All MR 59 (NOC): ILR 2008 Kant (SC) 697: (2008) 3 SCC 1: 2008 (1) SCT 80: (2007) 13 SCALE 762; *Addl. Distt. Magistrate, Jabalpur* v. *Shivakant Shukla*, AIR 1976 SC 1207: (1976) 2 SCC 521: 1976 Cr LJ 945: 1976 UJ (SC) 610: 1976 SC Cr R 277: 1976 SCC (Cri) 448: 1976 Cr App R (SC) 298: (1976) 3 SCR 929: 1976 Supp SCR 172.

Excessive Delegation

Where the rule-making authority gives to itself the power to prescribe criteria and procedure for certain specific situations, there is no question of excessive delegation. (In fact, there is no delegation at all, in such cases); *Arun Tewari* v. *Zila Mansavi Shikshak Sangh*, AIR 1998 SC 331: 1997 AIR SCW 4310: JT 1997 (9) SC 593: 1998 (1) Jab LJ 114: (1998) 2 SCC 332: 1998 SCC (L&S) 541: 1998 (1) SCT 533: (1997) 7 SCALE 461: 1997 (10) Supreme 281.

For the meaning and scope of delegated legislation see *Agricultural Market Committee* v. *Shalimar Chemical Works Ltd.*, AIR 1997 SC 2502: (1997) 5 SCC 516: 1997 AIR SCW 2443: 1997 (3) APLJ 10: JT 1997 (5) SC 272: (1997) 4 SCALE 93: 1997 (4) Supreme 575.

The power to alter the applicability of the Act, by amending the Schedule, according to the change in local conditions, may be delegated, provided standards for guidance are provided in the Act; *Kishan* v. *State of Rajasthan*, AIR 1990 SC 2269: 1990 Supp SCC 742: (1990) 183 ITR 433, paragraph 4.

The Legislature may leave it to the judgment of a local administrative body as to the necessity of applying or introducing the Act in a local area, or the determination of a contingency or even, upon the happening of which the legislative provisions are made to operate; this is known as conditional legislation; *Orient Paper and Industries Ltd.* v. *State of Orissa*, AIR 1991 SC 672: (1991) Supp 1 SCC 81: JT 1990 (4) SC 267: (1991) 1 UJ (SC) 75, paragraphs 27-29.

Incidental Provisions

While enacting a law in exercise of a particular legislative power, the legislature may make all incidental and ancillary provisions to make the law effective, but it would not extend to purposes which are not ancillary; *Tinsukhia Electric Supply Co. Ltd.* v. *State of Assam*, AIR 1990 SC 123: (1989) 3 SCC 709: JT 1989 (2) SC 217: (1989) 45 Taxman 29: (1989) 2 Comp LJ 377, paragraph 129.

But taxation is not an ancillary power and cannot be deduced from a regulatory law; *Synthetics & Chemicals Ltd.* v. *State of Uttar Pradesh*, (1990) 1 SCC 109: AIR 1990 SC 1927: JT 1989 (4) SC 267.

Legislation as the will of the People

An Act of the legislature represents the will of the people and cannot be lightly declared as unconstitutional; *State of Bihar* v. *Bihar Distillery Ltd.*, AIR 1997 SC 1511: (1997) 2 SCC 453: 1997 AIR SCW 259: 1997 (2) BLJ 640: 1997 (1) BLJR 551: JT 1996 (10) SC 854: 1997 (1) Supreme 121, paragraph 18.

Legislation Overriding Decision

Legislature can render a judicial decision by enacting a valid law—even retrospectively. But it cannot declare a particular judgment of the court as invalid as that would amount to exercise of judicial power; *S.S. Bola* v. *B.D. Sardana*, AIR 1997 SC 3127: (1997) 8 SCC 522: 1997 AIR SCW 3172: 1997 (5) SCJ 278: 1997 (3) SCT 645: (1997) 5 SCALE 90: 1997 (7) Supreme 427.

Legislative Competence of State

It is within legislative competence of State of Maharashtra to enact provisions of "promoting insurgency" in section 2(1)(e) of MCOCA under Entries 1 and 2 of List II read with Entries 1, 2 and 12 of List III of Seventh Schedule of Constitution; *Zameer Ahmed Latifur Rehman Sheikh* v. *State of Maharashtra*, AIR 2010 SC 2633.

Legislative Powers of Parliament and State Legislatures

Legislative power under the Indian Constitution is subject to the following limitations:—

(a) The federal scheme of distribution of legislative powers.

(b) Fundamental rights and other provisions of the Constitution, as to what laws can be passed.

(c) Constitutional provisions as to prior sanction or subsequent approval of the President or Governor in respect of certain Bills.

(d) The rule that a State Legislature cannot legislate extra-territorially—though Parliament does not suffer from this limitation, by virtue of article 245(2).

(e) The doctrine that the Legislature cannot delegate matters of policy.

(f) The doctrine that the legislation must not be a fraud on the Constitution.

(g) The doctrine that the legislature must make a 'law'. Its function is not adjudicatory nor executive, but only legislative.

Limitation (a) above flows from article 246.

Limitation (b) above flows from articles 12 and 13.

Limitation (c) above flows (i) from the general doctrine that all authority and power must be exercised in conformity with the Constitution, and (ii) from the words 'Subject to the provisions of this Constitution' in article 245(1).

Limitation (d) above flows from the words 'for the whole or any of the State' in article 245(1) (as regards state Legislatures). *See* the undermentioned cases:

(i) *State of Bihar* v. *Charusila Dasi*, AIR 1959 SC 1002: (1959) Supp 2 SCR 601: (1959) 2 SCA 369: 1959 SCJ 1193: 1959 BLJR 785: 1960 Pat LR (SC) 1.

(ii) *Tata Iron & Steel Co.* v. *State of Bihar*, AIR 1958 SC 452: 1958 SCR 1355: (1958) 9 STC 267.

Limitation (e) above flows from the general principle that power given to a body by the Constitution must, in its essentials, be exercised by that body only.

Limitation (f) flows from another principle that all constitutional and statutory powers must be exercised for the purpose for which they are intended. This aspect has been discussed exhaustively in; *Dr. D.C. Wadhwa* v. *State of Bihar*, AIR 1987 SC 579: (1987) 1 SCC 378: JT 1987 (1) SC 70: 1986 (4) Supreme 465: 1987 BBCJ (SC) 46: 1987 IJR 116, paragraph 3. *See* also *Poona City Municipal Corporation* v. *Dattatraya Nagesh Deodhar*, AIR 1965 SC 555: (1964) 8 SCR 178: 1965 MPLJ 69: 1965 Mah LJ 105: (1965) 1 SCWR 221: 1965 (1) SCJ 626.

Limitation (g) above flows from interpretation of the word 'law' occurring in article 245(1), which confers the power to make 'laws'. On this point, *see* the undermentioned cases:

(i) *Basanta* v. *Emperor*, AIR 1944 FC 86.

(ii) *Indira Nehru Gandhi* v. *Raj Narain*, AIR 1975 SC 2299: 1975 Supp SCC 1: (1976) 2 SCR 347.

(iii) *Misri Lal* v. *State of Orissa*, AIR 1977 SC 1686: (1977) 3 SCC 212: (1977) 3 SCR 714.

(iv) *Government of Andhra Pradesh* v. *Hindustan Machine Tools Ltd.*, AIR 1975 SC 2037: (1975) 2 SCC 274: (1975) 1 APLJ (SC) 41: 1975 Tax LR 2013: (1975) 2 SCWR 293: 1975 Supp SCR 394.

(v) *Municipal Corporation of the City of Ahmedabad* v. *New Shrock Spg. and Wvg. Co. Ltd.*, AIR 1970 SC 1292: (1970) 2 SCC 280: (1971) 1 SCR 288.

(vi) *Tirath Ram* v. *State of Uttar Pradesh*, AIR 1973 SC 405: (1973) 3 SCC 585: 1973 Tax LR 1951: (1973) 2 CTR 123 (SC).

Motive of Legislature

If the legislature is competent to make a particular law, its motive in enacting it, or the fact that the law would operate harshly on some persons, or that it failed to enact a connected legislation, is irrelevant; *Ashok* v. *Union of India*, AIR 1991 SC 1792: (1991) 3 SCC 498: (1991) 3 Crimes 185: 1991 Cr LJ 2483, paragraph 6.

Power of Legislature

Power of a legislature to enact a law with a reference to a topic entrusted to it, is, unqualified subject only to any limitation imposed by the Constitution. In the exercise of such a power, it will be competent for the legislative to enact a law, which is either prospective or retrospective. Uttar Pradesh Tea Validation Act, 1958 is not *ultra vires* the powers of the legislative under entry 54, for the reasons that it operates retrospectively, *J.K. Jute Mills Co. Ltd.* v. *State of Uttar Pradesh*, AIR 1961 SC 1534: 1961 (12) STC 429: (1962) 2 SCR 1.

Under the Constitutional scheme the Parliament exercises sovereign power to enact laws and no outside power or authority can issue a direction to enact a particular piece of legislation; *Union of India* v. *Prakash P. Hinduja*, AIR 2003 SC 2562: (2003) 6 SCC 195: 2003 SCC (Cri) 1314.

Rule-making Power

The State's power to make rules under a Central Act extends only to the extent provided for under the Central Act; *V.V.S. Rama Sharma* v. *State of Uttar Pradesh*, (2009) 7 SCC 234.

Sub-judice

If a legislature has the power to amend a provision, there is nothing colourable if it uses that power during the pendency of a writ petition challenging the validity of that provision in order to avoid possible adverse verdict in that writ petition; *Hotel Balaji* v. *State of Andhra Pradesh*, AIR 1993 SC 1048: (1993) Supp 4 SCC 536: (1993) 88 STC 98, paragraph 32.

Transgression of Limits of Power by Legislature

In a federal Constitution, transgression of its limits of power by a legislature may be (i) open, direct and overt, or (ii) disguised, indirect and covert. The latter is called 'colourable legislation'. Entries in the seventh Schedule should be construed so as to avoid conflict. On applying this test the Expenditure Tax Act is not colourable legislation. It is within the competence of Parliament; *Federation of Hotel and Restaurant* v. *Union of India*, AIR 1990 SC 1637: (1989) 3 SCC 634: (1989) 178 ITR 97: (1989) 74 STC 102.

Validating Act

Legislature may validate an unlawful executive Act, including an unauthorised assessment of tax, and with retrospective effect, subject to constitutional limitation; *Yadlapati Venkateswarlu* v. *State of Andhra Pradesh*, AIR 1991 SC 704: (1992) Supp 1 SCC 74: 1991 (190) ITR 375: JT 1990 (4) SC 19, paragraph 7.

246. Subject-matter of laws made by Parliament and by the Legislatures of States.—(1) Notwithstanding anything in clauses (2) and (3), Parliament has exclusive power to make laws with respect to any of the matters enumerated in List I in the Seventh Schedule (in this Constitution referred to as the "Union List").

(2) Notwithstanding anything in clause (3), Parliament and, subject to clause (1), the Legislature of any State [1][***] also, have power to make laws with respect to any of the matters enumerated in List III in the Seventh Schedule (in this Constitution referred to as the "Concurrent List").

(3) Subject to clauses (1) and (2), the Legislature of any State [1][***] has exclusive power to make laws for such State or any part thereof with respect to any of the matters enumerated in List II in the Seventh Schedule (in this Constitution referred to as the 'State List').

---

1. The words and letters "specified in Part A or Part B of the First Schedule" omitted by the Constitution (Seventh Amendment) Act, 1956, sec. 29 and Sch. (w.e.f. 1-11-1956).

(4) Parliament has power to make laws with respect to any matter for any part of the territory of India not included ¹[in a State] notwithstanding that such matter is a matter enumerated in the State List.

Notes on Article 246

Co-operative Societies

Under State List, Entry 32, legislation can be passed for providing for nomination by Government of the Chairman and members of the Committee of Management of co-operative societies. It is open to the State to legislate on any or all aspects of co-operative societies including their managements; *Sheetal Prasad Gupta* v. *State of Bihar*, AIR 1990 Pat 64: 1990 (1) Pat LJR 133 (FB).

Doctrine of Pith and Substance

In no field of constitutional law is the comparative approach more useful than in regard to the doctrine of pith and substance. This is a doctrine which has come to be established in India and derives its genesis from the approach adopted by the courts (including the Privy Council) in dealing with controversies arising in other federations. Briefly stated, what the doctrine means is this. Where the question arises of determining whether a particular law relates to a particular subject mentioned in one list or another, the court looks to the substance of the matter. Thus, if the substance falls within Union List, then the incidental encroachment by the law on the State List does not make it invalid. This principle had come to be established by the Privy Council when it determined appeals from Canada or Australia involving the question of legislative competence of the federation or the States in those countries. In India, the doctrine came to be established in the pre-independence period under the Government of India Act, 1935. The classical example is the Privy Council judgment in *Prafulla* v. *Bank of Commerce*, AIR 1947 PC 60, holding that a State law dealing with money lending (a State subject) is not invalid merely because it incidentally affects promissory notes (Union List, entry 46). The doctrine is sometimes expressed in terms of ascertaining the true character of legislation and it is also emphasised that the name given by the Legislature to the legislation in the short title is immaterial. Again, for applying the doctrine of pith and substance, regard is to be had (i) to the enactment as a whole, (ii) to its main objects, and (iii) to the scope and effect of its provisions—

The undermentioned decisions illustrate the above proposition:

(i) *Southern Pharmaceuticals & Chemicals, Trichur* v. *State of Kerala*, AIR 1981 SC 1863: (1981) 4 SCC 391: 1981 Tax LR 2838: (1982) 1 SCR 519, paragraph 15 (Incidental encroachment to be disregarded).

(ii) *Prem* v. *Chhabra*, (1984) 2 SCC 302: 1984 SCC (Cri) 233: 1984 Cr LJ 668, paragraph 8.

(iii) *State of Rajasthan* v. *Chawla*, AIR 1959 SC 544 (547): (1959) Supp 1 SCR 904: 1959 Cr LJ 660.

(iv) *Amar Singh* v. *State of Rajasthan*, (1955) 2 SCR 803 (extent of invasion immaterial).

(v) *Delhi Cloth and General Mills Co. Ltd.* v. *Union of India*, AIR 1983 SC 937: (1983) 9 SCC 166: 1983 Tax LR 2584: (1983) 2 Comp LJ 281: 1983 UJ (SC) 699: (1983) 54 Comp Cas 674, paragraph 33 (Incidental encroachment immaterial).

(vi) *United Provinces* v. *Atiqua Begum*, AIR 1941 FC 16.

No question of conflict between two lists will arise if the impugned legislation by the application of the doctrine of 'pith and substance' appears to fall exclusively under one list, and the encroachment upon another list is only incidental; *B. Viswanathiah & Co.* v. *State of Karnataka*, (1991) 3 SCC 358: 1991 AIR SCW 455, paragraph 9.

In every case where the legislative competence of a Legislature in regard to a particular enactment is challenged with reference to the entries in the various lists, it is necessary to examine the pith and substance of the Act and to find out if the matter comes substantially

---

1. Subs. by the Constitution (Seventh Amendment) Act, 1956, sec. 29 and Sch., for "in Part A or Part B of the First Schedule" (w.e.f. 1-11-1956).

within an item in the list. The express words employed in an entry would necessarily include incidental and ancillary matters so as to make the legislation effective; *Welfare Assocn. A.R.P., Maharashtra* v. *Ranjit P. Gohil*, AIR 2003 SC 1266: 2003 AIR SCW 1663: JT 2003 (2) SC 335: (2003) 9 SCC 358: (2003) 2 SCR 139: 2003 (4) SRJ 381: (2003) 2 SCALE 288.

Effect of Declaration

Even when Parliament makes a declaration under Entry 52 of List 1 that the control of a particular industry by the Union is expedient in the public interest, the State Legislature shall retain its power to legislate in regard to the raw materials used in that industry; *B. Viswanathiah & Co.* v. *State of Karnataka*, (1991) 3 SCC 358: 1991 AIR SCW 455, paragraph 6 (3 Judge Bench).

Even when Parliament legislates under Entry 7 or 52 of List I, the exclusion of the State Legislature is not total, it would be confined only to those aspects of the industry which are brought under the control of the Union by the relevant legislation; *Orissa Cement Ltd.* v. *State of Orissa*, (1991) Supp 1 SCC 430: AIR 1991 SC 1676: 1991 AIR SCW 1375: 1991 (34) ECR 497: (1991) 2 SCR 105: (1991) Supp 1 SCC 430, paragraphs 42 and 43.

Effect of the Words 'subject to'

When one Entry is made subject to another Entry, it means that out of the scope of the former Entry, a field of legislation covered by the latter Entry has been reserved to be specially dealt with by the appropriate Legislature; *Mahabir Prasad Jalan* v. *State of Bihar*, AIR 1991 Pat 40: (1991) 2 BLJR 915: 1991 BBCJ 227, paragraph 46.

Entry of Goods

State Legislature cannot levy taxes on the entry of goods into local area which are not meant for consumption, use or sale therein. If in the exercise of its authority, the State Legislature uses wide words, such words are construed in such a manner that it is held that the State Legislature had intended to restrict those words and phrases in their meaning within the parameters of the competence of the State Legislature. The State Legislature cannot empower municipal committees to levy tax, only on the entry of goods within the local areas, when those goods are not meant for consumption, sale or use within that area; *Indian Oil Corporation* v. *Municipal Corporation, Jullunder*, AIR 1990 P&H 99: 1989 (2) Land LR 192.

Essential Commodities

Our legislation in relation to essential commodities illustrates the position. What is an essential commodity has to be determined not merely from the terms of the Essential Commodities Act, 1955, but also with reference to section 2(a)(xi) read with notifications issued thereunder from time to time, section 2(a)(xi) provides as under:

> Any other class of commodity which the Central Government may, by notified order declare to be an essential commodity for the purposes of this Act, being a commodity with respect to which Parliament has power to make laws by virtue of Entry 33 in List III in the Seventh Schedule of the Constitution.

Thus, for determining the scope of the Act, one has to refer to the entry in this Constitution relating to the subject. Now, the Constitution, in the Concurrent List, Entry 33, provides as under:

Trade and Commerce in, and the production, supply and distribution of,—

> The products of any industry where the control of such industry by the Union is declared by Parliament by law to be expedient in the public interest, and imported goods of the same kind as such products.

It may further be mentioned that section 2 of the Industries (Development and Regulation) Act, 1951 declares that it is expedient in the public interest that the Union should take under its control the commodities specified in the schedule to the Act, which includes cement. On this basis the Delhi High Court in *Trans Yamuna Cement Dealers Association* v. *Lt. Governor of Delhi*, AIR 1988 Del 247: 1988 Raj LR 134: (1988) 21 Reports 537: (1988) 14 DRJ 275: (1988) 25 STL 25, has held that the Delhi Cement and Licensing and Control Order, 1982 is valid.

Industries

The power of the State Legislature as regards industries other than those falling under the Union List is exclusive; *B. Viswanathiah & Co.* v. *State of Karnataka*, (1991) 3 SCC 358: 1991 AIR SCW 455, paragraphs 6 and 8.

Legislative List: Entries

Entries in the legislative lists are to be construed according to pith and substance. Bombay Money-Lenders Act, 1946 is enacted under the State List, Entry 30 relating to "Money-lending and money-lenders; relief of agricultural indebtedness". It does not fall within Union List, Entry 46 (Bills of Exchange, etc.); *Bhanushankar Jatashankar Bhatt* v. *Kamal Tara Builders Pvt. Ltd.*, AIR 1990 Bom 140 (141): 1989 Mah LJ 440: (1989) 2 Bom CR 526: 1989 Mah LR 1526 (DB).

As observed by the Supreme Court in *Ujagar Prints (II)* v. *Union of India*, AIR 1989 SC 516: (1989) 3 SCC 488: (1989) 179 ITR 317: (1989) 74 STC 401, paragraph 23:

> Entries in the legislative lists, it may be recalled, are not sources of the legislative power, but are merely topics or fields or legislation and must receive a liberal construction inspired by a broad and generous spirit and not in a narrow pedantic sense. The expression with respect to article 246 brings in the doctrine of pith and substance in the understanding of the exertion of the legislative power and wherever the question of legislative competence is raised, the test is whether the legislation looked at as a whole is substantially with respect to the particular topic of legislation. If the legislation has a substantial and not merely a remote connection with the entry, the matter may well be taken to be legislation on the topic.

Mala Fides

Under the unamended Income Tax Act, 1961 the Legislature had already classified Income Tax Officer into grades and given power to Government to appoint and sanction their appointments. The amendment of 1987 redesignated these posts and made certain other provisions. It was held that it can hardly be argued that the amended Act was passed *mala fide* to destroy the cause of action in the present petitions. This is apart from the fact that no legislation can be challenged on the ground that it is *mala fide*; *Hundraj Kanyalal Sajnani* v. *Union of India*, AIR 1990 SC 1106: 1990 Supp SCC 577: 1990 Lab IC 890.

Mines

Union List, Entry 54 reads "Regulation of mines and mineral development to the extent to which such regulation and development under the control of the Union is declared by Parliament by law to be expedient in the public interest. Such a law was passed in 1957—The Mines and Minerals (Regulation and Development) Act, 1957. The Act of 1957 covers all mineral oils, including minor. State List, Entry 23 reads—"Regulation of mines and mineral development, subject to the provisions of List I with respect to regulation and development under the control of the Union". Any legislation by the State after such declaration by Parliament is unconstitutional, because that field is abstracted from the legislative competence of the State Legislature; *Nanjanayaka* v. *State of Karnataka*, AIR 1990 Kant 97 (103, 104): (1989) 2 Kant LJ 202, paragraphs 10-13. *See* the undermentioned cases:

    (i) *Baijnath Kedia* v. *State of Bihar*, AIR 1970 SC 1436 (1443, 1444, 1445): (1969) 3 SCC 838: (1969) 2 SCA 335: 1970 (1) SCJ 913: (1970) 2 SCR 100: 1970 Pat LJR 661 (reviews case law).

    (ii) *State of Tamil Nadu* v. *Hind Stone*, AIR 1981 SC 711: (1981) 2 SCC 205: (1981) 2 SCR 742.

Preventive Detention

With reference to legislative entries relating to preventive detention (Union List, Entry 9 and Concurrent List 1, Entry 3) the expressions (i) 'security of State' and 'security of India' are different expressions. It has been held that Parliament can enact legislation for preventive detention of smugglers (COFEPOSA) and for the forfeiture of assets obtained by smuggling; *Attorney-General of India* v. *Amratlal Pranjivandas*, JT 1994 (3) SC 583: (1994) 5 SCC 54: AIR 1994 SC 2179.

Construing Union List, Entry 66, Supreme Court has held that the University. Grants Commission has jurisdiction to coordinate and maintain standards of higher education. The Regulation of 1991, made under section 26 of the University Grants Commission Act, 1956 regarding qualifications for teachers was held to be valid; *University of Delhi* v. *Raj Singh*, JT 1994 (6) SC 1: (1994) Supp 3 SCC 576: (1994) 28 ATC 541: AIR 1995 SC 336.

Reconciliation

It should be considered whether a fair reconciliation cannot be effected by giving to the language of the Union Legislative List a meaning which, if less wide than it might in another context bear, is yet one that can properly be given to it and equally giving to the language of the State Legislative list a meaning which it can properly bear; *Federation of Hotel and Restaurant* v. *Union of India*, AIR 1990 SC 1637: (1989) 3 SCC 634: (1989) 178 ITR 97: (1989) 74 STC 102, paragraph 12 (CB).

Stamp Duties

Article 25(b) of the Bombay Stamp Act, 1958 (as amended in 1985), which levies stamp duty on documents of transfer of shares in co-operative societies, falls within concurrent list, entry 44 (Stamp duties—but not including rates of stamp duty and State List, Entry 63) Rates of stamp duty in respect of document other than those specified in the provision of List 1 with regard to rates of stamp duty. It is therefore within the competence of the State Legislature. In any case the Act has received the assent of President and its validity cannot be questioned. *See* the undermentioned cases:

Hanuman Vitamins Foods Pvt. Ltd. v. *State of Maharashtra*, AIR 1990 Bom 204 (207, 208): 1989 Bank J 377: 1989 Mah LJ 935: (1989) 2 Bom CR 460 (DB), paragraphs 5 and 6 following; *Bar Council of Uttar Pradesh* v. *State of Uttar Pradesh*, AIR 1973 SC 231: (1973) 1 SCC 261: (1973) 2 SCR 1073, paragraph 12.

247. Power of Parliament to provide for the establishment of certain additional courts.—Notwithstanding anything in this Chapter, Parliament may by law provide for the establishment of any additional courts for the better administration of laws made by Parliament or of any existing laws with respect to a matter enumerated in the Union List.

248. Residuary powers of legislation.—(1) Parliament has exclusive power to make any law with respect to any matter not enumerated in the Concurrent List or State List.

(2) Such power shall include the power of making any law imposing a tax not mentioned in either of those Lists.

Notes on Article 248

Constitutionality of

The nature of the wealth tax imposed under the Wealth-tax Act, as originally stood, was different from that of a tax under Entry 49, List II, and it did not fall under this entry. However, assuming that the Wealth-tax Act, a originally enacted, is held to be legislation under Entry 86, List I, there is nothing in the Constitution to prevent Parliament from combining its powers under Entry 86, List I with its powers under Entry 97, List I; *Union of India* v. *Harbhajan Singh Dhillon*, AIR 1972 SC 1061: (1971) 2 SCC 779: (1972) 2 SCR 33: (1972) 83 ITR 582.

249. Power of Parliament to legislate with respect to a matter in the State List in the national interest.—(1) Notwithstanding anything in the foregoing provisions of this Chapter, if the Council of States has declared by resolution supported by not less than two-thirds of the members present and voting that it is necessary or expedient in national interest that Parliament should make laws with respect to any matter enumerated in the State List specified in the resolution, it shall be lawful for Parliament to make laws for the whole or any part of the territory of India with respect to that matter while the resolution remains in force.

(2) A resolution passed under clause (1) shall remain in force for such period not exceeding one year as may be specified therein:

Provided that, if and so often as a resolution approving the continuance in force of any such resolution is passed in the manner provided in clause (1), such resolution shall continue in force for a further period of one year from the date on which under this clause it would otherwise have ceased to be in force.

(3) A law made by Parliament which Parliament would not but for the passing of a resolution under clause (1) have been competent to make shall, to the extent of the incompetency, cease to have effect on the expiration of a period of six months after the resolution has ceased to be in force, except as respects things done or omitted to be done before the expiration of the said period.

250. Power of Parliament to legislate with respect to any matter in the State List if a Proclamation of Emergency is in operation.—(1) Notwithstanding anything in this Chapter, Parliament shall, while a Proclamation of Emergency is in operation, have, power to make laws for the whole or any part of the territory of India with respect to any of the matters enumerated in the State List.

(2) A law made by Parliament which Parliament would not but for the issue of a Proclamation of Emergency have been competent to make shall, to the extent of the incompetency, cease to have effect on the expiration of a period of six months after the Proclamation has ceased to operate, except as respects things done or omitted to be done before the expiration of the said period.

251. Inconsistency between laws made by Parliament under articles 249 and 250 and laws made by the Legislatures of States.—Nothing in articles 249 and 250 shall restrict the power of the Legislature of a State to make any law which under this Constitution it has power to make, but if any provision of a law made by the legislature of a State is repugnant to any provision of a law made by Parliament which Parliament has under either of the said articles power to make, the law made by Parliament, whether passed before or after the law made by the legislature of the State, shall prevail, and the law made by the Legislature of the State shall to the extent of the repugnancy, but so long only as the law made by Parliament continues to have effect, be inoperative.

252. Power of Parliament to legislate for two or more States by consent and adoption of such legislation by any other State.—(1) If it appears to the Legislatures of two or more States to be desirable that any of the matters with respect to which Parliament has no power to make laws for the States except as provided in articles 249 and 250 should be regulated in such States by Parliament by law, and if resolutions to that effect are passed by all the Houses of the Legislatures of those States, it shall be lawful for Parliament to pass an Act for regulating that matter accordingly, and any Act so passed shall apply to such States and to any other State by which it is adopted afterwards by resolution passed in that behalf by the House or, where there are two Houses, by each of the Houses of the Legislature of that State.

(2) Any Act so passed by Parliament may be amended or repealed by an Act of Parliament passed or adopted in like manner but shall not, as respects any State to which it applies, be amended or repealed by an Act of the Legislature of that State.

Notes on Article 252

The article makes it possible for Parliament to make such laws relating to State subjects as regards such States whose legislatures empower Parliament in this behalf by resolutions. Passing of the resolutions is a condition precedent for vesting the power in Parliament.

When only a distinct and separate part of a State Entry is transferred by the resolutions, the State Legislatures do not lose their power to legislate with respect to the rest of that Entry; *Krishna Bhimrao Deshpande* v. *Land Tribunal, Dharwad*, AIR 1993 SC 883: (1993) 1 SCC 287: 1992 AIR SCW 3407: 1993 Bom CJ 576: JT 1992 (6) SC 149: 1992 (3) SCJ 693, paragraph 3.

253. Legislation for giving effect to international agreements.—Notwithstanding anything in the foregoing provisions of this Chapter, Parliament has power to make any law for the whole or any part of the territory of India for implementing any treaty, agreement or convention with any other country or countries or any decision made at any international conference, association or other body.

254. Inconsistency between laws made by Parliament and laws made by the Legislatures of States.—(1) If any provision of a law made by the Legislature of a State is repugnant to any provision of a law made by Parliament which Parliament is competent to enact, or to any provision of an existing law with respect to one of the matters enumerated in the Concurrent List, then, subject to the provisions of clause (2), the law made by Parliament, whether passed before or after the law made by the Legislature of such State, or, as the case may be, the existing law, shall prevail and the law made by the Legislature of the State shall, to the extent of the repugnancy, be void.

(2) Where a law made by the Legislature of a State [1][***] with respect to one of the matters enumerated in the Concurrent List contains any provision repugnant to the provisions of an earlier law made by Parliament or an existing law with respect to that matter, then, the law so made by the Legislature of such State shall, if it has been reserved for the consideration of the President and has received his assent, prevail in that State:

Provided that nothing in this clause shall prevent Parliament from enacting at any time any law with respect to the same matter including a law adding to, amending, varying or repealing the law so made by the Legislature of the State.

Notes on Article 254

Article 254 contains mechanism for resolution of conflict between central and state legislations enacted with respect to any matter enumerated in List III of 7th Schedule of Constitution; *Central Bank of India* v. *State of Kerala*, (2009) 4 SCC 94.

The operation of article 254 is not complex. The real problem that in practice arises is the problem of determining whether a particular State law is repugnant to a Central Act. A number of judicial decisions (noted below) give guidance as to when repugnancy arises. The important rulings are:

(i) *Zaverbhai* v. *State of Bombay*, AIR 1954 SC 752: (1955) 1 SCR 799: 1954 Cr LJ 1822.

(ii) *Tika Ramji* v. *State of Uttar Pradesh*, (1956) SCR 393: AIR 1956 SC 676: 1956 SCA 979: 1956 SCJ 625: 1956 All WR (HC) 657.

(iii) *Municipal Corporation* v. *Shiv Shankar*, AIR 1971 SC 815: (1971) 1 SCC 442: 1971 Cr LJ 680.

(iv) *M. Karunanidhi* v. *Union of India*, AIR 1979 SC 898: (1979) 3 SCC 431: 1979 Cr LJ 773.

(v) *Western Coalfields Ltd.* v. *Special Area Development Authority, Korba*, AIR 1982 SC 697: (1982) 1 SCC 125: 1982 (2) SCJ 1: (1982) 2 Comp LJ 793.

(vi) *Raghubir* v. *State of Haryana*, AIR 1981 SC 2037: (1981) 4 SCC 210: 1981 Cr LJ 1497.

Repugnancy

A Tamil Nadu Act which is repugnant to section 10A of the Indian Medical Council Act, 1956 is void as repugnant to the latter. The latter Act covers the entire field for establishing new

---

1. The words and letters "specified in Part A or Part B of the First Schedule" omitted by the Constitution (Seventh Amendment) Act, 1956, sec. 29 and Sch. (w.e.f. 1-11-1956).

medical colleges, leaving no scope for State-legislation; *Thirumuruga Kirupananda Variyar Thavathiru Sundara Swamigal Medical Educational and Charitable Trust* v. *State of Tamil Nadu*, AIR 1996 SC 2384: (1996) 3 SCC 15: 1996 AIR SCW 926: JT 1996 (2) SC 692: 1996 (2) Mad LJ 10: (1996) 2 SCR 422.

Section 48(8) of the Karnataka Land Reforms Act, 1961 (as amended in 1974) prohibited the legal practitioners from appearing in proceedings before land tribunals. It was held to be repugnant to section 30 of the Advocates Act, 1961 and section 14 of the Bar Council Act, 1926. The Supreme Court held that Union List, Entries 77 and 78 are concerned with persons entitled to practice before the Supreme Court and High Court and these entries have been construed in; *O.N. Mohindroo* v. *Bar Council of Delhi*, AIR 1968 SC 888: (1968) 2 SCR 709: (1968) 1 SCA 618: (1968) 1 SCWR 986: 1968 Ker LJ 373: 1968 SCD 605: 1968 (2) SCJ 448 as applied in *Jaswant Kaur* v. *State of Haryana*, AIR 1977 P&H 221: 1977 Punj LJ 230: 1977 Cur LJ (Civ) 324: 1977 Rev LR 418: ILR (1977) 2 P&H 116, as regulating all aspects of the rights of advocates; *H.S. Srinivasa Raghavachar* v. *State of Karnataka*, (1987) 2 SCC 692: AIR 1987 SC 1518: JT 1987 (4) SC 26: ILR 1987 Kant 2059: 1987 (1) Supreme 642: 1987 (2) SCJ 611: (1987) 2 UJ (SC) 427: 1987 (2) Land LR 530.

The test of 'pith and substance' has been applied to determine whether the State law has *substantially* transgressed on the field occupied by the law of Parliament. There is no 'repugnance' where the encroachment is not substantial, or the subject-matter of the legislation is not the same; *State of Uttar Pradesh* v. *Synthetics and Chemicals Ltd.*, (1991) 4 SCC 139: JT 1991 (3) SC 268, paragraphs 18 and 28.

If the State Legislature enacts a law which is not covered by its exclusive List II but relates to a subject included in List-I, it is a patent case of *ultra vires*, because of article 246. It is beyond the competence of the State Legislature under clause (2) and pertains to the *exclusive* jurisdiction of Parliament under clause (1) of article 246; *Orissa Cement Ltd.* v. *State of Orissa*, (1991) Supp 1 SCC 430: AIR 1991 SC 1676: 1991 AIR SCW 1375: 1991 (34) ECR 497: (1991) 2 SCR 105, paragraph 61.

Union and State Legislation

The scheme of distribution of legislative powers under the Indian Constitution—such distribution being a necessary component of a federal political structure—raises interesting issues where the co-existence of Central and State laws in a particular area give rise to litigation. Such problem arises either because the Union or a State may illegally encroach upon the province of the other parallel legislature or it may arise because though there is no encroachment as such on each other's sphere, yet, the two laws clash with each other. The two situations are, strictly speaking, different from each other and they must be judged by two different tests. Where the subject-matter of the legislation in question falls within either the Union List or the State List only, the question is to be decided with reference to legislative competence. One of the two laws must necessarily be void because leaving aside matters in the Concurrent List, the Indian Constitution confers exclusive jurisdiction upon Parliament for matters in the Union List and upon a State Legislature for matters in the State List. The correct doctrine applicable is that of *ultra vires*.

The above is a case of exclusive jurisdiction and since one of the two laws must be void, the question of inconsistency between the two has no application. Only one law will survive and other law will not survive. In contrast, where the legislation passed by the Union and the State is on a subject-matter included in the Concurrent List, then the matter cannot be determined by applying the test of *ultra vires* because the hypothesis is that both the laws are constitutionally valid. In such a case, the test to be adopted will be that or repugnancy under article 254(2). It follows that it is only where the legislation is on a matter in the Concurrent List that it would be relevant to apply the test of repugnancy. Notwithstanding the contrary view expressed by some authors, this is the correct position. Such a view was expressed by Dr. D. Basu in his Commentary on the Constitution of India (1950), page 564 and it is this view that has been upheld by the Supreme Court in the undermentioned decisions:

    (i) *Deep Chand* v. *State of Uttar Pradesh*, AIR 1959 SC 648: (1959) Supp 2 SCR 8: 1959 SCA 377: 1959 SCJ 1069: ILR (1959) 1 All 293.

(ii) *Prem Nath Kaul* v. *State of Jammu & Kashmir*, AIR 1959 SC 749: (1959) Supp 2 SCR 270: (1959) 2 SCA 65: 1959 SCJ 797.

(iii) *Ukha* v. *State of Maharashtra*, AIR 1963 SC 1531: (1964) 1 SCR 926: (1963) 2 Cr LJ 418: 65 Bom LR 793, paragraph 20.

(iv) *Bar Council of Uttar Pradesh* v. *State of Uttar Pradesh*, AIR 1973 SC 231 (238): (1973) 1 SCC 261.

(v) *T. Barai* v. *Henry*, AIR 1983 SC 150: (1983) 1 SCC 177: 1983 Cr LJ 164, paragraph 15.

(vi) *Hoechst Pharmaceuticals Ltd.* v. *State of Bihar*, AIR 1983 SC 1019: (1983) 4 SCC 45: 1983 UJ (SC) 617: 1983 SCC (Tax) 248: (1983) 8 STL (SC) 1, paragraphs 68, 69 and 76.

(vii) *L.T.C.* v. *State of Karnataka*, (1985) Supp SCC 476, paragraph 29.

(viii) *Lingappa Pochanna Appealwar* v. *State of Maharashtra*, AIR 1985 SC 389: (1985) 1 SCC 479: (1985) 87 Bom LR 65: 1985 GOC (SC) 41: (1985) 2 SCR 224, paragraph 26.

255. Requirements as to recommendations and previous sanctions to be regarded as matters of procedure only.—No Act of Parliament or of the Legislature of a State [1][***] and no provision in any such Act, shall be invalid by reason only that some recommendation or previous sanction required by this Constitution was not given, if assent to that Act was given—

(a) where the recommendation required was that of the Governor, either by the Governor or by the President;

(b) where the recommendation required was that of the Rajpramukh, either by the Rajpramukh or by the President;

(c) where the recommendation or previous sanction required was that of the President, by the President.

Notes on Article 255

Neither the legislature nor the President has the power to declare that non-compliance with article 255, of the Constitution was of no effect; *Utkal Contractors and Joinery (P) Ltd.* v. *State of Orissa*, AIR 1987 SC 2310: 1987 Supp SCC 751: JT 1987 (5) SC 1: 1987 Raj LR 652. By giving his assent to a subsequent Bill, the President cannot validate, with retrospective effect an earlier Act which had failed for want of the President's assent under article 255 so as to validate acts done under the invalid statute, because it would amount to a declaration that non-compliance with article 255 was of no consequence, which is a declaration beyond the competence of the President; *Abdul Kadir* v. *State of Kerala*, AIR 1976 SC 182: (1976) 3 SCC 219: 1976 Tax LR 1293.

CHAPTER II
ADMINISTRATIVE RELATIONS

General

256. Obligation of States and the Union.—The executive power of every State shall be so exercised as to ensure compliance with the laws made by Parliament and any existing laws which apply in that State, and the executive power of the Union shall extend to the giving of such directions to a State as may appear to the Government of India to be necessary for that purpose.

Notes on Article 256

Comply with Article 256

A failure to comply with article 256 may attract serious consequences but no court is likely to entertain a grievance at the instance of a private party that article 256 has not been complied

---

1. The words and letters "specified in Part A or Part B of the First Schedule" omitted by the Constitution (Seventh Amendment) Act, 1956, sec. 29 and Sch. (w.e.f. 1-11-1956).

with by a State Government; *Addl. Distt. Magistrate, Jabalpur v. Shivakant Shukla,* AIR 1976 SC 1207: (1976) 2 SCC 521: 1976 Cr LJ 945: 1976 UJ (SC) 610: 1976 SC Cr R 277: 1976 SCC (Cri) 448: 1976 Cr App R (SC) 298: (1976) 3 SCR 929: 1976 Supp SCR 172.

257. Control of the Union over States in certain cases.—(1) The executive power of every State shall be so exercised as not to impede or prejudice the exercise of the executive power of the Union, and the executive power of the Union shall extend to the giving of such directions to a State as may appear to the Government of India to be necessary for that purpose.

(2) The executive power of the Union shall also extend to the giving of directions to a State as to the construction and maintenance of means of communication declared in the direction to be of national or military importance:

Provided that nothing in this clause shall be taken as restricting the power of Parliament to declare highways or waterways to be national highways or national waterways or power of the Union with respect to the highways or waterways so declared or the power of the Union to construct and maintain means of communication as part of its functions with respect to naval, military and air force works.

(3) The executive power of the Union shall also extend to the giving of directions to a State as to the measures to be taken for the protection of the railways within the State.

(4) Where in carrying out any direction given to a State under clause (2) as to the construction or maintenance of any means of communication or under clause (3) as to the measures to be taken for the protection of any railway, costs have been incurred in excess of those which would have been incurred in the discharge of the normal duties of the State if such direction had not been given, there shall be paid by the Government of India to the State such sum as may be agreed, or, in default of agreement, as may be determined by an arbitrator appointed by the Chief Justice of India, in respect of the extra costs so incurred by the State.

[1][**257A. Assistance to States by deployment of armed forces or other forces of the Union.**—[*Rep. by the Constitution (Forty-fourth Amendment) Act, 1978, sec. 33 (w.e.f. 20-6-1979).*]]

258. Power of the Union to confer powers, etc., on States in certain cases.—(1) Notwithstanding anything in this Constitution, the President may, with the consent of the Governor of a State, entrust either conditionally or unconditionally to that Government or to its officers functions in relation to any matter to which the executive power of the Union extends.

(2) A law made by Parliament which applies in any State may, notwithstanding that it relates to a matter with respect to which the Legislature of the State has no power to make laws, confer powers and impose duties, or authorise the conferring of powers and the imposition of duties, upon the State or officers and authorities thereof.

(3) Where by virtue of this article powers and duties have been conferred or imposed upon a State or officers or authorities thereof, there shall be paid by the Government of India to the State such sum as may be agreed, or, in default of agreement, as may be determined by an arbitrator appointed by the Chief Justice of

---

1. Article 257A was earlier inserted by the Constitution (Forty-second Amendment) Act, 1976, sec. 43 (w.e.f. 3-1-1977).

India, in respect of any extra costs of administration incurred by the State in connection with the exercise of those powers and duties.

[1][258A. **Power of the States to entrust functions to the Union.**—Notwithstanding anything in this Constitution, the Governor of a State may, with the consent of the Government of India, entrust either conditionally or unconditionally to that Government or to its officers functions in relation to any matter to which the executive power of the State extends.]

259. **Armed Forces in States in Part B of the First Schedule.**—[*Rep. by the Constitution (Seventh Amendment) Act, 1956, sec. 29 and Sch. (w.e.f. 1-11-1956).*]

260. **Jurisdiction of the Union in relation to territories outside India.**—The Government of India may by agreement with the Government of any territory not being part of the territory of India undertake any executive, legislative or judicial functions vested in the Government of such territory, but every such agreement shall be subject to, and governed by, any law relating to the exercise of foreign jurisdiction for the time being in force.

261. **Public acts, records and judicial proceedings.**—Full faith and credit shall be given throughout the territory of India to public acts, records and judicial proceedings of the Union and of every State.

(2) The manner in which and the conditions under which the acts, records and proceedings referred to in clause (1) shall be proved and the effect thereof determined shall be as provided by law made by Parliament.

(3) Final judgments or orders delivered or passed by civil courts in any part of the territory of India shall be capable of execution anywhere within that territory according to law.

Disputes relating to Waters

262. **Adjudication of disputes relating to waters of inter-State rivers or river valleys.**—(1) Parliament may by law provide for the adjudication of any dispute or complaint with respect to the use, distribution or control of the waters of, or in, any inter-State river or river valley.

(2) Notwithstanding anything in this Constitution, Parliament may by law provide that neither the Supreme Court nor any other court shall exercise jurisdiction in respect of any such dispute or complaint as is referred to in clause (1).

Notes on Article 262

The Inter State Water Disputes Act, 1956 (33 of 1956) is legislation passed under article 262 of the Constitution. Section 11 of the Act excludes the jurisdiction of the Supreme Court in respect of a water dispute referred to the Tribunal. But the Supreme Court can direct that Central Government to fulfil its statutory obligation under section 4 of the Act, which is mandatory, particularly when the State of Tamil Nadu supported the writ petition filed for the purpose by a registered society; *T.N. Cauvery Neerppasana Vilaiporulgal Vivasayigal Nala Urimai Padhugappu Sangam* v. *Union of India*, AIR 1990 SC 1316: (1990) 3 SCC 440: JT 1990 (2) SC 397.

Co-ordination between States

263. **Provisions with respect to an inter-State Council.**—If at any time it appears to the President that the public interests would be served by the establishment of a Council charged with the duty of—

---

1. Ins. by the Constitution (Seventh Amendment) Act, 1956, sec. 18 (w.e.f. 1-11-1956).

(a) inquiring into and advising upon disputes which may have arisen between States;

(b) investigating and discussing subjects in which some or all of the States, or the Union and one or more of the States, have a common interest; or

(c) making recommendations upon any such subject and, in particular, recommendations for the better co-ordination of policy and action with respect to that subject,

it shall be lawful for the President by order to establish such a Council, and to define the nature of the duties to be performed by it and its organisation and procedure.

Notes on Article 263

The Supreme Court has held that once the Central Government finds that the dispute referred to in the request received from the State Government cannot be settled by negotiations, it becomes mandatory for the Central Government to constitute a tribunal and to refer the dispute to it for adjudication.

If the Central Government fails to make such reference, the court may, on an application under article 32 by an aggrieved party issue *mandamus* to the Central Government to carry out its statutory obligation; *T.N. Cauvery Neerppasana Vilaiporulgal Vivasayigal Nala Urimai Padhugappu Sangam* v. *Union of India*, AIR 1990 SC 1316: (1990) 3 SCC 440: JT 1990 (2) SC 397, paragraph 18.

It is held by the Supreme Court that—

(a) It is the exclusive function and duty of a court to interpret a statute and to determine the limits of the Jurisdiction of any tribunal or statutory authority. This jurisdiction of the court is not barred by section 11 of the Act.

(b) What is barred is the question whether any party before the tribunal is entitled to any relief on the merits.

In this case the tribunal held that it had no jurisdiction to grant any interim relief under the Act. The Supreme Court, on appeal by Special leave, held that the jurisdiction to grant interim relief had been conferred by agreement between the parties before the tribunal and the Supreme Court directed the tribunal to decide on the merits whether the appellant was entitled to any interim relief on the facts of the case; *State of Tamil Nadu* v. *State of Karnataka*, (1991) Supp 1 SCC 240, paragraphs 12, 15 and 22.

PART XII
FINANCE, PROPERTY, CONTRACTS AND SUITS
CHAPTER I
FINANCE
General

¹[**264. Interpretation.**—In this Part, "Finance Commission" means a Finance Commission constituted under article 280.]

265. Taxes not to be imposed save by authority of law.—No tax shall be levied or collected except by authority of law.

Notes on Article 265

Article 265 requires that—

(i) there must be a law;

(ii) the law must authorise the tax; and

(iii) the tax must be levied and collected according to the law.

---

1. Subs. by the Constitution (Seventh Amendment) Act, 1956, sec. 29 and Sch., for article 264 (w.e.f. 1-11-1956).

Tax illegally levied must be refunded. Doctrine of "unjust enrichment has to be applied after having regard to the facts of each case; *New India Industries Ltd.* v. *Union of India*, AIR 1990 Bom 239: 1990 Mah LJ 5: (1990) 1 Bom CR 515 (FB) (case law reviewed).

Writ court can order refund of tax, paid under mistake of law; *Salonah Tea Co. Ltd.* v. *Superintendent of Taxes, Nowgong*, AIR 1990 SC 772 (774-776): (1988) 1 SCC 401: (1988) 69 STC 290: (1988) 173 ITR 42, paragraphs 6-13.

The authorisation made by the statute to levy a tax must be express. Taxing power cannot be derived from the delegation of mere regulating power, even though the tax was within the competence of the Legislature which made the delegation. The power to tax is not incidental or ancillary to the power to legislate on a matter; *Synthetics & Chemicals Ltd.* v. *State of Uttar Pradesh*, (1990) 1 SCC 109: AIR 1990 SC 1927: JT 1989 (4) SC 267; *Subash Chander* v. *State of Haryana*, AIR 1992 P&H 20: 1991 (2) LJR 580: 1992 (1) RRR 50: 1991 (2) RevLR 431.

Fee

The word "fee" does not have a rigid technical meaning. Its meaning depends on the subject-matter in relation to which the fee is imposed.

(i) *Secretary to Government of Madras* v. *P.R. Sriramulu*, AIR 1996 SC 676: (1996) 1 SCC 345: 1995 AIR SCW 4691: 1996 (1) CTC 235: JT 1995 (8) SC 305: 1996 (1) Mad LW 1: 1996 (1) UJ (SC) 612, paragraph 14.

(ii) *Corporation of Calcutta* v. *Liberty Cinema*, AIR 1965 SC 1107: 1965 1 SCA 657: 1965 2 SCR 477.

There should be a reasonable 'relationship' between levy of the fee and the service rendered. When there is no such correlation, the levy, despite its nomenclature is in fact a tax; *State of Uttar Pradesh* v. *Vam Organic Chemicals Ltd.*, AIR 2003 SC 4650: (2004) 1 SCC 225: 2003 AIR SCW 5463: JT 2003 (8) SC 1: 2004 (2) SRJ 125: (2003) 8 SCALE 775: 2003 (8) Supreme 165.

266. Consolidated Funds and public accounts of India and of the States.— (1) Subject to the provisions of article 267 and to the provisions of this Chapter with respect to the assignment of the whole or part of the net proceeds of certain taxes and duties to States, all revenues received by the Government of India, all loans raised by that Government by the issue of treasury bills, loans or ways and means advances and all moneys received by that Government in repayment of loans shall form one consolidated fund to be entitled "the Consolidated Fund of India", and all revenues received by the Government of a State, all loans raised by that Government by the issue of treasury bills, loans or ways and means advances and all moneys received by that Government in repayment of loans shall form one consolidated fund to be entitled "the Consolidated Fund of the State".

(2) All other public moneys received by or on behalf of the Government of India or the Government of a State shall be credited to the public account of India or the public account of the State, as the case may be.

(3) No moneys out of the Consolidated Fund of India or the Consolidated Fund of a State shall be appropriated except in accordance with law and for the purposes and in the manner provided in this Constitution.

267. Contingency Fund.—(1) Parliament may by law establish a Contingency Fund in the nature of an imprest to be entitled "the Contingency Fund of India" into which shall be paid from time to time such sums as may be determined by such law, and the said Fund shall be placed at the disposal of the President to enable advances to be made by him out of such Fund for the purposes of meeting unforeseen expenditure pending authorisation of such expenditure by Parliament by law under article 115 or article 116.

(2) The Legislature of a State may by law establish a Contingency Fund in the nature of an imprest to be entitled "the Contingency Fund of the State" into which shall be paid from time to time such sums as may be determined by such law, and the said Fund shall be placed at the disposal of the Governor [1][***] of the State to enable advances to be made by him out of such Fund for the purposes of meeting unforeseen expenditure pending authorisation of such expenditure by the Legislature of the State by law under article 205 or article 206.

Distribution of Revenues between the Union and the States

268. Duties levied by the Union but collected and appropriated by the States.— (1) Such stamp duties and such duties of excise on medicinal and toilet preparations as are mentioned in the Union List shall be levied by the Government of India but shall be collected—

(a) in the case where such duties are leviable within any [2][Union territory], by the Government of India, and

(b) in other cases, by the States within which such duties are respectively leviable.

(2) The proceeds in any financial year of any such duty leviable within any State shall not form part of the Consolidated Fund of India, but shall be assigned to that State.

[3][**268A. Service tax levied by Union and collected and appropriated by the Union and the States.—**(1) Taxes on services shall be levied by the Government of India and such tax shall be collected and appropriated by the Government of India and the States in the manner provided in clause (2).

(2) The proceeds in any financial year of any such tax levied in accordance with the provisions of clause (1) shall be—

(a) collected by the Government of India and the States;

(b) appropriated by the Government of India and the States,

in accordance with such principles of collection and appropriation as may be formulated by Parliament by law.]

269. Taxes levied and collected by the Union but assigned to the States.— [4][(1) Taxes on the sales or purchase of goods and taxes on the consignment of goods shall be levied and collected by the Government of India but shall be assigned and shall be deemed to have been assigned to the States on or after the 1st day of April, 1996 in the matter provided in clause (2).

Explanation.—For the purposes of this clause,—

(a) the expression "taxes on the sale or purchase of goods" shall mean taxes on sale or purchase of goods other than newspapers, where such sale or purchase takes place in the course of inter-State trade or commerce;

---

1. The words "or Rajpramukh" omitted by the Constitution (Seventh Amendment) Act, 1956, sec. 29 and Sch. (w.e.f. 1-11-1956).

2. Subs. by the Constitution (Seventh Amendment) Act, 1956, sec. 29 and Sch., for "State specified in Part C of the First Schedule" (w.e.f. 1-11-1956).

3. Ins. by the Constitution (Eighty-eighth Amendment) Act, 2003, sec. 2 (w.e.f. 19-2-2004).

4. Subs. by the Constitution (Eightieth Amendment) Act, 2000, sec. 2, for clause (1) (w.e.f. 9-6-2000). Earlier clause (1) was amended by the Constitution (Sixth Amendment) Act, 1956, sec. 3(a) (w.e.f. 11-9-1956) and by the Constitution (Forty-sixth Amendment) Act, 1982, sec. 2(a) (w.e.f. 2-2-1983).

(b) the expression "taxes on the consignment of goods" shall mean taxes on the consignment of goods (whether the consignment is to the person making it or to any other person), where such consignment takes place in the course of inter-State trade or commerce.]

[1](2) The net proceeds in any financial year of any such tax, except in so far as those proceeds represent proceeds attributable to Union territories, shall not form part of the Consolidated Fund of India, but shall be assigned to the States within which that tax is leviable in that year, and shall be distributed among those States in accordance with such principles of distribution as may be formulated by Parliament by law.]

[2](3) Parliament may by law formulate principles for determining when a [3][sale or purchase of, or consignment of, goods] takes place in the course of inter-State trade or commerce.]

Notes on Article 269

As to clause (1), sub-clauses (g) and (h) relating to inter-State purchases and consignments, see the Seventh Schedule, Union List, Entries 92A and 92B. Entry 92B was inserted by the Constitution (Forty-sixth Amendment) Act, 1982.

A law which, though purporting to impose tax on the price at which raw materials are purchased actually becomes effective with reference to manufactured goods on their despatch to a place outside the State, is a "Consignment tax", falling within the competence of Parliament under article 269(1)(g) and Union List, Entry 92B; *Goodyear India Ltd.* v. *State of Haryana*, AIR 1990 SC 781 (795, 796, 797, 798): (1990) 2 SCC 712: JT 1989 (4) SC 229, paragraphs 35-40 [History of the Constitution (Forty-sixth Amendment) Act, 1982 and Law Commission of India, 61st Report, referred].

By reason of the new Entry [Entry 92B, List 1, Seventh Sch. inserted by the Constitution (Forty-sixth Amendment) Act, 1982] it has been held that when a tax is imposed by a State on the mere despatch of goods by a manufacturer to his own branches outside the State, the tax is *ultra vires* because it is a consignment tax within the exclusive competence of parliament under Entry 92B of List I.

When a question arises as to the competence of a legislature to impose a tax, in a conflict between two competing jurisdictions, the nomenclature used by the taxing State is not conclusive. The court has to apply the doctrine of pith and substance in order to find out the real nature of the tax, with reference to its taxing event; *Goodyear India Ltd.* v. *State of Haryana*, AIR 1990 SC 781: (1990) 2 SCC 712: JT 1989 (4) SC 229, paragraphs 37-41 and 76; *Mukerian Papers Ltd.* v. *State of Punjab*, (1991) 2 SCC 580: 1991 AIR SCW 553, paragraphs 5 and 6.

[4][**270. Taxes levied and distributed between the Union and the States.**—(1) All taxes and duties referred to in the Union List, except the duties and taxes referred to in [5][articles 268, 268A and 269], respectively, surcharge on taxes and duties referred

---

1. Subs. by the Constitution (Eightieth Amendment) Act, 2000, sec. 2, for clause (2) (w.e.f. 9-6-2000). Earlier clause (2) was amended by the Constitution (Seventh Amendment) Act, 1956, sec. 29 and Sch. (w.e.f. 1-11-1956).

2. Ins. by the Constitution (Sixth Amendment) Act, 1956, sec. 3(b) (w.e.f. 11-9-1956).

3. Subs. by the Constitution (Forty-sixth Amendment) Act, 1982, sec. 2(b), for "sale or purchase of goods" (w.e.f. 2-2-1983).

4. Subs. by the Constitution (Eightieth Amendment) Act, 2000, sec. 3, for article 270 (w.r.e.f. 1-4-1996). Earlier article 270 was amended by the Constitution (Seventh Amendment) Act, 1956, sec. 29 and Sch. (w.e.f. 1-11-1956).

5. Subs. by the Constitution (Eighty-eighth Amendment) Act, 2003, sec. 3, for "articles 268 and 269" (w.e.f. 19-2-2004).

to in article 271 and any cess levied for specific purposes under any law made by Parliament shall be levied and collected by the Government of India and shall be distributed between the Union and the States in the manner provided in clause (2).

(2) Such percentage, as may be prescribed, of the net proceeds of any such tax or duty in any financial year shall not form part of the Consolidated Fund of India, but shall be assigned to the States within which that tax or duty is leviable in that year, and shall be distributed among those States in such manner and from such time as may be prescribed in the manner provided in clause (3).

(3) In this article, "prescribed" means,—

  (i) until a Finance Commission has been constituted, prescribed by the President by order, and

  (ii) after a Finance Commission has been constituted, prescribed by the President by order after considering the recommendations of the Finance Commission.]

271. Surcharge on certain duties and taxes for purposes of the Union.— Notwithstanding anything in articles 269 and 270, Parliament may at any time increase any of the duties or taxes referred to in those articles by a surcharge for purposes of the Union and the whole proceeds of any such surcharge shall form part of the Consolidated Fund of India.

*272. Taxes which are levied and collected by the Union and may be distributed between the Union and the States.—[*Rep. by the Constitution (Eightieth Amendment) Act, 2000, sec. 4 (w.e.f. 9-6-2000).*]

273. Grants in lieu of export duty on jute and jute products.—(1) There shall be charged on the Consolidated Fund of India in each year as grants-in-aid of the revenues of the States of Assam, Bihar, [1][Odisha] and West Bengal, in lieu of assignment of any share of the net proceeds in each year of export duty on jute and jute products to those States, such sums as may be prescribed.

(2) The sums so prescribed shall continue to be charged on the Consolidated Fund of India so long as any export duty on jute or jute products continues to be levied by the Government of India or until the expiration of ten years from the commencement of this Constitution, whichever is earlier.

(3) In this article, the expression "prescribed" has the same meaning as in article 270.

274. Prior recommendation of President required to Bills affecting taxation in which States are interested.—(1) No Bill or amendment which imposes or varies any tax or duty in which States are interested, or which varies the meaning of the expression "agricultural income" as defined for the purposes of the enactments relating to Indian Income-tax, or which affects the principles on which under any of the foregoing provisions of this Chapter moneys are or may be distributable to State, or which imposes any surcharge for the purposes of the Union as is mentioned in the foregoing provisions of this Chapter, shall be introduced or moved in either House of Parliament except on the recommendation of the President.

(2) In this article, the expression "tax or duty in which States are interested" means—

---

* The union duties of excise including additional duties and any other tax or duty collected and distributed by Central Government as grants-in-aid to States after 1-4-1996 and before 9-6-2000 shall be deemed to be distributed as if before 1-4-1996.

1. Subs. by the Orissa (Alteration of Name) Act, 2011 (15 of 2011), sec. 5, for "Orissa" (w.e.f. 1-11-2011, *vide* G.S.R. 791(E), dated 1st November, 2011).

(a) a tax or duty the whole or part of the net proceeds whereof are assigned to any State; or

(b) a tax or duty by reference to the net proceeds whereof sums are for the time being payable out of the Consolidated Fund of India to any State.

275. Grants from the Union to certain States.—(1) Such sums as Parliament may by law provide shall be charged on the Consolidated Fund of India in each year as grants-in-aid of the revenues of such States as Parliament may determine to be in need of assistance, and different sums may be fixed for different States:

Provided that there shall be paid out of the Consolidated Fund of India as grants-in-aid of the revenues of a State such capital and recurring sums as may be necessary to enable that State to meet the costs of such schemes of development as may be undertaken by the State with the approval of the Government of India for the purpose of promoting the welfare of the Scheduled Tribes in that State or raising the level of administration of the Scheduled Areas therein to that of the administration of the rest of the areas of that State:

Provided further that there shall be paid out of the Consolidated Fund of India as grants-in-aid of the revenues of the State of Assam sums, capital and recurring, equivalent to—

(a) the average excess of expenditure over the revenues during the two years immediately preceding the commencement of this Constitution in respect of the administration of the tribal areas specified in [1][Part I] of the table appended to paragraph 20 of the Sixth Schedule; and

(b) the costs of such schemes of development as may be undertaken by that State with the approval of the Government of India for the purpose of raising the level of administration of the said areas to that of the administration of the rest of the areas of that State.

[2][(1A) On and from the formation of the autonomous State under article 244A,—

(i) any sums payable under clause (a) of the second proviso to clause (1) shall, if the autonomous State comprises of all the tribal areas referred to therein, be paid to the autonomous State, and, if the autonomous State comprises only some of those tribal areas, be apportioned between the State of Assam and the autonomous State as the President may, by order, specify;

(ii) there shall be paid out of the Consolidated Fund of India as grants-in-aid of the revenues of the autonomous State sums, capital and recurring, equivalent to the costs of such schemes of development as may be undertaken by the autonomous State with the approval of the Government of India for the purpose of raising the level of administration of that State to that of the administration of the rest of the State of Assam.]

(2) Until provision is made by Parliament under clause (1), the powers conferred on Parliament under that clause shall be exercisable by the President by order and any order made by the President under this clause shall have effect subject to any provision so made by Parliament:

Provided that after a Finance Commission has been constituted no order shall be made under this clause by the President except after considering the recommendations of the Finance Commission.

---

1. Subs. by the North Eastern Areas (Reorganisation) Act, 1971 (81 of 1971), sec. 71(e), for "Part A" (w.e.f. 21-1-1972).

2. Ins. by the Constitution (Twenty-second Amendment) Act, 1969, sec. 3 (w.e.f. 25-9-1969).

276. Taxes on professions, trades, callings and employments.— (1) Notwithstanding anything in article 246, no law of the Legislature of a State relating to taxes for the benefit of the State or of a municipality, district board, local board or other local authority therein in respect of professions, trades, callings or employments shall be invalid on the ground that it relates to a tax on income.

(2) The total amount payable in respect of any one person to the State or to any one municipality, district board, local board or other local authority in the State by way of taxes on professions, trades, callings and employments shall not exceed ¹[two thousand and five hundred rupees] per annum:

²[***]

(3) The power of the Legislature of a State to make laws as aforesaid with respect to taxes on professions, trades, callings and employments shall not be construed as limiting in any way the power of Parliament to make laws with respect to taxes on income accruing from or arising out of professions, trades, callings and employments.

277. Savings.—Any taxes, duties, cesses or fees which, immediately before the commencement of this Constitution, were being lawfully levied by the Government of any State or by any municipality or other local authority or body for the purposes of the State, municipality, district or other local area may, notwithstanding that those taxes, duties, cesses or fees are mentioned in the Union List, continue to be levied and to be applied to the same purposes until provision to the contrary is made by Parliament by law.

Notes on Article 277
For meanings of 'tax' and 'fee' see notes on article 265.

278. Agreement with States in Part B of the First Schedule with regard to certain financial matters.—[*Rep. by the Constitution (Seventh Amendment) Act, 1956, sec. 29 and Sch. (w.e.f. 1-11-1956).*]

279. Calculation of "net proceeds", etc.—(1) In the foregoing provisions of this Chapter, "net proceeds" means in relation to any tax or duty the proceeds thereof reduced by the cost of collection, and for the purposes of those provisions the net proceeds of any tax or duty, or of any part of any tax or duty, in or attributable to any area shall be ascertained and certified by the Comptroller and Auditor-General of India, whose certificate shall be final.

(2) Subject as aforesaid, and to any other express provision of this Chapter, a law made by Parliament or an order of the President may, in any case where under this Part the proceeds of any duty or tax are, or may be, assigned to any State, provide for the manner in which the proceeds are to be calculated, for the time from or at which and the manner in which any payments are to be made, for the making of adjustments between one financial year and another, and for any other incidental or ancillary matters.

280. Finance Commission.—(1) The President shall, within two years from the commencement of this Constitution and thereafter at the expiration of every fifth year or at such earlier time as the President considers necessary, by order constitute a Finance Commission which shall consist of a Chairman and four other members to be appointed by the President.

---

1. Subs. by the Constitution (Sixtieth Amendment) Act, 1988, sec. 2(a), for "two hundred and fifty rupees" (w.e.f. 20-12-1988).
2. Proviso omitted by the Constitution (Sixtieth Amendment) Act, 1988, sec. 2(b) (w.e.f. 20-12-1988).

(2) Parliament may by law determine the qualifications which shall be requisite for appointment as members of the Commission and the manner in which they shall be selected.

(3) It shall be the duty of the Commission to make recommendations to the President as to—

(a) the distribution between the Union and the States of the net proceeds of taxes which are to be, or may be, divided between them under this Chapter and the allocation between the States of the respective shares of such proceeds;

(b) the principles which should govern the grants-in-aid of the revenues of the States out of the Consolidated Fund of India;

[1][(bb) the measures needed to augment the Consolidated Fund of a State to supplement the resources of the Panchayats in the State on the basis of the recommendations made by the Finance Commission of the State;]

[2][(c) the measures needed to augment the Consolidated Fund of a State to supplement the resources of the Municipalities in the State on the basis of the recommendations made by the Finance Commission of the State;]

[3][(d)] any other matter referred to the Commission by the President in the interests of sound finance.

(4) The Commission shall determine their procedure and shall have such powers in the performance of their functions as Parliament may by law confer on them.

281. Recommendations of the Finance Commission.—The President shall cause every recommendation made by the Finance Commission under the provisions of this Constitution together with an explanatory memorandum as to the action taken thereon to be laid before each House of Parliament.

Miscellaneous Financial Provisions

282. Expenditure defrayable by the Union or a State out of its revenues.—The Union or a State may make any grants for any public purpose, notwithstanding that the purpose is not one with respect to which Parliament or the Legislature of the State, as the case may be, may make laws.

283. Custody, etc., of Consolidated Funds, Contingency Funds and moneys credited to the public accounts.—(1) The custody of the Consolidated Fund of India and the Contingency Fund of India, the payment of moneys into such Funds, the withdrawal of moneys therefrom, the custody of public moneys other than those credited to such Funds received by or on behalf of the Government of India, their payment into the public account of India and the withdrawal of moneys from such account and all other matters connected with or ancillary to matters aforesaid shall be regulated by law made by Parliament, and, until provision in that behalf is so made, shall be regulated by rules made by the President.

(2) The custody of the Consolidated Fund of a State and the Contingency Fund of a State, the payment of moneys into such Funds, the withdrawal of moneys therefrom,

---

1. Ins. by the Constitution (Seventy-third Amendment) Act, 1992, sec. 3 (w.e.f. 24-4-1993).

2. Ins. by the Constitution (Seventy-fourth Amendment) Act, 1992, sec. 3 (w.e.f. 1-6-1993).

3. Sub-clause (c) relettered as sub-clause (d) by the Constitution (Seventy-fourth Amendment) Act, 1992, sec. 3 (w.e.f. 1-6-1993). Earlier sub-clause (c) was omitted and sub-clause (d) was re-lettered as clause (c) by the Constitution (Seventh Amendment) Act, 1956, sec. 29 and Sch. (w.e.f. 1-11-1956).

the custody of public moneys other than those credited to such Funds received by or on behalf of the Government of the State, their payment into the public account of the State and withdrawal of moneys from such account and all other matters connected with or ancillary to matters aforesaid shall be regulated by law made by the Legislature of the State, and, until provision in that behalf is so made, shall be regulated by rules made by the Governor [1][***] of the State.

284. Custody of suitors' deposits and other moneys received by public servants and courts.—All moneys received by or deposited with—

(a) any officer employed in connection with the affairs of the Union or of a State in his capacity as such, other than revenues or public moneys raised or received by the Government of India or the Government of the State, as the case may be, or

(b) any court within the territory of India to the credit of any cause, matter, account or persons,

shall be paid into the public account of India or the public account of the State, as the case may be.

285. Exemption of property of the Union from State taxation.—(1) The property of the Union shall, save in so far as Parliament may by law otherwise provide, be exempt from all taxes imposed by a State or by any authority within a State.

(2) Nothing in clause (1) shall, until Parliament by law otherwise provides, prevent any authority within a State from levying any tax on any property of the Union to which such property was immediately before the commencement of this Constitution liable or treated as liable, so long as that tax continues to be levied in that State.

Notes on Article 285

Property of a Union is exempted from State taxation under article 285 except for taxes which were imposed on the Central Government before the Constitution. In Punjab vehicles of railways were not being subjected to road tax before 1950 and they cannot be subjected to tax after the Constitution. Even though the relevant rules were there, the tax was not actually being levied against the Union of India's vehicles. Writ petition by the Union of India was accepted; *Union of India* v. *State of Punjab*, AIR 1990 P&H 183 (J.S. Sekhon, J.) (It is not clear how the High Court entertained a dispute between the Union of India and the State. Under the Constitution, the Supreme Court has, exclusive jurisdiction in such disputes).

Property owned by a Government company or a statutory corporation, which has a corporate personality of its own, cannot be said to be 'property of the Union' and may, therefore, be liable to State or municipal taxation; *International Airports Authority of India* v. *Municipal Corporation of Delhi*, AIR 1991 Del 302: 1991 (1) Comp LJ 337 Del: ILR 1991 (2) Del 265, paragraph 35.

286. Restrictions as to imposition of tax on the sale or purchase of goods.—(1) No law of a State shall impose, or authorise the imposition of, a tax on the sale or purchase of goods where such sale or purchase takes place—

(a) outside the State; or

(b) in the course of the import of the goods into, or export of the goods out of, the territory of India.

---

1. The words "or Rajpramukh" omitted by the Constitution (Seventh Amendment) Act, 1956, sec. 29 and Sch. (w.e.f. 1-11-1956).

¹[***]

²[(2) Parliament may by law formulate principles for determining when a sale or purchase of goods takes place in any of the ways mentioned in clause (1).]

³[(3) Any law of a State shall, in so far as it imposes, or authorises the imposition of,—

(a) a tax on the sale or purchase of goods declared by Parliament by law to be of special importance in inter-State trade or commerce; or

(b) a tax on the sale or purchase of goods, being a tax of the nature referred to in sub-clause (b), sub-clause (c) or sub-clause (d) of clause (29A) of article 366,

be subject to such restrictions and conditions in regard to the system of levy, rates and other incidents of the tax as Parliament may by law specify.]

Notes on Article 286

For the purposes of clause (a), a sale or purchase shall be deemed to have taken place in the State in which the goods have actually been delivered as a direct result of such sale or purchase for the purpose of consumption in that State, notwithstanding the fact that under the general law relating to sale of goods the property in the goods has by reason of such sale or purchase passed in another State; *Associated Cement Companies Ltd., Kymore* v. *Commissioner of Sales Tax, Indore*, (1991) Supp 1 SCC 251: AIR 1991 SC 1122: 1991 AIR SCW 1102: 1991 BRLJ 199: 1991 (5) Cor LA 374: JT 1991 (2) SC 144: (1991) 2 SCR 250: 1991 (82) STC 1, paragraphs 6-9.

A sale may be for the purpose of export but in the course of export, *e.g.*, the 'penultimate sale' for the purpose of export; *Murli Manohar & Co.* v. *State of Haryana*, (1991) 1 SCC 377: JT 1990 (4) SC 189, paragraphs 6-7 (3 judges).

Export sales become complete only after the goods reach the foreign destination; *State of Orissa* v. *M.M.T.C.*, JT 1994 (4) SC 628: (1994) 3 SCC 109: (1994) 95 STC 80.

287. Exemption from taxes on electricity.—Save in so far as Parliament may by law otherwise provide, no law of a State shall impose, or authorise the imposition of, a tax on the consumption or sale of electricity (whether produced by a Government or other persons) which is—

(a) consumed by the Government of India, or sold to the Government of India for consumption by that Government; or

(b) consumed in the construction, maintenance or operation of any railway by the Government of India or a railway company operating that railway, or sold to that Government or any such railway company for consumption in the construction, maintenance or operation of any railway,

and any such law imposing, or authorising the imposition of, a tax on the sale of electricity shall secure that the price of electricity sold to the Government of India for consumption by that Government, or to any such railway company as aforesaid for consumption in the construction, maintenance or operation of any railway, shall be less by the amount of the tax than the price charged to other consumers of a substantial quantity of electricity.

---

1. *Explanation* omitted by the Constitution (Sixth Amendment) Act, 1956, sec. 4(a) (w.e.f. 11-9-1956).

2. Subs. by the Constitution (Sixth Amendment) Act, 1956, sec. 4(b), for clause (2) (w.e.f. 11-9-1956).

3. Subs. by the Constitution (Forty-sixth Amendment) Act, 1982, sec. 3, for clause (3) (w.e.f. 2-2-1983). Earlier clause (3) was substituted by the Constitution (Sixth Amendment) Act, 1956, sec. 4(b) (w.e.f. 11-9-1956).

288. Exemption from taxation by States in respect of water or electricity in certain cases.—(1) Save in so far as the President may by order otherwise provide, no law of a State in force immediately before the commencement of this Constitution shall impose, or authorise the imposition of, a tax in respect of any water or electricity stored, generated, consumed, distributed or sold by any authority established by any existing law or any law made by Parliament for regulating or developing any inter-State river or river-valley.

Explanation.—The expression "law of a State in force" in this clause shall include a law of a State passed or made before the commencement of this Constitution and not previously repealed, notwithstanding that it or parts of it may not be then in operation either at all or in particular areas.

(2) The Legislature of a State may by law impose, or authorise the imposition of, any such tax as is mentioned in clause (1), but no such law shall have any effect unless it has, after having been reserved for the consideration of the President received his assent; and if any such law provides for the fixation of the rates and other incidents of such tax by means of rules or orders to be made under the law by any authority, the law shall provide for the previous consent of the President being obtained to the making of any such rule or order.

289. Exemption of property and income of a State from Union taxation.—(1) The property and income of a State shall be exempt from Union taxation.

(2) Nothing in clause (1) shall prevent the Union from imposing, or authorising the imposition of, any tax to such extent, if any, as Parliament may by law provide in respect of a trade or business of any kind carried on by, or on behalf of, the Government of a State, or any operations connected therewith, or any property used or occupied for the purposes of such trade or business, or any income accruing or arising in connection therewith.

(3) Nothing in clause (2) shall apply to any trade or business, or to any class of trade or business, which Parliament may by law declare to be incidental to the ordinary functions of Government.

290. Adjustment in respect of certain expenses and pensions.—Where under the provisions of this Constitution the expenses of any court or Commission, or the pension payable to or in respect of a person who has served before the commencement of this Constitution under the Crown in India or after such commencement in connection with the affairs of the Union or of a State, are charged on the Consolidated Fund of India or the Consolidated Fund of a State, then, if—

(a) in the case of a charge on the Consolidated Fund of India, the court or Commission serves any of the separate needs of a State, or the person has served wholly or in part in connection with the affairs of a State; or

(b) in the case of a charge on the Consolidated Fund of a State, the court or Commission serves any of the separate needs of the Union or another State, or the person has served wholly or in part in connection with the affairs of the Union or another State,

there shall be charged on and paid out of the Consolidated Fund of the State or, as the case may be, the Consolidated Fund of India or the Consolidated Fund of the other State, such contribution in respect of the expenses or pension as may be agreed, or as may in default of agreement be determined by an arbitrator to be appointed by the Chief Justice of India.

¹[**290A. Annual payment to certain Devaswom Funds.**—A sum of forty-six lakhs and fifty thousand rupees shall be charged on, and paid out of, the Consolidated Fund of the State of Kerala every year to the Travancore Devaswom Fund; and a sum of thirteen lakhs and fifty thousand rupees shall be charged on, and paid out of the Consolidated Fund of the State of ²[Tamil Nadu], every year to the Devaswom Fund established in that State for the maintenance of Hindu temples and shrines in the territories transferred to that State on the 1st day of November, 1956, from the State of Travancore-Cochin.]

³[**291. Privy purse sums of Rulers.**—[*Rep. by the Constitution (Twenty-sixth Amendment) Act, 1971, sec. 2 (w.e.f. 28-12-1971).*]]

CHAPTER II
BORROWING

292. Borrowing by the Government of India.—The executive power of the Union extends to borrowing upon the security of the Consolidated Fund of India within such limits, if any, as may from time to time be fixed by Parliament by law and to the giving of guarantees within such limits, if any, as may be so fixed.

293. Borrowing by States.—(1) Subject to the provisions of this article, the executive power of a State extends to borrowing within the territory of India upon the security of the Consolidated Fund of the State within such limits, if any, as may from time to time be fixed by the Legislature of such State by law and to the giving of guarantees within such limits, if any, as may be so fixed.

(2) The Government of India may, subject to such conditions as may be laid down by or under any law made by Parliament, make loans to any State or, so long as any limits fixed under article 292 are not exceeded, give guarantees in respect of loans raised by any State, and any sums required for the purpose of making such loans shall be charged on the Consolidated Fund of India.

(3) A State may not without the consent of the Government of India raise any loan if there is still outstanding any part of a loan which has been made to the State by the Government of India or by its predecessor Government, or in respect of which a guarantee has been given by the Government of India or by its predecessor Government.

(4) A consent under clause (3) may be granted subject to such conditions, if any, as the Government of India may think fit to impose.

CHAPTER III
PROPERTY, CONTRACTS, RIGHTS, LIABILITIES, OBLIGATIONS AND SUITS

294. Succession to property, assets, rights, liabilities and obligations in certain cases.—As from the commencement of this Constitution—

(a) all property and assets which immediately before such commencement were vested in His Majesty for the purposes of the Government of the Dominion of

---

1. Ins. by the Constitution (Seventh Amendment) Act, 1956, sec. 19 (w.e.f. 1-11-1956).
2. Subs by the Madras State (Alteration of Name) Act, 1968 (53 of 1968), sec. 4, for "Madras" (w.e.f. 14-1-1969).
3. Article 291 was earlier amended by the Constitution (Seventh Amendment) Act, 1956, sec. 29 and Sch. (w.e.f. 1-11-1956).

India and all property and assets which immediately before such commencement were vested in His Majesty for the purposes of the Government of each Governor's Province shall vest respectively in the Union and the corresponding State, and

(b) all rights, liabilities and obligations of the Government of the Dominion of India and of the Government of each Governor's Province, whether arising out of any contract or otherwise, shall be the rights, liabilities and obligations respectively of the Government of India and the Government of each corresponding State,

subject to any adjustment made or to be made by reason of the creation before the commencement of this Constitution of the Dominion of Pakistan or of the Provinces of West Bengal, East Bengal, West Punjab and East Punjab.

295. Succession to property, assets, rights, liabilities and obligations in other cases.—(1) As from the commencement of this Constitution—

(a) all property and assets which immediately before such commencement were vested in any Indian State corresponding to a State specified in Part B of the First Schedule shall vest in the Union, if the purposes for which such property and assets were held immediately before such commencement will thereafter be purposes of the Union relating to any of the matters enumerated in the Union List, and

(b) all rights, liabilities and obligations of the Government of any Indian State corresponding to a State specified in Part B of the First Schedule, whether arising out of any contract or otherwise, shall be the rights, liabilities and obligations of the Government of India, if the purposes for which such rights were acquired or liabilities or obligations were incurred before such commencement will thereafter be purposes of the Government of India relating to any of the matters enumerated in the Union List,

subject to any agreement entered into in that behalf by the Government of India with the Government of that State.

(2) Subject as aforesaid, the Government of each State specified in Part B of the First Schedule shall, as from the commencement of this Constitution, be the successor of the Government of the corresponding Indian State as regards all property and assets and all rights, liabilities and obligations, whether arising out of any contract or otherwise, other than those referred to in clause (1).

296. Property accruing by escheat or lapse or as *bona vacantia*.—Subject as hereinafter provided any property in the territory of India which, if this Constitution had not come into operation, would have accrued to His Majesty or, as the case may be, to the Ruler of an Indian State by escheat or lapse, or as *bona vacantia* for want of a rightful owner, shall, if it is property situate in a State, vest in such State, and shall, in any other case, vest in the Union:

Provided that any property which at the date when it would have so accrued to His Majesty or to the Ruler of an Indian State was in the possession or under the control of the Government of India or the Government of a State shall, according as the purposes for which it was then used or held were purposes of the Union or a State, vest in the Union or in that State.

Explanation.—In this article, the expressions "Ruler" and "Indian State" have the same meanings as in article 363.

¹[**297. Things of value within territorial waters or continental shelf and resources of the exclusive economic zone to vest in the Union.**—(1) All lands, minerals and other things of value underlying the ocean within the territorial waters, or the continental shelf, or the exclusive economic zone, of India shall vest in the Union and be held for the purposes of the Union.

(2) All other resources of the exclusive economic zone of India shall also vest in the Union and be held for the purposes of the Union.

(3) The limits of the territorial waters, the continental shelf, the exclusive economic zone, and other maritime zones, of India shall be such as may be specified, from time to time, by or under any law made by Parliament.]

²[**298. Power to carry on trade, etc.**—The executive power of the Union and of each State shall extend to the carrying on of any trade or business and to the acquisition, holding and disposal of property and the making of contracts for any purpose:

Provided that—

(a) the said executive power of the Union shall, in so far as such trade or business or such purpose is not one with respect to which Parliament may make laws, be subject in each State to legislation by the State; and

(b) the said executive power of each State shall, in so far as such trade or business or such purpose is not one with respect to which the State Legislature may make laws, be subject to legislation by Parliament.]

Notes on Article 298

Extra-territorial Operation

It has been held that the power of a State under article 298 extends to carrying on a trade in other States also; *Khazan Singh* v. *State of Uttar Pradesh*, AIR 1974 SC 669: (1974) 1 SCC 295: (1974) 2 SCR 562. This implies that article 298 has been treated as an independent source of executive power. For, otherwise, on a combined reading of article 162 and 245(1). The executive power of a State would be confined to the area of the State as its legislative power is so confined by virtue of article 245; *See* also *Mahabir Auto Stores* v. *Indian Oil Corporation*, AIR 1990 SC 1031: (1990) 3 SCC 752: (1990) 2 SLR 69 Reversing; *Mahabir Auto Stores* v. *Indian Oil Corporation Ltd.*, AIR 1989 Del 315.

Trade or Business

The leading case on this article is *H. Anraj* v. *State of Maharashtra*, AIR 1984 SC 781: (1984) 2 SCC 292: (1984) 1 SCWR 293: 1984 UJ (SC) 909. The case discusses, *inter alia*, the relationship between (a) articles 73 and 298, and also (b) articles 258 and 298.

The use of words "business" and "contracts for any purpose" and its title "power to carry on trade etc." makes the field of article 298 wider than article 301. This widening is for a purpose and not to restrict only to "trade". No doubt it includes "trade" also within its field of activity. So every "trade" what is covered by article 301 would be within the field of article 298; *B.R. Enterprises* v. *State of Uttar Pradesh*, AIR 1999 SC 1867: (1999) 9 SCC 700: 1999 AIR SCW 1526: JT 1999 (3) SC 431: 1999 (7) SRJ 95: 2000 (120) STC 302: 1999 SC Cr R 526: 1999 (4) Supreme 472.

299. Contracts.—(1) All contracts made in the exercise of the executive power of the Union or of a State shall be expressed to be made by the President, or by the

---

1. Subs. by the Constitution (Fortieth Amendment) Act, 1976, sec. 2, for article 297 (w.e.f. 27-5-1976). Earlier article 297 was amended by the Constitution (Fifteenth Amendment) Act, 1963, sec. 9 (w.e.f. 5-10-1963).

2. Subs. by the Constitution (Seventh Amendment) Act, 1956, sec. 20, for article 298 (w.e.f. 1-11-1956).

Governor [1][***] of the State, as the case may be, and all such contracts and all assurances of property made in the exercise of that power shall be executed on behalf of the President or the Governor [1][***] by such persons and in such manner as he may direct or authorise.

(2) Neither the President nor the Governor [2][***] shall be personally liable in respect of any contract or assurance made or executed for the purposes of this Constitution, or for the purposes of any enactment relating to the Government of India heretofore in force, nor shall any person making or executing any such contract or assurance on behalf of any of them be personally liable in respect thereof.

Notes on Article 299

The position resulting from article 299 can be stated in this form—

(a) Government contracts must be expressed as to be made by the President or the Governor.

(b) They shall be executed by the competent person and in the prescribed manner.

(c) If the above requirements are not complied with—

  (i) Government is not bound by the contract, because article 299 is mandatory;

  (ii) the officer executing the contract would be personally bound;

  (iii) the Government, however, if it enjoys the benefit of performance by the other party to the contract, would be bound to give recompense on the principle of *quantum merit or quantum valebat* (service or goods received). This is on quasi-contract (sections 65 and 70 of the Indian Contract Act, 1872).

  (iv) Besides this, the doctrine of promissory estoppel may apply on the facts.

(d) In any case, the President or the Governor is not personally liable on the contract.

Following are the important decisions supporting the above proposition—

(i) *State of West Bengal* v. *B.K. Mondal & Sons*, AIR 1962 SC 779: (1962) Supp 1 SCR 876: (1962) 2 SCA 375 (Article 299 is mandatory).

(ii) *Karamshi Jethabhai Somayya* v. *State of Bombay*, AIR 1964 SC 1714: (1964) 6 SCR 984: 1965 (2) SCJ 568 (Person executing must be authorised to enter into the control).

(iii) *Union of India* v. *A.L. Rallia Ram*, AIR 1963 SC 1685: (1964) 3 SCR 164 (Tender and acceptance).

(iv) *Bihar Eastern Gangetic Fishermen Co-operative Society Ltd.* v. *Sipahi Singh*, AIR 1977 SC 2149: (1977) 4 SCC 145: 1978 Pat LJR 60: 1978 BLJR 22: (1978) 1 SCWR 268: 1978 BLJ 60 (Quantum meruit).

(v) *M.P. Sugar Mills* v. *State of Uttar Pradesh*, AIR 1979 SC 627: 1980 Supp SCC 157: 1979 Cr LJ 1027 (Promissory estoppel).

(vi) *New Marine Coal Co. (Bengal) Private Ltd.* v. *Union of India*, AIR 1964 SC 152: (1964) 2 SCR 859: 1964 (1) SCA 491: (1964) 2 SCR 859.

The freedom of the Government to enter into business with anybody it likes is subject to the condition of reason and fair play as well as public interest; *Mahabir Auto* v. *I.O.C.*, AIR 1990 SC 1031: (1990) 3 SCC 752: (1990) 2 SCR 69.

Doctrine of Indoor Management

In the case of Government contracts and contracts of Government Corporations, where certain formalities are required to be observed under the Constitution or under the law, the doctrine of "indoor management" cannot be applied, so as to remove the need to observe the

---

1. The words "or the Rajpramukh" omitted by the Constitution (Seventh Amendment) Act, 1956, sec. 29 and Sch. (w.e.f. 1-11-1956).

2. The words "nor the Rajpramukh" omitted by the Constitution (Seventh Amendment) Act, 1956, sec. 29 and Sch. (w.e.f. 1-11-1956).

formalities regarding formation of the contract or essential terms of the contract; *U.P. Rajkiya Nirman Nigam Ltd.* v. *Indure Pvt. Ltd.*, AIR 1996 SC 1373: (1996) 2 SCC 667: 1996 AIR SCW 980: JT 1996 (2) SC 322: 1996 (1) LJR 323: 1996 (2) RRR 31: (1996) 2 SCR 386: 1996 (2) UJ (SC) 48, paragraph 18.

300. Suits and proceedings.—(1) The Government of India may sue or be sued by the name of the Union of India and the Government of a State may sue or be sued by the name of the State and may, subject to any provisions which may be made by Act of Parliament or of the Legislature of such State enacted by virtue of powers conferred by this Constitution, sue or be sued in relation to their respective affairs in the like cases as the Dominion of India and the corresponding Provinces or the corresponding Indian States might have sued or been sued if this Constitution had not been enacted.

(2) If at the commencement of this Constitution—

(a) any legal proceedings are pending to which the Dominion of India is a party, the Union of India shall be deemed to be substituted for the Dominion in those proceedings; and

(b) any legal proceedings are pending to which a Province or an Indian State is a party, the corresponding State shall be deemed to be substituted for the Province or the Indian State in those proceedings.

Notes on Article 300

Government Liability in Tort

(a) The ruling principle is that Government is not liable for torts of its employees committed in the course of performance of sovereign functions.

(b) The theoretical doctrine as per (a) above is still adhered to, but it is being applied in a liberal manner and the courts interpret "sovereign" narrowly, as is shown by recent law.

It is enough to cite the following cases of importance:—

(i) *P&O Steam Navigation Co.* v. *Secretary of State*, (1861) 5 Bom HCR App A. (This was really a Calcutta ruling, reported in the Bombay series).

(ii) *State of Rajasthan* v. *Vidhyawati*, AIR 1962 SC 933: (1962) Supp 2 SCR 989: (1962) 2 SCA 362.

(iii) *Shyam Sunder* v. *State of Rajasthan*, AIR 1974 SC 890: (1974) 1 SCC 690: (1974) 3 SCR 549, paragraph 21.

(iv) *Kasturi Lal* v. *State of Uttar Pradesh*, AIR 1965 SC 1039: (1965) 1 SCR 375: (1966) 2 LLJ 583.

(v) *Union of India* v. *Sugrabai Wife of Abdul Majid*, AIR 1969 Bom 13: 70 Bom LR 212: 1968 Mah LJ 468: ILR (1968) Bom 998.

(vi) *Virendra* v. *State of Uttar Pradesh*, (1955) 1 SCR 415 (436): AIR 1954 SC 447: (1954) 2 MLJ 369 (Act of State).

A suit lies against the Government for wrongs done by public servants in the course of business, such as death or injury caused to a person by Police atrocities; *Saheli* v. *Commissioner of Police*, AIR 1990 SC 513: (1990) 1 SCC 422: 1990 SCC (Cri) 145.

¹[*CHAPTER IV*

RIGHT TO PROPERTY

300A. Persons not to be deprived of property save by authority of law.—No person shall be deprived of his property save by authority of law.]

---

1. Chapter IV (containing article 300A) ins. by the Constitution (Forty-fourth Amendment) Act, 1978, sec. 34 (w.e.f. 20-6-1979).

Notes on Article 300A

Deprivation of Property

Bar under section 69(2A) (Maharashtra Amendment) of Partnership Act instituting suit for dissolution of unregistered firm or recovery of property as well are arbitrary and unreasonable; *V. Subramaniam* v. *Rajesh Raghuvandra Rao,* AIR 2009 SC 1858: 2009 AIR SCW 3329: 2009 (3) All MR 418: 2009 (3) Bom CR 790: 2009 (4) Mad LJ 120: 2009 (3) Mah LJ 946: 2009 (5) Mah LJ 120: (2009) 5 SCC 608: (2009) 4 SCALE 459.

Refusal of sanction to erect a building does not deprive a person of his property within the meaning of article 300A. He is not deprived of his possession of the property by reason thereof. Inability to construct on account of legal restriction is not a deprivation of right to enjoy. Inability to enjoy according to one's own will are subject to legal restrictions which can never be equated with the deprivation of property. Though however, prevention of user of a land without any legal sanction or freezing of user of land is contemplation of preparation of Land Use and Development Plan without any such provision provided in law is a deprivation within the meaning of article 300A. *Giridharilal Soni* v. *Municipal Commission, Calcutta Municipal Corporation,* AIR 2001 Cal 12: 2000 (2) Cal HN 578: 2001 CWN 310.

Nature of the Right

Right not to be deprived of property save by authority of law is no longer a fundamental right, though it is still a constitutional right; *Bishamber Dayal Chandra Mohan* v. *State of Uttar Pradesh,* AIR 1982 SC 33: (1982) 1 SCC 39: 1982 SCC (Cri) 53: 1982 Cr LR (SC) 99: (1982) 1 SCR 1137: 1982 IJR 67: 1982 UJ (SC) 802.

Right to property is a human right as also a Constitutional right. But it is not a fundamental right. Each and every claim to property would not be property right; *Indian Handicrafts Emporium* v. *Union of India,* AIR 2003 SC 3240: (2003) 7 SCC 589: (2003) 106 DLT 350.

Requisitioning

There was a dispute between the operators of mini buses and their workers. Instead of referring the dispute to the proper forum, the State Government purporting to act under section 3 of the West Bengal Requisition of Vehicles Act, 1979 requisitioned the buses. The buses were then run by the Municipality though the requisition order did not mention that they would be so run. It was held, that the requisition was illegal, Further, though the order was passed by the District Magistrate, he was actually acting under the orders of the State Transport Minister. Hence the requisitioning was *mala fide* and for extraneous purpose and void; *New Barrackppore Mini Bus Owners' Association* v. *District Magistrate,* AIR 1990 Cal 268 (290 to 293), paragraphs 42-55 (Mahitosh Majumdar, J.) (reviews case law).

As to the general effect of article 300A see *Elizebath Samuel Aaron* v. *State of Kerala,* AIR 1991 Ker 162: 1992 (75) Comp Cas 377: ILR 1991 (2) Ker 113: 1991 (1) Ker LJ 626: 1991 (1) Ker LT 475 (FB), paragraph 24; and *Tinsukhia Electric Supply Co. Ltd.* v. *State of Assam,* AIR 1990 SC 123 (138): (1989) 3 SCC 709: JT 1989 (2) SC 217: (1989) 45 Taxman 29: (1989) 2 Comp LJ 377.

After the Constitution (Forty-fourth Amendments) Act, 1978 the right to property is only a constitutional right. It is not a part of the basic structure. The Constitution (Sixty-sixth Amendment) Act, 1990 does not destroy the basic structure of the Constitution; *Jilubhai Nanbhai Khachar* v. *State of Gujarat,* JT 1994 (4) SC 473: AIR 1995 SC 142: 1994 (72) Taxman 435: 1994 (1) UPTC 603: 1994 AIR SCW 4181.

A letter written by Private Secretary to the Minister, to the General Manager, Railways confers no legal right, nor can it be said to raise 'Legitimate expectations; *Union of India* v. *Graphic Industries,* JT 1994 (5) SC 237: (1994) 5 SCC 398: AIR 1995 SC 409.

Right to Property

The right to property includes within it the right to use the property in accordance with the law as it stands at a particular time; *Chairman, Indore Vikas Pradhikaran* v. *Pure Industrial Coke & Chemicals Ltd.,* (2007) 8 SCC 705: AIR 2007 SC 2458: 2007 AIR SCW 4387: 2007 (4) MPHT 1: (2007) 8 SCALE 110.

State Finance Corporations Act, 1951

Section 29 of the State Finance Corporations Act, 1951 gives the Corporation power to take possession of the property of an individual concerned, if the latter makes the default in payment of any loan *etc.* The Finance Corporation Act does not violate articles 14, 19, 21 or 300A of the Constitution. The principles of natural justice have to be read into the section. The Board of the Corporation consists of high ranking officials. When the industrial Concern enters into an agreement with the Corporation it is fully aware of the provision. If the Corporation acts unfairly, the action can be challenged, but that does not vitiate the provision; *Alka Ceramics, Piplodi, Himatnagar v. Gujarat State Financial Corporation, Ahmedabad,* AIR 1990 Guj 105 (DB).

PART XIII
TRADE, COMMERCE AND INTERCOURSE WITHIN THE TERRITORY OF INDIA

301. Freedom of trade, commerce and intercourse.—Subject to the other provisions of this Part, trade, commerce and intercourse throughout the territory of India shall be free.

Notes on Article 301

Imposition of duty does not in every case tantamount to infringement of article 301. One has to determine whether the impugned provision amounts to a restriction directly and immediately on the movement of trade or commerce. *See* the undermentioned cases:

(i) *Atiabari Tea Co. Ltd. v. State of Assam,* AIR 1961 SC 232: (1961) 1 SCR 809: ILR (1961) 13 Assam 257.

(ii) *Automobile Transport (Rajasthan) Ltd. v. State of Rajasthan,* AIR 1962 SC 1406: (1963) 1 SCR 491: (1962) 2 SCA 35.

(iii) *Andhra Sugars Ltd. v. State of Andhra Pradesh,* AIR 1968 SC 599: (1968) 1 SCR 705: 21 STC 212: (1968) 1 SCA 213: (1968) 1 Mad LJ (SC) 117: 1968 (1) SCJ 694.

(iv) *State of Madras v. N.K. Nataraja Mudaliar,* AIR 1969 SC 147: (1968) 3 SCR 829: 22 STC 376.

(v) *State of Kerala v. A.B. Abdul Khadir,* AIR 1970 SC 1912: (1970) SCR 700: 1969 KLT 649.

(vi) *Goodyear India Ltd. v. State of Haryana,* AIR 1990 SC 781 (806): (1990) 2 SCC 712: JT 1989 (4) SC 229, paragraphs 74 and 75.

(vii) *Maharaja Tourist Service v. State of Gujarat,* AIR 1991 SC 1650: (1992) Supp 1 SCC 489: 1991 AIR SCW 1643: 1991 (2) Cur CC 479: (1991) 2 SCR 524: 1991 (2) UJ (SC) 251.

Freedom of Inter-state & Intra-state Trade & Commerce

(a) Article 301 provides freedom not from all laws but freedom from such laws which restrict or affect activities of trade and commerce among the States; *Jindal Stainless Ltd. v. State of Haryana,* AIR 2006 SC 2550: 2006 AIR SCW 3396: 2006 (2) All CJ 1216: 2006 (283) ITR 1: (2006) 7 SCC 241: (2006) 4 SCALE 300: 2006 (3) Supreme 593: 2006 (194) Taxation 525.

(b) Article 301 refers to freedom from laws which go beyond regulations which burdens, restricts or prevents the trade movements between states and within state; *Jindal Stainless Ltd. v. State of Haryana,* AIR 2006 SC 2550: 2006 AIR SCW 3396: 2006 (2) All CJ 1216: 2006 (283) ITR 1: (2006) 7 SCC 241: (2006) 4 SCALE 300: 2006 (3) Supreme 593: 2006 (194) Taxation 525.

302. Power of Parliament to impose restrictions on trade, commerce and intercourse.—Parliament may by law impose such restrictions on the freedom of trade, commerce or intercourse between one State and another or within any part of the territory of India as may be required in the public interest.

303. Restrictions on the legislative powers of the Union and of the States with regard to trade and commerce.—(1) Notwithstanding anything in article 302, neither Parliament nor the Legislature of a State shall have power to make any law giving, or authorising the giving of, any preference to one State over another, or making, or authorising the making of, any discrimination between one State and another, by virtue of any entry relating to trade and commerce in any of the Lists in the Seventh Schedule.

(2) Nothing in clause (1) shall prevent Parliament from making any law giving, or authorising the giving of, any preference or making, or authorising the making of, any discrimination if it is declared by such law that it is necessary to do so for the purpose of dealing with a situation arising from scarcity of goods in any part of the territory of India.

304. Restrictions on trade, commerce and intercourse among States.— Notwithstanding anything in article 301 or article 303, the Legislature of a State may by law—

(a) impose on goods imported from other States [or the Union territories] any tax to which similar goods manufactured or produced in that State are subject, so, however, as not to discriminate between goods so imported and goods so manufactured or produced; and

(b) impose such reasonable restrictions on the freedom of trade, commerce or intercourse with or within that State as may be required in the public interest:

Provided that no Bill or amendment for the purposes of clause (b) shall be introduced or moved in the Legislature of a State without the previous sanction of the President.

Notes on Article 304

The test of reasonableness for the purposes of clause (b) of article 304 would be the same as the test adopted for the purpose of article 19(6). *See* the undermentioned cases:

(i) *Tika Ramji* v. *State of Uttar Pradesh*, (1956) SCR 393: AIR 1956 SC 676: 1956 SCA 979: 1956 SCJ 625: 1956 All WR (HC) 657.

(ii) *Kalyani Stores* v. *State of Orissa*, AIR 1966 SC 1686: (1966) 1 SCR 865: (1966) 2 SCA 36: 1966 (2) SCJ 367: 1967 SCD 303: 33 Cut LT 356.

Taxation by a State on goods imported from outside is valid provided it is non-discriminatory and this includes sales tax so long as it is non-discriminatory. *See* the undermentioned cases:

(i) *State of Madras* v. *N.K. Nataraja Mudaliar*, AIR 1969 SC 147: (1968) 3 SCR 829: (1968) 22 STC 376.

(ii) *State of Rajasthan* v. *Mangilal*, (1969) 2 SCC 710.

(iii) *Indian Cement* v. *State of Andhra Pradesh*, AIR 1988 SC 567: (1988) 1 SCC 743: (1988) 69 STC 305.

A notification issued in exercise of legislative power under sections 24 and 25 of the U.P. Sales Tax Act, 1948, is a "law" within articles 304 and 306; *Video Electronics Pvt Ltd.* v. *State of Punjab*, AIR 1990 SC 820: (1990) 3 SCC 87: (1989) Supp 2 SCR 731.

An action which furthers the economic development of the whole of India and its unity by removing economic barriers cannot be said to be discriminatory; *Video Electronics Pvt Ltd.* v. *State of Punjab*, AIR 1990 SC 820: (1990) 3 SCC 87: (1989) Supp 2 SCR 731, paragraphs 20-28 (3 Judges).

Regulation and Prohibition must be Distinguished from Each Other

(a) A rule which totally prohibits the movement of forest produce between specified hours is prohibitory, (b) A rule which permits, transport, subject to specified conditions, for

---

1. Ins. by the Constitution (Seventh Amendment) Act, 1956, sec. 29 and Sch. (w.e.f. 1-11-1956).

preventing public injury or to serve the public good, *e.g.*, in pursuance of the directive under article 51A would be a reasonable restriction whether under article 19(1)(g) or under article 304; *State of Tamil Nadu* v. *Sanjeetha Trading Co.*, AIR 1993 SC 237: (1993) 1 SCC 236: 1992 AIR SCW 2934: 1993 (2) EFR 115: JT 1992 (Supp) 695: 1992 (3) SCJ 293: (1992) 4 SCR 840, paragraphs 17 and 18.

The illegal felling of trees may be regulated by requiring that no forest produce should be transported from one place to another without obtaining a permit from a specified officer; *Aramachine and Lakri Vikreta Sangh, Nagpur* v. *State of Rajasthan*, AIR 1992 Raj 7: 1991 (2) Raj LW 598, paragraphs 10, 14 and 17.

Where the State law does not offend against article 301 or article 303, it need not be examined whether the conditions imposed by article 304 are satisfied; *Video Electronics Pvt Ltd.* v. *State of Punjab*, AIR 1990 SC 820: (1990) 3 SCC 87: (1989) Supp 2 SCR 731, paragraphs 20, 28 (3 Judges).

Where an assessee purchases upon scrap from both local dealers in the State of Karnataka and dealers outside the State and the State of Karnataka imposes a tax on the sale of ingots manufactured out of scrap purchased from outside the State while ingots manufactured from locally purchased scrap would not be subjected to such a tax, the case would be hit by clause (a) of article 304; *Andhra Steel Corporation* v. *Commissioner of Commercial Taxes in Karnataka*, AIR 1990 SC 1912: 1990 Supp SCC 617: JT 1990 (2) SC 380, paragraphs 22-23.

A requirement to deposit a cash amount as security for realisation of the money due under a Chit Fund Scheme has been held to be in the public interest; *Subodhaya Chit Fund (P) Ltd.* v. *Director of Chits, Madras*, AIR 1991 SC 998: (1991) Supp 2 SCC 131: 1991 AIR SCW 271: 1991 (2) Bank CLR 243: 1993 (76) Comp Cas 873, paragraph 4.

Where the original act received the President's sanction under article 304(b), no fresh sanction is required where the Amending Act, without imposing any additional restriction merely varied the form of restriction; *Subodhaya Chit Fund (P) Ltd.* v. *Director of Chits, Madras*, AIR 1991 SC 998: (1991) Supp 2 SCC 131: 1991 AIR SCW 271: 1991 (2) Bank CLR 243: 1993 (76) Comp Cas 873, paragraph 5.

[1][**305. Saving of existing laws and laws providing for State monopolies.**— Nothing in articles 301 and 303 shall affect the provisions of any existing law except in so far as the President may by order otherwise direct; and nothing in article 301 shall affect the operation of any law made before the commencement of the Constitution (Fourth Amendment) Act, 1955, in so far as it relates to, or prevent Parliament or the Legislature of a State from making any law relating to, any such matter as is referred to in sub-clause (ii) of clause (6) of article 19.]

Notes on Article 305

Where a pre-existing State Act is amended by a post Constitution Act then the protection of article 305—

(a) is available to the amending Act also if it is merely clarificatory; but

(b) is not available in so far as the amending Act makes any additional provisions; *Punjab Traders* v. *State of Punjab*, AIR 1990 SC 2300: (1991) 1 SCC 86, paragraph 14.

306. Power of certain States in Part B of the First Schedule to impose restrictions on trade and commerce.—[*Rep. by the Constitution (Seventh Amendment) Act, 1956, sec. 29 and Sch. (w.e.f. 1-11-1956).*]

307. Appointment of authority for carrying out the purposes of articles 301 to 304.—Parliament may by law appoint such authority as it considers appropriate for carrying out the purposes of articles 301, 302, 303 and 304, and confer on the authority so appointed such powers and such duties as it thinks necessary.

---

1. Subs. by the Constitution (Fourth Amendment) Act, 1955, sec. 4, for article 305 (w.e.f. 27-4-1955).

PART XIV

SERVICES UNDER THE UNION AND THE STATES

CHAPTER I

SERVICES

308. Interpretation.—In this Part, unless the context otherwise requires, the expression "State" [1][does not include the State of Jammu and Kashmir].

309. Recruitment and conditions of service of persons serving the Union or a State.—Subject to the provisions of this Constitution, Acts of the appropriate Legislature may regulate the recruitment, and conditions of service of persons appointed, to public services and posts in connection with the affairs of the Union or of any State:

Provided that it shall be competent for the President or such person as he may direct in the case of services and posts in connection with the affairs of the Union, and for the Governor [2][***] of a State or such person as he may direct in the case of services and posts in connection with the affairs of the State, to make rules regulating the recruitment, and the conditions of service of persons appointed, to such services and posts until provision in that behalf is made by or under an Act of the appropriate Legislature under this article, and any rules so made shall have effect subject to the provisions of any such Act.

Notes on Article 309

Article 309 is expressly made subject to other provisions of the Constitution and subject to that, appropriate legislature or governor can regulate the recruitment and conditions of service of persons appointed to public services and posts in connection with the affairs of State concerned (Para 18); *State of Bihar* v. *Bal Mukund Sah*, AIR 2000 SC 1296: 2000 AIR SCW 1180: JT 2000 (3) SC 221: (2000) 4 SCC 640: 2000 SCC (L&S) 489: 2000 (2) SCJ 599: 2000 (3) SCT 459: (2000) 2 SCALE 415: 2000 (2) Supreme 409.

Administrative Instructions

Though non-statutory Rules cannot modify statutory Rules, there is nothing to prevent the Government from issuing administrative instructions on matters upon which the statutory Rules are silent; *Comptroller & Auditor General of India* v. *Mohan*, AIR 1991 SC 2288: (1992) 1 SCC 20: (1992) 1 LLJ 335: (1992) 1 SLJ 1.

Adverse Remarks in Confidential Report

Adverse remarks against which a representation is pending should not be taken into account when considering an employee's case for selection to the Selection Grade, *etc.*; *State of Madhya Pradesh* v. *Bani*, (1990) Supp SCC 736: AIR 1990 SC 1308: (1990) 1 LLN 780, paragraph 6.

If an adverse order is challenged in a court of law, it is always open to the competent authority to place before the court the reasons which may have led to the rejection of the representation; *Union of India* v. *E.G. Nambudri* , AIR 1991 SC 1216: (1991) 3 SCC 38: (1991) 17 ATC 104: (1991) 62 FLR 850.

A copy of the adverse entry is to be supplied to the employee within a reasonable time. This obligation to communicate does not extend to any observation in the entry which is not adverse to the employee; *Baikuntha* v. *C.D.M.O.*, (1992) 2 SCC 299: AIR 1992 SC 1020: (1992) 1 LLJ 784: (1992) 21 ATC 649, paragraph 33 (3 Judges).

---

1. Subs. by the Constitution (Seventh Amendment) Act, 1956, sec. 29 and Sch., for "means a State specified in Part A or Part B of the First Schedule" (w.e.f. 1-11-1956).

2. The words "or Rajpramukh" omitted by the Constitution (Seventh Amendment) Act, 1956, sec. 29 and Sch. (w.e.f. 1-11-1956).

Appointment

Though a person, by making an application for a post pursuant to an advertisement, does not acquire any vested right to be appointed to that post, he acquires a right to be *considered* for selection according to the terms of that advertisement. The eligibility of a candidate for selection for a post depends upon whether he is qualified in accordance with the relevant Rules as they existed at the date of the advertisement for recruitment; *N.T. Devin Katti* v. *Karnataka Public Service Commission,* (1990) 3 SCC 157: AIR 1990 SC 1233: 1990 Lab IC 1009.

Armed Forces

As regards retirees from the Armed forces, the Supreme Court has not accepted the demand of retirees of armed forces for "one rank one pension"; *Indian Ex-Service League* v. *Union of India,* AIR 1991 SC 1182: (1991) 2 SCC 104: (1991) 16 ATC 488: (1991) 1 LLN 387, paragraphs 8, 10 and 18.

It is legitimate for the State Government to announce special benefits of pension, increments *etc.,* to persons enrolled in the armed forces during emergency as contrasted with those enrolled before emergency. Older men, by joining the military service, lost the chance of joining other Government departments. The discrimination is reasonable; *Dhan Singh* v. *State of Haryana,* AIR 1991 SC 1047: (1991) Supp 2 SCC 190: (1991) 17 ATC 317: (1991) 2 LLN 8.

Compulsory Retirement

Compulsory retirement does not contain any stigma and is based on the subjective satisfaction of the authority. However, an order of compulsory retirement cannot be quashed under article 226, on the ground that the adverse entry was not communicated to the petitioner, or that rules of natural justice or the requirements of article 21 of the Constitution have not been complied with; *Union of India* v. *Reddy,* AIR 1990 SC 563, paragraph 27; *State of Sikkim* v. *Sonam,* (1991) Supp 1 SCC 179: AIR 1991 SC 534: (1991) 17 ATC 257, paragraphs 4 and 5.

Copywriters

The copywriters are mere licencees. They are not on establishment under the Rules formulated under article 309; *State of West Bengal* v. *West Bengal Regn. Copy Writers Assocn.,* AIR 2010 SC 2184.

Criminal Proceedings

Since article 20(2) has been held to be applicable only to punishment in judicial proceedings, there is no question of its applications where a prosecution or acquittal in a criminal proceeding is followed by a departmental proceeding against a Government servant and *vice versa.* Conversely, recovery of embezzled or other recovery due to the Government by departmental proceeding cannot bar a criminal prosecution for the offence, if any; *Bishwanath* v. *Union of India,* (1991) 16 ATC 912 (Cal), paragraphs 14-16 (FB).

Discrimination

Even as between employees of the same class of service, it would be permissible to give weightage to those who acquire a relevant higher qualification, which is reasonable, *e.g.,* giving accelerated promotion to the most meritorious in order to attract brilliant candidates to the public service; *Biswas* v. *State Bank of India,* (1991) 2 UJ SC 567:AIR 1991 SC 2039: (1991) Supp 2 SCC 354, paragraph 4. .

If the Rule be applicable to all classes of Government servants, it cannot be challenged as discriminatory, but if it is *mala fide,* or arbitrary or perverse, the order may be struck down; *Baikuntha* v. *C.D.M.O.,* (1992) 2 SCC 299: (1992) 21 ATC 649: AIR 1992 SC 1020: (1992) 1 LLJ 784, paragraphs 32 and 34 (3 Judges).

Examination

The court would not interfere with the comparative merits of candidates as assessed by the examining body, in the absence of bias or *mala fides* or material irregularity in the Constitution of the examining body or the procedure adopted by it—because these are matters requiring an expertise which the courts do not possess; *Dalpat Abasaheb Solunke* v. *Dr. B.S. Mahajan,* (1990) 1 SCC 305, paragraph 12 (3 Judges); *Jaswant* v. *State of Punjab,* (1991) Supp 1 SCC 313: (1991) 1 LLJ 580: (1991) 16 ATC 932, paragraph 6.

Exploitation

The State should not exploit its employees nor should it take advantage of the helplessness of either the employees or the unemployed persons. The State should act as a model employer and give equal pay for equal work. It should not keep a person in temporary or *ad hoc* status for long, and take steps for their regularisation; *State of Haryana* v. *Piara*, (1992) 4 SCC 118: AIR 1992 SC 2130: (1992) 21 ATC 403: 1992 Lab IC 2168.

The rule of equality of pay cannot be so applied as to give to an employee the higher emoluments of a post in which he has never worked; *Virender* v. *Avinash*, AIR 1991 SC 958: (1990) 3 SCC 472: (1991) 14 ATC 732.

In general, the grant of a higher pay to a junior in the same cadre would be violative of the rule of "equal pay for equal work". But to this there are exceptions founded on justifiable grounds or intelligible differential, *e.g.*, where the higher pay offered to a junior is personal to him, say, on account of additional duties; *Chief Engineer* v. *Jagdish*, AIR 1991 SC 2000: (1991) Supp 2 SCC 1: (1991) 17 ATC 398, paragraph 5.

Gratuity

Government has no longer any discretion to forfeit gratuity on any ground; *Jesuratnam* v. *Union of India*, (1990) Supp SCC 640: 1990 SCC (L&S) 370., paragraph 2.

High Court

In regard to making appointments to clerical posts in the subordinate courts, the Chief Justice of the High Court cannot depart from the constitutional and statutory provisions on the subject. If the Chief Justice takes upon himself the power of both the authorities mentioned above to make selections for, as well as appointments in, the establishments of the subordinate courts, such appointments shall be void; *Puttaswamy* v. *Chief Justice*, AIR 1991 SC 295: (1991) Supp 2 SCC 421: (1991) 1 LLN 352.

Interpretation

Subject to certain limitations, Government's interpretation of its own rules and the policy decisions made thereunder should be respected by the courts; *Ajeet Singh Singhvi* v. *State of Rajasthan*, (1991) Supp 1 SCC 343: 1991 SCC (L&S) 1026: (1991) 16 ATC 935, paragraph 12.

Interview

There is nothing contrary in preparing a select list based on the results of the written test alone and then to call for interview out of that list, depending upon the number of vacancies available; *Biswas* v. *State Bank of India*, (1991) 2 UJ SC 567: (1991) Supp 2 SCC 354: AIR 1991 SC 2039, paragraphs 4.

Where the Rules relating to recruitment do not require that both written and *viva voce* tests should be adopted, selection by interview alone cannot be held to be illegal. There is no inflexible standard as to the duration of an interview. A candidate cannot complain that the interview was too short, except in the case of a selection post, *i.e.*, of a higher category; *Sardara Singh* v. *State of Punjab*, AIR 1991 SC 2248: (1991) 4 SCC 555: 1991 SCC (L&S) 1357, paragraphs 6 and 7.

The court would not interfere where, in the absence of the Rules fixing any pass marks for the interview test, the examining body fixes a 40% pass marks for the interview as for the written test; *Manjeet* v. *E.S.I.C.*, AIR 1990 SC 1104: (1990) 2 SCC 367: (1990) 13 ATC 686: (1990) 1 CLR 777, paragraph 6 (3 Judge Bench).

Lien

When a Government servant's lien is suspended under the Rules, *e.g.*, while he is appointed to a deputation post, he loses all chances of being considered for promotion during the period of such suspension of lien. His lien in the patent cadre is revived only when he reverts to the parent cadre either on his own option, or on release from the deputation; *Ram Saran* v. *State of Punjab*, (1991) 2 SCC 253: (1991) 16 ATC 484: (1991) 1 LLJ 585, paragraphs 14, 19-21.

The lien on a post is acquired only when the employee has been confirmed and made permanent on that post and not earlier; *Triveni* v. *State of Uttar Pradesh*, AIR 1992 SC 496: (1992) Supp 1 SCC 524: (1992) 19 ATC 931, paragraphs 21-22.

Mandamus

Mandamus would issue to give the petitioner the same pay scale as has been given to employees of the same cadre, without any rational justification; *State of West Bengal* v. *Debdas*, (1991) 1 SCC 138: (1991) 17 ATC 261: 1991 SCC (L&S) 841, paragraph 15; *State of Rajasthan* v. *Gurcharan*, (1990) Supp SCC 778: AIR 1990 SC 1760: (1990) 2 LLN 278: (1990) 1 SLJ 151, paragraphs 10-11.

Officiating Post

Where an officer, substantively holding a post, is ordered merely to discharge the duties of a higher post in the exigencies of public service, he is not entitled to the emoluments of the higher post. He can claim only what is called the "charge allowance"; *Ramakant Shripad Sinai Advalpalkar* v. *Union of India*, AIR 1991 SC 1145: (1991) Supp 2 SCC 733: 1992 SCC (L&S) 115: 1993 (3) SCT 586: 1992 (6) Serv LR 290, paragraph 4.

Privacy

The L.I.C. cannot terminate the service of a lady employee who refuses to give particulars about her menstrual periods. To demand such information compulsorily violates the right of privacy flowing from article 21 of the Constitution. The L.I.C. can (if it so chooses) get the employee medically examined, if the information in question is required to check pregnancy, *etc.*; *Neera Mathur* v. *L.I.C.*, (1992) 1 SCC 286: (1992) 19 ATC 31: AIR 1992 SC 392: (1992) 1 LLJ 322.

Promissory Estoppel

A change of policy is also controlled by the doctrines of promissory estoppel; *Amrit Banaspati Co. Ltd.* v. *State of Punjab*, (1992) 2 SCC 411: AIR 1992 SC 1075: 1992 AIR SCW 953: JT 1992 (2) SC 217: (1992) 2 SCR 13: 1992 (85) STC 493: 1992 (110) Taxation 60: 1992 (1) UJ SC 599, paragraphs 4-6.

Promotion

Any change in the Rules which affects the right to be considered for promotion would offend articles 14 and 16 but not a change which merely affects the chances of promotion. Any change in the Rules will, therefore, not be applicable only to vacancies which occurred prior to the amendment. But the petitioner was given the benefit of a retrospective amendment which took place during the pendency of his litigation; *Sheshrao Jungluji Bagle* v. *Govindrao*, AIR 1991 SC 76: (1991) Supp 1 SCC 367: (1991) 16 ATC 938: (1991) 2 LLJ 109, paragraph 3.

In considering an employee for promotion, the relevant authority is entitled to take into consideration the penalties imposed on him, including censure upto the date when such consideration takes place; *Union of India* v. *K.V. Jankiraman*, AIR 1991 SC 2010: (1991) 4 SCC 109: 1991 Lab IC 2045: 1991 AIR SCW 2276: JT 1991 (3) SC 527: 1991 (2) LLJ 570: 1992 (1) LLN 24: 1993 SCC (L&S) 387: (1991) 3 SCR 790, paragraph 8 (3 Judges).

The mere pendency of a departmental proceeding at any stage is not sufficient for not considering an employee's case for promotion or to withhold his promotion; *Union of India* v. *Tajinder Singh*, (1991) 4 SCC 129: 1991 SCC (L&S) 387: (1986) 2 SCALE 860, paragraph 4.

Withholding of promotion on reasonable ground is permissible; *Arumugam* v. *State of Tamil Nadu*, (1991) Supp 1 SCC 199: (1991) 17 ATC 407, paragraph 5.

The consideration of an employee for promotion may be postponed if he is suspended in view of the initiation of disciplinary of criminal proceedings against him; *Union of India* v. *K.V. Jankiraman*, AIR 1991 SC 2010: (1991) 4 SCC 109: 1991 Lab IC 2045: 1991 AIR SCW 2276: JT 1991 (3) SC 527: 1991 (2) LLJ 570: 1992 (1) LLN 24: 1993 SCC (L&S) 387: (1991) 3 SCR 790, paragraphs 16, 17 and 26 (3 Judges).

Provident Fund

Under a pension scheme, Government has a continuing obligation so long as the retiree is alive. In a Provident Fund Scheme, the retiree's right is crystallised on the date of retirement and after that date Government has no obligation. Hence if, under the Provident Fund Scheme, option is given to the pensioner from a specified cut off date, there is no discrimination and it would not be hit by article 14 of the Constitution; *Krishena* v. *Union of India*, AIR 1990 SC 1782: (1990) 4

SCC 207: (1990) 4 SCR 716, paragraphs 30 and 31; *All India Reserve Bank Retired Officers Assocn.* v. *Union of India*, AIR 1992 SC 767: (1992) Supp 1 SCC 664: 1992 Lab IC 633, paragraphs 8 and 10.

Contributory Provident Fund retirees and Pension Scheme Optees form two different classes; *State of Rajasthan* v. *Rajasthan Pensioner Samaj*, AIR 1991 SC 1743: (1991) Supp 2 SCC 141: (1991) 17 ATC 342: 1991 Lab IC 1651.

Qualification

The court would not interfere with the propriety of particular qualification for a post laid down by the Government; *Rangaswamy* v. *Government of Andhra Pradesh*, (1990) 1 SCC 288: AIR 1990 SC 535: 1990 Lab IC 296: (1990) 1 LLJ 526, paragraph 6.

It is competent for the appropriate authority to prescribe relevant qualifications for appointment to a post, provided they are not unconstitutional. It is not for the courts to consider and assess whether they are proper. A person who is aggrieved, can move the appropriate authority for review of the prescribed qualifications; *Rangaswamy* v. *Government of Andhra Pradesh*, AIR 1990 SC 535: (1990) 1 SCC 288: 1990 Lab IC 296: (1990) 1 LLJ 526; *Mahendran* v. *State of Karnataka*, (1990) 1 SCC 411: AIR 1990 SC 405: 1990 Lab IC 369, paragraphs 4-5 (3 Judges).

Quota

When appointments are made from more than one source, it is permissible to fix the ratio (known as 'quota') for recruitment from the different sources, and if rules are framed in this regard, they must ordinarily be followed strictly; *Direct Recruit Class-II Engineering Officers' Association* v. *State of Maharashtra*, (1990) 2 SCC 715: AIR 1990 SC 1607: (1990) 13 ATC 348, paragraphs 21 and 47 (CB).

Railways

Employees in Railway Institutes and Railway Clubs are not railway employees and cannot be treated on par with employees in statutory railway canteens; *All India Railway Institute Employees' Association* v. *Union of India*, AIR 1990 SC 952: (1990) 2 SCC 542: (1990) 13 ATC 691.

Recruitment

In the absence of any constitutional bar (*e.g.* article 233), determination of the mode of recruitment to a service or post, say by promotion, transfer or direct appointment, is a matter of policy of the Government or other appropriate authority; *Union of India* v. *Syed*, (1992) 1 UJ SC 590: (1992) Supp 2 SCC 534: AIR 1994 SC 605: (1992) 2 CLR 38, paragraph 13 (3 Judges); *Rangaswamy* v. *Government of Andhra Pradesh*, AIR 1990 SC 535: (1990) 1 SCC 288: 1991 Lab IC 296: (1990) 1 LLJ 526.

Subject to constitutional provisions (*e.g.* article 233 of the Constitution), it is for the Government (or other appropriate authority) to decide as a matter of policy, whether recruitment to a particular service should be by (a) promotion, (b) direct recruitment, or (c) transfer; *Orissa J.S.A.* v. *State of Orissa*, AIR 1991 SC 382: (1992) Supp 1 SCC 187: (1992) 19 ATC 229, paragraph 3.

Retrenchment

(i) Where, owing to reduction of work or shrinkage of cadre, retrenchment becomes necessary, then the principle of "last come, first go" is applicable, subject to what is stated in (ii) below,

(ii) If, in disregard of this principle, a junior is retained in preference to a senior, article 14 of the Constitution is violated,

(iii) But the above principle does not apply where services of a temporary employee are terminated on an assessment of his merit in accordance with the conditions of his service,

(iv) In such a case, retaining a Junior with merit is no discrimination.

See the undermentioned cases:

(i) *Triveni* v. *State of Uttar Pradesh*, AIR 1992 SC 496: (1992) Supp 1 SCC 524: (1992) 19 ATC 931: (1992) 2 LLJ 23.

(ii) *State of Uttar Pradesh* v. *Kaushal,* (1991) 1 SCC 691 (1991) 16 ATC 498: (1991) 1 SLR 606, paragraph 5 (3 Judges).

Even where the restructuring of a service is necessitated by the mistake on the part of the Department, such change should not be so interpreted so as to prejudice those who were in service prior to the date when the change in the rule took place; *Nirmal* v. *Union of India,* (1991) Supp 2 SCC 363: (1991) 1 LLN 316: (1991) 1 SLR 761, paragraphs 3 and 5.

Rules

So long as a Rule framed under article 309 is not duly amended, it is binding on the Government and its action in matter covered by the rules must be regulated by the Rules; *Bhatnagar* v. *Union of India,* (1991) 1 SCC 544: (1991) 16 ATC 501: (1991) 1 SLR 191: (1991) 1 CLR 70, paragraph 13 (3 Judges).

A rule made in exercise of the power under the proviso to article 309 constitutes law within the meaning of article 235. For the same reason, such rule may be struck down only on such ground as may invalidate a legislative measure, *e.g.* violation of articles 14 and 16 of the Constitution, and not because the court considers it to be unreasonable; *Bansal* v. *Union of India,* AIR 1993 SC 978: (1992) Supp 2 SCC 318: (1992) 21 ATC 503: (1992) 4 SLR 445, paragraph 21; *Jaiswal* v. *Debi,* (1992) 1 UJ SC 731, paragraph 5; *Raghunath* v. *State of Karnataka,* AIR 1992 SC 81: (1992) 1 SCC 335: (1992) 19 ATC 507, paragraph 7.

Rule-making Power

Rules as to service matters may be made—

(a) under article 309, proviso, or

(b) subject to law made by competent legislation) by executive orders; *State of Haryana* v. *Piara,* (1992) 4 SCC 118: AIR 1992 SC 2130: (1992) 21 ATC 403, paragraph 21.

Salary

It has been laid down by a Constitution Bench, that the salary drawn on the date of retirement cannot be re-opened as a result of any enhancement made at a later date for persons retiring subsequently; *Indian Ex-Services League* v. *Union of India,* AIR 1991 SC 1182: (1991) 2 SCC 104: (1991) 16 ATC 488: (1991) 1 SLR 745, paragraphs 21 and 22.

Seniority

Fixation of seniority of the employees by placing them higher in seniority list by fixing their notional duty of confirmation on day of expiry of original period of probation is not contrary to law; *Om Prakash Shrivastava* v. *State of Madhya Pradesh,* AIR 2005 SC 2453: 2005 AIR SCW 2397: JT 2005 (4) SC 602: (2005) 11 SCC 488: 2005 (4) SCJ 323: 2005 (2) SCT 665: 2005 (5) SRJ 567: (2005) 4 SCALE 358: 2005 (4) Supreme 169.

Even where the order of appointment may have stated that the appointment was temporary or stop gap, *etc.,* yet, where it is established that the appointee has been working in that post for a long period (number of years) without break, the court may apply the principle of "continuous officiation" and hold that the appointee be deemed to have been regularised; *Nayar* v. *Union of India,* AIR 1992 SC 1574: (1992) Supp 2 SCC 508: (1992) 21 ATC 695; *State of Haryana* v. *Piara,* AIR 1992 SC 2130: (1992) 4 SCC 118: (1992) 21 ATC 403: 1992 Lab IC 2168, paragraph 12 (3 Judges).

A subsequent restructuring of the service or delay in holding the selection for which the employee was not responsible cannot take away his seniority for promotion; *Nirmal* v. *Union of India,* (1991) Supp 2 SCC 363, paragraphs 4-6.

It is open to the State to lay down any criteria which it thinks appropriate, for determining seniority in service and it is not competent for the court to strike down such Rule; *Dhan Singh* v. *State of Haryana,* (1991) 2 Supp SCC 190: (1991) 17 ATC 317: AIR 1991 SC 1407: (1991) 2 LLN 8, paragraph 10.

Where promotees have acquired a higher qualification or are selected by the Public Service Commission, Government can give them some weightage in seniority. There is no improper discrimination and court cannot interfere with such a policy decision of the Government;

State of Andhra Pradesh v. *Muralidhar,* AIR 1992 SC 922: (1992) 2 SCC 241: (1992) 20 ATC 226: 1992 Lab IC 855.

Where a person has been denied seniority by a wrong application of the rules or without any reasonable ground, the court may direct the competent authority to place him in the higher grade with effect from the date when his junior was placed therein, with consequential monetary benefits; *Dharam* v. *Administrator,* (1991) 17 ATC 925: AIR 1991 SC 1924: (1991) Supp 2 SCC 635: 1991 Lab IC 1695, paragraph 4.

In general, the court would not interfere with rules, or even executive instructions laying down the principles of seniority if they are 'reasonable, just and equitable', *Devdutta* v. *State of Madhya Pradesh,* (1992) 19 ATC 154: (1991) Supp 2 SCC 553: (1991) 1 LLJ 492: (1991) 1 SLJ 168 (SC), paragraph 17.

As between employees serving in the same service or cadre, seniority shall be determined by the Rules made under article 309. If there is no unconstitutionality in such Rules, the seniority *inter se* must be determined according to the criteria laid down in such rules, *e.g.,* rank and merit (where selected by the P.S.C.); the court cannot lay down any other criteria; *State of Tamil Nadu* v. *Pari,* 1991 (3) SCJ 302, paragraph 10 (3 Judges).

Service Matters: Judicial Interference

Judicial interference in service matters is called for only in order to examine that the action challenged before the court is from the point of—

  (a) fundamental rights,

  (b) statutory provisions,

  (c) rules and instructions,

  (d) fairness.

State of Haryana v. *Piara,* (1992) 4 SCC 118: AIR 1992 SC 2130: 1992 Lab IC 2168, para 21.

Temporary Service

The State should not keep a person in temporary or *ad hoc* service for a long period. It should take steps for his regularisation; *Dharwad District P.W.D. Literate Daily Wage Employees Association* v. *State of Karnataka,* (1990) 2 SCC 396: AIR 1990 SC 883: 1990 Lab IC 625, paragraph 23.

Termination

If the termination (of an employee) is arbitrary, it will be violative of article 16, even though the employee is of an *ad hoc,* temporary or officiating status, or even casual employee; *Shrilekha* v. *State of Uttar Pradesh,* (1991) 1 SCC 212: AIR 1991 SC 537: 1991 SCC (L&S) 742.

Transfer

When a person belongs to a service or cadre which is transferable, then, in the absence of any statutory restrictions, a person appointed to the cadre or service is transferable from one post to another, in the interests of public service. In such a case, transfer is an incident of the service and the employee cannot complain except where (a) it is ordered in violation of some mandatory statutory rule, (b) if it is actuated by *mala fides,* that is, some collateral purpose other than the interests of the administration. The court cannot, therefore, interfere on the mere ground that the transfer was made at the request of the employee and the competent authority granted it to avoid hardship; *Shilpi* v. *State of Bihar,* (1991) Supp 2 SCC 659: AIR 1991 SC 532: 1991 Lab IC 360, paragraphs 3-4.

Where employees are transferred from a Government Department to a statutory corporation and provision is made in the statute (or in the directions issued thereunder) that their existing conditions of service would not be adversely affected by the transfer, the court would interfere if the corporation frames regulations to change the conditions of service to the disadvantage of the employees, *e.g.,* in the matter of the age for retirement; *Dubey* v. *M.P.S.R.T.C.,* (1991) Supp 1 SCC 426: AIR 1991 SC 276: (1991) 16 ATC 939: (1991) 1 LLN 339, paragraph 11.

Vacancies

State is not bound to fill up a vacancy. But the decision not to fill up a vacancy has to be taken *bona fide* for good reasons. The mere fact that a person's name appears in the merit list does not give him a right to be appointed. But if the vacancy is filled up, the comparative merit (as reflected in the recruitment test) has to be respected and no discrimination is permissible; *Shankaran* v. *Union of India*, (1991) 3 SCC 47: (1991) 17 ATC 95: AIR 1991 SC 1612: (1991) 62 FLR 981: (1991) 2 LLN 65, paragraph 7a.

310. Tenure of office of persons serving the Union or a State.—(1) Except as expressly provided by this Constitution, every person who is a member of a defence service or of a civil service of the Union or of an all-India service or holds any post connected with defence or any civil post under the Union holds office during the pleasure of the President, and every person who is a member of a civil service of a State or holds any civil post under a State holds office during the pleasure of the Governor [1][***] of the State.

(2) Notwithstanding that a person holding a civil post under the Union or a State holds office during the pleasure of the President or, as the case may be, of the Governor [2][***] of the State, any contract under which a person, not being a member of a defence service or of an all-India service or of a civil service of the Union or a State, is appointed under this Constitution to hold such a post may, if the President or the Governor [3][***], as the case may be, deems it necessary in order to secure the services of a person having special qualifications, provide for the payment to him of compensation, if before the expiration of an agreed period that post is abolished or he is, for reasons not connected with any misconduct on his part, required to vacate that post.

Notes on Article 310

Contract

Clause (2) of article 310 is only an enabling provision which empowers the Governor to enter into the contract with specifically qualified person(s) providing for payment of compensation where no compensation is payable under the doctrine "service at the pleasure of the State". In absence of any specific term regarding compensation, it cannot be countenanced that the intention was to pay it; *J.P. Bansal* v. *State of Rajasthan*, AIR 2003 SC 1405: (2003) 5 SCC 134: (2003) 3 SLR 50: (2003) 2 LLN 405.

As to the effect of contract, *see State of Gujarat* v. *Kampavat*, (1992) 3 SCC 226: AIR 1992 SC 1685: 1992 Lab IC 1687: (1992) 21 ATC 112.

Expiry of Term

Where article 310 (2) applies and the service terminates on expiry of period then—

(a) no notice required.

(b) there is no question of premature retirement.

State of Gujarat v. *P.J. Kampavat*, (1992) 3 SCC 226: AIR 1992 SC 1685: 1992 AIR SCW 1866: JT 1992 (Supp) 102: 1992 SCC (L&S) 654: 1992 (2) SCJ 404: (1992) 2 SCR 845: 1993 (1) SCT 231: (1992) 5 Serv LR 524: (1992) 2 UJ SC 78; *Aggarwal* v. *Union of India*, (1992) 2 UJ SC 266.

Pleasure: Doctrine of

The doctrine of pleasure codified in article 310(1) of the Constitution is a legacy of the English. It means that a servant of the Crown holds office during the pleasure of the Sovereign. But in order to protect civil servant against the political interference, article 311 introduces certain safeguards. Moreover, a specific contract can override the doctrine of pleasure;

---

1. The words "or, as the case may be, the Rajpramukh" omitted by the Constitution (Seventh Amendment) Act, 1956, sec. 29 and Sch. (w.e.f. 1-11-1956).

2. The words "or Rajpramukh" omitted by the Constitution (Seventh Amendment) Act, 1956, sec. 29 and Sch. (w.e.f. 1-11-1956).

3. The words "or the Rajpramukh" omitted by the Constitution (Seventh Amendment) Act, 1956, sec. 29 and Sch. (w.e.f. 1-11-1956).

Purshottam v. *Union of India*, AIR 1958 SC 36 (41): 1958 SCR 828: (1958) 1 LLJ 544; *Moti Ram Deka* v. *Union of India*, AIR 1964 SC 600: (1964) 5 SCR 683: (1964) 2 SCA 372: (1964) 2 LLJ 467: ILR (1964) 2 All 717: ILR (1964) 16 Assam 81.

Where the doctrine of pleasure applies there are no limitations other than those flowing from the Constitution or from rules or orders under the Constitution; *Madhosingh Daulatsingh* v. *State of Bombay*, AIR 1960 Bom 285: 1959 Nag LJ 441: 61 Bom LR 1537: ILR (1959) Bom 1846: (1960) 1 LLJ 291.

Exceptions to the doctrine are found in the Constitution as illustrated by articles 124, 148, 217, 218 and 324. It is also subject to fundamental rights; *State of Orissa* v. *Dhirendranath*, AIR 1961 SC 1715; *Union of India* v. *More*, AIR 1962 SC 630 (633): (1961) 2 LLJ 427: (1961) 3 FLR 313.

311. Dismissal, removal or reduction in rank of persons employed in civil capacities under the Union or a State.—(1) No person who is a member of a civil service of the Union or an all-India service or a civil service of a State or holds a civil post under the Union or a State shall be dismissed or removed by an authority subordinate to that by which he was appointed.

[1][(2) No such person as aforesaid shall be dismissed or removed or reduced in rank except after an inquiry in which he has been informed of the charges against him and given a reasonable opportunity of being heard in respect of those charges [2][***]:

[3][Provided that where it is proposed after such inquiry, to impose upon him any such penalty, such penalty may be imposed on the basis of the evidence adduced during such inquiry and it shall not be necessary to give such person any opportunity of making representation on the penalty proposed:

Provided further that this clause shall not apply—]

(a) where a person is dismissed or removed or reduced in rank on the ground of conduct which has led to his conviction on a criminal charge; or

(b) where the authority empowered to dismiss or remove a person or to reduce him in rank is satisfied that for some reason, to be recorded by that authority in writing, it is not reasonably practicable to hold such inquiry; or

(c) where the President or the Governor, as the case may be, is satisfied that in the interest of the security of the State it is not expedient to hold such inquiry.

[4][(3) If, in respect of any such person as aforesaid, a question arises whether it is reasonably practicable to hold such inquiry as is referred to in clause (2), the decision thereon of the authority empowered to dismiss or remove such person or to reduce him in rank shall be final.]

Notes on Article 311

Abolition of Post

Even in the case of a permanent post, article 311(2) is not attracted, simply because abolition of a post for administrative exigencies could not be said to be a 'punishment' for some

---

1. Subs. by the Constitution (Fifteenth Amendment) Act, 1963, sec. 10, for clause (2) (w.e.f. 5-10-1963).
2. Certain words omitted by the Constitution (Forty-second Amendment) Act, 1976, sec. 44(a) (w.e.f. 3-1-1977).
3. Subs. by the Constitution (Forty-second Amendment) Act, 1976, sec. 44(b), for certain words (w.e.f. 3-1-1977).
4. Subs. by the Constitution (Fifteenth Amendment) Act, 1963, sec. 10, for clause (3) (w.e.f. 5-10-1963).

misconduct, and also because the creation and abolition of a post is the exclusive concern of the executive. The court thus upheld the abolition of the posts of Election Commissioners within 3 months of their creation; *S.S. Dhanoa* v. *Union of India,* AIR 1991 SC 1745: (1991) 3 SCC 567: (1991) 2 LLN 428.

Where a post (even if it is a permanent post) is abolished, article 311(2) is not attracted. There is no "punishment" and no "misconduct"; *Kamra* v. *N.I.A.,* (1992) 2 SCC 36: AIR 1992 SC 1072: (1992) 1 LLN 401: (1992) 1 LLJ 630, paragraphs 4 and 5.

Adverse Remarks

Where there is no rule requiring the competent authority to record or communicate reasons for rejecting a representation against adverse remarks, such order of rejection cannot be challenged merely on the ground of non-recording of reasons, provided it was passed in a fair and just manner, after considering the materials on record. The competent authority may show the reasons from the notings in the file and other materials on the record; *Union of India* v. *Nambudri,* AIR 1991 SC 1216: (1991) 3 SCC 38: 1991 SCC (L&S) 813: (1991) 17 ATC 104, paragraphs 10 and 11.

Administrative Tribunal

In view of section 14(1)(b) of the Specific Relief Act, 1963 the court cannot direct the employer to reinstate a dismissed employee, even though as a result of the declaration of the court that the dismissal was wrongful or unconstitutional, the Government may be obliged to put him back to his post or another post of the same status; *Om Prakash* v. *State of Uttar Pradesh,* (1991) Supp 2 SCC 436: AIR 1991 SC 425: 1991 Lab IC 303, paragraph 3.

There may be circumstances in which the court may not on equitable grounds, interfere with an order of reinstatement which has been already implemented; *Union of India* v. *Chhida,* (1991) Supp 2 SCC 16: 1991 SCC (L&S) 1362, paragraph 5.

The High Court, in writ jurisdiction, is not a court of appeal. It cannot interfere on the ground of inadequacy or unreliability of the evidence on which the disciplinary authority has acted. It cannot review the evidence and come to its own conclusions; *Maharashtra State Board of Secondary and Higher Secondary Education* v. *K.S. Gandhi,* (1991) 2 SCC 716: 1991 AIR SCW 879, paragraphs 10, 38.

After the establishment of an Administrative tribunal under the Administrative Tribunals Act, 1985 an application under section 19 of that Act would lie to the Tribunal, in place of the High Court under article 226 of the Constitution. *See* the undermentioned cases:

(i) *Union of India* v. *Deep,* (1992) 4 SCC 432: AIR 1993 SC 382: 1993 SCC (L&S) 21: (1993) 23 ATC 356, paragraphs 3 and 6.

(ii) *C.S.I.R.* v. *Labour Court,* (1992) 19 ATC 414, paragraph 2.

So far as employees of the Government or authorities coming under article 323A(1) of the Constitution and section 14 of the Administrative Tribunals Act, 1985 are concerned, the jurisdiction of the civil courts now belongs to the Tribunal set up under the Act [sec. 15(1)], and the remedy of the aggrieved employee is by an application under section 19 of the Act; *Ashok* v. *Union of India,* (1992) 20 ATC 501 (Pat).

Appeal

For article 311(2), proviso to apply, it is not necessary for the Government to wait until the disposal of appeal or revision presented against conviction. But if the conviction is subsequently set aside, on appeal or otherwise, the order of dismissal ceases to have effect and the employee is entitled to be reinstated forthwith and to recover arrears of salary from the date of the challenge of dismissal till he is properly dismissed in compliance with article 311(2); *Babu Lal* v. *State of Haryana,* (1991) 2 SCC 335: (1991) 16 ATC 481: AIR 1991 SC 1310: (1991) 1 SLR 756, paragraph 7.

Civil Post

The provisions of article 311 extend to all persons holding a civil post under the Union or a State, including members of the all India and State Service. Members of the Defence Services are thus excluded from the scope of this article, but not police officers. The only persons who are excluded from the purview of article 311(1) [which is in the nature of an exception to the general provision in article 310(1)] are—

(a) members of Defence Services, and

(b) persons holding any post connected with defence, but not Police Officers.

Central Bank v. *Bernard*, (1991) 1 SCC 319: (1991) 15 ATC 720: (1991) 1 LLN 1111, paragraph 5.

Compulsory Retirement

Compulsory retirement (if penal) must comply with article 311; *Ram Ekbal Sharma* v. *State of Bihar*, AIR 1990 SC 1368: (1990) 3 SCC 504: 1990 SCC (L&S) 491: (1990) 2 SLJ 98.

Even though the order of compulsory retirement may be couched in innocuous language without making any imputation against the Government servant, the court may, in appropriate cases, lift the veil to find out whether the order is based on any misconduct of the Government servant or whether it is *bona fide*; *Ram Ekbal Sharma* v. *State of Bihar*, AIR 1990 SC 1368: (1990) 3 SCC 504: (1990) 2 SLJ 98.

(i) Compulsory retirement in the public interest carries no stigma under rule 16(3) of the All India Services (Death-cum-Retirement) Rules, 1958 and the officer retains full pensionary benefits.

(ii) Loss of efficiency at that age is a ground of public interest. It is not a punishment. Hence article 311(2) is not attracted.

(iii) Even if adverse entries are not communicated, the order is valid if there are no *mala fides*.

Baikuntha v. *C.D.M.O.*, (1992) 2 SCC 299: (1992) 21 ATC 649: AIR 1992 SC 1020: (1992) 1 LLJ 784.

Even an adverse report for a *single* year may constitute sufficient material for the Government to come to a decision that the employee's standard of work was not satisfactory and should therefore be retired. The reason is that the nature of the delinquency, and whether it is of such a nature as to require compulsory retirement is for the departmental authorities to decide. The court will not interfere with the exercise of that power except on the ground of *mala fides etc.*; *Post and Telegraph Board* v. *Murthy*, (1992) 2 SCC 317:(1992) 21 ATC 664: AIR 1992 SC 1368: (1992) 1 LLN 948, paragraph 5.

Confirmation

Where the appointment of a temporary employee is made for an unspecified or indefinite period of time, he cannot claim that he has been automatically confirmed on the expiry of the period of appointment. It is true, that the period can be extended indefinitely. But that does not mean that the services of the incumbent holding the post would be extended; *Sri Dhiraj Ghosh* v. *Union of India*, AIR 1991 SC 73: (1991) Supp 2 SCC 203: 1990 Lab IC 1956: 1993 (24) ATC 541: 1993 SCC (L&S) 671: 1994 (2) SCT 736: (1993) 3 Serv LR 18.

Copy of Report

Where the action proposed is not based on a report, or the disciplinary authority itself is the Inquiry Officer, the omission to supply a copy thereof to the delinquent will not vitiate the proceedings; *Union of India* v. *Mohd. Ramzan Khan*, (1991) 1 SCC 588: (1991) 16 ATC 505: AIR 1991 SC 471, paragraphs 16-18 (3 Judges).

Criminal Proceedings

Where the employee was acquitted on the merits and was reinstated on the basis thereof, and thereafter allowed to retire on superannuation, it would be against the interest of justice, to re-start the disciplinary proceedings against him on the basis of certain observations of the High Court in the case relating to a co-accused; *Prafulla* v. *State of Maharashtra*, AIR 1992 SC 2209: (1993) Supp 1 SCC 564: (1993) 23 ATC 675: (1993) 1 LLJ 171.

Date of Birth

A question as to disputed age would not ordinarily be gone into in a writ petition because it is a question of fact. A decree passed against a University or Board to correct the date of birth is not binding on the Government if the State has not been made a party. It can only be treated as evidence; *Director* v. *Sitadevi*, AIR 1991 SC 308: (1991) Supp 2 SCC 378: (1991) 1 LLN 578.

Where an employee has throughout his career accepted a particular date as his date of birth, by his own statement, and near about the date of his superannuation, he makes a representation and files some documents, the order of the relevant authority, made upon a consideration of those documents, cannot be assailed on the ground that the order of rejection of his representation was made without giving him a personal hearing; *Executive Engineer Bhadrak (Rand B) Division, Orissa* v. *Rangadhar Mallik*, (1992) 2 UJ SC 453: (1993) Supp 1 SCC 763: (1993) 23 ATC 807: 1993 Lab IC 425, paragraph 3.

Disciplinary Enquiry
The uncommunicated past adverse entries in service record cannot be considered for imposition of punishment is respect of disciplinary enquiry; *Indu Bhushan Dwivedi* v. *State of Jharkhand*, AIR 2010 SC 2472.

The "authority" is a generic term and is used in different places with different meaning and purposes; *Union of India* v. *Alok Kumar*, AIR 2010 SC 2735.

Disciplinary Proceedings
Power of judicial review in respect of disciplinary proceedings by inquiry officer is confined to decision making process; *State of Uttar Pradesh* v. *Man Mohan Nath Sinha*, AIR 2010 SC 137.

Dismissal
When a government servant has been dismissed in contravention of either article 311(1) or article 311(2), or of a mandatory statutory rule, or of the principles of natural justice, he would be entitled to bring a suit against the Government; *State of Punjab* v. *Ram*, AIR 1992 SC 2188: (1992) 4 SCC 54: 1992 SCC (L&S) 793: (1992) 21 ATC 435, paragraph 11.

Whether any order discharging an employee, in exercise of the power conferred by the conditions of service amounts to an order of "dismissal" would depend upon several factors, such as—

(a) the nature of the enquiry, if any, that may have been held;
(b) the proceedings taken in the enquiry;
(c) the substance of the final order passed on such inquiry;
(d) material that existed prior to such order.

Double Jeopardy
Where a Government employee has been punished for the same misconduct both under the Army Act as also under the Central Civil Services (Classification and Control and Appeal) Rules, 1965, a question arises whether this would tentamount to 'double jeopardy'. The Supreme Court has held that the two proceedings operate in two different fields though the crime or misconduct may arise out of the same act. The Court-Martial proceedings deal with the personal aspect of the misconduct while proceedings under the Central Rules deal with the disciplinary aspect of the misconduct. The two proceedings do not overlap; *Union of India* v. *Sunil Kumar Sarkar*, AIR 2001 SC 1092: (2001) 3 SCC 414: 2001 Lab IC 1114: 2001 SCC (L&S) 600.

Fresh Inquiry
Where an order of dismissal is set aside by any court on the merits, but the competent authority decides to hold a fresh departmental proceedings against the delinquent officer, he will not be entitled to be reinstated or to recover arrears of pay since the date of the original order of dismissal on the ground that it was declared by administrative authority to be a nullity; *Nelson* v. *Union of India*, AIR 1992 SC 1981: (1992) 4 SCC 711: (1992) 5 SCR 394, paragraph 10.

Inquiry
The reasons recorded must *ex facie* show that it was not reasonably practicable to hold a disciplinary inquiry, and must not be vague or irrelevant; *C.S.O.* v. *Singasan*, (1991) 1 SCC 729: AIR 1991 SC 1043: (1991) 16 ATC 453, paragraph 5.

Article 311(1) does not require that the inquiry should be initiated or conducted by a particular level of authority; *P.V. Srinivasa* v. *Comptroller Auditor General*, (1993) 1 SCC 419: AIR 1993 SC 1321: 1993 Lab IC 421: (1993) 1 LLJ 824, paragraphs 4-6.

Legal Assistance

Ordinarily, natural justice does not postulate a right to be represented or assisted by a lawyer, in departmental inquiries. But in particular circumstances, the rules of natural justice or fairness, may require that the person charged should have professional help if he so desires; *I.I.T.* v. *Union of India*, (1991) Supp 2 SCC 12: 1991 SCC (L&S) 1137: (1991) 17 ATC 352, paragraph 15 (3 Judges).

Ordinarily, natural justice does not postulate a right to be represented or assisted by a lawyer, in departmental inquiries. But in particular circumstances, the rules of natural justice or fairness may require that the person charged should have professional help, if he so desires; *J.K. Aggarwal* v. *Haryana Seeds Development Corporation Ltd.*, (1991) 2 SCC 283: AIR 1991 SC 1221: 1991 (16) ATC 480: JT 1991 (5) SC 191: (1991) 2 Lab LJ 412: 1992 LLR 21: 1991 SCC (L&S) 483: (1991) 3 Serv LJ SC 161: (1991) 1 UJ (SC) 633, paragraphs 6 and 8.

No general principle regarding representation by a lawyer which is valid in all cases, can be enunciated. A decision has to be reached on a case to case basis on the situation particularities and the special requirement of justice of the case. Where the Presiding Officer is stated to be a man of law, justice would require that the other party who has no legal background is represented by a lawyer; *J.K. Aggarwal* v. *Haryana Seeds Development Corporation Ltd.*, (1991) 2 SCC 283: AIR 1991 SC 1221: 1991 (16) ATC 480: JT 1991 (5) SC 191: (1991) 2 Lab LJ 412: 1992 LLR 21: 1991 SCC (L&S) 483: (1991) 3 Serv LJ SC 161: (1991) 1 UJ (SC) 633.

Malice

Malice will be proved—

(i) where it is shown that the discretionary power was exercised for an unauthorised or extraneous purpose, *e.g.*, where there is nothing on the record to justify the order of premature retirement of the petitioner or the alleged 'public interest' is founder on non-existent facts or circumstances, or on no evidence;

(ii) where it is shown that the order is arbitrary or perverse or, in other words, no reasonable person could form such opinion on the given material.

In case of post for fixed tenure, malice will be presumed; *Baikuntha* v. *C.D.M.O.*, (1992) 2 SCC 299: (1992) 21 ATC 649: AIR 1992 SC 1020: (1992) 1 LLN 902, paragraph 34; *Aggarwal* v. *Union of India*, (1992) 3 SCC 526: AIR 1992 SC 1872: 1992 Lab IC 1807.

Misconduct

The Punjab Police Manual makes a distinction between 'misconduct' and 'gravest misconduct'. If the court objectively finds that the conduct in question is not of the gravest kind, then only a minor punishment can be awarded. In such a case, an order of dismissal would be set aside; *State of Punjab* v. *Ram*, (1992) 4 SCC 54: 1992 SCC (L&S) 793: (1992) 21 ATC 435: AIR 1992 SC 2188 (3 Judges).

Opportunity

Though the delinquent is no longer entitled to make any representation to the disciplinary authority as to the nature or quantum of the punishment proposed, the Constitution (Forty-second Amendment) Act, 1976 has not taken away the delinquent's right of appeal against the final order in the disciplinary proceedings, where he can show that the findings of the Inquiry Officer or any of them have not been established on the materials before the Inquiry Officer and that the Punishing Authority has been influenced by such findings; *Union of India* v. *Mohd. Ramzan Khan*, (1991) 1 SCC 588: (1991) 16 ATC 505: AIR 1991 SC 471, paragraphs 15-17.

Penal Order

Even where an order is innocuous on its face and purports to be an order of discharge in accordance with the terms and conditions of the appointment, the court can lift the veil and find out the real nature of the order and to set it aside if it is penal in nature and was made without giving the employee any opportunity to show cause why he should not be dismissed for the misconduct alleged; *Babu Lal* v. *State of Haryana*, AIR 1991 SC 1310: (1991) 2 SCC 335: (1991) 16 ATC 481: (1991) 1 SCR 756, paragraph 8.

Reinstated Employee

Where the reinstated employee has actually discharged his duties without any such fresh fixation of pay made in the order of reinstatement, he should get his full salary for that period; *Nelson* v. *Union of India*, AIR 1992 SC 1981: (1992) 4 SCC 711: (1992) 5 SLR 394, paragraph 14 (3 Judges).

Relief by Supreme Court

The extraordinary powers of the Supreme Court are not fettered by any limitation. The court can grant any relief to meet the interests of justice on equitable grounds, *e.g.*, to direct the State to make some *ex gratia* payment to an employee whose appeal has been dismissed. *See* the undermentioned cases:

(i) *Triveni* v. *State of Uttar Pradesh*, 1992 (1) SCJ 27: (1992) Supp 1 SCC 524: AIR 1992 SC 496, paragraph 31.

(ii) *Rajendra* v. *State of Madhya Pradesh*, (1992) Supp 2 SCC 513: (1992) 21 ATC 699.

(iii) *State of Uttar Pradesh* v. *Sani*, (1992) 19 ATC 264 (SC).

(iv) *Prabhuswamy* v. *K.S.R.T.C.*, AIR 1991 SC 1789: (1991) 19 ATC 266: (1991) Supp 2 SCC 433 (SC).

The court may reduce a punishment of 'removal' into that of compulsory retirement; *Mohal* v. *Sr. Supdt.*, (1991) Supp 2 SCC 503: AIR 1991 SC 328: (1991) 1 LLN 301, paragraph 6.

Removal

According to the Departmental Rules, there is some difference between dismissal and removal, as to their consequences. Thus, while a person 'dismissed' is ineligible for re-employment under the Government, no such disqualification attaches to person 'removed'; *Dattatraya Mahadev Nadkarni* v. *Corporation of Greater Bombay*, (1992) 2 SCC 547: AIR 1992 SC 786: (1992) 1 SCR 785, paragraphs 6-8.

Seniority

The court will not disturb a seniority after a long lapse of time from when it as fixed; *S.B. Dogra* v. *State of Himachal Pradesh*, (1992) 4 SCC 455, paragraphs 10 and 11.

Temporary Appointment

In *State of Uttar Pradesh* v. *Kaushal*, (1991) 1 SCC 691: 1991 SCC (L&S) 587: (1991) 16 ATC 498: (1991) 1 SCR 606, the court has summed up the position as under:

"(a) If, on the perusal of the character roll entries or on the basis of preliminary inquiry on the allegations made against an employee, the competent authority is satisfied that the employee is not suitable for the service whereupon the services of the temporary employees are terminated, no exception can be taken to such an order of termination. A Government servant has no right to hold the post; his services are liable to be terminated by giving him one month's notice without assigning any reason either under the terms of the contract providing for such termination or under the relevant statutory rules regulating the terms and conditions of temporary Government servants.

(b) However, this court has made it clear that if the competent authority decides to take punitive action, it may do (only) by holding a formal inquiry by framing charges and giving an opportunity to the Government servant in accordance with the provisions of article 311 of the Constitution; *Triveni* v. *State of Uttar Pradesh*, AIR 1992 SC 496: (1992) Supp 1 SCC 524: (1992) 1 LLN 889, paragraphs 26 and 27.

Where an appointment order states that the post was temporary, though likely to continue for an indefinite period, the person appointed does not acquire a legal right to extension, and his services may be terminated by issuing notice under the Civil Services (Temporary) Rules, 1949; *Sri Dhiraj Ghosh* v. *Union of India*, AIR 1991 SC 73: (1991) Supp 2 SCC 203: 1990 Lab IC 1956: 1993 (24) ATC 541: 1993 SCC (L&S) 671: 1994 (2) SCT 736: (1993) 3 Serv LR 18, paragraph 8; *See* also *State of Uttar Pradesh* v. *Kaushal*, (1991) 1 SCC 691; *Triveni* v. *State of Uttar Pradesh*, (1992) Supp 1 SCC 524 (534): AIR 1992 SC 496: (1992) 1 LLN 889.

Tenure Post

A "Tenure post" means a post held for a specified term. The appointment terminated on the expiry of that term. The question of superannuation or of premature retirement does not arise in the case of such post; *Aggarwal* v. *Union of India*, (1992) 2 UJ SC 266: AIR 1992 SC 1872: 1992 Lab IC 1807: (1992) 4 SLR 583, paragraphs 16-17.

Term : Expiry of

There is no question of application of article 311(2) where a person's services are sought to be terminated at the expiry of the term for which he was engaged or at the expiry of the period of notice by which, in accordance with the conditions of his services, his services could be terminated, provided of course, the contract itself is not unconstitutional, say, for contravention of article 311(2); *Triveni* v. *State of Uttar Pradesh*, AIR 1992 SC 496: (1992) Supp 1 SCC 524: (1992) 19 ATC 931: (1992) 1 LLN 889: (1992) 2 LLJ 23, paragraphs 26 and 27 (3 Judges).

312. All-India Services.—(1) Notwithstanding anything in [1][Chapter VI of Part VI or Part XI], if the Council of States has declared by resolution supported by not less than two-thirds of the members present and voting that it is necessary or expedient in the national interest so to do, Parliament may by law provide for the creation of one or more all-India services [2][(including an all-India judicial service)] common to the Union and the States, and, subject to the other provisions of this Chapter, regulate the recruitment, and the conditions of service of persons appointed, to any such service.

(2) The services known at the commencement of this Constitution as the Indian Administrative Service and the Indian Police Service shall be deemed to be services created by Parliament under this article.

[3][(3) The all-India judicial service referred to in clause (1) shall not include any post inferior to that of a district judge as defined in article 236.]

[3][(4) The law providing for the creation of the all-India judicial service aforesaid may contain such provisions for the amendment of Chapter VI of Part VI as may be necessary for giving effect to the provisions of that law and no such law shall be deemed to be an amendment of this Constitution for the purposes of article 368.]

Notes on Article 312

Central Staffing Scheme

The central staffing scheme as amended in 1996 is not *ultra vires* section of the All India Services Act, 1951 on ground of lack of consultation with State Governments. Section 3 is an enabling power of the Central Government to make rules for the regulation of recruitment and conditions of service for persons appointed to the All India Services; *Satya Narain Shukla* v. *Union of India*, AIR 2006 SC 2511: 2006 AIR SCW 2665: 2006 (4) ALJ 276: (2006) 9 SCC 69: 2006 (6) SCJ 272: 2006 (3) SCT 305: (2006) 5 SCALE 627: 2006 (5) Supreme 417.

[4][**312A. Power of Parliament to vary or revoke conditions of service of officers of certain services.**—(1) Parliament may by law—

(a) vary or revoke, whether prospectively or retrospectively, the conditions of service as respects remuneration, leave and pension and the rights as

---

1. Subs. by the Constitution (Forty-second Amendment) Act, 1976, sec. 45(a)(i), for "Part XI" (w.e.f. 3-1-1977).

2. Ins. by the Constitution (Forty-second Amendment) Act, 1976, sec. 45(a)(ii) (w.e.f. 3-1-1977).

3. Ins. by the Constitution (Forty-second Amendment) Act, 1976, sec. 45(b) (w.e.f. 3-1-1977).

4. Ins. by the Constitution (Twenty-eighth Amendment) Act, 1972, sec. 2 (w.e.f. 29-8-1972).

respects disciplinary matters of persons who, having been appointed by the Secretary of State or Secretary of State in Council to a civil service of the Crown in India before the commencement of this Constitution, continue on and after the commencement of the Constitution (Twenty-eighth Amendment) Act, 1972, to serve under the Government of India or of a State in any service or post;

(b) vary or revoke, whether prospectively or retrospectively, the conditions of service as respects pension of persons who, having been appointed by the Secretary of State or Secretary of State in Council to a civil service of the Crown in India before the commencement of this Constitution, retired or otherwise ceased to be in service at any time before the commencement of the Constitution (Twenty-eighth Amendment) Act, 1972:

Provided that in the case of any such person who is holding or has held the office of the Chief Justice or other Judge of the Supreme Court or a High Court, the Comptroller and Auditor-General of India, the Chairman or other members of the Union or a State Public Service Commission or the Chief Election Commissioner, nothing in sub-clause (a) or sub-clause (b) shall be construed as empowering Parliament to vary or revoke, after his appointment to such post, the conditions of his service to his disadvantage except in so far as such conditions of service are applicable to him by reason of his being a person appointed by the Secretary of State or Secretary of State in Council to a civil service of the Crown in India.

(2) Except to the extent provided for by Parliament by law under this article, nothing in this article shall affect the power of any Legislature or other authority under any other provision of this Constitution to regulate the conditions of service of persons referred to in clause (1).

(3) Neither the Supreme Court nor any other court shall have jurisdiction in—

(a) any dispute arising out of any provision of, or any endorsement on, any covenant, agreement or other similar instrument which was entered into or executed by any person referred to in clause (1), or arising out of any letter issued to such person, in relation to his appointment to any civil service of the Crown in India or his continuance in service under the Government of the Dominion of India or a Province thereof;

(b) any dispute in respect of any right, liability or obligation under article 314 as originally enacted.

(4) The provisions of the article shall have effect notwithstanding anything in article 314 as originally enacted or in any other provision of this Constitution.]

Notes on Article 312A

High Court Judge belonging to Indian Civil Service: Pension

Where the Judge of a High Court who was a member of Indian Civil Services had joined as a judge in 1959 he would be entitled to pension; *Union of India* v. *V.B. Raju*, AIR 1982 SC 1174: 1982 Lab IC 1487: 1982 UJ (SC) 312: (1982) 2 SCC 326: (1982) 1 Serv LJ 602: 1982 SCC (Lab) 247: (1982) 2 LLN 640.

313. Transitional provisions.—Until other provision is made in this behalf under this Constitution, all the laws in force immediately before the commencement of this Constitution and applicable to any public service or any post which continues to exist after the commencement of this Constitution, as an all-India Service or as service or post under the Union or a State shall continue in force so far as consistent with the provisions of this Constitution.

Notes on Article 313

Dismissal of High Court Staff

The power to dismiss High Court staff vests in chief justice; *Pradyat Kumar Bose* v. *Hon'ble Chief Justice of Calcutta High Court*, AIR 1956 SC 285: 1956 SCA 79: 1956 SCJ 259: (1955) 2 SCR 1331: 1956 SCC 402.

Promotion to Posts of Assistant Commissioner of Income Tax

Promotion of the posts of Assistant Commissioner of Income Tax in 1960 and 1970 showed that all promoters except 2 had completed at least 10 year's service. The field of choice was determined by Departmental promotion committee in 1974 was valid; *Union of India* v. *Majji Jangammayya*, AIR 1977 SC 757: 1977 Lab IC 295: 1977 Serv LJ 90: 1977 SCC (Lab) 191: 1977 SLWR 163: (1977) 1 SCC 606: (1977) 2 SCR 28.

314. Provision for protection of existing officers of certain services.—[*Rep. by the Constitution (Twenty-eighth Amendment) Act, 1972, sec. 3 (w.e.f. 29-8-1972).*]

CHAPTER II
PUBLIC SERVICE COMMISSIONS

315. Public Service Commissions for the Union and for the States.—(1) Subject to the provisions of this article, there shall be a Public Service Commission for the Union and a Public Service Commission for each State.

(2) Two or more States may agree that there shall be one Public Service Commission for that group of States, and if a resolution to that effect is passed by the House or, where there are two Houses, by each House of the Legislature of each of those States, Parliament may by law provide for the appointment of a Joint State Public Service Commission (referred to in this Chapter as Joint Commission) to serve the needs of those States.

(3) Any such law as aforesaid may contain such incidental and consequential provisions as may be necessary or desirable for giving effect to the purposes of the law.

(4) The Public Service Commission for the Union, if requested so to do by the Governor [1][***] of a State, may, with the approval of the President, agree to serve all or any of the needs of the State.

(5) References in this Constitution to the Union Public Service Commission or a State Public Service Commission shall, unless the context otherwise requires, be construed as references to the Commission serving the needs of the Union or, as the case may be, the State as respects the particular matter in question.

Notes on Article 315

Essential Qualification for Appointment

The public service Commission can relax essential qualification only if it is expressly given power of relaxation; *Sanjay Kumar Manjul* v. *Chairman, U.P.S.C.*, AIR 2007 SC 254: 2006 AIR SCW 6023: (2006) 8 SCC 42: 2006 (4) SCT 329: 2006 (10) SRJ 386: (2006) 9 SCALE 232: 2006 (7) Supreme 304.

Seniority

Candidates belonging to competitive examination of earlier year selected illegally by lowering norms cannot claim seniority over candidates selected legally from competitive examination held in subsequent year; *State of Uttar Pradesh* v. *Rafiquddin*, AIR 1988 SC 162: 1988 Lab IC 344: JT 1987 (5) SC 251: 1987 Supp SCC 401: (1988) 19 Reports 28: 1988 SCC (Lab) 183: (1988) 1 Serv LR 491: 1988 (2) SCJ 170.

---

1. The words "or Rajpramukh" omitted by the Constitution (Seventh Amendment) Act, 1956, sec. 29 and Sch. (w.e.f. 1-11-1956).

316. Appointment and term of office of members.—(1) The Chairman and other members of a Public Service Commission shall be appointed, in the case of the Union Commission or a Joint Commission, by the President, and in the case of a State Commission, by the Governor [1][***] of the State:

Provided that as nearly as may be one-half of the members of every Public Service Commission shall be persons who at the dates of their respective appointments have held office for at least ten years either under the Government of India or under the Government of a State, and in computing the said period of ten years any period before the commencement of this Constitution during which a person has held office under the Crown in India or under the Government of an Indian State shall be included.

[2][(1A) If the office of the Chairman of the Commission becomes vacant or if any such Chairman is by reason of absence or for any other reason unable to perform the duties of his office, those duties shall, until some persons appointed under clause (1) to the vacant office has entered on the duties thereof or, as the case may be, until the Chairman has resumed his duties, be performed by such one of the other members of the Commission as the President, in the case of the Union Commission or a Joint Commission, and the Governor of the State in the case of a State in the case of a State Commission, may appoint for the purpose.]

(2) A member of a Public Service Commission shall hold office for a term of six years from the date on which he enters upon his office or until he attains, in the case of the Union Commission, the age of sixty-five years, and in the case of a State Commission or a Joint Commission, the age of [3][sixty-two years], whichever is earlier:

Provided that—

(a) a member of a Public Service Commission may, by writing under his hand addressed, in the case of the Union Commission or a Joint Commission, to the President, and in the case of a State Commission, to the Governor [1][***] of the State, resign his office;

(b) a member of a Public Service Commission may be removed from his office in the manner provided in clause (1) or clause (3) of article 317.

(3) A person who holds office as a member of a Public Service Commission shall, on the expiration of his term of office, be ineligible for re-appointment to that office.

Notes on Article 316

The requirement in article 316(1) proviso, as to one-half members being persons who have held office under the Government is directory. Hence in a State Public Service Commission comprising eleven members, a challenge to the seventh member (who belongs to the non-service category) is not sustainable in law; *Jai Shankar Prasad* v. *State of Bihar*, (1993) 2 SCC 597: AIR 1993 SC 1906: (1993) 2 SCR 357: (1993) 24 ATC 584.

317. Removal and suspension of a member of a Public Service Commission.— (1) Subject to the provisions of clause (3), the Chairman or any other member of a Public Service Commission shall only be removed from his office by order of the

---

1. The words "or Rajpramukh" omitted by the Constitution (Seventh Amendment) Act, 1956, sec. 29 and Sch. (w.e.f. 1-11-1956).

2. Ins. by the Constitution (Fifteenth Amendment) Act, 1963, sec. 11 (w.e.f. 5-10-1963).

3. Subs. by the Constitution (Forty-first Amendment) Act, 1976, sec. 2, for "sixty years" (w.e.f. 7-9-1976).

President on the ground of misbehaviour after the Supreme Court, on reference being made to it by the President, has, on inquiry held in accordance with the procedure prescribed in that behalf under article 145, reported that the Chairman or such other member, as the case may be, ought on any such ground to be removed.

(2) The President, in the case of the Union Commission or a Joint Commission, and the Governor [1][***] in the case of a State Commission, may suspend from office the Chairman or any other member of the Commission in respect of whom a reference has been made to the Supreme Court under clause (1) until the President has passed orders on receipt of the report of the Supreme Court on such reference.

(3) Notwithstanding anything in clause (1), the President may by order remove from office the Chairman or any other member of a Public Service Commission if the Chairman or such other member, as the case may be,—

(a) is adjudged an insolvent; or

(b) engages during his term of office in any paid employment outside the duties of his office; or

(c) is, in the opinion of the President, unfit to continue in office by reason of infirmity of mind or body.

(4) If the Chairman or any other member of a Public Service Commission is or becomes in any way concerned or interested in any contract or agreement made by or on behalf of the Government of India or the Government of a State or participates in any way in the profit thereof or in any benefit or emolument arising therefrom otherwise than as a member and in common with the other members of an incorporated company, he shall, for the purposes of clause (1), be deemed to be guilty of misbehaviour.

Notes on Article 317

Important judgments as to Public Service Commissions are the following:—

(i) *Reference under article 317(1)*, AIR 1983 SC 996: (1983) 4 SCC 258: (1983) 2 Serv LJ 411: 1983 BLJR 529: 1983 UJ (SC) 860: (1983) 2 Serv LR 759: (1983) 47 FLR 371.

(ii) *U.P. Public Service Commission v. Suresh*, AIR 1987 SC 1953: (1987) 4 SCC 176: 1987 Lab IC 1644.

(iii) *K.P. Sen v. State of West Bengal*, AIR 1966 Cal 356: (1966) 2 LLJ 861: 71 CWN 622.

(iv) *Hargovind v. Raghukul*, AIR 1979 SC 1109: (1979) 4 SCC 358: 1979 Lab IC 818.

Misconduct

In article 124(4) the word 'proved' qualifies the word 'misconduct' while that qualification is absent in article 317(1).

Such proof in the case of a Supreme Court Judge, comes from [the law enacted by Parliament under clause (5) of article 124], the inquiry under the Judges (Inquiry) Act, 1968, which is absent in the case of a member of a Public Service Commission. In the case of a member of the Public Service Commission, the inquiry and proof of misbehaviour shall be made by the Supreme Court, while in the case of a Supreme Court Judge, that is to be done by the Committee set up under the Judges (Inquiry) Act, 1968; *Sub-Committee of Judicial Accountability v. Union of India*, AIR 1992 SC 320: (1991) 4 SCC 699: 1991 AIR SCW 3049: JT 1991 (6) SC 184, paragraph 45.

If the Chairman of a State Public Service Commission is slapped on the face by another, it is a case of misbehaviour under article 317(1) and renders the latter member liable to be removal.

---

1. The words "or Rajpramukh" omitted by the Constitution (Seventh Amendment) Act, 1956, sec. 29 and Sch. (w.e.f. 1-11-1956).

Infirmities under article 317(3)(c) must be such as to disable the member from the efficient discharge of his functions and must be of post—appointment origin. Where a university professor is appointed a member of State Public Service Commission and is known to be blind, he cannot be removed on the ground of infirmity; *Jai Shankar Prasad* v. *State of Bihar*, (1993) 2 SCC 597: AIR 1993 SC 1906: (1993) 1 SCR 357: (1993) 3 SLJ 32.

The provisions of proviso (b) to article 316 and the word 'only' in article 317(a) make it clear that the power to remove a Public Service Commission has been vested exclusively in the President.

Hence, no court can exercise this power even by means of the writ of *quo warranto*.

The determination as to whether a member should be removed on the ground of infirmity is left to the subjective satisfaction of the President as to whether the infirmity is such that it incapacitates the particular member for discharging the functions of his office; *Jai Shankar Prasad* v. *State of Bihar*, (1993) 2 SCC 597: AIR 1993 SC 1906: (1993) 1 SCR 357: (1993) 3 SLJ 32, paragraphs 13, 15 and 18.

In a reference under article 317 regulating enquiry and report on the allegations made against the Chairman Manipur State Public Service Commission, the Supreme Court directed that direct evidence in relation to the reference should be recorded by a sitting Judge of the High Court: *In Re* Art. 317 (1) of the Constitution of India; JT 1994 (2) SC 63: (1994) Supp 2 SCC 166.

Members of State Public Service Commission are not equal to the Chairman and cannot claim the same facilities as the Chairman; *Bihar Public Service Commission* v. *Dr. Shiv Jatan Thakur*, JT (1994) SC 681: (1994) Supp 3 SCC 220: AIR 1994 SC 2466: (1994) 4 SCR 582.

Object
The object of article 317(1) is to give protection to a Chairman or other member of the Public Service Commission in the matter of removal on the ground of misbehaviour and, therefore, the function of such determination is vested in the Supreme Court so that the Public Service Commission may be immune from political pressure; *Ravinder Pal Singh Sidhu* v. *Punjab Public Service Commission*, AIR 2003 SC 788: (2003) 2 SCC 147: 2003 SCC (L&S) 143.

Proportion
The validity of the appointment of a particular member cannot be challenged on the ground that he did not belong to the category which was required to make up the 50% proportion; *Jai Shankar Prasad* v. *State of Bihar*, (1993) 2 SCC 597: (1993) 24 ATC 584: AIR 1993 SC 1906: (1993) 2 SLR 357, paragraphs 9-12.

318. Power to make regulations as to conditions of service of members and staff of the Commission.—In the case of the Union Commission or a Joint Commission, the President and, in the case of a State Commission, the Governor [1][***] of the State may by regulations—

(a) determine the number of members of the Commission and their conditions of service; and

(b) make provision with respect to the number of members of the staff of the Commission and their conditions of service:

Provided that the conditions of service of a member of a Public Service Commission shall not be varied to his disadvantage after his appointment.

319. Prohibition as to the holding of offices by members of Commission on ceasing to be such members.—On ceasing to hold office—

(a) the Chairman of the Union Public Service Commission shall be ineligible for further employment either under the Government of India or under the Government of a State;

---

1. The words "or Rajpramukh" omitted by the Constitution (Seventh Amendment) Act, 1956, sec. 29 and Sch. (w.e.f. 1-11-1956).

(b) the Chairman of a State Public Service Commission shall be eligible for appointment as the Chairman or any other member of the Union Public Service Commission or as the Chairman of any other State Public Service Commission, but not for any other employment either under the Government of India or under the Government of a State;

(c) a member other than the Chairman of the Union Public Service Commission shall be eligible for appointment as the Chairman of the Union Public Service Commission or as the Chairman of a State Public Service Commission, but not for any other employment either under the Government of India or under the Government of a State;

(d) a member other than the Chairman of a State Public Service Commission shall be eligible for appointment as the Chairman or any other member of the Union Public Service Commission or as the Chairman of that or any other State Public Service Commission, but not for any other employment either under the Government of India or under the Government of a State.

320. Functions of Public Service Commissions.—(1) It shall be the duty of the Union and the State Public Service Commissions to conduct examinations for appointments to the services of the Union and the services of the State respectively.

(2) It shall also be the duty of the Union Public Service Commission, if requested by any two or more States so to do, to assist those States in framing and operating schemes of joint recruitment for any services for which candidates possessing special qualifications are required.

(3) The Union Public Service Commission or the State Public Service Commission, as the case may be, shall be consulted—

(a) on all matters relating to methods of recruitment to civil services and for civil posts;

(b) on the principles to be followed in making appointments to civil services and posts and in making promotions and transfers from one service to another and on the suitability of candidates for such appointments, promotions or transfers;

(c) on all disciplinary matters affecting a person serving under the Government of India or the Government of a State in a civil capacity, including memorials or petitions relating to such matters;

(d) on any claim by or in respect of a person who is serving or has served under the Government of India or the Government of a State or under the Crown in India or under the Government of an Indian State, in a civil capacity, that any costs incurred by him in defending legal proceedings instituted against him in respect of acts done or purporting to be done in the execution of his duty should be paid out of the Consolidated Fund of India, or, as the case may be, out of the Consolidated Fund of the State;

(e) on any claim for the award of a pension in respect of injuries sustained by a person while serving under the Government of India or the Government of a State or under the Crown in India or under the Government of an Indian State, in a civil capacity, and any question as to the amount of any such award, and it shall be the duty of a Public Service Commission to advise on any matter so referred to them and on any other matter which the President, or, as the case may be, the Governor [1][***] of the State, may refer to them:

Provided that the President as respects the all-India services and also as respects other services and posts in connection with the affairs of the Union, and the Governor [2][***], as respects other services and posts in connection with the affairs of a State, may make regulations specifying the matters in which either generally, or in any particular class of case or in any particular circumstances, it shall not be necessary for a Public Service Commission to be consulted.

(4) Nothing in clause (3) shall require a Public Service Commission to be consulted as respects the manner in which any provision referred to in clause (4) of article 16 may be made or as respects the manner in which effect may be given to the provisions of article 335.

(5) All regulations made under the proviso to clause (3) by the President or the Governor [1][***] of a State shall be laid for not less than fourteen days before each House of Parliament or the House or each House of the Legislature of the State, as the case may be, as soon as possible after they are made, and shall be subject to such modifications, whether by way of repeal or amendment, as both Houses of Parliament or the House or both Houses of the Legislature of the State may make during the session in which they are so laid.

Notes on Article 320

Some of the important decisions on article 320 are the following:—

(i) *Neelima* v. *State of Haryana*, AIR 1987 SC 169: (1986) 4 SCC 268: 1986 SCC (L&S) 759 (Commission's duty to forward names).

(ii) *Keshav Ram Pal (Dr.)* v. *Uttar Pradesh Higher Education Services Commission*, (1986) 1 SCC 671: 1986 SCC (L&S) 195: AIR 1986 SC 597: (1986) 1 LLJ 311: 1986 Lab IC 553 (Method of selection).

(iii) *State of Uttar Pradesh* v. *Rafiuddin*, AIR 1988 SC 162: 1987 Supp SCC 401: 1988 SCC (L&S) 153 (Re-opening selection).

(iv) *State of Punjab* v. *Manjit Singh*, AIR 2003 SC 4580: (2003) 11 SCC 559: (2003) 6 SLR 63.

If before the selection is held, the Government withdraws its requisition from the Public Service Commission, neither the candidate nor the Commission itself can insist on continuing the process of selection; *Dr. P.K. Jaiswal* v. *Debi Mukherjee*, AIR 1992 SC 749: 1992 Lab IC 580: 1992 AIR SCW 432: JT 1992 (1) SC 315l: (1992) 2 SCC 148: 1992 SCC (L&S) 377: (1992) 1 SCR 1: (1992) 1 Serv LR 593: (1992) 1 UJ (SC) 731, paragraph 5.

321. Power to extend functions of Public Service Commissions.—An Act made by Parliament or, as the case may be, the Legislature of a State may provide for the exercise of additional functions by the Union Public Service Commission or the State Public Service Commission as respects the services of the Union or the State and also as respects the services of any local authority or other body corporate constituted by law or of any public institution.

322. Expenses of Public Service Commissions.—The expenses of the Union or a State Public Service Commission, including any salaries, allowances and

---

1. The words "or Rajpramukh" omitted by the Constitution (Seventh Amendment) Act, 1956, sec. 29 and Sch. (w.e.f. 1-11-1956).

2. The words "or Rajpramukh, as the case may be" omitted by the Constitution (Seventh Amendment) Act, 1956, sec. 29 and Sch. (w.e.f. 1-11-1956).

pensions payable to or in respect of the members or staff of the Commission, shall be charged on the Consolidated Fund of India or, as the case may be, the Consolidated Fund of the State.

323. Reports of Public Service Commissions.—(1) It shall be the duty of the Union Commission to present annually to the President a report as to the work done by the Commission and on receipt of such report the President shall cause a copy thereof together with a memorandum explaining, as respects the cases, if any, where the advice of the Commission was not accepted, the reasons for such non-acceptance to be laid before each House of Parliament.

(2) It shall be the duty of a State Commission to present annually to the Governor [1][***] of the State a report as to the work done by the Commission, and it shall be the duty of a Joint Commission to present annually to the Governor [1][***] of each of the States the needs of which are served by the Joint Commission a report as to the work done by the Commission in relation to that State, and in either case the Governor [2][***], shall, on receipt of such report, cause a copy thereof together with a memorandum explaining, as respects the cases, if any, where the advice of the Commission was not accepted, the reasons for such non-acceptance to be laid before the Legislature of the State.

[3][PART XIVA

TRIBUNALS

323A. Administrative tribunals.—Parliament may, by law, provide for the adjudication or trial by administrative tribunals of disputes and complaints with respect to recruitment and conditions of service of persons appointed to public services and posts in connection with the affairs of the Union or of any State or of any local or other authority within the territory of India or under the control of the Government of India or of any corporation owned or controlled by the Government.

(2) A law made under clause (1) may—

(a) provide for the establishment of an administrative tribunal for the Union and a separate administrative tribunal for each State or for two or more States;

(b) specify the jurisdiction, powers (including the power to punish for contempt) and authority which may be exercised by each of the said tribunals;

(c) provide for the procedure (including provisions as to limitation and rules of evidence) to be followed by the said tribunals;

(d) exclude the jurisdiction of all courts, except the jurisdiction of the Supreme Court under article 136, with respect to the disputes or complaints referred to in clause (1);

---

1. The words "or Rajpramukh" omitted by the Constitution (Seventh Amendment) Act, 1956, sec. 29 and Sch. (w.e.f. 1-11-1956).
2. The words "or Rajpramukh, as the case may be" omitted by the Constitution (Seventh Amendment) Act, 1956, sec. 29 and Sch. (w.e.f. 1-11-1956).
3. Part XIVA (containing articles 323A and 323B) ins. by the Constitution (Forty-second Amendment) Act, 1976, sec. 46 (w.e.f. 3-1-1977).

(e) provide for the transfer to each such administrative tribunal of any cases pending before any court or other authority immediately before the establishment of such tribunal as would have been within the jurisdiction of such tribunal if the cause of action on which such suits or proceedings are based had arisen after such establishment;

(f) repeal or amend any order made by the President under clause (3) of article 371D;

(g) contain such supplemental, incidental and consequential provisions (including provisions as to fees) as Parliament may deem necessary for the effective functioning of, and for the speedy disposal of cases by, and the enforcement of the orders of, such tribunals.

(3) The provisions of this article shall have effect notwithstanding anything in any other provision of this Constitution or in any other law for the time being in force.

Notes on Article 323A

The Administrative Tribunals Act, 1985 is a legislation in terms of article 323A. By setting up a tribunal under that Act, for the resolution of service disputes, the jurisdiction of the High Court in regard to such matters is intended to be taken away and is intended to be vested in the Tribunal; *S.P. Sampath Kumar* v. *Union of India,* AIR 1987 SC 386: (1987) 1 SCC 124: (1987) 2 ATC 82: 1987 Lab IC 222: (1987) 1 LLJ 128.

Co-operative Societies

Under section 14(2) of the Administrative Tribunals Act, 1985, as amended, co-operative societies can be added to the list by notification. But until they are so notified by Government, jurisdiction of courts in regard to service matters relating to such societies remains unaffected. *See* the undermentioned cases:

(i) *Ashwani* v. *P.C.D.F.,* (1992) 4 SCC 17.

(ii) *Governing Council of Kidwai Memorial Institute of Oncology, Bangalore* v. *Dr. Pandurang Godwalkar,* (1992) 4 SCC 719: AIR 1993 SC 392: 1992 AIR SCW 3297: 1993 (23) ATC 389: (1993) 1 LLJ 308: 1993 SCC (L&S) 1: 1993 (1) SCT 267: (1993) 2 Serv LJ SC 174, paragraph 2.

Interference by the Tribunal

The Administrative Tribunal will not interfere with an order of rejection by the Tribunal, of an application for reinstatement on the grounds of inordinate and unexplained delay; *Bhoop* v. *Union of India,* AIR 1992 SC 1414: (1992) 3 SCC 136: (1992) 21 ATC 675: (1992) 4 SLR 761: 1992 Lab IC 1464, paragraph 2.

The Tribunal would not ordinarily interfere with the decision of the competent authority to compulsorily retire an employee on the ground of unfitness, in the absence of *mala fides,* or arbitrariness, or in the absence of any material on the record to show that compulsory retirement of the petitioner was not in the public interest.

Principles of natural justice are not attracted in the case of compulsory retirement under the relevant Rules; *Baikuntha* v. *C.D.M.O.,* AIR 1992 SC 1020: (1992) 2 SCC 299: (1992) 21 ATC 649: (1992) 1 LLN 902: (1992) 1 LLJ 784, paragraphs 29, 32 and 33 (3 Judges).

323B. Tribunals for other matters.—(1) The appropriate Legislature may, by law, provide for the adjudication or trial by tribunals of any disputes, complaints, or offences with respect to all or any of the matters specified in clause (2) with respect to which such Legislature has power to make laws.

(2) The matters referred to in clause (1) are the following, namely:—

(a) levy, assessment, collection and enforcement of any tax;

(b) foreign exchange, import and export across customs frontiers;

(c) industrial and labour disputes;

(d) land reforms by way of acquisition by the State of any estate as defined in article 31A or of any rights therein or the extinguishment or modification of any such rights or by way of ceiling on agricultural land or in any other way;

(e) ceiling on urban property;

(f) elections to either House of Parliament or the House or either House of the Legislature of a State, but excluding the matters referred to in article 329 and article 329A;

(g) production, procurement, supply and distribution of foodstuffs (including edible oilseeds and oils) and such other goods as the President may, by public notification, declare to be essential goods for the purpose of this article and control of prices of such goods;

[1][(h) rent, its regulation and control and tenancy issues including the rights, title and interest of landlords and tenants;]

[2][(i)] offences against laws with respect to any of the matters specified in sub-clauses (a) to [3][(h)] and fees in respect of any of those matters;

[2][(j)] any matter incidental to any of the matters specified in sub-clauses (a) to [4][(i)].

(3) A law made under clause (1) may—

(a) provide for the establishment of a hierarchy of tribunals;

(b) specify the jurisdiction, powers (including the power to punish for contempt) and authority which may be exercised by each of the said tribunals;

(c) provide for the procedure (including provisions as to limitation and rules of evidence) to be followed by the said tribunals;

(d) exclude the jurisdiction of all courts except the jurisdiction of the Supreme Court under article 136, with respect to all or any of the matters falling within the jurisdiction of the said tribunals;

(e) provide for the transfer to each such tribunal of any cases pending before any court or any other authority immediately before the establishment of such tribunal as would have been within the jurisdiction of such tribunal if the causes of action on which such suits or proceedings are based had arisen after such establishment;

(f) contain such supplemental, incidental and consequential provisions (including provisions as to fees) as the appropriate Legislature may deem necessary for the effective functioning of, and for the speedy disposal of cases by, and the enforcement of the orders of, such tribunals.

---

1. Ins. by the Constitution (Seventy-fifth Amendment) Act, 1993, sec. 2(a) (w.e.f. 15-5-1994).

2. Sub-clauses (h) and (i) relettered as sub-clauses (i) and (j) by the Constitution (Seventy-fifth Amendment) Act, 1993, sec. 2(a) (w.e.f 15-5-1994).

3. Subs. by the Constitution (Seventy-fifth Amendment) Act, 1993, sec. 2(b), for "(g)" (w.e.f. 15-5-1994).

4. Subs. by the Constitution (Seventy-fifth Amendment) Act, 1993, sec. 2(c), for "(h)" (w.e.f. 15-5-1994).

(4) The provisions of this article shall have effect notwithstanding anything in any other provision of this Constitution or in any other law for the time being in force.

Explanation.—In this article, "appropriate Legislature", in relation to any matter, means Parliament or, as the case may be, a State Legislature competent to make laws with respect to such matter in accordance with the provisions of Part XI.]

Notes on Article 323B

All Courts

Service Tribunals have been set up under the Administrative Tribunals Act, 1985. The words 'all courts' in article 323A(2)(d) and article 323B(3)(d) include the High Court and the jurisdiction of the High Court under articles 226-227 has been exclusively vested in the Administrative Tribunals set up under the Act; *Union of India* v. *Deep*, (1992) 4 SCC 432: AIR 1993 SC 382: (1993) 23 ATC 356: 1993 SCC (L&S) 21, paragraph 3 and 6 (3 Judges).

The State of West Bengal enacted the W.B. Taxation Tribunal Act, 1987, and set up a Tribunal with exclusive jurisdiction to adjudicate disputes or complaints or offences with respect to taxation under any of the State Acts specified therein. The Calcutta High Court has, however, struck down this Act in so far as it dealt with the case levied on the basis of the value of coal raised by mining companies, under the W.B. Primary Education Act, 1973, W.B. Rural Employment and Production Act, 1976, and the Bengal Cess Act, 1880 on the ground that the power to legislate relating to cess on coal or other minerals belonged to the Union Parliament and not the State Legislature.

The Explanation to article 323B makes it clear that the distribution of legislative powers as between the Union and the State legislatures, in Part XI of the Constitution is not in any way to be affected by the insertion of article 323B. Hence, a State Legislature shall be competent to set up a Tribunal under clause (a) of sub-section (2) of article 323B, only if the State Legislature has jurisdiction to legislate with respect to the assessment, collection or enforcement of the particular tax in relation to which the Tribunal is sought; *Kesoram Industries Ltd. (Textile Division)* v. *Coal India Ltd.*, AIR 1993 Cal 78: 1993 (1) CHN 488: 1993 (1) Cal LJ 13 (DB), paragraph 34.

Appeal to Supreme Court

Appeal lies to the Supreme Court from orders of an Administrative Tribunal by special leave under 136 on the following ground (*inter alia*) of error of law, *e.g.*, in the matter of determining the proper date of confirmation of seniority or age of retirement of the appellant, *See* the undermentioned cases:

  (i) *Union of India* v. *Sharma*, AIR 1992 SC 1188: (1992) 2 SCC 728: (1992) Lab IC 1136: (1992) 2 SCR 373, paragraphs 5 and 8.

  (ii) *Union of India* v. *Partap*, AIR 1992 SC 1363: (1992) 3 SCC 268: (1992) 20 ATC 756: (1992) 1 LLJ 446, paragraphs 8, 14.

  (iii) *Union of India* v. *Komal*, AIR 1992 SC 1479: (1992) Supp 3 SCC 186: 1992 Lab IC 1549: (1992) 4 SLR 575.

Scope

Articles 323A and 323B are enabling provisions which specifically enable the setting up of tribunals. Therefore, articles, however, cannot be interpreted to mean that they prohibit the legislature from establishing tribunals not covered by these articles, as long as there is legislative competence under an appropriate entry in the Seventh Schedule. Articles 323A and 323B do not take away that legislative competence; *State of Karnataka* v. *Vishwabarathi House Building Co-operative Society*, AIR 2003 SC 1043: (2003) 2 SCC 412: (2003) 11 Comp Cas 536.

Tribunals and Writs

Tribunals constituted under articles 323A and 323B of the Constitution are subject to the writ jurisdiction of the High Courts; *L. Chandra Kumar* v. *Union of India*, AIR 1997 SC 1125: (1997) 3 SCC 261: (1997) 1 CLR 778: 1997 Lab IC 1069: (1977) 2 SCR 1, paragraph 99.

PART XV
ELECTIONS

324. Superintendence, direction and control of elections to be vested in an Election Commission.—(1) The superintendence, direction and control of the preparation of the electoral rolls for, and the conduct of, all elections to Parliament and to the Legislature of every State and of elections to the offices of President and Vice-President held under this Constitution [1][***] shall be vested in a Commission (referred to in this Constitution as the Election Commission).

(2) The Election Commission shall consist of the Chief Election Commissioner and such number of other Election Commissioners, if any, as the President may from time to time fix and the appointment of the Chief Election Commissioner and other Election Commissioners shall, subject to the provisions of any law made in that behalf by Parliament, be made by the President.

(3) When any other Election Commissioner is so appointed the Chief Election Commissioner shall act as the Chairman of the Election Commission.

(4) Before each general election to the House of the People and to the Legislative Assembly of each State, and before the first general election and thereafter before each biennial election to the Legislative Council of each State having such Council, the President may also appoint after consultation with the Election Commission such Regional Commissioners as he may consider necessary to assist the Election Commission in the performance of the functions conferred on the Commission by clause (1).

(5) Subject to the provisions of any law made by Parliament, the conditions of service and tenure of office of the Election Commissioners and the Regional Commissioners shall be such as the President may by rule determine:

Provided that the Chief Election Commissioner shall not be removed from his office except in like manner and on the like grounds as a Judge of the Supreme Court and the conditions of service of the Chief Election Commissioner shall not be varied to his disadvantage after his appointment:

Provided further that any other Election Commissioner or a Regional Commissioner shall not be removed from office except on the recommendation of the Chief Election Commissioner.

(6) The President, or the Governor [2][***] of a State, shall, when so requested by the Election Commission, make available to the Election Commission or to a Regional Commissioner such staff as may be necessary for the discharge of the functions conferred on the Election Commission by clause (1).

Notes on Article 324

Abolition of post of Election Commissioners by the President and consequential termination of the service of the incumbent of the abolished post, cannot be made a ground of action. There is no illegality in such termination of service; *S.S. Dhanoa* v. *Union of India*, AIR 1991 SC 1745: (1991) 3 SCC 567: (1991) 2 LLN 428.

However wide the powers of the Election Commission relating to direction and control may be, its orders must be traceable to some existing law and cannot violate the provisions of any law

---

1. Certain words omitted by the Constitution (Nineteenth Amendment) Act, 1966, sec. 2 (w.e.f. 11-12-1966).

2. The words "or Rajpramukh" omitted by the Constitution (Seventh Amendment) Act, 1956, sec. 29 and Sch. (w.e.f. 1-11-1956).

including State Acts. But precautionary measures which can be taken without violating any statutory provision would not be illegal; *Dasappa & Brothers, Bangalore* v. *Election Commission, New Delhi*, AIR 1992 Kant 230: ILR 1991 Kant 3038: (1992) 1 Kant LJ 152, paragraph 10.

No election can be invalidated on the ground that the Electoral Officer failed to comply with the non-statutory directions issued by the Commission even though they are administratively binding upon the Electoral Officer; *Narayan* v. *Purshottam*, (1993) 1 UJ SC 297: (1993) Supp 2 SCC 90: AIR 1993 SC 1698, paragraph 37.

In October, 1989 the President notified that besides the Chief Election Commissioner the Commission should have two other members called 'Election Commissioners' with co-ordinate powers. On January 1, 1990 the President revoked his Notification of 1989 as a result of which, the two Election Commissioners who had been appointed, lost their office as Election Commissioners. One of them challenged the revocation of the Notification on various grounds. The Supreme Court rejected the petition under article 324 holding as under—

(i) Even though it was desirable that the highly vital functions of the Election Commission should be exercised by more than one individual, the creation and abolition of posts was a prerogative of the Executive and article 324(2) left to the President to fix and appoint such number of Election Commissioners as he may, from time to time determine. Hence, the abolition of the post of Election Commissioners, which was a consequence of such abolition gave rise to *no* cause of action.

(ii) While it was obligatory to appoint the Chief Election Commissioner, the appointment of other Election Commissioners [clause (2)] or Regional Commissioners [clause (4)] was left by the Constitution to the discretion of the President.

(iii) In the absence of any evidence that the abolition of the posts and the removal of the incumbents thereof was made on the recommendation of the Chief Election Commissioner, it could not be held that the President or the Chief Election Officer was actuated by *malice*: *Dhanoa* v. *Union of India*, AIR 1991 SC 1745: (1991) 3 SCC 567: (1991) 2 LLN 428.

Articles 174 *viz-a-viz* Article 324—Scope

The Provisions of the article 174 are mandatory in character so far as the time period between two sessions is concerned in respect of live Assemblies and not dissolved Assemblies. Article 174 and article 324 operate in different fields. Article 174 does not deal with elections which is primary function of the Election Commission under article 324. Therefore, the question of one yielding to the other does not arise; Special Reference No. 1 of 2002 [under article 143(1) of the Constitution], AIR 2003 SC 87: (2002) 8 SCC 237: 2002 AIR SCW 4492: JT 2002 (8) SC 389: (2002) 7 SCALE 614: 2002 (7) Supreme 437.

325. No person to be ineligible for inclusion in, or to claim to be included in a special, electoral roll on grounds of religion, race, caste or sex.—There shall be one general electoral roll for every territorial constituency for election to either House of Parliament or to the House or either House of the Legislature of a State and no person shall be ineligible for inclusion in any such roll or claim to be included in any special electoral roll for any such constituency on grounds only of religion, race, caste, sex or any of them.

326. Elections to the House of the People and to the Legislative Assemblies of States to be on the basis of adult suffrage.—The elections to the House of the People and to the Legislative Assembly of every State shall be on the basis of adult suffrage; that is to say, every person who is a citizen of India and who is not less than [1][eighteen years] of age on such date as may be fixed in that behalf by or under any law made by the appropriate Legislature and is not otherwise

---

1. Subs. by the Constitution (Sixty-first Amendment) Act, 1988, sec. 2, for "twenty-one years" (w.e.f. 28-3-1989).

disqualified under this Constitution or any law made by the appropriate Legislature on the ground of non-residence, unsoundness of mind, crime or corrupt or illegal practice, shall be entitled to be registered as a voter at any such election.

327. Power of Parliament to make provision with respect to elections to Legislatures.—Subject to the provisions of this Constitution, Parliament may from time to time by law make provision with respect to all matters relating to, or in connection with, elections to either House of Parliament or to the House or either House of the Legislature of a State including the preparation of electoral rolls, the delimitation of constituencies and all other matters necessary for securing the due constitution of such House or Houses.

Notes on Article 327

Power of Parliament to Legislate Election Laws

The amendment of section 79(b) of Representation of People Act, 1951 by section 7 read with section 10 of the Election Laws (Amendment) Act of 1975 is within the unquestionable powers of parliament; *Indira Nehru Gandhi* v. *Raj Narain*, AIR 1975 SC 2299: 1975 Supp SCC 1: (1976) 2 SCR 347.

328. Power of Legislature of a State to make provision with respect to elections to such Legislature.—Subject to the provisions of this Constitution and in so far as provision in that behalf is not made by Parliament, the Legislature of a State may from time to time by law make provision with respect to all matters relating to, or in connection with, the elections to the House or either House of the Legislature of the State including the preparation of electoral rolls and all other matters necessary for securing the due constitution of such House or Houses.

329. Bar to interference by courts in electoral matters.—[1][Notwithstanding anything in this Constitution [2][***]]

(a) the validity of any law relating to the delimitation of constituencies or the allotment of seats to such constituencies, made or purporting to be made under article 327 or article 328, shall not be called in question in any court;

(b) no election to either House of Parliament or to the House or either House of the Legislature of a State shall be called in question except by an election petition presented to such authority and in such manner as may be provided for by or under any law made by the appropriate Legislature.

Notes on Article 329

Bar of article 329(b) will not come into play when case falls under articles 191 and 193 and whole of the election process is over; *K. Venkatachalam* v. *A. Swamickan*, AIR 1999 SC 1723: (1999) 4 SCC 526: 1999 AIR SCW 1353: JT 1999 (3) SC 242: 1999 (5) SRJ 293: (1999) 3 SCALE 12: 1999 (4) Supreme 333: (1999) 2 UJ (SC) 1064.

[3][**329A. Special provision as to elections to Parliament in the case of Prime Minister and Speaker.**—[*Rep. by the Constitution (Forty-fourth Amendment) Act, 1978, sec. 36 (w.e.f. 20-6-1979).*]]

1. Subs. by the Constitution (Thirty-ninth Amendment) Act, 1975, sec. 3, for certain words (w.e.f. 10-8-1975).

2. The words, figures and letter "but subject to the provisions of article 329A" omitted by the Constitution (Forty-fourth Amendment) Act, 1978, sec. 35 (w.e.f. 20-6-1979).

3. Article 329A was earlier inserted by the Constitution (Thirty-ninth Amendment) Act, 1975, sec. 4 (w.e.f. 10-8-1975).

PART XVI
SPECIAL PROVISIONS RELATING TO CERTAIN CLASSES

330. Reservation of seats for Scheduled Castes and Scheduled Tribes in the House of the People.—(1) Seats shall be reserved in the House of the People for—

(a) the Scheduled Castes;

[1][(b) the Scheduled Tribes except the Scheduled Tribes in the autonomous districts of Assam; and]

(c) the Scheduled Tribes in the autonomous districts of Assam.

(2) The number of seats reserved in any State [2][or Union territory] for the Scheduled Castes or the Scheduled Tribes under clause (1) shall bear, as nearly as may be, the same proportion to the total number of seats allotted to that State [2][or Union territory] in the House of the People as the population of the Scheduled Castes in the State [2][or Union territory] or of the Scheduled Tribes in the State [2][or Union territory] or part of the State [2][or Union territory], as the case may be, in respect of which seats are so reserved, bears to the total population of the State [2][or Union territory].

[3][(3) Notwithstanding anything contained in clause (2), the number of seats reserved in the House of the People for the Scheduled Tribes in the autonomous districts of Assam shall bear to the total number of seats allotted to that State a proportion not less than the population of the Scheduled Tribes in the said autonomous districts bears to the total population of the State.]

[4][*Explanation.*—In this article and in article 332, the expression "population" means the population as ascertained at the last preceding census of which the relevant figures have been published:

Provided that the reference in this *Explanation* to the last preceding census of which the relevant figures have been published shall, until the relevant figures for the first census taken after the year [5][2026] have been published, be construed as a reference to the [6][2001] census.]

331. Representation of the Anglo-Indian community in the House of the People.—Notwithstanding anything in article 81, the President may, if he is of opinion that the Anglo-Indian community is not adequately represented in the House of the people, nominate not more than two members of that community to the House of the People.

---

1. Subs. by the Constitution (Fifty-first Amendment) Act, 1984, sec. 2(1), for sub-clause (b) (w.e.f. 16-6-1986). Earlier clause (b) was amended by the Constitution (Twenty-third Amendment) Act, 1969, sec. 2 (w.e.f. 23-1-1970) and by the Constitution (Thirty-first Amendment) Act, 1973, sec. 3(1)(a) (w.e.f. 17-10-1973).

2. Ins. by the Constitution (Seventh Amendment) Act, 1956, sec. 29 and Sch. (w.e.f. 1-11-1956).

3. Ins. by the Constitution (Thirty-first Amendment) Act, 1973, sec. 3(b) (w.e.f. 17-10-1973).

4. Ins. by the Constitution (Fourty-second Amendment) Act, 1976, sec. 47 (w.e.f. 3-1-1977).

5. Subs. by the Constitution (Eighty-fourth Amendment) Act, 2001, sec. 6, for "2000" (w.e.f. 21-2-2002).

6. Subs. by the Constitution (Eighty-seventh Amendment) Act, 2003, sec. 5, for '1991' (w.e.f. 22-6-2003). Earlier the figures "1991" were substituted by the Constitution (Eighty-fourth Amendment) Act, 2001, sec. 6, for the figures "1971" (w.e.f. 21-2-2002).

332. Reservation of seats for Scheduled Castes and Scheduled Tribes in the Legislative Assemblies of the States.—(1) Seats shall be reserved for the Scheduled Castes and the Scheduled Tribes, [1][except the Scheduled Tribes in the autonomous districts of Assam], in the Legislative Assembly of every State [2][***].

(2) Seats shall be reserved also for the autonomous districts in the Legislative Assembly of the State of Assam.

(3) The number of seats reserved for the Scheduled Castes or the Scheduled Tribes in the Legislative Assembly of any State under clause (1) shall bear, as nearly as may be, the same proportion to the total number of seats in the Assembly as the population of the Scheduled Castes in the State or of the Scheduled Tribes in the State or part of the State, as the case may be, in respect of which seats are so reserved bears to the total population of the State.

[3][(3A) Notwithstanding anything contained in clause (3), until the taking effect, under article 170, of the re-adjustment, on the basis of the first census after the year [4][2026], of the number of seats in the Legislative Assemblies of the States of Arunachal Pradesh, Meghalaya, Mizoram and Nagaland, the seats which shall be reserved for the Scheduled Tribes in the Legislative Assembly of any such State shall be,—

(a) if all the seats in the Legislative Assembly of such State in existence on the date of coming into force of the Constitution (Fifty-seventh Amendment) Act, 1987 (hereafter in this clause referred to as the existing Assembly) are held by members of the Scheduled Tribes, all the seats except one;

(b) in any other case, such number of seats as bears to the total number of seats, a proportion not less than the number (as on the said date) of members belonging to the Scheduled Tribes in the existing Assembly bears to the total number of seats in existing Assembly.]

[5][(3B) Notwithstanding anything contained in clause (3), until the re-adjustment, under article 170, takes effect on the basis of the first census after the year [6][2026], of the number of seats in the Legislative Assembly of the State of

---

1. Subs. by the Constitution (Fifty-first Amendment) Act, 1984, sec. 3(i), for "except the Scheduled Tribes in the triable areas of Assam, in Nagaland and in Meghalaya" (w.e.f. 16-6-1986). Earlier the words "except the Scheduled Tribes in the triable areas of Assam and Nagaland" were substituted by the Constitution (Twenty-third Amendment) Act, 1969, sec. 3, for the words "except the Scheduled Tribes in the triable areas of Assam" (w.e.f. 23-1-1970) and the words "except the Scheduled Tribes in the triable areas of Assam, in Nagaland and in Meghalaya" were substituted by the Constitution (Thirty-first Amendment) Act, 1973, sec. 4(1), for the words "except the Scheduled Tribes in the triable areas of Assam and Nagaland" (w.e.f. 17-10-1973).

2. The words and letters "specified in Part A or Part B of the First Schedule" omitted by the Constitution (Seventh Amendment) Act, 1956, sec. 29 and Sch. (w.e.f. 1-11-1956).

3. Ins. by the Constitution (Fifty-seventh Amendment) Act, 1987, sec. 2(i) (w.e.f. 21-9-1987).

4. Subs. by the Constitution (Eighty-fourth Amendment) Act, 2001, sec. 7(a), for "2000" (w.e.f. 21-2-2002).

5. Ins. by the Constitution (Seventy-second* Amendment) Act, 1992, sec. 2(1) (w.e.f. 5-12-1992).

6. Subs. by the Constitution (Eighty-fourth Amendment) Act, 2001, sec. 7(b), for "2000" (w.e.f. 21-2-2002).

Tripura, the seats which shall be reserved for the Scheduled Tribes in the Legislative Assembly shall be, such number of seats as bears to the total number of seats, a proportion not less than the number, as on the date of coming into force of the Constitution (Seventy-second Amendment) Act, 1992, of members belonging to the Scheduled Tribes in the Legislative Assembly in existence on the said date bears to the total number of seats in that Assembly.]

(4) The number of seats reserved for an autonomous district in the Legislative Assembly of the State of Assam shall bear to the total number of seats in that Assembly a proportion not less than the population of the district bears to the total population of the State.

(5) The constituencies for the seats reserved for any autonomous district of Assam shall not comprise any area outside that district [1][***].

(6) No person who is not a member of a Scheduled Tribe of any autonomous district of the State of Assam shall be eligible for election to the Legislative Assembly of the State from any constituency of that district [1][***]:

[2][Provided that for elections to the Legislative Assembly of the State of Assam, the representation of the Scheduled Tribes and non-Scheduled Tribes in the constituencies included in the Bodoland Territorial Areas District, so notified, and existing prior to the constitution of the Bodoland Territorial Areas District, shall be maintained.]

Notes on Article 332

Sub-section (3B) of this article shall not affect any representation in the Legislative Assembly of the State of Tripura until the dissolution of the Legislative Assembly existing at the commencement of this Act. [section 2 of Constitution (Seventy-second Amendment) Act, 1992.]

333. Representation of the Anglo-Indian community in the Legislative Assemblies of the States.—Notwithstanding anything in article 170, the Governor [3][***] of a State may, if he is of opinion that the Anglo-Indian community needs representation in the Legislative Assembly of the State and is not adequately represented therein, [4][nominate one member of that community to the Assembly].

334. Reservation of seats and special representation to cease after [5][seventy years].—Notwithstanding anything in the foregoing provisions of this Part, the provisions of this Constitution relating to—

1. Certain words omitted by the North-Eastern Areas (Reorganisation) Act, 1971 (81 of 1971), sec. 71(i) (w.e.f. 21-1-1972).

2. Ins. by the Constitution (Ninetieth Amendment) Act, 2003, sec. 2 (w.e.f. 28-9-2003).

3. The words "or Rajpramukh" omitted by the Constitution (Seventh Amendment) Act, 1956, sec. 29 and Sch. (w.e.f. 1-11-1956).

4. Subs. by the Constitution (Twenty-third Amendment) Act, 1969, sec. 4(1), for certain words (w.e.f. 23-1-1970).

5. Subs. by the Constitution (Ninety-fifth Amendment) Act, 2009, sec. 2, for "Sixty years" (w.e.f. 25-1-2010). Earlier the words "sixty years" were substituted by the Constitution (Seventy-ninth Amendment) Act, 1999, sec. 2, for the words "fifty years" (w.e.f. 25-1-2000), the words "fifty years" were substituted by the Constitution (Sixty-second Amendment) Act, 1989, sec. 2, for the words "forty years" (w.r.e.f. 20-12-1989) the words "forty years" were substituted by the Constitution (Forty-fifth Amendment) Act, 1980, sec. 2, for the words "thirty years" (w.e.f. 25-1-1980) and the words "thirty years" by the Constitution (Twenty-third Amendment) Act, 1969, sec. 5, for the words "twenty years" (w.e.f. 23-1-1970).

(a) the reservation of seats for the Scheduled Castes and the Scheduled Tribes in the House of the People and in the Legislative Assemblies of the States; and

(b) the representation of the Anglo-Indian community in the House of the People and in the Legislative Assemblies of the States by nomination,

shall cease to have effect on the expiration of a period of [1][seventy years] from the commencement of this Constitution:

Provided that nothing in this article shall affect any representation in the House of the People or in the Legislative Assembly of a State until the dissolution of the then existing House or Assembly, as the case may be.

335. Claims of Scheduled Castes and Scheduled Tribes to services and posts.—The claims of the members of the Scheduled Castes and the Scheduled Tribes shall be taken into consideration, consistently with the maintenance of efficiency of administration, in the making of appointments to services and posts in connection with the affairs of the Union or of a State:

[2][Provided that nothing in this article shall prevent in making of any provision in favour of the members of the Scheduled Castes and the Scheduled Tribes for relaxation in qualifying marks in any examination or lowering the standards of evaluation, for reservation in matters of promotion to any class or classes of services or posts in connection with the affairs of the Union or of a State.]

Notes on Article 335

Article 335 is to be read with article 46, which provides (as a directive principle) that the State shall promote with special care the educational and economic interests of the weaker sections of the people; *Comptroller v. Jagannathan*, AIR 1987 SC 537: (1986) 2 SCC 679: (1986) 1 ATC 1: (1986) 1 SLR 712.

There is need to maintain a balance between reservation and efficiency and not only with reference to Scheduled Castes and Scheduled Tribes but also with reference to other backward classes. Since sacrifice of merit may have to be made for social justice; *Indra Sawhney v. Union of India*, (1992) Supp 3 SCC 217: AIR 1993 SC 477: 1992 SCC (L&S) Supp 1: (1992) 22 ATC 385 (Mandal Commission Report Case).

Whether a particular class is adequately represented in the services under the State is a matter within the subjective satisfaction of the appropriate government based on the materials in the possession of the government and the existing conditions in the society; *Indra Sawhney v. Union of India*, (1992) Supp 3 SCC 217: AIR 1993 SC 477: 1992 SCC (L&S) Supp 1: (1992) 22 ATC 385 (Mandal Commission Report Case).

336. Special provision for Anglo-Indian community in certain services.— (1) During the first two years after the commencement of this Constitution, appointments of members of the Anglo-Indian community to posts in the railway,

---

1. Subs. by the Constitution (Ninety-fifth Amendment) Act, 2009, sec. 2, for "Sixty years" (w.e.f. 25-1-2010). Earlier the words "sixty years" were substituted by the Constitution (Seventy-ninth Amendment) Act, 1999, sec. 2, for the words "fifty years" (w.e.f. 25-1-2000), the words "fifty years" were substituted by the Constitution (Sixty-second Amendment) Act, 1989, sec. 2, for the words "forty years" (w.r.e.f. 20-12-1989) the words "forty years" were substituted by the Constitution (Forty-fifth Amendment) Act, 1980, sec. 2, for the words "thirty years" (w.e.f. 25-1-1980) and the words "thirty years" by the Constitution (Twenty-third Amendment) Act, 1969, sec. 5, for the words "twenty years" (w.e.f. 23-1-1970).

2. Ins. by the Constitution (Eighty-second Amendment) Act, 2000, sec. 2 (w.e.f. 8-9-2000).

customs, postal and telegraph services of the Union shall be made on the same basis as immediately before the fifteenth day of August, 1947.

_During every succeeding period of two years, the number of posts reserved for the members of the said community in the said services shall, as nearly as possible, be less by ten per cent. than the numbers so reserved during the immediately preceding period of two years:

Provided that at the end of ten years from the commencement of this Constitution all such reservations shall cease.

(2) Nothing in clause (1) shall bar the appointment of members of the Anglo-Indian community to posts other than, or in addition to, those reserved for the community under that clause if such members are found qualified for appointment on merit as compared with the members of other communities.

337. Special provision with respect to educational grants for the benefit of Anglo-Indian community.—During the first three financial years after the commencement of this Constitution, the same grants, if any, shall be made by the Union and by each State [1][***] for the benefit of the Anglo-Indian community in respect of education as were made in the financial year ending on the thirty-first day of March, 1948.

During every succeeding period of three years the grants may be less by ten per cent. than those for the immediately preceding period of three years:

Provided that at the end of ten years from the commencement of this Constitution such grants, to the extent to which they are a special concession to the Anglo-Indian community, shall cease:

Provided further that no educational institution shall be entitled to receive any grant under this article unless at least forty per cent. of annual admissions therein are made available to members of communities other than the Anglo-Indian community.

338. [2]**[National Commission for Scheduled Castes].**—[3][(1) There shall be a Commission for the Scheduled Castes to be known as the National Commission for the Scheduled Castes.]

[3][(2) Subject to the provisions of any law made in this behalf by Parliament, the Commission shall consist of a Chairperson, Vice-Chairperson and three other Members and the conditions of service and tenure of office of the Chairperson, Vice-Chairperson and other Members so appointed shall be such as the President may by rule determine.]

[4][(3) The Chairperson, Vice-Chairperson and other Members of the Commission shall be appointed by the President by warrant under his hand and seal.]

---

1. The words and letters "specified in Part A or Part B of the First Schedule" omitted by the Constitution (Seventh Amendment) Act, 1956, sec. 29 and Sch. (w.e.f. 1-11-1956).
2. Subs. by the Constitution (Eighty-ninth Amendment) Act, 2003, sec. 2(a), for the heading "**Special Officer for Scheduled Castes and Scheduled Tribes**" (w.e.f. 19-2-2004). Earlier the heading was substituted by the Constitution (Sixty-fifth Amendment) Act, 1990, sec. 2(a) (w.e.f. 12-3-1992).
3. Subs. by the Constitution (Eighty-ninth Amendment) Act, 2003, sec. 2(b), for clauses (1) and (2) (w.e.f. 19-2-2004). Earlier clauses (1) and (2) were substituted by the Constitution (Sixty-fifth Amendment) Act, 1990, sec. 2(b) (w.e.f. 12-3-1992).
4. Subs. by the Constitution (Sixty-fifth Amendment) Act, 1990, sec. 2(b), for clauses (1) and (2) (w.e.f. 12-3-1992).

[1][(4) The Commission shall have the power to regulate its own procedure.]

[1][(5) It shall be the duty of the Commission—

(a) to investigate and monitor all matters relating to the safeguards provided for the Scheduled Castes [2][***] under this Constitution or under any other law for the time being in force or under any order of the Government and to evaluate the working of such safeguards;

(b) to inquire into specific complaints with respect to the deprivation of rights and safeguards of the Scheduled Castes [2][***];

(c) to participate and advise on the planning process of socio-economic development of the Scheduled Castes [2][***] and to evaluate the progress of their development under the Union and any State;

(d) to present to the President, annually and at such other times as the Commission may deem fit, reports upon the working of those safeguards;

(e) to make in such reports recommendations as to the measures that should be taken by the Union or any State for the effective implementation of those safeguards and other measures for the protection, welfare and socio-economic development of the Scheduled Castes [2][***]; and

(f) to discharge such other functions in relation to the protection, welfare and development and advancement of the Scheduled Castes [2][***] as the President may, subject to the provisions of any law made by Parliament, by the rule specify.]

[1][(6) The President shall cause all such reports to be laid before each House of Parliament along with a memorandum explaining the action taken or proposed to be taken on the recommendations relating to the Union and the reasons for the non-acceptance, if any, of any of such recommendations.]

[1][(7) Where any such report, or any part thereof, relates to any matter with which any State Government is concerned, a copy of such report shall be forwarded to the Governor of the State who shall cause it to be laid before the Legislature of the State along with a memorandum explaining the action taken or proposed to be taken on the recommendations relating to the State and the reasons for the non-acceptance, if any, of any of such recommendations.]

[1][(8) The Commission shall, while investigating any matter referred to in sub-clause (a) or inquiring into any complaint referred to in sub-clause (b) of clause (5), have all the powers of a civil court trying a suit and in particular in respect of the following matters, namely:—

(a) summoning and enforcing the attendance of any person from any part of India and examining him on oath;

(b) requiring the discovery and production of any documents;

(c) receiving evidence on affidavits;

(d) requisitioning any public record or copy thereof from any court or office;

(e) issuing commissions for the examination of witnesses and documents;

(f) any other matter which the President may, by rule, determine.]

---

1. Subs. by the Constitution (Sixty-fifth Amendment) Act, 1990, sec. 2(b), for clauses (1) and (2) (w.e.f. 12-3-1992).

2. The words "and Scheduled Tribes" omitted by the Constitution (Eighty-ninth Amendment) Act, 2003, sec. 2(c) (w.e.f. 19-2-2004).

[1](9) The Union and every State Government shall consult the Commission on all major policy matters affecting Scheduled Castes [2][***].]

[3][(10)] In this article, references to the Scheduled Castes [2][***] shall be construed as including references to such other backward classes as the President may, on receipt of the report of a Commission appointed under clause (1) of article 340 by order specify and also to the Anglo-Indian community.

[4][**338A. National Commission for Scheduled Tribes.**—(1) There shall be a Commission for the Scheduled Tribes to be known as the National Commission for the Scheduled Tribes.

(2) Subject to the provisions of any law made in this behalf by Parliament, the Commission shall consist of a Chairperson, Vice-Chairperson and three other Members and the conditions of service and tenure of office of the Chairperson, Vice-Chairperson and other Members so appointed shall be such as the President may be rule determine.

(3) The Chairperson, Vice-Chairperson and other Members of the Commission shall be appointed by the President by warrant under his hand and seal.

(4) The Commission shall have the power to regulate its own procedure.

(5) It shall be the duty of the Commission—

(a) to investigate and monitor all matters relating to the safeguards provided for the Scheduled Tribes under this Constitution or under any other law for the time being in force or under any order of the Government and to evaluate the working of such safeguards;

(b) to inquire into specific complaints with respect to the deprivation of rights and safeguards of the Scheduled Tribes;

(c) to participate and advise on the planning process of socio-economic development of the Scheduled Tribes and to evaluate the progress of their development under the Union and any State;

(d) to present to the President, annually and at such other times as the Commission may deem fit, reports upon the working of those safeguards;

(e) to make in such reports recommendations as to the measures that should be taken by the Union or any State for the effective implementation of those safeguards and other measures for the protection, welfare and socio-economic development of the Scheduled Tribes; and

(f) to discharge such other functions in relation to the protection, welfare and development and advancement of the Scheduled Tribes as the President may, subject to the provisions of any law made by Parliament, by rule specify.

(6) The President shall cause all such reports to be laid before each House of Parliament along with a memorandum explaining the action taken or proposed to

---

1. Subs. by the Constitution (Sixty-fifth Amendment) Act, 1990, sec. 2(b), for clauses (1) and (2) (w.e.f. 12-3-1992).

2. The words "and Scheduled Tribes" omitted by the Constitution (Eighty-ninth Amendment) Act, 2003, sec. 2(c) (w.e.f. 19-2-2004).

3. Clause (3) renumbered as clause (10) by the Constitution (Sixty-fifth Amendment) Act, 1990, sec. 2(c) (w.e.f. 12-3-1992).

4. Ins. by the Constitution (Eighty-ninth Amendment) Act, 2003, sec. 3 (w.e.f. 19-2-2004).

be taken on the recommendations relating to the Union and the reasons for the non-acceptance, if any, of any of such recommendations.

(7) Where any such report, or any part thereof, relates to any matter with which any State Government is concerned, a copy of such report shall be forwarded to the Governor of the State who shall cause it to be laid before the Legislature of the State along with a memorandum explaining the action taken or proposed to be taken on the recommendations relating to the State and the reasons for the non-accpetance, if any, of any such recommendations.

(8) The Commission shall, while investigating any matter referred to in sub-clause (a) or inquiring into any complaint referred to in sub-clause (b) of clause (5), have all the powers of a civil court trying a suit and in particular in respect of the following matters, namely:—

(a) summoning and enforcing the attendance of any person from any part of India and examining him on oath;

(b) requiring the discovery and production of any document;

(c) receiving evidence on affidavits;

(d) requisitioning any public record or copy thereof from any court of office;

(e) issuing commissions for the examination of witnesses and documents;

(f) any other matter which the President may, by rule, determine.

(9) The Union and every State Government shall consult the Commission on all major policy matters affecting Scheduled Tribes.]

339. Control of the Union over the administration of Scheduled Areas and the welfare of Scheduled Tribes.—(1) The President may at any time and shall, at the expiration of ten years from the commencement of this Constitution by order appoint a Commission to report on the administration of the Scheduled Areas and the welfare of the Scheduled Tribes in the States [1][***].

The order may define the composition, powers and procedure of the Commission and may contain such incidental or ancillary provisions as the President may consider necessary or desirable.

(2) The executive power of the Union shall extend to the giving of directions to [2][a State] as to the drawing up and execution of schemes specified in the direction to be essential for the welfare of the Scheduled Tribes in the State.

340. Appointment of a Commission to investigate the conditions of backward classes.—(1) The President may by order appoint a Commission consisting of such persons as he thinks fit to investigate the conditions of socially and educationally backward classes within the territory of India and the difficulties under which they labour and to make recommendations as to the steps that should be taken by the Union or any State to remove such difficulties and to improve their condition and as to the grants that should be made for the purpose by the Union or any State and the conditions subject to which such grants should be made, and the order appointing such Commission shall define the procedure to be followed by the Commission.

---

1. The words and letters "specified in Part A or Part B of the First Schedule" omitted by the Constitution (Seventh Amendment) Act, 1956, sec. 29 and Sch. (w.e.f. 1-11-1956).

2. Subs. by the Constitution (Seventh Amendment) Act, 1956, sec. 29 and Sch., for "any such State" (w.e.f. 1-11-1956).

(2) A Commission so appointed shall investigate the matters referred to them and present to the President a report setting out the facts as found by them and making such recommendations as they think proper.

(3) The President shall cause a copy of the report so presented together with a memorandum explaining the action taken thereon to be laid before each House of Parliament.

341. Scheduled Castes.—(1) The President ¹[may with respect to any State ²[or Union territory], and where it is a State ³[***], after consultation with the Governor ⁴[***] thereof], by public notification⁵, specify the castes, races or tribes or parts of or groups within castes, races or tribes which shall for the purposes of this Constitution be deemed to be Scheduled Castes in relation to that State ²[or Union territory, as the case may be].

(2) Parliament may by law include in or exclude from the list of Scheduled Castes specified in a notification issued under clause (1) any caste, race or tribe or part of or group within any caste, race or tribe, but save as aforesaid a notification issued under the said clause shall not be varied by any subsequent notification.

Notes on Article 341

See notes on article 342.

342. Scheduled Tribes.—(1) The President ⁶[may with respect to any State ²[or Union territory], and where it is a State ³[***], after consultation with the Governor ⁴[***] thereof], by public notification⁷, specify the tribes or tribal communities or parts of or groups within tribes or tribal communities which shall for the purposes of this Constitution be deemed to be Scheduled Tribes in relation to that State ²[or Union territory, as the case may be].

---

1. Subs. by the Constitution (First Amendment) Act, 1951, sec. 10, for "may, after consultation with the Governor or Rajpramukh of a State" (w.e.f. 18-6-1951).

2. Ins. by the Constitution (Seventh Amendment) Act, 1956, sec. 29 and Sch. (w.e.f. 1-11-1956).

3. The words and letters "specified in Part A or Part B of the First Schedule" omitted by the Constitution (Seventh Amendment) Act, 1956, sec. 29 and Sch. (w.e.f. 1-11-1956).

4. The words "or Rajpramukh" omitted by the Constitution (Seventh Amendment) Act, 1956, sec. 29 and Sch. (w.e.f. 1-11-1956).

5. *See* the Constitution (Scheduled Castes) Order, 1950 (C.O. 19), the Constitution (Scheduled Castes) (Union Territories) Order, 1951, (C.O. 32), the Constitution (Jammu and Kashmir) Scheduled Castes Order, 1956 (C.O. 52), the Constitution (Dadra and Nagar Haveli) Scheduled Castes Order, 1962, (C.O. 64), the Constitution (Pondicherry) Scheduled Castes Order, 1964 (C.O. 68), the Constitution (Goa, Daman and Diu) Scheduled Castes Order, 1968 (C.O. 81) and the Constitution (Sikkim) Scheduled Castes Order, 1978 (C.O. 110).

6. Subs. by the Constitution (First Amendment) Act, 1951, sec. 11, for "may, after consultation with the Governor or Rajpramukh of a State" (w.e.f. 18-6-1951).

7. *See* the Constitution (Scheduled Tribes) Order, 1950 (C.O. 22), the Constitution (Scheduled Tribes) (Union Territories) Order, 1951, (C.O. 33), the Constitution (Andaman and Nicobar Islands) Scheduled Tribes Order, 1959 (C.O. 58), the Constitution (Dadra and Nagar Haveli) Scheduled Tribes Order, 1962 (C.O. 65), the Constitution (Scheduled Tribes) (Uttar Pradesh) Order, 1967 (C.O. 78), the Constitution (Goa, Daman and Diu) Scheduled Tribes Order, 1968 (C.O. 82), the Constitution (Nagaland) Scheduled Tribes Order, 1970 (C.O. 88) and the Constitution (Sikkim) Scheduled Tribes Order, 1978 (C.O. 111).

(2) Parliament may by law include in or exclude from the list of Scheduled Tribes specified in a notification issued under clause (1) any tribe or tribal community or part of or group within any tribe or tribal community, but save as aforesaid a notification issued under the said clause shall not be varied by any subsequent notification.

Notes on Articles 341 and 342

Conversion

A person who is converted to another religion cannot claim Scheduled Caste status; *Soosai* v. *Union of India*, AIR 1986 SC 733: 1985 Supp SCC 590: 1986 UJ (SC) 39: 1986 (1) Supreme 207: (1985) 87 Bom LR 652.

Finality of Presidential Order

Presidential Order under article 342 regarding Scheduled Tribes is final. Court cannot add or subtract any entry. Its enquiry is confined to interpreting what an entry in the Presidential Order is intended to mean. Court cannot add to, modify or subtract from the Order. *See* the following cases on the above point:—

(i) *B. Basavalingappa* v. *D. Munichinnappa*, AIR 1965 SC 1269 (1271): (1965) 1 SCR 316: 1965 (2) SCJ 153.

(ii) *Bhaiya Lal* v. *Harikishan Singh*, AIR 1965 SC 1557: (1965) 2 SCR 877: (1965) 1 SCWR 840: 1965 MPLJ 669: 1965 Jab LJ 860: (1965) 2 SCA 721: 1966 (2) SCJ 77 (Scheduled Tribes).

(iii) *Dina* v. *Narayan Singh*, (1968) 38 ELR 212 (Scheduled Tribes).

(iv) *Parsram* v. *Shivchand*, AIR 1969 SC 597: (1969) 1 SCC 20: (1969) 2 SCR 997 (Scheduled Castes).

(v) *Bhaiya Ram Munda* v. *Anirudh Patar*, (1971) 1 SCR 804: AIR 1971 SC 2533: (1970) 2 SCC 825 (Scheduled Tribes).

(vi) *Srish Kumar* v. *State of Tripura*, AIR 1990 SC 991: 1990 Supp SCC 220: 1990 Lab IC 707 (Scheduled Tribes).

(vii) *Dr. Virendra Mohan Rai Khangar* v. *Union of India*, AIR 1992 All 147: 1991 AWC 1089: 1992 (1) All CJ 193.

The entries in the Presidential Order have to be taken as final. It is not open to the court to make any addition or subtraction from the Presidential Order. Enquiry is contemplated before the Presidential Order is made but any amendment to the Presidential Order can only be by legislation. The court cannot assume jurisdiction and enter into an enquiry to determine whether the three terms indicated in the Presidential Order, *viz.* Tripura/Tripuri/Tippera in Entry 15 includes Deshi Tripura which according to some Government Circulars includes the Laskar Community.

The Order is made after a detailed inquiry as to the economic status, the level of education and the necessity of protection, inclusion into or exclusion from the Order is made. The material relating to the Laskar tribe in 1930 or 1941 may not have been considered sufficient before the respective Orders were made for including the Laskars, said to have been covered by the description of Deshi Tripura. Therefore, even if historically this tribe was covered by the general description that by itself may not justify its inclusion in the Order as a Scheduled Tribe; *Srish Kumar Chouhay* v. *State of Tripura*, AIR 1990 SC 991: 1990 Supp SCC 220: 1990 Lab IC 707, paragraphs 15-20.

It is open to the President to declare that a caste or sub-caste shall be deemed to be a Scheduled Caste in a particular part of a State and not in any other part. It follows that a person who wants to be elected from a Scheduled Caste constituency must show that he has been registered as a Scheduled Caste in his electoral roll; the fact that his caste is recognised as a Scheduled Caste in the constituency from which he is seeking election is of no avail.

Conversely, where the President's Notification declares a caste to be a SC for the purposes of certain specified States, no Court will direct that caste, to be declared SC in relation to another

State; *Dr. Virendra Mohan Rai Khangar* v. *Union of India*, AIR 1992 All 147: 1991 AWC 1089: 1992 (1) All CJ 193, paragraph 6.

Where the President's Order specifies 'Dhoba' as a Scheduled Caste in Orissa, its literal synonym 'Rajaka' would also be admitted in that S.C.; *Revenue Officer* v. *Prafulla Kumar Pati*, AIR 1990 SC 727: JT 1990 (1) SC 155, paragraph 12A.

Under a Circular of the Government of India, dated 6-8-1984, a person who is a Scheduled Tribe in a State, according to the President's Order, continues to be a Scheduled Tribe in another State to which he has migrated; *State of Gujarat* v. *R.L. Patel*, AIR 1992 Guj 42: 1991 (1) Civ LJ 128: (1990) 2 Guj LH 1: (1990) 2 Guj LR 1163: (1992) 1 LLJ 721: (1990) 6 Serv LR 782, paragraph 4.

Migrants Tribals

Bhils are recognized as Scheduled Tribes in Gujarat and Maharashtra. Petitioner's father had migrated to Bombay from Gujarat in 1961. There was reservation for Scheduled Tribes in medical colleges. But the petitioner was refused the facility of reservation on the ground that Government Instruction 17(a) disallowed reservation for migrants from other States. It was held that the relevant clauses of the instruction were violative of articles 14, 15, 16, 19 and 342 of the Constitution; *Rajesh Arjunbhai Patel* v. *State of Maharashtra*, AIR 1990 Bom 114 (117, 118): 1990 Mah LJ 55.

Scheduled Tribe –Acquisition of Status

The offshoots of the wedlock of a tribal woman married to a non-tribal husband cannot claim Scheduled Tribe Status; *Anjan Kumar* v. *Union of India*, AIR 2006 SC 1177: 2006 AIR SCW 888: 2006 (3) Jab LJ 42: (2006) 3 SCC 257: 2006 (2) SCJ 472: 2006 (3) SRJ 414: (2006) 2 SCALE 327: (2006) 2 Serv LR 487: 2006 (2) Supreme 59.

PART XVII

OFFICIAL LANGUAGE

CHAPTER I

LANGUAGE OF THE UNION

343. Official language of the Union.—(1) The official language of the Union shall be Hindi in Devanagari script.

The form of numerals to be used for the official purposes of the Union shall be the international form of Indian numerals.

(2) Notwithstanding anything in clause (1), for a period of fifteen years from the commencement of this Constitution, the English language shall continue to be used for all the official purposes of the Union for which it was being used immediately before such commencement:

Provided that the President may, during the said period, by order[1] authorise the use of the Hindi language in addition to the English language and of the Devanagari form of numerals in addition to the international form of Indian numerals for any of the official purposes of the Union.

(3) Notwithstanding anything in this article, Parliament may by law provide for the use, after the said period of fifteen years, of—

(a) the English language, or

(b) the Devanagari form of numerals,

for such purposes as may be specified in the law.

344. Commission and Committee of Parliament on official language.—(1) The

---

1. *See* C.O. 41.

President shall, at the expiration of five years from the commencement of this Constitution and thereafter at the expiration of ten years from such commencement, by order constitute a Commission which shall consist of a Chairman and such other members representing the different languages specified in the Eighth Schedule as the President may appoint, and the order shall define the procedure to be followed by the Commission.

(2) It shall be the duty of the Commission to make recommendations to the President as to—

(a) the progressive use of the Hindi language for the official purposes of the Union;

(b) restrictions on the use of the English language for all or any of the official purposes of the Union;

(c) the language to be used for all or any of the purposes mentioned in article 348;

(d) the form of numerals to be used for any one or more specified purposes of the Union;

(e) any other matter referred to the Commission by the President as regards the official language of the Union and the language for communication between the Union and a State or between one State and another and their use.

(3) In making their recommendations under clause (2), the Commission shall have due regard to the industrial, cultural and scientific advancement of India, and the just claims and the interests of persons belonging to the non-Hindi speaking areas in regard to the public services.

(4) There shall be constituted a Committee consisting of thirty members, of whom twenty shall be members of the House of the People and ten shall be members of the Council of States to be elected respectively by the members of the House of the People and the members of the Council of States in accordance with the system of proportional representation by means of the single transferable vote.

(5) It shall be the duty of the Committee to examine the recommendations of the Commission constituted under clause (1) and to report to the President their opinion thereon.

(6) Notwithstanding anything in article 343, the President may, after consideration of the report referred to in clause (5), issue directions in accordance with the whole or any part of that report.

CHAPTER II

REGIONAL LANGUAGES

345. Official language or languages of a State.—Subject to the provisions of articles 346 and 347, the Legislature of a State may by law adopt any one or more of the languages in use in the State or Hindi as the language or languages to be used for all or any of the official purposes of that State:

Provided that, until the Legislature of the State otherwise provides by law, the English language shall continue to be used for those official purposes within the State for which it was being used immediately before the commencement of this Constitution.

Notes on Article 345

Language for Right to Information

In case of supply of information, the public authority is under obligation to give information to citizen in language which he understands; *State Consumer Disputes Redressal Commission, Uttarakhand* v. *Uttarakhand State Information Commission,* AIR 2010 Uttra 55.

346. Official language for communication between one State and another or between a State and the Union.—The language for the time being authorised for use in the Union for official purposes shall be the official language for communication between one State and another State and between a State and the Union:

Provided that if two or more States agree that the Hindi language should be the official language for communication between such States, that language may be used for such communication.

347. Special provision relating to language spoken by a section of the population of a State.—On a demand being made in that behalf the President may, if he is satisfied that a substantial proportion of the population of a State desire the use of any language spoken by them to be recognised by that State, direct that such language shall also be officially recognised throughout that State or any part thereof for such purpose as he may specify.

CHAPTER III

LANGUAGE OF THE SUPREME COURT, HIGH COURTS, ETC.

348. Language to be used in the Supreme Court and in the High Courts and for Acts, Bills, etc.—(1) Notwithstanding anything in the foregoing provisions of this Part, until Parliament by law otherwise provides—

(a) all proceedings in the Supreme Court and in every High Court,

(b) the authoritative texts—

    (i) of all Bills to be introduced or amendments thereto to be moved in either House of Parliament or in the House or either House of the Legislature of a State,

    (ii) of all Acts passed by Parliament or the Legislature of a State and of all Ordinances promulgated by the President or the Governor [1][***] of a State, and

    (iii) of all orders, rules, regulations and bye-laws issued under this Constitution or under any law made by Parliament or the Legislature of a State,

shall be in the English language.

(2) Notwithstanding anything in sub-clause (a) of clause (1), the Governor [1][***] of a State may, with the previous consent of the President, authorise the use of the Hindi language, or any other language used for any official purposes of the State, in proceedings in the High Court having its principal seat in that State:

Provided that nothing in this clause shall apply to any judgment, decree or order passed or made by such High Court.

(3) Notwithstanding anything in sub-clause (b) of clause (1), where the Legislature of a State has prescribed any language other than the English language

---

1. The words "or Rajpramukh" omitted by the Constitution (Seventh Amendment) Act, 1956, sec. 29 and Sch. (w.e.f. 1-11-1956).

for use in Bills introduced in, or Acts passed by, the Legislature of the State or in Ordinances promulgated by the Governor [1][***] of the State or in any order, rule, regulation or bye-law referred to in paragraph (iii) of that sub-clause, a translation of the same in the English language published under the authority of the Governor [1][***] of the State in the Official Gazette of that State shall be deemed to be the authoritative text thereof in the English language under this article.

349. **Special procedure for enactment of certain laws relating to language.**— During the period of fifteen years from the commencement of this Constitution, no Bill or amendment making provision for the language to be used for any of the purposes mentioned in clause (1) of article 348 shall be introduced or moved in either House of Parliament without the previous sanction of the President, and the President shall not give his sanction to the introduction of any such Bill or the moving of any such amendment except after he has taken into consideration the recommendations of the Commission constituted under clause (1) of article 344 and the report of the Committee constituted under clause (4) of that article.

CHAPTER IV
SPECIAL DIRECTIVES

350. **Language to be used in representations for redress of grievances.**—Every person shall be entitled to submit a representation for the redress of any grievance to any officer or authority of the Union or a State in any of the languages used in the Union or in the State, as the case may be.

[2][**350A. Facilities for instruction in mother-tongue at primary stage.**—It shall be the endeavour of every State and of every local authority within the State to provide adequate facilities for instruction in the mother-tongue at the primary stage of education to children belonging to linguistic minority groups; and the President may issue such directions to any State as he considers necessary or proper for securing the provision of such facilities.]

[2][**350B. Special Officer for linguistic minorities.**—(1) There shall be a Special Officer for linguistic minorities to be appointed by the President.

(2) It shall be the duty of the Special Officer to investigate all matters relating to the safeguards provided for linguistic minorities under this Constitution and report to the President upon those matters at such intervals as the President may direct, and the President shall cause all such reports to be laid before each House of Parliament, and sent to the Governments of the States concerned.]

351. **Directive for development of the Hindi language.**—It shall be the duty of the Union to promote the spread of the Hindi language, to develop it so that it may serve as a medium of expression for all the elements of the composite culture of India and to secure its enrichment by assimilating without interfering with its genius, the forms, style and expressions used in Hindustani and in the other languages of India specified in the Eighth Schedule, and by drawing, wherever necessary or desirable, for its vocabulary, primarily on Sanskrit and secondarily on other languages.

---

1. The words "or Rajpramukh" omitted by the Constitution (Seventh Amendment) Act, 1956, sec. 29 and Sch. (w.e.f. 1-11-1956).
2. Ins. by the Constitution (Seventh Amendment) Act, 1956, sec. 21 (w.e.f. 1-11-1956).

PART XVIII

EMERGENCY PROVISIONS

352. Proclamation of Emergency.—(1) If the President is satisfied that a grave emergency exists whereby the security of India or of any part of the territory thereof is threatened, whether by war or external aggression or [1][armed rebellion,] he may, by Proclamation, make a declaration to that effect [2][in respect of the whole of India or of such part of the territory thereof as may be specified in the Proclamation].

[3][*Explanation.*—A Proclamation of Emergency declaring that the security of India or any part of the territory thereof is threatened by war or by external aggression or by armed rebellion may be made before the actual occurrence of war or of any such aggression or rebellion, if the President is satisfied that there is imminent danger thereof.]

[4][(2) A Proclamation issued under clause (1) may be varied or revoked by a subsequent Proclamation.

(3) The President shall not issue a Proclamation under clause (1) or a Proclamation varying such Proclamation unless the decision of the Union Cabinet (that is to say, the Council consisting of the Prime Minister and other Ministers of Cabinet rank appointed under article 75) that such a Proclamation may be issued has been communicated to him in writing.

(4) Every Proclamation issued under this article shall be laid before each House of Parliament and shall, except where it is a Proclamation revoking a previous Proclamation, cease to operate at the expiration of one month unless before the expiration of that period it has been approved by resolutions of both Houses of Parliament:

Provided that if any such Proclamation (not being a Proclamation revoking a previous Proclamation) is issued at a time when the House of the People has been dissolved, or the dissolution of the House of the People takes place during the period of one month referred to in this clause, and if a resolution approving the Proclamation has been passed by the Council of States, but no resolution with respect to such Proclamation has been passed by the House of the People before the expiration of that period, the Proclamation shall cease to operate at the expiration of thirty days from the date on which the House of the People first sits after its reconstitution, unless before the expiration of the said period of thirty days a resolution approving the Proclamation has been also passed by the House of the People.

(5) A Proclamation so approved shall, unless revoked, cease to operate on the expiration of a period of six months from the date of the passing of the second of the resolutions approving the proclamation under clause (4):

---

1. Subs. by the Constitution (Forty-fourth Amendment) Act, 1978, sec. 37(a)(i), for "internal disturbance" (w.e.f. 20-6-1979).
2. Ins. by the Constitution (Forty-second Amendment) Act, 1976, sec. 48(a) (w.e.f. 3-1-1977).
3. Ins. by the Constitution (Forty-fourth Amendment) Act, 1978, sec. 37(a)(ii) (w.e.f. 20-6-1979).
4. Subs. by the Constitution (Forty-fourth Amendment) Act, 1978, sec. 37(b), for clauses (2), (2A) and (3) (w.e.f. 20-6-1979). Earlier clause (2) was amended and clause (2A) was inserted by the Constitution (Forty-second Amendment) Act, 1976, sec. 48(b) and(c) (w.e.f. 3-1-1977).

Provided that if and so often as a resolution approving the continuance in force of such a Proclamation is passed by both Houses of Parliament the Proclamation shall, unless revoked, continue in force for a further period of six months from the date on which it would otherwise have ceased to operate under this clause:

Provided further that if the dissolution of the House of the People takes place during any such period of six months and a resolution approving the continuance in force of such Proclamation has been passed by the Council of States but no resolution with respect to the continuance in force of such Proclamation has been passed by the House of the People during the said period, the Proclamation shall cease to operate at the expiration of thirty days from the date on which the House of the People first sits after its reconstitution unless before the expiration of the said period of thirty days, a resolution approving the continuance in force of the Proclamation has been also passed by the House of the People.

(6) For the purposes of clauses (4) and (5), a resolution may be passed by either House of Parliament only by a majority of the total membership of that House and by a majority of not less than two-thirds of the members of that House present and voting.

(7) Notwithstanding anything contained in the foregoing clauses, the President shall revoke a Proclamation issued under clause (1) or a Proclamation varying such Proclamation if the House of the People passes a resolution disapproving, or, as the case may be, disapproving the continuance in force of, such Proclamation.

(8) Where a notice in writing signed by not less than one-tenth of the total number of members of the House of the People has been given, of their intention to move a resolution for disapproving, or, as the case may be, for disapproving the continuance in force of, a Proclamation issued under clause (1) or a Proclamation varying such Proclamation,—

(a) to the Speaker, if the House is in session; or

(b) to the President, if the House is not in session,

a special sitting of the House shall be held within fourteen days from the date on which such notice is received by the Speaker, or, as the case may be, by the President, for the purpose of considering such resolution.]

[1][[2][(9)] The power conferred on the President by this article shall include the power to issue different Proclamations on different grounds, being war or external aggression or [3][armed rebellion] or imminent danger of war or external aggression or [3][armed rebellion], whether or not there is a Proclamation already issued by the President under clause (1) and such Proclamation is in operation.]

[4][***]

---

1. Ins. by the Constitution (Thirty-eighth Amendment) Act, 1975, sec. 5 (retrospectively).

2. Clause (4) re-numbered as clause (9) by the Constitution (Fourty-fourth Amendment) Act, 1978, sec. 37(c) (w.e.f. 20-6-1979).

3. Subs. by the Constitution (Fourty-fourth Amendment) Act, 1978, sec. 37, for "internal disturbance" (w.e.f. 20-6-1979).

4. Clause (5) omitted by the Constitution (Fourty-fourth Amendment) Act, 1978, sec. 37(d) (w.e.f. 20-6-1979).

Notes on Article 352

Proclamation of Emergency

Neither article 352 nor any other article of Constitution contains any provision saying that a proclamation of emergency validly issued under clause (1) shall cease to operate as soon as the circumstances warranting its issuance have ceased to exist. Hence as long as the proclamation of emergency is not revoked by another proclamation, it would continue to be in operative irrespective of change of circumstances; *Minerva Mills Ltd.* v. *Union of India*, AIR 1980 SC 1789: (1980) 3 SCC 625: 1980 Ker LT 573: 1980 UJ (SC) 727.

353. Effect of Proclamation of Emergency.—While a Proclamation of Emergency is in operation, then—

(a) notwithstanding anything in this Constitution, the executive power of the Union shall extend to the giving of directions to any State as to the manner in which the executive power thereof is to be exercised;

(b) the power of Parliament to make laws with respect to any matter shall include power to make laws conferring powers and imposing duties, or authorising the conferring of powers and the imposition of duties, upon the Union or officers and authorities of the Union as respects that matter, notwithstanding that it is one which is not enumerated in the Union List:

[1][Provided that where a Proclamation of Emergency is in operation only in any part of the territory of India,—

(i) the executive power of the Union to give directions under clause (a), and

(ii) the power of Parliament to make laws under clause (b),

shall also extend to any State other than a State in which or in any part of which the Proclamation of Emergency is in operation if and in so far as the security of India or any part of the territory thereof is threatened by activities in or in relation to the part of the territory of India in which the Proclamation of Emergency is in operation.]

354. Application of provisions relating to distribution of revenues while a Proclamation of Emergency is in operation.—(1) The President may, while a Proclamation of Emergency is in operation, by order direct that all or any of the provisions of articles 268 to 279 shall for such period, not extending in any case beyond the expiration of the financial year in which such Proclamation ceases to operate, as may be specified in the order, have effect subject to such exceptions or modifications as he thinks fit.

(2) Every order made under clause (1) shall, as soon as may be after it is made, be laid before each House of Parliament.

355. Duty of the Union to protect States against external aggression and internal disturbance.—It shall be the duty of the Union to protect every State against external aggression and internal disturbance and to ensure that the Government of every State is carried on in accordance with the provisions of this Constitution.

356. Provisions in case of failure of constitutional machinery in States.—(1) If the President, on receipt of report from the Governor [2][***] of a State or otherwise, is

---

1. Ins. by the Constitution (Forty-second Amendment) Act, 1976, sec. 49 (w.e.f. 3-1-1977).
2. The words "or Rajpramukh" omitted by the Constitution (Seventh Amendment) Act, 1956, sec. 29 and Sch. (w.e.f. 1-11-1956).

satisfied that a situation has arisen in which the government of the State cannot be carried on in accordance with the provisions of this Constitution, the President may by Proclamation—

(a) assume to himself all or any of the functions of the Government of the State and all or any of the powers vested in or exercisable by the Governor [1][***] or any body or authority in the State other than the Legislature of the State;

(b) declare that the powers of the Legislature of the State shall be exercisable by or under the authority of Parliament;

(c) make such incidental and consequential provisions as appear to the President to be necessary or desirable for giving effect to the objects of the Proclamation, including provisions for suspending in whole or in part the operation of any provisions of this Constitution relating to any body or authority in the State:

Provided that nothing in this clause shall authorise the President to assume to himself any of the powers vested in or exercisable by a High Court, or to suspend in whole or in part the operation of any provision of this Constitution relating to High Courts.

(2) Any such Proclamation may be revoked or varied by a subsequent Proclamation.

(3) Every Proclamation under this article shall be laid before each House of Parliament and shall, except where it is a Proclamation revoking a previous Proclamation, cease to operate at the expiration of two months unless before the expiration of that period it has been approved by resolutions of both Houses of Parliament:

Provided that if any such Proclamation (not being a Proclamation revoking a previous Proclamation) is issued at a time when the House of the People is dissolved or the dissolution of the House of the People takes place during the period of two months referred to in this clause, and if a resolution approving the Proclamation has been passed by the Council of States, but no resolution with respect to such Proclamation has been passed by the House of the People before the expiration of that period, the Proclamation shall cease to operate at the expiration of thirty days from the date on which the House of the People first sits after its reconstitution unless before the expiration of the said period of thirty days a resolution approving the Proclamation has been also passed by the House of the People.

(4) A Proclamation so approved shall, unless revoked, cease to operate on the expiration of a period of [2][six months from the date of issue of the Proclamation]:

Provided that if and so often as a resolution approving the continuance in force of such a Proclamation is passed by both Houses of Parliament, the Proclamation

---

1. The words "or Rajpramukh, as the case may be" omitted by the Constitution (Seventh Amendment) Act, 1956, sec. 29 and Sch. (w.e.f. 1-11-1956).

2. Subs. by the Constitution (Forty-fourth Amendment) Act, 1978, sec. 38(a)(i), for "one year from the date of the passing of the second of the resolutions approving the Proclamation under clause (3)" (w.e.f. 20-6-1979). Earlier the words "one year" were substituted by the Constitution (Forty-second Amendment) Act, 1976, sec. 50, for the words "six months" (w.e.f. 3-1-1977).

shall, unless revoked, continue in force for a further period of [1][six months] from the date on which under this clause it would otherwise have ceased to operate, but no such Proclamation shall in any case remain in force for more than three years:

Provided further that if the dissolution of the House of the People takes place during any such period of [2][six months] and a resolution approving the continuance in force of such Proclamation has been passed by the Council of States, but no resolution with respect to the continuance in force of such Proclamation has been passed by the House of the People during the said period, the Proclamation shall cease to operate at the expiration of thirty days from the date on which the House of the People first sits after its reconstitution unless before the expiration of the said period of thirty days a resolution approving the continuance in force of the Proclamation has been also passed by the House of the People:

[3][Provided also that in the case of the Proclamation issued under clause (1) on the 11th day of May, 1987 with respect to the State of Punjab, the reference in the first proviso to this clause to "three years" shall be construed as a reference to [4][five years].]

[5][(5) Notwithstanding anything contained in clause (4), a resolution with respect to the continuance in force of a Proclamation approved under clause (3) for any period beyond the expiration of one year from the date of issue of such proclamation shall not be passed by either House of Parliament unless—

(a) a Proclamation of Emergency is in operation, in the whole of India or, as the case may be, in the whole or any part of the State, at the time of the passing of such resolution, and

(b) the Election Commission certifies that the continuance in force of the Proclamation approved under clause (3) during the period specified in such resolution is necessary on account of difficulties in holding general elections to the Legislative Assembly of the State concerned:]

[6][Provided that nothing in this clause shall apply to the Proclamation issued under clause (1) on the 11th day of May, 1987 with respect to the State of Punjab.]

---

1. Subs. by the Constitution (Forty-fourth Amendment) Act, 1978, sec. 38(a)(ii) , for "one year (w.e.f. 20-6-1979). Earlier the words "one year" were substituted by the Constitution (Forty-second Amendment) Act, 1976, sec. 50, for the words "six months" (w.e.f. 3-1-1977).

2. Subs. by the Constitution (Forty-fourth Amendment) Act, 1978, sec. 38(a)(iiii), for "one year" (w.e.f. 20-6-1979).

3. Ins. by the Constitution (Sixty-fourth Amendment) Act, 1990, sec. 2(a) (w.e.f. 16-4-1992).

4. Subs. by the Constitution (Sixty-eight Amendment) Act, 1991, sec. 2, for "four years" (w.e.f. 12-3-1991). Earlier the words "four years" were substituted by the Constitution (Sixty-seventh Amendment) Act, 1990, sec. 2, for the words "three years and six months" (w.e.f. 4-10-1990).

5. Subs. by the Constitution (Forty-fourth Amendment) Act, 1978, sec. 38(b), for clause (5) (w.e.f. 20-6-1979). Earlier clause (5) was inserted by the Constitution (Thirty-eighth Amendment) Act, 1975, sec. 6 (retrospectively).

6. Subs. by the Constitution (Fifty-ninth Amendment) Act, 1988, sec. 2, for the proviso (w.e.f. 30-3-1988). Earlier the proviso was inserted by the Constitution (Forty-eight Amendment) Act, 1984, sec. 2 (w.e.f. 26-8-1984) and was omitted by the Constitution (Sixty-third Amendment) Act, 1989, sec. 2 (w.e.f. 6-1-1990) and again inserted by the Constitution (Sixty-fourth Amendment) Act, 1990, sec. 2(b) (w.e.f. 16-4-1990).

357. Exercise of legislative powers under Proclamation issued under article 356.—(1) Where by a Proclamation issued under clause (1) of article 356, it has been declared that the powers of the Legislature of the State shall be exercisable by or under the authority of Parliament, it shall be competent—

(a) for Parliament to confer on the President the power of the Legislature of the State to make laws, and to authorise the President to delegate, subject to such conditions as he may think fit to impose, the power so conferred to any other authority to be specified by him in that behalf;

(b) for Parliament, or for the President or other authority in whom such power to make laws is vested under sub-clause (a), to make laws conferring powers and imposing duties, or authorising the conferring of powers and the imposition of duties, upon the Union or officers and authorities thereof;

(c) for the President to authorise when the House of the People is not in session expenditure from the Consolidated Fund of the State pending the sanction of such expenditure by Parliament.

[1][(2) Any law made in exercise of the power of the Legislature of the State by Parliament or the President or other authority referred to in sub-clause (a) of clause (1) which Parliament or the President or such other authority would not, but for the issue of a Proclamation under article 356, have been competent to make shall, after the Proclamation has ceased to operate, continue in force until altered or repealed or amended by a competent Legislature or other authority.]

Notes on Articles 356 and 357

Judicial Review

Dr. Basu, in the Constitutional law of India (1988), pages 403, 404, has pointed out that judicial review of a proclamation under article 356 would lie on any of the grounds upon which any executive determination which is founded on subjective satisfaction can be questionable. By way of example he has cited the following grounds:—

(a) That the Proclamation has been made upon a consideration which is wholly extraneous or irrelevant to the purpose for which the power under section 356 had been conferred by the Constitution, namely, a breakdown of the constitutional machinery in a State, or, in other words, where there is no 'reasonable nexus' between the reasons disclosed and the satisfaction of the President, because in such a case, it can be said that there has been no 'satisfaction' of the President which is a condition for exercise of the power under article 356.

(b) That the exercise of the power under article 356 has been *mala fide*, because a statutory order which lacks *bona fides* has no existence in law.

State of Rajasthan v. *Union of India*, AIR 1977 SC 1361: (1977) 3 SCC 592: (1978) 1 SCR 1: 1978 (1) SCJ 78, paragraphs 124, paragraph 124 (Chandrachud, J., paragraph 144 Bhagwati and Gupta, JJ.) (allowed in *A.K. Roy* v. *Union of India*, AIR 1982 SC 710: (1982) 1 SCC 271: 1982 Cr LJ 340, paragraph 27; *State of Rajasthan* v. *Union of India*, AIR 1977 SC 1361: (1977) 3 SCC 592, paragraph 123: (1978) 1 SCR 1: 1978 (1) SCJ 78 (Chandrachud, J.), 170 (Goswami, J.) 178-179 (Untwalia, J.), 203, 206, 208 (Fazl Ali, J.).

In the absence of *mala fides etc.* court cannot grant relief in law. But as a matter of propriety Minister should not be unseated without giving to the Legislative Assembly an opportunity expressing its confidence (or want of confidence) in the ministry; *S.R. Bommai* v. *Union of India*, AIR 1990 Kant 5: ILR 1989 Kant 2425 (FB), paragraph 33.

---

1. Subs. by the Constitution (Forty-second Amendment) Act, 1976, sec. 51, for clause (2) (w.e.f. 3-1-1977).

Mere dissolution of the Assembly on the advice of the Chief Minister does not bring the case within article 356 of the Constitution; *Arun Kumar Rai Chaudhary* v. *Union of India*, AIR 1992 All 1: 1992 All LJ 290, paragraph 7.

In *S.R. Bommai* v. *Union of India*, JT 1994 (2) SC 215: (1994) 3 SCC 1: AIR 1994 SC 1918 the following propositions have been laid down by the Supreme Court judgement dealing with article 356:—

(i) Presidential Proclamation dissolving a State Legislative Assembly is subject to judicial review.

(ii) Burden lies on the Government of India to prove that relevant material existed (to justify the issue of Proclamation).

(iii) Courts would not go into the correctness of the material.

(iv) If the court strikes down the proclamation it has power to restore the dismissed State Government to office.

(v) A State Government pursuing anti-secular politics is liable to action under article 356.

Judicial Review of Proclamation under Article 356
Proclamation under section 356 is open to judicial review only when the power is exercised *mala fide* or is based on wholly extraneous or irrelevant grounds; *Rameshwar Prasad* v. *Union of India*, AIR 2006 SC 980: 2006 AIR SCW 494: 2006 (3) CTC 209: (2006) 2 SCC 1: 2006 (1) SCJ 477: 2006 (3) SRJ 399: (2006) 1 SCALE 385: 2006 (1) Supreme 393.

358. Suspension of provisions of article 19 during emergencies.—[1][(1)] [2][While a Proclamation of Emergency declaring that the security of India or any part of the territory thereof is threatened by war or by external aggression is in operation], nothing in article 19 shall restrict the power of the State as defined in Part III to make any law or to take any executive action which the State would but for the provisions contained in that Part be competent to make or to take, but any law so made shall, to the extent of the incompetency, cease to have effect as soon as the Proclamation ceases to operate, except as respects things done or omitted to be done before the law so ceases to have effect:

[3][Provided that [4][where such Proclamation of Emergency] is in operation only in any part of the territory of India, any such law may be made, or any such executive action may be taken, under this article in relation to or in any State or Union territory in which or in any part of which the Proclamation of Emergency is not in operation, if and in so far as the security of India or any part of the territory thereof is threatened by activities in or in relation to the part of the territory of India in which the Proclamation of Emergency is in operation.]

[5][(2) Nothing in clause (1) shall apply—

(a) to any law which does not contain a recital to the effect that such law is in relation to the Proclamation of Emergency in operation when it is made; or

(b) to any executive action taken otherwise than under a law containing such a recital.]

---

1. Article 358 re-numbered as clause (1) thereof by the Constitution (Forty-fourth Amendment) Act, 1978, sec. 39 (w.e.f. 20-6-1979).

2. Subs. by the Constitution (Forty-fourth Amendment) Act, 1978, sec. 39(a)(i), for "While a Proclamation of Emergency is in operation" (w.e.f. 20-6-1979).

3. Ins. by the Constitution (Forty-second Amendment) Act, 1976, sec. 52 (w.e.f. 3-1-1977).

4. Subs. by the Constitution (Forty-fourth Amendment) Act, 1978, sec. 39(a)(ii), for "where a Proclamation of Emergency" (w.e.f. 20-6-1979).

5. Ins. by the Constitution (Forty-fourth Amendment) Act, 1978, sec. 39(b) (w.e.f. 20-6-1979).

359. Suspension of the enforcement of the rights conferred by Part III during emergencies.—(1) Where a Proclamation of Emergency is in operation, the President may by order declare that the right to move any court for the enforcement of such of [1][the rights conferred by Part III (except articles 20 and 21)] as may be mentioned in the order and all proceedings pending in any court for the enforcement of the rights so mentioned shall remain suspended for the period during which the Proclamation is in force or for such shorter period as may be specified in the order.

[2][(1A) While an order made under clause (1) mentioning any of [1][the rights conferred by Part III (except articles 20 and 21)] is in operation, nothing in that Part conferring those rights shall restrict the power of the State as defined in the said Part to make any law or to take any executive action which the State would but for the provisions contained in that Part be competent to make or to take, but any law so made shall, to the extent of the incompetency, cease to have effect as soon as the order aforesaid ceases to operate, except as respects things done or omitted to be done before the law so ceases to have effect:]

[3][Provided that where a Proclamation of Emergency is in operation only in any part of the territory of India, any such law may be made, or any such executive action may be taken, under this article in relation to or in any State or Union territory in which or in any part of which the Proclamation of Emergency is not in operation, if and in so far as the security of India or any part of the territory thereof is threatened by activities in or in relation to the part of the territory of India in which the Proclamation of Emergency is in operation.]

[4][(1B) Nothing in clause (1A) shall apply—

(a) to any law which does not contain a recital to the effect that such law is in relation to the Proclamation of Emergency in operation when it is made; or

(b) to any executive action taken otherwise than under a law containing such a recital.]

(2) An order made as aforesaid may extend to the whole or any part of the territory of India:

[5][Provided that where a Proclamation of Emergency is in operation only in a part of the territory of India, any such order shall not extend to any other part of the territory of India unless the President, being satisfied that the security of India or any part of the territory thereof is threatened by activities in or in relation to the part of the territory of India in which the Proclamation of Emergency is in operation, considers such extension to be necessary.]

(3) Every order made under clause (1) shall, as soon may be after it is made, be laid before each House of Parliament.

---

1. Subs. by the Constitution (Forty-fourth Amendment) Act, 1978, sec. 40(a), for "the rights conferred by Part III" (w.e.f. 20-6-1979).

2. Ins. by the Constitution (Thirty-eighth Amendment) Act, 1975, sec. 7 (retrospectively).

3. Ins. by the Constitution (Forty-second Amendment) Act, 1976, sec. 53(a) (w.e.f. 3-1-1977).

4. Ins. by the Constitution (Forty-fourth Amendment) Act, 1978, sec. 40(b) (w.e.f. 20-6-1979).

5. Ins. by the Constitution (Forty-second Amendment) Act, 1976, sec. 53(b) (w.e.f. 3-1-1977).

Notes on Article 359

Application of Article 359

The bar created by article 359 applies to petitions for the enforcement of fundamental rights mentioned in the presidential Order whether by way of an application under article 32 or by way of any application under article 226; *Addl. Distt. Magistrate, Jabalpur* v. *Shivakant Shukla*, AIR 1976 SC 1207: (1976) 2 SCC 521: 1976 Cr LJ 945: 1976 UJ (SC) 610: 1976 SC Cr R 277: 1976 SCC (Cri) 448: 1976 Cr App R (SC) 298: (1976) 3 SCR 929: 1976 Supp SCR 172.

¹[**359A. Application of this Part to the State of Punjab.**—[*Rep. by the Constitution (Sixty-third Amendment) Act, 1989, sec. 3 (w.e.f. 6-1-1990).*]]

360. Provisions as to financial emergency.—(1) If the President is satisfied that a situation has arisen whereby the financial stability or credit of India or of any part of the territory thereof is threatened, he may by a Proclamation make a declaration to that effect.

²[(2) A Proclamation issued under clause (1)—

(a) may be revoked or varied by a subsequent Proclamation;

(b) shall be laid before each House of Parliament;

(c) shall cease to operate at the expiration of two months unless before the expiration of that period it has been approved by resolutions of both Houses of Parliament:

Provided that if any such Proclamation is issued at a time when the House of the People has been dissolved or the dissolution of the House of the People takes place during the period of two months referred to in sub-clause (c), and if a resolution approving the Proclamation has been passed by the Council of States, but no resolution with respect to such Proclamation has been passed by the House of the People before the expiration of that period, the Proclamation shall cease to operate at the expiration of thirty days from the date on which the House of the People first sits after its reconstitution, unless before the expiration of the said period of thirty days a resolution approving the Proclamation has been also passed by the House of the People.]

(3) During the period any such Proclamation as is mentioned in clause (1) is in operation, the executive authority of the Union shall extend to the giving of directions to any State to observe such canons of financial propriety as may be specified in the directions, and to the giving of such other directions as the President may deem necessary and adequate for the purpose.

(4) Notwithstanding anything in this Constitution—

(a) any such direction may include—

   (i) a provision requiring the reduction of salaries and allowances of all or any class of persons serving in connection with the affairs of a State;

   (ii) a provision requiring all Money Bills or other Bills to which the provisions of article 207 apply to be reserved for the consideration of the President after they are passed by the Legislature of the State;

(b) it shall be competent for the President during the period any Proclamation issued under this article is in operation to issue directions for the reduction

---

1. Article 359A was earlier inserted by the Constitution (Forty-ninth Amendment) Act, 1988, sec. 3 (w.e.f. 30-3-1988).

2. Subs. by the Constitution (Forty-fourth Amendment) Act, 1978, sec. 41(a), for clause (2) (w.e.f. 20-6-1979).

of salaries and allowances of all or any class of persons serving in connection with the affairs of the Union including the Judges of the Supreme Court and the High Courts.

[1][***]

PART XIX

MISCELLANEOUS

361. Protection of President and Governors and Rajpramukhs.—(1) The President, or the Governor or Rajpramukh of a State, shall not be answerable to any court for the exercise and performance of the powers and duties of his office or for any act done or purporting to be done by him in the exercise and performance of those powers and duties:

Provided that the conduct of the President may be brought under review by any court, tribunal or body appointed or designated by either House of Parliament for the investigation of a charge under article 61:

Provided further that nothing in this clause shall be construed as restricting the right of any person to bring appropriate proceedings against the Government of India or the Government of a State.

(2) No criminal proceedings whatsoever shall be instituted or continued against the President, or the Governor [2][***] of a State, in any court during his term of office.

(3) No process for the arrest or imprisonment of the President, or the Governor [2][***] of a State, shall issue from any court during his term of office.

(4) No civil proceedings in which relief is claimed against the President, or the Governor [2][***] of a State, shall be instituted during his term of office in any court in respect of any act done or purporting to be done by him in his personal capacity, whether before or after he entered upon his office as President, or as Governor [2][***] of such State, until the expiration of two months next after notice in writing has been delivered to the President or the Governor [3][***], as the case may be, or left at his office stating the nature of the proceedings, the cause of action therefor, the name, description and place of residence of the party by whom such proceedings are to be instituted and the relief which he claims.

[4][**361A. Protection of publication of proceedings of Parliament and State Legislatures.**—(1) No person shall be liable to any proceedings, civil or criminal, in any court in respect of the publication in a newspaper of a substantially true report of any proceedings of either House of Parliament or the Legislative Assembly, or, as the case may be, either House of the Legislature, of a State, unless the publication is proved to have been made with malice:

Provided that nothing in this clause shall apply to the publication of any report of the proceedings of a secret sitting of either House of Parliament or the Legislative Assembly, or, as the case may be, either House of the Legislature, of a State.

---

1. Clause (5) omitted by the Constitution (Forty-fourth Amendment) Act, 1978, sec. 41(b) (w.e.f. 20-6-1979). Earlier clause (5) was inserted by the Constitution (Thirty-eighth Amendment) Act, 1975, sec. 8 (retrospectively).

2. The words "or Rajpramukh" omitted by the Constitution (Seventh Amendment) Act, 1956, sec. 29 and Sch. (w.e.f. 1-11-1956).

3. The words "or the Rajpramukh" omitted by the Constitution (Seventh Amendment) Act, 1956, sec. 29 and Sch. (w.e.f. 1-11-1956).

4. Ins. by the Constitution (Forty-fourth Amendment) Act, 1978, sec. 42 (w.e.f. 20-6-1979).

(2) Clause (1) shall apply in relation to reports or matters broadcast by means of wireless telegraphy as part of any programme or service provided by means of a broadcasting station as it applies in relation to reports or matters published in a newspaper.

Explanation.—In this article, "newspaper" includes a news agency report containing material for publication in a newspaper.]

[1][361B. Disqualification for appointment on remunerative political post.—A member of a House belonging to any political party who is disqualified for being a member of the House under paragraph 2 of the Tenth Schedule shall also be disqualified to hold any remunerative political post for duration of the period commencing from the date of his disqualification till the date on which the term of his office as such member would expire or till the date on which he contests an election to a House and is declared elected, whichever is earlier.

Explanation.—For the purpose of this article,—

(a) the expression "House" has the meaning assigned to it in clause (a) of paragraph 1 of the Tenth Schedule;

(b) the expression "remunerative political post" means any office—

(i) under the Government of India or the Government of a State where the salary or remuneration for such office is paid out of the public revenue of the Government of India or the Government of the State, as the case may be; or

(ii) under a body, whether incorporated or not, which is wholly or partially owned by the Government of India or the Government of a State and the salary or remuneration for such office is paid by such body,

except where such salary or remuneration paid is compensatory in nature.]

[2][362. Rights and privileges of Rulers of Indian States.—[*Rep. by the Constitution (Twenty-sixth Amendment) Act, 1971, sec. 2 (w.e.f. 28-12-1971).*]]

363. Bar to interference by courts in disputes arising out of certain treaties, agreements, etc.—(1) Notwithstanding anything in this Constitution but subject to the provisions of article 143, neither the Supreme Court nor any other court shall have jurisdiction in any dispute arising out of any provision of a treaty, agreement, covenant, engagement, *sanad* or other similar instrument which was entered into or executed before the commencement of this Constitution by any Ruler of an Indian State and to which the Government of the Dominion of India or any of its predecessor Governments was a party and which has or has been continued in operation after such commencement, or in any dispute in respect of any right accruing under or any liability or obligation arising out of any of the provisions of this Constitution relating to any such treaty, agreement, covenant, engagement, *sanad* or other similar instrument.

(2) In this article—

(a) "Indian State" means any territory recognised before the commencement of this Constitution by His Majesty or the Government of the Dominion of India as being such a State; and

---

1. Ins. by the Constitution (Ninety-first Amendment) Act, 2003, sec. 4 (w.e.f. 1-1-2004).

2. Article 362 was earlier amended by the Constitution (Seventh Amendment) Act, 1956, sec. 29 and Sch. (w.e.f. 1-11-1956).

(b)   "Ruler" includes the Prince, Chief or other person recognised before such commencement by His Majesty or the Government of the Dominion of India as the Ruler of any Indian State.

Notes on Article 363

Dispute Arising Out of Treaties

The Treaty of Mandsaur entered into in 1818 by Maharaja Holkar is not shown to have continued in operation after commencement of Constitution. Hence the source of right claimed does not relate specifically to Treaty of Mandsaur. Article 363 does not create bar for court to interfere; *Association of the Residents of Mhow* v. *Union of India*, AIR 2010 MP 40.

[1][**363A. Recognition granted to Rulers of Indian States to cease and privy purses to be abolished.**—Notwithstanding anything in this Constitution or in any law for the time being in force—

(a)   the Prince, Chief or other person who, at any time before the commencement of the Constitution (Twenty-sixth Amendment) Act, 1971, was recognised by the President as the Ruler of an Indian State or any person who, at any time before such commencement, was recognised by the President as the successor of such Ruler shall, on and from such commencement, cease to be recognised as such Ruler or the successor of such Ruler;

(b)   on and from the commencement of the Constitution (Twenty-sixth Amendment) Act, 1971, privy purse is abolished and all rights, liabilities and obligations in respect of privy purse are extinguished and accordingly the Ruler or, as the case may be, the successor of such Ruler, referred to in clause (a) or any other person shall not be paid any sum as privy purse.]

364. Special provisions as to major ports and aerodromes.—(1) Notwithstanding anything in this Constitution, the President may by public notification direct that as from such date as may be specified in the notification—

(a)   any law made by Parliament or by the Legislature of a State shall not apply to any major port or aerodrome or **shall** apply thereto subject to such exceptions or modifications as may be specified in the notification, or

(b)   any existing law shall cease to have effect in any major port or aerodrome except as respects things done or omitted to be done before the said date, or shall in its application to such port or aerodrome have effect subject to such exceptions or modifications as may be specified in the notification.

(2) In this article—

(a)   "major port" means a port declared to be a major port by or under any law made by Parliament or any existing law and includes all areas for the time being included within the limits of such port;

(b)   "aerodrome" means aerodrome as defined for the purposes of the enactments relating to airways, aircraft and air navigation.

365. Effect of failure to comply with, or to give effect to, directions given by the Union.—Where any State has failed to comply with, or to give effect to any directions given in the exercise of the executive power of the Union under any of the provisions of this Constitution, it shall be lawful for the President to hold that a situation has arisen in which the Government of the State cannot be carried on in accordance with the provisions of this Constitution.

---

1. Ins. by the Constitution (Twenty-sixth Amendment) Act, 1971, sec. 3 (w.e.f. 28-12-1971).

366. Definitions.—In this Constitution, unless the context otherwise requires, the following expressions have the meanings hereby respectively assigned to them, that is to say—

(1) "agricultural income" means agricultural income as defined for the purposes of the enactments relating to Indian income-tax;

(2) "an Anglo-Indian" means a person whose father or any of whose other male progenitors in the male line is or was of European descent but who is domiciled within the territory of India and is or was born within such territory of parents habitually resident therein and not established there for temporary purposes only;

(3) "article" means an article of this Constitution;

(4) "borrow" includes the raising of money by the grant of annuities, and "loan" shall be construed accordingly;

[1][***]

(5) "clause" means a clause of the article in which the expression occurs;

(6) "corporation tax" means any tax on income, so far as that tax is payable by companies and is a tax in the case of which the following conditions are fulfilled:—

(a) that it is not chargeable in respect of agricultural income;

(b) that no deduction in respect of the tax paid by companies is, by any enactments which may apply to the tax, authorised to be made from dividends payable by the companies to individuals;

(c) that no provision exists for taking the tax so paid into account in computing for the purposes of Indian income-tax the total income of individuals receiving such dividends, or in computing the Indian income-tax payable by, or refundable to, such individuals;

(7) "corresponding Province", "corresponding Indian State" or "corresponding State" means in cases of doubt such Province, Indian State or State as may be determined by the President to be the corresponding Province, the corresponding Indian State or the corresponding State, as the case may be, for the particular purpose in question;

(8) "debt" includes any liability in respect of any obligation to repay capital sums by way of annuity and any liability under any guarantee, and "debt charges" shall be construed accordingly;

(9) "estate duty" means a duty to be assessed on or by reference to the principal value, ascertained in accordance with such rules as may be prescribed by or under laws made by Parliament or the Legislature of a State relating to the duty, of all property passing upon death or deemed, under the provisions of the said laws, so to pass;

(10) "existing law" means any law, Ordinance, order, bye-law, rule or regulation passed or made before the commencement of this Constitution by any Legislature, authority or person having power to make such a law, Ordinance, order, bye-law, rule or regulation;

---

1. Clause (4A) omitted by the Constitution (Forty-third Amendment) Act, 1977, sec. 11 (w.e.f. 13-4-1978). Earlier clause (4A) was inserted by the Constitution (Forty-second Amendment) Act, 1976, sec. 54(a) (w.e.f. 1-2-1977).

(11) "Federal Court" means the Federal Court constituted under the Government of India Act, 1935;

(12) "goods" includes all materials, commodities, and articles;

(13) "guarantee" includes any obligation undertaken before the commencement of this Constitution to make payments in the event of the profits of an undertaking falling short of a specified amount;

(14) "High Court" means any court which is deemed for the purposes of this Constitution to be a High Court for any State and includes—

(a) any Court in the territory of India constituted or reconstituted under this Constitution as a High Court, and

(b) any other Court in the territory of India which may be declared by Parliament by law to be a High Court for all or any of the purposes of this Constitution;

(15) "Indian State" means any territory which the Government of the Dominion of India recognised as such a State;

(16) "Part" means a part of this Constitution;

(17) "pension" means a pension, whether contributory or not, of any kind whatsoever payable to or in respect of any person, and includes retired pay so payable, a gratuity so payable and any sum or sums so payable by way of the return, with or without interest thereon or any other addition thereto, of subscriptions to a provident fund;

(18) "Proclamation of Emergency" means a Proclamation issued under clause (1) of article 352;

(19) "public notification" means a notification in the Gazette of India, or, as the case may be, the Official Gazette of a State;

(20) "railway" does not include—

(a) a tramway wholly within a municipal area, or

(b) any other line of communication wholly situate in one State and declared by Parliament by law not to be a railway;

[1][***]

[2][(22) "Ruler" means the Prince, Chief or other person who, at any time before the commencement of the Constitution (Twenty-sixth Amendment) Act, 1971, was recognised by the President as the Ruler of an Indian State or any person who, at any time before such commencement, was recognised by the President as the successor of such Ruler;]

(23) "Schedule" means a Schedule to this Constitution;

(24) "Scheduled Castes" means such castes, races or tribes or parts of or groups within such castes, races or tribes as are deemed under article 341 to be Scheduled Castes for the purposes of this Constitution;

(25) "Scheduled Tribes" means such tribes or tribal communities or parts of or groups within such tribes or tribal communities as are deemed under article 342 to be Scheduled Tribes for the purposes of this Constitution;

---

1. Clause (21) omitted by the Constitution (Seventh Amendment) Act, 1956, sec. 29 and Sch. (w.e.f. 1-11-1956).

2. Subs. by the Constitution (Twenty-sixth Amendment) Act, 1971, sec. 4, for clause (22) (w.e.f. 28-12-1971).

(26) "securities" includes stock;

[1][***]

(27) "sub-clause" means a sub-clause of the clause in which the expression occurs;

(28) "taxation" includes the imposition of any tax or impost, whether general or local or special, and "tax" shall be construed accordingly;

(29) "tax on income" includes a tax in the nature of an excess profits tax;

[2][(29A) "tax on the sale or purchase of goods" includes—

(a) a tax on the transfer, otherwise than in pursuance of a contract, of property in any goods for cash, deferred payment or other valuable consideration;

(b) a tax on the transfer of property in goods (whether as goods or in some other form) involved in the execution of a works contract;

(c) a tax on the delivery of goods on hire-purchase or any system of payment by instalments;

(d) a tax on the transfer of the right to use any goods for any purpose (whether or not for a specified period) for cash, deferred payment or other valuable consideration;

(e) a tax on the supply of goods by any unincorporated association or body of persons to a member thereof for cash, deferred payment or other valuable consideration;

(f) a tax on the supply, by way of or as part of any service or in any other manner whatsoever, of goods, being food or any other article for human consumption or any drink (whether or not intoxicating), where such supply or service, is for cash, deferred payment or other valuable consideration,

and such transfer, delivery or supply of any goods shall be deemed to be a sale of those goods by the person making the transfer, delivery or supply and a purchase of those goods by the person to whom such transfer, delivery or supply is made;]

[3][(30)"Union territory" means any Union territory specified in the First Schedule and includes any other territory comprised within the territory of India but not specified in that Schedule.]

Notes on Article 366

Clause (10): 'Existing Law'

A grant made by a Ruler as a gift on the occasion of his daughter's marriage is an 'executive' act and is not an existing law within article 366(10); *Tej Singh Rao* v. *State of Maharashtra*, (1992) Supp 2 SCC 554: AIR 1993 SC 1227, paragraphs 6-8.

---

1. Clause (26A) omitted by the Constitution (Forty-third Amendment) Act, 1977, sec. 11 (w.e.f. 13-4-1978). Earlier clause (26A) was inserted by the Constitution (Forty-second Amendment) Act, 1976, sec. 54(b) (w.e.f. 1-2-1977).

2. Ins. by the Constitution (Forty-sixth Amendment) Act, 1982, sec. 4 (w.e.f. 2-2-1983).

3. Subs. by the Constitution (Seventh Amendment) Act, 1956, sec. 29 and Sch., for clause (30) (w.e.f. 1-11-1956).

Clause (17)

See *Jarnail* v. *Secretary*, (1993) 1 SCC 47: AIR 1994 SC 1484: (1993) 1 LLJ 962: (1993 1 SCR 23, paragraph 9.

Clause (29A)

Article 366(29)(A) explains the ambit of the expression "sale or purchase of goods" as occurring in article 286 (and in List II, Entry 56) and amplifies it by fiction but in other respects subject to the same restrictions as attach to the provisions referred to above; *Gannon Dunkerly & Co.* v. *State of Rajasthan*, (1993) 1 SCC 364: (1993) 88 STC 204, paragraphs 15-16, 25 and 31: 1993 AIR SCW 2621 (5 Judges). As to works contract, *etc.*; See *Builders Association* v. *State of Karnataka*, AIR 1993 SC 991: (1993) 1 SCC 409: (1993) 88 STC 248

367. Interpretation.—(1) Unless the context otherwise requires, the General Clauses Act, 1897, shall, subject to any adaptations and modifications that may be made therein under article 372, apply for the interpretation of this Constitution as it applies for the interpretation of an Act of the Legislature of the Dominion of India.

(2) Any reference in this Constitution to Acts or laws of, or made by, Parliament, or to Acts or laws of, or made by, the Legislature of a State [1][***], shall be construed as including a reference to an Ordinance made by the President or, to an Ordinance made by a Governor [2][***], as the case may be.

(3) For the purposes of this Constitution "foreign State" means any State other than India:

Provided that, subject to the provisions of any law made by Parliament, the President may by order[3] declare any State not to be a foreign State for such purposes as may be specified in the order.

PART XX
AMENDMENT OF THE CONSTITUTION

368. [4][**Power of Parliament to amend the Constitution and procedure therefor**].—[5][(1) Notwithstanding anything in this Constitution, Parliament may in exercise of its constituent power amend by way of addition, variation or repeal any provision of this Constitution in accordance with the procedure laid down in this article.]

[6][(2)] An amendment of this Constitution may be initiated only by the introduction of a Bill for the purpose in either House of Parliament, and when the Bill is passed in each House by a majority of the total membership of that House and by a majority of not less than two-thirds of the members of that House present

---

1. The words and letters "specified in Part A or Part B of the First Schedule" omitted by the Constitution (Seventh Amendment) Act, 1956, sec. 29 and Sch. (w.e.f. 1-11-1956).

2. The words "or the Rajpramukh" omitted by the Constitution (Seventh Amendment) Act, 1956, sec. 29 and Sch. (w.e.f. 1-11-1956).

3. *See* the Constitution (Declaration as to Foreign States) Order, 1950 (C.O. 2).

4. Subs. by the Constitution (Twenty-fourth Amendment) Act, 1971, sec. 3(a), for "**Procedure for amendment of the Constitution**" (w.e.f. 5-11-1971).

5. Ins. by the Constitution (Twenty-fourth Amendment) Act, 1971, sec. 3(b) (w.e.f. 5-11-1971).

6. Article 368 renumbered as clause (2) thereof by the Constitution (Twenty-fourth Amendment) Act, 1971, sec. 3 (w.e.f. 5-11-1971). Earlier article 368 was amended by the Constitution (Seventh Amendment) Act, 1956, sec. 29 and Sch. (w.e.f. 1-11-1956).

and voting, [1][it shall be presented to the President who shall give his assent to the Bill and thereupon] the Constitution shall stand amended in accordance with the terms of the Bill:

Provided that if such amendment seeks to make any change in—

(a) article 54, article 55, article 73, article 162 or article 241, or

(b) Chapter IV of Part V, Chapter V of Part VI, or Chapter I of Part XI, or

(c) any of the Lists in the Seventh Schedule, or

(d) the representation of States in Parliament, or

(e) the provisions of this article,

the amendment shall also require to be ratified by the Legislatures of not less than one-half of the States [2][***] by resolution to that effect passed by those Legislatures before the Bill making provision for such amendment is presented to the President for assent.

[3][(3) Nothing in article 13 shall apply to any amendment made under this article.]

[4][(4) No amendment of this Constitution (including the provisions of Part III) made or purporting to have been made under this article [whether before or after the commencement of section 55 of the Constitution (Forty-second Amendment) Act, 1976] shall be called in question in any court on any ground.]

[4][(5) For the removal of doubts, it is hereby declared that there shall be no limitation whatever on the constituent power of Parliament to amend by way of addition, variation or repeal the provisions of this Constitution under this article.]

Notes on Article 368

Clauses (4) and (5) of article 368 are *ultra vires* because they exclude judicial review which is a basic feature of the Constitution; *Minerva Mills Ltd.* v. *Union of India*, AIR 1980 SC 1789: (1980) 3 SCC 625: 1980 Ker LT 573: 1980 UJ (SC) 727. Compare—

(i) *Indira Nehru Gandhi* v. *Raj Narain*, AIR 1975 SC 2299: 1975 Supp SCC 1: (1976) 2 SCR 347.

(ii) *Keshavananda Bharati* v. *State of Kerala*, AIR 1973 SC 1461: (1973) 4 SCC 225: 1973 Supp SCR 1.

(iii) *S.P. Sampath Kumar* v. *Union of India*, AIR 1987 SC 386: (1987) 1 SCC 124: 1987 Lab IC 222.

(iv) *Waman Rao* v. *Union of India*, AIR 1981 SC 271: (1981) 2 SCC 362: (1981) 2 SCR 1.

(v) *Bhim Singhji* v. *Union of India*, AIR 1981 SC 234: (1981) 1 SCC 166: 1981 Raj LR 39: 1981 All CJ 38.

The power under this article is a constituent power not subject to the constitutional scheme as to distribution of legislative power according to entries in the Seventh Schedule; *Sasanka Sekhar Maity* v. *Union of India*, AIR 1981 SC 522: (1980) 4 SCC 716: (1980) 3 SCR 1209.

Basic Features

Some judgments deal with the following as basic features:—

---

1. Subs. by the Constitution (Twenty-fourth Amendment) Act, 1971, sec. 3(c), for certain words (w.e.f. 5-11-1971).

2. The words and letters "specified in Parts A and B of the First Schedule" omitted by the Constitution (Seventh Amendment) Act, 1956, sec. 29 and Sch. (w.e.f. 1-11-1956).

3. Ins. by the Constitution (Twenty-fourth Amendment) Act, 1971, sec. 3(d) (w.e.f. 5-11-1971).

4. Ins. by the Constitution (Forty-second Amendment) Act, 1976, sec. 55 (w.e.f. 3-1-1977).

(i) Elections free and fair; *Kihota Hollohan* v. *Zachillhu,* AIR 1993 SC 412: (1992) Supp (2) SCC 651: 1992 AIR SCW 3497: JT 1992 (1) SC 600: (1992) 1 SCR 686: (1992) Supp 2 SCC 651, paragraphs 18, 46 and 104.

(ii) The principle of equality, not every feature of equality, but (the quintessence of equal justice); *Raghunathrao Ganpatrao* v. *Union of India,* AIR 1993 SC 1267: (1994) Supp 1 SCC 191: 1993 AIR SCW 1044: JT 1993 (1) SC 374: (1993) 1 SCR 480 (CB), paragraphs 96, 176, 185 and 186.

(iii) Judicial review; *Subhesh Sharma* v. *Union of India,* AIR 1991 SC 631: (1991) Supp 1 SCC 574: 1991 AIR SCW 128: 1991 (2) Civ LJ 532: JT 1990 (4) SC 245: (1990) 6 Serv LR 36: 1991 (2) UPLBEC 826, paragraph 44 (3 Judges); *Shri Kumar* v. *Union of India,* (1992) 2 SCC 428: AIR 1992 SC 1213: (1992) 20 ATC 239: (1992) 1 LLN 951, paragraph 37.

(iv) Rule of law; *Indra Sawhney* v. *Union of India,* AIR 1993 SC 477: 1992 AIR SCW 3682: JT 1992 (6) SC 273: 1993 (1) SCJ 353: 1993 (1) SCT 448: (1992) Supp 3 SCC 217, paragraph 339.

(v) Sovereign, democratic, republican structure; *Kihota Hollohan* v. *Zachillhu,* AIR 1993 SC 412: (1992) Supp (2) SCC 651: 1992 AIR SCW 3497 : JT 1992 (1) SC 600: (1992) 1 SCR 686: (1992) Supp 2 SCC 651, paragraphs 18, 46 and 104.

(vi) Powers of the Supreme Court under articles 32, 136, 141, 142; *Delhi Judicial Service Association, Tis Hazari Court, Delhi* v. *State of Gujarat,* (1991) 4 SCC 406: AIR 1991 SC 2176: 1991 Cr LJ 3086: 1991 AIR SCW 2419: 1991 (3) Crimes 232: JT 1991 (3) SC 617: 1991 (3) Rec Cr R 566: (1991) 3 SCR 936, paragraph 37 (3 Judges).

(vii) Theory of basic structure; *Addl. Distt. Magistrate, Jabalpur* v. *Shivakant Shukla,* AIR 1976 SC 1207: (1976) 2 SCC 521: 1976 Cr LJ 945: 1976 UJ (SC) 610: 1976 SC Cr R 277: 1976 SCC (Cri) 448: 1976 Cr App R (SC) 298: (1976) 3 SCR 929: 1976 Supp SCR 172.

(viii) Fundamental Rights; fundamental rights is part of basic structure; *Indira Nehru Gandhi* v. *Raj Narain,* AIR 1975 SC 2299: 1975 Supp SCC 1: (1976) 2 SCR 347.

According to proviso (b) to sub-section (2) an amendment of the Constitution which takes away the powers of the Supreme Court (say, under article 136) or of a High Court (say, under article 226) shall be void unless it is ratified by the legislatures of not less than 1/2 of the States before being presented to the President for his assent.

Object of this Proviso is to Give Effect to the *Federal Principle*

The word 'change' at the beginning of the proviso means a change in the remedy while the right remains intact. But such change may not be a direct change in the language of any of the provisions specified in clauses (a) to (e) of the proviso, but may be a change 'in effect'.

An instance of a Constitution Amendment 'in effect' changing articles 136, 226, 227 is to be found in the judgment of the Constitution Bench where the validity of paragraph 7 inserted into Sch. X of the Constitution, by the Constitution (Fifty-second Amendment) Act, 1985 was challenged; *Kihota* v. *Zachilhu,* (1992) Supp 2 SCC 651: AIR 1993 SC 412, paragraphs 61-62.

PART XXI
[1][TEMPORARY, TRANSITIONAL AND SPECIAL PROVISIONS]

369. Temporary power to Parliament to make laws with respect to certain matters in the State List as if they were matters in the Concurrent List.— Notwithstanding anything in this Constitution, Parliament shall, during a period of five years from the commencement of this Constitution, have power to make laws with respect to the following matters as if they were enumerated in the Concurrent List, namely:—

(a) trade and commerce within a State in, and the production, supply and distribution of, cotton and woollen textiles, raw cotton (including ginned

---

1. Subs. by the Constitution (Thirteenth Amendment) Act, 1962, sec. 2(a), for "TEMPORARY AND TRANSITIONAL PROVISIONS" (w.e.f. 1-12-1963).

cotton and unginned cotton or *kapas*), cotton seed, paper (including newsprint), foodstuffs (including edible oilseeds and oil), cattle fodder (including oil-cakes and other concentrates), coal (including coke and derivatives of coal), iron, steel and mica;

(b) offences against laws with respect to any of the matters mentioned in clause (a), jurisdiction and powers of all courts except the Supreme Court with respect to any of those matters, and fees in respect of any of those matters but not including fees taken in any court,

but any law made by Parliament, which Parliament would not but for the provisions of this article have been competent to make, shall, to the extent of the incompetency, cease to have effect on the expiration of the said period, except as respects things done or omitted to be done before the expiration thereof.

[1]370. Temporary provisions with respect to the State of Jammu and Kashmir.—(1) Notwithstanding anything in this Constitution,—

(a) the provisions of article 238 shall not apply in relation to the State of Jammu and Kashmir;[†]

(b) the power of Parliament to make laws for the said State shall be limited to—

   (i) those matters in the Union List and the Concurrent List which, in consultation with the Government of the State, are declared by the President to correspond to matters specified in the Instrument of Accession governing the accession of the State to the Dominion of India as the matters with respect to which the Dominion Legislature may make laws for that State; and

   (ii) such other matters in the said Lists as, with the concurrence of the Government of the State, the President may by order specify.

   Explanation.—For the purposes of this article, the Government of the State means the person for the time being recognised by the President as the Maharaja of Jammu and Kashmir acting on the advice of the Council of Ministers for the time being in office under the Maharaja's Proclamation dated the fifth day of March, 1948;

(c) the provisions of article 1 and of this article shall apply in relation to that State;

(d) such of the other provisions of this Constitution shall apply in relation to that State subject to such exceptions and modifications as the President may by order[2] specify:

---

1. In exercise of the powers conferred by this article the President, on the recommendation of the Constituent Assembly of the State of Jammu and Kashmir, declared that, as from the 17th day of November, 1952, the said article 370 shall be operative with the modification that for the *Explanation* in clause (1) thereof, the following *Explanation* is substituted namely:—

   "*Explanation*—For the purposes of this article, the Government of the State means the person for the time being recognised by the President on the recommendation of the Legislative Assembly of the State as the *Sadar-i-Rayasat of Jammu and Kashmir, acting on the advice of the Council of Ministers of the State for the time being in office."

   * Now "Governor" (Ministry of Law Order No. C.O. 44, dated the 15th November, 1952).

† Article 238 which was included in PART VII has been repealed by the Constitution (Seventh Amendment) Act, 1956, sec. 29 and Sch. (w.e.f. 1-11-1956).

2. *See* the Constitution (Application to Jammu and Kashmir) Order, 1954 (C.O. 48) as amended from time to time.

Provided that no such order which relates to the matters specified in the Instrument of Accession of the State referred to in paragraph (i) of sub-clause (b) shall be issued except in consultation with the Government of the State:

Provided further that no such order which relates to matters other than those referred to in the last preceding proviso shall be issued except with the concurrence of that Government.

(2) If the concurrence of the Government of the State referred to in paragraph (ii) of sub-clause (b) of clause (1) or in the second proviso to sub-clause (d) of that clause be given before the Constituent Assembly for the purpose of framing the Constitution of the State is convened, it shall be placed before such Assembly for such decision as it may take thereon.

(3) Notwithstanding anything in the foregoing provisions of this article, the President may, by public notification, declare that this article shall cease to be operative or shall be operative only with such exceptions and modifications and from such date as he may specify:

Provided that the recommendation of the Constituent Assembly of the State referred to in clause (2) shall be necessary before the President issues such a notification.

¹[371. Special provision with respect to the States of ²[***] Maharashtra and Gujarat.—³[***]

(2) Notwithstanding anything in this Constitution, the President may by order made with respect to ⁴[the State of Maharashtra or Gujarat], provide for any special responsibility of the Governor for—

(a) the establishment of separate development boards for Vidarbha, Marathwada, ⁵[and the rest of Maharashtra or, as the case may be,] Saurashtra, Kutch and the rest of Gujarat with the provision that a report on the working of each of these boards will be placed each year before the State Legislative Assembly;

(b) the equitable allocation of funds for developmental expenditure over the said areas, subject to the requirements of the State as a whole; and

(c) an equitable arrangement providing adequate facilities for technical education and vocational training, and adequate opportunities for employment in service under the control of the State Government, in respect of all the said areas, subject to the requirements of the State as a whole.]

⁶[371A. Special provision with respect to the State of Nagaland.— (1) Notwithstanding anything in this Constitution,—

---

1. Subs. by the Constitution (Seventh Amendment) Act, 1956, sec. 22, for article 371 (w.e.f. 1-11-1956).
2. The words "Andhra Pradesh," omitted by the Constitution (Thirty-second Amendment) Act, 1973, sec. 2 (w.e.f. 1-7-1974).
3. Clause (1) omitted by the Constitution (Thirty-second Amendment) Act, 1973, sec. 2 (w.e.f. 1-7-1974).
4. Subs. by the Bombay Reorganisation Act, 1960 (11 of 1960), sec. 85(a), for "the State of Bombay" (w.e.f. 1-5-1960).
5. Subs. by the Bombay Reorganisation Act, 1960 (11 of 1960), sec. 85(b), for "the rest of Maharashtra" (w.e.f. 1-5-1960).
6. Ins. by the Constitution (Thirteenth Amendment) Act, 1962, sec. 2(b) (w.e.f. 1-12-1963).

(a) no Act of Parliament in respect of—
   (i) religious or social practices of the Nagas,
   (ii) Naga customary law and procedure,
   (iii) administration of civil and criminal justice involving decisions according to Naga customary law,
   (iv) ownership and transfer of land and its resources,

   shall apply to the State of Nagaland unless the Legislative Assembly of Nagaland by a resolution so decides;

(b) the Governor of Nagaland shall have special responsibility with respect to law and order in the State of Nagaland for so long as in his opinion internal disturbances occurring in the Naga Hills-Tuensang Area immediately before the formation of that State continue therein or in any part thereof and in the discharge of his functions in relation thereto the Governor shall, after consulting the Council of Ministers, exercise his individual judgment as to the action to be taken:

   Provided that if any question arises whether any matter is or is not a matter as respects which the Governor is under this sub-clause required to act in the exercise of his individual judgment, the decision of the Governor in his discretion shall be final, and the validity of anything done by the Governor shall not be called in question on the ground that he ought or ought not to have acted in the exercise of his individual judgment:

   Provided further that if the President on receipt of a report from the Governor or otherwise is satisfied that it is no longer necessary for the Governor to have special responsibility with respect to law and order in the State of Nagaland, he may by order direct that the Governor shall cease to have such responsibility with effect from such date as may be specified in the order;

(c) in making his recommendation with respect to any demand for a grant, the Governor of Nagaland shall ensure that any money provided by the Government of India out of the Consolidated Fund of India for any specific service or purpose is included in the demand for a grant relating to that service or purpose and not in any other demand;

(d) as from such date as the Governor of Nagaland may by public notification in this behalf specify, there shall be estalished a regional council for the Tuensang district consisting of thirty-five members and the Governor shall in his discretion make rules providing for—
   (i) the composition of the regional council and the manner in which the members of the regional council shall be chosen:

      Provided that the Deputy Commissioner of the Tuensang district shall be the Chairman *ex officio* of the regional council and the Vice-Chairman of the regional council shall be elected by the members thereof from amongst themselves;
   (ii) the qualifications for being chosen as, and for being, members of the regional council;
   (iii) the term of office of, and the salaries and allowances, if any, to be paid to members of, the regional council;

(iv) the procedure and conduct of business of the regional council;

(v) the appointment of officers and staff of the regional council and their conditions of services; and

(vi) any other matter in respect of which it is necessary to make rules for the constitution and proper functioning of the regional council.

(2) Notwithstanding anything in this Constitution, for a period of ten years from the date of the formation of the State of Nagaland or for such further period as the Governor may, on the recommendation of the regional council, by public notification specify in this behalf,—

(a) the administration of the Tuensang district shall be carried on by the Governor;

(b) where any money is provided by the Government of India to the Government of Nagaland to meet the requirements of the State of Nagaland as a whole, the Governor shall in his discretion arrange for an equitable allocation of that money between the Tuensang district and the rest of the State;

(c) no Act of the Legislature of Nagaland shall apply to the Tuensang district unless the Governor, on the recommendation of the regional council, by public notification so directs and the Governor in giving such direction with respect to any such Act may direct that the Act shall in its application to the Tuensang district or any part thereof have effect subject to such exceptions or modifications as the Governor may specify on the recommendation of the regional council:

Provided that any direction given under this sub-clause may be given so as to have retrospective effect;

(d) the Governor may make regulations for the peace, progress and good government of the Tuensang district and any regulations so made may repeal or amend with retrospective effect, if necessary, any Act of Parliament or any other law which is for the time being applicable to that district;

(e) (i) one of the members representing the Tuensang district in the Legislative Assembly of Nagaland shall be appointed Minister for Tuensang affairs by the Governor on the advice of the Chief Minister and the Chief Minister in tendering his advice shall act on the recommendation of the majority of the members as aforesaid;[1]

(ii) the Minister for Tuensang affairs shall deal with, and have direct access to the Governor on, all matters relating to the Tuensang district but he shall keep the Chief Minister informed about the same;

(f) notwithstanding anything in the foregoing provisions of this clause, the final decision on all matters relating to the Tuensang district shall be made by the Governor in his discretion;

---

1. Paragraph 2 of the Constitution (Removal of Difficulties) Order, No. X provides (w.e.f. 1-12-1963) that article 371A of the Constitution of India shall have effect as if the following proviso were added to paragraph (i) of sub-clause (e) of clause (2) thereof, namely:—

"Provided that the Governor may, on the advice of the Chief Minister, appoint any person as Minister for Tuensang affairs to act as such until such time as persons are chosen in accordance with law to fill the seats allocated to the Tuensang district in the Legislative Assembly of Nagaland".

(g) in articles 54 and 55 and clause (4) of article 80, references to the elected members of the Legislative Assembly of a State or to each such member shall include references to the members or member of the Legislative Assembly of Nagaland elected by the regional council established under this article;

(h) in article 170—

    (i) clause (1) shall, in relation to the Legislative Assembly of Nagaland, have effect as if for the word "sixty", the words "forty-six" had been substituted;

    (ii) in the said clause, the reference to direct election from territorial constituencies in the State shall include election by the members of the regional council established under this article;

    (iii) in clauses (2) and (3), references to territorial constituencies shall mean references to territorial constituencies in the Kohima and Mokokchung districts.

(3) If any difficulty arises in giving effect to any of the foregoing provisions of this article, the President may by order do anything (including any adaptation or modification of any other article) which appears to him to be necessary for the purpose of removing that difficulty:

Provided that no such order shall be made after the expiration of three years from the date of the formation of the State of Nagaland.

Explanation.—In this article, the Kohima, Mokokchung and Tuensang districts shall have the same meanings as in the State of Nagaland Act, 1962 (27 of 1962).]

Notes on Article 371A

The Limitation Act, 1963 does not involve customary law. Hence it can apply to Nagaland; *Temjenkaba* v. *Temjenwati*, AIR 1992 Gau 8: 1991 (2) Gau LR 200.

[1][**371B. Special provision with respect to the State of Assam.**— Notwithstanding anything in this Constitution, the President may, by order made with respect to the State of Assam, provide for the constitution and functions of a committee of the Legislative Assembly of the State consisting of members of that Assembly elected from the tribal areas specified in [2][Part I] of the table appended to paragraph 20 of the Sixth Schedule and such number of other members of that Assembly as may be specified in the order and for the modifications to be made in the rules of procedure of that Assembly for the constitution and proper functioning of such committee.]

[3][**371C. Special provision with respect to the State of Manipur.**— (1) Notwithstanding anything in this Constitution, the President may, by order made with respect to the State of Manipur, provide for the constitution and functions of a committee of the Legislative Assembly of the State consisting of members of that Assembly elected from the Hill Areas of that State, for the modifications to be made in the rules of business of the Government and in the rules of procedure of the Legislative Assembly of the State and for any special

---

1. Ins. by the Constitution (Twenty-second Amendment) Act, 1969, sec. 4 (w.e.f. 25-9-1969).

2. Subs. by the North-Eastern Areas (Reorganisation) Act, 1971 (81 of 1971), sec. 71, for "Part A" (w.e.f. 21-1-1972).

3. Ins. by the Constitution (Twenty-seventh Amendment) Act, 1971, sec. 5 (w.e.f. 15-2-1972).

responsibility of the Governor in order to secure the proper functioning of such committee.

(2) The Governor shall annually, or whenever so required by the President, make a report to the President regarding the administration of the Hill Areas in the State of Manipur and the executive power of the Union shall extend to the giving of directions to the State as to the administration of the said areas.

Explanation.—In this article, the expression "Hill Areas" means such areas as the President may, by order, declare to be Hill Areas.]

¹[**371D. Special provisions with respect to the State of Andhra Pradesh.**—(1) The President may, by order made with respect to the State of Andhra Pradesh provide, having regard to the requirements of the State as a whole, for equitable opportunities and facilities for the people belonging to different parts of the State, in the matter of public employment and in the matter of education, and different provisions may be made for various parts of the State.

(2) An order made under clause (1) may, in particular,—

(a) require the State Government to organise any class or classes of posts in a civil service of, or any class or classes of civil posts under, the State into different local cadres for different parts of the State and allot in accordance with such principles and procedure as may be specified in the order the persons holding such posts to the local cadres so organised;

(b) specify any part or parts of the State which shall be regarded as the local area—

(i) for direct recruitment to posts in any local cadre (whether organised in pursuance of an order under this article or constituted otherwise) under the State Government;

(ii) for direct recruitment to posts in any cadre under any local authority within the State; and

(iii) for the purposes of admission to any University within the State or to any other educational institution which is subject to the control of the State Government;

(c) specify the extent to which, the manner in which and the conditions subject to which, preference or reservation shall be given or made—

(i) in the matter of direct recruitment to posts in any such cadre referred to in sub-clause (b) as may be specified in this behalf in the order;

(ii) in the matter of admission to any such University or other educational institution referred to in sub-clause (b) as may be specified in this behalf in the order,

to or in favour of candidates who have resided or studied for any period specified in the order in the local area in respect of such cadre, University or other educational institution, as the case may be.

(3) The President may, by order, provide for the constitution of an Administrative Tribunal for the State of Andhra Pradesh to exercise such jurisdiction, powers and authority [including any jurisdiction, power and authority which immediately before the commencement of the Constitution (Thirty-

---

1. Ins. by the Constitution (Thirty-second Amendment) Act, 1973, sec. 3 (w.e.f. 1-7-1974).

second Amendment) Act, 1973, was exercisable by any court (other than the Supreme Court) or by any tribunal or other authority] as may be specified in the order with respect to the following matters, namely:—

(a) appointment, allotment or promotion to such class or classes of posts in any civil service of the State, or to such class or classes of civil posts under the State, or to such class or classes of posts under the control of any local authority within the State, as may be specified in the order;

(b) seniority of persons appointed, allotted or promoted to such class or classes of posts in any civil service of the State, or to such class or classes of civil posts under the State, or to such class or classes of posts under the control of any local authority within the State, as may be specified in the order;

(c) such other conditions of service of persons appointed, allotted or promoted to such class or classes of civil posts in any civil service of the State or to such class or classes of civil posts under the State or to such class or classes of posts under the control of any local authority within the State, as may be specified in the order.

(4) An order made under clause (3) may—

(a) authorise the Administrative Tribunal to receive representations for the redress of grievances relating to any matter within its jurisdiction as the President may specify in the order and to make such orders thereon as the Administrative Tribunal deems fit;

(b) contain such provisions with respect to the powers and authorities and procedure of the Administrative Tribunal (including provisions with respect to the powers of the Administrative Tribunal to punish for contempt of itself) as the President may deem necessary;

(c) provide for the transfer of the Administrative Tribunal of such classes of proceedings, being proceedings relating to matters within its jurisdiction and pending before any court (other than the Supreme Court) or tribunal or other authority immediately before the commencement of such order, as may be specified in the order;

(d) contain such supplemental, incidental and consequential provisions (including provisions as to fees and as to limitation, evidence or for the application of any law for the time being in force subject to any exceptions or modifications) as the President may deem necessary.

(5) The order of the Administrative Tribunal finally disposing of any case shall become effective upon its confirmation by the State Government or on the expiry of three months from the date on which the order is made, whichever is earlier:

Provided that the State Government may, by special order made in writing and for reasons to be specified therein, modify or annul any order of the Administrative Tribunal before it becomes effective and in such a case, the order of the Administrative Tribunal shall have effect only in such modified form or be of no effect, as the case may be.

(6) Every special order made by the State Government under the proviso to clause (5) shall be laid, as soon as may be after it is made, before both Houses of the State Legislature.

(7) The High Court for the State shall not have any powers of superintendence over the Administrative Tribunal and no court (other than the Supreme Court) or tribunal shall exercise any jurisdiction, power or authority in respect of any matter subject to the jurisdiction, power or authority of, or in relation to, the Administrative Tribunal.

(8) If the President is satisfied that the continued existence of the Administrative Tribunal is not necessary, the President may by order abolish the Administrative Tribunal and make such provisions in such order as he may deem fit for the transfer and disposal of cases pending before the Tribunal immediately before such abolition.

(9) Notwithstanding any judgment, decree or order of any court, tribunal or other authority,—

(a) no appointment, posting, promotion or transfer of any person—

(i) made before the 1st day of November, 1956, to any post under the Government of, or any local authority within, the State of Hyderabad as it existed before that date; or

(ii) made before the commencement of the Constitution (Thirty-second Amendment) Act, 1973, to any post under the Government of, or any local or other authority within, the State of Andhra Pradesh; and

(b) no action taken or thing done by or before any person referred to in sub-clause (a),

shall be deemed to be illegal or void or ever to have become illegal or void merely on the ground that the appointment, posting, promotion or transfer of such person was not made in accordance with any law, then in force, providing for any requirement as to residence within the State of Hyderabad or, as the case may be, within any part of the State of Andhra Pradesh, in respect of such appointment, posting, promotion or transfer.

(10) The provisions of this article and of any order made by the President thereunder shall have effect notwithstanding anything in any other provision of this Constitution or in any other law for the time being in force.]

Notes on Article 371D

Article 371D does not militate against basic structure of Constitution; *C. Surekha (Dr.)* v. *Union of India*, AIR 1989 SC 44: (1988) 3 ITJ 694: (1988) 4 SCC 526: 1988 (3) SCJ 514: (1988) 2 UJ (SC) 539; *Dr. Fazal Ghafoor* v. *Union of India*, AIR 1989 SC 48: JT 1988 (3) SC 698: (1988) 2 UJ (SC) 613.

Article 371D(1) of the Constitution unequivocally indicates that the said article and any order made by the President thereunder shall have effect notwithstanding anything in any other provision of the Constitution or in any other law for the time being in force; *V. Jagannadha Rao* v. *State of Andhra Pradesh*, AIR 2002 SC 77: (2001) 10 SCC 401: (2002) 92 FLR 512.

In article 371D(1) the expression 'public employment' includes direct recruitment as well as promotion. Article 371D(2) does not restrict the scope of article 371D(1) but particularises it in relation to direct recruitment. It is complementary to clause (1); *Government of Andhra Pradesh* v. *A. Suryanarayanarao*, AIR 1991 SC 2113: (1991) Supp 2 SCC 367: 1991 AIR SCW 2404: JT 1991 (4) SC 206: 1992 SCC (L&S) 62: (1991) Supp 2 SCC 367: (1991) 2 UJ (SC) 623, paragraph 7.

A.P. Panchayati Raj Engineering Service Rules, 1963, rule 2A, (introduced in 1979) has to be given retrospective effect, so that promotions abroad do not have to be required as provisional and as subject to review and readjustment; *Government of Andhra Pradesh* v. *A. Suryanarayanarao*, AIR 1991 SC 2113: (1991) Supp 2 SCC 367: 1991 AIR SCW 2404: JT 1991 (4) SC 206: 1992 SCC (L&S) 62: (1991) Supp 2 SCC 367: (1991) 2 UJ (SC) 623, paragraph 7.

Once the President makes an order under article 371D(1) and (2) the State Government loses its inherent power to deal with matters relating to services, it may exercise its powers on matters dealt within the Presidential order only in the manner specified in the order; *Prakasha* v. *C.C.T.*, (1990) 2 SCC 259: AIR 1990 SC 997: (1990) SCC (L&S) 235: (1990) 4 SLR 215 (3 Judges).

Appeal by special leave lies to the Supreme Court from orders of the Andhra Pradesh Administrative Tribunal, *inter alia*—

    (i) where the order of the Tribunal is without jurisdiction; *A.P.S.E.B.* v. *Azami*, AIR 1992 SC 1542: (1992) Supp 1 SCC 660: (1992) 19 ATC 862: (1992) 1 LLN 381, paragraph 7.

   (ii) where the order of the Tribunal is without jurisdiction; *A.P.S.E.B.* v. *Azami*, (1992) Supp 1 SCC 660: (1992) 19 ATC 862: AIR 1992 SC 1542: (1992) 1 LLN 381, paragraphs 5-7.

[1][371E. Establishment of Central University in Andhra Pradesh.—Parliament may by law provide for the establishment of a University in the State of Andhra Pradesh.]

[2][371F. Special provisions with respect to the State of Sikkim.—Notwithstanding anything in this Constitution,—

   (a) the Legislative Assembly of the State of Sikkim shall consist of not less than thirty members;

   (b) as from the date of commencement of the Constitution (Thirty-sixth Amendment) Act, 1975 (hereafter in this article referred to as the appointed day)—

      (i) the Assembly for Sikkim formed as a result of the elections held in Sikkim in April, 1974 with thirty-two members elected in the said elections) hereinafter referred to as the sitting members) shall be deemed to be the Legislative Assembly of the State of Sikkim duly constituted under this Constitution;

     (ii) the sitting members shall be deemed to be the members of the Legislative Assembly of the State of Sikkim duly elected under this Constitution; and

    (iii) the said Legislative Assembly of the State of Sikkim shall exercise the powers and perform the functions of the Legislative Assembly of a State under this Constitution;

   (c) in the case of the Assembly deemed to be the Legislative Assembly of the State of Sikkim under clause (b), the references to the period of [3][five years] in clause (1) of article 172 shall be construed as references to a period of [4][four years] and the said period of [4][four years] shall be deemed to commence from the appointed day;

   (d) until other provisions are made by Parliament by law, there shall be allotted to the State of Sikkim one seat in the House of People and the State of Sikkim

---

1. Ins. by the Constitution (Thirty-second Amendment) Act, 1973, sec. 3 (w.e.f. 1-7-1974).

2. Ins. by the Constitution (Thirty-sixth Amendment) Act, 1975, sec. 3 (w.e.f. 26-4-1975).

3. Subs. by the Constitution (Forty-fourth Amendment) Act, 1978, sec. 43, for "six years" (w.e.f. 6-9-1979). Earlier the words "six years" were substituted by the Constitution (Forty-second Amendment) Act, 1976, sec. 56, for the words "six years" (w.e.f. 3-1-1977).

4. Subs. by the Constitution (Forty-fourth Amendment) Act, 1978, sec. 43, for "five years" (w.e.f. 6-9-1979). Earlier the words "five years" were substituted by the Constitution (Forty-second Amendment) Act, 1976, sec. 56, for the words "four years" (w.e.f. 3-1-1977).

shall form one Parliamentary constituency to be called the Parliamentary constituency for Sikkim;

(e) the representative of the State of Sikkim in the House of the people in existence on the appointed day shall be elected by the members of the Legislative Assembly of the State of Sikkim;

(f) Parliament may, for the purpose of protecting the rights and interests of the different sections of the population of Sikkim make provision for the number of seats in the Legislative Assembly of the State of Sikkim which may be filled by candidates belonging to such sections and for the delimitation of the Assembly constituencies from which candidates belonging to such sections alone may stand for election to the Legislative Assembly of the State of Sikkim;

(g) the Governor of Sikkim shall have special responsibility for peace and for an equitable arrangement for ensuring the social and economic advancement of different sections of the population of Sikkim and in the discharge of his special responsibility under this clause, the Governor of Sikkim shall, subject to such directions as the President may, from time to time, deem fit to issue, act in his direction;

(h) all property and assets (whether within or outside the territories comprised in the State of Sikkim) which immediately before the appointed day were vested in the Government of Sikkim or in any other authority or in any person for the purposes of the Government of Sikkim shall, as from the appointed day, vest in the Government of the State of Sikkim;

(i) the High Court functioning as such immediately before the appointed day in the territories comprised in the State of Sikkim shall, on and from the appointed day, be deemed to be the High Court for the State of Sikkim;

(j) all courts of civil, criminal and revenue jurisdiction, all authorities and all officers, judicial, executive and ministerial, throughout the territory of the State of Sikkim shall continue on and from the appointed day to exercise their respective functions subject to the provision of this Constitution;

(k) all laws in force immediately before the appointed day in the territories comprised in the State of Sikkim or any part thereof shall continue to be in force therein until amended or repealed by a competent Legislature or other competent authority;

(l) for the purpose of facilitating the application of any such law as is referred to in clause (k) in relation to the administration of the State of Sikkim and for the purpose of bringing the provisions of any such law into accord with the provisions of this Constitution, the President may, within two years from the appointed day, by order, make such adaptations and modifications of the law, whether by way of repeal or amendment, as may be necessary or expedient, and thereupon, every such law shall have effect subject to the adaptations and modifications so made, and any such adaptation or modification shall not be questioned in any court of law;

(m) neither the Supreme Court nor any other court shall have jurisdiction in respect of any dispute or other matter arising out of any treaty, agreement, engagement or other similar instrument relating to Sikkim which was entered into or executed before the appointed day and to which the

Government of India or any of its predecessor Governments was a party, but nothing in this clause shall be construed to derogate from the provisions of article 143;

(n) the president may, by public notification, extend with such restrictions or modifications as he thinks fit to the State of Sikkim any enactment which is in force in a State in India at the date of the notification;

(o) if any difficulty arises in giving effect to any of the foregoing provisions of this article, the President may, by order[1], do anything (including any adaptation or modification of any other article) which appears to him to be necessary for the purpose of removing the difficulty:

Provided that no such order shall be made after the expiry of two years from the appointed day;

(p) all things done and all actions taken in or in relation to the State of Sikkim or the territories comprised therein during the period commencing on the appointed day and ending immediately before the date on which the Constitution (Thirty-sixth Amendment) Act, 1975, receives the assent of the President shall, in so far as they are in conformity with the provisions of this Constitution as amended by the Constitution (Thirty-sixth Amendment) Act, 1975, be deemed for all purposes to have been validly done or taken under this Constitution as so amended.]

[2][**371G. Special provision with respect to the State of Mizoram.**— Notwithstanding in this Constitution,—

(a) no Act of Parliament in respect of—

   (i) religious or social practices of the Mizos,

   (ii) Mizo customary law and procedure,

   (iii) administration of civil and criminal justice involving decisions according to Mizo customary law,

   (iv) ownership and transfer of land,

     shall apply to the State of Mizoram unless the Legislative Assembly of the State of Mizoram by a resolution so decides:

     Provided that nothing in this clause shall apply to any Central Act in force in the Union Territory of Mizoram immediately before the commencement of the Constitution (Fifty-third Amendment) Act, 1986;

(b) the Legislative Assembly of the State of Mizoram shall consist of not less than forty members.]

[3][**371H. Special provision with respect to the State of Arunachal Pradesh.**— Notwithstanding anything in this Constitution,—

(a) the Governor of Arunachal Pradesh shall have special responsibility with respect to law and order in the State of Arunachal Pradesh and in the discharge of his functions in relation thereto, the Governor shall, after consulting the Council of Ministers, exercise his individual judgment as to the action to be taken:

---

1. *See* the Constitution (Removal of Difficulties) Order XI (C.O. 99).
2. Ins. by the Constitution (Fifty-third Amendment) Act, 1986, sec. 2 (w.e.f. 20-2-1987).
3. Ins. by the Constitution (Fifty-fifth Amendment) Act, 1986, sec. 2 (w.e.f. 20-2-1987).

Provided that if any question arises whether any matter is or is not a matter as respects which the Governor is under this clause required to act in the exercise of his individual judgment, the decision of the Governor in his discretion shall be final, and the validity of anything done by the Governor shall not be called in question on the ground that he ought or ought not to have acted in the exercise of his individual judgment:

Provided further that if the President on receipt of a report from the Governor or otherwise is satisfied that it is no longer necessary for the Governor to have special responsibility with respect to law and order in the State of Arunachal Pradesh, he may by order direct that the Governor shall cease to have such responsibility with effect from such date as may be specified in the order;

(b) the Legislative Assembly of the State of Arunachal Pradesh shall consist of not less than thirty members.]

¹[**371-I. Special provision with respect to the State of Goa.**—Notwithstanding anything in this Constitution, the Legislative˙ Assembly of the State of Goa shall consist of not less than thirty members.]

372. Continuance in force of existing laws and their adaptation.— (1) Notwithstanding the repeal by this Constitution of the enactments referred to in article 395 but subject to the other provisions of this Constitution, all the laws in force in the territory of India immediately before the commencement of this Constitution shall continue in force therein until altered or repealed or amended by a competent legislature or other competent authority.

(2) For the purpose of bringing the provisions of any law in force in the territory of India into accord with the provisions of this Constitution, the President may by order² make such adaptations and modifications of such law, whether by way of repeal or amendment, as may be necessary or expedient and provide that the law shall, as from such date as may be specified in the order, have effect subject to the adaptations and modifications so made, and any such adaptation or modification shall not be questioned in any court of law.

(3) Nothing in clause (2) shall be deemed—

(a) to empower the President to make any adaptation or modification of any law after the expiration of ³[three years] from the commencement of this Constitution; or

(b) to prevent any competent Legislature or other competent authority from repealing or amending any law adapted or modified by the President under the said clause.

Explanation I.—The expression 'law in force' in this article shall include a law passed or made by a Legislature or other competent authority in the territory of India before the commencement of this Constitution and not previously repealed,

---

1. Ins. by the Constitution (Fifty-sixth Amendment) Act, 1987, sec. 2 (w.e.f. 30-5-1987).

2. *See* the Adaptation of Laws Order, 1950, dated 26th January, 1950, Gazette of India, Extra., p. 449 as amended by Notification S.R.O. 115, dated the 5th June, 1950, Gazette of India, Extra., Pt. II, Sec. 3, p. 51, Notification S.R.O. 870, dated the 4th November, 1950, Gazette of India, Extra., Pt. II, Sec. 3, p. 903, Notification S.R.O. 508, dated the 4th April, 1951, Gazette of India, Extra., Pt. II, Sec. 3, p. 287, Notification S.R.O. 1140 B, dated 2nd July, 1952, Gazette of India, Extra., Pt. II, Sec. 3, p. 661/I and the Adaptation of the Travancore-Cochin Land Acquisition Laws Order, 1952, dated the 20th November, 1952, Gazette of India, Extra., Pt. II, Sec. 3, p. 923.

3. Subs. by the Constitution (First Amendment) Act, 1951, sec. 12, for "two years" (w.e.f. 18-6-1951).

notwithstanding that it or parts of it may not be then in operation either at all or in particular areas.

Explanation II.—Any law passed or made by a Legislature or other competent authority in the territory of India which immediately before the commencement of this Constitution had extra-territorial effect as well as effect in the territory of India shall, subject to any such adaptations and modifications as aforesaid, continue to have such extra-territorial effect.

Explanation III.—Nothing in this article shall be construed as continuing any temporary law in force beyond the date fixed for its expiration or the date on which it would have expired if this Constitution had not come into force.

Explanation IV.—An Ordinance promulgated by the Governor of a Province under section 88 of the Government of India Act, 1935, and in force immediately before the commencement of this Constitution shall, unless withdrawn by the Governor of the corresponding State earlier, cease to operate at the expiration of six weeks from the first meeting after such commencement of the Legislative Assembly of that State functioning under clause (1) of article 382, and nothing in this article shall be construed as continuing any such Ordinance in force beyond the said period.

Notes of Article 372

Expression: "All the Laws in Force"

The expression "all the laws in force" includes not only the enactments of the Indian Legislature but also the common law of the land which was being administered by the courts in India. This includes not only the personal law, *viz.* the Hindu and Mohammedan laws, but also the rules of the English Common law, *e.g.*, the law of torts as well as customary laws, the rules of interpretation of statutes; *Amina (in re:)*, AIR 1992 Bom 214: 1991 (3) Bom CR 531: 1992 (1) Mah LR 873.

There is no bar to an executive act or a grant or a contract made by such Ruler (the absolute Ruler of an Indian State) being modified by an executive act of the appropriate successor Government, *e.g.*, where the Ruler purported to act under certain administrative Rules framed by himself and not in the exercise of sovereign power; *Tej Singh Rao* v. *State of Maharashtra*, (1992) Supp 2 SCC 554: AIR 1993 SC 1227: 1992 AIR SCW 3228: JT 1992 (4) SC 520: 1993 (2) Mah LR 693: 1992 (3) SCJ 483: (1992) 3 SCR 929: (1992) 2 UJ (SC) 677, paragraphs 6 and 8.

[1][**372A. Power of the President to adapt laws.**—(1) For the purposes of bringing the provisions of any law in force in India or in any part thereof, immediately before the commencement of the Constitution (Seventh Amendment) Act, 1956, into accord with the provisions of this Constitution as amended by that Act, the President may by order[2] made before the first day of November, 1957, make such adaptations and modifications of the law, whether by way of repeal or amendment, as may be necessary or expedient, and provide that the law shall, as from such date as may be specified in the order, have effect subject to the adaptations and modifications so made, and any such adaptation or modification shall not be questioned in any court of law.

(2) Nothing in clause (1) shall be deemed to prevent a competent Legislature or other competent authority from repealing or amending any law adapted or modified by the President under the said clause.]

373. Power of President to make order in respect of persons under preventive detention in certain cases.—Until provision is made by Parliament under clause

---

1. Ins. by the Constitution (Seventh Amendment) Act, 1956, sec. 23 (w.e.f. 1-11-1956).
2. *See* the Adaptation of Laws Orders of 1956 and 1957.

(7) of article 22, or until the expiration of one year from the commencement of this Constitution, whichever is earlier, the said article shall have effect as if for any reference to Parliament in clauses (4) and (7) thereof there were substituted a reference to the President and for any reference to any law made by Parliament in those clauses there were substituted a reference to an order made by the President.

374. Provisions as to Judges of the Federal Court and proceedings pending in the Federal Court or before His Majesty in Council.—(1) The Judges of the Federal Court holding office immediately before the commencement of this Constitution shall, unless they have elected otherwise, become on such commencement the Judges of the Supreme Court and shall thereupon be entitled to such salaries and allowances and to such rights in respect of leave of absence and pension as are provided for under article 125 in respect of the Judges of the Supreme Court.

(2) All suits, appeals and proceedings, civil or criminal, pending in the Federal Court at the commencement of this Constitution shall stand removed to the Supreme Court, and the Supreme Court shall have jurisdiction to hear and determine the same, and the judgments and orders of the Federal Court delivered or made before the commencement of this Constitution shall have the same force and effect as if they had been delivered or made by the Supreme Court.

(3) Nothing in this Constitution shall operate to invalidate the exercise of jurisdiction by His Majesty in Council to dispose of appeals and petitions from, or in respect of, any judgment, decree or order of any court within the territory of India in so far as the exercise of such jurisdiction is authorised by law, and any order of His Majesty in Council made on any such appeal or petition after the commencement of this Constitution shall for all purposes have effect as if it were an order or decree made by the Supreme Court in the exercise of the jurisdiction conferred on such Court by this Constitution.

(4) On and from the commencement of this Constitution the jurisdiction of the authority functioning as the Privy Council in a State specified in Part B of the First Schedule to entertain and dispose of appeals and petitions from or in respect of any judgment, decree or order of any court within that State shall cease, and all appeals and other proceedings pending before the said authority at such commencement shall be transferred to, and disposed of by, the Supreme Court.

(5) Further provision may be made by Parliament by law to give effect to the provisions of this article.

375. Courts, authorities and officers to continue to function subject to the provisions of the Constitution.—All courts of civil, criminal and revenue jurisdiction, all authorities and all officers, judicial, executive and ministerial, throughout the territory of India, shall continue to exercise their respective functions subject to the provisions of this Constitution.

376. Provisions as to Judges of High Courts.—(1) Notwithstanding anything in clause (2) of article 217, the Judges of High Court in any Province holding office immediately before the commencement of this Constitution shall, unless they have elected otherwise, become on such commencement the Judges of the High Court in the corresponding State, and shall thereupon be entitled to such salaries and allowances and to such rights in respect of leave of absence and pension as are provided for under article 221 in respect of the Judges of such High Court. [1][Any such Judge shall, notwithstanding that he is not a citizen of India, be eligible for appointment as Chief Justice of such High Court, or as Chief Justice or other Judge of any other High Court.]

---

1. Added by the Constitution (First Amendment) Act, 1951, sec. 13 (w.e.f. 18-6-1951).

(2) The Judges of a High Court in any Indian State corresponding to any State specified in Part B of the First Schedule holding office immediately before the commencement of this Constitution shall, unless they have elected otherwise, become on such commencement the Judges of the High Court in the State so specified and shall, notwithstanding anything in clauses (1) and (2) of article 217 but subject to the proviso to clause (1) of that article, continue to hold office until the expiration of such period as the President may by order determine.

(3) In this article, the expression 'Judge' does not include an acting Judge or an additional Judge.

377. Provisions as to Comptroller and Auditor-General of India.—The Auditor-General of India holding office immediately before the commencement of this Constitution shall, unless he has elected otherwise, become on such commencement the Comptroller and Auditor-General of India and shall thereupon be entitled to such salaries and to such rights in respect of leave of absence and pension as are provided for under clause (3) or article 148 in respect of the Comptroller and Auditor-General of India and be entitled to continue to hold office until the expiration of his term of office as determined under the provisions which were applicable to him immediately before such commencement.

378. Provisions as to Public Service Commissions.—(1) The members of the Public Service Commission for the Dominion of India holding office immediately before the commencement of this Constitution shall, unless they have elected otherwise, become on such commencement the members of the Public Service Commission for the Union and shall, notwithstanding anything in clauses (1) and (2) of article 316 but subject to the proviso to clause (2) of that article, continue to hold office until the expiration of their term of office as determined under the rules which were applicable immediately before such commencement to such members.

(2) The members of a Public Service Commission of a Province or of a Public Service Commission serving the needs of a group of Provinces holding office immediately before the commencement of this Constitution shall, unless they have elected otherwise, become on such commencement the members of the Public Service Commission for the corresponding State or the members of the Joint State Public Service Commission serving the needs of the corresponding States, as the case may be, and shall, notwithstanding anything in clauses (1) and (2) of article 316 but subject to the proviso to clause (2) of that article, continue to hold office until the expiration of their term of office as determined under the rules which were applicable immediately before such commencement to such members.

²[**378A. Special provisions as to duration of Andhra Pradesh Legislative Assembly.**—Notwithstanding anything contained in article 172, the Legislative Assembly of the State of Andhra Pradesh as constituted under the provisions of section 28 and 29 of the States Reorganisation Act, 1956, shall, unless sooner dissolved, continue for a period of five years from the date referred to in the said section 29 and no longer and the expiration of the said period shall operate as a dissolution of that Legislative Assembly.]

379. Provisions as to provincial Parliament and the Speaker and Deputy Speaker thereof.—[*Rep. by the Constitution (Seventh Amendment) Act, 1956, sec. 29 and Sch. (w.e.f. 1-11-1956).*]

380. Provisions as to President.—[*Rep. by the Constitution (Seventh Amendment) Act, 1956, sec. 29 and Sch. (w.e.f. 1-11-1956).*]

381. Council of Ministers of the President.—[*Rep. by the Constitution (Seventh Amendment) Act, 1956, sec. 29 and Sch. (w.e.f. 1-11-1956).*]

---

1. Ins. by the Constitution (Seventh Amendment) Act, 1956, sec. 24 (w.e.f. 1-11-1956).

382. Provisions as to provisional Legislatues for States in Part A of the First Schedule.—[*Rep. by the Constitution (Seventh Amendment) Act, 1956, sec. 29 and Sch. (w.e.f. 1-11-1956).*]

383. Provisions as to Governors of Provinces.—[*Rep. by the Constitution (Seventh Amendment) Act, 1956, sec. 29 and Sch. (w.e.f. 1-11-1956).*]

384. Council of Ministers of Governors.—[*Rep. by the Constitution (Seventh Amendment) Act, 1956, sec. 29 and Sch. (w.e.f. 1-11-1956).*]

385. Provisions as to provisional Legislatures in States in Part B of the First Schedule.—[*Rep. by the Constitution (Seventh Amendment) Act, 1956, sec. 29 and Sch. (w.e.f. 1-11-1956).*]

386. Council of Ministers for States in Part B of the First Schedule.—[*Rep. by the Constitution (Seventh Amendment) Act, 1956, sec. 29 and Sch. (w.e.f. 1-11-1956).*]

387. Special provision as to determination of population for the purposes of certain elections.—[*Rep. by the Constitution (Seventh Amendment) Act, 1956, sec. 29 and Sch. (w.e.f. 1-11-1956).*]

388. Provisions as to the filling of casual vacancies in the provisional Parliament and provisional Legislature of the States.—[*Rep. by the Constitution (Seventh Amendment) Act, 1956, sec. 29 and Sch. (w.e.f. 1-11-1956).*]

389. Provisions as to Bills pending in the Dominion Legislature and in the Legislatures of Provinces and Indian States.—[*Rep. by the Constitution (Seventh Amendment) Act, 1956, sec. 29 and Sch. (w.e.f. 1-11-1956).*]

390. Moneys received or raised or expenditure incurred between the commencement of the Constitution and the 31st day of March, 1950.—[*Rep. by the Constitution (Seventh Amendment) Act, 1956, sec. 29 and Sch. (w.e.f. 1-11-1956).*]

391. Power of the President to amend the First and Fourth Schedules in certain contingencies.—[*Rep. by the Constitution (Seventh Amendment) Act, 1956, sec. 29 and Sch. (w.e.f. 1-11-1956).*]

392. Power of the President to remove difficulties.—(1) The President may, for the purpose of removing any difficulties, particularly in relation to the transition from the provisions of the Government of India Act, 1935, to the provisions of this Constitution, by order direct that this Constitution shall, during such period as may be specified in the order, have effect subject to such adaptations, whether by any of modification, addition or omission, as he may deem to be necessary or expedient:

Provided that no such order shall be made after the first meeting of Parliament duly constituted under Chapter II of Part V.

(2) Every order made under clause (1) shall be laid before Parliament.

(3) The powers conferred on the President by this article, by article 324, by clause (3) of article 367 and by article 391 shall, before the commencement of the Constitution, be exercisable by the Governor-General of the Dominion of India.

Notes on Article 392
Adaptations to Provisions of the Constitution
The power given to President under article 392 to make adaptations to the provisions of the Constitution for the purposes of provisions in the Constitution was very wide and it cannot be said that he could make the adaptation in one way and not in another *i.e.*, either by modification addition or omission; *D.S. Garewal* v. *State of Punjab*, AIR 1959 SC 512: 1959 SCJ 399: 1959 SCA 364: ILR 1959 Punj 827: (1959) Supp 1 SCR 792.

Provision for President
There is nothing in article 392 to suggest that the President should wait, before adapting a particular article, till an occasion actually arose for the provisional Parliament to exercise the

power conferred by that article; *Shankari Prasad Singh Deo* v. *Union of India*, AIR 1951 SC 458: 64 MLW 1005: 1951 ALJ 740: (1951) 2 MLJ 683: 88 Cal LJ 281: 1951 SCJ 775: 30 Pat 1176: 1952 SCR 89.

PART XXII

SHORT TITLE, COMMENCEMENT, [1][AUTHORITATIVE TEXT IN HINDI] AND REPEALS

393. Short title.—This Constitution may be called the Constitution of India.

394. Commencement.—This article and articles 5, 6, 7, 8, 9, 60, 324, 366, 367, 379, 380, 388, 391, 392 and 393 shall come into force at once, and the remaining provisions of this Constitution shall come into force on the twenty-sixth day of January, 1950, which day is referred to in this Constitution as the commencement of this Constitution.

Notes on Article 394

Article 394 is the commencement provision for all articles in two parts. The judicial reference of such article is given only in one leading case *viz-a-viz.*; *S. Raghbir Singh Gill* v. *S. Gurcharan Singh Tohra*, AIR 1980 SC 1362: 1980 Supp SCC 53: (1980) 3 SCR 1302.

[2][**394A. Authoritative text in the Hindi language.**—(1) The President shall cause to be published under his authority,—

(a) the translation of this Constitution in the Hindi language, signed by members of the Constituent Assembly, with such modifications as may be necessary to bring it in conformity with the language, style and terminology adopted in the authoritative texts of Central Acts in the Hindi language, and incorporating therein all the amendments of this Constitution made before such publication; and

(b) the translation in the Hindi language of every amendment of this Constitution made in the English language.

(2) The translation of this Constitution and of every amendment thereof published under clause (1) shall be construed to have the same meaning as the original thereof and if any difficulty arises in so construing any part of such translation, the President shall cause the same to be revised suitably.

(3) The translation of this Constitution and of every amendment thereof published under this article shall be deemed to be, for all purposes, the authoritative text thereof in the Hindi language.]

395. Repeals.—The Indian Independence Act, 1947 and the Government of India Act, 1935, together with all enactments amending or supplementing the latter Act, but not including the Abolition of Privy Council Jurisdiction Act, 1949 are hereby repealed.

Notes on Article 395

Appeal Maintainable to Federal Court: Suit filed before Adoption of Constitution: Right of Appeal

Where the suit was instituted on April 22, 1949, the right of appeal vested in the parties thereto at that date and is to be governed by the law as it prevailed on that date, *i.e.*, on that date the parties acquired the right, if unsuccessful, to go up in appeal from the sub-court to the High Court and from the High Court to federal court under the federal Court (Enlargement of Jurisdiction) Act, 1947; *Garikapati Veeraya* v. *N. Subbiah Choudhry*, AIR 1957 SC 540: 1957 SCA 495: 1957 SCJ 439: (1957) 2 Mad LJ (SC) 1: (1957) 2 Andh WR (SC) 1: 1957 SCR 399.

---

1. Ins. by the Constitution (Fifty-eighth Amendment) Act, 1987, sec. 2 (w.e.f. 9-12-1987).

2. Ins. by the Constitution (Fifty-eighth Amendment) Act, 1987, sec. 3 (w.e.f. 9-12-1987).

¹[FIRST SCHEDULE

(*Articles 1 and 4*)

I. THE STATES

Name	Territories
1. Andhra Pradesh	²[The territories specified in sub-section (1) of section 3 of the Andhra State Act, 1953, sub-section (1) of section 3 of the States Reorganisation Act, 1956, the First Schedule to the Andhra Pradesh and Madras (Alteration of Boundaries) Act, 1959, and the Schedule to the Andhra Pradesh and Mysore (Transfer of Territory) Act, 1968, but excluding the territories specified in the Second Schedule to the Andhra Pradesh and Madras (Alteration of Boundaries) Act, 1959.]
2. Assam	The territories which immediately before the commencement of this Constitution were comprised in the Province of Assam, the Khasi States and the Assam Tribal Areas, but excluding the territories specified in the Schedule to the Assam (Alteration of Boundaries) Act, 1951, ³[and the territories specified in sub-section (1) of section 3 of the State of Nagaland Act, 1962] ⁴[and the territories specified in sections 5, 6 and 7 of the North-Eastern Areas (Reorganisation) Act, 1971.]
3. Bihar	⁵[The territories which immediately before the commencement of this Constitution were either comprised in the Province of Bihar or were being administered as if they formed part of that Province and the territories specified in clause (a) of sub-section (1) of section 3 of the Bihar and Uttar Pradesh (Alteration of Boundaries) Act, 1968, but excluding the territories specified in sub-section (1) of section 3 of the Bihar and West Bengal (Transfer of Territories) Act, 1956, and the territories specified in clause (b) of sub-section (1) of section 3 of the first mentioned Act] ⁶[and the territories specified in section 3 of the Bihar Reorganisation Act, 2000]].

1. Subs. by the Constitution (Seventh Amendment) Act, 1956, sec. 2(2), for the FIRST SCHEDULE (w.e.f. 1-11-1956).
2. Subs. by the Andhra Pradesh and Mysore (Transfer of Territory) Act, 1968 (36 of 1968), sec. 4(a), for the former entry (w.e.f. 1-10-1968). Earlier the entry was substituted by the Andhra Pradesh and Madras (Alteration of Boundaries) Act, 1959 (56 of 1959), sec. 6(a) (w.e.f. 1-4-1960).
3. Added by the State of Nagaland Act, 1962 (27 of 1962), sec. 4(a) (w.e.f. 1-12-1963).
4. Added by the North-Eastern Areas (Reorganisation) Act, 1971 (81 of 1971), sec. 9(a)(i) (w.e.f. 21-1-1972).
5. Subs. by the Bihar and Uttar Pradesh (Alteration of Boundaries) Act, 1968 (24 of 1968), sec. 4(a), for the former entry (w.e.f. 10-6-1970).
6. Added by the Bihar Reorganisation Act, 2000 (30 of 2000), sec. 5(a) (w.e.f. 15-11-2000).

Name	Territories
[1][4. Gujarat	The territories referred to in sub-section (1) of section 3 of the Bombay Reorganisation Act, 1960.]
5. Kerala	The territories specified in sub-section (1) of section 5 of the States Reorganisation Act, 1956.
6. Madhya Pradesh	The territories specified in sub-section (1) of section 9 of the States Reorganisation Act, 1956 [2][and the First Schedule to the Rajasthan and Madhya Pradesh (Transfer of Territories) Act, 1959] [3][but excluding the territories specified in section 3 of the Madhya Pradesh Reorganisation Act, 2000].
[4][7. Tamil Nadu]	The territories which immediately before the commencement of this Constitution were either comprised in the Province of Madras or were being administered as if they formed part of that Province and the territories specified in section 4 of the States Reorganisation Act, 1956, [5][and the Second Schedule to the Andhra Pradesh and Madras (Alteration of Boundaries) Act, 1959] but excluding the territories specified in sub-section (1) of section 3 and sub-section (1) of section 4 of the Andhra State Act, 1953 and [6][the territories specified in clause (b) of sub-section (1) of section 5, section 6 and clause (d) of sub-section (1) of section 7 of the States Reorganisation Act, 1956 and the territories specified in the First Schedule to the Andhra Pradesh and Madras (Alteration of Boundaries) Act, 1959].
[7][8. Maharashtra	The territories specified in sub-section (1) of section 8 of the States Reorganisation Act, 1956, but excluding the territories referred to in sub-section (1) of section 3 of the Bombay Reorganisation Act, 1960.]

---

1. Subs. by the Bombay Reorganisation Act, 1960 (11 of 1960), sec. 4(a), for entry 4 (w.e.f. 1-5-1960).

2. Ins. by the Rajasthan and Madhya Pradesh (Transfer of Territories) Act, 1959 (47 of 1959), sec. 4(a) (w.e.f. 1-10-1959).

3. Added by the Madhya Pradesh Reorganisation Act, 2000 (28 of 2000), sec. 5(a) (w.e.f. 1-11-2000).

4. Subs. by the Madras State (Alteration of Name) Act, 1968 (53 of 1968), sec. 5(1), for "7. Madras" (w.e.f. 14-1-1969).

5. Ins. by the Andhra Pradesh and Madras (Alteration of Boundaries) Act, 1959 (56 of 1959), sec. 6(b)(i) (w.e.f. 1-4-1960).

6. Subs. by the Andhra Pradesh and Madras (Alteration of Boundaries) Act, 1959 (56 of 1959), sec. 6(b)(ii), for certain words (w.e.f. 1-4-1960).

7. Ins. by the Bombay Reorganisation Act, 1960 (11 of 1960), sec. 4(b) (w.e.f. 1-5-1960).

Name	Territories
[1][2][9.] Karnataka]	The territories specified in sub-section (1) of section 7 of the States Reorganisation Act, 1956 [3][but excluding the territory specified in the Schedule to the Andhra Pradesh and Mysore (Transfer of Territory) Act, 1968].
[1][10.] [4][Odisha]	The territories which immediately before the commencement of this Constitution were either comprised in the Province of Orissa or were being administered as if they formed part of that Province.
[1][11.] Punjab	The territories specified in section 11 of the States Reorganisation Act, 1956 [5][and the territories referred to in Part II of the First Schedule to the Acquired Territories (Merger) Act, 1960] [6][but excluding the territories referred to in Part II of the First Schedule to the Constitution (Ninth Amendment) Act, 1960] [7][and the territories specified in sub-section (1) of section 3, section 4 and sub-section (1) of section 5 of the Punjab Reorganisation Act, 1966].
[1][12.] Rajasthan	The territories specified in section 10 of the States Reorganisation Act, 1956 [8][but excluding the territories specified in the First Schedule to the Rajasthan and Madhya Pradesh (Transfer of Territories) Act, 1959].
[1][13.] Uttar Pradesh	[9][The territories which immediately before the commencement of this Constitution were either comprised in the Province known as the United Provinces or were being administered as if they formed part of that Province, the territories specified in clause (b) of sub-section (1) of section 3 of the Bihar and Uttar Pradesh (Alteration of Boundaries) Act, 1968 and the territories specified in clause (b) of sub-section (1) of section 4 of the Haryana and Uttar Pradesh (Alteration of Boundaries) Act, 1979, but

---

1. Entries 8 to 14 renumbered as entries 9 to 15 by the Bombay Reorganisation Act, 1960 (11 of 1960), sec. 4(c) (w.e.f. 1-5-1960).
2. Subs. by the Mysore State (Alteration of Name) Act, 1973 (31 of 1973), sec. 5(1), for "9. Mysore" (w.e.f. 1-11-1973).
3. Ins. by the Andhra Pradesh and Mysore (Transfer of Territory) Act, 1968 (36 of 1968), sec. 4(b) (w.e.f. 1-10-1968).
4. Subs. by the Orissa (Alteration of Name) Act, 2011 (15 of 2011), sec. 6, for "Orissa" (w.e.f. 1-11-2011, *vide* G.S.R. 791(E), dated 1st November, 2011).
5. Ins. by the Acquired Territories (Merger) Act, 1960 (64 of 1960), sec. 4(b) (w.e.f. 17-1-1961).
6. Added by the Constitution (Ninth Amendment) Act, 1960, sec. 3 (w.e.f. 17-1-1961).
7. Ins. by the Punjab Reorganisation Act, 1966 (31 of 1966), sec. 7(a)(i) (w.e.f. 1-11-1966).
8. Ins. by the Rajasthan and Madhya Pradesh (Transfer of Territories) Act, 1959 (47 of 1959), sec. 4(b) (w.e.f. 1-10-1959).
9. Subs. by the Haryana and Uttar Pradesh (Alteration of Boundaries) Act, 1979 (31 of 1979), sec. 5(a), for the former entry (w.e.f. 15-9-1983).

Name	Territories
	excluding the territories specified in clause (a) of sub-section (1) of section 3 of the Bihar and Uttar Pradesh (Alteration of Boundaries) Act, 1968, [1][and the territories specified in section 3 of the Uttar Pradesh Reorganisation Act, 2000], and the territories specified in clause (a) of sub-section (1) of section 4 of the Haryana and Uttar Pradesh (Alteration of Boundaries) Act, 1979.]
[2][14.] West Bengal	The territories which immediately before the commencement of this Constitution were either comprised in the Province of West Bengal or were being administered as if they formed part of that Province in the territory of Chandernagore as defined in clause (c) of section 2 of the Chandernagore (Merger) Act, 1954, and also the territories specified in sub-section (1) of section 3 of the Bihar and West Bengal (Transfer of Territories) Act, 1956.
[2][15.] Jammu and Kashmir	The territory which immediately before the commencement of this Constitution was comprised in the Indian State of Jammu and Kashmir.
[3][16. Nagaland	The territories specified in sub-section (1) of section 3 of the State of Nagaland Act, 1962.]
[4][17. Haryana	[5][The territories specified in sub-section (1) of section 3 of the Punjab Reorganisation Act, 1966 and the territories specified in clause (a) of sub-section (1) of section 4 of the Haryana and Uttar Pradesh (Alteration of Boundaries) Act, 1979, but excluding the territories specified in clause (b) of sub-section (1) of section 4 of that Act.]]
[6][18. Himachal Pradesh	The territories which immediately before the commencement of this Constitution were being administered as if they were Chief Commissioners' Provinces under the names of Himachal Pradesh and Bilaspur and the Territories specified in sub-section (1) of section 5 of the Punjab Reorganisation Act, 1966.]

1. Ins. by the Uttar Pradesh Reorganisation Act, 2000 (29 of 2000), sec. 5(a) (w.e.f. 9-11-2000).
2. Entries 8 to 14 renumbered as entries 9 to 15 by the Bombay Reorganisation Act, 1960 (11 of 1960), sec. 4(c) (w.e.f. 1-5-1960).
3. Ins. by the State of Nagaland Act, 1962 (27 of 1962), sec. 4(b) (w.e.f. 1-12-1963).
4. Ins. by the Punjab Reorganisation Act, 1966 (31 of 1966), sec. 7(a)(ii) (w.e.f. 1-11-1966).
5. Subs. by the Haryana and Uttar Pradesh (Alteration of Boundaries) Act, 1979 (31 of 1979), sec. 5(b), for the former entry (w.e.f. 15-9-1983).
6. Ins. by the State of Himachal Pradesh Act, 1970 (53 of 1970), sec. 4(a) (w.e.f. 25-1-1971).

Name	Territories
[1][19. Manipur	The territory which immediately before the commencement of this Constitution was being administered as if it were a Chief Commissioner's Province under the name of Manipur.]
[1][20. Tripura	The territory which immediately before the commencement of this Constitution was being administered as if it were a Chief Commissioner's Province under the name of Tripura.]
[1][21. Meghalaya	The territories specified in section 5 of the North-Eastern Areas (Reorganisation) Act, 1971.]
[2][22. Sikkim	The territories which immediately before the commencement of the Constitution (Thirty-sixth Amendment) Act, 1975, were comprised in Sikkim.]
[3][23. Mizoram	The territories specified in section 6 of the North Eastern Areas (Reorganisation) Act, 1971.]
[4][24. Arunachal Pradesh	The territories specified in section 7 of the North Eastern Areas (Reorganisation) Act, 1971.]
[5][25. Goa	The territories specified in section 3 of the Goa, Daman and Diu Reorganisation Act, 1987.]
[6][26. Chhattisgarh	The territories specified in section 3 of the Madhya Pradesh Reorganisation Act, 2000.]
[7][27. [8][Uttarakhand]	The territories specified in section 3 of the Uttar Pradesh Reorganisation Act, 2000.]
[9][28. Jharkhand	The territories specified in section 3 of the Bihar Reorganisation Act, 2000.]

II. THE UNION TERRITORIES

Name	Extent
1. Delhi	The territory which immediately before the commencement of this Constitution was comprised in the Chief Commissioner's Province of Delhi.

[10][***]

---

1. Ins. by the North-Eastern Areas (Reorganisation) Act, 1971 (81 of 1971), sec. 9(a)(ii) (w.e.f. 21-1-1972).
2. Ins. by the Constitution (Thirty-sixth Amendment) Act, 1975, sec. 2 (w.e.f. 26-4-1975).
3. Ins. by the State of Mizoram Act, 1986 (34 of 1986), sec. 4(a) (w.e.f. 20-2-1987).
4. Ins. by the State of Arunachal Pradesh Act, 1986 (69 of 1986), sec. 4(a) (w.e.f. 20-2-1987).
5. Ins. by the Goa, Daman and Diu Reorganisation Act, 1987 (18 of 1987), sec. 5(a) (w.e.f. 30-5-1987).
6. Ins. by the Madhya Pradesh Reorganisation Act, 2000 (28 of 2000), sec. 5(b) (w.e.f. 1-11-2000).
7. Ins. by the Uttar Pradesh Reorganisation Act, 2000 (29 of 2000), sec. 5(b) (w.e.f. 9-11-2000).
8. Subs. by the Uttaranchal (Alteration of Name) Act, 2006 (52 of 2006), sec. 4, for "Uttaranchal" (w.e.f. 1-1-2007).
9. Ins. by the Bihar Reorganisation Act, 2000 (30 of 2000), sec. 5(b) (w.e.f. 15-11-2000).
10. Entry relating to "Himachal Pradesh" omitted by the State of Himachal Pradesh Act, 1970 (53 of 1970), sec. 4(b) (w.e.f. 25-1-1971).

Name	Territories
1[***]	
†2. The Andaman and Nicobar Islands	The territory which immediately before the commencement of this Constitution was comprised in the Chief Commissioner's Province of the Andaman and Nicobar Islands.
†3. 3[Lakshadweep]	The territory specified in section 6 of the States Reorganisation Act, 1956.
†4[4. Dadra and Nagar Haveli	The territory which immediately before the eleventh day of August, 1961 was comprised in Free Dadra and Nagar Haveli.]
†5[6[5. Daman and Diu	The territories specified in section 4 of the Goa, Daman and Diu Reorganisation Act, 1987.]]
†7[6. 8[Puducherry]	The territories which immediately before the sixteenth day of August, 1962, were comprised in the French Establishments in India known as Pondicherry, Karikal, Mahe and Yanam.]
†9[7. Chandigarh	The territories specified in section 4 of the Punjab Reorganisation Act, 1966.]
10[***]	
11[***]	

1. Entries relating to Manipur and Tripura omitted by the North-Eastern Areas (Reorganisation) Act, 1971 (81 of 1971), sec. 9(b)(i) (w.e.f. 21-1-1972).

† Entry numbers have been re-numbered by the State of Himachal Pradesh Act, 1970 (53 of 1970), sec. 4(b) (w.e.f. 25-1-1971); by the North-Eastern Areas (Reorganisation) Act, 1971 (81 of 1971), sec. 9(b)(i) (w.e.f. 21-1-1972) and by the State of Mizoram Act, 1986 (34 of 1986), sec. 4(b) (w.e.f. 20-2-1987).

3. Subs. by the Laccadive, Minicoy and Amindivi Islands (Alteration of Name) Act, 1973 (34 of 1973), sec. 5, for "The Laccadive, Minicoy and Amindivi Islands" (w.e.f. 1-11-1973).

4. Ins. by the Constitution (Tenth Amendment) Act, 1961, sec. 2 (w.e.f. 11-8-1961).

5. Ins. by the Constitution (Twelfth Amendment) Act, 1962, sec. 2 (w.e.f. 20-12-1961).

6. Subs. by the Goa, Daman and Diu Reorgnisation Act, 1987 (18 of 1987), sec. 5(b), for entry 5 (w.e.f. 30-5-1987).

7. Ins. by the Constitution (Fourteenth Amendment) Act, 1962, sec. 3 and sec. 7 (w.r.e.f. 16-8-1962).

8. Subs. by the Pondicherry (Alteration of Name) Act, 2006 (44 of 2006), sec. 4, for "Pondicherry" (w.e.f. 1-10-2006).

9. Ins. by the Punjab Reorganisation Act, 1966 (31 of 1966), sec. 7(b)(ii) (w.e.f. 1-11-1966).

10. Entry 8 relating to Mizoram omitted by the State of Mizoram Act, 1986 (34 of 1986), sec. 4(b) (w.e.f. 20-2-1987). Earlier entry 8 relating to Mizoram was inserted by North-Eastern Areas Reorganisation Act, 1971 (81 of 1971), sec. 9(b)(ii) (w.e.f. 21-1-1972).

11. Entry 8 relating to Arunachal Pradesh omitted by the State of Arunachal Pradesh Act, 1986 (69 of 1986), sec. 4(b) (w.e.f. 20-2-1987). Earlier entry 9 relating to Arunachal Pradesh was inserted by the North-Eastern Areas (Reorganisation) Act, 1971 (81 of 1971), sec. 2(b)(ii) (w.e.f. 21-1-1972) and later entry 9 relating to Arunachal Pradesh was re-numbered as entry 8 by the State of Mizoram Act, 1986 (34 of 1986), sec. 4(b) (w.e.f. 20-2-1987).

SECOND SCHEDULE

[Articles 59(3), 65(3), 75(6), 97, 125, 148(3), 158(3), 164(5), 186 and 221]

PART A

PROVISIONS AS TO THE PRESIDENT AND
THE GOVERNORS OF STATES [1][***]

1. There shall be paid to the President and to the Governors of the States [1][***] the following emoluments per mensem, that is to say:—

The President	[2][10,000 rupees]
The Governor of a State	[3][5,500 rupees]

2. There shall also be paid to the President and to the Governors of the States [4][***] such allowances as were payable respectively to the Governor-General of the Dominion of India and to the Governors of the corresponding Provinces immediately before the commencement of this Constitution.

3. The President and the Governors of [5][the States] throughout their respective terms of office shall be entitled to the same privileges to which the Governor-General and the Governors of the corresponding Provinces were respectively entitled immediately before the commencement of this Constitution.

4. While the Vice-President or any other person is discharging the functions of, or is acting as, President, or any person is discharging the functions of the Governor, he shall be entitled to the same emoluments, allowances and privileges as the President or the Governor whose functions he discharges or for whom he acts, as the case may be.

[6][***]

PART C

PROVISIONS AS TO THE SPEAKER AND THE DEPUTY SPEAKER OF THE HOUSE OF THE PEOPLE AND THE CHAIRMAN AND THE DEPUTY CHAIRMAN OF THE COUNCIL OF STATES AND THE SPEAKER AND THE DEPUTY SPEAKER OF THE LEGISLATIVE ASSEMBLY [7][***] AND THE CHAIRMAN AND THE DEPUTY CHAIRMAN OF THE LEGISLATIVE COUNCIL OF [8][A STATE].

7. There shall be paid to the Speaker of the House of the People and the Chairman of the Council of States such salaries and allowances as were payable to the Speaker of the

---

1. The words and letter "specified in Part A of the First Schedule" omitted by the Constitution (Seventh Amendment) Act, 1956, sec. 29 and Sch. (w.e.f. 1-11-1956).
2. Raised to 1,50,000 rupees per mensem by the President's Emoluments and Pension (Amendment) Act, 2008 (28 of 2008) (w.r.e.f. 1-1-2006). Earlier 10,000 rupees were raised to 15,000 rupees per mensem by the President's Pension (Amendment) Act, 1985 (77 of 1985) (w.e.f. 26-12-1985) and again raised to 20,000 rupees per mensem by the President's Emoluments and Pension (Amendment) Act, 1990 (16 of 1990) (w.e.f. 29-6-1990) and further raised to 50,000 rupees per mensem by the President's Emoluments and Pension (Amendment) Act, 1998 (25 of 1998) (w.r.e.f. 1-1-1996).
3. Raised to 1,10,000 rupees per mensem by the Governor's (Emoluments, Allowances and Privileges) (Amendment) Act, 2008 (1 of 2009) (w.r.e.f. 1-1-2006). Earlier 5,500 rupees were raised to 11,000 rupees per mensem by the Governor's Emoluments, Allowances and Privileges (Amendment) Act, 1987 (17 of 1987) (w.r.e.f. 1-4-1986) and again raised to 36,000 rupees per mensem by the Governor's (Emoluments, Allowances and Privileges) Amendment Act, 1998 (27 of 1998) (w.r.e.f. 1-1-1996).
4. The words "so specified" omitted by the Constitution (Seventh Amendment) Act, 1956, sec. 29 and Sch. (w.e.f. 1-11-1956).
5. Subs. by the Constitution (Seventh Amendment) Act, 1956, sec. 29 and Sch., for "such States" (w.e.f. 1-11-1956).
6. Part B omitted by the Constitution (Seventh Amendment) Act, 1956, sec. 29 and Sch. (w.e.f. 1-11-1956).
7. The words and letter "of a State in Part A of the First Schedule" omitted by the Constitution (Seventh Amendment) Act, 1956, sec. 29 and Sch. (w.e.f. 1-11-1956).
8. Subs. by the Constitution (Seventh Amendment) Act, 1956, sec. 29 and Sch., for "any such State" (w.e.f. 1-11-1956).

Constituent Assembly of the Dominion of India immediately before the commencement of this Constitution, and there shall be paid to the Deputy Speaker of the House of the People and to the Deputy Chairman of the Council of States such salaries and allowances as were payable to the Deputy Speaker of the Constituent Assembly of the Dominion of India immediately before such commencement.

8. There shall be paid to the Speaker and the Deputy Speaker of the Legislative Assembly [1][***] and to the Chairman and the Deputy Chairman of the Legislative Council of [2][a State] such salaries and allowances as were payable respectively to the Speaker and the Deputy Speaker of the Legislative Assembly and the President and the Deputy President of the Legislative Council of the corresponding Province immediately before the commencement of this Constitution and, where the corresponding Province had no Legislative Council immediately before such commencement, there shall be paid to the Chairman and the Deputy Chairman of the Legislative Council of the State such salaries and allowances as the Governor of the State may determine.

PART D
PROVISIONS AS TO THE JUDGES OF THE SUPREME COURT AND OF THE HIGH COURTS [3][***]

9. (1) There shall be paid to the Judges of the Supreme Court, in respect of time spent on actual service, salary at the following rates per mensem, that is to say:—

The Chief Justice   [4][10,000 rupees]

Any other Judge   [5][9,000 rupees]:

Provided that if a Judge of the Supreme Court at the time of his appointment is in receipt of a pension (other than a disability or wound pension) in respect of any previous service under the Government of India or any of its predecessor Governments or under the Government of a State or any of its predecessor Governments, his salary in respect of service in the Supreme Court [6][shall be reduced—

(a) by the amount of that pension, and

(b) if he has, before such appointment, received in lieu of a portion of the pension due to him in respect of such previous service the commuted value thereof, by the amount of that portion of the pension, and

(c) if he has, before such appointment, received a retirement gratuity in respect of such previous service, by the pension equivalent of that gratuity].

---

1. The words and letter "of a State specified in Part A of the First Schedule" omitted by the Constitution (Seventh Amendment) Act, 1956, sec. 29 and Sch. (w.e.f. 1-11-1956).

2. Subs. by the Constitution (Seventh Amendment) Act, 1956, sec. 29 and Sch., for "such State" (w.e.f. 1-11-1956).

3. The words and letter "in States in Part A of the First Schedule" omitted by the Constitution (Seventh Amendment) Act, 1956, sec. 25(a) (w.e.f. 1-11-1956).

4. Subs. by the Constitution (Fifty-fourth Amendment) Act, 1986, sec. 4(a)(i), for "5,000 rupees" (w.r.e.f. 1-4-1986). Raised to Rs. 33,000 per mensem *vide* the High Court and Supreme Court Judges (Conditions of Service) Amendment Act, 1998 (18 of 1998), sec. 7(b) (w.r.e.f. 1-1-1996). Raised to Rs. 1,00,000 per mensem *vide* High Court and Supreme Court Judges (Salaries and Conditions of Service) Amendment Act, 2009 (23 of 2009), sec. 8(a) (w.r.e.f. 1-1-2006).

5. Subs. by the Constitution (Fifty-fourth Amendment) Act, 1986, sec. 4(a)(ii), for "4,000 rupees" (w.r.e.f. 1-4-1986). Raised to Rs. 30,000 per mensem *vide* the High Court and Supreme Court Judges (Conditions of Service) Amendment Act, 1998 (18 of 1998), sec. 7(b) (w.r.e.f. 1-1-1996). Raised to Rs. 90,000 per mensem *vide* the High Court and Supreme Court Judges (Salaries and Conditions of Service) Amendment Act, 2009 (23 of 2009), sec. 8(b) (w.r.e.f. 1-1-2006).

6. Subs. by the Constitution (Seventh Amendment) Act, 1956, sec. 25(b), for "shall be reduced by the amount of that pension" (w.e.f. 1-11-1956).

(2) Every Judge of the Supreme Court shall be entitled without payment of rent to the use of an official residence.

(3) Nothing in sub-paragraph (2) of this paragraph shall apply to a Judge who, immediately before the commencement of this Constitution,—

(a) was holding office as the Chief Justice of the Federal Court and has become on such commencement the Chief Justice of the Supreme Court under clause (1) of article 374, or

(b) was holding office as any other Judge of the Federal Court and has on such commencement become a Judge (other than the Chief Justice) of the Supreme Court under the said clause,

during the period he holds office as such Chief Justice or other Judge, and every Judge who so becomes the Chief Justice or other Judge of the Supreme Court shall, in respect of time spent on actual service as such Chief Justice or other Judge, as the case may be, be entitled to receive in addition to the salary specified in sub-paragraph (1) of this paragraph as special pay an amount equivalent to the difference between the salary so specified and the salary which he was drawing immediately before such commencement.

(4) Every Judge of the Supreme Court shall receive such reasonable allowances to reimburse him for expenses incurred in travelling on duty within the territory of India and shall be afforded such reasonable facilities in connection with travelling as the President may from time to time prescribe.

(5) The rights in respect of leave of absence (including leave allowances) and pension of the Judges of the Supreme Court shall be governed by the provisions which, immediately before the commencement of this Constitution, were applicable to the Judges of the Federal Court.

10. [1][(1). There shall be paid to the Judges of High Courts, in respect of time spent on actual service, salary at the following rates per mensem, that is to say,—

The Chief Justice	[2][9,000 rupees]
Any other Judge	[3][8,000 rupees]:

Provided that if a Judge of a High Court at the time of his appointment is in receipt of a pension (other than a disability or wound pension) in respect of any previous service under the Government of India or any of its predecessor Governments or under the Government of a State or any of its predecessor Governments, his salary in respect of service in the High Court shall be reduced—

(a) by the amount of that pension, and

(b) if he has, before such appointment, received in lieu of a portion of the pension due to him in respect of such previous service the commuted value thereof, by the amount of that portion of the pension, and

---

1. Subs. by the Constitution (Seventh Amendment) Act, 1956, sec. 25(c)(i), for sub-paragraph (1) (w.e.f. 1-11-1956).

2. Subs. by the Constitution (Fifty-fourth Amendment) Act, 1986 (34 of 1986), sec. 4(b)(i), for "4,000 rupees" (w.r.e.f. 1-4-1986). Raised to Rs. 30,000 per mensem *vide* the High Court and Supreme Court Judges (Conditions of Service) Amendment Act, 1998 (18 of 1998), sec. 4(b) (w.r.e.f. 1-1-1996). Raised to Rs. 90,000 per mensem *vide* High Court and Supreme Court Judges (Salaries and Conditions of Service) Amendment Act, 2009 (23 of 2009), sec. 2(a) (w.r.e.f. 1-1-2006).

3. Subs. by the Constitution (Fifty-fourth Amendment) Act, 1986 (34 of 1986), sec. 4(a)(ii), for "3,500 rupees" (w.r.e.f. 1-4-1986). Raised to Rs. 26,000 per mensem *vide* the High Court and Supreme Court Judges (Conditions of Service) Amendment Act, 1998 (18 of 1998), sec. 4(b) (w.r.e.f. 1-1-1996). Raised to Rs. 80,000 per mensem *vide* the High Court and Supreme Court Judges (Salaries and Conditions of Service) Amendment Act, 2009 (23 of 2009), sec. 2(b) (w.r.e.f. 1-1-2006).

(c) if he has, before such appointment, received a retirement gratuity in respect of such previous service, by the pension equivalent of that gratuity.]

(2) Every person who immediately before the commencement of this Constitution—

(a) was holding office as the Chief Justice of a High Court in any Province and has on such commencement become the Chief Justice of the High Court in the corresponding State under clause (1) of article 376, or

(b) was holding office as any other Judge of a High Court in any Province and has on such commencement become a Judge (other than the Chief Justice) of the High Court in the corresponding State under the said clause,

shall, if he was immediately before such commencement drawing a salary at a rate higher than that specified in sub-paragraph (1) of this paragraph, be entitled to receive in respect of time spent on actual service as such Chief Justice or other Judge, as the case may be, in addition to the salary specified in the said sub-paragraph as special pay an amount equivalent to the difference between the salary so specified and the salary which he was drawing immediately before such commencement.

¹[(3) Any person who, immediately before the commencement of the Constitution (Seventh Amendment) Act, 1956, was holding office as the Chief Justice of the High Court of a State specified in Part B of the First Schedule and has on such commencement become the Chief Justice of the High Court of a State specified in the said Schedule as amended by said Act, shall, if he was immediately before such commencement drawing any amount as allowance in addition to his salary, be entitled to receive in respect of time spent on actual service as such Chief Justice, the same amount as allowance in addition to the salary specified in sub-paragraph (1) of this paragraph.]

11. In this Part, unless the context otherwise requires—

(a) the expression "Chief Justice" includes an acting Chief Justice, and a "Judge" includes an *ad hoc* Judge;

(b) "actual service" includes—

(i) time spent by a Judge on duty as a Judge or in the performance of such other functions as he may at the request of the President undertake to discharge;

(ii) vacations, excluding any time during which the Judge is absent on leave; and

(iii) joining time on transfer from a High Court to the Supreme Court or from one High Court to another.

PART E

PROVISIONS AS TO THE COMPTROLLER AND AUDITOR-GENERAL OF INDIA

12. (1) There shall be paid to the Comptroller and Auditor-General of India a salary at the rate of four thousand rupees* per mensem.

---

1. Subs. by the Constitution (Seventh Amendment) Act, 1956, sec. 25(c)(ii), for sub-paragraphs (3) and (4) (w.e.f. 1-11-1956).

* *Vide* section 3 of the Comptroller and Auditor General's (Duties, Powers and Conditions of Service) Act, 1971 (56 of 1971) the Comptroller and Auditor-General of India shall be paid a salary equal to the salary of the Judge of Supreme Court. The salary of Judges of the Supreme Court was raised to Rs. 9,000 per mensem by the Constitution (Fifty-fourth Amendment) Act, 1986, sec. 4(a)(ii) (w.r.e.f. 1-4-1986) and was again raised to Rs. 30,000 p.m. by the High Court and Supreme Court Judges (Conditions of Service) Amendment Act, 1998 (18 of 1998), sec. 7(b) (w.r.e.f. 1-1-1996) and further raised to Rs. 90,000 per mensem by the High Court and Supreme Court Judges (Salaries and Conditions of Service) Amendment Act, 2009 (23 of 2009), sec. 8(b) (w.r.e.f. 1-1-2006).

(2) The person who was holding office immediately before the commencement of this Constitution as Auditor-General of India and has become on such commencement the Comptroller and Auditor-General of India under article 377 shall in addition to the salary specified in sub-paragraph (1) of this paragraph be entitled to receive as special pay an amount equivalent to the difference between the salary so specified and the salary which he was drawing as Auditor-General of India immediately before such commencement.

(3) The rights in respect of leave of absence and pension and the other conditions of service of the Comptroller and Auditor-General of India shall be governed or shall continue to be governed, as the case may be, by the provisions which were applicable to the Auditor-General of India immediately before the commencement of this Constitution and all references in those provisions to the Governor-General shall be construed as references to the President.

THIRD SCHEDULE

[Articles 75(4), 99, 124(6), 148(2), 164(3), 188 and 219][1]

FORMS OF OATHS OR AFFIRMATIONS

I

Form of oath of office for a Minister for the Union:

"I, A.B., do $\dfrac{\text{swear in the name of God}}{\text{solemnly affirm}}$ that I will bear true faith and allegiance to the Constitution of India as by law established, [2][that I will uphold the sovereignty and integrity of India,] that I will faithfully and conscientiously discharge my duties as a Minister for the Union and that I will do right to all manner of people in accordance with the Constitution and the law, without fear or favour, affection or ill-will."

II

Form of oath of secrecy for a Minister for the Union:

"I, A.B., do $\dfrac{\text{swear in the name of God}}{\text{solemnly affirm}}$ that I will not directly or indirectly communicate or reveal to any person or persons any matter which shall be brought under my consideration or shall become known to me as a Minister for the Union except as may be required for the due discharge of my duties as such Minister."

[3][III

A

Form of oath or affirmation to be made by a candidate for election to Parliament:

"I, A.B., having been nominated as a candidate to fill a seat in the Council of States (or the House of the People) do $\dfrac{\text{swear in the name of God}}{\text{solemnly affirm}}$ that I will bear true faith and allegiance to the Constitution of India as by law established and that I will uphold the sovereignty and integrity of India."

---

1. *See* also articles 84(a) and 173(a).

2. Ins. by the Constitution (Sixteenth Amendment) Act, 1963, sec. 5(a), (w.e.f. 5-10-1963)..

3. Subs. by the Constitution (Sixteenth Amendment) Act, 1963, sec. 5(b), for Form III (w.e.f. 5-10-1963).

B

Form of oath or affirmation to be made by a member of Parliament:

"I, A.B., having been elected (or nominated) a member of the Council of States (or the House of the People) do $\frac{\text{swear in the name of God}}{\text{solemnly affirm}}$ that I will bear true faith and allegiance to the Constitution of India as by law established, that I will uphold the sovereignty and integrity of India and that I will faithfully discharge the duty upon which I am about to enter."]

IV

Form of oath or affirmation to be made by the Judges of the Supreme Court and the Comptroller and Auditor-General of India:

"I, A.B., having been appointed Chief Justice (or a Judge) of the Supreme Court of India (or Comptroller and Auditor-General of India) do $\frac{\text{swear in the name of God}}{\text{solemnly affirm}}$ that I will bear true faith and allegiance to the Constitution of India as by law established, [1][that I will uphold the sovereignty and integrity of India,] that I will duly and faithfully and to the best of my ability, knowledge and judgment perform the duties of my office without fear or favour, affection or ill-will and that I will uphold the Constitution and the laws."

V

Form of oath of office for a Minister for a State:

"I, A.B., do $\frac{\text{swear in the name of God}}{\text{solemnly affirm}}$ that I will bear true faith and allegiance to the Constitution of India as by law established, [1][that I will uphold the sovereignty and integrity of India,] that I will faithfully and conscientiously discharge my duties as a Minister for the State of.................. and that I will do right to all manner of people in accordance with the Constitution and the law without fear or favour, affection or ill-will."

VI

Form of oath of secrecy for a Minister for a State:

"I, A.B., do $\frac{\text{swear in the name of God}}{\text{solemnly affirm}}$ that I will not directly or indirectly communicate or reveal to any person or persons any matter which shall be brought under my consideration or shall become known to me as a Minister for the State of.................. except as may be required for the due discharge of my duties as such Minister."

[2][**VII**

A

Form of oath or affirmation to be made by a candidate for election to the Legislature of a State:

"I, A.B., having been nominated as a candidate to fill a seat in Legislative Assembly (or Legislative Council), do $\frac{\text{swear in the name of God}}{\text{solemnly affirm}}$ that I will bear true faith

---

1. Ins. by the Constitution (Sixteenth Amendment) Act, 1963, sec. 5(c) (w.e.f. 5-10-1963).
2. Subs. by the Constitution (Sixteenth Amendment) Act, 1963, sec. 5(d), for Form VII (w.e.f. 5-10-1963).

and allegiance to the Constitution of India as by law established and that I will uphold the sovereignty and integrity of India."

B

Form of oath or affirmation to be made by a member of the Legislature of a State:

"I, A.B., having been elected (or nominated) a member of the Legislative Assembly (or Legislative Council), do $\frac{\text{swear in the name of God}}{\text{solemnly affirm}}$ that I will bear true faith and allegiance to the Constitution of India as by law established, that I will uphold the sovereignty and integrity of India and that I will faithfully discharge the duty upon which I am about to enter."]

VIII

Form of oath or affirmation to be made by the Judges of a High Court:

"I, A.B., having been appointed Chief Justice (or a Judge) of the High Court at (or of) ... do $\frac{\text{swear in the name of God}}{\text{solemnly affirm}}$ that I will bear true faith and allegiance to the Constitution of India as by law established, [1][that I will uphold the sovereignty and integrity of India,] that I will duly and faithfully and to the best of my ability, knowledge, and judgment perform the duties of my office without fear or favour, affection or ill-will and that I will uphold the Constitution and the laws."

[2][FOURTH SCHEDULE

[Articles 4(1) and 80(2)]

ALLOCATION OF SEATS IN THE COUNCIL OF STATES

For each State or Union territory specified in the first column of the following table, there shall be allotted the number of seats specified in the second column thereof opposite to that State or that Union territory, as the case may be.

TABLE

1. Andhra Pradesh	18
2. Assam	7
3. Bihar	[3][16]
[4][4. Jharkhand	6]
[5][*5. Goa	1]
[6][*6. Gujarat	11]

---

1. Ins. by the Constitution (Sixteenth Amendment) Act, 1963, sec. 5(c) (w.e.f 5-10-1963).
2. Subs. by the Constitution (Seventh Amendment) Act, 1956, sec. 3(2), for the Fourth Schedule (w.e.f. 1-11-1956).
3. Subs. by the Bihar Reorganisation Act, 2000 (30 of 2000), sec. 7(b), for "22" (w.e.f. 15-11-2000).
4. Ins. by the Bihar Reorganisation Act, 2000 (30 of 2000), sec. 7(c) (w.e.f. 15-11-2000).
5. Ins. by Goa, Daman and Diu Reorganisation Act, 1987 (18 of 1987), sec. 6(b) (w.e.f. 30-5-1987).
6. Subs. by the Bombay Reorganisation Act, 1960 (11 of 1960), sec. 6(a), for entry 4 (w.e.f. 1-5-1960).

[1][*7. Haryana   5]
  *8. Kerala   9
  *9. Madhya Pradesh   [2][11]
[3][*10. Chattisgarh   5]
[4][*11. Tamil Nadu]   [5][18]
[6][*12. Maharashtra   19]
[7][*13. Karnataka]   12
  *14. [8][Odisha]   10
  *15. Punjab   [9][7]
  *16. Rajasthan   10
  *17. Uttar Pradesh   [10][31]
[11][18. [12][Uttarakhand]   3]
  *19. West Bengal   16
  *20. Jammu and Kashmir   4
[13][*21. Nagaland   1]
[14][*22. Himachal Pradesh   3]
[15][*23. Manipur   1]
  *24. Tripura   1
  *25. Meghalaya   1
[16][*26. Sikkim   1]
  *27. Mizoram   1

---

1. Ins. by the Punjab Reorganisation Act, 1966 (31 of 1966), sec. 9(b) (w.e.f. 1-11-1966).
2. Subs. by the Madhya Pradesh Reorganisation Act, 2000 (28 of 2000), sec. 7(b), for "16" (w.e.f. 1-11-2000).
3. Ins. by Madhya Pradesh Reorganisation Act, 2000 (28 of 2000), sec. 7(c) (w.e.f. 1-11-2000).
4. Subs. by the Madras State (Alteration of Name) Act, 1968 (53 of 1968), sec. 5(2), for "8. Madras" (w.e.f. 14-1-1969).
5. Subs. by the Andhra Pradesh and Madras (Alteration of Boundaries) Act, 1959 (56 of 1959), sec. 8(a), for "17" (w.e.f. 1-4-1960).
6. Ins. by the Bombay Reorganisation Act, 1960 (11 of 1960), sec. 6(b) (w.e.f. 1-5-1960).
7. Subs. by the Mysore State (Alternation of Name) Act, 1973 (31 of 1973), sec. 5(2), for "10. Mysore" (w.e.f. 1-11-1973).
8. Subs. by the Orissa (Alteration of Name) Act, 2011 (15 of 2011), sec. 7, for "Orissa" (w.e.f. 1-11-2011, *vide* G.S.R. 791(E), dated 1st November, 2011).
9. Subs. by the Punjab Reorganisation Act, 1966 (31 of 1966), sec. 9(c), for "11" (w.e.f. 1-11-1966).
10. Subs. by the Uttar Pradesh Reorganisation Act, 2000 (29 of 2000), sec. 7(b), for "34" (w.e.f. 9-11-2000).
11. Ins. by the Uttar Pradesh Reorganisation Act, 2000 (29 of 2000), sec. 7(c) (w.e.f. 9-11-2000).
12. Subs. by the Uttaranchal (Alteration of Name) Act, 2006 (52 of 2006), sec. 5, for "Uttaranchal" (w.e.f. 1-1-2007).
13. Ins. by the State of Nagaland Act, 1962 (27 of 1962), sec. 6(b)(ii) (w.e.f. 1-12-1963).
14. Ins. by the State of Himachal Pradesh Act, 1970 (53 of 1970), sec. 5(a) (w.e.f. 25-1-1971).
15. Subs. by the North Eastern Areas (Reorganisation) Act, 1971 (81 of 1971), sec. 10(a) for entries 19 to 22 (w.e.f. 21-1-1972).
16. Ins. by the Constitution (Thirty-sixth Amendment) Act, 1975, sec. 4(a) (w.e.f. 26-4-1975).

*28. Arunachal Pradesh	1
*29. Delhi	3
1[*30. 2[Puducherry].	1]

Total 3+[233]]

FIFTH SCHEDULE

[Article 244(1)]

PROVISIONS AS TO THE ADMINISTRATION AND CONTROL OF SCHEDULED AREAS AND SCHEDULED TRIBES

PART A

GENERAL

1. Interpretation.—In this Schedule, unless the context otherwise requires, the expression 'State' 4[***] does not include the 5[States of Assam, Meghalaya, Tripura and Mizoram].

2. Executive power of a State in Scheduled Areas.—Subject to the provisions of this Schedule, the executive power of a State extends to the Scheduled Areas therein.

3. Report by the Governor 6[***] **to the President regarding the administration of Scheduled Areas.**—The Governor 6[***] of each State having Scheduled Areas therein

---

* Entry numbers have been re-numbered by (i) the Bombay Reorganisation Act, 1960 (11 of 1960), sec. 6(c) (w.e.f. 1-5-1960); (ii) the State of Nagaland Act, 1962 (27 of 1962), sec. 6(b)(i) (w.e.f. 1-12-1963); (iii) the Punjab Reorganisation Act, 1966 (31 of 1966), sec. 9(a) (w.e.f. 1-11-1966); (iv) the State of Himachal Pradesh Act, 1970 (53 of 1970), sec. 5(a) (w.e.f. 25-1-1971); (v) the North Eastern Areas (Reorganisation) Act, 1971 (81 of 1971), sec. 10(a) (w.e.f. 21-1-1972); (vi) the Constitution (Thirty-sixth Amendment) Act, 1975, sec. 4(b) (w.e.f. 26-4-1975); (vii) the State of Mizoram Act, 1986 (34 of 1986), sec. 5(a) (w.e.f. 20-2-1987); (viii) the Goa, Daman and Diu Reorganisation Act, 1987 (18 of 1987), sec. 6(a) (w.e.f. 30-5-1987); (ix) the Madhya Pradesh Reorganisation Act, 2000 (28 of 2000), sec. 7(a) (w.e.f. 1-11-2000); (x) the Uttar Pradesh Reorganisation Act, 2000 (29 of 2000), sec. 7(a) (w.e.f. 9-11-2000) and (xi) the Bihar Reorganisation Act, 2000 (30 of 2000), sec. 7(a) (w.e.f. 15-11-2000).

1. Ins. by the Constitution (Fourteenth Amendment) Act, 1962, sec. 6(a) (w.e.f. 28-12-1962).

2. Subs. by the Pondicherry (Alteration of Name) Act, 2006 (44 of 2006), sec. 4, for "Pondicherry" (w.e.f. 1-10-2006).

3. Subs. by the Goa, Daman and Diu Reorganisation Act, 1987, sec. 6(c), for "232" (w.e.f. 30-5-1987).

† The figures have been changed by (i) the Bombay Reorganisation Act, 1960 (11 of 1960), sec. 6(d) (w.e.f. 1-5-1960); (ii) the State of Nagaland Act, 1962 (27 of 1962), sec. 6(b)(iii); (iii) the Punjab Reorganisation Act, 1966 (31 of 1966), sec. 9(c) (w.e.f. 1-11-1966); (iv) the North-Eastern Areas (Reorganisation) Act, 1971 (81 of 1971), sec. 10(b) (w.e.f. 21-1-1972); (v) the Constitution (Thirty-sixth Amendment) Act, 1975, sec. 4(c) (w.e.f. 26-4-1975); (vi) Goa, Daman and Diu Reorganisation Act, 1987 (18 of 1987), sec. 6(c) (w.e.f. 30-5-1987).

4. The words and letters "means a State specified in Part A or Part B of the First Schedule but" omitted by the Constitution (Seventh Amendment) Act, 1956, sec. 29 and Sch. (w.e.f. 1-11-1956).

5. Subs. by the State of Mizoram Act, 1986 (34 of 1986), sec. 39(e), for "Meghalaya and Tripura" (w.e.f. 20-2-1987). Earlier the words "States of Assam and Meghalaya" were substituted by the North-Eastern Areas (Reorganisation) Act, 1971, sec. 71(4), for the words "State of Assam" (w.e.f. 21-1-1972), and the words ", Meghalaya and Tripura" were substituted by the Constitution (Forty-ninth Amendment) Act, 1984, sec. 3, for the words "and Meghalaya" (w.e.f. 1-4-1985).

6. The words "or Rajpramukh" omitted by the Constitution (Seventh Amendment) Act, 1956, sec. 29 and Sch. (w.e.f. 1-11-1956).

shall annually, or whenever so required by the President, make a report to the President regarding the administration of the Scheduled Areas in that State and the executive power of the Union shall extend to the giving of directions to the State as to the administration of the said areas.

PART B

ADMINISTRATION AND CONTROL OF SCHEDULED AREAS AND SCHEDULED TRIBES

4. Tribes Advisory Council.—(1) There shall be established in each State having Scheduled Areas therein and, if the President so directs, also in any State having Scheduled Tribes but not Scheduled Areas therein, a Tribes Advisory Council consisting of not more than twenty members of whom, as nearly as may be, three-fourths shall be the representatives of the Scheduled Tribes in the Legislative Assembly of the State:

Provided that if the number of representatives of the Scheduled Tribes in the Legislative Assembly of the State is less than the number of seats in the Tribes Advisory Council to be filled by such representatives, the remaining seats shall be filled by other members of those tribes.

(2) It shall be the duty of the Tribes Advisory Council to advise on such matters pertaining to the welfare and advancement of the Scheduled Tribes in the State as may be referred to them by the Governor [1][***].

(3) The Governor [1][***] may make rules prescribing or regulating, as the case may be,

(a) the number of members of the Council, the mode of their appointment and the appointment of the Chairman of the Council and of the officers and servants thereof,

(b) the conduct of its meetings and its procedure in general; and

(c) all other incidental matters.

5. Law applicable to Scheduled Areas.—(1) Notwithstanding anything in this Constitution, the Governor [1][***] may by public notification direct that any particular Act of Parliament or of the Legislature of the State shall not apply to a Scheduled Area or any part thereof in the State or shall apply to a Scheduled Area or any part thereof in the State subject to such exceptions and modifications as he may specify in the notification and any direction given under this sub-paragraph may be given so as to have retrospective effect.

(2) The Governor [1][***] may make regulations for the peace and good government of any area in a State which is for the time being a Scheduled Area.

In particular and without prejudice to the generality of the foregoing power, such regulations may—

(a) prohibit or restrict the transfer of land by or among members of the Scheduled Tribes in such area;

(b) regulate the allotment of land to members of the Scheduled Tribes in such area;

(c) regulate the carrying on of business as money-lender by persons who lend money to members of the Scheduled Tribes in such area.

---

1. The words "or Rajpramukh, as the case may be" omitted by the Constitution (Seventh Amendment) Act, 1956, sec. 29 and Sch. (w.e.f. 1-11-1956).

(3) In making any such regulation as is referred to in sub-paragraph (2) of this paragraph, the Governor [1][***] may repeal or amend any Act of Parliament or of the Legislature of the State or any existing law which is for the time being applicable to the area in question.

(4) All regulations made under this paragraph shall be submitted forthwith to the President and, until assented to by him, shall have no effect.

(5) No regulation shall be made under this paragraph unless the Governor [2][***] making the regulation has, in the case where there is a Tribes Advisory Council for the State, consulted such Council.

PART C
SCHEDULED AREAS

6. Scheduled Areas.—(1) In this Constitution, the expression 'Scheduled Areas' means such areas as the President may by order[3] declare to be Scheduled Areas.

(2) The President may at any time by order[4]—

(a) direct that the whole or any specified part of a Scheduled Area shall cease to be a Scheduled Area or a part of such an area;

[5][(aa) increase the area of any Scheduled Area in a State after consultation with the Governor of that State;]

(b) alter, but only by way of rectification of boundaries, any Scheduled Area;

(c) on any alteration of the boundaries of a State or on the admission into the Union or the establishment of a new State, declare any territory not previously included in any State to be, or to form part of, a Scheduled Area;

[6][(d) rescind, in relation to any State or States, any order or orders made under this paragraph, and in consultation with the Governor of the State concerned, make fresh orders redefining the areas which are to be Scheduled Areas,]

and any such order may contain such incidental and consequential provisions as appear to the President to be necessary and proper, but save as aforesaid, the order made under sub-paragraph (1) of this paragraph shall not be varied by any subsequent order.

PART D
AMENDMENT OF THE SCHEDULE

7. Amendment of the Schedule.—(1) Parliament may from time to time by law amend by way of addition, variation or repeal any of the provisions of this Schedule and, when

---

1. The words "or Rajpramukh" omitted by the Constitution (Seventh Amendment) Act, 1956, sec. 29 and Sch. (w.e.f. 1-11-1956).
2. The words "or the Rajpramukh" omitted by the Constitution (Seventh Amendment) Act, 1956, sec. 29 and Sch. (w.e.f. 1-11-1956).
3. *See* the Scheduled Areas (Part A States) Order, 1950 (C.O. 9), the Scheduled Areas (Part B States) Order, 1950 (C.O. 26), the Scheduled Areas (Himachal Pradesh) Order, 1975 (C.O. 102) and the Scheduled Areas (States of Bihar, Gujarat, Madhya Pradesh and Orissa) Order, 1977 (C.O. 109).
4. *See* the Madras Scheduled Area (Cesser) Order, 1951 (C.O. 30) and the Andhra Scheduled Areas (Cesser) Order, 1955 (C.O. 50).
5. Ins. by the Fifth Schedule to the Constitution (Amendment) Act, 1976 (101 of 1976), sec. 2(1) (w.e.f. 7-9-1976).
6. Ins. by the Fifth Schedule to the Constitution (Amendment) Act, 1976 (101 of 1976), sec. 2(2) (w.e.f. 7-9-1976).

the Schedule is so amended, any reference to this Schedule in this Constitution shall be construed as a reference to such Schedule as so amended.

(2) No such law as is mentioned in sub-paragraph (1) of this paragraph shall be deemed to be an amendment of this Constitution for the purposes of article 368.

SIXTH SCHEDULE

[Articles 244(2) and 275(1)]

PROVISIONS AS TO THE ADMINISTRATION OF TRIBAL AREAS IN ¹[THE STATES OF ASSAM, MEGHALAYA, TRIPURA AND MIZORAM]

1. Autonomous districts and autonomous regions.—(1) Subject to the provisions of this paragraph, the tribal areas in each item of ²[³[Parts I, II and IIA] and in Part III] of the table appended to paragraph 20 of this Schedule shall be an autonomous district.

(2) If there are different Scheduled Tribes in an autonomous district, the Governor may, by public notification, divide the area or areas inhabited by them into autonomous regions.⁴

(3) The Governor may, by public notification,—

(a) include any area in ²[any of the Parts] of the said table,

(b) exclude any area from ²[any of the Parts] of the said table,

(c) create a new autonomous district,

(d) increase the area of any autonomous district,

(e) diminish the area of any autonomous district,

(f) unite two or more autonomous districts or parts thereof so as to form one autonomous district,

⁵[(ff) alter the name of any autonomous district,]

(g) define the boundaries of any autonomous district:

Provided that no order shall be made by the Governor under clauses (c), (d), (e) and (f) of this sub-paragraph except after consideration of the report of a Commission appointed under sub-paragraph (1) of paragraph 14 of this Schedule:

---

1. Subs. by the State of Mizoram Act, 1986 (34 of 1986), sec. 39(f), for "the States of Assam, Meghalaya and Tripura and in the Union Territory of Mizoram" (w.e.f. 20-2-1987). Earlier the words "The States of Assam and Meghalaya and in the Union Territory of Mizoram" were substituted by the North-Eastern Areas (Reorganisation) Act, 1971 (81 of 1971), sec. 71(i) and Eighth Sch., for the word "Assam" (w.e.f. 21-1-1972) and the words ", Meghalaya and Tripura" were substituted by the Constitution (Forty-ninth Amendment) Act, 1984, sec. 4(a), for the words "and Meghalaya" (w.e.f. 1-4-1985).

2. Subs. by the North-Eastern Areas (Reorganisation) Act, 1971 (81 of 1971), sec. 71(i) and Eighth Sch., for "Part A" (w.e.f. 21-1-1972).

3. Subs. by the Constitution (Forty-ninth Amendment) Act, 1984, sec. 4(b), for "Parts I and II" (w.e.f. 1-4-1985).

4. Paragraph 1 has been amended in its application to the State of Assam by the Sixth Schedule to the Constitution (Amendment) Act, 2003 (44 of 2003), sec. 2(1) (w.e.f. 7-9-2003) so as to insert after sub-paragraph (2) the following proviso; namely:—

    "Provided that nothing in this sub-paragraph shall apply to the Bodoland Territorial Areas District."

5. Ins. by the Assam Reorganisation (Meghalaya) Act, 1969 (55 of 1969), sec. 74 and Fourth Sch. (w.e.f. 2-4-1970).

¹[Provided further that any order made by the Governor under this sub-paragraph may contain such incidental and consequential provisions (including any amendment of paragraph 20 and of any item in any of the Parts of the said table) as appear to the Governor to be necessary for giving effect to the provisions of the order.]

2. Constitution of District Councils and Regional Councils.—²[(1) There shall be a District Council for each autonomous district consisting of not more than thirty members, of whom not more than four persons shall be nominated by the Governor and the rest shall be elected on the basis of adult suffrage.]³

(2) There shall be a separate Regional Council for each area constituted an autonomous region under sub-paragraph (2) of paragraph 1 of this Schedule.

(3) Each District Council and each Regional Council shall be a body corporate by the name respectively of 'the District Council of (*name of district*)' and 'the Regional Council of (*name of region*)', shall have perpetual succession and a common seal and shall by the said name sue and be sued.⁴ *

(4) Subject to the provisions of this Schedule, the administration of an autonomous district shall, in so far as it is not vested under this Schedule in any Regional Council within such district, be vested in the District Council for such district and the administration of an autonomous region shall be vested in the Regional Council for such region.

(5) In an autonomous district with Regional Councils, the District Council shall have only such powers with respect to the areas under the authority of the Regional Council as may be delegated to it by the Regional Council in addition to the powers conferred on it by this Schedule with respect to such areas.

(6) The Governor shall make rules for the first constitution of District Councils and Regional Councils in consultation with the existing tribal Councils or other representative

---

1. Ins. by the North-Eastern Areas (Reorganisation) Act, 1971 (81 of 1971), sec. 71(i) and Eighth Sch. (w.e.f. 21-1-1972).
2. Subs. by the Assam Reorganisation (Meghalaya) Act, 1969 (55 of 1969), sec. 74 and Fourth Sch., for paragraph (1) (w.e.f. 2-4-1970).
3. Paragraph 2 has been amended in its application to the State of Assam by the Sixth Schedule to the Constitution (Amendment) Act, 2003 (44 of 2003), sec. 2(2) (w.e.f. 7-9-2003), so as to insert after sub-paragraph (1), the following proviso, namely:—
   "Provided that the Bodoland Territorial Council shall consist of not more than forty-six members of whom forty shall be elected on the basis of adult suffrage, of whom thirty shall be reserved for the Scheduled Tribes, five for non-tribal communities, five open for all communities and the remaining six shall be nominated by the Governor having same rights and privileges as other members, including voting rights, from amongst the un-represented communities of the Bodoland Territorial Areas District, of which at least two shall be women."
4. Paragraph 2 has been amended in its application to the State of Assam by the Sixth Schedule to the Constitution (Amendment) Act, 1995 (42 of 1995), sec. 2(1) (w.e.f. 12-9-1995), so as to insert in sub-paragraph (3), the following proviso, namely:—
   "Provided that the District Council constituted for the North Cachar Hills District shall be called as the North Cachar Hills Autonomous Council and the District Council constituted for the Karbi Anglong District shall be called as the Karbi Anglong Autonomus Council."
* Paragraph 2 has been amended in its application to the State of Assam by the Sixth Schedule to the Constitution (Amendment) Act, 2003 (44 of 2003), sec. 2(3) (w.e.f. 7-9-2003), so as to insert in sub-paragraph (3), after the proviso, the following proviso, namely:—
   "Provided further that the District Council constituted for the Bodoland Territorial Areas District shall be called the Bodoland Territorial Council."

tribal organisations within the autonomous districts or regions concerned, and such rules shall provide for—

(a) the composition of the District Councils and Regional Councils and the allocation of seats therein;

(b) the delimitation of territorial constituencies for the purpose of elections to those Councils;

(c) the qualifications for voting at such elections and the preparation of electoral rolls therefor;

(d) the qualifications for being elected at such elections as members of such Councils;

(e) the term of office of members of ¹[Regional Councils];

(f) any other matter relating to or connected with elections or nominations to such Councils;

(g) the procedure and the conduct of business ²[including the power to act notwithstanding any vacancy] in the District and Regional Councils;

(h) the appointment of officers and staff of the District and Regional Councils.

²[(6A) The elected members of the District Council shall hold office for a term of five years from the date appointed for the first meeting of the Council after the general elections to the Council, unless the District Council is sooner dissolved under paragraph 16 and a nominated member shall hold office at the pleasure of the Governor:

Provided that the said period of five years may, while a Proclamation of Emergency is in operation or if circumstances exist which, in the opinion of the Governor, render the holding of elections impracticable, be extended by the Governor for a period not exceeding one year at a time and in any case where a Proclamation of Emergency is in operation not extending beyond a period of six months after the Proclamation has ceased to operate:

Provided further that a member elected to fill a casual vacancy shall hold office only for the remainder of the term of office of the member whom he replaces.]

(7) The District or the Regional Council may after its first constitution make rules ²[with the approval of the Governor] with regard to the matters specified in sub-paragraph (6) of this paragraph and may also make rules ²[with like approval] regulating—

(a) the formation of subordinate local Councils or Boards and their procedure and the conduct of their business; and

(b) generally all matters relating to the transaction of business pertaining to the administration of the district or region, as the case may be:

Provided that until rules are made by the District or the Regional Council under this sub-paragraph the rules made by the Governor under sub-paragraph (6) of this paragraph shall have effect in respect of elections to, the officers and staff of, and the procedure and the conduct of business in, each such Council.

³[***]

---

1. Subs. by the Assam Reorganisation (Meghalaya) Act, 1969 (55 of 1969), sec. 74 and Fourth Sch., for "such Councils" (w.e.f. 2-4-1970).

2. Ins. by the Assam Reorganisation (Meghalaya) Act, 1969 (55 of 1969), sec. 74 and Fourth Sch. (w.e.f. 2-4-1970).

3. Second proviso omitted by the Assam Reorganisation (Meghalaya) Act, 1969 (55 of 1969), sec. 74 and Fourth Sch. (w.e.f. 2-4-1970).

3. Powers of the District Councils and Regional Councils to make laws.—(1) The Regional Council for an autonomous region in respect of all areas within such region and the District Council for an autonomous district in respect of all areas within the district except those which are under the authority of Regional Councils, if any, within the district shall have power to make laws with respect to—

(a) the allotment, occupation or use, or the setting apart, of land, other than any land which is a reserved forest for the purposes of agriculture or grazing or for residential or other non-agricultural purposes or for any other purpose likely to promote the interests of the inhabitants of any village or town:

Provided that nothing in such laws shall prevent the compulsory acquisition of any land, whether occupied or unoccupied, for public purposes [1][by the Government of the State concerned] in accordance with the law for the time being in force authorising such acquisition;

(b) the management of any forest not being a reserved forest;

(c) the use of any canal or water-course for the purpose of agriculture;

(d) the regulation of the practice of *jhum* or other forms of shifting cultivation;

(e) the establishment of village or town committees or councils and their powers;

(f) any other matter relating to village or town administration, including village or town police and public health and sanitation;

(g) the appointment or succession of Chiefs or Headmen;

(h) the inheritance of property;

[2][(i) marriage and divorce;]

(j) social customs.

(2) In this paragraph, a 'reserved forest' means any area which is a reserved forest under the Assam Forest Regulation, 1891, or under any other law for the time being in force in the area in question.

(3) All laws made under this paragraph shall be submitted forthwith to the Governor and, until assented to by him, shall have no effect.[3] * †

1. Subs. by the North-Eastern Areas (Reorganisation) Act, 1971 (81 of 1971), sec. 71(i) and Eighth Sch., for certain words (w.e.f. 21-1-1972).

2. Subs. by the Assam Reorganisation (Meghalaya) Act, 1969 (55 of 1969), sec. 74 and Fourth Sch., for clause (i) (w.e.f. 2-4-1970).

3. Paragraph 3 has been amended in its application to the State of Assam by the Sixth Schedule to the Constitution (Amendment) Act, 2003 (44 of 2003), sec. 2(4) (w.e.f. 7-9-2003), so as to substitute for sub-paragraph (3), the following sub-paragraph, namely:—

"(3) Save as otherwise provided in sub-paragraph (2) of paragraph 3A or sub-paragraph (2) of paragraph 3B, all laws made under this paragraph or sub-paragraph (1) of paragraph 3A or sub-paragraph (1) of paragraph 3B shall be submitted forthwith to the Governor and, until assented to by him, shall have no effect."

Earlier sub-paragraph (3) was substituted by the Sixth Schedule to the Constitution (Amendment) Act, 1995 (42 of 1995), sec. 2(2) (w.e.f. 12-9-1995).

* After paragraph 3, the following paragraph has been inserted in its application to the State of Assam by the Sixth Schedule to the Constitution (Amendment) Act, 1995 (42 of 1995), sec. 2(3) (w.e.f. 12-9-1995), namely:—

"3A. *Additional powers of the North Cachar Hills Autonomous Council and the Karbi Anglong Autonomous Council to make law.*—(1) Without prejudice to the provisions of paragraph 3, the North Cachar Hills Autonomous Council and the Karbi Anglong Autonomous Council within their respective districts, shall have power to make laws with respect to—

(*Contd. on next page*)

4. Administration of justice in autonomous districts and autonomous regions.—(1) The Regional Council for an autonomous region in respect of areas within such region

(Contd. from previous page)

   (a) industries, subject to the provisions of entries 7 and 52 of List I of the Seventh Schedule;
   (b) communications, that is to say, roads, bridges, ferries and other means of communication not specified in List I of the Seventh Schedule; municipal tramways, ropeways, inland waterways and traffic thereon subject to the provisions of List I and List III of the Seventh Schedule with regard to such waterways; vehicles other than mechanically propelled vehicles;
   (c) preservation, protection and improvement of stock and prevention of animal diseases; veterinary training and practice; cattle pounds;
   (d) primary and secondary education;
   (e) agriculture, including agricultural education and research, protection against pests and prevention of plant diseases;
   (f) fisheries;
   (g) water, that is to say, water supplies, irrigation and canals, drainage and embankments, water storage and water power subject to the provisions of entry 56 of List I of the Seventh Schedule;
   (h) social security and social insurance; employment and unemployment;
   (i) flood control schemes for protection of villages, paddy fields, markets, towns, etc. (not of technical nature);
   (j) theatre and dramatic performances, cinemas subject to the provisions of entry 60 of List I of the Seventh Schedule; sports entertainments and amusements;
   (k) public health and sanitation, hospitals and dispensaries;
   (l) minor irrigation;
   (m) trade and commerce in, and the production, supply and distribution of, food stuffs, cattle fodder, raw cotton and raw jute;
   (n) libraries, museums and other similar institutions controlled or financed by the State; ancient and historical monuments and records other than those declared by or under any law made by Parliament to be of national importance; and
   (o) alienation of land.

(2) All laws made by the North Cachar Hills Autonomous Council and the Karbi Anglong Autonomous Council under paragraph 3 or under this paragraph shall, in so far as they relate to matters specified in List III of the Seventh Schedule, be submitted forthwith to the Governor who shall reserve the same for the consideration of the President.

(3) When a law is reserved for the consideration of the President, the President shall declare either that he assents to the said law or that he withholds assent therefrom:

Provided that the President may direct the Governor to return the law to the North Cachar Hills Autonomous Council or the Karbi Anglong Autonomous Council, as the case may be, together with a message requesting that the said Council will reconsider the law or any specified provisions thereof and, in particular, will, consider the desirability of introducing any such amendments as he may recommend in his message and, when the law is so returned, the said Council shall consider the law accordingly within a period of six months from the date of receipt of such message and, if the law is again passed by the said Council with or without amendments it shall be presented again to the President for his consideration."

   † After paragraph 3A, the following paragraph has been inserted in its application to the State of Assam by the Sixth Schedule to the Constitution (Amendment) Act, 2003 (44 of 2003), sec. 2(5) (w.e.f. 7-9-2003), namely:—

"3B. Additional powers to the Bodoland Territorial Council to make laws.—(1) Without prejudice to the provisions of paragraph 3, the Bodoland Territorial Council within its areas shall have power to make laws with respect to—(i) Agriculture, including agricultural education and research, protection against pests and prevention of plant diseases; (ii)

(Contd. on next page)

and the District Council for an autonomous district in respect of areas within the district other than those which are under the authority of the Regional Councils, if any, within the district may constitute village councils or courts for the trial of suits and cases between the parties all of whom belong to Scheduled Tribes within such areas, other than suits and cases to which the provisions of sub-paragraph (1) of paragraph 5 of this

---

(Contd. from previous page)

Animal husbandry and verterinary, that is to say, preservation, protection and improvement of stock and prevention of animal diseases, veterinary training and practice, cattle pounds; (iii) Co-operation; (iv) Cultural affairs; (v) Education, that is to say, primary education, higher secondary including vocational training, adult education, college education (general); (vi) Fisheries; (vii) Flood control for protection of village, paddy fields, markets and towns (not of technical nature); (viii) Food and civil supply; (ix) Forests (other than reserved forests); (x) Handloom and textile; (xi) Health and family welfare; (xii) Intoxicating liquors, opium and derivatives, subject to the provisions of entry 84 of List I of the Seventh Schedule; (xiii) Irrigation; (xiv) Labour and employment; (xv) Land and Revenue; (xvi) Library services (financed and controlled by the State Government); (xvii) Lotteries (subject to the provisions of entry 40 of List I of the Seventh Schedule), theatres, dramatic performances and cinemas (subject to the provisions of entry 60 of List I of the Seventh Schedule); (xviii) Markets and fairs; (xix) Municipal corporation, improvement trust, district boards and other local authorities; (xx) Museum and archaeology institutions controlled or financed by the State, ancient and historical monuments and records other than those declared by or under any law made by Parliament to be of national importance; (xxi) Panchayat and rural development; (xxii) Planning and development; (xxiii) Printing and stationery; (xxiv) Public health engineering; (xxv) Public works department; (xxvi) Publicity and public relations; (xxvii) Registration of births and deaths; (xxviii) Relief and rehabilitation; (xxix) Sericulture; (xxx) Small, cottage and rural industry subject to the provisions of entries 7 and 52 of List I of the Seventh Schedule; (xxxi) Social welfare; (xxxii) Soil conservation; (xxxiii) Sports and youth welfare; (xxxiv) Statistics; (xxxv) Tourism; (xxxvi) Transport (roads, bridges, ferries and other means of communications not specified in List I of the Seventh Schedule, municipal tramways, ropeways, inland waterways and traffic thereon subject to the provision of List I and List III of the Seventh Schedule with regard to such waterways, vehicles other than mechanically propelled vehicles); (xxxvii) Tribal research institute controlled and financed by the State Government; (xxxviii) Urban development—town and country planning; (xxxix) Weights and measures subject to the provisions of entry 50 of List I of the Seventh Schedule; and (xl) Welfare of plain tribes and backward classes:

Provided that nothing in such laws shall—

(a) extinguish or modify the existing rights and privileges of any citizen in respect of his land at the date of commencement of this Act; and

(b) disallow any citizen from acquiring land either by way of inheritance, allotment, settlement or by any other way of transfer if such citizen is otherwise eligible for such acquisition of land within the Bodoland Territorial Areas District.

(2) All laws made under paragraph 3 or under this paragraph shall in so far as they relate to matters specified in List III of the Seventh Schedule, be submitted forthwith to the Governor who shall reserve the same for the consideration of the President.

(3) When a law is reserved for the consideration of the President, the President shall declare either that he assents to the said law or that he withholds assent therefrom:

Provided that the President may direct the Governor to return the law to the Bodoland Territorial Council, together with the message requesting that the said Council will reconsider the law or any specified provisions thereof and, in particular, will consider the desirability of introducing any such amendments as he may recommend in his message and, when the law is so returned, the said Council shall consider the law accordingly within a period of six months from the date of receipt of such message and, if the law is again passed by the said Council with or without amendments it shall be presented again to the President for his consideration."

Schedule apply, to the exclusion of any court in the State, and may appoint suitable persons to be members of such village councils or presiding officers of such courts, and may also appoint such officers as may be necessary for the administration of the laws made under paragraph 3 of this Schedule.

(2) Notwithstanding anything in this Constitution, the Regional Council for an autonomous region or any court constituted in that behalf by the Regional Council or, if in respect of any area within an autonomous district there is no Regional Council, the District Council for such district, or any court constituted in that behalf by the District Council, shall exercise the powers of a court of appeal in respect of all suits and cases triable by a village council or court constituted under sub-paragraph (1) of this paragraph within such region or area, as the case may be, other than those to which the provisions of sub-paragraph (1) of paragraph 5 of this Schedule apply, and no other court except the High Court and the Supreme Court shall have jurisdiction over such suits or cases.

(3) The High Court [1][***] shall have and exercise such jurisdiction over the suits and cases to which the provisions of sub-paragraph (2) of this paragraph apply as the Governor may from time to time by order specify.

(4) A Regional Council or District Council, as the case may be, may with the previous approval of the Governor make rules regulating—

(a) the constitution of village councils and courts and the powers to be exercised by them under this paragraph;

(b) the procedure to be followed by village councils or courts in the trial of suits and cases under sub-paragraph (1) of this paragraph;

(c) the procedure to be followed by the Regional or District Council or any court constituted by such Council in appeals and other proceedings under sub-paragraph (2) of this paragraph;

(d) the enforcement of decisions and orders of such Councils and courts;

(e) all other ancillary matters for the carrying out of the provisions of sub-paragraphs (1) and (2) of this paragraph.

[2][(5) On and from such date as the President may, [3][after consulting the Government of the State concerned], by notification appoint in this behalf, this paragraph shall have effect in relation to such autonomous district or region as may be specified in the notification, as if—

(i) in sub-paragraph (1), for the words "between the parties all of whom belong to Scheduled Tribes within such areas, other than suits and cases to which the provisions of sub-paragraph (1) of paragraph 5 of this Schedule apply,", the words "not being suits and cases of the nature referred to in sub- paragraph (1) of paragraph (5) of this Schedule, which the Governor may specify in this behalf," had been substituted;

(ii) sub-paragraphs (2) and (3) had been omitted;

(iii) in sub-paragraph (4)—

(a) for the words "A Regional Council or District Council, as the case may be, may with the previous approval of the Governor make rules regulating", the

---

1. The words "of Assam" omitted by the North-Eastern Areas (Reorganisation) Act, 1971 (81 of 1971), sec. 71(i) and Eighth Sch. (w.e.f. 21-1-1972).

2. Ins. by the Assam Reorganisation (Meghalaya) Act, 1969 (55 of 1969), sec. 74 and Fourth Sch. (w.e.f. 2-4-1970).

3. Subs. by the North-Eastern Areas (Reorganisation) Act, 1971 (81 of 1971), sec. 71(i) and Eighth Sch., for certain words (w.e.f. 21-1-1972).

words "the Governor may make rules regulating" had been substituted; and

(b) for clause (a), the following clause had been substituted, namely:—

(a) the constitution of village councils and courts, the powers to be exercised by them under this paragraph and the courts to which appeals from the decisions of village councils and courts shall lie;";

(c) for clause (c), the following clause had been substituted, namely:—

"(c) the transfer of appeals and other proceedings pending before the Regional or District Council or any court constituted by such Council immediately before the date appointed by the President under sub-paragraph (5);" and

(d) in clause (e), for the words, brackets and figures "sub-paragraphs (1) and (2)", the word, brackets and figure "sub-paragraph (1)" had been substituted.][1]

5. Conferment of powers under the Code of Civil Procedure, 1908, and the Code of Criminal Procedure, 1898,[2] on the Regional and District Councils and on certain courts and officers for the trial of certain suits, cases and offences.—(1) The Governor may, for the trial of suits or cases arising out of any law in force in any autonomous district or region being a law specified in that behalf by the Governor, or for the trial of offences punishable with death, transportation for life, or imprisonment for a term of not less than five years under the Indian Penal Code or under any other law for the time being applicable to such district or region, confer on the District Council or the Regional Council having authority over such district or region or on courts constituted by such District Council or on any officer appointed in that behalf by the Governor, such powers under the Code of Civil Procedure, 1908, or, as the case may be, the Code of Criminal Procedure, 1898[2], as he deems appropriate, and thereupon the said Council, court or officer shall try the suits, cases or offences in exercise of the powers so conferred.

(2) The Governor may withdraw or modify any of the powers conferred on a District Council, Regional Council, court or officer under sub-paragraph (1) of this paragraph.

(3) Save as expressly provided in this paragraph, the Code of Civil Procedure, 1908, and the Code of Criminal Procedure, 1898[2], shall not apply to the trial of any suits, cases or offences in an autonomous district or in any autonomous region to which the provisions of this paragraph apply.

[3][(4) On and from the date appointed by the President under sub-paragraph (5) of paragraph 4 in relation to any autonomous district or autonomous region, nothing contained in this paragraph shall, in its application to that district or region, be deemed to authorise the Governor to confer on the District Council or Regional Council or on courts constituted by the District Council any of the powers referred to in sub-paragraph (1) of this paragraph.]

---

1. Paragraph 4 has been amended in its application to the State of Assam by the Sixth Schedule to the Constitution (Amendment) Act, 2003 (44 of 2003), sec. 2(6) (w.e.f. 7-9-2003), so as to insert after sub-paragraph (5), the following sub-paragraph, namely:—

   "(6) Nothing in this paragraph shall apply to the Bodoland Territorial Council consituted under the proviso to sub-paragraph (3) of paragraph 2 of this Schedule."

2. *See* now the Code of Criminal Procedure, 1973 (2 of 1974).

3. Ins. by the Assam Reorganisation (Meghalaya) Act, 1969 (55 of 1969), sec. 74 and Fourth Sch. (w.e.f. 2-4-1970).

¹[**6. Powers of the District Council to establish primary schools, etc.**—(1) The District Council for an autonomous district may establish, construct, or manage primary schools, dispensaries, markets, ²[cattle pounds], ferries, fisheries, roads, road transport and waterways in the district and may, with the previous approval of the Governor, make regulations for the regulation and control thereof and, in particular, may prescribe the language and the manner in which primary education shall be imparted in the primary schools in the district.

(2) The Governor may, with the consent of any District Council, entrust either conditionally or unconditionally to that Council or to its officers functions in relation to agriculture, animal husbandry, community projects, co-operative societies, social welfare, village planning or any other matter to which the executive power of the State ³[***] extends.]

7. District and Regional Funds.—(1) There shall be constituted for each autonomous district, a District Fund for each autonomous region, a Regional Fund to which shall be credited all moneys received respectively by the District Council for that district and the Regional Council for that region in the course of the administration of such district or region, as the case may be, in accordance with the provisions of this Constitution.

⁴[(2) The Governor may make rules for the management of the District Fund, or, as the case may be, the Regional Fund and for the procedure to be followed in respect of payment of money into the said Fund, the withdrawal of moneys therefrom, the custody of moneys therein and any other matter connected with or ancillary to the matters aforesaid.

(3) The accounts of the District Council or, as the case may be, the Regional Council shall be kept in such form as the Comptroller and Auditor-General of India may, with the approval of the President, prescribe.

(4) The Comptroller and Auditor-General shall cause the accounts of the District and Regional Councils to be audited in such manner as he may think fit, and the reports of the Comptroller and Auditor General relating to such accounts shall be submitted to the Governor who shall cause them to be laid before the Council.]

8. Powers to assess and collect land revenue and to impose taxes.—(1) The Regional Council for an autonomous region in respect of all lands within such region and the District Council for an autonomous district in respect of all lands within the district except those which are in the areas under the authority of Regional Councils, if any, within the district, shall have the power to assess and collect revenue in respect of such lands in accordance with the principles for the time being followed ⁵[by the Government of the State in assessing lands for the purpose of land revenue in the State generally].

(2) The Regional Council for an autonomous region in respect of areas within such region and the District Council for an autonomous district in respect of all areas in the

---

1. Subs. by the Assam Reorganisation (Meghalaya) Act, 1969 (55 of 1969), sec. 74 and Fourth Sch., for paragraph 6 (w.e.f. 2-4-1970).

2. Subs. by the Repealing and Amending Act, 1974 (56 of 1974), sec. 4 , for "cattle ponds" (w.e.f. 20-12-1974).

3. The words "of Assam or Meghalaya, as the case may be," omitted by the North-Eastern Areas (Reorganisation) Act, 1971 (81 of 1971), sec. 71(i) and Eighth Sch. (w.e.f. 21-1-1972).

4. Subs. by the Assam Reorganisation (Meghalaya) Act, 1969 (55 of 1969), sec. 74 and Fourth Sch., for sub-paragraph (2) (w.e.f. 2-4-1970).

5. Subs. by the North-Eastern Areas (Reorganisation) Act, 1971 (81 of 1971), sec. 71(i) and Eighth Sch., for certain words (w.e.f. 21-1-1972).

district except those which are under the authority of Regional Councils, if any, within the district, shall have power to levy and collect taxes on lands and buildings, and tolls on persons resident within such areas.

(3) The District Council for an autonomous district shall have the power to levy and collect all or any of the following taxes within such district, that is to say—

(a) taxes on professions, trades, callings and employments;

(b) taxes on animals, vehicles and boats;

(c) taxes on the entry of goods into a market for sale therein, and tolls on passengers and goods carried in ferries; and

(d) taxes for the maintenance of schools, dispensaries or roads.

(4) A Regional Council or District Council, as the case may be, may make regulations to provide for levy and collection of any of the taxes specified in sub-paragraphs (2) and (3) of this paragraph [1][and every such regulation shall be submitted forthwith to the Governor and, until assented to by him, shall have no effect].

[3]**9. Licences or leases for the purpose of prospecting for, or extraction of, minerals.**— (1) Such share of the royalties accruing each year from licences or leases for the purpose of prospecting for, or the extraction of, minerals granted by [2][the Government of the State] in respect of any area within an autonomous district as may be agreed upon between [2][the Government of the State] and the District Court of such district shall be made over to that District Council.

(2) If any dispute arises as to the share of such royalties to be made over to a District Council, it shall be referred to the Governor for determination and the amount determined by the Governor in his discretion shall be deemed to be the amount payable under sub-paragraph (1) of this paragraph to the District Council and the decision of the Governor shall be final.

[4]**10. Power of District Council to make regulations for the control of money-lending and trading by non-tribals.**—(1) The District Council of an autonomous district may make regulations for the regulation and control of money-lending or trading within the district by persons other than Scheduled Tribes resident in the district.

---

1. Ins. by the Assam Reorganisation (Meghalaya) Act, 1969 (55 of 1969) sec. 74 and Fourth Sch. (w.e.f. 2-4-1970).

2. Subs. by the North-Eastern Areas (Reorganisation) Act, 1971 (81 of 1971), sec. 71(i) and Eighth Sch., for "the Government of Assam" (w.e.f. 21-1-1972).

3. Paragraph 9 has been amended in its application to the States of Tripura and Mizoram by the Sixth Schedule to the Constitution (Amendment) Act, 1988 (67 of 1988), sec. 2(1) (w.e.f. 16-12-1988), so as to insert after sub-paragraph (2), the following sub-paragraph namely:—

    "(3) The Governor may, by order, direct that the share of royalties to be made over to a District Council under this paragraph shall be made over to that Council within a period of one year from the date of any agreement under sub-paragraph (1) or, as the case may be, of any determination under sub-paragraph (2)."

4. Paragraph 10 has been amended in its application to the States of Tripura and Mizoram by the Sixth Schedule to the Constitution (Amendment) Act, 1988 (67 of 1988), sec. 2(2) (w.e.f. 16-12-1988), as under:

    (a) in the heading, the words "by non-tribals" shall be omitted;

    (b) in sub-paragraph (1), the words "other than Scheduled Tribes" shall be omitted;

    (c) in sub-paragraph (2), for clause (d), the following clause shall be substituted, namely:—

    "(d) prescribe that no person resident in the district shall carry on any trade, whether wholesale or retail, except under a licence issued in that behalf by the District Council."

(2) In particular and without prejudice to the generality of the foregoing power, such regulations may—

(a) prescribe that no one except the holder of a licence issued in that behalf shall carry on the business of money-lending;

(b) prescribe the maximum rate of interest which may be charged or be recovered by a money-lender;

(c) provide for the maintenance of accounts by money-lenders and for the inspection of such accounts by officers appointed in that behalf by the District Council;

(d) prescribe that no person who is not a member of the Scheduled Tribes resident in the district shall carry on wholesale or retail business in any commodity except under a licence issued in that behalf by the District Council:

Provided that no regulations may be made under this paragraph unless they are passed by a majority of not less than three-fourths of the total membership of the District Council:

Provided further that it shall not be competent under any such regulations to refuse the grant of a licence to a money-lender or a trader who has been carrying on business within the district since before the time of making of such regulations.

(3) All regulations made under this paragraph shall be submitted forthwith to the Governor and, until assented to by him, shall have no effect.[1]

11. Publication of laws, rules and regulations made under the Schedule.—All laws, rules and regulations made under this Schedule by a District Council or a Regional Council shall be published forthwith in the Official Gazette of the State and shall on such publication have the force of law.

[2][**12. [3][Application of Acts of Parliament and of the Legislature of the State of Assam to autonomous districts and autonomous regions in the State of Assam].**—(1) Notwithstanding anything in this Constitution—

(a) no Act of the [4][Legislature of the State of Assam] in respect of any of the matters specified in paragraph 3 of this Schedule as matters with respect to which a District Council or a Regional Council may make laws, and no Act of the [4][Legislature of the State of Assam] prohibiting or restricting the consumption of any non-distilled alcoholic liquor shall apply to any autonomous district or autonomous region [5][in the State] unless in either case the District Council for

---

1. Paragraph 10 has been amended in its application to the State of Assam by the Sixth Schedule to the Constitution (Amendment) Act, 2003 (44 of 2003), sec. 2(7) (w.e.f. 7-9-2003), so as to insert after sub-paragraph (3), the following sub-paragraph, namely:—

   "(4) Nothing in this paragraph shall apply to the Bodoland Territorial Council constituted under the proviso to sub-paragraph (3) of paragraph 2 of this Schedule."

2. Paragraph 12 has been amended in its application to the State of Assam by the Sixth Schedule to the Constitution (Amendment) Act, 1995 (42 of 1995), sec. 2(4) (w.e.f. 12-9-1995), so as to substitute in sub-paragraph (1), for the words and figure "matters specified in paragraph 3 of this Schedule", the words, figures and letter "matters specified in paragraph 3 or paragraph 3A of this Schedule".

3. Subs. by the North-Eastern Areas (Reorganisation) Act, 1971 (81 of 1971), sec. 71(i) and Eighth Sch., for the heading (w.e.f. 21-1-1972).

4. Subs. by the North-Eastern Areas (Reorganisation) Act, 1971 (81 of 1971), sec. 71(i) and Eighth Sch., for "Legislature of the State" (w.e.f. 21-1-1972).

5. Ins. by the North-Eastern Areas (Reorganisation) Act, 1971 (81 of 1971), sec. 71(i) and Eighth Sch., (w.e.f. 21-1-1972).

such district or having jurisdiction over such region by public notification so directs, and the District Council in giving such direction with respect to any Act may direct that the Act shall in its application to such district or region or any part thereof have effect subject to such exceptions or modifications as it thinks fit;[1]

(b) the Governor may, by public notification, direct that any Act of Parliament or of the [2][Legislature of the State of Assam] to which the provisions of clause (a) of this sub-paragraph do not apply shall not apply to an autonomous district or an autonomous region [3][in that State], or shall apply to such district or region or any part thereof subject to such exceptions or modifications as he may specify in the notification.

(2) Any direction given under sub-paragraph (1) of this paragraph may be given so as to have retrospective effect.

[4][**12A. Application of Acts of Parliament and of the Legislature of the State of Meghalaya to autonomous districts and autonomous regions in the State of Meghalaya.**—Notwithstanding anything in this Constitution,—

(a) if any provision of a law made by a District or Regional Council in the State of Meghalaya with respect to any matter specified in sub-paragraph (1) of paragraph 3 of this Schedule or if any provision of any regulation made by a District Council or a Regional Council in that State under paragraph 8 or paragraph 10 of this Schedule, is repugnant to any provision of a law made by the Legislature of the State of Meghalaya with respect to that matter, then, the law or regulation made by the District Council or, as the case may be, the Regional Council whether made before or after the law made by the Legislature of the State of Meghalaya, shall, to the extent of repugnancy, be void and the law made by the Legislature of the State of Meghalaya shall prevail;

(b) the President may, with respect to any Act of Parliament, by notification, direct that it shall not apply to an autonomous district or an autonomous region in the State of Meghalaya, or shall apply to such district or region or any part thereof subject to such exceptions or modifications as he may specify in the notification and any such direction may be given so as to have retrospective effect.]

[5][**12AA. Application of Acts of Parliament and of the Legislature of the State of Tripura to the autonomous district and autonomous regions in the State of Tripura.**— Notwithstanding anything in this Constitution,—

(a) no Act of the Legislature of the State of Tripura in respect of any of the matters specified in paragraph 3 of this Schedule as matters with respect to which a

---

1. Paragraph 12 has been amended in its application to the State of Assam by the Sixth Schedule to the Constitution (Amendment) Act, 2003 (44 of 2003), sec. 2(8) (w.e.f. 7-9-2003), so as to substitute in sub-paragraph (1), in clause (a), for the words, figures and letter "matters specified in paragraph 3 or paragraph 3A of this Schedule the words, figures and letters "matters specified in paragraph 3 or paragraph 3A or paragraph 3B of this Schedule".

2. Subs. by the North-Eastern Areas (Reorganisation) Act, 1971 (81 of 1971), sec. 71(i) and Eighth Sch., for "Legislature of the State" (w.e.f. 21-1-1972).

3. Ins. by the North-Eastern Areas (Reorganisation) Act, 1971 (81 of 1971), sec. 71(i) and Eighth Sch., (w.e.f. 21-1-1972).

4. Subs. by the North-Eastern Areas (Reorganisation) Act, 1971 (81 of 1971), sec. 71(i) and Eighth Sch., for paragraph 12A (w.e.f. 21-1-1972). Earlier paragraph 12A was inserted by the Assam Reorgnisation (Meghalaya) Act, 1969 (55 of 1969), sec. 74 and Fourth sch. (w.e.f. 2-4-1970).

5. Subs. by the Sixth Schedule to the Constitution (Amendment) Act, 1988 (67 of 1988), sec. 2(3) (w.e.f. 16-12-1988), for paragraph 12AA. Earlier paragraph 12AA was inserted by the Constitution (Forty-ninth Amendment) Act, 1984, sec. 4(c) (w.e.f. 1-4-1985).

District Council or a Regional Council may make laws, and no Act of the Legislature of the State of Tripura prohibiting or restricting the consumption of any non-distilled alcoholic liquor shall apply to the autonomous district or an autonomous region in that State unless, in either case, the District Council for that district or having jurisdiction over such region by public notification so directs, and the District Council in giving such direction with respect to any Act direct that the Act shall, in its application to that district or such region or any part thereof, have effect subject to such exceptions or modifications as it thinks fit;

(b) the Governor may, by public notification, direct that any Act of the Legislature of the State of Tripura to which the provisions of clause (a) of this sub-paragraph do not apply, shall not apply to the autonomous district or any autonomous region in that State, or shall apply to that district or such region, or any part thereof, subject to such exceptions or modifications, as he may specify in the notification;

(c) the President may, with respect to any Act of Parliament, by notification, direct that it shall not apply to the autonomous district or an autonomous region in the State of Tripura, or shall apply to such district or region or any part thereof, subject to such exceptions or modifications as he may specify in the notification and any such direction may be given so as to have retrospective effect.]

¹[**12B. Application of Acts of Parliament and of the Legislature of the State of Mizoram to autonomous districts and autonomous regions in the State of Mizoram.**— Notwithstanding anything in this Constitution,—

(a) no Act of the Legislature of the State of Mizoram in respect of any of the matters specified in paragraph 3 of this Schedule as matters with respect to which a District Council or a Regional Council may make laws, and no Act of Legislature of the State of Mizoram prohibiting or restricting the consumption of any non-distilled alcoholic liquor shall apply to any autonomous district or autonomous region in that State unless, in either case, the District Council for such district or having jurisdiction over such region, by public notification, so directs, and the District Council, in giving such direction with respect to any Act, may direct that the Act shall, in its application to such district or region or any part thereof, have effect subject to such exceptions or modifications as it thinks fit;

(b) the Governor may, by public notification, direct that any Act of the Legislature of the State of Mizoram to which the provisions of clause (a) of this sub-paragraph do not apply, shall not apply to an autonomous district or an autonomous region in that State, or shall apply to such district or region, or any part thereof, subject to such exceptions or modifications, as he may specify in the notification;

(c) the President may, with respect to any Act of Parliament, by notification, direct that it shall not apply to an autonomous district or an autonomous region in the State of Mizoram, or shall apply to such district or region or any part thereof, subject to such exceptions or modifications as he may specify in the notification and any such direction may be given so as to have retrospective effect.]

13. Estimated receipts and expenditure pertaining to autonomous districts to be shown separately in the annual financial statement.—The estimated receipts and expenditure pertaining to an autonomous district which are to be credited to, or is to be

---

1. Subs. by the Sixth Schedule to the Constitution (Amendment) Act, 1988 (67 of 1988), sec. 2(3), for paragraph 12B (w.e.f. 16-12-1988). Earlier paragraph 12B was substituted by the North-Eastern (Reorganisation) Act, 1971 (81 of 1971), sec. 71(i) and Eighth Sch. (w.e.f. 21-1-1972) and again substituted by the Government of Union Territories (Amendment) Act, 1971 (83 of 1971), sec. 13(i) (w.e.f. 29-4-1972).

made from, the Consolidated Fund of the State ¹[***] shall be first placed before the District Council for discussion and then after such discussion be shown separately in the annual financial statement of the State to be laid before the Legislature of the State under article 202.

²14. Appointment of Commission to inquire into and report on the administration of autonomous districts and autonomous regions.—(1) The Governor may at any time appoint a Commission to examine and report on any matter specified by him relating to the administration of the autonomous districts and autonomous regions in the State, including matters specified in clauses (c), (d), (e) and (f) of sub-paragraph (3) of paragraph 1 of this Schedule, or may appoint a Commission to inquire into and report from time to time on the administration of autonomous districts and autonomous regions in the State generally and in particular on—

(a) the provision of educational and medical facilities and communications in such districts and regions;

(b) the need for any new or special legislation in respect of such districts and regions; and

(c) the administration of the laws, rules and regulations made by the District and Regional Councils,

and define the procedure to be followed by such Commission.

(2) The report of every such Commission with the recommendations of the Governor with respect thereto shall be laid before the Legislature of the State by the Minister concerned together with an explanatory memorandum regarding the action proposed to be taken thereon by ³[the Government of the State].

(3) In allocating the business of the Government of the State among his Ministers the Governor may place one of his Ministers specially in charge of the welfare of the autonomous districts and autonomous regions in the State.

⁴15. Annulment or suspension of acts and resolutions of District and Regional Councils.—(1) If at any time the Governor is satisfied that an act or resolution of a District or a Regional Council is likely to endanger the safety of India ⁵[or is likely to be prejudicial to public order], he may annul or suspend such act or resolution and take such steps as he may consider necessary (including the suspension of the Council and the assumption to himself of all or any of the powers vested in or exercisable by the Council) to prevent the commission or continuance of such act, or the giving of effect to such resolution.

---

1. The words "of Assam" omitted by the North-Eastern Areas (Reorganisation) Act, 1971 (81 of 1971), sec. 71(i) and Eighth Sch. (w.e.f. 21-1-1972).
2. Paragraph 14 has been amended in its application to the State of Assam by the Sixth Schedule to the Constitution (Amendment) Act, 1995 (42 of 1995), sec. 2(5) (w.e.f. 12-9-1995), so as to omit in sub-paragraph (2), the words "with the recommendations of the Governor with respect thereto".
3. Subs. by the North-Eastern Areas (Reorganisation) Act, 1971 (81 of 1971), sec. 71(i) and Eighth Sch., for "the Government of Assam" (w.e.f. 21-1-1972).
4. Paragraph 15 has been amended in its application to the States of Tripura and Mizoram by the Sixth Schedule to the Constitution (Amendment) Act, 1988 (67 of 1988), sec. 2(4) (w.e.f. 16-12-1988), so as to—
   (a) in sub-paragraph (2), for the words "by the Legislature of the State", the words "by him" shall be substituted.
   (b) the proviso shall be omitted.
5. Ins. by the Assam Reorganisation (Meghalaya) Act, 1969 (55 of 1969), sec. 74 and Fourth Sch. (w.e.f. 2-4-1970).

(2) Any order made by the Governor under sub-paragraph (1) of this paragraph together with the reasons therefor shall be laid before the Legislature of the State as soon as possible and the order shall, unless revoked by the Legislature of the State, continue in force for a period of twelve months from the date on which it was so made:

Provided that if and so often as a resolution approving the continuance in force of such order is passed by the Legislature of the State, the order shall unless cancelled by the Governor continue in force for a further period of twelve months from the date on which under this paragraph it would otherwise have ceased to operate.

[1]**16. Dissolution of a District or a Regional Council.**—[2][(1)] The Governor may on the recommendation of a Commission appointed under paragraph 14 of this Schedule by public notification order the dissolution of a District or a Regional Council, and—

(a) direct that a fresh general election shall be held immediately for the reconstitution of the Council, or

(b) subject to the previous approval of the Legislature of the State assume the administration of the area under the authority of such Council himself or place the administration of such area under the Commission appointed under the said paragraph or any other body considered suitable by him for a period not exceeding twelve months:

Provided that when an order under clause (a) of this paragraph has been made, the Governor may take the action referred to in clause (b) of this paragraph with regard to the administration of the area in question pending the reconstitution of the Council on fresh general election:

Provided further that no action shall be taken under clause (b) of this paragraph without giving the District or the Regional Council, as the case may be, an opportunity of placing its views before the Legislature of the State.

[3][(2) If at any time the Governor is satisfied that a situation has arisen in which the administration of an autonomous district or region cannot be carried on in accordance with the provisions of this Schedule, he may, by public notification assume to himself all or any of the functions or powers vested in or exercisable by the District Council or, as the case may be, the Regional Council and declare that such functions or powers shall be exercisable by such person or authority as he may specify in this behalf, for a period not exceeding six months:

Provided that the Governor may by a further order or orders extend the operation of the initial order by a period not exceeding six months on each occasion.

(3) Every order made under sub-paragraph (2) of this paragraph with the reasons therefor shall be laid before the Legislature of the State and shall cease to operate at the expiration of thirty days from the date on which the State Legislature first sits after the

---

1. Paragraph 16 has been amended in its application to the States of Tripura and Mizoram by the Sixth Schedule to the Constitution (Amendment) Act, 1988 (67 of 1988), sec. 2(5) (w.e.f. 16-12-1988), as under:

    (a) in sub-paragraph (1), the words "subject to the previous approval of the Legislature of the State" occurring in clause (b), and the second proviso shall be omitted;

    (b) for sub-paragraph (3), the following sub-paragraph shall be substituted, namely:—
        "(3) Every order made under sub-paragraph (1) or sub-paragraph (2) of this paragraph, along with the reasons therefor shall be laid before the Legislature of the State."

2. Paragraph 16 renumbered as sub-paragraph (1) thereof by the Assam Reorganisation (Meghalaya) Act, 1969 (55 of 1969), sec. 74 and Fourth Sch. (w.e.f. 2-4-1970).

3. Ins. by the Assam Reorganisation (Meghalaya) Act, 1969 (55 of 1969), sec. 74 and Fourth Sch. (w.e.f. 2-4-1970).

issue of the orders, unless, before the expiry of that period it has been approved by that State Legislature.]

¹**17. Exclusion of areas from autonomous districts in forming constituencies in such districts.**—For the purposes of elections to ²[the Legislative Assembly of Assam or Meghalaya] ³[or Tripura] ⁴[or Mizoram], the Governor may by order declare that any area within an autonomous district ⁵[in the State of Assam or Meghalaya ³[or Tripura] ⁴[or Mizoram], as the case may be,] shall not form part of any constituency to fill a seat or seats in the Assembly reserved for any such district but shall form part of a constituency to fill a seat or seats in the Assembly not so reserved to be specified in the order.

⁶[***]

⁷**19. Transitional provisions.**—(1) As soon as possible after the commencement of this Constitution the Governor shall take steps for the constitution of a District Council for each autonomous district in the State under this Schedule and, until a District Council is so constituted for an autonomous district, the administration of such district shall be vested in the Governor and the following provisions shall apply to the administration of the areas within such district instead of the foregoing provisions of this Schedule, namely:—

(a) no Act of Parliament or of the Legislature of the State shall apply to any such area unless the Governor by public notification so directs; and the Governor in giving such a direction with respect to any Act may direct that the Act shall, in its application to the area or to any specified part thereof, have effect subject to such exceptions or modifications as he thinks fit;

(b) the Governor may make regulations for the peace and good government of any such area and any regulations so made may repeal or amend any Act of Parliament or of the Legislature of the State or any existing law which is for the time being applicable to such area.

(2) Any direction given by the Governor under clause (a) of sub-paragraph (1) of this paragraph may be given so as to have retrospective effect.

(3) All regulations made under clause (b) of sub-paragraph (1) of this paragraph shall be submitted forthwith to the President and, until assented to by him, shall have no effect.

---

1. Paragraph 17 has been amended in its application to the Sate of Assam by the Sixth Schedule to the Constitution (Amendment) Act, 2003 (44 of 2003), sec. 2(9) (w.e.f. 7-9-2003), so as to insert the following proviso, namely:—

    "Provided that nothing in this paragraph shall apply to the Bodoland Territorial Areas District."

2. Subs. by the North-Eastern Areas (Reorganisation) Act, 1971 (81 of 1971), sec. 71(i) and Eighth Sch., for "the Legislative Assembly of Assam" (w.e.f. 21-1-1972).

3. Ins. by the Constitution (Forty-ninth Amendment) Act, 1984, sec. 4(d) (w.e.f. 1-4-1985).

4. Ins. by the State of Mizoram Act, 1986 (34 of 1986), sec. 39(f) (w.e.f. 20-2-1987).

5. Ins. by the North-Eastern Areas (Reorganisation) Act, 1971 (81 of 1971), sec. 71(i) and Eighth Sch. (w.e.f. 21-1-1972).

6. Paragraph 18 omitted by the North-Eastern Areas (Reorganisation) Act, 1971 (81 of 1971), sec. 71(i) and Eighth Sch. (w.e.f. 21-1-1972). Earlier paragraph 18 was amended by the Constitution (Seventh Amendment) Act, 1956 (1 of 1956), sec. 29 and Sch. (w.e.f. 1-11-1956).

7. Paragraph 19 has been amended in its application to the State of Assam by the Sixth Schedule to the Constitution (Amendment) Act, 2003 (44 of 2003), sec. 2(10) (w.e.f. 7-9-2003), so as to insert after sub-paragraph (3), the following sub-paragraph, namely:—

(Contd. on next page)

[1][20. Tribal areas.—(1) The areas specified in Parts I, II [2][,IIA] and III of the table below shall respectively be the tribal areas within the State of Assam, the State of Meghalaya [3][, the State of Tripura] and the [4][State] of Mizoram.

(2) [5][Any reference in Part I, Part II or Part III of the table below] to any district shall be construed as a reference to the territories comprised within the autonomous district of that name existing immediately before the day appointed under clause (b) of section 2 of the North-Eastern Areas (Reorganisation) Act, 1971:

Provided that for the purposes of clauses (e) and (f) of sub-paragraph (1) of paragraph 3, paragraph 4, paragraph 5, paragraph 6, sub-paragraph (2), clauses (a), (b) and (d) of sub-paragraph (3) and sub-paragraph (4) of paragraph 8 and clause (d) of sub-paragraph (2) of paragraph 10 of this Schedule, no part of the area comprised within the municipality of Shillong shall be deemed to be within the [6][Khasi Hills District].]

[7][(3) The reference in Part IIA in the table below to the "Tripura Tribal Areas District" shall be construed as a reference to the territory comprising the tribal areas specified in the First Schedule to the Tripura Tribal Areas Autonomous District Council Act, 1979.]

TABLE
[8]PART I

1. The North Cachar Hills District.
2. [9][The Karbi Anglong District.]

(Contd. from previous page)

"(4) As soon as possible after the commencement of this Act, an Interim Executive Council for Bodoland Territorial Areas District in Assam shall be formed by the Governor from amongst leaders of the Bodo movement, including the signatories to the Memorandum of Settlement, and shall provide adequate representation to the non-tribal communities in that area:

Provided that the Interim Council shall for a period of six months during which endeavour to hold the election to the Council shall be made.

Explanation.—For the purposes of this sub-paragraph, the expression "Memorandum of Settlement" means the Memorandum signed on the 10th day of February, 2003 between Government of India, Government of Assam and Bodo Liberation Tigres."

1. Subs. by the North-Eastern Areas (Reorganisation) Act, 1971 (81 of 1971), sec. 71(i) and Eighth Sch., for paragraphs 20 and 20A (w.e.f. 21-1-1972). Earlier paragraph 20 was amended by the State of Nagaland Act, 1962 (27 of 1962), sec. 5 (w.e.f. 1-12-1963) and paragraph 20A was inserted by the Assam Reorganisation (Meghalaya) Act, 1969 (55 of 1969), sec. 74 and Eighth Sch. (w.e.f. 2-4-1970).
2. Ins. by the Constitution (Forty-ninth Amendment) Act, 1984, sec. 4(e)(i)(A) (w.e.f. 1-4-1985).
3. Ins. by the Constitution (Forty-ninth Amendment) Act, 1984, sec. 4(e)(i)(B) (w.e.f. 1-4-1985).
4. Subs. by the State of Mizoram Act, 1986 (34 of 1986), sec. 39(f), for "Union territory" (w.e.f. 20-2-1987).
5. Subs. by the Constitution (Forty-ninth Amendment) Act, 1984, sec. 4(ii), for "Any reference in the table below" (w.e.f. 1-4-1985).
6. Subs. by the Government of Meghalaya Notification DCA 31/72/11, dated the 14th June, 1973, published in the Gazette of Meghalaya, Pt. VA, dated 23rd June, 1973, p. 200.
7. Ins. by the Constitution (Forty-ninth Amendment) Act, 1984, sec. 4(e)(iii) (w.e.f. 1-4-1985).
8. Paragraph 20 has been amended in its application to the State of Assam by the Sixth Schedule to the Constitution (Amendment) Act, 2003 (44 of 2003), sec. 2(11) (w.e.f. 7-9-2003), so as to insert in Part I of the Table, after entry 2, the following, namely:—
   "3. The Bodoland Territorial Areas District.".
9. Subs. by the Government of Assam Notification T-A D/R/115/74/47, dated 14th October, 1976, for "The Mikir Hills District".

PART II

¹[1. Khasi Hills District.

2. Jaintia Hills District.]

3. The Garo Hills District.

²[PART IIA

Tripura Tribal Areas District.]

PART III

³[***]

⁴[1. The Chakma District.

⁵[2. The Mara District.

3. The Lai District.]]

⁶[**20A. Dissolution of the Mizo District Council.**—(1) Notwithstanding anything in this Schedule, the District Council of the Mizo District existing immediately before the prescribed date (hereinafter referred to as the Mizo District Council) shall stand dissolved and cease to exist.

(2) The Administrator of the Union territory of Mizoram may, by one or more orders, provide for all or any of the following matters, namely:—

(a) the transfer, in whole or in part, of the assets, rights and liabilities of the Mizo District Council (including the rights and liabilities under any contract made by it) to the Union or to any other authority;

(b) the substitution of the Union or any other authority for the Mizo District Council, or the addition of the Union or any other authority, as a party to any legal proceedings to which the Mizo District Council is a party;

(c) the transfer or re-employment of any employees of the Mizo District Council to or by the Union or any other authority, the terms and conditions of service applicable to such employees after such transfer or re-employment;

(d) the continuance of any laws, made by the Mizo District Council and in force immediately before its dissolution, subject to such adaptations and modifications, whether by way of repeal or amendment, as the Administrator may make in this behalf, until such laws are altered, repealed or amended by a competent Legislature or other competent authority;

(e) such incidental, consequential and supplementary matters as the Administrator considers necessary.

---

1. Subs. by the Government of Meghalaya Notification DCA 31/72/11, dated 14th June, 1973, published in the Gazette of Meghalaya, Pt. VA, dated 23rd June, 1973, p. 200.
2. Ins. by the Constitution (Forty-ninth Amendment) Act, 1984, sec. 4(f) (w.e.f. 1-4-1985).
3. The words "The Mizo District" omitted by the Government of Union Territories (Amendment) Act, 1971 (83 of 1971), sec. 13 (w.e.f. 29-4-1972).
4. Ins. by the Mizoram District Councils (Miscellaneous Provisions) Order, 1972, published in the Mizoram Gazette, 1972, dated the 5th May, 1972, Vol. 1, Pt. II, p. 17 (w.e.f. 29-4-1972).
5. Subs. by the Sixth Schedule to the Constitution (Amendment) Act, 1988 (67 of 1988), sec. 2(6) (w.e.f. 16-12-1988), for serial numbers 2 and 3 and the entries relating thereto.
6. Subs. by the Government of Union Territories (Amendment) Act, 1971 (83 of 1971), sec. 13(iii), for paragraph 20A (w.e.f. 29-4-1972). Earlier paragraph 20A was inserted by the Assam Reorganisation (Meghalaya) Act, 1969 (55 of 1969), sec. 74 and Fourth Sch. (w.e.f. 2-4-1970).

Explanation.—In this paragraph and in paragraph 20B of this Schedule, the expression "prescribed date" means the date on which the Legislative Assembly of the Union territory of Mizoram is duly constituted under and in accordance with the provisions of the Government of Union Territories Act, 1963 (20 of 1963).

[1][20B. **Autonomous regions in the Union territory of Mizoram to be autonomous districts and transitory provisions consequent thereto.**—(1) Notwithstanding anything in this Schedule,—

(a) every autonomous region existing immediately before the prescribed date in the Union territory of Mizoram shall, on and from that date, be an autonomous district in that Union territory (hereafter referred to as the corresponding new district) and the Administrator thereof may, by one or more orders, direct that such consequential amendments as are necessary to give effect to the provisions of this clause shall be made in paragraph 20 of this Schedule (including Part III of the table appended to that paragraph) and thereupon the said paragraph and the said Part III shall be deemed to have been amended accordingly;

(b) every Regional Council of an autonomous region in the Union territory of Mizoram existing immediately before the prescribed date (hereafter referred to as the existing Regional Council) shall, on and from that date and until a District Council is duly constituted for the corresponding new district, be deemed to be the District Council of that district (hereafter referred to as the corresponding new District Council).

(2) Every member whether elected or nominated of an existing Regional Council shall be deemed to have been elected or, as the case may be, nominated to the corresponding new District Council and shall hold office until a District Council is duly constituted for the corresponding new district under this Schedule.

(3) Until rules are made under sub-paragraph (7) of paragraph 2 and sub-paragraph (4) of paragraph 4 of this Schedule by the corresponding new District Council, the rules made under the said provisions by the existing Regional Council and in force immediately before the prescribed date shall have effect in relation to the corresponding new District Council subject to such adaptations and modifications as may be made therein by the Administrator of the Union territory of Mizoram.

(4) The Administrator of the Union territory of Mizoram may, by one or more orders, provide for all or any of the following matters, namely:—

(a) the transfer in whole or in part of the assets, rights and liabilities of the existing Regional Council (including the rights and liabilities under any contract made by it) to the corresponding new District Council;

(b) the substitution of the corresponding new District Council for the existing Regional Council as a party to the legal proceedings to which the existing Regional Council is a party;

(c) the transfer or re-employment of any employees of the existing Regional Council to or by the corresponding new District Council, the terms and conditions of service applicable to such employees after such transfer or re-employment;

(d) the continuance of any laws made by the existing Regional Council and in force immediately before the prescribed date, subject to such adaptations and modifications, whether by way of repeal or amendment, as the Administrator may

---

1. Subs. by the Government of Union Territories (Amendment) Act, 1971 (83 of 1971), sec. 13(iii), for paragraph 20A (w.e.f. 29-4-1972).

make in this behalf until such laws are altered, repealed or amended by a competent Legislature or other competent authority;

(e) such incidental, consequential and supplementary matters as the Administrator considers necessary.[1]

[2][**20C. Interpretation.**—Subject to any provision made in this behalf, the provisions of this Schedule shall, in their application to the Union territory of Mizoram, have effect—

(1) as if references to the Governor and Government of the State were references to the Administrator of the Union territory appointed under article 239, references to State (except in the expression "Government of the State") were references to the Union territory of Mizoram and references to the State Legislature were references to the Legislative Assembly of the Union territory of Mizoram;

(2) as if—

(a) in sub-paragraph (5) of paragraph 4, the provision for consultation with the Government of the State concerned had been omitted;

(b) in sub-paragraph (2) of paragraph 6, for the words "to which the executive power of the State extends", the words "with respect to which the Legislative Assembly of the Union territory of Mizoram has power to make laws" had been substituted;

(c) in paragraph 13, the words and figures "under article 202" had been omitted.]

21. Amendment of the Schedule.—(1) Parliament may from time to time by law amend by way of addition, variation or repeal any of the provisions of this Schedule and, when the Schedule is so amended, any reference to this Schedule in this Constitution shall be construed as a reference to such Schedule as so amended.

---

1. After paragraph 20B, the following paragraph has been inserted in its application to the State of Assam by the Sixth Schedule to the Constitution (Amendment) Act, 1995 (42 of 1995), sec. 2(6) (w.e.f. 12-9-1995), namely:—

   "20BA. *Exercise of discretionary powers by the Governor in the discharge of his functions.*—The Governor in the discharge of his functions under sub-paragraphs (2) and (3) of paragraph 1, sub-paragraphs (1), (6), sub-paragraph (6A) excluding the first proviso and sub-paragraph (7) of paragraph 2, sub-paragraph (3) of paragraph 3, sub-paragraph (4) of paragraph 4, paragraph 5, sub-paragraph (1) of paragraph 6, sub-paragraph (2) of paragraph 7, sub-paragraph (4) of paragraph 8, sub-paragraph (3) of paragraph 9, sub-paragraph (3) of paragraph 10, sub-paragraph (1) of paragraph 14, sub-paragraph (1) of paragraph 15 and sub-paragraphs (1) and (2) of paragraph 16 of this Schedule, shall, after consulting the Council of Ministers and the North Cachar Hills Autonomous Council or the Karbi Anglong Autonomous Council, as the case may be, take such action as he considers necessary in his discretion."

   After paragraph 20B, the following paragraph has been inserted in its application to the State of Tripura and Mizoram, by the sixth Schedule to the Constitution (Amendment) Act, 1988 (67 of 1988), sec. 2(7) (w.e.f. 12-9-1995), namely:—

   "20BB. *Exercise of discretionary powers by the Governor in the discharge of his functions.*—The Governor, in the discharge of his functions under sub-paragraphs (2) and (3) of paragraph 1, sub-paragraphs (1) and (7) of paragraph 2, sub-paragraph (3) of paragraph 3, sub-paragraph (4) of paragraph 4, paragraph 5, sub-paragraph (1) of paragraph 6, sub-paragraph (2) of paragraph 7, sub-paragraph (3) of paragraph 9, sub-paragraph (1) of paragraph 14, sub-paragraph (1) of paragraph 15 and sub-paragraphs (1) and (2) of paragraph 16 of this Schedule, shall, after consulting the Council of Ministers, and if he thinks it necessary, the District Council or the Regional Council concerned, take such action as he considers necessary in his discretion."

2. Subs. by the Government of Union Territories (Amendment) Act, 1971 (83 of 1971), sec. 13(iii), for paragraph 20A (w.e.f. 29-4-1972).

(2) No such law as is mentioned in sub-paragraph (1) of this paragraph shall be deemed to be an amendment of this Constitution for the purposes of article 368.

SEVENTH SCHEDULE

(Article 246)

LIST I—UNION LIST

1. Defence of India and every part thereof including preparation for defence and all such acts as may be conducive in times of war to its prosecution and after its termination of effective demobilisation.

2. Naval, military and air forces; any other armed forces of the Union.

¹[2A. Deployment of any armed force of the Union or any other force subject to the control of the Union or any contingent or unit thereof in any State in aid of the civil power; powers, jurisdiction, privileges and liabilities of the members of such forces while on such deployment.]

3. Delimitation of cantonment areas, local self-government in such areas, the constitution and powers within such areas of cantonment authorities and the regulation of house accommodation (including the control of rents) in such areas.

4. Naval, military and air force works.

5. Arms, firearms, ammunition and explosives.

6. Atomic energy and mineral resources necessary for its production.

7. Industries declared by Parliament by law to be necessary for the purpose of defence or for the prosecution of war.

8. Central Bureau of Intelligence and Investigation.

9. Preventive detention for reasons connected with Defence, Foreign Affairs, or the security of India; persons subjected to such detention.

10. Foreign affairs; all matters which bring the Union into relation with any foreign country.

11. Diplomatic, consular and trade representation.

12. United Nations Organisation.

13. Participation in international conferences, associations and other bodies and implementing of decisions made thereat.

14. Entering into treaties and agreements with foreign countries and implementing of treaties, agreements and conventions with foreign countries.

15. War and peace.

16. Foreign jurisdiction.

17. Citizenship, naturalisation and aliens.

18. Extradition.

19. Admission into, and emigration and expulsion from, India; passports and visas.

20. Pilgrimages to places outside India.

21. Piracies and crimes committed on the high seas or in the air; offences against the law of nations committed on land or the high seas or in the air.

22. Railways.

---

1. Ins. by the Constitution (Forty-second Amendment) Act, 1976, sec. 57(a) (w.e.f. 3-1-1977).

23. Highways declared by or under law made by Parliament to be national highways.

24. Shipping and navigation on inland waterways, declared by Parliament by law to be national waterways, as regards mechanically propelled vessels; the rule of the road on such waterways.

25. Maritime shipping and navigation, including shipping and navigation on tidal waters; provision of education and training for the mercantile marine and regulation of such education and training provided by States and other agencies.

26. Lighthouses, including lightships, beacons and other provisions for the safety of shipping and aircraft.

27. Ports declared by or under law made by Parliament or existing law to be major ports, including their delimitation and the constitution and powers of port authorities therein.

28. Port quarantine, including hospitals connected therewith; seamen's and marine hospitals.

29. Airways; aircraft and air navigation; provision of aerodromes; regulation and organisation of air traffic and of aerodromes; provision for aeronautical education and training and regulation of such education and training provided by States and other agencies.

30. Carriage of passengers and goods by railway, sea or air, or by national waterways in mechanically propelled vessels.

31. Posts and telegraphs; telephones, wireless, broadcasting and other like forms of communication.

32. Property of the Union and the revenue therefrom, but as regards property situated in a State [1][***] subject to legislation by the State, save in so far as Parliament by law otherwise provides.

[2][***]

34. Courts of wards for the estates of Rulers of Indian States.

35. Public debt of the Union.

36. Currency, coinage and legal tender; foreign exchange.

37. Foreign loans.

38. Reserve Bank of India.

39. Post Office Savings Bank.

40. Lotteries organised by the Government of India or the Government of a State.

41. Trade and commerce with foreign countries; import and export across customs frontiers; definition of customs frontiers.

42. Inter-State trade and commerce.

43. Incorporation, regulation and winding up of trading corporations, including banking, insurance and financial corporations but not including co-operative societies.

44. Incorporation, regulation and winding up of corporations, whether trading or not, with objects not confined to one State, but not including universities.

---

1. The words and letters "specified in Part A or Part B of the First Schedule" omitted by the Constitution (Seventh Amendment) Act, 1956, sec. 29 and Sch. (w.e.f. 1-11-1956).

2. Entry 33 omitted by the Constitution (Seventh Amendment) Act, 1956, sec. 26 (w.e.f. 1-11-1956).

45. Banking.

46. Bills of exchange, cheques, promissory notes and other like instruments.

47. Insurance.

48. Stock exchanges and futures markets.

49. Patents, inventions and designs; copyright; trade-marks and merchandise marks.

50. Establishment of standards of weight and measure.

51. Establishment of standards of quality for goods to be exported out of India or transported from one State to another.

52. Industries, the control of which by the Union is declared by Parliament by law to be expedient in the public interest.

53. Regulation and development of oil fields and mineral oil resources; petroleum and petroleum products; other liquids and substances declared by Parliament by law to be dangerously inflammable.

54. Regulation of mines and mineral development to the extent to which such regulation and development under the control of the Union is declared by Parliament by law to be expedient in the public interest.

55. Regulation of labour and safety in mines and oilfields.

56. Regulation and development of inter-State rivers and river valleys to the extent to which such regulation and development under the control of the Union is declared by Parliament by law to be expedient in the public interest.

57. Fishing and fisheries beyond territorial waters.

58. Manufacture, supply and distribution of salt by Union agencies, regulation and control of manufacture, supply and distribution of salt by other agencies.

59. Cultivation, manufacture, and sale for export, of opium.

60. Sanctioning of cinematograph films for exhibition.

61. Industrial disputes concerning Union employees.

62. The institutions known at the commencement of this Constitution as the National Library, the Indian Museum, the Imperial War Museum, the Victoria Memorial and the Indian War Memorial, and any other like institution financed by the Government of India wholly or in part and declared by Parliament by law to be an institution of national importance.

63. The institutions known at the commencement of this Constitution as the Banaras Hindu University, the Aligarh Muslim University and the ¹[Delhi University; the University established in pursuance of article 371E;] any other institution declared by Parliament by law to be an institution of national importance.

64. Institutions for scientific or technical education financed by the Government of India wholly or in part and declared by Parliament by law to be institutions of national importance.

65. Union agencies and institutions for—

(a) professional, vocational or technical training, including the training of police officers; or

(b) the promotion of special studies or research; or

(c) scientific or technical assistance in the investigation or detection of crime.

---

1. Subs. by the Constitution (Thirty-second Amendment) Act, 1973, sec. 4, for "Delhi University and" (w.e.f. 1-7-1974).

66. Co-ordination and determination of standards in institutions for higher education or research and scientific and technical institutions.

67. Ancient and historical monuments and records, and archaeological sites and remains, [1][declared by or under law made by Parliament] to be of national importance.

68. The Survey of India, the Geological, Botanical, Zoological and Anthropological Surveys of India; Meteorological organisations.

69. Census.

70. Union Public Services; All-India Services; Union Public Service Commission.

71. Union pensions, that is to say, pensions payable by the Government of India or out of the Consolidated Fund of India.

72. Elections to Parliament, to the Legislatures of States and to the offices of President and Vice-President; the Election Commission.

73. Salaries and allowances of members of Parliament, the Chairman and Deputy Chairman of the Council of States and the Speaker and Deputy Speaker of the House of the People.

74. Powers, privileges and immunities of each House of Parliament and of the members and the Committees of each House; enforcement of attendance of persons for giving evidence or producing documents before committees of Parliament or commissions appointed by Parliament.

75. Emoluments, allowances, privileges, and rights in respect of leave of absence, of the President and Governors; salaries and allowances of the Ministers for the Union; the salaries, allowances, and rights in respect of leave of absence and other conditions of service of the Comptroller and Auditor-General.

76. Audit of the accounts of the Union and of the States.

77. Constitution, organisation, jurisdiction and powers of the Supreme Court (including contempt of such Court), and the fees taken therein; persons entitled to practise before the Supreme Court.

78. Constitution and organisation [2][(including vacations)] of the High Courts except provisions as to officers and servants of High Courts; persons entitled to practise before the High Courts.

[3][79. Extension of the jurisdiction of a High Court to, and exclusion of the jurisdiction of a High Court from, any Union territory.]

80. Extension of the powers and jurisdiction of members of a police force belonging to any State to any area outside that State, but not so as to enable the police of one State to exercise powers and jurisdiction in any area outside that State without the consent of the Government of the State in which such area is situated; extension of the powers and jurisdiction of members of a police force belonging to any State to railway areas outside that State.

81. Inter-State migration; inter-State quarantine.

82. Taxes on income other than agricultural income.

---

1. Subs. by the Constitution (Seventh Amendment) Act, 1956, sec. 27, for "declared by Parliament by law" (w.e.f. 1-11-1956).

2. Ins. by the Constitution (Fifteenth Amendment) Act, 1963, sec. 12 (with retrospective effect).

3. Subs. by the Constitution (Seventh Amendment) Act, 1956, sec. 29 and Sch., for entry 79 (w.e.f. 1-11-1956).

83. Duties of customs including export duties.

84. Duties of excise on tobacco and other goods manufactured or produced in India except—

(a) alcoholic liquors for human consumption.

(b) opium, Indian hemp and other narcotic drugs and narcotics,

but including medicinal and toilet preparations containing alcohol or any substance included in sub-paragraph (b) of this entry.

85. Corporation tax.

86. Taxes on the capital value of the assets, exclusive of agricultural land, of individuals and companies; taxes on the capital of companies.

87. Estate duty in respect of property other than agricultural land.

88. Duties in respect of succession to property other than agricultural land.

89. Terminal taxes on goods or passengers, carried by railway, sea or air; taxes on railway fares and freights.

90. Taxes other than stamp duties on transactions in stock exchanges and futures markets.

91. Rates of stamp duty in respect of bills of exchange, cheques, promissory notes, bills of lading, letters of credit, policies of insurance, transfer of shares, debentures, proxies and receipts.

92. Taxes on the sale or purchase of newspapers and on advertisements published therein.

[1][92A. Taxes on the sale or purchase of goods other than newspapers, where such sale or purchase takes place in the course of inter-State trade or commerce.]

[2][92B. Taxes on the consignment of goods (whether the consignment is to the person making it or to any other person), where such consignment takes place in the course of inter-State trade or commerce.]

[3][92C. Taxes on services.]

93. Offences against laws with respect to any of the matters in this List.

94. Inquiries, surveys and statistics for the purpose of any of the matters in this List.

95. Jurisdiction and powers of all courts, except the Supreme Court, with respect to any of the matters in this List; admiralty jurisdiction.

96. Fees in respect of any of the matters in this List, but not including fees taken in any court.

97. Any other matter not enumerated in List II or List III including any tax not mentioned in either of those Lists.

LIST II—STATE LIST

1. Public order (but not including [4][the use of any naval, military or air force or any other armed force of the Union or of any other force subject to the control of the Union or of any contingent or unit thereof] in aid of the civil power).

---

1. Ins. by the Constitution (Sixth Amendment) Act, 1956, sec. 2(a) (w.e.f. 11-9-1956).
2. Ins. by the Constitution (Forty-sixth Amendment) Act, 1982, sec. 5 (w.e.f. 2-2-1983).
3. Ins. by the Constitution (Eighty-eighth Amendment) Act, 2003, sec 4 (w.e.f. 19-2-2004).
4. Subs. by the Constitution (Forty-second Amendment) Act, 1976, sec. 57(b)(i), for certain words (w.e.f. 3-1-1977).

[1][2. Police (including railway and village police) subject to the provisions of entry 2A of List I.]

3. [2][***] Officers and servants of the High Court; procedure in rent and revenue courts; fees taken in all courts except the Supreme Court.

4. Prisons, reformatories, Borstal institutions and other institutions of a like nature, and persons detained therein; arrangements with other States for the use of prisons and other institutions.

5. Local government, that is to say, the constitution and powers of municipal corporations, improvement trusts, district boards, mining settlement authorities and other local authorities for the purpose of local self-government or village administration.

6. Public health and sanitation; hospitals and dispensaries.

7. Pilgrimages, other than pilgrimages to places outside India.

8. Intoxicating liquors, that is to say, the production, manufacture, possession, transport, purchase and sale of intoxicating liquors.

9. Relief of the disabled and unemployable.

10. Burials and burial grounds; cremations and cremation grounds.

[3][***]

12. Libraries, museums and other similar institutions controlled or financed by the State; ancient and historical monuments and records other than those [4][declared by or under law made by Parliament] to be of national importance.

13. Communications, that is to say, roads, bridges, ferries, and other means of communication not specified in List I; municipal tramways; ropeways; inland waterways and traffic thereon subject to the provisions of List I and List III with regard to such waterways; vehicles other than mechanically propelled vehicles.

14. Agriculture, including agricultural education and research, protection against pests and prevention of plant diseases.

15. Preservation, protection and improvement of stock and prevention of animal diseases; veterinary training and practice.

16. Pounds and the prevention of cattle trespass.

17. Water, that is to say, water supplies, irrigation and canals, drainage and embankments, water storage and water power subject to the provisions of entry 56 of List I.

18. Land, that is to say, right in or over land, land tenures including the relation of landlord and tenant, and the collection of rents; transfer and alienation of agricultural land; land improvement and agricultural loans; colonization.

[5][***]

---

1. Subs. by the Constitution (Forty-second Amendment) Act, 1976, sec. 57(b)(ii), for entry 2 (w.e.f. 3-1-1977).

2. Certain words omitted by the Constitution (Forty-second (Amendment) Act, 1976, sec. 57(b)(iii) (w.e.f. 3-1-1977).

3. Entry 11 omitted by the Constitution (Forty-second Amendment) Act, 1976, sec. 57(b)(iv) (w.e.f. 3-1-1977).

4. Subs. by the Constitution (Seventh Amendment) Act, 1956, sec. 27, for "declared by Parliament by law" (w.e.f. 1-11-1956).

5. Entries 19 and 20 omitted by the Constitution (Forty-second Amendment) Act, 1976, sec. 57(b)(iv) (w.e.f. 3-1-1977).

21. Fisheries.

22. Courts of wards subject to the provisions of entry 34 of List I; encumbered and attached estates.

23. Regulation of mines and mineral development subject to the provisions of List I with respect to regulation and development under the control of the Union.

24. Industries subject to the provisions of ¹[entries 7 and 52] of List I.

25. Gas and gas-works.

26. Trade and commerce within the State subject to the provisions of entry 33 of List III.

27. Production, supply and distribution of goods subject to the provisions of entry 33 of List III.

28. Markets and fairs.

²[***]

30. Money-lending and money-lenders; relief of agricultural indebtedness.

31. Inns and inn-keepers.

32. Incorporation, regulation and winding up of corporation, other than those specified in List I, and universities; unincorporated trading, literary, scientific, religious and other societies and associations; co-operative societies.

33. Theaters and dramatic performances; cinemas subject to the provisions of entry 60 of List I; sports, entertainments and amusements.

34. Betting and gambling.

35. Works, lands and buildings vested in or in the possession of the State.

³[***]

37. Elections to the Legislature of the State subject to the provisions of any law made by Parliament.

38. Salaries and allowances of members of the Legislature of the State, of the Speaker and Deputy Speaker of the Legislative Assembly and, if there is a Legislative Council, of the Chairman and Deputy Chairman thereof.

39. Powers, privileges and immunities of the Legislative Assembly and of the members and the committees thereof, and, if there is a Legislative Council, of that Council and of the members and the committees thereof; enforcement of attendance of persons for giving evidence or producing documents before committees of the Legislature of the State.

40. Salaries and allowances of Ministers for the State.

41. State public services; State Public Service Commission.

42. State pensions, that is to say, pensions payable by the State or out of the Consolidated Fund of the State.

43. Public debt of the State.

44. Treasure trove.

---

1. Subs. by the Constitution (Seventh Amendment) Act, 1956, sec. 28, for "entry 52" (w.e.f. 1-11-1956).

2. Entry 29 omitted by the Constitution (Forty-second Amendment) Act, 1976, sec. 57(b)(iv) (w.e.f. 3-1-1977).

3. Entry 36 omitted by the Constitution (Seventh Amendment) Act, 1956, sec. 26 (w.e.f. 1-11-1956).

45. Land revenue, including the assessment and collection of revenue, the maintenance of land records, survey for revenue purposes and records of rights, and alienation of revenues.

46. Taxes on agricultural income.

47. Duties in respect of succession to agricultural land.

48. Estate duty in respect of agricultural land.

49. Taxes on lands and buildings.

50. Taxes on mineral rights subject to any limitations imposed by Parliament by law relating to mineral development.

51. Duties of excise on the following goods manufactured or produced in the State and countervailing duties at the same or lower rates on similar goods manufactured or produced elsewhere in India:—

(a) alcoholic liquors for human consumption;

(b) opium, Indian hemp and other narcotic drugs and narcotics,

but not including medicinal and toilet preparations containing alcohol or any substance included in sub-paragraph (b) of this entry.

52. Taxes on the entry of goods into a local area for consumption, use or sale therein.

53. Taxes on the consumption or sale of electricity.

[54. Taxes on the sale or purchase of goods other than newspapers, subject to the provisions of entry 92A of List I.]

55. Taxes on advertisements other than advertisements published in the newspapers [and advertisements broadcast by radio or television].

56. Taxes on goods and passengers carried by road or on inland waterways.

57. Taxes on vehicles, whether mechanically propelled or not, suitable for use on roads, including tramcars subject to the provisions of entry 35 of List III.

58. Taxes on animals and boats.

59. Tolls.

60. Taxes on professions, trades, callings and employments.

61. Capitation taxes.

62. Taxes on luxuries, including taxes on entertainments, amusements, betting and gambling.

63. Rates of stamp duty in respect of documents other than those specified in the provisions of List I with regard to rates of stamp duty.

64. Offences against laws with respect to any of the matters in this List.

65. Jurisdiction and powers of all courts, except the Supreme Court, with respect to any of the matters in this List.

66. Fees in respect of any of the matters in this List, but not including fees taken in any court.

---

1. Subs. by the Constitution (Sixth Amendment) Act, 1956, sec. 2(b), for entry 54 (w.e.f. 11-9-1956).
2. Ins. by the Constitution (Forty-Second Amendment) Act, 1976, sec. 57(b)(v) (w.e.f. 3-1-1977).

LIST III—CONCURRENT LIST

1. Criminal law, including all matters included in the Indian Penal Code at the commencement of this Constitution but excluding offences against laws with respect to any of the matters specified in List I or List II and excluding the use of naval, military or air forces or any other armed forces of the Union in aid of the civil power.

2. Criminal procedure, including all matters included in the Code of Criminal Procedure at the commencement of this Constitution.

3. Preventive detention for reasons connected with the security of a State, the maintenance of public order, or the maintenance of supplies and services essential to the community; persons subjected to such detention.

4. Removal from one State to another State of prisoners, accused persons and persons subjected to preventive detention for reasons specified in entry 3 of this List.

5. Marriage and divorce; infants and minors; adoption; wills, intestacy and succession; joint family and partition; all matters in respect of which parties in judicial proceedings were immediately before the commencement of this Constitution subject to their personal law.

6. Transfer of property other than agricultural land; registration of deeds and documents.

7. Contracts, including partnership, agency, contracts of carriage, and other special forms of contracts, but not including contracts relating to agricultural land.

8. Actionable wrongs.

9. Bankruptcy and insolvency.

10. Trust and Trustees.

11. Administrators-general and official trustees.

[1][11A. Administration of justice; constitution and organisation of all courts, except the Supreme Court and the High Courts.]

12. Evidence and oaths; recognition of laws, public acts and records, and judicial proceedings.

13. Civil procedure, including all matters included in the Code of Civil Procedure at the commencement of this Constitution, limitation and arbitration.

14. Contempt of court, but not including contempt of the Supreme Court.

15. Vagrancy; nomadic and migratory tribes.

16. Lunacy and mental deficiency, including places for the reception or treatment of lunatics and mental deficients.

17. Prevention of cruelty to animals.

[2][17A. Forests.]

[2][17B. Protection of wild animals and birds.]

18. Adulteration of foodstuffs and other goods.

19. Drugs and poisons, subject to the provisions of entry 59 of List I with respect to opium.

20. Economic and social planning.

---

1. Ins. by the Constitution (Forty-second Amendment) Act, 1976, sec. 57(c)(i) (w.e.f. 3-1-1977).

2. Ins. by the Constitution (Forty-second Amendment) Act, 1976, sec. 57(c)(ii) (w.e.f. 3-1-1977).

¹[20A. Population control and family planning.]

21. Commercial and industrial monopolies, combines and trusts.

22. Trade unions; industrial and labour disputes.

23. Social security and social insurance; employment and unemployment.

24. Welfare of labour including conditions of work, provident funds, employers' liability, workmen's compensation, invalidity and old age pensions and maternity benefits.

²[25. Education, including technical education, medical education and universities, subject to the provisions of entries 63, 64, 65 and 66 of List I; vocational and technical training of labour.]

26. Legal, medical and other professions.

27. Relief and rehabilitation of persons displaced from their original place of residence by reason of the setting up of the Dominions of India and Pakistan.

28. Charities and charitable institutions, charitable and religious endowments and religious institutions.

29. Prevention of the extension from one State to another of infectious or contagious diseases or pests affecting men, animals or plants.

30. Vital statistics including registration of births and deaths.

31. Ports other than those declared by or under law made by Parliament or existing law to be major ports.

32. Shipping and navigation on inland waterways as regards mechanically propelled vessels, and the rule of the road on such waterways, and the carriage of passengers and goods on inland waterways subject to the provisions of List I with respect to national waterways.

³[33. Trade and commerce in, and the production, supply and distribution of,—

(a) the products of any industry where the control of such industry by the Union is declared by Parliament by law to be expedient in the public interest, and imported goods of the same kind as such products;

(b) foodstuffs, including edible oilseeds and oils;

(c) cattle fodder, including oilcakes and other concentrates;

(d) raw cotton, whether ginned or unginned, and cotton seed; and

(e) raw jute.]

⁴[33A. Weights and measures except establishment of standards.]

34. Price control.

35. Mechanically propelled vehicles including the principles on which taxes on such vehicles are to be levied.

36. Factories.

37. Boilers.

38. Electricity.

---

1. Ins. by the Constitution (Forty-second Amendment) Act, 1976, sec. 57(c)(iii) (w.e.f. 3-1-1977).
2. Subs. by the Constitution (Forty-second Amendment) Act, 1976, sec. 57(c)(iv), for entry 25 (w.e.f. 3-1-1977).
3. Subs. by the Constitution (Third Amendment) Act, 1954, sec. 2, for entry 33 (w.e.f. 22-2-1955).
4. Ins. by the Constitution (Forty-second Amendment) Act, 1976, sec. 57(c)(v) (w.e.f. 3-1-1977).

39. Newspapers, books and printing presses.

40. Archaeological sites and remains other than those [1][declared by or under law made by Parliament] to be of national importance.

41. Custody, management and disposal of property (including agricultural land) declared by law to be evacuee property.

[2][42. Acquisition and requisitioning of property.]

43. Recovery in a State of claims in respect of taxes and other public demands, including arrears of land-revenue and sums recoverable as such arrears, arising outside that State.

44. Stamp duties other than duties or fees collected by means of judicial stamps, but not including rates of stamp duty.

45. Inquiries and statistics for the purposes of any of the matters specified in List II or List III.

46. Jurisdiction and powers of all courts, except the Supreme Court, with respect to any of the matters in this List.

47. Fees in respect of any of the matters in this List, but not including fees taken in any court.

EIGHTH SCHEDULE
[Articles 344(1) and 351]

LANGUAGES

1. Assamese.
2. Bengali.
[3][3. Bodo.]
[4][4. Dogri.]
*5. Gujarati.
*6. Hindi.
*7. Kannada.
*8. Kashmiri.
[4][*9. Konkani.]
[5][*10. Mathilli.]
*11. Malayalam.
[6][*12. Manipuri.]
*13. Marathi.
[7][*14. Nepali.]

---

1. Subs. by the Constitution (Seventh Amendment) Act, 1956, sec. 27, for "declared by the Parliament by law" (w.e.f. 1-11-1956).
2. Subs. by the Constitution (Seventh Amendment) Act, 1956, sec. 26, for entry 42 (w.e.f. 1-11-1956).
3. Ins. by the Constitution (Ninety-second Amendment) Act, 2003, sec. 2(a) (w.e.f. 7-1-2004).
4. Ins. by the Constitution (Seventy-first Amendment) Act, 1992, sec. 2(a) (w.e.f. 31-8-1992).
5. Ins. by the Constitution (Ninety-second Amendment) Act, 2003, sec. 2(c) (w.e.f. 7-1-2004).
6. Ins. by the Constitution (Seventy-first Amendment) Act, 1992, sec. 2(b) (w.e.f. 31-8-1992).
7. Ins. by the Constitution (Seventy-first Amendment) Act, 1992, sec. 2(c) (w.e.f. 31-8-1992).

*15. ¹[Odia].

*16. Punjabi.

*17. Sanskrit.

²[*18. Santhali.]

³[*19. Sindhi.]

*20. Tamil.

*21. Telugu.

*22. Urdu.

⁴[*NINTH SCHEDULE*

(Article 31B)

1. The Bihar Land Reforms Act, 1950 (Bihar Act XXX of 1950).

2. The Bombay Tenancy and Agricultural Lands Act, 1948 (Bombay Act LXVII of 1948).

3. The Bombay Maleki Tenure Abolition Act, 1949 (Bombay Act LXI of 1949).

4. The Bombay Taluqdari Tenure Abolition Act, 1949 (Bombay Act LXII of 1949).

5. The Panch Mahals, Mehwassi Tenure Abolition Act, 1949 (Bombay Act LXIII of 1949).

6. The Bombay Khoti Abolition Act, 1950 (Bombay Act VI of 1950).

7. The Bombay Paragana and Kulkarni Watan Abolition Act, 1950 (Bombay Act LX of 1950).

8. The Madhya Pradesh Abolition of Proprietary Rights (Estates, Mahals, Alienated Lands) Act, 1950 (Madhya Pradesh Act I of 1951).

9. The Madras Estates (Abolition and Conversion into Ryotwari) Act, 1948 (Madras Act XXVI of 1948).

10. The Madras Estates (Abolition and Conversion into Ryotwari) Amendment Act, 1950 (Madras Act I of 1950).

11. The Uttar Pradesh Zamindari Abolition and Land Reforms Act, 1950 (Uttar Pradesh Act I of 1951).

12. The Hyderabad (Abolition of Jagirs) Regulation, 1358F (No. LXIX of 1358, Fasli).

13. The Hyderabad Jagirs (Commutation) Regulation, 1359F (No. XXV of 1359, Fasli).]

⁵[14. The Bihar Displaced Persons Rehabilitation (Acquisition of Land) Act, 1950 (Bihar Act XXXVIII of 1950).

15. The United Provinces Land Acquisition (Rehabilitation of Refugees) Act, 1948 (U.P. Act XXVI of 1948).

16. The Resettlement of Displaced Persons (Land Acquisition) Act, 1948 (Act LX of 1948).

---

1. Subs. by the Constitution (Ninety-sixth Amendment) Act, 2011, sec. 2, for "Oriya" (w.e.f. 23-9-2011).

2. Ins. by the Constitution (Ninety-second Amendment) Act, 2003, sec. 2(e) (w.e.f. 7-1-2004).

3. Ins. by the Constitution (Twenty-first Amendment) Act, 1967, sec. 2(b) (w.e.f. 10-4-1967).

* Entry numbers have been re-numbered by (i) the Constitution (Twenty-first Amendment) Act, 1967, sec. 2(a) (w.e.f. 10-4-1967); (ii) by the Constitution (Seventy-first Amendment) Act, 1992, sec. 2 (w.e.f. 31-8-1992) and (iii) by the Constitution (Ninety-second Amendment) Act, 2003, sec. 2 (w.e.f. 7-1-2004).

4. Added by the Constitution (First Amendment) Act, 1951, sec. 14 (w.e.f. 18-6-1951).

5. Added by the Constitution (Fourth Amendment) Act, 1955, sec. 5 (w.e.f. 27-4-1955).

17. Sections 52A to 52G of the Insurance Act, 1938 (Act IV of 1938), as inserted by section 42 of the Insurance (Amendment) Act, 1950 (Act XLVII of 1950).

18. The Railway Companies (Emergency Provisions) Act, 1951 (Act LI of 1951).

19. Chapter IIIA of the Industries (Development and Regulation) Act, 1951 (Act LXV of 1951), as inserted by section 13 of the Industries (Development and Regulation) Amendment Act, 1953 (Act XXVI of 1953).

20. The West Bengal Land Development and Planning Act, 1948 (West Bengal Act XXI of 1948), as amended by West Bengal Act XXIX of 1951.]

[1][21. The Andhra Pradesh Ceiling on Agricultural Holdings Act, 1961 (Andhra Pradesh Act X of 1961).]

22. The Andhra Pradesh (Telangana Area) Tenancy and Agricultural Lands (Validation) Act, 1961 (Andhra Pradesh Act XXI of 1961).

23. The Andhra Pradesh (Telangana Area) Ijara and Kowli Land Cancellation of Irregular Pattas and Abolition of Concessional Assessment Act, 1961 (Andhra Pradesh Act XXXVI of 1961).

24. The Assam State Acquisition of Lands belonging to Religious or Charitable Institution of Public Nature Act, 1959 (Assam Act IX of 1961).

25. The Bihar Land Reforms (Amendment) Act, 1953 (Bihar Act XX of 1954).

26. The Bihar Land Reforms (Fixation of Ceiling Area and Acquisition of Surplus Land) Act, 1961 (Bihar Act XII of 1962), (except section 28 of this Act).

27. The Bombay Taluqdari Tenure Abolition (Amendment) Act, 1954 (Bombay Act I of 1955).

28. The Bombay Taluqdari Tenure Abolition (Amendment) Act, 1957 (Bombay Act XVIII of 1958).

29. The Bombay Inams (Kutch Area) Abolition Act, 1958 (Bombay Act XCVIII of 1958).

30. The Bombay Tenancy and Agricultural Lands (Gujarat Amendment) Act, 1960 (Gujarat Act XVI of 1960).

31. The Gujarat Agricultural Lands Ceiling Act, 1960 (Gujarat Act XXVII of 1961).

32. The Sagbara and Meshwassi Estates (Proprietary Rights Abolition, etc.) Regulation, 1962 (Gujarat Regulation I of 1962).

33. The Gujarat Surviving Alienations Abolition Act, 1963 (Gujarat Act XXXIII of 1963), except in so far as this Act relates to an alienation referred to in sub-clause (d) of clause (3) of section 2 thereof.

34. The Maharashtra Agricultural Lands (Ceiling on Holdings) Act, 1961 (Maharashtra Act XXVII of 1961).

35. The Hyderabad Tenancy and Agricultural Lands (Re-enactment, Validation and Further Amendment) Act, 1961 (Maharashtra Act XLV of 1961).

36. The Hyderabad Tenancy and Agricultural Lands Act, 1950 (Hyderabad Act XXI of 1950).

37. The Jenmikaram Payment (Abolition) Act, 1960 (Kerala Act III of 1961).

38. The Kerala Land Tax Act, 1961 (Kerala Act XIII of 1961).

39. The Kerala Land Reforms Act, 1963 (Kerala Act I of 1964).

40. The Madhya Pradesh Land Revenue Code, 1959 (Madhya Pradesh Act XX of 1959).

---

1. Added by the Constitution (Seventeenth Amendment) Act, 1964, sec. 3 (w.e.f. 20-6-1964).

41. The Madhya Pradesh Ceiling on Agricultural Holdings Act, 1960 (Madhya Pradesh Act XX of 1960).

42. The Madras Cultivating Tenants Protection Act, 1955 (Madras Act XXV of 1955).

43. The Madras Cultivating Tenants (Payment of Fair Rent) Act, 1956 (Madras Act XXIV of 1956).

44. The Madras Occupants of Kudiyiruppu (Protection from Eviction) Act, 1961 (Madras Act XXXVIII of 1961).

45. The Madras Public Trust (Regulation of Administration of Agricultural Lands) Act, 1961 (Madras Act LVII of 1961).

46. The Madras Land Reforms (Fixation of Ceiling on Land) Act, 1961 (Madras Act LVIII of 1961).

47. The Mysore Tenancy Act, 1952 (Mysore Act XIII of 1952).

48. The Coorg Tenants Act, 1957 (Mysore Act XIV of 1957).

49. The Mysore Village Offices Abolition Act, 1961 (Mysore Act XIV of 1961).

50. The Hyderabad Tenancy and Agricultural Lands (Validation) Act, 1961 (Mysore Act XXXVI of 1961).

51. The Mysore Land Reforms Act, 1961 (Mysore Act X of 1962).

52. The Orissa Land Reforms Act, 1960 (Orissa Act XVI of 1960).

53. The Orissa Merged Territories (Village Offices Abolition) Act, 1963 (Orissa Act X of 1963).

54. The Punjab Security of Land Tenures Act, 1953 (Punjab Act X of 1953).

55. The Rajasthan Tenancy Act, 1955 (Rajasthan Act III of 1955).

56. The Rajasthan Zamindari and Biswedari Abolition Act, 1959 (Rajasthan Act VIII of 1959).

57. The Kumaun and Uttarakhand Zamindari Abolition and Land Reforms Act, 1960 (Uttar Pradesh Act XVII of 1960).

58. The Uttar Pradesh Imposition of Ceiling on Land Holdings Act, 1960 (Uttar Pradesh Act I of 1961).

59. The West Bengal Estates Acquisition Act, 1953 (West Bengal Act I of 1954).

60. The West Bengal Land Reforms Act, 1955 (West Bengal Act X of 1956).

61. The Delhi Land Reforms Act, 1954 (Delhi Act VIII of 1954).

62. The Delhi Land Holdings (Ceiling) Act, 1960 (Central Act 24 of 1960).

63. The Manipur Land Revenue and Land Reforms Act, 1960 (Central Act 33 of 1960).

64. The Tripura Land Revenue and Land Reforms Act, 1960 (Central Act 43 of 1960).]

¹[65. The Kerala Land Reforms (Amendment) Act, 1969 (Kerala Act 35 of 1969).

66. The Kerala Land Reforms (Amendment) Act, 1971 (Kerala Act 25 of 1971).]

²[67. The Andhra Pradesh Land Reforms (Ceiling on Agricultural Holdings) Act, 1973 (Andhra Pradesh Act I of 1973).]

68. The Bihar Land Reforms (Fixation of Ceiling Area and Acquisition of Surplus Land) (Amendment) Act, 1972 (Bihar Act I of 1973).

---

1. Ins. by the Constitution (Twenty-ninth Amendment) Act, 1972, sec. 2 (w.e.f. 9-6-1972).
2. Ins. by the Constitution (Thirty-fourth Amendment) Act, 1974, sec. 2 (w.e.f. 7-9-1974).

69. The Bihar Land Reforms (Fixation of Ceiling Area and Acquisition of Surplus Land) (Amendment) Act, 1973 (Bihar Act IX of 1973).

70. The Bihar Land Reforms (Amendment) Act, 1972 (Bihar Act V of 1972).

71. The Gujarat Agricultural Lands Ceiling (Amendment) Act, 1972 (Gujarat Act 2 of 1974).

72. The Haryana Ceiling on Land Holdings Act, 1972 (Haryana Act 26 of 1972).

73. The Himachal Pradesh Ceiling on Land Holdings Act, 1972 (Himachal Pradesh Act 19 of 1973).

74. The Kerala Land Reforms (Amendment) Act, 1972 (Kerala Act 17 of 1972).

75. The Madhya Pradesh Ceiling on Agricultural Holdings (Amendment) Act, 1972 (Madhya Pradesh Act 12 of 1974).

76. The Madhya Pradesh Ceiling on Agricultural Holdings (Second Amendment) Act, 1972 (Madhya Pradesh Act 13 of 1974).

77. The Mysore Land Reforms (Amendment) Act, 1973 (Karnataka Act 1 of 1974).

78. The Punjab Land Reforms Act, 1972 (Punjab Act 10 of 1973).

79. The Rajasthan Imposition of Ceiling on Agricultural Holdings Act, 1973 (Rajasthan Act 11 of 1973).

80. The Gudalur Janmam Estates (Abolition and Conversion into Ryotwari) Act, 1969 (Tamil Nadu Act 24 of 1969).

81. The West Bengal Land Reforms (Amendment) Act, 1972 (West Bengal Act XXII of 1972).

82. The West Bengal Estates Acquisition (Amendment) Act, 1964 (West Bengal Act XXII of 1964).

83. The West Bengal Estates Acquisition (Second Amendment) Act, 1973 (West Bengal Act XXXIII of 1973).

84. The Bombay Tenancy and Agricultural Lands (Gujarat Amendment) Act, 1972 (Gujarat Act 5 of 1973).

85. The Orissa Land Reforms (Amendment) Act, 1974 (Orissa Act 9 of 1974).

86. The Tripura Land Revenue and Land Reforms (Second Amendment) Act, 1974 (Tripura Act 7 of 1974).]

[1][***]

[2][88. The Industries (Development and Regulation) Act, 1951 (Central Act 65 of 1951).

89. The Requisitioning and Acquisition of Immovable Property Act, 1952 (Central Act 30 of 1952).

90. The Mines and Minerals (Regulations and Development) Act, 1957 (Central Act 67 of 1957).

91. The Monopolies and Restrictive Trade Practices Act, 1969 (Central Act 54 of 1969).

[3][***]

---

1. Entry 87 omitted by the Constitution (Forty-fourth Amendment) Act, 1978, sec. 44 (w.e.f. 20-6-1979). Earlier entry 87 was inserted by the Constitution (Thirty-ninth Amendment) Act, 1975, sec. 5 (w.e.f. 10-8-1975).

2. Ins. by the Constitution (Thirty-ninth Amendment) Act, 1975, sec. 5 (w.e.f. 10-8-1975).

3. Entry 92 omitted by the Constitution (Forty-fourth Amendment) Act, 1978, sec. 44 (w.e.f. 20-6-1979). Earlier entry 92 was inserted by the Constitution (Thirty-ninth Amendment) Act, 1975, sec. 5 (w.e.f. 10-8-1975).

93. The Coking Coal Mines (Emergency Provisions) Act, 1971 (Central Act 64 of 1971).

94. The Coking Coal Mines (Nationalisation) Act, 1972 (Central Act 36 of 1972).

95. The General Insurance Business (Nationalisation) Act, 1972 (Central Act 57 of 1972).

96. The Indian Copper Corporation (Acquisition of Undertaking) Act, 1972 (Central Act 58 of 1972).

97. The Sick Textile Undertakings (Taking Over of Management) Act, 1972 (Central Act 72 of 1972).

98. The Coal Mines (Taking Over of Management) Act, 1973 (Central Act 15 of 1973).

99. The Coal Mines (Nationalisation) Act, 1973 (Central Act 26 of 1973).

100. The Foreign Exchange Regulation Act, 1973 (Central Act 46 of 1973).

101. The Alcock Ashdown Company Limited (Acquisition of Undertakings) Act, 1973 (Central Act 56 of 1973).

102. The Coal Mines (Conservation and Development) Act, 1974 (Central Act 28 of 1974).

103. The Additional Emoluments (Compulsory Deposit) Act, 1974 (Central Act 37 of 1974).

104. The Conservation of Foreign Exchange and Prevention of Smuggling Activities Act, 1974 (Central Act 52 of 1974).

105. The Sick Textile Undertakings (Nationalisation) Act, 1974 (Central Act 57 of 1974).

106. The Maharashtra Agricultural Lands (Ceiling on Holdings) (Amendment) Act, 1964 (Maharashtra Act XVI of 1965).

107. The Maharashtra Agricultural Lands (Ceiling on Holdings) (Amendment) Act, 1965 (Maharashtra Act XXXII of 1965).

108. The Maharashtra Agricultural Lands (Ceiling on Holdings) (Amendment) Act, 1968 (Maharashtra Act XVI of 1968).

109. The Maharashtra Agricultural Lands (Ceiling on Holdings) (Second Amendment) Act, 1968 (Maharashtra Act XXXIII of 1968).

110. The Maharashtra Agricultural Lands (Ceiling on Holdings) (Amendment) Act, 1969 (Maharashtra Act XXXVII of 1969).

111. The Maharashtra Agricultural Lands (Ceiling on Holdings) (Second Amendment) Act, 1969 (Maharashtra Act XXXVIII of 1969).

112. The Maharashtra Agricultural Lands (Ceiling on Holdings) (Amendment) Act, 1970 (Maharashtra Act XXVII of 1970).

113. The Maharashtra Agricultural Lands (Ceiling on Holdings) (Amendment) Act, 1972 (Maharashtra Act XIII of 1972).

114. The Maharashtra Agricultural Lands (Ceiling on Holdings) (Amendment) Act, 1973 (Maharashtra Act L of 1973).

115. The Orissa Land Reforms (Amendment) Act, 1965 (Orissa Act 13 of 1965).

116. The Orissa Land Reforms (Amendment) Act, 1966 (Orissa Act 8 of 1967).

117. The Orissa Land Reforms (Amendment) Act, 1967 (Orissa Act 13 of 1967).

118. The Orissa Land Reforms (Amendment) Act, 1969 (Orissa Act 13 of 1969).

119. The Orissa Land Reforms (Amendment) Act, 1970 (Orissa Act 18 of 1970).

120. The Uttar Pradesh Imposition of Ceiling on Land Holdings (Amendment) Act, 1972 (Uttar Pradesh Act 18 of 1973).

121. The Uttar Pradesh Imposition of Ceiling on Land Holdings (Amendment) Act, 1974 (Uttar Pradesh Act 2 of 1975).

122. The Tripura Land Revenue and Land Reforms (Third Amendment) Act, 1975 (Tripura Act 3 of 1975).

123. The Dadra and Nagar Haveli Land Reforms Regulation, 1971 (3 of 1971).

124. The Dadra and Nagar Haveli Land Reforms (Amendment) Regulation, 1973 (5 of 1973).]

¹[125. Section 66A and Chapter IVA of the Motor Vehicles Act, 1939 (Central Act 4 of 1939).]

126. The Essential Commodities Act, 1955 (Central Act 10 of 1955).

127. The Smugglers and Foreign Exchange Manipulators (Forfeiture of Property) Act, 1976 (Central Act 13 of 1976).

128. The Bonded Labour System (Abolition) Act, 1976 (Central Act 19 of 1976).

129. The Conservation of Foreign Exchange and Prevention of Smuggling Activities (Amendment) Act, 1976 (Central Act 20 of 1976).

²[***]

131. The Levy Sugar Price Equalisation Fund Act, 1976 (Central Act 31 of 1976).

132. The Urban Land (Ceiling and Regulation) Act, 1976 (Central Act 33 of 1976).

133. The Departmentalisation of Union Accounts (Transfer of Personnel) Act, 1976 (Central Act 59 of 1976).

134. The Assam Fixation of Ceiling on Land Holdings Act, 1956 (Assam Act 1 of 1957).

135. The Bombay Tenancy and Agricultural Lands (Vidarbha Region) Act, 1958 (Bombay Act XCIX of 1958).

136. The Gujarat Private Forests (Acquisition) Act, 1972 (Gujarat Act 14 of 1973).

137. The Haryana Ceiling on Land Holdings (Amendment) Act, 1976 (Haryana Act 17 of 1976).

138. The Himachal Pradesh Tenancy and Land Reforms Act, 1972 (Himachal Pradesh Act 8 of 1974).

139. The Himachal Pradesh Village Common Lands Vesting and Utilization Act, 1974 (Himachal Pradesh Act 18 of 1974).

140. The Karnataka Land Reforms (Second Amendment and Miscellaneous Provisions) Act, 1974 (Karnataka Act 31 of 1974).

141. The Karnataka Land Reforms (Second Amendment) Act, 1976 (Karnataka Act 27 of 1976).

142. The Kerala Prevention of Eviction Act, 1966 (Kerala Act 12 of 1966).

143. The Thiruppuvaram Payment (Abolition) Act, 1969 (Kerala Act 19 of 1969).

144. The Sreepadam Lands Enfranchisement Act, 1969 (Kerala Act 20 of 1969).

145. The Sree Pandaravaka Lands (Vesting and Enfranchisement) Act, 1971 (Kerala Act 20 of 1971).

---

1. Ins. by the Constitution (Fortieth Amendment) Act, 1976, sec. 3 (w.e.f. 27-5-1976).
2. Entry 130 omitted by the Constitution (Forty-fourth Amendment) Act, 1978, sec. 44 (w.e.f. 20-6-1979).

146. The Kerala Private Forests (Vesting and Assignment) Act, 1971 (Kerala Act 26 of 1971).

147. The Kerala Agricultural Workers Act, 1974 (Kerala Act 18 of 1974).

148. The Kerala Cashew Factories (Acquisition) Act, 1974 (Kerala Act 29 of 1974).

149. The Kerala Chitties Act, 1975 (Kerala Act 23 of 1975).

150. The Kerala Scheduled Tribes (Restriction on Transfer of Lands and Restoration of Alienated Lands) Act, 1975 (Kerala Act 31 of 1975).

151. The Kerala Land Reforms (Amendment) Act, 1976 (Kerala Act 15 of 1976).

152. The Kanam Tenancy Abolition Act, 1976 (Kerala Act 16 of 1976).

153. The Madhya Pradesh Ceiling on Agricultural Holdings (Amendment) Act, 1974 (Madhya Pradesh Act 20 of 1974).

154. The Madhya Pradesh Ceiling on Agricultural Holdings (Amendment) Act, 1975 (Madhya Pradesh Act 2 of 1976).

155. The West Khandesh Mehwassi Estates (Proprietary Rights Abolition, etc.) Regulation, 1961 (Maharashtra Regulation 1 of 1962).

156. The Maharashtra Restoration of Lands to Scheduled Tribes Act, 1974 (Maharashtra Act XIV of 1975).

157. The Maharashtra Agricultural Lands (Lowering of Ceiling on Holdings) and (Amendment) Act, 1972 (Maharashtra Act XXI of 1975).

158. The Maharashtra Private Forests (Acquisition) Act, 1975 (Maharashtra Act XXIX of 1975).

159. The Maharashtra Agricultural Lands (Lowering of Ceiling on Holdings) and (Amendment) Act, 1975 (Maharashtra Act XLVII of 1975).

160. The Maharashtra Agricultural Lands (Ceiling on Holdings) (Amendment) Act, 1975 (Maharashtra Act II of 1976).

161. The Orissa Estates Abolition Act, 1951 (Orissa Act I of 1952).

162. The Rajasthan Colonisation Act, 1954 (Rajasthan Act XXVII of 1954).

163. The Rajasthan Land Reforms and Acquisition of Landowners' Estates Act, 1963 (Rajasthan Act 11 of 1964).

164. The Rajasthan Imposition of Ceiling on Agricultural Holdings (Amendment) Act, 1976 (Rajasthan Act 8 of 1976).

165. The Rajasthan Tenancy (Amendment) Act, 1976 (Rajasthan Act 12 of 1976).

166. The Tamil Nadu Land Reforms (Reduction of Ceiling on Land) Act, 1970 (Tamil Nadu Act 17 of 1970).

167. The Tamil Nadu Land Reforms (Fixation of Ceiling on Land) Amendment Act, 1971 (Tamil Nadu Act 41 of 1971).

168. The Tamil Nadu Land Reforms (Fixation of Ceiling on Land) Amendment Act, 1972 (Tamil Nadu Act 10 of 1972).

169. The Tamil Nadu Land Reforms (Fixation of Ceiling on Land) Second Amendment Act, 1972 (Tamil Nadu Act 20 of 1972).

170. The Tamil Nadu Land Reforms (Fixation of Ceiling on Land) Third Amendment Act, 1972 (Tamil Nadu Act 37 of 1972).

171. The Tamil Nadu Land Reforms (Fixation of Ceiling on Land) Fourth Amendment Act, 1972 (Tamil Nadu Act 39 of 1972).

172. The Tamil Nadu Land Reforms (Fixation of Ceiling on Land) Sixth Amendment Act, 1972 (Tamil Nadu Act 7 of 1974).

173. The Tamil Nadu Land Reforms (Fixation of Ceiling on Land) Fifth Amendment Act, 1972 (Tamil Nadu Act 10 of 1974).

174. The Tamil Nadu Land Reforms (Fixation of Ceiling on Land) Amendment Act, 1974 (Tamil Nadu Act 15 of 1974).

175. The Tamil Nadu Land Reforms (Fixation of Ceiling on Land) Third Amendment Act, 1974 (Tamil Nadu Act 30 of 1974).

176. The Tamil Nadu Land Reforms (Fixation of Ceiling on Land) Second Amendment Act, 1974 (Tamil Nadu Act 32 of 1974).

177. The Tamil Nadu Land Reforms (Fixation of Ceiling on Land) Amendment Act, 1975 (Tamil Nadu Act 11 of 1975).

178. The Tamil Nadu Land Reforms (Fixation of Ceiling on Land) Second Amendment Act, 1975 (Tamil Nadu Act 21 of 1975).

179. Amendments made to the Uttar Pradesh Zamindari Abolition and Land Reforms Act, 1950 (Uttar Pradesh Act I of 1951) by the Uttar Pradesh Land Laws (Amendment) Act, 1971 (Uttar Pradesh Act 21 of 1971) and the Uttar Pradesh Land Laws (Amendment) Act, 1974 (Uttar Pradesh Act 34 of 1974).

180. The Uttar Pradesh Imposition of Ceiling on Land Holdings (Amendment) Act, 1976 (Uttar Pradesh Act 20 of 1976).

181. The West Bengal Land Reforms (Second Amendment) Act, 1972 (West Bengal Act XXVIII of 1972).

182. The West Bengal Restoration of Alienated Land Act, 1973 (West Bengal Act XXIII of 1973).

183. The West Bengal Land Reforms (Amendment) Act, 1974 (West Bengal Act XXXIII of 1974).

184. The West Bengal Land Reforms (Amendment) Act, 1975 (West Bengal Act XXIII of 1975).

185. The West Bengal Land Reforms (Amendment) Act, 1976 (West Bengal Act XII of 1976).

186. The Delhi Land Holdings (Ceiling) Amendment Act, 1976 (Central Act 15 of 1976).

187. The Goa, Daman and Diu Mundkars (Protection from Eviction) Act, 1975 (Goa, Daman and Diu Act I of 1976).

188. The Pondicherry Land Reforms (Fixation of Ceiling on Land) Act, 1973 (Pondicherry Act 9 of 1974).]

¹[189. The Assam (Temporarily Settled Areas) Tenancy Act, 1971 (Assam Act XXIII of 1971).

190. The Assam (Temporarily Settled Areas) Tenancy (Amendment) Act, 1974 (Assam Act XVIII of 1974).

191. The Bihar Land Reforms (Fixation of Ceiling Area and Acquisition of Surplus Land) (Amendment) (Amending) Act, 1974 (Bihar Act 31 of 1975).

192. The Bihar Land Reforms (Fixation of Ceiling Area and Acquisition of Surplus Land) (Amendment) Act, 1976 (Bihar Act 22 of 1976).

---

1. Ins. by the Constitution (Forty-seventh Amendment) Act, 1984, sec. 2 (w.e.f. 26-8-1984).

193. The Bihar Land Reforms (Fixation of Ceiling Area and Acquisition of Surplus Land) (Amendment) Act, 1978 (Bihar Act VII of 1978).

194. The Land Acquisition (Bihar Amendment) Act, 1979 (Bihar Act 2 of 1980).

195. The Haryana Ceiling on Land Holdings (Amendment) Act, 1977 (Haryana Act 14 of 1977).

196. The Tamil Nadu Land Reforms (Fixation of Ceiling on Land) Amendment Act, 1978 (Tamil Nadu Act 25 of 1978).

197. The Tamil Nadu Land Reforms (Fixation of Ceiling on Land) Amendment Act, 1979 (Tamil Nadu Act 11 of 1979).

198. The Uttar Pradesh Zamindari Abolition Laws (Amendment) Act, 1978 (Uttar Pradesh Act 15 of 1978).

199. The West Bengal Restoration of Alienated Land (Amendment) Act, 1978 (West Bengal Act XXIV of 1978).

200. The West Bengal Restoration of Alienated Land (Amendment) Act, 1980 (West Bengal Act LVI of 1980).

201. The Goa, Daman and Diu Agricultural Tenancy Act, 1964 (Goa, Daman and Diu Act 7 of 1964).

202. The Goa, Daman and Diu Agricultural Tenancy (Fifth Amendment) Act, 1976 (Goa, Daman and Diu Act 17 of 1976).]

¹[203. The Andhra Pradesh Scheduled Areas Land Transfer Regulation, 1959 (Andhra Pradesh Regulation I of 1959)

204. The Andhra Pradesh Scheduled Areas Laws (Extension and Amendment) Regulation, 1963 (Andhra Pradesh Regulation 2 of 1963).

205. The Andhra Pradesh Scheduled Areas Land Transfer (Amendment) Regulation, 1970 (Andhra Pradesh Regulation 1 of 1970).

206. The Andhra Pradesh Scheduled Areas Land Transfer (Amendment) Regulation, 1971 (Andhra Pradesh Regulation 1 of 1971).

207. The Andhra Pradesh Scheduled Areas Land Transfer (Amendment) Regulation, 1978 (Andhra Pradesh Regulation 1 of 1978).

208. The Bihar Tenancy Act, 1885 (Bihar Act 8 of 1885).

209. The Chhota Nagpur Tenancy Act, 1908 (Bengal Act 6 of 1908) (Chapter VIII— sections 46, 47, 48, 48A and 49; Chapter X—sections 71, 71A and 71B; and Chapter XVIII—sections 240, 241 and 242).

210. The Santhal Parganas Tenancy (Supplementary Provisions) Act, 1949 (Bihar Act 14 of 1949) except section 53.

211. The Bihar Scheduled Areas Regulation, 1969 (Bihar Regulation 1 of 1969).

212. The Bihar Land Reforms (Fixation of Ceiling Area and Acquisition of Surplus Land) (Amendment) Act, 1982 (Bihar Act 55 of 1982).

213. The Gujarat Devasthan Inams Abolition Act, 1969 (Gujarat Act 16 of 1969).

214. The Gujarat Tenancy Laws (Amendment) Act, 1976 (Gujarat Act 37 of 1976).

215. The Gujarat Agricultural Lands Ceiling (Amendment) Act, 1976 (President's Act 43 of 1976).

216. The Gujarat Devasthan Inams Abolition (Amendment) Act, 1977 (Gujarat Act 27 of 1977).

217. The Gujarat Tenancy Laws (Amendment) Act, 1977 (Gujarat Act 30 of 1977).

---

1. Ins. by the Constitution (Sixty-sixth Amendment) Act, 1990, sec. 2 (w.e.f. 7-6-1990).

218. The Bombay Land Revenue (Gujarat Second Amendment) Act, 1980 (Gujarat Act 37 of 1980).

219. The Bombay Land Revenue Code and Land Tenure Abolition Laws (Gujarat Amendment) Act, 1982 (Gujarat Act 8 of 1982).

220. The Himachal Pradesh Transfer of Land (Regulation) Act, 1968 (Himachal Pradesh Act 15 of 1969).

221. The Himachal Pradesh Transfer of Land (Regulation) (Amendment) Act, 1986 (Himachal Pradesh Act 16 of 1986).

222. The Karnataka Scheduled Castes and Scheduled Tribes (Prohibition of Transfer of certain Lands) Act, 1978 (Karnataka Act 2 of 1979).

223. The Kerala Land Reforms (Amendment) Act, 1978 (Kerala Act 13 of 1978)

224. The Kerala Land Reforms (Amendment) Act, 1981 (Kerala Act 19 of 1981).

225. The Madhya Pradesh Land Revenue Code (Third Amendment) Act, 1976 (Madhya Pradesh Act 61 of 1976).

226. The Madhya Pradesh Land Revenue Code (Amendment) Act, 1980 (Madhya Pradesh Act 15 of 1980).

227. The Madhya Pradesh Akrishik Jot Uchachatam Seema Adhiniyam, 1981 (Madhya Pradesh Act 11 of 1981).

228. The Madhya Pradesh Ceiling on Agricultural Holdings (Second Amendment) Act, 1976 (Madhya Pradesh Act I of 1984).

229. The Madhya Pradesh Ceiling on Agricultural Holdings (Amendment) Act, 1984 (Madhya Pradesh Act 14 of 1984).

230. The Madhya Pradesh Ceiling on Agricultural Holdings (Amendment) Act, 1989 (Madhya Pradesh Act 8 of 1989).

231. The Maharashtra Land Revenue Code, 1966 (Maharashtra Act 41 of 1966), sections 36, 36A and 36B.

232. The Maharashtra Land Revenue Code and the Maharashtra Restoration of Lands to Scheduled Tribes (Second Amendment) Act, 1976 (Maharashtra Act 30 of 1977).

233. The Maharashtra Abolition of Subsisting Proprietary Rights to Mines and Minerals in certain Lands Act, 1985 (Maharashtra Act 16 of 1985).

234. The Orissa Scheduled Areas Transfer of Immovable Property (By Scheduled Tribes) Regulation, 1956 (Orissa Regulation 2 of 1956).

235. The Orissa Land Reforms (Second Amendment) Act, 1975 (Orissa Act 29 of 1976).

236. The Orissa Land Reforms (Amendment) Act, 1976 (Orissa Act 30 of 1976).

237. The Orissa Land Reforms (Second Amendment) Act, 1976 (Orissa Act 44 of 1976).

238. The Rajasthan Colonisation (Amendment) Act, 1984 (Rajasthan Act 12 of 1984).

239. The Rajasthan Tenancy (Amendment) Act, 1984 (Rajasthan Act 13 of 1984).

240. The Rajasthan Tenancy (Amendment) Act, 1987 (Rajasthan Act 21 of 1987).

241. The Tamil Nadu Land Reforms (Fixation of Ceiling on Land) Second Amendment Act, 1979 (Tamil Nadu Act 8 of 1980).

242. The Tamil Nadu Land Reforms (Fixation of Ceiling on Land) Amendment Act, 1980 (Tamil Nadu Act 21 of 1980).

243. The Tamil Nadu Land Reforms (Fixation of Ceiling on Land) Amendment Act, 1981 (Tamil Nadu Act 59 of 1981).

244. The Tamil Nadu Land Reforms (Fixation of Ceiling on Land) Second Amendment Act, 1983 (Tamil Nadu Act 2 of 1984).

245. The Uttar Pradesh Land Laws (Amendment) Act, 1982 (Uttar Pradesh Act 20 of 1982).

246. The West Bengal Land Reforms (Amendment) Act, 1965 (West Bengal Act 18 of 1965).

247. The West Bengal Land Reforms (Amendment) Act, 1966 (West Bengal Act 11 of 1966).

248. The West Bengal Land Reforms (Second Amendment) Act, 1969 (West Bengal Act 23 of 1969).

249. The West Bengal Estate Acquisition (Amendment) Act, 1977 (West Bengal Act 36 of 1977).

250. The West Bengal Land Holding Revenue Act, 1979 (West Bengal Act 44 of 1979).

251. The West Bengal Land Reforms (Amendment) Act, 1980 (West Bengal Act 41 of 1980).

252. The West Bengal Land Holding Revenue (Amendment) Act, 1981 (West Bengal Act 33 of 1981).

253. The Calcutta Thikka Tenancy (Acquisition and Regulation) Act, 1981 (West Bengal Act 37 of 1981).

254. The West Bengal Land Holding Revenue (Amendment) Act, 1982 (West Bengal Act 23 of 1982).

255. The Calcutta Thikka Tenancy (Acquisition and Regulation) (Amendment) Act, 1984 (West Bengal Act 41 of 1984).

256. The Mahe Land Reforms Act, 1968 (Pondicherry Act 1 of 1968).

257. The Mahe Land Reforms (Amendment) Act, 1980 (Pondicherry Act 1 of 1981).]

[1][257A. The Tamil Nadu Backward Classes, Scheduled Castes and Scheduled Tribes (Reservation of Seats in Educational Institutions and of appointments or posts in the Services under the State) Act, 1993 (Tamil Nadu Act 45 of 1994).]

[2][258. The Bihar Privileged Persons Homestead Tenancy Act, 1947 (Bihar Act 4 of 1948).

259. The Bihar Consolidation of Holdings and Prevention of Fragmentation Act, 1956 (Bihar Act 22 of 1956).

260. The Bihar Consolidation of Holdings and Prevention of Fragmentation (Amendment) Act, 1970 (Bihar Act 7 of 1970).

261. The Bihar Privileged Persons Homestead Tenancy (Amendment) Act, 1970 (Bihar Act 9 of 1970).

262. The Bihar Consolidation of Holdings and Prevention of Fragmentation (Amendment) Act, 1973 (Bihar Act 27 of 1975).

263. The Bihar Consolidation of Holdings and Prevention of Fragmentation (Amendment) Act, 1981 (Bihar Act 35 of 1982).

264. The Bihar Land Reforms (Fixation of Ceiling Area and Acquisition of Surplus Land) (Amendment) Act, 1987 (Bihar Act 21 of 1987).

265. The Bihar Privileged Persons Homestead Tenancy (Amendment) Act, 1989 (Bihar Act 11 of 1989).

266. The Bihar Land Reforms (Amendment) Act, 1989 (Bihar Act 11 of 1990).

---

1. Ins. by the Constitution (Seventy-sixth Amendment) Act, 1994, sec. 2 (w.e.f. 31-8-1994).

2. Ins. by the Constitution (Seventy-eighth Amendment) Act, 1995, sec. 2 (w.e.f. 30-8-1995).

267. The Karnataka Scheduled Castes and Scheduled Tribes (Prohibition of Transfer of Certain Lands) (Amendment) Act, 1984 (Karnataka Act 3 of 1984).

268. The Kerala Land Reforms (Amendment) Act, 1989 (Kerala Act 16 of 1989).

269. The Kerala Land Reforms (Second Amendment) Act, 1989 (Kerala Act 2 of 1990).

270. The Orissa Land Reforms (Amendment) Act, 1989 (Orissa Act 9 of 1990).

271. The Rajasthan Tenancy (Amendment) Act, 1979 (Rajasthan Act 16 of 1979).

272. The Rajasthan Colonisation (Amendment) Act, 1987 (Rajasthan Act 2 of 1987).

273. The Rajasthan Colonisation (Amendment) Act, 1989 (Rajasthan Act 12 of 1989).

274. The Tamil Nadu Land Reforms (Fixation of Ceiling on Land) Amendment Act, 1983 (Tamil Nadu Act 3 of 1984).

275. The Tamil Nadu Land Reforms (Fixation of Ceiling on Land) Amendment Act, 1986 (Tamil Nadu Act 57 of 1986).

276. The Tamil Nadu Land Reforms (Fixation of Ceiling on Land) Second Amendment Act, 1987 (Tamil Nadu Act 4 of 1988).

277. The Tamil Nadu Land Reforms (Fixation of Ceiling on Land) Amendment Act, 1989 (Tamil Nadu Act 30 of 1989).

278. The West Bengal Land Reforms (Amendment) Act, 1981 (West Bengal Act 50 of 1981).

279. The West Bengal Land Reforms (Amendment) Act, 1986 (West Bengal Act 5 of 1986).

280 The West Bengal Land Reforms (Second Amendment) Act, 1986 (West Bengal Act 19 of 1986).

281. The West Bengal Land Reforms (Third Amendment) Act, 1981 (West Bengal Act 35 of 1986).

282. The West Bengal Land Reforms (Amendment) Act, 1989 (West Bengal Act 23 of 1989).

283. The West Bengal Land Reforms (Amendment) Act, 1990 (West Bengal Act 24 of 1990).

284. The West Bengal Land Reforms Tribunal Act, 1991 (West Bengal Act 12 of 1991).]

Explanation.—Any acquisition made under the Rajasthan Tenancy Act, 1955 (Rajasthan Act III of 1955), in contravention of the second proviso to clause (1) of article 31A shall, to the extent of the contravention, be void.

¹[*TENTH SCHEDULE*

[Articles 102(2) and 191(2)]

PROVISIONS AS TO DISQUALIFICATION ON GROUND OF DEFECTION

1. Interpretation.—In this Schedule, unless the context otherwise requires,—

(a) "House" means either House of Parliament or the Legislative Assembly or, as the case may be, either House of the Legislature of a State;

(b) "legislature party", in relation to a member of a House belonging to any political party in accordance with the provisions of paragraph 2 or ²[***] paragraph 4, means the group consisting of all the members of that House for the time being belonging to that political party in accordance with the said provisions;

---

1. Added by the Constitution (Fifty-second Amendment) Act, 1985, sec. 6 (w.e.f. 1-3-1985). Earlier the Tenth Schedule was omitted by the Constitution (Thirty-sixth Amendment) Act, 1975, sec. 5(d) (w.e.f. 28-4-1975).

2. The words "paragraph 3, or as the case may be," omitted by the Constitution (Ninety-first Amendment) Act, 2003, sec. 5(a) (w.e.f. 1-1-2004).

(c) "original political party", in relation to a member of a House, means the political party to which he belongs for the purposes of sub-paragraph (1) of paragraph 2;

(d) "paragraph" means a paragraph of this Schedule.

2. Disqualification on ground of defection.—(1) Subject to the provisions of ¹[paragraphs 4 and 5], a member of a House belonging to any political party shall be disqualified for being a member of the House—

(a) if he has voluntarily given up his membership of such political party; or

(b) if he votes or abstains from voting in such House contrary to any direction issued by the political party to which he belongs or by any person or authority authorised by it in this behalf, without obtaining, in either case, the prior permission of such political party, person or authority and such voting or abstention has not been condoned by such political party, person or authority within fifteen days from the date of such voting or abstention.

Explanation.—For the purposes of this sub-paragraph,—

(a) an elected member of a House shall be deemed to belong to the political party, if any, by which he was set up as a candidate for election as such memb

(b) a nominated member of a House shall,—

(i) where he is a member of any political party on the date of his nomination as such member, be deemed to belong to such political party;

(ii) in any other case, be deemed to belong to the political party of which he becomes, or, as the case may be, first becomes, a member before the expiry of six months from the date on which he takes his seat after complying with the requirements of article 99 or, as the case may be, article 188.

(2) An elected member of a House who has been elected as such otherwise than as a candidate set up by any political party shall be disqualified for being a member of the House if he joins any political party after such election.

(3) A nominated member of a House shall be disqualified for being a member of the House if he joins any political party after the expiry of six months from the date on which he takes his seat after complying with the requirements of article 99 or, as the case may be, article 188.

(4) Notwithstanding anything contained in the foregoing provisions of this paragraph, a person who, on the commencement of the Constitution (Fifty-second Amendment) Act, 1985, is a member of a House (whether elected or nominated as such) shall,—

(i) where he was a member of political party immediately before such commencement, be deemed, for the purposes of sub-paragraph (1) of this paragraph, to have been elected as a member of such House as a candidate set up by such political party;

(ii) in any other case, be deemed to be an elected member of the House who has been elected as such otherwise than as a candidate set up by any political party for the purposes of sub-paragraph (2) of this paragraph or, as the case may be, deemed to be a nominated member of the House for the purposes of sub-paragraph (3) of this paragraph.

²[***]

---

1. Subs. by the Constitution (Ninety-first Amendment) Act, 2003, sec. 5(b), for "paragraphs 3, 4 and 5" (w.e.f. 1-1-2004).

2. Paragraph 3 omitted by the Constitution (Ninety-first Amendment) Act, 2003, sec. 5(c) (w.e.f. 1-1-2004).

4. Disqualification on ground of defection not to apply in case of merger.—(1) A member of a House shall not be disqualified under sub-paragraph (1) of paragraph 2 where his original political party merges with another political party and he claims that he and any other members of his original political party—

(a) have become members of such other political party or, as the case may be, of a new political party formed by such merger; or

(b) have not accepted the merger and opted to function as a separate group,

and from the time of such merger, such other political party or new political party or group, as the case may be, shall be deemed to be the political party to which he belongs for the purposes of sub-paragraph (1) of paragraph 2 and to be his original political party for the purpose of this sub-paragraph.

(2) For the purposes of sub-paragraph (1) of this paragraph, the merger of the original political party of a member of a House shall be deemed to have taken place if, and only if, not less than two-thirds of the members of the legislature party concerned have agreed to such merger.

5. Exemption.—Notwithstanding anything contained in this Schedule, a person who has been elected to the office of the Speaker or the Deputy Speaker of the House of the People or the Deputy Chairman of the Council of States or the Chairman or the Deputy Chairman of the Legislative Council of a State or the Speaker or the Deputy Speaker of the Legislative Assembly of a State, shall not be disqualified under this Schedule,—

(a) if he, by reason of his election to such office, voluntarily gives up the membership of the political party to which he belonged immediately before such election and does not, so long as he continues to hold such office thereafter, rejoin that political party or become a member of another political party; or

(b) if he, having given up by reason of his election to such office his membership of the political party to which he belonged immediately before such election, rejoins such political party after he ceases to hold such office.

6. Decision on questions as to disqualification on ground of defection.—(1) If any question arises as to whether a member of a House has become subject to disqualification under this Schedule, the question shall be referred for the decision of the Chairman or, as the case may be, the Speaker of such House and his decision shall be final:

Provided that where the question which has arisen is as to whether the Chairman or the Speaker of a House has become subject to such disqualification, the question shall be referred for the decision of such member of the House as the House may elect in this behalf and his decision shall be final.

(2) All proceedings under sub-paragraph (1) of this paragraph in relation to any question as to disqualification of a member of a House under this Schedule shall be deemed to be proceedings in Parliament within the meaning of article 122 or, as the case may be, proceedings in the Legislature of a State within the meaning of article 212.

*7. Bar of jurisdiction of courts.—Notwithstanding anything in this Constitution, no court shall have any jurisdiction in respect of any matter connected with the disqualification of a member of a House under this Schedule.

8. Rules.—(1) Subject to the provisions of sub-paragraph (2) of this paragraph, the Chairman or the Speaker of a House may make rules for giving effect to the provisions of this Schedule, and in particular, and without prejudice to the generality of the foregoing, such rules may provide for—

---

* Paragraph 7 declared invalid for want of ratification in accordance with the proviso to clause (2) of article 368 as per majority opinion in *Kihoto Hollohon v. Zachilhu*, (1992) 1 SCC 309.

(a) the maintenance of registers or other records as to the political parties if any, to which different members of the House belong;

(b) the report which the leader of a legislature party in relation to a member of a House shall furnish with regard to any condonation of the nature referred to in clause (b) of sub-paragraph (1) of paragraph 2 in respect of such member, the time within which and the authority to whom such report shall be furnished;

(c) the reports which a political party shall furnish with regard to admission to such political party of any members of the House and the officer of the House to whom such reports shall be furnished; and

(d) the procedure for deciding any question referred to in sub-paragraph (1) of paragraph 6 including the procedure for any inquiry which may be made for the purpose of deciding such question.

(2) The rules made by the Chairman or the Speaker of a House under sub-paragraph (1) of this paragraph shall be laid as soon as may be after they are made before the House for a total period of thirty days which may be comprised in one session or in two or more successive sessions and shall take effect upon the expiry of the said period of thirty days unless they are sooner approved with or without modifications or disapproved by the House and where they are so approved, they shall take effect on such approval in the form in which they were laid or in such modified form, as the case may be, and where they are so disapproved, they shall be of no effect.

(3) The Chairman or the Speaker of a House may, without prejudice to the provisions of article 105 or, as the case may be, article 194, and to any other power which he may have under this Constitution direct that any wilful contravention by any person of the rules made under this paragraph may be dealt with in the same manner as a breach of privilege of the House.]

¹[ELEVENTH SCHEDULE
(Article 243G)

1. Agriculture, including agricultural extension.
2. Land improvement, implementation of land reforms, land consolidation and soil conservation.
3. Minor irrigation, water management and watershed development.
4. Animal husbandry, dairying and poultry.
5. Fisheries.
6. Social forestry and farm forestry.
7. Minor forest produce.
8. Small scale industries, including food processing industries.
9. Khadi, village and cottage industries.
10. Rural housing.
11. Drinking water.
12. Fuel and fodder.
13. Roads, culverts, bridges, ferries, waterways and other means of communication.
14. Rural electrification, including distribution of electricity.
15. Non-conventional energy sources.
16. Poverty alleviation programme.

---

1. Added by the Constitution (Seventy-third Amendment) Act, 1992, sec. 4 (w.e.f. 24-4-1993).

17. Education, including primary and secondary schools.
18. Technical training and vocational education.
19. Adult and non-formal education.
20. Libraries.
21. Cultural activities.
22. Markets and fairs.
23. Health and sanitation, including hospitals, primary health centres and dispensaries.
24. Family welfare.
25. Women and child development.
26. Social welfare, including welfare of the handicapped and mentally retarded.
27. Welfare of the weaker sections, and in particular, of the Scheduled Castes and the Scheduled Tribes.
28. Public distribution system.
29. Maintenance of community assets.]

¹[TWELFTH SCHEDULE
(Article 243W)

1. Urban planning including town planning.
2. Regulation of land-use and construction of buildings.
3. Planning for economic and social development.
4. Roads and bridges.
5. Water supply for domestic, industrial and, commercial purposes.
6. Public health, sanitation conservancy and solid waste management.
7. Fire services.
8. Urban forestry, protection of the environment and promotion of ecological aspects.
9. Safeguarding the interests of weaker sections of society, including the handicapped and mentally retarded.
10. Slum improvement and upgradation.
11. Urban poverty alleviation.
12. Provision of urban amenities and facilities such as parks, gardens, play-grounds.
13. Promotion of cultural, educational and aesthetic aspects.
14. Burials and burial grounds; cremations, cremation grounds and electric crematoriums.
15. Cattle ponds; prevention of cruelty to animals.
16. Vital statistics including registration of births and deaths.
17. Public amenities including street lighting, parking lots, bus stops and public conveniences.
18. Regulation of slaughter houses and tanneries.]

---

1. Ins. by the Constitution (Seventy-fourth Amendment) Act, 1992, sec. 4 (w.e.f. 1-6-1993).

THE CONSTITUTION (APPLICATION TO JAMMU AND KASHMIR) ORDER, 1954[1]

C.O. 48

In exercise of the powers conferred by clause (1) of article 370 of the Constitution, the President, with the concurrence of the Government of the State of Jammu and Kashmir, is pleased to make the following Order:—

1. (1) This Order may be called the Constitution (Application to Jammu and Kashmir) Order, 1954.

(2) It shall come into force on the fourteenth day of May, 1954, and shall thereupon supersede the Constitution (Application to Jammu and Kashmir) Order, 1950.

2. [2][The provisions of the Constitution as in force on the 20th day of June, 1964 and as amended by the Constitution (Nineteenth Amendment) Act, 1966, the Constitution (Twenty-first Amendment) Act, 1967, section 5 of the Constitution (Twenty-third Amendment) Act, 1969, the Constitution (Twenty-fourth Amendment) Act, 1971, section 2 of the Constitution (Twenty-fifth Amendment) Act, 1971, the Constitution (Twenty-sixth Amendment) Act, 1971, the Constitution (Thirtieth Amendment) Act, 1972, section 2 of the Constitution (Thirty-first Amendment) Act, 1973, section 2 of the Constitution (Thirty-third Amendment) Act, 1974, sections 2, 5, 6 and 7 of the Constitution (Thirty-eighth Amendment) Act, 1975, the Constitution (Thirty-ninth Amendment) Act, 1975, the Constitution (Fortieth Amendment) Act, 1976, sections 2, 3 and 6 of the Constitution (Fifty-second Amendment) Act, 1985 and the Constitution (Sixty-first Amendment) Act, 1988 which, in addition to article 1 and article 370, shall apply in relation to the State of Jammu and Kashmir and the exceptions and modifications subject to which they shall so apply shall be as follows:—]

(1) THE PREAMBLE

(2) PART I

To article 3, there shall be added the following further proviso, namely:—

"Provided further that no Bill providing for increasing or diminishing the area of the State of Jammu and Kashmir or altering the name or boundary of that State shall be introduced in Parliament without the consent of the Legislature of that State."

(3) PART II

(a) This Part shall be deemed to have been applicable in relation to the State of Jammu and Kashmir as from the 26th day of January, 1950.

---

1. Published with the Ministry of Law Notification No. S.R.O. 1610, dated the 14th May, 1954, Gazette of India, Extra., Pt. II, Sec. 3, p. 821.

2. The opening words have been successively amended by C.O. 56, C.O. 74, C.O. 76, C.O. 79, C.O. 89, C.O. 91, C.O. 94, C.O. 98, C.O. 103, C.O. 104, C.O. 105, C.O. 108, C.O. 136 and C.O. 141 to read as above.

(b) To article 7, there shall be added the following further proviso, namely:—

"Provided further that nothing in this article shall apply to a permanent resident of the State of Jammu and Kashmir who, after having so migrated to the territory now included in Pakistan, returns to the territory of that State under a permit for resettlement in that State or permanent return issued by or under the authority of any law made by the Legislature of that State, and every such person shall be deemed to be a citizen of India."

(4) PART III

(a) In article 13, references to the commencement of the Constitution shall be construed as references to the commencement of this Order.

[1][***]

(c) In clause (3) of article 16, the reference to the State shall be construed as not including a reference to the State of Jammu and Kashmir.

(d) In article 19, for a period of [2][[3][twenty-five] years] from the commencement of this Order—

(i) in clauses (3) and (4) after the words "in the interests of", the words "the security of the State or" shall be inserted;

(ii) in clause (5), for the words "or for the protection of the interests of any Scheduled Tribe", the words "or in the interests of the security of the State" shall be substituted; and

(iii) the following new clause shall be added, namely:—

'(7) The words "reasonable restrictions" occurring in clauses (2), (3), (4) and (5) shall be construed as meaning such restrictions as the appropriate Legislature deems reasonable.'

(e) In clauses (4) and (7) of article 22, for the word "Parliament", the words "the Legislature of the State" shall be substituted.

(f) In article 31, clauses (3), (4) and (6) shall be omitted; and for clause (5) , there shall be substituted the following clause, namely:—

"(5) Nothing in clause (2) shall affect—

(a) the provisions of any existing law; or

(b) the provisions of any law which the State may hereafter make—

(i) for the purpose of imposing or levying any tax or penalty; or

(ii) for the promotion of public health or the prevention of danger to life or property; or

(iii) with respect to property declared by law to be evacuee property."

(g) In article 31A, the proviso to clause (1) shall be omitted; and for sub-clause (a) of clause (2), the following sub-clause shall be substituted, namely:—

'(a) "estate" shall mean land which is occupied or has been let for agricultural purposes or for purposes subservient to agriculture, or for pasture, and includes—

---

1. Clause (b) omitted by C.O. 124 (w.e.f. 4-12-1985).
2. Subs. by C.O. 69, for "ten years".
3. Subs. by C.O. 97, for "twenty".

(i) sites of buildings and other structures on such land;

(ii) trees standing on such land;

(iii) forest land and wooded waste;

(iv) area covered by or fields floating over water;

(v) sites of *Jandars* and *gharats*;

(vi) any *Jagir, inam, muafi* or *mukarrari* or other similar grant,

but does not include—

(i) the site of any building in any town, or town area or village *abadi* or any land appurtenant to any such building or site;

(ii) any land which is occupied as the site of a town or village; or

(iii) any land reserved for building purposes in a municipality or notified area or cantonment or town area or any area for which a town planning scheme is sanctioned.'.

[1][(h) In article 32, clause (3) shall be omitted.]

(i) In article 35—

(i) references to the commencement of the Constitution shall be construed as references to the commencement of this Order;

(ii) in clause (a)(i), the words, brackets and figures "clause (3) of article 16, clause (3) of article 32" shall be omitted; and

(iii) after clause (b), the following clause shall be added, namely:—

"(c) no law with respect to preventive detention made by the Legislature of the State of Jammu and Kashmir, whether before or after the commencement of the Constitution (Application to Jammu and Kashmir) Order, 1954, shall be void on the ground that it is inconsistent with any of the provisions of this Part, but any such law shall, to the extent of such inconsistency, cease to have effect on the expiration of [2][[3][twenty-five] years] from the commencement of the said Order, except as respects things done or omitted to be done before the expiration thereof."

(j) After article 35, the following new article shall be added, namely:—

"35A. *Saving of laws with respect to permanent residents and their rights—* Notwithstanding anything contained in this Constitution, no existing law in force in the State of Jammu and Kashmir, and no law hereafter enacted by the Legislature of the State,—

(a) defining the classes of persons who are, or shall be, permanent residents of the State of Jammu and Kashmir; or

(b) conferring on such permanent residents any special rights and privileges or imposing upon other persons any restrictions as respects—

(i) employment under the State Government;

---

1. Subs. by C.O. 89, for clause (h).
2. Subs. by C.O. 69, for "ten years".
3. Subs. by C.O. 97, for "twenty".

(ii) acquisition of immovable property in the State;

(iii) settlement in the State; or

(iv) right to scholarships and such other forms of aid as the State Government may provide,

shall be void on the ground that it is inconsistent with or takes away or abridges any rights conferred on the other citizens of India by any provision of this Part".

(5) PART V

[1][(a) For the purposes of article 55, the population of the State of Jammu and Kashmir shall be deemed to be sixty-three lakhs.

(b) In article 81, for clauses (2) and (3), the following clauses shall be substituted, namely:—

"(2) For the purposes of sub-clause (a) of clause (1),—

(a) there shall be allotted to the State six seats in the House of the People;

(b) the State shall be divided into single member territorial constituencies by the Delimitation Commission constituted under the Delimitation Act, 1972, in accordance with such procedure as the Commission may deem fit;

(c) the constituencies shall, as far as practicable, be geographically compact areas, and in delimiting them regard shall be had to physical features, existing boundaries of administrative units, facilities of communication and public convenience; and

(d) the constituencies into which the State is divided shall not comprise the area under the occupation of Pakistan.

(3) Nothing in clause (2) shall affect the representation of the State in the House of the People until the dissolution of the House existing on the date of publication in the Gazette of India of the final order or orders of the Delimitation Commission relating to the delimitation of parliamentary constituencies under the Delimitation Act, 1972.

(4)(a) The Delimitation Commission shall associate with itself for the purpose of assisting it in its duties in respect of the State, five persons who shall be members of the House of the People representing the State.

(b) The persons to be so associated from the State shall be nominated by the Speaker of the House of the People having due regard to the composition of the House.

(c) The first nominations to be made under sub-clause (b) shall be made by the Speaker of the House of the People within two months from the commencement of the Constitution (Application to Jammu and Kashmir) Second Amendment Order, 1974.

(d) None of the associate members shall have a right to vote or to sign any decision of the Delimitation Commission.

(e) If owing to death or resignation, the office of an associate member falls vacant, it shall be filled as soon as may be practicable by the Speaker of the

---

1. Subs. by C.O. 98, for clauses (a) and (b).

House of the People and in accordance with the provisions of sub-clauses (a) and (b)."]

¹[(c) In article 133, after clause (1), the following clause shall be inserted, namely:—

'(1A) The provisions of section 3 of the Constitution (Thirtieth Amendment) Act, 1972, shall apply in relation to the State of Jammu and Kashmir subject to the modification that references therein to "this Act", "the commencement of this Act", "this Act had not been passed" and "as amended by this Act" shall be construed respectively as references to "the Constitution (Application to Jammu and Kashmir) Second Amendment Order, 1974", "the commencement of the said Order", "the said Order had not been made" and "as it stands after the commencement of the said Order". '].

²[(d)] In article 134, clause (2), after the words "Parliament may", the words "on the request of the Legislature of the State" shall be inserted.

²[(e)] Articles 135, ³[***] and 139 shall the omitted.

⁴[***]

⁵[(5A) PART VI

⁶[(a) Articles 153 to 217, article 219, article 221, articles 223, 224, 224A and 225 and articles 227 to 237 shall be omitted.]

(b) In article 220, references to the commencement of the Constitution shall be construed as references to the commencement of the Constitution (Application to Jammu and Kashmir) Amendment Order, 1960.

⁷[(c) In article 222, after clause (1), the following new clause shall be inserted, namely:—

'(1A) Every such transfer from the High Court of Jammu and Kashmir or to that High Court shall be made after consultation with the Governor.'.]]

(6) PART XI

⁸[(a) In article 246, for the words, brackets and figures "clauses (2) and (3)" occurring in clause (1), the word, brackets and figure "clause (2)" shall be substituted, and the words, brackets and figure "Notwithstanding anything in clause (3)," occurring in clause (2) and the whole of clauses (3) and (4) shall be omitted.]

⁹[¹⁰[(b) For article 248, the following article shall be substituted, namely:—

"248 *Residuary powers of legislation.*—Parliament has exclusive power to make any law with respect to—

---

1. Ins. by C.O. 98.
2. Clauses (c) and (d) relettered as clauses (d) and (e) by C.O. 98.
3. The figures "136" omitted by C.O. 60.
4. Clauses (f) and (g) omitted by C.O. 56.
5. Ins. by C.O. 60 (w.e.f. 26-1-1960).
6. Subs. by C.O. 89, for clause (a).
7. Subs. by C.O. 74, for clause (c) (w.e.f. 24-11-1965).
8. Subs. by C.O. 66, for clause (a).
9. Clauses (b) and (bb) subs. by C.O. 85, for original clause (b).
10. Subs. by C.O. 93, for clause (b).

[1][(a) prevention of activities involving terrorist acts directed towards over-awing the Government as by law established or striking terror in the people or any section of the people or alienating any section of the people or adversely affecting the harmony amongst different sections of the people.]

[2][(aa)] [3][prevention of other activities] directed towards disclaiming, questioning or disrupting the sovereignty and territorial integrity of India or bringing about cession of a part of the territory of India or secession of a part of the territory of India from the Union or causing insult to the Indian National Flag, the Indian National Anthem and this Constitution; and

(b) taxes on—

    (i) foreign travel by sea or air;

    (ii) inland air travel;

    (iii) postal articles, including money orders, phonograms and telegrams".

    [1][*Explanation.*—In this article, "terrorist act" means any act or thing by using bombs, dynamite or other explosive substances or inflammable substances or firearms or other lethal weapons or poisons or noxious gases or other chemicals or any other substances (whether biological or otherwise) of a hazardous nature.]

[4][(bb) In article 249, in clause (1), for the words "any matter enumerated in the State List specified in the resolution," the words "any matter specified in the resolution being a matter which is not enumerated in the Union List or in the concurrent List" shall be substituted.]]

(c) In article 250, for the words "to any of the matters enumerated in the State List", the words "also to matters not enumerated in the Union List" shall be substituted.

    [5][***]

(e) to article 253, the following proviso shall be added, namely:—

    "Provided that after the commencement of the Constitution (Application to Jammu and Kashmir) Order, 1954, no decision affecting the disposition of the State of Jammu and Kashmir shall be made by the Government of India without the consent of the Government of that State."

[6][***]

[7][(f)] Article 255 shall be omitted.

[7][(g)] Article 256 shall be re-numbered as clause (1) of that article, and the following new clause shall be added thereto, namely:—

---

1. Ins. by C.O. 122.
2. Clause (a) relettered as clause (aa) by C.O. 122.
3. Subs. by C.O. 122, for "prevention of activities".
4. Subs. by C.O. 129, for clause (bb).
5. Clause (d) omitted by C.O. 129.
6. Clause (f) omitted by C.O. 66.
7. Clauses (g) and (h) relettered as clauses (f) and (g) by C.O. 66.

"(2) The State of Jammu and Kashmir shall so exercise its executive power as to facilitate the discharge by the Union of its duties and responsibilities under the Constitution in relation to that State; and in particular, the said State shall, if so required by the Union, acquire or requisition property on behalf and at the expense of the Union, or if the property belongs to the State, transfer it to the union on such terms as may be agreed, or in default of agreement, as may be determined by an arbitrator appointed by the Chief Justice of India".

[1][***]

[2][(h) In clause (2) of article 261, the words "made by Parliament" shall be omitted.

(7) PART XII

[3][***]

[4][(a)] Clause (2) of article 267, article 273, clause (2) of article 283 [5][and article 290] shall be omitted.

[4][(b)] In articles 266, 282, 284, 298, 299 and 300, references to the State or States shall be construed as not including references to the State of Jammu and Kashmir.

[4][(c) In articles 277 and 295, references to the commencement of the Constitution shall be construed as references to the commencement of this Order.

(8) PART XIII

[6][***] In clause (1) of article 303, the words "by virtue of any entry relating to trade and commerce in any of the Lists in the Seventh Schedule" shall be omitted.

[7][***]

(9) PART XIV

[8][In article 312 after the words "the States", the brackets and words "(including the State of Jammu and Kashmir)" shall be inserted.]

[9][(10) PART XV

(a) In clause (1) of article 324, the reference to the Constitution shall, in relation to elections to either House of the Legislature of Jammu and Kashmir be construed as a reference to the Constitution of Jammu and Kashmir.

[10][(b) In articles 325, 326, 327 and 329, the reference to a State shall be construed as not including a reference to the State of Jammu and Kashmir.

(c) Article 328 shall be omitted.

---

1. Clause (i) omitted by C.O. 56.
2. Clause (j) relettered as clause (i) by C.O. 56 and again relettered as clause (h) by C.O. 66.
3. Clauses (a) and (b) inserted by C.O. 55 and omitted by C.O. 56.
4. Clauses (a), (b) and (c) relettered as (c), (d) and (e) respectively by C.O. 55 and been relettered as clauses (a), (b) and (c) respectively by C.O. 56.
5. Subs. by C.O. 94, for "articles 290 and 291".
6. Brackets and letter "(a)" omitted by C.O. 56.
7. Clause (b) omitted by C.O. 56.
8. Subs. by C.O. 56, for the previous modification.
9. Subs. by C.O. 60, for sub-paragraph (10) (w.e.f. 26-1-1960).
10. Subs. by C.O. 75, for clauses (b) and (c).

(d) In article 329, the words and figures "or article 328" shall be omitted.]]

¹[(e) In article 329A, clauses (4) and (5) shall be omitted.]

(11) PART XVI

²[***]

³[(a)] Articles 331, 332, 333 ⁴[336 and 337] shall be omitted.

³[(b)] In articles 334 and 335, references to the State or the States shall be construed as not including references to the State of Jammu and Kashmir.

⁵[(c) In clause (1) of article 339, the words "the administration of the Scheduled Areas and" shall be omitted.]

(12) PART XVII

The provisions of the Part shall apply only in so far as they relate to—

(i) the official language of the Union;

(ii) the official language for communication between one State and another, or between a State and the Union; and

(iii) the language of the proceedings in the Supreme Court.

(13) PART XVIII

(a) To article 352, the following new clause shall be added, namely:—

"⁶[(6)] No Proclamation of Emergency made on grounds only of internal disturbance or imminent danger thereof shall have effect in relation to the State of Jammu and Kashmir (except as respects article 354) ⁷[unless—

(a) it is made at the request or with the concurrence of the Government of that State, or

(b) where it has not been so made, it is applied subsequently by the President to that State at the request or with the concurrence of the Government of that State.]".

⁸[(b) In clause (1) of article 356, references to provisions or provision of this Constitution shall, in relation to the State of Jammu and Kashmir, be construed as including references to provisions or provision of the Constitution of Jammu and Kashmir.

⁹[(bb) In clause (4) of article 356, after the second proviso, the following proviso shall be inserted, namely:—

'Provided also that in the case of the Proclamation issued under clause (1) on the 18th day of July, 1990 with respect to the State of Jammu and Kashmir,

---

1. Ins. by C.O. 105.
2. Clause (a) omitted by C.O. 124.
3. Clauses (b) and (c) relettered as clauses (a) and (b) by C.O. 124.
4. Subs. by C.O. 124, for "336, 337, 339 and 342".
5. Ins. by C.O. 124.
6. Subs. by C.O. 104, for "(4)".
7. Subs. by C.O. 100, for certain words.
8. Clauses (b) and (c) subs. by C.O. 71, for original clause (b).
9. Added by C.O. 151.

the reference in the first proviso to this clause to "three years" shall be construed as a reference to [1]["seven years"]'].

(c) Article 360 shall be omitted.]

(14) PART XIX

[2][***]

[3][(a)] [4][Article 365] shall be omitted.

[5][***]

[6][(b)] To article 367, there shall be added the following clause, namely:—

"(4) For the purposes of this Constitution as it applies in relation to the State of Jammu and Kashmir—

(a) references to this Constitution or to the provisions thereof shall be construed as references to the Constitution or the provisions thereof as applied in relation to the said State;

[6][(aa) references to the person for the time being recognised by the President on the recommendation of the Legislative Assembly of the State as the *Sadar-i-Riyasat* of Jammu and Kashmir, acting on the advice of the Council of Ministers of the State for the time being in office, shall be construed as references to the Governor of Jammu and Kashmir;

(b) references to the Government of the said State shall be construed as including references to the Governor of Jammu and Kashmir acting on the advice of his Council of Ministers:

Provided that in respect of any period prior to the 10th day of April, 1965, such references shall be construed as including references to the *Sadar-i-Riyasat* acting on the advice of his Council of Ministers;]

(c) references to a High Court shall include references to the High Court of Jammu and Kashmir;

[7][***]

[8][(d)] references to the permanent residents of the said State shall be construed as meaning persons who, before the commencement of the Constitution (Application to Jammu and Kashmir) Order, 1954 were recognised as State subjects under the laws in force in the State or who are recognised by any law made by the Legislature of the State as permanent residents of the State; and

---

1. Subs. by C.O. 154, for "four years" and successively substituted by C.O. 160, for "five years" and C.O. 162, for "six years"
2. Original clause (a) omitted by C.O. 74.
3. Clauses (b) and (c) relettered as clauses (a) and (b) by C.O. 74.
4. Subs. by C.O. 94, for "Articles 362 and 365".
5. Original clause (c) omitted by C.O. 56.
6. Subs. by C.O. 74, for clause (b).
7. Clause (d) omitted by C.O. 56.
8. Clauses (e) and (f) relettered as clauses (d) nad (e) respectively by C.O. 56.

[1][(e) references to a Governor shall include references to the Governor of Jammu and Kashmir:

Provided that in respect of any period prior to the 10th day of April, 1965, such references shall be construed as references to the person recognised by the President as the *Sadar-i-Riyasat* of Jammu and Kashmir and as including references to any person recognised by the President as being competent to exercise the powers of the *Sadar-i-Riyasat*.].

(15) PART XX

[2][(a)] [3][To clause (2) of article 368], the following proviso shall be added, namely:—

"Provided further that no such amendment shall have effect in relation to the State of Jammu and Kashmir unless applied by order of the President under clause (1) of article 370.";

[4][(b) After clause (3) of article 368, the following clause shall be added, namely:—

"(4) No law made by the Legislature of the State of Jammu and Kashmir seeking to make any change in or in the effect of any provision of the Constitution of Jammu and Kashmir relating to—

(a) appointment, powers, functions, duties, emoluments, allowances, privileges or immunities of the Governor; or

(b) superintendence, direction and control of elections by the Election Commission of India, eligibility for inclusion in the electoral rolls without discrimination, adult suffrage and composition of the Legislative Council, being matters specified in sections 138, 139, 140 and 150 of the Constitution of Jammu and Kashmir,

shall have any effect unless such law has, after having been reserved for the consideration of the President, received his assent."].

(16) PART XXI

(a) Articles 369, 371, [5][371A], [6][372A], 373, clauses (1), (2), (3) and (5) of article 374 and [7][articles 376 to 378A and 392] shall be omitted.

(b) In article 372—

(i) clauses (2) and (3) shall be omitted;

(ii) references to the laws in force in the territory of India shall include references to *hidayat, ailans, ishtihars,* circulars, *robkars, irshads, yadashts,* State Council Resolutions, Resolutions of the Constituent Assembly, and other instruments having the force of law in the territory of the State of Jammu and Kashmir; and

(iii) references to the commencement of the Constitution shall be construed as references to the commencement of this Order;

---

1. Subs. by C.O. 74, for clause (e).
2. Numbered as clause (a) by C.O. 101.
3. Subs. by C.O. 91, for "To article 368".
4. Ins. by C.O. 101.
5. Ins. by C.O. 74.
6. Ins. by C.O. 56.
7. Subs. by C.O. 56, for "articles 376 to 392".

(c) In clause (4) of the article 374, the reference to the authority functioning as the Privy Council of a State shall be construed as a reference to the Advisory Board constituted under the Jammu and Kashmir Constitution Act, 1996 and references to the commencement of the Constitution shall be construed as references to the commencement of this Order.

(17) PART XXII

Articles 394 and 395 shall be omitted.

(18) FIRST SCHEDULE

(19) SECOND SCHEDULE

[1][***]

(20) THIRD SCHEDULE

Forms V, VI, VII and VIII shall be omitted.

(21) FOURTH SCHEDULE

[2][(22) SEVENTH SCHEDULE

(a) In the Union List—

(i) for entry 3, the entry "3. Administration of cantonments" shall be substituted;

[3][(ii) entries 8, 9 [4][and 34], [5][***] entry 79, and the words "Inter-State migration" in entry 81 shall be omitted;]

[6][***]

[7][(iii) in entry 72, the reference to the States shall be construed,—

    (a) in relation to appeals to the Supreme Court from any decision or order of the High Court of the State of Jammu and Kashmir made in an election petition whereby an election to either House of the Legislature of that State has been called in question, as including a reference to the State of Jammu and Kashmir;

    (b) in relation to other matters, as not including a reference to that State]; [8][and]

[9][(iv) for entry 97, the following entry shall be substituted, namely:—

    [10][97. Prevention of activities—

    (a) involving terrorist acts directed towards overawing the Government as by law established or striking terror in the people or any section of the

---

1. Modification relating to paragraph 6 omitted by C.O. 56.
2. Subs. by C.O. 66 of 1963, for sub-paragraph (22).
3. Item (ii) subs. by C.O. 85. It was previously subs. by C.O. 72.
4. Subs. by C.O. 92, for "34 and 60".
5. The words and figures 'the words "and records" in entry 67' omitted by C.O. 95.
6. Original item (iii) omitted by C.O. 74.
7. Subs. by C.O. 83, for item (iii).
8. Ins. by C.O. 85.
9. Subs. by C.O. 93, for item (iv).
10. Subs. by C.O. 122 for entry 97 (w.e.f. 4-6-1985).

people or alienating any section of the people or adversely affecting the harmony amongst different sections of the people;

(b) directed towards disclaiming, questioning or disrupting the sovereignty and territorial integrity of India or bringing about cession of a part of the territory of India or secession of a part of the territory of India from the Union or causing insult to the Indian National Flag, the Indian National Anthem and this Constitution,

taxes on foreign travel by sea or air, on inland air travel and on postal articles, including money orders, phonograms and telegrams.

Explanation.—In this entry, "terrorist act" has the same meaning as in the *Explanation* to article 248.]]

(b) The State List shall be omitted.

¹[(c) In the Concurrent List—

²[(i) for entry 1, the following entry shall be substituted, namely:—

"1. Criminal law (excluding offences against laws with respect to any of the matters specified in List I and excluding the use of naval, military or air forces or any other armed forces of the Union in aid of the civil power) in so far as such criminal law relates to offences against laws with respect to any of the matters specified in this List."];

³[⁴[(ia) for entry 2, the following entry shall be substituted, namely:—

"2. Criminal procedure (including prevention of offences and constitution and organisation of criminal courts, except the Supreme Court and the High Court) in so far as it relates to,—

(i) offences against laws with respect to any matters being matters with respect to which Parliament has power to make laws; and

(ii) administration of oaths and taking of affidavits by diplomatic and consular officers in any foreign country".

(ib) for entry 12, the following entry shall be substituted, namely:—

"12. Evidence and oaths in so far as they relate to,—

(i) administration of oaths and taking of affidavits by diplomatic and consular officers in any foreign country; and

(ii) any other matters being matters with respect to which Parliament has power to make laws.];

(ic) for entry 13, the entry "13. Civil procedure in so far as it relates to administration of oaths and taking of affidavits by diplomatic and consular officers in any foreign country." shall be substituted;]

⁵[***]

---

1. Subs. by C.O. 69, for clause (c).
2. Subs. by C.O. 70, for item (i).
3. Ins. by C.O. 94.
4. Subs. by C.O. 122, for sub-clauses (ia) and (ib) (w.e.f 4-6-1985).
5. Items (ii) and (iii) omitted by C.O. 74.

[1][[2][(ii)] for entry 30, the entry "30. Vital statistics in so far as they relate to births and deaths including registration of births and deaths." shall be substituted;]

[3][***]

[4][(iii) entry 3, entries 5 to 10 (both inclusive), entries 14, 15, 17, 20, 21, 27, 28, 29, 31, 32, 37, 38, 41 and 44 shall be omitted;

(iiia) for entry 42, the entry "42. Acquisition and requisitioning of property, so far as regards acquisition of any property covered by entry 67 of List I or entry 40 of List III or of any human work of art which has artistic or aesthetic value." shall be substituted; and]

[5][(iv)] in entry 45, for the words and figures "List II or List III", the words "this List" shall be substituted.]

(23) EIGHTH SCHEDULE

[6][(24) NINTH SCHEDULE

[7][(a)] After entry 64, the following entries shall be added, namely:—

[8][64A.] The Jammu and Kashmir State Kuth Act (No. I of Svt. 1978).

[8][64B.] The Jammu and Kashmir Tenancy Act (No. II of Svt. 1980).

[8][64C.] The Jammu and Kashmir Alienation of Land Act (No. V of Svt. 1995).

[9][***]

[10][64D.] The Jammu and Kashmir Big Landed Estates Abolition Act (No. XVII of Svt. 2007).

[10][64E.] Order No. 6H of 1951, dated the 10th March, 1951, regarding Resumption of Jagirs and other assignments of land revenue, etc.]

[11][64F. The Jammu and Kashmir Restitution of Mortgaged Properties Act, 1976 (Act XIV of 1976).

64G. The Jammu and Kashmir Debtor's Relief Act, 1976 (Act XV of 1976).]

[12][(b) Entries 87 to 124, inserted by the Constitution (Thirty-ninth Amendment) Act, 1975, shall be renumbered as entries 65 to 102 respectively.]

[13][(c) Entries 125 to 188 shall be renumbered as entries 103 to 166 respectively.]

---

1. Ins. by C.O. 70.
2. Item (iv) renumbered as item (ii) by C.O. 74.
3. Items (v) and (vi) omitted by C.O. 72.
4. Subs. by C.O. 95, for item (iii).
5. Item (vii) renumbered as item (iv) by C.O. 74.
6. Subs. by C.O. 74, for sub-paragraph (24)
7. Numbered by C.O. 105.
8. Renumbered by C.O. 98.
9. Omitted by C.O. 106.
10. Renumbered by C.O. 106.
11. Ins. by C.O. 106.
12. Ins. by C.O. 105.
13. Ins. by C.O. 108 (w.e.f. 31-12-1977).

¹f(25) *TENTH SCHEDULE*

(a) for the brackets, words and figures "[Articles 102(2) and 19(2)]", the brackets, word and figures "[Article 102(2)]" shall be substituted;

(b) in clause (a) of paragraph 1, the words "or the Legislative Assembly or, as the case may be, either House of the Legislature of a State" shall be omitted;

(c) in paragraph 2,—

(i) in sub-paragraph (1), in sub-clause (ii) of clause (b) of the *Explanation*, the words and figures "or, as the case may be, article 188" shall be omitted;

(ii) in sub-paragraph (3) , the words and figures "or, as the case may be, article 188" shall be omitted;

(iii) in sub-paragraph (4), the reference to the commencement of the Constitution (Fifty-second Amendment) Act, 1985 shall be construed as a reference to the commencement of the Constitution (Application to Jammu and Kashmir) Amendment Order, 1989;

(d) in paragraph 5, the words "or the Chairman or the Deputy Chairman of the Legislative Council of a State or the Speaker or the Deputy Speaker of the Legislative Assembly of a State", shall be omitted;

(e) in sub-paragraph (2) of paragraph 6, the words and figures "or, as the case may be, proceedings in the Legislature of a State within the meaning of article 212" shall be omitted;

(f) in sub-paragraph (3) of paragraph 8, the words and figures "or, as the case may be, article 194" shall be omitted.]

---

1. Ins. by C.O. 136.

RE-STATEMENT, WITH REFERENCE TO THE PRESENT TEXT OF THE CONSTITUTION, OF THE EXCEPTIONS AND MODIFICATIONS SUBJECT TO WHICH THE CONSTITUTION APPLIES TO THE STATE OF JAMMU AND KASHMIR

[*Note.*—The exceptions and modifications subject to which the Constitution applies to the State of Jammu and Kashmir are either those provided in the Constitution (Application to Jammu and Kashmir) Order, 1954 or those consequential to the non-application to the State of Jammu and Kashmir of certain amendments to the Constitution. All the exception and modifications which have a practical significance are included in the re-statement which is only for facility of quick reference. For ascertaining the exact position, reference will have to be made to the Constitution (Application to Jammu and Kashmir) Order, 1954 and to the text of the Constitution on the 20th June, 1964, as amended by the subsequent amendments to the Constitution mentioned in clause 2 of the said Order.]

(1) THE PREAMBLE

(a) In the first paragraph, omit "SOCIALIST SECULAR";

(b) in the penultimate paragraph, omit "and integrity".

(2) PART I

Article 3—

(a) Add the following further proviso, namely:—

"Provided further that no Bill providing for increasing or diminishing the area of the State of Jammu and Kashmir or altering the name or boundary of that State shall be introduced in Parliament without the consent of the Legislature of that State.";

(b) omit *Explanation I* and *Explanation II*.

(3) PART II

(a) This Part shall be deemed to have been applicable in relation to the State of Jammu and Kashmir as from the 26th day of January, 1950.

(b) *Article 7*—Add the following further proviso, namely:—

"Provided further that nothing in this article shall apply to a permanent resident of the State of Jammu and Kashmir who, after having so migrated to the territory now included in Pakistan, returns to the territory of that State under a permit for resettlement in that State or permanent return issued by or under the authority of any law made by the Legislature of that State, and every such person shall be deemed to be a citizen of India.".

(4) PART III

(a) *Article 13*—References to the commencement of the Constitution shall be construed as references to the commencement of the Constitution (Application to Jammu and Kashmir) Order, 1954 (C.O. 48), *i.e.*, the 14th day of May, 1954.

* * * * * *

(c) *Article 16*—In clause (3), reference to the State shall be construed as not including a reference to the State of Jammu and Kashmir.

(d) *Article 19*—

(A) In clause (1),—

(i) in sub-clause (e), omit "and" at the end;

(ii) after sub-clause (e), insert the following clause, namely:—

"(f) to acquire, hold and dispose of property; and";

(B) in clause (5), for "sub-clauses (d) and (e)", substitute "sub-clauses (d), (e) and (f)".

(e) *Article 22*—In clauses (4) and (7), for "Parliament", substitute "the Legislature of the State".

(f) *Article 30*—Omit clause (1A).

(g) After article 30, insert the following, namely:—

"*Right to Property*

31. *Compulsory acquisition of property.*—(1) No person shall be deprived of his property save by authority of law.

(2) No property shall be compulsorily acquired or requisitioned save for a public purpose and save by authority of a law which provides for acquisition or requisitioning of the property for an amount which may be fixed by such law or which may be determined in accordance with such principles and given in such manner as may be specified in such law; and no such law shall be called in question in any court on the ground that the amount so fixed or determined is not adequate or that the whole or any part of such amount is to be given otherwise than in cash:

Provided that in making any law providing for the compulsory acquisition of any property of an educational institution established and administered by a minority, referred to in clause (1) of article 30, the State shall ensure that the amount fixed by or determined under such law for the acquisition of such property is such as would not restrict or abrogate the right guaranteed under that clause.

(2A) Where a law does not provide for the transfer of the ownership or right to possession of any property to the State or to a Corporation owned or controlled by the State, it shall not be deemed to provide for the compulsory acquisition or requisitioning of property, notwithstanding that it deprives any person of his property.

(2B) Nothing in sub-clause (f) of clause (1) of article 19 shall affect any such law as is referred to in clause (2).

* * * * * *

(5) Nothing in clause 2 shall affect—

(a) the provisions of any existing law; or

(b) the provisions of any law which the State may hereafter make—

(i) for the purpose of imposing or levying any tax or penalty; or

(ii) for the promotion of public health or the prevention of danger to life or property; or

(iii) with respect to property declared by law to be evacuee property".

*　　　*　　　*　　　*　　　*　　　*

(h) After article 31, omit the following sub-heading, namely:—

"Saving of Certain Laws"

(i) *Article 31A—*

(A) In clause (1),—

(i) for "article 14 or article 19", substitute "article 14, article 19 or article 31";

(ii) omit the first proviso to clause (1);

(iii) in the second proviso omit "further";

(B) in clause (2), for sub-clause (a), substitute the following sub-clause, namely:—

'(a) "estate" shall mean land which is occupied or has been let for agricultural purposes or for purposes subservient to agriculture, or for pasture, and includes—

(i) sites of buildings and other structures on such land;

(ii) trees standing on such land;

(iii) forest land and wooded waste;

(iv) area covered by or fields floating over water;

(v) sites of *jandars* and *gharats*;

(vi) any *jagir, inam* or *muafi* or *mukarrari* or other similar grant,

but does not include—

(i) the site of any building in any town, or town area or village *abadi* or any land appurtenant to any such building or site;

(ii) any land which is occupied as the site of a town or village; or

(iii) any land reserved for building purposes in a municipality or notified area or cantonment or town area or any area for which a town planning scheme is sanctioned;'.

(j) *Article 31C*—This article is not applicable to the State of Jammu and Kashmir.

(k) *Article 32*—Omit clause (3).

(l) Article 35—

(A) References to the commencement of the Constitution shall be construed as references to the commencement of the Constitution (Application to Jammu and Kashmir) Order, 1954 (C.O. 48), *i.e.*, the 14th day of May, 1954;

(B) in clause (a)(i), omit "clause (3) of article 16, clause (3) of article 32";

(C) after clause (b), add the following clause, namely:—

"(c) no law with respect to preventive detention made by the Legislature of the State of Jammu and Kashmir [whether before or after the commencement of the Constitution (Application to Jammu and Kashmir) Order, 1954] shall be void on the ground that it is inconsistent with any of the provisions of this

Part, but any such law shall, to the extent of such inconsistency, cease to have effect on the expiration of twenty-five years from the commencement of the said Order, except as respects things done or omitted to be done before the expiration thereof."

(m) After article 35, add the following article, namely:—

"35A. *Saving of laws with respect to permanent residents and their rights*— Notwithstanding anything contained in this Constitution, no existing law in force in the State of Jammu and Kashmir, and no law hereafter enacted by the Legislature of the State,—

(a) defining the classes of persons who are, or shall be permanent residents of the State of Jammu and Kashmir; or

(b) conferring on such permanent residents any special rights and privileges or imposing upon other persons any restrictions as respects—

(i) employment under the State Government;

(ii) acquisition of immovable property in the State;

(iii) settlement in the State; or

(iv) right to scholarships and such other forms of aid as the State Government may provide,

shall be void on the ground that it is inconsistent with or takes away or abridges any rights conferred on the other citizens of India by any provision of this Part".

(5) PART IV

This Part is not applicable to the State of Jammu and Kashmir.

(6) PART IVA

This Part is not applicable to the State of Jammu and Kashmir.

(7) PART V

(a) *Article 55*—

(A) For the purposes of this article, the population of the State of Jammu and Kashmir shall be deemed to be sixty-three lakhs;

(B) in the *Explanation* omit the proviso.

(b) *Article 81*—for clauses (2) and (3), substitute the following clauses, namely:—

"(2) for the purposes of sub-clause (a) of clause (1),—

(a) there shall be allotted to the State six seats in the House of the People;

(b) the State shall be divided into single-member territorial constituencies by the Delimitation Commission constituted under the Delimitation Act, 1972, in accordance with such procedure as the Commission may deem fit;

(c) the constituencies shall, as far as practicable, be geographically compact areas, and in delimiting them regard shall be had to physical features, existing boundaries of administrative units, facilities of communication and public convenience; and

(d) the constituencies into which the State is divided shall not comprise the area under the occupation of Pakistan.

(3) Nothing in clause (2) shall affect the representation of the State in the House of the People until the dissolution of the House existing on the date of publication in the Gazette of India of the final order or orders of the Delimitation Commission relating to the delimitation of parliamentary constituencies under the Delimitation Act, 1972.

(4)(a) The Delimitation Commission shall associate with itself for the purpose of assisting it in its duties in respect of the State, five persons who shall be members of the House of the People representing the State.

(b) The persons to be so associated from the State shall be nominated by the Speaker of the House of the People having due regard to the composition of the House.

(c) The first nominations to be made under sub-clause (b) shall be made by the Speaker of the House of the People within two months from the commencement of the Constitution (Application to Jammu and Kashmir) Second Amendment Order, 1974.

(d) None of the associate members shall have a right to vote or to sign any decision of the Delimitation Commission.

(e) If owing to death or resignation, the office of an associate member falls vacant, it shall be filled as soon as may be practicable by the Speaker of the House of the People and in accordance with the provisions of sub-clauses (a) and (b)."

(c) *Article 82*—Omit the second and third provisos.

(d) *Article 105*—In clause (3), for "shall be those of that House and of its members and committees immediately before the coming into force of section 15 of the Constitution (Forty-fourth Amendment) Act, 1978" substitute "shall be those of the House of Commons of the Parliament of the United Kingdom, and of its members and committees, at the commencement of this Constitution".

(e) For article 132, substitute the following article, namely:—

'132. *Appellate jurisdiction of Supreme Court in appeals from High Courts in certain cases*—(1) An appeal shall lie to the Supreme Court from any judgment, decree or final order of a High Court in the territory of India, whether in a civil, criminal or other proceeding, if the High Court certifies that the case involves a substantial question of law as to the interpretation of this Constitution.

(2) Where the High Court has refused to give such a certificate, the Supreme Court may, if it is satisfied that the case involves a substantial question of law as to the interpretation of this Constitution, grant special leave to appeal from such judgment, decree or final order.

(3) Where such a certificate is given, or such leave is granted, any party in the case may appeal to the Supreme Court on the ground that any such question as aforesaid has been wrongly decided and, with the leave of the Supreme Court, on any other ground.

Explanation.—For the purposes of this article, the expression "final order" includes an order deciding an issue which, if decided in favour of the appellant, would be sufficient for the final disposal of the case.'

(f) *Article 133—*

    (A) In clause (1), omit "under article 134A";

    (B) after clause (1), insert the following clause, namely:—

        '(1A) The provisions of section 3 of the Constitution (Thirtieth Amendment) Act, 1972, shall apply in relation to the State of Jammu and Kashmir subject to the modification that references therein to "this Act", "the commencement of this Act", "this Act had not been passed" and "as amended by this Act" shall be construed respectively as references to "the Constitution (Application to Jammu and Kashmir) Second Amendment Order, 1974", "the commencement of the said Order", "the said Order had not been made" and "as it stands after the commencement of the said Order".

(g) *Article 134—*

    (A) In clause (1), in sub-clause (c), omit "under article 134A";

    (B) in clause (2), after "Parliament may" insert "on the request of the Legislature of the State".

(h) *Articles 134A, 135, 139 and 139A*—These articles are not applicable to the State of Jammu and Kashmir.

(i) *Article 145*—In clause (1), omit sub-clause (cc).

(j) *Article 150*—For "as the President may, on the advice of the Comptroller and Auditor-General of India, prescribe" substitute "as the Comptroller and Auditor-General of India may, with the approval of the President prescribe".

(8) PART VI

(a) Omit articles 153 to 217, article 219, article 221, articles 223, 224, 224A and 225, articles 227 to 233, article 233A and articles 234 to 237.

(b) *Article 220*—References to the commencement of the Constitution shall be constructed as references to the commencement of the Constitution (Application to Jammu and Kashmir) Amendment Order, 1960, i.e., the 26th January, 1960.

(c) *Article 222*—After clause (1), insert the following clause, namely:—

    "(1A) Every such transfer from the High Court of Jammu and Kashmir or to that High Court shall be made after consultation with the Governor."

(d) *Article 226—*

(A) Renumber clause (2) as clause (1A);

(B) Omit clause (3);

(C) renumber clause (4) as clause (2); and in clause (2) as so renumbered, for "this article" substitute "clause (1) or clause (1A)".

(9) PART VIII

This Part is not applicable to the State of Jammu and Kashmir.

(10) PART X

This Part is not applicable to the State of Jammu and Kashmir.

(11) PART XI

(a) *Article 246—*

    (A) In clause (1), for "clauses (2) and (3)" substitute "clause (2)";

    (B) in clause (2), omit "Notwithstanding anything in clause (3)";

    (C) omit clauses (3) and (4).

(b) For article 248, substitute the following article, namely:—

> "248. *Residuary powers of legislation.*—Parliament has exclusive power to make any law with respect to—

>   (a) prevention of activities involving terrorist acts directed towards over-awing the Government as by law established or striking terror in the people or any section of the people or alienating any section of the people or adversely affecting the harmony amongst different sections of the people;

>   (aa) prevention of other activities directed towards disclaiming, questioning or disrupting the sovereignty and territorial integrity of India or bringing about cession of a part of the territory of India or secession of a part of the territory of India from the Union or causing insult to the Indian National Flag, the Indian National Anthem and this Constitution; and

>   (b) taxes on—

>   (i) foreign travel by sea or air;

>   (ii) inland air travel;

>   (iii) postal articles, including money orders, phonograms and telegrams.

> *Explanation*—In this article, "terrorist act" means any act or thing by using bombs, dynamite or other explosive substances or inflammable substances or firearms or other lethal weapons or poisons or noxious gases or other chemicals or any other substances (whether biological or otherwise) of a hazardous nature.

(bb) Article 249, in clause (1), for "any matter enumerated in the State List specified in the resolution", substitute "any matter specified in the resolution, being a matter which is not enumerated in the Union List or in the Concurrent List".

(c) *Article 250—*For "to any of the matters enumerated in the State List" substitute "also to matters not enumerated in the Union List".

(d) Omit clause (d).

(e) *Article 253—*Add the following proviso, namely:—

> "Provided that after the commencement of the Constitution (Application to Jammu and Kashmir) Order, 1954, no decision affecting the disposition of the State of Jammu and Kashmir shall be made by the Government of India without the consent of the Government of that State."

(f) Omit articles 255.

(g) *Article 256—*Renumber this article as clause (1) thereof, and add the following new clause thereto, namely:—

> "(2) The State of Jammu and Kashmir shall so exercise its executive power as to facilitate the discharge by the Union of its duties and responsibilities under the Constitution in relation to that State; and in particular, the said

State shall, if so required by the Union, acquire or requisition property on behalf and at the expense of the Union, or if the property belongs to the State, transfer it to the Union on such terms as may be agreed, or in default of agreement, as may be determined by an arbitrator appointed by the Chief Justice of India.

(h) *Article 261*—In clause (2), omit "made by Parliament".

(12) PART XII

(a) *Article 266, 282, 284, 298, 299 and 300*—In these articles references to the State or States shall be construed as not including references to the State of Jammu and Kashmir;

(b) omit clause (2) of article 267, article 273, clause (2) of article 283 and article 290;

(c) *Articles 277 and 295*—In these articles references to the commencement of the Constitution shall be construed as references to the commencement of the Constitution (Application to Jammu and Kashmir) Order, 1954, *i.e.*, the 14th day of May, 1954.

(d) omit the sub-heading "CHAPTER IV—RIGHT TO PROPERTY" and article 300A.

(13) PART XIII

In article 303, in clause (1), omit "by virtue of any entry relating to trade and commerce in any of the Lists in the Seventh Schedule".

(14) PART XIV

Except in article 312, reference to "State" in this part does not include the State of Jammu and Kashmir.

(15) PART XIVA

This Part is not applicable to the State of Jammu and Kashmir.

(16) PART XV

(a) *Article 324*—In clause (1), the reference to the Constitution shall, in relation to elections to either House of the Legislature of Jammu and Kashmir be construed as a reference to the Constitution of Jammu and Kashmir.

(b) *Articles 325, 326 and 327*—In these articles the references to a State shall be construed as not including a reference to the State of Jammu and Kashmir.

(c) Omit article 328.

(d) *Article 329*—

    (A) Reference to a State shall be construed as not including a reference to the State of Jammu and Kashmir;

    (B) Omit "or article 328".

(17) PART XVI

Original clause (a) omitted and clauses (b) and (c) relettered as clauses (a) and (b).

(a) Omit articles 331, 332, 333, 336 and 337.

(b) *Articles 334 and 335*—References to the State or the States shall be construed as not including references to the State of Jammu and Kashmir.

(c) *Article 339*, in clause (1) omit "the administration of the Scheduled Areas and".

(18) PART XVII

The provisions of this Part shall apply to the State of Jammu and Kashmir only in so far as they relate to—

  (i) the official language of the Union;

 (ii) the official language for communication between one State and another, or between a State and the Union; and

(iii) the language of the proceedings in the Supreme Court.

(19) PART XVIII

(a) For article 352, substitute the following article, namely:—

"352. *Proclamation of Emergency.*—(1) If the President is satisfied that a grave emergency exists whereby the security of India or of any part of the territory thereof is threatened, whether by war or external aggression or internal disturbance, he may, by Proclamation, make a declaration to that effect.

(2) A Proclamation issued under clause (1)—

  (a) may be revoked by a subsequent Proclamation;

  (b) shall be laid before each House of Parliament;

  (c) shall cease to operate at the expiration of two months unless before the expiration of that period it has been approved by resolutions of both Houses of Parliament:

Provided that if any such Proclamation is issued at a time when the House of the People has been dissolved or the dissolution of the House of the People takes place during the period of two months referred to in sub-clause (c), and if a resolution approving the Proclamation has been passed by the Council of States but no resolution with respect to such Proclamation has been passed by the House of the People before the expiration of the period, the Proclamation shall cease to operate at the expiration of thirty days from the date on which the House of the People first sits after its reconstitution unless before the expiration of the said period of thirty days a resolution approving the Proclamation has been also passed by the House of the People.

(3) A Proclamation of Emergency declaring that the security of India or of any part of the territory thereof is threatened by war or by external aggression or by internal disturbance may be made before the actual occurrence of war or of any such aggression or disturbance if the President is satisfied that there is imminent danger thereof.

(4) The power conferred on the President by this article shall include the power to issue different Proclamations on different grounds, being war or external aggression or internal disturbance or imminent danger of war or external aggression or internal disturbance, whether or not there is a Proclamation already issued by the President under clause (1) and such Proclamation is in operation.

(5) Notwithstanding anything in this Constitution,—

  (a) the satisfaction of the President mentioned in clause (1) and clause (3) shall be final and conclusive and shall not be questioned in any court on any ground;

(b) subject to the provisions of clause (2), neither the Supreme Court nor any other Court shall have jurisdiction to entertain any question, on any ground, regarding the validity of—

(i) a declaration made by Proclamation by the President to the effect stated in clause (1); or

(ii) the continued operation of such Proclamation.

(6) No Proclamation of Emergency made on grounds only of internal disturbance or imminent danger thereof shall have effect in relation to the State of Jammu and Kashmir (except as respects article 354) unless—

(a) it is made at the request or with the concurrence of the Government of that State; or

(b) where it has not been so made, it is applied subsequently by the President to that State at the request or with the concurrence of the Government of that State".

(b) *Article 353*—omit the proviso.

(c) *Article 356*—

(A) In clause (1), reference to provisions or provision of this Constitution shall, in relation to the State of Jammu and Kashmir, be construed as including references to provisions or provision of the Constitution of Jammu and Kashmir;

(B) in clause (4),—

(i) for the opening portion, substitute the following, namely:—

"A Proclamation so approved shall, unless revoked, cease to operate on the expiration of a period of six months from the date of the passing of the second of the resolution approving the Proclamation under clause (3)";

(ii) after the second proviso, the following proviso shall be inserted, namely:—

'Provided also that in the case of the Proclamation issued under clause (1) on the 18th day of July, 1990 with respect to the State of Jammu and Kashmir, the reference in the first proviso to this clause to "three years" shall be construed as a reference to "seven years".

(C) for clause (5), substitute the following clause, namely:—

"(5) Notwithstanding anything in this Constitution, the satisfaction of the President mentioned in clause (1) shall be final and conclusive and shall not be questioned in any court on any ground.".

(d) *Article 357*—For clause (2), substitute the following clause, namely:—

"(2) Any law made in exercise of the power of the Legislature of the State by Parliament or the President or other authority referred to in sub-clause (a) of clause (1) which Parliament or the President or such other authority would not, but for the issue of a Proclamation under article 356, have been competent to make shall, to the extent of the incompetency, cease to have effect on the expiration of a period of one year after the Proclamation has ceased to operate except as respects things done or omitted to be done before the expiration of the said period, unless the provisions which shall so cease to have effect are sooner repealed or re-enacted with or without modification by Act of the appropriate Legislature.".

(e) For article 358, substitute the following article, namely:—

"358. *Suspension of provisions of article 19 during emergencies.*—While a Proclamation of Emergency is in operation, nothing in article 19 shall restrict the power of the State as defined in Part III to make any law or to take any executive action which the State would but for the provisions contained in that Part be competent to make or to take, but any law so made shall, to the extent of the incompetency, cease to have effect as soon as the Proclamation ceases to operate, except as respects things done or omitted to be done before the law so ceases to have effect."

(f) *Article 359—*

(A) In clause (1) omit "(except articles 20 and 21)";

(B) in clause (1A),—

(i) omit "(except articles 20 and 21)";

(ii) omit the proviso;

(C) omit clause (1B);

(D) in clause (2), omit the proviso.

(g) omit article 360.

(20) PART XIX

(a) Article 361A—This article is not applicable to the State of Jammu and Kashmir.

(b) Omit article 365.

(c) *Article 367*—After clause (3), add the following clause, namely:—

"(4) For the purposes of this Constitution as it applies in relation to the State of Jammu and Kashmir—

(a) references to this Constitution or to the provisions thereof shall be construed as references to the Constitution or the provisions thereof as applied in relation to the said State;

(aa) references to the person for the time being recognised by the President on the recommendation of the Legislative Assembly of the State as the *Sadar-i-Riyasat* of Jammu and Kashmir, acting on the advice of the Council of Ministers of the State for the time being in office, shall be construed as references to the Governor of Jammu and Kashmir;

(b) references to the Government of the said State shall be construed as including references to the Governor of Jammu and Kashmir acting on the advice of his Council of Ministers:

Provided that in respect of any period prior to the 10th day of April, 1965, such references shall be construed as including references to the *Sadar-i-Riyasat* acting on the advice of his Council of Ministers;

(c) references to a High Court shall include references to the High Court of Jammu and Kashmir;

(d) references to the permanent residents of the said State shall be construed as meaning persons who, before the commencement of the Constitution

(Application to Jammu and Kashmir) Order, 1954, were recognised as State subjects under the laws in force in the State or who are recognised by any law made by the Legislature of the State as permanent residents of the State; and

(e) references to a Governor shall include references to the Governor of Jammu and Kashmir:

Provided that in respect of any period prior to the 10th day of April, 1965, such references shall be construed as references to the person recognised by the President as the *Sadar-i-Riyasat* of Jammu and Kashmir and as including references to any person recognised by the President as being competent to exercise to the powers of the *Sadar-i-Riyasat*".

(21) PART XX

Article 368—

(a) In clause (2), add the following further proviso, namely:—

"Provided further that no such amendment shall have effect in relation to the State of Jammu and Kashmir unless applied by order of the President under clause (1) of article 370.".

(b) omit clauses (4) and (5) and after clause (3) add the following clause, namely:—

"(4) No law made by the Legislature of the State of Jammu and Kashmir seeking to make any change in or in the effect of any provision of the Constitution of Jammu and Kashmir relating to—

(a) appointment, powers, functions, duties, emoluments, allowances, privileges or immunities of the Governor; or

(b) superintendence, direction and control of elections by the Election Commission of India eligibility for inclusion in the electoral rolls without discrimination, adult suffrage and composition of the Legislative Council, being matters specified in sections 138, 139, 140 and 150 of the Constitution of Jammu and Kashmir,

shall have any effect unless such law has, after having been reserved for the consideration of the President, received his assent."

(22) PART XXI

(a) omit articles 369, 371, 371A, 372A, 373 and articles 376 to 378A and 392.

(b) *Article 372—*

(A) Omit clauses (2) and (3);

(B) references to the laws in force in the territory of India shall include references to *hidayats, ailans, ishtihars,* circulars, *robkars, irshads, yadashts,* State Council Resolutions, Resolutions of the Constituent Assembly, and other instruments having the force of law in the territory of the State of Jammu and Kashmir;

(C) references to the commencement to the Constitution shall be construed as references to the commencement of the Constitution (Application to Jammu and Kashmir) Order, 1954 (C.O. 48), *i.e.,* the 14th day of May, 1954.

(c) *Article 374—*

    (A) Omit clauses (1), (2), (3) and (5).

    (B) in clause (4), the reference to the authority functioning as the Privy Council of a State shall be construed as a reference to the Advisory Board constituted under the Jammu and Kashmir Constitution Act Svt. 1996, and references to the commencement of the Constitution shall be construed as references to the commencement of the Constitution (Application to Jammu and Kashmir) Order, 1954, *i.e.*, the 14th day of May 1954.

(23) PART XXII

Omit articles 394 and 395.

(24) THIRD SCHEDULE

Omit Forms V, VI, VII and VIII.

(25) FIFTH SCHEDULE

This Schedule is not applicable to the State of Jammu and Kashmir.

(26) SIXTH SCHEDULE

This Schedule is not applicable to the State of Jammu and Kashmir.

(27) SEVENTH SCHEDULE

(a) List I—Union List—

    (A) Omit entry 2A;

    (B) for entry 3, substitute the following entry, namely:—

        "3. Administration of cantonments";

    (C) omit entries 8, 9, 34 and 79;

    (D) in entry 72, the reference to the States shall be construed,—

        (i) in relation to appeals to the Supreme Court from any decision or order of the High Court of the State of Jammu and Kashmir made in an election petition whereby an election to either House of the Legislature of that State has been called in question, as including a reference to the State of Jammu and Kashmir;

        (ii) in relation to other matters, as not including a reference to that State;

    (E) in entry 81, omit "Inter-State migration";

    (F) for entry 97, substitute the following entry, namely:—

        '97. Prevention of activities—

        (a) involving terrorist acts directed towards overawing the Government as by law established or striking terror in the people or any section of the people or alienating any section of the people or adversely affecting the harmony amongst different sections of the people;

        (b) directed towards disclaiming, questioning or disrupting the sovereignty and territorial integrity of India or bringing about cession of a part of the territory of India or secession of a part of the territory of India from the Union or causing insult to the Indian National Flag, the Indian National Anthem and this Constitution,

taxes on foreign travel by sea or air, on inland air travel and on postal articles, including money orders, phonograms and telegrams.

Explanation—In this entry, "terrorist act" has the same meaning as in the *Explanation* to article 248'.

(b) Omit List II—State List.

(c) List III—Concurrent List—

    (A) For entry 1, substitute the following entry, namely:—

        "1. Criminal law (excluding offences against laws with respect to any of the matters specified in List I and excluding the use of naval, military or air forces or any other armed forces of the Union in aid of the civil power) in so far as such criminal law relates to offences against laws with respect to any of the matters specified in this List".

    (B) for entry 2, substitute the following entry, namely:—

        "2. Criminal procedure (including prevention of offences and constitution and organisation of criminal courts, except the Supreme Court and the High Court) in so far as it relates to—

        (i) offences against laws with respect to any matters being matters with respect to which Parliament has power to make laws; and

        (ii) administration of oaths and taking of affidavits by diplomatic and consular officers in any foreign country";

(C) omit entry 3, entries 5 to 10 (both inclusive) entries 14, 15, 17, 20, 21, 27, 28, 29, 31, 32, 37, 38, 41 and 44;

(D) entries 11A, 17A, 17B, 20A and 33A are not applicable to the State of Jammu and Kashmir;

(E) for entry 12, substitute the following entry, namely:—

    "12. Evidence and oaths in so far as they relate to,—

    (i) administration of oaths and taking of affidavits by diplomatic and consular officers in any foreign country; and

    (ii) any other matter being matters with respect to which Parliament has power to make laws";

(F) for entry 13, substitute the following entry, namely:—

    "13. Civil procedure in so far as it relates to administration of oaths and taking of affidavits by diplomatic and consular officers in any foreign country.";

(G) for entry 25, substitute the following entry, namely:—

    "25. Vocational and technical training of labour.";

(H) for entry 30, substitute the following entry, namely:—

    "30. Vital statistics in so far as they relate to births and deaths including registration of births and deaths.";

(I) for entry 42, substitute the following entry, namely:—

    "42. Acquisition and requisitioning of property, so far as regards acquisition of any property covered by entry 67 of List I or entry 40 of List III or of any human work of art which has artistic or aesthetic value.";

(J) in entry 45, for "List II or List III" substitute "this List".

(28) NINTH SCHEDULE

(a) After entry 64, add the following entries, namely:—

"64A. The Jammu and Kashmir State Kuth Act (No. I of Svt. 1978).

64B. The Jammu and Kashmir Tenancy Act (No. II of Svt. 1980).

64C. The Jammu and Kashmir Alienation of Land Act (No. V of Svt. 1995).

64D. The Jammu and Kashmir Big Landed Estates Abolition Act (No. XVII of Svt. 2007).

64E. Order No. 6H of 1951, dated the 10th March, 1951, regarding Resumption of *Jagirs* and other assignments of land revenue, etc.

64F. The Jammu and Kashmir Restitution of Mortgaged Properties Act, 1976 (Act XIV of 1976).

64G. The Jammu and Kashmir Debtors' Relief Act, 1976 (Act XV of 1976)".

(b) entries 65 to 86 are not applicable to the State of Jammu and Kashmir;

(c) after entry 86, insert the following entry, namely:—

"87. The Representation of the People Act, 1951 (Central Act 43 of 1951), the Representation of the People (Amendment) Act, 1974 (Central Act 58 of 1974) and the Election Laws (Amendment) Act, 1975 (Central Act 40 of 1975).";

(d) after entry 91, insert the following entry, namely:—

"92. The Maintenance of Internal Security Act, 1971 (Central Act 26 of 1971).";

(e) after entry 129, insert the following entry, namely:—

"130. The Prevention of Publication of Objectionable Matter Act, 1976 (Central Act 27 of 1976).";

(f) after insertion of the entries 87, 92 and 130 as indicated above, renumber entries 87 to 188 as entries 65 to 166 respectively.

(29) TENTH SCHEDULE

(a) for the brackets, words and figures "[Articles 102(2) and 191(2)]", the brackets, word and figures "[Article 102(2)]" shall be substituted;

(b) in clause (a) of paragraph 1, the words "or the Legislative Assembly or, as the case may be, either House of the Legislature of a State" shall be omitted.

(c) in paragraph 2,—

(i) in sub-paragraph (1), in sub-clause (ii) of clause (b) of the *Explanation*, the words and figures "or, as the case may be, article 188" shall be omitted.

(ii) in sub-paragraph (3), the words and figures "or, as the case may be, article 188" shall be omitted;

(iii) in sub-paragraph (4), the reference to the commencement of the Constitution (Fifty-second Amendment) Act, 1985 shall be construed as a reference to the commencement of the Constitution (Application to Jammu and Kashmir) Amendment Order, 1989;

(d) in paragraph 5, the words "or the Chairman or the Deputy Chairman of the Legislative Council of a State or the Speaker or the Deputy Speaker of the Legislative Assembly of a State", shall be omitted;

(e) in sub-paragraph (2) of paragraph 6, the words and figures "or, as the case may be, proceedings in the Legislature of a State within the meaning of article 212" shall be omitted;

(f) in sub-paragraph (3) of paragraph 8, the words and figures "or, as the case may be, article 194," shall be omitted.

EXTRACTS FROM THE CONSTITUTION (FORTY-FOURTH AMENDMENT) ACT, 1978

1. Short title and commencement.—*   *   *   *   *

(2) It shall come into force on such date as the Central Government may, by notification in the Official Gazette, appoint and different dates may be appointed for different provisions of this Act.

*   *   *   *   *

3. Amendment of article 22.—In article 22 of the Constitution,—

(a) for clause (4), the following clause shall be substituted, namely:—

"(4) No law providing for preventive detention shall authorise the detention of a person for a longer period than two months unless an Advisory Board constituted in accordance with the recommendations of the Chief Justice of the appropriate High Court has reported before the expiration of the said period of two months that there is in its opinion sufficient cause for such detention:

Provided that an Advisory Board shall consist of a Chairman and not less than two other members, and the Chairman shall be a serving Judge of the appropriate High Court and the other members shall be serving or retired Judges of any High Court:

Provided further that nothing in this clause shall authorise the detention of any person beyond the maximum period prescribed by any law made by Parliament under sub-clause (a) of clause (7).

Explanation.—In this clause, "appropriate High Court" means,—

(i) in the case of the detention of a person in pursuance of an order of detention made by the Government of India or an officer or authority subordinate to that Government, the High Court for the Union territory of Delhi;

(ii) in the case of the detention of a person in pursuance of an order of detention made by the Government of any State (other than a Union territory), the High Court for that State; and

(iii) in the case of the detention of a person in pursuance of an order of detention made by the administrator of a Union territory or an officer or authority subordinate to such administrator, such High Court as may be specified by or under any law made by Parliament in this behalf.';

(b) in clause (7),—

(i) sub-clause (a) shall be omitted;

(ii) sub-clause (b) shall be re-lettered as sub-clause (a); and

(iii) sub-clause (c) shall be re-lettered as sub-clause (b) and in the sub-clause as so re-lettered, for the words, brackets, letter and figure "sub-clause (a) of clause (4)", the word, brackets and figure "clause (4)" shall be substituted.

SUBJECT INDEX

A

Advocate-General for State, 167
  appointment of, 167
All-India Services, 290
  central staffing scheme, 290
Amendment of Constitution
  power of Parliament to amend, 335
Amendment of First and Fourth Schedule
  legislative power of State, 10
  levy of penalty, 10
  new High Court for States, 10
  power of Parliament, 10
  scope and applicability of article 4, 10
  State re-organisation, 9
Amendment to Constitution
  article-368, 335
  1st Amendment, 31, 41, 83, 85, 125, 126, 172, 173, 174, 313, 348, 350, 402
  2nd Amendment, 23
  3rd Amendment, 400
  4th Amendment, 83, 84, 275, 402
  5th Amendment, 8
  6th Amendment, 258, 259, 265, 395, 398
  7th Amendment, 6, 8, 35, 84, 107, 113, 115, 117, 119, 123, 124, 129, 137, 145, 158, 161, 162, 163, 169, 170, 188, 189, 190, 191, 192, 220, 221, 223, 227, 228, 241, 245, 246, 251, 253, 255, 256, 258, 259, 263, 264, 267, 269, 270, 274, 276, 283, 292, 293, 294, 295, 297, 298, 302, 305, 306, 307, 309, 312, 313, 317, 318, 321, 322, 328, 329, 332, 333, 334, 335, 337, 338, 349, 351, 360, 361, 362, 363, 366, 368, 369, 370, 386, 392, 394, 396, 397, 401
  9th Amendment, 356
  10th Amendment, 227
  11th Amendment, 115, 116
  12th Amendment, 227
  13th Amendment, 336, 338
  14th Amendment, 124, 223, 227, 368
  15th Amendment, 142, 144, 189, 190, 191, 192, 193, 269, 284, 293
  16th Amendment, 41, 125, 172, 364, 365, 366
  17th Amendment, 84, 403
  18th Amendment, 9
  19th Amendment, 302
  20th Amendment, 221
  21st Amendment, 402
  22nd Amendment, 241, 261, 341
  23rd Amendment, 305, 306, 307, 308
  24th Amendment, 17, 334, 335
  25th Amendment, 83, 86
  26th Amendment, 330, 332
  27th Amendment, 223, 226, 227, 228, 341
  28th Amendment, 290
  29th Amendment, 404

30th Amendment, 147
31st Amendment, 123, 124, 305, 306
32nd Amendment, 338, 342, 345, 393
33rd Amendment, 129, 130, 177
34th Amendment, 404
35th Amendment, 123
36th Amendment, 123, 345, 367, 368, 413
37th Amendment, 223, 227
38th Amendment, 140, 188, 226, 320, 323, 326, 328
39th Amendment, 116, 304, 405
40th Amendment, 269, 407
41st Amendment, 293
42nd Amendment, 1, 83, 86, 86, 95, 100, 102, 104, 107, 109, 112, 119, 122, 124, 125, 131, 139, 145, 153, 158, 159, 161, 167, 170, 171, 178, 190, 193, 217, 218, 220, 254, 284, 290, 298, 305, 319, 321, 322, 323, 324, 325, 326, 331, 333, 335, 345, 391, 395, 396, 397, 398, 399, 400
43rd Amendment, 158, 159, 193, 220, 331, 333
44th Amendment, 41, 67, 79, 83, 84, 86, 100, 116, 119, 122, 125, 131, 132, 139, 140, 146, 147, 148, 153, 161, 167, 171, 178, 179, 188, 190, 193, 194, 217, 218, 226, 271, 304, 319, 320, 322, 323, 325, 326, 327, 328, 345, 405, 407
45th Amendment, 307, 308
46th Amendment, 258, 259, 265, 333, 395
47th Amendment, 409
48th Amendment, 323
49th Amendment, 241, 368, 371, 386, 387, 388
50th Amendment, 1984, 95
51st Amendment, 305, 306
52nd Amendment, 129, 130, 177, 178, 413
53rd Amendment, 347
54th Amendment, 143, 191, 361, 362, 363
55th Amendment, 347
56th Amendment, 348
57th Amendment, 306
58th Amendment, 353
59th Amendment, 323
60th Amendment, 262
61st Amendment, 303
62nd Amendment, 307, 308
63rd Amendment, 323
64th Amendment, 323
65th Amendment, 309, 310, 311
66th Amendment, 410
67th Amendment, 323
68th Amendment, 323
69th Amendment, 224, 225
70th Amendment, 112, 225
71st Amendment, 401, 402
72nd Amendment, 306
73rd Amendment, 228, 263, 416
74th Amendment, 234, 263, 417

75th Amendment, 300
76th Amendment, 412
77th Amendment, 35
78th Amendment, 412
79th Amendment, 307, 308
80th Amendment, 258, 259
81st Amendment, 35
82nd Amendment, 308
83rd Amendment, 233
84th Amendment, 112, 124, 125, 170, 305, 306
85th Amendment, 35
86th Amendment, 67, 106, 109
87th Amendment, 124, 125, 170, 305
88th Amendment, 258, 259, 395
89th Amendment, 309, 310, 311
90th Amendment, 307
91st Amendment, 120, 166, 329, 413, 414
92nd Amendment, 401, 402
93rd Amendment, 31
94th Amendment, 166
95th Amendment, 307, 308
Arrest and detention: Freedom, 67
    article *21*, 69
    article *22*, 69
    consideration of representation, 69
    delay, 69
    documents, 69
    grounds of arrest, 69
    language, 70
    preventive detention, 70
    production of accused before nearest magistrate, 70
    right of detenu, 71
    right to consult and defence by legal practitioner, 71
Attorney-General for India, 121

B

Borrowing
    Government of India, 267
    States, 267

C

Chairman or Deputy Chairman, 175
    Deputy Chairman to perform as Chairman, 175
    not to preside while a resolution for removal is under consideration, 175
    salaries and allowances, 176
    Secretariat of State Legislature, 176
    vacation and resignation, 175
Children employment in factories, 72
    construction industry, 72
    hazardous employment, 72
    observation home, 72
    prohibition of child labour, 72
    random home, 72
Citizenship
    article *7*, 12
    article 8 and citizenship, 13

article *11*, 14
at commencement of Constitution, 10
catch-up rule, 11
Citizenship Act, 1955, sec. *9(2)*, 13
citizenship and domestic law, 13
continuance of the rights of citizenship, 13
continuing to be in India, 12
determination of, 10
domicile on date of Constitution, 12
every person, 11
Indian origin residing outside India, 12
migrants to Pakistan, 12, 13
migrated from Pakistan, 11
migrated to territory of India, 11
migration: meaning of, 12
obtaining passport, 13
of foreign State, 11
of India, 12
one domicile, 11
Parliament to regulate the right of, 13
question of, 14
retrospective operation of the Citizenship Act, 14
voluntarily acquiring citizenship of foreign State, 13
Comptroller and Auditor-General of India, 160
    audit reports, 161
    duties and powers, 161
    form of accounts of Union and States, 161
Conduct of Business of Parliament
    oath or affirmation by members, 128
    quorum, 129
    vacancies, 129
    voting in houses, 129
Conduct of Government business
    Cabinet secrecy, 122
    duties of Chief Minister, 167
    duties of Prime Minister, 122
    individual officers, 168
    information to President, 122
    of State, 167
Contracts, 269
    doctrine of indoor management, 270
Conviction for Offences: Freedom, 52
    article *20*, 54
    clash between fundamental rights, 52
    commencement of protection, 52
    compulsion to be witness, 52
    double jeopardy, 53
    FERA, 53
    no right in procedure at law, 53
    penalty not prescribed, 54
    protection against self-incrimination, 54
    testimonial compulsion for accused, 54
    to be a witness, 54
Council of Ministers
    advice of Cabinet, 119
    aid and advise President, 119
    Cabinet Government, 119

classification of orders, 165
confidentiality of Cabinet decisions, 120
continue until its successor assumes
    charge, 165
governor and cabinet, 165
other provisions as to ministers, 166
to aid and advise governor, 165

Cultural and Educational Rights
compulsory acquisition of property, 83

D

Directive Principles of State Policy
agriculture and animal husbandry, 107
appointment of judges in higher judiciary,
    108
bonded labour, 103
casual labour, 100, 104
child labour: employment of parent, 101
court and Legislature, 108
early childhood care, 106
education to children below age of six
    years, 106
educational and economic interests of
    scheduled castes, scheduled tribes and
    other weaker sections, 106
environment protection, 107
equal justice, 102
equal pay for equal work, 101
equality before law, 100
extradition, 108
fundamental rights under article 37, 99
grant of liquor licence, 107
harmony, 99
humane conditions of work and maternity
    relief, 103
improve public health, 106
improvement of environment, 107
international law and national law
    (municipal law), 108
international peace and security, 108
legal aid, 102
level of nutrition, 106
living wage for workers, 104
maternity benefits, 103
monuments and places protection, 107
museum trust: public interest litigation,
    108
non-workman directors: banking, 104
object of article 39A, 102
organisation of village Panchayats, 103
participation of workers in management of
    industries, 104
personal law, 104
prices, 102
religious freedom, 105
religious trusts, 105
reservation, 103
revised pension formula, 104
right to education, 103, 106
right to public assistance, 103
right to work, 103

safeguarding of forests and wild life, 107
separation of powers, 108
slaughter of cows and calves, 107
social development, 107
standard of living, 106
UN Convention, 98
uniform civil code, 105
validity of 42nd Amendment, 99

**Disqualifications of Members State
    Legislature**
decision on questions as to
    disqualifications, 178
disqualifications for membership, 178
election Commission's opinion as to
    disqualifications, 179
penalty for sitting and voting before
    making oath, 179
powers, privileges and immunities, 179
salaries and allowances, 179
vacation of seats, 177

E

Elections
adult suffrage, 303
articles 174 *viz-a-viz* article 324— scope,
    303
bar to interference by courts in electoral
    matters, 304
Election Commission, 302
ineligible on grounds of religion, race, caste
    or sex, 303
Legislature of a State to make provision,
    304
Parliament to legislate election laws, 304
Parliament to make provision, 304
superintendence, direction and control, 302

Emergency Provisions
proclamation of emergency, 319, 321
effect of proclamation of emergency, 321
distribution of revenues, 321
Union to protect States against external
    aggression, 321
failure of constitutional machinery in
    States, 321
proclamation issued under article 356, 324
judicial review of proclamation under
    article 356, 325
suspension of provisions of article 19, 325

Employment: Equal opportunity, 34
All India Services, 35
appointment, 35
arbitrariness, 36
article 16, 37
article 18, 39
Constitution (Seventy-seventh
    Amendment) Act, 1995, 36
discrimination, 36
employment, 37
grant of opportunity of hearing, 37
medical colleges, 37
other safeguards, 37

pay scales, 38
qualifying minimum marks, 38
recruitment test, 38
relaxation in standard of eligibility, 38
reservation, 38
reservation and promotion, 38
reservation to single post, 38
revision of pay scales, 38
right to go anywhere and live with any
person, 39
seniority, 39

Executive
Central Govt.'s executive power, 162
duty of high officers, 164
executive instructions, 165
executive power of State, 162
extent of executive power of State, 164

F

Finance and Financial Provisions
adjustment in expenses and pensions, 266
annual payment to certain Devaswom
funds, 267
consolidated funds and public accounts,
257
contingency fund, 257
custody of consolidated funds, 263
custody of suitors' deposits, 264
exemption from State taxation, 264
exemption from taxation by States, 266
exemption from taxes on electricity, 265
expenditure defrayable, 263
fee, 257
income of State from Union taxation, 266
moneys credited to public accounts, 263
moneys received by public servants and
courts, 264
restrictions as to imposition of tax, 264
taxes not to be imposed, 256

Freedom, 41
aids patient, 42
arbitrariness, 42
ban on slaughter, 42
bandhs, 42
burden of proof, 42
business aspects of media, 42
business with government, 42
constitutionality, 43
contempt of court, 43
convicts, 43
Co-operative Societies Act, 1965 (U.P.), 43
corporations as citizens, 44
criteria of validity of law, 44
false news item about judges, 44
freedom of association, 44
freedom of expression, 45
freedom of movement, 45
freedom of profession, 46
freedom of residence, 46
government advertisements, 47
ivory import, 47

judicial officers, 47
letter by employee against the organisation,
47
licences and permits for carrying trade, 47
press, 48
price fixation, 48
reasonable restrictions, 48
relationship with articles 21 and 22, 48
right of minority to administer educational
institution, 49
right to carry on business, 49
right to know, 49
right to practise medicine, 49
right to practise profession, 50
right to pray, 50
State Acts: educational institution, 50
substantive and procedural aspects, 50
test of reasonableness, 50
total prohibition, 51
trial by media, 51
unincorporated associations, 51

**Freedom from attendance at religious
instruction, 77**
religious instructions, 77
right to administer minority institutions, 77

Freedom from payment of taxes
imposition of fee, 77
promotion of any religion, 77

Fundamental duties, 109
enforcement of duties, 110
environment, 109
striving towards excellence, 110
use and interpretation, 110

Fundamental Rights
Act of Parliament, 18
Act of State, 18
agency outside India, 14
basic features, 18
BCCI, 14
Constitution Amendment Acts declared as
unconstitutional, 19
co-operative societies, 14
laws inconsistent with or in derogation of,
16
local authorities: writ, 15
other authorities, 15
private body, 16
severability, 19
State, 16
State action, 16
statutory and other bodies held to be State,
14
treaties on human rights, 19
voidness of existing laws, 20
working of Act, 20

G

Governor
appointment of, 162
conditions of governor's office, 163
discharge of functions, 163

oath or affirmation, 163
of States, 162
power to grant pardons, 163
promulgate ordinances during recess of
    Legislature, 187
qualifications for appointment, 163
suspend, remit or commute sentences, 163
term of office of, 162

H

High Courts
appointment and conditions of a judge,
    189
appointment of acting Chief Justice, 192
appointment of additional and acting
    judges, 192
appointment of retired judges at sittings of
    High Courts, 192
Constitution of, 189
contempt power, 189
courts of record, 189
for States, 188
jurisdiction, 192
oath or affirmation by judges, 191
provisions relating to Supreme Court, 191
restriction on practice, 191
salaries, 191
status of additional judge, 190
transfer, 191, 192

I

Interests of minorities, 78
minorities, 78
regional language, 79

L

Law declared by SC: Binding, 154
binding jurisdiction, 154
doctrine of *stare decisis*, 154
foreign case law – precedent, 154
judicial discipline, 154
law declared, 154
obiter dicta, 155
precedent, 155
procedure value of decision, 155
reconsideration, 155
retrospective operation, 156
stare decisis, 156

Legislative Powers of President
effect of duration, 140
promulgate ordinances during recess of
    Parliament, 140
re-promulgation, 141

Legislative Procedure of Parliament
assent to bills, 136
introduction and passing of bills, 133
joint sitting of both houses, 134
special procedure in respect of money bills,
    135

Legislative Procedure of State Council
assent to bills, 182

bills reserved for consideration, 182
governor's assent to bills, 182
introduction and passing of bills, 180
restriction on powers of Legislative Council,
    180
special procedure in respect of money bills,
    181

M

Members of Parliament
33rd Amendment Act, 132
42nd Amendment Act, 132
44th Amendment Act, 132
code of conduct, 130
decision on questions as to
    disqualifications, 131
disqualifications for membership, 130
freedom of speech, 132
material date, 130
office of profit, 131
penalty for sitting and voting before
    making oath, 131
powers, privileges and immunities, 131,
    133
principle debarring holders of office of
    profit, 131
publication of proceedings, 133
salaries and allowances, 133
vacation of seats, 129

Miscellaneous Provisions
administration and control of Scheduled
    Areas and Scheduled Tribes, 368
administration of justice in autonomous
    districts and autonomous regions, 375
administration of tribal areas in States of
    Assam, Meghalaya, Tripura and
    Mizoram, 371
amendment of schedule, 390
annulment or suspension of Acts and
    resolutions, 384
appointment of Commission to inquire, 384
assess and collect land revenue, 379
autonomous districts and autonomous
    regions, 371
autonomous regions, 389
Bar of jurisdiction of courts, 415
Chairman and Deputy Chairman of
    Council of States, 360
Chairman and Deputy Chairman of
    Legislative Council, 360
Comptroller and Auditor-General of India,
    363
conferment of powers under the CPC and
    CrPC, 378
constitution of District Councils and
    Regional Councils, 372
dispute arising out of treaties, 329, 330
disqualification for appointment on
    remunerative political post, 329
disqualification on ground of defection,
    413, 414, 415

dissolution of a District or a Regional Council, 385
dissolution of Mizo District Council, 388
district and regional funds, 379
District Council to establish primary schools, 379
District Councils and Regional Councils to make laws, 374
estimated receipts and expenditure pertaining to autonomous districts, 383
exclusion of areas from autonomous districts, 386
judges of Supreme Court and High Courts, 361
licences or leases, 380
major ports and aerodromes, 330
President and Governors of States, 360
protection of publication of proceedings of house, 328
publication of laws, rules and regulations, 381
recognition granted to rulers, 330
regulations for control of money-lending and trading, 380
Speaker and Deputy Speaker of house, 360
Speaker and Deputy Speaker of Legislative Assembly, 360
tribal areas, 387

Municipalities
application to Union Territories, 238
audit of accounts, 238
committee for district planning, 239
committee for metropolitan planning, 240
composition, 235
Constitution, 235
continuance of existing laws, 240
disqualifications for membership, 237
duration, 236
elections, 238
finance commission, 238
interference by courts in electoral matters, 241
powers, authority and responsibilities, 237
reservation of seats, 236
to impose taxes, 237
Wards Committees, 236

N

New States, 8
admission of, 8
agreements between India and Bangladesh, 9
alteration of areas, 8
boundaries, 8
formation of, 8
inter-State agreement on water, 9
names of existing States, 8
reference of Central Bills to States, 9
re-organisation of territory under existing laws, 9

O

Officers of Parliament
Chairman and Deputy Chairman of Council of States, 126
not to preside while resolution for removal is under consideration, 127, 128
power of Deputy Chairman, 127
power of the Deputy Speaker, 128
salaries and allowances, 128
Secretariat of Parliament, 128
Speaker and Deputy Speaker, 127
vacation and resignation of Deputy Chairman, 126
vacation and resignation of Speaker and Deputy Speaker, 127

Official Language
Commission and Committee of Parliament on, 315
communication between State and Union, 317
directive for development of Hindi language, 318
enactment of laws relating to language, 318
for Acts, Bills, 317
instruction in mother-tongue at primary stage, 318
language for right to information, 317
language spoken by a section of population, 317
of a State, 316
of Union, 315
representations for redress of grievances, 318
special officer for linguistic minorities, 318
used in High Courts, 317
used in Supreme Court, 317

P

Panchayats
application to union territories, 233
audit of accounts, 232
Bar to interference by courts in electoral matters, 234
composition of, 229
Constitution of, 229
Constitution of Finance Commission, 232
continuance of existing laws, 233
disqualifications for membership, 231
duration of, 230
election process, 234
elections, 232
Gram Sabha, 229
impose taxes, 231
powers, authority and responsibilities, 231
reservation of seats, 230

Parliament
composition of Council of States, 123
composition of House of People, 123
Constitution of, 122
dissolution, 125

duration of Houses, 125
prorogation, 125
qualification for membership, 125
readjustment after census, 124
right of President, 126
rights of Ministers and Attorney- General, 126
sessions of, 125
special address by President, 126
Parliament's General Procedure
courts not to inquire into proceedings, 140
language to be used, 139
regulation by law of procedure, 139
restriction on discussion, 140
rules of procedure, 139
Parliament's Procedure in Financial Matters
annual financial statement, 136
appropriation bills, 137
exceptional grants, 138
special provisions as to financial bills, 138
supplementary, additional or excess grants, 137
votes of credit, 138
votes on account, 138
with respect to estimates, 137
Personal Life and Liberty: Freedom, 54
AIDS patient and employment, 54
arrest, 54
assault on child, 54
atomic energy, 55
bail, 55
beauty contests, 55
child offenders, 55
compensation, 55
cruel punishment, 55
custodial death, 55
death sentence, 55
debtor and article 21, 56
delay in bringing to trial, 56
delay in execution, 56
ecological balance, 56
ecology and "public trust" doctrine, 56
environment, 56
environment: hazardous chemicals, 56
environment: precautionary principle, 57
fair procedure, 57
fair trial, 57
foreign travel, 57
forests, 57
handcuffing, 57
health, 57
housing, 57
illegal detention, 58
illegal encroachment, 58
inhuman treatment, 58
insane person, 58
Irish Constitution, 58
legal aid, 59
livelihood, 59
medical aid in government hospitals, 59

medical confidentiality, 59
medical test, 59
minimum punishment, 60
natural justice, 60
non-revision of pay scale, 60
obstruction of movement, 60
oppression of peasants, 60
passport, 60
paternity of child, 60
personal liberty: women, 60
police atrocities, 61
position in USA, 61
preventive detention, 61
prison restrictions, 61
prisoners: classification, 61
prisoners: interview, 61
prisoners: torture, 61
prisoners: wrongful detention, 62
privacy, 62
private industries and pollution, 62
prostitution, 62
public hanging, 62
public trial, 62
punishment for attempted suicide, 63
radiation (X-ray), 63
right of appeal, 63
right of convict, 63
right to die (provision in I.P.C.), 63
right to fair trial, 63
right to life and liberty, 65
right to life and personal liberty, 63
right to life: various rights included, 63
right to livelihood or work, 65
right to speedy trial, 65
right to work, 65
scheduled tribes women, 66
scope of article 21, 65
sexual harassment, 66
smoking in public place, 66
solitary confinement, 66
speedy justice, 66
speedy trial, 66
summary dismissal of appeal, 66
telephone tapping, 66
traffic control, 67
undertrial prisoners, 67
water, 67
Power to carry on trade, 269
extra-territorial operation, 269
trade or business, 269
Preamble
abolition of caste system, 1
as basic structure, 4
basic structure of Constitution, 2
constitutional philosophy, 2
duty of citizen, 2
features of basic structure, 2
federal structure, 2
fundamental law, 3
idealism, 3

interpretation of Preamble, 3
interpretation of statutes, 3
parents *patriae*, 4
part of Constitution, 4
powers from constitutional provision, 4
res extra commercium, 4
secularism, 4
social justice, 5
socialistic concept, 5
sovereign, 5
structural sources of the Constitution, 5
structure of government and fundamental
    aspects of Constitution, 6
unity of nation, 6

President
conditions of President's office, 113
election of, 111
eligibility for re-election, 113
executive power, 111
holding election to fill vacancy, 114
manner of election, 112
martial law and Presidential order, 111
oath or affirmation, 113
President of India, 110
procedure for impeachment, 113
qualifications, 113
term of office, 112
term of office of person elected to fill casual
    vacancy, 114

President's power
grant pardons, 116
new commonwealth, 117
position elsewhere, 118
Presidential clemency and death sentence,
    118
remission of sentence, 118
stay, 118
suspend, remit or commute sentences, 116
to consult Supreme Court, 119

Prohibition of discrimination, 31
acquiring of scheduled caste status, 34
area-wise reservation, 31
backward class, 31
constitutional 93rd amendment, 32
discrimination, 32
grounds of sex, 33
horizontal and vertical reservation, 33
medical colleges reservation, 33
relationship to article *14*, 33
reservation for SCs and STs, 33
reservation on basis of domicile, 33
reservation within reservation, 34
University-wise reservation, 34
women and sexual harassment, 34
women: reservation, 34

Provisions Relating to Classes
claims of services and posts, 308
Commission to investigate conditions of
    backward classes, 312
control of Union over administration, 312

conversion, 314
educational grants for benefit of Anglo-
    Indian community, 309
finality of Presidential order, 314
migrants tribals, 315
National Commission for Scheduled
    Castes, 309
representation of Anglo-Indian community,
    305, 307
reservation after seventy years, 307
reservation of seats in house of people, 305,
    306
scheduled castes, 313
scheduled tribe-acquisition of status, 315
scheduled tribes, 313
special provision for Anglo-Indian
    community, 308

Public Service Commissions
appointment and term of office members,
    293
expenses, 297
for Union and States, 292
functions, 296
misconduct, 294
power to extend functions, 297
power to make regulations, 295
proportion, 295
qualification for appointment, 292
removal and suspension of office member,
    293
reports, 298
seniority, 292

R

Religion and religious affairs
administration of property of religious
    endowments, 75
affairs of religion, 76
Ananda marg, 73
charity, 73
denomination, 76
loudspeaker, 75
minority institutions, 73
priests, 73
profession, practice and propagation of
    religion, 72
regulation by State, 73
religion, 74
religious freedom, 74
restrictions that can be imposed, 75
right to own property, 76
rituals, 76
speedy trial, 77

Revenues between Union and States
calculation of "net proceeds", 262
duties, 258
Finance Commission, 262
grants from Union to States, 261
grants in export duty, 260
recommendation of President required to
    Bills, 260

recommendations of Finance Commission, 263

service tax, 258

surcharge on duties and taxe, 260

taxes levied and collected by Union, 258

taxes levied and distributed, 259

taxes on professions, trades, callings and employments, 262

Right against Exploitation, 71, 72

Right of minorities

condition as to admission fees, 79

conditions for aid or recognition, 79

conditions: void, 79

crucial words, 80

educational standards, 80

establish and administer educational institutions, 79

mal-administration, 80

minorities based on religion or language, 81

regulation by State, 81

regulatory laws, 81

requirements of regulation, 82

right to receive aid, 82

Right to Constitutional Remedies

article 35 and Jammu and Kashmir Constitution, 98

certiorari, 87

child prostitution, 87

closure of industry, 87

Commissioner, 87

compensation, 88

composite petition, 88

contempt, 88

continuing *mandamus*, 88

counter-affidavits: detention, 88

damages, 88

death in custody, 88

detention, 88

determine age of Chief Justice of India, 95

doctrine of *parens patriae*, 88

earlier decision, 89

estoppel against petitioner, 89

estoppel against State, 89

false plea, 89

infringement of fundamental right, 89

introduction of Bill in Legislature, 89

laches, 89

law making power, 90

legislation on personal law, 90

limits of writ jurisdiction, 90

locus standi, 90

mandamus, 90

misuse of PIL, 90

natural justice, 91

Parliamentary legislation and fundamental rights, 96

pleadings, 91

policy of government, 91

political question, 91

pollution, 91

price fixation, 91

prostitutes' children, 92

public interest litigation, 91, 92

public safety: preventive detention, 98

relief, 92

res judicata, 93

scope of article 32, 93

service matters, 93

sovereign power of Legislature, 94

stock exchange, 94

workers in winding-up proceedings, 95

writ jurisdiction, 95

writ petition, 95

writs against courts martial, 96

Right to education, 67

Right to Equality: before law, 20

administrative order, 20

admission in college and reservations, 20

arbitrary action and discretion, 21

article 14, 27, 28

backward areas, 21

ban on sex selection, 22

BCCI, 22

bias and *mala fide* allegations, 22

change of name, 22

citizenship, 22

concept of equality, 22

defection, 22

discrimination, 22

disinvestment, 22

doctrine of natural justice, 22

education, 23

equal citizens, 23

equal pay for equal work, 23

equality, 23

equality in promotion, 23

equals and unequals, 23

executive action, 24

flexibility, 24

grant-in-aid, 24

illegal action, 24

illegalities cannot be perpetuated, 24

interpretation, 24

land acquisition, 24

land ceiling, 25

legitimate expectations, 25

limitations, 25

mala fide, 25

newspapers, 25

Panchayat: removal of members, 25

pension, 25

principles of natural justice, 26

procedural discrimination, 26

Rajasthani language, 26

reasonable restriction, 26

reasonableness, 26

right to have reasoned order, 27

royalties for industries, 27

rule for termination of service, 27

Scheduled Castes, 27

service, 28

service rules, 28

State policy, 29
tax exemptions, 29
taxation laws, 29
taxing statutes, 30
test of equality, 30
uncanalised discretion, 30
zone-wise merit list for recruitment, 31
Right to Property, 272
deprivation of property, 272
nature of right, 272
requisitioning, 272
State Finance Corporations Act, *1951*, 273

S

Saving of Certain Laws
anti-national activities, 86
constitutional validity of a statute, 86
land reform legislation, 84
laws providing for acquisition of estates, 83
validity of article *31B*, 86
Service: Dismissal, removal or reduction in rank, 284
abolition of post, 284
administrative tribunal, 285
adverse remarks, 285
appeal, 285
civil post, 285
compulsory retirement, 286
confirmation, 286
copy of report, 286
criminal proceedings, 286
date of birth, 286
disciplinary enquiry, 287
disciplinary proceedings, 287
dismissal, 287
double jeopardy, 287
fresh inquiry, 287
inquiry, 287
legal assistance, 288
malice, 288
misconduct, 288
opportunity, 288
penal order, 288
reinstated employee, 289
relief by Supreme Court, 289
removal, 289
seniority, 289
temporary appointment, 289
tenure post, 290
term : expiry of, 290
Service: Recruitment and conditions, 276
administrative instructions, 276
adverse remarks in Confidential Report, 276
appointment, 277
armed forces, 277
compulsory retirement, 277
copywriters, 277
criminal proceedings, 277
discrimination, 277
examination, 277

exploitation, 278
gratuity, 278
High Court, 278
interview, 278
lien, 278
mandamus, 279
officiating post, 279
privacy, 279
promissory estoppel, 279
promotion, 279
provident fund, 279
qualification, 280
quota, 280
railways, 280
recruitment, 280
retrenchment, 280
rule-making power, 281
rules, 281
salary, 281
seniority, 281
service matters: judicial interference, 282
temporary service, 282
termination, 282
transfer, 282
vacancies, 282
Service: Tenure of office, 283
contract, 283
expiry of term, 283
pleasure: doctrine of, 283
Speaker and Deputy Speaker, 174
Deputy Speaker to perform as Speaker, 174
not to preside while a resolution for removal is under consideration, 175
salaries and allowances, 176
Secretariat of State Legislature, 176
vacation and resignation, 174
Special leave to appeal by Supreme Court, 149
appeal, 149
criminal cases, 149
effect, 149
fraud, 150
grounds, 150
leave granted, 151
leave refused, 152
maintenance claim by illegitimate child, 150
question of fact, 150
re-appreciation of evidence, 151
relief, 151
remand of matter, 151
service matter, 150, 151
special leave petition, 151
Special Provisions with respect to
Andhra Pradesh, 342
Arunachal Pradesh, 347
Assam, 341
determination of population for elections, 352
duration of Andhra Pradesh Legislative Assembly, 351

Goa, 348
Maharashtra and Gujarat, 338
Manipur, 341
Mizoram, 347
Nagaland, 338
Sikkim, 345
**State Council Procedure in Financial
Matters**
annual financial statement, 183
appropriation Bills, 184
procedure in Legislature with respect to
estimates, 183
special provisions as to Financial Bills, 185
supplementary, additional or excess grants,
184
votes on account, votes of credit and
exceptional grants, 184
State Council's General Procedure
courts not to inquire into proceedings, 186
defects of competence, 187
language to be used, 186
regulation by law of procedure, 186
restriction on discussion, 186
rules of procedure, 185
State Legislature
abolition or creation of Councils, 169
composition of Assemblies, 169
composition of Councils, 170
conduct of business, 176
Constitution of, 168
dissolution of Assembly, 172
duration of, 171
endorsement of legislative Bill, 173
governor to address and send messages,
173
ground for dissolution of assembly, 173
oath or affirmation by members, 176
qualification for membership, 172
rights of Ministers and Advocate-General,
174
sessions of, 172
special address by governor, 173
vacancies and quorum, 176
voting in houses, 176
Suits and proceedings, 271
government liability in tort, 271
Supreme Court
ancillary powers of, 153
appeal against conviction, 148
appellate jurisdiction of, 145, 147, 148
application of constitutional right, 147
appointment of acting Chief Justice, 144
appointment of *ad hoc* judges, 144
appointment of judge, 142
article *31*, 145
building plan, 147
certificate for appeal to, 148
civil and judicial authorities to act in aid of,
158
conferment on, 153

consultation, 143
contempt of, 144
contempt power, 144
dispute between two States, 145
enforcement of decrees and orders, 157
enlargement of jurisdiction, 153
establishment and Constitution of, 141
Federal Court, 149
interlocutory appeal, 147
jurisdiction of, 147
officers and servants and expenses of, 160
original jurisdiction of, 145
power of President to consult, 157
retired judges at sittings of, 144
review of judgments or orders, 152
salaries of judges, 143
seat of, 145
to be a court of record, 144
transfer of certain cases, 153

T

Temporary and Transitional Provisions
Bills pending in dominion Legislature, 352
Comptroller and Auditor-General of India,
351
continuance in force of existing laws, 348
Council of Ministers for States, 352
Council of Ministers or governors, 352
courts, authorities and officers to continue
to function, 350
establishment of Central University in
Andhra Pradesh, 345
filling of casual vacancies, 352
Governors of provinces, 352
judges of Federal Court, 350
judges of High Courts, 350
President order for persons under
detention, 349
President to adapt laws, 349
President to amend first and fourth
schedules, 352
President to remove difficulties, 352
proceedings pending before *His Majesty* in
Council, 350
proceedings pending in Federal Court, 350
Public Service Commissions, 351
temporary power to Parliament to make
laws, 336
temporary provisions to State of Jammu
and Kashmir, 337
Territory of Union, 6
acquisition of foreign territory, 7
action subsequent to acquisition, 7
boundaries of State, 7
law applicable to acquired territory, 7
meaning of territory of India, 7
territorial waters, 7
territory of India, 8
Union of India, 6
Titles Abolition, 40
Central Civil Service: pension, 40

equality, 40
national awards, not titles, 40
Trade, Commerce and Intercourse within India
freedom of, 273
inter-State & intra-State, 273
laws providing for State monopolies, 275
Parliament to impose restrictions, 273
restrictions among States, 274
restrictions on legislative powers of Union and States, 273
saving of existing laws, 275
Traffic Prohibition, 71
child labour, 71
children of prostitutes, 71
traffic in human beings, 72
Tribunals
administrative tribunals, 298
all courts, 301
appeal to Supreme Court, 301
co-operative societies, 299
interference by tribunal, 299
tribunals and writs, 301
tribunals for other matters, 299

U

Union and States: Administrative Relations
assistance to States by deployment of forces, 254
comply with article 256, 253
control of the Union over States, 254
co-ordination between States, 255
disputes relating to waters, 255
jurisdiction of union, 255
obligation of States and Union, 253
public Acts, records and judicial proceedings, 255
States to entrust functions to Union, 255
Union to confer powers on States, 254
Union and States: Legislative Relations
conditional legislation, 242
conflict between statutes, 243
constitutional validity of law, 243
constitutionality of, 249
co-operative societies, 246
doctrine of pith and substance, 246
effect of declaration, 247
entry of goods, 247
essential commodities, 247
excessive delegation, 243
extent of laws, 242
incidental provisions, 243
inconsistency between laws, 250, 251
industries, 248
international agreements, 251
legislation overriding decision, 243
legislative competence of State, 244
legislative list: entries, 248
mala fides, 248
mines, 248

motive of Legislature, 245
Parliament to legislate for two or more States, 250
Parliament to legislate in national interest, 249
power of Legislature, 245
preventive detention, 248
proclamation of emergency is in operation, 250
reconciliation, 249
repugnancy, 251
residuary powers of legislation, 249
rule-making power, 245
stamp duties, 249
subject-matter of laws, 245
sub-judice, 245
transgression of limits of power, 245
Union and State Legislation, 252
validating Act, 245
Union Territories
administration, 223
Coorg, 228
Council of Ministers, 223
failure of constitutional machinery, 225
High Courts for, 228
local Legislatures, 223
ordinances during recess of Legislature, 226
President to make regulations, 227
special provisions with respect to Delhi, 224
Untouchability Abolition, 39
article 17, 39
religious freedom, 39

V

Vice-President
act as President during casual vacancies, 114
discharge of President's functions, 116
during absence of President, 114
election of, 115
ex-officio chairman of Council of States, 114
holding election to fill vacancy, 115
oath or affirmation, 116
term of office, 115
term of office of person elected to fill casual vacancy, 115
Vice-President of India, 114

W

Writs and Students
circumstantial evidence, 215
cross-examination, 215
difference from criminal trials, 215
disciplinary action, 215
disciplinary proceedings, 215
discretion of institution, 216
examinations, 216
illustrations of *quasi*-judicial acts, 216
inquiry when not necessary, 216
natural justice, 216

procedure, 217
punishment, 217
standard of proof, 217
writ jurisdiction, 217
Writs and Superintendence, 217
   correction of facts, 218
   jurisdiction of court, 219
   jurisdictional defects, 219
   locus standi, 219
   petition – maintainability, 219
   reasons, 219
   scope and nature of article 227, 219
   supervisory jurisdiction, 219
Writs: High Courts power, 193
   acquiescence, 194
   administrative action, 194
   allotment of land, 194
   alternative remedy, 195
   amenability, 195
   arbitrariness, 195
   arrest, 195
   bail, 195
   bias, 195
   cases of non-statutory matters, 195
   certiorari, 195
   certiorari and prohibition, 195
   civil consequences, 198
   Code of Civil Procedure, 198
   compensation, 198
   concession: withdrawal, 199
   Consumer Disputes Redressal
      Commission, 199
   court martial, 199
   criminal investigation, 199
   delay and lachas, 199
   discretion, 199
   discrimination, 200
   domestic inquiry, 200
   education: medical colleges, 200
   encroachment and natural justice, 200
   enforcement of an Act, 201
   error of law, 201
   exercise of power, 201
   exercise of writ jurisdiction, 201
   extraordinary jurisdiction, 201
   facts, 201
   factual inaccuracy, 202
   fairness, 202
   fraud, 202
   futile writ, 202
   geographical limits, 202
   habeas corpus, 202
   illegal order, 204
   image of judiciary, 204
   interim orders, 204

joint petitions, 204
judicial activism, 204
judicial review *vis-à-vis* legislative policy,
   204
jurisdiction, 204
jurisdiction of High Court, 204
jurisdictional limitations, 205
laches, 205
legal assistance, 205
legal binding, 205
legitimate expectation, 205
local authority, 205
locus standi, 206
maintenance of internal security, 206
mala fides, 206
mandamus, 206
mining lease, 207
natural justice, 207
nemo judex in causa sua, 208
notification, 208
order of arbitral tribunal, 208
particular writs, 208
parties, 208
plea before single judge of High Court, 208
policy and discretion, 208
pollution: disposal of petition by consent,
   209
premature petition, 209
preventive detention, 209
preventive detentions: stay, 209
prisons, 209
prohibition, 209
promissory estoppel, 210
public interest legislation, 211
public interest litigation, 210
quasi-judicial authority, 211
quo warranto, 211
reasonableness, 211
registered or unregistered Association, 212
relief, 212
remedy: extraordinary and discretionary,
   212
res judicata, 213
restoration of writ petition, 213
scope of article 226: High Court power, 213
service matters, 214
State Government, 214
statutory authority, 214
statutory instrument, 214
suppression of facts, 214
tender forms, 214
tribunal, 214
unincorporated Association, 214
violation of fundamental rights, 215
writ petition – maintainability, 215

RECENT CASE-LAWS ON CONSTITUTION OF INDIA

Artificial inequality or illusory equality under article 14: The classification must rest on a reasonable and intelligible basis. The court always has to bear in mind the facts and circumstances of the particular case in order to judge the validity of a classification; *B. Manmad Reddy* v. *Chandra Prakash Reddy,* (2010) 3 SCC 314.

Supreme Court v. Supreme Court under article 141: The decision of smaller Bench cannot overrule the decision of larger Bench; *National Small Industries Corporation Ltd.* v. *Harmeet Singh Paintal,* (2010) 3 SCC 330.

Judicial discipline and comity: The courts should avoid temptation to become authoritarian. There have been several instances, where in their anxiety for justice, the courts have gone overboard, which results in injustice, rather than justice. All power is trust and with greater power comes greater responsibility; *S. Palani Velayutham* v. *District Collector, Tirunelveli, Tamil Nadu,* (2009) 10 SCC 664.

Judicial review: The doctrine of proportionality is well recognized concept of judicial review; *Chairman-cum-Managing Director, Coal India Ltd.* v. *Mukul Kumar Choudhary,* AIR 2010 SC 75.

Basic features of democracy: The readjustment of extent and boundaries of delimitation constituencies cannot be said to be basic feature of democracy; *Jammu and Kashmir National Panthers Party* v. *Union of India,* AIR 2010 J&K 47.

Criminal contempt in face of Supreme Court: The summary proceedings punishing alleged contemnors, when deliberate and willful criminal contempt committed by disrupting court proceedings by using very offensive, intemperate and abusive language and while contemnors, instead of expressing any regret, sought to justify the contumacious act, the summary proceedings in such a case is permissible; *Leila David* v. *State of Maharashtra,* (2009) 10 SCC 337.

Right to development: Every person has a right to develop his or her potential. In fact a right to development is a basic human right; *Vikram Vir Vohra* v. *Shalini Bhalla,* (2010) 4 SCC 409.

Liberty: Liberty is one of the most precious and cherished possession of a human being and he would resist forcefully any attempt to diminish it; *State of Haryana* v. *Jagdish,* (2010) 4 SCC 216.

Caste system: It is absolutely imperative to abolish the caste system as expeditiously as possible for the smooth functioning of Rule of Law and Democracy in our country; *State of Uttar Pradesh* v. *Ram Sajivan,* AIR 2010 SC 1738.

Criminal Trials to be public: All criminal trials have to be public trials where public and press have complete access. Public access is essential if trial adjudication is to achieve the objective of maintaining public confidence in the administration of justice. An open trial serves an important prophylactic purpose, providing an outlet for community concern, hostility, and emotions. Public trial restores the balance in cases when shocking crime occurs in the society. People have inherent distrust for the secret trials; *Mohd. Shahabuddin* v. *State of Bihar,* (2010) 4 SCC 653.

Sovereign Power to Grant Remission: The power of the sovereign to grant remission is within its exclusive domain and it is for this reason that our Constitution makers went on to incorporate the provisions of article 72 and article 161 of the Constitution of India. This responsibility was cast upon the executive through a constitutional mandate to ensure that some public purpose may require fulfilment by grant of remission in appropriate cases. This power was never intended to be used or utilized by the executive as an unbridled power of reprieve; *State of Haryana* v. *Jagdish,* AIR 2010 SC 1690.

Right to Information: Information pertaining to documents of co-operative societies, cannot be refused on ground that document was more than 20 years old; *Greenhood Co-operative Housing Society Ltd.* v. *State of West Bengal,* AIR 2009 Cal 129: 2009 AIHC 519 (NOC): (2009) 4 ALJ (NOC) 649: (2009) 3 AKAR (NOC) 502: (2009) 2 Cal HN 472: 2009 (1) Cal LT 551.

Obiter dicta of Supreme Court: The *obiter dicta* of Supreme Court may not be binding upon judges of Supreme Court. But are binding upon all subordinate courts; *Bulbul Mondal* v. *National Insurance Company Ltd.,* AIR 2009 (NOC) 285 (All).

Judicial Review: At threshold stage of formation of contract, the scope of judicial review is wider than at stage of enforcement of terms of contract; *United India Insurance Co. Ltd.* v. *Manubhai Dharamsinhbhai Gajera,* AIR 2009 SC 446: 2008 AIR SCW 7532: 2008 (4) ACJ 2399: 2009 (2) Civ LJ 791: 2008 (5) Mad LJ 1006: (2008) 10 SCC 404: (2008) 7 SCALE 377.

Mandamus to Police: The *mandamus* can be issued to a police officer, if only it is shown that the officer has failed to discharge his statutory duties; *Suseela* v. *State of Kerala,* AIR 2009 (NOC) 377 (Ker).

Right to Trade: There is no fundamental right to carry on trade or business in liquor; *Jitendra Sharma* v. *State of Rajasthan,* AIR 2009 (NOC) 1520 (Raj).

Substitution of Legal Representative: No limitation period is prescribed for substitution for legal representative. The substitution has to be done within a reasonable time; *Ganpat* v. *Mangla Ram,* AIR 2009 (NOC) 1519 (Raj).

Power of Speaker: The Speaker functioning as Tribunal under Tenth Schedule and interim order passed by him suspending a Member from House and his voting right during pendency and before taking final decision in a proceeding under Tenth Schedule is without his authority; *Sanbor Shullai* v. *State of Meghalaya,* AIR 2009 (NOC) 1509 (Gau).

Judicial Review: It is a settled principle of law that the executive actions are tested under the judicial review on the touchstone of arbitrariness but the criteria for examining the arbitrariness in administrative or executive actions are not *pari materia* for examining arbitrariness in legislative act. The scope of Judicial review for examining arbitrariness in legislative act is much narrower; *P.B. Samant* v. *Union of India,* AIR 2009 (NOC) 1506 (Bom).

Formation of New State: The words "ascertain views of Legislature of State" cannot be read as "consent of State" for formation of new States and alteration of areas, boundaries and names of existing States. The formation of new State or alteration of boundaries does not require consent of State; *A. Srinath Reddy* v. *Union of India,* AIR 2009 (NOC) 1505 (AP).

Supervisory Jurisdiction: Where the High Court does not exercise appellate jurisdiction, it cannot review or reweigh evidence, nor it can correct error of law in decision of subordinate courts; *K.L. Diwan* v. *Mohan Malhotra,* AIR 2009 (NOC) 1582 (Del).

State: The Public Charitable Trust cannot be said to be "State" as defined under article 12 nor also instrumentality of State; *Mandeep Mishra* v. *Union of India,* AIR 2009 Cal 31: 2009 (2) ALJ (NOC) 269.

Equality Clause: The benefit of equality clause cannot be claimed on basis of illegality; *Kerala State Electricity Board* v. *Saratchandran, P.,* AIR 2009 SC 191: 2008 AIR SCW 7122: (2008) 4 Lab LN 991: (2008) 9 SCC 396: 2008 (4) SCT 378: (2008) 13 SCALE 29: (2009) 1 Serv LJ 306 SC: (2008) 3 Shim LC 272.

Policy Decision: The policy decisions/guidelines have no Statutory force hence cannot be enforced through the Courts; *I.T.C. Ltd.* v. *State of Uttar Pradesh,* AIR 2009 (NOC) 100 (All).

Change of Policy with Change of Government: The change of policy with change of government is not proper unless it is found that act done by authority earlier in existence is contrary to statutory provision or unreasonable or against public interest. The State should not change its stand merely because other political party has come to power; *I.T.C. Ltd.* v. *State of Uttar Pradesh,* AIR 2009 (NOC) 100 (All).

Discrimination on Ground of Sex: The post of Sarpanch reserved for candidate belonging to Scheduled Castes category can be contested by woman belonging to Scheduled Castes. The plea that she can contest only for post reserved for Scheduled Caste is not tenable; *Parmjit Singh* v. *State of Punjab,* AIR 2009 P&H 7.

Increase in Punishment through Amendment: The increase in punishment by amendment is not a creation of new offence; *Superintendent, Narcotic Control Bureau* v. *Parash Singh,* AIR 2009 SC 244: 2009 Cr LJ 386: 2008 AIR SCW 7206: 2008 (41) OCR 835: (2008) 13 SCC 499: (2008) 13 SCALE 372: 2009 (2) SCC (Cri) 1147.

Equal Pay for Equal Work: The concept of equal pay for equal work is not applicable to contract worker; *Steel Authority of India Ltd.* v. *State of West Bengal,* AIR 2009 SC 120: 2009 Lab IC 1389: 2008 AIR SCW 7019: (2008) 14 SCC 589: 2009 (1) SCT 35: (2008) 12 SCALE 869: (2009) 1 Serv LJ 279 SC.

Practice and Procedure for Filing Public Interest Litigation: The Division Bench of High Court under article 226 has no jurisdiction to lay down practice and procedure for filing Public Interest Litigation; *S.P. Anand* v. *Registrar General, M. P. High Court, Jabalpur,* AIR 2009 MP 1: 2008 (3) Jab LJ 361: 2008 (4) MPHT 279: (2008) 3 MPLJ 596: 2008 (4) SCT 352.

Quasi-Judicial Order: The *quasi*-judicial order is to be tested on basis of reasoning contained therein and not on basis of plea of person seeking to sustain order; *I.T.C. Ltd.* v. *State of Uttar Pradesh,* AIR 2009 (NOC) 100 (All).

Alternative Remedy: If the issues raised in writ petitions are purely legal and jurisdictional issues, the writ petitions cannot be thrown on the ground of non- exhaustion of alternative remedy; *Ashok Kumar* v. *State of Uttar Pradesh,* AIR 2009 (NOC) 161 (All).

Principle of *res judicata*: The principles of *res judicata* apply equally to writ proceedings; *Indu Bhusan Jana* v. *Union of India,* AIR 2009 Cal 24.

Review of Judgment: The provision of Civil Procedure Code will also apply to wit jurisdiction of High Court unless inconsistent with any Rule; *Union of India* v. *Zokailiana,* AIR 2009 (NOC) 72 (Gau).

Disputed Question of Fact: The disputed question of fact cannot be decided in writ; *Abhay Kumar* v. *Chief Manager, State Bank of Indore,* AIR 2009 MP 24: 2009 AIHC 154 NOC: 2009 (2) ALJ (NOC) 247: 2009 (2) Bank CLR 95: 2009 (2) Bank Cas 393: (2008) 4 MPLJ 33.

Award of Lok Adalat: The award of Lok Adalat is regarded as final and cannot be questioned in original suit; *Paras Holidays Pvt. Ltd.* v. *State of Haryana,* AIR 2009 P&H 9.

Claim for Compensation: The claim for compensation on account of medical negligence since the questions of fact have to be taken into consideration in order to arrive at actual compensation to be paid, the appropriate remedy is to file civil suit; *Seema Rana* v. *State of Rajasthan,* AIR 2009 (NOC) 108 (Raj).

Right to Live with Dignity: The wife has right guaranteed to live with dignity; *Kunji Lal Lodhi* v. *Smt. Bala Bai Lodhi,* AIR 2009 (NOC) 694 (M.P.).

Preventive Detention: If detenue at pre-execution stage satisfies the court that detention order is clearly illegal, there is no reason why court should stay its hands and compel the petitioner to go to jail even though he is bound to be released subsequently; *Deepak Bajaj* v. *State of Maharashtra,* AIR 2009 SC 628: 2008 AIR SCW 7788: (2008) 4 JCC 2951: 2009 (1) MPHT 234: (2009) 3 Mad LJ 708: (2008) 4 Raj LW 3631: (2008) 14 SCALE 62.

Obiter dictum: Well considered *obiter dictum* of Supreme Court is binding precedent; *Mahammed Saud* v. *Dr. (Maj) Shaikh Mahfooz,* AIR 2009 Ori 46: 2009 AIHC 1349: (2008) 2 CLR 593: (2009) 1 Cur CC 234: (2008) 2 Ori LR 725.

Executive Power of State: The creation of reservation benefits by State *qua* executive orders from time-to-time is legitimate exercise of State's power in terms of article 15(4) of Constitution; *Mahendra Kamprai* v. *State of Assam,* AIR 2009 (NOC) 734 (Gau).

Discrimination on Ground of Sex: The Councilor elected from seat reserved for women cannot be prohibited from contesting election for post of President reserved for general category; *Manoj* v. *State of Haryana,* AIR 2009 (NOC) 427 (P&H).

Citizen's Right to Know: The citizen's right to know under Right to Information Act emanates from citizen's fundamental right to freedom of speech and expression; *Tamil Nadu Road Development Company Ltd.* v. *Tamil Nadu Information Commission,* AIR 2009 (NOC) 542 (Mad).

Precedent: The law declared by Supreme Court is assumed to be law from inception. In absence of any declaration, the law declared by Supreme Court cannot be said to be prospective in operation; *Sulochana Damodar* v. *State Transport Authority, Karnataka,* AIR 2009 (NOC) 1653 (Karn).

Public Interest Litigation: The Public Interest Litigation not barred in furtherance of public interest; *Sundargarh Citizen's Forum* v. *Orissa State Road Transport Corporation,* AIR 2009 (NOC) 1690 (Ori).

Amendment of Pleadings: The amendment of pleadings is barred after trial commenced on date, issues are framed; *Vidyabai* v. *Padmalatha,* AIR 2009 SC 1433: 2009 AIR SCW 899: 2009 (1) CLR 406: 2009 (2) Civ LJ 608: 2009 (1) ICC 1: (2009) 2 SCC 409: (2009) 1 SCALE 202.

Writ Jurisdiction: The appointment of civil servant is prerogative of State. The court will not interfere particularly when the appointment is to sensitive post; *Citizens for Justice and Peace* v. *State of Gujarat,* AIR 2009 SC 1420: 2009 AIR SCW 883: 2009 (74) All Ind Cas 105: 2009 (74) All LR 664: 2009 (1) ESC 95: (2009) 1 SCALE 449: (2009) 2 Serv LR 46.

Gay Marriage, Homosexuality and Constitutional Validity of section 377 of IPC: The writ petition was filed to challenge the constitutional validity of section 377 of Indian Penal code which criminally penalises the unnatural offences, to the extent that said provision criminalises consensual sexual acts between adults in private. And it infringed the fundamental rights guaranteed under articles 14, 15, 19 and 21 of the Constitution of India.

Broadly it had been submitted that there was a case for consensual sexual intercourse *i.e.,* homosexuality between two willing adults in privacy to be saved and excepted from the penal provision contained in section 377 of Indian Penal Code.

It was declared by the Court that section 377 of Indian Penal Code, insofar it criminalises consensual sexual acts of adults in private was violative of article 21, 14 and 15 of the Constitution. And the provisions of section 377 of Indian Penal Code would continue to govern non-consensual penile non-vaginal sex and penile non-vaginal sex involving minors; *Naz Foundation* v. *Government of NCT of Delhi,* 2010 Cr LJ 94.

Requisites for Writ of *Mandamus*: The *mandamus* can be issued provided there exists a legal right in applicant and a corresponding legal duty in respondent; *Union of India* v. *Muralidhara Menon,* (2009) 9 SCC 304.

Doctrine of *Parens Patriae*: It is responsibility of State to take decisions to protect interests of those who are unable to take care of themselves; *Suchita Srivastava* v. *Chandigarh Administration,* (2009) 9 SCC 1: AIR 2010 SC 235.

Matter of Reservation of Seats of SC and STs: The writ cannot be issued to State to make reservation; *Gulshan Prakash (Dr)* v. *State of Haryana,* AIR 2010 SC 288.

Personal Liberty of Foreigner in India: The foreign national staying in India without renewing his residential permit cannot seek to enforce fundamental rights guaranted under article 21; *Mertinez Monstant Joan* v. *Union of India,* AIR 2010 (NOC) 87 (AP).

Protection on Conviction for Offences: The conviction and sentence in criminal proceedings under *ex post facto* law, is prohibited. The sentence imposable on date of commission of offence has to determine sentence imposable on completion of trial; *Ravinder Singh* v. *State of Himachal Pradesh,* AIR 2010 SC 199.

SELECT LANDMARK JUDGMENTS ON CONSTITUTION OF INDIA

• Speeches made in Constituent Assembly in course of Debates on Draft Constitution cannot be used as aids for interpreting any Article of Constitution; *State of Travancore-Cochin* v. *Bombay Company Ltd.*, (1952) SCR 1112: AIR 1952 SC 366: (1952) 3 STC 434: 1952 SCA 656: 1952 SCJ 527: (1953) 1 Mad LJ 1.

• Parole is not a suspension of sentence; *Dadu* alias *Tulsidas* v. *State of Maharashtra*, AIR 2000 SC 3203: (2000) 8 SCC 437: 2000 Cr LJ 4619: 2000 AIR SCW 3711: 2000 (4) Crimes 124: JT 2000 (1) SC (Supp) 449: 2000 (4) SCJ 197: (2000) 6 SCALE 746: 2000 SCC (Cri) 1528: 2001 (2) UJ (SC) 1245.

• No one not even a wisest Judge, is above a commission or omission which needs correction; *Palace Administration Board* v. *Rama Varma Bharathan Thampuran*, AIR 1980 SC 1187: (1980) 3 SCR 187.

• Right to form associations or unions is a fundamental right under article 19(1)(c) of Constitution; *B.R. Singh* v. *Union of India*, AIR 1990 SC 1: 1990 Lab IC 389: (1989) 17 DRJ 90: (1989) 2 Lab LJ 591: (1989) 2 Cur LR 619: JT 1989 (4) SC 21.

• A strike may be illegal by a technical violation, but need not be necessarily unjustified. It is a fundamental flaw to equate illegal with unjust strikes; *Gujarat Steel Tubes Ltd.* v. *Gujarat Steel Tubes Mazdoor Sabha*, (1980) 2 SCC 593: AIR 1980 SC 1896: 1980 Lab IC 1004: (1980) 1 Lab LJ 137: 1980 SCC (Lab) 197: (1980) 2 SCR 146.

• Not merely is equality guaranteed but discrimination in favour of women has found favour with the Constitution and the court; *Miss C.B. Muthamma* v. *Union of India*, AIR 1979 SC 1868: 1979 Lab IC 1307: 1979 Serv LJ 654: (1979) 4 SCC 260: 1979 SCC (Lab) 366: (1979) 2 Lab LN 586.

• To insist on corroboration except in the rarest of rare cases is to equate woman who is a victim of the lust of another with an accomplice to a crime and thereby insult womanhood; *State of Maharashtra* v. *Chandraprakash Kewalchand Jain*, (1990) 1 SCC 550: AIR 1990 SC 658: 1990 Cr LJ 889: JT 1990 (1) SC 61: 1990 (1) Crimes 724: 1990 (1) SCJ 601: 1990 SCC (Cri) 210.

• Even a woman of easy virtue is entitled to protect her person; *State of Maharashtra* v. *Madhukar Narayan Mardikar*, JT 1990 (4) SC 169: AIR 1991 SC 207: 1991 Lab IC 207: (1991) 1 Lab LJ 269: (1991) 1 SCC 57: 1994 SCC (L&S) 761: 1991 SCC (Cri) 1: (1991) 1 Serv LJ SC 164: 1991 (1) UJ (SC) 109.

• Maintenance necessarily must encompass a provision for residence; *Mangat Mal (dead)* v. *Punni Devi*, (1995) 5 SCALE 199: AIR 1996 SC 172: 1995 AIR SCW 3885: JT 1995 (7) SC 506: (1996) 1 Mad LJ 82: (1996) 1 Mad LW 135: (1995) 20 Marri LJ 80: (1995) 6 SCC 88.

• In absence of serious reasons, no man can justify a divorce either in the eye of religion or the law; *Fuzlunbi* v. *K. Khader Vali*, AIR 1980 SC 1730: 1980 Cri App R (SC) 246: (1980) 2 APLJ (SC) 26: 1980 Cr LJ 1249: (1980) 4 SCC 125: 1980 LS (SC) 61: 1930 Cr LR (SC) 524.

• Supreme Court in any event has inherent jurisdiction to pass any order it considers fit and proper in the interest of justice; *Delhi Domestic Working Women's Forum* v. *Union of India*, (1995) 1 SCC 14.

• Speaker or Chairman acting under Tenth Schedule of Constitution is a Tribunal; *Kihota Hollohan* v. *Zachillhu*, (1992) Supp (2) SCC 651: AIR 1993 SC 412: 1992 AIR SCW 3497: JT 1992 (1) SC 600: (1992) 1 SCR 686: (1992) Supp 2 SCC 651.

• Proof of legislative intent can best be found in the language which the Legislature uses; *Gurbaksh Singh Sibbia* v. *State of Punjab*, AIR 1980 SC 1632: 1980 Cur LJ (Cri) 95: (1980) 2 SCC 565: 1980 2 APLJ (SC) 1: 1980 SCC (Cri) 465: 1980 Cr LJ 1125: 1980 Cr LR (SC) 475.

• Speedy and reasonably expeditious trial is an integral and essential part of the fundamental right to life and liberty; *Madheshwardhari Singh* v. *State of Bihar*, AIR 1986 Pat 324: 1986 Cr LJ 1771: 1986 Pat LJR (HC) 767: 1986 BBCJ (HC) 529: 1986 BLJ 503: 1986 BLJR 624.

• Life and liberty of a citizen guaranteed under article 21 includes life with dignity and liberty with dignity; *Lt. Col. S.J. Chaudhary* v. *State (Delhi Administration)*, AIR 1984 SC 618: 1984 Cr LJ 340: 1984 Cr LR (SC) 68: (1984) 1 SCC 722: 1984 Cur Cr J 63: 1984 SCC (Cri) 163: (1984) 1 SCWR 253: 1984 Chand Cr C 30.

• Justice that comes too late has no meaning to the person it is meant for; *Moti Lal Jain* v. *State of Bihar*, AIR 1968 SC 1509: 1969 Cr LJ 33: (1968) 2 SCA 535: 1969 (1) SCJ 68: (1969) Mad LJ (Cri) 49: 1969 BLJR 375: (1969) 3 SCR 587: ILR 47 Pat 808.

• No fair justice delivery system can keep persons on trial for their lives under infinite suspension; *Machander* v. *State of Hyderabad*, AIR 1955 SC 792: 1955 Cr LJ 1644: 1956 SCJ 34: 1956 SCA 12: (1956) 1 Mad LJ (SC) 25: (1955) 2 SCR 524: 1956 All LJ 76: 1956 BLJR 93.

• Even a delay of one year in the commencement of trial is bad enough; *Frances Coralie Mullin* v. *W.C. Khambra*, AIR 1980 SC 849: (1980) 2 SCC 275: 1980 Cr LJ 548: 1980 Cri App R (SC) 143: 1980 SCC (Cri) 419.

• It is a well-settled rule of interpretation that a document must be construed as a whole; *State of Madhya Pradesh* v. *Orient Paper Mills Ltd.*, (1977) 2 SCR 149: AIR 1977 SC 687: 40 STC 603: 1977 Tax LR 1781: (1977) 2 SCC 77.

• When a question is whether a provincial legislation is repugnant to an existing Indian law, the onus of showing its repugnancy should be on the party attacking its validity; *Tika Ramji* v. *State of Uttar Pradesh*, (1956) SCR 393: AIR 1956 SC 676: 1956 SCA 979: 1956 SCJ 625: 1956 All WR (HC) 657.

• In order to pass a valid law validating past transactions, the Legislature must have power over the subject-matter; *Shri Prithvi Cotton Mills Ltd* v. *Broach Borough Municipality*, AIR 1970 SC 192: 1970 (1) SCJ 288: 11 Guj LR 226: (1970) 1 SCA 448: (1970) 1 SCR 388.

• Principles of interpretation of statutes, apply to the interpretation of Constitution; *Mithilesh Kumari* v. *Prem Behari Khare*, AIR 1989 SC 1247: JT 1989 (1) SC 275: (1989) 1 Ker LJ 424: 1989 BBCJ (SC) 54: (1989) 2 SCC 95: (1989) 1 LS (SC) 14: (1989) 1 Civ LJ 635: 1989 (2) Land LR 97.

• An earlier statute prescribing a period of limitation may be altered by a later statute; *Maxmel* v. *Murphy*, (1957) 96 CLR 261.

• Doubt to the constitutionality of a law is to resolve it in favour of its validity; *V.M.Syed Mohammad & Co.* v. *State of Andhra Pradesh*, AIR 1954 SC 314: 1954 SCA 400: 1954 SCJ 390: (1954) 1 Mad LJ 619: 67 Mad LW 611: 1954 SCR 1117.

• Unitary features in Constitution are so many that the federal features disappear; *State of West Bengal* v. *Union of India*, AIR 1963 SC 1241: (1963) 2 SCA 448: (1964) 1 SCR 371.

• The powers conferred by Article 356 have been gravely abused and if it is desired to prevent, constitutional amendments would have to be made; *State of Rajasthan* v. *Union of India*, AIR 1977 SC 1361: (1978) 1 SCR 1: 1978 (1) SCJ 78.

• A law prohibiting the exercise of a fundamental right is in no case saved, cannot therefore be accepted; *Narendra Kumar* v. *Union of India*, AIR 1960 SC 430: 1960 SCJ 214: (1960) 2 SCR 375.

• Article 19(1)(a) has no applicability to a law which confers certain statutory rights subject to certain statutory restrictions, including restrictions on the freedom of speech; *Jamuna Prasad Mukhariya* v. *Lacchi Ram*, AIR 1954 SC 686: 1954 SCJ 835: (1954) 2 Mad LJ 711: 1955 Nag LJ 112: 1955 SCA 151: 1955 SCR 608.

• Right to stand as a candidate for an election is not a fundamental right; *Sakhawant Ali* v. *State of Orissa*, AIR 1955 SC 166: 21 Cut LT 88: 1955 SCA 353: 1955 SCJ 262: 1955 SCR 1004.

• Object and form of the State action determine the extent of the protection which the aggrieved party may claim is not consistent with the constitutional scheme; *R.C. Cooper* v. *Union of India*, AIR 1970 SC 564: (1970) 3 SCR 530.

Discrimination in Criminal Trial: The discrimination in criminal trials offends article 14 of Constitution of India; *State of West Bengal* v. *Anwar Ali Sarkar*, AIR 1952 SC 75: (1952) SCR 284: 1952 Cr LJ 510: 1952 SCJ 55: 1952 Mad WN 460: 1952 SCA 148.

Conception of Mahantship: In the conception of mahantship and shabaitship, both in office and property of duties and personal interest are blended together and neither can be detached from the other. *Commissioner, Hindu Religious Endowments, Madras* v. *Lakshmindra Thirtha Swamiar of Sri Shirur Mutt*, (1954) SCR 1005: AIR 1954 SC 282: 1954 SCJ 335: (1954) 1 Mad LJ 596: 20 Cut LT 250: 1954 SCA 415: 1954 Mad WN 363.

Advisory Jurisdiction of Supreme Court: While under clause 2 of article 143, it is obligatory on Supreme Court to entertain a reference and to report to President its opinion thereon, that court has under clause (1) a discretion in the matter and may in a proper case and for good reasons decline to express any opinion on the questions submitted to it. *In re* Kerala Education Bill 1957, AIR 1958 SC 956: 1959 SCR 995: 1958 Ker LT 465: ILR 1958 Ker 1167: 1959 SCA 450: 1959 SCJ 321.

Characteristic of Citizenship: Citizen includes only natural person and not juristic person like corporations; *State Trading Corporation of India Ltd.* v. *Commercial Tax Officer*, AIR 1963 SC 1811: (1964) 4 SCR 99: 1963 Cur LJ (SC) 126: (1963) 33 Com Cas 1057: 1963 (2) SCJ 605: (1964) 2 SCA 201.

Reference of matter to Supreme Court: Any question of law or fact can be referred to Supreme Court and on such reference Court may report but is not bound to "report".

Special Reference of 1 of 1964, Dt. 30-9-1964. AIR 1965 SC 745: (1965) 1 SCR 413: 1965 (1) SCJ 847: (1965) 1 SCA 441 in article 143 of the Constitution of India.

Fundamental Right of Company and its shareholders: Infringement of fundamental rights and shareholders of the company is distinctive. *Rustom Covasji Cooper* v. *Union of India*, AIR 1971 SC 564: (1970) 3 SCR 530.

Power of Courts under articles 32 and 226 is part of basic structure of Constitution: Power of judicial review of Supreme Court and High Courts under articles 32 and 226 is part of basic structure of Constitution. *L. Chandra Kumar* v. *Union of India*, AIR 1997 SC 1125: (1997) 2 SCR 1186: 1997 AIR SCW 1345: JT 1997 (3) SC 589: (1997) 2 Lab LN 482: 1997 (1) MPLJ 621: (1997) 3 SCC 261: 1997 SCC (L&S) 577: (1997) 3 SCALE 40: 1997 (3) Supreme 147: 1997 Writ LR 358.

First and Fourth Amendment of Constitution of India: The 1st and 4th Amendment of Constitution of India in 1951 and 1955 do not damage basic structure of Constitution and is also valid. *Waman Rao* v. *Union of India*, AIR 1981 SC 271: (1981) 2 SCC 362: 1980 Ker LT 573: 1980 UJ (SC) 742: (1981) 2 SCR 1.

Appointment and removal of subordinate judicial officers: The Governor and President act on aid and advice of Council of Ministers in executive action and not required by Constitution to act personally without aid and advice of Council of Ministers in appointment of and removal of subordinate judicial officers within the framework of Constitution *Samsher Singh* v. *State of Punjab*, AIR 1974 SC 2192: (1975) 1 SCR 814: 1974 Lah IC 1380: 1974 Serv LR 701: 1974 SCC (Lab) 550: 1976 All Serv Rep 269.

Unconstitutionality of Legislation and Duty of Court: When examining a legislation from the angle of vires the court has to be resilient, not rigid, forward looking, not static, liberal, not verbal in interpreting the organic law of the nation: and the courts do not substitute their social and economic belief for the judgment of legislative bodies. *R.S. Joshi* v. *Ajit Mills Ltd.,* AIR 1977 SC 2279: (1978) 1 SCR 338: 1978 (1) SCJ 239: 1978 CSNR 163.

Definition of Industry: The Bangalore Water Supply and Sewage Board, is an industry. *Bangalore Water Supply and Sewage Board* v. *A. Rajjappa,* AIR 1978 SC 548: (1978) 3 SCR 207: 1978 Lab IC 467: (1978) 1 Lab LJ 349: (1978) 1 Lab LN 376: 1978 SCC (Lab) 215: 1978 CLNR 96: 1978 (1) SCJ 481: (1978) 2 SCC 213.

Question of Fact and Supreme Court and Reference of President of India: The Supreme Court can decline to answer the reference of President even on question of fact. *In re the Special Court Bill, 1978,* AIR 1979 SC 478: (1979) 2 SCR 476: (1979) 1 SCC 380: 1979 (2) SCJ 35.

Power of CJI in appointment of judges: In the appointment of High Court and Supreme Court judges the opinion of Chief Justice of India is of primary importance. *Supreme Court Advocates-on-Record Association* v. *Union of India,* (1993) 4 SCC 441: AIR 1994 SC 268: 1993 AIR SCW 4101: JT 1993 (5) SC 479: 1993 (5) Serv LR 337: (1993) Supp 2 SCR 659.

MPs and MLAs as Public Servant: The MPs and MLAs are public servants *P.V. Narsimha Rao* v. *State (CBI/SPE),* (1990) 2 SCR 870: AIR 1998 SC 2120: 1998 Cr LJ 2930: 1998 AIR SCW 2001: 1998 (2) Crimes 124: JT 1998 (3) SC 318: (1998) (4) SCC 626: 1998 (1) SCJ 529: 1998 SCC (Cri) 1108: 1998 (4) Supreme 1.

Power of Supreme Court to Complete Justice: Article 142 vests power in Supreme Court to pass such decree or make such order as is necessary for doing complete justice in any case or matter pending before it. There is no provision for limitation regarding causes and circumstances for it. *E.S.P. Rajaram* v. *Union of India,* (2001) 1 SCR 203: AIR 2001 SC 581: 2001 AIR SCW 200: 2002 (1) JCR SC 430: JT 2001 (1) SC 573: (2001) 2 SCC 186: 2001 SCC (L&S) 352: 2001 (2) SCJ 458: 2001 (1) SCT 759: (2001) 1 SCALE 146: 2001 (1) Supreme 169.

Long Hand of Contempt of Court: Only weapon available to judiciary against the contemnor attempting to tarnish, diminish, or wipe out the confidence of people in judiciary is the long hand of contempt of court.

Relationship between Fundamental Rights and Directive Principles: Directive principles are relevant consideration in deciding reasonableness on restriction imposed on Fundamental Rights. *State of Gujarat* v. *Mirzapur Moti Kureshi Kassab Jamat,* AIR 2006 SC 212: (2005) 8 SCC 534: 2005 AIR SCW 5723: 2006 (2) JCR SC 272: 2005 (7) SCJ 701: 2005 (8) SLT 349: 2006 (1) SRJ 223: (2005) 8 SCALE 661: 2005 (8) Supreme 697.

Power of CJI in Constitution of Arbitral Tribunal: The power of Chief Justice of India or his designate in constitution of Administrative Tribunal is not an administrative power but is a judicial power; *S.B.P. & Co.* v. *Patel Engineering Ltd.,* AIR 2006 SC 450: 2005 AIR SCW 5932: 2005 CLC 1546: 2006 (1) JCR SC 190: JT 2005 (9) SC 219: (2005) 8 SCC 618: 2005 (7) SCJ 461: 2005 (8) SLT 405: 2006 (1) SRJ 25: (2005) 9 SCALE 1: 2005 (7) Supreme 610.

Right to Life Die: The Right to life under article 21 also includes right to die; *Gian Kaur* v. *State of Punjab,* AIR 1996 SC 946: 1996 Cr LJ 1660: 1996 AIR SCW 1336: 1996 (1) Crimes 197: JT 1996 (3) SC 339: (1996) 2 SCC 648: (1996) 3 SCR 697: 1996 SCC (Cri) 374.

SALARY OF FIVE PILLARS OF INDIA APPOINTED BY PRESIDENT UNDER HIS HAND AND SEAL

Designation	Salary	Constitutional/Statutory Provision
Chief Justice	Rs. 1,00,000 per month	Schedule 2, Part-D, Entry 9 of High Court and Supreme Court Judges (Salaries and Conditions of Service) Amendment Act, 2009 (23 of 2009)
Attorney General	Determined by President	Article 76(4)
Comptroller and Auditor General	Rs. 90,000 per month (Equal to salary of a judge of Supreme Court)	Schedule, 2 Part-E entry 12 and High Court and Supreme Court Judges (Salaries and Conditions of Service) Amendment Ordinance, 2009
Chief Election Commissioner	Determined by President	
Chairman, Public Service Commission	Charged on Consolidated Fund of India	Article 322

Note.—*The Salary of Chief Justice once determined cannot be reduced rather than in Financial Emergency.*

Glossary of Constitutional Terms

Act of God, is a direct, violent, sudden and irresistible act of nature, which could not, by any reasonable care have been foreseen or resisted, *Wharton's Law Lexicon, 14th Edn., p. 19. See also Nugent v. Smith, (1876) 1 CPD 423.*

Act of Parliament, means a Bill passed by the two Houses of Parliament and assented to by the President and in the absence of an express provision to the contrary, operative from the date of notification in the Gazette, *Commentary on the Constitution of India, Durga Das Basu, p. 637.*

Act of State, means the act of sovereign power of a country or its agent (if acting *intra-vires*). By its very nature such an act cannot be questioned by any Court of Law. *Wharton's Law Lexicon, 15th Edn., p. 32.*

— the plea of Act of State is not available against subjects, *Jahangir v. Secretary of State of India*, 6 Bom LR 31; *Virender v. State of Uttar Pradesh*, 1995 SCR 415; *Secretary of State for India in Council v. Kamachee Boye Saheba*, 7 MIA 476.

Address of President, is the prepared speech delivered by the President of India to both Houses of Parliament assembled together at the commencement of the first Session after each general election to Lok Sabha and at the commencement of the first Session of each year informing Parliament of the causes of its summons which is later laid before and discussed on a formal Motion of Thanks in each House of Parliament or an address by the President of India to either House of Parliament or both Houses assembled together on any other occasion, *Rules of Procedure and Conduct of Business in Lok Sabha, 10th Edn., 2002, Rule 16.*

Adjournment Motion, if Speaker gives his consent after satisfying himself that the matter to be raised is definitely urgent and of public importance and holds that the matter prepared to be discussed is in order, he shall call the member concerned who shall rise in his place and ask for leave to move the adjournment of the House. If objection to leave being granted is taken, the Speaker shall request those members who are in favour of leave being granted to rise in their places, and if not less than fifty members rise accordingly, the Speaker shall intimate that leave is granted, if not, he shall inform the House that the members have not to leave the House, *Rules of Procedure and Conduct of Business in Lok Sabha, 10th Edn., 2002, Rules 56 & 60.*

Adjournment of House, in Lok Sabha the Speaker determines when sitting of House is to adjourn *sine die* or to a particular day or to an hour or part of same day while in Rajya Sabha it is the Chairman who determines, *Rules of Procedure and Conduct of Business in Lok Sabha, 10th Edn., 2002, rule 15 read with rules 11 and 13 of Rules of Procedure and Conduct of Business in Council of States (Rajya Sabha), 5th Edn., 2000.*

Admonition, is a judicial or ecclesiastic censure or reprimand. *Wharton's Law Lexicon, 15th Edn., p. 51.*

Advocate-General, the Attorney-General and after him, the Advocate-General of a State have precedence over other advocates *Practice and Procedure of Parliament, M.N. Kaul and S.L. Shakdher, 5th Edn., 2001, p. 154.*

Affirmation, is a solemn declaration without oath, *Wharton's Law Lexicon, 15th Edn., p. 65.*

Amendment, is a device to alter a motion moved or question under discussion in the Legislature, includes omission, substitution, addition and insertion of certain words, figures or marks to the clause of a Bill, a resolution or a motion or to an amendment made thereof, *Practice and Procedure of Parliament, M.N. Kaul and S.L. Shakdher, 5th Edn., 2001, p. 664.*

— is a structural improvement, *Stroud's Judicial Dictionary, pp. 128 & 498.*

Anglo-Indian, is of a British birth but living or having lived long in India, *Concise Oxford Dictionary, H.W. Fowler and F.G. Fowler, p. 51.*

— is a person of both English and Indian ancestry, *Webster American Dictionary, p. 81.*

Appeal, is the judicial examination of the decision by a higher court or the decision of an inferior court, *Wharton's Law Lexicon, 15th Edn., p. 105.*

Appropriation Bill, is the act of devoting or reserving for a special or distinct purpose or of destining to a particular end; anything set aside especially money for a specific use, *Webster American Dictionary, p. 72.*

Arrest, is the restraining of the liberty of a man's person in order to compel obedience to the order of a court of justice, or to prevent the commission of a crime, or to ensure that a person charged or suspected of a crime may be forth-coming to answer it, *Wharton's Law Lexicon, 15th Edn., p. 126.*

— is when one is taken into custody and restrained from his liberty, *Stroud's Judicial Dictionary, Vol. 1, p. 175.*

Assent to Bill, is ratification, sovereign's formal acquiescence in a measure passed by Legislature, *A Dictionary of Law, Willium C. Anderson, 1889, p. 79.*

Attorney-General, is the Chief Law Officer of a country, legal adviser to the Chief Executive, *Webster American Dictionary, p. 95.*

Backward classes, the list of OBCs are prepared by the Central Government and are revised after the expiry of every 10 years, *National Commission for Backward Classes Act, 1993, section 11.*

— are the classes slow in development, *Webster American Dictionary, p. 106.*

Ballot, is a small ball, ticket or paper used in secret voting, *The Concise Oxford Dictionary, H.W. Fowler and F.G. Fowler, p. 89.*

Begar, is a labour or service exacted by court or a person in power without giving remuneration, *Vasudevan v. Mittal,* AIR 1962 Bom 35.

Bill, is a draft of a law proposed to a lawmaking body, *Webster American Dictionary, p. 146.*

— is the draft or form of an Act presented to a Legislature but not enacted, *A Dictionary of Law, Willium C. Anderson, 1889, p. 120.*

Breach of privilege, disregard of any of the privileges, rights and immunities either of the members of Parliament individually or of either House of Parliament in its collective capacity or of its committees, also includes action which obstruct the House in the performance in its functions and thereby lower its dignity and authority such as disobedience of its legitimate order or libel upon itself, or its member or officers which are called contempt of the House. *Practice and Procedure of Parliament, M.N. Kaul and S.L. Shakdher, 5th Edn., 2001, p. 212.*

Budget, refers to the statement of the estimated receipts and expenditure of the Government of India known as annual financial statement; it is caused to be laid before both Houses of Parliament by the President in respect of every financial year on such day as he may direct. *Rules of Procedure and Conduct of Business in Lok Sabha, 10th Edn., 2002, Rule 204.*

Bulletin, is an official notice of a public transaction or matter of public importance, *Wharton's Law Lexicon, 15th Edn., p. 231.*

Business of the House, is the relative order of the items of business in the House of a Legislature to be taken up on a particular day, *The Office of the Speaker in the Parliaments of Commonwealth, Wilding and Philip Laundy, p. 64.*

Cabinet, is a private and confidential assembly of the most considerable minister of State to concert measures for the administration of public affairs, *Wharton's Law Lexicon, 15th Edn., p. 241.*

Censure Motion, is a motion moved against the government censuring its policy in some direction or an individual minister or minister of the Government, *The Office of the Speaker in the Parliaments of Commonwealth, Wilding and Philip Laundy, p. 775.*

Certiorari, is a writ of High Court to an inferior court to call up the records of a cause therein depending that conscionable justice may be therein administered, *Stroud's Judicial Dictionary, Vol. 1, p. 487.*

— is issued by the superior Court to inferior judicial or quasi-judicial body, grounds for invoking are excess of jurisdiction, violation of natural justice, fraud and terms on the face of the record. Conditions for issuing this writ are: (i) a body of persons having legal authority, (ii) to determine questions altering rights of subjects, (iii) having the duty to act judicially, (iv) act in excess of their legal authority, (v) issued on constitutional grounds also. *Province of Bombay v. Kushal Das,* AIR 1960 SC 222; *Ujjan Bai v. State of Uttar Pradesh,* AIR 1962 SC 1621.

Chief whip, is the chief of the whips of different political parties in Parliament (generally the Minister of Parliamentary Affairs), *Dictionary of Constitutional and Parliamentary Terms, Lok Sabha Secretariat, 2005, 2nd Edn., p. 48.*

Citizen, is a member of a State or nation, especially one with a republican form of government, who owes allegiance to it by birth or naturalisation and is entitled to full civil rights, *Webster American Dictionary, p. 267.*

Closure, is the Parliamentary procedure by which debate is closed and the measure under discussion brought up for an immediate vote, *Webster American Dictionary, p. 276.*

— is the procedure in deliberative assemblies whereby debate is closed, *Wharton's Law Lexicon, 15th Edn., p. 319.*

Coalition, usually takes place in multi-party system in which no single party is able to command support of a working majority, *Dictionary of Political Science, Joseph Dunner, 1965, p. 101.*

Comptroller and Auditor-General, is the officer who is responsible for the auditing of all public accounts, *The Office of the Speaker in the Parliaments of Commonwealth, Wilding and Philip Laundy, p. 161.*

Concurrent List, is a list of subjects appended to a Federal Constitution in respect of which the Federal Legislature and the State or regional Legislatures have power to make laws, federal law prevailing in case of conflict, *The Office of the Speaker in the Parliaments of Commonwealth, Wilding and Philip Laundy, p. 132.*

Consolidated fund, is a repository of public money which now comprises the produce of customs, excise, stamps and several other taxes, and some small receipts from the royal hereditary revenue surrendered to its public use, *Wharton's Law Lexicon, 15th Edn., p. 375.*

Constituent Assembly, is a legislative body charged with the task of framing or revising a Constitution, set up for India after it became independent in 1947 for the purpose of framing its Constitution, *The Office of the Speaker in the Parliaments of Commonwealth, Wilding and Philip Laundy, p. 273.*

Constitution, is the system of fundamental laws and principles of a government written or unwritten, *Webster American Dictionary, p. 315.*

— is the basic law defining and delimiting the principal organs of Government and their jurisdiction as well as the basic rights of men and citizens, *Dictionary of Political Science, Joseph Dunner, 1965, p. 118.*

Constitutionality of law, is the law being in accordance with the provisions of the Constitution of a country, *Dictionary of Constitutional and Parliamentary Terms, Lok Sabha Secretariat, 2nd Edn., 2005, p. 94.*

— can be challenged only by the person directly affected, *Chiranji Lal* v. *Union of India,* AIR 1951 SC 41.

Contempt of court, is a disobedience to or disregard of the rules, orders, process, or dignity of a court, which has power to punish for such offence by committal, *Wharton's Law Lexicon, 15th Edn., p. 387.*

Contingency fund, is placed at the disposal of the executive to meet the unforeseen expenditure, *Dictionary of Constitution and Parliamentary Terms, Lok Sabha Secretariat, 2005, Edn., p. 98.*

Court, is a place where justice is judicially administered, *Stroud's Judicial Dictionary, Vol. 1, p. 561.*

Cut Motion, during the discussion on the demands for grants, motion can be moved to reduce the amount of a demand, such a motion is called cut motion, *Practice and Procedure of Parliament, M.N. Kaul and S.L. Shakdher, 5th Edn., 2001, p. 713.*

Debate, is a Parliamentary discussion, *Dictionary of Constitutional and Parliamentary Terms, Lok Sabha Secretariat, 2nd Edn., 2005, p. 107.*

Defection, is abandonment of loyalty, duty, principle etc., *Webster American Dictionary, p. 301.*

Delegated legislation, is rules and regulations with the effect of law made by the executive under statutory sanction by Parliament, *The Office of the Speaker in the Parliaments of Commonwealth, Wilding and Philip Laundy, p. 199.*

Deprivation, is a loss of dismissal from office, *Webster American Dictionary, p. 310.*

— refers to property taken under the power of eminent domain, *A Dictionary of Law, Willium C. Anderson, 1889, p. 347.*

Deputy Speaker, is the Officer of the House of a Legislature who takes the Chair during the absence of the Speaker and performs his duties in relation to all proceedings in the House, *Parliamentary Practice, Erskine May, 22nd Edn., 1997, p. 194.*

Directive Principles of State Policy, lay down guidelines which can be implemented only by passing legislation, *Commentary on the Constitution of India, Durga Das Basu, Vol. 11, p. 303.*

Discrimination, is a difference in treatment of two or more persons or subject, *Stroud's Judicial Dictionary, Vol. 1, p. 695.*

— is an act of depriving an individual or a group of equality of opportunity, *Dictionary of Political Science, Joseph Dunner, 1965, p. 148.*

Dissolution, is the civil death of Parliament, *Wharton's Law Lexicon, 15th Edn., p. 533.*

Doctrine of severability, is a rule of interpretation; it means that where some particular provision of statute offends against a constitutional limitation, but that provision is severable from the rest of the statute, only that offending provision will be declared void by the court and not the entire statute, *R.M.D.C. v. Union of India,* AIR 1957 SC 628.

Double jeopardy, is subjection of an accused person to repeated trial for the same alleged offence, *Dictionary of Political Science, Joseph Dunner, 1965, p. 154.*

Due process of law, is the law in conformity with due process a concept adopted by the American Constitution; the process of law which hears before it condemns; judiciary can declare a law bad, if it is not in accordance with due process even though the legislation may be within the competence of the Legislature concerned, *Commentary on the Constitution of India, Durga Das Basu, 6th Edn., Vol. D, p. 83.*

Election, is act of selecting one or more from a greater number for an office, *Wharton's Law Lexicon, 15th Edn., p. 572.*

Election Commission, is a constitutional body created for the purpose of holding elections to Parliament, State Legislatures and Offices of President and Vice-President, *Constitution of India, Article 324.*

Electoral college, is an intermediary body chosen by electors to choose the representatives in an indirect election, *The Office of the Speaker in the Parliaments of Commonwealth, Wilding and Philip Laundy, p. 235.*

Electoral roll, is known as voter's list in common parlance; is the basic document on which the whole electoral process is founded, *Election Law Practice and Procedure, V.S. Rama Devi, p. 249.*

Equal protection, all individuals and classes will be equally subjected to the ordinary law of the land administered by the law courts, *Commentary on the Constitution of India, Durga Das Basu, Vol. B, p. 7.*

Equality, is the state of being equal in political, economic and social rights, *Webster American Dictionary, p. 391.*

Existing law, is the law in force at the passage of an Act, *A Dictionary of Law, Willium C. Anderson, 1889, p. 434.*

Expulsion, is the unseating of members for offences committed against the House or for grave misdemeanours, *The Office of the Speaker in the Parliaments of Commonwealth, Wilding and Philip Laundy, p. 263.*

Extradition, is the surrender by a foreign State of a person accused of a crime to the State where it was committed, *Wharton's Law Lexicon, 15th Edn., p. 642.*

Financial memorandum, is a memorandum required to accompany all Bills involving expenditure, *The Office of the Speaker in the Parliaments of Commonwealth, Wilding and Philip Laundy, p. 272.*

Fundamental duties, are certain obligations on the part of a citizen which he or she owes towards the State so that the individual may not overlook his duties to the community while exercising his fundamental right or commit wanton destruction of public property or life, *Shorter Constitution, Durga Das Basu, p. 465.*

Fundamental rights, is protected and guaranteed by the written Constitution of a State, *Commentary on the Constitution of India, Durga Das Basu, Vol. 1, p. 126.*

Gazette, is the official newspaper of the Government, *Wharton's Law Lexicon, 15th Edn., p. 730.*

— is known as the Gazette of India or the Official Gazette of a State, *General Clauses Act, 1897, section 3(39)*.

Government, is a established system of political administration by which State is governed, *Webster American Dictionary, p. 826.*

Guillotine, is the most drastic method of curtailing debate in a Legislature, *Parliamentary Practice, Erskine May, 22nd Edn., 1997, p. 410.*

Habeas corpus, commands a Judge of the inferior court to produce the body of the defendant with a statement of the cause of his detention, to do and to receive whatever the higher court shall decree, *A Dictionary of Law, Willium C. Anderson, 1889, p. 580.*

Hung Parliament, is a Parliament wherein no party has won a working majority, *Reader's Digest Dictionary, p. 823.*

Impeachment, a person found guilty may be removed from his office, *Dictionary of Political Science, Joseph Dunner, 1965, p. 252.*

Joint sitting, is a joint sitting of both Houses of a Bicameral Legislature for setting a disagreement between them, *The Office of the Speaker in the Parliaments of Commonwealth, Wilding and Philip Laundy, p. 412.*

Judgment, order or sentence given by a judge or law court, *Webster American Dictionary, p. 1036.*

Judicial review, is the power of the court to review statutes or administrative acts and determine their constitutionality. The examination of Federal and State Legislature statutes and the acts of executive officials by the Courts to determine their validity according to written Constitutions, *Dictionary of Political Science, Joseph Dunner, 1965, p. 285.*

Judiciary, is the body of officers who administer the law, *A Dictionary of Law, Willium C. Anderson, 1889, p. 579.*

Law, all the rules of conduct established and enforced by the authority, *Webster American Dictionary, p. 828.*

Legislative relations, in case of conflict the Union law prevails, *Prafulla Kumar v. Bank of Commerce,* AIR 1947 PC 60.

Legislature, is the body of persons in a State authorised to make, alter and repeal law. It may consist of one or two Houses with similar or different powers, *The Office of the Speaker in the Parliaments of Commonwealth, Wilding and Philip Laundy, p. 429.*

Liberty, is something which results from a permission given to or something enjoyed under sufferance by a particular person or body of persons as opposed to enjoyment by all and sundry, *Stroud's Judicial Dictionary, Vol. 2, p. 1459.*

Locus standi, means a place for standing, right to be heard, *A Dictionary of Law, Willium C. Anderson, 1889, p. 637.*

Maiden speech, is one's first or earliest speech especially in Parliament, *Webster American Dictionary, p. 883.*

Mandamus, is an established remedy to oblige inferior Courts and Magistrates to do that justice which they are in duty, and by virtue of their office, bound to do; compels officers and others to act in the discharge of the duties and impose upon them, *A Dictionary of Law, Willium C. Anderson, 1889, p. 651.*

Martial law, is arbitrary in its decisions and is not built on any settled principles, *Stroud's Judicial Dictionary, Vol. 2, p. 1563.*

Migration, means coming to India with the intention of residing here permanently, *Sanno Devi v. Mangal Sain,* AIR 1961 SC 810.

Minority, is racial, religious or political groups smaller than and differing from larger, controlling group of which it is a party, *Webster American Dictionary, p. 936; D.A.V. College v. State of Punjab,* AIR 1971 SC 137.

Money Bill, is a bill which contains only provisions dealing with the imposition, repeal, remission, alteration or regulation of taxes etc., *Parliamentary Practice, Erskine May, 22nd Edn., 1997, p. 807.*

Motion, is a proposal made in the House of a Legislature to elicit its decision on a subject, *The Office of the Speaker in the Parliaments of Commonwealth, Wilding and Philip Laundy, p. 481.*

Oath, is a ritualistic declaration, based on an appeal to God or some revered person or object that one will speak the truth, keep a promise, remain faithful etc., *Webster American Dictionary, p. 1011.*

Office of profit, is an employment with fees and emoluments attached to it; where pay or salary is attached to an office, it immediately and indisputably makes the office an "office of profit", *Practice and Procedure of Parliament, M.N. Kaul and S.L. Shakdher, 5th Edn., 2001, p. 76.*

Official gazette, means the Gazette of India or the Official Gazette of a State, *General Clauses Act, 1897, section 3(39).*

Ordinance, is a State paper, operative as a fundamental law, yet not describable as either a Constitution or a statute, *A Dictionary of Law, Willium C. Anderson, 1889, p. 738.*

Personal liberty, consists in the power of locomotion, of changing situation or moving one's person to whatever place one's own inclination may direct, without imprisonment or restraint unless by due course of law, *A Dictionary of Law, Willium C. Anderson, 1889, p. 620.*

Petition, is a solemn, earnest supplication or request to a superior or to a person or group in authority, *Webster American Dictionary, p. 327.*

Pith and substance, is a doctrine relating to the interpretation of statutes, evolved by the Privy Council, to solve the problem of two competing Legislatures, *Gallaghar* v. *Lymm,* 1937 AC 863; *Prafulla* v. *Bank of Commerce,* AIR 1947 PC 28; *State of Rajasthan* v. *V.G. Chowla,* AIR 1959 SC 544; *Sajjan Singh* v. *State of Rajasthan,* AIR 1985 SC 845.

Preamble, is an introduction, especially one to a constitutional statute etc., stating its reason and purpose, *Webster American Dictionary, p. 1147.*

President, is Chief executive of a Republic, *Webster American Dictionary, p. 1153.*

Presumption of constitutionality, is an assumption made failing proof of the contrary that an enactment is in accordance with the Constitution. The presumption is always in favour of the constitutionality of an enactment and the burden is upon him who attacks it to show that there has been a clear transgression of the constitutional principles, *Charanjit Lal* v. *Union of India,* AIR 1951 SC 41.

Privilege, is an exceptional right or advantage, *Wharton's Law Lexicon, 15th Edn., p. 1346.*

Privy purse, is the sum fixed by the Government of India for covering the expenses of each of the rulers of former Indian States and their families in consideration of their agreement of merger in the Indian Union, *Commentary on the Constitution of India, Durga Das Basu, Vol. 4, p. 369.*

Probationer, is one who is on probation or trial, *Chambers Concise 20th Century Dictionary, Davidson, Seaton and Simpson, p. 786.*

Procedure established by law, is the procedure prescribed by the law of the State. It does not mean the due process of law, *A.K. Gopalan* v. *State of Madras,* AIR 1950 SC 27.

Prohibition, is a remedy provided by the Common Law against the encroachment of jurisdiction, *Wharton's Law Lexicon, 15th Edn., p. 1361.*

Proportional representation, is a method of representation designed to secure the election of candidates in proportion to the numerical strength of each section of political opinion thus accurately reflecting the political feeling of the country in Parliament, *The Office of the Speaker in the Parliaments of Commonwealth, Wilding and Philip Laundy, p. 602.*

Question hour, is the time fixed for asking and answering oral questions in a sitting in a Legislature; it is fixed under the rules of the House or standing orders, *Dictionary of Constitutional and Parliamentary Terms, Lok Sabha Secretariat, 2005, Edn., p. 371.*

Quo warranto, is a writ ordering a person to show by what right he exercises an office, franchise or privilege, *Webster American Dictionary, p. 1196.*

Quorum, is a minimum number required to be present at an assembly before it can validly proceed to transact business, *Webster American Dictionary, p. 1196.*

Reasonable restriction, is restrictions imposed by State on the enjoyment of the fundamental rights, *Dictionary of Constitutional and Parliamentary Terms, Lok Sabha Secretariat, 2nd Edn., 2005, p. 379.*

Religion, is the specific system of belief, worship, conduct involving a Code of ethics and philosophy, *Webster American Dictionary, p. 1228.*

Repugnancy, is contradictory of each other, set of clauses in statutes, Will, etc., *A Dictionary of Law, Willium C. Anderson, 1889, p. 885.*

Res judicata, is final judgment already decided between the same parties or their privies on the same question by a legally constituted court having jurisdiction is conclusive between the parties, and the issue cannot be raised again, *Wharton's Law Lexicon, 14th Edn., p. 875; Daryao v. State, AIR 1964 SC 1457; Amalgamated Coal Fields v. Janapad Sabha, AIR 1964 SC 1013.*

Rule, is an established guide or regulation for action, conduct, *Webster American Dictionary, p. 1274.*

Rule of law, is absolute supremely or predominance of regular law as opposed to the influence of arbitrary power's; equality before the law or the equal subjection of all classes to the ordinary law courts; Constitution is the result of the ordinary law of the land, *Introduction to the Study of the Law of the Constitution, A.V. Dicey, 2003, p. 202.*

Session, connotes the sitting together of the legislative body for the transaction of business, *Saradhakar v. Orissa Legislative Assembly, AIR 1952 Ori 234.*

Shadow cabinet, is a body of opposition leaders meeting from time to time and ready to take office, *Chambers Concise 20th Century Dictionary, Davidson, Seaton and Simpson, p. 914.*

State, comprises people, territory, government through which its policies are implemented and sovereignty having authority to make final legal decisions and having physical power to enforce them, *Dictionary of Political Science, Joseph Dunner, 1965, p. 498.*

State Act, is an Act passed by Legislature of a State established or continued by the Constitution, *General Clauses Act, 1897, section 3(59).*

Statute, is synonymous with Act of Parliament, *Stroud's Judicial Dictionary, Vol. 3, p. 2544.*

Subordinate legislation, is a making of statutory instruments or orders by a body subordinate to the Legislature in exercise of the power within specific limits conferred by the Legislature, also covers statutory instruments themselves, *Practice and Procedure of Parliament, M.N. Kaul and S.L. Shakdher, 5th Edn., 2001, p. 630.*

Swear, is to make a solemn declaration or affirmation with an appeal to God or to some one or something held sacred for confirmation, *Webster American Dictionary, p. 1472.*

Untouchability, is social disabilities historically imposed on certain classes of people by reason of their birth in certain castes, *Commentary on the Constitution of India, Durga Das Basu, Vol. I, p. 540.*

Vote, is a decision by one or more persons on a proposal, resolution expressed by ticket, ballot or voice, *Webster American Dictionary, p. 1637.*

Vote on account, is estimate of an advance payment to enable Government Departments to carry on their work from beginning of financial year till the passing of Appropriation Act, *Parliamentary Dictionary, L.A. Abraham and S.C. Hawtrey, 1965 and H.M. Barclay, 3rd Edn., 1970, p. 223.*

Walk out, is a strike, an informal or unauthorised strike, an action of leaving a meeting or organisation as an expression of disapproval; continued absence from the meetings of an organisation as an expression of disapproval, *Webster American Dictionary, p. 2572.*

Zero hour, is a time set for the beginning of an attack or other military operation; any crucial or decisive moment, *Webster American Dictionary, p. 1698.*

— is usually noisy interregnum between the Question Hour and the beginning of the rest of the day's business in a Legislature; members raise often without notice various matters during this period, *Dictionary of Constitutional and Parliamentary Terms, Lok Sabha Secretariat, 2nd Edn., 2005, p. 491.*

• • •

Notes

Notes

CIVIL, CRIMINAL, COMMERCIAL, LABOUR & SERVICES

A

A-17. Actuaries Act, 2006 alongwith Allied Rules 65.00

A-1. Administration of Evacuee Property Act, 1950 with Rules, 1950   70.00

A-2. Administrative Tribunals Act, 1985 along with CAT (Procedure) Rules, 1987, CAT Rules of Practice, 1993 and Contempt of Courts (C.A.T.) Rules, 1992   110.00

A-3. Advocates Act, 1961   40.00

A-4. Advocates' Welfare Fund Act, 2001   30.00

A-5. Aircraft Act, 1934 along with allied Rules   155.00

A-6. Air Force Act, 1950 along with allied Act and Rules   150.00

A-7. Air (Prevention and Control of Pollution) Act,1981 along with Rules, 1982   55.00

A-15. Airport Authority of India Act, 1994 along with Rules and Regulations   70.00

A-8. Ancient Monuments and Archaeological Sites and Remains Act, 1958 along with allied Acts & Rules   110.00

A-9. Antiquities and Art Treasures Act, 1972 along with Rules, 1973   35.00

A-10. Apprentices Act, 1961 along with allied Act and Rules   100.00

A-11. Arbitration and Conciliation Act, 1996 along with Scheme, 1996   35.00

A-12. Armed Forces (Special Power) Act, 1958 along with allied Acts   30.00

A-18. Armed Forces Tribunal Act, 2007 along with allied Rules   120.00

A-13. Arms Act, 1959 along with Rules, 1962   100.00

A-14. Army Act, 1950 with Rules, 1954   195.00

A-16. Atomic Energy Act, 1962   30.00

B

B-1. Bankers' Books Evidence Act, 1891   25.00

B-2. Banking Companies (Acquisition and Transfer of Undertakings) Act, 1970 along with allied Act and Schemes   80.00

B-3. Banking Regulation Act, 1949 along with allied Rules and Scheme   150.00

B-4. Bar Council of India Rules along with allied Rules and Advocates Act, 1961   125.00

B-5. Beedi and Cigar Workers (Conditions of Employment) Act, 1966 along with Welfare Cess and Welfare Fund Act and Rules   60.00

B-6. Benami Transactions (Prohibition) Act, 1988   30.00

B-7. Biological Diversity Act, 2002 along with Rules, 2004   70.00

B-8. Boilers Act, 1923 along with allied Rules   55.00

B-9. Bonded Labour System (Abolition) Act, 1976 along with Rules, 1976   30.00

B-10. Border Security Force Act, 1968 along with allied Rules   140.00

B-11. Building and Other Construction Workers (Regulation of Employment and Conditions of Service) Act, 1996 along with Rules, 1998 with Cess Act and Rules   130.00

B-12. Bureau of Indian Standards Act, 1986 along with Rules and Regulations   80.00

C

C-1. Cable Television Networks (Regulation) Act, 1995 along with allied Rules & Regulations 50.00

C-2. Cantonments Act, 2006   110.00

C-4. Carriage by Air Act, 1972 *see* Carrier Laws (Land • Sea • Air)   75.00

C-44. Carriage by Road Act, 2007   40.00

C-4. Carriage of Goods by Sea Act, 1925 *see* Carrier Laws (Land • Sea • Air)   75.00

C-4. Carriers Act, 1865 *see* Carrier Laws (Land • Sea • Air)   75.00

C-4. Carrier Laws (Land • Sea • Air)   75.00

C-5. Cattle Trespass Act, 1871   30.00

C-43. Central Educational Institutions (Reservation in Admission) Act, 2006   30.00

C-48. Central Electricity Authority Regulations 320.00

C-49. Central Electricity Regulatory Commission Rules and Regulations   195.00

C-6. Central Excise Act, 1944 as amended by Finance Act, 2011   100.00

C-7. Central Industrial Security Force Act, 1968 along with Rules   60.00

C-8. Central Reserve Police Force Act, 1949 along with Rules, 1955   75.00

C-9. Central Sales Tax Act, 1956 as amended by Finance Act, 2011 along with Rules, 1957 60.00

C-10. Central Vigilance Commission Act, 2003 along with related Acts   50.00

C-11. Charitable and Religious Trusts Act, 1920 along with Charitable Endowments Act, 1890 and Religious Endowments Act, 1863   45.00

C-11. Charitable Endowments Act, 1890 *see* Charitable and Religious Trusts Act, 1920   45.00

C-42. Chemical Weapons Convention Act, 2000 along with Rules, 2005   110.00

C-12. Child Labour (Prohibition and Regulation) Act, 1986 along with Rules, 1988 and Children (Pledging of Labour) Act, 1933   30.00

C-13. Child Marriage Restraint Act, 1929   25.00

C-14. Chit Funds Act, 1982   40.00

C-15. Christian Marriage Act, 1872   40.00

C-16. Cigarettes and Other Tobacco Products (Prohibition of Advertisement and Regulation of Trade and Commerce, Production, Supply and Distribution) Act, 2003 along with allied Rules   30.00

C-17. Cine-Workers and Cinema Theatre Workers (Regulation of Employment) Act, 1981 along with Rules, 1984, Welfare Cess Act, 1981 along with Rules, 1984, Welfare Fund Act, 1981 and Rules, 1984 65.00

C-18. Cinematograph Act, 1952 along with Cinematograph (Certification) Rules, 1983   60.00

C-19. Citizenship Act, 1955 along with Citizenship Rules, 2009   85.00

C-20. Civil Defence Act, 1968 along with Rules and Regulations   35.00

C-50. Civil Liability for Nuclear Damage Act, 2010 with Rules, 2011   50.00

C-47. Clinical Establishments (Registration and
Regulation) Act, 2010   35.00

C-21. Code of Civil Procedure, 1908 (Hb)   195.00

C-23. Code of Civil Procedure, 1908 with
State Amendments (Hb)   295.00

C-45. Code of Civil Procedure, 1908 with
State & High Court Amendments with
Letters Patent (Hb)   375.00

C-24. Code of Criminal Procedure, 1973   165.00

C-25. Code of Criminal Procedure, 1973 (Hb)   195.00

C-26. COFEPOSA Act, 1974 and
SAFEMFOP Act, 1976 with Rules, 2006   35.00

C-46. Collection of Statistics Act, 2008 with
Rules, 2011   40.00

C-41. Commission for Protection of
Child Rights Act, 2005 along with Rules   35.00

C-27. Commissions of Inquiry Act, 1952
along with Rules, 1972   25.00

C-28. Commission of Sati (Prevention) Act,
1987 along with Rules   25.00

C-29. Companies Act (Hb)   395.00

C-30. Competition Act, 2002 with allied Rules   175.00

C-31. Constitution of India   130.00

C-33. Consumer Protection Act, 1986 along
with Rules, 1987 and Regulations, 2005   50.00

C-34. Contempt of Courts Act, 1971 along
with Rules to Regulate Proceedings for
Contempt of the Supreme Court, 1975   30.00

C-35. Contract Act, 1872   50.00

C-36. Contract Labour (Regulation and Abolition)
Act, 1970 along with Rules, 1971   55.00

N-6. Control of National Highways (Land and
Traffic) Act, 2002 *see* National
Highways Act, 1956   110.00

C-37. Copyright Act, 1957 along with
Rules, 1958 and International
Copyright Order, 1999   65.00

C-38. Court Fees Act, 1870   40.00

C-39. Credit Information Companies
(Regulation) Act, 2005 along with
Rules and Regulations, 2006   55.00

C-40. Customs Act, 1962 as amended by
Finance Act, 2011   120.00

M-18. Cutchi Memons Act, 1938
see Muslim laws   50.00

D

D-1. Dangerous Machines (Regulation)
Act, 1983 along with Rules, 2007   25.00

D-11. Dentists Act, 1948   70.00

D-2. Depositories Act, 1996 along with
Rules, 1998   40.00

D-3. Designs Act, 2000 along with
Rules, 2001   60.00

D-10. Disaster Management Act, 2005
along with allied Rules   60.00

M-18. Dissolution of Muslim Marriages
Act, 1939 *see* Muslim laws   50.00

D-4. Divorce Act, 1869   25.00

D-5. Dock Workers (Regulation of
Employment) Act, 1948 along with
Rules, 1962, Advisory Committee Rules,
1962, Safety, Health and Welfare
Act, 1986, Regulation of Employment
(Inapplicability of Major Ports) Act, 1997   45.00

D-6. Dowry Prohibition Act, 1961 along with
Rules and Relevant Provisions of IPC
& Evidence and CrPC relating to Dowry   30.00

D-12. Dramatic Performances Act, 1876   25.00

D-7. Drugs & Cosmetics Act, 1940   65.00

D-8. Drugs & Cosmetics Act, 1940
along with Rules, 1945   310.00

D-9. Drugs & Magic Remedies (Objectionable
Advertisements) Act, 1954 along with
Rules, 1955   25.00

E

E-1. Easements Act, 1882   30.00

E-2. Electricity Act, 2003 along with
Rules, 2005 and allied Rules and Orders   130.00

E-3. Electricity (Supply) Act, 1948   50.00

E-5. Electricity Rules, 2005
along with allied Rules and Orders   165.00

E-6. Emblems and Names (Prevention of
Improper use) Act, 1950 along
with allied Act and Rules   25.00

E-7. Emigration Act, 1983 along with
Rules, 1983   50.00

E-19. Employee's Compensation Act, 1923
along with allied Rules   70.00

E-8. Employees' Provident Funds and
Miscellaneous Provisions Act, 1952,
along with E.P.F. Scheme, 1952
with allied Schemes, Rules and Forms   160.00

E-9. Employees' Provident Funds and
Miscellaneous Provisions Act, 1952   55.00

E-10. Employees' State Insurance Act, 1948
along with Rules and Regulations   130.00

E-11. Employment Exchanges (Compulsory
Notification of Vacancies) Act, 1959
along with Rules, 1960   25.00

E-12. Employers' Liability Act, 1938   25.00

E-13. Energy Conservation Act, 2001
along with allied Rules   120.00

E-14. Environment (Protection) Act, 1986
along with allied Rules   240.00

E-15. Equal Remuneration Act, 1976
along with allied Rules   25.00

E-16. Essential Commodities Act, 1955
along with allied Acts   40.00

E-17. Evidence Act, 1872   50.00

E-18. Explosives Act, 1884 along with The
Explosive Substances Act, 1908 and
The Explosives Rules, 2008   160.00

F

F-1. Factories Act, 1948   60.00

F-2. Family Courts Act, 1984   30.00

F-3. Fatal Accidents Act, 1855   25.00

P-24. Flag Code of India, 2002 *see* Prevention
of Insult to National Honour Act, 1971   40.00

F-16. Food Safety and Standards Act, 2006   75.00

F-15. Food Safety and Standards Act, 2006
along with allied Rules, Regulations
and order   410.00

F-5. Foreign Contribution (Regulation) Act, 2010
along with Rules and Regulations   65.00

F-6. Foreign Exchange Management Act, 1999   35.00

F-7. Foreign Exchange Management
Act, 1999 along with allied
Rules and Regulations & Orders   175.00

F-8. Foreign Exchange Regulation Act, 1973 along with Rules, 1974 — 50.00

F-9. Foreign Marriage Act, 1969 along with Foreign Marriage Rules, 1970 — 25.00

F-10. Foreign Trade (Development and Regulation) Act, 1992 along with Rules, 1993 — 55.00

F-11. Foreigners Act, 1946 along with Foreigners Orders, 1948 with Registration of Foreigners Act, 1939 and Rules, 1992 — 45.00

F-12. Forest Act, 1927 along with The Forest (Conservation) Act, 1980 and Rules, 2003 — 85.00

F-14. Freedom of Information Act, 2002 along with Provisions of Relevant Documents and The Official Secrets Act, 1923 — 25.00

G

G-1. Gas Cylinders Rules, 2004 along with Rules, 1981 and allied Orders — 125.00

G-2. General Clauses Act, 1897 — 25.00

I-12. General Insurance Business (Nationalisation) Act, 1972 *see* Insurance Act, 1938 — 240.00

G-5. Geographical Indications of Goods (Registration and Protection) Act, 1999 along with Rules, 2002 — 80.00

G-7. Government Securities Act, 2006 along with Regulations — 55.00

G-8. Gram Nyayalayas Act, 2008 — 40.00

G-6. Guardians and Wards Act, 1890 — 25.00

H

H-1. Hindu Laws (Containing 5 Acts) — 50.00

H-2. Hindu Adoption & Maintenance Act, 1956 — 30.00

H-1. Hindu Disposition of Property Act, 1916 *see* Hindu Laws (containing 5 Acts) — 50.00

H-3. Hindu Marriage Act, 1955 — 25.00

H-4. Hindu Minority & Guardianship Act, 1956 — 25.00

H-5. Hindu Succession Act, 1956 — 30.00

H-6. Hire-Purchase Act, 1972 along with Hire-Purchase (Repeal) Act, 2005 — 25.00

I

I-1. Identification of Prisoners Act, 1920 — 25.00

I-2. Immoral Traffic (Prevention) Act, 1956 — 30.00

I-18. Income Tax Act as amended by Finance Act, 2011 (Pb) — 575.00

I-3. Indecent Representation of Women (Prohibition) Act, 1986 along with Rules, 1987 — 25.00

I-4. Indian Penal Code, 1860 with Classifications of offences and State Amendments — 100.00

I-6. Industrial Employment (Standing Orders) Act, 1946 along with Rules, 1946 — 35.00

I-7. Industrial Disputes Act, 1947 along with (Central) Rules, 1957 and allied Rules — 90.00

I-8. Industries (Development and Regulation) Act, 1951 — 45.00

I-9. Infant Milk Substitutes, Feeding Bottles and Infant Foods (Regulation of Production, Supply and Distribution) Act, 1992 along with Rules, 1993 — 25.00

I-10. Information Technology Act, 2000 along with Rules & Regulations — 160.00

I-19. Inland Vessels Act, 1917 — 70.00

I-11. Insecticides Act, 1968 along with Rules and Order — 70.00

I-12. Insurance Act, 1938 along with allied Act and Rules — 240.00

I-13. Insurance Regulatory and Development Authority Act, 1999 along with allied Rules and Regulations — 260.00

I-14. Insurance Regulatory and Development Authority Act, 1999 — 30.00

I-15. Inter-State Migrant Workmen (Regulation of Employment and Conditions of Service) Act, 1979 along with Rules, 1980 — 60.00

I-16. Interest Act, 1978 — 25.00

I-17. Interest on Delayed Payments to Small Scale and Ancillary Industrial Undertakings Act, 1993 — 25.00

J

J-1. Juvenile Justice (Care and Protection of Children) Act, 2000 along with Rules, 2007 — 110.00

K

M-18. Kazis Act, 1880 *see* Muslim laws (containing 9 Acts & Rules) — 50.00

L

L-1. Land Acquisition Act, 1894 — 85.00

L-7. Legal Metrology Act, 2009 along with Allied Rules — 350.00

L-2. Legal Services Authorities Act, 1987 along with allied Rules and Regulations — 75.00

L-3. Life Insurance Corporation Act, 1956 along with Rules, 1956 — 45.00

L-4. Limitation Act, 1963 — 30.00

L-6. Limited Liability Partnership Act, 2008 along with Notification and Allied Rules — 210.00

L-8. Limited Liability Partnership Act, 2008 — 55.00

L-5. Lotteries (Regulation) Act, 1998 — 25.00

M

A-8. Madras Ancient and Historical Monuments and Archaeological Sites and Remains Act, 1966 *see* Ancient Monuments and Archaeological Sites and Remains Act, 1958 — 110.00

M-22. Major Port Trusts Act, 1963 — 65.00

M-1. Majority Act, 1875 along with Guardian and Wards Act, 1890 — 30.00

M-24. Maintenance and Welfare of Parents and Senior Citizens Act, 2007 — 25.00

M-2. Maternity Benefit Act, 1961 along with Rules, 1963 — 30.00

M-3. Medical Council Act, 1956 along with Allied Act, Rules and Regulations — 225.00

M-4. Medical Termination of Pregnancy Act, 1971 along with Rules and Regulations — 30.00

M-5. Medicine Central Council Act, 1970 — 55.00

M-6. Medicinal and Toilet Preparations (Excise Duties) Act, 1955 — 30.00

M-7. Mental Health Act, 1987 along with Central Mental Health Authority Rules, 1990 and State Mental Health Rules, 1990 — 55.00

M-8. Merchant Shipping Act, 1958 along with allied Rules — 310.00

M-21. Micro, Small and Medium Enterprises Development Act, 2006 along with allied Act and Rules — 55.00

M-10. Mineral Concession Rules, 1960 *see* Mines & Minerals (Development and Regulation) Act, 1957 — 275.00

M-9. Mines Act, 1952 along with Rules, 1955 and The Mines Rescue Rules, 1985 — 110.00

M-10. Mines and Minerals (Regulation and Development) Act, 1957 along with Mineral Concession Rules, 1960 and allied Rules — 275.00

M-11. Minimum Wages Act, 1948 along with
Central Rules, 1950 — 60.00

M-12. Monopolies and Restrictive Trade
Practices Act, 1969 — 45.00

M-13. Motor Transport Workers Act, 1961 — 25.00

M-14. Motor Vehicles Act, 1988 — 110.00

M-15. Motor Vehicles Rules, 1989 along with
allied Material — 240.00

M-16. Multimodal Transportation of Goods
Act,1993 along with allied Rules — 30.00

M-17. Multi-State-Co-operative Societies
Act, 2002 along with Rules, 2002 — 95.00

M-18. Muslim Laws (Containing 9 Acts & Rules) — 50.00

M-19. Muslim Personal Law (*Shariat*)
Application Act, 1937 — 25.00

M-20. Muslim Women (Protection of Rights
on Divorce) Act. 1986 along with
Rules, 1986 — 30.00

M-18. Mussalman Wakf Act, 1923,
Mussalman Wakf Validating Act, 1913
& 1930 *see* Muslim Laws — 50.00

N

N-1. Narcotic Drugs & Psychotropic Substances Act,
1985 along with allied Act, Rules and Order 110.00

N-2. National Commission Acts [Containing
4 Acts-Women Act, 1990, Minorities Act,
1992, Backward Classes Act, 1993,
Safai Karamcharis Act, 1993 and allied
Information] — 50.00

N-3. National Commission for Minority Educational
Institutions Act, 2004 along with allied
Rules, 2006 — 35.00

N-5. National Environmental Tribunal Act, 1995 25.00

N-6. National Highways Act, 1956 along
with allied Acts & Rules — 110.00

N-6. National Highway Authority of India Act,
1988 *see* National Highways Act, 1956 110.00

N-15. National Green Tribunal Act, 2010 with Order,
2010 alongwith The National Green Tribunal
(Practice and Procedure) Rules, 2011 50.00

N-14. National Investigation Agency Act, 2008 30.00

N-11. National Rural Employment
Guarantee Act, 2005 with allied Rules — 50.00

N-7. National Security Act, 1980 — 25.00

N-13. National Security Guard Act, 1986 — 50.00

N-12. National Tax Tribunal Act, 2005 — 30.00

P-9. National Trust for Welfare of Persons
with Autism, Cerebal Palsy, Mental
Retardation with Multiple Disabilities Act,
1999 *see* Persons with Disabilities
(Equal Opportunities......) Act, 1995 — 80.00

N-8. Navy Act, 1957 — 60.00

N-9. Negotiable Instruments Act, 1881 — 50.00

N-10. Notaries Act, 1952 along with
Rules, 1956 — 35.00

O

O-1. Oaths Act, 1969 — 25.00

O-2. Official Languages Act, 1963 — 35.00

O-3. Official Secrets Act, 1923 — 25.00

P

P-1. Partition Act, 1893 — 25.00

P-2. Parsi Marriage and Divorce Act, 1936 — 25.00

P-3. Partnership Act, 1932 — 40.00

P-4. Passports Act, 1967 along with
Rules, 1980 — 90.00

P-5. Patents Act, 1970 along
with Rules, 2003 — 160.00

P-46. Payment and Settlement
Systems Act, 2007 — 40.00

P-6. Payment of Bonus Act, 1965
along with Rules, 1975 — 35.00

P-7. Payment of Gratuity Act, 1972
along with Rules, 1972 — 40.00

P-8. Payment of Wages Act, 1936 along with
(Procedure) Rules, 1937 — 50.00

P-9. Persons with Disabilities (Equal Opportunities,
Protection of Rights and Full Participation)
Act, 1995 along with Rules, 1996 and National
Trust for Welfare of Persons with
Disabilities Act, 1999 with Rules, 2000 80.00

P-10. Petroleum Act, 1934 along with
Rules, 2002 — 150.00

P-11. Pharmacy Act, 1948 — 30.00

P-12. Places of Worship (Special Provisions)
Act, 1991 — 25.00

P-13. Police Acts (6 Acts in 1) — 55.00

P-13. Police (Incitement of Disaffection) Act, 1992
see Police Acts (6 Acts in 1) — 55.00

P-13. Police Forces (Restriction of Rights)
Act, 1966 *see* Police Acts — 55.00

P-14. Post Office Act, 1898 — 30.00

P-15. Powers of Attorney Act, 1882 — 30.00

P-16. Prasar Bharti (Broadcasting Corporation
of India) Act, 1990 — 35.00

P-17. Pre-conception and Pre-natal Diagnostic
Techniques (Prohibition of Sex
Selection) Act, 1994 along with Rules — 50.00

P-18. Press & Registration of Books Act, 1867
along with Rules & Order — 40.00

P-19. Press Council Act, 1978 along with allied
Rules and Regulations — 35.00

E-16. Prevention of Blackmarketing and
Maintenance of Supplies of Essential
Commodities Act, 1980 *see* Essential
Commodities Act, 1955 — 40.00

P-20. Prevention of Corruption Act,1988 — 25.00

P-21. Prevention of Cruelty to Animals
Act, 1960 along with allied Rules — 80.00

P-22. Prevention of Damage to Public
Property Act, 1984 along with The Delhi
Prevention of Defacement of Property
Act, 2007 — 25.00

P-23. Prevention of Food Adulteration Act,
1954 along with Rules, 1955 — 285.00

P-27. Prevention of Illicit Traffic in NDPS
Act, 1974 *see* Preventive Detention Laws 40.00

P-24. Prevention of Insults to National
Honour Act, 1971 along with Emblems
and Names (Prevention of Improper
Use) Act, 1950 with Rules, 1982 — 40.00

P-25. Prevention of Money Laundering Act, 2002
along with allied Rules — 110.00

P-27. Preventive Detention Laws
(Containing 4 Acts) — 40.00

P-29. Prisoners Acts (Containing 6 Acts & Rules) 50.00

P-29. Prisoners (Attendance in Courts) Act,
1955 *see* Prisoners Acts — 50.00

P-30. Private Security Agencies
(Regulation) Act, 2005 with Rules, 2006 30.00

P-31. Prize Chits and Money Circulation
Schemes (Banning) Act, 1978 — 25.00

P-32. Probation of Offenders Act, 1958 — 30.00

P-45. Prohibition of Child Marriage Act, 2006
along with Allied Acts — 25.00

P-33. Protection of Civil Rights Act, 1955 along with Rules, 1977 — 25.00

P-34. Protection of Human Rights Act, 1993 along with Regulations and Rules — 45.00

P-35. Protection of Plant Varieties and Farmers' Rights Act, 2001 along with Rules & Regulations — 120.00

P-44. Protection of Women from Domestic Violence Act, 2005 along with Rules 2006 — 70.00

P-36. Provincial Insolvency Act, 1920 — 60.00

P-37. Provincial Small Cause Courts Act, 1887 — 30.00

P-38. Public Gambling Act, 1867 — 30.00

P-39. Public Liability Insurance Act, 1991 along with Rules, Forms & Notification — 35.00

P-40. Public Premises (Eviction of Unauthorised Occupants) Act, 1971 along with Rules, 1971 — 35.00

P-41. Public Provident Fund Act, 1968 — 25.00

P-42. Public Records Act, 1993 along with Rules, 1997 — 25.00

P-43. Public Servants (Inquiries) Act, 1850 — 25.00

R

R-1. Railways Act, 1989 along with allied Acts and Rules — 95.00

R-13. Railway Claims Tribunal Act, 1987 along with allied Rules — 65.00

R-2. Railway Protection Force Act, 1957 along with Rules, 1987 — 125.00

R-3. Recovery of Debts Due to Banks and Financial Institutions Act, 1993 along with allied Rules — 50.00

R-4. Registration Act, 1908 — 55.00

R-5. Registration of Births and Deaths Act, 1969 and The Births, Deaths and Marriages Registration Act, 1886 — 30.00

F-11. Registration of Foreigners Act, 1939 along with Rules, 1992 *see* Foreigners Act, 1946 — 45.00

C-11. Religious Endowments Act, 1863 *see* Charitable and Religious Trusts Act, 1920 — 45.00

R-6. Representation of the People Act, 1950 and Representation of the People Act, 1951 along with allied Act & Rules — 260.00

R-7. Repatriation of Prisoners Act, 2003 along with allied Acts — 50.00

R-12. Requisitioning and Acquisition of Immovable Property Act, 1952 — 35.00

R-8. Research and Development Cess Act, 1986 along with Rules, 1996 — 30.00

R-10. Reserve Bank of India Act, 1934 — 70.00

R-14. Right of Children to Free and Compulsory Education Act, 2009 — 45.00

R-9. Right to Information Act, 2005 along with allied Rules and Regulations — 50.00

R-11. Road Transport Corporation Act, 1950 — 30.00

S

C-26. SAFEMFOP Act, 1976 *see* COFEPOSA Act, 1974 — 35.00

S-1. Sale of Goods Act, 1930 — 25.00

S-2. Sales Promotion Employees (Conditions of Service) Act, 1976 along with Rules, 1976 — 25.00

S-23. Sarais Act, 1867 — 25.00

S-26. Sashastra Seema Bal Act, 2007 along with Rules, 2009 — 140.00

S-3. Scheduled Castes and Scheduled Tribes (Prevention of Atrocities) Act, 1989 along with Rules — 65.00

S-25. Scheduled Tribes and Other Traditional Forest Dwellers (Recognition of Forest Rights) Act, 2006 — 30.00

S-4. Securities and Exchange Board of India Act, 1992 — 40.00

S-5. Securities Contracts (Regulation) Act, 1956 along with Allied Rules — 60.00

S-6. Securitisation and Reconstruction of Financial Assets and Enforcement of Security Interest Act, 2002 along with Allied Rules and Orders — 120.00

S-7. Seeds Act, 1966 along with Rules, & Orders, 1983 — 40.00

S-8. Semiconductor Integrated Circuits Layout-Design Act, 2000 along with Rules, 2001 — 85.00

S-9. Sick Industrial Companies (Special Provisions) Act, 1985 along with BIFR and other allied Rules — 70.00

S-10. Slum Areas (Improvement and Clearance) Act, 1956 along with Rules, 1957 — 30.00

S-11. Small Industrial Development Bank of India Act, 1989 along with Rules, 2003 — 70.00

S-12. Societies Registration Act, 1860 with State Amendments — 40.00

S-13. Special Economic Zones Act, along with Rules, 2006 — 120.00

S-14. Special Marriage Act, 1954 — 30.00

S-24. Special Protection Group Act, 1988 — 25.00

S-15. Specific Relief Act, 1963 — 25.00

S-16. Stamp Act, 1899 — 40.00

S-17. Standards of Weights and Measures Act, 1976 along with allied Rules and Act, 1985 — 95.00

P-13. State Armed Police Forces (Extension of laws) Act, 1952 *see* Police Acts — 55.00

S-18. State Bank of India Act, 1955 — 45.00

S-19. State Financial Corporations Act, 1951 along with Rules, 2003 — 40.00

S-20. Succession Act, 1925 — 85.00

S-21. Suits Valuation Act, 1887 with State Amendments — 30.00

S-22. Supreme Court Rules, 1966 along with Regulations Regarding Advocate-on-Record Examination and Rules to Regulate Proceedings for Contempt of Supreme Court 1975 and The Supreme Court (Enlargement of Criminal Appellate Jurisdiction) Act, 1970 — 90.00

T

T-1. Telecom Regulatory Authority of India Act, 1997 along with Rules & Regulations — 295.00

T-2. Telegraph Act, 1885 with The Indian Wireless Telegraphy Act, 1933 along with allied Rules — 40.00

T-10. Terrorist Affected Areas (Special Courts) Act, 1984 — 25.00

T-3. Trade Marks Act, 1999 — 75.00

T-4. Trade Marks Act, 1999 along with allied Rules — 180.00

T-5. Trade and Merchandise Marks Act, 1958   40.00
T-6. Trade Unions Act, 1926 along with Central Trade Unions Regulations, 1938   35.00
P-29. Transfer of Prisoners Act, 1950 *see* Prisoners Acts   50.00
T-7. Transfer of Property Act, 1882   50.00
T-8. Transplantation of Human Organs and Tissues Act, 1994 along with Rules, 1995   55.00
T-9. Trusts Act, 1882   40.00

U

U-1. Unlawful Activities (Prevention) Act, 1967 along with Rules, 1968   45.00
U-3. Unorganised Workers' Social Security Act, 2008 alongwith Rules, 2009   35.00
U-2. Urban Land (Ceiling and Regulation) Act, 1976 along with Repeal Act, 1999   50.00

W

W-1. Wakf Act, 1995 along with Central Wakf Council Rules, 1998   65.00
W-9. Warehousing (Development and Regulation) Act, 2007 with allied Rules and Regulations   75.00
W-2. Water (Prevention and Control of Pollution) Act, 1974 along with Rules, 1975, Cess Act, 1977 and Cess Rules, 1978   75.00
W-3. Wealth-tax Act, 1957 as amended by Finance Act, 2011   120.00
W-4. Weapons of Mass Destruction and their Delivery Systems (Prohibition of Unlawful Activities) Act, 2005   25.00
W-5. Weekly Holidays Act, 1942   30.00
W-6. Wild Life (Protection) Act, 1972 along with allied Rules   120.00
W-7. Working Journalists and Other Newspaper Employees (Conditions of Service) and Miscellaneous Provisions Act, 1955 along with allied Acts & Rules   50.00

Y

Y-1. Young Persons (Harmful Publications) Act, 1956   25.00

BARE ACTS FOR DELHI

DL-2. Bombay Prevention of Begging Act, 1959 (As extended to U.T. of Delhi) with Rules, 1960   40.00
DL-33. Chit Funds Act, 1982 along with Delhi Chit Funds Rules, 2007   80.00
DL-3. Delhi Building and Other Construction Workers (Regulation of Employment and Conditions of Service) Rules, 2002 along with Act, 1996   175.00
DL-4. Delhi Co-operative Societies Act, 2003 along with Delhi Co-operative Societies Act, 1972   80.00
DL-5. Delhi Development Act, 1957 along with allied Act, Rules & Regulations   110.00
DL-6. Delhi Electricity Reforms Act, 2000 along with Regulations   185.00
DL-34. Delhi Excise Act, 2009 along with Rules, 2010   140.00

DL-32. Delhi Fire Service Act, 2007   45.00
DL-7. Delhi Land Reforms Act, 1954   65.00
DL-8. Delhi Lands (Restrictions on Transfer) Act, 1972 *see* Delhi Land Revenue Act, 1954   25.00
DL-8. Delhi Land Revenue Act, 1954 along with Delhi Lands (Restrictions on Transfer) Act, 1972   25.00
DL-10. Delhi Metro Railway (Operation and Maintenance) Act, 2002 along with allied Rules   140.00
DL-11. Delhi Municipal Corporation Act, 1957 along with allied Rules and Bye-Laws   240.00
DL-12. Delhi Police Act, 1978   50.00
DL-13. Delhi Preservation of Trees Act, 1994   20.00
P-22. Delhi Prevention of Defacement of Property Act, 2007 *see* The Prevention of Damage to Public Property Act, 1984   25.00
DL-15. Delhi Prohibition of Smoking and Non-Smokers Health Protection Act, 1996   25.00
DL-16. Delhi Public Gambling Act, 1955   25.00
DL-17. Delhi Rent Act, 1995 with Comparative Chart along with The Delhi Rent (Amendment) Bill, 1997   45.00
DL-18. Delhi Rent Control Act, 1958 along with Rules, 1959   90.00
DL-35. Delhi (Right of Citizen to Time Bound Delivery of Services) Act, 2011 with Rules   40.00
DL-19. Delhi Right to Information Act, 2001 along with Rules, 2001   40.00
DL-31. Delhi Special Police Establishment Act, 1946   25.00
DL-23. Government of NCT of Delhi Act, 1991   30.00
DL-25. Maharashtra Control of Organised Crime Act, 1999 As Extended to NCT of Delhi   30.00
DL-29. New Delhi Municipal Council Act, 1994   150.00
DL-26. New Minimum Rates of Wages in Delhi   60.00
DL-30. Sealings & Demolitions in Delhi [Delhi Laws (Special Provisions)] Act, 2006   30.00
DL-27. Stamp Duty, Registration Fees & Court Fees in Delhi along with Notifications & Delhi Registration Rules, 1976   65.00

POCKET SIZE EDITIONS

- Code of Civil Procedure, 1908 with State Amendments (Hb)   190.00
- Code of Civil Procedure, 1908 (Pb)   130.00
- Companies Act (Hb)   220.00
- Constitution of India with Selective Comments by P.M. Bakshi (Pb)   110.00
- Income Tax Act as amended by Finance Act, 2011 (Pb)   350.00

Prices are subject to change without notice.

Publishers

UNIVERSAL LAW PUBLISHING CO. PVT. LTD.

■ *(Hb) Hardbound, (Pb) Paperback (TBA) To be Announced*